Pension Claims
Rights and Obligations

Pension Claims

Rights and Obligations

Stephen R. Bruce

The Bureau of National Affairs, Inc., Washington, D.C.

Library of Congress Cataloging-in-Publication Data

Bruce, Stephen R.
Pension claims : rights and obligations / Stephen R. Bruce.
p. cm.
Includes index.
ISBN 0-87179-550-7
1. Pension trusts—Law and legislation—United States. 2. Pension trusts—Termination—Law and legislation—United States. I. Title.
KF3512.B75 1988
344.73'01252—dc19 87-32022
[347.3041252] CIP

International Standard Book Number: 0-87179-550-7
Printed in the United States of America

For my father Willis Bruce, 1915–1968,
and mother Lenecia Layman Bruce

Preface

This is a reference book on the types of pension claims that employees are most likely to have after denials of benefits from private pension plans. It is intended to be useful for persons specializing in employee benefits and for others who have not had the time or the resources to keep up with this field. While endeavoring to make the material accessible to persons who are not employee benefit specialists, this is not an introduction to the law on pension benefit claims, but is a detailed and, at times, complicated, treatment of the subject.

The table of contents directs a reader to chapters and sections related to a particular kind of benefit dispute. Each chapter is designed to be self-contained and cross-referenced to other relevant areas. For someone who is not familiar with ERISA's structure, Internal Revenue Code tax advantages and qualification requirements, and basic classifications of plans, the Introduction and Chapter 1 should be read first. In addition, Chapter 14 could be scanned to obtain an overview of how ERISA's and the Code's requirements are enforced.

Following the Introduction and Chapter 1, the book is structured into four parts. Chapters 2 through 6 first describe the minimum standards for private pension and profit-sharing plans under the Internal Revenue Code and the labor parts of ERISA on coverage of employees (Chapter 2), a plan's benefit or contribution formula (Chapter 3), the accrual of pension benefits for years of participation under a plan (Chapter 4), the vesting of a right to immediate or deferred receipt of accrued benefits (Chapter 5), and the commencement of benefits, the payment of benefits to survivors, and the amount of benefits under optional forms of payment (Chapter 6). Federal common law issues and issues arising under other federal statutory law are discussed in these chapters when specifically related to the subject area.

The second part covers the federal common law on employee benefit claims and overriding federal statutory protection. Chapter 7 thus discusses plan interpretation, factual findings related to benefit claims, and exercises of discretionary authority under a plan. Chapter 8 covers estoppel, separate contracts with employers, misrepresentation, unjust enrichment, and reform in equity. Chapter 9 discusses limits on plan amendments under the federal common law that can go beyond the the minimum standards established under ERISA. Antidiscrimination protections available under ERISA, the Internal Revenue Code, the ADEA, and Title VII of the Civil Rights Act are discussed in Chapter 10.

The third part focuses on more specialized issues related to plant closings and pension plan terminations. Chapter 11 covers pension issues in plant closings and work force reductions, emphasizing, in particular, the Internal Revenue Code requirement that every tax-qualified plan must contain a plan provision making benefits accrued vested, or nonforfeitable, on a partial termination. Chapter 12 discusses terminations of single-employer plans, and Chapter 13 discusses reorganization and insolvency rules for multiemployer plans.

The fourth part—all contained in Chapter 14—covers procedural issues and required disclosure to plan participants.

The focus of this book is on the contractual and statutory claims for pension benefits that employees have in different situations, and the strengths and weaknesses of those claims. It does not cover actuarial funding methods for defined benefit plan obligations. Nor does it cover fiduciary duties and prohibited transactions in investments of a pension or profit-sharing plan's assets. Claims that a plan was inadequately funded or that plan assets were misinvested are discussed in contexts where they can have a direct impact on a participant's benefits, e.g., in Chapter 12's discussion of defined benefit plan terminations in which all promised benefits cannot be paid from the plan's assets. Claims for breach of fiduciary duty in investments can, of course, always have a direct impact on the amount in a participant's individual account under a defined contribution plan.

This book also does not deal with pension plans of federal or state governments; pension plans of self-employed individuals (called Keogh or H.R. 10 plans), although the rules for these plans are prospectively the same as for corporate plans; or tax-deferred annuities available to public school employees and employees of certain tax-exempt organizations.

In writing this book, statutory provisions, regulations, and published court decisions up to June 1, 1987, have been followed. Included within the text is substantial new material digesting and analyzing the pension provisions of the 1986 Tax Reform Act.

As often happened in the long course of writing this book, the cited authorities will continue to change. Although I expect that future developments under ERISA will begin to become more interstitial, pension law is still obviously a fast moving area. Therefore, the need to check each point in the text or footnotes for new developments remains acute.

STEPHEN R. BRUCE

Washington, D.C.
November 1987

Acknowledgments

David A. Sayre, now the Managing Editor of *BNA Pension Reporter, Benefits Today,* and *Employee Benefits Cases*, provided extensive guidance and steady encouragement throughout the long drafting and redrafting of this manuscript as consulting editor on this project. In 1983, my idea was to apply ERISA's minimum standards and the federal common law to several then-current topics (plan amendments reducing early retirement benefits, pension rights after plant closings or corporate sales, and pension claims after plan terminations). These topics remain in the manuscript, but David pushed for, helped structure, and obtained a more comprehensive book covering all of ERISA's minimum standards and the developing federal common law. His substantive editorial comments and suggestions are also reflected throughout.

* * * * * * * * * * * *

A number of other persons contributed valuable substantive comments and suggestions. Dan McIntyre, Dan Brandenburg, Charles Pillsbury and Claude Poulin offered detailed comments on selected chapters. Tom Geoghegan, Lee Irish, Nell Hennessey, Ann Franke, and Joel Nomkin reviewed and commented on drafts of other chapters. Bill Payne of the United Steelworkers provided a large number of insights into the federal common law of pensions, which found their way into Chapters 7–10 and 14.

I am also in debt to Dan McGill for his *Fundamentals of Private Pensions* for numerous points in Chapters 1–6—as the footnotes show. Don Grubbs' "In-Depth Re-Examination of Integration," James Ray's and Samuel Halpern's "The Common Law of ERISA," Neal Dudovitz's and Gill Deford's "Representing Workers and Retirees in Private Pension Litigation," and Charles Pillsbury's "Employee Benefit Plan Claims Under ERISA" were also instrumental in getting started on Chapters 3, 7, 8, and 14.

Any list of everyone who has answered particular questions along the way runs the risk of omission. But Steve Zaleznick of AARP, Don Reynolds, Mark Borenstein, David Preminger, Don Grubbs, Ray Schmitt, Sam Berger, Jim Holland, Eric Raps, Susan Hoffman (the latter four all then at the IRS), Bob Doyle at the Department of Labor, and Al Rettig and Steve Caflisch at the PBGC, all were helpful on particular points.

I am also grateful to Richard Stanger, Dan Brandenburg, and Mort Klevan for allowing me to attend their graduate pension classes at Georgetown University Law Center in 1982–83, and to Karen Ferguson for introducing me to a number of pension policy issues in 1981–82 when I was attorney for the Pension Rights Center. Hundreds of letters from individual participants that I reviewed throughout that time helped inform my initial sense of which topics are of importance to plan participants. My review in June 1987 of close to two thousand letters from participants and beneficiaries commenting on the class action settlement of *Rettig v. PBGC* and *Piech v. PBGC* reinforces the selection of topics as it has developed.

Mary Hughes copyedited the manuscript and made it markedly less repetitious and more understandable. Since readers only see the final product, they may not fully appreciate where she started from and how much she improved the manuscript. I am also grateful to Louise R. Goines for her supervision, editorial skill, and advice as senior editor on this project, and to Tim Darby, Mildred Cary, Mary Miner, Georgia Love, and John Jones at BNA Books, who have all been extraordinarily helpful to me as a first-time author over a three-year period.

My mother Lenecia Bruce deserves my lasting thanks for having typed a large part of the original manuscript when I did not have the resources to do so. She has also been steadfast in her encouragement of this book, as has my brother Charles Bruce.

Any mistakes remaining in this book are, of course, my own.

S.R.B.

Summary Contents

Detailed Contents

Introduction: The Complexity of Pension Plans and Law

Thirty million American employees currently participate in more than 500,000 private pension plans. These plans hold assets exceeding $948 billion and receive additional employer contributions of close to $70 billion annually.[1] The coverage and size of private pension plans are astounding when it is considered that less than 700 private pension plans existed before World War II.[2] Since that time, pension plan participation has become a standard employment benefit. As a provider of retirement income, these plans now rank second only to Social Security.[3]

However, while Social Security is administered by one public administrative agency, according to a single, relatively uniform set of rules, private pension plans are administered individually, generally by employer-appointed plan administrators. Except for compliance with certain minimum standards established under ERISA and the Internal Revenue Code, each plan can have slightly different rules whose terminology alone is often enough to bewilder plan participants and lawyers

---

[1] See Statistical Abstract of the United States: 1986, at 368 and 369 (1983 estimate of participants and 1984 estimate of assets), and A. Munnell, *The Economics of Private Pensions* (Brookings 1982), at 11 (1980 estimates of number of plans and annual contributions). Pension contributions averaged 5.2% of covered payroll for 1,000 companies surveyed by the Chamber of Commerce in 1985. See 13 BNA Pens. Rep. 1920 (Nov. 17, 1986).

[2] See Congressional Research Service, 98th Cong., 2d Sess., "Designing a Retirement System for Federal Workers Covered by Social Security," at 37 (Comm. Print for the House Committee on Post Office and Civil Service 1985) (only 639 plans existed in 1939). Almost all major collectively bargained pension plans were established in or after the late 1940's, triggered in part by the Seventh Circuit's affirmance of a 1948 NLRB decision in *Inland Steel Co. v. NLRB,* 170 F.2d 247, 1 EBC 1008 (7th Cir. 1948), *cert. denied,* 336 U.S. 960 (1949), holding that pension benefits are a mandatory subject for collective bargaining. See *id.*

Since many plans initially required long periods of continuous service for vesting or only provided vested benefits upon retirement, the first wave of private pension retirees does not seem to have occurred until the early 1960's, almost coincident with the time when Congress first began taking notice of problems under such plans.

[3] See Washington Post, Oct. 31, 1985, at A-17 ("34.2 Million Get Pensions") (summarizing U.S. Bureau of the Census report that 30 million Americans receive Social Security old age or disability pensions, 7.9 million people receive private pensions, 2.9 million individuals receive state or local government pensions, and 1.3 million people receive military pensions). Benefit payments to individuals receiving private pensions averaged $360 per month in 1984, for a total payout of $35 billion annually. *Id.*, and see A. Munnell, *supra*, at 11 (citing identical figure for payments made in 1980).

alike. Senator Barry Goldwater could have served as spokesman for most of the private bar when he stated:

> "'Complicated' sums up this entire area. My staff and I have made forays into the world of private pension plans and ERISA, and after several briefings, have come to the conclusion that for every assumption or rule, there are at least 200 exceptions."[4]

Similarly, in *Riley v. MEBA Pension Trust,* Judge Henry Friendly, writing for the Second Circuit, stated that a lower court had fallen "victim to the not uncommon error of reading technical pension language as if it were ordinary English speech."[5] Later, the Second Circuit was forced to reverse its own decision when it found that its reading of the "technical pension language" had not been correct either.[6]

Most of this complexity arises under so-called defined benefit plans. The differences between defined benefit and defined contribution plans are examined more in Chapter 1. But it is sufficient here to say that defined benefit plans are more intricate contracts in which the employer is promising to pay set amounts of benefits under different, often detailed conditions, rather than promising merely to make annual contributions to an individual profit-sharing or savings plan account. Accordingly, the law regulating defined benefit plans is more complex than for defined contribution plans.[7] In addition, more attention naturally focuses on the abstruse aspects of defined benefit plans because more employees participate in them and more money is generally at stake in the benefits promised under them.

Federal administrative agencies are frequently cited as a primary source for the complexity of pension law. This is in part true. Federal regulation adds a layer of regulatory standards that were not present before ERISA. This is compounded by the need to reference the regulations and opinions of two different agencies (the Department of Labor and the Internal Revenue Service), and sometimes a third (the Pension Benefit Guaranty Corporation), to resolve a single pension question. But, in a time when legislators and regulators are sometimes seen as the inventors of complexity, it is worth observing that ERISA and the Internal Revenue Code, and the regulations under each, often merely codify pension practices and terminology developed in the private sector by pension specialists. Congress thus did not invent participation requirements, benefit accrual methods, vesting or break-in-

---

[4] 126 Cong. Rec. 12179 (May 22, 1980) (speaking in support of the Multiemployer Pension Plan Amendments Act of 1980).

[5] 570 F.2d 406, 1 EBC 1757, at 1759 (2d Cir. 1977). See also *Gediman v. Anheuser Busch, Inc.,* 299 F.2d 537, at 546 (2d Cir. 1962) (Friendly, J.) (in describing an employee's options at early retirement: " [n]either the Plan nor the employee's booklet, so beautifully clear to the experienced [pension plan] draftsman, used the kind of language that is fully understandable by even an intelligent layman").

[6] 586 F.2d 968, 1 EBC 1768 (2d Cir. 1978).

[7] And see, e.g., 126 Cong. Rec. 12179 (May 22, 1980) (statement of Senator Goldwater) ("every problem" Congress faces from "lack of portability" to "lack of early vesting" to "unfunded liabilities" is primarily, or exclusively, a defined benefit plan problem).

service rules, or even "summary plan descriptions," but rather it established minimum standards applicable to each of these existing practices. As a practical matter, the minimum standards generally ameliorate more extreme practices, while accommodating most other existing practices with only slight alterations.[8] But one consequence of regulating pension plans in this manner is that the law itself and the regulations appear to be an almost endless catalog of rules, permissible alternatives, and accommodating exceptions—which in many respects they are.

The complexity of pension law can also be overdone. Perhaps the major theme of this book is the continuing application of basic common law principles to plan interpretation, particularly when examining the understanding of employees of the terms of a plan as developed by the description of benefits provided in the summary plan description. Examining employee pension rights and employer obligations from a common law perspective was virtually ignored after the enactment of ERISA, as the courts, the private bar, and the federal agencies charged with enforcing ERISA all struggled to understand the full implications of the Act. However, as the courts have increasingly recognized, despite ERISA's "comprehensive and reticulated" detail,[9] a federal common law examination of pension rights and obligations remains an essential adjunct in resolving many close statutory questions under ERISA and is the mainstay in determining the perennial question of whether an employer has contracted under a plan or by other representations to abide by higher standards than required under ERISA.

The diversity in the terms of plans generated by the existence of over 500,000 separate plans can also be overestimated. More than 75 percent of all plan participants are in just two percent, or only 10,000, of these plans.[10] Apart from this statistic, all plans have more continuity among them than would appear at first. Unions establish a great deal of continuity among collectively bargained plans by negotiating basically the same pattern plan with each employer with whom the international union bargains, subject in many instances only to real negotiation on the dollar amounts of benefits and slight changes in drafting. More continuity between plans is introduced because they are drafted by a relatively small group of banks, insurance companies, law firms, and benefits consultants who, like most lawyers, have their favorite form language. A third source of continuity among plans stems from the IRS's publication of master and prototype plans and sample

---

[8] ERISA's minimum funding standards for defined benefit plans also illustrate this. Congress did not invent the actuarial funding methods named in ERISA §3(31), but rather codified all existing actuarial funding methods except two, "pay-as-you-go" and "terminal" funding, which it considered unacceptable. Congress neither simplified the actuarial nomenclature nor the funding methods themselves nor did it make them more complicated.

[9] *Nachman Corp. v. PBGC,* 446 U.S. 359, 2 EBC 1431, at 1432 (1980).

[10] Congressional Research Service, 98th Cong., 2d Sess., "Designing a Retirement System for Federal Workers Covered by Social Security," at 37 (Comm. Print for the House Committee on Post Office and Civil Service 1985).

paragraphs that will, in most circumstances, conform a plan with ERISA's requirements and qualify it for the tax advantages available under the Code.

Perhaps the most significant point of diversity among pension plans is in their benefit formulas. Many plans only provide very low benefits. A "pension" from one of these plans may therefore be no more than a small monthly allowance. A related word of caution for lawyers representing employees: Do not overestimate the power of ERISA, or of the common law, to redress benefit formulas that are inescapably meager. Even if a participant is entitled to *more* benefits, the claim may have a relatively small value. As a benchmark, a claim for $100 per month in benefits beginning at age 65 (without any cost of living adjustments thereafter) is worth $11,520 in a lump sum present value for an employee who is 65 (or very close to it).[11] When a $100 per month benefit will not begin until age 65 and the employee is age 55, the present value of the claim is a little less than one-half of $11,520 (more exactly $5,650).[12] For an employee age 45, the present value of $100 per month payable at age 65 is about one-fourth of the age 65 present value, or more exactly $3,003.[13]

The amount at stake can be still less when a claim for benefits involves whether a participant is entitled, for example, to one additional year of participation for benefit accruals. In 1984, an additional year of participation credit added $17 per month on average to a salaried participant's age 65 benefits.[14] The values mentioned above would therefore be reduced by roughly one-sixth at each of the respective ages if this was an employee's only claim for additional benefits.

The present value of an employee's benefit claim is not as much of a barrier to being able to bring suit under ERISA (including to enforce federal common law rights) as it is with some other contractual rights because prevailing attorneys in ERISA actions may be entitled to attorney's fee awards in the discretion of the court—without regard to the amount of benefits at issue (as in Civil Rights cases).[15]

---

[11] Assuming a 6% interest rate and the "UP-1984" mortality table with a one-year setback to reflect a 40% female workforce. If the assumed interest rate is 8%, the present value of the benefit claim is $10,068.

[12] Assuming a 6% interest rate and the UP-1984 mortality table with a one-year setback.

[13] Assuming a 6% interest rate and the UP-1984 mortality table with a one-year setback.

[14] See U.S. Department of Labor, Findings from the Survey of Private Pension Amounts (1985), at 3 and 50 (estimate in text obtained by projecting mean benefit levels per year of credited service in 1978 forward to 1984 in step with changes in the Consumer Price Index).

[15] See *City of Riverside v. Rivera*, 477 U.S. ___ (1986). However, such an award assumes that the claimant prevails and that the court does not limit the attorney's fee award, in its discretion, when the amount of benefits at stake is not large and the prevailing claimant has not established an important principle applicable to other plan participants. The exercise of a court's discretion in such cases under ERISA has not been fully resolved. See generally ch. 14, sec. II.G.

1

ERISA and Internal Revenue Code Basics

I. ERISA: Purposes and Structure

The Employee Retirement Income Security Act of 1974 (ERISA)[1] is a comprehensive, landmark reform of employee benefit law. It is also a statute with numerous statutory, common law, and regulatory antecedents. Primary among these are the Internal Revenue Code requirements for tax-qualified pension and profit-sharing plans, most notably, the requirement first adopted in the 1942 Revenue Act, and applied in an extensive series of regulations and rulings, that pension and profit-sharing plans are not to "discriminate" in favor of employees who are officers, shareholders, or highly compensated employees of the company sponsoring the plan. In addition, Section 302(c)(5) of the Labor Management Relations Act of 1947 (the Taft-Hartley Act) requires employee benefit plans administered by unions to have an equal number of management-appointed trustees, and mandates that such plans be structured for the "sole and exclusive benefit" of covered employees and their families. Disclosure, bonding, and criminal provisions for employee benefit plans were established by the Welfare and Pension Plans Disclosure Act of 1958. Finally, antecedents to ERISA are also found throughout the common law of trusts and contracts.

[1] P.L. 93-406, codified in 29 U.S.C. §§1001–1461, and codified in and amending the Internal Revenue Code, 26 U.S.C. §§401–418E, 4971, 4975, 6057-59, and 7476, as amended by the Multiemployer Pension Plan Amendments Act of 1980 (MPPAA), P.L. 96-364; the 1984 Retirement Equity Act (REA), P.L. 98-397; the Consolidated Omnibus Budget Reconciliation Act of 1985, P.L. 99-272; the Tax Reform Act of 1986, P.L. 99-514; and the Omnibus Budget Reconciliation Act of 1986, P.L. 99-509. The Code's rules have also been amended by the Revenue Act of 1978, P.L. 95-600, the Tax Equity and Fiscal Responsibility Act of 1982 (TEFRA), P.L. 97-248; and the Deficit Reduction Act of 1984, P.L. 98-369.

Beginning with President Kennedy's appointment in 1962 of a President's Committee on Corporate Pension Funds and the Committee's subsequent final report in 1965, however, a consensus began developing that this existing federal regulation, along with the nonuniform state common law regulation of plans, was not sufficient. Too often, as Senator Vance Hartke put it:

> "The pension promise shrinks to this: 'If you remain in good health and stay with the company until you are sixty-five years old, and if the company is still in business, and if your department has not been abolished, and if you haven't been laid off for too long a period, and if there's enough money in the fund, and if that money has been prudently managed, you will get your pension.' "[2]

In other instances, legal technicalities hidden in full plan documents reduced or narrowed broader pension promises made in booklets provided employees. Senator Jacob Javits stated:

> "Many workers are led to believe they are covered by a good pension plan because of nicely phrased booklets and other assurances handed them by their employers. When the time comes for the payoff, they learn that the cold legal phrasing in pension contracts says otherwise."[3]

Following nearly a decade of hearings and study, and with extensive, unorganized constituent support, Congress enacted the reforms embodied in ERISA in August of 1974 by a vote of 407 to 2 in the House and unanimously in the Senate. President Gerald Ford signed the Act into law on Labor Day of 1974.

A. Principal Minimum Standards and Coverage

Congress found in Section 2(a) of ERISA that

> "the continued well-being and security of millions of employees and their beneficiaries are directly affected by these plans; . . . that employees with long years of employment are losing anticipated retirement benefits owing to the lack of vesting provisions in such plans; . . . that owing to the termination of plans before requisite funds have been accumulated, employees and their beneficiaries have been deprived of anticipated benefits; . . . and that it is . . . in the interest of employees and their beneficiaries . . . that minimum standards be provided assuring the equitable character of such plans and their financial soundness."[4]

In ERISA, Congress established minimum standards for pension plans as federal labor law. In most cases, the same standards were enacted by parallel amendments as tax-qualification requirements

---

[2] Hearings Before the Senate Subcommittee on Private Pension Plans of the Committee on Finance, 93d Cong., 1st Sess., at 451 (1973) (statement of Senator Hartke).

[3] 3 ERISA Leg. Hist. 4750. ___ ERISA Leg. Hist ___ refers to the volume number and page number of the 3-volume *Legislative History of the Employee Retirement Income Security Act of 1974*, prepared by the Subcommittee on Labor of the Senate Committee on Labor and Public Welfare and published by the U.S. Government Printing Office.

[4] 29 U.S.C. §1001(a).

under the Internal Revenue Code. These minimum standards establish:

- Permissible age and service conditions for beginning participation in benefit accruals under pension plans, Section 202 (paralleled in Code Section 410(a));[5]
- Methods for the accrual of pension benefits across years of participation in a defined benefit plan, Section 204 (paralleled in Code Section 411(b));[6]
- Rules for the vesting of pension benefits and limits on break-in-service rules that can cancel years of service toward vesting, Section 203 (paralleled in Code Section 411(a));[7]
- Requirements for survivor's annuity options, and standards on the commencement and assignability of pension benefits, Sections 205 and 206 (paralleled in Code Sections 401(a)(11), (13), and (14), 414(p), and 417;[8]
- Funding standards for defined benefit plan obligations, Section 302 (paralleled in Code Section 412);[9]
- Standards for the conduct of fiduciaries who administer plans and invest plan assets, Sections 401–414 (partially paralleled in Code Section 4975);[10]
- Requirements for disclosure to participants and to the federal government of understandable and accurate descriptions of the terms of plans and of information on the financial status and operations of plans, Sections 101–111 and Section 209 (and see Code Section 6057);[11] and
- Insurance for pension promises made by defined benefit plans against insufficiencies of plan assets on plan termination, Sections 4001-4303.[12]

In recognition of ERISA's remedial purposes, the courts have uniformly held that ERISA is to be liberally construed, with the guiding principles being the findings and policies in Section 2 of the Act.[13]

---

[5] 29 U.S.C. §1052 (and 26 U.S.C. §410(a)).

[6] 29 U.S.C. §1054 (and 26 U.S.C. §411(b)).

[7] 29 U.S.C. §1053 (and 26 U.S.C. §411(a)).

[8] 29 U.S.C. §§1055 and 1056 (and 26 U.S.C. §§401(a)(11), (13) and (14), 414(p), and 417).

[9] 29 U.S.C. §1082 (and 26 U.S.C. §412).

[10] 29 U.S.C. §§1101–1114 (and 26 U.S.C. §4975).

[11] 29 U.S.C. §§1021–1031 and §1059 (and 26 U.S.C. §6057).

[12] 29 U.S.C. §1301–1461.

[13] See *Smith v. CMTA-IAM Pension Trust*, 746 F.2d 587, 5 EBC 2428 (9th Cir. 1984) ("ERISA, like the Civil Rights Acts . . . is remedial legislation [to] be liberally construed in favor of protecting [employee benefit plan] participants"); *Amato v. Western Union Int'l, Inc.*, 773 F.2d 1402, 6 EBC 2226 (2d Cir. 1985) (ERISA "employee-oriented" and designed to assure that "they would not be deprived of their reasonably anticipated pension benefits; an employer [is] to be prevented from 'pulling the rug out from under' promised retirement benefits upon which . . . employees [have] relied during their long years of service"); *Rettig v. PBGC*, 744 F.2d 133, 5 EBC 2025 (D.C. Cir. 1984) ("remedial purpose of ERISA must be given due weight in construing provisions whose language and legislative history are susceptible of varying interpretations"); *Leigh v. Engle*, 727 F.2d 113, 4 EBC 2702 (7th Cir. 1984) ("reluctant to construe narrowly any

With certain express exceptions, ERISA's coverage extends to *all* employee benefit plans "established or maintained" by any employer engaged in commerce or any employee organization representing employees engaged in commerce, and also any plan established or maintained by any employer or employee organization engaged in any industry or activity "affecting commerce."[14]

The "affecting commerce" language is "an expression of Congress' intent to regulate within the full sweep of its constitutional authority."[15] Express exceptions to ERISA's coverage apply to government-sponsored pension and welfare plans;[16] church plans;[17] so-called top hat plans that provide benefits in excess of the maximum benefits allowed for tax-qualified plans on an unfunded basis to select groups of employees (usually top management);[18] plans maintained outside the United States primarily for nonresident aliens;[19] and plans maintained solely for the purpose of complying with workmen's compensation, unemployment compensation, or disability insurance laws.[20]

ERISA also covers so-called welfare plans, for example, health, vacation, sick pay, day care, prepaid legal services, severance pay, and death benefit plans.[21] However, ERISA's substantive application to these types of plans is limited to the disclosure requirements, the

---

protective provisions of the Act" in light of "Congress' overriding concern with the protection of plan beneficiaries"); *Kross v. Western Elec. Co.*, 701 F.2d 1238, 4 EBC 1265 (7th Cir. 1983) (ERISA a "remedial statute to be liberally construed in favor of employee benefit fund participants"); *Duchow v. New York Teamsters Pension Fund*, 691 F.2d 74, 3 EBC 2312 (2d Cir. 1982) "ERISA . . . a remedial statute . . . to protect beneficiaries of retirement plans by reducing the risk of loss of pension benefits"; "[i]nterpreting [in favor of] additional vesting furthers this goal"); *Connolly v. PBGC*, 581 F.2d 729, 1 EBC 1410 (9th Cir. 1978), *cert. denied*, 440 U.S. 935 (1979) ("[c]onsistent with ERISA's remedial function" of assuring that retirement benefits are "available when needed," coverage of Act to be liberally construed); *Eaves v. Penn*, 587 F.2d 453, 1 EBC 1592 (10th Cir. 1978) (ERISA a "comprehensive remedial statute" to protect interests of participants and beneficiaries, a "central and fundamental" part of which is the fiduciary standard in §404(a)(1)).

See also *Brock v. Self*, 632 F.Supp. 1509, 7 EBC 1512 (W.D. La. 1986); *Folz v. Marriott Corp.*, 594 F.Supp. 1007, 5 EBC 2244 (W.D. Mo. 1984); *Hollenbeck v. Falstaff Brewing Corp.*, 605 F.Supp. 421 (E.D. Mo. 1984); *Marshall v. Davis*, 517 F.Supp. 551, 2 EBC 1721 (W.D. Mich. 1981); *Gilliam v. Edwards*, 492 F.Supp. 1255, 2 EBC 2475 (D.N.J. 1980); *Marshall v. Kelly*, 465 F.Supp. 341, 1 EBC 1850 (W.D. Okla. 1978); *Freund v. Marshall & Ilsley Bank*, 485 F.Supp. 629, 1 EBC 1898 (W.D. Wis. 1979); *Corley v. Hecht Co.*, 530 F.Supp. 1155, 2 EBC 2397 (D.D.C. 1982); *Eaton v. D'Amato*, 581 F.Supp. 743, 3 EBC 1003 (D.D.C. 1980); *United Paper Workers v. Bowater Pension Plan*, 2 EBC 1154 (E.D. Tenn. 1981); *In re M&M Trans. Co.*, 3 B.R. 722, 2 EBC 2486 (S.D.N.Y. 1980); *Donovan v. Daugherty*, 550 F.Supp. 390, 3 EBC 2079 (S.D. Ala. 1982); *Bostic v. Ohio River Co. Basic Pension Plan*, 517 F.Supp. 627, 2 EBC 1670 (S.D. W.Va. 1981); *Western Washington Cement Masons Trust Funds v. Hillis Homes, Inc.*, 612 P.2d 436 (Wash. App. 1980).

[14] ERISA §4(a).

[15] *Winterrowd v. Freedman & Co.*, 724 F.2d 823, 5 EBC 1221 (9th Cir. 1984) (coverage extends to plans of employers engaged in agricultural work). And see S. Rep. 93-127, at 18, 1 ERISA Leg. Hist. 604 ("[i]t is intended that coverage . . . be construed liberally to provide the maximum degree of protection to working men and women covered by private retirement programs").

[16] ERISA §3(32) and §4(b)(1).

[17] ERISA §3(33) and §4(b)(2).

[18] ERISA §3(36) and §4(b)(5).

[19] ERISA §4(b)(4).

[20] ERISA §4(b)(3).

[21] See ERISA §3(1).

fiduciary standards, the federal common law of employee benefits, and the enforcement provisions.[22]

B. Structure

ERISA is divided into four titles. Title I contains the "labor" provisions of the Act, which in turn are divided into five parts. Part 1 contains the disclosure requirements; Part 2 contains the minimum standards for beginning plan participation, accruing benefits, vesting, and offering survivor's annuity options; Part 3 sets minimum funding standards; Part 4 covers fiduciary duties, and Part 5 covers enforcement. A Part 6, added in 1986, requires continuation of group health insurance coverage in certain circumstances.

Title II amends and makes additions to the Internal Revenue Code to include parallel "mirror image" tax-qualification requirements on plan participation, benefit accruals, vesting, and survivor's annuity options. Title II also added the minimum funding requirements to the Code and established limitations on deductible employer contributions to and maximum individual benefits from tax-qualified plans. It also established the first version of the Individual Retirement Account. Although contained in ERISA, the Title II provisions, as well as the preexisting Code sections are still generally, and are hereafter, referred to as "Code" provisions.

Title III of ERISA primarily concerns the division and coordination of enforcement jurisdiction between the Labor and Treasury Departments.[23] It also sets up an Enrolled Actuaries Board to certify pension actuaries. Title IV establishes the Pension Benefit Guaranty Corporation and sets the terms for the PBGC's insurance of benefits promised under terminated defined benefit pension plans.

II. Tax Advantages of Qualified Plans

The tax advantages offered in the Internal Revenue Code are the bedrock on which all employer-sponsored pension and profit-sharing plans rest. Plans that meet certain requirements in the Code become

---

[22] ERISA's preemption of virtually all state law from the regulation of covered employee "welfare" plans without setting more than general standards continues to be one of its more surprising features and is the subject of much litigation. Compare *Metropolitan Life Ins. Co. v. Massachusetts*, 471 U.S. 724, 6 EBC 1545 (1985), with *Pilot Life Ins. v. Dedeaux*, 481 U.S. ___, 8 EBC 1409 (1987).

Statutory provisions requiring continuation of group health insurance (at the employee's or other person's expense) after termination of employment, death of the employee, retirement, divorce or legal separation, or the cessation of a child's status as a dependent were added to ERISA as §§601—608 by Title X of the Consolidated Omnibus Budget Reconciliation Act of 1985, P.L. 99-272.

[23] The statutory division of enforcement jurisdiction between the Labor and Treasury Departments was altered by President Carter's 1978 Reorganization Plan No. 4. See 5 U.S.C.A. Appendix 1.

"qualified" for these tax advantages. Senator Carl Curtis, the Nixon Administration's spokesman in the final debates over ERISA, summed up the significance of the tax advantages when he stated that "without the tax provisions, they [private pension plans] would all fall."[24]

The lost federal tax revenues from these tax advantages were estimated to be $4 billion when ERISA was enacted.[25] For fiscal year 1985, the Treasury Department estimated that the lost revenues attributable to the tax advantages were in excess of $71 billion, or roughly $2,000 annually for each individual participant.[26] The incidence of these tax expenditures is not spread evenly among plan participants. This is because the essence of the tax advantages is a business expense deduction for the employer for contributions made to a qualified plan without accompanying income for the employees on whose behalf the contributions are made until the benefits from the plan, based on contributions plus investment earnings, are later received. This deferral of taxation is more valuable for a high-income bracket employee than for a low-income bracket employee. In addition, the pension benefits of highly compensated employees are generally greater in dollar amount (and even as a percentage of compensation) than for low or average income employees.

More specifically, the tax advantages that flow from tax qualification of a plan are:

- Contributions by sponsoring employers to the plan are deductible *when made*, even though the employee-participants are not taxed until their benefits are received—usually many years later. Code Section 404(a).
- Earnings on contributions are tax exempt until received as benefits. Code Section 501(a).
- When employees vest in benefits, even if they have immediate rights to withdrawal of the money (which usually would result in taxation under the constructive receipt doctrine), benefits are not taxed until actually received. Code Section 402(a)(1).
- When benefits from a qualified plan become subject to taxation, employee-participants have usually retired and generally are in lower tax brackets than if taxation of the contributions and earnings had not been deferred.
- Contributions of employer stock to Employee Stock Ownership Plans (ESOPs) are encouraged by a further, ever-changing panoply of special tax provisions.[27]

---

[24] 3 ERISA Leg. Hist. 4784.

[25] S. Rep. 93-383, at 11, 1 ERISA Leg. Hist. 1079.

[26] See 13 BNA Pens. Rep. 359 (Feb. 24, 1986) (reporting figures in Reagan Administration's fiscal year 1987 budget request). The assumptions in the Treasury Department's estimates of the tax expenditures from qualified pension plans have changed over the years so that the pre-ERISA $4 billion may not be exactly comparable to the 1985 $71 billion estimate.

[27] Code §1042 allows a tax-free sale of stock that is not readily tradable on an established market to an ESOP (as defined in Code §4975(e)(7)) if the ESOP owns at least 30% of the

A number of narrower provisions in the Code can diminish the tax to participants when benefits are received from a qualified plan:

- To determine the tax on lump sum distributions, 10-year forward averaging can apply *as if* an individual had no other income over a 10-year period and received the distribution in 10 equal annual installments. Code Section 402(e).
- The portion of a lump sum distribution attributable to service before 1974 may be taxed at capital gains rates. Code Section 402(a)(2).
- Lump sum distributions of benefits may be rolled over tax-free into an IRA (or into another tax-qualified plan) without regard to the normal limits on contributions to an IRA (or on contributions to a qualified plan). Code Sections 402(a)(5), (6), and (7).
- No gift tax applies to an irrevocable designation of a beneficiary for benefits under a qualified plan. Code Section 2517(a). Until 1985, a $100,000 exclusion from a decedent's gross estate applied to benefits going to a nonspouse.[28] An unlimited exclusion from the gross estate still applies, as it does for all other property, for benefits going to a spouse.[29]

Effective in 1987, the 1986 Tax Reform Act reduces the forward averaging allowed on a lump sum distribution to five-year forward averaging, and repeals capital gains treatment on the portion of a lump sum distribution attributable to pre-1974 service.[30]

---

company's stock after the sale, and the seller reinvests the proceeds within 12 months in stock of another domestic corporation. The 1986 Tax Reform Act also allows an exclusion from the value of a stockholder's gross estate for 50% of the proceeds from the sale of employer securities to an ESOP (as defined in Code §4975(e)(7)) by the estate's executor. Code §2057, as added by §1172 of P.L. 99-514.

A deduction from the taxable income of an employer sponsoring an ESOP applies to dividends paid on stock held by an ESOP which are in turn applied to repay ESOP acquisition loans. A deduction for such dividends is also allowed if they are immediately distributed to participants. Code §404(k)(2), as amended by §1173 of the TRA. The Tax Reform Act continues an exclusion from taxation of 50% of the interest income received by banks and insurance companies on loans made to ESOPs to acquire employer securities, and extends the exclusion to interest on loans to ESOPs made by regulated investment companies. Code §133(a), as amended by §1173 of the TRA. See also Code §4980, as amended by §1132 of the TRA (allowing exception from 10% excise tax on reversions of excess assets to employers upon plan termination for money or stock that is transferred to an ESOP).

[28] Code §2039(c). The $100,000 exclusion was repealed by the Deficit Reduction Act of 1984. The Tax Equity and Fiscal Responsibility Act of 1982 (TEFRA) had limited the exclusion to $100,000. Before then, the estate tax exclusion for benefits provided a nonspouse was unlimited, making this a valuable estate planning device.

[29] Up to $5,000 in death benefits, whether from a qualified plan or from any other type of program maintained by an employer, may also be excluded from a beneficiary's income. However, this does not apply to benefits to which the employee-participant had a nonforfeitable right prior to his or her death, including survivor's benefits provided under a joint and survivor's form of annuity, unless the benefits are distributed in lump sum form within the meaning of Code §402(e)(4). Code §101(b).

[30] §1122 of P.L. 99-514, amending Code §402(e)(4)(B) and repealing Code §402(a)(2). Extensive transition rules are provided for individuals who attained age 50 by Jan. 1, 1987.

The Tax Reform Act also repeals the prior law's 3-year basis recovery rule. This rule allowed employees in contributory plans to treat their initial annuity payments as a return of their already-taxed employee contributions, provided that all employee contributions were recovered within the first 3 years. See §1122 of P.L., 99-514, repealing Code §72(d) and amending §72(b).

Because these tax advantages have a considerable cost to the federal treasury, Section 415 of the Code sets maximum upper limits on the amount of benefits that can be provided to an individual through a qualified plan. The dollar amounts of these limits are generous, however. Under Section 415, the benefits that can be provided from a qualified defined benefit plan are "limited" to $90,000 per year, or 100 percent of an individual's highest three years of compensation if this is less.[31] No adjustment is made in the defined benefit plan limits when benefits begin as early as age 62, or when benefits are provided in a joint and survivor form that continues to pay up to 100 percent of the participant's annuity benefit to a surviving spouse. Effective in 1987, the Tax Reform Act reduces the $90,000 limit if retirement occurs between the retirement age for unreduced Social Security benefits (currently, age 65) and age 62, using the factors used for reducing Social Security benefits. As a result, instead of an unreduced $90,000 limit at age 62, $72,000 is the maximum annual benefit. For retirement prior to 62, the age 62 limit is actuarially reduced.[32]

For defined contribution plans, the maximum Section 415 limit is $30,000 in annual contributions to a plan, or 25 percent of a participant's compensation if this is less.[33] Effective in 1987, elective deferrals

---

Without this provision, each annuity payment from a contributory plan is treated as in part a return of after-tax employee contributions based on the ratio of those contributions to the total expected annuity payments (as determined under IRS life expectancy tables). However, if employee contributions are placed in separate accounts and the plan provides for withdrawal of those contributions first on retirement, similar results to those allowed under the 3-year basis recovery rule can continue to be produced. See IRS Notice 87-13, reprinted in 14 BNA Pens. Rep. 59 (Jan. 12, 1987), at Q&A-14.

[31] A defined benefit plan may, however, provide an annual benefit of $10,000, even if this is more than 100% of an individual's highest 3 years of compensation. Code §415(b)(4). Both the maximum $90,000 limit and this $10,000 limit are prorated if a participant has less than 10 years of service with the employer. Code §415(b)(5).

Effective in 1987, the Tax Reform Act divides the $90,000 limit by years of participation if a participant has less than 10 years of participation under a plan. Code §415(b)(5), as amended by §1106 of P.L. 99-514. The 100% of compensation limit and $10,000 minimum for defined benefit plans continue to be prorated only when a participant's "years of service" with an employer (whether or not under a plan) are less than 10.

The $90,000 individual annual benefits limit for defined benefit plans increases with changes in the Consumer Price Index (CPI) beginning in 1988.

[32] Using a 5% interest assumption and a relatively standard mortality table, the new limit is $39,885 at age 55, in contrast to the old law's $75,000 limit. Benefits accrued before 1987 are, however, grandfathered at the old §415 levels for early retirement. See Code §§415(b)(2)(C), (D), and (b)(8), as amended by §1106 of P.L. 99-514, and Price Waterhouse, "Analysis of Pension and Welfare Benefit Plan Provisions of Tax Reform Act of 1986," 13 BNA Pens. Rep. Spec. Supp., at S-40 (Oct. 27, 1986) (computing the age 55 limit under a 5% interest assumption and the UP-1984 mortality table).

[33] The Tax Reform Act freezes the $30,000 limit on annual contributions to defined contribution plans until the $90,000 limit for annual benefits from defined benefit plans reaches $120,000 under its CPI escalator (assuming 6% annual increases in the CPI, this will not be until 1993). Code §415(c)(1)(A), as amended by §1106 of P.L. 99-514. Beginning in 1987, the Tax Reform Act also counts all employee contributions toward the $30,000 limit, in contrast to the prior law's inclusion of the lesser of (1) total employee contributions in excess of 6% of compensation or (2) one-half of the employee's contributions. Code §415(c)(2)(B), as amended by §1106 of P.L. 99-514.

When ERISA was originally enacted, the §415 limits were $75,000 in annual benefits under a defined benefit plan and $25,000 in annual contributions to a defined contribution plan, but under an annual cost of living escalator, the limits had risen to $136,425 per year in benefits or $45,475 per year in contributions by 1982. The 1982 Tax Equity and Fiscal Responsibility Act lowered the dollar amounts back to $90,000 per year in benefits or $30,000 per year in contributions, and froze

of salary to Code Section 401(k) plans are separately capped at $7,000, in addition to being included under the $30,000 or 25 percent of compensation limits on contributions on a participant's behalf to defined contribution plans.[34] A separate limit on deductible contributions under Code Section 404 limits contributions to profit-sharing or stock bonus plans to 15 percent of the total compensation of covered participants.[35]

When an employer has both a defined benefit and a defined contribution plan, a combined plan rule is used to determine the Section 415 limits.[36] Effective January 1, 1987, the Tax Reform Act places a 15 percent excise tax on distributions to an individual in any year from one or more qualified plans, IRAs, or tax-sheltered annuities exceeding $112,500.[37]

Effective in 1989, the Tax Reform Act also limits the compensation base for computing benefits or contributions under any qualified plan to $200,000 as a condition for qualification, completely apart from whether any employee is a participant in two or more plans.[38]

---

further application of the cost-of-living escalator until Jan. 1, 1986. This freeze was extended until Jan. 1, 1988, under the Deficit Reduction Act of 1984. See Code §415(d)(3), as amended.

[34] Code §402(g), as amended by §1105 of P.L. 99-514. The $7,000 limit increases with increases in the CPI beginning in 1988. Deferrals in excess of this limit are subject to tax as current income of the employee and are subject to certain other restrictions unless refunded by the plan within a statutorily prescribed period.

[35] Code §404(a)(3). The Tax Reform Act disallows carryforwards of unused deductible contribution limits from years in which contributions to a profit-sharing or stock bonus plan were less than 15% of aggregate compensation. Code §404(a)(3)(A), as amended by §1131 of P.L. 99-514. ESOPs are permitted to use a higher deductible contribution limit of 25% of compensation of covered employees. Code §404(a)(9).

[36] Code §415(e)(1) thus provides that "the sum of the defined benefit plan fraction and the defined contribution plan fraction for any year may not exceed 1.0 " for an individual who is a participant in both a defined benefit and a defined contribution plan maintained by the same employer. The defined benefit plan fraction is the projected annual benefit of the participant under the plan (determined as of the close of the plan year) divided by the product of 1.25 times the dollar limitation in effect for such year (or, if less, 1.4 times the 100% of compensation limit). The defined contribution plan fraction is the sum of all the annual additions to the participant's account under the plan for the current and prior years as of the close of the plan year divided by 1.25 times the sum of the defined contribution plan dollar limitations in effect for each year of the participant's service with the employer (or, if less in any year, 1.4 times the 25% of compensation limit).

Code §404(a)(7) can also effectively limit individual benefits or contributions from two or more plans by providing that an employer's total deductible contributions on behalf of all participants in defined benefit and defined contribution plans may not exceed the *greater* of 25% of aggregate compensation or the contributions required by the minimum funding standards if any employee is a participant under both the defined benefit and defined contribution plans.

[37] Code §4981, as added by §1133; and see Conf. Rep., H.R. Rep. 99-841, at II-477-78, [1986] U.S. Code Cong. & Ad. News 4565-66. The dollar amount is adjusted beginning in 1988 for increases in the CPI. Detailed grandfather rules are provided for benefits accrued before Aug. 1, 1986.

If distributions to an individual include, or are comprised of, a lump sum distribution eligible for 5-year forward averaging, the excise tax applies to the lump sum distribution only to the extent it is in excess of five times the $112,500 limit. Code §4981(c)(4). A separate excess distribution limit applies to distributions to a beneficiary after a participant's death, with the tax on any excess amount being added to the federal estate tax. Code §4981(d).

[38] Code §401(a)(17), as added by §1106(d)(1) of P.L. 99-514. In computing deductible contributions, the Tax Reform Act simultaneously limits includible compensation for any participant to $200,000. Code §404(l), as added by §1106(d)(2) of P.L. 99-514.

III. The Code's Additional Qualification Requirements

To obtain a comprehensive picture of the legal regulation of pension plan benefits, the tax-qualification requirements in the Internal Revenue Code must still be read in conjunction with the ERISA minimum standards. Since ERISA's coverage is not limited to tax-qualified plans, a few plans are subject to ERISA's standards but not to the Code's qualification requirements. However, for virtually all participants, both the ERISA standards and the tax-qualification requirements apply. This synchronization, or overlap, was recognized by Congress in its debates, and in the findings and policy of ERISA. For example, Representative Martha Griffiths stated:

> "The real effort in this bill [ERISA] is to see to it that the money that has been set aside from the tax stream is used so that the people who are supposed to get pensions really do get them."[39]

Similarly, the findings on which ERISA is based state:

> "The Congress finds . . . that [employee benefit plans] substantially affect the revenues of the United States because they are afforded preferential Federal tax treatment . . . ."[40]

ERISA Section 2(c) then states the policy of ERISA as:

> "[T]o protect . . . the Federal taxing power, and the interests of participants in private pension plans . . . by improving the equitable character and the soundness of such plans . . . ."

More important for purposes of this discussion, Congress, in largely *implicit* recognition of the Code's requirements for tax-qualified status, created in the labor title of ERISA an Act that leaves the regulation of pension plans incomplete *unless* the Code's qualification requirements are considered. Two crucial issues—the extent of a plan's *coverage* and the plan's *benefit formula*—are not addressed by ERISA's Title I minimum standards, but are addressed in the Code.

First, although ERISA sets minimum standards on the age and service that may be required by a plan as a condition of beginning participation in benefit accruals, it does not address the threshold question of how many employees, apart from those requirements, must be covered by a plan. Thus, ERISA does not address whether a company with two divisions can cover only the employees in one division.[41] The Code, on the other hand, addresses this question, although its focus is limited to ensuring that the plan's coverage does not discriminate in favor of employees who are officers, shareholders, or highly compensated employees. It does not necessarily require that the employees in both divisions be covered.

---

[39] 3 ERISA Leg. Hist. 3552. And see 3 ERISA Leg. Hist. 4784 (statement of Sen. Carl Curtis) ("without the tax provisions, they [private pension plans] would all fall").

[40] ERISA §2(a).

[41] See, e.g., 26 C.F.R. 1.410(a)-3(d).

Second, a plan's benefit formula is not addressed under ERISA's minimum standards. This is a somewhat tricky distinction because ERISA contains minimum standards on how a defined benefit plan's benefits must "accrue" for years of participation in a plan. But as the Supreme Court stated in *Alessi v. Raybestos-Manhattan, Inc.*, ERISA does not regulate the plan's initial "method for calculating" the benefits which are required to "accrue" under ERISA's minimum standards.[42] The Code's qualification requirements, on the other hand, address the plan's benefit formula by requiring that it not "discriminate" in favor of employees who are "officers, shareholders, or highly compensated."[43] Benefits as determined under a "nondiscriminatory" formula must then "accrue" according to the ERISA accrual standards, and "vest" according to the ERISA vesting standards. As discussed in Chapters 3 and 4, the accrual rules can have a reverse, indirect impact on what types of benefit formulas are acceptable, but ERISA does not directly regulate the benefit formula itself.

Additional tax-qualification requirements that are not found in the Title I labor provisions of ERISA require vesting of benefits to the extent funded on the termination or partial termination of a plan, and provide special vesting standards and benefit formula rules for "top-heavy" plans, Code Section 401(k) plans, Employee Stock Ownership Plans (ESOPs), and plans under which there is a tendency for discrimination in favor of highly compensated employees. This is not an all-inclusive list, but they are the major Code provisions that can benefit rank and file participants that are not contained in ERISA Title I.

An important distinction between the Code's tax-qualification requirements and the ERISA minimum standards is in enforcement. Plan participants and other employees can directly enforce ERISA Title I requirements in federal court. On the other hand, plan participants have no direct private cause of action to enforce the Code's requirements. Instead, they must generally depend on the IRS for enforcement. Participants and other employees can, however, call violations of the qualification requirements to the attention of the IRS. Participants can also obtain Tax Court review of certain adverse IRS determinations if they file comments contesting a plan's compliance with the Code's requirements at the time a sponsoring employer submits an application for a favorable determination of the plan's qualified status to the IRS. Typically, such applications are filed when an employer establishes, amends, or terminates a plan. A favorable determination letter from the IRS assures the employer that the plan is qualified under current law and will not be retroactively disqualified, unless the plan is found to have been discriminatory in operation.[44]

---

[42] 451 U.S. 504, 2 EBC 1297, at 1300 (1981).

[43] Code §401(a)(4).

[44] Even if a favorable determination letter has been previously issued, it may be revoked prospectively if it was issued erroneously or if the law or the regulations have changed.

Plan participants can also enforce many tax-qualification requirements by enforcing terms of the plan that incorporate the language used in the Code. For example, Code Section 411(d)(3) requires that every tax-qualified plan contain a plan provision providing that benefits will become nonforfeitable on the termination or partial termination of the plan. With such a plan provision, a participant can enforce the Code requirement in state or federal court under the ERISA Section 502(a)(1)(B) cause of action "to enforce his rights under the terms of the plan." In other instances, Code requirements may be enforced by interpreting specific plan provisions, such as on coverage, in light of general plan provisions stating the employer's intention that all plan provisions be interpreted so that the plan will be tax-qualified.

References to the Code's "qualification" requirements can be misleading if they connote initial, one-time satisfaction. The Code's qualification requirements, like the ERISA minimum standards, are continuing requirements. For example, a tax-qualified plan must satisfy the Code's requirements for coverage initially, and then also on at least one day in each quarter of each calendar year.[45] Similarly, the Code's qualification requirement that a plan not "discriminate" in contributions or benefits in favor of officers, shareholders, or other highly compensated employees is an initial and continuing requirement.[46]

IV. Higher Contractual and Other Federal Law Standards

The relationship of both ERISA's minimum standards and the Code's qualification requirements to higher contractual standards and other federal law may also need preliminary explanation. The Code's qualification requirements and ERISA's standards establish *minimum* requirements, much like the federal minimum wage and hour laws, except that the Code and ERISA do not generally set minimum dollar amounts of benefits. Like the minimum wage and hour laws, however, they do not rule out higher standards, or generally indicate whether higher conduct is required under other federal statutory law, under a contract, e.g., a collective bargaining agreement, or under quasi-contractual obligations. Thus, when ERISA establishes a minimum standard or the Code establishes a qualification requirement, it does not mean that every, or in some cases, very many, plans precisely parallel the minimum standard or qualification requirement.

Doing more than the minimum standard or qualification requirement is permissible and may be required under a general common law rule or other federal statutory law. ERISA often permits a plan to use an exception, for example, to disregard years of service for vesting *if* the years of service occurred before the employer established the plan.

---

[45] Code §401(a)(6).

[46] 26 C.F.R. 1.401-1(b)(3).

However, if a plan provides that *all* years of service with the employer will count for vesting, it cannot fall back on the permissible exception later simply because ERISA would have permitted it had the plan originally provided for it.

Even when more than a minimum standard or qualification requirement is not required by another legal or contractual rule, many employers still provide more to maintain good personnel relations, for administrative convenience, or to make a plan more understandable to employees and administrative personnel than if the limits of some of the more complex ERISA or Code rules were used.

V. Classifications of Plans

ERISA Section 3(2)(A) defines the term pension plan to mean "*any* plan, fund or program . . . established or maintained by an employer or by an employer organization, or by both," which

> "(i) provides retirement income to employees, or
>
> "(ii) results in a deferral of income by employees for periods extending to the termination of employment or beyond, *regardless* of the method of calculating the contributions made to the plan, the method of calculating the benefits under the plan, or the method of distributing benefits from the plan."[47]

This broad definition encompasses defined benefit and defined contribution plans and what the Internal Revenue Code alternatively classifies as pension plans (which include all defined benefit plans and one type of defined contribution plan), and what the Code terms profit-sharing or stock bonus plans. Also encompassed within this overall definition are plans generally known by more specific names, such as Code Section 401(k) cash or deferred arrangements (also known as salary reduction plans), which are a type of profit-sharing plan, and ESOPs, which are generally a type of stock bonus plan.[48]

A. Defined Benefit and Defined Contribution Plans

1. Functional Differences

a. The benefit or contribution promise. The major functional distinction between pension plans is between defined benefit and defined contribution plans. A defined benefit plan is the type of plan most people think about when they think of a pension plan. A defined

---

[47] Emphasis added.

[48] Certain types of severance pay and supplemental retirement income plans which might otherwise be considered "pension plans" under the ERISA definition are specifically excepted. See ERISA §3(2)(B) and 29 C.F.R. 2510.3-2(b), (e) and (g). As a result, they are regulated under ERISA only as welfare plans.

benefit plan promises a participant a specific amount of pension benefits at retirement determined under a formula based on years of participation in the plan, and in most nonbargained plans, based on an average of compensation. For example, a defined benefit plan may promise a benefit at retirement of one percent of a final, or highest, five-year average of salary multiplied by years of participation in the plan. This is known as a final or highest average pay formula. Alternatively, a defined benefit plan may promise a percentage of each year's compensation, such as 1½ percent, for each year of participation in the plan. This is called a career average formula because the resulting pension benefit is the same as if the career average of compensation during all years of participation in the plan was multiplied by the same percentage and the total years of participation. If a defined benefit plan is collectively bargained, it often simply promises a dollar amount per month at retirement, such as $20 per month, multiplied by each year of participation in the plan. This is a flat dollar formula.

There are variations on all of these formulas. In particular, some defined benefit plans:

- Offset a percentage of the participant's Social Security primary insurance amount or use a formula which provides a lower percentage benefit on compensation below a figure related to an average of the Social Security wage base;
- Contain alternative formulas for computing benefits, with one formula, usually on a flat dollar basis, functioning as a minimum benefit; or
- Use a flat overall percentage or dollar benefit at retirement, such as 30 percent of a final five-year average of compensation or $600 per month, and then accrue these benefits before retirement on a basis which may vary from the uniform year-by-year rates described above.

Whichever type or combination of formulas is used, the point remains the same: a defined benefit plan promises defined benefits at retirement.

Defined contribution plans, on the other hand, promise that an employer will contribute to the plan on a specified basis, but do not promise that the contributions will produce specific benefits at retirement. Instead, the benefits available at retirement are the accumulation of contributions made to the plan and allocated to the individual's account, plus earnings and appreciation, and less losses and administrative costs (if administrative costs are not paid by the employer).[49] A share of the plan's earnings must be allocated to the participant's

[49] See ch. 4, sec. II.A, on the "accrued benefit" under a defined contribution plan. If a money purchase pension plan so provides, forfeitures can be reallocated to other participants' accounts in plan years beginning after Dec. 31, 1985. Code §401(a)(8), as amended by §1119 of the Tax Reform Act, P.L. 99-514.

account until the account balance is distributed even when new contribution allocations to the account have stopped.

As an example, a savings (or thrift) plan might promise that a sponsoring employer will contribute up to three percent of each participant's salary if the participant makes a matching contribution. Benefits at retirement depend on how much those contributions amount to in dollars and how much is earned on the contributions before the participant's retirement. In a money purchase pension plan without matching employee contributions, the employer might simply contribute six percent of the employee's salary annually. Benefits at retirement again depend on how much those contributions amount to and the plan's investment earnings before the participant's retirement.

Profit-sharing plans are also a type of defined contribution plan. However, in a profit-sharing plan, the sponsoring employer's promise to contribute to the plan is conditioned on the existence and extent of profits.[50] For example, the employer may promise to contribute a specified percentage of profits, e.g., 10 percent, with the contributions required under that formula then being allocated to each participant's account, usually on the basis of compensation. Since contributions are dependent on profits, the employer may in some years make *no* contributions to the plan, and in other years, 10 percent of profits may be very little. The promise contained in a profit-sharing plan can be still less definite. A profit-sharing plan can define profits and the basis on which contributions will be allocated among participants' accounts when contributions are made, but then leave the percentage of profits to be contributed, or whether *any* percentage of profits will be contributed, to the discretion of the employer. In the 1970's organizing drive at J. P. Stevens' textile mills, one of the employees' major complaints was that under a discretionary formula J. P. Stevens was making no contributions to the profit-sharing plan even in years in which it had profits.[51] Another distinctive feature of profit-sharing plans is that they are permitted to reallocate account balances of participants who separate from service before vesting to the accounts of the participants still in the plan, usually with the forfeited accounts reallocated on the same basis as new contributions.[52] Benefits at retirement are then based on contributions, plus reallocated accounts, plus earnings.

A stock bonus plan is another type of defined contribution plan. In a stock bonus plan, the employer's contributions to the plan are typically in the form of stock in the sponsoring employer (or they can be in cash with which to purchase company stock). The stock contributions

---

[50] Effective in plan years beginning after Dec. 31, 1985, contributions to profit-sharing plans need not be restricted to current or accumulated profits. Code §401(a)(27), as added by §1136 of the Tax Reform Act, P.L. 99-514.

[51] See M. Conway, *Rise Gonna Rise* (Anchor Press 1979), at 5 and 22. Consequences of not making recurring and substantial contributions are summarized in ch. 3, sec. III.

[52] If a money purchase pension plan so provides, forfeitures can be reallocated to other participants' accounts in plan years beginning after Dec. 31, 1985. Code §401(a)(8), as amended by §1119 of the Tax Reform Act, P.L. 99-514.

may be made dependent on profits, as in a profit-sharing plan, or they may be independent of profits.[53]

At retirement, the stock in the participant's account is distributed, generally with an option for repurchase of the stock by the employer if the stock is not widely traded. The benefits a stock bonus plan yields are again not specified, but are a function of the amount of stock contributed to the participant's account, reallocated forfeitures from other participants' accounts (if the plan provides for them), and dividends and appreciation prior to retirement or withdrawal.

b. Past service credits. In addition to the specification of benefits at retirement, defined benefits are distinguished from defined contribution plans in that defined benefit plans often provide "past service" credits for years of service before the plan was established (or if the plan is a multiemployer plan, for years of service with an employer before the employer signed an agreement to contribute to the plan). Past service credits are advantageous for older workers who would otherwise not receive substantial retirement benefits under a benefit formula, such as one that offers one percent of a final average of pay for each year of participation under the plan. But past service can be a mixed blessing for other employees: The past service credits provided older workers must, of course, be paid for, and in many small nonbargained plans, past service is a device for discrimination in favor of highly compensated employees who have more years of past service than rank and file employees. The basic point here, however, is that past service credits are a feature of many defined benefit plans that is rarely found in defined contribution plans—in part because the potential for discrimination in operation is more closely examined by the IRS when contribution allocations are based on or weighted by years of service instead of being allocated on the basis of current compensation.[54]

c. Arrays of benefits. A defined benefit plan, at least of the kind commonly adopted by medium and large-sized employers, is also likely to contain a wider array of benefits than found in a defined contribution plan. It may thus contain special benefit provisions for disabled participants and early retirement benefits that are either unreduced from the benefits available at normal retirement or that are only slightly reduced. In the Bureau of Labor Statistics' 1982 survey of defined benefit plans of medium and large firms, 89 percent of all defined benefit plan participants were in plans with disability provisions that entitled a disabled participant to begin receiving his or her normal retirement benefits immediately, usually with no reduction for early retirement, or to continue receiving credit toward benefits at early or normal retirement during the period of disability (with immediate disability income provided through insurance offered outside the

---

[53] See 26 C.F.R. 1.401-1(b)(iii).

[54] See, e.g., Rev. Rul. 84-155.

pension plan).[55] Similarly, in the BLS's survey, 53 percent of all defined benefit plan participants were in plans where it was possible to retire before age 65 without an actuarial reduction in benefits.[56] A significant number of other participants are in defined benefit plans where early retirement benefits are only partially reduced.[57] Some defined benefit plans also contain joint and survivor's benefit options that are "subsidized" in the sense that benefits in a joint and survivor's form are worth more than the actuarial equivalent of the participant's benefits on a single-life basis. Defined benefit plans also sometimes contain preretirement lump sum death benefits that are only partially based on the participant's accrued benefits, and occasionally contain special health benefits for retirees.[58] In short, a defined benefit plan is often a complicated contract that provides benefits on different contingencies and under different options that are not always actuarially equivalent to each other.

Defined contribution plans, on the other hand, often provide for withdrawals of a participant's account balance at early retirement or on disability and some vest otherwise nonvested account balances on disability. But in each instance, the amount payable is the participant's individual account balance, without special adjustment or subsidy. Some defined contribution plans also provide for withdrawals from an account balance for hardship, and in many profit-sharing and stock bonus plans, for withdrawals from the individual's account for *any* reason after a very short number of years of participation. When death occurs before a participant's retirement or withdrawal of funds, defined contribution plans generally provide that the participant's account balance goes to his or her survivor, but again with no special subsidy. Some defined contribution plans do, however, permit a participant to use part of his or her account balance for the purchase of life, accident, and health insurance, which is held by the plan for the participant's benefit.[59]

d. Funding. The manner in which obligations are funded also distinguishes defined benefit plans from defined contribution plans. In a defined contribution plan, the employer completely "funds" each year's obligation by making contributions on the promised basis. Once the employer makes the contribution, its contribution obligation for

---

[55] BLS, Employee Benefits in Medium and Large Firms, 1984, at 14 and 52.

[56] *Id.*, at 50. In some cases, a supplement is added to early retirement benefits until the participant reaches the age when he or she becomes eligible to draw Social Security benefits.

[57] *Id.*, at 52.

[58] The inclusion of disability, death, and health benefits (for retirees) is specifically approved by IRS regulations. 26 C.F.R. 1.401-1(b)(i). Death benefits must remain "incidental" to the plan's retirement income purpose, as defined in IRS rulings. See generally Rev. Rul. 85-15.

[59] Life, accident, and health insurance is specifically permitted to be offered under profit-sharing and stock bonus plans, but with the limit again that such benefits must be "incidental," as spelled out in Revenue Rulings. 26 C.F.R. 1.401-1(b)(ii) and (iii). And see Rev. Ruls. 60-83, 66-143, and 85-15.

that year is at an end. The responsibility is the plan trustee's to manage the money, or stock, wisely and pay it out as provided under the terms of the plan.

The funding of defined benefits, on the other hand, is not as simple or so easily concluded. When an employer promises a benefit of 1½ percent of final average pay for each year of participation to a participant who is 20, 30, or more years away from retirement, the present cost of that future obligation can only be estimated. Under ERISA, the employer must fund what it estimates to be the present value of the future benefit obligations arising from each year's service. If experience proves that this cost estimate was too low—which usually occurs because the plan does not earn as much on its investments as estimated—the employer must amortize this "experience loss" over a fixed number of years. In addition, if the plan provides past service credits and thus has benefit liabilities from service before the plan's establishment, or if the employer increases the plan's benefits for years of service already rendered and thus creates a different type of past service liability, those liabilities, too, can be amortized. The result for the employer is that it may have continuing contribution obligations from past years' benefit promises. For participants, the result is that a defined benefit plan is often not fully funded should the plan be terminated (or partially terminated) at any point in time.

It is important to recognize that the distinctions between defined benefit and defined contribution plans frequently do not lead to an either/or choice for participants. Many employers, particularly medium and large-sized employers, offer both defined benefit and defined contribution plans to their employees. Thus, a large corporation may have a defined benefit plan based on a final or highest average of salary, a savings or salary reduction plan, and a profit-sharing plan. Usually participation in the defined benefit and profit-sharing plans is automatic, and the employee's only choice is the extent of his or her participation in the savings or salary reduction plan.

2. Differences Under ERISA

When ERISA draws distinctions between pension plans, the chief distinction it draws is between "defined benefit" plans[60] and "individual account" plans.[61] "Individual account" plans are commonly called defined contribution plans, and are referred to as such here. The rules under ERISA for defined benefit and defined contribution plans are different in a number of respects. First, ERISA's minimum standards for benefit accruals, vesting, breaks in service, and survivor's benefits apply to both types of pension plans, but all have special rules for defined contribution plans. Second, ERISA's funding requirements apply to defined benefit plans, but generally do not apply to, or have no

---

[60] ERISA §3(35) (Code §414(j)).

[61] ERISA §3(34) (Code §414(i)).

significance for, defined contribution plans.[62] Third, the PBGC's program of pension insurance does not cover defined contribution plans.

B. Pension Plans and Profit-Sharing/Stock Bonus Plans

Rather than using the defined benefit/defined contribution distinction throughout, the Internal Revenue Code sorts plans into "pension" plans on the one hand, and "profit-sharing" or "stock bonus" plans on the other, for purposes of certain tax-qualification requirements. Where the Code requirements parallel the minimum standards in ERISA, the same defined benefit/defined contribution plan distinction is used. Under the Code, "pension plans" include defined benefit plans and also "money purchase" pension plans. A money purchase pension plan is a defined contribution plan in which the employer's annual contribution obligation is in no manner dependent on profits.

The classification of a plan under the Code as a pension plan or as a profit-sharing/stock bonus plan has three major consequences:

- A pension plan must provide definitely determinable benefits. For a money purchase pension plan, this means definitely determinable contributions that are not dependent on profits. A profit-sharing plan, on the other hand, may make contributions dependent on profits. As described before, a profit-sharing plan can also define profits and specify the basis on which contributions will be allocated among participants when contributions are made, but leave the percentage of profits to be contributed, or whether any percentage of profits will be contributed, to the discretion of the employer.[63] Contributions to a stock bonus plan may or may not be dependent on profits.[64] Effective in plan years beginning after December 31, 1985, contributions to profit-sharing plans also need not be restricted to current or accumulated profits.[65]
- Under a pension plan, forfeitures are used to reduce future employer contributions to the plan. Generally, in a defined benefit plan, the employer's contributions are based on estimates of the

[62] Technically, the funding requirements apply to money purchase plans, which are defined contribution plans under which employer contributions are not dependent on profits. However, the application of the funding requirements to money purchase plans has only slight significance—whereas it is very significant for defined benefit plans.

[63] Consequences of not making recurring and substantial contributions are summarized in ch. 3, sec. III.

[64] 26 C.F.R. 1.401-1(b)(1)(iii).

[65] Code §401(a)(27), as added by §1136 of the Tax Reform Act, P.L. 99-514. The distinction between pension plans and profit-sharing plans was never as sharp as it sounded. Savings or thrift plans could be qualified as either money purchase pension plans or profit-sharing plans depending on their drafting. The requirement that profit-sharing contributions must come out of profits could be designed around, if desired, by providing that contributions would be from accumulated profits. See Rev. Rul. 66-174 (contributions may be from accumulated profits). The "great majority" of savings or thrift plans were, in fact, qualified as profit-sharing plans, presumably because of the greater flexibility this permits in withdrawals of employer contributions. D. McGill, with D. Grubbs, Jr., *Fundamentals of Private Pensions* (Richard D. Irwin 5th ed.), at 644.

forfeitures that will occur, so that, in a sense, the employer's contributions are reduced by expected forfeitures at the start. Under the 1986 Tax Reform Act, a money purchase pension plan, although classified as a pension plan under the Code, is permitted to reallocate forfeitures to other participants' accounts in plan years beginning after December 31, 1985.[66] Profit-sharing or stock bonus plans have always been permitted to reallocate forfeitures to other participants' accounts (or to use the forfeitures to reduce the employer's future contributions to the plan).[67]

- Under a pension plan, benefits attributable to employer contributions can only commence on the participant's separation from service, disability, death, or retirement.[68] Under a profit-sharing or stock bonus plan, employer contributions, plus earnings, may be distributed on all these occasions, and also after a fixed number of years of participation.[69] Under Revenue Ruling 71-295, profit-sharing contributions, plus related earnings, may be distributed two years after the contribution is made. All contributions, including those made within two years, can be withdrawn once a participant has five years of participation if the plan so provides.[70] However, if a profit-sharing or stock bonus plan is "integrated" with Social Security by providing higher percentage contributions on compensation in excess of a certain level, the plan may only provide benefits on the same occasions as a pension plan.[71] A 10 percent tax on "early" withdrawals from all plans, including profit-sharing and stock bonus plans, enacted under the 1986 Tax Reform Act further counteracts this distinction for plan years beginning in 1987.[72]

1. Code Section 401(k) Plans

Code Section 401(k) plans are qualified under the Code as profit-sharing or stock bonus plans, but they must comply with special rules. In a Section 401(k) plan, participants specify whether they will take a percentage of their salary in cash or whether they will defer it as a contribution to the plan. While technically forfeitures might be reallocated to other participant accounts (because a Section 401(k) plan is a

---

[66] Code §401(a)(8), as amended by §1119 of the Tax Reform Act, P.L. 99-514. Forfeitures can also continue to be used to reduce future employer contributions to the money purchase plan, as under prior law.

[67] 26 C.F.R. 1.401-1(b)(1) and 1.401-7.

[68] 26 C.F.R. 1.401-1(b)(1)(i). Plan termination may also be a permissible circumstance for distribution of benefits from a pension plan. See Conf. Rep. on the 1986 Tax Reform Act, H.R. Rep. 99-841, at II-452, [1986] U.S. Code Cong. & Ad. News 4540, and compare PLR 8536042 (June 11, 1985), reprinted in CCH Pension Plan Guide, at ¶17,377C-3 (same does not apply to profit-sharing and stock bonus plans, except where specially provided).

[69] 26 C.F.R. 1.401-1(b)(1)(ii).

[70] Rev. Rul. 68-24.

[71] Rev. Rul. 71-446, sec. 15.03.

[72] See ch. 6, sec. I.B.

profit-sharing plan), no forfeitures will generally exist to be reallocated since Code Section 401(k)(2)(C) requires all contributions to be nonforfeitable when made.[73] Section 401(k) plans are also required to adhere to slightly more restrictive rules on withdrawals than profit-sharing plans generally, with withdrawals permitted only on a separation from service, disability, death, retirement, or plan termination (as under a pension plan), *or* at any time after age 59½, after certain earlier asset or stock sales, or on an earlier finding of "hardship."[74]

2. ESOPs

An Employee Stock Ownership Plan (ESOP) is generally qualified as a stock bonus plan. Any stock bonus plan could be called an ESOP, but the term is usually reserved for leveraged plans, i.e., plans that have acquired a block of employer stock through a loan from a bank or other lender that is repaid basically by passing employer contributions to the plan through to the bank or other lender. Even if the ESOP could as a stock bonus plan provide that employer contributions are dependent on the existence of profits, the bank or other lender will in all likelihood require repayment of the loan proceeds used to acquire the stock on a regular payment schedule. Special rules for leveraged ESOPs to safeguard against overappraisal of the value of employer stock and to provide participants with repurchase options when the participant retires or separates from service and the stock is not widely traded are contained in Internal Revenue Code and Department of Labor regulations.[75] The rules on the reallocation of forfeitures to other participants' accounts and on the withdrawal of funds from participant accounts follow those for stock bonus plans if the ESOP is qualified as such.

A tax credit ESOP is a special, limited type of ESOP that may be established as a stock bonus plan or as a combination stock bonus and money purchase pension plan. However, the tax credits on contributions to tax credit ESOPs were repealed effective at the end of 1986.[76] Code Section 41 had previously provided a dollar-for-dollar tax credit on contributions of employer stock to a tax credit ESOP up to a limit of .5 percent of compensation of plan participants. To obtain this tax credit, the ESOP had to adhere to special rules contained in Code Section 409 in addition to complying with the normal tax-qualification

---

[73] Code §401(k)(2)(C). Nonelective employer contributions to a Code §401(k) plan can be subject to the normal ERISA and Code standards on vesting, *but only* if the contributions are not needed to meet a special §401(k) nondiscrimination test which compares elective contributions (i.e., deferrals of salary) by highly compensated employees with those of all other eligible employees. See ch. 5, sec. II.E.

[74] Code §401(k)(2)(B). And see ch. 6, sec. I.B, for §401(k) withdrawal rule changes effected by the 1986 Tax Reform Act.

[75] See 26 C.F.R. 54.4975-7 and -11 and 29 C.F.R. 2550.407d-6 and 2520.408b-3. And see ch. 6, secs. I.A and B for withdrawal rule changes effected by the 1986 Tax Reform Act for stock bonus plans, including ESOPs. Additional tax advantages for ESOPs are summarized in sec. II above.

[76] §1171(a) of the Tax Reform Act, P.L. 99-514, repealing Code §41.

requirements. The special Section 409 rules require immediate vesting of all benefits derived from employer contributions and also restrict withdrawals from the plan to eight years after contributions are made, except in the event of an earlier death, disability, separation from service, retirement, certain earlier asset or stock sales affecting the sponsoring employer, or plan termination.[77]

C. Noncontributory and Contributory Plans

The distinction between defined benefit and defined contribution plans is sometimes confused with whether a plan requires employee contributions. A plan that requires employee contributions is a contributory plan and one that does not is a noncontributory plan. Part of the confusion with the defined benefit/defined contribution classification stems from the fact that most defined benefit plans do not require employee contributions, and are thus noncontributory plans, whereas many defined contribution plans, primarily savings (or thrift) plans, require employee contributions, and are thus contributory.

A further source of confusion about employee contributions lies in the distinction under ERISA and in the Code between "mandatory" and "voluntary" employee contributions. A mandatory employee contribution under ERISA and the Code is a contribution that is required either: (1) as a condition of employment, (2) as a condition of participation in the plan, or (3) as a condition of obtaining employer contributions, or benefits attributable to employer contributions.[78]

Voluntary employee contributions must be purely voluntary. That is, no club in the form of loss of employment or participation in the plan, or even the loss of matching employer contributions, can be wielded if the employee does not make contributions. While the employee contributions will be from after-tax income, as with any mandatory employee contributions, the incentive for making voluntary employee contributions is that the earnings on those contributions are tax exempt until received. In addition, saving through payroll deduction may be more convenient than saving outside a plan. Voluntary employee contributions are rarely allowed in defined benefit plans, but are frequently permitted in savings and other individual account plans on top of any mandatory employee contributions.[79]

Under a Code Section 401(k) salary reduction plan, participants elect to reduce their salaries in order to make contributions to a plan. Such contributions are not considered employee contributions under

[77] Code §§409(c) and (d).

[78] ERISA §204(c)(2)(C) (Code §411(c)(2)(C)) and 26 C.F.R. 1.411(c)-1(c)(4).

[79] Certain voluntary employee contributions (VDECs or QVECs) can be deducted from personal income up to the IRA limits with a commensurate reduction in the amount that can be contributed to an IRA. See Code §219. However, effective for taxable years beginning in 1987, this deduction is repealed by the Tax Reform Act in accordance with the Act's simultaneous restriction of deductible IRA contributions by active participants in qualified plans. §1101(b) of P.L. 99-514, repealing and then redesignating other material as Code §219(e)(2).

the Code or ERISA, nor are they considered employee contributions for purposes of federal income taxation (although they are taxed as a part of the employee's wage base for FICA and FUTA).

D. Single-Employer and Multiemployer Plans

A single-employer plan is a plan sponsored by one employer (or by one "controlled group" of employers).[80] The term single-employer plan encompasses both defined benefit and defined contribution plans, but the term is usually reserved for defined benefit plans. This is because the major consequence under ERISA of whether a plan is a single-employer or a multiemployer plan is in the PBGC's insurance program—which only applies to defined benefit plans.

Multiemployer plans are plans to which more than one employer contributes pursuant to collective bargaining agreements.[81] Perhaps the best-known examples of multiemployer plans are the United Mine Workers' Health and Retirement Fund and the Teamsters' Central States, Southeast and Southwest Areas Pension Fund. Multiemployer pension plans are also common in unionized sectors of the building and construction trades, the garment industry, the printing and publishing trades, the lumber industry, the maritime industry, the entertainment trades, the retail and food industries, and the hotel and restaurant industries.

Multiemployer plans have four primary characteristics that distinguish them from single-employer plans. The first is that the union is involved both in the administration of the plan and the investment of its assets by appointment of half of the plan trustees. Whenever an employee benefit plan has union-appointed trustees, Section 302(c)(5) of the Labor Management Relations Act of 1947 (the Taft-Hartley Act) requires, primarily as an anticorruption measure, that at least an equal number of the trustees be appointed by management.[82] In contrast, in collectively bargained single-employer plans, such as the plan the United Auto Workers negotiates with General Motors, the union negotiates the levels of the plan's benefits and all other benefit terms, but generally does not negotiate for the appointment of any of the trustees who administer the plan and invest its assets.[83]

---

[80] ERISA §210(c) (Code §414(b)).

[81] ERISA §3(37) and Code §414(f). The definition of multiemployer plan was amended by the Multiemployer Pension Plan Amendments Act in 1980. Previously, when one employer contributed over 50% of the plan's contributions, the plan was *not* considered a multiemployer plan even if it otherwise fit the definition. Such a plan is now a multiemployer plan unless a one-time election to maintain the plan's previous status was made. ERISA §3(37)(E) (Code §414(f)(5)), as amended.

[82] 29 U.S.C. §186(c)(5).

[83] Although rare in practice, it is permissible for a union to appoint up to half of the trustees to administer a single-employer plan. See *UAW v. Greyhound Lines, Inc.*, 701 F.2d 1181, 4 EBC 1105 (6th Cir. 1983), for an example of a jointly administered single-employer plan. When the union appoints plan trustees, the plan must have an equal number of management-appointed trustees and it is also subject to the "sole and exclusive" benefit requirement of §302(c)(5) of the Labor Management Relations Act.

A second characteristic of multiemployer plans is that the plan's trustees, rather than collective bargaining representatives, generally establish the levels of the plan's benefits and the terms for benefit eligibility. Collective bargaining establishes the contributions that employers will make, but the trustees generally set the terms and conditions for benefits under the plan according to estimates of what those contributions can support. In a collectively bargained single-employer plan, by contrast, collective bargaining focuses on the benefits to be provided under the plan. The collective bargaining agreement for a single-employer plan will rarely specify a contribution rate, although it may establish a funding standard, such as that past service liabilities must be amortized within 25 years.

A third characteristic of multiemployer plans is that they offer at least a limited degree of portability in the sense that a participant's service with different employers can be pieced together under one plan in determining the amount of the participant's benefits and whether the participant is vested. A construction carpenter, for example, might work for a large number of employers on a project-by-project basis during his career, but if each employer has an agreement to contribute to the same multiemployer plan, the carpenter's service will be treated as if it were with one employer. Reciprocity agreements may also apply to service under different multiemployer plans outside the geographic area covered by a participant's original plan if the plans are associated with the same international union. It is estimated that 80 to 90 percent of multiemployer plans are parties to reciprocity agreements.[84] Reciprocity agreements are usually either: (1) a "money transfer" agreement under which credit for service under another multiemployer plan is returned to a "home" plan, along with an agreed amount of contributions,[85] or (2) a "*pro rata*" agreement under which a combined pension is determined according to the participant's years under the benefit formula of each plan, with each plan bearing its share of the costs of the benefits due to service under its formula.[86] Reciprocity agreements between different single-employer plans are, in contrast, practically nonexistent.

A fourth characteristic of multiemployer plans is that they generally have a degree of financial stability or durability that is not quite as common among single-employer plans, particularly those sponsored by small employers. Since a multiemployer plan's funding is not tied to the fortunes of one employer, and the plan may, moreover, take in new employers as some of its old contributors go out of business, a multiemployer plan generally has a broader, more durable contribution base, and thus a longer period of expected existence than a single-

---

[84] See D. McGinn, *Joint Trust Pension Plans* (Richard D. Irwin 1978), at 142.

[85] D. McGinn, *supra*, at 140. And see *Nichols v. Trustees of Asbestos Workers Pension Plan*, 3 EBC 1726 (D.D.C. 1982).

[86] D. McGinn, *supra*, at 137–40. And see *Bianco v. Teamsters Local 816 Pension Trust*, 494 F.Supp. 206 (E.D.N.Y. 1980); *Hoover v. Cumberland, Md. Area Teamsters Pension Fund*, 756 F.2d 977, 6 EBC 1401 (3d Cir. 1985), *cert. denied*, 474 U.S. 845 (1985).

employer plan. When ERISA was enacted, Congress' view was, in fact, that multiemployer plans were virtually indestructible. This view was revised in the late 1970's as it became apparent that some multiemployer plans were in serious financial difficulty because of industry-wide downturns and the decline of unions within some industries. The result was withdrawal liability whenever an employer withdraws from a multiemployer plan and the special reorganization and insolvency rules and insurance limits for multiemployer plans, all of which were enacted under the Multiemployer Pension Plan Amendments Act of 1980. With the exception of withdrawal liability, these rules are discussed in Chapter 13.

Plans to which more than one employer contributes are termed *multiple*-employer plans, whether the plan was or was not established pursuant to collective bargaining.[87] Collectively bargained multiemployer plans are thus one subset of multiple-employer plans. But they are a subset that nearly occupies the whole. Nonbargained multiple-employer plans are not common, but they may be found among employer groups with strong associational ties, such as religious, charitable, and educational organizations, and to a lesser extent among banks.[88] Nonbargained multiple-employer plans may also be found among some employers that have a degree of common ownership, but not the extent required to be a "controlled group" under ERISA. The largest and best-known example of a nonbargained multiple-employer plan is the Teachers Insurance and Annuity Association and College Retirement Equities Fund (TIAA-CREF) which covers more than 800,000 staff members of over 3,500 colleges, universities, independent schools, libraries, and nonprofit research and educational institutions across the country. As in multiemployer plans, participants in multiple employer plans can have their service with the different employers contributing to the plan pieced together for purposes of vesting and determining the amount of their benefits. However, with a few exceptions (such as under the TIAA-CREF plan), the chances of a participant working for another employer covered by the same multiple-employer plan are not as great as in a multiemployer plan where one of the primary reasons for the plan's establishment as a multiemployer plan is the mobility of union members among different employers within a particular trade or craft.

---

[87] See Code §§413(b) and (c), and 26 C.F.R. 1.413-1 and -2. See also 29 C.F.R. 2530.210(c)(3)(i).

[88] See D. McGill, *Fundamentals of Private Pensions* (5th ed.), at 78.

2

Coverage of Employees

To many people, it comes as a surprise that an employer can have a pension plan, but not cover certain job classifications or departments or, if the company is large enough, not cover entire plants, divisions, or subsidiaries. However, ERISA does not address the adequacy of a plan's coverage. To qualify for the tax advantages under the Code, the plan need only meet an objective "percentage" test or a nondiscriminatory "classification" test for coverage. A qualified plan must meet either test when it is established and must continue to meet one test or the other—but not necessarily the same test as initially—on at least one day in each quarter of each calendar year.[1] Neither test, however, requires that an employer cover *all* employees and, as described below, the percentage covered may in fact be very low. Many companies, particularly larger employers, exceed the coverage required under these standards.

Two slightly different uses of the term "coverage" appear below. A plan's "coverage" is often used in a broad sense here and in other texts to mean the employees whose job classifications or divisions are covered under the terms of a plan, regardless of whether they have met any minimum age and service requirements established by the plan's terms for participation. Although Code Section 410(b) is generally described as establishing "coverage" tests, it actually requires a qualified plan to do somewhat more, namely, to "benefit" either a percentage or a nondiscriminatory classification of all employees. An employee benefits from a plan within the meaning of this Section only when he or she is *covered* by the plan *and* actually *participates* in it.[2] Because of the participation requirement, it may thus be more accurate to say that

[1] Code §401(a)(6).

[2] Employees who have the minimum age and service to participate in contributory plans, but who have not made employee contributions required for participation, are included as "benefiting" from plans in certain instances, described below.

Code Section 410(b) establishes tests for both coverage and participation. However, alteration of the breadth of the plan's coverage, in the sense of the covered job classifications, is the main variable in achieving compliance with the Code's tests.

ERISA independently establishes minimum standards on the permissible age and service conditions for beginning participation in a plan when an employee's job is covered by the plan. These minimum standards apply regardless of whether or not a plan is in compliance with the Code's Section 410(b) tests for adequate coverage and participation and are discussed in Chapter 4.

I. Highly Compensated Employees

A. Before 1989

For the purposes of the Code's coverage tests, as well as all other nondiscrimination tests under the Code, the employees who are "officers, shareholders, or highly compensated" constitute a group of employees in whose favor discrimination is prohibited.[3] Employees who are officers or shareholders are usually objectively determinable, but an employee who is only a nominal officer or a shareholder who only owns one or two shares of stock is not an officer or a shareholder employee for this purpose.[4] Who is a "highly compensated" employee is a more relative determination that is made by the IRS on a "facts and circumstances" basis for each plan.[5] On this basis whether an employee is highly compensated depends on the employee's standing within the salary structure of the particular employer.[6] Highly compensated thus does not necessarily mean highly compensated by local, regional, or national standards.[7] For example, if over 90 percent of an employer's employees make less than $15,000 per year, a salary of over $20,000 may be highly compensated for that employer for purposes of the Code's nondiscrimination tests.[8]

B. After 1989

The 1986 Tax Reform Act substitutes the term "highly compensated employees" throughout the Code to replace longer prior law

---

[3] Code §401(a)(4).

[4] See Rev. Rul. 80-314 (employee given title of secretary-treasurer but with no voice in management or administration is not an "officer" under Code §410(b) or §401(a)(4)).

[5] 26 C.F.R. 1.410(b)-1(d). And see *Commissioner v. Pepsi-Cola Niagara Bottling Corp.*, 399 F.2d 390 (2d Cir. 1968).

[6] *Id.*

[7] *Id.*

[8] See *Seekonk Lace Co. v. Commissioner*, 45 T.C.M. 951, 4 EBC 1441 (1983); *Fujinon Optical, Inc. v. Commissioner*, 76 T.C. 499, 2 EBC 1145 (1981).

phrases describing employees who are "officers, shareholders, or highly compensated."[9] The most important substantive change accompanying this is the replacement of the facts and circumstances test for determining old law "highly compensated" employees with objective rules. The new rules also establish objective standards for determining the prohibited group status of employees who are only nominally officers or shareholders. These rules apply for purposes of the coverage tests and for purposes of the Code's general nondiscrimination test in plan years beginning after December 31, 1988.[10]

A highly compensated employee under the new Tax Reform Act rules is an employee who during the year, or the preceding year, is, or was:

(1) An officer of the employer who receives annual compensation in excess of $45,000;[11]

(2) A five percent shareholder or other owner of the employer;

(3) A member of the top-paid 20 percent of the employer's employees who receives compensation in excess of $50,000;[12] or

(4) Any employee who receives in excess of $75,000 in annual compensation.[13]

A special rule excludes an employee, other than a five percent owner, from being considered highly compensated if the employee, although highly compensated in the current year, was not highly compensated in the preceding year *and* is currently not among the employer's 100 highest paid employees.[14] Compensation is defined as total compensation, including elective deferrals to Code Section 401(k) plans.[15]

---

[9] See §1114(b) of P.L. 99-514, making conforming changes throughout the Code.

[10] §1114(c) of P.L. 99-514. The rules apply at earlier dates for certain other purposes, *inter alia*, the special contributory plan and Code §401(k) plan nondiscrimination tests. See *id.*

[11] Code §414(q)(1), as added by §1114. No more than 50 employees, or, if less, the greater of 3 employees or 10% of all the employer's employees, can be officers under this rule. At the same time, regardless of the $45,000 earnings test, every employer is considered to have at least one officer.

The $45,000 test is based on 150% of the §415 contribution limit for a defined contribution plan (currently $30,000). The dollar amount will automatically increase when the §415 limit increases sometime in the 1990's.

[12] In determining the top-paid 20% of employees, employees under age 21, and certain short-service, seasonal, and part-time employees are excluded. Code §414(q)(8), as amended. The $50,000 compensation test is indexed to the CPI beginning in 1988.

[13] The $75,000 test is indexed to the CPI beginning in 1988.

[14] Code §414(q)(2). Another special rule treats the compensation and contributions or benefits of certain family members of 5% owner-employees or the employer's 10 most highly compensated employees *as if* they were earned and accrued by the related 5% owners or most highly compensated employees, with the family member also not being treated as a separate employee, under all Code tests for nondiscrimination, including the coverage tests. Code §414(q)(6), as added by §1114 of P.L. 99-514.

[15] Code §414(q)(7), as amended by §1114 of P.L. 99-514 (referencing Code §415(c)(3), and thus, 26 C.F.R. 1.415-2(d); and separately including elective deferrals to §401(k) plans).

II. The Percentage and Classification Tests

A. The Percentage Test

Under the percentage test in Code Section 410(b)(1)(A), a plan is considered to have nondiscriminatory coverage if at least 70 percent of all of the employees of the sponsoring employer participate, excluding (1) employees who are included in a unit covered by a collective bargaining agreement "if there is evidence that retirement benefits were the subject of good faith bargaining,"[16] and (2) employees who have not satisfied any minimum age and service requirements for plan participation that are permitted under ERISA's minimum standards.[17] For example, if an employer has 150 employees, 90 of whom are bargaining unit employees and another 10 of whom have not met minimum age and service requirements for participation, the 70 percent test applies to only the remaining 50 employees. The test is satisfied if 35 (70 percent × 50) or more of those employees participate in the plan. When 70 percent of the nonexcluded employees participate in the plan, the percentage test is satisfied, and coverage is considered nondiscriminatory, regardless of the proportion of the participating employees who are officers, shareholders, or highly compensated.[18]

Code Section 410(b)(1)(A) provides a variant on the basic 70 percent test for plans that require employee contributions.[19] Under this variant, a contributory plan is considered to cover a nondiscriminatory group of employees if 70 percent of all employees, with the previous exclusions, are eligible to participate in the plan, and 80 percent or more of the eligible employees actually make the employee contributions required to participate. Thus, if a contributory plan under the facts given above makes 70 percent or more of the 50 nonexcluded employees eligible to participate (35 or more), and 80 percent or more

---

[16] Code §410(b)(3)(A). According to ERISA's legislative history, the bargaining unit employees must be offered a pension program. While it need not be exactly "comparable" to that provided the salaried or other nonbargaining unit employees, the employer thus has to do more than just discuss pensions with an open mind. See 3 ERISA Leg. Hist. 3540-41 (exchange between Reps. Thompson and Ullman), S. Rep. 93-383, 42, 1 ERISA Leg. Hist. 1110, H.R. Rep. 93-770, 48, 2 ERISA Leg. Hist. 2637, and H.R. Rep. 93-807, 49, 2 ERISA Leg. Hist. 3169. This was to "ease" the pre-ERISA Code requirement of "comparability" of benefits under the collectively bargained plan with benefits under the salaried employees' plan if the salaried employees' plan could not qualify as covering a nondiscriminatory group by itself. See *Boggs v. Commissioner*, 83 T.C. 132, 5 EBC 2006 (1984), *vacated and remanded on other grounds*, 784 F.2d 1166, 7 EBC 1113 (4th Cir. 1985), for an example of the pre-ERISA Code rule. The IRS's regulations may have weakened Congress' intent. See 26 C.F.R. 1.410(b)-1(c)(1) (requiring only that "retirement benefits" have been a subject of bargaining).

[17] Code §410(b)(1)(A). Certain nonresident aliens who have no earned income from an employer constituting income from sources within the United States are also excluded from consideration; a special rule also applies to coverage under collectively bargained plans for air line pilots. Code §§410(b)(3)(B) and (C).

[18] See Rev. Rul. 79-348.

[19] This variant is not expressly described as a contributory plan rule, but it only makes sense in that context. See, e.g., D. McGill, *Fundamentals of Private Pensions* (Richard D. Irwin 5th ed.), at 78.

of those employees (28 or more) actually make the contributions required to participate, the plan is considered to provide nondiscriminatory coverage. Again, if this percentage test is satisfied, coverage is considered nondiscriminatory regardless of the proportion of the participating employees who are members of the prohibited group.

B. The Classification Test

When a plan does not meet the basic 70 percent test, or the contributory plan variant, it may still qualify under Code Section 410(b) if the employer can show that a classification of employees that does not discriminate in favor of the prohibited group participates in the plan.[20]

Whether the plan covers a classification of employees that does *not* discriminate in favor of the prohibited group is determined by the IRS on the basis of a facts and circumstances test. Employees under a collective bargaining agreement with respect to which retirement benefits were the subject of good faith bargaining are once again excluded from consideration *per se*, but employees who have not satisfied the plan's minimum age and service requirements are included in determining whether a nondiscriminatory classification of employees participates in the plan.[21] Particular consideration is given to whether a "fair cross-section" of employees participate, or more specifically, whether (1) employees in all salary ranges participate and (2) employees in lower and middle income brackets participate in more than nominal numbers.[22] This fair cross-section test is not, however, the exclusive test if a classification can otherwise be shown to be nondiscriminatory.[23]

It is possible for a plan to qualify under the classification test with substantially less than the 70 percent participation required under the objective percentage test.[24] Moreover, a plan is not foreclosed from qualification under the classification test "merely because" it excludes

---

[20] Code §410(b)(1)(B).

[21] See 26 C.F.R. 1.410(b)-1(b)(2); *Fujinon Optical, Inc. v. Commissioner, supra*; *Seekonk Lace Co. v. Commissioner, supra*. But compare Rev. Rul. 83-94 and Rev. Rul. 84-150.

[22] See Rev. Ruls. 83-58 and 84-150.

[23] See *Federal Land Bank Ass'n v. Commissioner*, 74 T.C. 1106, 2 EBC 2385 (1980); *Fujinon Optical, Inc. v. Commissioner*, 76 T.C. 499, 2 EBC 1145 (1981).

[24] See, e.g., Rev. Rul. 83-58 (nondiscriminatory classification resulted in participation of only 27% of the employees) and *Federal Land Bank Ass'n v. Commissioner*, 74 T.C. 1106, 2 EBC 2385 (1980) (participation of only 8.7% of employees acceptable when contributory plan was open to all employees, but only 2 elected to participate—one of whom was lower paid and the other of whom was highly compensated). But see Rev. Rul. 83-94 (participation of 43% of employees unacceptable where plan covered 5 of 5 employees in high compensation ranges and excluded all hourly paid employees); Rev. Rul. 84-150 (participation of 8.7% of employees unacceptable when 4 out of the 7 participants were highly compensated and none of the 73 employees in middle compensation ranges participated); *Seekonk Lace Co. v. Commissioner, supra* (participation of 16% of employees unacceptable when 9 out of 9 highly compensated employees participated, compared to 12 out of 130 nonhighly compensated employees); *Fujinon Optical, Inc. v. Commissioner, supra* (participation of 4% of employees unacceptable when 25% of highly compensated employees participated compared to less than 1% of other employees).

all hourly-rated employees from coverage (even if they are nonunion employees for whom the good faith bargaining exclusion does not apply).[25] If a broad enough classification of salaried workers who are not "officers, shareholders, or highly compensated" participate, a plan may still be able to meet the classification test despite even a *per se* exclusion of hourly rated employees.[26]

C. Controlled and Affiliated Service Groups and Leased Employees

Before ERISA, employers could limit a plan's coverage by setting up separate corporations. They could then satisfy the Code's coverage tests only with respect to the employees of one corporation. With changes in the Code made under ERISA, all of the employees in a controlled group of corporations (or controlled group of trades or businesses, whether or not incorporated) are treated as employed by "one employer" to determine whether the percentage or classification tests for coverage are met.[27] This applies, moreover, whether or not the separate corporate entities or trades or businesses were set up for "manipulative" or for functional reasons.[28] The treatment of all employees in a controlled group as employed by "one employer" goes beyond coverage; for example, it also means that service with any of the employers within the controlled group must count for satisfying conditions for beginning participation in benefit accruals under the plan and also for vesting requirements, if and when an employee within a controlled group ever comes under the plan's coverage.[29]

Under Code Section 414(b) and ERISA Section 210(c), whether corporations are members of a controlled group is determined by reference to Code Section 1563(a).[30] Generally, controlled groups are either parent-subsidiary or brother-sister groups. A parent-subsidiary controlled group requires that 80 percent or more of the voting power, or total stock value, of a corporation be owned directly or through a chain by a common parent.[31] A brother-sister controlled group requires that

---

[25] Code §401(a)(5).

[26] Compare Rev. Rul. 83-94 (exclusion of all hourly paid employees unacceptable where salaried employees were predominantly highly compensated) with Rev. Rul. 83-58 (exclusion of all hourly paid employees acceptable where salaried employees included employees in all compensation ranges). Part of the reason for leniency concerning *per se* exclusions of lower paid hourly workers may be that a plan can nominally cover lower paid workers, but then through Social Security integration often effectively excludes them from most or, in some cases, all of the plan's benefits. See ch. 3, sec. VIII (on Social Security integration).

[27] Code §414(b).

[28] *Fujinon Optical, Inc. v. Commissioner*, 76 T.C. 499, 2 EBC 1145 (1981). But see *Sutherland v. Commissioner*, 78 T.C. 395, 3 EBC 1182 (1982) (rejecting treatment of all employees as employed by one employer when two of three companies in a controlled group were on the verge of failing).

[29] See ch. 5, sec. III.A.1 (on what years of service count for vesting).

[30] Code §1563(a) is applied without regard to §1563(a)(4) (containing a special rule for insurance companies) and §1563(e)(3)(C) (containing an exception in the rules on stock attribution for stock owned by an employee benefit trust).

[31] Code §1563(a)(1).

80 percent or more of the voting power, or total stock value, of two or more corporations be owned by five or fewer individuals, estates, or trusts. These individuals, estates, or trusts must also own more than 50 percent of the voting power, or stock value, of the same corporations when only identical interests of each individual in each corporation are considered.[32] Rules on computing voting power and stock value, and constructive ownership and attribution rules, are detailed in Code Sections 1563(c)-(e). Under Code Section 414(c) and ERISA Section 210(d) and IRS regulations, the same principles apply to determine whether unincorporated trades or businesses constitute a controlled group.

Some groups of corporations, or trades or businesses, that do not have a sufficient ownership relation to be controlled groups under the Code may nevertheless be "affiliated service" groups under Section 414(m).[33] Affiliated service groups are groups of corporations or partnerships that are joined by common ownership and regularly perform services for one of the corporations or partnerships, or regularly associate in performing services for third persons.[34]

Code Section 414(n) also requires employers to include "leased" employees in satisfying the coverage tests and and to count their service as leased employees for meeting conditions for participation, vesting, and certain other qualification requirements and ERISA minimum standards. A leased employee is a person who provides services to an employer under contract on a substantially full-time basis for a period of at least one year that are of a type historically performed in the field of business by employees.[35]

---

[32] Code §1563(a)(2). And see *U.S. v. Vogel Fertilizer Co.*, 455 U.S. 16, 3 EBC 1041 (1982) (invalidating the IRS's regulations insofar as they permitted different individuals' interests to be used to satisfy the 80% test and the 50% test). A controlled group can also be a combined parent-subsidiary and brother-sister group as defined in Code §1563(a)(3).

[33] As added to the Code in 1980 and amended in 1984.

[34] More precisely, an affiliated service group is a group of organizations composed of a service organization (a corporation, partnership, or other business organization that has its principal business in the performance of services) and one or more (1) service organizations that are shareholders or partners in the first organization and that regularly perform services for the first organization, or regularly associate with the first organization in performing services for third persons, or (2) organizations that are 10% or more owned by officers, highly compensated employees, or owners of the first organization, or another organization in the service group, and that have a significant portion of their business in the performance of services for the first organization, or for other organizations in the service group, that are of a type historically performed in the field by employees.

See also Prop. Regs. 1.414(m)-1, 48 Fed. Reg. 8293 (Feb. 28, 1983), Rev. Rul. 81-105 (guidelines on affiliated service groups), and Rev. Proc. 85-43 (procedures for qualification of affiliated service group plans).

[35] As added in 1982 and amended in 1984. See also IRS Notice 84-11, I.R.B. 1984-29 (questions and answers on employee leasing) and Rev. Proc. 85-43.

Code §414(n)(5) provides a safe harbor from including leased employees under the coverage tests and subjecting their service with an employer to the minimum standards listed in Code §414(n)(3) if the leased employees are covered by a money purchase pension plan sponsored by the leasing organization that provides immediate participation and vesting, and a nonintegrated annual contribution of 7.5% of compensation. Effective Dec. 31, 1986, the 1986 Tax Reform Act amends this to require coverage under the leasing organization's plan of virtually all of the leasing organization's employees and a nonintegrated annual contribution of 10% of compensation. The safe harbor is unavailable, regardless of satisfaction of these standards, if more than 20% of an employer's nonhighly compensated employees are leased employees. Code §414(n)(5), as amended by §1146 of P.L. 99-514.

The affiliated service group and employee leasing rules are designed primarily to prevent arrangements under which employers avoid the coverage and other benefit requirements by splitting up their employees in ways not subject to Sections 414(b) or (c) (although employee leasing is favored by many employers for other reasons). Under the Deficit Reduction Act of 1984, the IRS was given additional authority to develop such rules "as may be necessary to prevent the avoidance" of the affiliated service group and employee leasing rules through still more esoteric devices involving separate organizations, employee leasing, or other arrangements.[36]

D. Separate Lines of Business

In a departure from prior law, the 1986 Tax Reform Act allows employers, beginning in 1987, to separate employees in each "separate line of business" maintained by the employer in applying the Code Section 410(b) coverage tests.[37] This is allowed regardless of whether the employees in two or more separate lines of business are employed by the same corporation or by separate members of a controlled group of corporations.

Separate lines of business are determined under a largely subjective facts and circumstances test described in a new Code Section 414(r).[38] The basic rule is that a separate line of business must be separate, self-sustaining, and maintained for bona fide business reasons, and must employ at least 50 persons.[39] A separate line of business can be just one operating unit within a separate line of business, e.g., a single store or factory, if the operating unit employs at least 50 persons, and the employer does not have any similar operating units in the same line of business within the same geographic area.[40]

However, a separate line of business cannot be comprised of company headquarters' employees. Nor can job classifications, such as all hourly employees or leased employees, or all secretaries, clerks, nurses, or laboratory personnel, ordinarily pass as bona fide separate lines of

---

[36] Code §414(o), as added by the 1984 Deficit Reduction Act.

[37] An employer can use separate lines of business in meeting the old law coverage tests beginning with the first plan year after Dec. 31, 1986. §1115(b) of P.L. 99-514. Separate lines of business can also be used in meeting the new coverage tests enacted by the Tax Reform Act that become effective in 1989. See sec. III.B, below.

[38] In *Fujinon Optical, Inc. v. Commissioner*, 76 T.C. 499, 2 EBC 1145 (1981), the Tax Court noted the IRS's position that allowing employers to separate lines of business that are not functionally related would create an "administrative nightmare." 2 EBC 1151. However, Code §414(r), as amended, effectively adopts such a rule.

[39] Code §§414(r)(1) and (2)(A), as added by §1115 of P.L. 99-514. Employees who are in a collective bargaining unit and employees who are (1) not age 21, (2) do not have 6 months of service, or (3) normally work less than 17½ hours per week or less than 6 months per year, do not count toward the 50 employee requirement. Further guidance on facts and circumstances bearing on the bona fideness of a claimed separate line of business is provided in the Conference Report on the Tax Reform Act and is to be provided in Treasury regulations. See Conf. Rep., H.R. Rep. 99-841, at II-523-26.

[40] Code §414(r)(7).

business.[41] A safe harbor from additional Treasury guidelines is allowed if the percentage of highly compensated employees in a bona fide separate line of business, or operating unit, is not less than one-half, nor more than twice, the percentage of highly compensated employees in the employer's entire workforce.[42]

E. Aggregation of Coverage Under Comparable Plans

Many corporations with multiplant, multidivision, or multisubsidiary operations have different plans for different groups of employees. Separate plans are also found among small employers, sometimes as an attempt to cover enough employees to meet the Code's coverage requirements while providing different benefit terms with lower costs to rank and file employees.

For purposes of meeting the percentage or nondiscriminatory classification tests, coverage under different plans may be aggregated if the two or more plans do not discriminate in contributions or benefits in favor of the prohibited group of employees. Revenue Ruling 81-202 provides extensive technical guidelines for normalizing benefits or contributions in different plans so that they can be compared to determine whether benefits or contributions under a two or more plan arrangement discriminate in favor of the prohibited group.[43]

Alternatively, the coverage of each of the two or more plans may be tested separately under the classification test (without regard to whether the plans' terms would be considered to discriminate if considered together). When different plans of one employer are tested separately under the classification test, it is possible that one plan will be found to have nondiscriminatory coverage, while another plan, e.g., the plan covering upper management, will be found to discriminate. It is also possible, of course, that both plans will be determined to cover nondiscriminatory classifications of employees. In contrast, it is generally not possible for two plans of an employer to qualify separately under the percentage test (unless at least some of the same employees are covered under both plans) because to qualify each plan has to

---

[41] Code §§414(r)(1) and (6), and Conf. Rep., H.R. Rep. 99-841, at II-522-24, [1986] U.S. Code Cong. & Ad. News 4610-12.

[42] Code §§414(r)(3) and (4). A line of business is treated *as if* it employs not less than one-half of the percentage of highly compensated employees in the employer's entire work force whenever it employs at least 10% of all of the employer's highly compensated employees. Code §414(r)(3).

[43] And see Rev. Rul. 83-110. See also Rev. Rul. 81-5 (using a more abbreviated test for discrimination when an employer maintained a profit-sharing plan for highly compensated employees and a defined benefit plan for rank and file employees, and coverage under the profit-sharing plan "standing alone" could not meet either the percentage or classification test for qualified plan coverage), and *Boggs v. Commissioner, supra*, at n.16.

Differences in vesting schedules are not considered in comparing contributions to two plans, e.g., contributions to two defined contribution plans. See Rev. Rul. 74-165. However, differences in vesting schedules are weighed if an employer seeks to establish that two plans are comparable on the basis of benefits. See Rev. Rul. 74-166 (providing examples of two methods for weighing differences in vesting in valuing two plans' benefits).

separately cover 70 percent or more of the employer's *total* employees (with the exclusions described before).

In addition to different plans that cover wholly different groups of employees, employers often have two or more plans that cover at least some of the same employees. For example, an employer may have a defined benefit plan that covers all employees, and then a defined contribution plan, such as a profit-sharing plan, that covers a more restricted group, e.g., only salaried workers. Given these facts, coverage under the defined benefit plan should pass under either the percentage or the classification test since the plan covers *all* employees. However, coverage under the salaried-only defined contribution plan may or may not be satisfactory under the percentage or classification test.[44]

III. Coverage Tests for Plan Years Beginning in 1989

The 1986 Tax Reform Act establishes a new minimum coverage and participation rule and three more general tests for the adequacy of a plan's coverage, effective for plan years beginning after December 31, 1988.[45] Congress' intent is to broaden coverage under plans. But the rules may not substantially broaden coverage because of the authority conferred under the same Act allowing employers to exclude employees in "separate lines of business" in applying the three general tests.

A. Minimum Coverage and Participation Rule

As a minimum overall coverage and participation rule, the Tax Reform Act requires every qualified plan (on each day of each plan year) to cover enough employees to result in the participation of the *lesser* of 50 employees or 40 percent of all the employer's employees—excluding employees in a collective bargaining unit and those not meeting any minimum age and service conditions for participation under the plan.[46] This rule may not be satisfied by aggregating participation

---

[44] Even if a plan for salaried employees, or only upper management, is not qualified, it can still be maintained as a nonqualified plan. The difference is in the tax advantages. A nonqualified plan may still be subject to ERISA's minimum participation, vesting, benefit accrual, funding, and fiduciary standards unless it is restricted to "a select group of management or highly compensated employees," and is maintained as a completely unfunded plan. See ERISA §201(2), §301(a)(3), and §401(a)(1).

[45] A later effective date can apply to collectively bargained plans. See sec. IV.B below. The IRS is to issue final regulations implementing the coverage amendments by Feb. 1, 1988.

[46] Code §401(a)(26), as amended by §1112 of P.L. 99-514. Employees who are eligible to participate in a Code §401(k) plan or a defined contribution plan requiring employee contributions are counted as participants for purposes of this rule so long as the special nondiscrimination rules applicable to such plans are satisfied. Code §401(a)(26)(C). Employees who are eligible to participate in defined benefit plans requiring employee contributions may also be counted if the employee contributions, when made, are allocated to separate accounts on behalf of the employees and such employee contributions meet the special nondiscrimination rules. See Conf. Rep., H.R. Rep. 99-841, at II-394. And see ch. 3, sec. VII, for descriptions of the nondiscrimination tests applicable to these plans.

under comparable plans.[47] The exclusion of employees in separate lines of business also cannot be used as a means to satisfy the percentage of employees element of the rule.[48]

B. Three General Tests: The Percentage, Ratio, and Classification and Average Benefits

Beyond this minimum, a plan must satisfy one of three tests (on at least one day of each quarter of each taxable year of the plan). These tests require participation[49] under the plan, or under the plan and one or more comparable plans, of:

(1) 70 percent or more of the employer's employees who are not highly compensated;[50]

(2) A percentage of the employer's nonhighly compensated employees that is equal to, or greater than, 70 percent of the percentage of highly compensated employees who are participating; or

(3) A nondiscriminatory classification of the employer's employees, as described in prior rulings and cases;[51] if this test is used, the average benefit percentage of the employer's nonhighly compensated employees (whether or not covered under the plan or any comparable plan of the employer) must also be at least 70 percent of the average benefit percentage of the employer's highly compensated employees (whether or not covered).[52]

The minimum coverage and participation rule is primarily aimed at stemming the formation by small businesses of several pension plans covering different groups of employees which satisfy the coverage rules through comparability of benefits or contributions and aggregation of coverage.

[47] Conf. Rep., H.R. Rep. 99-841, at II-421, [1986] U.S. Code Cong. & Ad. News 4509.

[48] Conf. Rep., H.R. Rep. 99-841, at II-421.

[49] Employees who are eligible to participate in a Code §401(k) plan or a defined contribution plan requiring employee contributions are counted as participants for purposes of these rules so long as the special nondiscrimination rules applicable to such plans are satisfied. Code §410(b)(6)(E). Employees who are eligible to participate in contributory defined benefit plans may also be counted if the employee contributions, when made, are allocated to separate accounts on behalf of the employees and such employee contributions meet the special nondiscrimination rules. Conf. Rep., H.R. Rep. 99-841, at II-394. See ch. 3, sec. VII, for descriptions of the nondiscrimination tests applicable to these plans.

[50] Unlike the prior law 70% test, this test looks only at the coverage and participation of the employer's nonhighly compensated employees. No variant is provided analogous to the one available under prior law for contributory plans (requiring that 70% of the employer's employees be eligible to participate and that 80% of those eligible actually participate). However, as described in n. 49 above, employees in contributory plans who are eligible to participate are counted as participating under this rule, and also under the two other tests described below, if the plan meets certain nondiscrimination tests.

[51] Code §410(b)(2)(A)(i), as amended, and Conf. Rep., at II-413. However, in applying the classification test, the 1986 Tax Reform Act's definition of highly compensated employees applies. In a further departure from prior law, employees who have not met minimum age and service requirements for participation under the plan are excluded from consideration. Compare Conf. Rep., at II-413, with 26 C.F.R. 1.410(b)-1(b)(2).

[52] Code §410(b)(2)(A)(ii), as amended by §1112 of P.L. 99-514.

The average benefit percentage under the third test is the contributions or benefits of the employee group in question expressed as a percentage of compensation.[53] An employer can perform this test using either benefits or contributions. If benefits are used, contributions to defined contribution plans must be converted to a benefit basis. If contributions are used, benefits must be converted to a contributions basis.[54] Benefits for this purpose are not just accrued benefits, but are the most valuable projected benefits of the employee under any plan or plans (assuming, if the employee is covered by a plan, that he or she will continue to work until retirement and will continue to earn the same rate of compensation earned in the current year).[55] The average benefit (or contribution) percentage of the respective groups of employees is the sum of the benefit (or contribution) percentages of each individual in the group divided by the number of employees in the group.[56]

Employees in bargaining units for which retirement benefits have been the subject of good faith bargaining are excluded in determining if a plan meets any one of these three coverage tests, as under prior law.[57] Employees who have not satisfied minimum age and service conditions for participation under plans are also excluded except under the average benefit test.[58] Under the average benefit test, such employees can be excluded on a restricted basis, if an employer elects. This election allows the exclusion of those employees who have not satisfied the *lowest* age and service requirements for participation under *any* plan maintained by the employer.[59]

As described before, in a departure from prior law, an employer can also exclude employees in "separate lines of business" in applying the three coverage tests.[60] With respect to employees in the nonexcluded separate line of business, the plan must satisfy one of the three

---

[53] Under the Tax Reform Act's definition of highly compensated employees, the compensation and contributions or benefits earned and accrued by certain family members of 5% owners or of the employer's 10 most highly compensated employees are treated *as if* they were earned and accrued by the related 5% owners or most highly compensated employees for purposes of the average benefit percentage test. Code §414(q)(6), as added by §1114 of TRA. Such family members are also not treated as separate employees for purposes of the other tests. *Id.*

[54] Conf. Rep., H.R. Rep. 99-841, at II-413. The conversion to either benefits or contributions is to follow the methods set out in Rev. Rul. 81-202. *Id.*

[55] See Conf. Rep., at II-413 (stating that Rev. Rul. 81-202 provides the method for making this determination). And see Rev. Rul. 81-202, sec. 4.

[56] Conf. Rep., H.R. Rep. 99-841, at II-414.

[57] Code §410(b)(3)(A), as amended. Nonresident aliens who have no income from the employer which constitutes income from sources within the U.S. are also excluded under all three tests, as under prior law. Code §410(b)(3)(C), as amended by §1112.

[58] Code §410(b)(4), as amended. If some employees who could be excluded under minimum age and service requirements which are permissible under ERISA nevertheless participate under a plan, i.e., if the plan allows employees to participate who are not age 21 or who do not have one year of service, the employer can still exclude all employees who have not satisfied the permissible minimum age and service requirements as long as one of the three tests for coverage is satisfied in looking at participation of this excludable group of employees alone. Code §410(b)(4)(B), as amended by §1112.

[59] Code §410(b)(2)(D), as amended by §1112.

[60] Code §410(b)(5), as amended. Separate lines of business are described in sec. II.D above.

tests, as well as, in every case, the nondiscriminatory classification test for coverage on an employer-wide basis.[61]

Aggregation of coverage under comparable plans is allowed in meeting the three tests.[62] Revenue Ruling 81-202's method for testing whether different plans provide comparable benefits or contributions is to be used after being modified according to instructions in the Conference Report.[63]

IV. Collectively Bargained Plans

A. Before 1989

Adequacy of coverage is usually not an issue for collectively bargained plans. Under a union's duty of fair representation, all employees in a bargaining unit should be covered under any plan negotiated by the union, without regard to whether the bargaining unit employees are union members.[64] As discussed in more detail in Chapter 3, the Code's standard of nondiscrimination in favor of the prohibited group applies to collectively bargained plans, but in most cases, there are no "officers" or "shareholders" of the employer in the plan. Nor are there likely to be many "highly compensated" employees because this is determined by reference to *all* of the employer's employees, whether or not they are in the plan. Coverage of a nondiscriminatory classification under the collectively bargained plan is, therefore, usually a foregone conclusion. The percentage test for coverage may also be met if the collective bargaining unit contains a high enough percentage of all the employer's employees.[65] The comparability of the plan's contributions or benefits with those offered under an employer's salaried employees' plan was, but is no longer, a part of the test for determining whether the salaried employees' plan covers a nondiscriminatory classification of employees.[66]

---

[61] Code §410(b)(5), as amended, and Conf. Rep., H.R. Rep. 99-841, at II-523. This nondiscriminatory classification test does not require satisfaction of the average benefit percentage subtest described above.

[62] Code §410(b)(6)(B), as amended. Aggregation of coverage is not directly relevant in meeting the average benefit percentage test since that test effectively provides its own aggregation rules (which are, in turn, drawn from the aggregation rules in Rev. Rul. 81-202).

[63] See Conf. Rep., at II-413-15.

[64] See §§8(a)(3) and (b)(2) of the National Labor Relations Act.

[65] Adequacy of coverage can be an issue if the employees in the collectively bargained plan are more highly compensated than the employer's employees who are not in the plan. The exception in §410(b)(3)(B) for the collectively bargained plans of air line pilots was, in fact, designed to ensure that the IRS would not continue to raise this issue, as it apparently had been doing. See 3 ERISA Leg. Hist. 3541-42.

[66] See *Boggs v. Commissioner, supra,* at n.16 (testing comparability of benefits under pre-ERISA tests for coverage when coverage under an employer's salaried plan was not nondiscriminatory standing alone), and see n. 16 above (on ERISA's exclusion of bargaining unit employees from consideration under the coverage tests if pension benefits have been the subject of good faith collective bargaining).

B. After 1989

The Tax Reform Act's revised coverage rules apply to collectively bargained plans, but generally with a later effective date than for other plans.[67]

To satisfy the minimum coverage and participation test (requiring participation of 50 employees or 40 percent of all employees), a collectively bargained single-employer plan can exclude those employees who are not in the bargaining unit, as well as those bargaining unit employees who have not met the plan's minimum age and service requirements for participation.[68] The minimum coverage and participation test does not apply to multiemployer plans, except as provided in Treasury regulations.[69] The Conference Report, however, states that neither this special rule for single-employer plans nor the exception for multiemployer plans is to apply to a collectively bargained plan covering *any* employee who is a professional.[70]

To test a collectively bargained plan's coverage under the first of the three general coverage rules, i.e., the percentage test, all of the employer's nonhighly compensated employees, except those in other collective bargaining units and those employees who are excluded because of minimum age and service requirements, are included in determining whether or not 70 percent of the nonhighly compensated employees are participating in the plan.[71] As a result of this formulation, the first test may not be satisfied by every collectively bargained plan. However, the second, ratio test only looks at whether the percentage of the employer's nonhighly compensated employees who are participating in the plan is at least 70 percent of the percentage of highly compensated employees who are participating in the plan. Since the latter percentage is generally zero under a collectively bargained plan, satisfaction of this test is nearly automatic. If the nondiscriminatory classification and average benefit percentage test is needed to qualify a collectively bargained plan, the average benefit test is applied looking at the benefits of all nonexcluded nonhighly compensated employees (whether or not under the collectively bargained plan) compared to the average benefit percentage of all nonexcluded highly compensated employees (whether or not under the plan).

---

[67] The effective date for a collectively bargained plan is the first plan year after the *earlier* of Jan. 1, 1991, or the date of expiration of the collective bargaining agreement under which the the plan is maintained if the collective bargaining agreement was ratified before March 1, 1986, and has not expired by the general effective date of Jan. 1, 1988. §1112(e) of P.L. 99-514.

[68] Code §401(a)(26)(D), as amended by §1112.

[69] Code §401(a)(26)(E), as amended.

[70] Conf. Rep., H.R. Rep. 99-841, at II-422, [1986] U.S. Code Cong. & Ad. News 4510. A collective bargaining agreement must also always be a bona fide agreement with bona fide employee representatives to come under any of the special Code provisions for collectively bargained plans. Code §7701(a)(46), as amended by §1137.

[71] Code §410(b)(1)(A), as amended, and Conf. Rep., at II-415-16.

V. Other Legal Considerations on Coverage

ERISA's minimum age and service requirements for participation can have an indirect impact on coverage. Even if coverage is otherwise adequate under Code Section 410(b), it is impermissible for employees to be excluded from coverage for what amount to age or service related reasons in excess of ERISA's minimum age and service requirements for beginning participation in a plan. For example, if a corporation is divided into two divisions, with employment in the second division in effect depending on service within the first division in excess of the ERISA minimum service requirement of one year, excluding the first division from coverage under the plan could have the indirect effect of requiring service in excess of the minimum standards as a condition for participation.[72]

Additional considerations on coverage are whether exclusions from coverage are based on race, sex, national origin, or religion, and thus violate the Civil Rights Act.[73] Exclusions that predominantly rule out older workers are also suspect; however, until 1988, ERISA expressly permits the exclusion from participation in a defined benefit plan of employees who are hired within five years of the plan's normal retirement age.[74]

The scope of a plan's coverage can also be subject to varying interpretations. In *Crouch v. Mo-Kan Iron Workers Welfare Fund,* the Tenth Circuit followed a standard plan interpretation proviso stating that the plan was to be interpreted in favor of tax qualification to find that a secretary was to be covered under a multiemployer plan that covered a local union's staff when the plan had been interpreted by its trustees to cover only the local union's officers and one secretary in another office.[75]

Another type of coverage question that arises in collectively bargained plans, especially in multiemployer plans, is whether an individual is within the bargaining unit, and thus is covered by the plan, or is a supervisor, independent contractor, or other nonbargaining unit employee not eligible for coverage.[76] In some cases, the legal issue of an employee's status within the bargaining unit is complicated by a union

---

72 See 26 C.F.R. 1.410(a)-3(d) and (e).

73 See ch. 10, sec. IV (on Title VII protections), and *Simmons v. S.C. State Ports Authority,* 495 F.Supp. 1239 (D.S.C. 1980), *aff'd,* 3 EBC 2413 (4th Cir. 1982) (plan excluded temporary employees, most of whom were black, but statute of limitations barred claim because practice discontinued long before action instituted, although effects lingered).

74 See ch. 4, sec. I.B (on maximum age exclusions from participation), and ch. 10, sec. III (on age discrimination).

75 740 F.2d 805, 5 EBC 1971 (10th Cir. 1984). See also *Sanchez v. Trustees of Pension Plan,* 359 So.2d 1279 (La. 1979) (interpreting plan in favor of coverage, without regard to tests for discrimination in coverage, based on acceptance of contributions on certain employees' behalf); *Reiherzer v. Shannon,* 581 F.2d 1266, 1 EBC 1175 (7th Cir. 1978).

76 See, e.g., *Reiherzer v. Shannon, supra; Richardson v. Central States Pension Fund,* 645 F.2d 660 (8th Cir. 1981).

business agent's representations that the individual will be covered by the plan, or by the trustees' knowing acceptance of contributions on the individual's behalf and their refusal to return those contributions, with interest, if the individual is determined not to be covered.[77]

---

[77] See, e.g., *Aitken v. IP & GCU-Employer Retirement Fund*, 604 F.2d 1261 (9th Cir. 1979); *McHugh v. Teamsters Pension Trust Fund of Philadelphia*, 638 F.Supp. 1036 (E.D. Pa. 1986). And see ch. 8, secs. II.B (on estoppel of multiemployer plans) and VI.B (on unjust enrichment from mistaken contributions).

3

Benefit or Contribution Formulas

I. Examples

Benefit formulas, particularly of larger companies, may involve a variety of alternatives that use slightly varying percentages and benefit amounts. For example, the U.S. Steel noncontributory plan provides a benefit of the *greater of:*

> "1.1 percent of final average pay times credited service up to 30 years, plus 1.2 percent of final average pay times credited service in excess of 30 years, all times 1.05; or
>
> "$198 times credited service up to 15 years, plus $216 times credited service between 15 and 30 years, plus $234 times credited service in excess of 30 years;"

but not more than the greater of:

> "70 percent of final two-year average pay, plus 1.0 percent of such pay times credited service in excess of 15 years, less 100 percent of the primary Social Security benefit; or
>
> "$156 times credited service up to 15 years, plus $168 times credited service between 15 and 30 years, plus $180 times credited service in excess of 30 years."[1]

More often, formulas are less complex than this. The most common type of defined benefit plan formula is a unit benefit formula. It multiplies years of credited service under the plan by (1) a percentage of final or highest pay (e.g., one percent of a highest five consecutive year average of pay), (2) a percentage of a career average of pay (e.g., 1½ percent of career average pay), or (3) a dollar amount (e.g., $15 per month).

---

[1] This is still just a summary of the U.S. Steel noncontributory pension plan formula taken from the Wyatt Company's "A Survey of Retirement, Thrift and Profit Sharing Plans Covering Salaried Employees of 50 Large U.S. Industrial Companies as of January 1, 1982."

The other major type of defined benefit formula uses a flat percentage or dollar amount that is independent of years of credited service, except for a minimum years requirement, such as 15 years. For example, a flat percentage formula could offer 50 percent of final or highest average pay, or 70 percent of a career average of pay, assuming a participant has a minimum of 15 years of credited service. For service below 15 years, the percentage would usually be prorated. But for service above 15 years, the percentage would stay the same. A flat benefit can also be provided as a flat dollar amount, such as $600 per month, again usually with a minimum service requirement, for example, of 15 or 20 years, and a prorated benefit for lesser service.

In a defined contribution plan, the plan's formula is basically a contribution rate. For example, a money purchase pension plan may offer annual contributions to individual accounts of six percent of each participant's compensation. Similarly, a savings or thrift plan might match employee contributions of up to a certain percentage of pay, such as five percent, with employer contributions either on a dollar-for-dollar basis or at a lower rate, such as fifty cents for each dollar an employee contributes. The contribution rate for a profit-sharing plan may involve two elements: First, a percentage of profits, such as 10 percent, that determines the employer's overall contribution to the plan, and second, an allocation formula that allocates among participants' accounts whatever contributions this percentage of profits yields—using, for example, the ratio of the individual's compensation to all participants' compensation.

II. Overview of Nondiscrimination Requirements for Benefit or Contribution Formulas

It is easy to confuse the Code's rules on a plan's benefit formula with the ERISA accrual rules because many unit benefit plans' accrual and benefits formulas are exactly the same. But it is useful to keep in mind that ERISA does *not* directly regulate benefit or contribution formulas. The distinction between the plan's benefit formula and the ERISA accrual rules is established in *Alessi v. Raybestos-Manhattan, Inc.* In *Alessi*, the U.S. Supreme Court approved a benefit formula that offset workmen's compensation awards from pension benefits, despite the argument that such an offset constituted a forfeiture of accrued benefits.[2] The Court stated:

> "[R]etirees' argument overlooks a threshold issue: what defines the content of the benefit that once vested cannot be forfeited? . . . [T]he statutory definition of 'nonforfeitable' assures that an employee's claim to the protected benefit is legally enforceable, but it does not guarantee a particular amount or a method for calculating the benefit. . . .

---

[2] 451 U.S. 504, 2 EBC 1297 (1981).

> "Rather than imposing mandatory pension levels or methods for calculating benefits, Congress in ERISA set outer bounds on permissible accrual practices ... and specified three alternative schedules for the vesting of pension rights .... In so doing, Congress limited the variation permitted in accrual rates applicable across the entire period of an employee's participation in the plan. And Congress disapproved pension practices unduly delaying an employee's acquisition of a right to enforce payment of the portion of benefits already accrued, without further employment."[3]

The Supreme Court thus concluded that ERISA left pension "calculation practices" to the discretion of plan designers, and to the constraints, largely on discrimination, in the Internal Revenue Code. ERISA's accrual rules require a portion of the plan's normal retirement benefits, as determined by the plan's method for calculating benefits, to accrue across the employee's years of participation in the plan, and to vest after significant periods of service.

The demarcation in *Alessi* between the pension calculation technique or method and the benefit accrual rules can be overdrawn. ERISA's benefit accrual rules do affect permissible formulas for initially calculating benefits by the statutory definition of the "normal retirement benefit" that must accrue and by the focus of the rules on preventing backloading of accrued benefits to later years of plan participation under any type of benefit formula. As a practical matter, the benefit accrual rules thus constrain benefit formulas to certain types. Moreover, as suggested earlier, under plans with unit benefit formulas, the plan's benefit formula and its accrual formula are often exactly the same. Although it is thus blurred as a matter of law in certain situations and awkward because of common practice, the distinction between the plan's benefit formula and the ERISA accrual rules remains a necessary separation for legal analysis, as demonstrated by *Alessi*.

The Internal Revenue Code, as distinct from ERISA, directly addresses a plan's benefit or contribution allocation formula in a number of respects. While a plan's benefits or contributions are generally not required to be a certain dollar level to satisfy the Code's requirements, Section 415 establishes maximum dollar and percentage limits on the benefits or contributions that a qualified plan may provide. More important for this discussion, within these maximum limits, the Code provides that a qualified plan's benefits or contributions must not discriminate in favor of officers, shareholders, or highly compensated employees. This nondiscrimination standard is pervasive and is still considered the cornerstone of pension law by most tax lawyers—even after ERISA. The specific language of the standard is set forth in Section 401(a)(4) which states that a pension, profit-sharing or stock bonus plan will constitute a qualified trust for tax purposes if and only if:

---

[3] 2 EBC at 1299-1300.

> "[T]he contributions or benefits provided do not discriminate in favor of employees who are—
>
> "(A) officers,
>
> "(B) shareholders or
>
> "(C) highly compensated."

Section 401(a)(5) goes on to provide that a plan shall not be considered discriminatory "merely because" the contributions or benefits for the employees covered under the plan bear a "uniform relationship" to the "total compensation," or the "basic or regular rate of compensation" of all employees. That is, a plan does not discriminate in favor of the employees who are officers, shareholders, or highly compensated "merely because" it provides benefits, for example, of 10 percent of compensation to employees who make $100,000 ($10,000 benefits) and 10 percent of compensation benefits for employees who make $10,000 ($1,000 benefits)—although the dollar amounts of benefits for the highly compensated employees are obviously much larger under such a formula. Under Social Security offset and excess formulas, which are permitted under Code Section 401(a)(5) and discussed in detail below, a plan's benefits may be further skewed so that they are in fact disproportionate, even as a percentage of compensation, in favor of the highly compensated employees.

The general test for discrimination is thus whether a plan's benefit or contribution allocation formula produces differences between (1) the highly compensated employees' benefits or contributions and (2) the nonhighly compensated employees' benefits or contributions, when both are expressed as a percentage of their compensation—beyond those differences expressly permitted by Social Security integration. For this purpose, compensation is defined as total compensation or as the basic or regular rate of compensation.[4] It is defined only as total compensation includible in the gross income of the employee for any plan year beginning after December 31, 1988.[5] Compensation and contributions or benefits of certain family members of five percent owners or of the employer's 10 most highly compensated employees are treated *as if* earned and accrued by the owners or most highly compensated employees, effective in 1989.[6] The top heavy plan minimum benefit or contribution rules that are discussed in section III below establish additional nondiscrimination requirements that can require rank and file employees' benefits or contributions to exceed certain highly compensated employees' benefits or contributions as a percentage of compensation.

---

[4] Code §401(a)(5).

[5] Code §401(a)(5)(B), as amended by §1111 of P.L. 99-514, and Code §414(s), as amended by §1115. Effective at the same time, the Tax Reform Act establishes a $200,000 cap on the annual compensation that may be included under *any* qualified plan's benefit or contribution allocation formula. Code §401(a)(17), as added by §1106(d)(1).

[6] Code §414(q)(6), as added by §1114 of P.L. 99-514. See §1114(c)(3) for effective date.

The discussion that follows examines the application of the nondiscrimination standard to common elements of benefit or contribution formulas within the general framework of requiring benefits or contributions to be a uniform percentage of compensation for all employees. More specifically, it examines:

(1) The determinability of benefits or contribution allocations under a plan's formula;
(2) The definition of compensation, if compensation is used in the formula;
(3) The use of years, including years of past service, under a defined benefit plan's formula;
(4) The use of years or other service-weighting for contribution allocations under a defined contribution plan; and
(5) Employee contribution requirements, including elective deferrals of salary under Code Section 401(k) plans.

Limits on Social Security integration under defined benefit and defined contribution plans are discussed thereafter.

A useful point to keep in mind is that the Code's nondiscrimination requirement is not directly enforceable by participants. Indirect enforcement avenues are discussed in Chapter 14. A second point to remember is that even a rank and file employee's interests in nondiscrimination can shift as he or she nears retirement. For example, assume a rank and file participant is considering whether past service years should be included in a plan's benefit formula, and knows that officers, shareholders, and highly compensated employees have a much greater number of past service years than he or she. Logically, the participant may want those past service years excluded from the plan's formula since the exclusion would force the so-called prohibited group to attain their benefit objectives through a higher percentage multiplier on years of future service alone—where all employees start with the same base. However, if the participant is at or near retirement, and has *any* past service, he or she may want the past years of service to count, unless the effect of their exclusion can be shown to be an immediate increase in the percentage multiplier.

III. Definitely Determinable Benefit and Contribution Allocation Terms

A qualified pension plan must provide "definitely determinable" benefits.[7] This requirement aids in preventing discrimination but it also applies regardless of whether noncompliance favors the prohibited group. The definitely determinable benefits requirement means that it

---

[7] 26 C.F.R. 1.401-1(b)(1)(i).

must be possible to determine and compute the benefits of each participant under express terms and according to an express formula that is not within the discretion of the employer.[8] Similarly, although the percentage of profits to be contributed to a profit-sharing or stock bonus plan is permitted to remain discretionary, the Code requires that these plans provide a "definite predetermined formula" for allocating whatever contributions are made from profits among the participants under the plan.[9]

The requirement that benefits or contribution allocations under a plan must be definitely determinable does not prevent an employer from amending the plan's terms, but it forces the employer to put the terms of the plan on record, with plan amendments then subject to other safeguards.[10] The basic point of the definitely determinable requirement, namely, that a plan must be a written, nondiscretionary document, is not a Code requirement alone. Under ERISA, all plans, whether or not qualified, must be written and must "specify the basis on which payments are made to and from the plan."[11] Similarly, under Section 302(c)(5) of the Labor Management Relations Act, a jointly administered trust must specify the "detailed basis" on which payments are to be made to and from the trust.[12]

The definitely determinable requirement covers not only benefits under a plan's normal retirement benefit formula, but also the terms and conditions under which benefits will be paid under all benefit options the plan offers, such as early retirement, lump sum, or disability benefits.[13] Consequently, Revenue Ruling 79-90 and, as of 1984, Code Section 401(a)(25) require that the actuarial assumptions under which any optional forms of benefits are paid must be specified in the plan in express, absolute terms (e.g., a percentage interest rate and a specific mortality table), or by reference to a variable standard outside

---

[8] See Rev. Ruls. 74-385, 79-90, and 85-130. If discretion is instead placed in the hands of a plan "trustee," the lack of definite determinability can similarly cause the trust to fail to qualify. See Rev. Ruls. 79-90 and 71-296.

[9] 26 C.F.R. 1.401-1(b)(1)(ii). Contributions to a profit-sharing plan must also be "recurring and substantial" for the plan to remain a tax-qualified plan. 26 C.F.R. 1.401-1(b)(2). Failure to make contributions with "sufficient regularity" in years in which the sponsoring employer has profits can cause a plan to be retroactively disqualified. See J. Mamorsky, *Employee Benefits Law* (Law Journal Seminars-Press 1984 ed.), at 2-10. When contributions are not made from profits, the plan may also be considered discontinued, or terminated, requiring full vesting of all participant account balances. Code §411(d)(3) and 26 C.F.R. 1.411 (d)-2(a)(1) and (d). And see ch. 9, sec. VIII.A, and ch. 12, sec. III. A discretionary commitment to make contributions out of profits, without a substantial nondiscretionary minimum, can also affect whether contributions to the plan, when made, are considered a part of the employee's regular rate of pay for the purpose of determining overtime compensation under the Fair Labor Standards Act. See secs. IV and VI.

[10] See e.g., Rev. Rul. 81-12, and ch. 4, sec. IV.B (on protection of accrued benefits) and ch. 5, sec. IV (on vesting schedule changes). The record of the plan's terms and amendments also enables the IRS to determine more readily whether a plan has been operated in a manner which discriminates in favor of the prohibited group of employees.

[11] ERISA §402(b)(4).

[12] See *Aitken v. IP & GCU-Employer Retirement Fund*, 604 F.2d 1261, at 1266 (9th Cir. 1979).

[13] See Rev. Ruls. 69-427, 74-385, and 79-90.

the employer's control, such as a percentage of the prime interest rate of a named bank.[14]

IV. Compensation Under a Benefit or Contribution Allocation Formula

When employee compensation is used under a plan's benefit or contribution formula in determining a participant's benefits, compensation must be defined in the plan in a manner that is definitely determinable. Moreover, the definition must not produce discrimination in favor of the employees who are officers, shareholders or highly compensated. In making this test in any plan year beginning after December 31, 1988, compensation is expressly defined as *total* compensation includible in the gross income of the employee.[15]

Generally, nondiscrimination in a compensation definition requires that a plan use at least a three-year average of compensation when it bases benefits on an average of compensation.[16] A three-year average is to ensure that compensation will not be artificially adjusted in one or two years to produce higher benefits for the select few. As discussed below, where a plan's benefits are integrated with Social Security on an "excess" basis, at least a five-year average of compensation is required, or else the maximum level of permissible integration is reduced.

The IRS has also ruled that definitions of "compensation" are discriminatory when compensation is defined to include unfunded deferred compensation available primarily to officers and highly compensated employees,[17] bonuses largely available to the same group,[18] and

---

[14] Despite the definite determinability requirement, employer discretion has been allowed to exist under plans in regard to whether early retirement, lump sum benefits, or other benefit options are allowed an employee so long as the benefits available under such options do not exceed the actuarial equivalent of the participant's normal retirement benefits and prohibited discrimination does not occur in the exercise of the discretion. See Rev. Ruls. 85-59, 58-151, and 58-604.

The future status of early retirement, lump sum, and other benefit options requiring consent of an employer, or "mutually satisfactory" conditions, is at the time of this writing clouded by proposed IRS regulations that would require plans to eliminate such provisions in order to satisfy both the Code's definitely determinable benefit requirement and ERISA §204(g), as amended by the Retirement Equity Act. See Prop. Regs. 1.401(a)-4 and 1.411(d)-4, 51 Fed. Reg. 3798 (Jan. 30, 1986). In lieu of open-ended discretion, plans could adopt objective and clearly ascertainable criteria, for example, on the insurability of an employee or the existence of extreme financial need if the purpose of the discretion has been to ensure that only employees in good health receive lump sum benefits or that only employees with extreme financial hardship receive early withdrawals of benefits. This antidiscretion regulation is proposed to become effective for nonbargained plans in the second plan year after Jan. 30, 1986, and for collectively bargained plans, in the earlier of the third plan year after Jan. 30, 1986, or the second plan year after the expiration of the collective bargaining agreement in effect on Jan. 30, 1986.

[15] Code §401(a)(5)(B), as amended by §1111 of the Tax Reform Act, P.L. 99-514, and Code §414(s), as amended by §1115. Elective deferrals to §401(k) plans may be included as compensation for this purpose if an employer so elects. Code §414(s)(3), as amended.

[16] Rev. Rul. 71-330.

[17] Rev. Rul. 80-359 (inclusion of unfunded deferred compensation is discriminatory, unless proportion of compensation actually deferred by rank and file employees equals or exceeds proportion deferred by employees who are officers, shareholders, or highly compensated).

[18] *Epstein v. Commissioner*, 70 T.C. 439 (1978).

dividends from corporate profits payable only to employee-shareholders.[19] Definitions of compensation have also been ruled to discriminate when compensation is imputed to officers and shareholders who have little or no actual compensation.[20] Elective employee contributions to a Section 401(k) plan that may otherwise be received in cash may be included as compensation under a second plan's formula. Nonelective employer contributions to a Section 401(k) or any other profit-sharing or stock bonus plan may not be included as compensation unless the contributions are fully vested at all times, allocated on the basis of current compensation, and discrimination does not otherwise result.[21]

A compensation definition can function to produce discrimination based on other compensation characteristics of the participants. In Revenue Ruling 85-34, a plan provided that participants were to receive 15 percent of either their current compensation or their compensation during the first year the plan was established, whichever was higher. The one officer-employee under the plan had very high compensation in the year the plan was established relative to his current compensation and to the compensation of the rank and file employee in both the current year and the year of plan establishment. Use of this formula therefore produced discrimination in operation because it resulted in the employer's contributions on behalf of the officer exceeding the contributions on behalf of the rank and file employee when both were "expressed as a percentage of total compensation in [the current] year."

In certain situations, the question is not whether certain items should be excluded from a definition of compensation, but whether other items, such as overtime and commissions, which are within the particular province of the rank and file, must be included in a plan's definition of compensation for it to be nondiscriminatory. In Revenue Ruling 81-74, the issue was whether a profit-sharing plan's definition of compensation was discriminatory when it defined compensation to include regular salary and bonuses, but excluded sales commissions and overtime pay. To determine whether the definition was discriminatory, the Revenue Ruling looked at the relationship of the included items to the total compensation of the rank and file employees and to the total compensation of the prohibited group of employees. Because under the facts presented, the definition actually favored the rank and file—rank and file employees had 65 percent of their total compensation covered by the definition as compared to 55 percent for the prohibited group—the definition was found not to be discriminatory. The clear implication, however, was that if the percentages were reversed, discrimination would have resulted.

---

[19] Rev. Rul. 71-26.

[20] Rev. Rul. 62-206.

[21] Rev. Ruls. 59-13, 83-89, and 84-74.

The effect of the Code's nondiscrimination constraints, as mentioned before, is usually to indirectly require the plan to provide a little more to lower paid employees. For example, if the objective of the plan is to provide the owner and certain highly compensated employees with benefits equal to $50,000 per year in retirement, the effect of leaving out bonuses or dividends from the definition of "compensation" is to require the plan's benefit percentage to be somewhat higher. Thus, if an owner makes $100,000 in salary and also pays himself a year-end bonus of $50,000 per year, the effect of leaving the bonus out may be to require the plan to provide benefits of 50 percent of compensation to meet the owner's benefit objective, rather than 33⅓ percent of compensation. Either way, the owner can receive the same benefits, but lower paid employees may receive more when the items which they do not generally receive are excluded from the plan's definition.

Special constraints on permissible compensation definitions apply to "top-heavy" plans and tax credit ESOPs. For a top-heavy plan, which is described below, the maximum compensation permitted to be plugged into a plan's benefit or contribution formula for any employee is $200,000.[22] For a tax credit ESOP, the maximum compensation permitted is $100,000.[23]

Effective in 1989, the Tax Reform Act establishes a $200,000 cap on the annual compensation that may be included in computing benefits or contribution allocations under *any* qualified plan's formula.[24]

Profit-sharing plans that cover employees subject to the Fair Labor Standards Act and that provide only discretionary contributions out of profits, or an unsubstantial nondiscriminatory minimum contribution, may effectively be required to include overtime pay in their definition of compensation. This is because the FLSA excludes contributions to a "bona fide" plan from an employee's regular rate of pay for the purpose of computing overtime pay.[25] However, for a profit-sharing plan to be considered bona fide, it must provide substantial nondiscretionary contributions;[26] otherwise whatever contributions are made to the plan and allocated to the employee's account must be included in the employee's regular rate of pay in computing overtime compensation.[27] However, as an alternative, the Wage and Hour Administrator will allow discretionary profit-sharing plan contributions to be excluded from the regular rate of pay in computing overtime, so long as

---

[22] Code §416(d). Sec. VIII. F.4 below describes the tests for determining if a plan is top heavy.

[23] Code §409(b)(2). The Tax Reform Act repealed the special tax credits for contributions to tax credit ESOPs made after the end of 1986. As a result, tax credit ESOPs have generally been frozen or terminated. See §1171(a) of the Tax Reform Act, P.L. 99-514, repealing Code §41.

[24] Code §401(a)(17), as added by §1106(d)(1) of P.L. 99-514. Compensation is also limited to $200,000 in computing deductible contributions to a qualified plan, effective at the same time. See Code §404(l), as added by §1106(d)(2).

[25] 29 U.S.C. §207(e).

[26] 29 C.F.R. 778.215(a)(3). A substantial and nondiscretionary minimum percentage is illustrated in the regulations as 5% of profits. *Id.*

[27] 29 C.F.R. 778.214(c).

the basis for allocating contributions under the plan among participants is a percentage of compensation, defined as including overtime pay.[28]

The term compensation, even if relatively specifically defined in a plan, is also sometimes subject to different interpretations. In *Korn v. Levine Bros. Iron Works Corp.*, plan trustees interpreted the term compensation to exclude certain quarterly payments made to a participant. A district court held that where the plan defined compensation as including "bonuses, overtime and commissions," and in its application for determination to the IRS to obtain tax-qualified status stated that benefits were based on "total compensation," the exclusion of these quarterly payments was arbitrary and capricious.[29] In *Hepler v. CBS, Inc.*, it was arbitrary and capricious to construe "basic monthly earnings" to mean an artificially constructed low salary when an employee was paid entirely on commission because if the trustees' interpretation was upheld, the plan would have failed to disclose the "basis on which payments are made ... from the plan," as required by ERISA Section 402(b)(4).[30]

Of perhaps more general application, the *Korn* court also held that the trustees' interpretation of "the highest five consecutive years" in determining the participant's average compensation under the benefit formula could not mean, as the trustees contended, the highest five consecutive "*plan* years" when that was not expressly called for under the plan. Rather, the court held, the highest five consecutive years must mean the highest five consecutive 12-month periods, including the last months of employment. The court noted that typically salaries are rising, so that the substitution of "plan years" for years would tend to decrease the highest five consecutive year average, and found no justification for doing so when the plan simply referred to "years."[31]

ERISA's benefit accrual rules can also have an effect on the computation of averages of compensation under a plan's benefit formula, as discussed in Chapter 4.

---

[28] See Wage and Hour Opinion 190 (Jan. 8, 1973) and Wage and Hour Opinion 241 (Nov. 26, 1973), both reprinted in BNA Wage & Hour Man., at 94:575 and 94:576. And see D. McGill, *Fundamentals of Private Pensions* (Richard D. Irwin 5th ed.), at 611.

[29] 574 F.Supp. 836, 4 EBC 2533 (S.D.N.Y. 1983).

[30] 696 P.2d 596, 6 EBC 1426, at 1430 (Wash. Ct.App. 1985). But see *Bruder v. Holscher-Wernig Pension Plan,* 599 F.Supp. 347 (E.D. Mo. 1984) (commissions not included in "compensation" under benefit formula even though past plans had specifically excluded commissions and current plan did not, and even though exception had been made for one participant to enable him to receive at least some pension benefits); *Rosenthal v. National Life Ins. Co.*, 486 F.Supp. 1018 (S.D.N.Y. 1980) (denying participant's claim that renewal commissions received after termination from employment should be included in compensation definition).

[31] 574 F.Supp. 836, 4 EBC 2533 (S.D.N.Y. 1983).

V. Years, Including Past Service, in Defined Benefit Plan Formulas

When benefit formulas vary the amount of benefits with a participant's length of service, as occurs under almost all defined benefit plans, a wide variety of terms can be used to refer to the service element of the plan's benefit formula. For example, a plan may refer to "years of service," "continuous service," "pension credit," "benefit service," and, perhaps most commonly, "credited service." As there are variations in the names given to the service element, there are also variations in what is contained in the definition—even under the same name. Thus, an employer can define credited service to include periods of disability, approved leaves of absence (e.g., time spent on leave as a paid union officer, or on corporate loan), and military service. Credited service may also include past service—service with the employer before the plan was established; reciprocal service—service under a related multiemployer plan; or preparticipation service—any service before the employee became a participant in the plan.

ERISA requires certain periods of service, termed years of participation, to be included in any length of service element used in determining a defined benefit plan's normal retirement benefit and then also bases the accrual of a portion of the plan's normal retirement benefit before retirement on those years of participation.[32] Other legislation, such as the Veterans' Readjustment Assistance Act and the Pregnancy Discrimination Act, can also require that certain periods of service be included both in the credited service component of the plan's benefit formula and in the basis for determining the benefits that have accrued. The discussion below, however, focuses on the Code's requirements concerning credited service under a benefit formula. The requirements of ERISA, other federal law, and federal common law on what years count as years of participation for benefit accruals are discussed in Chapter 4.[33]

Under the Code, the first question is whether the service credited in a benefit formula is "definitely determinable." Any service term is, of course, open to interpretation, but certain terms, such as leave of absence, are more nebulous than others. When leaves of absence are credited, the purposes for which leaves are granted are not absolutely required to be expressed in the plan, but the employer must have an established policy on leaves of absence, and it must be applied in a uniform manner to all participants under similar circumstances.[34] Similarly, if the plan credits periods of disability or layoff, the service

[32] The opposite may not be true, i.e., when service that is not included in ERISA's "years of participation," e.g., years of past service, is included in the service component of a plan's benefit formula, the service is not necessarily required to be included in years of participation for benefit accruals—although it may be. See ch. 4, sec. III.B.6.

[33] See ch. 4, sec. III.

[34] Rev. Rul. 81-106, and see *Hardy v. H.K. Porter Co.*, 417 F.Supp. 1175 (E.D. Pa. 1976), *aff'd in part, rev'd in part*, 562 F.2d 42 (3d Cir. 1977).

included under these terms must be definitely determinable and the employer's policy on disability or layoffs applied in a uniform manner.

The second question under the Code is whether a service element in a benefit formula "discriminates" by including credit that is within the particular domain of employees who are officers, shareholders, or highly compensated. For example, if leaves of absence are largely restricted to the prohibited group employees, it may be insufficient that the employer's leave policy is established and applied uniformly to employees in similar circumstances, if those circumstances on their face or in operation result in discrimination.[35]

Although generally favorably regarded by pension planners, the biggest source of potential discrimination in the credited service component of a benefit formula among small plans comes from the inclusion of years of "past service." When defined benefit plans are established, past service, i.e., years with the employer before the plan was established, is often credited under the plan's benefit formula, because older workers otherwise might not have enough service credit to receive more than a small pension. In a small plan, and in some larger plans, however, the older employees who are officers, shareholders, and highly compensated are the employees who have the most past service. Moreover, they control the benefit formula, so that regardless of whether they are credited with their past service or with only future service, they can still obtain the benefits they want by varying the percentage of compensation that is to be multiplied by those years. In these cases, past service credit can be a device for discrimination. For example, a small employer might set up a plan to benefit the principal owner and the vice-president, both age 55 and with 25 years of past service. The rank and file employees may have at most five years of past service. If the plan provides benefits on a unit basis of one percent of final pay, the result of crediting the past service is that the owner and vice-president both have benefits of 25 percent of final pay at the inception of the plan, while the most any of the other employees have is five percent of pay benefits. If the plan is terminated on the retirement of the owner and vice-president 10 years later, as is common, their benefits will then be 35 percent of pay, while the other employees—if they are still employed—will have 15 percent of pay. Thus, rather than providing a benefit that is actually an equal percentage of pay to all employees, the owner and vice-president have obtained a much larger percentage of pay benefit compared to the other employees. The same benefits could be obtained by the owner and vice-president if only future service was used, but to do this, the plan's benefit formula would have to be 3½ percent of final pay for each year of future service, and the same percentage of pay benefits would have to be provided the other employees.

Generally, the IRS does not appear to object to the use of past

---

[35] Rev. Rul. 81-106.

service even if prohibited group employees have slightly more past service than other employees because this is seen as a needed incentive to the establishment of small plans. At some point, though, the resulting disproportion in benefits as a percentage of pay can become so great that the IRS will find discrimination from use of the past service. In Revenue Ruling 81-248, the IRS found discrimination when a plan at its inception was limited to benefits based entirely on past service years and the two employees who were officers and shareholders had 12 and 11 years of past service, while the six rank and file employees had from three to nine years of past service. The benefits under the plan were seven percent of a three-year average of compensation for each of the past service years reduced by the maximum percentage offset permitted under Social Security integration. (As discussed below, Social Security integration, by itself, results in a lower per year percentage pension benefit for lower paid employees than for the more highly compensated.) Revenue Ruling 81-248 found the plan discriminatory because it provided "both larger total benefits and larger benefits per year of service (in each case measured as a percentage of compensation), for participants in whose favor discrimination is prohibited." The fact that the plan was, at its inception, limited to benefits based only on past service years was not dispositive, except that it enabled the IRS to conclusively determine at the plan's inception that the discrimination would "not be remedied by the continued operation of the plan."

More commonly, a plan's benefits are based on past service and future service, as in the first example. In this situation, whether the discrimination from the use of past service credits will be "remedied by the continued operation of the plan" depends on the facts and circumstances. Chief among these may be whether the plan uses Social Security integration to lower the benefits of rank and file employees as a percentage of pay both in terms of benefits per year of service and the likely benefit total, and also how long the plan may reasonably be expected to continue. It may be noted that if the plan in the first example above was fully integrated, and then was continued for only 10 years, both of which are common among small employer plans, the results might actually be worse than in Revenue Ruling 81-248.

A plan with past service may also discriminate if it does not restrict the benefits from past service credits to benefits based on past service compensation. In Revenue Rulings 81-248 and 81-49, the compensation used in computing past service benefits was limited to a three-year average based on compensation immediately *preceding* the plan's establishment.

When a plan credits years of past service to original plan participants, past service credit must generally also be extended on the same basis to subsequent participants in the plan. In Revenue Ruling 70-77, past service credit for original, but not subsequent, participants in a plan was ruled to be discriminatory, unless the employer affirmatively demonstrates a lack of discrimination from the distinction. Most subsequent participants, of course, don't have past service in the sense of service with the employer before the establishment of the plan. However, they will often have one to three years of preparticipation service as a result of conditions for participation, and sometimes will have more years of preparticipation service from work with the employer in job classifications or divisions not covered by the plan. In Revenue Ruling 70-77, past service credits were required to be provided subsequent participants for preparticipation years under a pre-ERISA plan requiring five years and age 25 as conditions for participation. Revenue Ruling 70-77 suggested that such past service credit would not ordinarily be required to be extended to subsequent participants if a plan used just a one year waiting period as a condition for participation. It is unclear whether this exception still applies after ERISA, but clearly any longer preparticipation service (such as in an uncovered job classification or division) must be subject to the same past service grant afforded original participants, unless a lack of discrimination from such a distinction can be affirmatively demonstrated.

Another factor in whether past service credits discriminate in favor of the prohibited group is whether the past service years count for vesting. Usually, prohibited group employees will be in a position to vest regardless, but many rank and file employees may need the past service credits to vest. As discussed in Chapter 5, the IRS's regulations on vesting do not require that past service years credited for benefit accruals necessarily count for vesting, but the IRS can require this to diminish the potential discrimination from the past service grant.

Collectively bargained plans also frequently provide past service credits for years before the plan is established, or in the case of collectively bargained multiemployer plans, for years before an employer joins the plan. This is generally not discriminatory under the Internal Revenue Code. First, one major difference between nonbargained and collectively bargained plans is that very few members of the Code's "prohibited group" of employees are likely to be in a collectively bargained plan. Union officers are not generally "officers" for purposes of nondiscrimination under the Code.[36] The "shareholders" designation is likewise inapplicable because bargaining unit employees generally do

---

[36] However, if a union's paid staff are included in a plan, the union's officers may be considered "officers" for purposes of Code nondiscrimination as if the union were just another employer maintaining the plan. Code §413(b)(8), 26 C.F.R. 1.413-1(i), and Conf. Rep., at 384, 3 ERISA Leg. Hist. 4651. But if a union officer's participation in a plan is based on service with an employer, for example, when he or she is not paid on a full-time basis by the union and continues to work for the employer, or when a union official continues to receive benefit credits under a collectively bargained provision that provides for continuing pension credits during the period when he or she is a union officer, the "officer" designation does not apply.

Parenthetically, the pensions of union officers that are comparable to those of corporate executives are usually offered through separate plans for union staff alone. For an example, see *Hoffa v. Fitzsimmons*, 673 F.2d 1345, 3 EBC 1261 (D.C. Cir. 1982) (union staff plan provided 100% of final average salary for 20 years of service; Hoffa's pension was worth from $1.2 to $1.7 million in lump sum form). In plans for union staff, the union's officers are "officers" for purposes of the Code's nondiscrimination tests, and are also likely to be "highly compensated" vis-a-vis the lower paid union staff. See Rev. Rul. 71-438.

not have significant individual ownership interests in the employer. Participants in a collectively bargained plan may be "highly compensated" for purposes of the Code's nondiscrimination test, but only if their compensation is high relative to the compensation of *all* employees of the employer maintaining the plan, rather than just those employees who are covered under the collectively bargained plan.[37] The result is that few, if any, participants in a collectively bargained plan are likely to be considered officers, shareholders, or highly compensated employees under Code Section 401(a)(4).[38] Second, even if there are highly compensated employees within a collectively bargained plan, the past service credits are likely to be extended to enough other nonhighly compensated employees with similar past service records that discrimination would not exist at the inception of the plan or would be remedied by its continued operation.[39]

Similar constraints to those applying under the Code could arise under Section 302(c)(5) of the Labor Management Relations Act (if the plan is jointly administered), and under ERISA Section 404(a)(1)'s fiduciary standard, if plan provisions unduly favor or otherwise restrict the plan's benefits to the "class of employees from which union officers are commonly drawn."[40] Under the Supreme Court's holding in *UMW Health & Retirement Funds v. Robinson*, jurisdiction under Section 302(c)(5) and, by extension, under ERISA's fiduciary standard is not present if the provisions in question are the product of collective bargaining, as opposed to "trustee" decisions,[41] but the NLRA duty of fair representation could still provide a remedy in a particularly egregious case.

VI. Years Under Defined Contribution Plan Allocation Formulas

The IRS is more suspicious of potential discrimination when a defined contribution plan's formula for the allocation of contributions (or for the reallocation of forfeitures) takes years of service into account in any form—whether they are past service years or years after the establishment of the plan. In Revenue Ruling 84-155, the IRS

---

[37] 26 C.F.R. 1.413-1(c)(2).

[38] Rev. Rul. 71-438.

[39] The concept of discrimination could have some application if the base of employees actually benefiting from the past service is, by other factors, gradually and substantially narrowed. However, the application of the Code's nondiscrimination requirements is, as stated before, generally limited in a collectively bargained plan because of the absence of employees who are either officers or highly compensated within the meaning of the Code.

[40] In *Riley v. MEBA Pension Trust*, Judge Friendly of the Second Circuit stated that while §302(c)(5) does not give courts "a roving jurisdiction over . . . the structure of pension plans . . . a case might stand differently if, e.g., it were shown . . . that the plan was heavily weighted in favor of a class of employees from which union officers were commonly drawn." 570 F.2d 406, 1 EBC 1757, at 1763 (2d Cir. 1978).

[41] 455 U.S. 562, 3 EBC 1129 (1982).

examined a series of profit-sharing formulas that allocated contributions based on compensation units, e.g., one point for every $100 in compensation, that were: (1) multiplied by years of service, (2) added to years of service, and (3) weighted by years of service. Although none of these types of formulas was discriminatory or nondiscriminatory *per se*, the results were closely scrutinized for discrimination in operation in contributions as a percentage of compensation tending to favor highly compensated employees.

In the first situation, compensation units were multiplied by years of service. Even though the compensation units were capped at $20,000, so that participants in the very highest salary range actually received lower percentage contributions than participants in some of the lower salary ranges, the IRS still found discrimination because highly compensated employees in salary brackets directly below the very highest bracket were receiving higher percentage contributions under the formula than any other group of employees. In the second situation, contributions were allocated based on compensation units to which years of service were added as additional units. Discrimination was not found because the results produced under the formula, given the facts set forth in the ruling, were contributions as a percentage of compensation that increased uniformly as salary decreased. If these results were reversed in the plan's later operation, it is clear that the allocation formula would then be discriminatory.[42] In the third situation, contributions were allocated based on compensation units weighted by years of service. The IRS found discrimination, not based on the form of the formula *per se*, but based on the results for employees in different salary brackets.

Reallocations of forfeited profit-sharing accounts on the basis of account balances, rather than on the basis of each year's current compensation, is another means by which years of service can be taken into account in a profit-sharing plan formula. Again, as established in Revenue Ruling 81-10, the IRS does not flatly prohibit reallocations on this basis, but it examines the results on a "year-by-year basis" to determine whether the reallocation of forfeitures on the basis of account balances discriminates "as a percentage of compensation" in favor of highly compensated employees. Usually such a formula will produce discrimination. "Accordingly, the great majority of [profit-sharing] plans use [current] compensation, rather than account balances to reallocate forfeitures."[43]

The Fair Labor Standards Act can limit the use of years of service under a profit-sharing plan's contribution allocation formula when the employer's contribution commitment is completely discretionary, or is partially discretionary without a "substantial" nondiscretionary minimum. When such a profit-sharing plan covers FLSA employees, it is not considered a "bona fide" plan within the meaning of 29 U.S.C.

---

[42] See Rev. Ruls. 84-155 and 81-10.

[43] D. McGill, *Fundamentals of Private Pensions* (5th ed.), at 622-23.

Section 201(e)(4). Therefore, whatever contributions are made to the plan must be included in the employees' regular rates of pay for purposes of determining overtime compensation. As an alternative to this, the Wage and Hour Administrator allows employers to avoid this requirement if overtime pay is included in the definition of compensation on which profit-sharing contributions are allocated. However, if the allocation of contributions is then weighted by years of service, account balances, or other service-related factors, the basis for this alternative is undercut. Like the IRS, the Wage and Hour Administrator does not flatly prohibit these types of formulas, but the employer must be able to show that the allocation of contributions compensates overtime in the required relationship to regular time pay.[44] This is difficult to do when contribution allocations are based in large part on an unrelated years of service or account balance factor, except by happenstance.

Many defined contribution plans make the allocation of contributions to employees for any given year contingent on employment on a certain date. For example, a profit-sharing plan might provide for employer contributions of up to 10 percent of profits to be allocated according to the ratio of individual compensation in the year to total compensation, but only for participants who are employed on December 31 of the year. A participant who works nearly the entire year, but who is terminated on December 15, would then miss out on the entire year's contribution allocation because of a few days. As discussed in Chapter 4 on the measurement of years of participation, the IRS does not rule out such a provision flatly, but it will examine whether the provision results in discrimination. Under Revenue Ruling 76-250, to determine whether discrimination results, all participants who had over 1,000 hours of service in the yearly period are considered. Thus, if the group of participants who miss out on contributions for the year because of the December 31 employment requirement are primarily rank and file employees who had over 1,000 hours of service, the IRS may find prohibited discrimination from the use of an all or nothing employment date under the plan.[45]

VII. Employee Contribution Requirements and Elective Section 401(k) Deferrals

A. Employee Contribution Requirements

The general rule on employee contributions has been that a rate of mandatory employee contributions of up to six percent of compensation is not so burdensome to rank and file employees as to make a plan

---

[44] See Wage and Hour Opinion Letter 190 (Jan. 8, 1973), reprinted in BNA Wage & Hour Man., at 94:575. And see BNA Wage & Hour Man., at 94:702 (summarizing other opinions).

[45] This nondiscrimination requirement and also interpretation of ambiguous plan terms on whether employment on a certain date is required are discussed further in ch. 4, sec. III.E.

discriminatory under Code Section 401(a)(4), provided that the percentage or classification coverage tests in Code Section 410(b)(1) are met by the employees actually making the required contributions.[46] In Revenue Ruling 80-307, however, the IRS recognized that when a plan provides for optional rates of employee contributions with matching employer contributions, a much higher rate of employer contributions can effectively be delivered to officers, shareholders, or highly compensated employees because they are more likely to make the employee contributions at the plan's maximum rate. For example, if a thrift plan provides for dollar-for-dollar employer matching of employee contributions of up to six percent of compensation, the results may be sufficient participation by rank and file employees to meet the Section 410(b)(1) coverage tests, but much larger employer contributions as a percentage of pay on behalf of the prohibited group employees. The average rate of contributions by lower paid employees might, for example, be one percent, because of the burden of making employee contributions from a limited income, while the average rate of employee contributions for highly compensated employees might be the full six percent. The result is a plan that effectively provides employer contributions that are six times as much as a percentage of compensation for highly compensated employees as for other employees. Revenue Ruling 80-307 recognizes that discrimination *may* result in such a case.

The 1986 Tax Reform Act establishes an objective nondiscrimination test for defined contribution plans requiring employee contributions (generally know as thrift or savings plans) that is virtually identical to the actual deferral percentage test used for Code Section 401(k) plans.[47] The test is effective for plan years beginning after December 31, 1986.[48] Under it, the contribution percentage for highly compensated employees is compared to the contribution percentage of all other eligible employees. An employee's contribution percentage is the sum of employee contributions and matching employer contributions divided by the employee's compensation. The contribution percentages for individual highly compensated and other eligible employees are then separately summed and divided by the number of employees in the respective groups. To meet the nondiscrimination test, the contribution percentage of highly compensated employees must not exceed the *greater* of:

(1) 1.25 times the contribution percentage of all other eligible employees, or

(2) The contribution percentage of all other eligible employees

---

[46] Rev. Ruls. 69-421 and 72-58, and see *Federal Land Bank of Asheville v. Commissioner*, 74 T.C. 1106, 2 EBC 2385 (1980).

[47] Employee contributions to defined benefit plans are subject to the same test if the employee contributions are allocated to a separate account on behalf of the employee. Conf. Rep., H.R. Rep. 99-841, at II-394.

[48] §1117(d) of P.L. 99-514. A later effective date can apply to a collectively bargained plan.

plus two percent, or twice the contribution percentage of all other eligible employees, whichever of these two is *less*.[49]

B. Elective Salary Deferrals

Special nondiscrimination rules also apply to Section 401(k) salary reduction plans. Under the regular nondiscrimination rules, a defined contribution plan can provide up to 5.7 percent higher contributions on compensation above the Social Security wage base than below. Under Section 401(k), instead of this limit, the percentage of compensation deferred by the highest paid one-third of the employees covered by the plan must not be in excess of 1.5 times the percentage of compensation deferred by the lowest paid two-thirds of the employees under the plan. Alternatively, a Section 401(k) plan is not considered discriminatory if the deferral percentage for the highest paid one-third of the employees is neither (1) more than 2.5 times the deferral percentage for the lower two-thirds, nor (2) equal to or more than three percent above the deferral percentage of the lower two-thirds.

In making these tests, the deferral percentage for a group is the sum of the percentages of compensation deferred by each employee divided by the number of employees in the group.[50] An employer concerned about whether lower paid employees will defer enough of their compensation to meet either test can ensure compliance by providing nonelective employer contributions, or matching employer contributions on elective deferrals up to a certain percentage, which will be treated as elective salary deferrals in determining whether the special nondiscrimination tests are satisfied.[51]

Effective in 1987, the maximum actual deferral percentage (ADP) for highly compensated employees is changed by the Tax Reform Act from no more than 1.5 times the ADP of all other eligible employees to no more than 1.25 times their ADP.[52] The alternate ADP test is amended to provide that the ADP of highly compensated employees may be neither more than twice the ADP of all other eligible employees (instead of not more than 2.5 times their ADP), nor more than two

---

[49] Code §401(m), as amended by §1117 of P.L. 99-514. In meeting these tests, an employer can aggregate elective deferrals to §401(k) plans and "qualified" nonelective contributions to the same or other defined contribution plans. See Code §§401(m)(3) and (4), as amended.

[50] §401(k)(3)(B). The 1984 Deficit Reduction Act amended §401(k)(3) to clarify that these special rules are in lieu of the regular nondiscrimination rules for defined contribution plans. Proposed IRS regulations had provided that the regular nondiscrimination rules might be substituted for the special §401(k) rules. See Prop. Regs. 1.401(k)-1(a)(3). 44 Fed. Reg. 55544 (Nov. 10, 1981). Reliance on the proposed regulations was authorized by IRS Notice 82-1. The 1984 Deficit Reduction Act amendment clarifies that only the special §401(k) test applies for plan years after Dec. 31, 1984.

[51] Provided that the nonelective contributions are immediately nonforfeitable and subject to the same rules on withdrawals as the elective contributions. See Prop. Regs. 1.401(k)-1(c) and (d), 44 Fed. Reg. 55544 (Nov. 10, 1981), and Conference Report on DEFRA, H.R. Rep. 98-861, at 1144-45, [1984] U.S. Code Cong. & Ad. News, at 1832-33.

[52] Code §401(k)(3)(A)(ii)(I), as amended by §1116 of P.L. 99-514. A later effective date can apply to a collectively bargained §401(k) plan.

percent above the ADP of all other eligible employees (instead of not more than three percent).[53] The group of highly compensated employees used under these tests is altered from the highest paid one-third of all eligible employees to highly compensated employees as defined by the Tax Reform Act.[54] The compensation used in the denominator of the ADP tests is also expressly defined as total compensation (not including the elective deferrals themselves).[55]

Effective in 1989, the Tax Reform Act specifically prohibits elective deferrals to a Section 401(k) plan from being taken into account in determining if any other plan of the employer meets the Code's nondiscrimination standard.[56] The Act further provides that no other benefits, except matching employer contributions under the Section 401(k) plan, can be conditioned on whether an employee makes elective deferrals.[57]

VIII. Formulas With Social Security Integration

In designing a plan that provides disproportionately higher benefits for highly compensated employees than for lower and average paid employees, which is the express purpose of many pension plan designers, no more generally effective device exists than Social Security integration.[58] As a result of Social Security offsets and excess formulas, the pension benefits of many lower and average paid employees who are covered by a plan are much lower under the plan's formula, even as a percentage of pay for each credited year of service, than for more highly paid employees. This is done through formulas that "integrate" the plan's benefits by offsetting a percentage of Social Security benefits, or by paying a higher percentage benefit on compensation above an average related to the Social Security wage base. According to the Bureau of Labor Statistics' 1984 survey of the plans of medium and

---

[53] Code §401(k)(3)(A)(ii)(II), as amended.

[54] Code §401(k)(5), as amended.

[55] Code §401(k)(9), as amended by §1116, and §414(s), as amended by §1115. However, elective deferrals may be included for this purpose if the employer elects, Code §414(s)(3), and elective deferrals to the §401(k) plan are always included in determining who the highly compensated employees are.

[56] Code §401(k)(4)(C), as amended. This prohibits use of elective deferrals to a §401(k) plan in determining whether the §401(k) plan is comparable to another plan for the purpose of aggregating the two plans' coverage to meet the Code §410(b) coverage tests. An exception allows such deferrals to be taken into account under the average benefits test for coverage.

[57] Code §401(k)(4)(A), as amended. This provision prohibits floor-offset arrangements in which elective deferrals to a §401(k) plan are converted to annuity form and used as an offset from benefits under a defined benefit plan. See Conf. Rep., H.R. Rep. 99-841, at II-390, and Price Waterhouse, "Analysis of Pension and Welfare Benefit Plan Provisions of Tax Reform Act," 13 BNA Pens. Rep. Spec. Supp., at S-19 (Oct. 27, 1986). See also sec. VIII.F.4 on the application of this rule to top-heavy plans.

[58] Crediting past service can be equally or more effective in creating disproportionate benefits as a percentage of compensation if the officers, shareholders, and highly compensated employees have more past service than the rank and file. Vesting requirements can also increase disparities between the benefits of rank and file and highly compensated employees if rank and file employees have higher turnover.

large firms, 56 percent of all participants are in plans that integrate the plan's benefits with Social Security.[59] Among smaller plans, Social Security integration is even more prevalent.[60] Plans that are not integrated with Social Security at all are largely collectively bargained plans or defined contribution plans.

Social Security integration permits an employer to provide more substantial benefits or contributions as a percentage of pay to highly compensated employees than to employees who are in lower or average pay classes. An "integrated plan" is, in fact, defined by the IRS as:

> "[A] plan [with] differences in proportionate benefits ... which favor more highly paid employees. . . ."[61]

As mentioned, these "differences in proportionate benefits" are created through two basic types of benefit formulas:

(1) "Offset" formulas in which a percentage of the participant's primary Social Security benefit is subtracted from the participant's benefits; and

(2) "Excess" formulas under which a higher percentage benefit or contribution is offered on the portion of a participant's compensation which is above a breakpoint related to the Social Security wage base.

In an excess plan that provides benefits based on a final or highest average of pay, this breakpoint can be the average of the taxable wage base for Social Security over a full career, e.g., $15,000 for a worker reaching age 65 in 1986. In career average pay plans (i.e., plans where each year's benefits are determined separately based on compensation in that year) and in defined contribution plans, the breakpoint can be as high as the Social Security wage base in the current year, e.g., $42,000 in 1986.

Social Security integration can, in some cases, wipe out all benefits or contributions for rank and file participants, despite the fact that they are "covered" by a "nondiscriminatory" plan and have the number of years of service required to "vest." In effect, participants may vest in nothing. In most cases, however, Social Security integration formulas are designed to skew the plan's benefits or contributions toward highly compensated employees, while leaving lower and average paid employees with at least some pension benefits, but not as much on a percentage basis.

---

[59] BLS, Employee Benefits in Medium and Large Firms, 1984, at 47.

[60] See J. Schulz, T. Leavitt, and J. Strate, "The Incidence of Integration Provisions in Private Pension Plans," 9 J. Pens. Plan. & Compl. 399, at 404 (Oct. 1983).

[61] Rev. Rul. 71-446, §2.02.

A. Examples

An offset formula can be illustrated by the benefit formula of the J.C. Penney Company pension plan. It provides 1.5 percent of the highest five consecutive year average of pay in a participant's last 10 years of participation *less* 1.67 percent of the participant's primary Social Security benefit, multiplied by years of participation. For two participants retiring in 1986 with 15 years of participation, but the first with a $20,000 highest five-year average and the second with a $75,000 highest five-year average, the effect of this formula is as follows (with primary Social Security benefits estimated[62]):

((1.5% × $20,000) − (1.67% × $8,239))
× 15 years of participation = $2,436;
((1.5% × $75,000) − (1.67% × $9,121))
× 15 years of participation = $14,590.

The $20,000 participant thus receives 12.2 percent of his highest five-year average of pay under the formula, while the $75,000 participant receives 19.5 percent. The reason for this is that by subtracting a percentage of primary Social Security benefits, the plan has in effect removed a higher percentage of the lower paid person's salary from the benefit formula.

An excess formula that produces roughly comparable results can be illustrated by a formula that provides a benefit of 1.5 percent on the portion of a highest five-year average of pay above a breakpoint of $15,000 (established by the average of the maximum Social Security taxable wage base for someone reaching age 65 in 1986), and .75 percent on the portion of the five-year salary average below $15,000. Under this formula, two participants each with 15 years of participation, but one with a $20,000 highest average and the other with a $75,000 average, would receive:

((1.5% × ($20,000 − $15,000)) + (.75% × $15,000))
× 15 years of participation = $2,812.50;
((1.5% × ($75,000 − $15,000)) + (.75% × $15,000))
× 15 years of participation = $15,187.50.

As a percentage of the highest five-year average, the $20,000 participant thus receives 14.1 percent, while the $75,000 participant receives 20.3 percent. The reason for this difference is obvious: The higher paid participant has the greater proportion of his salary above the breakpoint, where it is multiplied by the higher percentage, while the $20,000 participant has only a small portion of salary above that point.

Among the plans of medium and large firms, the more prevalent

---

[62] Estimates of primary Social Security benefits were produced using a computer program supplied by the Office of the Actuary of the Social Security Administration. It was assumed that the $20,000 wage earner's salary had risen to its final level in tandem with increases in the average wage on which Social Security taxes are paid. The $75,000 wage earner was assumed to have always had earnings at or above the maximum taxable wage for Social Security.

form of Social Security integration is an offset formula.[63] Among the plans of smaller employers, excess formulas are somewhat more prevalent (presumably because of the lower administrative cost from not having to calculate Social Security benefits with the adjustments described below).[64] These, however, are only rough indicia, with excess formulas being found in the plans of many large employers, and offset formulas often found in small employer plans.

If a defined contribution plan is to be integrated, it can only be integrated on an excess basis, i.e., with contributions made at a higher level for salary above a breakpoint.[65]

B. Statutory and Regulatory Basis

Statutory support for Social Security integration is found in Code Section 401(a)(5), the basic language of which was first enacted in 1942.[66] The rule in Code Section 401(a)(4) is that a pension, profit-sharing, or stock bonus plan must not discriminate in contributions or benefits in favor of officers, shareholders, and highly compensated employees. However, Section 401(a)(5) first establishes that a plan is not considered to discriminate in their favor "merely because" the contributions or benefits bear a "uniform relationship," as a percentage of pay, to total compensation or to the participants' basic or regular rates of pay. Thus, a plan does not discriminate in favor of highly compensated employees "merely because" it provides the same 1½ percent of compensation benefit to employees making $75,000 as it does for employees making $20,000—even though this results in a higher dollar pension for the more highly compensated employee. Section 401(a)(5) then takes nondiscrimination a critical step further by providing that the plan's contributions or benefits will *also* not be considered discriminatory "merely because" contributions or benefits "differ" because Social Security benefits or other retirement benefits created under federal or state law are taken into account, *or* "merely because" contributions or benefits based on that part of compensation above the Social Security wage base "differ" from contributions or benefits on compensation below the Social Security wage base.

The policy rationale generally offered for Social Security integration is, in brief, that since Social Security benefits replace a higher percentage of lower paid employees' preretirement income, employers ought to be able to correct or retilt these percentages through private

---

[63] BLS, Employee Benefits in Medium and Large Firms, 1984, at 47.

[64] See J. Schulz, T. Leavitt and J. Strate, "The Incidence of Integration Provisions in Private Pension Plans," 9 J. Pens. Plan. & Compl. 399, at 405 (Oct. 1983).

[65] Except for so-called target benefit plans, which are allowed to use an offset in determining the benefits to which contributions are targeted. See Rev. Rul. 76-464.

[66] For a history of the statutory authority and rules on Social Security integration up to 1968, see J. Dyer, "Concept of Pension Social Security Integration," in D. McGill, ed., *Social Security and Private Pension Plans* (Richard D. Irwin 1977), at 122-133. For a more recent discussion, see B. Wolk, "Discrimination Rules for Qualified Plans," 70 Va. L. Rev. 419 (April 1984).

pensions to favor more highly compensated employees. Phillip Alden, a consulting actuary, thus writes:

> "Integration is a way of correcting part—not all—of Social Security's inherent bias in favor of low wage earners .... [A]n integrated plan discriminates in favor of higher-paid plan participants."[67]

It is alternatively sometimes argued that without Social Security coordination or integration, some lower and average paid workers might be "overpensioned," i.e., they might receive in excess of 100 percent of their preretirement income from Social Security and a private pension plan. Although this is a more subtle argument, the stark fact is that Social Security integration, as permitted and practiced, does more than is needed to prevent this.

Over the years, it has become rarer, except in general articles and texts by pension actuaries, to find anyone defending Social Security integration as sound retirement income or tax policy. Rather, the major basis for defending the practice now is that it is a long-standing part of the tax law for private plans and that its elimination or curtailment would alter sharply the costs and incentives for plans and might result in the termination of many smaller plans (which are set up to primarily benefit highly compensated employees). In enacting ERISA, Congress was prepared to temporarily freeze permissible integration based on the 1974 Social Security benefit and taxable wage base levels, but because of last minute lobbying, the freeze was deleted in conference, leaving only a slight change in the rules on Social Security integration after a separation from service. In doing this, it was clear that Congress had not had second thoughts in favor of the policies behind Social Security offset and excess formulas, but rather withdrew because of heavy lobbying concerning the costs to employers of the freeze and the threat that many plans would be terminated as a result. As Senator Williams stated in explaining the deletion:

> "We have been told that this will greatly increase the costs of private pension plans, something that I am sure none of the Senators would like to see occur. This is particularly true if these increased pension costs result in the termination of private pension plans."[68]

Since ERISA, proposals to curtail Social Security integration have

---

[67] P. Alden, "Calculating the Social Security Offset in Defined Benefit Plans," Pension World (Sept. 1984), at 59. And see, e.g., T. Stuchiner, *How to Integrate a Retirement Plan with Social Security* (Prentice-Hall 1982 ed.), at 7, D. McGill, *Fundamentals of Private Pensions* (5th ed.), at 177-78, and J. Mamorsky, *Employee Benefits Law* (Law Journal Seminars-Press 1983 ed.), at 7-3.

[68] 3 ERISA Leg. Hist. 4732. Similarly, the House Ways and Means Committee in reporting out the same freeze provision stated:

"Your committee ... believes that [integration] practices raise important issues. On the one hand, the objective of the Congress in increasing Social Security benefits might be considered to be frustrated to the extent that individuals with low and moderate incomes have their private retirement benefits reduced as a result of the integration procedures. On the other hand, your committee is very much aware that many present plans are fully or partly integrated and that elimination of the integration procedures could substantially increase the cost of financing private plans. Employees, as a whole, might be injured rather than aided if such cost increases resulted in slowing down the growth or perhaps even eliminated private retirement plans." H.R. Rep. 93-807, at 69, 2 ERISA Leg. Hist. 3189.

reappeared during the Carter Administration,[69] and in a 1982 bill endorsed by the Reagan Administration that led to the TEFRA changes for top-heavy plans.[70] In both instances, the same type of opposition on the grounds of costs and threatened plan terminations surfaced. In 1982, however, Congress proceeded to adopt major changes for top-heavy plans, requiring minimum nonintegrated benefits for these plans, and a slightly lower integration limit for all defined contribution plans. Effective for benefits that are attributable to plan years beginning after December 31, 1988, the 1986 Tax Reform Act lowers the maximum percentage allowed for all defined benefit plan offsets and prorates the lower maximum limit across 35 years of potential plan participation. The Act also reduces the disparities permitted under excess formulas used by defined benefit and defined contribution plans.[71]

Until the Tax Reform Act's rules begin to become effective in 1989, the general framework within which Social Security integration is permitted is developed in the IRS's regulations at 26 C.F.R. 1.401-3(e). Under the regulations, the IRS attributes one-half of an employee's Social Security benefits to the employer because of the employer's one-half FICA contributions. The value of this one-half attribution is estimated to be a pension benefit that is worth the equivalent of 37½ percent of a career average wage at the maximum taxable wage base, or 83⅓ percent of the participant's primary Social Security benefit.[72] Because the employer is said to have provided this, the IRS regulations permit employers to use formulas that take account of these benefits before providing private pension benefits.

The sophistry on which the regulations are based is that Social Security is a funded system, rather than a pay-as-you-go program. The employer's contributions, as well as the employee's, are actually providing current retirees with Social Security benefits, with the employee's future Social Security benefits being paid for entirely by future employers and employees. The wages on which contributions are made today are, of course, used as credits in determining tomorrow's benefits, but the money to pay for these benefits is entirely contingent on future employers and employees. Moreover, even if one-half of the

---

[69] See H.R. 12078 (proposed Revenue Act of 1978, introduced April 12, 1978 by Rep. Al Ullman for the Carter Administration), reprinted in 185 BNA Pens. Rep. at R-14 (April 24, 1978). And see 180 BNA Pens. Rep. A-4 and A-7 (March 20, 1978) (describing hearings on this proposal).

[70] See H.R. 6410 (proposed Pension Equity Tax Act, introduced by Rep. Charles Rangel on March 19, 1982, and generally endorsed by the Reagan Administration), section-by-section analysis reprinted in 394 BNA Pens. Rep. 781 (May 24, 1982), and see 9 BNA Pens. Rep. 840 (June 14, 1982) (reporting hearings on the proposed act).

[71] See sec. VIII.G below.

[72] In an offset plan, the offset is based on a percentage of the *primary* Social Security benefit, that is, the Social Security benefit without the spousal benefit. But the spousal benefit is taken into account in computing the *percentage* of this primary benefit that may be offset. Thus, the IRS regulations estimate the total benefit from Social Security, including spousal benefits, survivor's benefits, and disability insurance as 162% of the primary benefit. Then taking one-half of this, with a margin added for post-1971 Social Security increases, the employer's half is considered to be 83⅓% of the primary benefit.

participant's Social Security benefits were properly attributable to the employer's current FICA contributions, it is generally agreed, as a matter of labor economics, that the employee actually bears most of the cost of the employer's contributions to Social Security through reduced wage increases.[73]

The Social Security offset and excess percentages allowed under the existing regulations are also outdated. If the principles used in the regulations were applied today, the result would be a decrease in the maximum permissible Socials Security offset from 83⅓ percent of the Social Security primary benefit to 69.6 percent, and a still steeper decrease in the permissible excess percentage from 37½ percent of compensation above an average of the Social Security wage base to 19.8 percent.[74] The Tax Reform Act lowers the maximum percentage limits "to reflect the current [S]ocial [S]ecurity system," effective in 1989.[75]

On a more detailed level, the IRS's regulations also fail to apportion Social Security benefits among *all* of the employers who have contributed to Social Security on behalf of an employee. Instead, in both offset and flat percentage excess plans, the current employer is effectively allowed to take credit for all past employers' contributions. Benefits from future employers' contributions, on the other hand, are prorated. As stated by Donald Grubbs, the IRS's former chief actuary:

> "Although the Service requires this proration of the maximum offset to reflect the portion of the social security benefit earned after termination of employment, it requires no similar adjustment for the portion earned while working for prior employers."[76]

Proration of the maximum limits is required under the Tax Reform Act, effective in 1989.[77]

C. Maximum Limits for Defined Benefit Plans

Until the Tax Reform Act rules begin becoming effective in the first plan year beginning after December 31, 1988, Revenue Ruling 71-446 is the central source of law on the limits of Social Security integration. It is likely to remain so for many years thereafter because the Tax

---

[73] See B. Wolk, "Discrimination Rules for Qualified Plans," 70 Va. L. Rev. 419 (April 1984), at 432 n.62 (citing other sources).

[74] Congressional Research Service, "Updated Limits for Integration of Private Pensions with Social Security Benefits" (June 30, 1982), at CRS-2. But compare D. Grubbs, "In Depth Re-Examination of Integration," 38 Inst. on Fed. Tax'n—ERISA Supp. (1980), 2-1, at 2-22, and D. Halperin, "Retirement Security and Tax Equity: An Evaluation of ERISA," 17 B.C. Ind. & Com. L.R. 739, at 763 n. 128 (June 1976), both indicating that revision of the IRS's computations would have the opposite effect. The 1983 Social Security Amendments would apparently further lower the percentages computed in the Congressional Research Service study.

[75] Conf. Rep., H.R. Rep. 99-841, at II-435, [1986] U.S. Code Cong. & Ad. News 4523.

[76] D. Grubbs, "In Depth Re-Examination of Integration," 38 Inst. on Fed. Tax'n—ERISA Supp. (1980), at 2-12.

[77] See sec. VIII.G.

Act's rules are only effective for the "benefits attributable" to plan years after that date.

Revenue Ruling 71-446 translates the general theoretical framework and estimates in the regulations into more specific guidelines within which Social Security integration is permitted. It converts the estimates of employer-attributable Social Security benefits into detailed limits for offset plans and for unit benefit excess plans—using either a final or highest average of salary, or a career average of pay—and also establishes integration limits for defined contribution plans. Revenue Ruling 71-446 has been changed slightly by later revenue rulings, but overall, it remains the central source of information on the limits of Social Security integration. The only major departures from Revenue Ruling 71-446 are the rules for minimum nonintegrated benefits when a plan is top heavy and a lower limit on integration under all defined contribution plans, both of which were enacted in the 1982 Tax Equity and Fiscal Responsibility Act. Revenue Ruling 78-252 also effects a major departure from the rules in Revenue Ruling 71-446 for offset plans by showing that certain types of commonly found, nonprorated offsets can violate the ERISA accrued benefit rules.

The maximum integration limits of Revenue Ruling 71-446 are what many smaller (and some larger) plans look to in designing their benefit formulas. Use of the maximum limits can produce even greater disparities than those in the examples given before. Under Revenue Ruling 71-446, an employer can adopt an offset of as much as 83⅓ percent of a participant's primary Social Security benefit.[78] If the offset is not prorated according to potential years of credited service, this is a "hard" maximum offset.[79] Under a hard maximum offset, such as 1.5 percent of a final average of pay multiplied by years of credited service less 83⅓ percent of the primary Social Security benefit, it has been estimated that a participant with 10 years of credited service would have to have compensation above $40,000 per year to receive any benefits from the plan.[80] Under a "soft" offset, a plan might use the maximum 83⅓ percent offset, but the offset is prorated over potential years of credited service. For example, if the potential years of credited service under a plan are 40, the prorated offset may be slightly more than two percent of the primary Social Security benefit for each year of credited service. J.C. Penney's soft offset described before is 1.67 percent of offset per year, and thus slightly less than this maximum, but still on the worse end of the spectrum as far as offset formulas of larger companies are concerned. A soft offset will not usually completely wipe

---

[78] Rev. Rul. 71-446, sec. 7.

[79] Partial proration of the offset is always required on a separation from service, even under a hard offset. See sec. VIII.E.3, below.

[80] Joint Economic Committee, Special Study on Economic Change: Vol. 8, Social Security and Pensions, 96th Cong., 2d Sess., at 106. And see D. Grubbs, "In Depth Re-Examination of Integration," 38 Inst. on Fed. Tax'n—ERISA Supp. (1980), at 2-11. An employee with 20 years of service under such a formula would need a salary of at least $20,000 to receive any benefits. See JEC, Special Study, *supra*.

out benefits in the same way that a hard offset does, but if the prorated offset is based on the maximum 83⅓ percent limit, the result is an even greater skewing of benefits than illustrated above under the J.C. Penney formula.

Excess formulas can similarly go further than in the example given above.[81] To illustrate, a plan using the maximum limits of Social Security integration under an excess formula might provide benefits of up to one percent of the portion of a final five-year average of compensation above a breakpoint of $15,000, with *no* benefits provided on the portion of salary below.[82] This is a pure final average excess formula that uses the maximum integration limit. More commonly, plans use a "step-rate" formula like that illustrated above. For example, a plan maintaining the *maximum* one percent differential between benefits based on compensation above and below the breakpoint might use a step-rate formula providing 1.5 percent on the portion of a final average of compensation above a breakpoint of $15,000, and only .5 percent on compensation below. Such a plan provides some benefits to lower paid employees, but it is still integrated at the maximum level because it uses the maximum differential in stepping up benefits on compensation above the breakpoint. Any step-rate excess formula can be tested against the maximum integration limits by dividing the formula into two elements: a pure excess element, which in the example above is one percent on wages above the breakpoint, and a uniform element, which in the example is .5 percent on wages both above and below the breakpoint. The pure excess element is the part that is measured against the maximum limits for Social Security integration.[83]

An excess plan using a career average of pay can increase the maximum excess percentage to 1.4 percent, as compared to the one percent differential allowed for final or highest pay plans.[84] Thus, an excess plan with benefits based on a career average of salary can provide benefits each year that are equal to 1.4 percent of the portion of current year compensation above its breakpoint or integration level with *no* benefits on the portion of compensation below. Alternatively, a plan might use a step-rate formula that provides some benefits on compensation below, but still maintains the maximum 1.4 percent differential for compensation above the integration level, e.g., 2.4 percent on compensation above the integration level and one percent of compensation below.

A flat percentage benefit plan—one that offers a flat percentage

---

[81] Larger companies, on the other hand, tend to use less steep excess formulas than in that example. See Wyatt Co., "A Survey of Retirement, Thrift and Profit Sharing Plans Covering Salaried Employees of 50 Large U.S. Industrial Companies as of January 1, 1982."

[82] See. Rev. Rul. 71-446, sec. 6.03. The $15,000 breakpoint results from updating the covered compensation table in Rev. Rul. 71-446 to reflect the career average of the maximum Social Security wage bases that have applied to persons reaching age 65 in 1986. See IRS Notice 85-4, Notice 85-4, I.R.B. 1985-9, 21, reprinted in 12 BNA Pens. Rep. 386 (March 11, 1985).

[83] Rev. Rul. 71-446, sec. 16.

[84] Rev. Rul. 71-446, sec. 6.03.

benefit regardless of years of participation above a minimum number—can provide a flat percentage excess benefit of 37½ percent of the highest five consecutive year average of an employee's compensation above an integration level, with *no* benefits below.[85] Alternatively, on a step rate basis, a flat percentage benefit plan can maintain the maximum 37½ percent differential, while providing some benefits on compensation below the breakpoint, e.g., 57½ percent of the average of compensation above the breakpoint, and 20 percent of the average compensation below. In either case, the "pure" excess percentage must be prorated if a participant has less than 15 years of service at a rate of 2½ percent per year (37½ percent ÷ 15).[86]

The point at which the benefit percentage increases in an excess plan is called the breakpoint or integration level.[87] For an excess plan with benefits based on career average pay (a plan in which each year's benefits are determined separately based on that year's compensation), the integration level for any year is permitted to be as high as the Social Security wage base at the beginning of that year,[88] e.g., in 1986, $42,000. For an excess plan based on a final or highest average of pay, how high the breakpoint can be is determined by "covered compensation."[89] Covered compensation is defined as the average wage an employee who always earned at the maximum taxable wage base for Social Security would have over his or her career at age 65.[90] For a worker who is 35 in 1986 and who will thus not reach age 65 for another 30 years, the covered compensation average is projected as $38,400, or nearly identical to the 1985 taxable wage base of $39,600. For a worker reaching age 65 in 1986, this average, on the other hand, is $15,000, because it includes a large number of years in which the taxable wage base was much lower than it is currently. Covered compensation can thus vary substantially between employees depending on age. Many employers that integrate plans on an excess basis, however, use a single breakpoint applicable to all participants based on the covered compensation of a participant reaching age 65 in the current year, and then move this level up each year as covered compensation increases.[91] Other employers use a set figure, such as $6,000, which was established

[85] Rev. Rul. 71-446, sec. 5.

[86] Rev. Rul. 71-446, sec. 5.02.

[87] See Rev. Rul. 71-446, sec. 2.

[88] Rev. Rul. 71-446, sec. 6.012.

[89] Rev. Rul. 71-446, secs. 5 and 6. A plan can use a higher breakpoint than the covered compensation level (or than the current Social Security wage base, under a career average pay plan), but if it does, the excess percentage must be adjusted down. For example, if an excess plan with benefits based on final or highest average pay uses a breakpoint which is 1½ times the highest covered compensation level for any individual who is or may become a participant, then the excess percentage could be no more than 1% ÷ 1½, or .66%. Rev. Rul. 71-446, secs. 5.03 and 6.04.

[90] See Rev. Rul. 71-446, sec. 3, and IRS Notice 85-4, I.R.B. 1985-9, 21, reprinted in 12 BNA Pens. Rep. 386 (March 11, 1985) (updating the covered compensation tables in Rev. Rul. 71-446 for changes in the Social Security wage base through 1985). Tables of covered compensation are also published privately by actuarial firms. See 11 BNA Pens. Rep. 67 (Jan. 16, 1984) (reprinting a privately published table).

[91] D. McGill, *Fundamentals of Private Pensions* (5th ed.), at 186.

sometime before, often based on the covered compensation level at that time, but which has not been adjusted up each time that level changed.[92]

D. Defined Contribution Plan Integration Limits

If they are integrated at all, defined contribution plans can only be integrated on a different type of excess basis. For a defined contribution plan, the maximum excess percentage sets a limit on contributions, as opposed to benefits. The maximum percentage limit is determined by the Old Age, Survivors, and Disability Insurance (OASDI) component of Social Security tax (FICA) contributions. Revenue Ruling 71-446 originally permitted excess contributions of up to seven percent on compensation above the Social Security wage base applicable at the beginning of the plan year in which the contributions were made.[93] But the 1982 Tax Equity and Fiscal Responsibility Act (TEFRA) reduced the percentage to the OASDI component.[94] The OASDI rate is slated to remain at 5.7 percent through 1987.[95]

An integrated defined contribution plan can thus provide contributions (including reallocated forfeitures, if applicable)[96] of up to 5.7 percent of compensation above the Social Security wage base applicable at the beginning of the plan year with *no* contributions on compensation below. Again, more commonly than a pure excess formula, a defined contribution plan using the maximum excess percentage will provide contributions on a step-rate basis. If the maximum percentage is used, the plan might, for example, provide employer contributions of up to 7.7 percent on compensation above the Social Security wage base, with two percent of compensation contributions on compensation below the wage base, thus maintaining the full 5.7 percent differential.

As discussed below, the primary limitation on Social Security integration under defined contribution plans is that when participants are also covered under an integrated defined benefit plan, the maximum integration limits must be split between the two plans. One other limitation on profit-sharing and stock bonus plan integration (which includes savings plans qualified as profit-sharing plans) is that when

---

[92] An upward adjustment is not permitted when a plan uses a lower breakpoint than the covered compensation level, or taxable wage base, for any individual who is or may become a participant. For example, if an excess plan based on final or highest average pay uses a breakpoint of one-half the highest covered compensation level, the plan is not permitted to double the 1% maximum excess percentage. See Rev. Rul. 71-446, secs. 5 and 6.

Contributory plans are permitted to adjust the excess percentages upwards based on the employee contributions to the plan. Rev. Rul. 71-446, sec. 13. For example, a contributory defined benefit plan requiring employee contributions of 2.4% of compensation might adjust the excess percentage under a career average pay formula up from 1.4% to 1.8%. *Id.*

[93] See Rev. Rul. 71-446, secs. 14 and 15.

[94] Code §401(l), as amended by TEFRA. And see Rev. Rul. 83-110.

[95] See 26 U.S.C. §3111(a).

[96] Rev. Rul. 71-446, sec. 15.

such plans are integrated to any extent, they can no longer provide withdrawals of employer contributions and earnings after a fixed number of years, but, like pension plans, must permit withdrawals only on a separation from service, disability, death, or retirement.[97]

E. Downward Adjustments in the Maximum Social Security Integration Limits

The maximum percentage integration limits are subject to a series of downward adjustments unless the plan precisely fits the mold on which the limits in Revenue Ruling 71-446 are based—which is unlikely except for a defined contribution plan that is the only plan of an employer. The maximum integration limits in Revenue Ruling 71-446 presume a plan that is:

(1) The employer's only integrated plan.

If the plan in question is a defined benefit plan, Revenue Ruling 71-446 further presumes the plan:

(2) Uses at least a five consecutive year average in computing compensation under any excess formula based on final or highest pay;
(3) Does not provide vested benefits on a separation from service before age 65;
(4) Pays benefits no earlier than age 65 under any option;
(5) Includes no participants born after January 1, 1938, who will have to wait until after age 65 to receive unreduced Social Security benefits;
(6) Pays benefits only in the form of a single life annuity;
(7) Provides no preretirement death benefits; and
(8) Provides no preretirement disability benefits.

In a slight understatement, Jeffrey Mamorsky states that a defined benefit plan such as this is "the exception rather than the rule."[98] In fact, such a plan would be in violation of ERISA because of the lack of preretirement vesting, the lack of a joint and survivor's annuity form, and the lack of a preretirement survivor's benefit. Thus, adjustments in the maximum integration limits are required for all defined benefit plans.

It is important to note at the outset, however, that although few defined benefit plans fit the Revenue Ruling 71-446 mold, the required adjustments are often readily satisfied, or are insubstantial, except for the adjustment when an employer has another integrated plan. For example, if an offset or excess formula is already on a unit basis, the

---

[97] Rev. Rul. 71-446, sec. 15.03.

[98] J. Mamorsky, *Employee Benefits Law* (1983 ed.), at 7-12.

separation from service adjustment described below is satisfied. Additionally, if full actuarial adjustments are made for benefit payments before age 65, or payments in a form other than a single life annuity, these adjustments are similarly satisfied. In some instances, however, the adjustments can be more significant. Moreover, when two or more adjustments are required, the adjustments are cumulative.[99]

Preliminarily, it may also be noted that the downward adjustments also differ in the effects they produce under an offset plan and for an excess plan. In an offset plan, the adjustments are required to lower the Social Security offset. Thus, an adjustment can result in a lower or average paid participant receiving *more* pension benefits because of a lower permissible offset.[100] In an excess plan, however, the adjustments only lower the excess percentage, and thus result in less benefits for those participants with compensation above the excess breakpoint. The only advantage to rank and file participants from these adjustments is indirect. As with restrictions on compensation that may be used in a plan's formula, if an employer is not able to meet the benefit objectives of highly compensated employees with a lower adjusted excess percentage, it may meet those objectives by upgrading benefits on compensation both above and below the integration level.

Determining whether a plan complies with all the adjustments described below is complex. For a lawyer representing a participant, a useful place to start may be the plan's Application for Determination, namely, the Form 5300 (for defined benefit plans) or Form 5301 (for defined contribution plans). When a plan is integrated, the Form 5300 series instructions require an attachment explaining the plan's integration formula, and if "necessary," showing exactly how the formula complies with the integration rules, including the adjustments required in the situations described below.

1. Two or More Plans

If an employer maintains two or more plans covering *any* of the same employees, the integration of the two plans is significantly constrained by the rule that the "extent of integration" for both plans cannot exceed 100 percent of the maximum for one plan. In short, the maximum integration limits must be split between the two plans, or one of the plans must be left unintegrated.[101] The extent of integration for a plan is determined by "the ratio (expressed as a percentage)

---

[99] It is partly because of these adjustments and partly for reasons of simplicity that offsets in excess of 50% are rarely found.

[100] However, as mentioned above and discussed further below, the adjustments required for an offset plan can often be satisfied by an adjustment in *both* the offset component and the salary component of a formula. In these cases, a participant may not necessarily receive more benefits because of an adjustment.

[101] Rev. Rul. 71-446, sec. 17. Whether two plans cover "any" of the same employees is interpreted strictly. In Rev. Rul. 79-236, a controlled group with two plans was required to divide the integration limits between its two plans where there was only a possibility that the two plans might cover some of the same employees.

which the actual benefits, benefit rate, offset rate, or employer contribution rate under the plan bears to the limitation applicable to such plan."[102] For example, if an employer has two plans, one a defined benefit plan with a 83⅓ percent offset, and the other a profit-sharing plan with a contribution rate of 2.85 percent on the excess of compensation above the current year's Social Security wage base, the extent of integration under the two plans is 150 percent. However, if the defined benefit plan had a 41⅔ percent offset, and the profit-sharing plan had the same 2.85 percent excess contribution rate, and none of the other adjustments described below in the maximum integration limits were required, the extent of integration for the two plans does not exceed 100 percent, and thus is acceptable.

Typically, when an employer has both a defined benefit plan and one or more defined contribution plans, the defined benefit plan is integrated, and whether or not the integration for the defined benefit plan is close to the maximum permissible limits, the defined contribution plan, or plans, is not. Another rule mentioned before which adds to this tendency is that when a profit-sharing plan (which includes a savings or thrift plan qualified as a profit-sharing plan) is integrated, the plan may not provide for withdrawals after a fixed number of years, but, like a pension plan, must allow withdrawals only on a separation from service, disability, death, or retirement.[103]

2. *Excess Formulas With Final or Highest Average Pay Based on Less Than Five Consecutive Years*

The one percent per year unit benefit and 37½ percent flat percentage excess limits for defined benefit plans basing benefits on final or highest average pay in excess of covered compensation are predicated on a plan using at least a five consecutive year average of compensation.[104] When a plan uses a consecutive three- or four-year average instead, the maximum excess percentage must be reduced by multiplying by 90 percent or 95 percent, respectively.[105] Thus, if a three consecutive year average is used in determining salary above the integration level, the one percent maximum excess limit is reduced to .9 percent. On a step-rate basis, the excess percentage could thus not be more than .9 percent higher than the percentage used on compensation below the integration level, e.g., 1.4 percent and .5 percent, rather than 1.5 percent and .5 percent.

Offset plans that use final or highest average pay are not subject to a similar adjustment because the limits in Revenue Ruling 71-446 are

---

[102] Rev. Rul. 71-446, sec. 17.

[103] Rev. Rul. 71-446, sec. 15.03.

[104] Rev. Rul. 71-446, sec. 3.

[105] Rev. Rul. 72-276.

not based on a five consecutive year average. As a general nondiscrimination requirement, however, no less than a three-year average of compensation may be used.[106]

3. Separations From Service Before Age 65

a. Offset plans. When an employee separates from service before age 65 with a vested benefit, ERISA Section 206(b) and Code Section 401(a)(15) create an "overriding" requirement that any Social Security offset be computed using the Social Security benefit rules then in effect.[107] In addition, under Revenue Ruling 71-446, the plan must either (1) assume in computing the offset that the employee will earn *no* covered wages after the separation from service, or (2) assume that the employee will continue to receive wages until 65, but at no more than the rate of pay he or she was making before the separation from service.[108] *If* further wages are assumed at this constant rate, the maximum offset percentage must be prorated based on the ratio of the employee's years of service at separation to those years plus the years until age 65 for which further wages have been assumed. For example, if a plan provides a benefit of 50 percent of average annual compensation less 50 percent of the primary Social Security benefit at age 65, the offset for a participant who terminates employment at age 55 with a vested benefit based on 10 years of participation could not exceed 10/20 of the 83⅓ percent limit, or 41⅔ percent.[109] However, as Don Grubbs points out:

> "If the plan uses an offset per year of service [which is within the maximum percentage limit when multiplied by potential years of credited service], e.g., 1.25 percent of the [primary Social Security benefit] per year, it is not necessary to multiply the projected social security benefit by the ratio of service."[110]

b. Excess plans. When an employee in an excess plan separates from service before age 65 with a vested benefit, ERISA Section 206(b) (Code Section 401(a)(15)) requires that the plan's breakpoint or integration level for the employee be frozen at the taxable wage base in effect on the separation from service. Under Revenue Ruling 71-446, no further adjustments are required if the plan complies with the maximum unit benefit limits of one percent for a final or highest average pay plan, or 1.4 percent for a career average pay plan, since these are already prorated. However, if the plan provides excess benefits on a flat percentage excess basis, the maximum integration limit of 37½ percent must be adjusted based on the ratio of the participant's

---

[106] Rev. Rul. 71-330.

[107] Rev. Rul. 76-76.

[108] Rev. Rul. 71-446, sec. 11.01. And see Rev. Rul. 76-76.

[109] See Rev. Rul. 71-446, sec. 11 (example).

[110] D. Grubbs, "In Depth Re-Examination of Integration," 38 Inst. on Fed. Tax'n—ERISA Supp., at 2-12.

years of service with the employer at separation to the total years of service he or she would have had at retirement.[111]

4. Benefits Commencing Before Age 65

a. Offset plans. When an offset plan either (1) has a normal retirement age that is earlier than age 65, or (2) offers an early retirement option before age 65, the maximum offset percentage must be actuarially adjusted if benefits commence before age 65—in addition to applying the pre-age 65 separation from service rules described above. The actuarial adjustment requirement is presumed satisfied if the plan reduces the maximum offset by 1⁄15 for each of the first five years before age 65 that benefits commence, and by 1⁄30 for each of the next five years.[112] In making this adjustment, however, a plan is not required to adjust *only* the offset component, but rather it may adjust both the salary component and the offset component by the same factor. For example, a plan with a formula providing 50 percent of final pay less 83⅓ percent of the primary Social Security benefit might actuarially adjust both parts, or in other words, the net benefit, to reflect early retirement at age 62. The significance of Revenue Ruling 71-446 is that it requires at least the offset component of the formula to be adjusted to reflect early retirement. If an employer does not want to impose a full actuarial reduction for benefits payable before age 65, this adjustment still must be made for the offset component. Thus, if a plan provides a 50 percent of final pay less 83⅓ percent of the primary Social Security benefit at age 65, it can provide benefits at age 62 on a partially unreduced basis, but it must do so with a full actuarial reduction in the offset component of the formula.

When benefits are payable before age 65, the adjustments for a separation from service before age 65 must also be made. Thus, a plan can assume wages to age 65 at the same rate as at separation in computing the Social Security offset, but if it does this, it must prorate the offset based on the ratio of the participant's years of service with the employer at separation to those years plus the years of service between the separation and age 65.

Cumulatively, the adjustments in the maximum permissible offset when benefits are paid before age 65 can be fairly sharp when both the early retirement and separation from service adjustments are required. For example, if a plan offers early retirement at age 60, the maximum permissible offset for a participant with 15 years of service at age 60 is 83⅓ percent of the primary Social Security benefit multiplied first by 15⁄20 (the separation from service adjustment if additional wages are assumed in computing the amount of the offset), and then multiplied

---

[111] Rev. Rul. 71-446, sec. 10.01. For participants with less than 15 years of service, the 37½% flat excess limit must always be prorated, whether or not the separation from service occurs before age 65. See Rev. Rul. 71-446, sec. 5.022.

[112] Rev. Rul. 71-446, secs. 11.02 and 10.02.

by 10⁄15 (the early retirement adjustment), for an adjusted maximum permissible offset of 44 percent of primary Social Security benefits. As Don Grubbs has indicated, however, a plan is not ordinarily required to make the separation from service adjustment if the offset is already on a unit basis and the total offset for any participant under the unit basis formula is less than the maximum permissible limit.[113]

b. Excess plans. In an excess plan, the excess percentage is required to be actuarially adjusted for normal retirement earlier than age 65, or for an early retirement option before age 65. The actuarial adjustment requirement is again presumed satisfied if the excess limits are reduced by at least 1⁄15 for each of the first five years before age 65 that benefits commence, and by at least 1⁄30 for each of the next five years.[114] Thus, if an excess plan provides benefits of two percent per year multiplied by the highest five consecutive year average of compensation above the plan's integration level, and one percent on the compensation average below, the excess percentage must be adjusted actuarially, or the fractions given before must be used, when payments commence before age 65. However, again, a plan may actuarially reduce both parts of the formula to satisfy this requirement. For example, if the two percent excess portion and the one percent portion are both multiplied by 80 percent to reflect age 62 retirement, the result is a 1.6 percent and .8 percent formula for the age 62 retiree. The differential, or pure "excess" percentage, is then .8 percent which is satisfactorily adjusted for early retirement.

If a plan provides benefits on a flat percentage excess basis, the maximum excess percentage for payments commencing before age 65 must also be adjusted to reflect the early retirement. Because they are not already on a unit basis, flat percentage excess benefits that commence before age 65 must be further adjusted to reflect a pre-age 65 separation from service.

5. *Participants Born After January 1, 1938*

a. Offset plans. Revenue Ruling 71-446 assumed that age 65 is the age at which unreduced Social Security benefits commence. However, for individuals born after January 1, 1938, the 1983 Social Security Amendments Act provides for a gradual increase in the age at which their unreduced Social Security benefits will begin, up to age 67. Accordingly, in Revenue Ruling 86-74, the IRS adjusted the integration rules for offset plans to reflect this change. Under Revenue Ruling 86-74, an offset plan must limit its offset of primary Social Security benefits (1) based on the unreduced Social Security benefit that is expected to be payable to the participant at the later Social Security eligibility age, *assuming* no wages are earned after age 65, or (2) based

---

[113] D. Grubbs, "In Depth Re-Examination of Integration," 38 Inst. on Fed. Tax'n—ERISA Supp., at 2-12.

[114] Rev. Rul. 71-446, sec. 10.02.

on the unreduced Social Security benefit that is expected to be payable to the participant at the later age, *assuming* wages after age 65 at a rate of pay no higher than that applicable at age 65. If the second option is used, the maximum offset percentage for the plan must be multiplied by a fraction the numerator of which is the potential years of service until age 65, and the denominator of which is the potential years of service until the later retirement age. Under both options, the maximum offset percentage must also be reduced by 1⁄15 for each year between the later retirement age and a normal retirement age of 65 under the plan.

For early retirement before age 65, reduction in the maximum permissible offset must first be made in accordance with this rule. Then a second round of reductions must be made for the early retirement and separation from service before age 65 following the Revenue Ruling 71-446 rules described in the previous sections (except that in determining the period for which the 1⁄15 reduction in the maximum offset for early retirement serves as a safe harbor, the number of years, including portions thereof, by which the age at which unreduced Social Security benefits begin exceeds age 65 is subtracted from five).

Revenue Ruling 86-74 became effective with the first plan year beginning after December 31, 1986, for plans in existence on May 27, 1986, and otherwise satisfying the IRS's Social Security integration limits. The Ruling applies to all plan participants who were born before January 1, 1938, and who have any service after December 31, 1986. Compliance with the Ruling for those participants is not only prospective, but can require an increase in their previously accrued benefits.

b. Excess plans. No changes are required under Revenue Ruling 86-74 in the integration limits for excess plans.

6. *Benefits in Forms Other Than Single Life Annuities*

a. Offset plans. Actuarial adjustments in the maximum offset percentage are also required when benefits are paid in forms other than a single life annuity. Section 9 of Revenue Ruling 71-446 provides a table of adjustments that are presumed to satisfy this actuarial equivalence requirement. The adjustments for the most common forms of benefits are:

Life annuity with one-half continued to surviving spouse	80 percent
Annuity for 10 years certain and life thereafter	90 percent
Annuity for five years certain and life thereafter	97 percent

For example, if an offset plan provides a single life annuity of 50 percent of final pay less 83⅓ percent of the Social Security PIA, the benefit in the ERISA-required joint and survivor form must reflect an adjusted offset of 80 percent, or another actuarial equivalent, of the 83⅓ percent maximum. A plan can comply with this requirement by actuarially reducing both components of its formula, in essence, the net benefit. However, if an employer wants to provide joint and survivor's benefits that are only partially reduced actuarially, it must, nevertheless, comply with the full actuarial adjustment requirement with respect to the offset component.

b. Excess plans. Actuarial adjustments for forms of benefits other than a single life annuity are also required for excess plans, with the requirement being presumed satisfied if an adjustment is made according to the same table.[115] Thus, if a unit benefit excess plan provides a single life annuity of two percent of a final five-year consecutive average of compensation above an integration level, and one percent of compensation below, the excess percentage must be actuarially adjusted when benefits are paid in joint and survivor form.[116] Under the IRS's table, the adjusted excess percentage could be no more than 80 percent of the one percent maximum excess percentage. Similarly, on a flat percentage excess basis, the excess percentage may not exceed 80 percent of 37½ percent when benefits are in a joint and 50 percent survivor's form.

7. Preretirement Death Benefits

a. Offset plans. If an offset plan provides preretirement death benefits for death occurring before retirement, fractional adjustments in the maximum permissible offset are required. These range from 7/9, to 9/10, to 8/9 of the otherwise permissible maximum, depending on the amount of the preretirement death benefit.[117] One significant difference between these adjustments and those described above is that these adjustments are required in the plan's normal retirement benefit formula regardless of whether the event—in this case, death—occurs. Thus, if an offset plan provides lump sum death benefits of 100 times the anticipated monthly benefit if death occurs before retirement, the maximum permissible offset for the entire plan must not exceed 7/9 of the otherwise permissible limit.[118]

No adjustment is required when a plan provides the ERISA-required qualified preretirement survivor's annuity for death before retirement.[119]

b. Excess plans. Excess plans that provide death benefits before

---

[115] Rev. Rul. 71-446, sec. 9.

[116] Actuarially reducing the entire benefit satisfies this requirement. For example, if both parts of the benefit in a step-rate excess plan offering 2% benefits on the part of a final average of compensation above an integration level and 1% benefits on the part below are reduced by 80%, the result is a step-rate excess benefit of 1.6% on compensation above the integration level and .8% on compensation below. The excess differential of .8% is satisfactorily reduced.

[117] Rev. Rul. 71-446, sec. 8. And see Rev. Rul. 83-53. As an alternative to the fractions in sec. 8, a plan can actuarially reduce the offset using the value of the normal retirement benefit divided by the value of both the normal retirement benefit and the death benefits at the age at which the death benefits are most valuable in relation to the retirement benefits. Rev. Rul. 71-446, sec. 8.03.

[118] Rev. Rul. 71-446, sec. 8.013.

[119] IRS News Release IR-1646, July 28, 1976, reprinted in 97 BNA Pens. Rep. at A-6 (Aug. 2, 1976). An ERISA preretirement survivor's annuity can range from 50% to 100% of the amount of the participant's annuity.

retirement are required to make the same 7/9, 8/10, or 8/9 fractional adjustments in the excess percentage depending on the amount of the death benefit provided, with the same exception applying for the ERISA preretirement survivor's annuity.[120]

8. Disability Benefits

When an offset or an excess plan provides disability benefits, "disability" must be defined in the plan, and the plan's rules on disability must be uniformly and consistently applied. Disability benefits may then only be paid from the pension plan for the period of time when an employee is eligible for and receiving disability benefits under the Social Security Act (or is awaiting a decision on eligibility).[121] Additional rules apply depending on whether the plan is an offset or an excess plan.

a. Offset plans. When an offset plan provides disability benefits before age 65, the maximum permissible offset at age 65 is reduced to 90 percent of its otherwise permissible limit. As with the adjustment for preretirement death benefits, this adjustment is required regardless of whether disability occurs. The disability benefits before age 65 may themselves be subject to an offset, but not exceeding 64 percent of the employee's actual Social Security disability benefit (as in effect at the start of the employee's disability retirement).[122]

No adjustment in the maximum permissible offset is required if a plan provides additional pension credits, which assume no change in compensation, during a period of disability toward a pension benefit payable at age 65.[123] When this is done, immediate disability benefits are usually provided from a source outside the pension plan.

b. Excess plans. When an excess plan provides a disability pension before age 65, the integration level for benefits payable at 65 is reduced to 90 percent of its otherwise permissible level. Under a unit benefit excess formula, the disability benefit can also be no greater than the participant's accrued normal retirement benefit before the disability—unreduced for payment before age 65.[124] In a flat percentage excess benefit plan, the disability benefit may be no greater than the normal retirement benefit had the employee remained in service at the same salary, multiplied by the greater of 7/10 or the fraction produced by dividing the employee's years of service with the employer before the

---

[120] Rev. Rul. 71-446, sec. 8, and IRS News Release IR-1646, *supra.*

[121] Rev. Rul. 71-446, sec. 12, and Rev. Rul. 72-492. If a plan provides integrated disability benefits to participants who are *not* within the Social Security definition of disability, the benefits are treated as early retirement benefits and are subject to the rules in Rev. Rul. 71-446 for benefits payable before age 65. Rev. Rul. 71-446, sec. 12.03.

[122] Rev. Rul. 71-446, sec. 12.02, and see sec. X below.

[123] Rev. Rul. 72-492.

[124] Rev. Rul. 71-446, sec. 12.011(a).

disability by those years of service plus the years remaining until age 65.[125]

For either a unit benefit or a flat percentage benefit excess plan, no adjustment in the integration limits is required if the plan provides additional pension credits, assuming constant salary during the period of disability, toward a benefit payable at age 65.[126]

F. Other Constraints on Social Security Integration

In addition to the adjustments in the maximum limits described above, a number of other constraints can reduce permissible integration regardless of how close the plan is to the maximum integration percentages.

1. Separation From Service, Participants Born After January 1, 1938, and Post-Normal Retirement Age Service Rules

Regardless of how close or how far a plan is from the maximum integration percentages, two constraints apply on a separation from service. First, under ERISA Section 206(b) (Code Section 401(a)(15)), a plan must freeze any offset upon a separation from service according to the Social Security Act benefit formula then in effect. Similarly, the integration level for an excess plan may not be increased after a separation from service because of any later increase in the Social Security taxable wage base. Second, under Revenue Rulings 71-446 and 76-76, a plan must follow the rules described before on assuming wages during a postseparation period in determining an offset—regardless of how near or far the plan is to the maximum percentage offset.[127]

For participants born after January 1, 1938, the 1983 Social Security Amendments Act gradually increases the age at which unreduced Social Security benefits begin. In determining offsets of primary Social Security benefits for such participants, wage assumptions after age 65 must always be adjusted as required by Revenue Ruling 86-74 and described above.[128]

Under the Age Discrimination in Employment Act, post-normal retirement age service may not result in any increase in a Social Security offset or in the integration level under an excess plan unless the plan credits service after the plan's normal retirement age under its benefit and accrual formulas.[129]

---

[125] Rev. Rul. 71-446, sec. 12.011(b).

[126] Rev. Rul. 71-446, sec. 12.012.

[127] See Rev. Rul. 71-446, sec. 11, and sec. VIII.E.3., above.

[128] See sec. VIII.E.5., above.

[129] 29 C.F.R. 860.120(f)(1)(iv)(B)(8). See also ERISA §204(b)(1)(G), Code §411(b)(1)(G).

2. Estimated Wage Histories Used in Determining Social Security Benefit Amounts

In practice, many plans estimate wage histories for the period before a participant began work for the sponsoring employer to generate Social Security amounts for offsets. In Revenue Ruling 84-45, the IRS cracked down on the use of salary assumptions that are likely to lead to wage histories that are higher than the participant's actual earnings, and thus to improperly high offsets. Revenue Ruling 84-45 sets a floor under the salary increase assumptions that may be used to generate estimates of past wages and also requires plans to adjust offsets based on actual wage histories if a participant supplies this information.

Under Revenue Ruling 84-45, if a participant has any service during a plan year after December 31, 1983, the use of an estimated wage history is limited by a requirement that the participant's wage history must be estimated by either projecting back from compensation at the participant's date of hire, separation from service, or retirement, using a salary increase assumption of not less than either six percent per year or the actual change in average wages over the period (as determined and published by the Social Security Administration). In addition, the participant must have the opportunity to supply his or her actual wage history for the period (generally this may be done by obtaining an individual earnings history from the Social Security Administration and supplying it to the plan).

Postseparation wage estimates were limited before Revenue Ruling 84-45's effective date by the requirement in Revenue Ruling 71-446 that either no wages can be assumed for the period after a separation from service in determining the amount of an offset, or if wages are assumed, that they may only be assumed at the same rate of pay as at separation, with the maximum permissible offset then prorated based on the years the participant had with the employer divided by those years plus the years for which wages are assumed. However, when a participant remains out of the work force for several years after a separation from service or has low earnings with a new employer, assumption of wages at the same level may be too high. Revenue Ruling 84-45 provides that in this situation, too, the employer must adjust the Social Security estimate to actual wages during the post-separation period if the participant supplies this information.

As a matter of sound practice and employee relations, many plans have already permitted participants the opportunity to supply actual wage histories for preemployment and postseparation periods and to have their Social Security amounts for offsets adjusted accordingly.[130] One difficulty has been, and still is, that the participant may not be able to readily detect when a higher wage history is being used. One

---

[130] See D. Grubbs, "In Depth Re-Examination of Integration," 38 Inst. on Fed. Tax'n—ERISA Supp. (1980), at 2-12.

might think that all the participant would have to do is to compare the amount of his or her actual primary Social Security benefits with the amount used in an offset. The problem is that this is a faulty basis for comparison if, for example, a participant separated from service at age 55. On such a separation, the offset a plan uses should be limited to Social Security benefits determined under the levels *then in effect* under the Social Security Act, either with no wages assumed after the separation, or with wages assumed at the same rate as at the separation from service, with the required proration provided in Revenue Ruling 71-446.

These limits mean that the permissible Social Security amount for an offset should generally be lower than what the participant actually receives. The question then is whether the difference between the amount used in an offset and the amount the participant actually receives has been impermissibly narrowed by the use of a higher estimated wage history for work before or after employment with the employer than the participant actually had. To make this determination, the participant would have to make a special calculation using the Social Security Act benefit levels in effect at the separation, the Revenue Ruling 71-446 assumptions on wages for the postseparation period, and his or her actual wage history for employment prior to and after service with the employer.[131] As an alternative to some of this work, the participant could assume the plan has done the computations correctly and merely ask for the assumed wage history for comparison with his or her actual wage history. Finally, the participant could simply submit the actual wage history and assume that the plan will properly make any necessary adjustments. The risk in the final alternative is that the adjustments will not be properly made, or that the actual wage history will turn out to be higher than had been assumed and that this will permit a higher offset than the wage history the plan had been using. Revenue Ruling 84-45 does not address whether a plan could make such an upward adjustment in an offset based on a participant's voluntary submission of a wage history, but one article states that the IRS has indicated it is permissible for a plan to do so.[132]

In *Dameron v. Sinai Hospital of Baltimore, Inc.*, a class action was certified on claims predating Revenue Ruling 84-45 that estimates of participants' Social Security benefits for use under an 83⅓ percent offset were higher than the Social Security benefits the participants actually received.[133] On motion for summary judgment, the district court held that ERISA's nonforfeitability requirement was violated by

---

[131] Detailed statements of quarterly earnings with past and current employers (called Type I earnings statements) can be obtained from the Social Security Administration. Participants also have a right to obtain any tables or manuals used by the plan in estimating Social Security benefit amounts from such statements of earnings. See *Lee v. Dayton Power & Light Co.*, 604 F.Supp. 987 (S.D. Ohio 1985).

[132] P. Alden, "Calculating the Social Security Offset in Defined Benefit Plans," Pension World (Sept. 1984), 59, at 62.

[133] 595 F.Supp. 1404, 5 EBC 2321 (D. Md. 1984).

the employer's offset from pension benefits of Social Security benefit amounts that in two instances were over $200 more per month than the participants actually received due to faulty assumptions about the participants' past wage histories.[134]

3. Hard or Weighted Offsets Under the ERISA Accrual Rules

ERISA's benefit accrual rules can require substantial adjustments to avoid impermissible "backloading" of benefit accruals in hard offsets—for example, 1.25 percent of pay times years of credited service, less 50 percent of the primary Social Security benefit regardless of years of credited service—and also in weighted offsets—for example 1.25 percent of pay times years of credited service, less two percent of the primary Social Security benefit for each year of credited service up to 25. The effect of the benefit accrual rules on these types of formulas is described in Revenue Ruling 78-252 and discussed fully below in Chapter 4 on ERISA's benefit accrual methods.

4. Minimum Benefits From Top-Heavy Plans

The Tax Equity and Fiscal Responsibility Act of 1982 sharply limited Social Security integration for those plans which, through Social Security integration and other elements of plan design and operation, are top heavy. Top-heavy plans are generally small plans, but plans with 200 or more participants may be top heavy, particularly if they are using Social Security integration at its maximum limits.[135] If a plan is top heavy, the permissible Social Security integration limits for the plan are altered by a requirement that the plan provide minimum nonintegrated benefits, generally equal to two percent of the participant's highest five consecutive year average of pay for up to the first 10 years of service, or minimum nonintegrated contributions, generally equal to three percent of pay for each year, for all non-"key" employees.

TEFRA defines a top-heavy plan as any plan under which more than 60 percent of the present value of accrued benefits have been accrued by certain key employees. If an employer has more than one plan, aggregation of benefits or contributions under all plans of the employer that include any key employee as a participant is required in testing for top-heaviness.[136] As a result of aggregation, a plan that is top heavy standing alone may not be treated as top heavy if it is

---

[134] 626 F.Supp. 1012, 6 EBC 2742 (D. Md. 1986), *aff'd*, 815 F.2d 975 (4th Cir. 1987).

[135] See New York Times, Aug. 31, 1982, at D-1 ("Pension Plans: Major Changes") (describing a plan with over 200 participants where, presumably because of Social Security integration, contributions were actually only required for 20 participants, and 75% of those contributions went to just one man).

[136] See Code §416(g) and 26 C.F.R. 1.416-1, Q&A T-6. Any other plan of the employer that does not have a key employee in it, but that has been aggregated as a comparable plan to enable a key employee plan to meet the Code's coverage rules, must also be included in the aggregation group. *Id.*

required to be included in an aggregation group that is not top heavy overall.[137] Conversely, if a plan is not top heavy standing alone, it may still be treated as top heavy if it is required to be included in an aggregation group that is top heavy.

Key employees, as defined in Section 416(i)(1), as amended by the Deficit Reduction Act of 1984, are any employees, or former employees, who are, or in the preceding four years were:

- Officers of the employer earning more than $45,000;
- One of up to 10 employees with the largest ownership interests (among employees) in the employer who also earn more than $30,000;
- A five percent or more owner of the employer regardless of earnings; or
- A one percent or more owner earning more than $150,000.[138]

Generally, this is a somewhat narrower group than the prohibited group of employees.

Once the key employees in a plan are identified, whether a plan is top heavy is decided based on whether the present value of the key employees' accrued benefits represents 60 percent or more of the present value of the total accrued benefits of the plan, or plans. The present value of distributions of accrued benefits made during the year and the preceding four years is included. The present value of accrued benefits of participants who have not earned compensation from the employer in the current year and the preceding four years is not included.[139]

For a defined contribution plan, the present value of any key or non-key employee's accrued benefits is his or her account balance. Adjustments must be made to include any distributions made during the year or the preceding four years, and any contributions to the individual's account that are due, but that have not been contributed as of the determination date.[140]

Determining the present value of accrued benefits under a defined benefit plan is less straightforward. Monthly or yearly amounts of accrued benefits must be converted to the present value that would be

---

[137] An employer can include a plan within an aggregation group that is not required to be aggregated under the above rules in order to make the group not top heavy so long as the plan's inclusion does not cause the group to fail to meet the Code's coverage tests or overall nondiscrimination requirement. See Code §416(g)(2) and 26 C.F.R. 1.416-1, Q&A T-7. Collectively bargained plans may be included in a permissive aggregation group for purposes of making the group of the employer's key employee plans not top heavy so long as they provide comparable benefits. 26 C.F.R. 1.416-1, Q&A T-7.

[138] The $45,000 and $30,000 limits are based on the §415 limit for contributions to a defined contribution plan. This limit may be adjusted in the future, but it is expected to remain at $30,000 until the early 1990's. See Code §416(i)(1) and §415(c)(1)(A).

[139] Code §416(g) and 26 C.F.R. 1.416-1, Q&A T-1(d). Effective in 1987, testing for top-heaviness is performed under the fractional rule for benefit accruals if an employer has two or more defined benefit plans that use different benefit accrual methods. Code §416(g)(4)(F), as amended by §1118 of the Tax Reform Act, P.L. 99-514.

[140] 26 C.F.R. 1.416-1, Q&A T-24 and T-30.

necessary to cash out those obligations. The plan must use reasonable interest and mortality assumptions to determine the present value of each participant's accrued benefits.[141] Then it must compare the present value of the key employees' accrued benefits to the total present value of all accrued benefits under the plan to determine whether the plan is top heavy.

When a defined benefit plan is top heavy, the plan must provide minimum nonintegrated benefits to all non-key employees in each year that the plan remains top heavy. The minimum nonintegrated benefit for a non-key employee is defined as two percent of the employee's highest five consecutive year compensation average multiplied by each year of service during the period when the plan is top heavy, up to a maximum of 10 years. After 10 years of service under a top-heavy plan, this minimum nonintegrated benefit is capped at 20 percent of the non-key employee's highest five consecutive year average of compensation (if compensation increases, the highest five consecutive year compensation average is required to continue to increase after the 10 years so long as the plan remains top heavy). Any accruals of employer-derived benefits, whether or not attributable to years for which the plan is top heavy, may be used to satisfy the defined benefit minimums. Thus, if a non-key employee has already accrued a benefit of 20 percent of his or her highest five-year compensation average, no additional minimum accruals are required.[142] Conversely, a participant must continue to earn benefits under the plan's regular benefit formula during the years in which the plan is top heavy for comparison against this minimum benefit, and to generate additional benefits when the minimum benefit caps out.

Each non-key employee with at least 1,000 hours of service in the 12-month computation period a plan uses for benefit accruals must accrue a full year's minimum nonintegrated benefit (without any proration even if 2,000 hours is the norm for credit for a full year of participation under the plan). If the plan does not use an accrual computation period, minimum benefits must be credited for all periods of service required to be credited for benefit accruals under a reasonable and consistent method as provided in 26 C.F.R. 1.410(a)-7.[143]

The minimum nonintegrated benefits must not only be earned under the plan's benefit formula, but they must also "accrue." Thus, a plan cannot provide the minimum nonintegrated benefits under its benefit formula, and then accrue the benefits under a method, such as the fractional rule (described in Chapter 4), that might result in a lesser amount of immediate benefit accruals.[144]

---

[141] The actuarial assumptions are required to be stated in the plan, so that their reasonableness, and the accuracy of the computation, may be tested. 26 C.F.R. 1.416-1, at Q&A T-25, T-26, and T-36.

[142] *Id.*, at Q&A M-2.

[143] *Id.*, at Q&A M-4.

[144] *Id.*, at Q&A M-5.

For top-heavy defined contribution plans, minimum nonintegrated contributions are required. The minimum nonintegrated contribution must be at least three percent of a non-key employee's compensation in each plan year.[145] However, if key employees themselves do not receive three percent contributions, non-key employees can receive a minimum contribution equal to the largest percentage of pay contribution allocation provided any key employee.[146] If a defined contribution plan requires employee contributions, the minimum employer contributions may not be limited to those employees who have made the employee contributions. But the defined contribution minimums can generally be restricted to participants who have not separated from service before the end of a plan year.[147]

If a non-key employee participates in a defined benefit and a defined contribution plan maintained by the same employer, the employer may generally choose whether the employee is to receive the minimum contribution or benefit. As a benchmark, the regulations state that the defined benefit minimum is the "more valuable" of the two minimums. Under the regulations, the employer is allowed to choose between:

(1) Providing the defined benefit minimum to all non-key employees who are in both plans;

(2) Using a floor offset arrangement in which the defined benefit minimum is provided subject to an offset of the benefits, expressed in annuity form, that are provided under the defined contribution plan;

(3) Providing the defined contribution minimum if the benefits, expressed in annuity form, provided by the defined contribution plan can be proven to be at least equal to the defined benefit minimum, or

(4) Providing a special defined contribution minimum of five percent of compensation.[148]

In certain instances, higher minimum benefits or contributions are required. Employers who have both defined benefit and defined contribution plans and who want to provide combined benefits and contributions to individuals using the 1.25 multiplier in Code Section 415(e) are

---

[145] Effective in 1989, a non-key employee's elective deferrals under a §401(k) plan cannot be used as an offset to reduce the minimum defined benefit or contribution required under these rules. Code §401(k)(4)(C), as amended by §1116 of the Tax Reform Act of 1986, P.L. 99-514, and Conf. Rep., H.R. 99-841, at II-390.

[146] 26 C.F.R. 1.416-1, at Q&A M-7. The rule allowing the defined contribution plan minimum to drop below 3% only applies if contributions to *all* defined contribution plans in which the key employees participate are below 3%. It also cannot be applied to any defined contribution plan which is aggregated with a defined benefit plan under the Code's comparability rules to enable the defined benefit plan to meet the Code's coverage requirements. Code §§416(c)(2)(B)(ii) and (iii).

[147] 26 C.F.R. 1.416-1, at Q&A M-10.

[148] *Id.*, at Q&A M-12. Effective in 1989, a non-key employee's elective deferrals under a §401(k) plan cannot be used as an offset to reduce the minimum defined benefit or contribution required under these options. Code §401(k)(4)(C), as amended by §1116 of the Tax Reform Act of 1986, P.L. 99-514, and Conf. Rep., H.R. 99-841, at II-390.

required to increase the minimum contribution or benefit by one percentage point. In this situation, the minimum benefit must thus be increased to three percent of each non-key employee's five-year average compensation (up to a minimum of 30 percent after 10 years), or the minimum contribution for the defined contribution plan must be increased to four percent of compensation.[149]

5. Contributory Defined Contribution Plan, Section 401(k), and ESOP Rules

The nondiscrimination rules discussed in section VII above for contributory plans and Section 401(k) plans can function as special Social Security integration limits.

Tax credit ESOPs (which are a type of defined contribution plan) may not be integrated with Social Security. Instead, "the allocation to each participant [must be] an amount which bears substantially the same proportion to the amount of all [employer] securities allocated to all participants in the plan for that year as the amount of compensation paid to such participant during that year bears to the compensation paid to all such participants during that year." Compensation for this purpose is limited to $100,000 per participant.[150]

Leveraged ESOPs may not be integrated with Social Security unless they were already integrated before November 1, 1977, and both the integration level and the excess percentage remain frozen at their November 1, 1977, levels.[151] A nondiscrimination incentive in Code Section 415(c)(6) also increases the annual limit on contributions to an individual's account under an ESOP described in Code Section 4975(e)(7) to $60,000 if *no more* than one-third of employer contributions are allocated to officers, shareholder-employees owning more than 10 percent of the employer stock, and employees earning more than $60,000.[152]

The top-heavy plan rules described immediately above can also apply if a contributory plan, a Section 401(k) plan, or any ESOP is top heavy, or is a part of a top-heavy aggregation group.[153]

---

[149] See Code §416(h) and 26 C.F.R. 1.416-1, Q&A T-33 and M-14. If a non-key employee is covered under both the defined benefit and defined contribution plans, the employer can decide which minimum to provide—subject to the rules described before—except that the defined contribution minimum is in this instance further increased to 7½% of pay. 26 C.F.R. 1.416-1, Q&A M-14.

[150] In addition, no more than one-third of the stock may be allocated to officers, employee-shareholders owning more than 10% of the employer's stock, and employees earning more than $60,000 annually. Code §§409(b)(1)(B) and (b)(2), and Code §41(c)(1)(A)(ii).

Prospectively, all special tax credits for contributions to tax credit ESOPs have been repealed. See §1171(a) of the Tax Reform Act, P.L. 99-514, repealing Code §41.

[151] 26 C.F.R. 54.4975-11(a)(7)(ii).

[152] The Tax Reform Act amends this test to look at whether no more than one-third of the plan's contributions go to highly compensated employees as defined under the TRA. Code §415(c)(6), as amended by §1174(d) of P.L. 99-514.

[153] See 26 C.F.R. 1.416-1, Q&A T-29.

6. Integration Combined With Other Discriminatory Elements

The rules in Revenue Ruling 71-446 do not constitute a blanket endorsement of the results they produce under all circumstances. As the Internal Revenue regulations state:

> "[S]ection 401(a)(5) specifies certain provisions which *of themselves* are not discriminatory. However, this does not mean that a plan containing these provisions may not be discriminatory in actual operation."[154]

What this means is that while a plan is not discriminatory "merely because" it uses Social Security integration,[155] in combination with other circumstances, it may be. As an example, in Revenue Ruling 81-248, maximum use of Social Security integration in conjunction with past service credits that went predominantly to shareholder-employees and officers resulted in discrimination. This was because the plan provisions produced benefits which, as a percentage of compensation, were larger in terms of total benefits and benefits per year of credited service for officers, shareholders, and highly compensated employees.

An excess benefit formula based on a covered compensation table that varies the integration level according to the employee's year of retirement combined with benefit accruals under the fractional rule (described in Chapter 4) could also produce discrimination in operation if prohibited group employees are generally older than rank and file employees because covered compensation tables and the fractional rule both favor older workers.

7. Decreases in Accrued Benefits

An increase in an excess plan's integration level or in a Social Security offset may not so outrun a participant's benefits that a decrease in accrued benefits is produced compared to the amount of accrued benefits that a participant had the year before. Such a decrease in accrued benefits violates ERISA Section 204(b)(1)(G) and Code Section 411(b)(1)(G), which prohibit any decrease in a participant's accrued benefits because of an increase in service or age under a plan.[156] In an excess plan, such a decrease may also constitute a forfeiture of vested accrued benefits.[157]

A plan amendment either increasing the integration level at which benefits under an excess plan step up or increasing the percentage of Social Security benefits to be offset under an offset plan must also not

---

[154] 26 C.F.R. 1.401-1(b)(3) (emphasis added).

[155] Code §401(a)(5).

[156] See also 26 C.F.R. 1.411(b)-1(d)(3), Conf. Rep. on the 1986 Tax Reform Act, H.R. Rep. 99-841, at II-428, [1986] U.S. Code Cong. & Ad. News 4516, and D. Grubbs, "In-Depth Re-Examination of Integration," 38 Inst. on Fed. Tax'n—ERISA Supp. (1980), at 2-10 and 2-17.

[157] See 12 BNA Pens. Rep. 175 (Feb. 4, 1985) (reporting remarks by Ira Cohen, the IRS's chief actuary, concerning the consequences in terms of ERISA's nonforfeitability requirement of automatically adjusting breakpoints under excess formulas to reflect the steep recent and expected future increases in the Social Security taxable wage base).

have the effect of decreasing any participant's accrued benefits up to the date of adoption of the plan amendment.[158] In addition, benefits must thereafter accrue in a manner that complies with one of ERISA's three acceptable benefit accrual methods.[159]

Estoppel can also bar the introduction of or an increase in Social Security integration under a plan. In *Weesner v. Electric Power Board of Chattanooga*, oral and written assurances to employees that their retirement benefits would not be altered if they voted to come under Social Security estopped an employer from amending its pension plan two years later to offset their primary Social Security benefits from the plan's pension benefits.[160]

8. Adequacy of Disclosure

Although not a *per se* constraint, inadequate disclosure of an integrated benefit formula can result in appropriate equitable relief. For example, if a plan uses a "hard" offset, and the summary plan description illustrates the formula only with examples where participants have long service so that the effect of not prorating the offset on a short-service participant is undisclosed, the summary plan description may violate Section 102 of ERISA because it may have the "effect of misleading, misinforming, or failing to inform" participants of limitations in benefits that they might otherwise reasonably expect to receive.[161] Similarly, if the plan uses a unit basis offset, such as J.C. Penney's 1.5 percent of final pay less 1.67 percent of the primary Social Security amount, but illustrates it only with examples of highly paid participants, so that high percentage of pay pension benefits are always produced, the effect may again be "misleading, misinforming, or failing to inform" lower paid participants of the effect of the plan's benefit formula.[162] Both of these types of disclosure problems might be overcome if participants are provided with individual benefit statements clearly indicating the amount of pension plan benefits which they individually will be actually entitled to *after* the offset.

G. Social Security Integration Limits Beginning in 1989

Effective for benefits that are attributable to plan years beginning after December 31, 1988,[163] the 1986 Tax Reform Act lowers the maximum percentage limitation for defined benefit plan offsets of Social Security benefits and requires equal proration of the reduced limit

[158] See ch. 4, sec. IV.B.1.

[159] See ch. 4, sec. IV.B.2.

[160] 344 S.W.2d 766 (Tenn. Ct.App. 1961).

[161] 29 C.F.R. 2520.102-2(b); and see 2520.102-3(l) and ch. 8, sec. I.

[162] *Id.*

[163] The IRS is to issue final regulations implementing all the integration changes by Feb. 1, 1988. §1141(1) of P.L. 99-514. A later effective date of the earlier of Jan. 1, 1991, or the expiration

across 35 years of participation (in contrast to the partial proration of Social Security offsets required under ERISA's benefit accrual rules). The Act also reduces the disparities in benefits and contributions permitted under excess formulas used by defined benefit and defined contribution plans.

1. Offsets

For offsets of Social Security benefits, the Tax Reform Act provides that a participant's accrued benefits (as determined based on the greater of a final or highest consecutive three-year average compensation) must not be reduced by an offset that is greater than the "maximum offset allowance." The maximum offset allowance is the *lesser* of:

(1) 50 percent of the pension benefit that would have accrued in any year without regard to any offset, or

(2) An offset equal to .75 percent of the participant's current final three-year average of compensation for each year in which the participant accrues benefits under the plan, with the total offset not in excess of .75 percent of this compensation average multiplied by the participant's years of credited service under the plan up to 35 years.[164]

In computing the final three-year average under the second element of the maximum offset allowance, compensation is limited to the taxable wage base for each year.[165] If a plan provides unreduced early retirement benefits, the .75 percent factor is to be reduced under Treasury regulations that follow the existing early retirement factors in Revenue Ruling 71-446, but no reduction is to apply because a plan provides reduced early retirement benefits or preretirement disability or death benefits.[166]

Regardless of the benefits provided under these new rules, a plan can cap a participant's accrued benefits, when added to primary Social Security benefits attributable to service with the employer, at no more than the participant's highest single year's pay in his or her final five-year period of work. Social Security benefits are treated as accruing ratably over 35 years for this purpose.[167]

By use of a percentage of compensation as the offset, the amended

---

of the collective bargaining agreement applies to integrated plans maintained pursuant to collective bargaining agreements that were ratified before March 1, 1986, and that have not expired by the general effective date.

[164] Code §§401(l) and 401(a)(5), as amended by §1111 of P.L. 99-514. And see Conf. Rep., H.R. Rep. 99-841, at II-437-38, [1986] U.S. Code Cong. & Ad. News 4525-26. In contrast to the prior rules, the Tax Reform Act's rules require the employee's accrued benefits to satisfy the integration rules. Prior law allowed a plan to determine the integrated benefit under the Code rules and then to accrue the normal retirement benefit under a benefit accrual method that is permissible under ERISA. The Tax Reform Act short circuits this two-step process and requires the accrued benefit to be at certain levels.

[165] Code §401(l)(5)(D)(ii), as amended.

[166] Code §401(l)(5)(F) and Conf. Rep., H.R. Rep. 99-841, at II-439.

[167] Code §401(a)(5)(D), as amended.

rules generally "eliminate the need for offset plans to determine an employee's actual [primary] [S]ocial [S]ecurity benefit."[168] A plan presumably can still offset a percentage of the primary Social Security benefit, but it must test the offset against the maximum offset allowance each year under the new rules. Because the new rules are on a different basis than the old ones, they are also not directly comparable to the old limits. But as a rough measure of the differences produced, in the first example in section VIII above, the participant's primary Social Security benefit of $829 was equal to 39.3 percent of a final three-year average of compensation of $20,975. In this instance, an 83.3 percent offset of the primary Social Security benefit is equivalent to an offset of 32.7 percent of the final three-year average of pay (39.3% x 83.3%). In contrast, the Tax Reform Act's maximum total offset allowance is 26.25 percent of final pay (.75 x 35 years).[169]

2. Excess Formulas

For defined benefit plan excess formulas, the Tax Reform Act's integration limits provide that any accrued benefit based on a percentage of compensation above a plan's integration level must not exceed the percentage benefit provided on compensation below the integration level by more than a "maximum excess allowance." The maximum excess allowance is the *lesser* of:

(1) The percentage benefit provided on compensation below the integration level, or

(2) .75 percent of the participant's final or highest-consecutive three-year average of compensation (whichever is greater) for each year in which the participant accrues benefits under the plan, with the total excess percentage benefit not in excess of .75 percent of this average multiplied by the participant's years of credited service under the plan up to 35 years.[170]

As under prior law, a uniform integration level based on the covered compensation of the oldest participant in the plan can apply to all participants, or the integration level may be determined by a covered

---

[168] Conf. Rep., H.R. Rep., at II-435.

[169] For middle-income participants, the Tax Reform Act's requirement of equal proration of the maximum total offset over 35 years may make a greater difference than the reduction in the maximum overall limit.

[170] Code §§401(l) and 401(a)(5), as amended by §1111 of P.L. 99-514. And see Conf. Rep., H.R. Rep. 99-841, at II-437. The participant's compensation is not capped at the Social Security wage base for the year as it is in computing the maximum offset allowance. See Code §401(l)(5)(C), and compare Code §401(l)(5)(D)(ii). Also in contrast to the offset rules, the benefits referred to are not necessarily accrued benefits. See Conf. Rep., at II-437 (using example of plan with flat benefit formula providing benefits in conformity with these rules, and accruing the benefits under the ERISA fractional rule). The .75% maximum excess allowance is, however, less than the .9% excess percentage allowed under Rev. Rul. 71-446, with no limit on total credited years of service, for excess plans using 3-year final or highest averages of pay.

compensation table that varies the plan's integration level by each participant's age.[171]

The maximum excess allowance of .75 percent of final or highest average pay is not converted to an equivalent percentage of career average pay. Instead, a career average pay plan must apparently make the final or highest average pay computations necessary to comply with the same tests.[172]

The .75 percent factor is to be reduced under Treasury regulations if an excess plan provides unreduced early retirement benefits, as under Revenue Ruling 71-446, but no reduction is to apply because a plan provides reduced early retirement benefits or preretirement disability or death benefits.[173] Any optional form of preretirement benefit or other feature provided with respect to compensation in excess of the integration level is, however, required to be provided with respect to compensation below.

Regardless of the benefits otherwise required under the new maximum excess allowance, a plan can cap a participant's accrued benefits, when added to primary Social Security benefits attributable to service with the employer, at no more than the participant's highest single year's pay in his or her final five-year period of work. Social Security benefits are treated as accruing ratably over 35 years for this purpose.[174]

3. Defined Contribution Plans

The Tax Reform Act's integration rules provide that the percentage contribution under a defined contribution plan on compensation above an integration level must not exceed the percentage contribution provided on compensation below by more than the *lesser* of:

(1) The percentage contribution on compensation below the integration level, or

(2) 5.7 percent (as provided under current law), or the percentage OASDI contribution attributable solely to old age insurance, whichever of these two is greater.[175]

The plan's integration level can continue to be up to the Social Security wage base applicable at the beginning of the plan year in which the contributions are made.[176] Target benefit plans, which previously had

---

[171] Code §401(l)(5)(A), as amended by §1111, and Conf. Rep., H.R. Rep. 99-841, at II-437-38.

[172] See Conf. Rep., H.R. Rep. 99-841, at II-435 and 437.

[173] Conf. Rep., H.R. Rep. 99-841, at II-439.

[174] Code §401(a)(5)(D), as amended.

[175] Code §401(l)(2), as amended by §1111 of P.L. 99-514. In 1986, the old age insurance component of OASDI was less than 5%. Thus, 5.7% is the greater of these two percentages currently. See Conf. Rep., at II-436. The Social Security Administration is to notify the Secretary of Treasury when the old age insurance component of FICA exceeds 5%. *Id.*

[176] Conf. Rep., H.R. Rep. 99-841, at II-432 and 436. A uniform integration level must apply to all participants. Code §401(l)(5)(A), as amended by §1111. Rev. Rul. 71-446, section 19, previously permitted defined contribution plans to use two integration levels under certain circumstances.

been permitted to be integrated as if they were defined benefit plans, are required to adhere to these defined contribution plan limits.

The new nondiscrimination rules for contributory defined contribution plans may, in some instances, require more contributions for lower paid employees than required under these rules.[177]

4. Two or More Plans

IRS regulations are to provide rules for splitting the new integration limits if any employee is covered under two or more integrated plans, following the principles of prior regulations and rulings.[178]

5. Indirect Rules

In some instances, the Tax Reform Act's average benefit test for plans covering a nondiscriminatory classification of employees can place a further limit on Social Security integration as a result of the requirement that the average benefit (or contribution) percentage of nonhighly compensated employees must be no less than 70 percent of the highly compensated employees' average benefit (or contribution) percentage.

IX. Offsets of Public Program Benefits Other Than Social Security

In addition to offsets of primary Social Security benefits, the IRS's regulations and rulings allow pension plans to offset other types of public program benefits. Thus, Social Security disability benefits may be offset from a qualified pension plan's disability benefits. If the plan is integrated, this requires a downward adjustment in the plan's overall permissible Social Security integration limit, and the offset of Social Security disability benefits may also not exceed 64 percent of the employee's Social Security disability benefit amount.[179] A further limitation on offsets of Social Security disability benefits is that they may be offset only when the participant is actually receiving them.[180] In *Holmes v. Oxford Chemicals, Inc.*, a plan administrator was held liable for $25,000 in damages under the tort of outrage when he offset Social Security disability benefits before a participant actually began receiving them as a means to encourage the participant to be diligent in

---

The IRS has authority to reintroduce such multiple integration levels under new regulations. Code §401(l)(5)(A)(iv), as amended.

[177] See Conf. Rep., H.R. Rep., 99-841, at II-432 and 436. The special rules for top heavy plans and for §401(k) plans can also require more than required under these rules.

[178] Code §401(l)(5)(F) and Conf. Rep., H.R. Rep. 99-841, at II-439, [1986] U.S. Code Cong. & Ad. News 4527. And see sec. VIII.E.1 above.

[179] Rev. Rul. 71-446, sec. 12.

[180] *Id.*

applying.[181] It should also be noted that under the Social Security Act, "disability" benefits end at age 65, and "old age" benefits begin. Therefore, after age 65, any offset that applies must be the offset applicable to other participants' old age benefits.[182] In some cases, this will be a higher percentage offset, but in other cases, the offset may be less.

In *Alessi v. Raybestos-Manhattan, Inc.*, the Supreme Court permitted another type of public program benefit offset that the IRS had previously allowed in a Revenue Ruling. The *Alessi* Court permitted a plan to offset an award of workmen's compensation benefits provided under state law (except for fixed payments for bodily impairment and payments for medical expenses) from nondisability pension benefits, as well as from disability-based pension benefits, drawing on the "particularly pertinent" practice of Social Security integration for support.[183]

Limits on acceptable offsets of public program benefits are set out in Revenue Ruling 78-178. In this Ruling, the issue was whether unemployment compensation benefits constituted "retirement benefits created under State or Federal law" within the meaning of Code Section 401(a)(5) and thus could be used as an offset against benefits from a qualified plan. Unemployment compensation benefits met the preliminary test of being "public program" benefits in that they were benefits from programs that require employer contributions and were available to the general public. The next question was whether unemployment compensation benefits together with private pension benefits established an "integrated and correlated retirement system." In ruling that such an offset is not acceptable under this criteria, the IRS stated a broader principle:

> "There are many types of benefits under public programs that do not lend themselves to integration with private pension plan benefits.... Only those programs which provide benefits that may be provided under a qualified pension plan may be used as an offset since only then could a correlated retirement system exist. For example, the benefits payable under State or Federal programs because of sickness and maternity, and which include cash benefits and medical services, may not be used as an offset to pension plan benefits because such benefits may not be provided under a qualified plan....
>
> "Unemployment compensation benefits are paid for temporary periods of layoff. Under Section 1.401-1(b)(1)(i) of the regulations, a qualified plan may not provide layoff benefits. Consequently unemployment compensation falls into the broad category of State and Federal programs that may not be used as an offset to qualified pension plan benefits since such type of benefits may not be provided under a qualified plan."[184]

---

[181] 510 F.Supp. 915, 2 EBC 1167 (M.D. Ala. 1981), *aff'd*, 3 EBC 1667 (11th Cir. 1982).

[182] See Rev. Rul. 71-446, sec. 12.02 (example). Cf. *Massengill v. Aetna Life Ins. Co.*, 405 So.2d 516 (La. 1981).

[183] 451 U.S. 504, 2 EBC 1297, at 1300 (1981). And see Rev. Rul. 68-243. See also *Alessi v. Raybestos-Manhattan, Inc.*, 2 EBC at 1303 and Rev. Rul. 78-178 on the portions of an award of workmen's compensation that may *not* be offset under a qualified plan.

[184] Rev. Rul. 78-178. There is now another reason why offsets of unemployment benefits are unacceptable: Since 1980, federal law has required the states to offset pension benefits from unemployment benefits. See 26 U.S.C. §3304(a)(15). See also *Rivera v. Patino*, 524 F.Supp. 136, 2

Revenue Ruling 78-178 distinguished the permissibility of offsets of benefits payable under workmen's compensation laws on the basis that the same section of the regulations specifically allows pension plans to pay benefits on disability; therefore, workmen's compensation benefits, as well as Social Security disability benefits, are generally acceptable offsets.

The extent of a workmen's compensation or other public program offset can also depend on interpretation of the plan. In *Kowalczyk v. Flintkote Co.*, a plan provided that benefits of "similar kind" to pension and annuity benefits would be offset. Under the IRS's rulings, benefits of "similar kind" include workmen's compensation benefits. But in *Kowalczyk*, while the court declined to hold that a lump sum settlement of a workmen's compensation claim was different in "kind," it also would not rubber-stamp the plan administrator's more fundamental decision that workmen's compensation benefits were generally within the ambit of benefits of "similar kind," and instead sent the case back to the lower court for a hearing on the intent of the parties in using this phrase.[185] Summary plan descriptions of offsets can bear on such interpretations. In *Gladden v. Pargas, Inc.*, an offset of disability benefits by "any amount available from other legislated or group wage benefit plans available to the participant" was restricted based on an SPD description stating that the offset was of "Social Security benefits (primary), Workmen's Compensation, or other legislated benefits" for which the employer made contributions. An offset of benefits the participant was receiving from the Air Force and that his family was receiving from Social Security above the primary Social Security benefit was therefore not allowed.[186]

X. Offsets of Benefits From Other Private Plans

The IRS also permits certain offsets of benefits from other private plans. "Floor plans" are (1) defined benefit plan formulas that offset the vested amount of the participant's profit-sharing plan account balance (expressed as an actuarially equivalent annuity for purposes of the offset), and (2) profit-sharing contribution allocation formulas that offset contributions to money purchase pension plans. Both of these

---

EBC 1925 (N.D. Cal. 1981), and 543 F.Supp. 1160 (N.D. Cal. 1982), *aff'd in part, rev'd in part sub nom. Rivera v. Becerra*, 714 F.2d 887, 5 EBC 1917 (9th Cir. 1984), *cert. denied sub nom. UAW v. Donovan*, 465 U.S. 1099 (1984). Obviously, once pension benefits are subtracted from unemployment compensation, an offset going in the other direction cannot also be permitted.

[185] 405 N.Y.S.2d 852 (Sup.Ct. App.Div. 1978). See also *Wilken v. AT&T Technologies, Inc.*, 632 F.Supp. 772 (E.D. Mo. 1984) (offset of workmen's compensation benefits under disability benefit plan language authorizing offset of benefits of the "same general character" not permissible when employer's nationwide practice under this language was not to make such offsets, with the practice only excepted in Missouri).

[186] 575 F.2d 1091, at 1094 (4th Cir. 1978). See also *Lee v. Dayton Power & Light Co.*, 604 F.Supp. 987 (S.D. Ohio 1985) (long-term disability benefit plan could not offset benefits received by three daughters of a disabled participant from Social Security because of similar employee booklet description).

types of plans have been approved by the IRS, so long as the arrangement does not result in prohibited discrimination.[187]

Offsets of benefits from nonqualified plans stand on a different footing and will more commonly be found to result in discrimination. In Revenue Ruling 81-33, the IRS disapproved an offset of a qualified pension plan's disability benefits by benefits provided under a nonqualified disability benefit insurance contract when the benefits under the disability contract replaced a percentage of pay but then were capped at $500 per month. The result of such an offset would have been to make the remaining tax-qualified plan benefits a greater percentage of pay for highly compensated employees, and thus discriminatory under Code Section 401(a)(4).

Offsets of severance pay benefits by the amount of pension benefits have been held to violate the ADEA.[188] Presumably, an offset of pension benefits by the amount of severance pay would also violate the ADEA. It may also violate Revenue Ruling 78-178 (providing that only certain types of benefits may be offset from pension benefits), and potentially Revenue Ruling 81-33 (relating to discrimination from offsets of nonqualified plan benefits).

Offsets of benefits from one employer's plan by pension benefits received or due from the plan of another employer have been approved by one court,[189] but the IRS has never passed on such offsets. Statutory support for these offsets appears weaker than for public program offsets or offsets of benefits from other plans maintained by the *same* employer. As discussed in Chapters 4 and 10, such offsets may also run afoul of the ERISA benefit accrual rules, or may result in age discrimination.

---

[187] See Rev. Rul. 76-259 (approving offset of defined benefit plan benefits by amount of vested profit-sharing account balance expressed as an annuity) and Rev. Rul. 81-201 (approving offset of profit-sharing plan contribution allocations by amount of money purchase plan contributions). But see sec. VII.B for a special rule applying to §401(k) plans after 1988.

[188] See cases cited in ch. 10, sec. III.C.

[189] See *Quinn v. Burlington Northern Pension Plan*, 664 F.2d 675, 3 EBC 1137 (8th Cir. 1981). Cf. *Holliday v. Xerox Corp.*, 732 F.2d 548, 5 EBC 1705 (6th Cir. 1984).

4

Benefit Accruals

I. Beginning Participation

If an employee's job classification is covered by a pension plan, the plan can still have age and service requirements that must be fulfilled before participation may begin. Even with the age and service, an employee may still be subject to a waiting period before actually commencing participation in accruals of the plan's benefits or contributions.

The significance of ERISA's minimum "participation" standards can easily be mistaken. The standards are significant if and only if the employee later vests (which is determined independently of when participation begins). If an employee later vests, the minimum participation standards mean that the employee's accrued benefits will be based on a larger part of the employee's total period of employment than they might have been under pre-ERISA standards for beginning participation. On the other hand, if an employee does not vest, how early he or she began participation in a plan is of no consequence because the employee does not have a right to the accrued benefits.

A. Minimum Age and Service Conditions

Before the enactment of ERISA, Internal Revenue Code Section 401(a)(3) permitted service requirements of as many as five years as a condition of beginning participation; age requirements of as high as age 30 were also found in some plans.[1] ERISA generally provides that a plan may not require more as a condition of participation than the

[1] See, e.g., Rev. Rul. 73-265.

attainment of age 25 and the completion of one year of service.[2] The one year of service may be completed before the age is attained so that an employee hired at age 24 can satisfy both conditions immediately on reaching age 25.[3] The 1984 Retirement Equity Act (REA) amends ERISA to further lower the permissible age requirement from age 25 to age 21 effective in plan years beginning after December 31, 1984.[4]

One major drawback to the minimum participation standards is that they are not retroactive. If participation began before the ERISA effective date (which was not until the first plan year beginning after December 31, 1975, for plans in existence before January 1, 1974), the participant's commencement of participation can remain under a pre-ERISA standard.[5] The REA's lowering of the minimum participation age to age 21 similarly does not apply if an employee's participation in a plan began before the first plan year beginning after December 31, 1984.[6] The beginning of participation, and thus, the amount of benefit accruals, of many persons who are vested and now reaching retirement are therefore still under pre-ERISA standards, which may have required age 30 and three or five years' service as a condition to beginning participation.[7]

In contrast to the carryover of pre-ERISA requirements for many participants, it is important to recognize that ERISA minimum participation requirements are one of the minimum standards that many employers exceed, and that some employers exceeded even before ERISA. Many larger companies and collectively bargained plans do not use age 21 or one year of service as conditions for participation, even though they are permitted to do so under the ERISA standards. According to the Bureau of Labor Statistics' 1982 survey of plans of medium and large firms, 62 percent of plan participants were in plans without an age requirement as a condition for participation, and 39 percent were in plans that did not have either an age or service requirement.[8]

---

[2] ERISA §202(a)(1)(A) (Code §410(a)(1)(A)).

[3] *Id.*, and see 26 C.F.R. 1.410(a)-3(a).

[4] ERISA §202(a)(1)(A) (Code §410(a)(1)(A)), as amended by §§102(a) and 202(a) of the Retirement Equity Act, P.L. 98-397. Effective dates are in §§302(a) and (b) of P.L. 98-397. The effective date for a collectively bargained plan is the first plan year after the expiration of the collective bargaining agreement in effect on Aug. 23, 1984 (or the last collective bargaining agreement then in effect if there are more than one), or the first plan year beginning on or after Jan. 1, 1987, if that is earlier.

[5] ERISA §211(b)(2). For plans established after Jan. 1, 1974, the ERISA effective date was the first plan year beginning after Sept. 2, 1974. ERISA §211(a).

[6] See n. 4 above, and S. Rep. 98-575, 98th Cong., 2d Sess., at 10, reprinted in [1984] U.S. Code Cong. & Ad. News 2547, at 2556.

[7] See above. Although as many as 5 years were permitted as a condition of participation before ERISA, 3 years seems to have been a common requirement.

[8] Bureau of Labor Statistics, Employee Benefits in Medium and Large Firms, 1982, at 47 (another 4% of participants were in plans with an age requirement, but with no service requirement). See also Bureau of Labor Statistics, Employee Benefits in Medium and Large Firms, 1984, at 59 (37% in plans with neither an age nor a service requirement, 22% in plans with only a service requirement, and 3% in plans with age but no service requirement). One of the reasons for dispensing with at least the permissible service requirement relates to the rules on when actual participation in a plan must commence. A plan that does not have a service requirement may use

Under ERISA, a longer requirement of three years of service is permitted as a condition of participation if a plan provides full vesting in accrued benefits after three or less years of service. Under this exception, a plan is permitted to require a longer period before an employee begins participation—and thus begins to accrue benefits—if the plan, in implicit exchange, provides a shorter period for obtaining a vested right to accrued benefits than normally permitted.[9] Before 1983, this exception did not have very wide application because few plans, outside of H.R. 10 plans (plans of self-employed individuals) and some defined contribution plans, offered vesting after three or less years of service.

With the enactment of the top-heavy plan rules in the 1982 Tax Equity and Fiscal Responsibility Act (TEFRA), the three-year exception became more important. A top-heavy plan, as explained in Chapter 3, is a plan in which 60 percent or more of the plan's benefits have been accrued by certain key employees who are usually either officers, part owners, or very highly compensated employees of the business sponsoring the plan.[10]

Top-heavy plans are required to provide minimum nonintegrated benefits to non-key employees, and more pertinent to this discussion, are required to vest all employees' accrued benefits either under a schedule offering full vesting after three years of service, with no vesting required before, or under a graded vesting schedule providing 20 percent vesting in accrued benefits after two years of service and 20 percent increments in the vested percentage for each additional year of service thereafter, up to 100 percent, or full, vesting after six years of service. Under the exception described above, a top-heavy plan that provides full vesting after three years of service can require three years of service as a condition of participation in the plan. In contrast, a top-heavy plan using the graded 20 percent schedule cannot use the exception because full vesting does not occur after three or less years of service. Because top-heaviness is usually not an accident, but reflects the employer's design of the plan in a manner that provides most of the plan's benefits to key employees, many top-heavy plans may choose to provide full vesting after three years, even though this generally results in faster vesting than under the graded schedule, since it enables the plan to use the longer three years of service requirement as a condition for beginning participation in benefit accruals.[11]

---

a longer waiting period—effectively a service requirement—before participation actually commences. See sec. I.C (on actual commencement of participation).

[9] ERISA §202(a)(1)(B)(i) (Code §410(a)(1)(B)(i)), and see 26 C.F.R. 1.410(a)-3(b).

[10] See ch. 3, sec. VIII.F.4 (describing the top heavy determination and the rules on minimum nonintegrated benefits).

[11] See 26 C.F.R. 1.416-1, Q&A V-4. However, delaying participation in a top-heavy plan through use of the 3-year exception does not have as full an effect on benefits accruals as it does for other plans. Under the top-heavy rules, the plan's regular benefit accruals based on years of participation may be delayed by use of the exception, but the minimum nonintegrated benefits required for non-key employees must be provided based on years of service with the employer, and thus without regard to use of the exception. See Code §416(c).

Full vesting is also required on the commencement of participation in Code Section 401(k) "cash or deferred arrangements" (popularly known as salary reduction plans) and in tax credit ESOPs. Because these plans, too, are required to provide full vesting after three or less years of service, they are also permitted to require three years of service as a condition of participation in the plan.

Another, still more specialized exception on conditions for participation applies to plans of tax-exempt educational institutions. If such plans provide full vesting after one year of service, they are permitted to use the three year of service requirement as a condition of participation. Under a special alternate, such plans may instead substitute 30 years of age for the age 25 condition of participation standard.[12] If the higher age is used, it must be in conjunction with a one year of service requirement for participation, i.e., the plan cannot use *both* the higher age and the three year exception.[13] Along with the Retirement Equity Act's lowering of the general minimum participation age from 25 to 21, the age requirement permitted under this exception has been lowered to age 26 for plan years beginning after December 31, 1984.[14] The largest and most prominent plan using this exception is the TIAA-CREF plan for college teachers and other staff members.

Effective in 1989, the exception allowing plans with full and immediate vesting to use three years of service as a condition for participation is restricted to only allow two years of service as a participation condition.[15] Effective at the same time, a Section 401(k) plan cannot require more than one year of service as a condition for participation.[16]

1. Satisfaction of Age Conditions

When a plan uses a minimum age requirement as a condition of participation, satisfaction of the age requirement should be evident. Under the minimum standards, an age requirement is met as of the exact day the age is attained.[17] A one year of service requirement, or a three years of service requirement under the exception, may be completed before or after the employee reaches the required age.

2. Counting Service

In determining whether, and exactly when, a years of service requirement for participation has been completed, the rules on what

---

[12] ERISA §202(a)(1)(B)(ii) (Code §410(a)(1)(B)(ii)), and see 26 C.F.R. 1.410(a)-3(c).

[13] *Id.*

[14] ERISA §202(a)(1)(B)(ii) (Code §410(a)(1)(B)(ii)), as amended by P.L. 98-397, §102(a)(2) and §202(a)(2).

[15] ERISA §202(a)(1)(B)(i) and Code §410(a)(1)(B)(i), as amended by §§1113(c) and (e)(3) of the Tax Reform Act, P.L. 99-514.

[16] Code §401(k)(2)(D), as amended by §1116.

[17] 26 C.F.R. 1.410(a)-3(a)(1) and (b)(1). The same applies to the higher age requirement permitted educational institutions that provide full vesting after one year. 26 C.F.R. 1.410(a)-3(c)(1).

years of service with an employer or employers count for vesting should be consulted.[18] For example, a year of service in a job classification or division not covered under a plan must count for vesting, and must also count for any service requirement for beginning participation, if the employee later comes under a job classification or division that is covered by the plan. Years of service with any employer in a controlled group of employers are also required to count toward both vesting and conditions of participation requirements, as are years of service in an affiliated group or as a leased employee. One notable, and for employees, favorable, difference between the rules on counting years of service for vesting and years of service for participation is that a year of service with an employer before establishment of the plan is also required to count for conditions of participation.[19]

a. 1,000 hours of service method. Within periods of service that are required to be considered for meeting service requirements for participation, a year of service is more exactly measured by the completion of 1,000 hours of service within a 12-month computation period, which must initially start with the employment commencement date of the employee. Because the issues concerning whether an employee has completed a year of service within a 12-month period tend to arise more with vesting, "hours of service," and equivalencies that may be used in lieu of counting service on an hour-by-hour basis, are discussed in more detail in Chapter 5.[20] It may be noted in this context that the regulations require up to 501 hours to be credited during which no duties are performed, but for which an employee is paid, or entitled to payment, such as for paid vacation, sickness, and disability leave.[21] Also, if certain equivalencies are used in counting hours, less than 1,000 hours—i.e., 870 or 750 hours, depending on the equivalency used—must constitute a year of service.[22] Employment at the end of the 12-month computation period is not required for a "year of service" if 1,000 hours of service, or its equivalent, have been completed during the computation period.[23] However, if an employee is not reemployed for a long enough period of time, the "year of service" could be cancelled under the ERISA break-in-service rules, and until an employee is reemployed, actual participation in the plan, and thus the accrual of benefits, is not required to commence.

When a plan has a one year of service requirement, or a three years of service requirement under the exception, the 1,000 hours standard provides that an employee who does not have 1,000 hours of service, or its equivalent, by the end of the 12-month computation period beginning with the commencement date of employment simply

---

[18] See ch. 5, sec. III.

[19] Compare ERISA §202(b)(1) (Code §410(a)(5)) and ERISA §203(b)(1)(C) (Code §411(a)(4)(C)).

[20] See ch. 5, sec. III.B.1.

[21] 29 C.F.R. 2530.200b-2(a).

[22] 29 C.F.R. 2530.200b-3(d).

[23] 29 C.F.R. 2530.200b-1(b).

starts over. Whatever hours of service were counted in the computation period are not aggregated with hours of service in the next computation period.[24] When an employee comes up short of the 1,000 hours requirement for a year of service for commencing participation, some plans switch to a different computation period based on the plan year, rather than continuing with a 12-month computation period based on the date of employment. ERISA provides that when such a switch in computation periods is made, the new period must begin *before* the end of the initial employment commencement date period so that there is no gap in which an employee's hours of service are not counted toward the minimum service requirement for participation.[25]

b. Elapsed time method. As an alternative to counting 1,000 hours, or to using one of the set of equivalencies provided in the regulations, a plan may use the "elapsed time" method to measure a year of service for a one year or three years of service requirement for beginning participation. The elapsed time method is discussed in more detail in Chapter 5.[26] But here it may be sufficient to note that the elapsed time method permits an employer to require a full 12-month period of service before counting a year of service, whereas 1,000 hours can often be completed within a shorter period. However, under the elapsed time method, a plan is required to count as a period of service up to 12 months of absence, whether or not paid, by reason of layoff, sickness, accident, or any other type of leave.[27] A plan must also count as a period of service the period after a quit or discharge if an employee returns to do an hour of service within 12 months of the day of the quit or discharge.[28] Some plans that use the elapsed time method for computing years of vesting service do not use it for computing years of service for beginning participation, partly because of these features.[29]

An employee who does not have a 12-month period of service under these rules at the end of the first 12-month period beginning with his or her employment commencement date, retains the period of service he or she has (unless the breaks in service rules, described below, apply to cancel the service). That service is then aggregated with the employee's next period of service.[30] Under a one year of service requirement, this aggregation will normally not be required because if an employee separates from service by reason of a quit or

---

[24] Conf. Rep., at 263, 3 ERISA Leg. Hist. 4530.

[25] ERISA §202(a)(3)(A) (Code §410(a)(3)(A)), and 29 C.F.R. 2530.202-2(b). And see *Gennamore v. Buffalo Sheet Metals, Inc., Pension Plan*, 568 F.Supp. 931, 5 EBC 1268 (W.D.N.Y. 1983), for an illustration of how a change in computation periods is handled in counting years of service for vesting.

[26] See ch. 5, sec. III.B.2.

[27] 26 C.F.R. 1.410(a)-7(b)(2)(ii).

[28] 26 C.F.R. 1.410(a)-7(c)(2)(iii)(A). But see 26 C.F.R. 1.410(a)-7(c)(2)(iii)(B) (12-month period starts from the beginning of the absence if a quit or discharge occurs after a period of absence has begun).

[29] The use of the elapsed time method for determining vesting years of service, but not years of service for participation is permitted under 26 C.F.R. 1.410(a)-7(a)(4)(i).

[30] 26 C.F.R. 1.410(a)-7(c)(2)(iv).

discharge and returns to service within 12 months, or is absent for less than 12 months for any reason other than a quit or discharge, the entire period must count as a period of service, and therefore the one year of service for participation will be satisfied.[31]

Whether a plan uses the 1,000 hours standard, one of the equivalencies, or the elapsed time method in measuring a year of service for participation should be clear from the plan document. A plan that credits service on the basis of hours must state the definition of hours of service and at least incorporate by reference the regulatory citation for any equivalency it uses to count hours.[32]

A plan that uses the elapsed time method should define the basis for determining periods of service and should contain the special rules on crediting absences and periods of severance of less than 12 months. If a plan fails to specify the method it uses, the courts have used the 1,000 hours standard, or one of the equivalencies related to it, rather than the elapsed time method.[33]

c. Breaks in service. ERISA's "break-in-service" rules can be relevant to whether participation requirements have been met. Break-in-service rules are discussed in Chapter 5,[34] but briefly, the chief ERISA break-in-service rule is the "rule of parity." It provides that if an employee without *any* vested rights has a series of consecutive one-year breaks in service equal to or exceeding his or her prior years of service for vesting (whether or not those years are accumulated consecutively), the prior years of service for vesting may be cancelled.[35] Under the 1984 Retirement Equity Act amendments to ERISA, a floor of five consecutive one-year breaks in service (or a consecutive 60-month period of severance under the elapsed time method) is established for plan years beginning after December 31, 1984, before the rule of parity can be used to cancel any prior years of service.[36]

The rule of parity, as amended by the five-year floor in REA for plan years beginning after December 31, 1984, applies to counting years of service for minimum participation requirements.[37] However, since most plans have just a one year of service requirement, the rule of parity generally has no application to satisfaction of the service requirement for participation, except in determining whether an employee who already has one or more years of service and who separates

---

[31] 26 C.F.R. 1.410(a)-7(b)(2)(ii) and (c)(2)(iii).

[32] 29 C.F.R. 2530.200b-2(f).

[33] See *Gennamore v. Buffalo Sheet Metals, Inc., Pension Plan, supra*; *Tucci v. Edgewood Country Club*, 459 F.Supp. 940 (W.D. Pa. 1978).

[34] See ch. 5, secs. III.A.4 and III.C.

[35] ERISA §203(b)(3)(D) (Code §411(a)(6)(D)), as amended by the Retirement Equity Act, P.L. 98-397.

[36] *Id.*

[37] ERISA §202(b)(4) (Code §410(a)(5)(D)), as amended by the Retirement Equity Act, P.L. 98-397. Note that the special one-year break-in-service rule applicable to counting vesting service under defined contribution plans before 1985 does not apply to meeting conditions of participation. Compare *id.* and ERISA §203(b)(3)(C) (Code §411(a)(6)(C)). The years of service which the break must equal or exceed may also include some years of service not required to be included for vesting. See sec. I.A.2 above.

from service retains the credit on a return to service (which is discussed separately below).

The rule of parity can have a wider application if a plan is permitted to use a three years of service requirement as a condition of participation, but its application there is largely overridden by a more stringent break-in-service rule. Under ERISA Section 202(b)(2) (Code Section 410(a)(5)(B)), such plans are permitted to use a one-year break in service (or a one-year period of severance) to cancel years of service before the break, regardless of whether the effect is to cancel two prior years of service for just one year of break. This special one-year break rule was not changed by the REA.[38]

B. Maximum Age Exclusions

In addition to minimum age and service requirements for beginning participation, ERISA allows defined benefit plans to exclude employees from participation entirely if they are hired when they are over a certain maximum age. Under ERISA Section 202(a)(2) (Code Section 410(a)(2)), employees who are *hired* within five years of a defined benefit plan's "normal retirement age" may be excluded from participation. Unlike use of the minimum age and service requirements for participation, this exclusion is in wide use. In the BLS's survey of pension plans of medium and large employers, 61 percent of participants were in plans that use a maximum age exclusion for beginning participation.[39] Since the normal retirement age for most defined benefit plans is age 65, this means that employees who are age 60 or over when hired are often excluded from participation.

Three instances when this exclusion cannot apply may be stressed. First, if a defined benefit plan's normal retirement age is the *later* of age 65 or from the fifth up to the tenth anniversary of participation in the plan, an employee hired after age 60 can never be excluded from participation because, under this type of normal retirement age definition, no employee is ever within five years of the plan's normal retirement age *when hired*.[40] Second, any exclusions of employees because of their age when hired must be nondiscretionary under the terms of the plan to comply with the Age Discrimination in Employment Act. That is, a plan's terms must not allow the employer, or the plan's trustees, to

---

[38] A break in service delaying participation under a top-heavy plan that uses the 3-year exception cannot have as full an effect on benefits accruals as it does for other plans. Under the top-heavy rules, the plan's regular benefit accruals based on years of participation may be delayed by use of the exception, but the minimum nonintegrated benefits required for non-key employees must be provided based on years of service with the employer, and thus without regard to when participation began under this rule. See Code §416(c).

[39] Bureau of Labor Statistics, Employee Benefits in Medium and Large Firms, 1984, at 59.

[40] ERISA Conf. Rep., at 262, 3 ERISA Leg. Hist. 4529. Also note that a defined benefit plan with an age 65 normal retirement age which provides that an employee will become a participant on completion of one year of service if *at that time* he or she is less than 60 is not in compliance with this standard. Such a plan provision would permit an employee who was hired at age 59—more than 5 years before the plan's normal retirement age—to be excluded. See 26 C.F.R. 1.410(a)-4(a)(2).

make discretionary exceptions that are not enjoyed by all individuals hired at older ages.[41] Third, the exclusion of employees within five years of the normal retirement age has no application in defined contribution plans, except for so-called target benefit plans, which are not in wide use.[42]

The exclusion of employees from a defined benefit plan because of their age when hired has become politically unpalatable, but the limitation of such exclusions to only those employees who were hired within five years of a plan's normal retirement age was, when enacted, a significant *reform* compared to plan provisions that had existed before. The ERISA effective dates, moreover, have an interesting application in this area. The regulations give this example:

> "Prior to the effective date of section 410, a defined benefit plan with a normal retirement age of age 65 contained a maximum age 55 requirement for participation. Because of the maximum age requirement, an employee hired at age 58 was excluded from the plan. This employee is age 61 at the time that section 410 first applies to the plan. The employee cannot be excluded from participation because of age. The exclusion under section 410(a)(2) is not applicable in this instance because the employee's age at the time of hire, 58, was not within five years of the normal retirement age specified in the plan."[43]

Effective in 1988, the 1986 Omnibus Budget Reconciliation Act repeals the ERISA and Code rules allowing defined benefit plans to exclude employees from participation if they are hired within five years of a plan's normal retirement age.[44] Service prior to the effective date counts for any one year, or three years, of service condition for beginning participation if an employee who is in service at the effective date was previously permissibly excluded under the old law.[45] A plan can still provide that the normal retirement age for such participants is the *later* of age 65 or the fifth anniversary of the time the individual commences participation for purposes of vesting at normal retirement age, benefit accruals, and the commencement of benefits—even if age 65 applies to all other participants.[46]

---

[41] 29 C.F.R. 860.120(c).

[42] See 26 C.F.R. 1.410(a)-4(a)(1). On the permissibility of such an exclusion under a target benefit plan, see *id.* and 29 C.F.R. 860.120(f)(1)(iv)(A).

[43] 26 C.F.R. 1.410(a)-4(a)(2) (example (3)). And see *White v. Distributors Ass'n Warehousemen's Pension Trust,* 751 F.2d 1068 (9th Cir. 1985).

[44] ERISA §202(a)(2) and Code §410(a)(2), as amended by §9203 of P.L. 99-509.

[45] §9204(b) of P.L. 99-509, and Conf. Rep., H.R. Rep. 99-1012, at 382, [1986] U.S. Code Cong. & Ad. News 3868, at 4027. The effective date for this repeal is the first plan year starting on or after Jan. 1, 1988. For collectively bargained plans, the effective date is the *earlier* of Jan. 1, 1990, or the date on which the last collective bargaining agreement ratified before March 1, 1986, expires.

[46] ERISA §3(24)(B) and Code §411(a)(8)(B), as amended by §9203 of P.L. 99-509.

C. Waiting Periods for Commencement of Participation

Once an employee covered by a plan meets any age and service requirements for participation (and is not excluded by his or her age when hired), the actual commencement of participation in the plan can still be postponed, if a plan so provides, but not beyond a limited additional waiting period. Under ERISA Section 202(a)(4) (Code Section 410(a)(4)), the commencement of actual participation in a plan may be delayed after age and service requirements are met, but not beyond the *earlier* of:

(1) The start of the next plan year after any age and service requirements are satisfied, or

(2) Six months after the age and service requirements are satisfied.

To meet the latter requirement, plans typically provide for a semi-annual date of entry into the plan, in addition to entry at the beginning of each plan year.[47] Another alternative is allowed if a plan's requirements for participation are less stringent than permitted under the ERISA minimum standards, for example, a plan that has no age or service requirements for beginning participation. These plans may allow entry only at the start of each plan year following the date of employment, and may thus dispense with a semi-annual entry date, so long as the effective service requirement for any employee is no longer than the one year of service requirement that the plan could have used as a condition of participation.[48]

Entry dates other than at the start of a plan year and semi-annually are required for employees who satisfy the minimum age and service requirements for beginning participation, but are separated from service on their applicable entry date. Under these circumstances the employee must be admitted to participation immediately on returning to covered employment, provided that a one-year break in service has not occurred before the return.[49] When a plan uses the elapsed time method and an employee is absent on the applicable entry date for any reason other than a quit or discharge—e.g., because of a layoff or sick leave—and returns to active service before the end of the 12-month period that began with the start of the absence, the employee also must begin participation after the return to service. The commencement date of participation, moreover, must be retroactively

---

[47] Alternatively, some plans satisfy this requirement without using semi-annual entry dates by providing that an employee who satisfies the age and service requirements on or before the *middle* of a plan year will be considered to have entered the plan at the first of the plan year, and an employee who satisfies the age and service requirements after the middle of the plan year, will enter the plan at the start of the next plan year.

[48] See Rev. Rul. 80-360.

[49] 26 C.F.R. 1.410(a)-4(b) and 1.410(a)-7(c)(3)(ii)(B).

effective to the first applicable entry date occurring during the absence.[50]

When an employee misses an applicable entry date and incurs a one or more year break in service (or under elapsed time, a one or more year "period of severance"), a plan can use a "one-year hold-out" rule on the employee's return to service.[51] Under this rule, prebreak service, although not cancelled, need not be credited to the employee until he or she completes one year of service after returning from the break. However, once one year of service is completed, the employee is required to retroactively participate in benefit accruals under the plan beginning with the date when he or she returned.[52] Since the net effect is the same, many plans do not use the one-year hold-out rule, in which case participation commences immediately after the employee's return from a one or more year break in service.

The other possibility when an employee is separated from service on an applicable entry date and has a one or more year break in service (or a one or more year period of severance under the elapsed time method) is that the service already completed for satisfaction of a one year of service requirement for participation may be cancelled under the ERISA "rule of parity," with the employee forced to start over toward meeting that requirement.[53]

The rule of parity cannot apply to cancel years of service for participation requirements when a plan is permitted to have a three years of service requirement as a condition of participation and an employee satisfies the requirement but is then separated from service before the applicable entry date. The reason for this is that for a plan to be permitted to use three years of service as a condition of participation, it must provide full vesting after three or less years of service. Thus, an employee who satisfies the service requirement for participation must already have a nonforfeitable right. Once an employee has any nonforfeitable rights, neither the special one-year break rule for these plans nor the rule of parity can apply to cancel years of service, regardless of the number of consecutive one-year breaks in service.

---

[50] 26 C.F.R. 1.410(a)-7(c)(3)(ii)(B). Under the elapsed time method, it is also possible that an employee who did not meet the minimum service requirement when an absence first began will meet it during the absence and will also pass an applicable entry date. The same rule on retroactive commencement of participation applies in this case. *Id.*

[51] ERISA §202(b)(3) (Code §410(a)(5)(C)), and see 26 C.F.R. 1.410(a)-5(c)(3) and 1.410(a)-7(c)(5).

[52] *Id.*

[53] Prior to 1985 this meant that an employee's one year of service in satisfaction of a participation requirement could be cancelled after just a one-year break in service. Similarly, under the elapsed time method, an employee's one-year period of service for participation could be cancelled after just a one-year period of severance. However, beginning with plan years after Dec. 31, 1984, the rule of parity was amended to establish a floor requiring a minimum of 5 or more consecutive one-year breaks in service (or one-year periods of severance) before even *one* prior year of service may be cancelled. ERISA §202(b)(4) (Code §410(a)(5)(D)), as amended by the Retirement Equity Act, P.L. 98-397. See §302 and §303 of P.L. 98-397 for effective dates. The effective date for a collectively bargained plan is the first plan year beginning after the expiration of the collective bargaining agreement in effect on Aug. 23, 1984 (or the last of the collective bargaining agreements then in effect if there are more than one), or the first plan year beginning after Jan. 1, 1987, if that is earlier.

D. Employee Contributions

In addition to minimum age and service and waiting periods, employee contributions can be required to actually participate in benefit accruals. Defined benefit plans usually do not require employee contributions, but many defined contribution plans do.[54]

II. Year-by-Year Accruals of Benefits

Benefits must begin to accrue when an employee actually commences participation in a plan.[55] The significance of having an "accrued benefit" is that it is the amount that must vest under ERISA's vesting schedules, and that can then survive a separation from service before retirement. Thus, if a participant has an accrued benefit of $4,800 per year payable beginning at age 65, and is vested, the right to receive the accrued benefit at retirement is secure regardless of whether the participant quits, is permanently laid off, or is discharged before the plan's retirement age. Whether or not a benefit is an accrued benefit also has other ramifications. The most notable is that once a benefit becomes an accrued benefit, ERISA generally prohibits its reduction by plan amendment. *Future* benefit accruals may be reduced, but the benefits that have already accrued must be protected.

A. Defined Contribution Plans

In a defined contribution plan, the process by which benefits accrue is relatively straightforward. Once an employee commences participation, contributions to the plan must be allocated to an individual account for the participant according to a definite, predetermined formula stated in the plan on an at least annual date specified in the plan.[56] Earnings or losses on those contributions must then also be allocated to each individual account at least annually.[57] A share of the

---

[54] The effect of not making required employee contributions, or of withdrawing them after contribution, is discussed in secs. III.C.3 and 4 below. Limits on employee contribution requirements are discussed in ch. 3, sec. VII, and ch. 2, secs. II and III.

[55] More technically, even when an employee commences participation, a defined benefit plan can still defer the computation of his or her accrued benefits until the employee has 2 continuous years of service. ERISA §204(b)(1)(E) (Code §411(b)(1)(E)). The regulations provide that the computation of when these 2 years have passed shall be based on 1,000 hours of service within 2 computation periods beginning with the employment commencement date. 29 C.F.R. 2530.204-4. Generally, this should mean that a participant will have satisfied this requirement under a plan that uses it and that has a one-year service requirement for participation before the end of his or her first year of participation in the plan. In a plan with a 3 years of service requirement for participation, the 2 years should be completed well before the employee begins participation.

[56] See 26 C.F.R. 1.401-1(b)(1)(ii) and Rev. Rul. 80-155. And see *Steidtmann v. Koelbel & Co.*, 506 P.2d 1247 (Colo. App. 1973) (if allocation date is not fixed, discriminatory potential in ability to vary date of allocation until after a participant leaves can make denial of allocation for lack of employment on date that is finally set arbitrary and capricious).

[57] Rev. Ruls. 80-155 and 73-103.

plan's earnings, or losses, must continue to be allocated to a participant's individual account after active participation in the plan ends—unless and until the nonforfeitable portion of the account balance is distributed.[58]

The participant's accrued benefit in a defined contribution plan is thus the individual account balance, composed of contributions, earnings or losses, and if applicable under the terms of a plan, reallocations to the participant's account of forfeitures of other participants' account balances (generally forfeitures occur because other participants leave before vesting).[59] If contributions to a defined contribution plan are not made as promised, the plan sponsor is in breach of contract, and plan fiduciaries may also be in breach of fiduciary duty if they fail to take appropriate steps to secure the promised contributions.[60] Imprudent investments of a defined contribution plan's assets, e.g., through loans to the plan sponsor or other related parties at below market rates or without adequate security, are actionable as breaches of fiduciary duty.[61]

If a defined contribution plan so provides, a participant can be required to be employed on a specified date, e.g., December 31, to receive any contribution allocation for the year.[62] Thus, if a participant works nearly all year and then quits, is discharged, or even retires before the allocation date, the participant could miss an entire year's

---

[58] Rev. Ruls. 80-155 and 73-103. And see *Dennard v. Richards Group, Inc.*, 681 F.2d 306, 3 EBC 1769 (5th Cir. 1982). See also *Hickerson v. Velsicol Chem. Corp.*, 778 F.2d 365, 6 EBC 2545 (7th Cir. 1985), *cert. denied*, 479 U.S. ___ (1986) (right to allocation of investment earnings not a part of a participant's "accrued benefit" insofar as establishing *per se* protection against plan amendment, but employer has fiduciary duty in converting profit-sharing plan to defined benefit plan to ensure that existing account balances continue to earn at least a market rate of interest until distribution). But cf. *Ganze v. Dart Indus., Inc.*, 741 F.2d 790, 5 EBC 2309 (5th Cir. 1984) (quarterly dividends on company stock held in profit-sharing plan not required to be allocated to participants whose employment terminated before the end of the quarter; opinion unclear on whether the participants' account balances had been distributed before the end of the quarter).

[59] See ERISA §3(23) (Code §411(a)(7)) (accrued benefit in an individual account plan is the balance in the individual's account), and ERISA §3(34) (Code §414(i)) (an individual account plan means a plan which provides an individual account for each participant with benefits based solely on the amount contributed to the participant's account and any income, expenses, gains or losses, and forfeitures of accounts of other participants' account balances which may be reallocated under the terms of the plan to the participant's account). See also *Hickerson v. Velsicol Chemical Corp., supra.*

[60] See *Monson v. Century Mfg. Co.*, 739 F.2d 1293, 5 EBC 1625 (8th Cir. 1984) (employer who promised to contribute one-half of pretax profits to profit-sharing plan breached contract when it only contributed one-third over period of years; employer also liable for fraud when it continued to tell participants that it was contributing one-half; plan fiduciaries who knew the employer was not making the promised contributions and who took no steps to secure them liable for breach of fiduciary duty); *Chambers v. Kaleidoscope, Inc. Profit Sharing Plan*, 650 F.Supp. 359, 7 EBC 2628, at 2634 (N.D. Ga. 1986) (fiduciaries failed to protect profit-sharing plan's assets or to ensure that the plan received the money required to be contributed).

[61] See, e.g., *Freund v. Marshall & Ilsley Bank*, 485 F.Supp. 629, 1 EBC 1898 (W.D. Wis. 1979). A related problem under ESOPs is overappraisal of the value of employer stock purchased by plan fiduciaries from a business' owners. See *Donovan v. Cunningham*, 716 F.2d 1455, 4 EBC 2329 (5th Cir. 1983), *cert. denied*, 467 U.S. 1251 (1984). Undervaluation of stock in an individual account at the time of the individual's retirement or separation from service can also be in breach of fiduciary duty. See *Foltz v. U.S. News & World Report*, 613 F.Supp. 634, 6 EBC 1761 (D.D.C. 1985).

[62] See Rev. Rul. 76-250, 26 C.F.R. 1.411(b)-1(f), and 29 C.F.R. 2530.200b-1(b).

contribution allocation. Investment earnings must continue to be allocated to the participant's account until the account balance is distributed, but if the distribution of the account balance occurs before the date for allocation of the plan's earnings, an entire year's allocation of earnings could also be withheld.[63]

B. Defined Benefit Plans

In a defined benefit plan, benefits accrue based on "years of participation." A participant receives at least a partial year's credit for any year in which he or she has over 1,000 hours of service, or its equivalent, regardless of whether the participant is employed on a certain year-end date. The methods under which benefits may accrue for these years of participation can, however, be much more complicated than in a defined contribution plan. The problem is that benefits do not always necessarily "accrue" on a year-by-year basis under a defined benefit plan. For example, a plan that promises a benefit of 50 percent of an average of final pay at age 65 need not specify the portion of that benefit that is accrued at age 55 after 10 years of participation. Although an accrual rate might be implied, the nature of the plan does not compel the employer to provide one.

Congress, therefore, saw that without methods requiring benefits in defined benefit plans to accrue before retirement according to certain minimum standards, a plan would not necessarily have an amount that could be vested before retirement. In addition, Congress saw that if benefits were required to accrue, but allowed to accrue in any manner, defined benefit plans could be designed to backload accrued benefits to later years of service, thereby making preretirement vesting ineffective. As the House Ways and Means Committee stated:

> "[O]therwise a plan which wishes to evade the vesting requirements could provide for de minimis accruals until an employee's last years of employment, at which point very large accruals would be produced."[64]

The purpose of ERISA's benefit accrual requirements is thus to require that a defined benefit plan's normal retirement benefits accrue across a participant's years of participation in a fairly ratable manner that prevents excessive backloading and that enables preretirement vesting to be effective. However, as illustrated by Social Security integration, the benefit accrual methods do not necessarily ensure that there is a very substantial normal retirement benefit to accrue in the first place.[65] Moreover, none of the accrual rules prevent a plan from backloading benefits through the use of a final or highest average pay

---

[63] See sec. III.E below for a further discussion of limitations on these rules.

[64] H.R. 93-807, at 61, 2 ERISA Leg. Hist. 3181; and see 3 ERISA Leg. Hist. 4736 (statement of Sen. Williams) (accrual rules provided so employers cannot "subvert statutory intent to provide meaningful vested rights").

[65] The accrual rules do have an effect on the use of certain types of Social Security integration formulas. See sec. II.B.7 (on the effect of the accrual rules on hard or weighted offsets).

formula. Benefits under final or highest average pay formulas are effectively backloaded because increases in later years' salary raise benefits for all past years of participation under the plan. Under each of the ERISA accrual rules, the normal retirement benefit that must accrue is based on the participant's salary on the date in question. The participant is, therefore, not required to accrue a portion of a normal retirement benefit that anticipates later years' salary increases.

1. Normal Retirement Benefit

The ERISA accrual rules require a part of the plan's normal retirement benefit to accrue for each year of participation according to one of three benefit accrual methods set out in ERISA Sections 204(b)(1)(A)-(C) (Code Sections 411(b)(1)(A)-(C)). The normal retirement benefit is defined in ERISA Section 3(22) (Code Section 411(a)(9)) as the greater, in dollar amount, of the benefit payable at the plan's normal retirement age or at any earlier retirement age of the plan.[66] Since the dollar amount, rather than actuarial value, is considered, and since the early retirement benefit is defined to exclude any Social Security supplements that do not continue throughout the participant's retirement, the benefit at the plan's normal retirement age is almost invariably the normal retirement benefit that is required to accrue.

The regulations provide one example where the dollar amount of the benefit available at an early retirement age might be greater than at the normal retirement age. In this example, a plan provides a benefit of one percent per year multiplied by a participant's compensation average over the final five years before retirement. Early retirement benefits are available after age 60 with a four percent reduction in benefits for each year before age 65 that the retirement occurs. In such a plan, the dollar amount of the normal retirement age benefit would generally be greater. However, in the example, the participant suffers a sharp cut in pay from $50,000 per year to $33,000 per year at age 60. Because of this cut in pay and the use of a *final* average of pay, the participant's final average of compensation is dropping in each year after age 60 at a rate that outruns the four percent reduction factor for early retirement. Therefore, in this example, the early retirement benefit the participant has at age 62 is greater in dollar amount than the normal retirement age benefit at age 65, even with the four percent reduction for early retirement.[67]

---

[66] Under ERISA §3(24) (Code §411(a)(8)), a plan's normal retirement age is whenever the plan says it is, but *no later than* age 65 or the 10th anniversary of the participant's commencement of participation in the plan. The normal retirement age can thus be age 60, even if most participants retire later, or it can be age 65 or the later of the 10th anniversary of plan participation, even if most participants retire sooner.

[67] See 26 C.F.R. 1.411(a)-7(c)(6) (example (4)). See also *Keystone Automobile Club*, 85-2 ARB (CCH) ¶8468 (DiLauro, 1985).

Note the manner in which the compensation average is defined in the example above. It is the average of compensation in the 5 years immediately prior to retirement, in other words, a

The plan's normal retirement age benefit is still generally the benefit that is required to accrue. Knowing this does not, however, lead to a normal retirement benefit *amount*. For example, if a plan's normal retirement benefit is a flat 50 percent of a highest five-year average of pay, and a participant is age 40, an assumption about pay has to be made to generate a normal retirement benefit amount. If the normal retirement benefit is on a unit basis, e.g., two percent of final average pay for each year of participation, assumptions about both pay and years of participation have to be made before an amount is generated. These assumptions, in fact, vary slightly among the three benefit accrual methods in ERISA Section 204(b)(1), so that the amount of the normal retirement benefit can vary depending on which of the three benefit accrual methods a plan complies with.

Setting this aside for a moment, the three benefit accrual methods require that a portion of this normal retirement benefit becomes an accrued benefit based on the participant's years of participation in the plan. This accrued benefit is expressed in the form of an annual benefit commencing at the plan's normal retirement age; if the plan provides early retirement benefits, the annual early retirement benefit must be at least the actuarial equivalent of the normal retirement age accrued benefit.[68]

2. *Compensation in Determining the Normal Retirement Benefit*

As described in Chapter 3, the inclusion or omission of items, such as overtime pay or bonuses, from the definition of compensation used to determine a salary-based plan's benefits can be examined for whether the definition discriminates in favor of the prohibited group of employees. In certain cases, compensation definitions may simply be open to interpretation, for example, on whether sales commissions are included.

ERISA's benefit accrual rules also have an effect on a salary-based plan's definition of compensation. As described further below, two of the benefit accrual methods—the three percent method and the fractional rule—effectively rule out the use of a career average of compensation because the normal retirement benefit under both those methods must be determined based on an average of compensation over 10 years or less. A career average pay plan, therefore, can only comply with one benefit accrual method—the 133⅓ percent method.

Although the compensation base used in determining the normal retirement benefit can vary between benefit accrual methods, a common denominator is that the compensation used in determining the

---

final average. If the compensation average had been defined as the *highest* average of compensation, the participant's average would have stayed the same despite the pay cut, and the normal retirement age benefits would have remained greater in terms of dollar amount.

[68] ERISA §204(c)(3) (Code §411(c)(3)). But see sec. IV.B.3 (on indirect elements of the accrued benefit that may be more than the actuarial equivalent, but may still fall under the ERISA §204(g) (Code §411(d)(6)) protection against reduction by plan amendment).

normal retirement benefit under all three accrual methods can never be lower than the participant's compensation during the period before the *earlier* of the participant's separation from service or retirement.[69] ERISA also effectively prohibits a decrease in a participant's compensation in later years while still in service from ever decreasing accrued benefits under a salary-based formula below the amount that he or she would have had without the additional year, or years, of service.[70]

A rule against double proration of benefits under salary-based formulas prohibits a plan from multiplying a partial year of participation by a partial year of compensation.[71] When a participant is to be credited with a partial year of participation under a salary-based benefit formula, a special IRS regulation also requires the imputation of a full year's compensation for purposes of any final average of pay, or any highest average of pay over, for example, five of the last 10 or less years.[72]

Amendments to a plan's definition of compensation trigger ERISA's protections against decreases in the amount of accrued benefits from amendments of the plan.[73]

3. *Three Benefit Accrual Methods*

ERISA Section 204(b)(1) (Code Section 411(b)(1)) sets out three acceptable methods for the accrual of a portion of a plan's normal retirement benefit across years of plan participation. These are: (1) the three percent method, (2) the 133⅓ percent method, and (3) the fractional rule. A plan must comply with at least one of these methods. A

---

[69] See ERISA §§204(b)(1)(A)-(C). In *Chambless v. Masters, Mates & Pilots Pension Plan,* 772 F.2d 1032, 6 EBC 2209 (2d Cir. 1985), *cert. denied,* 475 U.S. 1012 (1986), the Second Circuit held that a plan amendment forfeiting early retirement benefits was arbitrary and capricious largely because of the interaction of the forfeiture with a definition of compensation that used the participant's highest 5 consecutive year average of salary in the 10 years before retirement (instead of in the 10 years before the earlier of retirement or a separation from service). Because the forfeiture of early retirement rights postponed retirement until age 65, a participant's accrued benefits under this formula could actually decrease in dollar amount down to a minimum benefit if no compensation or lower compensation was earned during this 10-year period. The compensation used for this purpose included compensation from employment with employers who were not parties to the plan. While finding the forfeiture of early retirement benefits arbitrary largely because of this interaction, the Second Circuit apparently overlooked the ERISA accrued benefit violation from a definition of compensation that looked beyond compensation up to the date of the participant's separation from service.

The *Chambless* plan's definition could also cause accrued benefits to decrease below the dollar amount available at early retirement in violation of the ERISA definition of the normal retirement benefit as the "greater of" the dollar amount available at normal retirement or at early retirement age. See 26 C.F.R. 1.411(a)-7(b)(6) (example (4)).

[70] See ERISA §204(b)(1)(G) (Code §411(b)(1)(G)), and 26 C.F.R. 1.411(b)-1(d)(3) and 1.411(a)-7(b)(6) (example (4)).

However, in *Edwards v. Wilkes-Barre Publishing Co. Pension Trust,* 757 F.2d 52, 6 EBC 1395 (3d Cir. 1985), *cert. denied,* 474 U.S. 843 (1985), the Third Circuit found that it was not arbitrary and capricious for employer-appointed trustees to credit permanently replaced strikers with completely uncompensated years of participation for their time on strike, with the result that their accrued benefits under a final 5-year average pay formula decreased for each year of the strike. The court did not discuss ERISA §204(b)(1)(G).

[71] See 29 C.F.R. 2530.204-2(d), and sec. III.D.1.

[72] See 26 C.F.R. 1.411(a)-7(c)(5), and sec. III.D.2.

[73] See secs. IV.B.1 and 2.

plan's terms, however, need not parallel the terms in which the methods are set out in ERISA as long as the rates of benefit accruals under the plan satisfy one of the three methods. As the IRS states:

> "Plans that meet the accrual rules are divided into two categories—plans that parallel the language of the statute and plans that otherwise satisfy the requirements though they do not contain specific statutory language."[74]

Learning the details of the benefit accrual methods may often seem unnecessary because many plans with unit benefit formulas provide that benefits accrue at the same even rate, e.g., one percent of final pay for each year of participation, or $15 per month for each year, as is used to determine the plan's normal retirement benefit. These are the type of plans the IRS is referring to that otherwise satisfy the requirements though they often do not contain specific statutory language. Both of these accrual rates comply with the 133⅓ percent method and also the fractional rule.

The need to understand the benefit accrual rules becomes more obvious when a plan provides a *flat* percentage normal retirement age benefit, such as 40 percent of an average of final pay above a covered compensation level and 20 percent on final pay below that level, and then uses the fractional rule to accrue those benefits before retirement. One only has to work through the differences the fractional rule produces in this instance according to a participant's age on beginning participation to see the importance of knowing how the accrual rules operate. Understanding the accrual rules is also essential when:

(1) A plan provides a normal retirement benefit on a unit basis, such as one percent of salary per year of participation, but uses a Social Security offset that is on a flat percentage basis, such as 50 percent of the participant's primary Social Security benefit amount, without prorating the offset according to years of participation;

(2) A plan provides a normal retirement age benefit with a Social Security offset, both parts of which are on a unit basis, such as one percent of salary less 1.5 percent of the primary Social Security benefit, but with the offset capped after a lesser number of years, e.g., after 25 years, than applies to the salary component;

(3) A plan provides a normal retirement age benefit and accruals based on different rates for different years of participation, e.g., one percent of salary for the first 10 years of participation and 1⅓ percent of salary for each year of participation thereafter (or on a dollar basis, $15 per month for the first 10 years of participation, and $20 per month for each year of participation thereafter); or

---

[74] IRS Doc. 6390 (5-82), reprinted in 456 BNA Pens. Rep. Spec. Supp. (Aug. 8, 1983), at S-35.

(4) A plan's normal retirement benefit is amended to increase or decrease benefits.

a. Three percent method. The three percent method is described in ERISA Section 204(b)(1)(A). With the fractional rule, it is distinctive in terms of the range of benefit formulas that can comply with it. Under the three percent method, a participant must accrue benefits at a rate of at least three percent of the plan's normal retirement benefit for each year of participation under the plan, up to 33⅓ years. The normal retirement benefit under the three percent method is determined *as if* a participant entered the plan at the earliest possible entry age—age 21 after the 1984 Retirement Equity Act amendments—whether or not the participant actually entered the plan at that age, and served continuously until the earlier of age 65 or the normal retirement age specified in the plan. If the plan's normal retirement benefit is based on a percentage of salary, the salary used in the determination of the three percent method normal retirement benefit must be the average salary that the participant has earned over a period of consecutive years of service, not in excess of 10 years, when his or her compensation is highest. A participant's accrued benefit must equal or exceed three percent of this normal retirement benefit multiplied by the participant's actual years of participation (not in excess of 33⅓).

To illustrate, if a plan offers a normal retirement age benefit of 1.5 percent of the average of compensation over the participant's highest five consecutive years, with a limit of 30 years on the years of participation credited under the benefit formula, a participant with 10 years of participation and a *current* highest consecutive five-year compensation average of $20,000 is required to have an accrued benefit of at least $2,700 per year for the plan to comply with the three percent method. The first step is to determine the normal retirement benefit: $20,000 × 1.5% × 30 years of potential participation = $9,000 normal retirement benefit. The next step is to determine the accrued benefit: $9,000 × 3% × 10 years of participation = $2,700 in accrued benefits.

Under the three percent method, if a plan is amended to increase the normal retirement benefit, the participant's accrued benefit must be increased to reflect three percent of the new normal retirement benefit times the current year and all of the participant's previous years of participation.[75]

Certain features are characteristic of plans that comply with the three percent method. The first is that the three percent method is incompatible with any unit benefit formula that does not by its terms

---

[75] 26 C.F.R. 1.411(b)-1(b)(1)(iii) (example (6)). Note that if a plan does not contain a cap on credited years of participation of 33⅓ or less years, the lowering of the minimum participation age for plans under the Retirement Equity Act amendments from age 25 to age 21 could effect an increase in the 3% method normal retirement benefit subject to this rule since the 3% method normal retirement benefit is determined by the earliest age when *any* employee can enter the plan, and not the age when a participant actually entered the plan.

limit the years of credited service under the plan's benefit formula to 33⅓ years or less. This is because the method's normal retirement benefit is determined by the years of participation the participant would have *if* he or she began participation at the earliest possible entry age under the plan and served continuously until the normal retirement age, which is usually a period of at least 40 years. This normal retirement benefit is then required to fully accrue over 33⅓ years of participation. Unless there is a commensurate cap on the years that can be credited under the plan's normal retirement benefit formula, the three percent method will accrue benefits at a higher rate than the plan's stated unit rate.

As an example, suppose a plan has an entry age of 25, a normal retirement age of 65, and a normal retirement benefit of one percent of a final average of salary for *all* years of participation. The three percent method normal retirement benefit is then 40 percent of the final average of salary. The three percent method would require this normal retirement benefit to accrue in full over a period of 33⅓ years of participation, which would work out to a higher unit rate of 1.2 percent of final average salary.[76]

The three percent method is also inconsistent with a benefit formula based on a career average of salary, e.g., a benefit formula of one percent of each year's salary for each year of participation. This is because the three percent method requires the normal retirement benefit to be determined based on the participant's salary over a period "not in excess of 10" years.[77] Compliance with the three percent method would effectively change a career average pay formula to a 10-year highest average formula.

A third feature of the three percent method is that it does not permit a plan to exclude years of participation after normal retirement age for benefit accruals unless the participant already has 33⅓ years of participation and thus has accrued the plan's full normal retirement benefit.[78] Under the other accrual methods (as in effect until 1988), employees are permitted to be excluded from participation after they reach the plan's normal retirement age, even if they continue to work for the employer.[79]

Finally, Revenue Ruling 75-480 points out that if a plan seeks to comply with the three percent method, it cannot be fully integrated with Social Security and still satisfy the separation from service and

---

[76] The inconsistency is greater if the plan does not have a minimum age requirement for participation, as is the case under many collectively bargained plans. For purposes of the 3% method, the earliest possible entry age is then assumed to be 0. See 26 C.F.R. 1.411(b)-1(b)(1)(iii) (example (3)). With a normal retirement age of 65, the 3% method normal retirement benefit for a plan providing $15 per month for each year of participation is then $11,700 per year ($15 per month x 12 months x 65 potential years of participation). Under the 3% method, this normal retirement benefit is required to accrue at a rate of at least $351 per year of participation (3% x $11,700), which works out to an accrual rate of $29.95 per month for each year of participation, almost twice the plan's stated unit benefit rate.

[77] ERISA §204(b)(1)(A) (Code §411(b)(1)(A)).

[78] 26 C.F.R. 1.411(b)-1(b)(1)(i).

[79] See sec. III.C.1 (on crediting years of participation after the plan's normal retirement age).

early retirement adjustments required under Revenue Ruling 71-446. This is because the three percent method accrues the plan's full normal retirement benefit over a period of not more than 33⅓ years of participation. For example, if a plan provides for participation beginning at age 21 and is fully integrated, the fully integrated benefit would accrue by age 54⅓. But under Revenue Ruling 71-446, the maximum integration limits for an offset formula (or a flat percentage excess formula) must be prorated for a separation from service before age 65, and the limits for all integrated plans must be adjusted down if a participant can begin receiving benefits before age 65. Because of these adjustments, a plan accruing a fully integrated normal retirement benefit by age 54⅓ cannot comply with Revenue Ruling 71-446.

b. 133⅓ percent method. The 133⅓ percent method assumes that a plan states an annual unit rate, or rates, of benefit accruals, e.g., one percent of final or career average pay per year of participation, or $15 per month per year. It essentially requires that there either be just one rate of benefit accruals under the plan or, if there is more than one rate, that the rate in any later year be not more than 133⅓ percent of the accrual rate in any earlier year. A plan that uses the full permissible variation in accrual rates that the name of the method implies might, for example, provide that benefit accruals for the first 10 years of participation are .9 percent of final salary, and that benefit accruals thereafter are 1.2 percent of final salary, or under a flat dollar formula, $13.50 per month for the first 10 years of participation, with $18 per month thereafter. The normal retirement benefit under the 133⅓ percent method is the sum of the accrued benefits under the annual rate, or rates, for years of actual participation. Unlike the three percent method and the fractional rule, the 133⅓ percent rule is amenable to either a career average pay formula or a final or highest average salary formula.[80] The 133⅓ percent method also does not require a cap of less than 33⅓ years of participation as the three percent method does.

When a plan complying with the 133⅓ percent method is amended to change its accrual rate, e.g., from $15 per month to $20 per month for each year of participation, the new rate of benefit accruals is presumed in effect for all prior years for testing whether the plan, as amended, is in compliance with the 133⅓ percent method.[81] However, no actual adjustment in the benefits accrued in prior years under the old rate is required (although many plans provide for such adjustments).

c. Fractional rule. Under the fractional rule, the normal retirement benefit is computed using the years of participation the participant would have from his or her actual date of entry under the plan until

---

[80] To test either a final average pay or career average pay formula's compliance with the 133⅓% method, compensation in earlier years is assumed equal to compensation in the current year. Thus, if a plan provides 1% of each year's salary, and a participant's salary doubles from $15,000 to $30,000, the accrual rate for both the current year and the prior years is tested based on the $30,000 salary to determine compliance with the 133⅓% method.

[81] ERISA §204(b)(1)(B)(i) (Code §411(b)(1)(B)(i)) and 26 C.F.R 1.411(b)-1(b)(2)(ii)(A).

normal retirement age, assuming continuous service, and assuming the same rate of compensation for future years as earned currently. A participant's accrued benefit is determined by multiplying this normal retirement benefit by the fraction that the participant's years of participation in the plan bears to the total number of years of participation the participant would have from the date of his or her actual entry into the plan until the plan's normal retirement age. The fractional rule, like the three percent method, does not accommodate a career average pay formula because the compensation used in computing the normal retirement benefit may look back over no more than the 10 years of service immediately preceding a separation from service.

The fractional rule is satisfied if benefits accrue at the same unit rate as under a plan's normal retirement benefit formula, e.g., one percent of a final average of pay, or $15 per month per year of service—as is the 133⅓ percent method. However, the fractional rule is also satisfied in one other important instance. A plan can offer a flat percentage or dollar normal retirement benefit, such as 50 percent of final pay, or $600 per month, and then accrue benefits before retirement under the fractional rule. In this form, the accrued benefit rate under the fractional rule works out to be *higher* for workers who start under the plan at older ages. This is because the denominator of their fraction is based on a smaller number of years from their actual entry until their normal retirement age than applies to workers who enter the plan at younger ages, with the normal retirement benefit remaining the same in both cases.

For example, if a plan offers a flat percentage benefit at age 65 of 50 percent of a final average of pay, and two workers, one age 45 and the other age 25, commence participation in the same year and earn the same salary, after 10 years of participation, the age 45 worker, then age 55, will have accrued one-half of his or her normal retirement benefit, based on the fraction produced by dividing years of participation (10) by years of potential participation from entry to normal retirement age (20). In contrast, the age 25 worker, then age 35, will have accrued only one-fourth of his or her normal retirement benefit, based on the fraction produced by dividing years of participation (10) by years of potential participation from entry to normal retirement age (40).[82] The accrual rate produced in this situation for each year of participation is a constant rate for each individual, e.g., the worker who enters the plan at age 45 accrues benefits at a constant rate of 5.0 percent (1⁄20) of the normal retirement benefit for each year of participation, and the worker who enters the plan at age 25 accrues benefits at a constant rate of 2.5 percent (1⁄40) in each year. But, as shown, the accrual rates vary substantially *between* participants depending on their age at entry.

---

[82] If final average pay for both workers is projected to be $20,000, the worker now age 55 has accrued a retirement benefit of $5,000 based on 10 years of participation, while the worker now age 35 has accrued a retirement benefit of $2,500 based on 10 years of participation.

The fractional rule is designed so a participant will accrue the normal retirement benefit ratably over a continuous period of participation from actual entry under the plan to normal retirement age. When a participant has a break in service, or is otherwise not credited with a full year of participation, an adjustment in the fraction must be made to take account of the break in service, or missing partial year of participation. Revenue Ruling 81-11 sets out two alternatives for this adjustment. The simplest is to subtract the year, or missing part of the year, of participation from the years of participation in the denominator of the fraction. Thus, if an employee enters a plan with a normal retirement age of 65 at age 35, his or her initial fraction has a denominator based on 30 potential years of participation. However, if the participant separates from service after 10 years of continuous service in the plan, and returns to service after another five years, the denominator on return is 30 - 5 = 25, with the numerator based on the 10 years already rendered, plus each additional year of participation.

Under Revenue Ruling 81-11, a plan alternatively can hedge closer to the lower limit of compliance with the fractional rule by protecting accrued benefits in the first period of continuous participation and then composing a new fraction for additional years of participation, based on years of participation in the second continuous period divided by the remaining years until normal retirement age, with this new fraction being multiplied by the number of years from the separation from service until retirement divided by the number of years from initial entry into the plan until retirement. According to Revenue Ruling 81-11, this alternative results in a lower accrual rate than the first.[83] Whichever of the two alternatives is used, an adjustment clearly must be made under the fractional rule to reflect the decrease in potential years of participation from a break in service or credit for only a partial year of participation.

When a plan amendment increases the fractional rule normal retirement benefit, the fractional rule, like the three percent method, effectively requires accrued benefits for all past years of participation in the plan to be recomputed in terms of the new normal retirement benefit. The ERISA Conference Report explains:

> "Assume an individual begins participation at age 25 in a plan which provides 1 percent of high-three-years pay during his first 10 years of service. In the 11th year the plan amends to provide 2 percent of pay for all future years of service. The employee separates from service at the end of the 11th year (and is 100 percent vested). His accrued benefit

---

[83] For example, if the normal retirement benefit at age 65 is determined on the basis of 2% of final pay for each year of credited service, a participant who enters the plan at age 35 has a normal retirement benefit of 60% of final pay (30 × 2%). If the participant separated from service after 10 years and then returned after another 5 years, either of the two alternatives described above could be used to determine accrued benefits for each year of participation thereafter. Under the first method, the total accrued benefits after one additional year of participation are ((11 years of participation ÷ 25 potential years of participation) × the normal retirement benefit of 60% of final pay =) 26.4% of final pay. Under the second method, the accrued benefits are ((10 years ÷ 30 years) + ((1 year ÷ 15 years) × (20 ÷ 30)) × 60% of final pay =) 22.66% of final pay.

would equal 19.25 percent of average high-three-years pay (10 (years of participation) times 1 percent per year + 30 (years of projected participation) times 2 percent per year, [multiplied by] 11⁄40ths (11 years of participation over 40 total years between age 25 and age 65))."[84]

4. ERISA's Exclusion of Early Retirement and Ancillary Benefits From the Accrual Requirements

"In order not to impose an undue cost burden on plans," Congress determined that certain types of benefits would not be required to accrue on a year-by-year basis.[85] The ERISA Conference Report provides perhaps the most informal description of the benefits that are not required to accrue on a year-by-year basis:

> "[T]he term 'accrued benefit' refers to pension or retirement benefits. The term does not apply to ancillary benefits such as payment of medical expenses (or insurance premiums for such expenses), or disability benefits which do not exceed the normal retirement benefit payable at age 65 to an employee with comparable service under the plan, or to life insurance benefits payable as a lump sum.
>
> "Also, the accrued benefit does not include the value of the right to receive early retirement benefits, or the value of social security supplements or other benefits under the plan which are not continued for any employee after he has attained normal retirement age."[86]

The IRS's regulations provide a still more specific list of benefits that are not included in the "accrued benefit." Under the regulations, the accrued benefit expressly does not include Social Security supplements, disability benefits, health benefits (such as payment through a pension plan of Medicare Part B premiums for retirees), life insurance benefits payable as a lump sum, "incidental" death benefits, or any "subsidized" value (i.e., excess actuarial value over benefits in a single-life form) provided under a joint and survivor's annuity form of payment of benefits.[87] The regulations also expressly provide that unless the dollar amount of an early retirement benefit is greater than the dollar amount of the normal retirement age benefit, exclusive of any Social Security supplement, any greater actuarial value under the provision for early retirement benefits is not taken into account in determining the participant's accrued benefit.[88]

Although unreduced, or only slightly reduced, early retirement benefits are not required to accrue, or to vest, according to the statutory methods and schedules, they are considered a part of the accrued

---

[84] Conf. Rep., at 275 n.3, 3 ERISA Leg. Hist. 4542 n.3.

[85] H.R. 93-807, at 60-61, 2 ERISA Leg. Hist. 3180-81.

[86] Conf. Rep., at 273, 3 ERISA Leg. Hist. 4540. See also H.R. Rep. 93-807, at 60, 2 ERISA Leg. Hist. 3180.

[87] 26 C.F.R. 1.411(a)-7(a)(1)(ii) (with certain exceptions, which seem to be relevant only in unusual cases).

[88] 26 C.F.R. 1.411(a)-7(a)(1)(ii).

benefit under the ERISA Section 204(g) (Code Section 411(d)(6)) protection against reduction of accrued benefits by plan amendment. Essentially, Section 204(g) requires a limited degree of grandfathering of an old reduction factor, or lack thereof, if a plan amendment is adopted that increases the reduction factor or eliminates an unreduced early retirement benefit option.[89]

5. Pre-ERISA Accrual Rules

For years of participation in a plan before the first plan year beginning after December 31, 1975,[90] ERISA permits the accrued benefit of a participant to be determined under the plan as in effect before that time, provided that the resulting accrued benefit for those years of participation is not less the one-half of the amount that would have accrued had any one of the Section 204(b)(1) accrual methods applied to the years of participation.[91] To come under this rule, a plan must specifically carryover its pre-ERISA accrual method.

As discussed below at sec. III.C.2, this not less than one-half test applies to years of participation determined without regard to any cancellations of years of participation under pre-ERISA break-in-service rules that were stricter than the ERISA rule of parity. When a plan's rate of benefit accruals for years of participation before ERISA is less than if the ERISA accrual rules applied, the plan must also provide that the difference can be accrued in the years after the effective date.[92] Exactly how this is done seems to be almost a science, with IRS regulations providing specific guidance for plans complying with the three percent method or the fractional rule.[93]

6. Accrued Benefits Under Individual Insurance Contract Plans

A special accrued benefit rule can apply for years of participation before or after ERISA under plans in which benefits are provided exclusively through individual insurance contracts that are guaranteed by an insurer and funded by level dollar annual premiums. Typically, these are plans of very small employers. Under ERISA Section 204(b)(1)(F) (Code Section 411(b)(1)(F)), a participant's accrued benefit under such a plan need not be determined under the methods

---

[89] See sec. IV.B.3 below.

[90] If the plan was not in existence on Jan. 1, 1974, "before the first plan year after Sept. 2, 1974," should be substituted in the text.

[91] ERISA §204(b)(1)(D) (Code §411(b)(1)(D)), and see 26 C.F.R. 1.411(b)-1(c). Before ERISA, some plans did not accrue benefits at all before retirement, but just offered flat benefits on retirement. For these plans, an accrual rate for pre-ERISA years of participation is not implied; instead accrued benefits can be simply one-half of the amount determined under either §§204(b)(1)(A), (B) or (C). *Janowski v. Teamsters Local No. 710 Pension Fund*, 673 F.2d 931, 3 EBC 2050 (7th Cir. 1982), *cert. denied*, 459 U.S. 858 (1982), *vacated and remanded on standing and attorney's fees*, 463 U.S. 1222 (1983).

[92] 26 C.F.R. 1.411(b)-1(c)(2)(v). And see IRS Doc. 6390 "Minimum Vesting Standards: Defined Benefit Plans" (5-82).

[93] 26 C.F.R. 1.411(b)-1(b)(1)(ii)(C) and 1.411(b)-1(b)(3)(ii)(D).

described above, but rather is required only to be not less than the cash surrender value of the individual insurance contracts issued on behalf of the employees, determined as if all premiums due at the applicable date have been paid and no policy loans are outstanding.[94]

7. Accrual Rules and Hard or Weighted Offsets of Social Security

Special problems in compliance with the ERISA accrual rules can arise when a plan uses a "hard" or "weighted" offset of Social Security under its benefit formula. A hard offset can be illustrated by a benefit formula that offers 1½ percent of salary (on either a career or final average salary basis) for each year of participation, less 50 percent of the participant's primary Social Security benefit regardless of years of participation. The effect of such a formula can be to wipe out benefits for low, average, and even relatively high-paid workers who have "shorter" periods of service under the plan, e.g., 10 to 15 years.[95] Basically, an offset such as this produces extreme backloading in the plan's benefits to later years of service. A weighted offset can be illustrated by a formula that offers 1½ percent of salary for each year of participation up to 40, less two percent of the participant's primary Social Security benefit for each year of participation *up to* 25 years. The effect of such an offset is not as drastic as a hard offset, but the result is again to load the offset onto the front end of the participant's service, and thus to backload the plan's benefits to later years of service. In contrast, a soft offset of Social Security prorates the offset over the same period as applies to the salary component of the formula, e.g., 1½ percent of salary less 1¼ percent of the primary Social Security benefit, both times years of participation in the plan. The total offset under such a formula can be just as high as under a hard or weighted offset after 40 years of participation, but the offset is spread ratably over all potential years of participation in the plan.

Under the IRS's Social Security integration rules, it is permissible for a plan to use a hard or a weighted offset, so long as the adjustments described in Chapter 3 are made when a participant separates from service before retirement with a vested benefit.[96] The ERISA accrual rules, however, have generally made hard and weighted offsets unlawful. Although this is not widely recognized, it is thoroughly established in Revenue Ruling 78-252. The ERISA accrual rules limit such offsets because a participant in a plan with a hard offset may actually accrue *no* benefits for a large number of years before the effect of the offset diminishes sufficiently for benefits to actually accrue under the terms of the plan. Under a weighted offset, the backloading may be less extreme, but when the period over which the offset increases expires,

[94] See 26 C.F.R. 1.411(b)-1(d)(2).

[95] See ch. 3, sec. VIII.C (on Social Security integration and offsets).

[96] See Rev. Rul. 71-446, secs. 7 and 11.

e.g., after 25 years, the rate of benefit accruals jumps substantially, thus backloading benefits under the plan.

Revenue Ruling 78-252 addressed whether a plan with a minimum participation age of 25, a normal retirement age of 65, and a normal retirement benefit formula of 2.4 percent of a participant's five highest consecutive years of compensation for all years of participation, less 2 percent of the participant's primary Social Security benefit for each of the first 25 years of participation, satisfied any of the ERISA benefit accrual methods. To test compliance with the three percent method, the Ruling first determined that the three percent method "normal retirement benefit" under this benefit formula is 96 percent of the final average of salary (2.4 percent × 40 potential years of participation) less 50 percent of the primary Social Security benefit (2 percent × 25 years). To comply with the three percent method, the Ruling stated, three percent of this normal retirement benefit, or 2.88 percent of the final average of salary less 1.5 percent of the primary Social Security benefit, would have to accrue for each year of participation, up to 33⅓. Thus, to comply with the three percent method, the offset would have to be prorated over the same period as used in the salary component of the formula. Since the plan did not do this, it failed the three percent method.

To test compliance with the 133⅓ percent method, Revenue Ruling 78-252 simply observed that since a participant under the plan's formula would after 25 years accrue benefits at a much higher rate than 133⅓ percent of the rate in prior years, the 133⅓ percent method was not satisfied. The Ruling noted in particular that a "low paid" participant would, in fact, accrue "virtually no benefit" until after the first 25 years of participation.

To test compliance with the fractional rule, Revenue Ruling 78-252 first determined that the fractional rule "normal retirement benefit" for a participant who actually entered the plan at age 25 would be 96 percent of the final average of salary less 50 percent of the primary Social Security benefit. For benefit accruals to comply with the fractional rule, 1⁄40 of this normal retirement benefit, or 2.4 percent of the final average of salary less 1.25 percent of the primary Social Security benefit, would have to accrue for each year of participation. Because the offset component of the plan's formula was higher than this in the first 25 years of participation, the formula did not comply with the fractional rule. The formula thus failed under all three of the ERISA benefit accrual methods.

While Revenue Ruling 78-252 addressed weighted offsets, it applies with equal force to hard offsets, which constitute a still more extreme form of backloading. For example, assume a plan with a minimum participation age of age 25, a normal retirement age of age 65, and a normal retirement benefit formula of 2.4 percent of a final average of salary for each year of participation, less 50 percent of the primary Social Security benefit regardless of years of participation (instead of two percent for each of the first 25 years of participation as in Revenue Ruling 78-252). Under the three percent method, the normal retirement benefit would again be 96 percent of the final average of salary less 50 percent of the primary Social Security benefit. Three percent of this normal retirement benefit, or 2.88 percent of the final average of salary less 1.5 percent of the primary Social Security benefit, would have to accrue for each year of participation, up to 33⅓. Thus, as in Revenue Ruling 78-252, the hard offset formula would not comply with the three percent accrual method.

Under the 133⅓ percent method, the same reasoning as in Revenue Ruling 78-252 also applies. In this case, not only would low-paid workers accrue no benefit for early years of participation under the formula, but even average or higher paid workers would accrue virtually no benefit for a large number of years. The variation in accruals between later and earlier years would therefore be in excess of 133⅓ percent and the formula could not comply with the 133⅓ percent method.[97]

Under the fractional rule, the normal retirement benefit for a participant who enters the plan at age 25 would, as in Revenue Ruling 78-252, be 96 percent of the final average of salary less 50 percent of the primary Social Security amount. For the plan to satisfy the rule, 1⁄40 of this amount, or 2.4 percent of the final average less 1.25 percent of the primary Social Security benefit, has to accrue for each year of participation. The hard offset formula would thus not comply with the fractional rule either.[98]

Hard and weighted offsets are still so common in plans that it may be difficult to believe that the ERISA accrual rules have generally made them unlawful. For example, the Bureau of Labor Statistics' 1984 survey of plans of medium and large firms indicates that one out of five participants in plans with an offset are in plans with "hard" offsets.[99] Similarly, the Wyatt Company's 1982 survey of the plans of

---

[97] Technically, under the 133⅓% method, the normal retirement benefit must equal the sum of the plan's benefit accruals at the plan's annual rate(s), with the rate of accrual in any later year not exceeding 133⅓% of the rate in any earlier year. Under the formula given above, a participant starting at age 25 would have at age 65 a normal retirement benefit of 96% of the final average of salary less 50% of the primary Social Security benefit. For the sum of the participant's annual rates of accruals to equal this normal retirement benefit and yet never exceed 133⅓% of the rate in any earlier year, the average rate of accrual would have to be 1⁄40 of the normal retirement benefit, or 2.4% of the final average less 1.25% of the primary Social Security benefit. Since the 133⅓% method permits some variation in rates of accruals, this average rate could be varied slightly between earlier and later years, but at no where near the variation appearing under a hard offset formula.

[98] The fractional rule works somewhat differently if the participant enters a plan at a later age, for example, age 45. Using the same example, the fractional rule normal retirement benefit would be only 48% of the final average less 50% of the Social Security amount. The fractional rate of accruals for the participant age 45 at entry would be 1⁄20, or 2.4% of the final average less 2.5% of the Social Security amount. For an age 55 entrant, the fractional rule normal retirement benefit would be 24% of the final average of salary less 50% of the Social Security amount. The rate of accruals in this case would be 1⁄10, or 2.4% of the final average less 5% of the Social Security amount. Thus, the fractional rule permits a higher percentage offset from each year of accrual, which, although not quite as high as under a hard offset, may as a practical matter be high enough to wipe out any benefit for a late entrant—unless the employee is very highly compensated.

[99] BLS, Employee Benefits in Medium and Large Firms, 1984, at 47.

50 large industrial companies shows a number of major corporate plans with weighted offsets.[100] However, Revenue Ruling 78-252 was issued in 1978, and by 1979 Dan McGill was also warning, in *Fundamentals of Private Pensions*, that both hard and weighted offsets of Social Security violate the accrual rules:

> "For determining [accrued] benefits, the period for prorating the offset cannot be less than the years of service that would have been used to calculate the participant's accrued benefit at normal retirement age; otherwise 'backloading' may violate the accrued benefit rates."[101]

8. *Top-Heavy Plan Rules on Benefit Accruals*

TEFRA requires that minimum nonintegrated benefits be provided under defined benefit plans that are top-heavy. These minimum benefits must not only be provided under the plan's normal retirement benefit formula, but they must accrue in each year the plan is top-heavy at the rate described in Code Section 416(c)(1), which is generally two percent of the participant's highest five-year compensation average for each year of service up to 10. The IRS's regulations specifically address whether a plan might satisfy the minimum nonintegrated benefit requirement by providing the minimum benefit in its normal retirement benefit formula, and then accruing those benefits under the fractional rule. If a plan could do this, the effect in certain cases would be to reduce a minimum benefit—based on 10 years of service—of 20 percent of the highest five-year average of compensation to an "accrued benefit" of five percent of the same highest five-year average.[102] Section 416(c)(1) and the regulations, however, require that the accrued benefit of each non-key employee must be no less than the minimum top-heavy benefit. Therefore, use of the fractional rule to accrue the minimum benefit violates Code Section 416(c)(1). Similarly, a plan cannot provide that the two percent per year of service minimum benefit is a part of the normal retirement benefit, and then accrue the benefit under the three percent method. Finally, even the slight variation permitted under the 133⅓ percent method would not satisfy Code Section 416(c)(1).

9. *Prohibited Discrimination Under the Accrual Rules*

Prohibited discrimination under Code Section 401(a)(4) can occur from the use of certain of the ERISA minimum standard benefit accrual rules in circumstances that will inevitably produce disproportionate accrued benefits for prohibited group employees compared to the

---

[100] Wyatt Company, "A Survey of Retirement, Thrift and Profit Sharing Plans Covering Salaried Employees of 50 Large U.S. Industrial Companies as of January 1, 1982."

[101] D. McGill, *Fundamentals of Private Pensions* (Richard D. Irwin 5th ed.), at 181. See p. 182 in the 1979 4th edition.

[102] 26 C.F.R. 1.416-1, Q&A M-5.

accrued benefits of rank and file employees.[103] For example, assume a newly established plan covers 20 employees, one of whom is the age 55 owner of the company sponsoring the plan, and the other 19 of whom are rank and file employees no older than age 35. If the plan offers a flat 50 percent of final average pay benefit at age 65 and accrues the benefit under the fractional rule, after 10 years (which could be coincident with the termination of the plan if it marks the date of the owner's retirement and the closing or sale of the business), the owner will have accrued the full 50 percent of final pay benefit. But while they have an equal number of years of participation under the plan, the most any rank and file employee will have accrued will be 10/30 times 50 percent, or 16.6 percent, of their final average pay. In this example, the older age of the owner compared to the ages of the rank and file employees has been used in conjunction with the fractional rule to produce a rate of benefit accruals of five percent of final pay for each year of participation for the owner, compared to, at most, 1.66 percent of final pay for each year of participation for the younger rank and file employees.[104]

10. Adequate Disclosure and Benefit Accruals

Generally, when a plan's normal retirement age benefit formula is on a unit basis, e.g., one percent of an average of salary for each year of credited service, or $15 per month per year of credited service, the same unit basis serves as the basis for benefit accruals—thus conforming the plan with the 133⅓ percent method and, unless the plan uses a career average of salary, also with the fractional rule. A plan can, however, legally provide that its normal retirement benefit is determined on one unit basis, and then use an accrual method that more closely parallels the limits of the Section 204(b)(1) methods to actually accrue benefits under the plan. When a plan does this, adequate disclosure can be an issue.

An example of when one unit basis may appear in a plan's normal retirement benefit formula, with quite different results under an accrual method appearing in another part of the plan, arises when a plan provides past service benefits. Assume a participant has five years of past service and is age 40 when a plan is established and that the plan credits both past service years and future years of participation up to a normal retirement age of 65 at a rate of two percent of highest average

---

[103] See 26 C.F.R. 1.401-1(b)(3) (plan must not discriminate by "any device whatever") and Prop. Regs. 1.411(d)-1(e) (defined benefit plan satisfying one of ERISA's benefit accrual methods is subject to tests for nondiscrimination in benefit accruals in operation).

[104] Another example is a plan that accrues benefits under the 3% method at a rate "not less" than that required, but then in the last year before the plan's normal retirement age accrues the remaining portion of the plan's normal retirement benefit in full, as permitted under a very literal reading of ERISA §204(b)(1)(A). Such a plan might discriminate in operation if the only participant to ever benefit from the provision is a prohibited group employee.

salary. The participant works 10 more years, until age 50, and separates from service. Under ERISA Section 204, such a plan might provide that the normal retirement benefit accrues based only on years of actual participation in the plan, and will, moreover, accrue under the fractional rule. Thus, whereas the participant might expect that his or her accrued benefit would be 30 percent of the highest average of salary (2 percent × 15 years), under separate terms for benefit accruals, the participant's accrued benefit could be based on the fraction produced by actual years of participation in the plan divided by potential years of participation in the plan (10⁄25) multiplied by the normal retirement benefit of 60 percent (2 percent × (5 past service years + 25 potential future years)). Multiplying this fraction by the normal retirement benefit results in an accrued benefit of 24 percent of highest salary, rather than the 30 percent the participant might reasonably have expected looking at the normal retirement benefit formula alone.

When unexpected results such as this are produced using a legal distinction between the normal retirement benefit formula and the plan's benefit accrual method, the adequacy of disclosure of the distinction to participants may be examined. A summary plan description (SPD) that has the "effect of misleading, misinforming or failing to inform" participants of "limitations" in benefits they might reasonably expect to receive based on the description of benefits in the SPD violates Section 102 of ERISA.[105] Thus, if a plan promises one benefit under its normal retirement benefit formula, but accrues a lesser benefit, the summary plan description must understandably disclose the difference between how benefits are determined under the plan's normal retirement benefit formula and how benefits under the plan actually accrue. If it does not, a court may provide "appropriate equitable relief . . . to redress [the Section 102] violation[]" under ERISA Section 502(a)(3).

III. What Years Count for Benefit Accruals

ERISA uses a "year of participation" as the basic unit for determining accrued benefits under a defined benefit plan. This usage can, however, be somewhat confusing. First, the term "year of participation" is seldom found in plans. Plans more frequently talk about "credited service," "continuous service," or "pension credits." As with benefit accrual methods that do not parallel the statutory language, the key in this area is *compliance* with the minimum standards. A plan can use whatever term it wishes, but it must be able to show that the term it uses includes all years of participation required to be credited under ERISA. Second, depending on the exact definition of the term in the

---

[105] 29 C.F.R. 2520.102-2(b). And see ch. 8, sec. I.A (on remedies for misleading statements or omissions in SPDs).

plan, the description of years in the SPD, past practice, and any other representations, additional years or shorter periods not required to be credited under ERISA may also be required to be included.

Defined contribution plans are not required to use years of participation as the unit for determining whether an annual contribution allocation is due a participant's account, but may instead use employment on a specific date, e.g., December 31, as the determining factor. In other respects, however, the rules on what periods of service count under defined contribution plans generally follow the rules for defined benefit plans, except that additional, special rules may apply.

The discussion below covers the general ERISA rules on what periods count under both types of plans, as well as the special rules applicable to defined contribution plans. Also discussed below are the impact of other laws, namely, the Age Discrimination in Employment Act, the Pregnancy Discrimination Act, and the Veterans' Readjustment Assistance Act, on years of participation, as well as the possibility that other years may be included under a particular plan's definition, giving rise to greater contractual obligations than required under ERISA.

A. Years of Actual Participation

As a general rule, only those years in which an employee is an actual participant in a plan are required to count for benefit accruals. In defined benefit plans, pre-ERISA years of participation may occasionally be subject to the special rule described in section II.B.5 above for determining the amount of accrued benefits. The general rule is subject to exceptions and quasi-exceptions that add to or subtract from the years that count for benefit accruals.

B. Potential Additions

1. If Commencement of Participation Was Unlawfully Delayed

If a plan unlawfully delays the commencement of participation in violation of the applicable ERISA standards, the participant is entitled to a recomputation of his or her years of participation for benefit accruals based on the date that participation should have commenced.

2. Recommencement of Participation

Once an employee commences participation in a plan, he or she may not be required to remeet the minimum age and service requirements for participation after a separation from service, nor may the employee be required to wait for the six-month period previously described for participation in the plan to recommence. The only exception to this rule is when the ERISA rule of parity permits a cancellation of *all* years of service that the employee had. Thus, only if an employee commences participation, separates from service without *any* nonforfeitable rights to benefits, and incurs a series of consecutive one-year breaks in service equal to or exceeding the employee's prior years of service, can prior years of service be cancelled for purposes of meeting a plan's minimum service requirements for participation. Beginning with plan years after December 31, 1984, the five-year floor on the rule of parity established under the Retirement Equity Act further limits the possibility that an employee who has commenced participation will be required to remeet a plan's minimum service requirements for participation, and then, in addition, potentially wait up to six months for participation to recommence.[106]

All employees, including those with vested rights, can, however, be subject to a one-year hold-out rule on recommencing participation—if they are returning after a one or more year break in service and a plan so provides. But on the completion of the required one year of service, their participation in the plan must recommence effective with the date of their return to service, with no intervening waiting period for which service is not credited.[107]

3. Military Service Years

Under the Veterans' Readjustment Assistance Act, 38 U.S.C. Sections 2021-24, absences from service with an employer on account of military service, whether the military enlistment was voluntary or involuntary, and whether the service was in war or in peace, are required to be credited for benefit accruals (and for vesting) as one of the "prerequisites of seniority" due a returning veteran. To be entitled to this credit under the law, the veteran must reapply for his or her old job within 90 days of the discharge (if the job is not already being held open). The veteran must then be reinstated to his or her old job, unless it was a temporary job or the employer's circumstances have changed so as to make reinstatement unreasonable or impossible.

The inclusion of benefit accrual credit (and vesting credit) among the prerequisites of seniority due a veteran for the intervening years of military service is well-established. In *Alabama Power Co. v. Davis*, the U.S. Supreme Court held that a returning veteran was entitled to pension credit for time spent in the military because pensions are

---

[106] ERISA §202(b)(4) (Code §410(a)(5)(D)). And see 26 C.F.R. 1.410(a)-4(b)(2) (example (3)). Note that the special one-year break-in-service rule applicable in counting vesting service under defined contribution plans before 1985 does not apply to meeting conditions of participation. Compare *id.* and ERISA §203(b)(3)(C) (Code §411(a)(6)(C)). The years of service that the break must equal or exceed may also include some years of service not required to be included for vesting. See sec. I.A.2 above.

[107] See 26 C.F.R. 1.410(a)-4(b)(2) (examples (3) and (4)).

predominantly rewards for continuous service, and because the purpose of the law's rights for returning veterans is to place them back on the seniority ladder at exactly the point they would have occupied had they not responded to the nation's military needs.[108]

Benefit accrual credit for time spent in the military is a standard item in plans, but some plans can still be found that unlawfully limit it to wartime service, or to draftees.[109]

Even reserve duty in a state National Guard unit is required to be credited for benefit accruals (as well as for vesting).[110] Military service is also required to be included in past service, when a plan counts past service for benefit accruals.[111]

Whether profit-sharing plan contribution allocations are a perquisite of seniority due a returning veteran for military service years remains an open issue—at least for profit-sharing plans under which the employer has a nondiscretionary commitment to contribute a percentage of profits in each year in which there are profits. In *Raypole v. Chemi-Trol Chemical Co.*, a district court held that a returning veteran was entitled to profit-sharing plan contributions he would have received with reasonable certainty had he been continuously employed instead of serving in the military.[112] On appeal, the Sixth Circuit reversed, holding that the "real nature" of the profit-sharing contributions was "short-term compensation" for actual work, rather than a reward for length of service, and also that the contributions had not accrued with "reasonable certainty" since the employer's contribution commitment to this particular profit-sharing plan was entirely discretionary, rather than a set percentage of each year's profits.[113]

4. Years When an Employer Was Delinquent in Contributions to a Multiemployer Plan

Before ERISA, some multiemployer plans denied benefit accrual and vesting credit to employees for years when their employer was delinquent in making contributions to the plan. Such periods are particularly likely to occur before a plant closing, union decertification, or any other type of employer withdrawal from a multiemployer plan. Under ERISA, such periods or years must be credited for both benefit accrual and vesting purposes because hours of service for use in determining such years are determined solely on the basis of hours of work,

---

[108] 431 U.S. 581, 1 EBC 1158 (1977).

[109] See *Bunnell v. New England Teamsters Pension Fund*, 655 F.2d 451, 2 EBC 1654 (1st Cir. 1981), *cert. denied*, 455 U.S. 908 (1982).

[110] 38 U.S.C. §2024(d). And see *U.S. v. New England Teamsters Pension Fund*, 737 F.2d 1274, 5 EBC 1824 (2d Cir. 1984).

[111] See *Smith v. Industrial Employers & Distributors Assoc.*, 546 F.2d 314, 1 EBC 1154 (9th Cir. 1977); *U.S. v. New England Teamsters Pension Fund, supra*; *Grzyb v. New River Co.*, 793 F.2d 590, 7 EBC 2134 (4th Cir. 1986) (5 years of military service required to be included in past service, even though participant only claimed the credit 31 years later when he retired).

[112] 4 EBC 2204 and 5 EBC 1038 (N.D. Ohio 1983).

[113] 754 F.2d 169, 6 EBC 1058, at 1064 and 1065 (6th Cir. 1985).

or hours for which payment is due the employee from the employer, without reference to the delinquency or nondelinquency of the employer's contributions to the plan.[114] The plan's recourse in these situations is to collect the delinquent contributions, and then kick the employer out of the plan *after* its contribution obligation expires.[115]

5. Periods of Layoff, Disability, or Other Leave

It is possible for a plan to comply with ERISA without crediting any hours of service for benefit accruals in which an employee is laid off, disabled, or on other leave.[116] However, plans often provide under their terms that such periods count for benefit accruals through parallel drafting or other adoption of ERISA's hours of service or elapsed time period of service definitions for measuring years of vesting service.[117]

Longer periods of layoff, disability, or other types of leaves of absence than required under the ERISA definitions may also count for benefit accruals under the terms of plans (subject to the overriding Code requirement that the additional periods a plan credits must not by design or operation discriminate in favor of the prohibited group of

---

[114] 29 C.F.R. 2530.200b-2. See also Rev. Rul. 85-130 (benefit credits contingent on employer's contributions puts benefits in the discretion of the employer and thus causes plan to fail to satisfy the Code's definitely determinable benefits requirement).

In *McCarthy v. Marshall,* 4 EBC 2545 (1st Cir. 1983), the trustees of the New England Teamsters Pension Fund attempted to invalidate the Department of Labor's regulation on crediting hours of service for participation regardless of an employer's delinquency in making contributions. The First Circuit dismissed the suit for lack of subject matter jurisdiction on finding that the trustees' "primary purpose" in challenging the rule necessarily related to maintenance of the plan's tax-qualified status, which, under ERISA, is a determination for the IRS to make in the first instance, subject to Tax Court review on an adverse determination.

Even for periods before ERISA, credit has been required when plan participants were not given notice of their employer's contribution delinquency. See *Rosen v. Hotel & Restaurant Pension Fund,* 637 F.2d 592, 2 EBC 1054 (3d Cir. 1981) (denial of credit arbitrary and capricious when employee not provided with notice by plan trustees of his employer's delinquency). Accord *Taylor v. Amalgamated Meat Cutters,* 619 S.W.2d 120 (Tenn. Ct.App. 1981) (trustees had duty to notify participant of employer's delinquencies when he had right under the plan to make up the contributions himself).

[115] See General Counsel Memorandum (GCM) 39048 (June 30, 1983) (multiemployer plan must continue to credit service with an employer as long as the employer has a contribution obligation to the plan; a trustee policy of kicking out an employer who is delinquent in making contributions for more than 60 days cannot override continuing contribution obligations under the terms of the employer's collective bargaining agreement).

This rule is bolstered by §§502(g)(2) and 515 of ERISA, as added by MPPAA in 1980, which provides trustees with express statutory authority to collect delinquent contributions, plus liquidated damages and attorneys fees.

[116] ERISA requires up to 501 hours in which no duties are performed, but which are compensated by an employer, such as for sick leave, vacation, and severance pay, to count as hours of service in determining whether a participant meets a threshold 1,000 hours of service that a plan can require for entitlement to at least a partial year of participation credit during a 12-month computation period. However, such hours are technically not required to count for determining the exact portion of a year of participation to which a participant is entitled, e.g., a plan may count such hours for the threshold requirement, but then count only "hours worked" in determining the portion of a year to which the participant is entitled. Similarly, plans may modify the alternative elapsed time method for computing years of participation to exclude unpaid periods of absence for purposes of benefit accruals. See secs. III.D.1 and D.2 below.

[117] See J. MacDonald and A. Bingham, *Pension Handbook for Union Negotiators* (BNA 1986), at 62 ("[m]ost negotiated plans pick one service counting system and use that system to determine vesting and eligibility service as well as benefit service"; using two service counting systems is "confusing"). Also see secs. III.D.1 and D.2 below.

employees). Many collectively bargained plans do, in fact, provide benefit accrual credit for extended periods of layoff. In *Fitzsimons Steel Co., Youngstown, Ohio,* for example, an arbitrator determined that a collectively bargained plan provision that required up to two years of benefit accrual credit for a layoff applied even when prospects for reemployment were nil.[118] Nonbargained plans that are patterned after collectively bargained plans may provide similar layoff credit. Both collectively bargained and nonbargained plans also frequently provide for continuing benefit accrual credit during periods of disability.

Some plans also provide credit during leaves of absence. When leaves of absence are credited, the employer must have an established leave policy that is uniformly applied to employees under similar circumstances and that does not discriminate on its face or in operation in favor of the prohibited group of employees, e.g., because leave is only granted for managerial sabbaticals.[119] There may be a question even then about whether such leaves can be credited for benefit accruals, as opposed to solely for vesting,[120] but some plans provide such credit.

---

[118] 81-2 ARB (CCH) ¶8408 (Ruben, 1981). On the use of the term "layoff" to cover separations from service in which prospects for reemployment are nil, see also *Faunce v. American Can Co.*, 407 A.2d 733 (Me. 1979) (permanently laid-off employees continued to accrue additional two years' benefits under provision for "layoffs"); *Union Central Life Ins. Co. v. Hamilton Steel Prod., Inc.*, 448 F.2d 501 (7th Cir. 1971) (mass terminations based on economic factors are in the nature of "layoffs," rather than dismissals for cause); *Roberts' Dictionary of Industrial Relations* (BNA 3d ed.) (layoff means "temporary or indefinite separation from service," usually with retention of certain seniority rights if recalls occur; a reduction in force is synonymous with a layoff); B. Aaron, *Legal Status of Employee Benefit Rights Under Private Pension Plans* (Richard D. Irwin 1961), at 37 (the term "layoff" "also covers . . . permanent reductions of available work"); *Galesburg Printing and Publishing Co.*, 82-2 ARB (CCH) ¶8538 (Nathan, 1982) (a job termination is a permanent layoff); PLR 8031091 (May 9, 1980), reprinted at ¶17,372E CCH Pension Plan Guide. But see *Radio Station WFDF,* 79 LA 424 (Ellman, 1982) (whether a separation from service is considered a layoff depends on whether there is a reasonable expectation of returning to work); *Formisano v. Blue Cross of Rhode Island,* 478 A.2d 167, 6 EBC 2244, at 2246 (R.I. 1984) ("layoff" does not include permanent reduction of employment by reason of employer going out of business, citing other authorities); *Dockray v. Phelps Dodge Corp.*, 801 F.2d 1149, 7 EBC 2327 (9th Cir. 1986) (layoff does not include permanently replaced strikers, even though a written notice from the employer stated that the employees were not working on account of the unavailability of work).

Apart from labor relations authorities and the case law, another consideration on the use of the term "layoff" is the increasing use of the term by newspapers, magazines, and television to encompass permanent reductions in force. See, e.g., "AT&T-Labor Talks to Focus on Disconnected Workers," Washington Post, April 1, 1986, at A-1 ("[Cheryl] Hoffer, a lifelong West Virginian, and her husband and son moved 472 miles to Virginia Beach, Va., in 1984 so that she could become a saleswoman at a new AT&T facility. What she did not know then, however, was that AT&T would close the Chesapeake customer service office two years later. On March 1, [1986] she was laid off after 10 years of service.").

In interpreting a pension plan provision providing additional accrual credits for employees on layoff in the context of a permanent work force reduction, the *alternative* classifications for the employee's status under the terms of the plan must also be considered. If the only alternatives are classifying the employee as having "quit" or having been "discharged," the layoff status may win almost by default. See *Roberts' Dictionary of Industrial Relations* (3d ed.) (discharge means "dismissal of an employee, usually for some infraction of the rules . . . , incompetence, or other good reason"). Cf. *Cook v. Pension Plan for Salaried Employees of Cyclops,* C.A. No. C-1-82-615 (S.D. Ohio, Oct. 5, 1984) (employees whose services were terminated by plant closing cannot be considered "discharged" within meaning of a plan because "discharge" in labor-management relations means a discharge "for cause" or the "individual fault" of the employee), *rev'd,* 801 F.2d 865, 7 EBC 2278 (6th Cir. 1986) ("discharge" ambiguous enough to be susceptible to plan administrator's interpretation).

[119] Rev. Rul. 81-106.

[120] Rev. Rul. 81-106 concerned a plan that provided credit for leaves of absence for vesting and conditions for commencing participation, but not for benefit accruals. The Ruling, therefore,

Under the 1978 Pregnancy Discrimination Amendments to Title VII of the Civil Rights Act, "women affected by pregnancy, childbirth or related medical conditions [are required to be] treated the same for all employment-related purposes, including receipt of benefits under fringe benefit programs, as other persons [with] similar [temporary or long-term inabilities to work]."[121] This amendment requires coverage of pregnancy or childbirth under health, disability, sick leave, and extended leave of absence plans or policies if similar conditions are covered under such plans. If accumulation of pension credits is provided under a pension or profit-sharing plan during such periods of disability, illness, or leave, then such credits are required for women who are disabled or on sick or other leave because of pregnancy or childbirth.[122]

Even when a plan is required to credit an additional period of layoff or other absence for benefit accruals, this may do a participant in a salary-based plan little good without some compensation to go with the credit. For example, under a career average pay plan, i.e., a plan in which benefits for each year of participation are a percentage of that year's compensation, obtaining an additional year or partial year of credit may, in fact, do a participant no good without at least some compensation to include under the benefit formula. In such cases, the definition of compensation under the plan may be examined to determine whether severance pay or any other payments to an employee that are related to a period of absence are included as compensation.[123]

Under a plan that bases benefits on an average of final pay—for example, the average of pay over the final five years of service—there may even be situations where an additional year with little or no compensation not only does a participant no good, but ostensibly *decreases* the participant's accrued benefits because of the inclusion in the final average of a year in which the participant earned little or no compensation. The IRS's regulations on benefit accruals, however, prohibit a decrease in benefits from the inclusion of uncompensated or low compensation years, and in many cases, ensure that the participant's benefits will still increase.

When a participant is credited with a partial year of participation and has some compensation in a period, the IRS's regulations require that the compensation be imputed to a full year's compensation for inclusion in any final average of the participant's compensation, or any highest average of compensation over a period of 10 years or less.[124] The regulatory definition of the normal retirement benefit as the

---

did not pass on the issue of whether approved leaves of absence could be credited for benefit accruals.

[121] 42 U.S.C. §2000e(k), as amended by P.L. 95-555.

[122] See *Zichy v. Philadelphia,* 36 FEP Cases 1637 (E.D. Pa. 1979), and 29 C.F.R. 1604, Appendix, Q&A 17.

[123] See also 29 C.F.R. 2530.204-2(d) (prohibiting plans from "double-prorating" a partial year by using both a partial year of credit and a partial year of compensation under a salary-based formula).

[124] 26 C.F.R. 1.411(a)-7(c)(5), and see 29 C.F.R. 2530.204-2(d).

greater of the benefit available at the normal retirement age or at any earlier age can also prevent any drop in benefits below the amount previously available as an early retirement benefit, and in some cases, can ensure an improvement in benefits for a final credited year in which compensation is low or nonexistent.[125] The bottom line is that ERISA Section 204(b)(1)(G) and Code Section 411(b)(1)(G) prohibit a plan from ever reducing a participant's accrued benefits because of an increase in service under the plan.[126]

In a plan in which benefits are based on an average of highest pay in *any* year, rather than a final average, credit for an additional period of layoff or other absence does not run into these problems because the highest average of compensation remains the same, despite any drop in compensation in a final year, and thus always results in increased benefits when multiplied by any additional period of credited service.

6. Past Service and Preparticipation Service

As discussed in Chapter 3, sec. V, many defined benefit plans provide past service credits for years before a plan is established, or under a multiemployer plan, for years of service with an employer before the employer joins the multiemployer plan.

Legally, it may be possible for past service credits for participants to be credited under a plan's normal retirement benefit formula, but then not to be credited in determining the participants' accrued benefits from years of participation. In so doing, a plan may effectively increase the participants' normal retirement benefit by crediting the past service under the normal retirement benefit formula, but then slow down the rate at which those past service benefits actually accrue by using only years of participation for benefit accruals. One consequence of this is that if a participant separates from service prior to accruing the entire normal retirement benefit, the participant will not actually receive all of the past service benefits. Plans that grant past service credit generally appear to provide that past service counts both under the normal retirement benefit formula and as years of participation for accruals. If a plan draws a distinction between the two, adequate disclosure to participants of the difference between the years credited under the normal retirement benefit formula and years of participation under the plan's benefit accrual method is critical, as is any resulting discrimination in favor of the prohibited group of employees.

When a plan credits years of past service for plan participants who

---

[125] See 26 C.F.R. 1.411(a)-7(c)(6) (example (4)).

[126] And see 26 C.F.R. 1.411(b)-1(d)(3). However, in *Edwards v. Wilkes-Barre Publishing Co. Pension Trust,* 757 F.2d 52, 6 EBC 1395 (3d Cir. 1985), *cert. denied,* 474 U.S. 843 (1985), the Third Circuit permitted employer-appointed plan trustees to credit permanently replaced strikers with completely uncompensated years of credited service during their time on strike, with the result that their accrued benefits under a final average pay formula actually decreased for each year of the strike. The court did not discuss ERISA §204(b)(1)(G).

were in the plan when it was established, the past service credit must generally be extended to all subsequent participants unless the sponsoring employer can demonstrate that the denial is nondiscriminatory within the meaning of the Code. This is established by Revenue Ruling 70-77, which is discussed in Chapter 3, sec. V. Most subsequent participants, of course, do not have past service in the sense of service with the employer before the establishment of the plan. But they do often have one to three years of preparticipation service as a result of a plan's conditions for participation, and in some cases, they may have additional years of service with the employer, such as from having previously worked in a job classification or division not covered by the plan.

When a plan is top-heavy, Code Section 416(c)(1) requires minimum two percent of highest pay benefits to be provided based on a non-key employee's "years of service" (up to 10 years), rather than based on his or her "years of participation." Thus, years of service with the employer before participation commences must be included.[127]

7. Years Under a Predecessor Employer's Plan

Under ERISA Section 210(b)(1) (Code Section 414(a)(1)), years of participation under a plan must be carried over if a different employer assumes and maintains the plan of a predecessor employer, or merges the predecessor's plan with a plan of its own. Such years of participation must also be carried over if a predecessor employer's plan is only nominally discontinued before being reestablished by a different employer.[128]

Under ERISA Section 210(b)(2) (Code Section 414(a)(2)), the IRS is also authorized to issue regulations requiring years of participation under a predecessor employer's plan to be carried over under a *different* plan of a successor employer. These regulations have never been issued. Without the regulations, a participant appears to be without recourse since the statutory section is contingent on the IRS's determination of the "extent" and circumstances under which such credit is to be required.[129] Draft regulations that have been circulated, but never formally proposed, would reportedly not require benefit accrual credit in any such situation, but would only require the new employer to

---

[127] But years of service before Jan. 1, 1984, and years of service when the plan was not in existence, or was not a top-heavy plan, are not included. Code §416(c)(1)(C)(ii).

The distinction between years of service and years of participation also means that if a non-key employee has 1,000 hours of service, or its equivalent, in a year, he or she must be credited with a full year's minimum benefit—whereas the employee might be credited with only one-half year under the years of participation rules. See sec. III.D.

[128] Conf. Rep., at 264, 3 ERISA Leg. Hist. 4531.

[129] *Phillips v. Amoco Oil Co.*, 614 F.Supp. 694 (N.D. Ala. 1985), *aff'd*, 799 F.2d 1464, 7 EBC 2246 (11th Cir. 1986), *cert. denied*, 481 U.S. ___ (1987).

credit years of service under the predecessor employer's plan for vesting.[130]

8. Years Subject to Estoppel

Particularly in periods before corporate acquisitions, union mergers, or changes in international union affiliations, representations may be made to employees about credit they will receive for benefit accruals (and also for vesting) under a new pension plan. In some instances, such representations are made, but then are not included in the terms of the plan. In single-employer plans, estoppel generally has been held to apply in such instances,[131] unless there is insufficient proof that the representations were made, an absence of actual or apparent authority of the person making the representations, or another shortcoming in establishing reasonable reliance by the employee.[132] In multiemployer plans, the courts have generally rejected estoppel because of a perceived special potential for corruption of jointly administered plans and because resulting actuarial imbalances might fall on nonculpable employers if estoppel was applied to the plan.[133] More recently, however, some courts have begun to examine estoppel claims involving jointly administered plans more closely, at least when the plan's actuarial soundness is not a significant issue.[134]

Past service years can also be required to be credited under ambiguous plan language if oral or written assurances of credit for past service support a broad interpretation of the plan. In *Walker v. Western-Southern Life Ins. Co.*, oral assurances that years a participant had rendered with an insurance company would count "for all purposes connected with employment benefits" under the plans of a successor employer supported a broad interpretation of a plan's definition of credited service.[135]

---

[130] See "Case Study: Handling Employee Benefits in Mergers and Acquisitions, A Panel Discussion," 37 Inst. on Fed. Tax'n—ERISA Supp. (1979), at 11-18 (remarks of Theresa Stuchiner, partner in Kwasha Lipton, a pension and actuarial services consulting firm).

[131] See *Landro v. Glendenning Motorways, Inc.*, 625 F.2d 1344 (8th Cir. 1980); *Anthony v. Ryder Truck Lines, Inc.*, 611 F.2d 944, 1 EBC 1961 (3d Cir. 1979); *Oates v. Teamster Affiliates Pension Plan*, 482 F.Supp. 481 (D.D.C. 1979). And see *Vastoler v. American Can Co.*, 700 F.2d 916 (3d Cir. 1983) (reversing employer's motion for summary judgment).

[132] See ch. 8, sec. II.D (on estoppel).

[133] See *Aitken v. IP & GCU-Employer Retirement Fund*, 604 F.2d 1261 (9th Cir. 1979), and ch. 8, sec. II.B.

[134] See *Novembre v. Local 584 Pension Fund*, 4 EBC 1286 (D.N.J. 1981), *aff'd*, 4 EBC 1289 (3d Cir. 1982), *cert. denied*, 459 U.S. 1172 (1983), and ch. 8, sec. II.B.

[135] 391 So.2d 925, at 927 (La.App. 1980). But see *Miles v. New York Teamsters Pension Fund*, 698 F.2d 593, 4 EBC 2160 (2d Cir. 1983), *cert. denied*, 464 U.S. 829 (1983); *Vorpahl v. Union Oil Co. Retirement Plan*, 4 EBC 2565 (D. Minn. 1983). When neither plan interpretation nor estoppel provides credit, a remedy may still be available under a separate contract formed with the employer by the promise of credit, or through a misrepresentation action against the person who made the statement that past service years would be credited. See ch. 8, secs. III, IV, and V.

9. Years Under Reciprocity Agreements

Reciprocity agreements between multiemployer plans can require years of service that are not with the employers contributing to a multiemployer plan to be credited for benefit accruals (and often for vesting). It is estimated that "80 to 90" percent of multiemployer plans are parties to reciprocity agreements, with the common denominator generally being that the plans are sponsored by the same international union.[136] The exact terms of reciprocity agreements vary, but basically fall into two types: (1) a "money transfer" agreement under which credit for service under another plan is returned to a "home" plan, along with an appropriate amount of the contributions made on the participant's behalf,[137] and (2) a "pro-rata" agreement under which a combined pension is determined by combining the participant's benefits from the years under the benefit formula of each plan—with each plan then bearing its share of the costs of the benefits due to service under its formula.[138]

C. Potential Deductions

1. Years After Normal Retirement Age

Under ERISA as in effect until 1988, years of participation are not required to be credited under defined benefit pension plans after a participant reaches a plan's "normal retirement age," which is usually age 65. This exclusion is largely by implication. ERISA's benefit accrual rules are directed to accruing a plan's normal retirement benefit by the plan's normal retirement age. Implicitly, years of participation are not required to be credited after that age.[139] Unlike some ERISA exceptions, the exclusion of years after a plan's normal retirement age is in wide use. In the Bureau of Labor Statistics' survey of plans of medium and large firms, 56 percent of defined benefit plan participants were in plans that did not count such years.[140]

Before reviewing the change in ERISA that is effective in 1988, and the more controversial issue of whether such an exclusion complied with the Age Discrimination in Employment Act after 1978, it

---

[136] D. McGinn, *Joint Trust Pension Plans* (Richard D. Irwin 1978), at 142.

[137] *Id.*, at 140, and see *Nichols v. Trustees of Asbestos Workers Pension Plan*, 3 EBC 1726 (D.D.C. 1982).

[138] D. McGinn, *supra*, at 137-40, and see *Bianco v. Teamsters Local 816 Pension Trust*, 494 F.Supp. 206 (E.D.N.Y. 1980); *Hoover v. Cumberland, Md. Area Teamsters Pension Fund*, 756 F.2d 977, 6 EBC 1401 (3d Cir. 1985), *cert. denied*, 474 U.S. 845 (1985); *Tanzillo v. Teamsters Local 617*, 769 F.2d 140 (3d Cir. 1985).

[139] See ERISA §§204(b)(1)(B) and (C) (Code §§411(b)(1)(B) and (C)).

[140] BLS, Employee Benefits in Medium and Large Firms, 1984, at 53. Plans are permitted to count years after the plan's normal retirement age. Smaller plans where the owner intends to keep working to age 70 or 75 may be inclined to do so to effect a benefit formula with a lower per year rate of benefit accruals for other employees.

may be best to examine when the exclusion unquestionably has not applied under ERISA and the ADEA:

- If a defined benefit plan complies with the ERISA benefit accrual rules through the three percent method, years of participation must be credited after the plan's normal retirement age until the participant has 33⅓ years of participation.[141]
- If a defined benefit plan defines its normal retirement age as the *later* of age 65 or the tenth anniversary of participation, years of participation must be credited until the participant reaches age 65 or, if *later*, his or her tenth anniversary of participation. Although not as significant as when the three percent method applies, this can mean that at least several years after age 65 can be required to count for benefit accruals when a participant has less than 10 years of participation at age 65.
- For benefit accruals to stop at a plan's normal retirement age, the ADEA also requires that the plan actually prescribe the cessation of accruals at the normal retirement age in nondiscretionary terms, i.e., neither the employer nor the plan's trustees can be permitted to offer discretionary exceptions to the rule that are not enjoyed by all similarly situated older employees.[142]
- Apart from whether years of participation after a plan's normal retirement age are credited for benefit accruals, a plan can still be examined for whether (1) salary increases after age 65 are to be used in an average of final or highest compensation, or (2) benefit improvements, such as an increase from $15 to $20 per month for each year of participation, are to apply up to the date of the participant's actual retirement.[143]
- As discussed further below, contribution allocations under a "supplemental" *defined contribution* plan may not stop at the plan's normal retirement age.

The 1978 amendments to the Age Discrimination in Employment Act raised the age at which retirement may be mandatory from 65 to 70, and also increased from 65 to 70 the age before which other forms of age discrimination in hiring, firing, and the terms and conditions of employment are prohibited. Since that time, whether the widespread exclusion under defined benefit plans of years of participation after age 65, but before age 70, constitutes age discrimination in terms and

---

[141] 26 C.F.R. 1.411(b)-1(b)(1)(i). A plan complying with the 3% method is usually indicated by a cap on credited years of service for benefit accruals of 33⅓ years or less—however, a plan with such a cap could potentially be in compliance with the 133⅓% rule or the fractional rule, which do not require years after the normal retirement age to be credited.

[142] 29 C.F.R. 860.120(c).

[143] When service after a plan's normal retirement age is not credited for benefit accruals, the dollar amounts used in any offset of Social Security benefits provided under the terms of the plan may also not be increased because of improvements in Social Security benefits or because of the participant's post normal retirement age service under the Social Security system. See 29 C.F.R. 860.120(f)(1)(iv)(B)(8).

conditions of employment before age 70 has been debated. The Department of Labor, which originally had jurisdiction to enforce the ADEA, took the position in a 1979 interpretive bulletin that years after a plan's normal retirement age, but before age 70, could still be excluded for purposes of benefit accruals based on the ADEA's legislative history and the higher costs of accruing a percentage or dollar defined benefit for older workers.[144] In 1985, the EEOC, which has had enforcement authority over the ADEA since 1979, announced that it intended to rescind this interpretation and would soon issue regulations, subject to the approval of the Office of Management and Budget, requiring benefit accruals after age 65—at least in instances when a participant has not already accrued a full career's benefits, e.g., 30 years of benefit accruals, before the plan's normal retirement age.[145]

Benefit accruals under defined contribution plans are not directed to accruing a defined benefit by a plan's normal retirement age, nor are there any cost differences under defined contribution plans that relate to the age of an employee. Nevertheless, based on the legislative history of the 1978 ADEA amendments, the Department of Labor's 1979 interpretive bulletin permitted defined contribution plans to deny additional contributions to participants after age 65, unless the defined contribution plan was "supplemental" to another plan.[146] A defined contribution plan was considered supplemental to a defined benefit plan for any employees who were participants in both plans.[147] If an employer had no defined benefit plan, but maintained two or more defined contribution plans, the interpretive bulletin permitted the employer to designate which of the plans was supplemental, and to discontinue contribution allocations after the normal retirement age to the nonsupplemental plan.[148] If an employer had only one plan that was a defined contribution plan, the interpretive bulletin provided that the plan was not supplemental to any other plan, and contributions could

---

[144] 29 C.F.R. 860.120(a)(1) and (f)(1)(iv)(B)(3). And see *Von Aulock v. Smith*, 720 F.2d 176, 4 EBC 2274 (D.C. Cir. 1983), 293 BNA Pens. Rep. R-8 (June 2, 1980), and 315 BNA Pens. Rep. R-1 (Oct. 17, 1980) for a history of the interpretive bulletin and of a 1980 EEOC attempt to override it.

[145] See 12 BNA Pens. Rep. 365 and 368 (March 11, 1985). Issuance of the regulations was delayed; in June 1986, the American Association of Retired Persons filed a lawsuit to compel their issuance. See 13 BNA Pens. Rep. 1163 (June 30, 1986). Judge Harold Greene ruled on Feb. 26, 1987, that the EEOC's failure to issue regulations requiring accruals after normal retirement age was an unlawful delay of its rulemaking duties. He ordered the EEOC to rescind the Interpretive Bulletin within 20 days and to issue final regulations within 80 days (apparently without retroactive effect). *AARP v. EEOC*, 8 EBC 1227 (D.D.C. 1987). The Interpretive Bulletin was rescinded on March 18, 1987. 52 Fed. Reg. 8448 (March 18, 1987). But see *Bell v. Trustees of Purdue Univ.*, 8 EBC 1529 (N.D. Ind. 1987) (based on statutory language and legislative history, absence of benefit accruals after normal retirement age does not violate ADEA).

[146] 29 C.F.R. 860.120(f)(1)(iv)(B)(1), and see 124 Cong. Rec. 8218 (March 23, 1978) (remarks of Sen. Javits) and 124 Cong. Rec. 7882 (March 21, 1978) (statement of Rep. Dent). Note, however, that investment gains and losses and forfeitures must be allocated to older workers' accounts on the same basis as for younger workers, whether or not a defined contribution plan is "supplemental." 29 C.F.R. 860.120(f)(1)(iv)(B)(2).

[147] 29 C.F.R. 860.120(f)(1)(iv)(B)(1).

[148] *Id.*

thus be denied for employees working past the plan's normal retirement age.[149]

In 1985, the EEOC announced that it intended to rescind this bulletin and propose regulations requiring contributions under all defined contribution plans for employees who work past age 65.[150] The basic argument against the distinction in the interpretive bulletin is that the legislative history supporting it is insufficient in light of the express language of the ADEA and the absence of any actuarial cost differences under *either* supplemental or nonsupplemental defined contribution plans. In addition, while the ADEA interpretive bulletin lent support to a denial of contribution allocations when a defined contribution plan was not supplemental to another plan, the support for this under ERISA was never clear. While ERISA's benefit accrual methods for defined benefit plans implicitly endorse the cessation of benefit accruals at a plan's normal retirement age, ERISA contains no parallel implicit endorsement for excluding employees from participation under a defined contribution plan after a normal retirement age.[151]

Effective in 1988, the Omnibus Budget Reconciliation Act of 1986 amends ERISA, the Code, and the ADEA to provide that neither benefit accruals nor contribution allocations can be stopped (or reduced) because a participant has attained a plan's normal retirement age. An exception is allowed if the participant has reached a generally applicable limit (that applies without regard to age) on the dollar amount or percentage of pay benefits that are provided under a defined benefit plan, or on the number of years of participation that are taken into account under a defined benefit plan's benefit accrual formula.[152] Actuarial increases in benefits provided by some defined benefit plans for individuals who postpone retirement past the normal retirement age can also be deducted from the required accruals. Also, if a defined benefit plan allows a participant to begin receipt of benefits after its normal retirement age without separating from service, the actuarial equivalent of the benefits received can be deducted from the required accruals.[153]

---

[149] *Id.*

[150] See 12 BNA Pens. Rep. 365 and 368 (March 11, 1985).

[151] See R. Blum and C. Kolm, 363 Tax Mgmt. (BNA), Age and Sex Discrimination and Employee Benefit Plans, at A-22. And cf. Rev. Rul. 76-250 (distinguishing the ERISA rules on counting years of participation as not applicable to defined contribution plans). The IRS, however, has taken the position that contribution allocations can be stopped when a defined contribution plan participant reaches the plan's normal retirement age except when prohibited discrimination results under such a provision. See Rev. Rul. 81-210, sec. 5, and R. Blum and C. Kolm, *supra* (citing PLR 7950025, Sept. 12, 1979).

[152] ADEA §4(i), as amended by §9201 of P.L. 99-509, ERISA §§204(b)(1)(H) and 204(b)(2), as amended by §9202(a), and Code §§411(b)(1)(H) and 411(b)(2), as amended by §9202(b). The effective date for this amendment is the first plan year starting on or after Jan. 1, 1988. For collectively bargained plans, the effective date is the *earlier* of Jan. 1, 1990, or the date on which the last collective bargaining agreement ratified before March 1, 1986, expires. P.L. 99-509, §9204.

[153] See Conf. Rep., H.R. Rep. 99-1012, at 381, [1986] U.S. Code Cong. & Ad. News, 3868, at 4026. The benefit accrual requirement may also be subject to exception as set out in IRS regulations if the accruals cause discrimination in favor of highly compensated employees. Conf. Rep., at 380, [1986] U.S. Code Cong. & Ad. News, at 4025.

2. Years Before Breaks in Service

a. Post-ERISA breaks in service. The major ERISA rule on breaks in service is the rule of parity. The rule of parity provides that if and only if a completely nonvested participant incurs a series of consecutive one-year breaks in service that equals or exceeds the number of years of service that the participant has toward vesting (whether or not those years of service were accumulated consecutively) can the plan provide that the participant's years of participation for benefit accruals are cancelled.[154] Amendments to ERISA enacted under the 1984 Retirement Equity Act establish a floor on the ERISA rule of parity requiring at least five consecutive one-year breaks in service before any cancellation of prior years of participation for accruals (or years of service for vesting) can occur.[155] This five-year floor became effective with the first plan year after December 31, 1984, except for collectively bargained plans.[156] The effective date means that if a participant's years of participation have not been cancelled under the ERISA rule of parity before the first *day* of that plan year, the rule, as modified, must apply.[157]

Before 1985, ERISA permitted defined contribution plans to use a more stringent break-in-service rule under which just a one-year break in service could forfeit all nonvested accrued benefits that were earned in years before the break.[158] The 1984 Retirement Equity Act amends the special defined contribution plan break rule, effective for plan years beginning after December 31, 1984, to establish a floor of five consecutive one-year breaks in service before any cancellation of nonvested accrued benefits earned before a break in service can occur.[159] As stated above, the effective date means that if nonvested prebreak accrued benefits have not already been cancelled under the old rule before the first day of that plan year, the new rule must apply.[160]

Other limits on break-in-service rules, discussed in more detail below and in Chapter 5, are:

- The plan must clearly provide for the application of the break-in-service rule, i.e., it must provide for the loss of *both* years of

---

154 See 29 C.F.R. 2530.204-1(b)(2).

155 ERISA §202(b)(4) (Code §410(a)(5)(D)), as amended by §102(d)(1) and §202(d)(1) of P.L. 98-397.

156 P.L. 98-397, §302(a). The effective date for a plan maintained pursuant to a collective bargaining agreement is the first plan year beginning after the expiration of the agreement in effect on Aug. 23, 1984 (or the first plan year after the expiration of the last of the collective bargaining agreements then in effect if there are more than one), *or* if earlier, the first plan year beginning after Jan. 1, 1987. See P.L. 98-397, §302(b).

157 P.L. 98-397, §303(a)(2).

158 ERISA §203(b)(3)(C) (Code §411(a)(6)(C)).

159 ERISA §203(b)(3)(C) (Code §411(a)(6)(C)), as amended by §102(c) and §202(c) of P.L. 98-397. See §302 of P.L. 98-397 for effective dates. A later effective date can apply under a collectively bargained plan. *Id.*, at §302(b).

160 P.L. 98-397, §303(a)(2). And see Temp. and Prop. Regs. 1.410(a)-5T, 50 Fed. Reg. 29371 (July 19, 1985).

service for vesting and years of participation for accruals on such a break.[161]

- If a plan uses the limits of the permissible ERISA break rules, the series of five or more consecutive one-year breaks in service must equal or exceed the number of years of service the participant has for *vesting*, which often includes at least one more year than the participant's years of participation, and in some cases, several more years.[162]
- Even when ERISA's minimum standards do not restrain a break-in-service rule, the application of such a rule to an *involuntary* break in service, such as a break in service resulting from a layoff or disability, may still be arbitrary.[163]

b. Pre-ERISA breaks in service. In counting years of service for vesting, ERISA expressly permits pre-ERISA break-in-service rules to continue in force if the break in service, and consequent loss of years of service for vesting, occurred under a plan's terms before the first plan year beginning after December 31, 1975.[164] However, no similar exception is made in the rules on counting years of participation for benefit accruals. Rather, ERISA Section 204(b)(4)(A) provides that years of participation must include all years that are required to count under ERISA Section 202(b). This section in turn permits a plan to disregard only those years of service that may be cancelled under the ERISA rule of parity. However, as mentioned before, ERISA Section 204(b)(1)(D) separately permits accrued benefits from years of participation before ERISA's effective date to be determined under the terms of the plan as in effect prior to the date of ERISA's enactment, so long as the accrued benefits determined with respect to such years of participation are not less than one-half of the accrued benefits to which the participant would be entitled if Sections 204(b)(1)(A), (B), or (C) applied to the same years of participation. Combined with the Section 204 treatment of pre-ERISA breaks, the proper reading of Section 204(b)(1)(D) seems to be that a plan's pre-ERISA break rules can be given effect, *provided that* the result is not less than one-half of the benefit accruals that would have been accrued had the ERISA benefit accrual rules applied to all the participant's years of participation, as determined under the ERISA rule of parity.[165]

The application of a pre-ERISA break-in-service rule can also be

---

[161] See the section immediately below on pre-ERISA break-in-service rules (describing *Snyder v. Titus* and *McKnight v. Southern Life & Health Ins. Co.*).

[162] See 29 C.F.R. 2530.204-1(b)(2).

[163] See ch. 5, sec. III.A.4.

[164] ERISA §203(b)(1)(F) and §211(b)(2). But see ERISA §211(e)(2) (prohibiting any amendments making break-in-service rules more stringent between Jan. 1, 1974, and the ERISA effective dates).

[165] When a plan's rate of benefit accruals for years before ERISA became effective is less than if the ERISA accrued benefit methods applied to the years of participation, the plan may also have to provide that the difference can be accrued in the years after ERISA's effective date. See sec. II.B.5.

limited if a plan was amended to comply with ERISA, and as amended, does not carry over the pre-ERISA rule. In *Snyder v. Titus*, a district court held that a pre-ERISA break rule did not continue to apply to cancel a participant's prebreak service in the absence of a clear statement in the plan in effect at the time of the participant's application for benefits preserving the application of the pre-ERISA break rule to the earlier years of service.[166] In *Govoni v. Bricklayers Local 5 Pension Fund*, however, another court faced with a similar claim found sufficient ambiguity in a plan's terms to support the trustees' interpretation that the plan's pre-ERISA break rule continued in effect.[167] Along the same line as in *Snyder*, a pre-ERISA break-in-service rule is not presumed to apply to a break occurring during a period of past service before an employer joins a multiemployer plan if the plan only provides for the rule's application to service *after* an employer begins contributions to the plan.[168]

A slightly different type of reading was given a plan's break-in-service rules in *McKnight v. Southern Life & Health Ins. Co.* In *McKnight*, an employee was held to be entitled to benefit accrual credit for two early pre-ERISA periods of service that had been broken before the period in which the employee finally accumulated enough years of service to vest. The Eleventh Circuit found that once the employee vested independently of the earlier breaks, he was entitled under the terms of the plan to benefit accrual credit for all his earlier periods of service, or alternatively, that he was entitled to the credit based on the description of the break rules in the summary plan description.[169]

The application of pre-ERISA break-in-service rules has also frequently been constrained as arbitrary when a break in service is involuntary—e.g., due to disability or a reduction in force—as opposed to a discharge for cause, or a voluntary quit.[170]

3. Years When Employee Contributions Were Not Made

When a plan requires employee contributions as a condition of plan participation, it is implicit that in years when an employee does not make the required contributions, years of participation for benefit accruals are not credited, whether the plan is a contributory defined benefit plan or a contributory defined contribution plan—such as a thrift plan.

However, under a top-heavy defined benefit plan, every non-key

---

166 513 F.Supp. 926, 2 EBC 1269 (E.D. Va. 1981).

167 732 F.2d 250, 5 EBC 1389 (1st Cir. 1984).

168 *Carr v. Hotel & Restaurant Pension Fund,* 585 F.Supp. 949, 5 EBC 2051 (E.D. Pa. 1984).

169 758 F.2d 1566, 6 EBC 1707 (11th Cir. 1985).

170 See ch. 5, sec. III.A.4.

employee must accrue a minimum nonintegrated benefit of two percent of highest five-year average pay without regard to whether employee contributions are made as required under the plan's terms.[171] The same rule applies to the minimum nonintegrated contribution required under a top-heavy defined contribution plan.[172]

4. Years Before Employee Contributions Were Withdrawn

A participant in a contributory plan can lose accrued benefits from employer contributions on the withdrawal of mandatory employee contributions, if the plan so provides. Under ERISA, contributory plans are permitted to provide that on the withdrawal of any mandatory employee contributions *before* a participant has a nonforfeitable right to at least 50 percent of accrued benefits from employer contributions, accrued benefits from employer contributions may be forfeited.[173] In a defined contribution plan using class-year vesting, a withdrawal of employee contributions is "treated as a withdrawal of such contributions on a plan year by plan year basis in succeeding order of time."[174] The effect of this is to lessen the permissible forfeiture.

A plan with a provision for withdrawal of employee contributions is, however, required to contain a repayment option under which the participant can repay the withdrawn mandatory employee contributions (with interest permitted to be required under a defined benefit plan) and have the accrued benefits from employer contributions restored.[175] Until 1985, the plan could provide that this repayment must be made by the *earlier* of:

(1) The end of the five-year period beginning with the date of the withdrawal of employee contributions;

(2) The end of the two-year period beginning with a resumption of employment under the plan (assuming there has been a separation from service); or

(3) Only for a defined contribution plan, the close of the first vesting computation period in which the participant has a one-year break in service.[176]

Beginning with the first plan year after December 31, 1984, the period for repayment of mandatory contributions that are withdrawn upon a separation from service must be at least as long as the earlier of:

---

[171] 26 C.F.R. 1.416-1, Q&A M-4.

[172] 26 C.F.R. 1.416-1, Q&A M-10.

[173] ERISA §203(a)(3)(D)(i) (Code §401(a)(19) and §411(a)(3)(D)(i)).

[174] ERISA §203(a)(3)(D)(iv) (Code §411(a)(3)(D)(iv)). And see 26 C.F.R. 1.411(d)-3(a)(2).

[175] ERISA §203(a)(3)(D)(ii) (Code §411(a)(3)(D)(ii)). Under a defined contribution plan, the accrued benefit required to be restored is the amount at the time of the withdrawal, unadjusted for any subsequent gains or losses. 26 C.F.R. 1.411(a)-7(d)(2)(iii). Hence, no interest is required to be repaid.

[176] 26 C.F.R. 1.411(a)-7(d)(2)(ii)(C) and (D).

(1) The five year period after any resumption of reemployment, or
(2) The end of five consecutive one-year breaks in service beginning with the date of withdrawal.[177]

For any withdrawal of contributions without a separation from service, the repayment period must be at least five years after the date of withdrawal.[178]

5. Years Before Voluntary or Involuntary Cash-Outs

When a participant separates from service, a plan may provide for an involuntarily cash-out of the participant's nonforfeitable benefits if they have a present value of $3,500 or less ($1,750 or less for plan years beginning before December 31, 1984).[179] Larger benefits may be voluntarily cashed-out on a separation from service if a plan so provides and the participant elects the cash-out.[180]

When benefits are involuntarily or voluntarily cashed-out, a plan may provide that on a subsequent return to employment, the years taken into account in computing the cashed-out benefits will not count in computing benefits under the plan.[181] In certain cases, however, the cashed-out benefits are less than all of the participant's accrued benefits under the plan. This can occur if the participant's accrued benefits were not 100 percent vested at the time of the cash-out. For example, if an employee in a defined contribution plan is 50 percent vested in an account balance of $1,000 after 10 years of service (under a 5-to-15 year graded vesting schedule), the plan can cash-out the participant's entire nonforfeitable benefit by paying the participant $500. Similarly, if a defined benefit plan offers benefits at age 65 equal to one percent of each year's compensation and an employee is 50 percent vested, the plan may cash-out the entire nonforfeitable benefit with a lump sum payment equal to the present value of a retirement benefit of one-half of one percent of each year's compensation.

When a participant receives an involuntary or voluntary distribution of nonforfeitable benefits that is less than the present value of all of his or her accrued benefits, the plan must contain a "buy back" option under which the participant can repay the amount distributed (with interest permitted to be required under a defined benefit plan) within a certain period of time, and have the entire accrued benefit restored.[182] Until 1985, a plan could provide that such repayment must be made by the *earlier* of:

---

[177] ERISA §203(a)(3)(D)(ii) and Code §411(a)(3)(D)(ii), as amended by §1898(a)(4) of P.L. 99-514.

[178] *Id.*

[179] ERISA §204(d)(1) (Code §411(a)(7)(B)(i)), as amended by the Retirement Equity Act, P.L. 98-397.

[180] ERISA §204(d)(2) (Code §411(a)(7)(B)(ii)).

[181] ERISA §204(d) (Code §411(a)(7)(B)).

[182] ERISA §204(e) (Code §411(a)(7)(C)). For a defined contribution plan, "the employer-derived accrued benefit required to be restored [must] be not less than the amount in the account

(1) The end of the five-year period beginning with the date of the cash-out;

(2) The end of the two-year period beginning with any resumption of employment under the plan; or

(3) Only for a defined contribution plan, the close of the vesting computation period in which the participant has a one-year break in service.[183]

Beginning with the first plan year after December 31, 1984, the period for repayment of any cash-out upon a separation from service must be at least as long as the earlier of:

(1) The five year period after any resumption of reemployment, or

(2) The end of five consecutive one-year breaks in service beginning with the date of withdrawal.[184]

For any cash-out without a separation from service, the repayment period must be at least five years after the date of withdrawal.[185]

6. *Cancellations of Past Service Years on an Employer's Complete Cessation of Contributions to a Multiemployer Plan*

When an employer completely ceases contributions to a multiemployer plan, some multiemployer plans cancel past service credits, i.e., credits for service with the employer before the employer signed an agreement to contribute to the plan. The purpose of such cancellations is generally stated to be to remove any actuarial imbalance to the plan from the extension of past service credits to employees of an employer who has not made sufficient contributions before the withdrawal to pay for those benefits. Cancellations of past service credits can result in sharp reductions in accrued benefits. In one case, a participant's benefits were reduced from $89.50 per month to $45 per month with the loss of the past service credits.[186]

ERISA Section 203(a)(3)(E) (and Code Section 411(a)(3)(E)) specifically permits multiemployer plans to cancel accrued benefits from past service with an employer "if the employer ceases contributions to the multiemployer plan" without violating ERISA's nonforfeitability

---

balance of the employee, both the amount distributed and the amount forfeited, unadjusted for any subsequent gains or losses. Thus, for example, if an employee received a distribution of $250 when he was 25% vested in an account balance of $1,000, upon repayment of $250, the account balance may not be less than $1,000 even if, because of plan losses, the account balance, if not distributed, would have been reduced to $500." 26 C.F.R. 1.411(a)-7(d)(4)(v).

[183] 26 C.F.R. 1.411(a)-7(d)(4)(iv)(B).

[184] ERISA §204(e) and Code §411(a)(7)(C), as amended by REA, P.L. 98-397, and as corrected by §1898(a)(4) of P.L. 99-514. But compare Temp. & Prop. Regs. 1.411(a)-7(d)(4)(iv)(B), 50 Fed. Reg. 29371 (July 19, 1985) (repayment may not be required earlier than the end of a period of 5 consecutive one-year breaks in service).

[185] *Id.*

[186] See *Stewart v. Nat'l Shopmen Pension Fund,* 563 F.Supp. 773, 4 EBC 1680 (D.D.C. 1983), *rev'd,* 730 F.2d 1552, 5 EBC 1518 (D.C. Cir. 1984), *cert. denied,* 469 U.S. 834 (1984).

requirement.[187] This does not allow such cancellations on an employer's partial withdrawal from a multiemployer plan because the employer continues then to have at least some contribution obligations to the plan, even though it may be for work at a completely different facility or under a different collective bargaining agreement.[188] Plan provisions cancelling past service credits on an employer's complete withdrawal are never mandatory under ERISA except in one instance—cancellation of past service credits is mandatory when a multiemployer plan uses the six-year "free look" provision in the Multiemployer Pension Plan Amendments Act (MPPAA) under which employers can join a multiemployer plan and withdraw within six years without incurring any withdrawal liability.[189]

The courts have not viewed the harsh effects of permissive past service cancellations sanguinely. In *Winpisinger v. Aurora Corp.*, a district court held that plan trustees' cancellation of past service credits on an employer's withdrawal from a plan violated ERISA Section 404(a)(1)'s requirement that fiduciaries act "solely in the interest" of participants and beneficiaries. The court emphasized the lack of adequate prior disclosure to participants of the potential cancellation and the fact that the cancellation was in this case structured to apply only to nonunion plan participants who were employed by the withdrawing employer.[190] In *Elser v. IAM National Pension Fund,* the Ninth Circuit also found a past service cancellation arbitrary, emphasizing the trustees' lack of actuarial evidence on the extent the contributions made by the employer paid for the promised past service benefits and also the inconsistency of an exception under which employees with less contributory service under the plan who left service with the employer 24 months before the withdrawal preserved all of their past service benefits.[191]

---

[187] ERISA §203(a)(3)(E) and the parallel Code section were added by the Multiemployer Pension Plan Amendments Act of 1980 (MPPAA). But even before MPPAA, ERISA §3(37)(A)(IV) and Code §414(f)(1)(D), both now deleted in favor of the MPPAA-amended sections, tolerated past service cancellations as not in violation of the ERISA minimum standards. See also 26 C.F.R. 1.414(f)-1(b)(2)(i).

[188] See ch. 5, sec. III, on the difference between a partial and a complete withdrawal from a multiemployer plan.

[189] See ERISA §4210.

[190] 456 F.Supp. 559, 1 EBC 2201 (N.D. Ohio 1978).

[191] 684 F.2d 648, 3 EBC 2155 (9th Cir. 1982), *cert. denied,* 464 U.S. 813 (1983). When cancellations of past service credit are based on changes in union representation as in *Elser,* questions also exist concerning whether the plan provision for cancellation of the past service hinders freedom of choice in selecting a collective bargaining representative in violation of §8(a)(3) and §8(b)(1) and (2) of the National Labor Relations Act. Professor Clyde Summers states: "To deprive [a union member of his potential benefits from a pension or welfare fund] because he shifts allegiance to another union would seriously inhibit his freedom of choice, which is central to collective bargaining." C. Summers, "Union Schism in Perspective," 45 Va. L. Rev. 261, 279 n.84 (1959), quoted in *Alvares v. Erickson,* 514 F.2d 156, 1 EBC 1121, at 1127 (9th Cir. 1975), *cert. denied,* 423 U.S. 874 (1977). And see *Chambless v. Masters, Mates & Pilots Pension Plan,* 571 F.Supp. 1430, at 1444 n.21 (S.D.N.Y. 1983), *aff'd,* 772 F.2d 1032, 6 EBC 2209 (2d Cir. 1985), *cert. denied,* 475 U.S. 1012 (1986) (suggesting that such a plan provision, if collectively bargained, would violate the NLRA). But see *Elser, supra* (citing NLRB refusal to issue a complaint on this basis when past service cancellation provision was adopted by plan trustees).

Apart from the NLRA issue, the equities in favor of limiting past service cancellations could actually be seen as diminished when the cancellation is triggered by decertification because the

Subsequent to the facts in these decisions, Congress amended ERISA in the Multiemployer Pension Plan Amendments Act of 1980 to provide multiemployer plans with compensation for remaining vested benefit liabilities, including liabilities from vested past service credits, whenever an employer withdraws from a multiemployer plan. As described by the Supreme Court in *PBGC v. R.A. Gray & Co.*:

> "MPPAA . . . requires a withdrawing employer to compensate a plan for benefits that have already vested with the employees at the time of the employer's withdrawal."[192]

With this compensation for vested benefit liabilities, the only legitimate rationale for a plan's cancellation of past service credits, i.e., as a necessary measure to maintain a plan's actuarial soundness, would seem to be henceforth eliminated. ERISA Section 4235, as amended by MPPAA, also alters the statutory backdrop against which past service cancellations take place if an employer ceases contributions to a multiemployer plan because of a certified change in the bargaining unit employees' collective bargaining representative. It provides that the plan from which the employer withdraws as a result of such a change is to transfer assets and liabilities attributable to vested benefits of the employer's employees to the employees' new plan.[193] The new plan can appeal to the PBGC to prevent such a transfer if it would incur "substantial harm as a result," but the general rule is that both the assets and the liabilities are to be transferred to the new plan.[194]

Even with the compensation of MPPAA's withdrawal liability, however, employees have not always fared so well in resisting past service cancellations. In *Niagara Paper Corp. v. Paper Industry Pension Fund,* over $3 million in unfunded vested liabilities remained unpaid from past service benefits after an employer paid withdrawal liability calculated under the "presumptive" method established in MPPAA. The court held that since the plan's cancellation of past service benefits was tailored to just remove the residual actuarial imbalance from the excess of liabilities for past service credits over the employer's contributions to the plan plus its withdrawal liability, the cancellation of the employees' past service credits was not arbitrary and capricious under Section 302(c)(5) of the Labor Management Relations Act.[195]

---

cancellation can then be viewed as a voluntary forfeiture brought on by the actions of the employee/participants themselves in voting to decertify. But in *Elser,* the Ninth Circuit noted that past service cancellations are "hardly . . . voluntary . . . when those who stand to lose the most [from the past service cancellation] are but a small segment of a larger group of employees voting on decertification." 3 EBC at 2160.

[192] 467 U.S. 717, 5 EBC 1545, at 1553 (1984).

[193] And see generally *TIME-DC, Inc. v. ILA Local 1730 Management-Labor Welfare & Pension Funds,* 756 F.2d 939, 6 EBC 1374 (2d Cir. 1985).

[194] ERISA §4235(b)(3). Certain other exceptions are also provided. See §§4235(e)(1) and (f).

[195] 603 F.Supp. 1420, 5 EBC 1915 (D. Minn. 1984), *aff'd,* 800 F.2d 742, 7 EBC 2313 (8th Cir. 1986). In *Niagara,* the employees were actually not at risk because the employer was contractually obligated to make up any benefits that were lost from a past service cancellation. The *Niagara* court did not rule on whether the cancellation might still violate ERISA, as opposed to §302(c)(5) of the Labor Management Relations Act, because the employer was the plaintiff in the action and

Similarly, in *Adams v. New Jersey Brewery Employees' Pension Fund Trustees,* a pre-ERISA and pre-MPPAA case, the Third Circuit held that a plan amendment cancelling past service credits on an employer's withdrawal from a multiemployer plan was not arbitrary and capricious when the plan's unfunded liabilities provided substantial justification for the provision, the amendment drew rational lines for exactly how it would affect employees, and the employees did not show that their failure to obtain work with other contributing employers that would continue their participation in the plan and preserve their past service credits was "involuntary."[196] On remand, the district court found that the cancellation was still arbitrary because the employees lacked advance notice of the amendment, and with notice, could have preserved their past service credits by leaving work with the employer more than 90 days before the employer's withdrawal or subsequently going to work for another contributing employer. On appeal, the Third Circuit again reversed, holding that the employees had actual notice of the amendment, or adequate constructive notice as a matter of law, since they had ratified a collective bargaining agreement with the amendment in it.[197]

Along roughly the same line, in *Central Tool Co. v. IAM National Pension Fund,* a district court held that a cancellation of past service credits for vesting was arbitrary and capricious under Section 302(c)(5) of the Labor Management Relations Act. But although the court emphasized the lack of actuarial evidence on the actuarial imbalance created by the employer's withdrawal, the court still permitted the past service credits to be cancelled for purposes of benefit accruals.[198] On appeal, the U.S. Court of Appeals for the District of Columbia Circuit upheld the trustees' cancellation of *both* vesting and benefit accrual credits for a completely different reason. Since the plan provision authorizing the cancellation was in the plan at the time the employer agreed to the collective bargaining agreement requiring it to contribute to the plan, the plan provision was held to be collectively bargained and thus excepted from review for reasonableness under the LMRA under the Supreme Court's holding in *UMW Health & Retirement Funds v. Robinson.*[199]

Even though past service cancellations are not *per se* ERISA violations (and even if they are not otherwise arbitrary and capricious), ERISA minimum standard protections can still be triggered when a plan amendment installs a past service cancellation provision *after* an employer joins a plan that offers past service credits to the employer's

---

lacked standing to pursue ERISA claims. See *Niagara Paper Corp. v. Paper Industry Pension Fund,* 5 EBC 1496 (D. Minn. 1983).

[196] 670 F.2d 387, 3 EBC 1083 (3d Cir. 1982).

[197] 755 F.2d 330, 6 EBC 1161 (3d Cir. 1985), *sub nom. Michota v. Anheuser-Busch, Inc.*

[198] 523 F.Supp. 812, 2 EBC 2019, at 2024 (D.D.C. 1981). See also *Stewart v. Nat'l Shopmen Pension Fund,* 795 F.2d 1079, 7 EBC 1917 (D.C. Cir. 1986).

[199] 811 F.2d 651, 8 EBC 1268 (D.C. Cir. 1987). And see ch. 8, sec. VIII, and ch. 9, sec. II.A., on the *Robinson* decision. But compare n. 191 above.

employees. In *Fentron Industries v. Shopmen's Pension Fund,* the Ninth Circuit held that the adoption of a plan provision for cancellation of past service credits after an employer joins a plan constitutes a change in the plan's vesting schedule, and therefore, is prohibited under ERISA Section 203(c)(1)(B) (Code Section 411(a)(10)), unless each employee with five or more years of service is given the option of remaining under the preamendment vesting rule. While the amendment was structured so as not to completely divest any employee, but only to reduce the "amount" to which the employee would be entitled, the Ninth Circuit held the amendment changed what the employees were vested in and therefore had to be considered a vesting schedule amendment. The Ninth Circuit could also have handled the amendment as a decrease in accrued benefits in violation of ERISA Section 204(g) (Code Section 411(d)(6)), but the court did not need to reach this issue once it found that the amendment altered the vesting schedule.[200]

However, in *Stewart v. National Shopmen Pension Fund,* the U.S. Court of Appeals for the District of Columbia Circuit held that the identical National Shopmen's plan provision involved in *Fentron* could be invoked without violating ERISA. While the court emphasized that the plan provision affected only benefit accruals and did not completely divest any employee's vested status, the legal distinction which formed the basis for the decision was the court's finding, in direct opposition to *Fentron,* that the cancellation did not result from a plan amendment, or at least not from one occurring after ERISA became effective. The discrepancy between these two findings of fact was not explained, but it is clear from the *Stewart* opinion that had the court found such an amendment, the cancellation of past service would have been prohibited as a decrease in accrued benefits.[201]

Common law rules on vested rights and estoppel can also preclude past service cancellations. In *Norton v. IAM National Pension Fund,* the District of Columbia Circuit held that a cancellation of past service credits on an employer's withdrawal was arbitrary and capricious under the Labor Management Relations Act when the cancellation applied to an employee who had vested rights prior to the employer's

---

[200] 674 F.2d 1300, 3 EBC 1323 (9th Cir. 1982). For purposes of the vesting schedule election, an employee's 5 years of service is computed without regard to the permissible exceptions in ERISA §203(b)(1) (Code §411(a)(4)). Therefore, it must include the past service years with the employer that the plan trustees seek authority to cancel with the amendment. See 26 C.F.R. 1.411(a)-8(b)(3). See also *Collins v. Seafarers Pension Trust,* 641 F.Supp. 293 (D. Md. 1986) (cancellation of past service credits for early retirement benefits under plan amendment also states claim for prohibited decrease in accrued benefits).

[201] 730 F.2d 1552, 5 EBC 1518 (D.C. Cir. 1984), *cert. denied,* 469 U.S. 834 (1984). And see 130 Cong. Rec. H-8762 (daily ed. Aug. 9, 1984) (statement of Rep. Clay) (§204(g)'s protection against amendments, as amended by REA, does not encompass invocations of existing past service cancellation authority with no plan "amendment" as such). The *Stewart* court later held that the cancellations also were not arbitrary under the common law and LMRA §302(c)(5) grounds under which past service cancellations were stricken in *Winpisinger v. Aurora Corp., Elser v. IAM Nat'l Pension Fund, supra,* and *Norton v. IAM Nat'l Pension Fund,* 553 F.2d 1352 (D.C. Cir. 1977), because the cancellations were tailored to the actuarial imbalance to the plan resulting from the past service credits. 7 EBC 1917 (D.C. Cir. 1986).

withdrawal such that if he had left earlier and gone to work for any other noncontributing employer, he would not have lost any pension credits. The court also held that "[a]t a minimum," an employee who is eligible to retire, as the plaintiff was, must be given a choice between retiring at the time of the withdrawal, without the cancellation, or continuing to work for the employer after the withdrawal, with the cancellation.[202] The past service cancellation was also arbitrary in *Norton* because the amendment installing it was adopted after the employer in question had withdrawn from the plan.[203]

D. Measurement of a Year of Participation

Employees and their employers are rarely so cooperative with pension plan drafters and federal regulators as to always work "full time" years, or to precisely time quits, discharges, retirements, layoffs, and rehires at 12-month intervals. It is therefore necessary to be able to precisely measure a "year of participation." Under ERISA, the general rule for defined benefit plans is that when a participant has over "1,000 hours of service," or its equivalent, in a 12-month computation period designated by the plan for measuring years of participation, the participant must receive credit for at least a partial year of participation.[204] A full year's credit can be conditioned on the completion of, for example, 2,000 hours of service within the 12-month computation period, if that is no more than the customary number of hours of work in the industry involved.

The measurement of years of participation is, however, rarely found in the form that ERISA's general rule suggests. First, as mentioned before, very few plans use the term "year of participation."

---

[202] 553 F.2d 1352, at 1359 (D.C. Cir. 1977). Past service benefits of retirees and pension-eligible employees (i.e., employees who are eligible to retire but who continue working) were also left unaffected in *Adams v. New Jersey Brewery Employees' Pension Fund Trustees, supra*, 3 EBC at 1086-87 (cancellation provision did not apply to retirees or pension-eligible employees), *Niagara Paper Corp. v. Paper Industry Pension Fund, supra*, 5 EBC at 1498 (provision did not apply to retirees or employees who were eligible to retire and who actually retired within one year after the employer's withdrawal), *Central Tool Co. v. Nat'l Shopmen Pension Fund, supra*, 2 EBC at 2021 (exceptions for retirees and employees who retired within two months after employer's withdrawal), and *Elser, supra*, 3 EBC at 2157 (retirees' benefits unaffected; opinion does not indicate whether pension-eligible employees also excepted). But see *Stewart, supra*, 7 EBC at 1917 (one retiree's benefits reduced from $80 per month to $9 per month; the court of appeals upheld application of the past service cancellation to the retirees' benefits, but did not discuss its own decision in *Norton*).

[203] Estoppel also applied in *Lix v. Edwards*, 147 Cal. Rptr. 294, at 299 (Cal. Ct.App. 1978), when multiemployer plan trustees attempted two years after the sale of a business to designate an employer as a "new contributing employer." Under the *Lix* plan, if an employer was a "new contributing employer," as opposed to a successor employer, past service credits were cancelled if the employer withdrew from the plan within the next 48 months. The court held that not having made this designation immediately, the trustees were estopped from doing so two years later; they could not "lock the barn door after the horse got out."

And see *McDaniel v. Nat'l Shopmen Pension Fund*, 6 EBC 2700, at 2702 (W.D. Wash. 1985) (past service cancellation on employer's withdrawal "not authorized" under plan provision on which trustees relied).

[204] If certain equivalencies are used in counting hours, either 870 or 750 hours are substituted for 1,000. See below and ch. 5, sec. III.B.1.

Instead, most use terms such as credited service, pension credit, continuous service, year of service, or just service. Second, "hours of service" are rarely found in the definitions of such service, or credit, except under multiemployer plans, nor is a 12-month computation period for determining years of participation often designated in a non-multiemployer plan. Instead, most plans use alternate methods for measuring years of participation.

Defined contribution plans are not required to base annual contribution allocations on years of participation, but rather may generally require employment at the end of a 12-month period, provided that discrimination under the Code does not result.[205]

1. Conventional Method

The best approach to measuring years of participation under defined benefit plans is probably to start with the statutory rule and its application under the regulations and then to turn to what may be more commonly found. The statutory rule has been called the conventional method, and was summarized by the Tax Court in *Standard Oil Co. v. Commissioner:*

> "Under [the conventional] method, a year of participation is based on the number of hours of service during an accrual computation period—a period of 12 consecutive months designated for that purpose.[[206]] Generally, an employee receives credit during an accrual computation period for hours for which he is paid or entitled to payment for the performance of duties or for which he is entitled to payment by the employer on account of a period of time during which no duties are performed, such as vacation, holiday, illness, disability, layoff, jury duty, military duty, or leave of absence.[[207]] In general, an employee who completes 1,000 hours of service during an accrual computation period must be credited with at

---

205 See sec. III.E below.

206 See also 29 C.F.R. 2530.204-2.

207 29 C.F.R. 2530.200b-2(a). Hours of service for which an employee is entitled to payment—for example, for vacation, illness, layoff—are to be credited "irrespective of whether the employment relationship has terminated." 29 C.F.R. 2530.200b-2(a)(2). Hours of service can therefore include hours of accrued vacation or sick leave that are paid, or for which payment is due, on a termination of employment. But see *Hope v. IBEW Local 1245 Pension Trust*, 785 F.2d 826, 7 EBC 1313 (9th Cir. 1986) (terminated staff employees of a union not entitled to 2 weeks credit for vesting based on accrued vacation, even though employees were entitled to receive their accrued vacation pay irrespective of a termination of employment).

Hours of service that are compensated as severance pay may also be required to be credited for participation. See PLR 8031091 (May 9, 1980), reprinted at ¶17,372E CCH Pension Plan Guide. Cf. *Tyson v. Teamsters Local No. 710 Pension Fund*, 811 F.2d 1145, 8 EBC 1324 (7th Cir. 1987) (LMRA §302(c)(5) not a bar to crediting 4 weeks salary paid to participant after he ceased employment in recognition of his long years of service and disability for purposes of 15 year service requirement for disability pension); *Eagar v. Savannah Foods & Indus., Inc.*, 605 F.Supp. 415 (N.D. Ala. 1984) (raising severance pay credit issue, but not deciding it).

Hours of service for participation can also include periods for which back pay is awarded, for example in settlement of a labor law or age, race, or sex discrimination violation. See 29 C.F.R. 2530.200b-2(a)(3) (defining hours of service for determining both vesting years of service and benefit accrual years of participation), 29 C.F.R. 2530.200b-3(e)(1) (including such hours under equivalencies based on counting days, weeks, or months in which an employee has an hour of service). But compare 29 C.F.R. 2530.200b-3(f) (not specifically including such hours under equivalencies based on total earnings or total earnings from the performance of duties during a computation period).

least a partial year of participation.[[208]] However, a plan may require more than 1,000 hours during an accrual computation period for a full year of participation, and in such a situation, the employee who falls short of performing the hours of service required by the plan may be given credit for only a part of a year of participation.[[209]]"[210]

The 12-month computation period for a plan using the conventional method is generally based either on the date when the participant commenced participation under the plan or else the plan year (which in turn is often the calendar year or the corporation's fiscal year). If a plan counts only days or weeks in which a participant has at least one hour of service in determining years of participation, 10 hours per day or 45 hours per week must be credited for each such day or week in computing whether a participant has the 1,000 hours required for at least a partial year of participation.[211] If a plan uses an "hours of service" equivalency that excludes hours that are paid but for which no duties are performed or that uses total earnings divided by an hourly rate to count "hours," 870 of such hours must be substituted for 1,000 hours as the threshold for at least a partial year of participation.[212] When a plan counts only regular time hours, or else bases the determination of hours on earnings from the performance of duties divided by an imputed hourly rate, 750 of such hours are substituted for 1,000 as the threshold.[213] It is important to recognize that when a plan counts hours, directly or through use of an equivalency, but does not state a 12-month accrual computation period, the plan is considered to be using an alternate to the conventional method. The significance of this is that such a plan may not disregard service of less than 1,000 hours in any period.[214]

As stated by the Tax Court, a plan may require more than 1,000 hours for a full year of participation. For example, a plan may require 2,000 hours for a full year of participation, and may credit a participant with 1,000 hours with only one-half of a year of participation.[215] When a participant in such a plan has 1500 hours, he or she must receive credit on a "pro rata basis" of "*at least*" 75 percent of the benefit that would be received with 2,000 hours.[216] A plan may use hourly ranges as

---

[208] 29 C.F.R. 2530.200b-1(a) and 2530.204-2(c)(1).

[209] 29 C.F.R. 2530.200b-1(a) and 2530.204-2(c)(2).

[210] 78 T.C. 541, 3 EBC 1276, at 1280 (1982). Citations by the author are added in the footnotes above to those provided by the court.

[211] 29 C.F.R. 2530.200b-3(e)(1)(i) and (ii).

[212] 29 C.F.R. 2530.200b-3(d)(1) and 2530.200b-3(f)(1).

[213] 29 C.F.R. 2530.200b-3(d)(2) and 2530.200b-3(f)(2) and (3).

[214] See 29 C.F.R. 2530.204-3(a) and (b) (example (2)).

[215] 29 C.F.R. 2530.204-2(c)(4)(i).

[216] Conf. Rep., at 269, 3 ERISA Leg. Hist. 4536 (emphasis added). And see *Janowski v. Teamsters Local No. 710 Pension Fund,* 673 F.2d 931, 3 EBC 1225 (7th Cir. 1982), *vacated and remanded on standing and attorney's fee award,* 463 U.S. 1222 (1983) (plan violated ERISA by requiring a minimum of 20 weeks of work for one-half of a year of participation, with 35 weeks required for a full year, but with no proration provided in between, i.e., under the plan, a participant with any of the number of weeks between 20 and 35 received one-half of a year of participation, but on working 35 weeks a full year of participation was credited; query whether the plan also violated ERISA by providing one-half of a year's credit for 20 weeks of work when a full

long as no participant in any range receives less than a *pro rata* portion of a full year's credit as determined by dividing the participant's number of hours by the hours required for a full year of participation. For example, if 2,000 hours are required for a full year of participation, crediting participants with hours between 1,000 and 1,200 with 6/10 of a year of participation, crediting participants with between 1,201 and 1,400 hours with 7/10 of a year, crediting between 1,401 and 1,600 hours with 8/10 of a year, and crediting a full year of participation for hours in excess of 1,800 is satisfactory.[217] The number of hours required for a full year of participation under a plan "cannot exceed the customary work year for the industry involved."[218] Thus, if the customary work year is 1,500 hours, the number of hours required for a full year of participation cannot exceed 1,500; 1,000 hours of service then has to result in at least 2/3 of a year of participation, with 1,200 hours resulting in at least 3/4 of a year, and so on.[219]

A plan can follow the hours of service regulations, or their equivalencies, in determining whether a participant has the 1,000 hours required for at least a partial year of participation, but then can use a more limited definition of "hours" or "weeks," to determine the exact portion of a full year of participation to which the participant is entitled. The regulations illustrate this with an example in which "hours of service," including sick leave, vacation time, and so forth, are used to compute whether a participant meets the threshold 1,000 hours requirement, but then only "hours worked" are counted in determining the exact portion of a year of participation to which the participant is entitled. Thus, in the example in the regulations, 1,500 hours worked are required for a full year of participation, with a participant who has 1,000 hours worked and 500 other hours of service being credited with only two-thirds of a year of participation.[220] When a plan does this, disclosure to participants of the limitations on the hours or weeks counted in the computation of the partial year to which a participant is actually entitled is a primary consideration. The total number of such hours or weeks required for a full year of participation also must not exceed the customary work year when hours or weeks are computed *on that basis*.[221] Also to be considered is whether the hours or weeks definition is reasonable and consistent for all employees within the same job classification, and whether it produces discrimination in favor of the prohibited group of employees.[222] (As a matter of practice,

---

year of participation was credited with 35 weeks). On remand, the district court held that the plaintiffs lacked standing to raise the part-time service issue; the Seventh Circuit then denied any attorney's fee award. 812 F.2d 295, 8 EBC 1503 (7th Cir. 1987).

[217] 29 C.F.R. 2530.204-2(c)(4)(ii).

[218] Conf. Rep., at 269, 3 ERISA Leg. Hist. 4536, and IRS Doc. 6390 "Minimum Vesting Standards: Defined Benefit Plans" (5-82), reprinted in 456 BNA Pens. Rep. Spec. Supp. (Aug. 8, 1983), at S-33.

[219] 29 C.F.R. 2530.204-2(c)(4)(iii).

[220] *Id.*

[221] See nn. 207 and 208.

[222] 29 C.F.R. 2530.204-2(c)(2) and (c)(4)(iii) and 26 C.F.R. 1.411(b)-1(f)(2).

collectively bargained plans generally use the same hours of service definition for determining the portion of the year of participation to be credited for benefit accruals as for determining whether a participant meets the threshold 1,000 hours of service requirement and for determining the participant's hours of service for vesting.[223])

All hours of service in a computation period, including any hours of service before entry or reentry into a plan, must be credited for determining whether the employee has the threshold 1,000 hours for receiving credit for at least a partial year of participation if an employee enters or reenters a plan during a 12-month accrual computation period. The regulations illustrate this rule with an example of an employee who actually commences participation on July 1 under a plan that uses the calendar year as its accrual computation period and that requires 1,800 hours for a full year's accrual. In the example, the employee has 100 hours of service in each month during the computation period. For purposes of determining if the employee has 1,000 hours of service within the computation period, the hours of service *before* July 1—i.e., during the waiting period before actual commencement of participation—as well as those after July 1, are required to be credited. For this purpose, the employee then has 1,200 hours of service, well in excess of the 1,000 hours required. For determining the part of a full year's accrual to which the employee is entitled, however, the plan is only required to consider the hours *after* July 1 that are within the computation period. Therefore, in determining the part of a full year's accrual the employee is actually to be credited with, the plan need only consider 600 hours (from July 1 through December 31), and thus may only credit the employee with one-third of a full year of participation (600/1800).[224]

a. Seasonal and maritime worker rules. In any seasonal industry where the customary period of employment is less than 1,000 hours during a calendar year, ERISA directs the Secretary of Labor to redefine the threshold level of 1,000 hours of service that may be required to receive credit for at least a partial year of participation to a level that takes the customary hours in such industries into account.[225] These regulations have never been issued. Under a 1976 interpretive bulletin, the completion of 500 or more hours of service in a seasonal industry was to trigger at least a partial year of participation.[226] However, because of comments that the interpretive bulletin's definition of "seasonal industry" included plans that would "generally be recognized as nonseasonal," the bulletin was rescinded almost as soon as it was issued.[227] Since that time, no regulations or other interpretive guidance

---

[223] See J. MacDonald, *Pension Handbook for Union Negotiators,* at 62 ("[m]ost negotiated plans pick one service counting system and use that system to determine vesting and eligibility service as well as benefit service;" use of two or more different systems is "confusing").

[224] 29 C.F.R. 2530.204-2(c)(4)(iv).

[225] ERISA §204(b)(4)(D) (Code §411(b)(4)(D)).

[226] Interpretive Bulletin 76-1, 41 Fed. Reg. 3290 (Jan. 22, 1976).

[227] Interpretive Bulletin 76-2, 41 Fed. Reg. 7749 (Feb. 20, 1976).

has been issued to implement the statutory provision. As noted before, however, a plan cannot use a higher hours total for a *full* year of participation than is customarily worked in the industry involved.[228] But this requirement by itself may not be enough. For example, in an industry in which the customary number of hours worked per year is 1,200, a plan could not require more than 1,200 hours for a full year of participation, but it could still require 1,000 hours before providing credit for even a partial year of participation.[229]

In the maritime industry, 125 days of service is the minimum standard threshold for receiving credit for at least a partial year of participation.[230] The Secretary of Labor has issued regulations defining the "maritime industry," detailing the application of this rule, and also permitting use of the conventional method's 1,000 hours of service rule or other equivalencies in lieu of counting days.[231]

b. Top-heavy plan rules. Under a top-heavy plan, a participant must accrue a full year's minimum nonintegrated benefit after just 1,000 hours of service during the 12-month computation period the plan uses for determining years of participation. If the plan does not specify a 12-month computation period, the plan's alternative method must credit all periods that are required to be credited under this rule.[232]

c. Prohibited double proration of partial years of participation under salary-based formulas. In practice, the counting of hours within computation periods, and even the use of equivalencies to hours within 12-month computation periods, is likely to be found predominantly among plans that provide benefits on a flat dollar basis, e.g., $15 per month per year of credited service. But when a plan uses the conventional method for crediting years of participation and also bases its benefits on a percentage of salary, the major rule is that the plan may not "double prorate" partial years of participation. That is, the plan may not credit only a partial year of participation and then compound the fractional effect of the partial year's credit by multiplying it by only a partial year of salary in determining the participant's benefit accruals for the year.[233]

To illustrate, a plan that provides one percent of each year's salary multiplied by years of participation cannot credit a participant with one-half of a year of participation for a year in which the participant

---

[228] See the description of the conventional method for crediting years of participation immediately above.

[229] As mentioned in ch. 5, sec. III.D, on the absence of regulations to implement Congress' intent that seasonal workers be subject to a more liberal standard for measuring vesting years of service than the conventional 1,000 hour standard, a court could compel the issuance of implementing regulations if it finds that agency action is being "unlawfully withheld or unreasonably delayed." 5 U.S.C. §706(1). And see *Farmworkers Justice Fund, Inc. v. Brock,* 811 F.2d 613 (D.C. Cir. 1987); *AARP v. EEOC,* 8 EBC 1227 (D.D.C. 1987) (citing other decisions).

[230] ERISA §204(b)(4)(E) (Code §411(b)(4)(E)).

[231] 29 C.F.R. 2530.200b-6, 7, and 8.

[232] 26 C.F.R. 1.416-1, Q&A M-4.

[233] 29 C.F.R. 2530.204-2(d).

only worked six months, and then compound the partial year of credit by multiplying it by only six months of salary. The effect of doing so, assuming salary at an annual rate of $20,000, would be as follows:

1 percent × $10,000 (6-months' salary)
× ½ year of participation = $50 annual retirement benefit.

Compared to this, a participant who worked the full year at the same annual salary rate would receive:

1 percent × $20,000 (12-months' salary)
× 1 year of participation = $200 annual retirement benefit.

Thus, a participant who worked one-half of a year would receive only one-quarter of the benefits if double proration were permitted. To prevent this, a salary-based plan must choose between either using the part year's salary in the formula together with a full year of participation, or using a part year of participation with an imputed full year's salary.[234]

IRS regulations, described further below on double proration under alternate methods, also require salary-based plans using a final average of pay or a highest average of pay over a base period of 10 years or less to impute a full year's salary in computing the plan's compensation average whenever a participant is credited with a partial year of participation in a final period of service.

2. Alternate Methods

Salary-based plans and collectively bargained single-employer plans generally use other approaches than the conventional method to measure years of participation for purposes of benefit accruals. In *Standard Oil Co. v. Commissioner*, the Tax Court emphasized that a range of alternate methods are acceptable "provided that the method satisfies the requirements of 29 C.F.R. 2530.204-3(a)."[235] Specifically, the regulation states:

> "[A] defined benefit pension plan may determine an employee's service for purposes of benefit accrual on the basis of accrual computation periods, as specified in §2530.204-2, *or* on any other basis which is reasonable and consistent and which takes into account all covered service during the employee's participation in the plan which is included in a period of service required to be taken into account under section 202(b) of the Act and section 410(a)(5) of the Code. If, however, a plan determines an employee's service for purposes of benefit accrual on a basis other than computation periods, it must be possible to prove that, despite the fact that benefit accrual under the plan is not based on computation periods, the plan's provisions meet at least one of the three benefit accrual rules of section 204(b)(1) of the Act and section 411(b)(1) of the Code under all circumstances. Further, a plan which does not provide for benefit accrual

---

[234] *Id.*

[235] 78 T.C. 541, 3 EBC 1276, at 1279 (1982).

> on the basis of computation periods *may not* disregard service under section 204(b)[(4)](C) of the Act and section 411(b)[(4)](C) of the Code [which otherwise allow computation periods in which a participant had less than 1,000 hours of service to be disregarded]."

The requirements in the regulation for an alternate to the "conventional" method are thus threefold:

(1) The method must be "reasonable and consistent";

(2) The method must take into account "all covered service during the employee's participation in the plan which is included in a period of service required to be taken into account [under the conventional method];" if proof is necessary, the plan has the burden of proving that "despite the fact that benefit accrual under the plan is not based on computation periods, the plan's provisions meet at least one of the three benefit accrual rules . . . under all circumstances"; and

(3) When a plan does *not* designate a 12-month computation period, it may not disregard years of participation with less than 1,000 hours of service, as is permitted under the conventional method.

a. Three acceptable alternatives. Provided that these three requirements are met, the regulations illustrate methods that may be acceptable alternates to the conventional method for measuring years of participation:

- *Career Compensation.* A defined benefit formula based on a percentage of compensation earned in a participant's career or during participation, with no variation in benefits depending on hours completed in given periods.
- *Credited Hours.* A defined benefit formula under which an employee is credited with a specified amount of accrual for each hour of service (or hour worked or regular time hour) completed by the employee during his or her career.
- *Elapsed Time.* A defined benefit plan formula under which a participant's service with an employer is based on the total period of service beginning with the participation commencement date and ending with his or her "severance from service" date. This period is expressed in years, months, and days. The severance from service date is extended to include credit for up to 12 months of absence for any reason other than a quit, discharge, death, or retirement, e.g., a layoff or other leave of absence, whether or not paid.[236]

A career average pay plan is, as the name suggests, the most likely type of plan to use the career compensation method. Plans offering

---

[236] 29 C.F.R. 2530.204-3(b) (examples (1)-(3)), and see 26 C.F.R. 1.410(a)-7(e) and (b)(2), instead of the incorrect cross-reference appearing in these regulations, for a description of the elapsed time method.

fixed dollar benefits may be more likely to use the credited hours method (and as stated before, one significant consequence of using this method without a computation period is that the plan may not then disregard periods with less than 1,000 hours service). Final or highest average pay plans seem most likely to use the elapsed time method, which in its most basic form means that the plan credits years, months, and days from the participation commencement date to the severance from service date under the plan's benefit formula.

Under the elapsed time regulations, up to 12 months of absence "for any other reason" than a quit, discharge, death, or retirement must be included within a participant's years, months, and days of credited participation, whether or not the absence is paid. Until the end of such an absence, the participant is not considered to have a severance from service.[237] However, in *Standard Oil Co. v. Commissioner*, the Tax Court upheld Standard Oil's use of a modified elapsed time method, that, unlike the elapsed time method in the IRS's regulations, limited credit for unpaid absences to the first 31 days of absence and excluded *any* period of absence during which an employee was on strike or locked out. The court said that the regulatory elapsed time method was just an example of the methods that could be used. Since the Standard Oil elapsed time method did not disregard service of less than 1,000 hours, covered all periods of participation required to be covered under the conventional method regulations, and since the court could find nothing unreasonable or inconsistent about the specific method, it was deemed acceptable.[238] (While the *Standard Oil* decision thus permits the elapsed time regulation to be modified for purposes of benefit accruals, it may be noted that many plans do not do this, and instead use the same elapsed time service counting rule for both benefit accruals and vesting.[239])

To determine whether a plan using an alternate method is disregarding any service required to be included under the conventional method, a 12-month computation period must be implied. Following analogous cases on computing vesting service when a plan has not stated a 12-month computation period, the comparison would seem to be based on hours of service within the 12-month computation period beginning with the date of the participant's commencement of participation.[240] In addition to covering all periods of participation required to be covered under such a comparison, the key and most favorable

---

[237] 26 C.F.R. 1.410(a)-7(e)(1) and (b)(2). The breadth of "for any other reason" than a quit, discharge, death, or retirement is discussed in ch. 5, sec. III.B.2. See also sec. III.B.5 in this chapter on credit for periods of layoff or other absence.

[238] 78 T.C. 541, 3 EBC 1276, at 1279 (1982).

[239] See J. MacDonald, *Pension Handbook for Union Negotiators*, at 62 (most negotiated plans use the same system for both vesting and benefit accruals; when different systems are used, the result is "confusing" for participants).

[240] Cf. *Gennamore v. Buffalo Sheet Metals, Inc., Pension Plan*, 568 F.Supp. 931, 5 EBC 1268 (W.D.N.Y. 1983); *Tucci v. Edgewood Country Club*, 459 F.Supp. 940 (W.D. Pa. 1978) (both implying vesting computation periods based on the employee's date of hire, rather than some other period that an employer might conceivably have chosen). For years of participation, the analogous starting point is the date of actual commencement of participation.

point for participants is that under an alternate method, no partial years of participation can be ignored, whereas years in which a participant had less than 1,000 hours of service may be disregarded under the conventional method. The requirement that an alternate method must also be "reasonable and consistent" could have substance, but as the *Standard Oil* opinion demonstrates, courts may not be overly critical of some inconsistencies.

b. Prohibited double proration of partial years. In a plan using an alternate method for crediting years of participation, one remaining question is whether double proration has crept in through use of partial years of credit combined with partial years' compensation under the plan's accrued benefit formula. Career average pay plans are unlikely to use partial years of participation, but rather will simply give the participant the plan's promised percentage of whatever compensation is earned in a year. The question of double proration is more likely to arise in a highest or final average pay plan that uses elapsed time years, months, and days multiplied by a stated percentage of the participant's final or highest average salary. The issue in these cases is whether the plan is implicitly double prorating when it credits a participant with a fractional year of participation without adjusting salary earned during the fractional part of the year to a full year's salary in computing the final or highest average of salary.

The significance of this issue may best be illustrated. Assume an employee receives $2,000 annual salary increases. In 1980, his salary is $18,000; in 1981, $20,000; in 1982, $22,000; in 1983, $24,000; in 1984, $26,000; and in June of 1985, when he separates from service, his salary is $28,000 on an annual basis, having been increased to that level on January 1, 1985. If the plan provides a benefit of 1½ percent of a final five consecutive year average of salary multiplied by years of credited service, there are basically three options: First, the plan could use the 1980–1984 five-year average salary, in which case, the final five-year average is $22,000. Second, the plan could use the June 1980-June 1985 salary, in which case the final average is $23,000. Or third, the plan could impute a full year's salary for 1985 and use 1981-1985, in which case the final five consecutive year average would be $24,000. If the participant has 11.5 years of credited service, the difference between these options is an annual retirement benefit of $3,795 (using the $22,000 average), $3,967.50 (using the $23,000 average), or $4,140 (using the $24,000 average).

The Department of Labor's regulations on double proration do not directly address which of these options is to be used.[241] However, applying the principle of the regulations, it seems that the proper test for double proration is whether the additional benefits from the fractional year of credit are less than a commensurate fraction of the benefits

[241] See 29 C.F.R. 2530.204-2(d).

that would accrue from a full year of participation. Thus, in the example, at the end of 1984, the participant would have 11 years of participation and an average salary of $22,000, for a benefit of (11 years × 1.5 percent × $22,000 =) $3,630. If the participant continued work through the end of 1985, he or she would have 12 years of participation and a final average salary of $24,000, for a benefit of (12 years × 1.5 percent × $24,000 =) $4,320. An additional $690 in annual retirement benefits would thus accrue for a full year of participation. For one-half of a year of participation, the participant must then have at least one-half of that benefit accrual, or $345, to prevent double proration. Added to the benefit at the start of the year of $3,630, this produces a total of $3,975. Thus, the first alternative, which did not take any of the 1985 salary into account, is ruled out. This leaves the second and third alternatives as acceptable under the Department of Labor's double proration regulations.

The third alternative, which imputes a full year's salary based on the final annual rate for use under the salary average, may be required in two instances. Under 26 C.F.R. 1.411(a)-7(c)(5), the IRS requires that the normal retirement benefit for purposes of the three benefit accrual methods be based on an imputed full year of compensation if an employee is credited with less than a full year of participation and the plan's compensation average is based on (1) a final average of salary, or (2) a highest average of salary over a base period of 10 or less years.[242] Thus, under the IRS's benefit accrual regulations, an employee in a plan using the *final* five years' average salary, or a highest five-year average out of a final 10, is entitled to have his or her salary for the last fractional year imputed to a full year's salary for inclusion in the final or highest average. On the other hand, if the formula uses the highest consecutive years out of *any* years, the IRS regulations would not require this.

In *Korn v. Levine Bros. Iron Works Corp.*, a district court handled the double proration issue as a matter of plan interpretation. The plan in *Korn* stated that the "average of the highest five consecutive years" of compensation was to be multiplied by a flat percentage of 36½ percent to determine a participant's benefit. The plan's trustees argued that "years" referred to "plan years," and thus that Korn, who had retired in the middle of a plan year, was not entitled to have his last

---

[242] Specifically, 26 C.F.R. 1.411(a)-7(c)(5) provides:
"If a defined benefit plan bases its normal retirement benefits on employee compensation, the compensation must reflect the compensation which would have been paid for a full year of participation within the meaning of [ERISA §204]. If an employee works less than a full year of participation, the compensation used to determine benefits under the plan for such year of participation must be multiplied by the ratio of the number of hours for a complete year of participation to the number of hours worked in such year. A plan whose benefit formula is computed on a computation base which cannot decrease is not required to adjust employee compensation in [this] manner. Thus, for example, if a plan provided for a benefit based on an employee's compensation for his highest five consecutive years or a separate benefit for each year of participation based on the employee's compensation for such year, the plan would not have to so adjust compensation. However, if a plan provided a benefit based on an employee's compensation for the employee's last five years or the five highest consecutive years out of the last 10 years, the compensation would have to be so adjusted."

months' salary included in the computation unless compensation in those months by themselves constituted one of his highest five consecutive years. The court found that the trustees interpretation was arbitrary, stating that no justification had been offered for using "plan years" when "years" were referred to. Rather, the court held "years" must mean the highest five consecutive *12-month* periods of compensation, which would pick up Korn's final months of salary. As is typical, the court noted, Korn's salary had been increasing, and therefore the inclusion of the final months increased his benefits.[243]

E. Measuring Years for Contribution Allocations Under Defined Contribution Plans

As a matter of consistent policy, ERISA should require defined contribution plans to provide at least partial credit for annual contribution allocations if a participant has over 1,000 hours in the 12-month computation period ending with the annual allocation date designated by the plan (or *pro rata* credit for the part of the year worked, with no threshold for a partial year, if a plan uses a "reasonable and consistent" alternative). If contributions are allocated based on a percentage of salary—for example, six percent—contributions could then be prorated for the partial year, either through a partial year's credit with a full year's imputed salary, or a full year's credit with a partial year's salary.

Defined contribution plans are, however, not required to provide any partial credit for a participant with over 1,000 hours of service in a year. Rather they may provide that a participant is entitled to *no* contributions unless he or she is employed on the plan's contribution allocation date, for example, December 31 of each year. The inapplicability of the years of participation definition to defined contribution plans is founded on the fact that the term "years of participation" is used in Section 204 only with reference to benefit accruals under defined benefit plans. This distinction is firmly established in both Department of Labor and Treasury regulations,[244] and most fully articulated in Revenue Ruling 76-250.[245] Revenue Ruling 76-250 is remarkable in that that there are no *per se* exceptions. Thus, if a defined contribution plan provides annual allocations only to participants who are employed on December 31, and a participant is terminated on December 15 because of a downturn in business, or retires on

---

[243] 574 F.Supp. 836, 4 EBC 2533 (S.D.N.Y. 1983). In *Korn*, the IRS's regulation did not apply because the plan used the highest 5 consecutive years without limitation to a final period. The Department of Labor's double proration regulation was not relevant because Korn was entitled to the plan's full flat percentage normal retirement benefit, rather than a portion of that benefit based on a percentage of pay multiplied by years and *partial* years of participation.

[244] See 29 C.F.R. 2530.200b-1(b) and 26 C.F.R. 1.411(b)-1(f).

[245] Employees can also be required to be employed at year-end to receive the minimum contributions required under top-heavy plans, but if so employed, they must receive the minimum contribution even if they do not have 1,000 hours of service within the year. 26 C.F.R. 1.416-1, Q&A M-10.

December 15 because he or she has reached age 65 or age 70, no contribution is required to be allocated to the participant's account for the year. Following this rule, in *Ovitz v. Jefferies & Co.*, a participant separated from service less than a month before a plan's allocation date, but a district court held that the participant had no right to any part of that year's allocation.[246] Similarly, in *Aronson v. Servus Rubber Division*, participants were not entitled to year-end profit-sharing contributions when a plan amendment eliminated employment at their plant (which was in the process of being shut down) from coverage under the plan two months before the plan's year-end allocation of contributions.[247]

Revenue Ruling 76-250 holds out the possibility that a failure to allocate contributions to participants who are not employed on a specific date may in some cases result in Code Section 401(a)(4) discrimination by reason of a resulting disproportion in contributions, as a percentage of compensation, going to employees who are officers, shareholders, or highly compensated. For this purpose, "[t]he significance of an employee completing a 'year of participation' is that he or she must be included in the plan to determine whether or not there is discrimination in that year in contributions in favor of the prohibited group."[248] In smaller plans where there has been turnover of rank and file employees with a year of participation before the year-end date, discrimination may frequently result unless an allocation of contributions is made to these participants, as well as to the participants who were still employed on the specific allocation date.

Of perhaps more general utility for participants is the fact that many defined contribution plans either do not adhere to as arbitrary a rule as permitted or do not both provide for the rule in the plan and adequately describe it in the summary plan description. In *Dennard v. Richards Group, Inc.*, for example, it was undisputed that participants were entitled to contributions and reallocated forfeitures under the plan's terms unless they had a "break in service" in the year before the allocation date.[249] In other cases, a plan's terms may provide that any person who is a "participant" at the end of the year is entitled to contributions with much the same effect as in *Dennard.*

Still other plans are ambiguous. In *Elby v. Livernois Engineering Co.*, a profit-sharing plan participant was held to be entitled to a portion of the full year's contribution allocation when he had worked for part of the year and ambiguities in the plan were construed against the draftsman.[250] However, in *Budwig v. Natelson's Inc. Profit Sharing Retirement*, a profit-sharing plan ambiguously provided that an annual

---

[246] 574 F.Supp. 488, 4 EBC 2559 (N.D. Ill. 1983).

[247] 730 F.2d 12, 5 EBC 1343 (1st Cir. 1984), *cert. denied*, 469 U.S. 1017 (1984).

[248] IRS Doc. 6393 "Coverage and Discrimination" (5-82).

[249] 681 F.2d 306, 3 EBC 1769 (5th Cir. 1982).

[250] 194 N.W.2d 429 (Mich. Ct.App. 1972). See also *Lampley v. Celebrity Homes, Inc.*, 594 P.2d 605 (Colo.App. 1979) (employment on contribution allocation date not required for allocation absent clear expression); *Lemmon v. Cedar Point, Inc.*, 406 F.2d 94, at 97 (6th Cir. 1969)

allocation of profit-sharing contributions was due if an individual was a "participant" in the plan on the allocation date. A former employee contended that he was a "participant" in the plan on that date because he had 1,000 or more hours of service during the 12-month period ending on that date—even though he was not employed on the allocation date. The district court held, however, that the plaintiff's interpretation would have made redundant plan language providing that "You must be a participant on January 31 [the allocation date] *and* have worked at least one thousand (1,000) hours."[251]

Although a participant may or may not be entitled under a plan's terms to year-end contributions on account of a lack of year-end employment, the participant must still be entitled to an allocation of the plan's earnings, based on an at least annual valuation, until the account balance is distributed.[252] However, here again, if a participant accepts a complete distribution of his or her account balance on December 15, and the plan's annual allocation of the year's earnings does not take place until December 31, the plan may deny the participant a *pro rata* share of that year's earnings, if the plan so provides and if prohibited discrimination does not result.

IV. Protection of Accrued Benefits Against Decreases

A. From Increases in Service or Age

Despite what may be otherwise permitted under the benefit accrual rules, ERISA Section 204(b)(1)(G) (Code Section 411(b)(1)(G)) prohibits a participant's accrued benefits under a defined benefit plan from ever decreasing on account of an increase in service or age under the plan.[253] Basically, Section 204(b)(1)(G) assures that a participant never has less in accrued benefits than he or she would have had upon an earlier separation from service because of having continued to work or having grown older. The application of this bottom-line constraint has been illustrated above concerning the effect credits for uncompensated years, or years after a cut in pay, might otherwise have under

---

(ambiguity in stock option agreement on whether employment at the end of year required for stock options to be construed in employee's favor since rights "almost earned").

Vacation pay plans are also generally construed to require payment of a prorated portion of an employee's annual vacation period on a termination from employment before the year's end "[a]bsent contrary indication." See *Schneider v. Electric Auto Lite Co.*, 456 F.2d 366, at 371 (6th Cir. 1972); *Telescope Folding Furniture Co.*, 49 LA 837 (Cox, 1967) (citing numerous other decisions to the same effect).

[251] 576 F.Supp. 661, at 666 (D. Neb. 1982), *aff'd,* 720 F.2d 977 (8th Cir. 1983) (emphasis added).

[252] Rev. Ruls. 73-103 and 80-155. See also *Dennard v. Richards Group, Inc., supra,* but cf. *Ganze v. Dart Indus., Inc.*, 741 F.2d 790, 5 EBC 2309 (5th Cir. 1984) (quarterly dividends on company stock held in a profit-sharing plan not required to be allocated to participants whose employment terminated before the end of the quarter; opinion unclear on whether the participants' account balances had been distributed before the end of the quarter).

[253] See also 26 C.F.R. 1.411(b)-1(d)(3) and Conf. Rep. on the 1986 Tax Reform Act, H.R. Rep. 99-841, at II-428, [1986] U.S. Code Cong. & Ad. News 4516.

final average pay formulas.[254] Excess formulas based on a percentage of a participant's final or highest average pay above a moving average related to an average of the Social Security taxable wage base also might otherwise decrease a participant's accrued benefits below their level the year before if the steep recent increases in the Social Security taxable wage base have outrun increases in the participant's average compensation.[255]

B. From Plan Amendments

1. Protection Under ERISA Section 204(g)

ERISA prohibits plan amendments that decrease or otherwise cut back on accrued benefits. ERISA Section 204(g) (Code Section 411(d)(6)) provides:

> "The accrued benefit of a participant under a plan may not be decreased by an amendment of a plan. . . ."

Prime examples of amendments contemplated by Section 204(g) are amendments decreasing a unit benefit formula from 1½ percent of final pay for each year of participation to one percent of final pay, or decreasing a flat dollar unit benefit from $15 per month at retirement for each year of participation to $10 per month. Under Section 204(g), such amendments can be made with prospective effect, i.e., they can apply to benefits accrued in future years of participation, but they cannot decrease the accrued benefits that a participant has already earned from prior years of participation.[256] A similar type of plan amendment might decrease a flat percentage normal retirement benefit from 45 percent of final pay to 30 percent of final pay. Again, such a change would be permitted to take effect prospectively, but under Section 204(g), it would not be permitted to decrease the portion of the 45 percent of final pay benefit that had already accrued under the benefit accrual method the plan uses.

Related types of amendments that have the potential to decrease accrued benefits of participants, unless Section 204(g) is applied, include changes in a plan's definition of "compensation," changes in the number of years of salary used in a compensation average (or a more major amendment, such as from a final pay formula to a career average formula), an increase in the percentage of a Social Security benefit offset or in the covered compensation level used under an excess plan, an increase in employee contributions under a plan, or a change in a

---

[254] See sec. III.B.5 above.

[255] See ch. 3, sec. VIII.F.7.

[256] See *Hoover v. Cumberland Md. Area Teamsters Pension Fund,* 756 F.2d 977, 6 EBC 1401 (3d Cir. 1985), *cert. denied,* 474 U.S. 845 (1985).

plan's benefit accrual method.[257] Still more subtle types of changes that can decrease accrued benefits include a change to a later "normal retirement age,"[258] new restrictions on the receipt of accrued benefits at retirement,[259] or a decrease in an automatic cost-of-living adjustment previously offered under a plan.[260] The IRS's regulations also establish that the types of amendments subject to Section 204(g) are not limited to those which directly modify a percentage or dollar amount in the formula. Rather, Section 204(g) covers all amendments that "directly or indirectly" affect the computation of accrued benefits under the plan. To illustrate indirect changes, the regulations state that:

> "Plan provisions indirectly affecting accrued benefits include, for example, provisions relating to years of service and breaks in service for determining benefit accrual, and to actuarial factors for determining optional or early retirement benefits."[261]

When a plan amendment decreases a participant's accrued benefits, Section 204(g)'s prohibition is read strictly. In Revenue Ruling 79-325, Section 204(g) was ruled applicable when a plan amendment was adopted and placed in effect in the middle of a plan year reducing participants' accrued benefits to the benefits accrued as of the first of the plan year. Under Revenue Ruling 79-325, the amendment could only apply to benefits earned after the precise date of adoption.[262] Effective at the beginning of 1986, ERISA Section 204(h) also provides that a "single-employer plan may not be amended so as to provide for a significant reduction in the rate of future benefit accrual" unless advance written notice of the amendment is provided to participants not less than 15 days before its effective date.[263]

The right to an allocation of a defined contribution plan's investment earnings is not considered a part of the participant's accrued

---

[257] See 26 C.F.R. 1.416-1, Q&A T-41 and 42 (changes in compensation definition) and IRS Doc. 6678 "Plan Termination Standards" (4-81) (changes in a plan's benefit accrual method included).

[258] Rev. Rul. 81-210, sec. 3 (finding that such a change might decrease accrued benefits under a plan complying with the fractional rule for benefit accruals). More generally, a plan amendment increasing a plan's normal retirement age decreases the value of the participant's accrued benefits because the participant loses years of benefit payments. For example, when the normal retirement age is increased to age 70 from age 65, a participant could lose as many as 5 years of benefit payments.

[259] See *Hauck v. Eschbacher*, 665 F.2d 843, 2 EBC 2202 (8th Cir. 1981) (new postemployment competition restriction for employees who vested under more liberal vesting standards than the ERISA-required schedules reduced accrued benefits in violation of plan provision which protected accrued benefits from amendment; no need to directly reach statutory issue).

[260] *Shaw v. IAM Pension Plan*, 750 F.2d 1458, 6 EBC 1193 (9th Cir. 1985), *cert. denied*, 471 U.S. 1137 (1985). It is rare for an automatic cost-of-living adjustment to be in a private pension plan.

[261] 26 C.F.R. 1.411(d)-3(b). When one amendment decreases benefits, e.g., when a definition of salary is changed from a 3- to a 10-year average, but another plan amendment simultaneously increases benefits in another respect, whether accrued benefits have been decreased under §204(g) is determined by looking at the combined effect of the plan amendments on each participant's accrued benefits. See 26 C.F.R. 1.411(d)-3(b).

[262] See also Rev. Rul. 79-215.

[263] ERISA §204(h), as amended by P.L. 99-272. For plan amendments adopted between Jan. 1, 1986, and April 7, 1986, notice was required within 60 days of April 7, 1986. §11006(b) of P.L. 99-272.

benefits insofar as triggering the protection of Section 204(g). But when a defined contribution plan is amended to convert the plan to a defined benefit plan, a fiduciary duty to avoid "self-interested plan administration" can require continued allocation of earnings at a market rate of interest to the account balances existing before the plan amendment until the date that the account balances are distributed.[264]

Limited exceptions to the general prohibition on defined benefit plan amendments decreasing accrued benefits are also provided for:

- Amendments pursuant to ERISA Section 302(c)(8) (Code Section 412(c)(8)), which permit plans to decrease accrued benefits retroactively to the first day of the plan year ending within two and a half months of the amendment (or to the first day of the plan year ending within two *years* of the amendment for a multiemployer plan) if necessitated by "substantial business hardship" with no other alternative, such as a funding waiver, that will allow the employer, or employers, to continue to maintain the plan;[265]
- Amendments pursuant to ERISA Section 4244A(a)(1), which permits reductions in benefits accrued under benefit increases granted within the previous five years if a multiemployer plan is in "reorganization" as defined in ERISA Section 4241;
- Amendments to multiemployer plans "terminated by mass withdrawal" under Section 4281, which requires reductions in accrued benefits resulting from benefit increases granted within the previous five years to the extent necessary to bring the plan's liabilities into equilibrium with its long-run resources; and
- Suspension of benefits, which are effectively amendments, for "insolvent" multiemployer plans under Section 4245(a), which requires reductions in pay status benefits down to the PBGC's insurance limits to the extent necessary to enable a plan to pay benefits as they come due in the plan year.[266]

Reductions in accrued benefits are also effectively permitted by plan amendments terminating single-employer plans at a time when the

---

[264] *Hickerson v. Velsicol Chem. Corp.*, 778 F.2d 365, 6 EBC 2545, at 2556 (7th Cir. 1985), *cert. denied*, 479 U.S. ___ (1986). Another alternative in *Hickerson* might have been to require the employer to determine the deferred annuities that could be purchased with the account balances on the open market before the amendment converting the plan to a defined benefit plan and then to protect the participants' account balances in that annuity form.

[265] "Substantial business hardship" is defined in ERISA §303(b) (Code §412(d)(2)). See also Conf. Rep., at 286, 3 ERISA Leg. Hist. 4553, and *Nichols v. Trustees of Asbestos Workers Pension Plan*, 3 EBC 1726 (D.D.C. 1982). Procedural rules for obtaining substantial business hardship determinations from the IRS for purposes of funding waivers are contained in Rev. Proc. 79-18. And see Rev. Rul. 79-215 (extending Rev. Proc. 79-18 to collectively bargained plans). To obtain approval for a retroactive reduction in accrued benefits, a separate application must be made to the Secretary of the Treasury and the Secretary must make the additional finding that no other course of action, such as a funding waiver, is viable. The statutory delegation of this authority to the Department of Labor was altered by Reorganization Plan No. 4 of 1978. See 5 U.S.C.A. App. 1.

[266] All of these exceptions are discussed in ch. 13 on special multiemployer plan termination rules and insurance limitations.

plan's benefits are not fully funded.[267] After ERISA was enacted, a special exemption from ERISA Section 204(g) was provided under Revenue Ruling 76-378 for plans that adopted interim plan provisions in accordance with temporary regulations issued for compliance with ERISA (collectively known as the ERISA Guidelines) if the plan was later amended to adopt plan provisions permitted under final regulations or rules.[268] For an amendment to fall under this exemption, use of the exemption must be conspicuously and specifically stated at the beginning of the plan document.[269]

As numerous as these exceptions may seem, they are relatively rare in practice. As a result, the general rule that accrued benefits may not be decreased by a plan amendment has considerable force. The courts have, however, read the "amendment" requirement strictly. In *Stewart v. National Shopmen Pension Fund*, the U.S. Court of Appeals for the District of Columbia Circuit held that a multiemployer plan could cancel accrued benefits based on past service credits by invoking an existing plan provision conditioning such credits on the continuation of the contribution obligation of the employer with respect to which the past service credits were granted. The court held that such a cutback was not a plan "amendment" within the meaning of Section 204(g) because it was done under authority that was in place before the past service credits were granted.[270]

2. *Benefit Accruals After an Amendment Decreasing the Normal Retirement Benefit*

When an accrued benefit is protected under Section 204(g), one major issue is what this means in terms of future benefit accruals under the plan's amended formula. This issue is seemingly simple: For example, when a plan's benefits are reduced from 1½ percent of pay to one percent of pay, the benefits accrued under the 1½ percent of pay formula are protected by Section 204(g), and thereafter, benefits accruing under the one percent of pay formula must add to the protected accrued benefits. Some practitioners, however, argue that the issue is not so simple, and that a second method is available, called the "greater of" method, under which the accrued benefit under the old, more favorable formula may be set off against accruals determined as if all years had been under the new formula, until all benefits under the old formula are in effect leveled off to the new, less favorable rate. Unless the participant separates from service before this leveling off

---

[267] Technically, the "accrued benefit" cannot be reduced by the termination of a single-employer plan. See Rev. Rul. 85-6. But the plan's funding can limit the amount of the accrued benefit that is actually paid.

[268] The same exemption extended to the election requirement under ERISA §203(c)(1)(B) (Code §411(a)(10)(B)) for changes in a plan's vesting schedule.

[269] Rev. Rul. 76-378.

[270] 730 F.2d 1552, 4 EBC 1518 (D.C. Cir. 1984), *cert. denied,* 469 U.S. 834 (1984). And see sec. III.C.6 (on past service cancellations).

process is complete, the greater of method would thus ultimately make the participant's accrued benefits equal to those that would have applied if the change in the plan's formula had originally been retroactive.

To illustrate how this works, assume a plan provides a benefit of 1½ percent of a highest five-year average of pay, and that on a year-end date, the sponsoring employer amends the plan to prospectively offer a reduced benefit of one percent of the same highest five-year average:

Participant A has 20 years under the old formula, and thus an accrued benefit of 30 percent of his highest five-year average of pay,

Participant B has 10 years under the old formula, and thus an accrued benefit of 15 percent of her highest average of pay, and

Participant C has 0 years under the old formula, and thus has an accrued benefit of 0 percent of his highest average of pay.

Under Section 204(g), it is undisputed that the "accrued benefits" of all three participants must be protected from any decrease on account of the amendment. However, if the greater of method is acceptable, instead of adding benefits accrued under the amended formula to the protected accrued benefits, the plan might provide that each participant's accrued benefit after the change is the greater of: (1) his or her accrued benefit before the change, or (2) his or her accrued benefit with all years computed on the new basis. The effect of this in terms of future benefits accruals would be:

Participant A accrues *no* new benefits for the next 10 years (assuming highest pay remains the same) before finally beginning to accrue new benefits at the one percent rate.

Participant B accrues *no* new benefits for the next five years (assuming highest pay remains the same) before finally beginning to accrue new benefits at the one percent rate, and

Participant C immediately begins to accrue benefits at the new one percent rate.

As this example shows, the greater of method discriminates against workers who have the most years of participation under the old formula, who, in turn, are generally older workers. On this basis alone, the greater of method may be a subterfuge for age discrimination sufficient to overcome the "bona fide" plan exception of the ADEA.[271]

The problem with the greater of method is that it may not comply with the ERISA benefit accrual methods. ERISA's legislative history and the IRS's regulations are not as clear as they could be on what constitutes compliance with the accrual rules after a benefit *decrease.*

---

[271] If the "greater of" method discriminates in favor of employees who are officers, shareholders or highly compensated, e.g., because rank and file employees are primarily affected by the use of the method, the method may be objectionable under Code §401(a)(4) as well. See S. Rep. 98-575, at 27, [1984] U.S. Code Cong. & Ad. News 2547, at 2573 (suggesting that the reduction of a benefit may result in Code discrimination).

All of the examples in the legislative history and regulations dealing with changes in benefit formulas deal with benefit increases (reflecting a more upbeat economic outlook). The inarguable point, however, is that in the example above, future benefit accruals for participants A and B are clearly backloaded by the greater of method because A accrues *no* new benefits for up to 10 years, and B accrues *no* new benefits for up to five years, before the new one percent formula begins adding to their accrued benefits. The second inarguable point is that all participants are not treated alike under the greater of method. Instead, each participant winds up with a different accrual pattern.

An examination of the three benefit accrual methods reveals that the pattern of benefit accruals produced under the greater of method does not comply with the 133⅓ method or the fractional rule, but may work under the three percent method, which is, however, a method that only a few plans comply with. The result of this is that use of the greater of method will generally cause a plan to fail to comply with ERISA's benefit accrual rules.

a. 133⅓ percent method. Under the 133⅓ percent method (which is the only benefit accrual method that a career average pay plan can normally satisfy), the greater of method would fail for two reasons: First, when a plan under the 133⅓ percent method is amended, the amendment is treated "as in effect for all other plan years" for testing compliance with the method.[272] Thus, when a plan is amended from a 1½ percent to a one percent rate, the 1½ percent rate goes out of the picture completely. Since participants A and B accrue *no* new benefits for a number of years after the amendment before beginning to accrue additional benefits at the one percent rate, the permissible variation under the 133⅓ percent method is infinitely exceeded. Second, even if the previous benefits at the 1½ percent rate remained in the picture, the pattern of accruals would still fail. For example, for participant B, the accrual pattern would be 1½ percent for the first 10 years, followed by 0 percent for the next five years, followed by one percent thereafter. The 133⅓ percent method requires that the accrual rate in any later year must not exceed 133⅓ percent of the annual rate in *any* prior year. Since participant B, accrues no benefits in years 10–15, the one percent rate in the later years is an infinite percentage increase, which causes the greater of method to fail.[273]

b. Fractional rule. The fractional rule can accommodate a pattern of no accruals in intermediate years of plan participation as produced under the greater of method. But over time, the fractional rule requires that the benefits that did not accrue in the intermediate years of plan participation have to be made up, until at the plan's normal retirement age, the same benefits are accrued as under a simple additive

---

[272] ERISA §204(b)(1)(B)(i) (Code §411(b)(1)(B)(i)), and see 26 C.F.R. 1.411(b)-1(b)(2)(ii)(A).

[273] See 26 C.F.R. 1.411(b)-1(b)(2)(iii) (example (3)).

method.[274] Rather than generalizing, this is best illustrated: Assume participant B entered a plan with an age 65 normal retirement age at age 45 and is age 55 with 10 years of participation when the plan is amended from a 1½ percent formula to a one percent formula. B's fractional rule normal retirement benefit is 10 years × 1½ percent + the remaining 10 years to normal retirement × 1 percent, for a 25 percent of pay normal retirement benefit. This normal retirement benefit is multiplied by B's fraction, determined by years of participation divided by potential years of participation from actual entry until the normal retirement age, to test whether benefits are accruing in compliance with the fractional rule.[275] Under this method, B's accruals in the years immediately after the amendment might be nil, as in the greater of method, but new accruals are required to start again sooner than under the greater of method, and the lost accruals are gradually made up, until at normal retirement age, the same benefits are accrued as under an additive method. The fractional rule accrual pattern and the patterns of benefit accruals under the greater of method and under a simple additive method are shown below for comparison:

YEAR	*FRACTIONAL RULE*	*GREATER OF*	*SIMPLE ADDITIVE*
11	15.00%	15%	16%
12	15.00%	15%	17%
13	16.25%	15%	18%
14	17.50%	15%	19%
15	18.75%	15%	20%
16	20.00%	16%	21%
17	21.25%	17%	22%
18	22.50%	18%	23%
19	23.75%	19%	24%
20	25.00%	20%	25%

In this example, it may be observed that the difference between the fractional rule benefit accruals and accruals under the greater of method is attributable to one factor, namely, that the greater of method implicitly determines the participant's "normal retirement benefit" *completely* under the new accrual rate. Thus, the greater of normal retirement benefit for this participant is 1 percent × 20 years,

---

[274] Also note that the fractional rule cannot generally be used by a career average pay plan. Another question is whether compliance with the fractional rule is permitted if a plan has not used it for benefit accrual compliance before, for example, when it increased benefits, which under the fractional rule requires *upward* adjustments in accrued benefits for participants with years of participation under an old, lower formula. See Conf. Rep., at 275 n.3, 3 ERISA Leg. Hist. 4542 n.3.

A change from compliance with one benefit accrual method to another, e.g., from the 133⅓% method to the fractional rule, is considered a plan amendment requiring protection of the participant's accrued benefits as determined under the old method up to the date of the adoption of the new benefit accrual method. See IRS Doc. 6678 "Plan Termination Standards" (4-81). And see Rev. Rul. 79-325 (on preserving accrued benefits when a plan is amended in the middle of a year).

[275] See Conf. Rep., at 275 n.3, 3 ERISA Leg. Hist. 4542 n.3, quoted in sec. II.B.3, above, for an example where this method was used to test compliance with the fractional rule after a benefit increase.

or 20 percent. The legislative history on the fractional rule, however, shows that the fractional rule "normal retirement benefit" in this situation is a composite of the old rate multiplied by years of participation up to the date of the change plus the new rate multiplied by potential years of participation after the change. As the example shows, this is an important distinction.

c. Three percent method. The greater of method may be accommodated under the three percent benefit accrual method *if* the same approach is followed as applies to a benefit increase. This is because when a plan is amended under the three percent method to increase benefits, the new normal retirement benefit is determined *entirely* under the new rate.[276] If the same can apply on a benefit decrease, using the example before, the new three percent normal retirement benefit would be one percent times the years of participation the participant would have if he or she entered the plan at the earliest possible entry age and served continuously until retirement. Assuming the potential number of credited years of participation during this period is capped at 33⅓ (so that compliance with the three percent method does not alter the plan's unit benefit formula rate), this means that participants are only required to have accrued benefits of at least one percent (1 percent of final pay × 33⅓ years of participation x 3 percent) times all their years of participation. If the protected accrued benefit under the 1½ percent rate can be used to satisfy this accrued benefit requirement, as can be done on a benefit increase, the greater of formulation satisfies the three percent method.[277]

The chief distinguishing characteristic of the three percent method is that so few plans comply with it because: (1) it is inconsistent with a unit benefit formula where more than 33⅓ years of participation can be credited for any plan participant, (2) it is inconsistent with a career average pay formula, (3) it is violated by any plan that does not credit years of participation after the plan's normal retirement age, unless and until the full three percent method normal retirement benefit has accrued, and (4) it requires benefits for earlier years of participation to be increased on a plan amendment increasing the plan's normal retirement benefits.[278]

General across-the-board support for the greater of method is sometimes sought based on Revenue Ruling 81-12 where the greater of method is expressly set out as an acceptable means for protecting a rate or factor used in determining an optional benefit against a decrease by plan amendment in violation of Section 204(g).[279] The distinguishing feature of Revenue Ruling 81-12, however, is that amounts

---

276 See C.F.R. 1.411(b)-1(b)(1)(iii) (example (6)).

277 See *id.*

278 See sec. II.B.3 above (on the features of the 3% method).

279 Specifically, Rev. Rul. 81-12 states that when a rate or factor for a benefit option to the plan's normal form of benefits is changed:
"One acceptable method is to provide that the actuarial equivalent of the accrued benefit on or after the date of the change is determined as the sum of (1) the actuarial equivalent of the accrued

under benefit options are *not* required to accrue in accordance with the ERISA accrual methods. Thus, the issue in Revenue Ruling 81-12 was only whether such a plan amendment decreases the a participant's current accrued benefit, rather than whether ERISA's benefit accrual methods are *thereafter* satisfied. When an amendment alters a plan's normal retirement benefit, the second issue of benefit accrual compliance after the amendment is unavoidable.[280]

3. Protection of Early Retirement Benefits and Benefit Options

Early retirement benefits and benefits under benefit options are not required to accrue from year-to-year under the ERISA benefit accrual methods, but the reduction factors or interest rates used for determining the amount of such benefits are protected under Section 204(g) (Code Section 411(d)(6)) against retroactive decreases by plan amendment. This is established in the IRS's regulations, in more detail in Revenue Ruling 81-12, and is codified in the 1984 Retirement Equity Act amendments (adding ERISA Section 204(g)(2) and Code Section 411(d)(6)(B)).

Revenue Ruling 81-12 requires a plan to protect accrued benefits under an old interest rate or reduction factor used for a benefit option against a decrease from a plan amendment by adding benefits in the optional form as determined by applying the old rate or factor to benefits accrued up to the date of the change to benefits in the optional form as determined by applying the new rate or factor to benefits accrued after the amendment. Alternatively, the plan may use the greater of method described in the previous section. In this context, the greater of method does not appear to be subject to legal challenge.[281]

The problem in reaching the protection offered under Revenue Ruling 81-12 is that many plans have not, until relatively recently, expressly stated their interest rates for determining benefits under benefit options. Instead, benefits under options, such as a joint and survivor's form of annuity or a lump sum option, were often stated as the "actuarial equivalent" of the accrued benefit in single-life annuity form with no reference to the specific actuarial assumptions to be used.

---

benefit as of the date of change computed on the old basis and (2) the actuarial equivalent, computed on the new basis, of the excess of (a) the total accrued benefit over (b) the accrued benefit as of the date of change.

"Another acceptable method is to provide that the actuarial equivalent of the accrued benefit on or after the date of the change is determined as the *greater of* (1) the actuarial equivalent of the accrued benefit as of the date of the change computed on the old basis or (2) the actuarial equivalent of the total accrued benefit computed on the new basis."

[280] A second distinguishing characteristic of Rev. Rul. 81-12 that may account for its allowance of the greater of method for benefits under benefit options is that the IRS's authority under §204(g) for protecting a rate or factor used for a benefit option was considerably weaker than for when a plan amendment changed the normal retirement benefit. The IRS's authority in this area was "clarified" by amendments in the Retirement Equity Act, which are discussed next.

[281] The greater of method was specifically described as sufficient protection for changes to early retirement benefits and benefit options in the legislative history to the Retirement Equity Act. See S. Rep. 98-575, at 29, [1984] U.S. Code Cong. & Ad. News 2547, at 2575.

Without an express rate or factor under the terms of the plan, changes in the underlying assumptions could be made without a plan "amendment," and thus without triggering the protection of Section 204(g).[282] Under Revenue Ruling 79-90, plans were required to begin expressly stating the actuarial assumptions used in determining all benefits options under the plan as of the first plan year after December 31, 1983, to meet the "definitely determinable" benefit requirement of the Code.[283] As a result, changes in the actuarial assumptions for benefit options from 1984 on require an amendment of the plan, and thus are subject to Section 204(g), as applied in Revenue Ruling 81-12.[284] Under Revenue Ruling 79-90, plans are, however, still permitted to state the interest assumption used in determining benefits under a benefit option as a variable standard, such as 75 percent of the prime rate of a named, unrelated bank, as long as the variable standard is outside of the control of the employer and the plan's fiduciaries. If a variable standard is used, changes in an interest assumption can continue to occur without an amendment of the plan, unless a change is made to a different variable standard.

Before the effective date of Revenue Ruling 79-90, express rates or factors were already in more widespread use for early retirement benefits than "actuarially equivalent" phrasing.[285] When a change in such a percentage or fractional reduction factor is made, the change, therefore, must come through a plan amendment, before or after 1984, and

---

[282] It would seem that even prior to the effective date for Rev. Rul. 79-90, a rate or factor used under "actuarially equivalent" phrasing could be so well-established by past practice or oral or written representations that a plan "amendment" would be deemed to have occurred when the rate or factor was changed, despite the absence of plan "amendment" formalities. The courts, however, have fastened on a strict reading of the "amendment" requirement in §204(g). See *Dooley v. American Airlines, Inc.*, 797 F.2d 1447 (7th Cir. 1986) (no "amendment" of plan—even though change in interest assumptions was evidenced by written bulletins distributed to employees); *Stewart v. Nat'l Shopmen Pension Fund,* 730 F.2d 1552, 5 EBC 1518 (D.C. Cir. 1984), *cert. denied,* 469 U.S 834 (1984); *Lewis v. Fulton Federal Savings & Loan Pension Plan,* 4 EBC 2072, at 2080-81 (N.D. Ga. 1983). This may be wrong since contracts often contain general terms that are defined by past practice and other representations, with a unilateral change in the meaning of the general term being considered a breach of contract. Specifically, courts have enforced phrases such as "sound actuarial basis" in pension plans according to past practice and other representations. A failure to fund a plan in the manner required by that usage is then a breach of contract. See *IAM Lodge No. 1194 v. Sargent Indus.*, 522 F.2d 280 (6th Cir. 1975). See also *Ingram Mfg. Co.*, 72 LA 47 (Caraway, 1978) (change in interest assumption for lump sum option from 3½% to 6½% violated employer's contractual obligation to "continue to maintain a pension program with benefits comparable to the program presently in effect;" arbitrator emphasized that lump sum option played a "vital role" in the pension program as all retiring employees had previously chosen it over an annuity).

[283] The requirement that actuarial assumptions must be stated in a plan for benefits to be "definitely determinable" is codified in Code §401(a)(25), as a result of the 1984 Retirement Equity Act amendments. And see *Dooley v. American Airlines, Inc., supra* (discretion under plan to change interest rate used for actuarially equivalent lump sums from a fixed rate to a varying standard not barred either by ERISA §402(b)(4) written plan or by definite determinability requirement of the Code when it occurred *before* the effective date of Rev. Rul. 79-90).

[284] If the actuarial assumptions stated in the plan to comply with Revenue Ruling 79-90 deviate from those previously used in practice, this could also be a plan "amendment" requiring protection under §204(g).

[285] In the BLS's 1982 survey of plans of medium and large firms, 21% of participants in plans permitting early retirement were in plans that used "actuarially equivalent" reductions, while 79% were in plans that used fractional or percentage reductions. BLS, Employee Benefits in Medium and Large Firms, 1982, at 43.

thus must be subject to Revenue Ruling 81-12's protection of benefits under the old rate or factor up to the date of the amendment.

The issue on early retirement benefits that was implicitly addressed in Revenue Ruling 81-12, and now is explicitly addressed in ERISA Section 204(g)(2) (Code Section 411(d)(6)(B)), as amended by the 1984 Retirement Equity Act, is how the Section 204(g) protection applies when an amendment reduces or completely eliminates so-called subsidized early retirement benefits or early retirement benefit reduction factors that over time have become favorable for participants as interest rates increased while the reduction factor remained the same. The complete elimination of an early retirement benefit is in essence but a further step in reducing an early retirement benefit, amounting to a 100 percent decrease in the rate or factor previously used for the benefit. Thus, under Revenue Ruling 81-12, if a plan eliminated an unreduced early retirement benefit, it can be considered a reduction in the rate or factor for the early retirement benefit option, from 1 × the accrued benefit to 0 × the accrued benefit. The change therefore may be subject to the Revenue Ruling 81-12 alternatives for protecting the accrued benefit under the old rate or factor.

However, in *Bencivenga v. Western Pennsylvania Teamsters Pension Fund,* the Third Circuit rejected this view when an early retirement benefit that was already reduced by ⅓ of one percent for each month that early retirement preceded age 60 was amended to a reduction of 7/10 of one percent for each such month. In *Bencivenga,* the Third Circuit recognized that Revenue Ruling 81-12 applies in this situation, but it refused to "accept the full breadth of the IRS's theory," holding that ERISA was designed to protect no more than the "bona fide" actuarial equivalent of an early retirement benefit, which the court found was still protected under the amended reduction factor.[286]

On the other hand, in *Amato v. Western Union International, Inc.*, the Second Circuit accepted the full breadth of Revenue Ruling 81-12, applying it to an amendment that eliminated a completely unreduced early retirement benefit, with only an actuarially reduced early retirement option left under the plan. The Second Circuit first held that the plan's early retirement benefits were accrued benefits because they were "expressed in the form of an annual benefit commencing at normal retirement age," even though the benefits actually commenced at an earlier age. Alternatively, the court held that the benefits were required to be protected against decrease because of the indirect effect that permitting such an amendment had on the accrued benefits of the participants. In so holding, the court emphasized that ERISA is " 'employee-oriented' and designed to assure that when private parties set

[286] 763 F.2d 574, 6 EBC 1799, at 1805 (3d Cir. 1985). One problem with *Bencivenga*'s distinction of "bona fide" actuarial equivalents from others is that actually drawing this line is not easy or objective. The IRS avoided this problem by establishing a mechanical rule under Rev. Rul. 81-12 that does not lessen participant protections by using necessarily subjective judgments.

higher standards [for providing benefits], as they have the right to do . . . 'employees with long years of employment and contributions [will] realize [those] anticipated pension benefits.' " The court thus found that ERISA was designed to require that a plan assure a retiree of "at least as much as [an] actuarially-reduced equivalent [of his or her normal retirement age benefits], but not [to] permit the employer to deprive him of any more [that] might be provided by the plan." In this light, the IRS's ruling was entitled to "great deference." The Second Circuit distinguished *Bencivenga* as "simply assur[ing] that employees qualifying for an actuarially reduced early retirement benefits would not receive pensions of greater actuarial value than those received at normal retirement age." Although this would seem to cover *Amato* as well (because the employer left an actuarially equivalent early retirement benefit in the plan), the court's distinction may have been that the early retirement benefit in *Bencivenga* had never been presented as more than an actuarial equivalent—or it may simply have been avoiding open disagreement with the Third Circuit.[287]

The REA clarifies this apparent division among the circuits for plan amendments made after July 30, 1984,[288] with "no inference . . . to be made on the basis of the clarification as to the scope of the prohibition before the effective date of the provision."[289] Under ERISA Section 204(g)(2) (Code Section 411(d)(6)(B)), as added by the REA, the elimination or reduction of a subsidized early retirement benefit or a "retirement-type subsidy" is prohibited to the extent that the elimination or reduction decreases benefits attributable to service before the date of the change. Regulations are to define the term "retirement-type subsidy," but it appears that Congress meant a subsidized benefit form, such as a joint and survivor's benefit that is not subject to a full actuarial reduction from the benefits available in a single-life annuity form. At the same time, the Senate Report specifically states that so-called Social Security supplements (which add to a participant's early retirement benefits until he or she becomes eligible for Social Security), disability benefits, medical benefits, and plant shutdown benefits that do not continue after retirement age are not to be considered "retirement-type subsidies" under the regulations.[290]

In addition to the elimination or reduction of early retirement benefits, or retirement-type subsidies, Section 204(g)(2), as amended,

---

[287] 773 F.2d 1402, 6 EBC 2226, at 2232-33, 2235, and 2237 (2d Cir. 1985) (citations omitted). See also *Collins v. Seafarers Pension Trust*, 641 F.Supp. 293 (D. Md. 1986) (cancellation of past service credits for early retirement benefits under plan amendment states claim for prohibited decrease in accrued benefits). The *Amato* court also distinguished the affirmance in *Sutton v. Weirton Steel Division*, 724 F.2d 406, 5 EBC 1033 (4th Cir. 1983), *cert. denied*, 467 U.S. 1205 (1984), of an amendment eliminating an early retirement benefit available on a "plant shutdown" as only involving an amendment to an "unfunded, contingent early retirement severance benefit[]," and not an option to an accrued benefit.

[288] P.L. 98-397, §302(d)(1). For collectively bargained pension agreements expiring between July 30, 1984, and Jan. 1, 1985, the effective date was generally for plan amendments adopted after April 1, 1985. See P.L. 98-397, §302(d)(2).

[289] S. Rep. 98-575, at 28, [1984] U.S. Code Cong. & Ad. News 2547, at 2574.

[290] S. Rep. 98-575, at 30, [1984] U.S. Code Cong. & Ad. News 2547, at 2576.

may more clearly restrict the addition of new conditions for such benefits, such as a longer years of service requirement for eligibility for the benefits or a plan amendment adding a forfeiture of early retirement benefits for competition with an employer, or for reemployment within the jurisdiction of a multiemployer plan.[291]

The REA also amended Section 204(g) to more specifically prevent the *elimination* of benefit options that are not subsidized in actuarial value, but that may be valuable parts of the accrued benefit for some participants.[292] Certain benefit options that reflect full actuarial reductions may, however, be exempted from this protection under to-be-issued Treasury regulations. As an example of the type of benefit option that might be exempted, the Senate Report specifically mentions the elimination of an actuarially reduced joint and 66.6 percent survivor annuity under a plan that continues to offer a joint and 100 percent survivor's benefit and a joint and 50 percent survivor's benefit, thus providing comparable alternatives. However, the Senate Report states:

> "The committee expects that the regulations will not permit the elimination of a 'lump sum distribution' option because, for a participant or beneficiary with substandard mortality, the elimination of that option could eliminate a valuable right even if a benefit of equal actuarial value (based on standard mortality) is available under the plan."[293]

When an early retirement benefit, a retirement-type subsidy, or a benefit option is protected against reduction or elimination, the protection is for the benefits that would be provided under the benefit option based on the accrued benefits *up to* the date of change, *assuming* that the participant has met, or later meets, any special eligibility (or vesting) requirements for the benefit. For example, if a plan with a one percent of average pay formula offers an unreduced early retirement benefit at age 55 to participants who complete 30 years of service, and as of a certain date the employer eliminates that benefit, leaving only an actuarially reduced early retirement benefit under the plan, the

---

[291] Although based on facts occurring before the REA effective dates, *Helmetag v. Consolidated Rail Corp.*, 5 EBC 1617 (E.D. Pa. 1984), might have been decided as a reduction in accrued benefits under Rev. Rul. 81-12 and certainly could be so decided under REA. In *Helmetag,* unreduced early retirement benefits requiring 30 years service and the attainment of age 60 were denied eligible employees because Conrail, after acquiring a bankrupt company's railroad assets and taking over control of its pension plan, added a condition that the employees who stayed with the bankrupt company, instead of taking employment with Conrail, could not draw their early retirement benefits—even though those employees could no longer accrue benefits under the plan and early retirees were not otherwise forbidden from employment while receiving early retirement benefits. The *Helmetag* district court treated the addition of this condition on receipt of benefits as a breach of fiduciary duty, without discussion of the REA amendments or Rev. Rul. 81-12, because the employees were not provided with notice of the condition before the time when they decided whether to take employment with Conrail and because the condition penalized the employees without offering them the opportunity to continue to accrue benefits under the plan.

[292] Protection against reduction of benefits under benefit options is not codified because Congress recognized that such protection was already extended by Rev. Rul. 81-12, and was presumably not subject to the same type of challenge as when Rev. Rul. 81-12 is applied to the elimination or reduction of early retirement subsidies that are more than any reasonable actuarial equivalent of benefits in normal retirement benefit form.

[293] S. Rep. 98-575, at 30, [1984] U.S. Code Cong. & Ad. News 2547, at 2576.

plan is required to preserve the unreduced 30-year benefit to a limited extent for participants who already have service toward the benefit and who later complete the required 30 years. The Senate Report on the REA illustrates the mechanics of the computation of benefits:

> "If as of January 1, 1985, [the date the benefit was eliminated] employee B was age 50, had completed 25 years of service, and had average pay of $10,000, then the plan amendment could not reduce B's benefit below $2,500 ($10,000 × 1 percent × 25 years). If B's average pay increased at 6 percent annually until age 55, then B's accrued benefit at age 55 under the plan as amended would be $4,016 ($13,382 × 1 percent × 30 years). But for the bill and prior law, [a 50%] actuarial reduction [at age 55] would reduce B's benefit to $2,008. Under the bill, the amendment could not reduce B's benefit payable at age 55 below $2,500."[294]

The same result can be reached under Revenue Ruling 81-12 (which is presumably the reference to "prior law") without the effective date limitation of the REA provision.

4. Other Considerations on Plan Amendments

Independent of Section 204(g), a plan amendment can constitute a vesting schedule change subject to ERISA Section 203(c)(1)(B) (Code Section 411(a)(10)(B)). This requires that all nonforfeitable benefits be protected and also requires that an election be provided all nonvested or partially vested participants who have five or more years of service in which they can choose to remain under the old vesting rule or schedule.[295]

A host of other common law and more specialized ERISA and Code rules can apply to plan amendments not covered under Section 204(g) (for example, because a reduction or elimination of a benefit option or an ancillary benefit is not covered by Revenue Ruling 81-12 or by the Retirement Equity Act). Arthur Kroll thus sagely states that:

> "Tender care is required where participants' rights, regardless of whether vested or accrued in the ERISA sense, are ... being reduced substantially...."[296]

The need for "tender care" is obvious once the legitimate expectations of participants in *all* benefits offered under a plan are recognized, and once it is considered that only a handful of participants know which benefits offered in a plan are protected as "accrued benefits," and then also know the limits of that protection. The other legal considerations on plan amendments are discussed in Chapters 9 and 10.

---

[294] S. Rep. 98-575, at 29, [1984] U.S. Code Cong. & Ad. News 2547, at 2575.

[295] Vesting schedule elections are discussed in ch. 5, sec. IV.

[296] A. Kroll, *Employee Benefits and ERISA Case Law Service* (Warren, Gorham & Lamont Jan. 1979 release), at §4.3[1] (service updating discont'd 1980).

5

Vesting

In drafting ERISA, Congress used the terms "vested" and "nonforfeitable" interchangeably.[1] When a participant has a vested, or nonforfeitable, right to accrued benefits, it means the participant has a claim to payment, on either an immediate or deferred basis, of at least a percentage of his or her accrued benefits that arises from the participant's service and that is "unconditional, and ... legally enforceable against the plan."[2]

Vesting is the "cornerstone" of pension reform because a vested, or nonforfeitable, right is indispensable to actual receipt of benefits.[3] Congress recognized that unless chances for becoming entitled to benefits from private pension plans were "substantially increased, there [would] be no meaningful reform in the eyes of the public."[4] Until benefits vest, dollar amounts of accrued benefits are credited to what is essentially a paper account, but the participant still lacks an unconditional right to receive the accrued benefits on retirement. For example, a participant with five years of participation under a plan offering $15 per month in retirement benefits beginning at age 65 for each year of participation may have "accrued benefits" of $75 per month at age 65, but the participant may still have no contractual right to receive those accrued benefits at age 65 unless and until he or she completes several more years of service needed to "vest." If the participant is permanently laid off or discharged before completing those years of service, he or she may never obtain a vested right to the accrued benefits.

Before ERISA, many plans only vested an employee's pension

[1] *Nachman Corp. v. PBGC*, 446 U.S. 359, 2 EBC 1431, at 1439 (1980) (finding that Congress used the two terms synonymously).

[2] ERISA §3(19).

[3] 2 ERISA Leg. Hist. 1773 (statement of Sen. Hartke).

[4] *Id.* And see 3 ERISA Leg. Hist. 3592 (Rep. Fascell) (vesting is "single most important aspect of the bill") and 2 ERISA Leg. Hist. 1634 (Sen. Bentsen) (Congress must establish minimum vesting standards because "countless numbers of American working men and women have been tragically victimized by unreasonable vesting provisions").

benefits if and when the employee reached the plan's normal retirement age. Other plans provided preretirement vesting after the employee had 15, 20, or more years of service (or a combination of age and years of service, such as age 40 and 15 years of service). Against this background, Congress found that:

> "[D]espite the enormous growth in [pension] plans many employees with long years of employment are losing anticipated retirement benefits owing to the lack of vesting provisions in such plans."[5]

Congress' policy was therefore:

> "[T]o protect the interests of participants in private pension plans . . . by requiring them to vest the accrued benefits of employees with significant periods of service."[6]

To accomplish this, Congress introduced preretirement vesting into all plans and generally shortened the period required to vest in accrued benefits under those plans that already had preretirement vesting.

When a participant becomes vested, the vested right is to the benefits accrued to that date and to any benefits that accrue in the future. It is not, however, a right to a full career pension, unless the participant actually accrues a full career pension. Confusion can arise when a vesting schedule provides for graduated increases in a participant's vested percentage up to 100 percent, or full, vesting. As then-Representative John Erlenborn stated:

> "[I]t is important to point out . . . how people can misconstrue this . . . [W]hen they look at vesting and we talk about . . . 30 percent, 50 percent, they believe we mean that percentage of the final pension. But it is important to note that that is not what is meant. If a person is 50 percent vested, that means that he [has a vested right to the accrued benefits from] one-half of the time he has accumulated as a participant in the plan."[7]

When a participant is 100 percent vested (i.e., fully vested), the accrued benefits to which the vested right attaches may still be based on a relatively small number of years of participation.[8] Even with more years of participation, a participant's accrued benefits can still be far from an adequate pension because the plan's benefit formula is meager generally, or because it uses Social Security integration.

---

[5] ERISA §2(a).

[6] ERISA §2(c).

[7] 2 ERISA Leg. Hist. 3387.

[8] See, e.g., *Greenfield v. IBEW Local 1783 Pension Trust,* 82 Civ. 2199 (S.D.N.Y. April 16, 1985) (participant had 5 years needed to vest under plan when years before participation began were counted, but still only had 2 years of participation for the purpose of determining the *amount* of benefits he was vested in).

I. ERISA's Vesting Rules

The chief means by which Congress implemented its goal of reforming vesting under private plans was the enactment of the alternative preretirement vesting schedules in ERISA Sections 203(a)(2)(A)-(C). The most commonly used of these is the "10-year cliff" vesting schedule under which accrued benefits vest fully after 10 years of service, with no vesting before 10 years. Although the ERISA preretirement vesting schedules are the best known of the minimum vesting standards, there are actually a number of other vesting rules under ERISA and also under the Internal Revenue Code that have relatively wide application. These other rules, as well as the ERISA preretirement vesting schedules, are discussed below.

A. Normal Retirement Age Vesting

A basic vesting rule is that accrued benefits must become nonforfeitable when a participant who is still in service with an employer reaches a plan's "normal retirement age."[9] This vesting requirement is *regardless* of whether the participant has the number of years of service otherwise required under ERISA's minimum preretirement vesting schedules. For example, if an employee begins service with an employer at age 57, and the plan's normal retirement age is age 65, the employee must become fully vested in his or her accrued benefits on reaching age 65 while still in service—even though he or she may only have eight or less "years of service" under the plan's preretirement vesting schedule. When a participant vests because of reaching the plan's normal retirement age, the benefits to which the vested right relates are often small—in this example, based on eight or less years of participation—but it is preferable for the participant to have a right to a small amount of benefits rather than no vested right at all.[10]

A number of plans have in the past attempted to insert an additional service requirement as a condition for vesting on reaching the normal retirement age. For example, in *Caterpillar Tractor Co. v. Commissioner*, a plan provided that its normal retirement age was 65, but in another plan provision limited any vested right on reaching that age to participants with 10 years of service (thus making vesting on reaching the normal retirement age the same as vesting under the 10-year

---

[9] Vesting on normal retirement age is not an ERISA reform, but is a continuation of a preexisting Code requirement for qualification. See pre-ERISA Code §401(a)(7), and see, e.g., *Caterpillar Tractor Co. v. Commissioner*, 72 T.C. 1088, 1 EBC 1830 (1979); *Duchow v. New York Teamsters Pension Fund*, 691 F.2d 74, 3 EBC 2312 (2d Cir. 1982), *cert. denied*, 461 U.S. 918 (1983).

[10] Technically, the benefit which must become nonforfeitable at normal retirement age is the plan's "normal retirement benefit." While the "normal retirement benefit" has a distinct meaning from the "accrued benefit" under the accrued benefit requirements, for purposes of §203(a)'s nonforfeitability on reaching normal retirement age, the term has been ruled to mean the "accrued benefit." See Rev. Rul. 84-69, and *Caterpillar Tractor Co. v. Commissioner, supra.*

cliff vesting schedule). The Tax Court held that this violates ERISA. The amount of benefits becoming nonforfeitable at the normal retirement age could be limited based on the participant's years of credited service, but the vested right on reaching the normal retirement age could not be conditioned on a particular number of years of service.[11]

When a participant reaches a plan's normal retirement age is also construed strictly. In Revenue Ruling 81-211, the requirement of vesting on reaching a plan's normal retirement age was not satisfied when a plan defined that age as age 65, but then only made benefits nonforfeitable for otherwise nonvested participants on the first day of the calendar month following the day when the participant reached age 65. The Service ruled that this violated ERISA because ERISA Section 203(a), and the parallel Code Section 411(a), require that benefits become nonforfeitable on the precise day when a participant reaches the plan's normal retirement age.[12]

The right of nonforfeitability on reaching a plan's normal retirement age may be diluted if a plan defines its normal retirement age as the later of age 65 or "the 10th anniversary of the time a participant commences participation in the plan," as is permitted under ERISA.[13] But when a plan uses this formulation, the "10th *anniversary* of the time [the] participant commences participation" is construed strictly. In *Duchow v. New York Teamsters Pension Fund*, a participant terminated his employment at age 69; at that time he did not have the 10 years of service required under the plan's vesting schedule and had not passed the tenth anniversary of the time he commenced participation.[14] At age 71 he returned to work for two months, and at the end of those two months celebrated the tenth anniversary of the date he commenced participation in the plan. He then reapplied for his pension benefits. It was undisputed that he still did not have 10 years of service, but he had been in service at the tenth anniversary of his commencement of participation in the plan (and he was also well past age 65). The plan trustees still denied his pension, contending that a service requirement was implicit in the tenth anniversary requirement. The Second Circuit rejected this and held that "anniversary" was

---

[11] 72 T.C. 1088, 1 EBC 1830 (1979).

[12] As discussed in ch. 4, sec. I.B, defined benefit plans are permitted, until 1988, to exclude employees from participation who are hired within 5 years of a plan's normal retirement age, and thus also from any benefits from the vesting at normal retirement age requirement.

[13] See ERISA §3(24) (Code §411(a)(8)). If a defined benefit plan does this, it may not exclude employees from participation who are hired within 5 years of age 65 because under this type of definition no employee is within 5 years of the plan's "normal retirement age" when hired. A plan that defines its normal retirement age in this way also may not halt benefit accruals at age 65 unless the participant's 10th anniversary of participation occurs before age 65. Some plans use a shorter period, for example, the later of age 65 or the 5th anniversary of participation in the plan. The discussion above applies to these plans as well, as does the requirement that the plan may not exclude employees hired within 5 years of age 65, and may not halt benefit accruals at age 65, unless the participant has, in this case, reached the 5th anniversary of participation before age 65.

[14] 691 F.2d 74, 3 EBC 2312 (2d Cir. 1982), *cert. denied*, 461 U.S. 918 (1983).

intended to have its normal dictionary meaning as the "annual return of the day of a past event" and that Duchow was therefore vested.[15]

The only exception to the tenth anniversary rule occurs when a nonvested participant incurs a series of one-year breaks in service equal to or exceeding his or her prior years of service for vesting before celebrating the tenth anniversary. In this case, participation may be required to recommence; consequently, the date participation commenced may be moved forward.[16] For example, if Duchow had started work at age 60 under a plan providing for immediate participation on starting work, worked three years until age 63, quit, and then came back six years later at age 69 for a two-month period to achieve his tenth anniversary of participation, his date of commencement could be moved forward to when his participation commenced again at age 69 after the disqualifying break in service. Even if the plan did not provide for this break-in-service rule, the benefits he would obtain would be very small because they would be based on only three years and two months of participation.

A plan's stated "normal retirement age" controls for vesting at retirement age as long as it is in compliance with ERISA and the ADEA. Thus, a plan can provide that its normal retirement age is 65 even though most employees retire at age 62.[17] A plan can also have two normal retirement ages. Effective in 1988, the 1986 Omnibus Budget Reconciliation Act repeals the ERISA and Code rules permitting defined benefit plans to exclude employees from participation who are hired within five years of the plan's normal retirement age. At the same time, the Act allows such plans to redefine the normal retirement age for these employees as the later of age 65 or the fifth anniversary of participation—even if the plan defines the normal retirement age as age 65 for all employees who commence participation earlier.[18]

However, whether a plan uses one age or two, the plan's normal retirement age may never exceed the employer's mandatory retirement age. Thus, if a plan defines its normal retirement age as the later of age 65 or the tenth anniversary of participation, but the employer uses a mandatory retirement age of 70, the tenth anniversary clause must be

---

[15] 3 EBC at 2317. See also *Taxicab Industry Pension Fund v. Commissioner*, T.C. Memo. 1981-651, 2 EBC 2101 (1981); *New York Hotel Pension Fund v. Commissioner*, T.C. Memo. 1981-597, 2 EBC 2097 (1981). Under the IRS's regulations, the 10th anniversary of the date a participant commences participation in a plan is interpreted, moreover, as "the 10th anniversary of the first *day* of the first year in which the participant commenced his participation in the plan." 26 C.F.R. 1.411(a)-7(b)(1) (emphasis added). For example, if a participant enters a plan that operates on a calendar year basis in the middle of a year, e.g., on June 1, the participant may claim a nonforfeitable right when the 10th January 1 rolls around, rather than the 10th June 1.

[16] 26 C.F.R. 1.411(a)-7(b)(1) and (2) (example (3)). Under the 1984 REA amendments, the series of one-year breaks in service have to equal at least 5 for this rule to apply. See ch. 4, sec. III.C.2.

[17] 26 C.F.R. 1.411(a)-7(b)(1).

[18] ERISA §3(24)(B) and Code §411(a)(8)(B), as amended by §9203 of P.L. 99-509. This amendment is effective with the first plan year beginning on or after Jan. 1, 1988. A later effective date of the *earlier* of Jan. 1, 1990, or the expiration date of the collective bargaining agreement in effect on March 1, 1986, applies if a plan is maintained pursuant to a collective bargaining agreement.

constrained by the employer's mandatory retirement age, and benefits therefore have to vest on reaching age 70.[19] Moreover, if an employer "consistently enforces a mandatory retirement age rule ... not set forth in the plan or any related document" at any earlier age than the normal retirement age stated under the plan—for example, a consistent policy of forcing employees to leave at age 62, rather than age 65—not only is the employer in violation of the ADEA, under which vesting may be a part of a remedy, but the vesting at retirement age requirement applies independently under ERISA at the earlier, unlawful mandatory retirement age.[20]

Finally, if the normal retirement age stated in the plan has been increased by plan amendment, participants in some instances are entitled to have the old, lower age applied for the purpose of vesting at normal retirement age. In Revenue Ruling 81-210, the Service ruled that when a plan increases its normal retirement age, such as from age 65 to age 70, or from age 65 to the later of age 65 or the tenth anniversary of participation, as many plans did in the wake of the 1978 ADEA amendments, the change is a vesting schedule amendment because of the vesting at normal retirement age requirement. When such a change is made, the ERISA Section 203(c)(1)(B) election must be provided all participants with five or more years of service insofar as the change affects their future opportunity to vest.[21]

Some plans do not specify a normal retirement age. In this case, vesting occurs at the earliest age stated in the plan when benefits can be received without a reduction for early retirement.[22] Thus, if a plan provides unreduced early retirement benefits and does not specify a later normal retirement age, vesting could be required for participants in service at the earlier age.[23] On the other hand, when a plan states that a later age is its normal retirement age, vesting is not required at any earlier retirement age even if benefits are available without reduction at the earlier age.[24]

B. Vesting in Employee Contributions

A second basic vesting rule under ERISA Section 203(a) is that *employee* contributions must be nonforfeitable at all times—whether the plan requires the employee contributions as a condition of participation or as a condition to obtaining matching employer contributions, or allows employee contributions on a completely voluntary basis.

---

[19] 26 C.F.R. 1.411(a)-7(b)(1).

[20] *Id.*

[21] Five or more years of service is specially defined for this purpose. See sec. IV below.

[22] 26 C.F.R. 1.411(a)-7(b)(1), and see *Nichols v. Board of Trustees,* 1 EBC 1868 (D.D.C. 1979).

[23] *Id.*

[24] 26 C.F.R. 1.411(a)-7(b), and see *Johnson v. Franco,* 727 F.2d 442, 5 EBC 1368 (5th Cir. 1984); *Geib v. New York Teamsters Pension Fund,* 758 F.2d 973, 6 EBC 1475 (3d Cir. 1985).

When a defined benefit plan requires mandatory employee contributions, distinguishing an otherwise nonvested participant's benefits that are attributable to the employee contributions from benefits attributable to employer contributions is more complicated than in defined contribution plans. Moreover, the ERISA rules downgrade the part attributable to employee contributions by permitting use of a low interest assumption. But the principle that benefits attributable to employee contributions must be nonforfeitable remains intact.[25]

C. Preretirement Vesting Schedules

The better-known preretirement vesting schedules for benefits derived from employer contributions are set forth in ERISA Section 203(a)(2) and the parallel Code Section 411(a)(2). ERISA Section 203(a)(2) sets out three alternate minimum preretirement vesting standards that an employer can choose among: the "10-year cliff" vesting schedule, the "5-to-15 year graded" vesting schedule, or the "Rule of 45" vesting schedule. Under these schedules, a participant obtains a vested right to accrued benefits at retirement that is "no longer contingent upon the individual's remaining in the service of the employer to normal retirement age."[26] The minimum vesting schedules required under each of these three standards are:

(1) *10-year cliff vesting.* The plan must provide 100 percent vesting after 10 years of service, but no vesting is required before then.[27]

(2) *5-to-15 year graded vesting.* The plan must provide 25 percent vesting after five years of service, with an additional five percent of the participant's accrued benefits becoming vested after each of the next five years, up to 50 percent vesting after 10 years of service, with another 10 percent of the participant's accrued benefits becoming vested after each of the next five years of service—up to 100 percent vesting after 15 years of service.[28]

(3) *Rule of 45 vesting.* The plan must provide 50 percent vesting in accrued benefits for all participants after 10 years of service with the vested right increasing by 10 percent after each of the next five years, to 100 percent vesting after 15 years of service. In addition, if a participant's age plus years of service equals or exceeds 45 points, e.g., age 40 plus five years of service, a special rule applies requiring 50 percent vesting after five

---

[25] See ERISA §204(c)(2)(B) (Code §411(c)(2)(B)). For the rules on separating employee-provided benefits from employer-provided benefits in contributory defined benefit plans, see *id.*, 26 C.F.R. 1.411(c)-1(c), and Rev. Ruls. 76-47 and 78-202. See also 29 C.F.R. 2618.12.

[26] *Nachman Corp. v. PBGC, supra*, 2 EBC at 1439 n.27, quoting D. McGill, *Preservation of Pension Benefit Rights* (Richard D. Irwin 1962), at 6.

[27] ERISA §203(a)(2)(A) (Code §411(a)(2)(A)).

[28] ERISA §203(a)(2)(B) (Code §411(a)(2)(B)).

years of service, with 10 percent increments to the vested right after each of the next five years.[29]

Of the three, the 10-year cliff schedule is predominant among defined benefit plans. In its 1984 survey of plans of medium and large firms, the Bureau of Labor Statistics found that over 85 percent of participants were in plans using the 10-year cliff vesting schedule.[30] More variety in vesting schedules is found among defined contribution plans, with many using a 5-to-15 year graded schedule, and many using the alternate "class-year" vesting standard described below. The Rule of 45 is seldom found among either defined benefit or defined contribution plans.

A plan can exceed the vesting required under any of the three schedules—for example, a plan may vest benefits under a 5-to-10 year graded vesting schedule or it may use a three-year cliff vesting schedule, but it must be able to show that the schedule it uses is in compliance with one or more of the minimum standard schedules. In practice, more liberal vesting schedules are seldom found outside of defined contribution plans and plans that are required to provide faster vesting under Internal Revenue Code requirements.

1. Faster Preretirement Vesting Beginning in 1989

The 1986 Tax Reform Act requires plans to adopt much *faster* preretirement vesting schedules than ERISA originally required effective as of the first plan year beginning after December 31, 1988.[31] As of this plan year, all plans, except multiemployer plans, are required to begin offering:

(1) Full (100 percent) vesting in accrued benefits after *five* years of service, with no vesting required before five years, or

(2) Graded vesting under a three-to-seven year schedule, requiring 20 percent vesting in accrued benefits after three years of service, with the vested percentage increasing in 20 percent increments to 100 percent vesting after seven years of service.

To vest under the new schedules, a participant must have at least one hour of service with the employer sponsoring the plan after the effective date.[32]

Multiemployer plans are excepted from these faster vesting schedules. But they are required to provide 100 percent vesting after 10 years

---

[29] ERISA §203(a)(2)(C) (Code §411(a)(2)(C)).

[30] BLS, Employee Benefits in Medium and Large Firms, 1984, at 56.

[31] §1113(e) of P.L. 99-514. A later effective date can apply to a plan maintained pursuant to a collective bargaining agreement that was ratified before March 1, 1986, and that has not expired before Jan. 1, 1989.

[32] ERISA §203(a)(2) and Code §411(a)(2), as amended by §1113 of P.L. 99-514.

of service in all cases, including those instances when the plan previously was using a 5-to-15 year graded or Rule of 45 vesting schedule that might only fully vest a participant after 15 years of service.[33]

2. Class-Year Vesting Alternate

Under ERISA Section 203(c)(3), and Code Section 411(d)(4), defined contribution plans have been permitted another vesting schedule alternate—"class-year" vesting. A class-year system of vesting is one in which each year's employer contributions vest separately and successively at the end of a set number of years after the year in which the employer contributions are made. Under ERISA Section 203(c)(3), defined contribution plans that use a class-year vesting schedule must vest contributions made in any plan year *no later* than the end of the fifth plan year following the plan year in which the contributions were made. For example, if the plan year is the calendar year, contributions made in plan year 1, 1981, must vest no later than the end of plan year 6, the end of 1986; contributions made in plan year 2, 1982, must vest no later than the end of plan year 7, the end of 1987; and so on. The vesting required under this rule includes the accumulated earnings on each year's contributions. Therefore, the past five years' earnings on the employer contributions made in plan year 1 must vest with the employer contributions by the end of plan year 6, but they need not vest before.

The major distinguishing characteristic of a class-year vesting schedule is that a participant is generally vested in some plan year contributions, plus earnings on those contributions, sooner than he or she might have been under the Section 203(a)(2) schedules, but the participant may never be fully vested in all years' contributions and earnings until he or she reaches the plan's normal retirement age. Thus, a participant separating from service after having been in a plan for 15 or 20 years may still forfeit the last five years' contributions, plus earnings, if the plan uses the maximum period permitted under Section 203(c)(3). Full vesting in all years' contributions is only required when a participant reaches the plan's normal retirement age.

The years needed for vesting in class-year contributions are also not counted as under the Section 203(a)(2) schedules. For example, years of service toward 10-year cliff vesting can include a number of years before an employee became a participant in a plan. In contrast, under the class-year vesting alternate, the five plan years required for vesting in employer contributions made in a previous plan year are computed beginning with the end of the plan year in which contributions were made to the participant's account—that is, five years after

---

[33] ERISA §203(a)(2)(C) and Code §411(a)(2)(C), as amended by §1113. The multiemployer exception to the vesting rules only applies to participants in the plan who are in a collective bargaining unit; it thus may not apply to union officers or union staff employees or employees of the plan who are sometimes covered under the plan. *Id.* And see Conf. Rep., H.R. Rep. 99-841, at II-427.

the end of a plan year in which the employee was already a plan participant.[34]

For top-heavy plans, class-year vesting is effectively overridden after 1983 by Code Section 416(b)'s requirement that top-heavy plans must vest *all* benefits or contributions 100 percent after three years of service, or must vest all benefits or contributions under a graded six-year schedule. Either schedule is incompatible with class-year vesting.[35]

Effective in 1989, the Tax Reform Act repeals the class-year vesting alternate for defined contribution plans.[36]

3. Vested Rights to Profit-Sharing Account Balances When Benefits Have Been Withdrawn

Many profit-sharing plans (including thrift plans that are qualified as profit-sharing plans) permit participants to withdraw benefits from employer contributions before their entire account balance is 100 percent vested. In these situations, questions can arise on how to determine the amount that is vested when a participant later separates from service with an increased, but still not fully vested, right to the remaining account balance. The IRS's regulations illustrate this issue as follows:

> "The plan distributes $250 to A when A's account balance prior to the distribution equals $1,000 and he is 25 percent vested. . . . Six years later, when A is 60 percent vested, he incurs a [one]-year break so that his vesting percentage cannot increase. At this time his separate account balance equals $1,500."[37]

The issue is what amount of the $1,500 account balance is vested? Since the vested percentage is 60 percent, the natural answer is $900. However, A has already received a distribution of $250, so that if he received $900 more, he would have received $1,150 out of a total of $1,750, or the equivalent of 68 percent of his total accrued benefits.

The IRS regulations provide two methods for handling the amount due A in this situation. The simplest is for the plan to add the previously distributed amount to the undistributed amount, multiply by the vested percentage, and then subtract the previously distributed

---

[34] 26 C.F.R. 1.411(d)-3(a)(1). Moreover, prior to 1984, all nonvested class year contributions could be forfeited if a participant separated from service prior to the end of the 5th plan year following the plan year for which contributions were made, and was not "reemployed in the plan year of separation." *Id.* The effect of the REA break-in-service reforms on this rule is summarized in n. 153 below.

[35] See 26 C.F.R. 1.416-1, Q&A V-6 (even if a plan provides class-year vesting at 3-year intervals, it does not satisfy the §416(b) vesting requirements unless *all* contributions vest after 3 years, or vest according to the graded 6-year schedule).

[36] §1113(b) and (e)(2) of the Tax Reform Act, P.L. 99-514, repealing ERISA §203(c)(3) and Code §411(d)(4).

[37] 26 C.F.R. 1.411(a)-7(d)(5). Beginning with the first plan year after Dec. 31, 1984, a one-year break can no longer stop the increase in vesting on accrued benefits accrued before the break. Instead, the break has to equal or exceed 5 consecutive one-year breaks in service. See ERISA §203(b)(3)(C) (Code §411(a)(6)(C)), as amended by REA, P.L. 98-397.

amount. Thus, for A, $250 would be added to $1,500, to yield $1,750, this would be multiplied by 60 percent to equal $1,050, and then with $250 already distributed, $800 would be left to be distributed.[38]

Under the second method, a plan can use the ratio of the account balance before the second distribution to the account balance after the first distribution. In the example, this ratio is $1,500 to $750 ($1,000 − $250), or a ratio of 2 to 1. This ratio is then multiplied by the earlier distribution (2 × $250), with the result added to the account balance before the second distribution ($500 + $1,500), and multiplied by the vested percentage ($2,000 × 60 percent = $1,200). The ratio is then also multiplied by the first distribution (2 × $250) with this amount subtracted from the last product ($1,200 − $500) to yield the vested amount to be distributed ($700).[39] The derivation of the second method is not obvious, but it is clear that it produces a $100 smaller second distribution. The adequacy of prior disclosure to participants on how their vested benefits are determined in this situation could be a crucial consideration in whether use of the second method is acceptable.

D. Vesting in Early Retirement and Ancillary Benefits

Defined benefit plans often offer benefits that are not within the ERISA Section 3(23), and Code Section 411(a)(7), definition of "accrued benefits," such as subsidized early retirement and joint and survivor's benefits, disability and death benefits, and health benefits for retirees. These benefits are not required to vest under the ERISA Section 203(a) vesting schedules. This is the means by which 25 and 30 years of service vesting requirements for early retirement benefits persist. As explained by the House Education and Labor Committee:

> "With respect to the term 'nonforfeitable right' or 'vested right,' it is not contemplated that vesting be required in benefits such as death benefits, disability benefits, or other forms of ancillary benefits provided by the plan. The plan may, of course, at its option, provide for vesting in such benefits."[40]

Depending on how a plan is drafted, some benefits, such as disability benefits, may be considered to never "vest" under a plan.[41] Usually, however, all benefits under a plan will vest at some point—for early retirement benefits, generally after a specified number of years or a

---

[38] 26 C.F.R. 1.411(a)-7(d)(5)(iii)(B) and (C) (example (2)).

[39] 26 C.F.R. 1.411(a)-7(d)(5)(iii)(A) and (C) (example (1)).

[40] 2 ERISA Leg. Hist. 3306 ("Material in the Nature of a Committee Report," introduced by Rep. Carl Perkins). Similarly, the House Ways and Means Committee's report stated:
"To require the vesting of these ancillary benefits [such as medical insurance or life insurance] would seriously complicate the administration and increase the cost of plans .... [W]here the employee moves from one employer to another, the ancillary benefits (which usually are on a contingency basis) would often be provided by the new employer, whereas the new employer normally would not provide pension benefits based on service with the old employer." H.R. Rep. 93-807, 60 2 ERISA Leg. Hist. 3180.

[41] See *Freeman v. IBEW Local 613 Pension Fund*, 3 EBC 1865 (N.D. Ga. 1982).

specified combination of age and service; for benefits such as disability or death benefits, after a specified number of years of service and the occurrence of the event, i.e., disability or death.[42]

Trustee and plan administrator interpretations of early retirement benefit vesting provisions have frequently been the subject of litigation, particularly on whether a participant who met a service requirement for a benefit but lacked the age is vested against an adverse amendment establishing new conditions for the benefit or providing less in benefits.[43] Litigation has also ensued over allegedly dissimilar treatment under early retirement benefit provisions requiring "consent" of the employer or allowing an early retirement under "mutually satisfactory" conditions.[44]

While neither ERISA nor the Code sets direct minimum standards on vesting in early retirement or other nonaccrued benefits, they can also have an effect on vesting under such provisions:

(1) Plan amendments altering the requirements for vesting in early retirement benefits are subject to the protection in ERISA Section 204(g) against amendments indirectly decreasing the accrued benefits of any participant under the plan.[45]

(2) Years of service toward early retirement or other special benefits need not be determined on the same basis as years of service for vesting in accrued normal retirement benefits. In most cases, however, the determination of years of service for these other benefits are not distinguished under the terms of the plan. As a result, a court may look to the ERISA rules on counting and measuring years of service, even though ERISA does not directly require that those rules apply.[46]

(3) ERISA and the Code do require one form of early retirement

---

[42] See ch. 9, sec. IV.A.

[43] *Apponi v. Sunshine Biscuits, Inc.*, 652 F.2d 643, 2 EBC 1534, at 1540 (6th Cir. 1981); *Hardy v. H.K. Porter Co.*, 417 F.Supp. 1175 (E.D. Pa. 1976), *aff'd in part, rev'd in part,* 562 F.2d 42 (3d Cir. 1977); *Van Fossan v. Teamsters Local 710 Pension Fund,* 649 F.2d 1243, 2 EBC 1457 (7th Cir. 1981); *Bencivenga v. Western Pennsylvania Teamsters Pension Fund,* 763 F.2d 574, 6 EBC 1799 (3d Cir. 1985); *Short v. UMW 1950 Pension Trust,* 728 F.2d 528, 5 EBC 1532 (D.C. Cir. 1984); *McCoy v. Mesta Machine Co.,* 260 BNA Pens. Rep. D-1 (W.D. Pa. 1979).

[44] See *Petrella v. NL Indus., Inc.*, 529 F.Supp. 1357, 3 EBC 1210 (D.N.J. 1982) (employer's refusal to consent to early retirement of employees younger than age 55 on plant closing was not irrational or inconsistent with past practice and did not result in prohibited discrimination under the Code); *U.S. Steel Pension Fund v. McSkimming,* 759 F.2d 269, 6 EBC 1621 (3d Cir. 1985) (employer's denial of consent for early retirement to an employee who was similarly situated with other employees who had been granted the consent ruled to be in breach of fiduciary duty under ERISA by arbitrator, but court denied enforcement of award as arbitrator lacked authority to decide ERISA questions). See also *Hackett v. PBGC,* 486 F.Supp. 1357, 2 EBC 2522 (D. Md. 1980) (although routinely granted in the past, employer's consent for early retirement still required for employees to be entitled to such benefits prior to plan termination); *Luli v. Sun Products Corp.,* 398 N.E.2d 553 (Ohio 1979) (employer's consent for early retirement benefit supplied by employer's act of closing the plant at which the employees worked).

[45] See ch. 4, sec. IV.B.3.

[46] See *Gennamore v. Buffalo Sheet Metals, Inc., Pension Plan,* 568 F.Supp. 931, 5 EBC 1268 (W.D.N.Y. 1983); *Cook v. Pension Plan for Salaried Employees of Cyclops,* C.A. No. C-1-82-615 (S.D. Ohio Oct. 5, 1984), *rev'd on other grounds,* 801 F.2d 865, 7 EBC 2278 (6th Cir. 1986).

benefit vesting. Under ERISA Section 206(a), and Code Section 401(a)(14), when a plan provides for the payment of an early retirement benefit, "a participant who satisfied the service requirement for the early retirement benefit, but separated . . . before satisfying any age requirement . . . is entitled upon satisfaction of [the] age requirement to receive a benefit *not less* than the benefit to which he would be entitled at the normal retirement age, actuarially reduced. . . ."[47] A district court in *Birmingham v. SoGen-Swiss International Corp.* stressed that this language requires a benefit of "not less" than the actuarial equivalent, and that a plan can be "more generous."[48] The court stated that "given that the acknowledged purpose of this section is the protection of employees, [the] defendants' argument that the section *demands* a[n] actuarial reduction of benefits can be seen as frivolous."[49] Following *Birmingham*, it appears that a plan providing an unreduced, or only slightly reduced, early retirement benefit for participants who separate from service having met both an age and service requirement must provide the same benefit to a participant who separates having satisfied the service but not the age requirement on the participant's later attainment of the required age—*unless* the plan specifically provides for a different, actuarially reduced benefit for such participants.

(4) In some instances, the Code's requirement that benefits vest on the termination or partial termination of a plan and the ERISA Section 4044 allocation of assets on termination can require vesting in early retirement benefits for participants who are short of either an age or service requirement on the date of termination or partial termination.[50]

(5) To prevent discrimination in favor of prohibited group employees within the meaning of the Code under consent requirements for early retirement or other benefits, a 1957 Revenue Ruling held that if benefits are conditioned on the employer's consent, the benefits must be worth *no more* than the actuarial equivalent of the plan's normal retirement benefit.[51] However, in two later Rulings, exceptions were provided for (a) plans that had favorable determination letters issued before April 22, 1957, on such provisions, so long as the consent power is not exercised in a discriminatory manner; (b) plans that include no "highly compensated" employees or other prohibited group members, such as hourly only plans; and (c) plans that have "set" standards for the exercise of such consent that are

---

[47] Emphasis added.

[48] 529 F.Supp. 86, at 91–92 (S.D.N.Y. 1981), *aff'd,* 718 F.2d 515, 4 EBC 2369 (2d Cir. 1983).

[49] *Id.* (emphasis added).

[50] See ch. 9, sec. VIII.A, ch. 11, sec. I.D, and ch. 12, secs. III and IV.A.

[51] See IRS Pub. 778, part 5(f), citing Rev. Rul. 57-163, part 5(f).

uniformly and consistently applied and that do not result in prohibited discrimination.[52]

The test for whether discrimination results under consent provisions is determined by whether the discretion is exercised "primarily" in favor of the prohibited group of employees, i.e., whether the percentage of prohibited group employees who receive consent is "significantly higher" than the percentage of rank and file employees receiving the consent.[53]

E. Vesting as a Remedy for Discrimination

ERISA Section 510 prohibits an employer or any other person from discharging or otherwise discriminating against a participant for the purpose of interfering with the attainment of benefit rights under a plan. Vesting can be required as a remedy when this prohibition is not observed. In *Ursic v. Bethlehem Mines*, a participant was discharged seven months before he would have attained a right to unreduced early retirement benefits requiring 30 years of service. Despite a "pretextual" reason for the discharge—he had borrowed wrenches without permission for work at home—the court found that the discharge was for the purpose of interfering with the attainment of his rights under the plan. Finding a violation of ERISA Section 510, the court ordered his early retirement benefits under the plan to be vested, along with making an award for other damages and attorney's fees.[54]

Ursic demonstrates that ERISA Section 510 can be applied to interference with the attainment of *any* right under the plan, including early retirement benefits that are not required to vest according to the ERISA schedules. As discussed in Chapter 10, particularly when a cliff vesting schedule is used, such as a 10-year cliff or a 30-year cliff for early retirement, where participants are fully vested on one day and

---

[52] Rev. Rul. 58-151, as amplified by Rev. Rul. 58-604.

[53] Rev. Rul. 85-59. The status of early retirement, lump sum, and other benefit options requiring consent of the employer, or "mutually satisfactory" conditions, is, at the date of this writing, clouded by a proposed IRS regulation that would require plans to eliminate any plan provision that requires employer consent or discretion with respect to the availability or payment of any alternative forms of benefits in order to satisfy the Code's definitely determinable benefit requirement and the ERISA §204(g) protection of early retirement benefits and benefit options against plan amendments. Under the regulation, plans could adopt objective and clearly ascertainable criteria in lieu of open-ended discretion, for example, on the existence of extreme financial need if the purpose of the consent requirement was to ensure that only employees experiencing extreme financial hardship receive early withdrawals of benefits. The regulation is not proposed to become effective until the *second* plan year after Jan. 30, 1986, for nonbargained plans, and for collectively bargained plans, not until the earlier of the third plan year after Jan. 30, 1986, or the second plan year after the expiration of the collective bargaining agreement in effect on Jan. 30, 1986. In a contradictory twist, if the proposed regulation becomes final, the IRS will then delay for the same transition periods the effectiveness of its previously issued Rev. Rul. 85-59 that looks at the respective percentages of rank and file participants and of prohibited group employees receiving benefits under a discretionarily available optional benefit form in examining the provision for discrimination in operation. Prop. Regs. 1.401(a)-4 and 1.411(d)-4, 51 Fed. Reg. 3798 (Jan. 30, 1986).

[54] 556 F.Supp. 571, 4 EBC 1537 (W.D. Pa. 1983), *aff'd*, 719 F.2d 670, 4 EBC 2297 (3d Cir. 1983), and see ch. 10, sec. I.

not vested at all the day before, there is a potential for abuse through timing a discharge, or, as in *Ursic*, creating a pretext for a discharge, just before vesting occurs.

Vesting in pension benefits can also be required as a part of a remedy for violations of other federal laws, such as Title VII of the Civil Rights Act or the ADEA, or for violations of non-preempted state law, such as in a suit alleging wrongful discharge.[55]

F. More Liberal Vesting Schedules

ERISA permits plans to exceed the minimum standards (just as employers are permitted to pay more than the minimum wage). ERISA thus specifically states that a "pension plan may allow for nonforfeitable benefits after a lesser period and in greater amounts than required by this part."[56] An employer may provide faster vesting than required under ERISA for a number of reasons, including as a matter of general personnel policy, as a measure to equal or outdo the plans of competitors, or because of a collective bargaining agreement.

Many defined contribution plans provide faster vesting schedules than required under ERISA, for example, by providing full and immediate vesting on commencement of participation; by using a faster graded vesting schedule than the 5-to-15 year graded schedule; or by using a shorter period than the five years allowed under a class-year system of vesting.

As a general rule of thumb, defined benefit plans are much less likely to provide faster vesting than required under the ERISA schedules. Instead, most defined benefit plans simply duplicate the 10-year cliff vesting schedule, or to a lesser extent, use the 5-to-15 year graded vesting schedule. Some do, however, provide for faster vesting on certain contingencies, for example, on the closing of a plant, the elimination of a job, or the disability of an employee.

One detraction from the general advantages for participants of a faster vesting schedule is that ERISA's protections against forfeitures for competition or for reemployment in the same industry covered by the plan need not apply to the benefits that vest under the faster schedule (but that would not be vested under ERISA's minimum standards).[57]

---

[55] See, e.g., *Berkman v. City of New York*, 580 F.Supp. 226 (E.D.N.Y. 1983) (back pay order under Title VII included order that employee be vested); *Loeb v. Textron, Inc.*, 600 F.2d 1003 (1st Cir. 1979) (even though employee would not have been vested before date of trial and reinstatement not ordered, pension benefits may be included in ADEA back pay award); *K Mart v. Ponsock*, 8 EBC 1548 (Nev. 1987) (unvested pension benefits included as compensatory damages in state law unjust dismissal action).

[56] ERISA §203(d).

[57] See sec. V below (on permitted forfeitures).

II. Vesting Requirements Under the Internal Revenue Code

The Internal Revenue Code requires faster vesting as a condition for tax-qualification in a number of situations. The Code requires:

- All tax-qualified plans to provide vesting on the occurrence of two related contingencies: the "termination" or any "partial termination" of the plan;[58]
- A vast number of small plans that are top-heavy to provide much faster vesting than required under ERISA;[59]
- Slightly faster vesting than the ERISA minimum standards for plans in which "there [has] been, or there is reason to believe there will be, an accrual of benefits or forfeitures tending to discriminate in favor of the highly compensated employees";[60]
- Faster vesting when there is a "pattern of abuse" in vesting, such as the dismissal of employees before their accrued benefits become vested, that tends to discriminate in favor of the prohibited group of employees;[61] and
- Immediate vesting for Section 401(k) plans (more popularly known as salary reduction plans) and tax credit ESOPs.[62]

A. Vesting on Termination or Partial Termination of a Plan

Code Section 411(d)(3) requires that benefits accrued must become nonforfeitable, regardless of a participant's place on the ERISA minimum standard vesting schedules, on the termination or partial termination of a plan—to the extent the benefits are funded under a termination basis allocation of plan assets. This potentially provides a powerful remedy for plan participants who are left short of vesting under the ERISA minimum standards because of a plant closing, large workforce reduction, or a plan amendment terminating a plan or sharply reducing its benefits. The caveat that benefits become vested on a termination or partial termination only "to the extent funded" is never a limitation under a defined contribution plan, and with improved plan funding and investment returns, it is much less of a limitation under defined benefit plans than it may have been prior to ERISA. Section 411(d)(3)'s vesting requirement is discussed in detail in other chapters. Vesting on termination (or for a profit-sharing plan, on the complete discontinuance of employer contributions) is discussed in Chapter 12, sec. III. Vesting on a partial termination because of the

---

[58] Code §411(d)(3).

[59] Code §416(b).

[60] Code §411(d)(1)(B).

[61] Code §411(d)(1)(A).

[62] Code §401(k)(2)(C) and Code §409(c).

exclusion of a significant percentage or number of participants is discussed in Chapter 11, sec. I. Vesting on a partial termination of a plan because of an amendment sharply reducing benefits or employer contributions is discussed in Chapter 9, sec. VIII.A.

B. Vesting Under Top-Heavy Plans

Starting with plan years beginning after December 31, 1983, the Tax Equity and Fiscal Responsibility Act of 1982 requires much faster vesting than under the ERISA schedules for top-heavy plans. A top-heavy plan is a plan in which over 60 percent of the present value of the plan's benefits have been accrued by certain "key" employees—who generally are a slightly narrower group than the Code Section 401(a)(4) group of highly compensated employees. The determination of when a plan is top-heavy is discussed in Chapter 3, sec. VIII.F.

When a plan is top-heavy, Code Section 416(b), as added by TEFRA, requires the plan to provide either 100 percent vesting after three years of service, or 20 percent vesting after two years of service, with 20 percent increments in the vested right after each of the next four years—up to 100 percent after six years of service. Years of service before the top-heavy rules became effective in 1984 are required to count under either schedule, as are years of service before a plan becomes top-heavy, if the plan becomes top-heavy after 1984. If the present value of a plan's benefits accrued by key employees drops below 60 percent, the top-heavy characterization of the plan disappears, but the vesting that has already occurred under these rules remains intact for accrued benefits and all future benefit accruals. Moreover, if any participants in the plan with five or more years of service (as specially defined in 26 C.F.R. 1.411(a)-8(b)(3)) are not fully vested, those participants are required to be given an election to remain under the top-heavy vesting schedule until they become fully vested.[63]

C. Vesting to Prevent Discrimination in Favor of Highly Compensated Employees

Before TEFRA's top-heavy rules became effective, the most significant source of faster vesting under the Code was a finding by the IRS under Section 411(d)(1) that "there has been, or there is reason to believe there will be, an accrual of benefits or forfeitures tending to discriminate in favor of highly compensated employees." This finding was generally based on higher turnover among rank and file employees than among the employees who are officers, shareholders or highly

---

[63] ERISA §203(c)(1)(B) (Code §411(a)(10)(B)). And see 26 C.F.R. 1.416-1, Q&A V-1, V-2, and V-7. See also sec. IV below on the years that must count in determining whether a participant has 5 years for purposes of this election.

compensated. Under Revenue Procedure 75-49, "high" turnover is a turnover rate among rank and file employees of six percent annually or, if greater, more than double the percentage turnover rate of prohibited group employees. For example, if the turnover rate among prohibited group employees is four percent, rank and file turnover has to be eight percent per year before turnover is considered "high" for this purpose. If the prohibited group turnover rate is two percent annually, the turnover rate among rank and file employees has to be six percent for "high" turnover to be found.[64]

The faster vesting the IRS can require in this situation is limited to a vesting schedule that provides 40 percent vesting after four years of service, an additional five percent vesting after each of the next two years, and 10 percent vesting increments after each of the following five years, up to 100 percent vesting after 11 years of service (so-called 4/40 vesting).[65] This is slightly, but not dramatically, faster than the ERISA 5-to-15 year graded vesting schedule. In certain cases, 4/40 vesting can be somewhat faster than it may at first appear because it does not permit the exclusion of years of service for vesting allowed under the ERISA schedules for years of service: (1) before age 22 (beginning in 1985, age 18), (2) during a period when an employee declined to make contributions to a contributory plan, or (3) before the employer established the plan, or a predecessor plan.[66]

As a practical matter, 4/40 vesting is generally restricted to small plans.[67] Even among small plans, 4/40 vesting is the exception. The

---

[64] If an employer has only employed one or more persons for a period of between 4 and 5 years, the rank and file employees' turnover rate has to be 6%, or more than 2½ times the prohibited group employee's rate; if the employer has had employees for less than 4 years, then rank and file turnover must be 6%, or more than 3 times the prohibited group's rate. Rev. Proc. 75-49.

When an employer has had one or more employees for more than 2 but less than 7 years, the employer also has to satisfy a "key employee" test, which sets a percentage limit on the participation of certain "key" employees. *Id.* If an employer has had one or more employees for less than 2 years, the key employee test is the only test that applies. *Id.* A small employer generally cannot satisfy the key employee test unless, for one reason or another, a high percentage of officers and highly compensated employees are not participating in the plan. If the owner of a small corporation is the only highly compensated employee, the key employee test cannot be satisfied unless he or she does not participate. The alternative to not participating is to provide the slightly faster 4/40 vesting schedules to lessen potential discrimination under the plan.

[65] See ERISA Conf. Rep., at 267, 3 ERISA Leg. Hist. 4543 (limiting the vesting that may be required under §411(d)(1) to 4/40 vesting except in cases of "actual misuse" in operation).

[66] Rev. Proc. 75-49.

[67] Despite "high" turnover, an employer is permitted to show the IRS "facts and circumstances" demonstrating that there has not been, and there is no reason to believe there will be, an accrual of benefits under the plan tending to discriminate in favor of the prohibited group. Rev. Proc. 76-11 and Prop. Regs. 1.411(d)-1(c)(2), 45 Fed. Reg. 39869 (June 12, 1980). As examples of "facts and circumstances" that suffice, 2 out of 3 illustrations contained in the preamble to proposed §411(d)(1) regulations indicate that 4/40 vesting will not be required, despite high turnover, if the present value of accrued benefits of officers and 5% shareholders is less than 50% of the total present value of benefits under the plan, or if a "fair cross section" of lower and average-paid employees are vested. See preamble to Prop. Regs. 1.411(d)-1, 45 Fed. Reg. 39869 (June 12, 1980), and IRS News Release, IR 80-85 (Aug. 4, 1980). The effect of this is to relegate 4/40 vesting to relatively small plans. Under the present value test, 4/40 vesting could take in a few plans that the top-heavy rules do not, because 60% is required for top-heaviness, but counteracting this is the fact that officers and 5% shareholders generally constitute a smaller group of employees than the group of "key" employees used under the test for top-heaviness in Code §416(i).

reason for this is a grandfather clause under which the high turnover test is *not* applied if an employer had previously obtained a favorable determination letter from the IRS on its vesting schedule. In addition, a plan without a favorable determination letter is permitted to seek a determination letter from the IRS on plan amendments without the IRS determining whether its vesting schedule satisfies this nondiscrimination requirement.[68]

For high turnover plans that are also top-heavy plans, 4/40 vesting has largely been supplanted by the much faster vesting now required under Code Section 416(b). In a few cases, however, 4/40 vesting can still improve on the vesting required for participants under a top-heavy plan because of the broader definition, described above, of the years of service that must count under the 4/40 schedule.

D. Pattern of Abuse Vesting

Code Section 411(d)(1) also provides that faster vesting may be required when there is a "pattern of abuse under the plan (such as a dismissal of employees before their accrued benefits become nonforfeitable) tending to discriminate in favor of [the prohibited group of employees]." Moreover, the ERISA Conference Report states:

> "[W]here there is a pattern of firing employees to avoid vesting, the [4/40] limitations . . . would not apply."[69]

Thus, if a pattern of abuse is shown, e.g., a "systematic dismissal of employees before their accrued benefits vest,"[70] the IRS can require much faster vesting than 4/40 as a remedy.

As discussed before, ERISA Section 510 can also lead to vesting as a remedy for a purposeful dismissal of participants shortly before the attainment of vested rights.[71] The differences between Section 510 and Section 411(d)(1) lie in:

(1) Who can enforce the provision: participants can enforce Section 510 directly, but only the IRS can enforce Code Section 411(d)(1);

(2) What must be shown to obtain the remedy: Section 411(d)(1) requires a pattern of abuse that tends to discriminate in favor of the prohibited group, whereas Section 510 requires only a showing that a dismissal was for the purpose of interfering with a participant's attainment of rights;[72] and

---

[68] Rev. Proc. 76-11.

[69] Conf. Rep., at 277, 3 ERISA Leg. Hist. 4544.

[70] See Prop. Regs. 1.411(d)-1(b)(2), 45 Fed. Reg. 24201 (April 9, 1980).

[71] See sec. I.E and ch. 10, sec. I.

[72] However, Code §411(d)(1) may not require a demonstration of purpose, as long as a "pattern" of abuse is shown.

(3) How sweeping the remedy is: Code Section 411(d)(1) can require faster vesting for participants who are still employed, as well as those who were discharged as a part of the pattern of abuse, whereas remedies under Section 510 appear to be limited to the specific participants who were discharged for the purpose of interfering with their rights.

E. Vesting Under Section 401(k) Plans and Tax Credit ESOPs

Section 401(k) plans (also known as cash or deferred, or salary reduction plans) are subject to a special vesting rule that requires full and immediate vesting of all accrued benefits beginning with an employee's commencement of participation in the plan.[73] The requirement of full and immediate vesting covers all elective deferrals of salary by the employee; it also covers nonelective employer contributions *if* nonelective employer contributions are used by the plan to satisfy the special nondiscrimination tests for Section 401(k) plans.[74]

Full and immediate vesting is also required for all employer contributions to tax credit ESOPs.[75]

III. Counting Years of Service for Vesting

There are a number of ways to vest that do not depend on "years of service"—i.e., vesting at normal retirement age or on termination or partial termination of a plan. Thus, it could be said that years of service are only relevant to certain types of vesting. But vesting under those other standards—namely, the preretirement vesting schedules in ERISA Section 203(a) and the faster preretirement vesting schedules required for top-heavy plans—is the most common way in which employees vest. Therefore, vesting is generally discussed in terms of years of service.

As it is important to distinguish how benefits accrue from how benefits vest, it is equally important to distinguish "years of participation" used for benefit accruals, from "years of service" used for preretirement vesting. Congress made the rules on what years count as years of service for vesting, as well as the rules on exactly how a year of service for vesting is measured, somewhat more liberal than the rules for years of participation. This reflects Congress' greater concern

---

[73] §401(k)(2)(c).

[74] Prop. Regs. 1.401(k)-1(c), 44 Fed. Reg. 55544 (Nov. 10, 1981), and see IRS Notice 82-1, I.R.B. 1982-8, 35 (approving reliance on the proposed regulations). See also Conf. Rep. on the 1984 Deficit Reduction Act, H.R. Rep. 98-861, at 1145, [1984] U.S. Code Cong. & Ad. News at 1833 (affirming the requirement of immediate nonforfeitability for nonelective employer contributions used to meet the special nondiscrimination tests).

[75] Code §409(c). The Tax Reform Act repealed the tax credits for contributions to tax credit ESOPs made after the end of 1986. As a result, tax credit ESOPs have generally been frozen or terminated. §1171(a) of the Tax Reform Act, P.L. 99-514, repealing Code §41.

throughout the deliberations leading to the enactment of ERISA with enhancing *entitlement* to anticipated benefits, rather than with requiring plans to necessarily increase the amount of benefits participants could anticipate.

One of the most important differences flowing from this is that years of service before ERISA became effective are required to count for vesting if a participant was still active under a plan after ERISA's effective dates, whereas pre-ERISA years of participation are required to be credited under the benefit accrual rules only to a limited extent provided in ERISA Section 204(b)(1)(D). On an ongoing, post-ERISA basis, the most important difference is that years of service for vesting are required to include years of service as a nonparticipant, such as the one year of service generally permitted as a condition for commencing participation, and any other nonparticipating years of service an employee has with an employer, such as in a job classification or division not covered by the plan. In contrast, years of participation for benefit accruals generally begin and end with actual participation in the plan.[76]

A. General Rule and Exceptions

ERISA Section 203(b)(1), and Code Section 411(a)(4), provide the general rule on what years of service count for vesting, and the permissible exceptions. Under Section 203(b)(1):

> "[A]ll of an employee's years of service with the employer or employers maintaining the plan shall be taken into account, except that the following may be disregarded:
>
> "(A) years of service before age 22 [lowered to age 18 by the Retirement Equity Act if an employee has one hour of service in a plan year beginning after Dec. 31, 1984] . . .;[77]
>
> "(B) years of service during a period for which the employee declined to contribute to a plan requiring employee contributions;
>
> "(C) years of service with an employer during any period for which the employer did not maintain the plan or a predecessor plan, [as] defined by the Secretary of Treasury;
>
> "(D) service not required to be taken into account under paragraph (3) [covering the one-year hold-out rule and cancellations of years of service under the break-in-service rule of parity or the special one-year break-in-service rule for defined contribution plans[78]];
>
> "(E) years of service before January 1, 1971, unless the employee has had at least 3 years of service after December 31, 1970;
>
> "(F) years of service before this part first applies to the plan [i.e., *before* the first plan year after Dec. 31, 1975, for plans in existence on Jan.

---

[76] See, e.g., *Greenfield v. IBEW Local 1783 Pension Trust,* 82 Civ. 2199 (S.D.N.Y. April 16, 1985) (participant had 5 years needed to vest under plan when years before participation began were counted, but still only had 2 years of participation for the purpose of determining *amount* of benefits he was vested in).

[77] The omitted language in (A) provides an exception to this exception when a plan uses the "Rule of 45" vesting schedule and an employee was a participant in the plan at any time during a year before attaining age 22. Use of the Rule of 45 is rare.

[78] Both the rule of parity and the special one-year break rule for defined contribution plans were modified by the Retirement Equity Act amendments. See sec. III.A.4.

1, 1974] if such service would have been disregarded under the rules of the plan with regard to breaks in service, as in effect on the applicable date[; and]

"(G) in the case of a multiemployer plan; years of service—

(i) with an employer after—

(I) a complete withdrawal of such employer from the plan (within the meaning of Section 4203), or

(II) to the extent permitted by regulations prescribed by the Secretary of Treasury, a partial withdrawal described in Section 4205(b)(2)(A)(i) in connection with the decertification of the collective bargaining representative; and

(ii) with any employer under the plan after the termination date of the plan under Section 4048."

While ERISA therefore tolerates seven exceptions, the general rule is that *all* years of service with an employer or employers maintaining a plan must count for vesting. For years of service to be excluded under any one of the exceptions, the years must fall within the exception, and the plan must specifically provide for its use. Many plans do not use the full range of permissible exceptions. For example, the Bureau of Labor Statistics' 1984 survey of employee benefit plans of medium and large employers found that over 66 percent of participants were in plans that did not use the exception, effective until 1985, permitting years of service before age 22 to be disregarded for vesting.[79]

Some of the exceptions to the general rule on what years must count for vesting are relatively self-explanatory:

- Years before age 22 need not be counted if the plan so provides (which, as mentioned, many do not). For participants who are still active in plan years beginning after December 31, 1984, only years before age 18 may be excluded (regardless of whether the years of service after age 18 occurred before or after 1984).[80]
- Years of service in which a participant was eligible to make, but did not make any required (i.e., "mandatory") employee contributions may be excluded under a contributory defined benefit or defined contribution plan.[81]
- Years of service before 1971 may be excluded for vesting under the ERISA minimum standards unless a participant had three years of service after 1970. Whether a participant has these three years of service must be determined without regard to any of the other exceptions permitted under Section 203(b)(1).[82] This is a

---

[79] BLS, Employee Benefits in Medium and Large Firms, 1984, at 56. If a participant has an hour of service in a plan year beginning after Dec. 31, 1984, this exception is limited to years before age 18.

[80] When a plan uses an age exclusion, e.g., excluding years of service before age 18, the computation of years of service after age 18 must begin with the year *in which* the employee reaches age 18 if the plan uses a computation period in determining years of service for vesting that is not synonymous with the participant's birth date. 26 C.F.R. 1.411(a)-5(b)(1)(iii).

[81] This exception covers only the years in which the employee was eligible to make contributions to the plan and did not make contributions in *any* part of the year in question. 26 C.F.R. 1.411(a)-5(b)(2).

[82] 26 C.F.R. 1.411(a)-5(b)(5).

transition provision which adds to the general transition requirement that a participant must be an active participant in a plan after the December 31, 1975, effective date of ERISA's minimum standards.[83] The plan must again provide for this exception for it to be effective.

The following discussion focuses on parts of the general rule and exceptions that may not be as self-explanatory, namely, (1) the scope of the general rule's requirement that all years of service "with the employer or employers maintaining the plan" must count for vesting, (2) the meaning of the permissible exception for "any period for which the employer did not maintain the plan or a predecessor plan," (3) veteran's law rules on crediting military service, and the possibility of greater contractual requirements under "the terms of a plan,"(4) the exceptions for years before certain breaks in service under defined benefit and defined contribution plans, and the special rule for pre-ERISA breaks in service, and (5) one-year hold-out rules.

1. Noncovered Service

Before dealing with any exceptions, the first step under Section 203(b)(1) and Code Section 411(a)(4) is to count *all* years of service an employee has "with the employer or employers maintaining the plan," including service in a job classification or division not covered under the plan. For example, if an employee is a participant in a collectively bargained plan, and is promoted to a nonbargaining unit supervisory or managerial position, the years of service with the employer while in the bargaining unit must count for vesting (and also for meeting any service requirements for beginning participation) under any plan for supervisory employees maintained by the employer. Similarly, the years of service as a supervisor must count back under the collectively bargained plan for vesting if the employee was not already vested under that plan. Under this same rule, service with an employer in a division of a business that is not covered by any plan must count for vesting (and for satisfying any service requirements for beginning participation) if the employee is ever transferred to a division that is covered by a pension plan. This is illustrated in the legislative history:

> "Assume that an employee begins work at age 25 for division A of a corporation, which does not have a pension plan, and, at age 40 he transfers to Division B, which does have a plan. Under all of the vesting standards the employee would immediately become fully vested in the benefits which accrue under the plan because of his 15 years of prior service with the employer. (Conversely, an employee who worked for 5 years in division B, and then shifted to division A, would continue to

[83] 26 C.F.R. 1.411(a)-2(f).

increase his percentage of vesting in the benefits which he had accrued under the division B plan, even though division A did not have a plan.)"[84]

As described below, this rule can be limited by the exception that years of service during which neither the plan nor a predecessor plan were maintained by the employer are not required to count for vesting. Thus, if an employee begins work in division A at age 25, and moves to division B at age 40, all of his or her years of service are required to count for vesting under any plan covering division B employees—*provided that* division B's plan or a predecessor plan existed during all of those years. If the plan was only established when the employee was age 35, the credit for the years in division A may be limited, if the plan so provides, to the years of service in division A after the plan's establishment.[85]

a. Within a controlled group of employers, or as a leased employee. When two or more corporations (or unincorporated trades or businesses) are members of a controlled group, the general rule that *all* years of service with the employer or employers must count for vesting (and for meeting conditions for participation requirements) means that all years of service with *any* employer who is a member of the controlled group count for vesting—provided that the employers were related in the controlled group sense during the period of time when the service occurred.[86] Thus, the rule, as stated in the legislative history, is:

> "Service for an employer is to be taken into account for purposes of placement on the vesting schedule, even though the service was in a different division of the corporation, *or with a different corporate member of the affiliated group.*"[87]

Years of service with members of an "affiliated service group," or as a leased employee from a "leasing organization," must also all count for vesting (and for conditions for beginning participation) under any plan maintained by any member of the affiliated service group or by the employer using the leased employee's services.[88]

b. With employers contributing to a multiemployer plan. Under ERISA Sections 210(a)(1) and (2), and Code Sections 413(b)(1) and (4), service in any capacity with any employer contributing to a multiemployer plan is to be treated "as if all employees of each of the

---

[84] H.R. Rep. 93-807, at 57, 2 ERISA Leg. Hist. 3177, and Material Explaining H.R. 12906, 2 ERISA Leg. Hist. 3325. The sentence in parentheses appears as a footnote in the legislative history. And see *Fraver v. North Carolina Farm Bureau Mut. Ins. Co.*, 643 F.Supp. 633, at 646 (E.D.N.C. 1985), *rev'd on other grounds*, 801 F.2d 675, 7 EBC 2137 (4th Cir. 1986), *cert. denied*, 480 U.S. ___ (1987) (3 years in another division of a company counted for vesting when employee moved into a job classification with a pension plan); *Holt v. Winpisinger*, 811 F.2d 1532, 8 EBC 1169 (D.C. Cir. 1987) (service for an employer characterized as being as an "independent contractor" included as years of employment when supervision, location, and control over details of work showed that the service was as an "employee" under common law agency principles).

[85] See sec. III.A.2. below.

[86] 26 C.F.R. 1.411(a)-5(b)(3)(iv), and see 29 C.F.R. 2530.210(d).

[87] H.R. Rep. 93-807, at 56, 2 ERISA Leg. Hist. 3176, and Material Explaining H.R. 12906, 2 ERISA Leg. Hist. 3325 (emphasis added).

[88] Code §§414(m)(1) and (4), and §§414(n)(1), (3), and (4).

employers were employed by a single employer, except that the application of break-in-service rules shall be made under regulations prescribed by the Secretary [of Labor]."[89] The Secretary of Labor's regulations seem, however, to go further than the intended "application of break-in-service rules," and instead restrict credit for service in any capacity with each of the employers contributing to a multiemployer plan to "contiguous" service. Under the regulations, noncovered service is only required to count for vesting if it is contiguous, i.e., if it "precedes or follows" covered service under the plan without an intervening "quit, discharge, or retirement."[90] If service is "noncontiguous," it need not count for vesting, and it may, in fact, count for the series of consecutive one-year breaks in service which under the ERISA rule of parity can cancel earlier covered or contiguous service under the plan.[91]

To illustrate how the contiguous service rule can require credit, if a union electrician moves from covered service under a multiemployer plan to noncovered service, e.g., as a supervisor, with the *same* employer without any intervening quit, discharge, or retirement, the service as a supervisor is required to count for vesting under the multiemployer plan. However, if the participant goes from covered service with one employer contributing to a plan to noncovered service with a different employer who also contributes to the plan, it would seem that the noncovered service would always be "noncontiguous" to the previous covered service because it necessarily involves an intervening quit or discharge. The only exception to this rule would seem to be if a distinction is drawn, as it is in labor agreements generally, between a "quit" or "discharge," and a layoff or other reduction in force, as when a construction project is completed. If this distinction is drawn, it may be possible for the noncovered work with a second employer to be contiguous to the preceding covered work.

In a few cases, "noncontiguous" service can later become "contiguous" service. For example, if an electrician goes from covered work with one employer contributing to a multiemployer plan to noncovered work as a supervisor with a second employer contributing to the same plan, the work with the second employer is generally noncontiguous under the regulations. However, if the electrician subsequently returns to covered service while working with the second employer without an intervening quit, discharge, or retirement, the service as a supervisor then becomes contiguous because it *precedes* later covered service; therefore, it is required to count for vesting.[92]

Neither the rule that credits noncovered contiguous service that

---

[89] See also H.R. Rep. 93-807, 58, 2 ERISA Leg. Hist. 3178, and Material Explaining H.R. 12906, 2 ERISA Leg. Hist. 3326.

[90] See 29 C.F.R. 2530.210(c)(3)(iv).

[91] 29 C.F.R. 2530.210(f).

[92] 29 C.F.R. 2530.210(c)(3)(iv) and see 29 C.F.R. 2530.210(g). However, if a plan using the rule of parity has already canceled prior covered service on account of the "noncontiguous" years as a supervisor, the cancellation is not reversed when and if the service as a supervisor becomes "contiguous" to later covered service. 29 C.F.R. 2530.210(g).

follows covered service nor the rule that credits noncovered service that precedes later covered service need apply if the noncovered service occurs during a period in which the employer did not have an agreement to contribute to the multiemployer plan. Such credit may be provided under the terms of the plan, but it is not required by ERISA.[93]

Even within the limited scope of the regulations, it is doubtful that many multiemployer plans properly credit contiguous service. According to Dan McGinn, multiemployer plan administrators generally lack knowledge of any service except covered service, and thus rarely credit contiguous service unless a participant brings it to their attention.[94]

c. Multiple-employer plans. The regulations on contiguous and noncontiguous service apply to multiple-employer plans (nonbargained plans to which more than one employer contributes), such as the TIAA-CREF plan.[95] For the TIAA-CREF plan, the application of these rules is inconsequential because the plan provides full vesting after one year of service. For other multiple-employer plans, such as plans of employers related by ownership interests that are not sufficient to make the group of employers a "controlled group," the regulations can have significance.[96]

d. Service with predecessor employers. Naturally enough, the inclusion of all years of service "with the employer or employers" maintaining a plan soon runs into the reality of corporate sales and mergers. ERISA deals with this problem largely through separate statutory provisions. Under ERISA Section 210(b)(1), and Code Section 414(a)(1), when a different employer assumes and maintains a plan of another employer, as may occur after an acquisition of another corporation or all of another corporation's assets, service with the predecessor employer is required to continue to count for *all* purposes under the plan. The same rule applies when a plan is only nominally discontinued before being assumed by a different employer.[97]

The more common situation is not an assumption of a plan by a different employer, but a change of employers *and* a change of plans. If the new employer is the product of a corporate merger, it is a continuation of both "employers," and no rule other than Section 203(b)(1) is needed to require earlier "years of service" with one of the merged employers to be credited for vesting, even if the employees are put

---

[93] 29 C.F.R. 2530.210(h), and see ERISA §203(b)(1)(C) (Code §411(a)(4)(C)). Thus, if an electrician works for an employer who joins a multiemployer plan, the service before the employer joined the plan is contiguous to covered service, but, under ERISA, it is not required to count for vesting. If the plan so provides, credit for this past service may be provided.

[94] D. McGinn, *Joint Trust Pension Plans* (Richard D. Irwin 1978), at 55-56. Under the recordkeeping obligations of ERISA §209 and general fiduciary duties to act in accordance with the terms of the plan and ERISA, a plan adminstrator has a duty to develop a system to obtain the information required to credit contiguous service, but McGinn suggests that it is rare for such a system to be found in practice. *Id.*, at 55-56 and 116.

[95] 29 C.F.R. 2530.210(b) and (c)(3)(i).

[96] If employers are members of a controlled group within the meaning of Code §1563(a), the more stringent rules on counting service with any member of a controlled group of employers override. 29 C.F.R. 2530.210(c)(3)(i) and (d).

[97] Conf. Rep., at 264, 3 ERISA Leg. Hist. 4531.

under a different pension or profit-sharing plan. Similarly, if an incorporated subsidiary is acquired by another company or is spun off on its own, the "employer" may remain the same.

Congress also contemplated regulations that would cover other business transactions that result in employees being placed under different plans. In ERISA Section 210(b)(2) and Code Section 414(a)(2), Congress provided:

> "[I]n any case in which the employer maintains a plan which is not the plan maintained by a predecessor employer, service for such predecessor [employer] shall, to the extent provided in regulations prescribed by the Secretary of the Treasury, be treated as service for the employer."

Twelve years after this was enacted, the IRS has not issued the regulations, although their draft content was discussed as early as 1979.[98] But Congress' intent that a carryover of years of service for vesting under a different plan should occur following a "business reorganization" is unmistakable. Three committee reports state identically:

> "Service with a predecessor of the employer would ... be counted, for purposes of the vesting rules, to the extent provided in regulations. Your committee anticipates that the regulations in this area will prevent a situation where an employee might lose his rights to vesting as a result of a business reorganization."[99]

Normally, without regulations, a statutory section such as Section 210(b)(2) may be impossible to enforce, but where the delay in promulgating the regulations is so long, it may be possible to enforce the section according to Congress' intent, or to obtain "appropriate equitable relief," such as an order that interim regulations be issued, from the Secretary of the Treasury under the Administrative Procedure Act or ERISA Section 502(a)(3)'s cause of action for participants "to enforce any provisions of this title."[100]

2. Period When a Plan, or a Predecessor Plan, Is Maintained

Under ERISA Section 203(b)(1)(C) and Code Section 411(a)(4)(C), years of service with an employer or employers maintaining a plan may be disregarded if the years of service occurred during a period of time when the employer or employers did not maintain the

---

[98] See "Case Study: Handling Employee Benefits in Mergers and Acquisitions, A Panel Discussion," 37 Inst. on Fed. Tax'n—ERISA Supp. (1979), at 11-18.

[99] H.R. Rep. 93-807, at 58, 2 ERISA Leg. Hist. 3178, Material Explaining H.R. 12906, 2 ERISA Leg. Hist. 3326, and H.R. Rep. 93-778, at 57, 2 ERISA Leg. Hist. 2646. And see 3 ERISA Leg. Hist. 3592 (statement of Rep. Fascell that the bill would protect working men and women from being deprived of benefits when a company changes ownership and "each time the new owner establishe[s] a different pension plan").

[100] ERISA does not place a deadline on the issuance of implementing regulations, but the Secretary of the Treasury's decision not to issue the regulations, or to continually delay their issuance, might be enjoined if it results from an arbitrary and capricious disregard of the duty the Secretary owes participants. The Administrative Procedure Act provides that a court may compel agency action "unlawfully withheld or unreasonably delayed." 5 U.S.C. §706(1). And see *Farmworkers Justice Fund, Inc. v. Brock*, 811 F.2d 613 (D.C. Cir. 1987); *AARP v. EEOC*, 8 EBC 1227 (D.D.C. 1987) (citing other decisions).

plan, or a predecessor plan. For this purpose, the period of maintenance of a plan begins with "the first day of the plan year in which the plan is adopted even though the plan is adopted after such first day."[101] For a multiemployer plan, the date of plan establishment is the first day of the plan year in which the particular employer adopts (or in other words, agrees to contribute to) the plan.[102]

The period during which a plan is maintained generally ends with the date the plan is terminated,[103] or in the case of a multiemployer plan, with the *earlier* of the date the employer completely withdraws from the plan or the date the entire plan is terminated.[104] When benefit accruals under a defined benefit plan are "frozen," i.e., the plan is amended to halt future benefit accruals, but it is not terminated under the ERISA Title IV plan termination rules, the plan continues to be maintained for purposes of counting service for vesting until the plan is in fact terminated as provided in Title IV.[105] For plans not subject to Title IV, e.g., defined contribution plans, service with the employer continues to count for vesting until the plan is terminated according to its own terms.[106]

a. When two plans merge. When two *plans* merge, as sometimes occurs after a corporate acquisition or merger (and as occasionally occurs with multiemployer plans), years of service for vesting must continue to count under the merged plan from the respective dates of establishment of each of the two plans.[107] Moreover, if a plan merger follows, rather than precedes, a corporate merger or acquisition, the earlier of the two dates of plan establishment may become the date of establishment for *all* participants for purposes of determining their years of service during the period when the plan was maintained.[108]

b. When a predecessor plan existed. Service with an employer or employers may not be disregarded for vesting during a period when a plan was *not* maintained if the service occurred during a period when a "predecessor plan" was maintained. Under IRS regulations, the term "predecessor plan" means any tax-qualified pension or profit-sharing plan which was "terminated" during a plan year after ERISA's Section

---

[101] 26 C.F.R. 1.411(a)-5(b)(3)(ii).

[102] *Id.*

[103] 26 C.F.R. 1.411(a)-5(b)(3)(iii). In a few cases, service with the employer may continue to count for vesting *after* a Title IV date of termination if the employer makes contributions to the plan that are in excess of its ERISA §4062 liability for any insufficiency of plan assets needed to pay the PBGC's guaranteed benefits. *Id.*

[104] ERISA §203(b)(1)(G) (Code §411(a)(4)(G)), and 26 C.F.R. 1.411(a)-5(b)(3)(iii).

[105] 26 C.F.R. 1.411(a)-5(b)(3)(iii). A partial termination requiring immediate vesting can also result from a "freeze" in benefit accruals. See ch. 9, sec. VIII.A.

[106] 26 C.F.R. 1.411(a)-5(b)(3)(iii).

[107] 26 C.F.R. 1.411(a)-5(b)(3)(ii). When two plans merge, service must continue to count for all purposes, not for just vesting. See ERISA §210(b)(1) (Code §414(a)(1)). Accrued benefits are also protected under ERISA §204(g) (Code §411(d)(6)) as the merger of two plans is a plan "amendment." The assets backing up the payment of accrued benefits under the better-funded of the two plans are also protected against dilution in the event of a subsequent termination of the merged plan under ERISA §208 (Code §414(l)). See ch. 9, sec. VIII.B.

[108] 26 C.F.R. 1.411(a)-5(b)(3)(ii).

211 effective dates and within a five-year period immediately preceding or following the date when the current plan was "established."[109]

In interpreting the scope of the "predecessor plan" rule, it is important to recognize that "terminated" includes a "partial termination,"[110] and that "established" can mean the date an employer "adopts" a plan that was previously "established" by another employer or group of employers.[111] For example, if A, a small employer, has a single-employer plan, and as of a certain date, its employees join a union and negotiate a collective bargaining agreement requiring the employer to contribute to a multiemployer plan, service with the employer during the period of time when the single-employer plan was maintained may be considered service under a "predecessor plan" for the purpose of vesting under the multiemployer plan if the exclusion of the bargaining unit employees from the single-employer plan caused a partial termination of that plan. Similarly, if employer B is a multisubsidiary company with a plan covering all salaried employees and, as of a certain date, one of the subsidiaries is sold to another company (or is spun off on its own), with a partial termination of employer B's plan occurring as a result, previous service with the subsidiary may be required to count for vesting under any new plan adopted by the subsidiary after the sale or spin off.

c. Past service credit as predecessor plan service. Most plans that credit past service for benefit accruals provide that the past service credits also count toward vesting.[112] A few small plans and some multiemployer plans may be found, however, that provide past service credits for benefit accruals, but not for vesting.[113] When Congress enacted ERISA, it directed the IRS to issue regulations defining the term "predecessor plan" as used in ERISA Section 203(b)(1)(C) and Code Section 411(a)(4)(C). As the prime example of the intended coverage of the regulations, the Conference Report states:

> "[I]f the plan provides past service credits for purposes of benefit accrual, it must also provide past service credits for purposes of participation and vesting."[114]

Congress' intent was therefore to require any period for which past service is credited to be included as a period during which a "predecessor plan" was maintained, with the result that any years of service with the employer during that period would count for vesting. The IRS's

---

[109] 26 C.F.R. 1.411(a)-5(b)(3)(v)(A) and (B). And see *Ricciardi v. Ricciardi Profit Sharing Plan*, 630 F.Supp. 914, 7 EBC 1470 (D.N.J. 1986) (requiring vesting credit for service under predecessor plan terminated after ERISA §211 effective date and within 5 years of establishment of new plan).

[110] 26 C.F.R. 1.411(a)-5(b)(3)(iii), and see Code §411(d)(3)(A) and 26 C.F.R. 1.411(d)-2(b).

[111] See 26 C.F.R. 1.411(a)-5(b)(3)(ii).

[112] See D. McGinn, *Joint Trust Pension Plans*, at 162.

[113] The New England Teamsters and Trucking Industry Pension Plan is an example of such a plan.

[114] Conf. Rep., at 268, 3 ERISA Leg. Hist. 4535. And see ch. 3, sec. V (on the discriminatory potential from grants of past service credits).

regulations defining a "predecessor plan," however, did not implement this intent, nor was the issue addressed in the preamble to the proposed or final regulations.[115]

The IRS's failure to implement Congress' intent that past service credit must always extend to vesting as a *per se* regulation does not bar consideration of whether vesting credit is required to prevent potential discrimination under the more general Code Section 401(a)(4) nondiscrimination rule.[116] A second issue when vesting credit is not provided is adequate disclosure—namely, whether participants were adequately informed that their past service credits would not count for vesting. A third issue is whether the employer had an actual "predecessor plan" within the meaning of the existing regulations during the period in which the past service occurred, and whether that plan was terminated or partially terminated in the five years immediately preceding or following the date the employer adopted, or agreed to make contributions to, the plan that is extending the past service credits.[117]

d. Complete withdrawal under a multiemployer plan. In determining the period when an employer contributing to a multiemployer plan "maintained the plan," a "complete withdrawal" generally substitutes for a plan termination as the concluding event in the employer's maintenance of the plan. An essential distinction for this purpose is between a complete and a partial withdrawal. Under ERISA Section 203(b)(1)(G)(i), and Code Section 411(a)(4)(G)(i), any years of service an employee has with an employer after a *partial* withdrawal from a multiemployer plan may not be disregarded for vesting—even, for example, if the employees are now in other service with the employer that is not covered by the plan—unless the partial withdrawal is the result of a decertification of the sponsoring union as the employees' collective bargaining representative (and then, the years may only be disregarded as permitted under as-yet-unissued Treasury regulations).[118] In contrast, any years of service with an employer after a "complete withdrawal" from a multiemployer plan may be disregarded for vesting.

An employer "completely" withdraws from a multiemployer plan when it ceases all operations that are covered under its agreement to

---

[115] See 26 C.F.R. 1.411(a)-5(b)(3)(v) (defining "predecessor plan"), 40 Fed. Reg. 51445 (Nov. 5, 1975) (proposed regulations), and 42 Fed. Reg. 42327 (Aug. 23, 1977) (final regulations).

[116] In multiemployer plans where the Code concept of nondiscrimination has limited application because no members of the prohibited group of employees are participants, the trustees' decision to deny vesting credit for years of past service might be examined under ERISA's fiduciary standard or §302(c)(5) of the Labor Management Relations Act to determine whether it tilts the real benefits of the grant of past service credits unduly in favor of the "class of employees from which union officers are commonly drawn," who may generally be long service employees who do not need the credits for vesting. See *Riley v. MEBA Pension Trust*, 570 F.2d 406, 1 EBC 1757, at 1763 (2d Cir. 1977) (Friendly, J.).

[117] See text at nn. 103 through 105, *supra*.

Declaration of a partial termination from an exclusion of nonvested participants on account of a plant closing, union decertification, or other employer withdrawal from a plan also prevents the forfeiture of benefits from the grant of past service credits, to the extent the benefits are funded at the time of the partial termination. See ch. 11, sec. I.

[118] ERISA §203(b)(1)(G)(i)(II) (Code §411(a)(4)(G)(i)(II)). However, MPPAA §405, 29 U.S.C. §1461, may apply. It permits plans to take "any reasonable action" until regulations or temporary instructions are issued by the named federal agency to put a statutory rule into effect.

contribute to the plan, or when its agreement to contribute to the plan expires and the employer does not negotiate a new contribution agreement with the union.[119] A "partial" withdrawal occurs when an employer ceases to have an obligation to contribute to a multiemployer plan under one or more, but not *all* of its collective bargaining agreements requiring contributions to the plan, while continuing to perform the type of work that was covered under the agreement (or agreements) within the geographic area covered by the plan (or outside this area if the work within the covered area was transferred to another location).[120] A partial withdrawal also occurs if an employer ceases to have an obligation to contribute to a plan for employment at one or more, but not *all* facilities covered by a collective bargaining agreement, while continuing to perform the same type of work at the facility, or facilities.[121] Finally, a partial withdrawal occurs if, for whatever reason, there has been a 70 percent or more decline in an employer's "contribution base units" under a plan, i.e., the number of hours of work or payroll dollars on which contributions to the plan are based, in each year in a consecutive three-year period as compared to the employer's highest average contribution base units in two years out of the preceding five-year period.[122]

The period in which an employer maintains a multiemployer plan may also be concluded by the termination of the entire plan.[123] However, multiemployer plan terminations are not nearly as common as single-employer plan terminations, and are far overshadowed in frequency by complete withdrawals of employers from multiemployer plans. Thus, the conclusion of the period during which an employer "maintains" a multiemployer plan for purposes of determining years of service for vesting is usually a complete withdrawal. Multiemployer plan terminations do, of course, occur and are discussed in Chapter 13.

---

[119] ERISA §4203. At least for purposes of assessing withdrawal liability, an employer may be determined to have completely withdrawn from a plan after it ceases all of its normal business operations, but still has a *de minimis* number of employees engaged in "clean-up work." See *Textile Workers Pension Fund v. Standard Dye & Finishing Co.*, 607 F.Supp. 570, 6 EBC 1562 (S.D.N.Y. 1985) ("complete withdrawal" occurred even though 3 employees still engaged in clean-up operations); *Speckmann v. Barford Chevrolet*, 535 F.Supp. 488, 3 EBC 1245 (E.D. Mo. 1982) (complete withdrawal when auto dealership closed and sold, but one employee still engaged in phase-out work); *F.H. Cobb Co. v. New York State Teamsters Conference*, 584 F.Supp. 1181 (N.D.N.Y. 1984) (complete withdrawal when all operations ceased, but "skeleton" crew of 9 to 16 employees stayed on to move inventory and equipment).

Special MPPAA rules can prevent a "complete" withdrawal from occurring in instances when it would otherwise occur if the plan in question is based in the building and construction industry, see ERISA §4203(b); the entertainment industry, ERISA §4203(c); the long and short-haul trucking, household moving, and public warehousing industries, ERISA §4203(d); or other industries which the PBGC determines display characteristics similar to those in the construction industry, ERISA §4203(f).

[120] ERISA §§4205(a)(2) and (b)(2)(A)(i).

[121] ERISA §4205(b)(2)(A)(ii).

[122] ERISA §§4205(a)(1) and (b)(1). Because the decline must be present in a 3 consecutive year period, there is a lag built in between an employer's first curtailment of operations and the determination that this type of partial withdrawal has occurred. Plans in the retail food industry can adopt a partial withdrawal rule under which a partial withdrawal occurs with only a 35% decline in an employer's contribution base units. See ERISA §4205(c).

[123] ERISA §203(b)(1)(G)(ii) (Code §411(a)(4)(G)(ii)).

3. Other Periods That May Count for Vesting

As with years of participation for benefit accruals, other years may be required to count for vesting beyond those required under ERISA:

a. Military service years. When a veteran is reinstated in his or her old job within 90 days after the end of a period of military service, the Veterans Readjustment Assistance Act requires employers to count the period of military service for vesting in pension and profit-sharing benefits (as well as to credit it for benefit accruals under pension plans).[124] Periods away from work for National Guard duty must also be credited.[125] Vesting credit under pension and profit-sharing plans for periods of military service is generally not contested because it is an even more obvious "perquisite of seniority" than benefit accruals.[126] Where it has been contested, it has been upheld,[127] including as credit toward any early retirement benefit vesting requirements established under a plan's terms.[128]

b. Periods of layoff, disability, or other leave. As described below on the exact measurement of a "year of service," ERISA requires up to 501 consecutive hours for which an employee is paid, or entitled to payment, while on layoff, disability, vacation, jury duty, or other absence to be credited toward the 1,000 "hours of service" required for a year of service for vesting. Under the elapsed time alternative for measuring a year of service, up to one year's absence for any reason other than a quit, discharge, retirement, or death is required to count for vesting, whether or not the absence is paid.

Beyond these minimum requirements, longer periods of layoff, disability, or other periods of absence may be credited under the terms of plans as years of service for vesting (and also as years of participation for benefit accruals). For example, under many collectively bargained plans, up to two years of layoff is credited for vesting, as well as for benefit accruals, whether or not any compensation is paid to the employee during the layoff.[129] Similarly, under both collectively bargained and nonbargained plans, longer periods of disability are commonly credited for both vesting and benefit accruals. Some plans also credit other types of employer-approved leaves of absence. When a

---

[124] 38 U.S.C. §§2021-24.

[125] See 38 U.S.C. §2024(d) and *U.S. v. New England Teamsters Pension Fund,* 737 F.2d 1274, 5 EBC 1824 (2d Cir. 1984).

[126] See, e.g., *Alabama Power Co. v. Davis,* 431 U.S. 581, 1 EBC 1158 (1977) (vesting credit not contested); *Raypole v. Chemi-Trol Chemical Co.,* 754 F.2d 169, 6 EBC 1058 (6th Cir. 1985) (upholding denial of benefit accrual credit under profit-sharing plan, but employer conceded vesting credit).

[127] See, e.g., *Beckley v. Lipe-Rollway Corp.,* 448 F.Supp. 563 (N.D. N.Y. 1978); *Horton v. Armour & Co.,* 98 LRRM 2651 (W.D. Mo. 1978); *Turnington v. Standard Register Co.,* 97 LRRM 2877 (S.D. Ohio 1977).

[128] See *Bunnell v. New England Teamsters Pension Fund,* 655 F.2d 451, 2 EBC 1654 (1st Cir. 1981).

[129] See ch. 4, sec. III.B.5, on the meaning of "layoff."

potentially nebulous term, such as leave of absence, is used, the employer must have an established policy on leaves that is applied uniformly to all similarly situated participants, and that does not otherwise result in prohibited discrimination, e.g., because leave is only granted for managerial sabbaticals.[130]

Under the 1978 Pregnancy Discrimination Amendments to Title VII of the Civil Rights Act, "women affected by pregnancy, childbirth, or related medical conditions [must be] treated the same for all employment-related purposes, including receipt of benefits under fringe benefit programs, as other persons [with] similar [inabilities to work]."[131] This amendment requires absences from work due to pregnancy, childbirth, or related medical conditions to be covered under health, disability, sick leave, or other extended leave of absence plans or policies if similar conditions are covered. When vesting credit is provided under the terms of a pension or profit-sharing plan for such absences, the credit is required to extend to women who are unable to work because of pregnancy or childbirth.[132]

c. Years subject to estoppel. When representations are made to employees that years of service will count for vesting, as may sometimes occur in the midst of a corporate acquisition or the merger of two unions, but the representations are not reduced to writing under the terms of the plan, estoppel may apply to credit the service, as discussed in Chapter 4.

d. Years under reciprocity agreements. Reciprocity agreements between multiemployer plans can create rights to have years of service under one multiemployer plan counted for vesting under another multiemployer plan, or combined with years of service under the other plan for the purpose of determining vesting in benefits accrued under both plans.[133] The precise terms of reciprocity agreements vary, and in some cases the reciprocal credit may be only partial for purposes of

---

[130] See Rev. Rul. 81-106, and see generally *Hardy v. H.K. Porter*, 417 F.Supp. 1175 (E.D. Pa. 1976), *aff'd in part, rev'd in part*, 562 F.2d 42 (3d Cir. 1977). In *Hardy*, some employees were granted extended "leaves of absence" by the employer "solely" to qualify them for early retirement benefits requiring service until age 60, but the same treatment was denied other participants in practically identical circumstances. The employer in *Hardy* argued that putting employees on a leave of absence was done within its discretion as an employer, and hence that it need not be done uniformly. The court, however, found that because the leaves were granted employees solely to qualify them for benefits under the plan, the employer's actions had to be considered an exercise of discretion under the plan. See also Rev. Rul. 81-106.

[131] 42 U.S.C. §2000e(k), as amended by P.L. 95-555.

[132] See *Zichy v. Philadelphia*, 36 FEP Cases 1637 (E.D. Pa. 1979), and 29 C.F.R. 1604, Appendix, Q&A 17.

[133] See D. McGinn, *Joint Trust Pension Plans*, at 135–40; and see, e.g., *Bianco v. Teamsters Local 816 Pension Trust*, 494 F.Supp. 206 (E.D.N.Y. 1980); *Hoover v. Cumberland, Md. Area Teamsters Pension Fund*, 756 F.2d 977, 6 EBC 1401 (3d Cir. 1985), *cert. denied*, 474 U.S. 845 (1985).

vesting.[134] Furthermore, as with contiguous service, many multiemployer plans do not have adequate systems for determining the existence of service subject to their reciprocity agreements, and instead may wait for participants to claim it.[135]

4. Break-In-Service Cancellations of Years of Service for Vesting

Before ERISA, many pension plans had harsh break-in-service rules. An employee might lose all of his or her accumulated years of service for vesting, and also for benefit accruals, because of a break in service which lasted only one year, or an even shorter period. John Daniel's forfeiture of over 10 years of service because of a four-month break in service is memorialized by the U.S. Supreme Court's 1979 decision in *Teamsters v. Daniel.* In *Daniel,* the Court held that omissions and misstatements about a plan's break-in-service rules do not violate the antifraud provisions of federal securities law because an interest in a noncontributory pension plan is not a security.[136]

a. Pre-ERISA break-in-service rules. Break-in-service rules as harsh as the rule applied to John Daniel's service were well-known and roundly condemned before ERISA.[137] However, ERISA Section 203(b)(1)(F) expressly permitted pre-ERISA break-in-service rules to continue in force if the years of service for vesting were lost under a plan's break-in-service rule before the first plan year beginning after December 31, 1975.[138] One quasi-exception to this is that the plan must provide for the continuing effectiveness of its pre-ERISA break provision. In *Snyder v. Titus,* a plan's pre-ERISA break rule was held to be inapplicable to a participant's pre-ERISA service when the plan in effect at the time the participant reached normal retirement age and applied for benefits failed to provide for its continued application to his pre-ERISA service.[139]

Another limit on the application of pre-ERISA break-in-service rules has developed in judicial decisions. The courts have shown a marked antipathy to forfeitures that result from *involuntary* breaks in service, such as a break due to unavailability of work or disability. In *Van Fossan v. Teamsters Local 710 Pension Fund,* for example, the Seventh Circuit noted:

---

[134] See D. McGinn, *supra,* at 135 and 140.

[135] See *Nichols v. Trustees of Asbestos Workers Pension Plan,* 3 EBC 1726 (D.D.C. 1982).

[136] *Teamsters v. Daniel,* 439 U.S. 551, 1 EBC 1620 (1979).

[137] See, e.g., 3 ERISA Leg. Hist. 4790 (statement of Sen. Bentsen).

[138] But the plan's break rules must not have been made harsher between Jan. 1, 1974, and the date ERISA's new rules on breaks in service became effective for the plan. ERISA §211(e)(2).

[139] 513 F.Supp. 926, 2 EBC 1269 (E.D. Va. 1981); but see *Govoni v. Bricklayers Local 5 Pension Fund,* 732 F.2d 250, 5 EBC 1389 (1st Cir. 1984).

> "[W]e do not consider a break in service provision arbitrary and capricious per se. It is only the application of such a rule to a circumstance *beyond the employee's control* that we find arbitrary."[140]

This distinction is recognized in the Third, Fourth, Seventh, Ninth, and District of Columbia Circuits.[141]

In *Saladino v. ILGWU Retirement Fund*, however, the Second Circuit suggested that the voluntary/involuntary distinction might be limited to a break in service that divested a participant from an already vested right (or from a conditional right to early retirement benefits for which the employee had the service but lacked the age).[142] The other decisions applying this distinction have not emphasized the participant's "vested" status as the critical element in making the application of a break-in-service rule to events beyond an employee's control arbitrary. In *Walker v. Construction Laborers Pension Trust*, a district court rejected the Second Circuit's argument in applying the voluntary/involuntary distinction to preserve 13½ years out of 15 years required for a benefit. The court observed that although the prior cases *could* be patterned along the line suggested in *Saladino* of protecting only vested rights:

> "There is no logic to a distinction between incurring an involuntary break in service before or after meeting a minimum employment requirement . . . and [the plan has] offered no reason why it *should* be made."[143]

A sounder limit on the voluntary/involuntary line of cases may arise when a participant's break in service, although *initially* involuntary, subsequently became voluntary because work was available well before the participant's eventual return to service. In *Saladino*, the Second Circuit stated that "more importantly" than its suggested vesting limit, the cases striking down the application of break-in-service rules to involuntary breaks all involved breaks of less than five years. Saladino, in contrast, had been absent from work for 13 years before he returned to work, and had not shown that he could not have returned earlier, even if his initial departure was involuntary.[144]

The application of break-in-service rules has also been struck

---

[140] 649 F.2d 1243, 2 EBC 1457, at 1462 n.21 (7th Cir. 1981) (emphasis added). See also *Vermeulen v. Central States Southeast and Southwest Pension Fund*, 490 F.Supp. 234 (M.D.N.C. 1980) (reviewing and summarizing cases on the distinction).

[141] See *Knauss v. Gorman*, 583 F.2d 82, 1 EBC 1491 (3d Cir. 1978); *Lee v. Nesbitt*, 453 F.2d 1309 (9th Cir. 1972); *Norton v. IAM Nat'l Pension Fund*, 553 F.2d 1352 (D.C. Cir. 1977), all using the distinction and finding involuntariness. And see *Van Fossan v. Teamsters Local 710 Pension Fund, supra* (remanding for a finding on involuntariness). See also *Wilson v. Board of Trustees*, 564 F.2d 1299 (9th Cir. 1977); *Giler v. Board of Trustees*, 509 F.2d 848, 1 EBC 1088 (9th Cir. 1975); *Eddington v. CMTA-Independent Tool & Die Craftsmen Pension Trust*, 794 F.2d 1383 (9th Cir. 1986); *Vermuelen v. Central States Southeast and Southwest Pension Fund, supra*, all using the voluntary/involuntary distinction, but not finding involuntariness.

[142] 754 F.2d 473, 6 EBC 1041, at 1045 n.4 (2d Cir. 1985) (distinguishing *Lee v. Nesbitt*, *Knauss v. Gorman*, and *Van Fossan v. Teamsters Local 710 Pension Fund* on this basis); and cf. *Harm v. Bay Area Pipe Trades Pension Fund*, 701 F.2d 1301, 4 EBC 1253, at 1256 (9th Cir. 1983).

[143] 6 EBC 1412, at 1416 n.5 (C.D. Cal. 1984) (emphasis added).

[144] 6 EBC at 1045 n.4.

down as arbitrary when the rule was inadequately disclosed to participants before the period in which the break occurred so that the participant lacked an opportunity to conform his actions to the rule.[145]

b. ERISA's rule of parity and Retirement Equity Act modification. The major ERISA reform on breaks in service, effective for plan years beginning after December 31, 1975, is the "rule of parity." Under ERISA Section 203(b)(3)(D), a participant cannot lose accumulated years of service for vesting, and consequently cannot lose accumulated years of participation for benefit accruals, unless he or she incurs a series of consecutive one-year "breaks in service" equal to or exceeding the number of years of service the participant had for *vesting* before the break began—regardless of whether or not those years were accumulated consecutively.[146] This is called the rule of parity because the number of consecutive one-year breaks in service must be on par with the years of service previously accumulated for vesting before a break-in-service forfeiture can occur. Thus, if a participant begins work at age 22, and has eight years of service for vesting by age 30, and five years of participation (because the plan used the age 25 minimum participation age permitted before 1985), a break in service cannot wipe out the participant's accumulated eight years of service for vesting (or the five years of participation for benefit accruals), *unless* the break in service extends to eight or more consecutive years.[147]

The 1984 Retirement Equity Act modified the rule of parity, generally effective with the first plan year beginning after December 31, 1984,[148] to establish a five consecutive year floor before the rule of parity can ever operate to cancel any prebreak service.[149] For example, if a participant has three years of service for vesting and incurs a series of three consecutive one-year breaks in service, under the amended rule of parity, the break in service is not long enough to cancel the prebreak service; instead, a minimum of five consecutive one-year breaks in service must occur, regardless of the number of years of service for vesting at stake.[150]

A major element of the ERISA rule of parity both before and after

---

[145] See *Burroughs v. Operating Engineers Pension Fund*, 542 F.2d 1128, 1 EBC 1258 (9th Cir. 1976), *cert. denied*, 429 U.S. 1096 (1977); *Hodgins v. Central States Pension Fund*, 624 F.2d 760 (6th Cir. 1980); *Reiherzer v. Shannon*, 581 F.2d 1266, 1 EBC 1175 (7th Cir. 1978); *Swackard v. Commission House Drivers Local 400*, 647 F.2d 712, 2 EBC 1317, at 1318 (6th Cir. 1981), *cert. denied*, 454 U.S. 1033 (1981). (But lack of disclosure does not create a Securities Act violation because an interest under a pension plan is not a "security." *Teamsters v. Daniel, supra.*)

[146] Paralleled in Code §411(a)(6)(D). And see ERISA §204(b)(4)(A) and Code §411(b)(4)(A) for the consequential rule on years of participation for benefit accruals.

[147] 29 C.F.R. 2530.204-1(b)(2). Because the rules on counting years of service for vesting are more liberal than the rules on counting years of participation, it is not uncommon for a participant to have several more years of service for vesting than years of participation for benefit accruals.

[148] A special rule delays the effective date for collectively bargained plans to the first plan year after the expiration of the bargaining agreement (or agreements) in effect on the date of enactment (Aug. 23, 1984), *or* the first plan year beginning after Jan. 1, 1987, if this is earlier. P.L. 98-397, §302(b).

[149] ERISA §203(b)(3)(D) (Code §411(a)(6)(D)), as amended by P.L. 98-397.

[150] The effective date of this modification means that unless a participant's prebreak service has already been canceled under a plan provision using the unmodified rule of parity by the day

the REA modification (but one that may often be overlooked) is that once a participant has any *nonforfeitable* right to benefits, even, for example, a 25 percent vested interest in accrued benefits, a break in service cannot wipe out the years of service the participant has for vesting, or the years of participation he or she has for benefit accruals. For example, if a participant is 25 percent vested, the vested right to 25 percent of the benefits accrued before a break cannot be forfeited no matter how long the break lasts. In addition, once the participant returns to service, years of service after the break must advance the participant toward a greater vested percentage in the benefits accrued both before and after the break, starting from the point of a 25 percent vested interest. An exception, discussed next, may be used by defined contribution plans to limit additional vesting in benefits accrued before the break.

c. *Defined contribution plan break rules and the REA reform.* In the case of a defined contribution plan (and a defined benefit plan funded exclusively by individual insurance contracts), a stricter break rule than the rule of parity was permitted before 1985 with respect to vesting in benefits accrued before a break in service. Under ERISA Section 203(b)(3)(C) and Code Section 411(a)(6)(C) as in effect before 1985, if a defined contribution plan participant had just a one-year break in service, years of service after the break were not required to be added to years of service before the break in determining the vested percentage of benefits accrued before the break. In other words, the nonforfeitable percentage of prebreak accruals could be frozen at its prebreak level after just a one-year break in service. Thus, if a participant did not have a vested interest in the account balance before the break, the benefits would be forfeited entirely. If a participant in a defined contribution plan was 25 percent vested in his or her account balance, and incurred a one-year break in service, the years after the break were not required to advance him or her on the vesting schedule insofar as increasing the vested percentage in the account balance accrued before the break. The years of service before the break, however, had to be (and continue to have to be) added to the years of service after the break for purposes of vesting in benefits accrued after the break—unless the normal ERISA rule of parity allows their cancellation.

Under a class-year system of vesting, a defined contribution plan participant can always lack a vested right to the five preceding years' employer contributions, along with earnings on those contributions—even if the participant has worked for the employer for 15 or 20 years. Until 1985, all nonvested contributions in a class-year plan could be forfeited if a participant separated from service prior to the end of the

---

before the first day of the first plan year beginning after Dec. 31, 1984, the rule of parity, as modified, must apply. See P.L. 98-397, §303(a)(2).

fifth plan year following the plan year for which contributions were made, and was not "reemployed *in the plan year* of separation."[151]

Under the 1984 Retirement Equity Act, the special one-year break rule for defined contribution plans is modified, generally effective with the first plan year beginning after December 31, 1984,[152] to require that the break in service must be for at least five consecutive years before the nonvested portion of a prebreak account balance can be forfeited.[153]

When the special one-year break rule was used before the REA effective date, the considerations discussed before on application of pre-ERISA break-in-service rules—concerning whether the break in service was voluntary or involuntary and whether the plan disclosed the break rule adequately—are both relevant. Discrimination under the Internal Revenue Code can also result from the operation of a break-in-service provision.[154]

5. One-Year Hold-Out Rule

A one-year hold-out rule in ERISA permits a plan to hold out, or not take into account, years of prebreak service in determining a participant's nonforfeitable rights after a one or more year break in service until the participant completes a year of service after returning from the break.[155] When a participant completes a year of service after the break, the prebreak service must be taken into account immediately along with the postbreak service (unless the ERISA rule of parity has applied to cancel the years of prebreak service).

---

[151] 26 C.F.R. 1.411(d)-3(a)(1) (emphasis added).

[152] A special rule delays the effective date for collectively bargained defined contribution plans to the first plan year after the date of expiration of the bargaining agreement (or agreements) in effect on the date of enactment, *or* the first plan year after Jan. 1, 1987, if this is earlier. P.L. 98-397, §302(b).

The effective date means that unless a plan's use of the unmodified rule had already operated to freeze the vested percentage, or lack thereof, in a prebreak account balance by the day before the first plan year beginning after Dec. 31, 1984, the rule, as modified, must apply. See P.L. 98-397, §303(a)(2), and Temp. and Prop. Regs. 1.410(a)-5T, 50 Fed. Reg. 29371 (July 19, 1985).

[153] ERISA §203(b)(3)(C) (Code §411(a)(6)(C)), as amended by P.L. 98-397. A technical correction in the Tax Reform Act clarifies the application of REA's 5-year floor to class-year plans, effective for contributions made in plan years beginning after Sept. 27, 1986. ERISA §203(c)(3) and Code §411(d)(4), as amended by §1898(a)(1) of P.L. 99-514. This correction basically follows the rule in Temp. and Prop. Regs. 1.411(d)-3T, 50 Fed. Reg. 29371 (July 19, 1985), which is effective in the interim period—with one critical difference. The temporary regulations defined a 5-year break under a class-year plan as 5 consecutive years in which the participant was not performing services as of the close of each plan year (the temporary regulations expressly provided that the close of any plan year in which the participant was on maternity or paternity leave did not count).

The *critical* difference, however, is that, read in conjunction with the preexisting regulations, the temporary regulations provided that a participant would vest in class year contributions at the end of the 5th plan year after the year in which the contributions were made as long as a disqualifying break in service did not occur prior to the end of the 5th plan year. See 26 C.F.R. 1.411(d)-3(a)(1). In contrast, the technical correction requires a participant to be "performing services for the employer as of the close of each of 5 plan years . . . after the plan year for which the contributions were made" in order to vest.

[154] For example, if a one-year forfeiture provision under a pre-REA profit-sharing plan significantly increases a plan's discrimination in terms of contributions, plus forfeitures, going to the prohibited group of employees as a percentage of pay, the break-in-service provision in operation may violate §401(a)(4) of the Code.

[155] ERISA §203(b)(3)(B) (Code §411(a)(6)(B)).

If a plan uses the 1,000 hours of service standard described below for measuring years of service for vesting, the significance of the one-year hold-out rule is minimal except for whatever administrative convenience it offers the plan. This is because the hours of service standard operates only in whole years. If a participant has nine years of service under a plan that requires 10 years for vesting and incurs a one-year break in service, a one-year hold-out rule allows the plan to wait until the participant completes a year of service after a return to service before vesting him in the accrued benefits. But this hold-out period is no longer than the participant would have had to wait in any event to complete the tenth year of service required for vesting.

However, when a plan uses the elapsed time alternative for measuring service for vesting, the use of a one-year hold-out rule can be more significant. Under the elapsed time method, periods of service that are measured in years, months, and days are aggregated in determining the number of whole years a participant has for vesting. Thus, if a plan uses the 10-year cliff vesting schedule and a participant has a nine year and three month period of service and incurs a one year and one day period of severance before returning to service, he or she would normally have 10 years under the elapsed time method after just nine more months of service. However, if the plan uses a one-year hold-out rule, the participant may effectively be required to work 10 years and three months before the prebreak service is aggregated to vest the participant's accrued benefits.[156]

B. Exact Measurement of a Year of Service for Vesting

As in measuring "years of participation," employees and their employers are rarely so cooperative as to end periods of employment precisely at 12-month intervals, or to always work "full time" years. Whether a "year of service" for vesting has occurred is, however, often more important than whether a year of participation has occurred because one additional year of service for vesting can make the difference between a right to receive accrued benefits from a large number of years of participation and no right to receive those accrued benefits.

ERISA Section 203(b)(2)(A), and Code Section 411(a)(5)(A), define a "year of service" for vesting as:

> "[A] calendar year, plan year, or other 12-consecutive month period designated by the plan during which the participant has completed 1,000 hours of service."

The vesting "year of service" definition applies to both defined benefit

---

[156] 26 C.F.R. 1.410(a)-7(d)(5). However, for the one-year hold-out rule to apply in this manner, the rule must be adequately disclosed to participants.

and defined contribution plans, even though years of participation only apply to the accrual of benefits under defined benefit plans.[157]

ERISA's hours-based definition of the term "year of service" (with special, more liberal rules for seasonal and maritime workers) contains no "reasonable and consistent" alternative authorization parallel to that contained in the definition of a year of participation.[158] Nevertheless, the agency regulations allow two completely different approaches to measuring years of service. The first is based on the 1,000 hours standard described in the statute (and numerous equivalencies directly related to hours), and is set forth in Department of Labor regulations. The second approach is the elapsed time method, which is set forth in Treasury regulations. The elapsed time method was promulgated because of employer complaints concerning the administrative inconvenience of counting hours under the 1,000 hours standard. By its terms, the elapsed time method disregards hours of service, and instead focuses on periods of service. It contains special rules on crediting layoffs, other absences, and short separations from service (called service-spanning rules).[159]

1. 1,000 Hours Standard and Equivalencies

While 2,000 hours can be required for a full "year of participation," if this is no more than the customary work year, 1,000 hours of service must result in a full "year of service" for vesting regardless of the customary work year. Any greater number of hours within a 12-month computation period is inconsequential. As Jeffrey Mamorsky states in *Employee Benefits Law*:

> "Three employees who complete 1,000, 1,500, and 2,000 hours, respectively, will each receive an identical one year of vesting service under this provision."[160]

For an employee working a 40-hour week, 1,000 hours of service can be completed approximately halfway through any 12-consecutive month period the plan designates as its vesting computation period (40 hours × 25 weeks = 1,000 hours). On the other hand, for a part-time, 20-hour per week worker, it can take nearly the entire 12-month period to obtain 1,000 hours of service. In either case, additional hours of service

---

[157] An exception to this is that the "year of service" definition does not apply to defined contribution plans that use "class-year" vesting. ERISA §203(c)(3), which provides the class-year vesting schedule alternative for defined contribution plans, does not use the term "year of service," but instead refers to vesting occurring "not later than the end of the 5th plan year following the plan year for which such contributions were made." Under the IRS's regulations, this language has been interpreted to permit forfeitures when a participant separates from service before the end of a plan year—regardless of the number of *hours* the participant had during the plan year. 26 C.F.R. 1.411(d)-3(a)(1).

And see n. 153 on the changes to this rule resulting from the REA break-in-service amendments and a technical correction in the 1986 Tax Reform Act.

[158] Compare ERISA §204(b)(4) and §203(b)(2)(A).

[159] 26 C.F.R. 1.410(a)-7(a)(1)(ii).

[160] J. Mamorsky, *Employee Benefits Law* (Law Journal Seminars-Press 1983 ed.), at 5-13.

within the 12-month computation period do not result in any additional year or part-year of service for vesting. At the same time, once 1,000 hours of service have been completed in the 12-month computation period, a participant must receive a full year of service for vesting, *whether or not* he or she is still employed at the end of the computation period.[161] When a participant has less than 1,000 hours within a plan's computation period, ERISA does not require a partial year of credit that can be aggregated with service in the next computation period. Instead, the lesser number of hours of are lost. The language of a plan, or of its SPD, could require that a lesser hours total, such as 500 hours, results in a partial year of vesting credit, to be aggregated with service in succeeding years, but ERISA does not require it.[162]

The 12-month computation period a plan uses for measuring vesting years of service must be specified in the plan.[163] Typically, it is based on each employee's date of hire, or else the plan year. The computation period may be any other 12-consecutive month period as long as the plan provision is uniformly applied and is not devised in a manner that results in artificial postponement of vesting credit, e.g., a computation period which begins four months after each individual is hired.[164] However, in determining years of service for meeting any condition of participation requirement, the initial 12-month computation period must be based on the employee's employment commencement date.[165] For example, if a plan uses a January 1 to December 31 computation period for determining vesting years of service, and an individual is hired on June 1, 1986, his or her hours from June 1 to December 31, 1986, determine whether he or she has a year of service for vesting in the first applicable vesting computation period, while his or her hours of service from June 1, 1986, to May 31, 1987, are required to be separately computed to determine whether he or she had a year of service for purpose of any one year of service condition of participation requirement.

In determining whether an employee has 1,000 hours of service during a 12-month computation period, an hour of service is each hour for which an employee is paid, or entitled to payment, for the performance of duties for the employer, and also each hour for which the employee is paid, or entitled to payment, during the 12-month period although no duties were performed, e.g., on account of paid vacation, holidays, sick leave, disability leave, jury duty, military leave, or any other paid absence, including a period for which severance payments

---

161 29 C.F.R. 2530.200b-1(b).

162 See ERISA §203(d).

163 29 C.F.R. 2530.200b-1.

164 29 C.F.R. 2530.203-2(a). If a plan excludes years prior to age 18 (previously age 22 was allowed), a special rule requires that the first 12-month vesting computation period either must begin with the date of the employee's 18th birthday, or else all hours of service in the 12-month computation period *in which* the employee reached age 18 must be counted. 26 C.F.R. 1.411(a)-5(b)(1)(iii).

165 29 C.F.R. 2530.202-2(a).

are made, irrespective of when the employment relationship terminated.[166] Hours of service can thus include hours of accrued vacation or sick leave that are paid, or for which payment is due, on a termination of employment.[167] They can also include hours which form the basis for severance pay, e.g., when one week of regular time pay is due for each two years of work on a severance of employment.[168] Hours of service also include periods for which back pay is awarded or agreed to by an employer because of labor law violations, or age, race, or sex discrimination.[169] However, no more than 501 consecutive hours of service which are paid, or entitled to payment, but for which no duties are performed, are required to be credited in a 12-month computation period.[170] Rules are provided for counting hours of service when no duties are performed and the rate of pay is on a different basis than the rate normally earned, e.g., when vacation pay is $200 per week and the regular rate of pay is $400 per week.[171]

Rather than counting each hour of service (including hours which are paid, or entitled to payment, but for which no duties are performed), a plan can adopt one of seven equivalencies set out in Department of Labor regulations. These permit plans to:

(1) Count only hours in which duties are performed; but then because of the exclusion of hours in which no duties are performed but which are paid, or entitled to payment, the plan must use 870 hours for which duties are performed as the equivalent of 1,000 hours of service;[172]

(2) Count only regular time hours; but then because of the exclusion of overtime hours and also the exclusion of hours for

---

[166] 29 C.F.R. 2530.200b-2(a)(1) and (2). If no duties are performed and payments to an employee are made under a plan maintained by the employer solely for the purpose of complying with applicable state workmen's compensation, disability insurance, or unemployment compensation laws, hours of service are not required to be credited. 29 C.F.R. 2530.200b-2(a)(2)(ii). Hours of service are also not required to be credited if the only payments to the employee are for medical expenses. 29 C.F.R. 2530.200b-2(a)(2)(iii).

[167] 29 C.F.R. 2530.200b-2(a)(1) and (2). But see *Hope v. IBEW Local 1245 Pension Trust*, 785 F.2d 826, 7 EBC 1313 (9th Cir. 1986) (terminated staff employees of a union not entitled to 2 weeks credit for vesting based on accrued vacation at termination of employment, even though the employees were entitled to receive the accrued vacation pay irrespective of the termination of employment). Vacation hours need not be credited if vacation pay is drawn while continuing to work normal hours and receive normal wages. See 29 C.F.R. 2530.200b-2(b)(3) and PLR 7946099 (undated), reprinted at ¶17,370J CCH Pension Plan Guide.

[168] See PLR 8031091 (May 9, 1980), reprinted at ¶17,372E CCH Pension Plan Guide. Cf. *Tyson v. Teamsters Local No. 710 Pension Fund*, 811 F.2d 1145, 8 EBC 1324 (7th Cir. 1987) (LMRA §302(c)(5) not a bar to crediting 4 weeks salary paid to participant after he ceased employment in recognition of his long years of service and disability for purposes of 15 year service requirement for disability pension); *Eagar v. Savannah Foods & Indus., Inc.*, 605 F.Supp. 415 (N.D. Ala. 1984) (raising severance pay credit issue, but not deciding it).

[169] 29 C.F.R. 2530.200b-2(a)(3).

[170] 29 C.F.R. 2530.200b-2(a)(2)(i). More than 501 consecutive hours for which no duties are performed are required to be credited for absences due to military service under the Veterans Readjustment Assistance Act.

[171] 29 C.F.R. 2530.200b-2(b).

[172] 29 C.F.R. 2530.200b-3(d)(1). Hours for which back pay is awarded, or agreed to, must be counted as hours for which duties are performed to the extent that is the basis of an award or settlement.

which no duties are performed, the plan must use 750 regular time hours as the equivalent of 1,000 hours of service;[173]

(3) Count days of employment in which at least one hour of service (whether with duties or without) would be required to be credited, with each such day then credited as the equivalent of 10 hours of service;[174]

(4) Count weeks of employment in which at least one hour of service (whether with duties or without) would be required to be credited, with each week then credited as the equivalent of 45 hours of service;[175]

(5) Count semi-monthly pay periods in which at least one hour of service (whether with duties or without) would be required to be credited, with each semi-monthly period then credited as the equivalent of 95 hours of service;[176]

(6) Count months of employment in which at least one hour of service (whether with duties or without) would be required to be credited, with each month then credited as the equivalent of 190 hours of service;[177] or

(7) Use total earnings in the 12-month period divided by the hourly rate from time to time, or the lowest hourly rate during the entire 12-month period, to determine hours, with 870 hours substituted for 1,000 hours of service as a year.[178] If the employee has no hourly rate, a plan can use earnings from the performance of duties divided by an imputed hourly rate based on regularly scheduled hours within the 12-month period, with 750 of such hours then substituted for 1,000 hours of service as a year of service.[179]

When a plan uses one of these equivalencies, it must set forth the equivalency that it is using in the plan document.[180] Similarly, a plan that uses the basic 1,000 hours-counting standard must state the regulatory definition of hours of service in the plan.[181]

2. Elapsed Time Alternative

Despite the equivalencies provided in the regulations, many employers urged the Department of Labor to promulgate a regulation that would allow them to use an elapsed time method of counting service in

---

[173] 29 C.F.R. 2530.200b-3(d)(2).

[174] 29 C.F.R. 2530.200b-3(e)(1)(i).

[175] 29 C.F.R. 2530.200b-3(e)(1)(ii).

[176] 29 C.F.R. 2530.200b-3(e)(1)(iii).

[177] 29 C.F.R. 2530.200b-3(e)(1)(iv).

[178] 29 C.F.R. 2530.200b-3(f)(1).

[179] 29 C.F.R. 2530.200b-3(f)(2) and (3).

[180] 29 C.F.R. 2530.200b-3(c).

[181] 29 C.F.R. 2530.200b-2(f).

lieu of either strict hours-counting or the equivalencies. In 1976, the Department issued such proposed and temporary regulations.[182] In 1980, under a transfer of jurisdictional authority effected by the President's 1978 Reorganization Plan No. 4,[183] the IRS made the regulations final.[184]

The elapsed time method is not based on hours of service, nor does it, like the equivalencies, translate other periods of service, such as days or weeks, back into hours. Instead, the elapsed time method looks at an employee's "period of service," i.e., the years, months, and days, from the employment commencement date.[185] When the employment relationship ends by reason of a quit, discharge, retirement, or death, the "period of service" ends, and no rounding up to the next highest whole year is required. Thus, to use an example in the regulations:

> "[I]f a plan provides for the statutory five to fifteen year graded vesting, an employee with a period (or periods) of service which yield 5 whole year periods of service and an additional 321-day period of service is twenty-five percent vested in his or her employer-derived accrued benefits (based solely on the 5 whole year periods of service)."[186]

The regulatory adoption of the elapsed time method has been justified on the grounds that it was used before ERISA by many single-employer plans, is administratively less cumbersome than the hours of service method (although comparison is seldom made to the equivalencies allowed under the hours method), and contains a number of compensating features that are said to make it generally "as equitable" as the statutory hours standard. The compensating features are:

(1) The period of service must always start with the employee's employment commencement date.[187] Under the hours standard, it is possible for employees to be hired at the end of a plan's vesting computation period and thus to have no real chance of obtaining 1,000 hours in the first 12-month computation period.

(2) When a participant returns to service following a one or more year break in service (called a "period of severance"), a new period of service must begin immediately on the date of reemployment, with this new period of service being added to the prior period, or periods, of service. Under the hours standard, it is possible for employees to be rehired after a one or more year break at the end of a plan's vesting computation period and thus to have no real chance of obtaining 1,000 hours in the

---

[182] 41 Fed. Reg. 56462 (Dec. 28, 1976).

[183] See §101(b) of Reorganization Plan No. 4 of 1978, 5 U.S.C.A. App. 1.

[184] 45 Fed. Reg. 40979 (June 17, 1980).

[185] See 26 C.F.R. 1.410(a)-7(a)(1).

[186] 26 C.F.R. 1.410(a)-7(d)(1)(iv), and see 26 C.F.R. 1.410(a)-7(d)(1)(i). The same rule applies in meeting year of service requirements that are conditions for beginning participation in benefit accruals. See 26 C.F.R. 1.410(a)-7(c)(2)(i).

[187] 26 C.F.R. 1.410(a)-7(b)(6).

first 12-month computation period during which the return to work occurs.

(3) Periods of service are required to be aggregated under elapsed time. Thus, if an employee works for four years and four months, has a one-year period of severance, and returns to work, the counting of the employee's period of service picks up at four years and four months.[188] Under the hours standard, if the employee has less than 1,000 hours in the last computation period before the break, he or she starts up on a return to service with an even four years.

(4) Up to one year of service, whether or not paid, is required to be credited for any absence, other than by reason of a quit, discharge, death, or retirement. Under the hours standard, this type of credit is limited to 501 consecutive hours credit (approximately one-half of a year of service under the 1,000 hours standard), and applies only to periods which are paid, or for which the employee is entitled to payment.[189]

(5) Up to one year's service is also required to be counted if an employee severs from service by reason of a quit, discharge, or retirement and returns to work *within* 12 months from the date of severance.[190]

The first three compensating features are actually equivocal. Thus, while the elapsed time period of service must always start with the employment commencement date (or reemployment commencement date), for some employees this is an advantage, as illustrated above, but for others it is a disadvantage. For example, if a plan uses a calendar year 12-month computation period, and an employee is hired on March 1, he or she might have one full year of service for vesting by December 31 under the hours standard, whereas under the elapsed time method, he or she would have a nine month period of service. Similarly, the use of partial year periods of service sometimes results in less credit than under the hours standard. For example, an employee with four years and six months of service might have five full years of service under the hours standard, while under the elapsed time method he or she would have four years and six months. On returning to service after a two-year break, the elapsed time method would aggregate the four year and six month period of service with the new period of service. Thus, after six months, the employee would have five years of service. But under the 1,000 hours standard, the employee may already have five years, and with six months additional service, might

[188] 26 C.F.R. 1.410(a)-7(d)(1)(ii).

[189] 26 C.F.R. 1.410(a)-7(d)(1)(iii).

[190] 26 C.F.R. 1.410(a)-7(d)(1)(iii)(A). A special rule applies when an employee is absent for any other reason, and then quits, is discharged, or retires during the absence. In this case, the 12-month period begins at the date when the employee was first absent. If the employee returns to service within 12 months from this date, credit is required for the period. 26 C.F.R. 1.410(a)-7(d)(1)(iii)(B).

have a sixth year of service based on 1,000 hours within the plan's 12-month computation period.

The only features of the elapsed time method that are clearly more advantageous are the service-spanning features, namely, (1) that any absence other than on account of a quit, discharge, death, or retirement results in up to one year's additional credit for vesting, whether or not the employee receives any pay during the period, and (2) when service is severed by a quit, discharge, or retirement, but the individual returns to service within 12 months, the service must be bridged and the entire period of severance credited.[191]

The chief disadvantage of the elapsed time method occurs when a participant is permanently separated from service with a fractional year in his or her last 12-month period of service with the employer, e.g., after nine years and 321 days, that, if rounded up, would result in a critical additional year of service for vesting. The elapsed time rule will not round up the 321 days to the tenth year of service, even though 321 days generally represents well in excess of 1,000 hours of service.[192] This disadvantage of the elapsed time rule can apply under a 10-year cliff vesting schedule, with the result that a participant is not vested at all and, also, under a graded vesting schedule, which is often used by defined contribution plans, with the result that either the participant is not vested at all or is vested in a lower percentage of the account balance than would otherwise be the case.

In the case of a defined contribution plan with class-year vesting, a requirement that a participant complete whole years can be justified because ERISA specifically provides that class-year contributions are only required to become nonforfeitable by "the *end* of the 5th plan year following the plan year for which such contributions were made."[193] However, for all other plans, the definition of a year of service is set out in Section 203(b)(2)(A). This definition specifically requires credit for a year of service whenever a participant has completed 1,000 hours of service in a 12-month computation period. In essence, the statute rounds up to a whole year of service for vesting when a participant completes more than the requisite 1,000 hours of service in a 12-month period chosen by the plan.

In *Swaida v. IBM Retirement Plan*, a plan participant who was employed by IBM for nine years, nine months, and 21 days challenged the elapsed time rule insofar as it required more than the statute

---

[191] See n. 190 above on the rule when a quit, discharge, or retirement occurs in the middle of an absence, e.g., when an employee removes himself from a recall list after a 3-month layoff.

[192] In an example in the elapsed time regulations, an employee is 25% vested under a 5-to-15 year graded vesting schedule based on 5 years and 321 days of service, whereas he or she would normally be 30% vested under the hours-counting method for computing years. The application of ERISA's break in service rule of parity and special defined contribution plan break rules can also be more disadvantageous for participants under the elapsed time method. See sec. III.C below. Another closely related feature of elapsed time that can be disadvantageous to participants is its delayed aggregation of periods of service after a one or more year break in service under the one-year hold-out rule. See sec. III.A.5 above.

[193] ERISA §203(c)(3) (Code §411(d)(4)) (emphasis added), and see 26 C.F.R. 1.411(d)-3(a)(1). The quoted language was altered by the 1986 Tax Reform Act amendments.

required (assuming, as the courts have generally assumed, that his date of hire would have marked the start of the applicable 12-month computation periods).[194] Despite the statutory 1,000 hours language, legislative history indicating that recordkeeping problems were to be handled by equivalencies to hours—such as equivalencies based on earnings data[195] —and lack of authority under the statute to promulgate or approve alternates, such as in the "year of participation" definition, the *Swaida* court held that the elapsed time regulations were in general terms "as equitable" as the statutory method. The court stated that it was "convinced" that "[h]ad Congress desired to preclude ... regulations permitting use of the elapsed time method ... [Congress] would have done so explicitly."[196]

In *Automated Packaging Systems, Inc. v. Commissioner*, on the other hand, the Tax Court expressly declined to pass on the legality of the elapsed time regulations in such situations in a case in which the compensatory, service-spanning features of the elapsed time rule were challenged by an employer as exceeding the IRS's authority.[197] In a concurring opinion, three judges indicated that they viewed the *Swaida* issue differently than the federal district court later did. The concurring opinion, written by Judge Chabot, who was on the staff of the Joint Committee on Internal Revenue Taxation at the time ERISA was enacted,[198] stated that the petitioner's plan must fail because:

> "[I]t is impossible, under the plan's provisions ... for a participant to be denied a nonforfeitable right to his or her accrued benefit derived from employer contributions even though the participant has completed 1,000 hours of service during each of that number of years which the plan is permitted to require under [the minimum vesting standards.] Since the statute forbids a plan to impose a greater obligation on a participant, I do not see how a regulation could validly permit a plan to impose a greater obligation on a participant. Consequently, I do not see how we could hold for petitioner in this case, even if we had agreed with petitioner's analysis of the regulations drawn in question."[199]

The *Swaida* decision also contrasts in terms of results with *Gennamore v. Buffalo Sheet Metals, Inc., Pension Plan* and *Tucci v. Edgewood Country Club*, in which an employee with nine years and 10 months from his date of hire and another employee with nine years and 11

---

[194] 570 F.Supp. 482, 4 EBC 2017 (S.D.N.Y. 1983), *aff'd per curiam*, 728 F.2d 159, 5 EBC 1120 (2d Cir. 1984), *cert. denied*, 469 U.S. 874 (1984).

[195] See 3 ERISA Leg. Hist. 4659 (statement of Rep. Dent) and 3 ERISA Leg. Hist. 4735 (statement of Sen Williams).

[196] 4 EBC at 2023. See also *Bruch v. Firestone Tire & Rubber Co.*, 640 F.Supp. 519 (E.D. Pa. 1986) (use of elapsed time method to determine vesting not arbitrary and capricious).

[197] 70 T.C. 214, 1 EBC 1834 (1978). The majority opinion also states, "We do not pass on the validity of the [elapsed time] regulations in a situation where application of the ... method results in more restrictive vesting than application of the 1,000 hour standard." 1 EBC at 1841 n.11.

[198] See 3 ERISA Leg. Hist. 4747 and 4774.

[199] 1 EBC at 1841.

months from his date of hire were both held to be vested under the hours of service definition in Section 203(b)(3)(A).[200]

When the elapsed time method is used, instead of challenging its validity, participants may seek to obtain the maximum credit under the features that are to compensate for the alteration of the statutory definition, namely, the required credit for up to 12 months of absence "for any reason other than" a quit, discharge, death, or retirement, and the required credit for up to 12 months of severance after a quit, discharge, or retirement if the employee returns to service before the 12-month period after the quit, discharge, or retirement ends. The latter feature is relatively straightforward and self-explanatory. The former is more open to interpretation, particularly on the difference between a layoff or other reduction in force, and a discharge. Under labor agreements, the term "discharge" is generally reserved for individual discharges for cause, with the terms "layoff," "reduction in force," or "termination" being used when a separation from service is the result of more general economic or business conditions.[201] Thus, "for any reason *other than*" a quit, discharge, retirement, or death can be interpreted to include permanent reductions in force, as well as temporary, short-term layoffs. In *Cook v. Pension Plan for Salaried Employees of Cyclops,* a pension plan used the elapsed time method for crediting service for vesting. When the sponsoring employer closed a plant, the employer-appointed plan administrator denied the separated employees the additional year of credit on the ground that they had been "discharged." The district court held that this interpretation was arbitrary and capricious since a discharge in labor-management relations means a discharge "for cause" or the "individual fault" of an employee. On appeal, however, the Sixth Circuit reversed, holding that "discharge" was ambiguous enough to be susceptible to the plan administrator's construction.[202]

---

[200] See *Gennamore v. Buffalo Sheet Metals, Inc., Pension Plan,* 568 F.Supp. 931, 5 EBC 1268 (W.D.N.Y. 1983); *Tucci v. Edgewood Country Club,* 459 F.Supp. 940 (W.D. Pa. 1978). See also *Tice v. Lampert Yards, Inc.,* 761 F.2d 1210 (7th Cir. 1985) (57 year old millshop foreman who was terminated failed to prove that termination was pretext to deny him pension benefits for which he had 9 years of service under plan requiring 10 years for vesting and thus was a violation of ADEA; however, independent plan administrator had determined subsequent to discharge that plaintiff did in fact have 10th year of service under ERISA's 1,000 hours standard for measuring a year of service).

The elapsed time regulations may also be subject to challenge because they were made final by the IRS under a transfer of jurisdiction from the Department of Labor effected by Reorganization Plan No. 4 of 1978. Reorganization Plan No. 4 contained a one-house veto provision identical to the one struck down by the Supreme Court in *I.N.S. v. Chadha,* 462 U.S. 919 (1983).

[201] See, e.g., *Fitzsimons Steel Co.,* 81-2 ARB (CCH) ¶8408 (Ruben, 1981).

[202] C.A. No. C-1-82-615 (S.D. Ohio, Oct. 5, 1984), *rev'd,* 801 F.2d 865, 7 EBC 2278 (6th Cir. 1986). But see PLR 8031091 (May 9, 1980), reprinted at ¶17,372E CCH Pension Plan Guide, *Roberts' Dictionary of Industrial Relations* (BNA 3d ed.) (discharge means "dismissal of an employee, usually for some infraction of the rules . . . , incompetence, or other good reason"), and ch. 4, sec. III.B.5 (on the meaning of "layoff"). And compare *Holt v. Winpisinger,* 811 F.2d 1532, 8 EBC 1169 (D.C. Cir. 1987) (administrator's interpretation of whether a person was employed or an independent contractor was entitled to no deference when issue was years of employment ERISA requires to count for vesting).

In *Cook,* the elapsed time rule applied to vesting in early retirement benefits because the plan provided, although it was not required to, that the same service-counting rule applied for all vesting requirements under the plan.

Beyond this issue, the Revenue Rulings and case law are clear that when an employer can place employees in a status, such as on layoff or leave of absence, which results in more vesting credit under the terms of a plan, or can use a characterization, such as discharge, which will stop credit, to describe the participant's status, the employer must have an established policy for drawing this line, and must apply it uniformly to similarly situated employees.[203] In addition, prohibited discrimination must not result under the policy. That is, it is not sufficient for an employer to have an established layoff or leave of absence "policy" that is uniformly applied if the policy is one that discriminates in operation in favor of employees who are primarily highly compensated, e.g., because leave is only granted for managerial sabbaticals.[204]

3. Measuring Pre-ERISA Years of Service

ERISA's vesting schedules require pre-ERISA "years of service" to count for vesting if a participant was still active under the plan after the applicable ERISA effective date.[205] If a plan was in existence on January 1, 1974, this means that years of service before the effective date must be computed and counted for vesting for participants who are active in any plan year beginning with the first plan year after December 31, 1975. ERISA's definition of a "year of service" as 1,000 hours of service within a 12-month computation period applies to these years, as well to years after the effective date. Since the necessary records for a determination of pre-ERISA years under the hours of service standard may not have been kept, the Department of Labor's regulations permit a plan to use:

> "[W]hatever records may be reasonably accessible to it and ... make whatever calculations are necessary to determine the approximate number of hours of service completed before such effective date. For example, if a plan ... has, or has access to, only the records of compensation of employees for the period before the effective date, it may derive the pre-effective date hours of service by using the hourly rate for the period or the hours customarily worked. If accessible records are insufficient to make an approximation of the number of pre-effective date hours of service for a particular employee or group of employees, the plan may make a reasonable estimate of the hours of service completed by such employee or employees during the particular period. For example, if records are available with respect to some employees, the plan may estimate the hours of other employees in the same job classification based on these records. A plan may use any of the equivalencies permitted ... or the elapsed time method of crediting service ... to determine hours of service completed before the effective date. ..."[206]

---

[203] Rev. Rul. 81-106 and see *Hardy v. H.K. Porter Co.*, 417 F.Supp. 1175 (E.D. Pa. 1976), *aff'd in part, rev'd in part*, 562 F.2d 42 (3d Cir. 1977).

[204] Rev. Rul. 81-106.

[205] Conf. Rep., at 268, 3 ERISA Leg. Hist. 4535, and 26 C.F.R. 1.411(a)-2(f).

[206] 29 C.F.R. 2530.200b-3(b).

The regulations are silent on the 12-month computation period to be used in determining years of service before ERISA's effective dates, but unless a different computation period is "specifically detailed" in the plan as it existed prior to ERISA's effective date, courts have used a computation period based on the employee's date of hire.[207] When a plan has been amended to "specifically designate" a different 12-month computation period as the computation period for vesting, the rules described below on crediting service after a change in computation periods apply.[208]

4. Changes in Computation Periods or in the Method for Measuring a Year of Service for Vesting

If a plan was amended with the effective dates of ERISA to specifically designate a 12-month computation period other than the anniversary date of hire as the vesting computation period, or is amended at any other time to change from one 12-month computation period to another for determining vesting years of service, Labor Department regulations provide:

> "[T]he first vesting computation period established under such amendment [must] begin before the last day of the preceding vesting computation period . . . [A]n employee who is credited with 1000 hours of service in both the vesting computation period under the plan before the amendment and the first vesting computation period under the amendment is credited with 2 years of service for those vesting computation periods. For example, a plan which has been using a calendar year vesting computation period is amended to provide for a July 1—June 30 vesting computation period starting in 1977. Employees who complete more than 1000 hours of service in both of the 12-month computation periods extending from January 1, 1977 to December 31, 1977 and from July 1, 1977 to June 30, 1978 [must be] advanced two years on the plan's vesting schedule."[209]

Special rules apply when a plan, instead of merely changing computation periods, changes from the 1,000 hours standard, or an equivalency based on hours, to the regulatory elapsed time alternative, or vice versa.[210]

Whenever a plan's computation period or its method of determining service is changed, consideration should also be given to whether an indirect change in the plan's vesting schedule has occurred, thereby necessitating a vesting schedule election for participants with five or more years of service, as defined in the regulations.[211]

---

[207] *Gennamore v. Buffalo Sheet Metals, Inc., Pension Plan*, and *Tucci v. Edgewood Country Club, supra.* A computation period based on the date of hire was used for pre-ERISA periods even when testimony was offered that the plan's practice had been to use employment during the plan's fiscal year as the basis for crediting years of service. *Gennamore, supra.*

[208] See *Gennamore, supra* (applying the rules on changes in computation periods and obtaining 2 years of service for employment during a 22-month period).

[209] 29 C.F.R. 2530.203-2(c)(1). *Gennamore, supra,* provides another example of how this rule works.

[210] 26 C.F.R. 1.410(a)-7(f)(1) and (g).

[211] See 26 C.F.R. 1.411(a)-8(c)(1) and 1.411(a)-8(b)(3).

C. Exact Measurement of a One-Year Break in Service

ERISA defines a one-year break in service as a 12-month computation period, which must be the same as the 12-month computation period the plan uses for computing years of service for vesting, in which a participant has 500 or less hours of service.[212] When a plan uses an equivalency related to hours, the critical number of hours may move down to 435 or less if the equivalency counts only hours for which duties are performed or is based on total earnings divided by an hourly rate. It may be reduced to 375 hours or less if the equivalency is based on counting only regular time hours, or dividing earnings from the performance of duties by an imputed hourly rate.[213] When a participant has 501 or more hours of service, or 436 or 376 under these equivalencies, a one-year break in service is avoided within the 12-month computation period. Although the service may be insufficient for a "year of service," ERISA leaves this intermediate terrain in which a participant may have neither a year of service nor a one-year break in service within the computation period.[214]

Under the alternate elapsed time method, the break-in-service concept is changed to a participant's period of severance. When a participant severs from service, a "period of severance" begins. For the period of severance to have any negative effect, it must be at least a "one-year period of severance," i.e., a period of 12 continuous full months. If the period of severance ends within 12 months, the participant's service must be bridged under the elapsed time service-spanning provisions.[215] Beyond this, however, the elapsed time method does not operate in whole years. Thus, while under the hours counting method, a participant can have only whole years of service and whole one-year breaks in service, under elapsed time, it is possible, and indeed likely, that the participant will have periods of service in years, months, and days, and periods of severance in years, months, and days. For example, a participant might have a five year, four months, and 10 day period of service followed by a period of severance. If the participant's period of severance equals or exceeds five years, four months, and 10 days, the ERISA rule of parity can operate to cancel the prior period of service (provided that the participant has no vested rights and the plan provides for the cancellation).

In certain circumstances, the elapsed time method can result in a quicker cancellation of accumulated service under the ERISA rule of parity and the special defined contribution plan break rule than under the hours of service standard. This is because an employee with, for example, four years and four months of service is likely to have the 501

---

[212] ERISA §203(b)(3)(A) (Code §411(a)(6)(A)), and 29 C.F.R. 2530.200b-4(a)(3).

[213] See 29 C.F.R. 2530.200b-3(d)(1) and (2) and (f)(1) and (2).

[214] See ERISA §203(b)(2)(A) (Code §411(a)(5)(A)) and ERISA §203(b)(3)(A) (Code §411(a)(6)(A)). And see, e.g., 26 C.F.R. 1.411(a)-6(d) (example (2)).

[215] 26 C.F.R. 1.410(a)-7(d)(7).

hours of service needed to prevent a one-year break in service in the fifth computation period, and thus enough hours to postpone the first possible one-year break in service until the sixth computation period. In contrast, under the elapsed time method, the period of severance which may be used to cancel prior years of service begins immediately. Under the special one-year break-in-service rule applicable to defined contribution plans before the 1984 Retirement Equity Act, a participant could thus have his or her nonvested percentage of an account balance forfeited after just over a one-year "period of severance" in circumstances when a one-year break in service under the 1,000 hours standard would not ordinarily have occurred. The 1984 Retirement Equity Act's establishment of a minimum floor of five consecutive one-year breaks in service, or five consecutive one-year periods of severance, before the rule of parity or the special defined contribution plan break rule can operate makes break-in-service rules less important prospectively, and with them, this disadvantage in the elapsed time rule.

Under the REA amendments to ERISA, beginning with plan years after December 31, 1984, an individual is also to be deemed to have up to 501 hours of service by reason of any absence from work on maternity or paternity leave—regardless of whether those hours are paid—in determining whether a one-year break in service has occurred in a 12-month computation period.[216] If this credit is not needed to prevent a one-year break in service in the year in which the leave begins, it can apply in the following year. "For example, an individual who completes at least 501 hours during a year before leaving employment by reason of pregnancy . . . is entitled to credit of up to 501 hours in the next year, because such credit is not needed in the year in which the absence begins."[217] The elapsed time regulations have been amended to provide commensurate additional credit against the onset of a period of severance.[218] The credit under the REA amendment is solely for the purpose of preventing a break in service from occurring during maternity or paternity leave. The deemed hours do not count for purposes of determining whether an individual has a year of service for vesting, or for determining whether the individual has a year of participation for benefit accruals, unless they are otherwise required to be credited under ERISA or the terms of the plan.[219]

When a participant returns to service following a one or more year break in service, the 12-month computation period under an hours-counting method generally remains the same as before. Thus, if a computation period is based on the original date of hire, it may remain

---

[216] ERISA §202(b)(5) (Code §410(a)(5)(E)) and ERISA §203(b)(3)(E) (Code §411(a)(6)(E)), as added by REA, P.L. 98-397.

[217] S. Rep. 98-575, at 9-10, [1984] U.S. Code Cong. & Ad. News 2547, at 2555-56.

[218] Temp. and Prop. Regs., 1.410(a)-7T, 50 Fed. Reg. 29371 (July 19, 1985).

[219] S. Rep. 98-575, at 9-10, [1984] U.S. Code Cong. & Ad. News 2547, at 2555-56.

so. Similarly, if it is based on the plan year, it may remain so. Alternatively, a plan may provide that on reemployment, the new date of hire will be the start of the next computation period. Under the elapsed time method, when an employee is rehired, a new "period of service" must begin with the employment commencement date with the new period of service then being added to the prior period, or periods, of service.

D. Seasonal and Maritime Worker Year of Service and Break in Service Rules

ERISA Section 203(b)(2)(C), and Code Section 411(a)(5)(C), provide:

> "In the case of any seasonal industry, where the customary period of employment is less than 1,000 hours during a calendar year, the term 'year of service' shall be such period as determined under the regulations of the Secretary [of Labor]."

Twelve years after enactment, regulations have not been proposed. In January 1976, the Department of Labor issued an interpretive bulletin that would have defined seasonal industry by (1) whether 50 percent or more of the employees covered by a plan complete less than 1,000 hours of service each year, and (2) whether the hours of service completed by employees in any three-month period vary by more than 150 percent from the hours completed in any other three-month period, thus demonstrating a "peak" period indicative of seasonal work.[220] Under this interpretive bulletin, when a worker is in a seasonal industry as defined above, the completion of 500 or more hours of service within the plan's 12-month computation period was to result in a year of service for vesting (and the completion of more than 250 hours in the period was to prevent a one-year break in service).[221]

However, less than a month after this interpretive bulletin was issued, it was rescinded.[222] The rescission was based on comments that the definition of "seasonal industries" would cover "a number of plans in industries which would generally be recognized as nonseasonal."[223] Since that time, no interpretive bulletins have been issued, and no regulations have been proposed. By inaction, the special ERISA rule for workers in seasonal industries has become a dead letter, even for plans in industries that would "generally be recognized" as seasonal.

Given the length and the effect of this delay, one senior citizens' organization has suggested a seasonal worker might be able to obtain a court order compelling the issuance of regulations or a determination

---

[220] IB 76-1, 41 Fed. Reg. 3290 (Jan. 22, 1976).

[221] *Id.* Similarly, the completion of 500 or more hours of service would have been required to trigger credit for at least a partial year of participation for benefit accruals.

[222] IB 76-2, 41 Fed. Reg. 7749 (Feb. 20, 1976).

[223] Preface to IB 76-2, *supra.*

of his or her vesting rights under this section of ERISA or the Administrative Procedure Act in view of Congress' intent that a more liberal "year of service" standard was to be established for seasonal workers.[224] Because seasonal workers are often women or minorities, another approach may be under Title VII of the Civil Rights Act if the number of hours customarily completed in a year by women or minority workers is below the number of hours required under a plan for a "year of service."[225]

In the case of the maritime industry, ERISA Section 203(b)(2)(D), and Code Section 411(a)(5)(D), provide:

> ". . . 125 days of service shall be treated as 1,000 hours of service. The Secretary [of Labor] may prescribe regulations to carry out the purposes of this subparagraph."

The Secretary of Labor has issued regulations defining the maritime industry and further clarifying the determination of days of service in the maritime industry. The regulations also allow maritime industry plans to use the hours-counting regulations, any of the equivalencies to hours, or the elapsed time method in lieu of counting days of service.[226]

IV. Vesting Schedule or Rule Change Elections

Analogous to the ERISA Section 204(g) protection of accrued benefits against decreases from plan amendments,[227] ERISA Section 203(c)(1)(A), and Code Section 411(a)(10)(A), provide that when a plan's vesting schedule is amended, the change must not have any detrimental effect on nonforfeitable rights to accrued benefits. ERISA Section 203(c)(1)(B) and Code Section 411(a)(10)(B) go one step further and provide that all participants without vested or fully vested benefits who have five or more years of service must also be given the option of remaining under the plan's old vesting schedule. For this purpose, whether a participant has five or more years of service is determined as of 60 days after the *later* of (1) the date the amendment is adopted, (2) the date the amendment becomes effective, or (3) the date on which notice of the amendment is furnished to participants.[228] Perhaps even more important, whether a participant has five or more years of service for this purpose is determined without regard to the

---

[224] National Senior Citizens Law Center, Representing Older Workers in Rural Areas (1982), at IX-21. Under the APA, a court may compel agency action "unlawfully withheld or unreasonably delayed." 5 U.S.C. §706(1). And see *Farmworkers Justice Fund, Inc. v. Brock*, 811 F.2d 613 (D.C. Cir. 1987); *AARP v. EEOC*, 8 EBC 1227 (D.D.C. 1987) (citing other decisions).

[225] See generally ch. 10, sec. IV. A similar argument can be made about the number of hours needed to trigger credit for a partial year of participation if a plan sets a threshold for receiving credit for a partial year of participation that is above the number of hours worked by women or minority workers. See ch. 4, sec. III.D.1.

[226] See 29 C.F.R. 2530.200b-6, -7, and -8.

[227] ERISA §204(g) (Code §411(d)(6)). And see ch. 4, sec. IV.B.

[228] 26 C.F.R. 1.411(a)-8(b)(2).

generally permissible exceptions in ERISA Section 203(b)(1) that a plan may otherwise use to disregard years of service before a participant reached age 18, years of service before the plan, or a predecessor plan, was established, or years of service before certain breaks in service.[229]

Vesting schedule amendments that are subject to this election include more than the most obvious vesting schedule changes, e.g., from 10-year cliff vesting to a 5-to-15 year graded vesting schedule. The regulations specifically provide:

> "[A]n amendment of a vesting schedule is each plan amendment which *directly or indirectly* affects the computation of the nonforfeitable percentage of employees' rights to employer-derived accrued benefits. Consequently, such an amendment, for example, includes each change in the plan which affects either the plan's computation of years of service or of vesting percentages for years of service."[230]

As an example, if a plan voluntarily provides that an up to two-year period of layoff counts for vesting, and the employer later decides to cut back on this provision, a vesting schedule election may be required for all participants with five or more years of service, as defined above. Another example of a less obvious vesting schedule change is a change in a plan's normal retirement age. In Revenue Ruling 81-210, the Service ruled that when a plan increases its normal retirement age, such as from age 65 to age 70, or from age 65 to the later of age 65 or the tenth anniversary of participation, as many plans did in the wake of the 1978 ADEA amendments, the change is a vesting schedule amendment because of ERISA's vesting at normal retirement age requirement. In *Fentron Industries v. Shopmen's Pension Fund,* a plan amendment adding a provision to cancel benefit accruals based on years of past service upon an employer's withdrawal from a multiemployer plan was also held to be a change in the plan's vesting schedule. Although the amendment was structured so as not to completely divest any employee of all accrued benefits, but rather only to reduce the "amount" to which the employee would be entitled, the Ninth Circuit held the amendment changed what the employees were vested in, and therefore, had to be considered a vesting schedule amendment.[231]

To avoid the Section 203(c)(1)(B) election procedure, which is regarded by some plan administrators as cumbersome, and also to avoid putting employees to difficult choices (such as between a 10-year

---

[229] 26 C.F.R. 1.411(a)-8(b)(3).

[230] 26 C.F.R. 1.411(a)-8(c)(1) (emphasis added).

[231] 674 F.2d 1300, 3 EBC 1323 (9th Cir. 1982). But compare *Stewart v. National Shopmen Pension Fund,* 730 F.2d 1552, 5 EBC 1518 (D.C. Cir. 1984), *cert. denied,* 469 U.S. 834 (1984) (not finding a plan amendment in another case involving the same plan and plan provision as in *Fentron*).

The addition of a new forfeiture provision for postemployment competition applicable to participants who had vested under a more liberal vesting schedule than ERISA requires might also have been handled as a vesting schedule change in *Hauck v. Eschbacher,* 665 F.2d 843, 2 EBC 2202 (8th Cir. 1981), had the Eighth Circuit not invalidated the amendment as a matter of contract.

cliff and 5-to-15 year graded vesting schedule) that might not work out as they expect, many plans merge a change in the plan's vesting schedule with the existing vesting schedule in a manner that preserves the advantages of the unamended schedule for all current participants in the plan. If a vesting schedule amendment is merged in this manner, no election is required to be offered.[232] It is doubtful, however, that all plans are providing these elections, or properly merging their schedules, when an amendment *indirectly* affects vesting under the plan.

Effective in 1989, the Tax Reform Act amends the vesting schedule election rules to provide that this election is required for all participants who have *three* years of service and are not fully vested.[233]

V. Permitted Forfeitures of Vested Benefits

A. Exceptions to Nonforfeitability

ERISA Section 203(a)(3), and Code Section 411(a)(3), permit six exceptions to the ERISA Section 3(19) definition that a "nonforfeitable" benefit is a benefit that is unconditional. Under Section 203(a)(3), a "nonforfeitable" right to accrued benefits is not abridged "solely because":

(1) A plan provides that benefits are lost if a participant dies before preretirement survivor's annuity coverage is required to be offered under ERISA Section 205, or after electing a form of benefits that does not continue payments to a survivor;[234]

(2) A plan provides that the payment of benefits is suspended during a period of reemployment with the employer sponsoring a single-employer plan or, for a multiemployer plan, is suspended during a period of reemployment within the same industry, trade or craft, and geographic area covered by the plan;[235]

(3) A defined benefit plan is amended within two and a half months after the close of a plan year or, for a multiemployer plan, is amended within two years after the close of a plan year, to reduce accrued benefits earned beginning from the first day of the plan year based on a finding by the Secretary of the Treasury of "substantial business hardship," with no

---

[232] 26 C.F.R. 1.411(a)-8(b)(1).

[233] ERISA §203(c)(1)(B) and Code §411(a)(10)(B), as amended by §1113 of P.L. 99-514.

[234] ERISA §203(a)(3)(A). ERISA §205's requirements on preretirement survivor's benefits and survivor's benefit elections are discussed below in ch. 6, sec. II.

[235] ERISA §203(a)(3)(B). Benefits may not be suspended beyond the period of reemployment. The Department of Labor's regulations define the period of reemployment for this purpose on a month-by-month basis, and exclude as minimal, reemployment for less than 40 hours a month. See 29 C.F.R. 2530.203-3(c)(1) and (2). See also Rev. Rul. 81-140 on the consequences of noncompliance with the limits of this rule.

other alternatives available to the employer (or employers), such as a funding waiver or extension of amortization periods, that would enable the employer (or employers) to otherwise continue to maintain the plan;[236]

(4) A contributory defined benefit or defined contribution plan provides that on the withdrawal by a participant of benefits attributable to mandatory employee contributions, benefits from employer contributions that are less than 50 percent nonforfeitable are forfeited;[237]

(5) A multiemployer plan provides that past service benefits are canceled if the employer for whom the past service was rendered withdraws from the multiemployer plan;[238]

(6) A multiemployer plan is amended to reduce benefits as permitted under the MPPAA "reorganization" rules for multiemployer plans in financial difficulty, or to suspend benefit payments as required on the "insolvency" of the multiemployer plan.[239]

Although not expressly stated in Section 203(a)(3), a seventh exception is that "nonforfeitable" benefits from single-employer plans may be lost if an employer terminates a plan without enough assets to pay all benefits and the PBGC's guarantee does not insure all the benefits offered under the plan.[240] The 1986 Single-Employer Pension Plan Amendments Act effectively narrows this implied exception to a "distress" termination of a plan.[241]

Because Section 203(a)(3) only provides exceptions to the minimum vesting standards for accrued benefits established in ERISA Section 203(a)(2), an eighth and ninth implied exception have been established in the regulations and in the courts to permit the forfeiture of benefits that are not required to accrue, such as unreduced early retirement benefits, and also of benefits that vested under more liberal vesting schedules than the ERISA minimum standards in circumstances that are not permitted under the above exceptions. Early retirement benefits that are not considered a part of the "accrued benefit" have thus been permitted to be forfeited, rather than merely being suspended for a limited period, for any reemployment within the same industry, trade or craft, and geographic area covered by a multiemployer plan. In a single-employer plan, such benefits may be forfeited

---

[236] ERISA §203(a)(3)(C), and see ERISA §302(c)(8) and Code §412(c)(8). Also see the citations on "substantial business hardship" amendments in ch. 4, sec. IV.B.1.

[237] ERISA §203(a)(3)(D). To use this exception, the plan (which will usually be a defined contribution plan) must provide a buy-back provision under which the forfeited benefits will be restored if the employee contributions are repaid to the plan within certain periods. See ch. 4, sec. III.C.4.

[238] ERISA §203(a)(3)(E)(i). Limits on past service cancellations are discussed in ch. 4, sec. III.C.6.

[239] ERISA §203(a)(3)(E)(ii). And see ch. 13, secs. I and IV.

[240] See ch. 12, sec. I.A.

[241] See ch. 12, secs. I.A and VII.

for competition with the employer or other "bad boy" reasons that could not result in any suspension of benefits if the benefits were "accrued benefits" (for single-employer plans, Section 203(a)(3)(B) permits suspensions of benefits only for reemployment with the same employer).[242]

The same reasoning has been applied to permit forfeitures for competition or other "bad boy" reasons of benefits that vest under standards more liberal than the ERISA minimum vesting standards (More liberal standards than ERISA requires are most prevalent in profit-sharing and stock bonus plans.) Although ERISA generally forbids "bad boy" clauses or noncompetition conditions from being attached to nonforfeitable pension benefits, this protection has been limited in these cases not because the benefits are not "accrued benefits," but because the plan's vesting schedule exceeds the ERISA minimum standards. Thus, if a profit-sharing plan provides 100 percent vesting in participants' individual account balances after five years of service, when it is not required to do so under ERISA until after 10 years, the plan is permitted to condition the rights which vested with less than 10 years of service on noncompetition with the employer.[243] However, if the faster vesting schedule is required because the plan is top-heavy, the vested rights are subject to the same forfeiture restrictions as provided in ERISA Section 203(a)(3).[244] In addition, any plan, such as a Code Section 401(k) plan, that uses the ERISA exception that permits three years of service to be used as a condition of participation must provide that benefits become "completely nonforfeitable (within the meaning of [Section 203] and the regulations thereunder)" after not more than three years of service.[245] However, plans that are required to provide "4/40" vesting to prevent discrimination under the Code can forfeit the benefits that are vested beyond the ERISA minimum standards, unless prohibited discrimination results from the forfeitures.[246]

---

[242] See *Johnson v. Franco,* 727 F.2d 442, 5 EBC 1368 (5th Cir. 1984); *Thompson v. Asbestos Workers Local 53 Pension Fund,* 716 F.2d 340, 4 EBC 2307 (5th Cir. 1983); *Riley v. MEBA Pension Trust,* 586 F.2d 968, 1 EBC 1763 (2d Cir. 1979); *Capocci v. General Motors,* 444 F.Supp. 1306 (D. Haw. 1978); and 29 C.F.R. 2530.203-3(a). Cf. *Morse v. Stanley,* 732 F.2d 1139, 5 EBC 1602 (2d Cir. 1984) (lump sum payment of benefits denied because of noncompetition policy; court permitted this as legitimate plan policy, but emphasized that no forfeiture of actuarial value occurred from the denial).

[243] See *Hummell v. S.E. Rykoff & Co.,* 634 F.2d 446, 2 EBC 1416 (9th Cir. 1980); *Hepple v. Roberts & Dybdahl, Inc.,* 622 F.2d 962, 2 EBC 2529 (8th Cir. 1980); *Ramirez v. Lowe,* 504 F.Supp. 21 (S.D. Tex. 1979), *aff'd,* 639 F.2d 306 (5th Cir. 1980); *Montgomery v. Lowe,* 507 F.Supp. 618 (S.D. Tex. 1981); *Nedrow v. MacFarlane & Hays Co. Profit Sharing Trust,* 476 F.Supp. 934, 1 EBC 1932 (E.D. Mich. 1979); 26 C.F.R. 1.411(a)-4(c).

[244] Code §416(b) states that "[e]xcept to the extent inconsistent . . . with this subsection, the rules of [ERISA §203] shall apply" to benefits vested under the top-heavy plan rules.

[245] 26 C.F.R. 1.410(a)-3(b).

[246] See Rev. Rul. 85-31.

B. Limitations on Forfeitures for Competition or Reemployment[247]

The oxymoron in "nonforfeitable" benefits still being subject to "forfeiture" is obvious. Because of this, adequate disclosure to participants of the nonforfeitable benefit exceptions a plan uses is crucial. In *Hillis v. Waukesha Title Co.*, a pension plan was estopped from asserting a forfeiture provision for competition with the sponsoring employer when an SPD describing the provision had not been distributed to the participant. The court stated:

> "[W]here a plan participant is reasonably unaware of a benefit forfeiture clause, and where the plan administrator fails to take any steps to advise the participant of the clause, the forfeiture may not be enforced against the participant."[248]

Summary plan description statements, and the reasonable understanding of employees, have also been used to narrowly interpret the scope of forfeiture provisions for competition. In *Gould v. Continental Coffee Co.*, a summary booklet's description of a forfeiture clause as limited to "direct competition" with the employer that is "detrimental to the employer's interest" was used to construe a forfeiture provision that was not so limited in the full plan document.[249]

ERISA also does not insulate Section 203(a)(3) forfeitures from

---

[247] Author's Note: Common law and other ERISA limitations on the other permissible forfeitures are discussed in other parts of the text (as indicated in the footnotes to each exception above). The approach to determining whether any permissible forfeiture is otherwise in violation of law is, however, basically the same as described in this section. Forfeitures of normal or early retirement benefits because of continued employment after a corporate sale or merger are also discussed in ch. 6, sec. I.D.

[248] 576 F.Supp. 1103, at 1109 (E.D. Wis. 1983). See also 29 C.F.R. 2520.102-2(b) (SPD shall not "minimize[]" exceptions and other limitations on a plan's benefits), 29 C.F.R. 2520.102-3(l) (circumstances which may result in forfeiture must be "clearly identified" in SPD), and *Stanger v. Gordon*, 244 N.W.2d 628 (Minn. 1976) (employer's statements that employee would have an absolute right to profit-sharing benefits on his termination of employment resulted in award of compensatory and punitive damages when there was, in fact, a forfeiture for competition clause in the plan). But see *Risch v. Waukesha Title Co.*, 588 F.Supp. 69 (E.D. Wis. 1984) (no estoppel of forfeiture for competition when employee received an SPD describing the forfeiture before he left to go to work for a competitor, even though the SPD had been prepared late in violation of ERISA so that the employee had no notice of the provision during a significant part of the time when he was rendering service under the plan); accord *Freund v. Gerson*, 610 F.Supp. 69, 6 EBC 1796 (S.D. Fla. 1985).

[249] 304 F.Supp. 1, at 3 (S.D.N.Y. 1969). And see *Hollenbeck v. Falstaff Brewing Corp.*, 605 F.Supp. 421, at 428 and 434-35 (E.D. Mo. 1984), *aff'd*, 780 F.2d 20 (8th Cir. 1985) (under "rigorous reasonableness test," plan provision for forfeiture of death benefits for "proper cause" not applicable when employee's firing was "over a difference in managerial styles" and not "some impropriety that would breach the sensibilities of a hypothetical 'reasonable' businessman"); *Paddock Pool Const. Co. v. Monseur*, 533 P.2d 1188 (Ariz. App. 1975) (using common law principle of interpreting plans "to avoid forfeiture," to determine that employee did not leave "for the purpose" of competing with the employer, but left because of a dispute over a new method of compensation for his work); *Fredericks v. Georgia Pacific Corp.*, 331 F.Supp. 422 (E.D. Pa. 1972), *app. dismissed*, 474 F.2d 1338 (3d Cir. 1972) (when plan provided for forfeiture on voluntary quit or discharge, and company forced employee's resignation, neither circumstance applied to permit forfeiture). And compare *Noell v. American Design, Inc., Profit Sharing Plan*, 764 F.2d 827, 6 EBC 1833 (11th Cir. 1985) (ambiguity in provision for forfeiture of benefits vested above the ERISA minimum requirements resolved against participant when SPD explained the forfeiture provision clearly).

other legal considerations. In *Central Tool Co. v. IAM National Pension Fund,* a district court thus recognized that "ERISA merely tolerates the use of forfeiture provisions."[250] This toleration without a blanket endorsement is demonstrated by the "solely because" language used in setting out each of the permissible exceptions. Because of these factors, courts faced with forfeitures tolerated under Section 203(a)(3), or outside the scope of Section 203(a)(3) because the benefits are not accrued benefits, have begun to look at the reasonableness of the forfeiture apart from its toleration under ERISA. In *Lojek v. Thomas,* the Ninth Circuit stated that a forfeiture of early retirement benefits for competition is arbitrary and capricious if the employee was discharged or constructively discharged from employment so that he or she may have had no alternative but to compete.[251] State court cases dealing with pre-ERISA forfeitures have also applied the constructive condition that the forfeiture for competition must not be precipitated by a discharge or constructive discharge of the employee.[252]

In *Hurn v. Plumbing, Heating and Piping Industry Trust,* the Ninth Circuit, reviewing a pre-ERISA forfeiture, also examined whether a participant was reemployed or competing in a job which could be a legitimate concern of a plan and found that a retiree running for a union's presidency was not competing within the industry covered by a multiemployer plan, nor would his employment in the office he was running for be likely to erode the plan's contribution base.[253] Similarly, in *Ellis v. Lionikis,* a state court found that a salesman's employment within an industry could not pose a significant threat to a plan when he carried with him no trade secrets, confidential information, or prior customer relationships. Instead, "Ellis was simply one more salesman . . . in an industry which is admittedly [already] highly competitive."[254] Along the same line, other cases have interpreted the term "competitive business" narrowly to prevent an unreasonable restraint of trade, or have considered the reasonableness of the forfeiture as a measure of damages to the plan or the employer.[255]

Inconsistent application of a forfeiture provision is another factor that courts have considered in examining the reasonability of a forfeiture. In *Associated Milk Producers v. Nelson,* a forfeiture based on dishonest conduct—a common "bad boy" forfeiture provision before

---

[250] 523 F.Supp. 812, 2 EBC 2019, at 2024 (D.D.C. 1981); and see *Elser v. IAM Nat'l Pension Fund,* 684 F.2d 648, 3 EBC 2155, at 2161 (9th Cir. 1982), *cert. denied,* 464 U.S. 813 (1983).

[251] 716 F.2d 675, 4 EBC 2321 (9th Cir. 1983). *Morse v. Stanley,* 732 F.2d 1139, 5 EBC 1602 (2d Cir. 1984), also suggests that the competition giving rise to a forfeiture must not be precipitated by a discharge or constructive discharge of the employee.

[252] See *Post v. Merrill Lynch, Pierce, Fenner & Smith,* 421 N.Y.S.2d 847 (N.Y. 1979); *Kroeger v. Stop & Shop Co.,* 432 N.E.2d 566 (Mass. App.Ct. 1982) (forfeiture limited because employee "asked to go").

[253] 703 F.2d 386, 4 EBC 1811 (9th Cir. 1983).

[254] 394 A.2d 116, at 119 (N.J. App.Div. 1978).

[255] See *Kamenstein v. Jordan Marsh Co.,* 623 F.Supp. 1109, 6 EBC 2611 (D. Mass. 1985); *Zimmerman v. Brennan,* 254 N.W.2d 719 (Wis. 1977); *Kroeger v. Stop & Shop Co., supra.*

ERISA—was impermissible when four other employees who had engaged in the same conduct (making political contributions in violation of federal election law) had not been similarly treated.[256] Prohibited discrimination under the Code can also result from a forfeiture provision, particularly under a profit-sharing or stock bonus plan in which forfeitures are reallocated to other participants' account balances according to their level of compensation, and thus, in substantial part to prohibited group employees.[257]

When a forfeiture provision is added to a plan by plan amendment after a participant has accrued benefits under the plan or after a participant has five years of service, a different light is cast on whether the forfeiture is permissible. The introduction of a new forfeiture provision raises issues of compliance with ERISA Section 204(g), because of the direct or indirect effect of the amendment on existing accrued benefits, and with ERISA Sections 203(c)(1)(A) and (B), because of the direct or indirect effect of the amendment on the plan's vesting rules. With the 1984 Retirement Equity Act amendments to ERISA Section 204(g), the addition of a new forfeiture provision for early retirement benefits is clearly prohibited, even if the benefits are not "accrued benefits."[258] In *Hauck v. Eschbacher,* a plan provided for vesting after a shorter period than required under the ERISA minimum standards. The employer later adopted a new postemployment competition restriction applicable to those participants who had vested under the liberal plan rules, but not under the ERISA minimum standards. The participants argued that the amendment violated a provision in the plan, which paralleled ERISA Section 204(g), that no plan amendment would reduce a participant's accrued benefits "to less than he would have been entitled to if he had resigned from the employ of the Employer on the day prior to the effective date of the amendment." Without needing to reach ERISA Section 204(g), or ERISA Sections 203(c)(1)(A) and (B), the court held, as a matter of contract, that the plan amendment was invalid insofar as it reduced participants' accrued benefits before the date of the amendment.[259]

Plan amendments introducing new forfeitures can also be in breach of fiduciary duty when they lack a reasoned basis or impose a disproportionate burden on particular employee groups. In *Chambless v. Masters, Mates & Pilots Pension Plan,* a plan amendment forfeiting early retirement benefits for reemployment with any company operating in the industry covered by a plan, but not contributing to it, was held to be arbitrary when the plan did not show a factual basis for determining that the amendment would benefit plan participants and when the amendment had a severely punitive effect on participants

---

[256] 624 S.W.2d 920 (Tex. Ct.App. 1981). See also *Terito v. John S. Swift Co.,* 444 N.Y.S.2d 423 (N.Y. Sup.Ct. 1981).

[257] See Rev. Rul. 85-31 (discrimination in favor of prohibited group employees may not result from a forfeiture provision, even if the forfeiture is otherwise permissible).

[258] See ch. 4, sec. IV.B.3.

[259] 665 F.2d 843, 2 EBC 2202, at 2206 (8th Cir. 1981).

who worked for such employers because of an interaction with the definition of compensation used in determining the benefits the participant would later receive at normal retirement age. The amendment was also arbitrary because "clear [and] timely" notice of this interaction was not provided to participants before they went to work with noncontributing competitors.[260]

A plan amendment can also be arbitrary because it diminishes vested rights in a broad common law sense. In *New York State Teamsters Conference Pension v. Hoh,* a plan amendment expanding a provision for a suspension of benefits for reemployment with contributing employers after retirement to a suspension of benefits for any reemployment in the industry, trade or craft, and geographic area covered by the plan, whether or not with a contributing employer, was arbitrary when applied to a participant who had already retired before the amendment was adopted. The court stated that "to be effective, notification of rule changes . . . must be made prior to retirement." Without such notice, application of the amendment would "retroactively divest [Hoh] of earned benefits."[261] However, in *Geib v. New York Teamsters Pension Fund,* the Third Circuit found that the same amended suspension of benefit rule struck down in *Hoh* was reasonable in its application to participants who retired before the rule was adopted.[262]

---

[260] 772 F.2d 1032, 6 EBC 2209, at 2217 (2d Cir. 1985).

[261] 561 F.Supp. 679, at 684-85 (N.D.N.Y. 1982). And see *Rochester Corp. v. Rochester,* 450 F.2d 118 (4th Cir. 1971) (pre-ERISA amendment introducing forfeiture for competition invalidated insofar as participants who had already vested before the amendment, even if they had not retired).

[262] 758 F.2d 973, 6 EBC 1475 (3d Cir. 1985).

6

Benefit Payments

I. Commencement of Benefits

A. How Soon Benefits Must Commence

1. Normal Retirement

Unless a participant elects to defer receipt of benefits further, ERISA's minimum standards require that payments of vested benefits commence "not later than the 60th day after" the *end* of the "plan year" in which the *later* of these events occurs: (1) the participant attains age 65, or any earlier normal retirement age specified under the plan, (2) the participant passes his or her tenth anniversary of the commencement of participation in the plan, or (3) the participant terminates from service with the employer.[1] Most employers provide more immediate terms for the commencement of benefits, for example, beginning payment of benefits on the first of the month after a participant reaches the plan's normal retirement age.

A plan may require a participant to file a claim for benefits before

---

[1] ERISA §206(a) (Code §401(a)(14)), and see 26 C.F.R. 1.401(a)-14(a) and (b). The time when benefits must commence may thus be later than when benefits must become nonforfeitable if an otherwise nonvested participant reaches a plan's normal retirement age. Benefits of otherwise nonvested participants must become nonforfeitable *precisely* when the participant reaches the plan's normal retirement age. See Rev. Rul. 81-211.

When an employee misrepresents his or her age in applying for employment, and does not later correct the misstatement, the employee may sometimes be held to the misstated age for the purpose of benefit commencement. See *Nass v. Teamsters Local 810 Staff Retirement Plan,* 515 F.Supp. 950, 2 EBC 1407, at 1409 (S.D.N.Y. 1981) (participant represented he was 10 years younger than he actually was "because he feared he would not be hired [as an accountant] if he stated his true age"); accord *Moore v. Gormin,* 321 So.2d 810 (La.App. 1975) (employee of public relations firm represented that she was 5 years younger than she actually was). The terms of other plans, however, provide for correction of the age and benefit commencement date.

benefits commence.[2] But once a claim is filed, benefits are due from the ERISA-required commencement date, regardless of any longer period it may take a plan to process the claim, or to make a final benefit determination.[3] Before ERISA, some plans forfeited benefits that went unclaimed for a period of years. Under ERISA, no forfeiture can occur because of a late claim for benefits.[4] However, it is not clear that a participant who is separated from service but who for some reason does not file a claim for benefits until, for example, age 65½ can obtain back payments from the ERISA-required commencement date.[5] Benefits can be withheld, with *no* actuarial increase in future benefits required, when a participant continues working for a sponsoring employer past a plan's normal retirement age, and for that reason defers receipt of benefits.[6] Under a defined contribution plan, however, earnings must continue to be allocated to a participant's account balance until it is actually distributed.[7]

2. Early Retirement

No minimum standard generally applies to the commencement of early retirement benefits because neither ERISA nor the Code requires a plan to offer early retirement benefits. Instead, the terms of the plan generally control. However, when a plan offers an early retirement benefit requiring service and the attainment of a certain age while in service, ERISA requires a participant who has the service, but not the age at the time he or she separates from service, to be offered "not less" than an actuarial equivalent of his or her benefits at the plan's normal retirement age on attaining the early retirement age.[8] These benefits must commence at the same time that benefits commence for participants who have *both* the service and age before separating from service.[9]

Plans also often provide that participants may be entitled to early retirement benefits with the "consent" of the employer, or under "mutually satisfactory" conditions. A 1957 Revenue Ruling held that to prevent discrimination under such consent requirements in favor of

---

[2] 26 C.F.R. 1.401(a)-14(a)(4); and see 29 C.F.R. 2560.503-1(d) (on what constitutes a "claim," when one is required).

[3] 26 C.F.R. 1.401(a)-14(d).

[4] 26 C.F.R. 1.411(a)-4(b)(6) and (c) (example 2).

[5] See *id.* Note, however, that the IRS considers a suspension of benefits to be a forfeiture. Rev. Rul. 81-140. Even if missed back payments are not required to be made up under ERISA, they may be required under the terms of a particular plan.

[6] 26 C.F.R. 1.411(c)-1(f)(2) and see Rev. Rul. 81-140. However, rules on the suspension of otherwise receivable benefits have to be followed. See sec. I.D. below. In addition, after 1987, either benefit accruals or actuarial increases in benefits are required in such instances. See ch. 4, sec. III.C.1.

[7] Rev. Ruls. 73-103 and 80-155.

[8] ERISA §206(a) (Code §401(a)(14)). If a plan does not limit this benefit to the actuarial equivalent, the amount of benefits that are due may be the same as for participants who have both the service and required age before separating from service. See ch. 5, sec. I.D.

[9] 26 C.F.R. 1.401(a)-14(c)(1).

the prohibited group of employees, the benefits available with the employer's consent must be worth *no more* than the actuarial equivalent of the plan's normal retirement benefit.[10] When consent for an early retirement benefit is permissible under the nondiscrimination standard, questions can still arise concerning whether a *standardless* consent requirement causes benefits under the plan to fail to be definitely determinable as required by the Code, or whether it causes the plan to fail to "specify [in writing] the basis on which payments are made . . . from the plan," as required under ERISA Section 402(b)(4).[11] Consent requirements for the commencement of early retirement benefits have also been the subject of litigation on compliance with ERISA's fiduciary standard of duty for consistency in exercises of discretionary authority under a plan.[12]

3. *Survivor's Benefits*

Survivor's benefits under a qualified joint and survivor annuity at retirement or under a preretirement survivor's annuity must be "immediately payable upon the death of the participant."[13] One exception to this rule is provided on the death of a participant before a plan's *earliest* retirement age. In this case, the commencement of the survivor's benefits may be deferred until "not later than the month in which the participant would have attained the earliest retirement age under the plan."[14]

4. *Stock Bonus Plan Benefits*

If it is earlier than is otherwise required, the 1986 Tax Reform Act requires distributions of a participant's account balance under any stock bonus plan, including an ESOP, to begin:

(1) Within one year after the end of the plan year in which disability, death, or retirement at the normal retirement age occurs, *or*

(2) Within five years after the end of the plan year in which any other separation from service occurs.

---

[10] See IRS Pub. 778, part 5(f), citing Rev. Rul. 57-163, part 5(f). However, in two later Rulings, exceptions were provided for (1) plans that had favorable determination letters issued before April 22, 1957, on such provisions, so long as the power is not exercised in a discriminatory manner, (2) plans that include no "highly compensated" employees or other prohibited group members, such as hourly only plans, and (3) plans that have "set" standards for the exercise of such consent that are uniformly and consistently applied and that do not result in prohibited discrimination. Rev. Rul. 58-151, as amplified by Rev. Rul. 58-604.

[11] For example, under the definite determinability requirement, when a plan grants credit for "leaves of absence," or uses a similarly nebulous term, the employer must have an *established* leave policy which, although not necessarily in writing, extends uniformly to all employees in similar circumstances, and does not otherwise primarily benefit the prohibited group of employees. See Rev. Rul. 81-106. See also Rev. Rul. 85-59.

[12] See cases cited at ch. 5, sec. I.D, on vesting in early retirement benefits.

[13] Rev. Rul. 81-9 (situation 1).

[14] ERISA §205(e)(1)(B) (Code §417(c)(1)(B)), as amended by P.L. 98-397.

These rules apply only to the extent the individual's account is comprised of stock acquired after December 31, 1986 (and if such stock was acquired with a loan, only if the loan has been repaid in full).[15] If a distribution is required, the participant's attributable account balance must then be completely distributed over a period of five years or less, unless the participant elects a longer distribution option.[16]

5. Lump Sum Benefits

Frequently, plan participants assume there is an ERISA or Code right to have their benefits distributed in lump sum form on a separation from service. In fact, no such statutory rights exist.[17] Under ERISA, the only statutory rights concerning lump sums actually run in favor of the plan. When the lump sum present value of a participant's benefits is less than $3,500, a plan can *involuntarily* cash-out the participant if he or she has separated from service, if the plan has terminated, or if the participant has retired.[18] However, apart from statutory rights, the terms of a plan may contractually provide a participant with an option of a lump sum payment of benefits on a separation from service (or on retirement). A lump sum payment on a separation from service, retirement, or even while in service, is the predominant form of payment for benefits accumulating under profit-sharing and stock bonus plans, and lump sum payments of benefits are also frequently offered under defined benefit plans with the consent of a plan administrator, plan trustees, or a retirement committee on a separation from service or retirement.[19]

---

[15] Code §409(o)(1)(A) and (B), as amended by §1174 of P.L. 99-514. And see §1174(b)(3) for effective date. Stock bonus plans, including ESOPs, are required to meet this requirement under Code §401(a)(23), as amended by §1174.

[16] Code §409(o)(1)(C). For stock acquired after Dec. 31, 1986, the Tax Reform Act also establishes new put option rules (put options are options to have the sponsoring employer repurchase employer securities that are not readily tradable using a fair valuation formula). It also extends the put option rules, which previously applied only to ESOPs described in Code §4975(e)(7) and tax credit ESOPs, to all stock bonus plans. Code §§409(h) and 401(a)(23), respectively, as amended by §1174.

Participants in ESOPs described in Code §4975(e)(7) (but not participants in all stock bonus plans), who are age 55 or over and have at least 10 years of participation must also be offered elections *before retirement* to have the investment of 25% of their individual account balance diversified to the extent the account balance is comprised of stock acquired after Dec. 31, 1986. If the account balance is undistributed at age 60, a participant with 10 years of participation must be able to elect to diversify 50% of the account balance attributable to such stock. Code §401(a)(28), as amended by §1175.

[17] On termination of a "sufficient" defined benefit plan, the PBGC's regulations require annuities to be purchased from an insurer for participants to cover all benefits payable from the plan's assets. But the annuities may be "non-surrenderable" so that even if certificates of the annuity are distributed to the participant, the participant may not be able to cash the annuity in. See 29 C.F.R. 2617.14(b)(1)(ii).

[18] ERISA §204(d)(1) (Code §411(a)(7)(B)(i)), as amended by P.L. 98-397 in 1984, and ERISA §203(e) (Code §411(a)(11)), as amended; and see P.L. 98-397, §§302(a) and (b) for effective dates.

[19] According to a survey by TIAA-CREF, 10% of defined benefit plans sponsored by Fortune 500 companies provide lump sum options on a termination of employment *prior to* retirement. About 20% permit participants to take lump sum options at retirement in lieu of annuities. However, in both instances, the lump sum options are generally conditioned on trustee or committee "approval." See T. Cook, "What Employers Are Saying About Lump-Sum Distributions," Pension World (June 1984), at 45–48 (summarizing survey results).

Analogously to early retirement benefits available with consent, when lump sum benefits are available on a separation from service or retirement—but *only* with the consent of a plan's trustees, or a retirement committee—the Code's Section 401(a)(4) nondiscrimination standard requires the lump sum value to be no more than the actuarial equivalent of the benefits available under the plan without such consent.[20] Furthermore, the discretion to grant lump sums must not be exercised "primarily" in favor of the prohibited group of employees, i.e., the percentage of prohibited group employees who receive lump-sums under the option must not be "significantly higher" than the percentage of rank and file employees receiving the consent.[21] Discretion to confer or not confer a lump sum option on a separation from service or retirement has resulted in much litigation concerning whether the discretion has been exercised in accordance with the ERISA fiduciary standard of duty.[22]

6. *Changes in Commencement Rules*

Changes in when a plan provides that benefits will commence are subject to the protection of ERISA Section 204(g), and may also be subject to federal common law protections against the abridgment of vested rights.[23]

The future status of early retirement, lump sum, and other benefit options requiring consent of the employer, or "mutually satisfactory" conditions, is, at the date of this writing, clouded by proposed IRS regulations that would require plans to eliminate any plan provision that allows employer consent or discretion with respect to the availability or payment of any alternative forms of benefits. Such discretion would be required to be eliminated to satisfy the Code's definitely determinable benefit requirement and the protection in ERISA Section 204(g), as amended by REA, against plan amendments reducing early retirement or other benefit options. Plans could adopt objective and clearly ascertainable criteria in lieu of open-ended discretion, for example, on the insurability of an employee if the purpose of the discretion was to ensure that only employees in good health receive lump sum benefits. This regulation is, however, not proposed to become effective until the second plan year after January 30, 1986, for nonbargained plans (and for collectively bargained plans, not until the earlier of the third plan year after January 30, 1986, or the second plan year after the expiration of the collective bargaining agreement in

---

A total anticipatory breach of a plan's terms may be another ground for securing a lump sum payment of benefits. See ch. 14, sec. II.F.

[20] See Rev. Rul. 85-59 (superseding Rev. Ruls. 71-296 and 71-540). Under a defined contribution plan, maintaining actuarial equivalence with a later distribution available without consent requires the plan to continue to allocate investment gains and losses to the participant's account if the exercise of discretion is denied. See Rev. Rul. 73-103.

[21] Rev. Rul. 85-59.

[22] See ch. 7, sec. III.C.

[23] See ch. 4, sec. IV.B, and ch. 9, sec. IV.

effect on January 30, 1986). In a contradictory twist, if the proposed regulation becomes final, the IRS would also delay for the same periods the effectiveness of its previously issued Revenue Ruling 85-59 that looked at the respective percentages of rank and file and prohibited group employees receiving benefits under a discretionarily available optional benefit form in examining a plan for discrimination in operation.[24]

B. Code Rules on How Soon Benefits May Commence

The Internal Revenue Code also contains restrictions on how soon benefits from a tax-qualified plan *may* commence. The Code provides that benefits from a pension plan, i.e., a defined benefit or money purchase plan, may *not* commence before the *earlier* of a participant's separation from service, disability, death, or retirement.[25] In contrast, a profit-sharing or stock bonus plan may provide for the commencement of benefits (i.e., the withdrawal of employer contributions, plus interest and appreciation, from a participant's account balance) at any time two years after the contributions are made, or if earlier, on death, retirement, illness, layoff, severance of employment, or the attainment of a stated age.[26] All employer contributions, including those made within the two previous years, may be withdrawn after five years of participation if a profit-sharing or stock bonus plan so provides.[27] However, if a profit-sharing or stock bonus plan is integrated with Social Security (through the provision of higher percentage contributions on a participant's compensation above a certain level of pay), the plan may only provide benefits on the same occasions as under a pension plan.[28]

Although qualified as profit-sharing plans, special rules restrict withdrawals from Code Section 401(k) plans to the same occasions as under pension plans, *plus* at any time after age 59½ or on an earlier finding of "hardship."[29] The 1986 Tax Reform Act adds two additional permissible circumstances for Section 401(k) withdrawals, effective from December 31, 1984: (1) plan terminations without establishment of a successor plan, and (2) sales of business assets or subsidiaries to a purchaser who reemploys the employee (provided, in each case, that the employee/participant receives a distribution of his or her entire

---

[24] Prop. Regs. 1.401(a)-4 and 1.411(d)-4, 51 Fed. Reg. 3798 (Jan. 30, 1986).

[25] 26 C.F.R. 1.401-1(b)(1)(i), and see Rev. Rul. 74-254. Plan termination may also be a permissible circumstance for distribution of benefits from a pension plan. See Conf. Rep. on the 1986 Tax Reform Act, H.R. Rep. 99-841, at II-452, [1986] U.S. Code Cong. & Ad. News 4540, and compare PLR 8536042 (June 11, 1985), reprinted in CCH Pension Plan Guide, at ¶17,377C-3 (same does not apply to profit-sharing and stock bonus plans, except where specially provided).

[26] Rev. Rul. 71-295 and 26 C.F.R. 1.401-1(b)(1)(ii). A profit-sharing or stock bonus plan may also provide for "hardship" withdrawals. Rev. Rul. 71-224.

[27] Rev. Rul. 68-24.

[28] Rev. Rul. 71-446, sec. 15.03.

[29] Code §401(k)(2)(B), and see Prop. Regs. 1.401(k)-1(d)(2), 44 Fed. Reg. 55544 (Nov. 10, 1981) (on the meaning of "hardship").

account balance). Hardship is retained by the Tax Reform Act as a permissible circumstance for withdrawal of elective deferrals; however, effective in 1989, the Act provides that hardship does not permit a withdrawal of earnings on elective deferrals, or a withdrawal of matching employer contributions and earnings thereon.[30]

Tax credit ESOPs are also subject to a special rule under which withdrawals may not be made until eight years after the employer's contributions are made.[31]

Beginning with plan years after December 31, 1984, a special restriction applies to how soon benefits from *any* type of plan may commence for employees who are five percent or more owners of the employer sponsoring the plan. Under this rule, a 10 percent penalty tax is imposed if distributions from a plan are made to a five percent or more employee-owner before age 59½ except on an earlier disability.[32] Survivor's benefits are not subject to this rule because they do not go to the employee-owner, but there is no exception for a separation from service or retirement before age 59½.

For plan years beginning in 1987, the Tax Reform Act imposes a 10 percent tax on withdrawals from a profit-sharing or stock bonus plan before a participant or beneficiary reaches age 59½, unless the participant has:

(1) Died;

(2) Become disabled;

(3) Separated from service after age 55 on account of early retirement under the plan; or

(4) Separated from service at an earlier age and is receiving the distribution in the form of a single life or joint life annuity (or in substantially equal payments over a term certain at least equal to the same life or joint life expectancies).[33]

Also excepted are:

(5) Involuntary cash-outs of less than $3,500;

(6) Certain distributions from ESOPs;

(7) Distributions not in excess of medical expense deductions allowed under Code Section 213; and

---

[30] Code §401(k)(2)(B), as amended by §§1116(b) and (f) of P.L. 99-514. A later effective date can apply to a hardship withdrawal from a collectively bargained §401(k) plan.
However, even if a withdrawal from a §401(k) plan is permissible, such as for hardship, it may still be subject to the 10% tax on early withdrawals, described below.

[31] Code §409(d). The 84-month restriction does not apply if a participant dies, becomes disabled, separates from service, or is reemployed by a purchaser following certain types of business sales. Code §409(d)(1). The Tax Reform Act also lifts the 84-month restriction on withdrawals when a tax credit ESOP is terminated, or partially terminated. Code §409(d)(1), as amended by §1174 of P.L. 99-514, and Conf. Rep., H.R. Rep. 99-841, at II-558.

[32] Code §72(m)(5), as amended by the Deficit Reduction Act of 1984, P.L. 98-369.

[33] Code §72(t)(2)(A), as amended by §1123 of P.L. 99-514.

(8) Distributions to an alternate payee under a qualified domestic relations order.[34]

Qualified rollovers of distributions into IRAs and withdrawals of after-tax employee contributions prior to age 59½ are excepted from the 10 percent tax because it only applies to withdrawals that are includible in gross income.[35]

The 10 percent tax also applies to distributions from defined benefit plans or money purchase pension plans prior to age 59½, with the same exceptions. This is generally not as significant a change because distributions from such plans are already restricted as a condition of qualification to retirement, separation from service, disability, or death. But the 10 percent tax can apply to participants in these plans who retire before age 55 and who receive a lump sum distribution in excess of $3,500.

C. Code Rules on How Late Benefits May Commence

To limit the potential for tax deferral by pushing back the date of benefit receipt, the Code also contains rules on how late benefits from a plan may commence. These rules apply regardless of whether a participant may desire to elect to defer benefits further. The general rule, effective for plan years beginning after December 31, 1984, is that benefits from any type of plan must commence not later than the April 1 following the calendar year in which a participant reaches age 70½ or retires, whichever comes later.[36] Benefits of five percent employee-owners must commence not later than the April 1 following the calendar year in which the employee attains age 70½—whether or not the employee has actually retired.[37] Under both of these rules, benefits must thereafter be distributed in a substantially even manner over the joint life expectancy of the participant and the beneficiary.[38]

Effective in 1989, the Tax Reform Act provides that benefits from any qualified plan must begin no later than April 1 of the calendar year following the calendar year in which any participant reaches age 70½ and must thereafter be distributed in a substantially even manner—whether or not the participant has separated from service or is a five-percent owner. A 50 percent excise tax is to be levied on the participant based on the amount by which his or her distributions in that year and each year thereafter are less than the required minimum distribution.[39]

---

[34] Code §§72(t)(2)(B)-(D), as amended by §1123. And see Conf. Rep., H.R. Rep. 99-841, at II-455, [1986] U.S. Code Cong. & Ad. News 4543 (expressing intent that tax not apply to involuntary cash-outs of less than $3,500).

[35] See Code §72(t), as amended.

[36] Code §401(a)(9)(C), as amended by the Deficit Reduction Act, P.L. 98-369.

[37] *Id.*

[38] See sec. III.A below.

[39] Code §§401(a)(9)(C) and 4974, as amended by §1121 of P.L. 99-514. Compliance with the minimum distribution rules also remains a condition of tax qualification. Conf. Rep., H.R. Rep. 99-841, at II-451, [1986] U.S. Code Cong. & Ad. News 4539.

The longstanding Code rule that death benefits under a qualified plan must be no more than "*incidental*" to the plan's primary purpose of providing retirement income to employees can also limit how late a plan may provide, or a participant may elect, for benefits to commence (and also the form in which benefits may be paid when they do commence).[40] The "incidental benefit" rule is an involved rule when it comes to its application to preretirement death benefits,[41] but at retirement, it means, as stated in Revenue Ruling 72-241, that:

> "A settlement option under ... a plan will [only] meet the requirement ... that benefits payable to the beneficiary must be incidental to the primary purpose of distributing accumulated funds to the employee, if it contains provisions whereby the present value of the payments to be made to the participant is more than 50 percent of the present value of the total payments to be made to the participant and his beneficiaries."

In accordance with this, the IRS's regulations on the commencement of benefits specifically provide that although a participant may elect to defer benefits until after the period when benefits *must* commence under ERISA:

> "An election may not be made ... if the exercise of such election will cause benefits ... with respect to the participant in the event of his death to be more than 'incidental'. ..."[42]

To illustrate how this rule can apply to the commencement of benefits, the IRS's Employee Plans Training Program handbook provides an example in which a participant age 65 defers receipt of any benefits from a defined contribution plan for 25 more years, naming his grandson as the beneficiary of the account balance if he dies in the interim. Since the participant's life expectancy at age 65 is only 15 years, the participant has effectively created a death benefit for the nonparticipant beneficiary that can be expected to be more than 50 percent of his total benefits.[43]

D. Reemployment Restrictions on Receipt of Benefits

ERISA permits the payment of normal retirement benefits to be "suspended" on a month-by-month basis if a participant is employed in excess of 40 hours per month after normal retirement age with the employer sponsoring the single-employer plan that is paying the benefits. In a multiemployer plan, such suspensions can be based on reemployment in excess of 40 hours per month within the same industry, trade or craft, and geographic area covered by the multiemployer plan,

---

[40] 26 C.F.R. 1.401-1(b)(1)(i) and (ii).

[41] See generally Rev. Rul. 85-15 and sec. III.A below.

[42] 26 C.F.R. 1.401(a)-14(b)(3).

[43] IRS Employee Plans Training Program, at 333 *(rev'd* 4-83), reprinted by Commerce Clearing House.

regardless of whether the employment is with an employer contributing to the multiemployer plan.[44]

Many plans, in particular, multiemployer plans, suspend early retirement benefits for much longer periods, or forfeit the benefits entirely, for reemployment or competitive reemployment after retirement. The legality of such suspensions or forfeitures depends on: (1) the proper interpretation of the suspension or forfeiture provision, as illuminated by the disclosure to participants in the plan's SPD, (2) whether the employee was discharged or constructively discharged from employment, (3) whether the provision is irrational or excessive, (4) whether prohibited discrimination results, and (5) whether the plan provision results from an amendment which has abridged ERISA minimum standard protections for accrued benefits or vested rights, or which has abridged vested rights in a common law sense.[45]

A unique problem with the commencement of early or normal retirement benefits can arise after a company sells a plant or division to another company. Many employees who were deferring receipt of early or normal retirement benefits may then apply for them. To avoid paying some of these benefits, the plan sponsor/seller may attempt to condition the immediate receipt of early or normal retirement benefits on the participant *not* taking a job with the new owner, a condition that would not apply to employment with any other employer after retirement. If such a provision is imposed as a condition on the receipt of normal retirement age benefits, it is a suspension of benefits for employment beyond the permissible ambit of ERISA Section 203(a)(3)(B). For early retirement benefits, such a condition could be satisfactory if it was in a plan all along. But the more likely situation is that the condition will only have been adopted in anticipation of the sale, or shortly thereafter. In these cases, the new condition may be arbitrary and capricious because it restricts the receipt of vested benefits without conferring any additional rights.[46] In addition, such a condition can be seen as a plan amendment indirectly reducing the amount of participants' accrued benefits in violation of ERISA Section 204(g).[47]

---

[44] ERISA §203(a)(3)(B) (Code §411(a)(3)(B)). See also 29 C.F.R. 2530.203-3 and Rev. Rul. 81-140. An employee who is foregoing receipt of normal retirement benefits because of continued employment after a plan's normal retirement age must be individually notified that he or she is passing up benefits until the conclusion of employment. 29 C.F.R. 2530.203-3(b)(4). If this notice is not provided, benefits may be required to be actuarially increased to account for the period over which receipt was foregone (which may actually result in a greater increase in benefits than if additional years of participation after a plan's normal retirement age were credited). See Rev. Rul. 81-140. But compare 46 Fed. Reg. 8896 (Jan. 27, 1981) (Department of Labor regulatory preamble suggesting that lack of notice just affects plan's entitlement to commence withholding benefits, not the amount it may later withhold if the participant's service permits a suspension of benefits and notice of the suspension is ultimately provided).

[45] See ch. 5, sec. V.B, on permissible forfeitures of vested benefits.

[46] See *Helmetag v. Consolidated Rail Corp.*, 5 EBC 1617 (E.D. Pa. 1984). And see ch. 9, secs. II.B, IV, and V (on arbitrary and capricious plan amendments, vested rights, and advance notice requirements for adverse plan amendments).

[47] See ch. 4, sec. IV.B.3.

II. Survivor's Benefits

ERISA Section 203(a)(3)(A), and Code Section 411(a)(3)(C), permit payments of "nonforfeitable" benefits from employer contributions to be forfeited (i.e., to stop) on a participant's death under the terms of a plan unless the plan is required to provide survivor's benefits under ERISA Section 205 and Code Section 401(a)(11).

As originally enacted, ERISA Section 205 required plans that offered life annuities to automatically provide benefits in the form of a "qualified joint and survivor annuity" on a participant's retirement, unless the participant elected to take benefits in another form. Before retirement, the participant was required to be offered an option on attaining the plan's "qualified early retirement age" of electing preretirement survivor's annuity coverage.

Under the 1984 REA amendments, the number of instances when survivor's benefits are required to be provided under ERISA Section 205 has dramatically increased. Basically, the REA amendments shore up ERISA's original requirement that joint and survivor's annuities must be the automatic form of benefit payment on retirement by providing that the participant's *spouse* must consent to the participant's election of any other form of benefits. Under REA, survivor's benefits are also automatic for death *at any time* before retirement if a participant has a nonforfeitable right to benefits, unless the participant has elected, again with the consent of the spouse, to waive the preretirement survivor's coverage.

Benefits attributable to *employee* contributions can never be forfeited on account of death before or after the REA amendments.[48] Employee contributions are, however, relatively rare under defined benefit plans.

A. Postretirement Deaths

1. Under Pension Plans

ERISA Section 205, as originally enacted, required every pension or profit-sharing plan that offered benefits in the form of a "life annuity," that is, a form of benefit payments where the continuation of benefits depends on someone's survival, to offer benefits in the form of a "qualified joint and survivor annuity."[49] Under the Internal Revenue Code, pension plans, including money purchase defined contribution plans, are required to offer benefits "over a period of years, usually for

---

[48] ERISA §§203(a)(1) and (a)(3)(A) (Code §§411(a)(1) and (a)(3)(A)), and see 26 C.F.R. 1.411(a)-4(b)(1)(ii).

[49] See 26 C.F.R. 1.401(a)-11(a)(1) and (b)(1) (definition of "life annuity"). For this purpose, a "life annuity" also includes a form of payment in which benefits are paid in only 10 installments if the completion of payment of *all* the installments is contingent on the participant's, or the participant's spouse's, survival. *Id.*

life, after retirement."[50] Most commonly, this requirement is met by offering benefits in "life annuity" form. Hence, a qualified joint and survivor's annuity was almost categorically required under all such plans.

A qualified joint and survivor annuity provides benefits during the joint lives of a participant and the participant's spouse, and after the death of the participant (assuming the spouse is still alive), provides survivor's benefits of not less than 50 percent, nor more than 100 percent, of the benefits payable during the joint lives of the couple.[51] To provide this survivor's benefit, the benefits payable during the joint lives of the couple, and hence the benefits payable to the survivor as a percentage of those benefits, may be actuarially reduced from the amount payable in a single-life annuity form so that the total "actuarially" expected value of the joint and survivor's annuity benefits is no more than that available when benefits are in a single-life annuity form.[52]

As an example, if a participant is entitled to a single-life annuity of $400 per month at age 65 and has a spouse who is five years younger than he or she is, under typical actuarial assumptions, a joint and 50 percent survivor's benefit form can "cost" the participant a 15 percent reduction in the benefits payable during the participant's retirement. Thus, as opposed to $400 per month on a single-life basis, a joint and 50 percent survivor's form can reduce the benefits payable during the participant's retirement to $340 per month ($400 − ($400 × 15%)), so that 50 percent of $340, or $170, per month will be payable during the surviving spouse's life (assuming the spouse outlives the participant).[53]

To comply with the "qualified joint and survivor annuity" requirement, plans often offer a life annuity with a 50 percent survivor's benefit, or a range of options, such as life annuity with a 75 percent or 100 percent survivor's benefit.[54] The actuarial reduction from the benefits in single-life form increases with the percentage of the survivor's

---

[50] 26 C.F.R. 1.401-1(b)(1)(i).

[51] ERISA §205(g)(3) (Code §401(a)(11)(G)(iii)), before the 1984 REA amendments, and ERISA §205(d) (Code §417(b)), after the 1984 amendments.

[52] *Id.*, and see 26 C.F.R. 1.401(a)-11(b)(2).

[53] See 29 C.F.R. 2621.4(d)(2) and (e) (setting out the reduction factors the PBGC uses for reducing its maximum guaranteed benefit amount from single-life form to joint and 50% survivor's form). The effect of different interest assumptions, and of unisex versus sex-distinct mortality assumptions, on the amount of reductions for joint and survivor's benefits is discussed in the next section on the amount of benefits under optional forms. The PBGC factors are based on unisex composite of the 1971 GAM mortality table for male and female lives and a 5% interest rate assumption.

Some plans offer a joint and survivor's annuity under which benefits are reduced after the *first* death—whether it is of the participant or his or her spouse. This is a qualified joint and survivor's annuity as well. See 26 C.F.R. 1.401(a)-11(b)(2). The actuarial reduction to provide such a benefit is less because the benefits will be reduced after the first death, rather than only after the death of the participant. See 29 C.F.R. 2621.4(d)(3).

[54] See BLS, Employee Benefits in Medium and Large Firms, 1984, at 56.

benefits.[55] Survivor's benefits may also be "subsidized" under the terms of a plan, so that, for example, there is no actuarial reduction to provide a basic 50 percent survivor's benefit, and less than a full actuarial reduction to provide higher percentage survivor options.[56]

Other forms of payment that are commonly offered by plans as elective options to a qualified joint and survivor form are: (1) the single-life annuity form in which accrued benefits are generally expressed prior to retirement, (2) a single-life annuity with a "term-certain" under which payments are assured for a minimum number of years, usually five or 10 years from commencement of the annuity, regardless of the participant's death, and (3) lump sum or installment payment options.[57]

Under ERISA Section 205 as originally enacted, payments were automatically provided in the form of a qualified joint and survivor annuity on retirement at the plan's normal retirement age or on a retirement after a plan's "qualified early retirement age"—which was defined as the *later* of early retirement under the plan or 10 years before the plan's normal retirement age. Payments in a qualified joint and survivor's annuity form did not have to be provided if the participant specifically elected to take benefits in another form.[58] As a condition to actual payment of survivor's benefits under a "qualified joint and survivor annuity," ERISA Section 205, as originally enacted, also permitted a plan to require the surviving spouse to have been married to the participant throughout the one-year period ending with the date of the participant's death.[59] The IRS's regulations added that the plan could also require the participant and the surviving spouse to have been married throughout the one-year period before the annuity starting date, and that the plan could require that the same spouse satisfy both conditions.[60]

The Retirement Equity Act amends Section 205 (the effective dates are detailed at the end of this section). The major change from

---

[55] If the survivor's benefit is 100% of the benefit during the participant's life, the actuarial reduction from benefits in single-life annuity form would be 25%, using the factors the PBGC uses and assuming the spouse is 5 years younger than the participant. See 29 C.F.R. 2621.4(d)(2).

[56] This may be the result of collective bargaining or general personnel policy. There is also some incentive in the Internal Revenue Code for an employer to provide survivor's benefits *without* an actuarial reduction and/or at a higher percentage than the 50% of a reduced benefit required as a minimum standard under ERISA §205. Under Code §415, the maximum benefit limitation for benefits from a qualified defined benefit plan is $90,000 per year if benefits are in the form of a single-life annuity. However, the maximum benefit limitation is also $90,000 if benefits are provided in a 100% joint and survivor's form without an actuarial reduction. By enhancing the joint and survivor's form over the minimum requirements, an employer can deliver more benefits to highly compensated employees and their families with tax-deductible dollars and tax-exempt earnings on contributions than under terms that more closely parallel the ERISA §205 minimum standard. Of course, when such "subsidized" survivor's benefits are provided to highly compensated employees, they must be provided to rank and file employees on the same basis, although not in the same dollar amounts.

[57] Plans requiring employee contributions may offer a cash or installment-type refund annuity under which a single-life, joint and survivor's, or other form of annuity is provided, with repayment of employee contributions guaranteed regardless of death.

[58] 26 C.F.R. 1.401(a)-11(a)(1)(i)(A) and (C), and 26 C.F.R. 1.401(a)-11(a)(1)(ii).

[59] ERISA §205(d) (Code §401(a)(11)(D)), before the 1984 REA amendments.

[60] 26 C.F.R. 1.401(a)-11(d)(3).

the preexisting requirements for joint and survivor's forms of annuity on retirement is spousal consent. The spouse of the participant must now consent to an election of any form of benefits other than a qualified joint and survivor annuity. The spouse's consent must be in writing, must "acknowledge[] the effect of [the] election [to waive the survivor's benefits]," and must be witnessed by either a notary public or a plan representative.[61]

The joint and survivor's annuity form on retirement is also no longer contingent on whether a plan offers a "life annuity" in the first place, although separate rules are established for profit-sharing and stock bonus plans. Money purchase pension plans are thus now categorically required to provide a qualified joint and survivor annuity (to be purchased with the participant's account balance) as the normal form of benefit payment under the plan. A participant may elect another form of payment, such as a lump sum distribution of the entire account balance, but only with the consent of his or her spouse.[62]

A qualified joint and survivor annuity is also no longer contingent on whether retirement takes place on or after a plan's "qualified early retirement age."[63] As an example, under ERISA as originally enacted, if a participant retired under a provision that permitted early retirement more than 10 years before the plan's normal retirement age (as might occur under a 30-and-out early retirement provision), the plan was not required to offer benefits in joint and survivor's form.[64] It is not clear how many plans used this exception, but REA prospectively provides that the qualified joint and survivor's benefit form must be provided *whenever* a participant "retires" under a plan.[65]

Under ERISA as originally enacted, a joint and survivor's annuity form was also not required to be offered on a disability retirement before a plan's normal retirement age.[66] However, under REA, a joint and survivor's annuity must be offered whenever a participant "retires" under a plan. This is defined by the "annuity starting date," which in turn means the first day of the period for which an amount is

---

[61] ERISA §205(c)(2) (Code §417(a)(2)), as amended by P.L. 98-397. And see sec. II.C.3 below, discussing the spousal consent requirement in more detail.

[62] ERISA §205(b)(1)(B) (Code §401(a)(11)(B)(ii)), as amended. However, ESOPs are subject to the separate rules described below for profit-sharing and stock bonus plans, even if the ESOP is qualified as a money purchase pension plan, so long as the plan's stock accounts are subject to the "put option" rules in Code §409(h). ERISA §205(b)(2) (Code §401(a)(11)(C)), as amended.

[63] ERISA §205(a)(1) (Code §401(a)(11)(A)(i)), as amended.

[64] 26 C.F.R. 1.401(a)-11(a)(3) (example (3)).

[65] ERISA §205(a)(1) (Code §401(a)(11)(A)(i)), as amended.

[66] See 26 C.F.R. 1.401(a)-11(b)(4), Rev. Rul. 81-9 (situations 5 and 6), *Sobie v. Typographical Union Pension Plan*, 4 EBC 2524 (N.D. Ohio 1983); *Heisler v. Jeep Corp.-UAW Retirement Income Plan*, 807 F.2d 505, 8 EBC 1209 (6th Cir. 1986). But even when a joint and survivor's benefit option was not offered on a disability retirement, if the disabled participant later became eligible for early retirement, with survivor's benefits required to be available under the early retirement provision, denying the participant the opportunity to switch to the early retirement benefit could be arbitrary and capricious, unless both the plan and the SPD clearly preclude such a change. See *Rhoton v. Central States Pension Fund*, 717 F.2d 988, 4 EBC 2233 (6th Cir. 1983). But compare *Heisler v. Jeep Corp.-UAW Retirement Income Plan, supra* (no survivor's benefit election required at age 57 early retirement age when employee became disabled and took a disability retirement at age 53 and was not an "employee" at age 57).

received as an annuity "whether by reason of retirement *or disability*."[67]

The one-year marriage requirement that plans can require is limited by REA to a permissible requirement of marriage throughout the one-year period ending on the *earlier* of the annuity starting date or the participant's death, but not *both*.[68] When a plan uses this requirement and a participant dies after his or her annuity starting date, the spouse to whom he or she was married during the one-year period before the annuity starting date is entitled to the survivor's benefit—whether or not he or she was still the spouse in the period before the participant's death.[69]

An exception to the permissible requirement of one year of marriage throughout the one-year period ending on the annuity starting date is also provided if a participant marries *within* the one-year period before the annuity starting date and has been married for at least one year before the date of death.[70] A second exception exists if a "qualified domestic relations order" directs that an ex-spouse be treated as the surviving spouse for purposes of survivor's benefits. In this case, one year of marriage at any time substitutes for a plan's requirement of one year of marriage immediately before the annuity starting date.[71]

2. Under Profit-Sharing and Stock Bonus Plans

Under the Code, profit-sharing and stock bonus plans are not required to offer benefits "over a period of years, usually for life, after retirement." Instead, they may offer only a lump sum or a several-installment form of payment, with no life annuity option.[72] As originally enacted, ERISA Section 205 provided that when no "life annuity" was offered, no qualified joint and survivor annuity was required to be offered either. In *BBS Associates, Inc. v. Commissioner*, the U.S. Tax Court held, moreover, that even when a life annuity was offered as an elective option, if the plan's "normal" form of payment was a lump

---

[67] ERISA §205(a)(1) (Code §401(a)(11)(A)(i)), as amended, and ERISA §205(h)(2) (Code §417(f)(2)), as amended (emphasis added) (defining "annuity starting date"). A technical correction to REA in the 1986 Tax Reform Act clarifies that the annuity starting date encompasses the starting date of disability benefits, but it also provides that the survivor's annuity requirement does not extend to "auxiliary" disability benefits, which it does not define. ERISA §205(h)(2) and Code §417(f)(2), as amended by §1898(b)(12) of P.L. 99-514.

[68] ERISA §205(f)(1) (Code §417(d)(1)), as amended by P.L. 98-397.

[69] S. Rep. 98-575, at 15-16, reprinted in [1984] U.S. Code Cong. & Ad. News 2547, at 2561-62. A qualified domestic relations order can alter this rule so that a later spouse is be covered instead. *Id.*

[70] ERISA §205(f)(2) (Code §417(d)(2)), as amended by P.L. 98-397. The participant may be required to notify the plan when he or she has been married for one year in order to come under this exception. S. Rep. 98-575, at 16, [1984] U.S. Code Cong. & Ad. News 2547, at 2562.

[71] ERISA §206(d)(3)(F) (Code §414(p)(5)), as amended.

[72] 26 C.F.R. 1.401-1(b)(1)(ii) and see Rev. Rul. 71-540.

sum, a qualified joint and survivor annuity was required only if the participant elected the life annuity option.[73]

While the Retirement Equity Act amendments end the "life annuity" antecedent to the qualified joint and survivor's annuity requirement, Section 205, as amended, provides that a joint and survivor's annuity is still not required to be offered under a profit-sharing or stock bonus plan if the plan provides that any undistributed nonforfeitable account balance at death will go to the participant's *spouse.*[74] If another beneficiary is to be elected, it must be with the consent of the spouse.[75] When a profit-sharing or stock bonus plan does offer an annuity, REA's consent requirements apply to the election of any form of annuity other than the qualified joint and survivor's form.[76]

3. Effective Dates of ERISA Rules and REA Amendments

ERISA Section 205's requirements became effective on the first day of the first plan year beginning after December 31, 1975, if an individual was still an active participant in the plan in this or a later plan year.[77]

The Retirement Equity Act amendments became effective with the beginning of a plan's first plan year after December 31, 1984. For collectively bargained plans, the effective date is the *earlier* of the first plan year beginning after December 31, 1987, or the beginning of the first plan year after the expiration of the collective bargaining agreement in effect on the date of REA's enactment (August 23, 1984) (or after the expiration of the last of the collective bargaining agreements then in effect when there are more than one).[78] The spousal consent requirement is effective for *all* plans for any election not to take a joint

---

[73] 74 T.C. 1118, 2 EBC 2413 (1980), *aff'd,* 661 F.2d 913, 2 EBC 2422 (3d Cir. 1981). And see IRS Notice 82-4 (acquiescing to the decision in *BBS Associates*).

[74] A technical correction to REA in the 1986 Tax Reform Act allows the spouse's receipt of a participant's undistributed account balance under a profit-sharing or stock bonus plan to be conditioned on one year of marriage during the year before the earlier of the annuity starting date or date of death. ERISA §205(b)(3) and Code §401(a)(11)(D), as amended by §1898(b)(14) of P.L. 99-514. The annuity starting date under a profit-sharing or stock bonus plan is the first day on which all events have occurred (e.g., separation from service and spousal consent to payment) which entitle the participant to a distribution of benefits—whether or not in annuity form. ERISA §205(h)(2) and Code §417(f)(2), as amended by §1898(b)(12) of P.L. 99-514, and Conf. Rep., H.R. Rep. 99-841, at II-857.

[75] ERISA §205(b)(1)(C)(i) (Code § 401(a)(11)(B)(iii)(I)), as amended. If a profit-sharing or stock bonus plan is the recipient (or "transferee") of assets from a plan required to provide a joint and survivor's annuity, i.e., the recipient of assets covering benefits accrued by a participant under a pension plan, the joint and survivor annuity rules apply as if the plan is a money purchase pension plan. ERISA §205(b)(1)(C)(iii) (Code §401(a)(11)(B)(iii)(III)), as amended. And see Temp. and Prop. Regs. 1.401(a)-11T, Q&A 7 and 8, 50 Fed. Reg. 29371 (July 19, 1985) (on the definition of a transferee plan).

[76] ERISA §205(b)(1)(C)(ii) (Code §401(a)(11)(B)(iii)(II)), as amended.

[77] ERISA §211(b)(1) and §205(i), before the 1984 amendments. Section 303(e)(1) of the Retirement Equity Act, P.L. 98-397, provides a new rule for persons who separated from service after ERISA's Sept. 2, 1974, date of enactment but before this first plan year, and whose annuity starting date had still not occurred as of Aug. 23, 1984. Under §303(e)(1), such participants may elect to have the original ERISA provisions apply, thereby requiring the plan to at least offer a joint and survivor annuity on retirement.

[78] P.L. 98-397, §§302(a) and (b).

and survivor's form of annuity, or to designate a person who is not the spouse as the beneficiary of an undistributed account balance under a profit-sharing or stock bonus plan, made after December 31, 1984.[79]

Under both REA effective dates, a participant must have at least one hour of service, which could be one hour of paid leave, under the plan on or after August 23, 1984 (the REA enactment date) for the new requirements to apply to that participant's benefits.[80]

B. Preretirement Deaths

ERISA Section 205 requires survivor's benefits for spouses of plan participants who die with a nonforfeitable right to benefits under a plan before retiring. However, under ERISA as originally enacted, such benefits could be restricted to deaths under a plan offering a "life annuity" occurring after the participant had attained the plan's "qualified early retirement age."

Under the REA amendments, a preretirement survivor's annuity is required under all pension plans *whenever* a deceased participant had a nonforfeitable right to benefits under the plan, unless an election to waive the coverage had been made with the consent of the spouse. Rights of survivoring spouses to the account balances of deceased participants are also enhanced under profit-sharing and stock bonus plans, regardless of whether a "life annuity" is offered.

1. Under Defined Benefit Plans

Prior to the REA amendments, ERISA provided that when a plan offered a life annuity at retirement, a participant who continued working after reaching the plan's qualified early retirement age had to be offered an opportunity to elect preretirement survivor's annuity coverage to apply in the event he or she died before retiring.[81] The qualified early retirement age was defined as the *later* of the plan's earliest retirement age *or* 10 years before the plan's normal retirement age. For a preretirement survivor's annuity election to be required, a plan did not have to call a benefit an "early retirement benefit." Rather it was sufficient that it offered any form of retirement benefits before its normal retirement age, including an early retirement benefit available

---

[79] P.L. 98-397, §302(c)(3). Consent is also required for an election made *before* Dec. 31, 1984, if the election had not "take[n] effect" because the annuity starting date did not occur until *after* Dec. 31, 1984. See Temp. and Prop. Regs. 1.401(a)-11T, Q&A 22, 50 Fed. Reg. 29371 (July 19, 1985).

[80] P.L. 98-397, §302(c)(1).

[81] ERISA §205(b) and (c) (Code §401(a)(11)(B) and (C)). In contrast to the survivor's form at retirement, the preretirement coverage was not provided automatically, but required an election by the participant. However, to verify that a participant received notice of the election, and thus to be able to prove compliance with the Treasury regulations, many plans required a participant to mark one box or another, date, and sign an election form. Thus, as a practical matter, participants rarely did nothing, but elected one way or another. But see *Kaszuk v. Bakery and Confectionery Union Pension Fund*, 791 F.2d 548, 7 EBC 1724 (6th Cir. 1986) (notice of election option provided by publication in union newspaper, no election required to be made).

only with the employer's consent, but not including a disability retirement.[82] Thus, when a plan with a normal retirement age of 65 offered any early retirement benefit beginning before age 55, its qualified early retirement age would be age 55.[83]

Besides attaining the qualified early retirement age and electing the coverage, a plan could provide that a participant's election of preretirement survivor's coverage was not effective if death occurred from nonaccidental causes, such as cancer or a heart attack, during an up to two-year period after the participant made the election.[84] Marriage throughout the one-year period ending on the date of the participant's death was also permitted as a further condition on benefits actually going to a surviving spouse.[85] In two instances, however, ERISA as originally enacted required a joint and survivor's annuity form to be automatic *before* retirement, and also prohibited any two-year waiting period for nonaccidental death. First, if a participant continued working for an employer past a plan's normal retirement age, survivor's benefits had to be automatic.[86] Second, if a participant separated from service with an employer after reaching a plan's qualified early retirement age, but died before applying for benefits, survivor's benefits were also automatic.[87]

The primary problem Congress found with ERISA's preretirement survivor's coverage was its failure to cover many "early" deaths. This resulted in "inequitable treatment of participants . . . who die before the normal [or qualified early] retirement age under the plan."[88] Thus, "the participant's spouse [could] be entitled to no survivor's benefits under the plan even though the participant had accrued significant vested benefits before death."[89]

---

[82] 26 C.F.R. 1.401(a)-11(b)(4) and Rev. Rul. 81-9 (situations 6 and 9), and see 185 BNA Pens. Rep. A-9 (April 24, 1978), reprinting IRS letter reversing prior position on whether early retirement benefits with consent are an early retirement benefit within the meaning of ERISA §205.

[83] See 26 C.F.R. 1.401(a)-11(b)(4) and (a)(3) (examples 2 and 3).

[84] ERISA §205(f) (Code §401(a)(11)(F)), before the 1984 REA amendments. However, if a plan contained such a waiting period, the IRS's regulations required that the participant be able to elect the preretirement survivor's coverage two years *before* reaching the plan's qualified early retirement age so that coverage for nonaccidental death could be effective immediately on reaching the qualified early retirement age. 26 C.F.R. 1.401(a)-11(c)(2)(ii). A participant in imminent danger of dying before the end of a two-year waiting period might also avoid the effect of such a rule by taking early retirement, since a joint and survivor's benefit on an actual early retirement after a plan's qualified early retirement age could not have a waiting period for nonaccidental death.

[85] ERISA §205(d) (Code §401(a)(11)(D)), before the 1984 amendments.

[86] 26 C.F.R. 1.401(a)-11(a)(i)(B). This is subject to an exception if the participant had already elected out of the joint and survivor's form. *Id.* But generally, if no claim for retirement benefits has been made, no election out of the joint and survivor's form will have been made either.

[87] 26 C.F.R. 1.401(a)-11(a)(i)(D). Again, this may be excepted if an election of another form has already been made before death, but generally, no such election will have been made unless the participant filed a claim for benefits prior to death. Even then, there may be a question about whether such an election was effective at the time of death or only when benefits actually commenced.

[88] S. Rep. 98-575, at 12, [1984] U.S. Code Cong. & Ad. News 2547, at 2558.

[89] *Id.*

The 1984 REA amendments make preretirement survivor's coverage automatic, rather than an elective option, and require it to begin once a participant has a nonforfeitable right to any portion of his or her accrued benefits, whether that right is obtained at age 35, 45, or later, and thus with no regard to a plan's qualified early retirement age. Moreover, once a participant has a nonforfeitable right to benefits, the preretirement survivor's coverage must continue "whether or not [the participant] is still employed by the employer."[90] The previously permissible two-year waiting period before an election of preretirement survivor's coverage became effective for nonaccidental deaths is also repealed.[91]

The permissible requirement of marriage throughout the one-year period before the participant's date of death for a preretirement survivor's annuity to be provided continues,[92] but a qualified domestic relations order may provide for continuing coverage of an ex-spouse who was married to the participant throughout any one-year period.[93]

Under both ERISA as originally enacted and the REA amendments, an actuarial charge for preretirement survivor's coverage, analogous to a premium for term-life insurance, may be assessed against the participant's retirement benefits when and if he or she does retire, or may be assessed against the survivor's benefits if the participant dies while under the coverage.[94] A typical charge is a one-half of one percent reduction in a participant's retirement benefits for each year of coverage between age 60 and 65. A smaller charge should apply for coverage at earlier ages because of the lesser chance of death.[95]

To avoid the charge against benefits when the participant later retires, an election to waive the preretirement survivor's coverage may be made. But under REA, it may *only* be made with the consent of the spouse. As discussed below, if a plan fully subsidizes the cost of preretirement survivor's coverage, no opportunity to elect to waive the coverage is required to be offered. Also, no opportunity to elect out of the coverage need be provided before age 35.[96]

The amount of a preretirement survivor's annuity under ERISA as originally enacted, and under REA, must be no less than *as if* the participant had retired on the day immediately preceding his or her death. If provided under the plan, reductions may thus be made for early retirement and for the actuarial cost of the joint and survivor's form as if the participant had retired. A charge may also be made

---

[90] *Id.* Under ERISA as originally enacted, a joint and survivor's annuity was *only* required after a separation from service if the separation from service occurred after the participant attained the qualified early retirement age under the plan, but, for one reason or another, postponed application for benefits. 26 C.F.R. 1.401(a)-11(a)(1)(i)(D).

[91] S. Rep. 98-575, at 16, [1984] U.S. Code Cong. & Ad. News 2547, at 2562.

[92] ERISA §205(f)(1) (Code §417(d)(1)), as amended.

[93] ERISA §206(d)(3)(F) (Code §414(p)(5)), as amended. See sec. IV.A. below.

[94] See 26 C.F.R. 1.401(a)-11(e). And see ERISA §205(i) (Code §417(f)(4)), as amended by REA.

[95] See D. McGill, *Fundamentals of Private Pensions* (Richard D. Irwin 5th ed.), at 127.

[96] See secs. II.C.1 and C.2 below.

against the survivor's benefits for the period of preretirement survivor's coverage before the date of death. Then, if applicable, the remaining benefits may be reduced by half for a 50 percent survivor's annuity.[97] Although a 75 percent or 100 percent preretirement survivor's annuity is permitted (with a greater actuarial charge for such coverage), as a matter of practice, a preretirement survivor's annuity is more likely to be set at the minimum level of 50 percent of an actuarially reduced single-life benefit, which is likely to also be reduced for early retirement.[98]

Under REA, a slight adaptation applies in determining the amount of the survivor's annuity if death occurs *before* a plan's earliest retirement age. As stated by the Senate Finance Committee:

> "[In the case of a participant who dies on or before the plan's earliest retirement age,] the amount of the payments . . . is not to be less than the payments that would have been made under the qualified joint and survivor annuity if . . . the participant had separated from service on the date of death [if he or she was not already separated from service], survived until the earliest retirement age, and retired at that time with a qualified joint and survivor annuity."[99]

In line with this, when survivor's benefits are payable due to death before a plan's *earliest* retirement age, the benefits are not required to commence for the survivor until "the month in which the participant would have attained the earliest retirement age under the plan."[100] For example, if a participant dies at age 50 under a plan with an earliest retirement age of 55, the surviving spouse's benefits are required to commence only when the participant *would have* reached age 55, that is, five years after the death occurred (unless the plan provides for earlier payment).

To deal with some of the administrative burden in preserving records for and paying relatively small benefits, while maintaining the greater equitable protection established under REA against complete forfeitures of vested benefits on account of early deaths, the REA amendments permit a plan to involuntarily cash-out a survivor's benefits if they are worth $3,500 or less in a lump sum present value and if payment of the benefits in the form of an annuity has not already

---

[97] See 26 C.F.R. 1.401(a)-11(b)(3) and ERISA §§205(c)(2) and (h) (Code §§401(a)(11)(C) and (G)), before the 1984 amendments. And see ERISA §§205(e)(1)(A)(i) and 205(i) (Code §§417(c)(1)(A)(i) and (f)(4)), as amended by REA. There is, in a sense, little logic to requiring an actuarial reduction for "*joint* and survivor's" benefits when the death of a participant has, by definition, occurred before benefits begin, and there is therefore only one remaining life expectancy at the outset, but ERISA clearly provides that benefits may be determined "as if" the participant had retired one day before his or her death, and had elected the joint and survivor's form—in which case an actuarial reduction would be permitted.

[98] See BLS, Employee Benefits in Medium and Large Firms, 1984, at 57. Ranges of survivor's annuity options, such as a choice between 50%, 75%, and 100% preretirement survivor's benefits, are also less common than at retirement. *Id.*

[99] S. Rep. 98-575, at 13, [1984] U.S. Code Cong. & Ad. News 2547, at 2559. And see ERISA §205(e)(1)(A)(ii) (Code §417(c)(1)(A)(ii)).

[100] ERISA §205(e)(1)(B) (Code §417(c)(1)(B)), and S. Rep. 98-575, at 13.

begun.[101] The interest assumption used in discounting a survivor's annuity to a present value, both to determine whether it falls into this range and to cash it out if it does, must be reasonable, and in no event, can it be higher than the interest rate the PBGC would use in "determining the present value of a lump sum distribution on plan termination."[102]

2. Under Money Purchase Pension Plans

Under ERISA as originally enacted, a money purchase pension plan was not required to offer preretirement survivor's annuity coverage even if it offered a life annuity at retirement. However, the plan was required to pay the participant's entire nonforfeitable account balance to a survivor (but not necessarily the spouse) in the event of the participant's death while in active service after reaching the plan's qualified early retirement age.[103]

Under the REA amendments, money purchase pension plans are required to provide preretirement survivor's annuities under the same rules that apply to defined benefit plans.[104] For a surviving spouse, a "qualified preretirement survivor's annuity" could actually be a poor substitute for receipt of the entire nonforfeitable account balance if a plan bases the preretirement survivor's annuity on only 50 percent of the participant's nonforfeitable account balance, as is permitted.[105] A money purchase pension plan can, however, still offer the entire nonforfeitable account balance as an elective option to a preretirement survivor's annuity, or it can offer a preretirement survivor's annuity based on 100 percent of the participant's account balance. Moreover, a plan may not use compliance with the REA amendment requiring a preretirement annuity option as the occasion for eliminating or reducing a previously available option to receive 100 percent of the account balance.[106]

3. Under Profit-Sharing and Stock Bonus Plans

Under ERISA as originally enacted, a preretirement survivor's annuity was not required to be offered under a profit-sharing or stock

---

[101] ERISA §205(g)(1) (Code §417(e)(1)), as amended.

[102] ERISA §205(g)(3) (Code §417(e)(3)), as amended. And see sec. III.B below on the interest rates the PBGC uses to discount a deferred benefit over the period before the benefit becomes payable.

[103] 26 C.F.R. 1.401(a)-11(c)(2)(i)(C)(2), and see Rev. Rul. 81-9 (situation 7).

[104] ERISA §205(b)(1)(B) (Code §401(a)(11)(B)(ii)), as amended. One year of marriage prior to the date of death can thus be required for receipt of this benefit. See nn. 92 and 93. ESOPs, even if qualified as money purchase pension plans, are subject to the same rules as profit-sharing and stock bonus plans (described next) to the extent a participant's accrued benefits are subject to the "put option" rules described in Code §409(h). ERISA §205(b)(2) (Code §401(a)(11)(C)), as amended.

[105] ERISA §205(e)(2) (Code §417(c)(2)), as amended.

[106] Temp. and Prop. Regs. 1.401(a)-11T, Q&A 9, 50 Fed. Reg. 29371 (July 19, 1985). See also sec. III.A below.

bonus plan as an elective option. However, if the plan provided a life annuity at retirement, the plan was required to pay the participant's entire nonforfeitable account balance to a survivor (but not necessarily the spouse) in the event of the participant's death while in active service after reaching the plan's qualified early retirement age.[107]

The REA amendments permit the payment of the participant's account balance to continue to substitute for a preretirement survivor's annuity, but *only if* the entire nonforfeitable account balance will go to the surviving spouse on death at any time before retirement.[108] Unlike the pre-REA rule, this requirement also extends to profit-sharing and stock bonus plans that do not offer a life annuity option at retirement.[109] If a participant elects, and the spouse consents, the account balance can still be designated to go to a nonspousal beneficiary.[110]

4. Effective Dates of ERISA Rules and REA Amendments

The effective dates for the ERISA preretirement survivor's benefit rules and REA amendments generally follow the effective dates set out above for survivor's benefits at retirement.[111]

However, insofar as the preretirement survivor's *annuity* rules (as opposed to the profit-sharing and stock bonus rules), the general REA effective dates are overridden by two special transition rules. The first provides that the preretirement survivor's annuity rules are "treated as in effect as of the time of the participant's death"—meaning that preretirement survivor's annuity coverage is automatic, and without regard to the attainment of a plan's "qualified early retirement age"—when a participant has at least one hour of service, including one hour of paid leave, after August 23, 1984, and dies before the REA effective date for the plan.[112]

The second transition rule provides that a participant must be able to elect to have the new preretirement survivor's annuity rules apply to his or her benefits in the event of death before retirement when the participant has at least one hour of service, including one

---

[107] 26 C.F.R. 1.401(a)-11(c)(2)(i)(C)(2), and see Rev. Rul. 81-9 (situation 7).

[108] A technical correction to REA in the 1986 Tax Reform Act allows the spouse's receipt of a participant's undistributed account balance under a profit-sharing or stock bonus plans to be conditioned on one year of marriage during the year before the earlier of the annuity starting date or date of death. ERISA §205(b)(3) and Code §401(a)(11)(D), as amended by §1898(b)(14) of P.L. 99-514. The annuity starting date under a profit-sharing or stock bonus plan is the first day on which all events have occurred (e.g., separation from service and spousal consent to payment) which entitle the participant to a distribution of benefits—whether or not in annuity form. ERISA §205(h)(2) and Code §417(f)(2), as amended by §1898(b)(12) of P.L. 99-514, and Conf. Rep., H.R. Rep. 99-841, at II-857.

[109] ERISA §205(b)(1)(C)(i) (Code §401(a)(11)(B)(iii)(I)), as amended. A qualified preretirement survivor's annuity is required to be provided if a profit-sharing or stock bonus plan is the transferee, i.e., recipient, of assets covering benefits accrued by a participant under a defined benefit or money purchase plan. ERISA §205(b)(1)(C)(iii) (Code §401(a)(11)(B)(iii)(III)), as amended. And see Temp. and Prop. Regs. 1.401(a)-11T, Q&A 7 and 8, 50 Fed. Reg. 29371 (July 19, 1985).

[110] ERISA §205(b)(1)(C)(i) (Code §401(a)(11)(B)(iii)(I)), as amended.

[111] See sec. II.A.3, on postretirement deaths.

[112] P.L. 98-397, §302(c)(2).

hour of paid leave, in a plan year beginning on or after January 1, 1976, and separates from service with at least 10 years of service under the plan and a nonforfeitable right to benefits *before* August 23, 1984.[113] By making this election, the participant can obtain preretirement survivor's coverage which starts immediately and continues without regard to the participant's separation from service. The election of coverage must be made before the participant's death (and the death must also have occurred after August 23, 1984). Plans are required to give notice of this election option "in such manner" as the Secretary of Treasury may prescribe.[114] Treasury regulations require such notice by the date the first summary annual report provided after September 17, 1985, is distributed to participants.[115]

One aspect of the application of the general REA effective dates to defined contribution plans that has drawn particular attention is their effect when a participant has already elected a nonspousal beneficiary for an account balance before the REA effective dates. In this case, spousal consent is not directly required when the spousal consent requirement becomes effective (because no "election" *after* the effective date has been made), but when the other substantive requirements of REA take effect for the plan, the prior designation of the nonspousal beneficiary is overridden by operation of law, unless and until a new election of the nonspousal beneficiary is made with the spouse's consent.[116]

C. Elections to Decline Survivor's Benefit Coverage

A participant must have a reasonable opportunity to elect *not* to take a joint and survivor's form of annuity at retirement. This applies both before and after the REA amendments. Before retirement, ERISA originally provided that a participant who continued working past a plan's qualified early retirement age had to have an opportunity, beginning at that time and continuing until death, retirement, or separation from service, to elect preretirement survivor's annuity coverage. After REA, this preretirement opportunity becomes an opportunity, as at retirement, to elect *not* to take the otherwise automatic preretirement survivor's annuity coverage.

Staying under a joint and survivor's form, instead of electing a single-life annuity, or a single life annuity with a term-certain, would seem to be an easy choice since a joint and survivor's annuity means

---

[113] P.L. 98-397, §§302(e)(2) and (3).

[114] P.L. 98-397, §302(e)(4)(A)(i).

[115] Temp. and Prop. Regs. 1.401(a)-11T, Q&A 28, 50 Fed. Reg. 29371 (July 19, 1985). But compare S. Rep. 98-575, at 18, [1984] U.S. Code Cong. & Ad. News 2547, at 2564.

[116] See Temp. and Prop. Regs. 1.401(a)-11T, Q&A 21 and 22, 50 Fed. Reg. 29371 (July 19, 1985). See also *Manitowoc Eng'g Co. v. Powalisz*, 7 EBC 1174 (E.D. Wis. 1987) (designation of 5 daughters as beneficiaries for account balance in the event of death before retirement overridden by REA's spousal consent requirement absent a new election and spousal consent). Accord *Art Builders Profit Sharing Plan v. Bosely*, 649 F.Supp. 848, 8 EBC 1582 (D. Md. 1986).

that benefits will continue for the surviving spouse for the remainder of his or her life. The problem participants confront in making this choice is the reduction most plans require in the benefits payable during the participant's life to cover the cost of the actuarially expected additional years of payments under a joint and survivor's form of benefits.

The reduction that can result on a retirement at a plan's normal retirement age has been illustrated above. When a participant takes early retirement, the total reduction may be greater still because the benefits may already be sharply reduced from the benefits that would be payable at normal retirement. An actuarial reduction is then permitted for the cost of providing benefits in the joint and survivor's form. Using typical reduction factors for early retirement, a $400 per month benefit payable at a normal retirement age of 65 might first be reduced by 35 percent for an early retirement at age 60, to $260 per month. Then for a 50 percent survivor's benefit to be payable to a spouse five years younger than the participant, the benefits might be reduced by another 14.5 percent—reducing the benefits payable during the participant's life to $222.30 per month, for $111.15 to be payable as the 50 percent survivor's benefit.[117]

Staying with preretirement survivor's coverage (or electing it before the REA effective dates) is much easier because the choice is not between permanently reduced joint and survivor's benefits or benefits in a single-life form, but is simply whether to take the preretirement survivor's coverage until the annuity starting date—at which time another election may be made. The preretirement survivor's coverage may have an actuarial charge against future benefits attached to it, but as mentioned before, even when not subsidized, a typical charge for preretirement survivor's coverage is only a one-half of one percent reduction in the participant's retirement benefits for each year of preretirement survivor's coverage between age 60 and 65.[118]

A participant's benefits may not be reduced more than is actuarially "reasonable" (e.g., at retirement, the plan should expect to pay out approximately the same whether a single-life or joint and survivor's annuity is chosen).[119] But confronted with the reduction in the amount of benefits payable under a joint and survivor's form, and generally

---

[117] See 29 C.F.R. 2621.4(c), (d)(2), and (e) (these are the factors the PBGC uses for reducing its maximum guaranteed benefit amount from an age 65 single-life annuity form for early retirement under a joint and survivor's form).

[118] D. McGill, *Fundamentals of Private Pensions* (5th ed.), at 127. For earlier years of coverage, the charge should decrease since the chance of death is less. *Id.*

The actuarial charge may be assessed against the participant's retirement benefits when and if he or she does retire, or it may be assessed against the survivor's benefits if the participant dies while under the coverage. A plan may also offer an option of paying the charge out-of-pocket, but this may not be the sole means by which the participant can obtain the coverage. 26 C.F.R. 1.401(a)-11(e).

[119] 26 C.F.R. 1.401(a)-11(b)(2) and 1.411(a)-4(a), and see S. Rep. 98-575, at 13, [1984] U.S. Code Cong. & Ad. News 2547, at 2559.

having thought of the amount of benefits that would be paid on retirement in terms of the "accrued benefit" expressed in a single-life annuity form, most participants have in the past elected out of the joint and survivor's form at retirement in favor of a single-life or another annuity form with higher immediate benefit payments. To a lesser extent, the charge for preretirement survivor's annuity coverage may also have discouraged participants from making this actuarially "equal" choice.

It was because of these practical problems, and the frequent resulting election of *no* survivor's coverage even after ERISA's reforms, that Congress determined that "the spouse should be involved in making choices with respect to retirement income on which the spouse may also rely."[120] Accordingly, under REA, Congress amended ERISA Section 205 to require "spousal consent when[ever] a participant elects not to take a survivor benefit."[121] With the spouse's consent, a participant may still elect to take benefits in a single-life form to avoid an actuarial reduction, or he or she may elect not to take preretirement coverage to avoid a small actuarial charge, but presumably fewer will do so with the new spousal consent requirements.

1. When No Election Is Required

Actuarial reductions to provide benefits in a joint and survivor's form are not required by ERISA or the Code.[122] In fact, many plans offer "subsidized" survivor's benefits at early or normal retirement with little or no actuarial reduction from the benefits payable in single-life form.[123] When a survivor's benefit is "fully subsidized" (that is, provided with no resulting decrease in benefits), a plan is not required to offer an election out of the joint and survivor's form to a single-life or other form since a participant has no cost reason for making such an election.[124] Employers commonly regard the preretirement election procedure as so administratively cumbersome compared to the small charges that may be assessed against benefits that they provide the preretirement survivor's coverage with no charge against future benefits.[125]

When a money purchase pension plan offers a preretirement survivor's annuity purchased with 50 percent or more of the participant's account balance, there is, by definition, no charge for the preretirement

---

[120] S. Rep. 98-575, at 12, [1984] U.S. Code Cong. & Ad. News 2547, at 2558.

[121] *Id.*

[122] See Rev. Rul. 81-9 (situation 4) and ERISA §205(c)(4) (Code §417(a)(4)), as amended by the Retirement Equity Act.

[123] See sec. II.A.1 and B.1 above.

[124] See 26 C.F.R. 1.401(a)-11(c)(i)(A) and ERISA §205(c)(4) (Code §417(a)(4)), as amended.

[125] In the Bureau of Labor Statistics' 1984 survey of plans of medium and large employers, over 57% of the participants were in plans that provided preretirement survivor's coverage at no charge, and therefore, presumably with no election to decline the coverage. BLS, Employee Benefits in Medium and Large Firms, 1984, at 57.

survivor's coverage since all of the payments come from the participant's account balance. Hence, no election out is required to be provided.[126] A money purchase pension plan may, however, still provide such an election, for example, if it wants to offer a lump sum option as an alternative to the annuity benefit, or if it offers participants the opportunity to elect a nonspousal beneficiary, with their spouse's consent.

Elections not to provide survivor's benefits are also not required when a profit-sharing or stock bonus plan provides that a participant's entire nonforfeitable account balance will go to the spouse on death before retirement because such a provision is also by definition without a charge or cost to the participant.[127] A profit-sharing or stock bonus plan may, however, still provide an election so that a participant may designate a nonspousal beneficiary, with the spouse's consent.[128]

2. Election Periods and Explanatory Material

When there is a cost for survivor's benefits, Treasury regulations prescribe election periods, and require explanatory material to be provided participants before any election. Under the pre-REA regulations, explanatory material on survivor's benefit elections must be furnished a participant on both the retirement and preretirement elections. This material must describe in "nontechnical" language[129] the "circumstances" in which the "survivor" part of the annuity is provided if the participant does not elect out of the survivor's form at retirement, or if the participant elects the coverage, as required for pre-REA preretirement coverage.[130] The explanatory material must also describe the "relative financial effect" of an election of the joint and survivor's form, i.e., it must describe the reduction in percentage or dollar amounts for the joint and survivor's form, or the charge against benefits for preretirement survivor's coverage.[131]

Under the REA amendments, the requirement of a written explanation of the effect of the joint and survivor's annuity form continues basically as before, except that the explanation must now cover the spousal consent required for an election to waive the joint and survivor's form or preretirement survivor's coverage. The explanation must also have a slightly more negative focus than before. It must describe "the effect of an election . . . to *waive* the joint and survivor annuity form of benefit."[132] In contrast, the pre-REA regulations permitted the explanation to describe only the positive side, i.e., the "circumstances

---

[126] See ERISA §205(c)(4) (Code §417(a)(4)) and ERISA §205(e)(2) (Code §417(c)(2)), as amended.

[127] See 26 C.F.R. 1.401(a)-11(c)(2)(i)(C)(2) of the pre-REA Treasury regulations.

[128] ERISA §205(b)(1)(C)(i) (Code §401(a)(11)(B)(iii)(I)), as amended.

[129] 26 C.F.R. 1.401(a)-11(c)(3)(i).

[130] 26 C.F.R. 1.401(a)-11(c)(3)(i)(A) and (B).

[131] 26 C.F.R. 1.401(a)-11(c)(3)(i)(C).

[132] ERISA §205(c)(3)(A)(ii) (Code §417(a)(3)(A)(ii)), as amended (emphasis added).

in which [the survivor annuity] *will be provided* unless the participant . . . elected not to have benefits provided in that form."[133]

a. At retirement. Under the pre-REA regulations, a participant must be provided with a written explanation on the effect, including the "relative financial effect," of the joint and survivor's form versus other options, nine months before the plan's qualified early or normal retirement age, with the participant having a period of at least 90 days before the commencement of benefits to make a decision.[134] Under the REA amendments, a written explanation of the joint and survivor's annuity form, and of the spousal consent now required to elect to waive it, must be provided within a "reasonable period of time" before the annuity starting date.[135] During the "applicable election period"—the 90-day period before the annuity starting date—the participant, with the spouse's consent, may elect out of the joint and survivor's form, and may at any time during the same period revoke any previous election.[136]

b. Preretirement. Under the pre-REA preretirement election regulations (where the election is an affirmative election of preretirement survivor's coverage), the preretirement election must be available 90 days before a participant first attains a plan's "qualified early retirement age," with explanatory material on the election furnished 90 days prior to that.[137] Even if not chosen at first, the election thereafter remains continuously available until the participant dies, retires, or separates from service.[138]

After the REA amendments, preretirement survivor's annuity coverage is automatic beginning with when a participant first obtains a nonforfeitable right to any portion of his or her benefits under the plan. Notice of the opportunity to elect *out* of the coverage and a written explanation of the preretirement coverage and the effect of waiving it are required to be provided at some point between the first day of the plan year in which a participant attains age 32 and the close of the plan year before the year in which the participant attains age 35—whether or not the participant is vested at that time.[139] The applicable election period, i.e., the period when a participant may elect not

---

[133] 26 C.F.R. 1.401(a)-11(c)(3)(i)(A) (emphasis added).

[134] See 26 C.F.R. 1.401(a)-11(c)(3)(ii) and 26 C.F.R. 1.401(a)-11(c)(1)(ii).

[135] ERISA §205(c)(3)(A) (Code §417(a)(3)(A)).

[136] ERISA §205(c)(1)(A) (Code §417(a)(1)(A)) and ERISA §205(c)(6)(A) (Code §417(a)(5)(A)). The election period may be less than 90 days, but it may not exceed the 90-day period before the annuity starting date. S. Rep. 98-575, at 3 and 15, [1984] U.S. Code Cong. & Ad. News 2547, at 2549 and 2561. No limit is placed on the number of times that a participant may change his or her mind during the 90-day period. S. Rep. 98-575, at 14.

[137] 26 C.F.R. 1.401(a)-11(c)(2)(ii) and (c)(3)(ii). However, if a plan provided that a preretirement survivor's election was ineffective for deaths from accidental causes within two years of the election, as permitted before the REA, the election had to be available two years plus 90 days before the qualified early retirement age, so that a participant could elect the option soon enough to immediately have both accidental and nonaccidental survivor's coverage on attaining the qualified early retirement age. 26 C.F.R. 1.401(a)-11(c)(2)(ii)(A).

[138] *Id.*

[139] ERISA §205(c)(3)(B) (Code §417(a)(3)(B)), as amended. And see Temp. and Prop. Regs. 1.401(a)-11T, Q&A 26, 50 Fed. Reg. 29371 (July 19, 1985).

to take the coverage, or may revoke an election not to take the coverage, begins on the first day of the plan year in which the participant attains age 35, and ends only on the earlier of the date of death or the annuity starting date.[140] When a participant obtains nonforfeitable benefits before age 35, the preretirement coverage may be provided with no opportunity to elect out until age 35 (even if there is a small charge for the coverage).[141] However, if a participant with nonforfeitable benefits separates from service before age 35, the applicable election period for the participant must begin not later than the date of the separation from service.[142] When an individual does not become a plan participant until after age 32, e.g., because he or she was not hired until age 40, a written explanation of the preretirement survivor's coverage must be provided no later than three years after the first day of the plan year in which the employee becomes a participant, with the applicable election period presumably starting at the same time.[143]

A significant change under REA related to revocations of elections not to take preretirement survivor's coverage is that unlike under the original ERISA provisions, plans are no longer permitted to place an up to two-year waiting period on the effectiveness of a new election of preretirement survivor's annuity coverage in the event of nonaccidental death. Judith Mazo, the director of research for the Martin E. Segal benefit consulting firm, thus observes that even if a participant at first elects out:

> "Unlike [in] the purchase of individual life insurance, [the participant] can always buy in at the last minute."[144]

This assumes, of course, that the participant knows when the "last minute" is.

3. *Spousal Consent*

The most profound change brought about by REA as far as elections of alternative benefit forms is the spousal consent requirement. For any election not to take a joint and survivor's annuity at retirement, not to take preretirement survivor's annuity coverage before retirement, or to designate a nonspousal beneficiary for an account balance before or after retirement under a profit-sharing or stock bonus plan, the participant's spouse must consent to the election.[145] To be

---

140 ERISA §205(c)(1)(A) (Code §417(a)(1)(A)), and ERISA §205(c)(6)(B) (Code §417(a)(5)(B)), as amended.

141 See S. Rep. 98-575, at 15, [1984] U.S. Code Cong. & Ad. News 2547, at 2561.

142 ERISA §205(c)(6) (Code §417(a)(5)), as amended. But see Temp. and Prop. Regs., *supra*, at Q&A 31 (permitting the explanation to be provided not later than one year after a separation from service).

143 Temp. and Prop. Regs., *supra*, at Q&A 32.

144 New York Times, March 24, 1985, at F-11.

145 ERISA §205(c)(1)(B) (Code §417(a)(1)(B)) and ERISA §205(b)(1)(C)(i) (Code §401(a)(11)(B)(iii)(I)), as amended. Technical corrections to REA in the 1986 Tax Reform Act clarify that the spousal consent requirement is applicable to a redesignation of a nonspousal beneficiary, to a change in an election of a form of benefits, and to a loan to a participant secured

effective, the spouse's consent must be in writing, must "acknowledge the effect of [the] election [to waive the survivor's benefits]," and must be witnessed by either a notary public or a plan representative.[146]

One wrinkle to the spousal consent requirement is that a spouse's consent to any election is effective only for *that* spouse. Given the long election period during which preretirement survivor's annuity coverage may be waived by an election, a participant may sometimes have two or more spouses over the period. If a participant is to continue an election *not* to take the coverage during the tenure of each spouse, spousal consent must be reobtained after each remarriage.[147] Similarly, a participant in a profit-sharing or stock bonus plan may have two or more spouses over the long period when he or she has a nonforfeitable account balance under a plan. If a participant has designated a child of the first marriage as the beneficiary for the account balance in the event of death, with the first spouse's consent, a second marriage overrides that designation, and requires the second spouse's consent for the child's interest to be continued.[148]

Consent is *not* required for an election out of the joint and survivor's form or a preretirement survivor's annuity when "it is established to the satisfaction of a plan representative [that] there is no spouse, [that] the spouse cannot be located, or because of such other circumstances as the Secretary of the Treasury may by regulation prescribe."[149] "If [a] plan administrator acts in accordance with the fiduciary standards of ERISA in securing spousal consent or in accepting representations of the participant that the spouse's consent cannot be obtained," but it turns out after the annuity starting date, or after the participant's death before retirement, that a spouse existed, or could be located (or that a properly notarized spousal consent was signed by someone other than the spouse), the plan will not be liable to the surviving spouse "to the extent of payments made."[150] The Senate Finance Committee report illustrates:

> "For example, if the plan administrator receives a notarized spousal consent, valid on its face, which the administrator [has] no reason to believe is invalid, the plan would certainly be allowed to rely on the consent even if it is, in fact, invalid."[151]

Although in this case a spouse's rights against the plan are limited "to

---

by the participant's accrued benefits. ERISA §205(c)(2)(A) and Code §417(a)(2)(A), and ERISA §§205(c)(4) and 205(j) and Code §§417(a)(4) and (5), as amended by §§1898(b)(6) and (b)(4) of P.L. 99-514.

[146] ERISA §205(c)(2)(A) (Code §417(a)(2)(A)), as amended.

[147] S. Rep. 98-575, at 14 and 15, [1984] U.S. Code Cong. & Ad. News 2547, at 2560 and 2561. And see ERISA §205(c)(2) (Code §417(a)(2)).

[148] *Id.*, and Temp. and Prop. Regs. 1.401(a)-11T, Q&A 23, 50 Fed. Reg. 29371 (July 19, 1985). A qualified domestic relations order calling for the child's interest to remain intact might overcome this problem. See ERISA §206(d)(3)(F) (Code §414(p)(5)), as amended.

[149] ERISA §205(c)(2)(B) (Code §417(a)(2)(B)), as amended.

[150] S. Rep. 98-575, at 14, [1984] U.S. Code Cong. & Ad. News 2547, at 2559; and ERISA §205(c)(5), as amended.

[151] S. Rep. 98-575, at 14.

the extent of payments made," the spouse may still have a claim against the plan for the payments *not* made, and against the participant, or the participant's estate, for the remainder.

The REA spousal consent requirement is effective for *any* election made after December 31, 1984.[152] But this single effective date can be misleading. For an election at retirement of a form of benefits *other than* the joint and survivor's annuity form, consent may be required even if an election was made before December 31, 1984, if the annuity starting date for the participant did not occur until after December 31, 1984.[153] For preretirement survivor's annuity coverage, the first transition rule under REA provides that the new preretirement rules, including the spousal consent requirement, are "treated as in effect" for any death before a participant's annuity starting date if the participant had one hour of service, including one hour of paid leave, after August 23, 1984.[154] Thus, preretirement survivor's annuities are automatic after this date *unless* an election has been made to waive the coverage, with the consent of the spouse. For a designation of a nonspousal beneficiary for an account balance under a profit-sharing or stock bonus plan, it has already been noted that even if the participant has a longstanding designation of a nonspousal beneficiary, when REA's effective dates for its substantive provisions occur, the spouse becomes the beneficiary by operation of law. Therefore, even if no "election" occurred after December 31, 1984, the spouse becomes the beneficiary under the plan unless a new election is made with the consent of the spouse.[155]

4. *Judicial Scrutiny of Elections*

The courts have interpreted ERISA's joint and survivor's benefit election notice requirements strictly. In *United Paper Workers v. Bowater Pension Plan,* a one-year waiting period on the effectiveness of a preretirement survivor's annuity coverage election if death occurred from nonaccidental causes was inapplicable because a participant was not provided with the election opportunity early enough.[156] In *Kaszuk v. Bakery & Confectionery Union Pension Fund,* a denial of survivor's benefits was arbitrary and capricious when general notice of the availability of the preretirement election was given through a union's newspaper, but was not "repeated" so as to make the election continuously

---

[152] P.L. 98-397, §303(c)(3).

[153] See C. Savage, et al, "Analysis of the Retirement Equity Act of 1984," 11 BNA Pens. Rep. Spec. Supp., at S-7 (Oct. 29, 1984).

[154] P.L. 98-397, §303(c)(2).

[155] ERISA §§205(b)(1)(C) and 205(c)(2) (Code §§401(a)(11)(B)(iii)(I) and 417(a)(2)), as amended. And see sec. II.B.4 above.

[156] 2 EBC 1154, at 1162 (E.D. Tenn. 1981).

available throughout the preretirement election period as required under the Treasury's regulations.[157]

Close examination of election forms to see what a participant has actually elected has also led to benefits for surviving spouses. In *Wolf v. National Shopmen Pension Fund,* a participant applying for a disability pension signed a form waiving 50 percent survivor's benefits on "retirement." After his death, the Third Circuit examined the terms used in the election form in relation to the meaning of "retirement" under the plan, and concluded that "retirement" was distinguished from a disability pension, and therefore that the participant had *not* waived survivor's benefits in the event of death while receiving the disability pension, but only had waived it if death occurred after his early or normal retirement age.[158]

Explanatory materials on election options, including information in a plan's SPD and other information supplied a participant, may also be inadequate if they do not enable a participant to make an intelligent choice based on his or her circumstances. In *Shea v. Teacher's Retirement System of the City of New York,* a participant who was dying selected a survivor's benefit option that would leave her estate with $65,000 less than was available under another option that would still have provided her with approximately the same benefits during her remaining life. The court found that the employer's description of the various options in a summary booklet distributed to employees was inadequate, and held that the employer, having undertaken to supply explanatory information (at a time before ERISA when such disclosure was not required, and under a public plan that would still not be subject to ERISA's requirements), was under a duty to act carefully, with the bounds of its duty "enlarged by knowledge of [the booklet's] prospective use." The duty to describe the options was so that "any . . . member of the class for whom it was intended could understand [the] privileges, restrictions and limitations."[159] In *Gediman v. Anheuser Busch, Inc.,* an employee sought individual advice from his employer about death benefits if he elected to defer a cash distribution available

---

[157] 791 F.2d 548, 7 EBC 1724 (6th Cir. 1986), and see 26 C.F.R. 1.401(a)-11(c)(3)(ii) (last sentence).

[158] 728 F.2d 182, 5 EBC 1257 (3d Cir. 1984).

[159] 381 N.Y.S.2d 266, at 269 (App. Div. 1976), *app. dismissed,* see 387 N.Y.S.2d 837 (Ct.App. 1976). But see *Lee v. Union Elec. Co.*, 789 F.2d 1303, 7 EBC 1636 (8th Cir. 1986), *cert. denied,* 479 U.S. ___ (1986) (SPD adequately explained the need for an *affirmative* election by the participant—before REA—to provide a survivor's annuity to his spouse in the event of death before retirement; Eighth Circuit suggested that even if the SPD explanation was inadequate, it would need evidence that the participant had an interest in providing survivor's benefits to his spouse to establish detrimental reliance on an inadequate explanation). In contrast, the *Shea* court provided relief to the deceased teacher's estate based on the most advantageous option, with a dissenting judge complaining that the teacher's reliance on the misleading booklet was entirely inferred since no direct evidence showed she had read the booklet, or relied on it, in making her choice. See also *Genter v. Acme Scale & Supply Co.*, 776 F.2d 1180 (3d Cir. 1985) (estate of employee awarded $10,000 in increased life insurance when SPD and written plan failed to disclose discretion exercised for certain other employees to increase benefits immediately upon a salary increase, rather than at the end of the year; although employee had died and it therefore could not be known whether he would have availed himself of this opportunity had it been disclosed, crucial point was that he would have had the opportunity to do so).

upon early retirement and his death occurred before the cash distribution was made. The employer referred the question to its pension consultants, who stated in a memo that the death benefit would not be "as much." In fact, the benefit was less that one-half of the amount otherwise available. The consultants were found not to have acted with care or competence in failing to state, or indicate, that the benefit would be reduced substantially in this circumstance. In view of having undertaken to advise the participant, the employer was liable for negligence.[160]

III. Other Optional Forms of Payment and Amounts of Benefits

A. Offers of Optional Benefit Forms

The Code requires "pension" plans (i.e., defined benefit plans and money purchase defined contribution plans) to offer benefits "over a period of years, usually for life, after retirement." This almost invariably results in benefits being offered in the form of a "life annuity."[161] Pension plans are required to offer a qualified joint and survivor's annuity as the automatic form of the life annuity, unless a participant elects another benefit form, with spousal consent required for any such other election after December 31, 1984.[162] Other annuity options which may be offered by pension plans include the single-life (or straight life) annuity form in which accrued benefits are generally expressed under a defined benefit plan, a single-life annuity with a five or 10-year term-certain feature, or a joint and survivor's annuity with the survivor's benefits going to a nonspousal beneficiary.

A profit-sharing or stock bonus plan is not required to offer benefits "over a period of years, usually for life," and thus is not required to offer benefits in life annuity form, although many do.[163] Profit-sharing and stock bonus plans are also not categorically required to offer a qualified joint and survivor's form of annuity. But when an annuity option is offered, a qualified joint and survivor's form must be offered and must, moreover, be the plan's automatic form of annuity, unless the participant specifically elects another annuity form, with his or her spouse's consent.[164]

Early retirement benefit options are, of course, commonplace under defined benefit pension plans, although neither ERISA nor the Code requires that they be offered. Likewise, lump sum options are

---

[160] 299 F.2d 537, at 545 (2d Cir. 1962) (Friendly, J.).

[161] 26 C.F.R. 1.401-1(b)(i).

[162] ERISA §205(c)(2) (Code §417(a)(2)), as amended by P.L. 98-397.

[163] See 26 C.F.R. 1.401-1(b)(ii).

[164] ERISA §205(b)(1)(C)(ii) (Code §401(a)(11)(B)(iii)(II)), as amended by P.L. 98-397.

often offered under the terms of plans, particularly under the terms of money purchase pension plans and profit-sharing plans.

Once offered, benefit options are subject to certain constraints. When an early retirement or lump sum option is subject to the consent or discretion of the employer, or a plan's trustees, as is common under defined benefit plans which offer lump sum options at all, the employer's or trustees' consent or discretion must not be exercised "primarily" in favor of the prohibited group of employees within the meaning of Code Section 401(a)(4).[165] The exercise of such consent or discretion is also subject to review for compliance with ERISA's fiduciary standard of duty.[166] To meet the Code's definitely determinable benefits requirement, and ERISA's requirement that plans "specify the basis on which payments are made," the consent or discretion may also be required to be exercised according to *established* criteria and policies.[167]

The addition of new conditions on the availability of any optional benefit form is considered an indirect reduction in the participant's accrued benefits subject to the protection of ERISA Section 204(g).[168] As of July 30, 1984, with a slightly later effective date for collectively bargained plans, optional benefit forms, including early retirement, lump sum, and joint and survivor's options, are also protected under ERISA Section 204(g) against complete *elimination*, unless the elimination does not eliminate a "valuable right" of participants, as defined under to-be-issued Treasury regulations.[169] According to the Senate Finance Committee's report, the Treasury regulations may exempt a benefit option from this protection against complete elimination, but only

> "if (1) the elimination of the option does not eliminate a valuable right of a participant or beneficiary, and (2) the option is not subsidized or a similar benefit with a comparable value subsidy is provided."[170]

As an example of the type of benefit option that might be exempted, the Committee's report mentions the elimination of an actuarially reduced joint and 66.6 percent survivor's annuity option from a plan which continues to offer a joint and 100 percent survivor's benefit option and a joint and 50 percent survivor's option, thus continuing to

---

165 Rev. Rul. 85-59. And see sec. I.A above (on the commencement of benefits) on the IRS's proposed antidiscretion regulations, which would eventually force all plans to adopt objective criteria, in lieu of open-ended discretion, on the availability of benefit options, but in the immediate future would delay the effectiveness of Rev. Rul. 85-59. See also ch. 5, I.D.

166 See ch. 7, sec. III.C.

167 See Rev. Ruls. 81-106 and 85-59, 26 C.F.R. 1.401-1(b)(1)(i), and ERISA §402(b)(4). See also sec. I.A above (on commencement of benefits) on the IRS's proposed antidiscretion regulations, and ch. 5, sec. I.D.

168 See ch. 4, sec. IV.B.3.

169 S. Rep. 98-575, at 30, [1984] U.S. Code Cong. & Ad. News 2547, at 2576, and ERISA §204(g)(2)(B) (Code §411(d)(6)(B)), as amended by P.L. 98-397, And see P.L. 98-397, §302(d), for effective dates. If a collectively bargained pension agreement expired between July 30, 1984, and Jan. 1, 1985, the provision is generally effective for plan amendments adopted after April 1, 1985. See P.L. 98-397, §302(d)(2).

170 S. Rep. 98-575, at 30, [1984] U.S. Code Cong. & Ad. News 2547, at 2576.

provide comparable alternatives.[171] However, the Senate report expressly states:

> "The committee expects that the regulations will *not* permit the elimination of a 'lump-sum distribution' option because, for a participant or beneficiary with substandard mortality, the elimination of that option could eliminate a valuable right even if a benefit of equal actuarial value (based on standard mortality) is available under the plan."[172]

Even before this, the elimination of a nondiscretionary right to an optional benefit form might be considered an abridgment or diminution of a participant's vested rights under the terms of the plan.[173]

In the opposite direction, the Internal Revenue Code contains rules that can limit a participant's benefit options in certain cases. To limit the potential for tax deferral by "commencing" benefits but then choosing an optional form that pushes back distribution of the bulk of the benefits until after a participant's death, the Code requires that benefits under any option offered by a qualified plan must be paid in a form which distributes a participant's entire interest by the end of the joint life expectancy of the participant and his or her spouse (or the participant and a designated beneficiary), and which does so in a "substantially nonincreasing," i.e., not backloaded, manner.[174]

The "incidental" benefit rule also limits the election of forms of benefits that create death benefits that are more than incidental to the plan's primary retirement income purpose. At retirement, the incidental benefit rule provides that under any settlement option provided by the plan, no more than 50 percent of the participant's total benefits may be actuarially expected to go to a nonparticipant beneficiary.[175] The incidental benefit rule is, however, always satisfied by a qualified joint and survivor's annuity, even though in some cases such a benefit may actually provide more than 50 percent of the present value of the participant's benefits to a spouse, e.g., under a joint and 100 percent survivor's benefit form when the participant has a much younger spouse.[176]

Before retirement, the incidental benefit rule generally requires that automatic or elective preretirement death benefits not exceed 100 times a participant's anticipated monthly lifetime pension benefits.[177] A qualified preretirement survivor's annuity can, however, provide up

---

[171] *Id.*

[172] *Id.*

[173] See ch. 9, sec. IV.B. And see ch. 9, sec. V, on advance notice requirements when a participant could have retired under an option before an amendment took effect.

[174] Code §401(a)(9), as amended by the Deficit Reduction Act, P.L. 98-369, and H. R. Rep. 98-861, at 1138, [1984] U.S. Code Cong. & Ad. News, at 1826.

[175] Rev. Rul. 72-241. And see sec. I.C., above.

[176] Rev. Rul. 72-240.

[177] Rev. Rul. 60-83. Some plans purchase life insurance to cover preretirement deaths. When life insurance is purchased, the limit of 100 times the participant's anticipated lifetime monthly benefit may be exceeded so long as the cost of the term life insurance is no more than 25% of the employer's total contributions for the employee, or so long as the cost of ordinary (or whole) life insurance is no more than 50% of the employer's total contributions. Rev. Rul. 66-143.

to 100 percent of the participant's current (as opposed to anticipated) accrued benefits without regard to this limit.[178]

B. Reasonableness and Consistency of an Interest Assumption

Under any optional benefit form, but perhaps most obviously under a lump sum option, the *amount* of benefits a participant receives depends in large measure on the particular interest and mortality assumptions the plan uses. As an example, if the assumed interest rate for an "actuarially equivalent" lump sum option is six percent, a participant age 65 receives $11,520 in cash for each $100 in monthly benefits. On the other hand, if the plan uses an eight percent interest rate, the participant may receive only $10,068 in cash for each $100 in monthly benefits.[179]

In addition to the conversion of benefits in annuity form into lump sum amounts—or the conversion of lump sum amounts into annuities—interest assumptions are also inherent in the conversion of benefits from a single-life annuity form to a joint and survivor's annuity form, and also in the conversion of normal retirement age benefits to "actuarially equivalent" early retirement benefits.

Even when set percentage or fractional factors are used in converting benefits to an optional form, as is common in determining the amount of early retirement benefits, an interest assumption and a mortality assumption are implicit in the percentage or fractional reduction factors. As an example, the reduction factors the PBGC uses to reduce its maximum guaranteed benefit from a benefit beginning at age 65 to an equivalent early retirement benefit call for a reduction of 7⁄12 of one percent for each month, up to 60 months, before age 65 that the participant begins to receive benefits—for a reduction of 35 percent if benefits commence at age 60. For each of the 60 months preceding age 60, the PBGC's reduction factor is 4⁄12 of one percent—for a total reduction of 55 percent when benefits commence at age 55.[180] These reduction factors reflect a five percent interest assumption with the resulting factors smoothed to produce even fractions over five-year periods.[181] If a seven percent interest assumption had been used, the reduction factor for benefits beginning at age 55 would be 63 percent.[182]

The effect of a higher or lower interest assumption on benefits

---

[178] Rev. Rul. 85-15. If a preretirement survivor's annuity has a present value of less than 100 times the participant's anticipated monthly lifetime pension, the difference may be provided the participant's spouse or a nonspousal beneficiary in a lump sum death benefit or other form without violating the incidental benefit rule. *Id.*

[179] Using the UP-1984 mortality assumptions with a one-year setback to reflect a 40% female workforce.

[180] 29 C.F.R. 2621.4(c).

[181] Assuming mortality under the PBGC's unisex composite of the 1971 GAM tables for male and female lives.

[182] *Id.*

under an optional form varies according to the benefit option in question. As indicated in the first example above, in converting benefits from an annuity to a lump sum, the lower the assumed rate of interest, the *higher* the lump sum. Similarly, in converting a normal retirement age benefit to an actuarially equivalent early retirement benefit, a lower interest assumption also results in higher early retirement benefits. On the other hand, in converting a lump sum, e.g., an individual's account balance under a defined contribution plan, into an annuity, a lower interest assumption works in the opposite direction, producing a *lower* annuity benefit. A similar effect occurs when converting a single-life annuity to joint and survivor's form, or to a single-life annuity with a "term-certain." Along the same line, when a plan "actuarially" increases benefits for a deferral of retirement past the plan's normal retirement age, the effect of a lower interest assumption is a lower increase in benefits for the period of deferral than if a higher interest rate was assumed.

In the past, when a plan did not use set percentage or fractional factors for converting benefits to optional forms, but stated that the benefits under an optional form were actuarially equivalent, the exact interest and mortality assumptions used in determining actuarial equivalence were often not stated anywhere in the plan. However, under Revenue Ruling 79-90, the interest rate and mortality assumption for determining any actuarially equivalent options must be stated in plans as of the first plan year beginning after December 31, 1983, to meet the Code's requirement that all benefits offered under a plan must be definitely determinable, and thus outside the discretion of the employer, or the plan's trustees, except by plan amendment.[183] For interest rates, the stated rate may be a specific interest rate, such as six percent, or a variable standard, such as 75 percent of the prime interest rate of a named and unrelated bank—but in either case, the interest rate must be definitely determinable from the plan's terms and must be outside the control of the employer, or the plan's trustees.[184]

Whatever the type of benefit option, the actuarial assumptions used in the computation of benefits in the optional form must also be reasonable. ERISA Section 204(c)(3) (Code Section 411(c)(3)) requires that any benefit option offered by a plan must be at least the actuarial equivalent of the participant's accrued benefits at the plan's normal retirement age. Conversions to benefits in an optional form based on

[183] See also Code §401(a)(25), as added by the Retirement Equity Act, P.L. 98-397. Some plans stated the interest rates for determining "actuarially equivalent" benefit options expressly before Rev. Rul. 79-90 took effect. A Hewitt Associates survey found that even before Rev. Rul. 79-90, 18% of group of plans expressly stated the interest rates used in computing lump sum benefits. See L. Brown and J. Mamorsky, "Playing Russian Roulette With Lump Sum Options," Pension World (April 1981), at 63 n.7 (summarizing survey results).

[184] See Rev. Rul. 79-90, and Rev. Rul. 81-12.

unreasonable actuarial factors will cause benefits to be "forfeited" in violation of ERISA's minimum standards for nonforfeitability.[185]

Generally, in determining the employer contributions required to fund deferred pension promises, the high interest rates of the late 1970's and early 1980's were not used by pension actuaries, and, in fact, were considered "unreasonable" rates for such purposes because they were unlikely to prevail over the long period of time that defined benefit plan obligations span:

> "[F]ew, if any, actuaries assume that the present high rates will endure for over 50 years and that is the appropriate time frame over which actuaries make their calculations."[186]

When it comes to benefit options, such as actuarially equivalent early retirement benefits, joint and survivor's benefits, or lump sum options, the appropriate time frame is shorter than in funding a plan, but is still longer than that underlying a money market interest rate. Life expectancy at age 65, for example, is approximately 16.5 years. In the case of a lump sum option at age 65, this means the issue is the present value of an annuity that would otherwise be paid out in fixed installments over this 16.5-year period. Similarly, in the case of an early retirement benefit beginning at age 60, the question is how much should benefits at normal retirement be reduced to make a stream of payments presently payable beginning at age 65 for a period of approximately 16.5 years equal to a stream of payments that starts five years sooner, and that may be expected to extend over approximately 20.5 years.

The rates the PBGC uses in determining the lump sum present value for immediate annuities on plan termination are a strong indicia of the upper bounds of reasonableness for interest rates spanning these periods. The PBGC's rates are based on a survey of the rates insurers are currently using as the basis for the sale of immediate group annuities, and are updated several times each year.[187] In *UAW District 65 v. Harper & Row Publishers, Inc.*, a district court thus questioned the reasonableness of a 15 percent interest rate Harper & Row was using to cash out participants with small annuity benefits at a time when the PBGC's interest rate for valuing immediate annuities was 10.75 percent and other indices also supported a lower rate.[188]

---

[185] 26 C.F.R. 1.411(a)-4(a). See also 26 C.F.R. 1.401(a)-11(b)(2) ("reasonable" and consistently applied actuarial assumptions must be the basis for reductions to provide benefits in qualified joint and survivor's form).

[186] Testimony of Lawrence N. Margel, vice-president and chief actuary, Towers, Perrin, Forster & Crosby, in House Select Committee on Aging, Hearings on Pension Funding Problems, at 210 (June 7, 1982).

[187] See 29 C.F.R. 2619.44 and 29 C.F.R. Part 2619 (Valuation of Benefits in Nonmultiemployer Plans), Appendix B.

[188] 576 F.Supp. 1468, 4 EBC 2586 (S.D.N.Y. 1983). And see *Dooley v. American Airlines, Inc.*, 797 F.2d 1447 (7th Cir. 1986) (summary judgment against plaintiffs reversed on claims that change in interest rates for lump sums to a 16% rate was unreasonable and in breach of fiduciary duty at time when PBGC's highest rate was 11%). But see *Lewis v. Fulton Federal Savings & Loan Pension Plan*, 4 EBC 2071 (N.D. Ga. 1983) (use of 13.65% and 14.5% interest rates for determining lump sum values of annuities not questioned closely even though PBGC's immediate annuity interest rates over the same periods were 10.5% and 10.75%).

The PBGC adjusts its immediate annuity rate when there is any period of deferral before an annuity will become payable. To value deferred annuities, the PBGC thus values the annuity as if payments were to begin immediately using its current immediate annuity rate, but then it discounts that value for the period of deferral using an interest rate that is adjusted to account for actuarial conservatism over the longer time frame. To illustrate, as of February 1, 1984, the PBGC used a 9.75 percent interest rate to value immediate annuities. But for the period of deferral, the PBGC rate on February 1, 1984, was 8.62 percent for an annuity under which payments were deferred for 10 years.[189] This difference in interest rates can be significant if a participant dies before a plan's earliest retirement age so that survivor's benefits are not immediately payable in annuity form, or if the question is the lump sum present value of a participant's benefits when he or she is a large number of years away from retirement. In both instances, application of the deferred annuity rate results in higher present values.[190]

Under the 1984 Retirement Equity Act amendments to ERISA, the amount of benefits that may be subject to an involuntary cash-out is raised to a present value of $3,500 (from $1,750), but the interest rate used in the computation of this present value, and in the actual involuntary cash-out of participants within this range, is now *expressly* limited at the upper end to the PBGC's current interest rate for "determining the present value of a lump sum distribution on a plan termination."[191] The IRS's implementing temporary and proposed regulations provide that the PBGC's immediate annuity interest rate sets the upper bounds for a reasonable interest rate for an involuntary cash-out of an immediate or deferred annuity from a defined benefit plan.[192] For deferred annuities, this may not go far enough because the statutory language refers to the rate the PBGC would use for "determining the present value of a lump sum distribution on plan termination." As a regulatory and factual matter, the interest rate the PBGC uses for valuing deferred annuities on a plan termination never rests solely on its immediate annuity rate.[193]

The temporary and proposed regulations also use the PBGC's immediate annuity interest rate to establish an upper bound of reasonableness for an interest rate for determining benefit amounts under any voluntary benefit options offered by a defined benefit plan.[194] The

---

[189] See 29 C.F.R. 2619.45 and 29 C.F.R. Part 2619, Appendix B, *supra.*

[190] See D. Walker, "The PBGC's Role in Protecting Lump Sum Benefit Values," 35 Lab. L.J. 667, at 670 (Nov. 1984), for further illustrations of this difference.

[191] ERISA §203(e)(2) (Code §411(a)(11)(B)), as amended by P.L. 98-397. The referenced PBGC interest rates would perhaps have been more accurately described as the PBGC's interest rates for valuing immediate and deferred annuities from trusteed nonmultiemployer plans, which appear at 29 C.F.R. Part 2619, Appendix B.

[192] Temp. and Prop. Regs. 1.417(e)-1T(b)(2)(ii), 50 Fed. Reg. 29371 (July 19, 1985).

[193] See 29 C.F.R. 2619.45 and Part 2619, Appendix B.

[194] Temp. and Prop. Regs. 1.417(e)-1T(e)(1), implementing ERISA §205(g)(3) (Code §417(e)(3)), as amended.

use of the PBGC's immediate annuity rate in computing the value of deferred benefits is again, however, highly questionable.[195]

The 1986 Tax Reform Act more clearly provides that, effective January 1, 1987, interest rates used in computing the present value of vested accrued benefits for an involuntary or a voluntary cash-out of a participant's annuity benefits must not exceed the PBGC's interest rates for valuing benefits in a lump sum form on plan termination—using the PBGC's *deferred* or *immediate* annuity interest rate, whichever conforms with the status of the benefit in question. If the present value of a participant's benefits is more than $25,000 (using the PBGC's rates), an interest rate not exceeding 120 percent of the appropriate PBGC rate can be used.[196]

To be "reasonable," an interest rate used for a benefit option should also be consistent with the rates for other actuarially equivalent options under a plan. Thus, if a low, but otherwise reasonable, interest rate is used in determining the reduction for benefits in joint and survivor's form (where it produces a higher reduction), the same low rate may be required to be used for an actuarially equivalent lump sum (where it produces a higher lump sum). It is implicit in ERISA Section 204(c)(3)'s requirement that *all* benefit options under a plan must be the actuarial equivalent of the normal retirement benefit that the same "reasonable" actuarial assumptions will be used under the plan for all such options.

C. Changes in Interest Rates or Percentage or Fractional Factors for Determining Benefits in Optional Forms

Once an interest rate, or a set percentage or fractional factor, for determining benefit amounts under a benefit option is stated in a plan, any change thereto triggers ERISA Section 204(g) (Code Section 411(d)(6)). ERISA Section 204(g) requires benefits to be preserved at the level that would have been computed under the optional form before the change. This is done by applying the old interest rate or factor to the participant's accrued benefits up to the date of the amendment. This rule is set out in Revenue Ruling 81-12, and is discussed in Chapter 4. When an interest rate for determining benefits

---

[195] The PBGC in draft regulations for all benefit options under terminated plans and in a cross-claim in the *UAW District 65 v. Harper & Row Publishers, Inc.* litigation has taken the position that an actuarially reasonable interest rate for valuing a deferred annuity must take into account the period of deferral, and thus the generally lower level of long-term interest rates than are available on immediate annuities. See 11 BNA Pens. Rep. 641 (May 7, 1984) (reprinting the PBGC's draft regulations), and 11 BNA Pens. Rep. 505 (April 16, 1984) (describing the PBGC's cross-claim in the *UAW District 65* litigation).

[196] ERISA §§203(e)(2) and 205(g)(3) and Code §§411(a)(11)(B) and 417(e)(3), as amended by §1139 of P.L. 99-514. And see Conf. Rep., H.R. Rep. 99-841, at II-488, [1986] U.S. Code Cong. & Ad. News 4576. An amendment before the close of the first plan year beginning on or before Jan. 1, 1989, to use the uppermost rate permitted under this rule in place of the PBGC immediate annuity rate is not considered a cutback in any participant's accrued benefits in violation of ERISA §204(g). §1139(d)(2). And see IRS Notice 87-20, reprinted in 14 BNA Pens. Rep. at 123 (Jan. 26, 1987).

in optional form is under a variable standard that is outside of the control of the employer, a change in the interest rate applying to all accrued benefits can, however, still occur without triggering Section 204(g) because a change under a variable standard does not require an "amendment" of the plan.[197]

When a benefit option is "subsidized," i.e., more is provided under a benefit option than any reasonable actuarial equivalent of the plan's normal retirement benefit, protection of the subsidy against reduction is expressly required by ERISA Section 204(g)(2), as amended by REA.[198] Subject to division among the circuits, protection of the subsidy against reduction may also be required under Revenue Ruling 81-12 for amendments made before REA's July 30, 1984, effective date for this amendment.[199] The protection under REA may be excepted only if a subsidy is determined under Treasury regulations not to be a "retirement-type subsidy." The Senate Finance Committee report illustrates subsidies that are not "retirement-type subsidies" as including Social Security supplements that are only payable between the time a person retires and reaches the Social Security eligibility age, disability benefits in excess of the actuarial equivalent of the participant's normal retirement benefit, medical benefits in excess of the normal retirement benefit, or its actuarial equivalent, and plant shutdown benefits that do not continue beyond retirement age.[200] A permanent lifetime subsidy on a joint and survivor's benefit, or on an early retirement benefit are, on the other hand, clearly retirement-type subsidies, and hence, are protected against reduction or elimination under Section 204(g)(2), as amended.

When an interest rate or factor for a benefit option has been changed before the effective dates for the REA amendments, and in circumstances where Revenue Ruling 81-12 is not applicable, reference may also be made to whether application of the amendment to participants with "vested" benefits abridges their contractual rights. There may also be a duty to give advance notice of an adverse change in an interest rate or reduction factor if participants could have retired to protect their rights under the old rate or factor.[201]

D. Mortality Assumptions and the *Norris* Decision

The use of one mortality table over another for determining benefit amounts under optional benefit forms is rarely as consequential as a

---

[197] Rev. Rul. 81-12, and see ch. 4, sec. IV.B.3.

[198] ERISA §204(g)(2) (Code §411(d)(6)(B)), as amended. And see S. Rep. 98-575, at 28, [1984] U.S. Code Cong. & Ad. News 2547, at 2574.

[199] See ch. 4, sec. IV.B.3. For a collectively bargained plan, the effective dates for the REA protection begin only with plan amendments adopted after Jan. 1, 1985 (or after April 1, 1985, if a collective bargaining agreement expired before Jan. 1, 1985, and negotiations carried over into 1985). See P.L. 98-397, §302(d)(2).

[200] S. Rep. 98-575, at 30, [1984] U.S. Code Cong. & Ad. News 2547, at 2576.

[201] See ch. 9, secs. IV.B and V.

slight increase or decrease in the interest assumption. An actuarial benchmark is that "a change from one mortality basis to another is generally of lesser importance than a ¼ percent change in the valuation rate of interest."[202] However, as opposed to the use of one mortality table over another, a plan's use of sex-distinct versus unisex mortality assumptions can make a very substantial difference in the calculation of benefits under optional forms.

The Supreme Court held in 1983 in *Arizona Comm. for Deferred Compensation Plans v. Norris* that Title VII of the Civil Rights Act of 1964 does *not* permit male and female employees who participate in pension or profit-sharing plans to be paid different benefits based on the use of sex-distinct mortality assumptions.[203] In *Norris*, the plaintiff had discovered that because of the use of sex-distinct mortality assumptions by a third-party insurer offering annuities to her plan, the money in her individual account would convert to an annuity of only $320 per month for life, compared with $354 per month for a man of the same age and with the same account balance.[204] In a 1978 decision in *Los Angeles Dept. of Water & Power v. Manhart*, the Supreme Court had held that a plan requiring mandatory employee contributions could not require 15 percent higher employee contributions from women to obtain the same monthly benefits at retirement as men.[205] In *Norris* the Court held that the "classification of employees on the basis of sex is no more permissible at the pay-out stage of a retirement plan than at the pay-in stage."[206] Justice Marshall quoted from *Manhart* in stating for the Court:

> "The use of sex-segregated actuarial tables to calculate retirement benefits violates Title VII whether or not the tables reflect an accurate prediction of the longevity of women as a class, for under the statute, '[e]ven a true generalization about a class' cannot justify class-based treatment."[207]

Thus, the Court concluded:

> "An individual woman may *not* be paid lower monthly benefits simply because women as [a] class live longer than men."[208]

1. Differences Sex-Distinct Mortality Assumptions Make Under Benefit Options

The outlawing in *Norris* of the use of sex-distinct mortality assumptions in determining benefit pay-outs makes a difference in five

---

[202] W. Fellers and P. Jackson, "Noninsured Pensioner Mortality—the UP-1984 Table," in *Proceedings of the Conference of Actuaries in Public Practice* (1976), at 485.

[203] 463 U.S. 1073, 4 EBC 1633 (1983).

[204] See *Norris v. Arizona Comm. for Deferred Compensation Plans*, 486 F.Supp. 645, 2 EBC 2440 (D. Ariz. 1980).

[205] 435 U.S. 702, 1 EBC 1813 (1978).

[206] *Norris, supra*, 4 EBC at 1638.

[207] 4 EBC at 1639.

[208] 4 EBC at 1639–40 (emphasis added).

common benefit pay-out situations, four of which involve defined benefit plans. In three of these situations, the use of unisex mortality assumptions favors male participants *as a class* because a longer life expectancy is predicted for men than under sex-distinct mortality assumptions.[209]

a. Conversions of defined contribution plan account balances to annuity form. In converting an individual account balance under a defined contribution plan to an annuity option, as occurred in *Norris,* the *Norris* decision means that the account balances of male and female participants cannot be converted to annuity forms using sex-distinct mortality assumptions. That is, a plan may no longer pay female participants any *less* than men under such annuity options because of the longer expected pay-out period for women as a class under sex-distinct mortality tables. The difference that sex-distinct mortality assumptions have made in this situation is illustrated by the facts in *Norris* given above.[210]

b. Defined benefit plan annuity to lump sum conversions. In converting a benefit expressed in annuity form, i.e., a benefit under a defined benefit plan, into a lump sum option, sex-distinct mortality assumptions also cannot be used. This prohibition has the opposite effect in terms of who it benefits: It means that a plan may no longer use sex-distinct mortality assumptions that previously had the effect of *lowering* the value of *male* participants' annuity benefits when converted to a lump sum form because of the shorter life expectancy for men predicted under sex-based mortality tables. As an example, if two participants in a defined benefit plan are age 65 and are both entitled to $5,000 per year in benefits in a single-life annuity form, using the same six percent assumed rate of interest but sex-distinct mortality assumptions, a male participant might be offered a lump sum of $45,450, while a female participant with the same annuity might be offered a lump sum of $51,762.[211] In this case, the male participant receives 12.2 percent *less* because of the use of sex-distinct mortality assumptions.

c. Single-life annuity to joint and survivor's form conversions. In converting a single-life annuity under a defined benefit plan into a joint and survivor's annuity option, the reduction for the survivor's

---

[209] It has often been observed that outside of defined contribution plans, *Norris* generally favors men as a class because under the basic benefit options applicable to defined benefit plans, sex-distinct mortality assumptions favored women as a class. See, e.g., R. Nagle, "Eliminating Sex-Based Pension Features After *Norris*," 9 J. Pens. Plan. & Compl. 341, at 354 (Oct. 1983), and R. Blum and C. Kolm, Age and Sex Discrimination in Employee Benefit Plans, 363 Tax Mgmt. (BNA), at A-29 and A-40 (citing Department of Labor estimates that men as a class will receive 55 to 95% of the benefits involved in complying with *Norris*).

[210] This difference may be further illustrated by the following example: Assume two participants in a defined contribution plan are both age 65 and have equal $50,000 account balances, but one is male and the other female. Using a 6% assumed interest rate, but sex-distinct mortality assumptions, the male participant might be offered $5,501 per year under an annuity option, while the female participant might only be offered an annuity of $4,830, or 12.2% less in annuity form, based on the *same* account balance (using the 1971 GAM Table).

[211] Using the same mortality assumptions.

benefit form also cannot be based on sex-distinct mortality assumptions. This means a plan may no longer reduce a male participant's single-life annuity *more* to provide a survivor's benefit for his wife because of the longer sex-distinct life expectancy added by her survivor's benefits, than it does for a female participant who chooses a survivor's benefit for her husband. To illustrate, using typical sex-distinct mortality assumptions and the same assumed interest rate, the reduction for a joint and survivor's benefit for a male participant age 65 with a wife the same age is 15 percent off of his normal retirement benefit on a single-life basis. In contrast, the reduction for a joint and survivor's benefit form for a female participant, also age 65, and with a husband the same age, is only six percent.[212] Thus, under sex-distinct mortality assumptions, if the normal retirement benefit on a single-life basis was $400 per month, the reduction for a male participant to provide a joint and survivor's benefit form would be to $340 per month, to leave a $170 per month survivor benefit for his wife, while a female participant's single-life annuity would only be reduced to $376 per month, to leave a $188 per month survivor's benefit for her husband.[213]

d. Normal retirement age annuity to early retirement annuity conversions. In converting a normal retirement age defined benefit into an "actuarially equivalent" early retirement benefit, the reduction for early retirement also must not be based on sex-distinct mortality assumptions. Most plans already use set percentage or fractional factors for reducing benefits for early retirement that apply equally to men and women.[214] But plans reducing benefits "actuarially" for early retirement may have been using sex-distinct mortality assumptions. *Norris* provides that a plan may no longer reduce a male participant's benefits *more* for early retirement than it would a female participant's benefits—even though sex-distinct mortality assumptions suggest that each year of early retirement benefits for a man has a higher relative actuarial value because of the shorter life expectancy for men after the normal retirement age. To illustrate, when early retirement benefits are reduced "actuarially" from an age 65 normal retirement age benefit for early retirement at age 60, using sex-distinct mortality assumptions with the same five percent interest assumption for both sexes can result in a 37 percent reduction in the normal retirement benefit for a male participant, as opposed to a 32.6 percent reduction in the normal

---

[212] See D. McGill, *Fundamentals of Private Pensions* (5th ed.), at 126–27 (not specifying the mortality table used).

[213] Along the same line, when a plan offers a life annuity with a "term-certain" as an option to a single-life annuity, it also must not convert a single-life annuity benefit to a life annuity with a term-certain using sex-distinct mortality assumptions. This means that a male participant's benefits may not be reduced more to provide a term-certain than a female participant's, even though sex-distinct mortality assumptions suggest that a term-certain has a higher added cost to the plan for a man.

[214] In the BLS's 1982 survey of plans of medium and large firms, 21% of participants in plans permitting early retirement were in plans that used "actuarially equivalent" reductions, while 79% were in plans that used fractional or percentage reductions. BLS, Employee Benefits in Medium and Large Firms, 1982, at 43.

retirement benefit for a female participant.[215] Using a $400 per month age 65 benefit, this means a difference between $252 per month beginning at age 60 for a man, as opposed to $269.60 per month for a woman.

e. Increasing normal retirement age annuity for service past normal retirement age. A fifth, but currently somewhat less common, payout situation in which *Norris* applies is to actuarial increases in benefits for employees who work past a plan's normal retirement age. When such actuarial increases are provided under the terms of a plan, use of sex-distinct mortality assumptions means that a female participant's benefits are increased *less* than a male colleague's for each month or year of work past normal retirement age. This is because sex-distinct mortality tables predict a smaller actuarial gain to the plan as a percentage of the total present value of an annuity benefit from postponing a woman's retirement.

The differences referred to above are split roughly in half if the unisex mortality assumptions adopted as a result of *Norris* are based on the male-female composition of the *national* workforce or population. For example, the reduction for joint and 50 percent survivor's benefits for both male and female participants is approximately 10 percent at age 65, assuming a five percent interest assumption and a spouse the same age.[216] However *exactly* what happens to these dollar differences as a result of *Norris* depends on three factors:

- The male-female composition of the lives used in determining the new unisex mortality assumption;
- The extent unisex mortality assumptions are required to be applied retroactively to benefits accrued before the *Norris* decision, or are made retroactive for administrative reasons; and
- Whether "topping up," that is, using the prior sex-distinct mortality assumption that produces the higher benefits under any option, is required as a remedy for sex discrimination under the Equal Pay Act.

2. Male-Female Composition of a Unisex Mortality Assumption

Although sex-based differences in benefits would be roughly split in half if unisex mortality assumptions were adopted based on the male-female composition of the national workforce, Robert Nagle, the former executive director of the PBGC, points out: "[M]ost actuaries . . . are likely to recommend assumptions that reflect the ratio of men and women either in the plan, or expected to elect the [particular]

---

[215] D. McGill, *Fundamentals of Private Pensions* (5th ed.), at 119 (using a 5% interest assumption and the 1971 GAM Table for males and females).

[216] See 29 C.F.R. 2621.3(d)(2) (setting out the PBGC's unisex reduction factors for reducing its maximum guaranteed benefit amount from a single-life to joint and survivor's annuity form). The PBGC's factors are based on a 5% interest assumption and a unisex composite of the 1971 GAM Table.

benefit option."[217] On this basis, if participants in a plan are, for example, 90 percent male, a new "unisex" mortality assumption may still basically be a sex-distinct male assumption. Conversely, if the participants in a plan are 90 percent women, the new "unisex" mortality assumption may be basically a sex-distinct female mortality assumption. In addition, an actuary could develop a unisex mortality assumption based on an estimate of who uses a benefit option. Thus, if women participants almost never elect a joint and survivor's form of annuity, the new unisex mortality assumption for joint and survivor reductions may reflect the old sex-distinct mortality assumption for men even more than the male-female composition of the employer's workforce would suggest.

3. *Norris' Retroactivity*

The effect of the *Norris* decision is clouded by the question of its retroactivity. *Norris* was "clearly foreshadowed"[218] by the Supreme Court's 1978 decision in *Los Angeles Dept. of Water & Power v. Manhart*, in which the Court held that requiring 15 percent *higher* employee contributions from women to obtain the same monthly retirement benefits as men violated Title VII.[219] Before *Manhart* and after, the lower courts and the EEOC had also specifically and almost unanimously held that distinctions on the basis of sex, including the use of sex-distinct mortality assumptions, were as unlawful at the pay-out stage as at the pay-in stage.[220]

But in *Norris*, a different 5-to-4 majority than the majority on the substantive issue came out *against* applying a remedy retroactively—even back to the 1978 date of the *Manhart* decision. Instead, this majority held that the remedy of requiring unisex mortality assumptions should be available in a defined contribution plan only as applied to contributions made to the plan after August 1, 1983, the date of the decision in *Norris*.[221] In a defined benefit plan, this prospective-only holding presumably means that unisex assumptions are only required to be applied to *benefits* accrued after the same August 1, 1983, date. The lack of retroactivity in *Norris* was based on the majority's perception that, despite *Manhart*, the decision was still somewhat unexpected, and might create a financial burden on plans that could "jeopardize ... entire pension fund[s]."[222] Justice Powell's opinion for the majority also stressed the uncertainty about the limits of the "open

[217] R. Nagle, "Eliminating Sex-Based Pension Features After *Norris*," 9 J. Pens. Plan. & Compl. 341, at 356 (Oct. 1983).

[218] 4 EBC at 1643 (Marshall, J.).

[219] See 435 U.S. 702, 1 EBC 1813 (1978).

[220] See the cases cited at note 9 of the *Norris* decision, 4 EBC at 1638 n.9. See also EEOC Decision No. 72-1919 (June 6, 1972); *Rosen v. Public Service Elec. & Gas Co.*, 477 F.2d 90 (3d Cir. 1973); *Fitzpatrick v. Bitzer*, 390 F.Supp. 278 (D. Conn. 1974); *Henderson v. State of Oregon*, 405 F.Supp. 1271 (D. Ore. 1975); *Chastang v. Flynn & Emrich Co.*, 541 F.2d 1040 (4th Cir. 1976).

[221] 4 EBC at 1650 (Powell, J., for the majority on relief).

[222] 4 EBC at 1652 (O'Connor, J., concurring).

market" exception that had been announced in *Manhart* for employers, such as the employer in *Norris*, who set aside equal amounts of money for men and women to use in purchasing annuities from insurers on the open market.[223]

Since *Norris*, the circuit courts have been divided on retroactivity. In *Spirt v. TIAA-CREF*, the Second Circuit distinguished the lack of retroactivity in *Norris* as predicated on the assumption that either the plan or employers would incur additional costs from retroactivity. In *Spirt*, however, the Second Circuit found *no* financial burden that would fall on the TIAA-CREF defined contribution plan, and hence, none on the sponsors of the plan, if both male and female participants' *entire* account balances were converted to annuities based on unisex mortality assumptions.[224] Although this meant that male participants would take a reduction in their annuities from what they would otherwise receive to pay for the higher annuities for women, the Second Circuit found this did not defeat any legitimate expectations of the male participants since "no employee could have settled expectations as to the amount of monthly benefits" nor was it "plausible to think that male plan participants relied upon [sex-distinct assumptions] in any meaningful way."[225]

However, in *Probe v. State Teachers' Retirement System*, the Ninth Circuit refused to remedy past use of sex-distinct mortality assumptions in determining benefits under lump sum and joint and survivor's options in a defined benefit plan. The Ninth Circuit focused on the lack of notice to the plan before the date of *Norris* that it could not provide benefit options on terms paralleling those offered on the open market by insurers. The Ninth Circuit did not focus on whether the costs of retroactive compliance could be shifted to the opposite sex participant group.[226]

Finally, in *Long v. Florida*, male employees who chose joint and survivor options under a defined benefit plan with reductions for the joint and survivor's form based on sex-distinct mortality tables were held to be discriminated against on the basis of sex under Title VII. The Eleventh Circuit provided a remedy increasing benefits for males who retired after the 1978 date of the *Manhart* decision to the benefit levels they would have obtained based on reductions under a unisex mortality table. This retroactive remedy was provided because the Eleventh Circuit found that the uncertainty mentioned in *Norris* about the open market exception was not involved. The joint and survivor's options in *Long* were offered by the employer, not on the open market by third-party insurers. Therefore, a remedy back to the date of *Manhart* was within the court's authority. Women who had obtained joint and survivor's benefits under still more favorable reductions produced

---

[223] 4 EBC at 1650.

[224] 735 F.2d 23, 5 EBC 1469 (2d Cir. 1984), *cert. denied*, 469 U.S. 881 (1984).

[225] 5 EBC at 1473.

[226] 780 F.2d 776, 6 EBC 2807 (9th Cir. 1986), *cert. denied*, 476 U.S. ___ (1986).

by sex-distinct mortality tables were allowed to keep their benefits at the pre-*Norris* levels.[227]

4. Retroactivity for Administrative Reasons

Whether or not *Norris* is legally required to be retroactive, administrative factors may weigh in favor of retroactive compliance. The most patent administrative factor is that making *Norris* retroactive may be less work: For a plan to draw a distinction between benefits accrued before and after August 1, 1983, and also comply with Revenue Ruling 79-90, it has to expressly provide for the continued application of sex-distinct mortality assumptions to the part of benefits accrued before *Norris* and for a unisex mortality assumption for benefits accrued after. Two computations are thus required for each participant using the option rather than one. If a plan administrator considers it unlikely that ERISA Section 204(g) or a vested rights theory can be successfully invoked by participants who are *disadvantaged* by the retroactive application of a unisex factor for benefits accrued before the date of *Norris*, and thus finds that the costs of retroactive compliance can effectively be shifted to the other sex participant group, administrative convenience may weigh in favor of applying unisex assumptions retroactively (except for those persons who were already in pay status, or who were already cashed-out, before August 1, 1983).

5. Topping-Up Under Title VII and the Equal Pay Act

"Topping up" in remedying discrimination from past use of sex-distinct mortality assumptions means using the previously used sex-distinct actuarial assumption that produces the higher benefits for men or women under each benefit option. Topping up was rejected as a prospective remedy in *Norris* under Title VII,[228] and is unlikely to be required under the Equal Pay Act.

A violation of the Equal Pay Act of 1963 was not alleged in *Norris*, or in *Manhart*, but Justice Marshall's opinion in *Norris* and Justice

---

[227] 805 F.2d 1542, 7 EBC 2648 (11th Cir. 1986) (the Eleventh Circuit stated that *Probe* was "wrong" in its limitation of remedies when the open market exception was not involved).

[228] In *Norris*, the Court did not really *discuss* whether to use a "topped-up" factor or an intermediate "unisex" factor as the remedy prospectively under Title VII, but simply assumed that an intermediate unisex factor would be the appropriate remedy. See R. Nagle, "Eliminating Sex-Based Pension Features After *Norris*," 9 J. Pens. Plan. & Compl. 341, at 343 (Oct. 1983), citing Justice Marshall's opinion, 4 EBC at 1644, Justice Powell's opinion, 4 EBC at 1650 n. 12, and Justice O'Connor's opinion, 4 EBC at 1652; see also *Los Angeles Dept. of Water & Power v. Manhart*, 1 EBC at 1820 n. 36.

There was actually more divergence among the Court on what would have been required *if* a retroactive remedy under Title VII had been provided. Justice Powell assumed that "topped up" payments would be required retroactively, not under a direct mandate from Title VII, but because he assumed that male participants' annuities could not be reduced, and that consequently, the past discrimination against women could not be eliminated unless their annuities were retroactively increased to the same level. See 4 EBC at 1650 n. 11. Justices Marshall and O'Connor did not make this assumption, see 4 EBC at 1644 (Marshall, J.), 4 EBC at 1652 (O'Connor, J.); and in *Manhart*, the Court also rejected it. 1 EBC at 1820 n. 36.

Stevens' opinion in *Manhart* expressly recognized the issue while refusing to decide it.[229] Based on the lack of guidance on this issue in opinions that were obviously directed to a larger audience, it seems to be assumed that the Court is not just saving Equal Pay Act topping up—both retroactively and prospectively—for a later day. Justice O'Connor expressed this view directly, stating that the Equal Pay Act would *not* be considered applicable to pension benefits, and even if it were, that topping up would not be required.[230]

IV. Anti-Assignment and Alienation Rules Prior to Benefit Receipt

Under ERISA Section 206(d) (Code Section 401(a)(13)), a participant's or beneficiary's pension benefits may not be assigned, including as collateral on a loan, or alienated before receipt. As enacted in 1974, Section 206(d) contained only two exceptions:

(1) Once a benefit is in pay status, a plan may permit a participant to make a voluntary, revocable assignment of up to 10 percent of each future benefit payment;[231] and
(2) Nonforfeitable benefits may be used as security for a loan from the plan itself, if the plan provides for such loans and if the requirements of ERISA Section 408(b)(1) and Code Section 4975(d)(1) are met on nondiscriminatory availability of loans from the plan, use of a reasonable rate of interest, and adequate security.

Section 206(d)'s anti-assignment and alienation rule has generally been strictly construed.[232] But one implied exception for domestic relations orders has been recognized in the courts, and is now codified in Section

[229] 463 U.S. 1073, 4 EBC 1633, at 1637 n.8 (1983), and 435 U.S. 702, 1 EBC 1813, at 1817 n.23 (1978).

[230] 4 EBC 1633, at 1652 n.4 (O'Connor, J., concurring). In *Probe v. State Teachers' Retirement System*, 780 F.2d 776, 6 EBC 2807 (9th Cir. 1986), *cert. denied*, 476 U.S. ___ (1986), the Ninth Circuit refused to decide whether pension benefits are a part of "wages" under the Equal Pay Act, but held that even if they were, the analysis of the inappropriateness of a retroactive remedy in *Norris* would still deny a retroactive remedy for the period before the date of the *Norris* decision.

[231] The IRS's regulations actually permit a voluntary, revocable assignment of up to *100%* of a participant's benefits once the participant is in pay status if certain conditions are met. 26 C.F.R. 1.401(a)-13(e).

[232] See, e.g., *General Motors Corp. v. Buha*, 623 F.2d 455, 2 EBC 2375 (6th Cir. 1980) (no garnishment of pension benefits permitted under ERISA); *Commercial Mortgage Ins., Inc. v. Citizens Nat'l Bank*, 526 F.Supp. 510, 2 EBC 2174 (N.D. Tex. 1981) (no garnishment of profit-sharing benefits allowed under ERISA); *Tenneco, Inc. v. First Virginia Bank*, 698 F.2d 688, 4 EBC 1091 (4th Cir. 1983) (benefits not subject to garnishment while in pension plan despite vested status and the availability of immediate withdrawal rights); *Smith v. Mirman*, 749 F.2d 181, 5 EBC 2689 (4th Cir. 1984) (assignment of benefits after a plan termination, but before actual distribution of plan assets, invalid). Benefits from welfare plans are not similarly protected. See *IBEW Local 212 Vacation Fund v. IBEW Local 212 Credit Union*, 549 F.Supp. 1299, 4 EBC 1340 (S.D. Ohio 1982) (permitting garnishment of an employee's interest in a vacation pay plan). However, for most health and welfare plans, a participant's interest in the plan is not of a type that is susceptible to garnishment or attachment.

206(d) by the Retirement Equity Act amendments, and another implied exception in bankruptcy appears to be established. Two other, less sweeping implied exceptions have also been recognized.

A. Qualified Domestic Relations Orders

The first implied exception to the anti-assignment and alienation rules was for court orders providing for alimony, child support, or the division of marital property on divorce. In numerous decisions, courts found that the purpose of ERISA Section 206 is to protect the employee against his or her own financial improvidence in dealings with third-parties, but not to protect the employee from *family* obligations. Therefore, an implied exception for state domestic relations orders was recognized.[233]

The 1984 Retirement Equity Act amendments codified this implied exception and detailed the contents of a "qualified domestic relations order" that a plan is required to honor. To be a qualified domestic relations order, an order, judgment, or decree (including approval of a property settlement) must relate to child support, alimony, or marital property rights under a state's domestic relations law,[234] *and* must specify:

- The name and last known mailing address of the participant, and the name and address of the "alternate payee," i.e., the spouse, former spouse, child, or other dependent who is to be paid;
- The amount or percentage of the participant's benefits to be paid the alternate payee, or the manner in which the amount is to be determined; and
- The number of payments, or the period for which payments are required.[235]

A domestic relations order is *not* a "qualified domestic relations order" if it requires a plan:

- To increase benefit beyond those provided under the plan;
- To pay benefits to an alternate payee that are already required to be paid another alternate payee under a previously qualified domestic relations order;[236] or

---

[233] See, e.g., *AT&T v. Merry*, 592 F.2d 118, 1 EBC 1585 (2d Cir. 1979); *Stone v. Stone*, 632 F.2d 740, 2 EBC 1463 (9th Cir. 1980); *Savings & Profit Sharing Fund of Sears Employees v. Gago*, 717 F.2d 1038 (7th Cir. 1983).

[234] ERISA §206(d)(3)(B) (Code §414(p)(1)), as added by P.L. 98-397.

[235] ERISA §206(d)(3)(C) (Code §414(p)(2)), as added by P.L. 98-397.

[236] In other words, the first ex-spouse to qualify a domestic relations order keeps the benefits unless more benefits are left, or unless more benefits have accrued since the first order, for the second ex-spouse to claim.

- To provide any type or form of benefits, or any benefit option, not provided in the plan.[237]

The contents of a qualified domestic relations order under the REA amendments are in most respects no more than a codification of sound practice under the preexisting implied exception. But in two respects Section 206(d), as amended, departs from the preexisting implied exception. First, Section 206(d)(3)(E) provides that payments under a qualified order may be required to begin at a plan's "earliest retirement age" *even if* a participant is still employed and does not have the option of receiving early retirement benefits himself (or herself) while still in service.[238] The earliest retirement age at which such payments may be ordered to begin is defined as the *later* of age 50 or the earliest date when the participant could elect to receive a distribution if he or she separated from service.[239] The amount of early retirement benefits that may be required to be paid under a qualified domestic relations order in these instances is limited to an actuarially reduced early retirement benefit.[240] Any higher, "subsidized" value available under an early retirement option cannot be included, but may be covered by the order when and if the participant does retire under the option.[241]

The second departure from judicially created law is that a qualified domestic relations order can preserve the rights of an ex-spouse to *survivor's* benefits, including to the exclusion of a future spouse who would otherwise be entitled to the benefits. ERISA Section 206(d)(3)(F),[242] as amended provides:

> "To the extent provided in any qualified domestic relations order—
>
> "(i) the former spouse of a participant shall be treated as a surviving spouse of such participant for purposes of section 205, and
>
> "(ii) if married for at least one year, the former spouse shall be treated as meeting the requirements of section 205(f) [which otherwise

---

[237] ERISA §206(d)(3)(D) (Code §414(p)(3)), as added by P.L. 98-397. See also 130 Cong. Rec. H-8761-62 (daily ed. Aug. 9, 1984) (statement of Rep. Clay) (providing examples of the operation of the QDRO rules when a divorced employee (1) dies before retirement, or (2) remarries, or when the employee's former spouse (3) wants a different benefit form for his or her court-awarded portion of the annuity, or (4) begins collecting at the plan's earliest retirement age before the employee actually retires).

[238] See ERISA §206(d)(3)(E) (Code §414(p)(4)), as amended by P.L. 98-397. Some courts would already order a participant to *elect* an early retirement benefit when the participant had separated from service, but was deferring application for benefits. See *Pepitone v. Pepitone*, 436 N.Y.S.2d 966, 2 EBC 1177 (N.Y. Sup.Ct. Queens Co. 1981) (ordering the former first baseman of the New York Yankees to elect early retirement benefits under his major league baseball players' pension). But the courts would not order the plan to pay the benefits in such instances without joinder of the participant so that he could be ordered to elect the option. See *Sochor v. IBM Corp.*, 5 EBC 1039 (N.Y. Ct.App. 1983); *Koelsch v. Koelsch*, 713 P.2d 1234 (Ariz. 1986).

[239] ERISA §206(d)(3)(E)(ii) and Code §414(p)(4)(B), as amended by §1898(c)(7) of the Tax Reform Act, P.L. 99-514. This applies to defined benefit and defined contribution plans. Before this technical correction, REA provided that the "earliest retirement age" under a defined contribution plan is the date on which the participant attains an age that is 10 years before the plan's normal retirement age (even if the plan provides for earlier withdrawals). ERISA §206(d)(3)(E)(ii) (Code §414(p)(4)(B)), as amended by P.L. 98-397.

[240] ERISA §206(d)(3)(E)(i)(II) (Code §414(p)(4)(A)(ii)), as amended by P.L. 98-397.

[241] See S. Rep. 98-575, at 21, [1984] U.S. Code Cong. & Ad. News 2547, at 2567.

[242] Code §414(p)(5).

permit a plan to require the participant to be married to the surviving spouse throughout the one-year period ending on the earlier of the date of death or the annuity starting date]."

Thus, under a qualified domestic relations order, a former spouse can displace the rights a current spouse would otherwise have under the survivor's benefit provisions, or if the participant has not remarried, can preserve rights as a surviving spouse that would otherwise no longer exist.

A qualified domestic relations order may not be needed to preserve survivor's benefits for an ex-spouse if the ex-spouse was married to a participant throughout the one-year period ending on the annuity starting date. The Senate Finance Committee report states that when a plan requires one year of marriage before the annuity starting date for survivor's benefits, the spouse to whom a participant was married during the one-year period "is entitled to the survivor annuity under the plan *whether or not* the participant and spouse are married on the date of the participant's death," unless a qualified domestic relations order "*otherwise* provides for the division or payment of the participant's retirement benefits."[243]

B. Personal Bankruptcy

A debtor's interest in pension or profit-sharing plan benefits is generally excluded from the bankruptcy estate under Bankruptcy Code Section 541(c)(2), and thus, is beyond the reach of creditors in personal bankruptcy proceedings, *unless* the debtor:

(1) Exercises dominion over the plan, e.g., as an owner of the sponsoring employer, or

(2) Has present access to the funds, e.g., through a right to withdraw all benefits from a savings plan immediately.[244]

If included, an interest in benefits under a plan may still be exempt from the reach of creditors, but generally only if a specific state law exemption applies or only to the extent the payments are reasonably

---

[243] S. Rep. 98-575, at 15-16. [1984] U.S. Code Cong. & Ad. News 2547, at 2561 (emphasis added).

[244] *Samore v. Graham*, 726 F.2d 1268, 5 EBC 2573 (8th Cir. 1984) (interest in profit-sharing plan not excluded from estate when debtor was sole stockholder in sponsoring employer and sole trustee for the plan; interest also not exempt under state and other federal law system of exemptions); *Goff v. Taylor*, 706 F.2d 574, 4 EBC 1653 (5th Cir. 1983) (interests in self-settled Keogh plans not excluded when plans would not be considered spendthrift trusts under state law because of debtor's control over plans and access to the funds); *Reagan v. Austin Municipal Federal Credit Union*, 6 EBC 1142 (5th Cir. 1984) (right to assign future interest in funds to secure loan sufficient to take interest out of the spendthrift trust category and thus into bankruptcy estate); *In re Lichtstrahl*, 750 F.2d 1488, 6 EBC 1583 (11th Cir. 1985) (interest in pension plan not excluded because physician's dominion over plan prevented it from being a spendthrift trust under state law; interest also not exempt under §522(b)(2)(A)); *McLean v. Central States Pension Fund*, 762 F.2d 1204, 7 EBC 1440 (4th Cir. 1985) (interest in pension plan excluded when debtor had no control over the plan); *In re Holt*, 32 B.R. 767, 4 EBC 2450 (Bankr. E.D. Tenn. 1983) (profit-sharing account balance excluded when debtor did not exercise dominion over plan and had no nondiscretionary withdrawal rights).

expected to be necessary for the debtor's support either currently or in old age.[245]

Some courts have gone farther in protecting debtors and have held that a debtor's interest in pension or profit-sharing benefits is *per se* excluded, or exempt under the state law and federal nonbankruptcy law system of exemptions—regardless of dominion or present access to the funds or the reasonable needs of the debtor—based largely on a stronger reading of Congress' intent in enacting ERISA's anti-alienation provisions.[246]

C. Felonies and Federal Taxes

The Eleventh Circuit has recognized a third implied exception to the anti-alienation rule for certain types of felonies, thus permitting a surety company for a bank to garnish pension benefits of an employee who was convicted of criminal mishandling of bank funds.[247] Somewhat similarly, in General Counsel Memorandum 39000, the IRS permitted a "killer" beneficiary exception when state law provided that a spouse who killed her husband, even if she was not guilty by reason of insanity, could not inherit from his estate or otherwise be his beneficiary.[248] However, the Second Circuit later rejected an implied criminal misconduct exception in a case in which commissions received from

---

[245] Under §522, there is an option between using a federal system of exemptions or a system of state law and federal nonbankruptcy law exemptions. Many states negate this option by prohibiting election of the federal system. If the federal system is available, §522(d)(10)(E) expressly exempts payments from tax-qualified pension and profit-sharing plans up to a level required for reasonable support of the debtor. See *In re Kochell*, 732 F.2d 564, 5 EBC 1289 (7th Cir. 1984) (given 44-year-old debtor's earning capacity as a doctor, interest in two pension plans was not reasonably necessary for support under federal exemption either immediately or in his old age); *In re Miller*, 33 B.R. 549, 4 EBC 2462 (Bankr. D. Minn. 1983) (under federal exemption and the facts, debtor's future pension benefits were reasonably necessary for support, but profit-sharing account was not; trustee authorized to apply to plan for "hardship" withdrawal); *In re Donaghy*, 11 B.R. 677, 4 EBC 1484 (Bankr. S.D.N.Y. 1981) (lump sum payment from pension plan to unemployed 62-year-old with emphysema who was existing on disability benefits and whose wife had cancer was reasonably necessary for support under federal exemption).

Under the state and other federal law system of exemptions in §522(b)(2)(A), pension or profit-sharing benefits may be exempt if exempted under a specific state law or federal law other than the Bankruptcy Code. See *Hovis v. Wright*, 751 F.2d 714, 5 EBC 2763 (4th Cir. 1985) (South Carolina law exempted state retirement system benefits).

[246] See *Barr v. Hinshaw*, 23 B.R. 233, 3 EBC 2535 (Bankr. D. Kan. 1982) (doctor's interest in pension plan and profit-sharing plan exempt *per se* because of ERISA's anti-alienation provision under other federal law part of state and federal exemptions in §522(b)(2)(A)); *Clotfelter v. CIBA-GEIGY Corp.*, 24 B.R. 927, 3 EBC 2634 (D. Kan. 1982) (interest in pension plan excluded from bankruptcy estate based on ERISA anti-alienation rule even though plan was not a spendthrift trust under state law based on the debtor's rights to immediate withdrawal of funds); *In re Pruitt*, 30 B.R. 330, 4 EBC 2130 (Bankr. D. Colo. 1983) (interest in thrift plan excluded on *per se* basis because of ERISA rules).

[247] *St. Paul Fire and Marine Ins. Co. v. Cox*, 752 F.2d 550, 6 EBC 1322 (11th Cir. 1985). See also *Crawford v. La Boucherie Bernard, Ltd.*, 815 F.2d 117 (D.C. Cir. 1987); *Guidry v. Nat'l Sheet Metal Workers Pension Fund*, 641 F.Supp. 360, 7 EBC 2044 (D. Colo. 1986) (narrow exception to anti-alienation appropriate to impose constructive trust on benefits of union officer who embezzled union funds).

[248] Dated Jan. 26, 1983, reprinted at ¶17,488 CCH Pens. Plan Guide.

allegedly fraudulent securities transactions had been contributed to a participant's savings account under a qualified plan.[249]

Not too suprisingly, a fourth exception is recognized by the Treasury in its ERISA regulations for the "enforcement of a federal tax levy" or the "collection by the United States of a judgment resulting from an unpaid tax assessment."[250]

---

[249] *Ellis Nat'l Bank v. Irving Trust Co.*, 786 F.2d 466, 7 EBC 1266 (2d Cir. 1986). See also *United Metal Products Corp. v. Nat'l Bank of Detroit*, 8 EBC 1244 (6th Cir. 1987) (no exception to anti-alienation to allow garnishment of $35,000 profit-sharing account of bookkeeper who embezzled $440,000 from the same plan).

[250] 26 C.F.R. 1.401(a)-13(b)(2).

7

Fiduciary Duties on Benefit Claims

I. The Federal Common Law Mandate

ERISA's immense detail, and in particular, the specificity of its minimum standards, initially led to a common, but mistaken, assumption that if a specific minimum standard did not prohibit a benefit denial or other action, the benefit denial or other action was permitted. An attorney practicing in the employee benefits area explains:

> "The Supreme Court's 1980 characterization of ERISA [in *Nachman Corp. v. PBGC*] as a 'comprehensive and reticulated statute' . . . captured the narrow perspective with which most practitioners, commentators and courts had viewed ERISA up to that time. The popular view was that the 200-page Act was the complete, if complex, answer to all of the questions about the regulation of employee benefit plans.
>
> . . . .
>
> "Whatever substantive rules could not be found in the statute itself would be created by regulations to be issued by one of the various administrative agencies vested with authority to implement aspects of ERISA . . . . Such has been the popular view and, accordingly, for most of ERISA's existence the focus of its implementation has been on the statute itself as interpreted and expanded by administrative agency regulations."[1]

This "popular" view would have been more supportable under earlier versions of ERISA that did not preempt state common law causes of action which could be used to resolve the questions of benefit rights and responsibilities not covered by ERISA's minimum standards. In *Shaw v. Delta Air Lines, Inc.*, the Supreme Court observed, "The bill that became ERISA originally contained a limited preemption clause,

---

[1] J. Ray, "ERISA and the Courts: The Developing Federal Common Law of Employee Benefits," at 4-5 (paper presented to AFL-CIO Lawyers Coordinating Committee, 1984).

applicable only to state laws relating to the specific subjects covered by ERISA. [But t]he Conference Committee rejected these provisions in favor of the present language, and indicated that the section's preemptive scope was as broad as its language."[2]

The conferees' agreement to this "virtually unique"[3] preemption provision was considered by some to be the "crowning achievement" of ERISA because it "reserv[ed] to Federal authority the sole power to regulate the field of employee benefits," without "the threat of conflicting and inconsistent State and local regulation."[4] However, ERISA's specific statutory provisions do not cover every question and, in particular, many contractual questions of benefit rights formerly resolved under state common law. Because of this, a "void" would be created[5]—in many instances with *less* protection than before ERISA—unless a uniform federal common law was simultaneously authorized to "round out the protection of participants."[6] In the final debate on ERISA, Senator Jacob Javits thus stated that Congress "intended that a body of Federal substantive law will be developed by the courts to deal with issues involving rights and obligations under private welfare and pension plans."[7]

The intent to develop a federal common law is also expressed in a Conference Report statement that all suits to enforce benefit rights that do not involve application of the Title I minimum standards, i.e., all actions to enforce the terms of individual plans, "are to be regarded as arising under the laws of the United States in similar fashion to those brought under Section 301 of the Labor Management Relations Act."[8] Under Section 301, the Supreme Court has held that the courts are authorized to develop a *substantive* federal common law over rights and obligations in labor contracts. In *Textile Workers v. Lincoln Mills of Ala.*, Justice William O. Douglas wrote:

> "The Labor Management Relations Act expressly furnishes some substantive law. It points out what the parties may or may not do in certain situations. Other problems will lie in the penumbra of express statutory mandates. Some will lack express statutory sanction but will be solved by looking at the policy of the legislation and fashioning a remedy that will

---

[2] 463 U.S. 85, 4 EBC 1593, at 1599 (1983).

[3] *Franchise Tax Board v. Construction Laborers Vacation Trust*, 463 U.S. 1, 4 EBC 1604, at 1614 n.26 (1983).

[4] 3 ERISA Leg. Hist. 4670 (statement of Rep. Dent), quoted in *Shaw v. Delta Air Lines, Inc.*, 463 U.S. 85, 4 EBC 1593, at 1599 (1983). And see S. Rep. 93-127, at 35, 1 ERISA Leg. Hist. 621, 3 ERISA Leg. Hist. 4746 (statement of Sen. Williams), and 3 ERISA Leg. Hist. 4770-71 (statement of Sen. Javits).

[5] "Where state law is preempted and no specific federal provisions govern, a 'court is forced to make law or leave a void where neither state nor federal law applies.'" *Hansen v. White Farm Equipment Co.*, 42 B.R. 1005, 5 EBC 2130, at 2139 (N.D. Ohio 1984), *rev'd on other grounds*, 788 F.2d 1186, 7 EBC 1411 (6th Cir. 1986), quoting *Wayne Chem. v. Columbus Agency Service Corp.*, 426 F. Supp. 316, at 322 (N.D. Ind. 1977), *aff'd as modified*, 567 F.2d 692, 1 EBC 1691 (7th Cir. 1977), in turn quoting, Note, "The Federal Common Law," 82 Harv. L. Rev. 1512, at 1522 (1969).

[6] 3 ERISA Leg. Hist. 4670 (statement of Rep. Dent).

[7] 3 ERISA Leg. Hist. 4771.

[8] Conf. Rep., at 327, 3 ERISA Leg. Hist. 4594, and see 3 ERISA Leg. Hist. 4745 (statement of Senator Williams).

effectuate that policy. The range of judicial inventiveness will be determined by the nature of the problem. Federal interpretation of the federal law will govern, not state law. But state law, if compatible with the purpose of §301, may be resorted to in order to find the rule that will best effectuate the federal policy. Any state law applied, however, will be absorbed as federal law and will not be an independent source of private rights."[9]

The judiciary's parallel role under ERISA in developing a federal common law of employee benefits to round out participant protections has been recognized in a large number of cases.[10] The rationale and guiding principles are described by the Ninth Circuit in *Menhorn v. Firestone Tire & Rubber Co.*:

> "Congress realized that the bare terms, however detailed, of [ERISA's] statutory provisions would not be sufficient to establish a comprehensive regulatory scheme. It accordingly empowered the courts to develop, in the light of reason and experience, a body of federal common law governing employee benefit plans. That federal common law serves three related ends. First, it supplements the statutory scheme interstitially. Second and more generally, it serves to ramify and develop the standards that the statute sets out in only general terms. For example, . . . Congress put [the detailed construction and application of the fiduciary standard] in the hands of the federal courts . . . . Third, Congress viewed ERISA as a grant of authority to the courts to develop principles governing areas of the law regulating employee benefit plans that had previously been the exclusive province of state law. For example, no provision of ERISA mentions the circumstances under which a plan participant or beneficiary is entitled to recover disputed benefits from a plan, but §[502](a)(1)(B) authorizes such a person to bring a civil action to recover benefits or to enforce or clarify rights to past or future benefits under the terms of a benefit plan. A Senate conferee noted Congress's 'inten[t] that a body of Federal substantive law will be developed by the courts to deal

---

[9] 353 U.S. 448, at 456–57 (1957) (citations omitted).

[10] See *Franchise Tax Board v. Construction Laborers Vacation Trust*, 463 U.S. 1, 4 EBC 1604, at 1614 n. 26 (1983) ("in light of [ERISA's] virtually unique preemption," body of federal substantive law to be developed by the courts); *Woodfork v. Marine Cooks & Stewards Union*, 642 F.2d 966, 2 EBC 1278 (5th Cir. 1981) (federal common law to augment ERISA's minimum standards). See also *Cowan v. Keystone Profit Sharing Fund*, 586 F.2d 888, 1 EBC 1184 (1st Cir. 1978); *Riley v. MEBA Pension Trust*, 570 F.2d 406, 1 EBC 1757 (2d Cir. 1977) (Friendly, J.), *rev'd on other grounds after remand*, 586 F.2d 968, 1 EBC 1763 (2d Cir. 1978); *Murphy v. Heppenstall Co.*, 635 F.2d 233, 2 EBC 1891 (3d Cir. 1980); *Grossmuller v. UAW*, 715 F.2d 853, 4 EBC 2082 (3d Cir. 1983); *Van Orman v. American Ins. Co.*, 680 F.2d 301, 3 EBC 1653 (3d Cir. 1982); *Martin v. Bankers Trust Co.*, 565 F.2d 1276, 1 EBC 1793 (4th Cir. 1977); *Paris v. Wolf, Inc., Profit Sharing Plan*, 637 F.2d 357, 2 EBC 1244 (5th Cir. 1981), *cert. denied*, 454 U.S. 836 (1981); *Hayden v. Texas-U.S. Chemical Co.*, 681 F.2d 1053, 3 EBC 2178 (5th Cir. 1982); *Authier v. Ginsberg*, 757 F.2d 796, 6 EBC 1420 (6th Cir. 1985), *reh. denied*, 6 EBC 1664 (6th Cir. 1985); *Jenkins v. Teamsters Local 705 Pension Plan*, 713 F.2d 247, 4 EBC 2315 (7th Cir. 1983); *Reiherzer v. Shannon*, 581 F.2d 1266, 1 EBC 1175 (7th Cir. 1978); *In re Vorpahl*, 695 F.2d 318, 3 EBC 2597 (8th Cir. 1982); *Landro v. Glendenning Motorways, Inc.*, 625 F.2d 1344 (8th Cir. 1980); *Amato v. Bernard*, 618 F.2d 559, 2 EBC 2536 (9th Cir. 1980); *Terpinas v. Seafarers Int'l Union*, 722 F.2d 1445 (9th Cir. 1984). See also *Ogden v. Michigan Bell Tel. Co.*, 595 F. Supp. 961, 5 EBC 2281 (E.D. Mich. 1984); *Hansen v. White Farm Equipment Co.*, 42 B.R. 1005, 5 EBC 2130 (N.D. Ohio 1984), *rev'd on other grounds*, 788 F.2d 1186, 7 EBC 1411 (6th Cir. 1986); *In re C.D. Moyer Co. Pension Trust*, 441 F.Supp. 1128, 1 EBC 1363 (E.D. Pa. 1977), *aff'd*, 582 F.2d 1273 (3d Cir. 1978); *Shaw v. Kruidenier*, 470 F.Supp. 1375 (S.D. Iowa 1979), *aff'd*, 620 F.2d 307 (8th Cir. 1980); *Whitaker v. Texaco, Inc.*, 566 F.Supp. 745, 4 EBC 1762 (N.D. Ga. 1983); *Holliday v. Xerox Corp.*, 555 F.Supp. 51, 4 EBC 1221 (E.D. Mich. 1982), *aff'd*, 732 F.2d 548, 5 EBC 1705 (6th Cir. 1984); *Brunt v. Charter Corp.*, 3 EBC 1201 (E.D. Pa. 1982); *Imler v. Southwestern Bell Tel. Co.*, 650 P.2d 712, 3 EBC 2147 (Kan. App. 1982).

with issues involving rights and obligations under private welfare and pension plans.' "[11]

The development of this federal common law is to be guided by Congress' policies in enacting ERISA.[12] Like the Title I minimum standards, the mandate to develop a federal common law is also recognized as *remedial* authority that is to be construed to "round out"[13] and "augment"[14] the minimum standards in dealing with the full range of problems Congress intended to address under ERISA.[15] In *Kross v. Western Electric Co.*, the Seventh Circuit found that Congress intended in ERISA to go beyond the vesting of "normal" retirement benefits, and deal, under the federal common law and general provisions such as Section 404(a)(1) and Section 510, with "a broad range of problems in the field of employee benefit plans," specifically including "malfeasance and maladministration in the plans" and lack of "adequate communication to participants."[16]

As in the federal common law developed under Section 301 of the Labor Management Relations Act, state common law, "if compatible" with the purposes of ERISA, "may be resorted to in order to find the rule that will best effectuate [the] federal policy."[17] In *Shaw v. Kruidenier*, a district court explained:

> "Congress did not intend to render prior law irrelevant where it fairly accommodates the interests of the parties and is not inconsistent with ERISA's purposes."[18]

Thus, although state common law is generally preempted by ERISA, it may be subsumed under the new federal common law of employee benefits if it is compatible with ERISA's purposes.

Substantively, the most important single component of the federal common law is the ERISA fiduciary standard of duty that governs *any* exercise of discretionary authority under an employee benefit plan, including authority to render plan interpretations and find facts necessary to decide benefit claims. The ERISA fiduciary standard of duty could be considered separately from the federal common law of rights and obligations authorized under ERISA Section 502(a)(1)(B) because it has a separate statutory basis in ERISA Section 404(a)(1), but in

---

[11] 738 F.2d 1496, 5 EBC 2193, at 2195 (9th Cir. 1984) (citations omitted).

[12] See *Menhorn v. Firestone Tire & Rubber Co., supra; Ogden v. Michigan Bell Tel. Co., supra; Hansen v. White Farm Equipment Co., supra; Hayden v. Texas-U.S. Chemical Co., supra; In re C.D. Moyer Co. Pension Trust, supra.*

[13] 3 ERISA Leg. Hist. 4670 (statement of Rep. Dent).

[14] *Woodfork v. Marine Cooks & Stewards Union, supra,* 2 EBC at 1284 (5th Cir. 1981).

[15] See ch. 1, sec. I, on the liberal construction accorded ERISA as a remedial statute.

[16] 701 F.2d 1238, 4 EBC 1265, at 1269 (7th Cir. 1983), quoting H.R. Rep. 93-533, at 9–10, 3 ERISA Leg. Hist. 2356–57.

[17] *Textile Workers v. Lincoln Mills of Alabama,* 353 U.S. 448, at 457 (1957).

[18] 470 F.Supp. 1375, at 1382 (S.D. Iowa 1979). See also *Menhorn v. Firestone Tire & Rubber Co., supra,* 5 EBC at 2196 (ERISA federal common law to be formulated "referring to and guided by principles of state law when appropriate, but governed by the federal policies at issue"); *Jenkins v. Teamsters Local 705 Pension Plan, supra; Terpinas v. Seafarers Int'l Union, supra; Woodfork v. Marine Cooks & Stewards Union, supra; Hansen v. White Farm Equipment Co., supra; Ogden v. Michigan Bell Tel. Co., supra; Holliday v. Xerox Corp., supra.*

this discussion and in practice, it is generally considered a part of the federal common law. The other basic parts of the substantive federal common law arise from the interpretive and equitable effects of ERISA Section 102's requirements for an understandable and accurate summary plan description and from common law principles of estoppel, intentional and negligent misrepresentation, unjust enrichment, and reform in equity. In spite of ERISA's broad preemption, non-preempted state law may still apply to contractual obligations of an employer beyond the terms of a plan, to intentional and negligent misrepresentations of benefits by nonfiduciaries, and to obligations under insurance contracts.

II. ERISA's Fiduciary Standard

ERISA Section 404(a)(1) establishes the fundamental fiduciary standard of duty for persons with discretionary authority under a pension or any other employee benefit plan:

> "[A] fiduciary shall discharge his duties with respect to a plan *solely in the interest* of the participants and beneficiaries and—
> "(A) for the *exclusive purpose* of:
> (i) providing benefits to participants and their beneficiaries;
> . . . .
> "(B) with the care, skill, prudence, and diligence under the circumstances then prevailing that a prudent man acting in a like capacity and familiar with such matters would use in the conduct of an enterprise of a like character and with like aims;
> . . . .
> "(D) in accordance with the documents and instruments governing the plan insofar as such documents and instruments are consistent with the provisions of [title I] or title IV."[19]

A plan fiduciary can be an officer, director, or other representative of a sponsoring employer or union, but despite any such dual role, the person must perform all fiduciary functions with respect to the plan "to the exclusion of the interests of *all* other parties."[20] Basically, the fiduciary standard follows the Golden Rule that "Whatsoever ye would that men should do to you, do ye even so to them."[21] A fiduciary, in other words, can't be just a "little bit" loyal,[22] but must act under an "unwavering duty . . . to make decisions with single-minded devotion to [the] plan's participants and beneficiaries,"[23] with "complete and

---

[19] Emphasis added. The omitted paragraph (C) relates to investments. It provides that fiduciaries shall discharge their duties "solely in the interest of participants and beneficiaries . . . (C) by diversifying the investments of the plan so as to minimize the risk of large losses, unless under the circumstances it is clearly prudent not to do so."

[20] *NLRB v. Amax Coal Co.*, 453 U.S. 322, 2 EBC 1489, at 1492 (1981).

[21] Matthew 7:12.

[22] *Blankenship v. Boyle*, 329 F.Supp. 1089, 1 EBC 1062, at 1066 (D.D.C. 1971).

[23] *Morse v. Stanley*, 732 F.2d 1139, 5 EBC 1602, at 1607 (2d Cir. 1984).

undivided loyalty to the beneficiaries of the trust,"[24] or put still another way, with an "eye single to the interests of the participants and beneficiaries."[25]

The ERISA Section 404(a)(1) fiduciary standard is a professional standard of conduct. The test of a fiduciary's actions is whether he or she acted with "the care, skill, prudence and diligence . . . that a prudent man acting *in a like capacity* and *familiar with such matters* would use in the conduct of an enterprise of a like character and with like aims."[26] "[A] pure heart and an empty head are not enough."[27] Moreover, as the "like capacity" and "enterprise of a like character" language suggests, the degree of skill required of a fiduciary may escalate for larger pension plans. Fiduciaries for a larger plan, for example, may be expected to have more sophisticated recordkeeping and claims procedures than may be required for a small plan. But the fiduciaries for even the smallest plan may not fall below the level of competence expected of a person "familiar with such matters . . . in the conduct of an enterprise of like character and with like aims."

A. Who Are a Plan's Fiduciaries

The first step in reaching the "solely in the interest," "exclusive benefit," and professional consideration standards established by Section 404(a)(1) is to determine whether an action, or lack of action, denying a participant's benefits is a "fiduciary" function. This depends not on the title or position of the person responsible for the action, i.e., not on whether the person or a committee responsible is denominated as a plan administrator, plan trustee, or retirement committee, although the issue may be conceded if they are, but on whether the action, or lack of action, is within the functions defined as "fiduciary" functions in ERISA Section 3(21)(A). Section 3(21)(A) provides:

> "[A] person is a fiduciary with respect to a plan to the extent (i) he exercises any discretionary authority or discretionary control respecting management of such plan or exercises any authority or control respecting management or disposition of its assets, (ii) he renders investment advice for a fee or other compensation, direct or indirect, with respect to any

---

[24] *Freund v. Marshall & Ilsley Bank*, 485 F.Supp. 629, 1 EBC 1898, at 1914 (W.D. Wis. 1979); *Donovan v. Mazzola*, 716 F.2d 1226, 4 EBC 1865, at 1876 (9th Cir. 1983), *cert. denied*, 464 U.S. 1040 (1984).

[25] *Donovan v. Bierwith*, 680 F.2d 263, 3 EBC 1417, at 1425 (2d Cir. 1982), *cert. denied*, 459 U.S. 1069 (1982). See also *Meinhard v. Salmon*, 249 N.Y. 458, at 464, 164 N.E. 545, at 546 (N.Y. 1928) (Cardozo, J.):
"Many forms of conduct permissible in a workaday world for those acting at arm's length, are forbidden to those bound by fiduciary ties. A trustee is held to something stricter than the morals of the market place. Not honesty alone, but the punctilio of an honor the most sensitive, is then the standard of behavior. . . . Uncompromising rigidity has been the attitude of courts of equity when petitioned to undermine the rule of undivided loyalty by the 'disintegrating erosion' of particular exceptions. . . . Only thus has the level of conduct for fiduciaries been kept at a level higher than that trodden by the crowd."

[26] ERISA §404(a)(1)(B) (emphasis added).

[27] *Donovan v. Cunningham*, 716 F.2d 1455, 4 EBC 2329, at 2339 (5th Cir. 1983).

moneys or other property of such plan, or has any authority or responsibility to do so, or (iii) he has any discretionary authority or discretionary responsibility in the administration of such plan."

In determining whether the Section 404(a)(1) standard applies to a denial of benefits, the statutory approach is thus to start, not with the hat or title of the person responsible, but with whether the decision, or any decision not made but within a person's authority, is "discretionary authority or discretionary control" over "management of [the] plan," "management or disposition of its assets," the "administration of the plan," or "investment advice . . . with respect to any moneys or other property" of the plan. These "functional realities," rather than a person's title, determine whether the person is a fiduciary.[28] The ERISA Conference Report specifically recognizes, moreover, that because of the nature of employee benefit plans, there may be many "situations where . . . consultants and advisors . . . because of their special expertise [will], *in effect*, be exercising discretionary authority or control under the plan, despite the formal authority of some other person.[29] For benefit decisions, the corporate employer may often "in effect" be supplanting a pension committee or plan administrator to make a benefit decision that the other party is formally charged with making. In such situations, the person with the formal authority *and* the person or entity who is informally making the fiduciary decision are both ERISA fiduciaries.[30]

B. Fiduciary Functions on Benefit Claims

"Administration" and "management" of a plan, and the "disposition of its assets," all cover the exercise of any discretionary authority over benefit entitlement under a plan, including exercises of express discretionary authority, interpretation of plan terms, and the finding of any facts necessary to determine individual benefit entitlement.[31] In

---

[28] See, e.g., *Donovan v. Williams*, 4 EBC 1237, at 1244 (N.D. Ohio 1983), and Conf. Rep., at 323, 3 ERISA Leg. Hist. 4590.

[29] Conf. Rep., at 323, 3 ERISA Leg. Hist. 4590 (emphasis added).

[30] *Id.* And see *Foulke v. Bethlehem 1980 Salaried Pension Plan*, 565 F.Supp. 882, 4 EBC 1848 (E.D. Pa. 1983) (if corporate employer played role along with pension committee in denial of lump sum benefits, then both are fiduciaries); *Genter v. Acme Scale & Supply Co.*, 776 F.2d 1180 (3d Cir. 1985).

[31] See 29 C.F.R. 2509.75-8, Q&A D-2 and D-3, and Department of Labor Advisory Opinion (AO) 79-66A (Sept. 14, 1979), reprinted in 260 BNA Pens. Rep. R-9 (Oct. 8, 1979) (decision on benefit entitlement is an exercise of discretionary authority respecting "management" and "administration" of plan). See also *Birmingham v. SoGen-Swiss Int'l Corp. Retirement Plan*, 718 F.2d 515, 4 EBC 2369 (2d Cir. 1983) ("management" of plan includes making plan interpretations); *Eaton v. D'Amato*, 581 F.Supp. 743, 3 EBC 1003 (D.D.C. 1980) ("management" and "administration" include final review of denied benefit claims); *Sixty-Five Security Plan v. Blue Cross of New York*, 583 F.Supp. 380, 5 EBC 1430 (S.D.N.Y. 1984) ("management" and "disposition of assets" include any discretion to grant or deny benefit claims); *Rehabilitation Institute v. Blue Cross & Blue Shield*, 5 EBC 2265 (W.D. Pa. 1984) ("administration" includes any discretionary authority over claims denials); *Eversole v. Metropolitan Life Ins. Co.*, 500 F.Supp. 1162 (C.D. Cal. 1980) ("administration" includes authority to grant or deny claims); *McLaughlin Estate v. Conn. Gen. Life Ins. Co.*, 565 F.Supp. 434, 4 EBC 1879 (N.D. Cal. 1983) ("administration" includes authority to grant or deny claims).

Birmingham v. SoGen-Swiss International Corp. Retirement Plan, the Second Circuit thus stated that the "rendering of interpretations as to the meaning of the provisions of the Plan" is a fiduciary function.[32] In *Rehabilitation Institute v. Blue Cross and Blue Shield,* a district court, following many others, similarly stated: "The bottom line . . . is that [a person] is a fiduciary if [he] exercises discretionary authority over claims denials."[33] The exercise of *any* other discretion under a plan, for example, whether to provide benefits in a lump sum form, or whether to grant or deny an early retirement benefit requiring employer consent is also a fiduciary function.[34]

A person who performs any of these functions is a fiduciary, regardless of his or her title. In *Foulke v. Bethlehem 1980 Salaried Pension Plan,* Bethlehem Steel moved to dismiss a claim that a denial of discretionary lump sum benefits was in breach of fiduciary duty on the ground that the Pension Board, not it as the employer, was responsible for the denial. The motion to dismiss was denied when the evidence suggested the employer, as an employer, had taken an active role in plan administration.[35] In addition to employers, the person or entity who is actually performing fiduciary functions on benefit grants and denials may also be an insurance company,[36] the plan's or company's

---

Instead of identifying the particular clause of the fiduciary definition that benefit decisions fall under, courts often simply conclude that such authority is a fiduciary function. See, e.g., *Paris v. Wolf, Inc., Profit Sharing Plan,* 637 F.2d 357, 2 EBC 1244 (5th Cir. 1981), *cert. denied,* 454 U.S. 836 (1981) (plan interpretation is fiduciary function); *Blue Cross v. Peacock's Apothecary, Inc.,* 567 F.Supp. 1258, 4 EBC 1833 (N.D. Ala. 1983) (final decision on benefit claim is fiduciary decision). See also cases cited below in the sections on review of exercises of discretion, plan interpretation, and fact-finding.

[32] 718 F.2d 515, 4 EBC 2369, at 2375 (2d Cir. 1983). And see *Paris v. Wolf, Inc., Profit Sharing Plan, supra*; *McLaughlin Estate v. Conn. Gen. Life Ins. Co., supra*; 29 C.F.R. 2509.75-8, Q&A D-2 and D-3. See also the cases in sec. III.A below on plan interpretation.

[33] 5 EBC 2265, at 2273 (W.D. Pa. 1984). And see *Sixty-Five Security Plan v. Blue Cross of New York, supra*; *Eaton v. D'Amato, supra*; *Eversole v. Metropolitan Life Ins. Co., supra*; *Blue Cross v. Peacock's Apothecary, Inc., supra*; and 29 C.F.R. 2509.75-8, Q&A D-2 and D-3. See also the cases in sec. III.B below on review of findings of fact. A person, or an entity such as an insurance company, who performs ministerial administrative services for a plan, but who does not have final review authority over denied claims is generally not a fiduciary. See 29 C.F.R. 2509.75-8, Q&A D-2 and D-3, *Austin v. General American Life Ins. Co.,* 498 F.Supp. 844 (N.D. Ala. 1980); *Wolfe v. J.C. Penney Co.,* 710 F.2d 388, 4 EBC 1795 (7th Cir. 1983).

[34] See, e.g., *Fine v. Semet,* 699 F.2d 1091, 4 EBC 1273, at 1275 (11th Cir. 1983); *Morse v. Stanley,* 732 F.2d 1139, 5 EBC 1602 (2d Cir. 1984); *Petrella v. NL Indus., Inc.,* 529 F.Supp. 1357, 3 EBC 1210 (D.N.J. 1982). See also sec. III.C on review of exercises of discretionary authority under a plan.

[35] 565 F.Supp. 882, 4 EBC 1848 (E.D. Pa. 1983). See also *Genter v. Acme Scale & Supply Co.,* 776 F.2d 1180 (3d Cir. 1985). But compare *Sommers Drug Stores Co. Profit Sharing Trust v. Corrigan Enters., Inc.,* 793 F.2d 1456, 7 EBC 1782 (5th Cir. 1986), *cert. denied,* 479 U.S. ___ (1987) (employer not fiduciary merely because of status as sponsoring employer or power to appoint plan's trustees, employer must have "caused the trustees to relinquish their independent discretion" over the decision).

[36] A few cases suggest that an insurer is not an ERISA fiduciary in making final determinations of claims under an insurance contract it has issued to a plan if the claims are payable from the insurer's general assets, as opposed to from separately managed plan assets under a deposit administration contract with the plan. See *American Federation of Unions, Local 102 Health & Welfare Fund v. Equitable Life Assur. Soc.,* 647 F.Supp. 947 (M.D. La. 1985) (insurer an ERISA fiduciary if it pays claims with plan money and makes final disposition of denied claims, but not if it uses its own general funds); *Lederman v. Pacific Mutual Life Ins. Co.,* 494 F.Supp. 1020, 2 EBC 2195 (C.D. Cal. 1980); *Cate v. Blue Cross & Blue Shield,* 434 F.Supp. 1187 (E.D. Tenn. 1977); *Sixty-Five Security Plan v. Blue Cross of New York,* 583 F.Supp. 380, 5 EBC 1430 (S.D.N.Y. 1984) (but not deciding issue). However, the more prevalent view is that an insurer is *both* an

attorney, actuary, or consulting benefit specialist,[37] or even an arbitrator.[38]

C. History of the Arbitrary and Capricious Standard of Review

Although discretionary authority over benefits, including through plan interpretation and individual factual determinations, are fiduciary functions, a major obstacle to a remedy for a fiduciary violation in a benefit denial arises because the courts generally use a different, lower standard to review performance of these benefit functions than for other fiduciary functions under a plan. Thus, while ERISA "imposes an unwavering duty on [a] trustee to make decisions with single-minded devotion to [the] plan's participants and beneficiaries,"[39] the increasingly reflexive standard of review for *benefit* claims is that a court will uphold a denial of benefits against a claim of breach of fiduciary duty unless the court finds that the action or decision is "(1) arbitrary and capricious, (2) not supported by substantial evidence, or (3) erroneous on a question of law."[40]

1. Pre-ERISA Use of the Arbitrary and Capricious Standard

The "arbitrary and capricious" standard of review is, of course, the standard for review of administrative agency determinations, but its use for pension and other employee benefit claims is founded on the common law of trusts and on employee benefit cases brought before and after ERISA under Section 302(c)(5) of the Labor Management

---

ERISA fiduciary and an insurer subject to state law in deciding claims under an insurance contract. See 29 C.F.R. 2560.503-1(g)(2), *LeFebre v. Westinghouse Elec. Co.*, 549 F.Supp. 1021, 3 EBC 2359 (D. Md. 1982), *rev'd on other grounds*, 747 F.2d 197, 5 EBC 2521 (4th Cir. 1984); *Austin v. General American Life Ins. Co.*, 498 F.Supp. 844, 2 EBC 2198 (N.D. Ala. 1980); *Eversole v. Metropolitan Life Ins. Co.*, 500 F.Supp. 1162 (C.D. Cal. 1980); *Presti v. Conn. Gen. Life Ins. Co.*, 605 F.Supp. 163 (N.D. Cal. 1985); *Benvenuto v. Conn. Gen. Life Ins. Co.*, 643 F.Supp. 87 (D.N.J. 1986); *McLaughlin Estate v. Conn. Gen. Life Ins. Co.*, 565 F.Supp. 434, 4 EBC 1879 (N.D. Cal. 1983) (citing other cases).

If an insurer's role in plan administration is *not* under an insurance contract, but is as a part of a service or deposit administration contract with a plan, the insurer is unquestionably an ERISA fiduciary, but it is not subject to potentially more stringent state insurance law on the determination of claims under insurance contracts. See *Powell v. Chesapeake & Potomac Tel. Co.*, 780 F.2d 419, 6 EBC 2754 (4th Cir. 1985), *cert. denied*, 476 U.S. ___ (1986); *Howard v. Parisian, Inc.*, 8 EBC 1033 (11th Cir. 1987). And compare cases cited in sec. III.A.5.c (applying more stringent state decisional law to the administration of insurance contracts), with *Pilot Life Ins. Co. v. Dedeaux*, 481 U.S. ___, 8 EBC 1409 (1987) (state common law tort and contract remedies for bad faith denial of a claim for benefits under an insured employee benefit plan are not saved from ERISA preemption by express savings provision for state laws and decisions regulating insurance when (1) state law remedies for bad faith breaches of contract were not "specifically directed toward [the insurance] industry," (2) the state law "does not define the terms of the relationship between the insurer and insured," and (3) Congress "clearly" intended "that the federal remed[ies] displace" state law remedies).

[37] See Conf. Rep., at 323, 3 ERISA Leg. Hist. 4590 (advisors and consultants may be fiduciaries if they are effectively exercising discretionary authority under the plan).

[38] See ch. 14, sec. I.B, on the division of authority concerning whether arbitrators are ERISA fiduciaries, or are subject to arbitral immunity.

[39] *Morse v. Stanley*, 732 F.2d 1139, 5 EBC 1602, at 1607 (2d Cir. 1984).

[40] *Peckham v. Painters Union Pension Fund Trustees*, 653 F.2d 424, 2 EBC 1323, at 1325 (10th Cir. 1981), and see sec. III below.

Relations Act. In *Dennard v. Richards Group, Inc.*, the Fifth Circuit explained that the arbitrary and capricious standard was "traditionally used for review of trusts."[41] On the other hand, in *Struble v. New Jersey Brewery Employees' Welfare Fund*, the Third Circuit focused on Section 302(c)(5) of the Labor Management Relations Act as the source of the standard, stating:

> "The 'arbitrary and capricious' standard derives from section 302(c)(5) of the LMRA. That section imposes a duty of loyalty on section 302 trustees by permitting employer contributions to a welfare [or pension] trust fund only if the contributions are used 'for the sole and exclusive benefit of the employees . . . .' Section [404] of ERISA imposes a similar duty of loyalty, and not surprisingly the courts have applied the 'arbitrary and capricious' standard under ERISA as well."[42]

While often cited as support, the use of the arbitrary and capricious standard under Section 302(c)(5) of the LMRA is generally not analogous to its use as the standard of review under ERISA. Although the distinction is blurred in some decisions, the "Taft-Hartley" Act cases are generally limited to review of plan rules for "structural defects." Thus, even if the terms of a plan are *unambiguous*, and their application to the facts free from doubt, a court can still strike down a plan provision, or its application to particular participants, as "arbitrary and capricious." At the same time, Section 302(c)(5) is generally not interpreted as extending to claims over the more routine day-to-day fiduciary functions of plan interpretation and fact-finding. In *Alvares v. Erickson*, the Ninth Circuit stated that Section 302(c)(5) distinguishes

> "between actions involving 'structural' deficiencies in the relevant trust which cause it to violate the 'sole and exclusive benefit' provision of §302(c)(5) and actions involving only questions of day-to-day fiduciary administration [with the courts finding jurisdiction under Section 302(c)(5)] over the former but not the latter."[43]

Within this "structural defect" purview, which essentially authorizes

---

[41] 681 F.2d 306, 3 EBC 1769, at 1775 (5th Cir. 1982). See also *Wardle v. Central States Pension Fund*, 627 F.2d 820, 2 EBC 1633 (7th Cir. 1980), *cert. denied*, 449 U.S. 1112 (1981) (arbitrary and capricious standard used because it was "traditional standard of review of the law of trusts used in diversity cases"); *Allen v. UMWA 1979 Benefit Plan & Trust*, 726 F.2d 352 (7th Cir. 1984) (arbitrary and capricious standard derives from cases "under state and federal common law").

[42] 732 F.2d 325, 5 EBC 1676, at 1682 (3d Cir. 1984).

[43] 514 F.2d 156, 1 EBC 1121, at 1128 (9th Cir. 1975), *cert. denied*. 423 U.S. 874 (1977). See also *Reiherzer v. Shannon*, 581 F.2d 1266, 1 EBC 1175, at 1178 (7th Cir. 1978); *Elser v. IAM Nat'l Pension Fund*, 684 F.2d 648, 3 EBC 2155 (9th Cir. 1982), *cert. denied*, 464 U.S. 813 (1983); *Riley v. MEBA Pension Trust*, 570 F.2d 406, 1 EBC 1757 (2d Cir. 1977) (dicta), *rev'd on other grounds after remand*, 586 F.2d 968, 1 EBC 1763 (2d Cir. 1978); *Insley v. Joyce*, 330 F.Supp. 1228 (N.D. Ill. 1971).

As suggested above, the sharpness of *Alvares'* distinction has not always been adhered to in practice: Many decisions do not distinguish between arbitrary and capricious holdings under §302(c)(5) based on structural defects in plan rules and arbitrary and capricious holdings under the common law of trusts based on misinterpretation or misapplication of a plan's terms in day-to-day administration. See Comment, "The Arbitrary and Capricious Standard Under ERISA," 23 Duq. L. Rev. 1033, at 1039-40 (Summer 1985).

reformation of plans, the arbitrary and capricious standard is considered appropriate because of the restraint it imposes. This restraint reflects both judicial recognition of the shaky legislative mandate for correcting structural defects in plan rules under Section 302(c)(5), and respect for the trustees need for discretion in "conceiving" plan rules.[44] The analogy drawn in *Struble* to these cases is not well-founded because in contrast (1) the jurisdictional support under ERISA for review of day-to-day fiduciary administration is unquestionable, and was, in fact, one of Congress' primary purposes,[45] and (2) the need for discretion in "conceiving" plan rules is not paralleled in the implementation of substantive benefit rules that have already been conceived and that participants have relied on by rendering their labor in anticipation of receiving benefits under the stated terms.

However, as *Dennard* and other cases suggest, the arbitrary and capricious standard was also used before ERISA for review of daytoday fiduciary administration issues in state courts and in federal courts under diversity jurisdiction. The foundation for the standard was the common law of trusts. The use of the standard for pension claims was, however, not as uniform as indicated in *Dennard* and other cases.[46] The history of judicial review of employee benefit claims is, in fact, a circular history that started with a very lax contractual view, progressed to a view of plans as trusts, with application of the arbitrary and capricious standard, and then circled back to a stricter contractual view. In *Mitzner v. Jarcho*, the New York Court of Appeals explained the first two steps:

> "The law governing the administration of pensions is a hybrid born of a marriage of contract and trust principles. Over the years both fields of law have vied for the dominant role. At first, courts fastened on the contractual nature of pensions. Because pensions presumably represented nothing more than agreements between employees or their unions and employers, an overwhelming demonstration of an improper denial of benefits was required before trustees would be judicially compelled to provide pension benefits to rejected applicants. Later cases, however, . . . accorded increasing weight to the fiduciary obligations borne by the trustees for the benefit of the employees. Even where the trustees are vested, by the terms of the trust indenture, with sole authority on matters relating to employees' rights to receive pension benefits, a denial of

---

[44] See *Hurn v. Plumbing, Heating & Piping Industry Trust*, 703 F.2d 386, 4 EBC 1811, at 1814 (9th Cir. 1983); *Alvares v. Erickson, supra.* In *UMW Health & Retirement Funds v. Robinson*, 455 U.S. 562, 3 EBC 1129 (1982), the Supreme Court cast doubt on whether even this "structural defect" jurisdiction exists under §302(c)(5). See 3 EBC at 1134 n.12.

[45] See ERISA §2(b). See also Student Symposium, "Judicial Review of Fiduciary Claim Denials Under ERISA," 71 Cornell L. Rev. 986, at 1000 n. 69 (July 1986) ("[p]articularly damaging to judicial perpetuation of the LMRA's arbitrary and capricious standard under ERISA [is] Congress' complaint [in enacting ERISA] that the LMRA was 'not intended to establish nor does it provide standards for . . . fiduciary conduct,' " quoting H.R. Rep. 93-533, at 4, 2 ERISA Leg. Hist. 2351).

[46] In 1962, for example, the District of Columbia Circuit noted that the "authorities are divided as to whether an applicant for a pension has a contractual interest or whether his interest is merely equitable." *Danti v. Lewis*, 312 F.2d 345, at 348 n.3 (D.C. Cir. 1962).

> benefits [would] be judicially set aside if the board's ruling was motivated by bad faith, or arrived at by fraud or arbitrary action."[47]

While the trust law standard for review of investments of trust assets or administrative expenses was set still higher at the level of "undivided loyalty," "exclusive benefit," or the highest "punctilio" of honor, the arbitrary and capricious standard was considered appropriate for benefit decisions. This was because a trustee's decision to pay or not pay benefits under discretion granted by a settlor was considered to involve a "twofold" obligation to (1) provide benefits to current beneficiaries, while (2) preserving the trust *res* against undue depletion for future beneficiaries.[48] This twofold obligation required a "balancing" of interests; hence, courts found it difficult to apply a higher standard than review for arbitrary and capricious action. In contrast, when a decision involved an investment of trust assets or administrative expenses, the interests of all of the trust's beneficiaries could be seen as singular, with the decision reviewed under the higher standards for breach of loyalty.[49]

The arbitrary and capricious standard for benefit claims was recognized as a "low" standard of judicial review.[50] For example, in *Lowenstern v. IAM*, an often-cited pre-ERISA case, the issue was whether an employee on an employer-approved leave of absence was still "employed" within the meaning of a plan, and thus entitled to pension credits for the period of leave. While not denying that the participant's interpretation of the plan was reasonable, and without attempting to determine if it was *more* reasonable than the trustees' contrary interpretation, the District of Columbia Circuit capsulized the arbitrary and capricious standard:

> "[A]s between two competing interpretations of the Plan, we are bound by that of the Administrators if it is not arbitrary and capricious."[51]

This view was also reflected in *Rehmar v. Smith*, perhaps the most-cited pre-ERISA pension case. In *Rehmar*, Lilian Yanks had lived with a participant for "many years" and had been named by him as his

---

[47] 403 N.Y.S.2d 490, at 492–93 (N.Y.Ct.App. 1978) (case citations omitted).

[48] *Mitzner v. Jarcho, supra*, 403 N.Y.S.2d at 493.

[49] *Id.* In *Struble v. New Jersey Brewery Employees' Welfare Fund*, 732 F.2d 325, 5 EBC 1676 (3d Cir. 1984), the Third Circuit offered a virtually identical explanation for the lowering of the ERISA standard of review for personal claims for benefits below the stringent level of review that applies when the interests of participants are more singular:

"The use of different fiduciary standards ... is justified by the different challenge to fiduciary loyalty that each type of action presents. In actions by individual claimants challenging the trustees' denial of benefits, the issue is not whether the trustees have sacrificed the interests of the beneficiaries as a class in favor of some third party's interests, but whether the trustees have correctly balanced the interests of present claimants against the interests of future claimants.... In such circumstances it is appropriate to apply the more deferential 'arbitrary and capricious' standard to the trustees' decisions. In the latter type of action, the gravamen of the plaintiff's complaint is not that the trustees have incorrectly balanced valid interests, but rather that they have sacrificed valid interests to advance the interests of non-beneficiaries."
5 EBC at 1683 (citations omitted).

[50] R. Thomas, "Due Process, Hearings, and Pension and Welfare Claims Denials Under ERISA," 28 Lab. L.J. 276, at 284 (1977).

[51] 479 F.2d 1211, at 1213 (D.C. Cir. 1973).

"beneficiary" and "wife" under a plan. After the participant's death, the trustees denied survivor's benefits to her under an interpretation of the plan that required a legally-valid marriage for benefits to go to someone as the surviving spouse. The Ninth Circuit found that the trustees' interpretation was "reasonable," and thus not "arbitrary and capricious." Whether Lilian Yanks' interpretation was equally or more reasonable was not an issue for the court, given its limited standard of review.[52]

For factual determinations by trustees or a plan administrator, the arbitrary and capricious standard could result in an even more wooden and insurmountable barrier for a participant. In *Matthews v. Swift & Co.*, a participant was denied disability benefits under a plan. The Fifth Circuit stated that for him to overcome the trustees' determination that he was *not* disabled, his obligation was to prove, not just disability, but:

> "[S]uch a clear case of permanent disability that no honest tribunal could reach any other decision and . . . that any other decision is or would be arbitrary, fraudulent or in bad faith."[53]

2. The Competing Contractual Standard

The problem with the twofold obligation model, and the resulting arbitrary and capricious standard of review, is that it provides a deference to a plan administrator's or trustee's decisions that is generally unwarranted. Employer-appointed administrators and trustees are typically not the loyal trustees for participants and beneficiaries that the common law of trusts envisions. Rather, they continue to act as "creatures" of the employer who appoints them, generally employs them, and who may remove them at will, with little pretense of acting independently under the high standards set by ERISA and the common law.[54] Even when a union appoints an equal number of plan trustees, with a professional administrator being chosen by all the trustees to administer a plan, the U.S. Court of Appeals for the District of Columbia Circuit has recognized that the plan administrator, with "no tenure" and little "job security," is "generally less well-insulated from outside pressures than those government employees whose decisions are more commonly reviewed under the arbitrary and capricious standard." As a result, the administrator may be "naturally disinclined to make [benefit] awards."[55]

The problem that compounds this lack of insulation from the employer's interests is that the twofold obligation model rests on a

---

[52] 555 F.2d 1362, 1 EBC 1799, at 1807 (9th Cir. 1977).

[53] 465 F.2d 814, at 821 (5th Cir. 1972).

[54] *Elby v. Livernois Eng'g Co.*, 194 N.W.2d 429, at 430 (Mich. Ct.App. 1972). See also *Gould v. Continental Coffee*, 304 F.Supp. 1, at 2 (S.D.N.Y. 1969) (distinction between the employer and plan administrator appointed by the employer and subject to removal by the employer is a "legal fiction").

[55] *Maggard v. O'Connell*, 671 F.2d 568, at 571 (D.C. Cir. 1982).

fiction about whose interests are actually pitted in benefit decisions under defined benefit plans. A fiduciary's grant of benefits to a current claimant depletes assets available for future claimants, as under the traditional trust law model, if present and future benefit payments under a benefit plan are dependent on a *fixed* trust *res*. But in a defined benefit pension plan, payment of current benefit obligations increases the employer's future funding obligations. If the trust *res* is depleted for future claimants, it is only temporarily. Conversely, if current benefit claims are denied, the trust *res* for other participants may be temporarily increased, but over the long run, the assets available for future claimants do not increase. Instead, the "beneficiary" of the restrictive interpretation is the employer by virtue of decreased future funding obligations.[56]

When forfeitures are reallocated under a profit-sharing or stock bonus plan, future claimants' may be the beneficiaries of a restrictive benefit decision, but the judicial deference called for under the twofold obligation model is countered by the direct and personal "dollar interest" in the outcome that a plan administrator or trustee has if he or she is also a participant in the plan, and the indirect dollar interest that the person has if they function as an appendage of corporate officers who have account balances under the plan.[57]

The initial difficulty the courts encountered in using a stricter contractual standard of review was that plan terms, or at least those of nonbargained and multiemployer plans, typically provide "sole" or "absolute" discretionary authority and finality to a plan administrator's or trustees' decision. Restraining "arbitrary and capricious" interpretations under trust law could thus be seen as an improvement over the absolute leeway that might be allowed under a literal reading of the plan's interpretation authority. However, faced with the trustees' or plan administrator's lack of loyalty to the interests of participants, many courts, in the years before ERISA and in cases since with pre-ERISA facts, shifted back to a contractual standard of review. These

---

[56] See R. Gilbert, "Fiduciary Duties Under ERISA," 43 Inst. on Fed. Tax'n, at 33-6 (1985) ("the conflicting interests of trust beneficiaries and remaindermen do not exist under [pension] plans"). The twofold obligation model could find more support before ERISA because employers were not required to fund plans systematically to ensure the payment of all accrued liabilities. Before ERISA, the Code rules for qualified plans were interpreted to require the funding of each year's normal costs, plus interest on unfunded past service liabilities. The unfunded past service liabilities were not required to be amortized. See D. McGill, *Fundamentals of Private Pensions* (Richard D. Irwin 5th ed.), at 31 (questioning whether even this level of funding was required).

[57] See *Russell v. Princeton Laboratories, Inc.*, 231 A.2d 800, at 804 (N.J. 1967) (judicial deference to decisions of a profit-sharing plan administrative committee is not encouraged if members of the administrative committee have a "dollar interest" in the outcome of their decisions through reallocation of forfeitures to their own accounts). Under money purchase pension plans, each participant has an individual account, as in a profit-sharing or stock bonus plan. But in contrast to those plans, forfeitures of participants' account balances cannot be reallocated to the accounts of other participants. Instead, any forfeitures must go to decrease the employer's future funding obligations. The 1986 Tax Reform Act amends the Code to allow money purchase plans to reallocate forfeitures to other participants' account balances effective in plan years beginning after Dec. 31, 1985. Code §401(a)(8), as amended by §1119 of P.L. 99-514.

courts overcame reservations of "sole" or "absolute" interpretive authority by treating them as boilerplate, or more commonly, by disregarding their ability to alter substantive rights under a plan.[58] This renewed contractual standard was further oriented to employees by the dual interpretive principles of construing plans "in favor of the employee" and "to avoid forfeiture."[59] Some courts adopted these employee-oriented interpretive principles, but applied them *under* the arbitrary and capricious standard, with the results under this previously low standard thus becoming closer to a contractual standard of review.[60]

Collectively bargained single-employer plans seldom grant "sole," "absolute," or "final" authority to an employer-appointed plan administrator's interpretation of the terms of a plan or to his or her findings of facts. Instead, an employer-appointed plan administrator *initially* determines facts or interprets the plan, but if there is a dispute, the facts and the plan interpretation are subject to *de novo* determination by an arbitrator. When such disputes reach the courts because of exceptions to the arbitration presumption established in the *Steelworkers Trilogy*, the standard of judicial review is also *de novo*.[61] Plan interpretation in these cases has also often been further oriented to employees by the principles of interpreting such plans "in favor of the employee" and "to avoid the forfeiture of rights."[62]

For pension plans that consist of individual or group insurance contracts and for other employee benefit plans, such as severance pay and vacation pay plans, that are not generally in the form of trusts, the

---

[58] See *Frietszche v. First Western Bank & Trust Co.*, 336 P.2d 589 (Cal. Dist. Ct.App. 1959); *Weesner v. Elec. Power Board of Chattanooga*, 344 S.W.2d 766 (Tenn. Ct.App. 1961); *Keding v. Barton*, 154 N.W.2d 172 (Iowa 1967); *Dierks v. Thompson*, 295 F.Supp. 1271 (D.R.I. 1969), *rev'd on other grounds*, 414 F.2d 453 (1st Cir. 1969); *Stopford v. Boonton Molding Co.*, 265 A.2d 657 (N.J. 1970); *Thornbery v. MGS Co.*, 176 N.W.2d 355 (Wis. 1970); *Rochester Corp. v. Rochester*, 450 F.2d 118 (4th Cir. 1971); *Elby v. Livernois Eng'g Co.*, 194 N.W.2d 429 (Mich. Ct. App. 1972); *Anger v. Bender*, 335 N.E.2d 122 (Ill.App. 1975); *Rosploch v. Alumatic Corp.*, 251 N.W.2d 838 (Wis. 1977); *Ruditys v. Wing*, 260 N.W.2d 794 (Wis. 1978); *Brulotte v. Cormier Hosiery Mills, Inc.*, 387 A.2d 1162 (N.H. 1978); *McCoy v. Mesta Machine Co.*, 213 BNA Pens. Rep. D-1 (W.D. Pa. 1978), *modified on other grounds*, 260 BNA Pens. Rep. D-1 (W.D. Pa. 1979); *Landro v. Glendenning Motorways, Inc.*, 625 F.2d 1344 (8th Cir. 1980).

[59] *Id.*, except *Keding v. Barton* (using "practical meaning" of the parties) and *Landro v. Glendenning Motorways, Inc.* (construing unilateral plan against the employer because of its role as draftsman of the plan).

[60] See *Sigman v. Rudolph Wurlitzer Co.*, 11 N.E.2d 878 (Ohio Ct.App. 1937); *Russell v. Princeton Laboratories, Inc.*, 231 A.2d 800 (N.J. 1967); *Levitt v. Billy Penn Corp.*, 283 A.2d 873 (Pa. Super.Ct. 1971); *Connell v. U.S. Steel*, 371 F.Supp. 991 (N.D. Ala. 1974); *Paddock Pool Const. Co. v. Monseur*, 533 P.2d 1188 (Ariz. App. 1975); *Ehrle v. Bank Bldg. & Equip. Corp.*, 530 S.W.2d 482 (Mo. Ct.App. 1975); *Baeten v. Van Ess*, 474 F.Supp. 1824, 1 EBC 2046 (E.D. Wis. 1979).

[61] See *Tolbert v. Union Carbide Corp.*, 495 F.2d 719 (4th Cir. 1974); *Union Central Life Ins. Co. v. Hamilton Steel Prod., Inc.*, 448 F.2d 501 (7th Cir. 1971); *Siss v. U.S. Steel Corp.*, 339 N.E.2d 279 (Ill. App. 1975); *Hoefel v. Atlas Tack Corp.*, 581 F.2d 1 (1st Cir. 1978); *Luli v. Sun Products Corp.*, 398 N.E.2d 553 (Ohio 1979); *Apponi v. Sunshine Biscuits, Inc.*, 652 F.2d 643, 2 EBC 1534 (6th Cir. 1981); *Terones v. Pacific States Steel Corp.*, 526 F.Supp. 1350 (N.D. Cal. 1981).

[62] See *Siss v. U.S. Steel Corp., supra*; *Hoefel v. Atlas Tack Corp., supra*; *Terones v. Pacific States Steel Corp., supra*; *Union Central Life Ins. Co. v. Hamilton Steel Prod., Inc., supra*, *Apponi v. Sunshine Biscuits, Inc., supra* (recognizing the principles, but not reaching whether they apply).

pre-ERISA standard of review was also always contractual, rather than an arbitrary and capricious standard.[63]

The only exception to the general movement to a new, stricter contractual view of pensions, or to the use of favorable plan interpretation principles *under* the arbitrary and capricious standard, was for benefit claims from jointly administered (Taft-Hartley Act) multiemployer plans. For these plans, where equal numbers of union- and management-appointed trustees are responsible for interpreting the terms of the plan, with an impartial arbiter required to resolve any deadlocked issues, the traditional trust law arbitrary and capricious standard held firm before ERISA.[64] In part, this may have reflected the equal representation of employee interests on the boards administering these plans.[65] At the same time, when this structure did not produce equitable results, courts before ERISA were increasingly reversing decisions of the trustees, even if the plan's language unambiguously called for a benefit denial, when the provision was itself arbitrary and capricious, or was arbitrary and capricious as applied to an individual or group of individuals.[66]

3. ERISA's Intended Policy

In enacting ERISA, Congress expressed sharp dissatisfaction with the ability of the traditional common law of trusts, i.e., the arbitrary and capricious standard, to "adjust inequities visited upon plan participants."[67] Both the Senate Committee on Labor and Public Welfare and the House Education and Labor Committee reports stated that under the traditional common law of trusts:

> "Courts strictly interpret the plan indenture and are reluctant to apply concepts of equitable relief or to disregard technical document wording. Thus, under present law, accumulated pension credits can be lost even when separated employees are within a few months, or even days, of qualifying for retirement."[68]

The congressional leaders on ERISA also uniformly viewed pensions as deferred compensation for the employee's labor, a view that is inherently undermined by a standard of review under which an employee

---

[63] See secs. III.A.5.c and d below.

[64] See, e.g., *Rehmar v. Smith*, 555 F.2d 1362, 1 EBC 1799 (9th Cir. 1977); *Lowenstern v. IAM*, 479 F.2d 1211 (D.C. Cir. 1973); *Beam v. Int'l Org. of Masters, Mates and Pilots*, 511 F.2d 975 (2d Cir. 1975). But see *Hart v. Carpenters Local 626*, 352 A.2d 423 (Del. Super. 1976) (using principles of interpreting plans in favor of the employee and to avoid forfeiture in interpreting multiemployer plan); *Dorward v. ILWU-PMA Pension Plan*, 452 P.2d 258 (Wash. 1969).

[65] See *Gaydosh v. Lewis*, 410 F.2d 262, at 266 (D.C. Cir. 1969):

"[U]nderlying all these determinations is the awareness that the employees are not at a disadvantage vis-a-vis the trustees. The Board of Trustees is chaired by the representative of the Union. He, as well as the other two members [one of whom is a neutral], is presumed to conscientiously serve the interests of all parties to the Fund."

[66] See ch. 8, sec. VIII.

[67] S. Rep. 93-127, at 5, 1 ERISA Leg. Hist. 591, and H.R. Rep. 93-533, at 5, 2 ERISA Leg. Hist. 2352.

[68] *Id.*

cannot prevail with a preponderantly *more* reasonable interpretation of a plan, but must instead prove that a plan administrator's or trustees' interpretation is "arbitrary and capricious." Senator Harrison Williams, one of the two chief Senate leaders and sponsors of ERISA, thus stated:

> "I would stress that pensions are not gratuities, like a gold watch bestowed as a gift by the employer on retirement.
>
> "They represent savings which the worker has earned in the form of deferred payment for his labors."[69]

Senator Jacob Javits, the other chief Senate leader and sponsor, similarly stated:

> "[T]he private pension plan is a means for transferring earnings during the working years into income for a decent living in the older years. The worker 'works' for that pension the same way he 'works' for his wages or salary and when he does not get it or some reasonable portion of it, he is angry, frustrated, and ultimately convinced that he has been robbed of a material recognition that was due him."[70]

Representative Carl Perkins, the chairman of the House Education and Labor Committee likewise stated:

> "It is unfair and inequitable and almost invariably, tragic as well, for workers to *defer income* from wages or salary in anticipation of retirement benefits they will never get.
>
> "The workers who fail to get expected pension benefits have reason to feel cheated just as they feel cheated if, having worked a week or a month, their employer refuses to pay them."[71]

Following the same view of pensions as deferred wages, legislators in both the House and Senate repeatedly referred to workers contributing to pension plans they received nothing back from—despite the fact that most pension plans do not require employee contributions.[72]

In addition to establishing minimum vesting and accrual rules, funding standards, and termination insurance, Congress accordingly took general steps to make pension plans more viable contracts for employees. Representative John Dent, the chairman of the House Subcommittee on Labor, emphasized this basic objective when he stated in the closing ERISA debates:

---

[69] 2 ERISA Leg. Hist. 1605. And see S. Rep. 93-127, at 9, 1 ERISA Leg. Hist. 595 (pensions are earned, deferred compensation for services).

[70] 2 ERISA Leg. Hist. 1609.

[71] 2 ERISA Leg. Hist. 3367 (emphasis added).

[72] See 3 ERISA Leg. Hist. 3591-93 (Rep. Fascell), 3 ERISA Leg. Hist. 4657 (Rep. Perkins), 3 ERISA Leg. Hist. 4698 and 4708 (Rep. Annunzio), 3 ERISA Leg. Hist. 4702 (Rep. Tiernan), 3 ERISA Leg. Hist. 4708 (Rep. Carney), 3 ERISA Leg. Hist. 4716 (Rep. Daniels), 2 ERISA Leg. Hist. 1865 (Sen. Kennedy), and 3 ERISA Leg. Hist. 4776 (Sen. Humphrey).

The trade-off between current wages and pensions and other fringe benefits is recognized in other federal legislation. In establishing priority among unsecured creditors for contributions to employee benefit plans under Bankruptcy Code §507(a)(4), Congress stated:

"The bill recognizes the realities of labor contract negotiations, where fringe benefits may be substituted for current wage demands."

S. Rep. 95-989, at 69, and see H.R. Rep. 95-595, at 187, 95th Cong., 2d Sess. (1978).

> "[W]e started out with only one aim in view and that was to give to a pension plan participant his entitlements under the contract of the pension plan he belonged to."[73]

Section 402(a)(1) of ERISA therefore requires that "[e]very benefit plan ... be established and maintained pursuant to a written instrument." More particularly, Section 402(b)(4) requires this written instrument to "specify the basis on which payments are [to be] made ... from the plan." As stated by the ERISA Conference Committee:

> "A written plan is ... required in order that every employee may, on examining the plan document, determine *exactly* what his rights and obligations are under the plan."[74]

To further establish precise communication of employees' benefit rights, ERISA Section 102 requires every plan to prepare and distribute to its participants a comprehensive and accurate summary plan description "written in a manner calculated to be understood by the average participant." The SPD is required to specifically describe the plan's provisions for attaining nonforfeitable benefits, and must also describe the "circumstances which may result in disqualification, ineligibility, or denial or loss of benefits" that a participant "*might otherwise reasonably expect* ... on the basis of the [SPD's] description of benefits"—however hidden or subsumed those drawbacks may be under the detailed and often technical language of the plan.[75] Both the House and Senate Labor committee reports thus stated:

> "Descriptions of plans furnished to participants should be presented in a manner that an average and reasonable worker participant can understand intelligently. It is grossly unfair to hold an employee accountable for acts which disqualify him from benefits, if he had no knowledge of these acts, or if these conditions were stated in a misleading or incomprehensible manner in plan booklets."[76]

The written plan and the SPD requirements are both undermined if plan trustees can prevail when they interpret a plan according to double meanings of terms and provisions that are at odds with a participant's reasonable understanding based on the plan and SPD. In combination, the written plan and SPD requirements thus must be considered to retilt plan interpretation toward the *more* reasonable interpretation of a plan's terms, and away from the view that a participant's interpretation can *only* prevail if the trustees' interpretation lacks rationality.

---

[73] 3 ERISA Leg. Hist. 4665.

[74] Conf. Rep., at 297, 3 ERISA Leg. Hist. 4564 (emphasis added).

[75] 29 C.F.R. 2520.102-3(l) (emphasis added). And see ERISA §102(a)(1) and (b).

[76] H.R. Rep. 93-533, at 8, 2 ERISA Leg. Hist. 2355, and S. Rep. 93-127, at 11, 1 ERISA Leg. Hist. 597.

Senator Javits decried the creation of benefit expectations by descriptions in summary booklets which are not fulfilled under strict constructions of plans, stating:

"Many workers are led to believe they are covered by a good pension plan because of nicely phrased booklets and other assurances handed them by their employers. When the time comes for the payoff, they learn that the cold legal phrasing in pension contracts says otherwise."

3 ERISA Leg. Hist. 4750.

Congress' establishment of a cause of action under Section 502(a)(1)(B) of ERISA to "enforce . . . the terms of the plan" and the mandate Congress gave the courts thereunder to develop a "body of Federal substantive law" "to deal with the issues involving rights and obligations under private pension and welfare plans" provide another indication of its intent to move away from the arbitrary and capricious standard.[77] The significance of Section 502(a)(1)(B) and this federal common law authorization is that it is set up separately from the cause of action for enforcement of fiduciary duties that could be expected to primarily draw its principles from the common law of trusts.[78]

In addition to the disclosure requirements and the Section 502(a)(1)(B) cause of action, the ERISA Section 404(a)(1) fiduciary standard is, moreover, to be a uniform, "strict,"[79] "more exacting"[80] standard of fiduciary responsibility. The committee reports thus emphasized that the ERISA fiduciary standard is to be interpreted by the courts "bearing in mind the special nature and purposes of employee benefit plans intended to be effectuated by the Act."[81] Accordingly, it has been recognized that in interpreting the fiduciary standard, "application of traditional trust law principles may, in some instances, conflict with Congress' desire to eliminate barriers to the protections and enforcement of rights in ERISA-covered benefit plans."[82] "Congress [thus] intended to codify the principles of trust law [but] with whatever alterations were needed to fit the needs of employee benefit plans."[83] The committee reports recognized that such alterations are required because employee benefit plans are in fact "quite different" both "in nature and purpose" from the testamentary and inter vivos trusts on which trust law is founded.[84] As a prime example, one authority points out that "the conflicting interests of trust beneficiaries and remaindermen [in a fixed trust *res*] do not exist" under pension plans because of ERISA's funding requirements.[85] Thus, the balancing of conflicting interests of current and future claimants that supported the arbitrary and capricious standard under traditional trust law is absent

---

[77] 3 ERISA Leg. Hist. 4771 (statement of Sen. Javits). And see Conf. Rep., at 327, 3 ERISA Leg. Hist. 4594.

[78] As mentioned above, the federal common law is also guided by Congress' policies in enacting ERISA, including promoting the receipt of "anticipated retirement benefits" and ensuring adequate communication of benefit requirements to participants. See sec. I above and ERISA §§2(a) and 2(b).

[79] *Struble v. New Jersey Brewery Employees' Welfare Fund,* 732 F.2d 325, 5 EBC 1676, at 1683 (3d Cir. 1984).

[80] *Donovan v. Mazzola,* 716 F.2d 1226, 4 EBC 1865, at 1870 (9th Cir. 1983) *cert. denied,* 464 U.S. 1040 (1984).

[81] S. Rep. 93-127, at 29, 1 ERISA Leg. Hist. 615, H.R. Rep. 93-533, at 29, 2 ERISA Leg. Hist. 2359. And see Conf. Rep., at 302, 3 ERISA Leg. Hist. 4569.

[82] *Thornton v. Evans,* 692 F.2d 1064, 3 EBC 2241, at 2255 (7th Cir. 1982).

[83] *Free v. Briody,* 732 F.2d 1331, 5 EBC 1442, at 1448 (7th Cir. 1984).

[84] S. Rep. 93-127, at 29, 1 ERISA Leg. Hist. 615, H.R. Rep. 93-533, at 29, 2 ERISA Leg. Hist. 2359. And see Conf. Rep., at 302, 3 ERISA Leg. Hist. 4569.

[85] R. Gilbert, "Fiduciary Duties Under ERISA," 43 Inst. on Fed. Tax'n, at 33-6 (1985).

under ERISA.[86] However, that has not foreclosed the courts from carrying that standard forward under ERISA.

III. Post-ERISA Judicial Review of Different Types of Benefit Decisions by Plan Fiduciaries

Despite the pre-ERISA movement to a more contractual standard of review and Congress' emphasis on more satisfactory adjustment of the inequities visited on plan participants than under the common law of trusts, every circuit that has addressed the issue has adopted the arbitrary and capricious standard of review for denied benefit claims. Some decisions set forth the full standard of "arbitrary and capricious, not supported by substantial evidence, or erroneous on a question of law,"[87] and others simply state the standard as the "arbitrary and capricious" standard, which from all indications is shorthand for the longer version.[88]

The only general alternative that has been offered to the arbitrary and capricious standard of review is a stricter standard that applies the precise language and duties in Section 404(a)(1). In *Winpisinger v. Aurora Corp.*, an exercise of discretionary authority to amend a plan (discussed in more detail in Chapter 9 below) was held not to be properly reviewed under the arbitrary and capricious standard because ERISA had superseded that standard with the higher, express duties of Section 404(a)(1).[89] Some courts have rejected the *Winpisinger* decision explicitly,[90] and most others have done so implicitly, presumably because the "arbitrary and capricious" standard also prevailed at common law for benefit decisions, despite the high common law duties of complete loyalty and exclusive benefit.[91]

In practice, however, the ERISA standard of review for plan interpretations is a more contractual standard, with emphasis on the exact

---

[86] See n. 56 above.

[87] *Wolfe v. J.C. Penney Co.*, 710 F.2d 388, 4 EBC 1795, at 1799 (7th Cir. 1983); *Wardle v. Central States Pension Fund*, 627 F.2d 820, 2 EBC 1633 (7th Cir. 1980); *Dennard v. Richards Group, Inc.*, 681 F.2d 306, 3 EBC 1769 (5th Cir. 1982); *Short v. Central States Pension Fund*, 729 F.2d 567, 5 EBC 2552 (8th Cir. 1984); *Elser v. IAM Nat'l Pension Fund*, 684 F.2d 648, 3 EBC 2155 (9th Cir. 1982), *cert. denied*, 464 U.S. 813 (1983); *Malhiot v. So. Cal. Retail Clerks Union*, 735 F.2d 1133 (9th Cir. 1984); *Peckham v. Painters Union Pension Fund Trustees*, 653 F.2d 424, 2 EBC 1323 (10th Cir. 1981).

[88] See, e.g., *Palino v. Casey*, 664 F.2d 854, 2 EBC 2169 (1st Cir. 1981); *Miles v. New York Teamsters Pension Fund*, 698 F.2d 593, 4 EBC 2160 (2d Cir. 1983), *cert. denied*, 464 U.S. 829 (1983); *Struble v. New Jersey Brewery Employees' Welfare Fund*, 732 F.2d 325, 5 EBC 1676 (3d Cir. 1984); *LeFebre v. Westinghouse Elec. Corp.*, 747 F.2d 197, 5 EBC 2521 (4th Cir. 1984); *Rhoton v. Central States Pension Fund*, 717 F.2d 988, 4 EBC 2233 (6th Cir. 1983); *Sharron v. Amalgamated Ins. Agency Services, Inc.*, 704 F.2d 562, 4 EBC 2178 (11th Cir. 1983); *Maggard v. O'Connell*, 671 F.2d 568 (D.C. Cir. 1982).

[89] 456 F.Supp. 559, 1 EBC 2201 (N.D. Ohio 1978).

[90] See *Petrella v. NL Indus., Inc.*, 529 F.Supp. 1357, 3 EBC 1210 (D.N.J. 1982); *Fine v. Semet*, 514 F.Supp. 34, 2 EBC 1103 (S.D. Fla. 1981), *aff'd*, 699 F.2d 1091, 4 EBC 1273 (11th Cir. 1983).

[91] See sec. II.C.1 above.

terms of the written plan and the description of the provision in question in the plan's summary plan description, than that which applied under the arbitrary and capricious standard before ERISA. Four exceptions have also been recognized when a contractual standard of review is, or may be, directly applicable.

Refinements have also developed to ensure procedural fairness in factual determinations, although absent procedural defects, determinations of fact are generally reviewed under a "substantial evidence" test. Exercises of other discretionary authority under a plan are stuck at the traditional arbitrary and capricious standard, but review of the purpose of the discretionary authority, and standards of consistency, rationality, and nondiscriminatory effects from discretionary criteria may give more substance to the post-ERISA arbitrary and capricious standard.

The discussion below focuses on the three basic types of nonstatutory benefit issues: (1) plan interpretation, (2) factual determinations, and (3) exercises of discretion—starting in each section with how the arbitrary and capricious standard applies in its traditional form, and then discussing refinements and exceptions.

As emphasized in each section below, if a legal issue enters into a trustee's or plan administrator's decision on a benefit claim, the legal issue must be separated out for *de novo* review. A plan administrator's, trustee's, or even a neutral arbitrator's opinion on a legal issue is not entitled to deference under the arbitrary and capricious standard of review. The fully articulated arbitrary and capricious standard makes this point by stating that a benefit denial must not be "arbitrary and capricious," "not supported by substantial evidence," *or* "erroneous on a question of law."[92] In *Amaro v. Continental Can Co.*, the Ninth Circuit thus stated that a court must always "consider [an] employee's [statutory] claim *de novo*."[93] Therefore, whether a plan provision complies with ERISA Section 203's vesting requirements, whether it complies with the benefit accrual requirements, whether the amount of a Social Security offset is determined in accordance with the Code and ERISA, or whether years of participation have been credited as required by ERISA based on the records required to be maintained by ERISA, are all legal issues on which a plan administrator's opinion is entitled to no deference.[94] Common law issues, such whether to apply

---

[92] *Wolfe v. J.C. Penney Co., supra*, 4 EBC at 1799. And see *Elser v. IAM Nat'l Pension Fund, supra*; *Malhiot v. So. Cal. Retail Clerks Union, supra*; *Peckham v. Painters Union Pension Fund, supra.*

[93] 724 F.2d 747, 5 EBC 1215, at 1221 (9th Cir. 1984), quoting *Alexander v. Gardner-Denver Co.*, 415 U.S. 36, at 60 (1974). See also *Holt v. Winpisinger*, 811 F.2d 1532, 8 EBC 1169 (D.C. Cir. 1987); *Riley v. MEBA Pension Trust*, 570 F.2d 406, 1 EBC 1757 (2d Cir. 1977), *rev'd on other grounds after remand*, 586 F.2d 968, 1 EBC 1763 (2d Cir. 1978); *Winer v. Edison Bros. Stores Pension Plan*, 593 F.2d 307, 1 EBC 1191 (8th Cir. 1979); *Quinn v. Burlington Northern Pension Plan*, 664 F.2d 675, 3 EBC 1137 (8th Cir. 1981); *Fentron Indus. v. Shopmen's Pension Fund*, 674 F.2d 1300, 3 EBC 1323 (9th Cir. 1982).

[94] See, e.g., *Duchow v. New York Teamsters Pension Fund*, 691 F.2d 74, 3 EBC 2312 (2d Cir. 1982); *Holt v. Winpisinger, supra.*

estoppel based on a misrepresentation by a person with actual or apparent authority over a plan, are also subject to *de novo* review.[95]

A. Plan Interpretations

1. Fiduciary and Contract Action Merger Under the Arbitrary and Capricious Standard

Every issue of plan interpretation can be framed as an action for breach of fiduciary duty. For example, in *Birmingham v. SoGen-Swiss International Corp. Retirement Plan*, the Second Circuit held that "the rendering of interpretations as to the meaning of the provisions of the Plan" is a fiduciary function.[96] Thus, whenever a claim for benefits is denied under a questionable plan interpretation, an action can be brought against the fiduciary responsible for the interpretation alleging that he or she acted in breach of fiduciary duty. Under the prevailing standard of review, the issue is then decided based on whether the court determines that the fiduciary's exercise of interpretive authority was "arbitrary and capricious."[97]

A unique aspect to any plan interpretation claim, however, is that the claim can also be framed as a cause of action under ERISA Section 502(a)(1)(B) to enforce the "terms of [the] plan." Construing ERISA to avoid redundancy, the Section 502(a)(1)(B) cause of action makes rights under the terms of a plan contractually enforceable, as some courts held before ERISA, while the Section 502(a)(3) action for breach of fiduciary duty preserves as a separate action the common law of trusts action for redress of arbitrary and capricious fiduciary conduct.

Given this statutory structure, it would seem that many interpretations of plans could be incorrect as a matter of contract under Section 502(a)(1)(B), without rising to the level of arbitrary and capricious fiduciary conduct under Section 502(a)(3).[98] Generally, however, the

---

[95] See ch. 8, secs. I and II.

[96] 718 F.2d 515, 4 EBC 2369, at 2375 (2d Cir. 1984). And see, e.g., *Paris v. Wolf, Inc., Profit Sharing Plan*, 637 F.2d 357, 2 EBC 1244 (5th Cir. 1981), *cert. denied*, 454 U.S. 836 (1981).

[97] See cases cited in introductory material in sec. III, adopting the arbitrary and capricious standard of review for actions alleging breaches of fiduciary duty in benefit denials.

[98] Differences between §502(a)(1)(B) actions and fiduciary actions are also found in ERISA's provision for concurrent state and federal court jurisdiction for claims to enforce the terms of a plan. In *Menhorn v. Firestone Tire & Rubber Co.*, the Ninth Circuit explained:

"Actions to recover benefits or enforce rights under the terms of a plan will typically involve the application of those general principles of *contract law* with which state courts have had substantial experience before ERISA; their expertise qualifies them to evaluate these rules in the light of ERISA's policies and apply federal common law. Congress simply increased the number of forums to which a claimant might have access in these cases, presumably both to increase the claimant's options and also to mitigate to some degree the burden on the federal courts resulting from ERISA."

738 F.2d 1496, 5 EBC 2193, at 2196 n. 2 (9th Cir. 1984) (emphasis added). In contrast, for actions alleging a breach of fiduciary duty, "[t]he U.S. district courts . . . have exclusive jurisdiction." Conf. Rep., at 327, 3 ERISA Leg. Hist. 4594.

courts have used the arbitrary and capricious standard for review of both whether a fiduciary violation has occurred and whether a plan interpretation is correct under Section 502(a)(1)(B). The merger of these two causes of action into a single fiduciary mold is effectively the position of every court that uses the "arbitrary and capricious" standard without regard to whether the participant is claiming the interpretation is incorrect under the terms of the plan or is arbitrary enough to be in breach of fiduciary duty.[99]

In determining whether an interpretation is arbitrary and capricious under this merged action, many courts will, moreover, not directly apply "ordinary principles of contract interpretation."[100] Rather, as the Fifth Circuit stated in *Paris v. Wolf, Inc., Profit Sharing Plan*:

> "Although the determination of eligibility for pension benefits *seems* to be a matter of contract law, 'the clear weight of federal authority' mandates that the trustee's determinations are to be upheld unless arbitrary and capricious."[101]

Despite the tenor of this statement, principles of contract interpretation indirectly enter into every court's analysis of whether a fiduciary's interpretation is arbitrary and capricious.[102] But the arbitrary and capricious standard does usually mean that somewhat more latitude is permitted the fiduciary in interpreting the terms of the plan than if the terms were directly reviewed to determine the *more* reasonable, or contractually "correct," of two interpretations.[103] The standard formulation of this difference is that:

> "Where both the trustees of a pension fund and a rejected applicant offer rational, though conflicting, interpretations of plan provisions, the trustees' interpretation must be allowed to control."[104]

Since an increasingly prevalent view before ERISA, except for review of interpretations of multiemployer plans, was that plan interpretation

---

Section 502(a)(1)(B) actions and actions for breach of fiduciary duty can also be distinguished on the basis of the potential personal liability of the fiduciary. A fiduciary is potentially personally liable for a breach of fiduciary duty, but only the plan is liable in an action to enforce the plan's terms.

[99] See, e.g., *Quinn v. Burlington Northern Pension Plan*, 664 F.2d 675, 3 EBC 1137 (8th Cir. 1981); *Paris v. Wolf, Inc., Profit Sharing Plan*, 637 F.2d 357, 2 EBC 1244 (5th Cir. 1981), *cert. denied*, 454 U.S. 836 (1981); *Harm v. Bay Area Pipe Trades Pension Fund*, 701 F.2d 1301, 4 EBC 1253 (9th Cir. 1983); *Miles v. New York Teamsters Pension Fund*, 698 F.2d 593, 4 EBC 2160 (2d Cir. 1983), *cert. denied*, 464 U.S. 829 (1983); *Martinez v. Swift Co.*, 656 F.2d 262, 2 EBC 1747 (7th Cir. 1981).

[100] *Quinn v. Burlington Northern Pension Plan*, 664 F.2d 675, 3 EBC 1137, at 1140 (8th Cir. 1981).

[101] 637 F.2d 357, 2 EBC 1244, at 1247 (5th Cir. 1981), *cert. denied*, 454 U.S. 836 (1981) (emphasis added).

[102] See *Dennard v. Richards Group, Inc.*, 681 F.2d 306, 3 EBC 1769 (5th Cir. 1982), and sec. III.A.3 below.

[103] See, e.g., *Rehmar v. Smith*, 555 F.2d 1362, 1 EBC 1799 (9th Cir. 1977).

[104] *Miles v. New York Teamsters Pension Fund*, 698 F.2d 593, 4 EBC 2160, at 2167 (2d Cir. 1983), *cert. denied*, 464 U.S. 829 (1983). And see, e.g., *Bruder v. Pension Plan for Employees of Holscher-Wernig, Inc.*, 599 F.Supp. 347, at 349 (E.D. Mo. 1984) (citing *Miles*); *Griffis v. Delta Family-Care Disability*, 723 F.2d 822, at 825 (11th Cir. 1984), *cert. denied*, 467 U.S. 1242 (1984).

was to be reviewed under a contractual standard, with the plan, moreover, interpreted "in favor of the employee" and "to avoid forfeiture," this standard, although now widely adopted, is ostensibly at the lower end of pre-ERISA practice.[105]

2. Problems With the Arbitrary and Capricious Standard of Review for Plan Interpretation

The justifications offered by the courts for the merger of the Section 502(a)(1)(B) and Section 502(a)(3) causes of action and for the use of the arbitrary and capricious standard of review thereunder have often been conclusory. In *Paris v. Wolf, Inc., Profit Sharing Plan*, the Fifth Circuit stated simply:

> "Although the determination of eligibility for pension benefits [under Section 502(a)(1)(B)] *seems* to be a matter of contract law, 'the clear weight of federal authority' mandates that the trustee's determinations of eligibility are to be upheld unless arbitrary or capricious."[106]

In *Dennard v. Richards Group, Inc.*, the Fifth Circuit revealed slightly more about the underlying reasons for the adoption of the arbitrary and capricious standard under ERISA by stating that it prevents "excessive judicial intervention" in pension plans.[107] Preventing excessive judicial intervention may in turn be read as meaning, in large part, that the standard keeps court dockets from becoming further overcrowded.[108]

The problem with the arbitrary and capricious standard, as described before, is that it may prevent "excessive judicial intervention" by providing a deference to plan administrators' interpretations that is unwarranted based on their loyalty to plan participants' interests over the employers'.[109] This lack of loyalty is compounded by the faulty presumption under the arbitrary and capricious standard that plan administrators are balancing the interests of present versus future claimants to a fixed trust *res*.[110] This is a fiction when applied to a pension plan under which payment of current benefit claims increases the employer's future contribution obligations while nonpayment of

---

[105] See sec. II.C.2 above.

[106] 2 EBC at 1247 (emphasis added).

[107] 681 F.2d 306, 3 EBC 1769, at 1775 (5th Cir. 1982). And see *Miles v. New York Teamsters Pension Fund*, 698 F.2d 593, 4 EBC 2160 (2d Cir. 1983), *cert. denied*, 464 U.S. 829 (1983); *Bayles v. Central States Pension Fund*, 602 F.2d 97, 1 EBC 1416 (5th Cir. 1979); *Ganze v. Dart Indus. Inc.*, 741 F.2d 790, 5 EBC 2309, at 2312 (5th Cir. 1984); *Rosen v. Hotel & Restaurant Pension Fund*, 637 F.2d 592, 2 EBC 1054, at 1057 (3d Cir. 1981), *cert. denied*, 454 U.S. 898 (1981).

[108] See *Lee v. Dayton Power & Light Co.*, 604 F.Supp. 987, at 1001 n. 11 (S.D. Ohio 1985). This is not necessarily the result. A lax arbitrary and capricious standard can send a message to plan administrators that it is permissible to deny benefits in instances when they have a barely rational reasons to do so, with the result being *more* lawsuits.

[109] See sec. II.C.2 above.

[110] See sec. II.C.1 and 2 above.

current claims decreases the employer's future contribution obligations—in both cases with the trust *res* available for future claimants remaining the same over the long run.[111]

An arbitrary and capricious standard in which the plan's or employer's interpretations always prevail between two intrinsically reasonable but opposite interpretations also undermines ERISA's disclosure requirements. Under ERISA, benefit payments are to be made on the basis of a written plan that allows a participant to determine "exactly" where he or she stands in advance of retirement.[112] The plan's terms are to be accurately and understandably described in a summary plan description so that "nicely phrased booklets" do not belie later restrictive interpretations of the "cold legal phrasing" of the plan.[113] Under a lax "arbitrary and capricious" standard, however, an employee can have a reasonable interpretation based on the written plan and the SPD, but still lose to a second, no more reasonable interpretation by the plan trustees. The result is often to make retirement planning a "best guess" process among rational interpretations that can be made under a plan provision,[114] and generally to shift the burden of dual meanings and understandable communication back onto the employee.

The equitable and legal problems with use of the arbitrary and capricious standard were summarized by the district court in *Hayden v. Texas-U.S. Chemical Co.*:

> "To an older worker, his pension rights may be more valuable than his salary. He can enforce those valued rights however, if and only if he can prove the contract's breach to be 'arbitrary and capricious'. . . .
>
> "The court believes that disputes over employment contracts—including pension and disability benefit plans—are most rationally, economically, and equitably resolved by the application of traditional contract principles. It is, after all, a contract that the court is being asked to interpret.
>
> " . . . Basic contract concepts and terms do not, of course, convey absolutely precise meaning. But they carry substantially more meaning than the slippery concept of 'arbitrary and capricious.' Requiring that 'standard' of review makes for a paucity of legal analysis. It substitutes conclusory phrases for specific supporting factual determinations."[115]

In *Lee v. Dayton Power & Light Co.*, another district court questioned

---

[111] See sec. II.C.2. In profit-sharing plans, a restriction in current benefit payments can benefit future claimants through reallocation of the current claimant's forfeiture to the remaining participants' accounts. But the "dollar interest" of a plan administrator or trustee who has an account under the plan, or who functions on behalf of highly paid employees who do, militates against using a deferential standard of review. See *id.* Effective in plan years beginning after Dec. 31, 1985, the Tax Reform Act amends the Code to also allow money purchase pension plans to reallocate forfeitures to other participants' account balances. Code §401(a)(8), as amended by §1119 of TRA, P.L. 99-514.

[112] Conf. Rep., at 297, 3 ERISA Leg. Hist. 4564.

[113] 3 ERISA Leg. Hist. 4750 (statement of Sen. Javits).

[114] *Cook v. Pension Plan for Salaried Employees of Cyclops Corp.*, C.A. C-1-82-615 (S.D. Ohio, Oct. 5, 1984), *rev'd*, 801 F.2d 865, 7 EBC 2278 (6th Cir. 1986).

[115] 557 F.Supp. 382, 4 EBC 1304, at 1310–11, *on remand from*, 681 F.2d 1053, 3 EBC 2178 (5th Cir. 1982).

the policies behind use of the arbitrary and capricious standard under ERISA:

> "This Court realizes that the limited security of this standard [for participants] discourages challenges to a denial of benefits, thereby, as a practical matter, preventing a further escalation in the number of complaints filed in federal courts. However, the Court questions whether those circuits which have adopted this standard of review have carefully considered its continued use. The District of Columbia Circuit developed the standard in a series of cases which evaluated individual's claims to benefits under pension trusts administered by the United Mine Workers in the early 1960's. Given the Congressional findings of inadequacy in the administration and understanding by participants of plans in the pre-ERISA era, . . . this Court must question the wisdom of the continued use of the arbitrary and capricious standard to review interpretations of pension plans qualified under ERISA when the statute expressly indicates a Congressional intent to provide safeguards in the administration of plans, standards of conduct for fiduciaries (including plan administrators), and ready access to federal courts."[116]

3. Refinements of the Arbitrary and Capricious Standard

The arbitrary and capricious standard under ERISA is steadily being refined away from the wooden application indicated in the general articulation of the standard. In *Dennard v. Richards Group, Inc.*, the Fifth Circuit expressly refined the standard in a manner that brings it much closer to contract analysis. Rather than separating Section 502(a)(1)(B)'s action to enforce the terms of the plan from review for a breach of fiduciary duty, the *Dennard* court continued to merge the two inquiries, but held that in applying the ERISA arbitrary and capricious standard, the proper approach is to first determine the " 'legally' correct meaning of the plan provision in question," using a "fair reading" of the provision that is internally consistent with the plan's other provisions, and only then to weigh this interpretation, if it is different, against the plan administrator's or trustee's interpretation, examining:

- "Plain meaning";
- The "internal consistency of [the] plan under the interpretation given by the administrators or trustees";
- The "uniformity" of the trustee's construction, i.e., whether the same interpretation has been made in the past, but without making "being consistently wrong" a virtue;
- "[A]ny relevant regulations or rulingsformulated by the appropriate administrative agencies [i.e.,] the IRS or Department of Labor";
- The extent of any unanticipated costs that would arise if the administrator's or trustee's interpretation is not followed; and

---

[116] 604 F.Supp. 987, at 1001 n.11 (S.D. Ohio 1985) (citations omitted).

- The "factual background of the determination by the plan and inferences of lack of good faith if any" on the trustee's part in making the determination.[117]

As demonstrated in the cases below, the Fifth Circuit did not create the *Dennard* factors. Rather, *Dennard* articulated criteria that have been widely accepted in pension cases before and after ERISA. Disagreement with the factors articulated in *Dennard* has been minimal. For example, in *Carr v. Hotel & Restaurant Pension Fund*, a district court in the Third Circuit stated:

> "Factors relevant to whether trustees of a pension plan acted arbitrarily and capriciously include: 1) uniformity of construction of the plan; 2) interpretation of the plan contrary to its terms; 3) fair interpretation and the reasonableness of the interpretation; and 4) unanticipated costs."[118]

In *Donovan v. Carlough*, the U.S. District Court for the District of Columbia Circuit accepted the validity of the *Dennard* factors, but emphasized that they are just factors, and that no one is necessarily dispositive.[119] In *Miles v. New York Teamsters Pension Fund*, the Second Circuit questioned a district court's use of the approach described in *Dennard* of first, and separately, finding the "legally correct" interpretation of a plan, but did not question the basic validity of the factors.[120]

Dennard can thus provide a useful checklist in considering whether an interpretation is arbitrary and capricious. In the discussion that follows, the *Dennard* factors are supplemented with additional factors that have proven equally critical in other decisions under the ERISA and pre-ERISA arbitrary and capricious standard.

a. Plain meaning, and conditions and exceptions not stated in a plan. A plan interpretation is arbitrary and capricious when it is inconsistent with the "plain meaning" of the plan. In *Cook v. Pension Plan for Salaried Employees of Cyclops*, a district court within the Sixth Circuit explained:

> "Few terms and conditions of employment are as important to employees as are pension rights. Long term financial decisions are made by workers on the basis of what they know or expect their postretirement income to be. With such monumental decisions being based on pension plans, it is imperative that the plans be interpreted in a manner which is consistent with their plain language. Otherwise financial planning would be reduced

---

[117] 681 F.2d 306, 3 EBC 1769, at 1775-76 and 1779-80 (5th Cir. 1982).

[118] 585 F.Supp. 949, 5 EBC 2051, at 2055 (E.D. Pa. 1984). Accord *Chicago Dist. Council of Carpenters Pension Fund v. Exhibition Contractors Co.*, 618 F.Supp. 234 (N.D. Ill. 1985).

[119] 576 F.Supp. 245, 5 EBC 1400 (D.D.C. 1983).

[120] 698 F.2d 593, 4 EBC 2160 (2d Cir. 1983), *cert. denied*, 464 U.S. 829 (1983). Although *Dennard*'s first step of independently determining a fair reading of the plan is not widely followed, it is discussed in sec. III.A.3.f.

Other courts, without questioning factors such as those in *Dennard*, continue to describe the arbitrary and capricious standard on a general basis as a standard that does not require the trustees' interpretation to be *more* reasonable than the plan participant's. See *Miles v. New York Teamsters Pension Fund, supra*, 4 EBC at 2167; *Bruder v. Pension Plan for Employees of Holscher-Wernig, Inc.*, 599 F.Supp. 347, at 349 (E.D.Mo. 1984); *Griffis v. Delta Family-Care Disability*, 723 F.2d 822, at 825 (11th Cir. 1984), *cert. denied*, 467 U.S. 1242 (1984).

to a best guess process. Therefore, an interpretation which is contrary to the plain wording of the plan must be considered arbitrary and capricious."[121]

The Second, Third, Fifth, and Eighth Circuits have likewise stated that an interpretation that is inconsistent with a plan's "plain words" is arbitrary and capricious, at least absent an extraordinary justification.[122]

Other circuits adopt essentially the same principle in holding that a plan interpretation is arbitrary and capricious when it imposes conditions not contained in a plan, or reads in exceptions to deny benefits that are not apparent from the literal plan provisions. In *Blau v. Del Monte Corp.*, the Ninth Circuit, which also decided *Rehmar v. Smith*, the classic "arbitrary and capricious" case, stated:

"With employee welfare plans, as with pension plans that are subject to the full panoply of ERISA requirements, imposition of a standard that is not contained in the terms of a plan amounts to an arbitrary and capricious decision."[123]

In so holding, *Blau* followed the Eighth Circuit's decision in *Morgan v. Mullins*, which held:

"Where the Trustees impose a standard not required by the pension plan itself, this court has stated that such action 'would result in an unwarranted and arbitrary construction of the Plan.' "[124]

In *Rhoton v. Central States Pension Fund*, the Sixth Circuit similarly examined whether a plan's terms "*preclude*[d]" a disability retiree from switching to receipt of early retirement benefits when he reached the early retirement age and otherwise had the required credited service. Finding that neither the plan nor the SPD supported the trustees' interpretation that such a switch was precluded, the court held that the

---

[121] C.A. No. C-1-82-615 (S.D. Ohio Oct. 5, 1984), *rev'd on other grounds*, 801 F.2d 865, 7 EBC 2278 (6th Cir. 1986) (Sixth Circuit concluded the language was ambiguous and susceptible to the plan's interpretation).

[122] *Miles v. New York Teamsters Pension Fund*, 698 F.2d 593, 4 EBC 2160, at 2165 (2d Cir. 1983), *cert. denied*, 464 U.S. 829 (1983); *Dennard v. Richards Group, Inc.*, 681 F.2d 306, 3 EBC 1769 (5th Cir. 1982); *Gaines v. Amalgamated Ins. Fund*, 753 F.2d 288 (3d Cir. 1985) (but the Third Circuit's "plain meaning" of being "eligible to receive" Social Security disability benefits within nine months of the last date of covered employment differed from the district court's); *Morgan v. Mullins*, 643 F.2d 1320, 2 EBC 1040, at 1043 (8th Cir. 1981) (inconsistency with "plain words" of the plan document); *Monson v. Century Mfg. Co.*, 739 F.2d 1293, 5 EBC 1625, at 1630 (8th Cir. 1984) (inconsistency with "common-sense reading" of the definition of profits in the plan). See also *Donovan v. Carlough*, 576 F.Supp. 245, 5 EBC 1400, at 1405 (D.D.C. 1983) (interpretation contrary to "literal meaning" of plan weighs heavily, although it is not necessarily dispositive).

[123] 748 F.2d 1348, 6 EBC 1264, at 1269 (9th Cir. 1984), *cert. denied*, 474 U.S. 865 (1985). In *Blau*, the additional standard the trustees attempted to impose under a severance pay plan was a requirement that participants must not only be severed from employment with the sponsoring employer, but also must not become employed by a company that has purchased the assets of a plant or division at which they worked. The Ninth Circuit emphasized that the plan referred to jobs "eliminated" by *Del Monte*, the sponsoring employer, and did not condition benefits on the heretofore "secret" second condition Del Monte urged. 6 EBC at 1270–71.

[124] 643 F.2d 1320, 2 EBC 1040, at 1041 (8th Cir. 1981), in turn quoting *Maness v. Williams*, 513 F.2d 1264, at 1267 (8th Cir. 1975). Accord *Miles v. New York Teamsters Pension Fund*, 698 F.2d 593, 4 EBC 2160, at 2165 (2d Cir. 1983), *cert. denied*, 464 U.S. 829 (1983).

trustees' "harsh" interpretation of the plan was arbitrary and capricious.[125] In *Swackard v. Commission House Drivers Local 400*, a plan rule was silent on whether the 15 years of service required for disability benefits had to be consecutive years, but the trustees interpreted the rule to require 15 years of consecutive service, thereby "effectively insert[ing] a new rule into the plan." The Sixth Circuit held that application of the new rule to a participant who already had 15 years of accumulated, but not consecutive, credited service was arbitrary and capricious because it "amount[ed] to a retroactive application of a [new] 'break in service' rule."[126] Along this same line, in *Reiherzer v. Shannon*, the Seventh Circuit found that employment as a corporate officer at the same time "an individual [was] doing classic teamster work, driving [a] truck, [was] not expressly *excluded* from [a plan's definition of] continuous employment," and therefore was required to be credited under the plan.[127] In *Snyder v. Titus*, a district court in the Fourth Circuit held that exceptions "not apparent on the face of the [current] plan" cannot be read in to deny benefits. In *Snyder*, a pre-ERISA break-in-service rule therefore could not be carried over by implication into a post-ERISA plan for application to an employee who had incurred a pre-ERISA break, but who did not retire until the more liberal post-ERISA rules went into effect.[128]

"Hidden power[s] to cancel express benefits," such as by broad interpretation of a plan's general amendment authority to permit an amendment cancelling previously granted past service credits on an employer's withdrawal from a multiemployer plan, are also not to be read as "subsume[d] in [a] detailed [written] Plan."[129]

b. Internal consistency under different interpretations. The internal consistency of a plan under a participant's versus a plan administrator's interpretations is a second factor in determining whether the administrator's interpretation is arbitrary and capricious. In *Morgan v. Mullins*, the Eighth Circuit emphasized that a requirement that a miner be employed after 1969 to receive credit for time receiving black lung benefits would be "superfluous" under a challenged trustee interpretation that would also have required employment after 1971 to receive the credit.[130] In deciding whether terminations of employment

---

[125] 717 F.2d 988, 4 EBC 2233, at 2234 and 2235 (6th Cir. 1983) (emphasis added).

[126] 647 F.2d 712, 2 EBC 1317, at 1318 (6th Cir. 1981), *cert. denied,* 454 U.S. 1033 (1981).

[127] 581 F.2d 1266, 1 EBC 1175, at 1181 (7th Cir. 1978) (emphasis added).

[128] 513 F.Supp. 926, 2 EBC 1269, at 1275 (E.D. Va. 1981). See also *Carr v. Hotel & Restaurant Pension Fund*, 585 F.Supp. 949, 5 EBC 2051 (E.D. Pa. 1984) (break-in-service rule not presumed to apply to a break occurring during a period of past service where express terms of break rule in plan apply only to interruptions in service *after* an employer begins contributions to a plan).

[129] *Winpisinger v. Aurora Corp.*, 456 F.Supp. 559, 1 EBC 2201, at 2209 (N.D. Ohio 1978).

[130] 643 F.2d 1320, 2 EBC 1040, at 1043 (8th Cir. 1981). See also *Dennard v. Richards Group, Inc.*, 681 F.2d 306, 3 EBC 1769, at 1778 (5th Cir. 1982) (other provisions of plan established that a "terminated" employee eligible to receive an annual allocation of the plan's earnings was not synonymous with a terminated employee who had already incurred a one-year break in service); *Miles v. New York Teamsters Pension Fund*, 698 F.2d 593, 4 EBC 2160 (2d Cir. 1983), *cert. denied*, 464 U.S. 829 (1983) (interpretations that render some provisions of a plan "superfluous" may be arbitrary and capricious).

due to a plant shutdown were for a reason "other than" a quit, discharge, or retirement, thereby requiring an additional year of credit for vesting and accruals under a plan's terms, a district court in *Cook v. Pension Plan for Salaried Employees of Cyclops* weighed a distinction in another part of the plan between a "discharge" and a "termination due to a plant shutdown." The court determined that a termination due to a plant shutdown was not within the plan's meaning of "discharge," as the plan administrator contended. However, on appeal, the Sixth Circuit reversed, holding that the plan had offered a reasonable explanation for how the inconsistency developed and that the plan's interpretation was still rational.[131]

The internal consistency of a plan under different interpretations can work against a participant's interpretation as well. In *Budwig v. Natelson's Inc. Profit Sharing Retirement,* a participant contended that he was entitled to an annual allocation of profit-sharing plan contributions when he was not employed but was still a "participant" in the plan on the allocation date based on having 1,000 or more hours of service in the plan year. The court held that this interpretation would make redundant other language in the plan providing that "[y]ou must be a participant on January 31 [the allocation date] *and* have worked at least one thousand (1,000) hours."[132]

c. Past practice. In *How Arbitration Works,* Frank and Edna Asper Elkouri emphasize that:

> "One of the most important standards used by arbitrators in the interpretation of ambiguous contract language is the custom or past practice of the parties."[133]

Past practice "need not be *absolutely* uniform" to carry interpretive weight; it may instead be a "consistent handling of repetitive or like situations."[134] However, mutuality, i.e., acceptance of, or acquiescence in, a past practice by both parties, must be present to establish past practice that carries significant weight in interpretation.[135]

Because of the mutuality requirement, past practice under nonbargained plans that is adverse to plan participants is rarely seen as having been acquiesced in by them. Without a union to represent all

---

[131] 801 F.2d 865, 7 EBC 2278 (6th Cir. 1986), *rev'g,* C.A. No. C-1-82-615 (S.D. Ohio Oct. 5, 1984).

[132] 576 F.Supp. 661, at 666 (D. Neb. 1982), *aff'd,* 720 F.2d 977 (8th Cir. 1983) (emphasis added).

[133] At 451 (BNA 1985 ed.). Similarly, Archibald Cox, Derek Bok, and Robert Gorman state:

> "Perhaps the most significant source of ... unwritten rules [under collective bargaining agreements] are the customs and usages—or past practices—which represent the accepted way that employees are treated . . . ."

Labor Law (Foundation Press 1973 ed.), at 623. The *Restatement of Contracts* likewise provides that "course of performance" carries "great weight" in contract interpretation. *Restatement (Second) of Contracts,* §202(4).

[134] Elkouri and Elkouri, *How Arbitration Works, supra,* at 453 (emphasis added).

[135] *Id.*, at 452.

participants, such acceptance or acquiescence would have to be demonstrated on an individual-by-individual basis. In *Blau v. Del Monte Corp.*, for example, a nonbargained severance pay plan had been consistently interpreted to deny severance benefits to employees when plants or divisions were sold and the new owners hired the former employees. The Ninth Circuit disregarded this unilateral past practice because "[i]mposition of conditions outside the plan amounts to arbitrary and capricious conduct in spite of how often it is practiced."[136] The consistency of a construction that is adverse to participants does, however, generally add some weight if other factors support a plan administrator's interpretation.[137]

Past practice under a nonbargained plan that is favorable to participants may, on the other hand, be dispositive. In *Associated Milk Producers v. Nelson*, a forfeiture of pension benefits based on dishonest conduct was impermissible when four other employees engaged in the same conduct—making political contributions in violation of federal election laws—without being similarly penalized.[138] In *Kann v. Keystone Resources, Inc. Profit Sharing Plan*, an employer raised a lack of formal corporate authorization for profit-sharing contributions made during the tenure of a prior corporate board as grounds for denying a distribution of a participant's benefits, but the court found this defect had been overlooked for other participants whose circumstances were "no different[] than Kann's."[139]

Inconsistencies in past plan interpretations can also demonstrate an interpretive malleability that undercuts a court's deference. In *Reiherzer v. Shannon*, a benefit denial was founded on classifying a period of the participant's work as in uncovered "self-employ[ment]." The Seventh Circuit held the interpretation was arbitrary and capricious when no specific plan language brought the participant, who was a corporate officer and shareholder as well as an employee during the period in question, into this status, and there was evidence that the trustees had blown "hot and cold" in the past on exactly how the term "self-employed" applied to employment with a corporation.[140]

---

[136] 748 F.2d 1348, 6 EBC 1264, at 1271 (9th Cir. 1984), *cert. denied*, 474 U.S. 865 (1985). See also *Dennard v. Richards Group, Inc.*, 681 F.2d 306, 3 EBC 1769, at 1779 (5th Cir. 1982) (unilateral past practice that is "consistently wrong" does not carry weight); *Snyder v. Titus*, 513 F.Supp. 926, 2 EBC 1269, at 1274 (E.D. Va. 1981) ("being consistently wrong can hardly be sanctioned as right").

[137] See, e.g., *Paris v. Wolf, Inc., Profit Sharing Plan*, 637 F.2d 357, 2 EBC 1244 (5th Cir. 1981), *cert. denied*, 454 U.S. 836 (1981); *Smith v. CMTA-IAM Pension Trust*, 654 F.2d 650, 2 EBC 1817 (9th Cir. 1981); *Bayles v. Central States Pension Fund*, 602 F.2d 97, 1 EBC 1416 (5th Cir. 1979).

[138] 624 S.W.2d 920 (Tex. Ct.App. 1981).

[139] 575 F.Supp. 1084, 5 EBC 1233, at 1242 (W.D. Pa. 1983). See also *Wilken v. AT&T Technologies, Inc.*, 632 F.Supp. 772 (E.D. Mo. 1984) (offset of workmen's compensation benefits under disability benefit plan language authorizing offset of benefits of the "same general character" not permissible when employer's nationwide practice under same plan was not to make such offsets, with exception to practice only recently imposed in Missouri).

[140] 581 F.2d 1266, 1 EBC 1175, at 1182 (7th Cir. 1978). In *Blau v. Del Monte Corp.*, 748 F.2d 1348, 6 EBC 1264 (9th Cir. 1984), *cert. denied*, 474 U.S. 865 (1985), the Ninth Circuit considered a statement by Del Monte's counsel that a severance pay plan could have been interpreted differently if the participant in question had been the president of Del Monte. The Ninth Circuit said it

The use of related discretionary authority under a plan to get select employees around certain requirements, while maintaining a harsh general interpretation, is another form of past practice that may be prevalent in nonbargained plans, and sometimes, in collectively bargained plans. In *Hardy v. H.K. Porter Co.*, some employees who were just short of a service until age 60 requirement for early retirement benefits were granted extended leaves of absence "solely" for the purpose of qualifying them for the benefits. The court held that the past exercise of this discretion dispensed with the service until age 60 condition for all other participants in the plan.[141] Although not cited by the court, this is in accord with the contract rule that:

> "Where it is unreasonable to interpret the contract in accordance with the course of performance, the conduct of the parties may be evidence of an agreed modification or of a waiver by one party."[142]

Past practice is likely to be most extensive, as well as better documented, under collectively bargained plans. In one labor arbitration, 28 years of past practice in extending the benefits of newly signed agreements to employees laid-off within the two-year period before the effective dates of new agreements required a new early retirement pension available on a plant shutdown to be extended to employees whose plants had already closed before the date of the agreement.[143] The practice of continuing health benefit coverage for retirees during strikes has also been used in interpreting whether retiree health coverage is only for the duration of the active workers' collective bargaining agreement or is for life.[144]

d. Relevant administrative agency regulations and rulings. In *Dennard v. Richards Group, Inc.*, the Fifth Circuit stated that it considers "any relevant regulations [and rulings] formulated by the appropriate administrative agencies [i.e.,] the IRS and Department of Labor" in determining whether a plan interpretation is arbitrary and capricious.[145] Of course, if a regulation or ruling applies directly to an issue, the question is not interpretation of the plan, but rather is compliance

---

could not countenance "secret" distinctions that could be so malleable as to produce "such widely disparate results." 6 EBC at 1271.

[141] 417 F.Supp. 1175, at 1184 (E.D. Pa. 1976), *aff'd in part, rev'd in part,* 562 F.2d 42 (3d Cir. 1977). In *Hardy*, the plan specifically provided that exercises of discretion were to be applied uniformly to all participants in substantially identical situations. Such a provision puts in contract form the basic fiduciary duty with respect to exercises of discretion under a plan. See, e.g., *Morse v. Stanley*, 732 F.2d 1139, 5 EBC 1602 (2d Cir. 1984). See also Rev. Rul. 81-106 (uniformity in exercises of discretion required by "definite determinability" requirement of the Code).

[142] *Restatement (Second) of Contracts,* §202, comment (g).

[143] *Arbitration Between Coordinating Committee Steel Companies and United Steelworkers of America,* 78-1 ARB (CCH) ¶8216 (Aaron, 1978).

[144] See *UAW v. Cadillac Malleable Iron Co.*, 3 EBC 1369 (W.D. Mich. 1982), *aff'd,* 728 F.2d 807, 5 EBC 1283 (6th Cir. 1984); *Bower v. Bunker Hill Co.*, 725 F.2d 1221, 5 EBC 1180 (9th Cir. 1984); *Food & Commercial Workers Local 150A v. Dubuque Packing Co.*, 756 F.2d 66, 6 EBC 1391 (8th Cir. 1985). A practice of continuing retiree health benefits after a plan provision specifically offering the benefits had been deleted, for unexplained reasons, has also been considered in determining whether benefits are for life or the duration of the bargaining agreement. *Food & Commercial Workers Local 150A v. Dubuque Packing Co., supra.*

[145] 681 F.2d 306, 3 EBC 1769, at 1776 (5th Cir. 1982).

with the authorized regulation or ruling. Attaching weight to Department of Labor and IRS regulations and rulings is also unquestioned when a persuasive analogy is to be found in regulations or rulings promulgated to implement sections of Title I of ERISA. Where a few courts have differed with *Dennard* is when the regulation or ruling is issued by the IRS to implement a tax-qualification requirement that is *not* duplicated under Title I of ERISA. Such requirements are not numerous, but are largely confined to the Code requirements of nondiscrimination in favor of the prohibited group, nonforfeitability on a termination or a partial termination of a plan, and after TEFRA, the top-heavy plan requirements for faster vesting and minimum nonintegrated benefits.

In *Dennard*, the Fifth Circuit relied on two Revenue Rulings under the Code's nondiscrimination requirement in requiring a plan to continue adjusting profit-sharing accounts for investment gains or losses after a participant was no longer employed, unless and until the account balance was completely distributed.[146] In suits by participants to enforce "partial termination" provisions under plans (which Code Section 411(d)(3) requires to be included in all tax-qualified plans), courts, including the Second Circuit, have similarly used the IRS's regulations and rulings almost exclusively to determine the meaning of "partial termination."[147] Along the same line, when a plan provides that an employer may recoup assets remaining after a plan termination if they are due to "actuarial error," courts have used the IRS's tax regulations to interpret the meaning of "actuarial error" under the plan.[148]

Plan provisions providing that a plan is to be interpreted, whenever possible, to be a tax-qualified plan under the Internal Revenue Code establish a second ground for using tax regulations and rulings in interpretation. In *Crouch v. Mo-Kan Iron Workers Welfare Fund*, the Tenth Circuit followed such a plan provision in construing a plan's coverage provisions to include a local union's secretary, who the plan and the union contended was not covered. The Tenth Circuit found that under the trustees' and the union's interpretation the plan ran afoul of the Code Section 410(b) requirement of nondiscriminatory coverage because the plan would then cover only the local union's officers and one secretary in another office. The Tenth Circuit stated:

> "Because the pension plan states that it is to be construed to meet the requirements of ERISA [including tax-qualification requirements], and there are obvious and significant benefits to meeting those requirements,

---

[146] *Id.*

[147] See *Weil v. Terson Co. Retirement Plan Committee*, 750 F.2d 10, 5 EBC 2537 (2d Cir. 1984), and ch. 11, sec. I, for other cases.

[148] See *UAW v. Dyneer Corp.*, 747 F.2d 335, 5 EBC 2605 (6th Cir. 1984); *UAW District 65 v. Harper & Row Publishers, Inc.*, 576 F.Supp. 1468, 4 EBC 2586 (S.D.N.Y. 1983). See also *Van Orman v. American Ins. Co.*, 680 F.2d 301, 3 EBC 1653 (3d Cir. 1982); *Bryant v. Int'l Fruit Products Co.*, 604 F.Supp. 890, 6 EBC 1623 (S.D. Ohio 1985), *rev'd on other grounds*, 793 F.2d 118, 7 EBC 1688 (6th Cir. 1986).

we conclude that we must construe the plan as including [the] plaintiff as a participant."[149]

Some courts have been more reluctant to rely on tax regulations or rulings in plan interpretation. In *United Steelworkers v. Harris & Sons Steel Co.*, an employer sought to reduce its liability to the Pension Benefit Guaranty Corporation (PBGC) for unfunded guaranteed benefits on plan termination by arguing that a series of "partial terminations" had occurred before the termination, and before the PBGC's guarantee of benefits from terminated plans became effective. Therefore, the employer argued, the unfunded benefits of participants affected by those partial terminations had been effectively discarded beforehand and were not subject to the PBGC's guarantees. The Third Circuit held that the Title IV question of employer liability for guaranteed benefits on a plan termination was not controlled by whether partial terminations had occurred earlier under the IRS's regulations and rulings. The court went on to add that "in most instances tax principles [also] do not control the interpretation of the terms of a pension plan" because the "contract, not the tax code, is the primary document."[150] The statement that tax principles do not "control" does not foreclose the use of tax regulations and rulings in plan interpretation, but the Third Circuit went still further in a footnote to state that "tax provisions normally do not *bear* on contract interpretation," citing a line of cases decided based on pre-ERISA facts in support.[151]

Besides being dicta, the major distinction to be drawn concerning the *Harris & Sons* footnote, and the cases it cites in support, is that they were all based on pre-ERISA facts. Before ERISA, plans were only required to provide in the plan's terms that benefits would vest on the "termination" of a plan. The IRS had, however, extended the term "termination" by regulation to include vesting on a "partial termination." While the IRS's regulations were enforceable for tax-qualification purposes, for the purpose of plan interpretation, they could be seen as departing from the plain meaning of the plan's provisions. Thus, not following the regulations in plan interpretation may at that time have been reasonable. However, when ERISA was enacted, tax-qualified plans were required to be amended to provide in express terms that benefits vest on a "termination" *or* a "partial termination" of a plan. The post-ERISA cases have recognized Congress' intent in making this change, and have followed the IRS's regulations as their almost exclusive source in interpreting the term "partial termination."

---

[149] 740 F.2d 805, 5 EBC 1971, at 1975 (10th Cir. 1984). See also *Dennard v. Richards Group, Inc., supra,* 3 EBC at 1779; *Chambers v. Kaleidoscope, Inc. Profit Sharing Plan,* 650 F.Supp. 359, 7 EBC 2628 (N.D. Ga. 1986) (using tax regulations on when a defined contribution plan terminated when tax definition incorporated in plan's terms); *Korn v. Levine Bros. Iron Works Corp.,* 574 F.Supp. 836, 4 EBC 2533 (S.D.N.Y. 1983) (a plan "cannot have it one way for the IRS and another way for [the] court"; therefore, statements by an employer in its application for determination of tax-qualified status may be used to interpret "compensation" under the plan).

[150] 706 F.2d 1289, 4 EBC 1396, at 1405 (3d Cir. 1983).

[151] *Id.,* 4 EBC at 1405 n.25 (emphasis added).

In *Amato v. Western Union International, Inc.*, a district court followed the *Harris & Sons* footnote and refused to consider the IRS's regulations in interpreting whether a "partial termination" occurred from a plan amendment completely eliminating an unreduced early retirement benefit.[152] On appeal, the Second Circuit reversed, holding, as it had before in *Weil v. Terson Corp. Retirement Plan Committee,* that the IRS's regulations and rulings are to be accorded "great weight" in interpretation of a plan.[153]

A different kind of distinction has been drawn concerning the relative weight or deference to be attached to IRS Revenue Rulings, as opposed to IRS regulations.[154] In *Bencivenga v. Western Pennsylvania Teamsters Pension Fund,* the Third Circuit found that "unlike authorized regulations, Revenue Rulings, as interpretive actions, do not have the force of law." For this reason, the Third Circuit found it was not required to "accept the full breadth of the IRS's theory," expressed in Revenue Ruling 81-12, that *any* change in a discount factor for an early retirement benefit triggered the ERISA Section 204(g) protection against decreases in the amount of accrued benefits.[155] However, in *Amato,* the Second Circuit followed the same Ruling, finding that Revenue Rulings, as well as regulations, are to be given "great deference," or "great weight."[156]

While weight is normally attached to analogous regulations and Revenue Rulings, it must always be considered whether adherence to an IRS or Labor Department regulation or ruling that a plan can exceed may defeat the "reasonable understanding" of participants. For example, if a plan says that benefits of "similar kind" may be offset from retirement benefits, the IRS's regulations and rulings would clearly permit the offset to extend to workmen's compensation without violating the Code's nondiscrimination prohibition, but few participants may understand workmen's compensation benefits to be within the scope of the similar benefits that can be offset from their pension benefits.[157]

e. Labor-management, common law, and other federal law use of terms. How a term is used in labor-management relations can weigh in whether an interpretation is arbitrary and capricious. In *Baeten v. Van Ess,* permanently replaced strikers were held not to have "quit" employment for purposes of a nonbargained profit-sharing plan's vesting requirements based on a district court's examination of the definition of "employee" under Section 2(3) of the NLRA and the meaning of a

---

[152] 596 F.Supp. 621, 5 EBC 2718, at 2725 (S.D.N.Y. 1984).

[153] 773 F.2d 1402, 6 EBC 2226, at 2238 (2d Cir. 1985), quoting *Weil v. Terson Co. Retirement Plan Committee,* 750 F.2d 10, 5 EBC 2537, at 2540 (2d Cir. 1984). And see cases in ch. 11, sec. I.

[154] If accepted, this distinction could apply regardless of whether the Rulings relate to tax-qualification requirements or to ERISA Title I provisions.

[155] 763 F.2d 574, 6 EBC 1799, at 1805 (3d Cir. 1985), citing *Baker v. Otis Elevator Co.,* 609 F.2d 686, at 691-92 (3d Cir. 1979), as support.

[156] 6 EBC at 2235 and 2238.

[157] See below on the "reasonable understanding" of employees as a guide in plan interpretation.

"quit" in labor-management relations.[158] Similarly, in *Cook v. Pension Plan for Salaried Employees of Cyclops*, a plan administrator asserted that salaried employees, whose services had been terminated due to a plant shutdown, had been "discharged," and thus were not entitled to the additional year's credit for vesting provided on a layoff. But the court found that "discharge" was distinguished in another part of the plan from a "termination" due to a plant shutdown, and further emphasized that in the general sphere of labor-management relations, the term "discharge" is synonymous with a "discharge for cause." On appeal, however, the Sixth Circuit reversed, holding that "discharge" was susceptible to the plan's interpretation. The court did not discuss the term's use in labor-management relations.[159]

The meaning in labor-management relations of terms that are commonly used in plans, such as "layoff" and "discharge," may often be found in arbitration decisions. Because the presumption of arbitrability established by the *Steelworkers Trilogy* has largely kept such contractual questions out of the courts, arbitration decisions may, in fact, often be the only authoritative "dictionary" for such questions of usage.

Some employers argue that interpretations of a term under collectively bargained plans should not be used for a nonbargained plan because an arbitrator's or a court's review of a collectively bargained plan is based directly on the contract, whereas for a nonbargained plan, the standard of review is whether the plan administrator's interpretation is "arbitrary and capricious." However, it would cause confusion if such a distinction were recognized because nonbargained and collectively bargained plans so often replicate the same terms.[160] In *Telescope Folding Furniture Co.*, Arbitrator Archibald Cox, in applying a settled interpretation of vacation pay plans, stated that while "each labor contract must stand on its own feet":

---

[158] 474 F.Supp. 1324, 1 EBC 2046 (E.D. Wis. 1979). And see *Edwards v. Wilkes-Barre Publishing Co. Pension Trust*, 757 F.2d 52, 6 EBC 1395 (3d Cir. 1985), *cert. denied*, 474 U.S. 843 (1985) (same interpretation used by plan trustees to decrease amount of accrued benefits of permanently replaced strikers under a plan in which benefits were based on an average of "final pay").

[159] 801 F.2d 865, 7 EBC 2278 (6th Cir. 1986), *rev'g*, C.A. No. C-1-82-615 (S.D. Ohio Oct. 5, 1984).

[160] Companies with unionized hourly workers frequently pattern their salaried employees' pension plan after the union plan. See, e.g., *Bower v. Bunker Hill Corp.*, 725 F.2d 1221, 5 EBC 1180 (9th Cir. 1984) (although not covered by the union agreement, nonunion employees had always received identical benefits). Other examples of salaried plans patterned after either the United Steelworkers or United Auto Workers' plans appear in *Cook v. Pension Plan for Salaried Employees of Cyclops Corp., supra*; *McCoy v. Mesta Machine Co.*, 260 BNA Pens. Rep. D-1 (W.D. Pa. 1979); *Amato v. Western Union Int'l, Inc.*, 773 F.2d 1402, 6 EBC 2226 (2d Cir. 1985). Terms, phrases, and entire paragraphs appearing in collectively bargained plans can also appear in nonbargained plans simply because both types of plans are drafted by specialists working in the same field who are conforming both types of plans to the same ERISA minimum standards and tax-qualification requirements. This duplication is furthered by the IRS's publication of sample paragraphs that generally permit plans to comply with the ERISA minimum standards and tax-qualification requirements. See 12 BNA Pens. Rep. Spec. Supp. (April 29, 1985) (reprinting IRS sample paragraphs, updated for compliance with the 1984 Retirement Equity Act amendments).

"In the long run only confusion and misunderstanding would result if different interpretations were given to substantially the same words."[161]

Plans also generally contain overall construction provisions. For example, the U.S. Steel plan states that all plan rules "shall be construed and enforced according to the laws of the Commonwealth of Pennsylvania." Such provisions can support use of state common law constructions of terms. In *Richardson v. Central States Pension Fund*, a multiemployer plan used the term "self-employed" to describe employees who were not included in a plan's coverage, and specifically provided that the term was to be construed under Illinois common law. Given this, the Eighth Circuit examined the interpretive issue following specific Illinois common law cases and concluded that the trustees' decision to deny credits to the plaintiff because of self-employment, while arguably not "arbitrary and capricious" in isolation, was erroneous as a matter of Illinois common law.[162]

Without reference to a construction provision, in *Helms v. Monsanto Co.*, the Eleventh Circuit used state law cases and Social Security disability benefit decisions as guides to determine whether "total disability" under a plan meant inability to follow any occupation from which a participant could earn a reasonably substantial income, as the participant contended, or meant inability to follow any occupation from which the participant could receive *any* income whatever, as the plan contended. The court held in favor of the participant.[163]

f. General interpretive principles. Common law principles of interpreting plans (1) in favor of the employee and to avoid forfeiture, (2) according to the reasonable understanding of employees, and (3) in favor of the plan's retirement income purpose, applied before ERISA. These principles have also been adopted under ERISA, either expressly or indirectly through consideration of related statutory policies and requirements.

(i) Interpretation in favor of the employee and to avoid forfeiture. Before ERISA, and in cases since with pre-ERISA facts, employee benefit plans, except multiemployer plans, were usually interpreted "in favor of the employee" and "to avoid forfeiture." These principles applied under either a direct contractual standard of review or *within* the arbitrary and capricious standard.[164] The adoption of these principles is consistent with the interpretation at common law of insurance

---

[161] 49 LA 837, at 839 (Cox, 1967).

[162] 645 F.2d 660, 2 EBC 1477 (8th Cir. 1981). See also *Short v. Central States Pension Fund*, 729 F.2d 567, 5 EBC 2552 (8th Cir. 1984) (interpreting the identical term); *Reiherzer v. Shannon*, 581 F.2d 1266, 1 EBC 1175 (7th Cir. 1978).

[163] 728 F.2d 1416 (11th Cir. 1984). And see *Danti v. Lewis*, 312 F.2d 345 (D.C. Cir. 1962) (looking to state law on whether an employee could be "retired" and still receive workmen's compensation benefits and unemployment compensation to determine that a plan's interpretation that an employee had "retired" before May 28, 1946, was arbitrary and capricious). But compare *Brown v. Retirement Committee of Briggs & Stratton Retirement Plan*, 797 F.2d 521 (7th Cir. 1986) (state law cases defining disability under disability insurance contracts not required to be followed by pension plan administrator).

[164] See cases cited in sec. II.C.2.

contracts providing health and life insurance benefits and annuity benefits in favor of the insured and to avoid forfeiture—whether the benefits are provided under individual insurance contracts or under group insurance contracts issued to employers to provide employee benefits.[165] The basis for applying these principles to pensions and other employee benefits was described by the New Jersey Supreme Court in *Russell v. Princeton Laboratories, Inc.*:

> "It must be remembered that we are not dealing with a mere gratuity, to be bestowed upon such objects of the donor's bounty as the donor or his trustee may select. On the contrary, the trust indenture represents a hard-headed business device to attract and to hold employees. . . . When the employee renders service in response to the promise of the trust plan, he acquires a right no less contractual than if the plan were expressly bargained for. . . . The question, then, is whether the employee should suffer a forfeiture of something he has earned. Forfeiture being disfavored we should take any tenable view of the indenture to avoid it. Indeed, these plans are to be liberally construed in favor of the employee."[166]

In *Roxbury Carpet Co.*, Arbitrator Clyde Summers explained the same principles, with emphasis on the "common understanding" that arises under employee plans that require labor to be rendered before deferred benefits actually become due:

> "[W]hen a man has worked over a period of time to earn certain rights, [the common understanding is that] he ought not be deprived of those rights by events beyond his control in the absence of clear contractual language requiring that result. When an employer has received the full value of his employees' services, he ought to provide the full value of the expected benefits. . . . In the absence of a clearly expressed intent to the contrary, compensation for services rendered in industrial employment is not to depend on contingencies, . . . men do not labor for chances on a roulette wheel and employers do not expect to pay wages with lottery tickets. [C]ontracts of employment will be read as reflecting this common understanding."[167]

The only plans for which these interpretive principles have generally been rejected are multiemployer plans where an equal number of union representatives sit with management representatives as trustees in all

---

[165] See, e.g., *Matter of Erie Lackawanna Railway Co.*, 548 F.2d 621 (6th Cir. 1977) (construing group life insurance plan to avoid forfeiture); *McLaughlin Estate v. Conn. Gen. Life Ins. Co.*, 565 F.Supp. 434, 4 EBC 1879 (N.D. Cal. 1983) (interpreting group health insurance plan in favor of the employee). The insurance contract analogy was, however, expressly rejected as a basis for construing multiemployer plans in favor of employees. See *Rehmar v. Smith*, 555 F.2d 1362, 1 EBC 1799 (9th Cir. 1976); *Beam v. Int'l Org. of Masters, Mates & Pilots*, 511 F.2d 975 (2d Cir. 1975). It was also rejected by some courts when plaintiffs have argued that insurance contract principles are directly applicable to single-employer plans, but no "insurance contract [actually] existed" within the meaning of the state's insurance laws. See *Mirigliano v. Local 259, UAW*, 396 N.Y.S.2d 685 (Sup. Ct. 1977).

[166] 231 A.2d 800, at 803 (N.J. 1967).

[167] 73-2 ARB (CCH) ¶8521, at page 4938 (Summers, 1973). See also *Union Central Life Ins. Co. v. Hamilton Steel Prod., Inc.*, 448 F.2d 501, at 508 (7th Cir. 1971).

matters of plan interpretation, with an impartial arbitrator required to resolve any deadlocks.[168]

Under ERISA, courts have been reticent to adopt interpretive principles. But the principles of interpreting plans "in favor of the employee" and "to avoid forfeiture," are built into ERISA for application to all plans, including multiemployer plans, by virtue of ERISA's overall policies and particularly its disclosure requirements. Thus, since ERISA's 1974 enactment, only a minority of courts have expressly adopted the principles of interpreting plans "in favor of the employee" and "to avoid forfeiture" as interpretive principles under ERISA's common law.[169] But almost identical principles have developed under ERISA based on its overall policies and disclosure requirements—even though the courts have generally adopted the arbitrary and capricious standard of review. For example, in *Helms v. Monsanto Co.*, the Eleventh Circuit used the arbitrary and capricious standard in interpreting a plan, but it was guided by the policy that "Congress wanted to assure that those who participate in the plans actually receive the benefits they are entitled to and do not lose them as a result of unduly restrictive provisions."[170] In *Amato v. Western Union International, Inc.*, the Second Circuit similarly stated that ERISA's purpose is to prevent employers from " 'pulling the rug out from under' promised retirement benefits upon which [the employer's] employees had relied during their long years of service." The court further found that ERISA is "employee-oriented" and designed to assure "that when private parties set higher standards" contractually than are required under the minimum standards, "employees with long years of employment and contributions [will] realize [their] anticipated benefits."[171]

Forfeiture provisions continue to be strictly construed. Thus, death benefits and other ancillary benefits, which are not protected on a *per se* basis as vested accrued benefits, have been held not to be forfeitable under "bad boy" clauses unless the clause can pass a "rigorous reasonableness test" to overcome the participant's "reasonable expectations" that his beneficiaries would receive the benefits. In *Hollenbeck v. Falstaff Brewing Corp.*, a district court thus found that Falstaff's former chief executive officer had not been fired because of "some impropriety that would breach the business sensibilities of a hypothetical 'reasonable' businessman," but had "actually [been] fired over a difference in managerial style." This did not translate into a

---

168 See sec. II.C.2, and, for specific examples, *Rehmar v. Smith*, 555 F.2d 1362, 1 EBC 1799 (9th Cir. 1976), and *Gordon v. ILWU-PMA Benefit Funds*, 616 F.2d 433 (9th Cir. 1980). Although the general principles of interpreting plans in favor of the employee and to avoid forfeiture were rejected for multiemployer plans, many decisions narrowly construing forfeiture provisions involve multiemployer plans—before and after ERISA. See sec. III.A.3.g.

169 See *Baeten v. Van Ess*, 474 F.Supp. 1324, 1 EBC 2046 (E.D. Wis. 1979); *Terones v. Pacific States Steel Corp.*, 526 F.Supp. 1350 (N.D. Cal. 1981); *Landro v. Glendenning Motorways, Inc.*, 625 F.2d 1344 (8th Cir. 1980).

170 728 F.2d 1416, at 1420 (11th Cir. 1984).

171 773 F.2d 1402, 6 EBC 2226, at 2232 and 2233 (2d Cir. 1985).

discharge for "proper cause" that would permit a forfeiture of death benefits for his beneficiaries.[172]

Guidance by the ERISA policies in favor of the receipt of "anticipated benefits" and adequate disclosure of benefit conditions and exceptions is also widely illustrated by decisions which rely on plain meaning and which refuse to impose conditions or exceptions not stated in the written plan, and by decisions emphasizing the SPD's description of benefit requirements and circumstances that may result in ineligibility or loss of benefits.[173]

(*ii*) *The reasonable understanding of employees.* Interpreting a plan in light of the "reasonable understanding" of employees, or the "practical meaning" of the parties, reiterates in part the principles of interpreting plans "in favor of the employee" and "to avoid forfeiture." But "reasonable understanding" places a sharper focus on the disclosure of a plan's terms and on the understanding of the plan that employees have developed. Under this principle, terms that carry dual meanings may be interpreted according to an employee's reasonable understanding, rather than a second, uncommunicated technical meaning that the specialist who drafted the plan may have.

Pre-ERISA cases illustrate this principle. In *Brulotte v. Cormier Hosiery Mills, Inc.*, the issue was whether an employee's termination because the volume of work for him had declined was a "job elimination" under a plan that provided a shorter vesting period on a "job elimination" than for other types of employee terminations. The court looked at what an employee would have "reasonably understood" the term "job elimination" to mean and found no significant difference between a job being "eliminated" and an employee being terminated because of lack of work for him.[174] In *Keding v. Barton*, the Iowa Supreme Court similarly looked at the "practical meaning" of the parties to determine whether the term "vested equitable interest" covered a right to an immediate distribution of a profit-sharing account balance on a termination of employment. Under the plan's terms, once a participant had a "vested equitable interest," his rights could not be altered by plan amendment. The court emphasized that a summary booklet said amendments would not affect any "existing rights." This showed that the "practical meaning" of the term was broad. Therefore, the employee's right to an immediate distribution on termination of employment was protected against amendment.[175] The contract law principle of construing contracts against the draftsman when the party drafting the agreement is more likely to know the "uncertainties of

---

[172] 605 F.Supp. 421, at 428 and 434–35 (E.D. Mo. 1984), *aff'd,* 780 F.2d 20 (8th Cir. 1985).

[173] See sec. III.A.3.a and sec. III.A.4.a.

[174] 387 A.2d 1162, at 1163 (N.H. 1978). Accord *Ruditys v. Wing,* 260 N.W.2d 794 (Wis. 1978) (interpreting vesting provision in profit-sharing plan contingent on lack of work in favor of the employee). See also *Weesner v. Elec. Power Board of Chattanooga,* 344 S.W.2d 766 (Tenn. Ct.App. 1961) (plan interpretation is not to defeat "reasonable expectations of receiving the promised reward").

[175] 154 N.W.2d 172, at 175 (Iowa 1967).

meaning" can also support interpretation according to the reasonable understanding of employees.[176] The *Restatement of Contracts* provides that when one party knows, or has reason to know, of a different meaning reasonably attached to a contract term by the other party, who does not know the first party's meaning, the promise or agreement is interpreted in accordance with the meaning attached by the second party.[177]

Another application of this principle to a common plan provision can be found in *Kowalczyk v. Flintkote Co.*, which concerned whether workmen's compensation benefits are benefits of "similar kind" to pension benefits for the purpose of offsetting them from pension benefits. Under IRS rulings, workmen's compensation benefits are considered of "similar kind" to pension benefits, and thus they can permissibly be offset without causing a plan to discriminate within the meaning of the Code.[178] But in the context of a particular plan, the issue is whether both parties understand benefits of "similar kind" to include workmen's compensation benefits. In *Kowalczyk*, the court rejected a plan participant's argument that receipt of workmen's compensation benefits in a lump sum should be treated any differently for purposes of such an offset if workmen's compensation benefits were included at all. But instead of rubber-stamping the plan administrator's decision that they were benefits of "similar kind," the court remanded for a hearing on the parties' intent concerning the term.[179]

Silence on a restrictive interpretation of an ambiguous plan provision until an employee reaches retirement and applies for benefits is a heavy factor in determining whether a restrictive plan interpretation is reasonable. In *Lowe v. Feldman*, an employee with over 29 years under a plan was denied benefits under a union-sponsored pension plan because of an interpretation that he was not "actively engaged" in the industry when he only regularly worked one day a week in the industry. The court stated that:

> "Having over . . . twenty-nine years accepted plaintiff's dues, in part turned over to the pension fund . . . all in silence [about the interpretation of the term], the union . . . is, in its present position of delinquency or indifference, estopped . . . from repudiating its contract after plaintiff . . . acted in good faith thereupon. . . . [T]he union falls within the axiom that 'he who has been silent when in conscience he ought to have spoken, shall be debarred from speaking when conscience [later] requires him to be silent.' "[180]

ERISA incorporates the reasonable understanding of employees

---

[176] *Restatement (Second) of Contracts*, §206, comment (a).

[177] *Restatement (Second) of Contracts*, §201(2)(a) and (b).

[178] See ch. 3, sec. IX.

[179] 405 N.Y.S.2d 852 (Sup.Ct. App.Div. 1978).

[180] 168 N.Y.S.2d 674, at 685 (Sup.Ct. 1957), *aff'd*, 174 N.Y.S.2d 949 (App.Div. 1958). See also *Carlsen v. Masters, Mates & Pilots Pension Plan*, 403 A.2d 880, at 884 (N.J. 1979) (duty to fully disclose "legal stance" on plan interpretation can preclude later assertion of rational, but previously undisclosed, position).

as an interpretive rule by virtue of its policies favoring receipt of "anticipated retirement benefits" and adequate disclosure to participants of all circumstances when they will not receive benefits.[181] These policies are implemented in the Section 402 requirement that a written plan specify the exact basis on which payments are to be made from the plan. As stated in the ERISA Conference Report:

> "A written plan is ... required in order that every employee may, on examining the plan document, determine *exactly* what his rights and obligations are under the plan."[182]

The post-ERISA decisions in the section above on not imposing conditions or exceptions not stated in the written plan to deny benefits can be seen as applications of the ERISA written plan requirements. For example, in *Blau v. Del Monte Corp.*, the Ninth Circuit stated that when a plan is subject to the "full panoply" of ERISA's requirements, imposition of a condition not stated in the written plan's terms constitutes an arbitrary and capricious benefit denial.[183] In *Hepler v. CBS, Inc.*, the Washington Court of Appeals held it to be arbitrary and capricious for a plan's trustees to construe "basic monthly earnings" as an artificial, low salary for a participant who was paid entirely on commission. If the trustees' interpretation were sustained, the court held, the plan would not be in compliance with the ERISA Section 402(b)(4) requirement that it specify the "basis on which payments are made . . . from the plan."[184]

A "fair reading" of a plan can be still another way of emphasizing the "reasonable understanding" of participants of the plan's terms. In *Dennard v. Richards Group, Inc.*, the Fifth Circuit first gave a "fair reading" to a plan provision requiring an allocation of a profit-sharing plan's earnings to accounts of "former Participants" until their account balances were distributed. That fair reading was then weighed against the plan administrator's interpretation, looking at the other factors described above. The Fifth Circuit thus determined that the provision for "former Participants," defined as all "terminated" employees, did not imply that a waiting period until the participant incurred a one-year break in service would be required before earnings began to be allocated to the account.[185] In *Bianco v. Teamsters Local 816 Pension Trust*, a district court gave a "fair reading" to a multiemployer plan's reciprocity provisions to overrule a plan interpretation

---

[181] See ERISA §§2(a) and (b).

[182] Conf. Rep., at 297, 3 ERISA Leg. Hist. 4564 (emphasis added).

[183] 748 F.2d 1348, 6 EBC 1264, at 1269 (9th Cir. 1984), *cert. denied*, 474 U.S. 865 (1985).

[184] 696 P.2d 596, 6 EBC 1426, at 1430 (Wash. Ct.App. 1985), *cert. denied*, 474 U.S. 946 (1985). Similarly, in *Reiherzer v. Shannon*, 581 F.2d 1266, 1 EBC 1175 (7th Cir. 1978), the Seventh Circuit found that an individual who was doing "classic teamster work," but who was also a corporate officer, was "not expressly excluded from the plan's definition of continuous employment." The written plan requirement under §302(c)(5) of the Labor Management Relations Act, which is less express than ERISA §§402(a)(1) and (b)(4), was a "strong indication" that an exception was not to be read in. 1 EBC at 1181.

[185] 681 F.2d 306, 3 EBC 1769 (5th Cir. 1982).

that parsed the plan's offer of reciprocal credit for service under "related plans." The plan had claimed that the same phrase referred to all plans under a national reciprocity agreement in one part of the plan, but only to those plans related under a narrower group of local reciprocity agreements for purposes of the disability benefit the participant was claiming.[186]

ERISA's policies in favor of adequate disclosure to participants and the receipt of anticipated benefits are also implemented in its Section 102 SPD requirements. Under Section 102, an SPD must understandably, accurately, and comprehensively describe the plan's benefit requirements, including all circumstances that "may result in disqualification, ineligibility, or denial, loss, forfeiture or suspension of any benefits that a participant might otherwise *reasonably expect* the plan to provide on the basis of the description of benefits."[187] Interpreting plans in accordance with the reasonable understanding of employees based on the disclosure in SPDs is extensively illustrated in the section below on the use of extrinsic evidence in plan interpretation.[188]

(iii) The plan's retirement income purpose. Before and after ERISA, interpretation of both single-employer and multiemployer plans is guided by the "fundamental purpose [of the plan], namely the provision of retirement income" to employees and their families.[189] For multiemployer plans, this purpose has often been stated still more strongly as to "insure that pension benefits are awarded to 'as many intended employees as is economically possible.' "[190] Use of the retirement income purpose as an interpretive guide parallels the *Restatement of Contracts* rule that "if the principal purpose of the parties is ascertainable, it is given great weight" in interpretation.[191] As an example, in *Hay v. South Central Bell Telephone Co.*, the Louisiana Supreme Court found that the purpose of a death benefits plan was to provide benefits after a participant's death to relatives by blood or marriage. Emphasizing this purpose, the court held that a denial of benefits to a surviving spouse because she was not "living with" the participant at the time of his death was arbitrary and capricious when they had been married for 26 years, had only separated for five months without filing any legal papers, and had reconciled before the participant's death (although the spouse had not physically moved back into

---

[186] 494 F.Supp. 206 (E.D.N.Y. 1980).

[187] 29 C.F.R. 2520.102-3(l) (emphasis added), and see ERISA §102(b). Emphasis on the "reasonable understanding" of employees is reinforced by the requirement that an SPD's description of the terms and conditions for benefits must be understandable to the "average" plan participant. This requires the elimination of "technical jargon" that may appear in the plan in favor of understandable terms or an understandable explanation in the SPD, or the use of clarifying examples or illustrations. See 29 C.F.R. 2520.102-2(a).

[188] See sec. III.A.4.a.

[189] *In re Washington Star Retirement Plan*, 4 EBC 2441, at 2442 (Gellhorn, 1983).

[190] *Elser v. IAM Nat'l Pension Fund*, 684 F.2d 648, 3 EBC 2155, at 2162 (9th Cir. 1982), *cert. denied*, 464 U.S. 813 (1983), quoting *Ponce v. Construction Laborers Pension Trust*, 628 F.2d 537, 2 EBC 1777 (9th Cir. 1980); *Gaydosh v. Lewis*, 410 F.2d 262 (D.C. Cir. 1969). See also *Struble v. New Jersey Brewery Employees' Welfare Fund*, 732 F.2d 325, 5 EBC 1676, at 1683 (3d Cir. 1984).

[191] *Restatement (Second) of Contracts*, §202(1).

the house).[192] Similarly, in *Morgan v. Mullins*, the trustees of the United Mine Workers' pension plan attempted to impose a standard restricting service credit for miners receiving black lung benefits that was not plainly required under the terms of the provision offering the credit. The Eighth Circuit found the interpretation would "frustrate the purpose [of the provision] to make fair provision for miners who have become incapacitated."[193]

A plan or plan provision's purpose can also work against an interpretation favorable to the employee. In *Sly v. P.R. Mallory Co.*, a severance pay plan was interpreted as "generally intended to tide an employee over while seeking a new job." This purpose was used in holding that severance pay was *not* due when a division of an employer was sold to another employer who hired all of the division's employees.[194]

g. Strict construction of forfeiture provisions. Any interpretation granting benefits is in a sense an interpretation "to avoid forfeiture." But forfeiture provisions that undercut age and service as the basic requirements for benefits and instead make benefits turn on narrower circumstances draw so much more scrutiny as to take them a step beyond the general interpretive principle. More specifically, plan rules are subject to particularly close scrutiny when they:

(1) Forfeit accrued or vested benefits because of *involuntary* breaks in service;[195]

(2) Forfeit vested benefits based on "bad boy" clauses or based on postseparation competition with the sponsoring employer (or in a multiemployer plan, based on work with noncontributing employers operating within the jurisdiction of the plan);[196]

(3) Forfeit previously granted past service credits because an employee's employer withdraws from a multiemployer plan;[197]

(4) Forfeit benefits to a surviving spouse after a participant's

---

[192] 6 EBC 2205 (La. 1985). See also *In re Washington Star Retirement Plan, supra* (analyzing whether "excess" assets are to revert to an employer after a plan's termination or be used to increase the participants' benefits in light of the plan's "retirement income" purpose).

[193] 643 F.2d 1320, 2 EBC 1040, at 1043 (8th Cir. 1981). See also *Shishido v. SIU-Pacific District-PMA Plan*, 587 F.Supp. 112, 5 EBC 1067, at 1073 (N.D. Cal. 1983) (plan provision enabling trustees to extend for "good cause" 30-year period during which 20 years of credited service had to be earned "manifest that the drafters of the Agreement contemplated that there could be extraordinary circumstances which would warrant extension of the period"; unconstitutional blacklist preventing participant from working in covered employment for 6-year period constituted such "good cause").

[194] 712 F.2d 1209, at 1211 (7th Cir. 1983). In *Blau v. Del Monte Corp.*, 748 F.2d 1348, 6 EBC 1264 (9th Cir. 1984), *cert. denied*, 474 U.S. 865 (1985), however, the Ninth Circuit distinguished narrow employer purposes, such as asserted in *Sly*, which are kept "secret," and are not necessarily shared by employees, and held under a very similar fact pattern that "unemployment" was not a condition for severance benefits.

[195] See ch. 5, sec. III.A.4.a, and ch. 4, sec. III.C.2.

[196] See ch. 5, sec. V.

[197] See ch. 4, sec. III.C.6.

death without an informed election by the participant that the benefits would not continue after death;[198] or

(5) Forfeit benefits of employees who have as much or more service as other employees, but lack a special characteristic, such as having their final year of service before retirement with a contributing employer.[199]

h. Deficiencies in procedural support for an interpretation. As a prerequisite to its deference, the arbitrary and capricious standard presumes that plan administrators or trustees interpret plans with exclusive loyalty to participants' interests following procedures designed to ensure reasoned decisionmaking, including consideration of alternative interpretations, disclosure previously provided participants, and past interpretations of the plan. Like an administrative agency, plan administrators or trustees must therefore derive support for the deference they seek for their interpretations by demonstrating that these basic procedures were followed. In *Struble v. New Jersey Brewery Employees' Welfare Fund*, the Third Circuit stated that to establish whether employer-appointed trustees acted prudently and loyally in voting for a plan interpretation that on its face served the employers' self-interest, the court would consider, *inter alia*:

> "[W]hether the [trustees] voted as they did on the instructions of the Employers; whether they took the time to investigate the merits of alternative courses of conduct; and whether they consulted with others, for example their attorneys."[200]

In *Maggard v. O'Connell*, the U.S. Court of Appeals for the District of Columbia Circuit similarly stated that judicial deference under the arbitrary and capricious standard must not slip into "inertia" and that the appearance of "danger signals," for example, of an "undue bias towards particular private interests" or evidence that the trustees have "not really taken a hard look at the salient problems," may result in more scrutiny of a decision, undertaken with a "stern hand and flinty eye."[201]

A lack of disclosure of plan provisions in a manner that foreshadows a plan interpretation can be considered a procedural shortcoming that modifies the application of the arbitrary and capricious standard. In *Blau v. Del Monte Corp.*, Del Monte failed to prepare a summary plan description for a severance pay plan, but nevertheless asked for deference to its interpretation of the plan under the arbitrary and capricious standard. The Ninth Circuit stated:

> "Despite its failure to assume any of ERISA's obligations, Del Monte urges upon us the deferential standard of review generally applicable to administrator's decisions under ERISA. . . . We do not decide that this is

---

[198] See ch. 6, sec. II.C.4.

[199] See ch. 8, sec. VIII.

[200] 732 F.2d 325, 5 EBC 1676, at 1684 (3d Cir. 1984).

[201] 671 F.2d 568, at 571 and 572 (D.C. Cir. 1982).

> the only applicable standard of review when ERISA's provisions have been flouted in such a wholesale and flagrant manner. We do, however, decide that [the trustee's decision in this case fails when judged by] even this deferential standard."[202]

In so holding, the court weighed the procedural violations under the arbitrary and capricious standard, stating:

> "Ordinarily, a claimant who suffers because of a fiduciary's failure to comply with ERISA's procedural requirements is entitled to no substantive remedy. . . .
>
> "[But w]hen procedural violations rise to the level that they have in this case, they alter the substantive relationship between employer and employee that disclosure, reporting and fiduciary duties sought to balance somewhat more equally. . . . [We therefore consider] continuing procedural violations in determining whether the decision to deny benefits in a particular case [is] arbitrary and capricious. We hold that the type of plan administration practiced by Del Monte is highly probative of whether the particular decision was infected by its having been made in conformity with the objectionable scheme."[203]

Not developing a "body of precedent" in administration of a plan can also weaken deference to an interpretation. In *Richardson v. Central States Pension Fund*, the Eighth Circuit stated that it was "troubled" that the trustees of the Central States Teamsters Pension Fund failed to state their reasons for benefit denials in writing and in sufficient detail for participants to be able to respond to them. The court stated that specific reasons were necessary not only for the particular participant, but also to build a "body of precedent" about the interpretation of a plan that will "ultimately bring about a form of consistency . . . in the [plan's] administration," and that will enable the courts and participants alike to police administration and the consistency of plan interpretations. According to the Eighth Circuit, this does not require "lengthy reasoned opinions," but it does require a brief statement of the facts and the "rationale."[204] In *Richardson*, the Eighth Circuit did not need to reach the issue of the remedy for this procedural violation because the court was able to find the trustees' interpretation erroneous as a matter of law, irrespective of the procedural shortcomings. But in *Short v. Central States Pension Fund*, the Eighth Circuit reiterated its emphasis on providing adequate rationales for benefit denials, and maintaining records of the rationales, to again impress on the same

---

[202] 748 F.2d 1348, 6 EBC 1264, at 1268 (9th Cir. 1984), *cert. denied*, 474 U.S. 865 (1985).

[203] 6 EBC at 1269. See also *Hancock v. Montgomery Ward Long Term Disability Plan*, 787 F.2d 1302, at 1308 (9th Cir. 1986) (substantive remedies are available under ERISA for procedural defects only when the defects cause a "substantive violation or themselves work[] a substantive harm," quoting *Ellenburg v. Brockway, Inc.*, 763 F.2d 1091 (9th Cir. 1985); *Hancock* plaintiff showed no prejudice from alleged inadequacy of letters from plan administrator explaining insufficiency of evidence plaintiff submitted on disability).

Under this standard, procedural support for the arbitrary and capricious standard may be weak if an SPD is prepared and distributed, but is as technical and ambiguous as the plan, e.g., because of repetition of the same phrasing, so that participants do not have the benefit of the *understandable* description that Congress intended as a substantive balance in plan administration.

[204] 645 F.2d 660, 2 EBC 1477, at 1480–81 (8th Cir. 1981).

plan the seriousness of its shortcomings in this regard—again without needing to reach the issue of an appropriate remedy.[205]

At the same time, in *Andersen v. CIBA-GEIGY, Inc.*, a procedural error in delegating administrative responsibilities for the interpretation of a plan from a committee named in the plan to an executive who was not named in the plan, in violation of ERISA Sections 402(a)(1) and (b)(2), did not weaken the support the Eleventh Circuit found for the arbitrary and capricious standard.[206]

i. Unanticipated costs from a different interpretation. The extent of unanticipated costs under contradictory plan interpretations is a less frequent interpretive factor in court decisions. In *Dennard v. Richards Group, Inc.*, the Fifth Circuit found that interest earned on assets in an individual's profit-sharing plan account after his termination of employment was not an "expense to the Plan," nor were "other participants entitled to the additional income." Hence, the trustees' interpretation that such earnings were not to be allocated to a terminated participant's account unless and until the participant incurred a one-year break in service could not find support in unanticipated costs to the plan.[207]

The anticipation of costs can also be weighed in interpretations affecting broad classes of participants. In *In re Washington Star Retirement Plan*, Arbitrator Walter Gellhorn analyzed whether employees or their employer were contractually to receive excess plan assets left after a plan's termination. Finding the plan document did not dictate the outcome, he resorted to the plan's purposes, and found that the plan "was structured not to produce the possibility of a monetary refund for the employer but to produce the assurance of retirement pay for the . . . employees." This "benefactory design," plus the "context of dealing" in which payments had been "costed out" and made to the fund only after exacting *quid pro quos* from the employees based on the anticipated costs, "strongly suggest[ed]"—in the absence of clear contrary expression—that any excess funds were to be dispersed in furtherance of the plan's retirement income purpose, rather than being returned to the employer.[208]

One difficulty with "unanticipated costs" as a factor in favor of a benefit denial is that in its crudest form "unanticipated costs" is a tautology. Once any benefit denial takes place, trustees can claim that the costs of later having to pay the benefit are unanticipated. But as a district court stated in *Donovan v. Carlough*:

"Every time the Trustees make a decision to deny benefit applications,

---

[205] 729 F.2d 567, 5 EBC 2553 (8th Cir. 1984). $100 per day penalties under ERISA §502(c) can provide a different type of substantive remedy for failure to respond to a participant's request for an explanation of a benefit denial. See ch. 14, sec. VII.

[206] 759 F.2d 1518, 6 EBC 1565 (11th Cir. 1985).

[207] 681 F.2d 306, 3 EBC 1769, at 1780 (5th Cir. 1982). See also *Rhoton v. Central States Pension Fund*, 717 F.2d 988, 4 EBC 2233 (6th Cir. 1983) (no evidence that costs of allowing disabled employee to switch from disability to early retirement benefits were unanticipated).

[208] 4 EBC 2441, at 2443-44 (Gellhorn, 1983).

they are preserving the Fund's financial resources [by the amount of the denial]. Were the Court to defer to this argument, Trustee denials of benefits could never be deemed arbitrary and capricious."[209]

A second difficulty in placing too much weight on unanticipated costs as a factor in favor of denials is that the extent to which costs are anticipated before an interpretation is made is largely in the control of one party, namely the plan's actuary—except to the extent that his or her actions are limited by ERISA's minimum funding requirements. Thus, if the anticipation of costs were dispositive, an actuary's views could silently defeat future interpretations of the plan. A third problem with anticipation of costs as a factor is that funding for pension benefits generally proceeds based on macro-level assumptions that are more general than the questions involved in benefit disputes, even though some individuals may be willing to testify to a greater degree of precision in retrospect than existed at the time the plan's funding requirements were determined.

j. The plan in effect at the time of retirement controls. A specific, but widely applicable, interpretive rule is that the plan in effect at the time of an employee's retirement application generally controls. For example, if a plan does not specifically carry over a pre-ERISA break-in-service rule into the post-ERISA plan, the pre-ERISA rule may not be applied to workers whose last service was before ERISA if their retirement applications are not filed until after the post-ERISA plan went into effect.[210] Similarly, when a plan rule is changed to restrict the conditions for benefits *after* a participant has filed his or her application for benefits, the rule in effect at the time of the application generally controls.[211]

---

[209] 576 F.Supp. 245, 5 EBC 1400, at 1405 (D.D.C. 1983), and see *Rhoton v. Central States Pension Fund, supra*, 4 EBC at 2236. But see *Bayles v. Central States Pension Fund*, 602 F.2d 97, 1 EBC 1416, at 1418 (5th Cir. 1979), for a case where this tautological argument carried weight. The actuary's testimony in *Bayles* was that it would cost the plan $750,000 more than it was currently paying if the benefits the trustees had denied were granted. This is not the same as whether costs were *anticipated* in funding the plan.

[210] *Snyder v. Titus*, 513 F.Supp. 926, 2 EBC 1269 (E.D. Va. 1981). And see *Budwig v. Natelson's, Inc. Profit Sharing Retirement*, 576 F.Supp. 661 (D. Neb. 1982), *aff'd*, 720 F.2d 977 (8th Cir. 1983); *Hicks v. Pacific Maritime Ass'n*, 567 F.2d 355 (9th Cir. 1978). But compare *Govoni v. Bricklayers Local No. 5 Pension Fund*, 732 F.2d 250, 5 EBC 1389 (1st Cir. 1984) (applying earlier break-in-service rule despite ambiguity in plan on whether it was carried over); *Kagarise v. Teamsters Pension Fund (Cumberland Md. Area)*, 661 F.2d 19, 2 EBC 2026 (3d Cir. 1981) (benefit levels at time of separation from service, rather than retirement, applied despite inconsistent extrinsic evidence on past interpretation of plan); *Tanzillo v. Teamsters Local 617*, 769 F.2d 140 (3d Cir. 1985) (plan expressly provided that provision in effect at the time of a break in service continued to apply to participants whose covered employment was broken); *Taylor v. Suburban Teamsters of N. Ill. Fringe Ben. Funds*, 613 F.Supp. 205 (N.D. Ill. 1985) (not applying plan in effect at time of application, which would have provided health benefits in retirement for the plaintiff, when consistent practice of applying plan in effect when employment ceased had been applied in interpreting plan; implicitly, court may have been holding that retirement is not as pivotal an event under a welfare plan as under a pension plan).

[211] See *Brug v. Carpenter's Pension Trust*, 669 F.2d 570, 3 EBC 1240 (9th Cir. 1982), *cert. denied*, 459 U.S. 861 (1982) (rescission of plan amendment covering clerical employees under a pension plan ineffective for participant who had already become disabled and applied for a disability pension, following *Danti v. Lewis*, 312 F.2d 345 (D.C. Cir. 1962), and *Kiser v. Huge*, 517 F.2d 1237 (D.C. Cir. 1974)). See also *Tilbert v. Eagle Lock Co.*, 165 A. 205 (Conn. 1933) (lack of notice of cancellation of death benefit prior to employee's death precluded denial of benefits to his survivor); *Schofield v. Zion's Co-op Mercantile Inst.*, 39 P.2d 342, at 347 (Utah 1934) (benefits

4. Extrinsic Evidence in Plan Interpretation

An employee benefit plan must be set out in a written document. But like all written documents, a number of ambiguous provisions can crop up when the plan is applied to individual facts. Like collective bargaining agreements, employee benefit plans are recognized as a "generalized code" for a "myriad of cases," which "by their very nature" may be ambiguous in a number of cases.[212] Plans are, moreover, to be treated as ambiguous so as to allow the introduction of extrinsic evidence on the meaning of plan terms more often than might be permitted with ordinary commercial contracts.[213] Thus, even when a plan provision appears unambiguous, extrinsic evidence is generally allowed to show a different meaning of the parties.[214]

The parol evidence rule does not preclude the introduction of extrinsic evidence on the meaning of a plan provision unless (1) the plan is completely integrated, (2) the plan provision is unambiguous, and (3) the extrinsic statement was made before the adoption of the written plan, or before the adoption of the particular plan provision.[215] The parol evidence rule does not apply at all when a statement, writing, or practice is made, or reiterated, *subsequent* to the adoption of the written document.[216] It also does not apply to usage or course of dealing (i.e., past practice) unless the prior usage or course of dealing is contradicted by the final plan terms, or final plan amendment, with no

---

may not be reduced after vesting). But compare *Geib v. New York Teamsters Pension Fund*, 758 F.2d 973, 6 EBC 1475 (3d Cir. 1985) (amendment suspending benefits for reemployed retirees could apply to persons who were already retired before amendment was adopted).

When a plan rule in effect at the time an employee retires is more restrictive than an earlier plan rule, whether the employee had a common law vested right in benefits under the preamendment provision, advance notice of the amendment, and whether benefits under the preamendment provision are statutorily protected as a part of the participant's accrued or vested benefits under ERISA must be considered. See ch. 9, secs. IV and V, ch. 4, sec. IV.B, and ch. 5, sec. IV. If a benefit improvement is pending at the time of a participant's retirement, employers or plan fiduciaries may also sometimes have a duty to disclose it to participants who could delay their retirements to take advantage of the amendment. See *Erion v. Timken Co.*, 368 N.E.2d 312 (Ohio Ct.App. 1976), and ch. 9, sec. V.

[212] *Brick Masons Pension Fund Trust v. F.K. Pullen Co.*, 4 EBC 1667, at 1668 (C.D. Cal. 1983) (quoting *United Steelworkers v. Warrior & Gulf Navigation Co.*, 363 U.S. 574 (1960), and *Pacific Northwest Bell Tel. Co. v. CWA*, 310 F.2d 244 (9th Cir. 1962)).

[213] *Id.*

[214] In *Mioni v. Bessemer Cement Co.*, 6 EBC 2677, at 2680 (W.D. Pa. 1985), a district court thus stated:
"[M]any courts are reluctant to hold words unambiguous without first examining the circumstances and facts in order to determine whether any variation of the words would be an impermissible rewriting of the contract."

[215] See *United Steelworkers v. North Bend Terminal Co.*, 752 F.2d 256, 6 EBC 1299 (6th Cir. 1985) (employer's obligation "to make contributions," while part of a final agreement, could be consistent with different interpretations and thus required a "look outside the contract" for interpretation); *Belland v. PBGC*, 4 EBC 1162 (D.D.C. 1983), *aff'd on other issues*, 726 F.2d 839, 5 EBC 1109 (D.C. Cir. 1984), *cert. denied*, 469 U.S. 880 (1984) (excluding parol evidence, but only when plan unambiguous and completely integrated, and alleged statements made before its adoption to individual employees, rather than to their collective bargaining representatives). And see *Restatement (Second) of Contracts*, §§214-215.

[216] Section 212, comment (c), of the *Restatement (Second) of Contracts* provides:
"Statements of a contracting party subsequent to the adoption of an integration are admissible against him to show his understanding of the meaning asserted by the other party."

reasonable possibility that it reveals a special meaning or adds a consistent term to an agreement that is not completely integrated.[217]

a. Summary plan descriptions. Summary plan descriptions, or SPD's, are the "key document in disputes over benefit entitlement."[218] As described in the preamble to the Department of Labor's final regulations on the SPD:

> "[T]he SPD is the basic document which informs a participant or beneficiary of the terms of his or her plan. It gives the participant . . . an understanding of how the plan works, what benefits it provides and how to get them. It also provides basic information for making decisions on things like changing jobs or retiring."[219]

The SPD is particularly crucial as it is the only description of the plan that most employees are likely to read and to have in their possession. This is because it is the only booklet that is required to be distributed to them. The plan itself is usually a longer, more legally phrased document. It must be kept available for inspection and copying in the plan administrator's offices; in some cases, it is contained at the back of the booklet with the SPD.

ERISA requires that the SPD accurately and comprehensively describe a plan's benefits and benefit requirements in a manner that is understandable to the average participant in the plan.[220] It also requires that the circumstances that may disqualify a participant from *any* benefits that he or she "might otherwise reasonably expect" on the basis of the description of benefits must be understandably described in the SPD—however hidden or jargon-laden they may be in the full plan document.[221] Because of these requirements, statements and omissions in an SPD frequently "illuminate the meaning and intent of the parties" under the plan.[222]

(*i*) *Statutory and regulatory requirements on the content of an SPD.* The importance Congress attached to the adequacy of disclosure in the SPD, including disclosure of negative circumstances, or drawbacks, in a plan's offer of benefits, cannot be overstated. The Senate Committee on Labor and Public Welfare and the House Education and Labor Committee both found that:

> "In almost every instance, participants lose their benefits not because of some violation of federal law, but rather because of the manner in which

---

[217] *Restatement (Second) of Contracts,* §§216 and 220.

[218] See, e.g., E. Miller and M. Dorenfeld, "ERISA: Adequate Summary Plan Descriptions," 14 Hous. L. Rev. 835, at 835 (1977).

[219] 42 Fed. Reg. 14266 (March 15, 1977) (preamble to final SPD regulations).

[220] ERISA §102(a)(1).

[221] 29 C.F.R. 2520.102-3(l), and see ERISA §102(b).

[222] *Anderson v. Alpha Portland Indus., Inc.*, 752 F.2d 1293, 6 EBC 1046, at 1051 (8th Cir. 1985) (*en banc*), *cert. denied,* 471 U.S. 1102 (1985).

the plan is executed with respect to its contractual requirements of vesting or funding. Courts strictly interpret the plan indenture and are reluctant to apply concepts of equitable relief or to disregard technical document wording."[223]

Senator Javits voiced Congress' concern with discrepancies between technical wording in plan documents and descriptions of benefits provided employees in summary booklets, stating:

> "Many workers are led to believe they are covered by a good pension plan because of nicely phrased booklets and other assurances handed them by their employers. When the time comes for the payoff, they learn that the cold legal phrasing in pension contracts says otherwise."[224]

Similarly, Representative John Erlenborn, the ranking minority member of the House Education and Labor Committee, firmly backed the SPD requirements, stating:

> "[I]f people ... have ... meaningful information ... I think some of the unwarranted expectations that gave rise to the horror stories that people were not getting what they anticipated will be a thing of the past, [people] anticipated getting [benefits] they never were entitled to because they honestly did not know what was in their pension plan; they did not honestly know what their rights would be."[225]

Both the House and Senate Labor committee reports thus determined:

> "Descriptions of plans furnished to employees should be presented in a manner that an average and reasonable worker participant can understand intelligently. It is grossly unfair to hold an employee accountable for acts which disqualify him from benefits, if he had no knowledge of these acts, or if these conditions were stated in a misleading or incomprehensible manner in plan booklets. Subcommittee findings were abundant in establishing that an average plan participant, even where he has been furnished an explanation of his plan's provisions, often cannot comprehend them because of the technicalities and complexities of the language used."[226]

The House and Senate Labor committees also stressed the need to increase the "scope and detail of information required to be disclosed":

> "Experience has ... demonstrated a need for a more particularized form of reporting so that the individual participant knows exactly where he stands with respect to the plan—what benefits he may be entitled to, what circumstances may preclude him from obtaining benefits, what procedures he must follow to obtain benefits, and who are the persons to whom the management and investment of his plan funds have been entrusted.... [T]he safeguarding effect of the fiduciary responsibility section will operate efficiently only if fiduciaries are aware that ... individual participants ... will be armed with enough information to enforce

---

[223] S. Rep. 93-127, at 5, 1 ERISA Leg. Hist. 591, and H.R. 93-533, at 5, 2 ERISA Leg. Hist. 2352.

[224] 3 ERISA Leg. Hist. 4750.

[225] 2 ERISA Leg. Hist. 3386-87.

[226] H.R. Rep. 93-533, at 8, 2 ERISA Leg. Hist. 2355, S. Rep. 93-127, at 11, 1 ERISA Leg. Hist. 597.

their own rights as well as the obligations owed by the fiduciary to the plan in general."[227]

In accord with the legislative history, Congress established adequate disclosure as one of ERISA's central policies,[228] and enacted the stringent summary plan description requirements in ERISA Section 102. The evils Congress intended these disclosure requirements to guard against were summarized by the Ninth Circuit in *Blau v. Del Monte Corp.* as "insecurity, lack of knowledge, and inability to police administration."[229]

• *Understandability*. As delineated in the Department of Labor's regulations, the Section 102(a) requirement that an SPD must "be calculated to be understood by the average participant" means that "technical jargon" and "the use of long, complex sentences" have to be limited or eliminated, or "clarifying examples and illustrations" and "clear cross references" used.[230] The Department's regulations further provide:

> "Any description of exceptions, limitations, reductions, and other restrictions on plan benefits shall not be minimized, rendered obscure, or otherwise made to appear unimportant."[231]

This requires that:

> "Such exceptions, limitations, reductions, or restrictions of plan benefits . . . be described in a manner not less prominent than the style, captions, printing type and prominence used to describe or summarize plan benefits. The advantages and disadvantages of the plan shall be presented without either exaggerating the benefits or minimizing the limitations. The description or summary of restrictive plan provisions need not be disclosed . . . in close conjunction with the description or summary of benefits, *provided that* adjacent to the benefit description the page on which the restrictions are described is noted."[232]

Even when a plan's fiduciaries could initially reasonably believe that a description of benefits in an SPD is adequate, if the description causes confusion among participants, e.g., as demonstrated by previous benefit claims, the fiduciaries may have a duty to clarify it through a summary of material modification, or other supplementary disclosure, rather than to continue to "disclose" the plan's meaning only through benefit denials. In short, to be in compliance with the understandability requirement in Section 102 and the regulations, an SPD must "not

---

[227] H.R. Rep. 93-533, at 11, 2 ERISA Leg. Hist. 2358, S. Rep. 93-127, at 27, 1 ERISA Leg. Hist. 613.

[228] ERISA §2(b). And see ERISA §2(a).

[229] 748 F.2d 1348, 6 EBC 1264, at 1271 (9th Cir. 1984), *cert. denied*, 474 U.S. 865 (1985).

[230] 29 C.F.R. 2520.102-2(a).

[231] 29 C.F.R. 2520.102-2(b).

[232] *Id.* (emphasis added).

have the effect of misleading, misinforming or failing to inform participants" about the plan's benefits.[233]

The duty of understandable disclosure can be illustrated by a pre-ERISA case in which an employer *voluntarily* undertook to disclose the plan's provisions in a summary booklet. In *Shea v. Teacher's Retirement System of the City of New York*, a participant who was dying selected a survivor's option that would provide her with a certain amount during her life but that would leave her estate with about $65,000 *less* than was available under another option with approximately the same lifetime benefits. The court found the employer's description of the survivor's options was inadequate. It held that having undertaken to supply the description, the employer had a duty to act carefully, with the bounds of its duty "enlarged by knowledge of [the booklet's] prospective use." The duty to describe the survivor's options was, therefore, so that any "member of the class for whom [the booklet] was intended could understand [the] privileges, restrictions and limitations."[234]

• *Comprehensiveness*. The second issue on compliance with the SPD requirements is whether an SPD is "sufficiently . . . comprehensive." Although "sufficiently comprehensive" seems to leave some room for omission, questions of comprehensiveness do not arise when a benefit requirement is one that must be described in the SPD under Section 102(b). Section 102(b) requires a description of *all* of the plan's provisions for nonforfeitable benefits. This is not limited to benefits which become nonforfeitable under ERISA's minimum standards, but includes any benefits that can become nonforfeitable under the terms of the plan, including early retirement benefits and so-called ancillary benefits, e.g., death and disability benefits.[235]

When a benefit is required to be described, circumstances that may result in ineligibility, loss, or denial of the benefit must be comprehensively described. The Labor Department's regulations emphasize that the SPD must "clearly identify[] circumstances which may result in disqualification, ineligibility, or denial, loss, forfeiture or suspension of any benefits that a participant or beneficiary *might otherwise reasonably expect* the plan to provide on the basis of the description of benefits."[236] The SPD regulations and past practice establish the extent that other nonbenefit provisions are required to be described in an

---

[233] 29 C.F.R. 2520.102-2(b), and *Corley v. Hecht Co.*, 530 F.Supp. 1155, 2 EBC 2397, at 2405 (D.D.C. 1982). See also 42 Fed. Reg. 14266 (March 15, 1977) (preamble to final SPD regulations: "[i]n short, the description of the plan must be fair and even-handed").

[234] 381 N.Y.S.2d 266, at 269 (App.Div. 1976), *app. dismissed*, see 387 N.Y.S.2d 837 (Ct.App. 1976).

[235] See DOL Advisory Opinion 85-05A (summary plan description must cover all vesting provisions under the plan to comply with the §102(b) requirement that it describe *all* "provisions providing for nonforfeitable benefits").

[236] 29 C.F.R. 2520.102-3(l) (emphasis added).

SPD.[237] But on the benefit offer itself, and its drawbacks, the intent of ERISA is comprehensiveness.[238] The only announced limit on an SPD's comprehensiveness in describing benefit provisions is when no "loss" of benefit value occurs from a lack of disclosure. Thus, a plan administrator's policy of denying discretionary lump sum options to participants who left for jobs in competition with the sponsoring employer was not required to be disclosed in an SPD when their benefits, increased by investment earnings, remained available to them at a later date.[239]

• *Accuracy.* When a summary plan description statement is "sufficiently accurate" is not addressed in the Department of Labor's regulations. Instead, the courts have been left as the arbiters of statutory compliance. Suffice it to say that no court has held that "sufficiently accurate" means less than "accurate."

(*ii*) *Judicial use of SPDs in plan interpretation.* Statements in summary plan descriptions were used in judicial review of plan interpretations before ERISA's more stringent statutory requirements for SPDs became effective. For example, in *Gould v. Continental Coffee Co.*, a federal district court used a summary booklet's description of a forfeiture for competition with the employer as the basis for limiting the forfeiture to "direct competition" that was "detrimental to the employer's interest," thus tracking the description of the forfeiture provision in the summary booklet.[240]

---

[237] See 29 C.F.R. 2520.102-3, and *Burud v. Acme Elec., Co.*, 591 F.Supp. 238, 5 EBC 1793 (D. Alas. 1984) (past practice established that plan amendment permitting increased investment in employer stock had to be disclosed).

[238] The comprehensiveness of the disclosure required in an SPD is also indicated by the use of ERISA disclosure as a substitute for securities law disclosure. In *Teamsters v. Daniel*, 439 U.S. 551, 1 EBC 1620 (1979), the Supreme Court stated:

"Whatever benefits employees might derive from the effect of the Securities Act are now provided in more definite form through ERISA."

1 EBC at 1628–29. The chief "benefit" the plaintiff in *Daniel* sought from the Securities Act was the protection of Rule 10b-5(b), which provides that in connection with the sale of any security, e.g., through a brochure or booklet:

"It shall be unlawful for any person, directly or indirectly, . . . [t]o make any untrue statement of material fact or to omit to state a material fact necessary in order to make the statements made, in light of the circumstances under which they were made, not misleading."

17 C.F.R. 240.10b-5(b).

[239] *Morse v. Stanley*, 732 F.2d 1139, 5 EBC 1602 (2d Cir. 1982). *Morse* was expressly limited to situations in which no loss of benefit value occurs in *Chambless v. Masters, Mates & Pilots Pension Plan*, 772 F.2d 1032, 6 EBC 2209 (2d Cir. 1985). See also *Hillis v. Waukesha Title Co.*, 576 F.Supp. 1103 (E.D. Wis. 1983) (non-compete policy required to be disclosed when profit-sharing benefits are forfeited for competition). In *Frary v. Shorr Paper Products, Inc.*, 494 F.Supp. 565, 2 EBC 2268 (N.D. Ill. 1980), a district court went farther than *Morse* and held that even if no loss in benefit value will occur, a circumstance that causes the loss of an actuarially equivalent lump sum option requires disclosure because:

"[B]asic notions of fairness dictate that *any* rule or policy of Plan administration be in a form which makes them knowable to the Plan's participants."

2 EBC at 2273 (emphasis added).

[240] 304 F.Supp. 1, at 3 (S.D.N.Y. 1969). See also *Gladden v. Pargas, Inc.*, 575 F.2d 1091, at 1094 (4th Cir. 1978) (offset from disability benefits of "other legislated or group wage benefit[s]" interpreted in light of description in employee booklet that the offset was of "Social Security

Since ERISA, the use of summary plan description statements and omissions in plan interpretation has increased. In *Anderson v. Alpha Portland Industries, Inc.*, a summary plan description stated that review of a benefit denial could be obtained either under a collectively bargained grievance and arbitration procedure *or* by filing a written complaint with the personnel department. This was used by the Eighth Circuit to interpret whether retirees were required to go to binding arbitration, or could proceed to court after filing and processing a claim with the personnel department.[241] In *Rhoton v. Central States Pension Fund*, the Sixth Circuit emphasized that "[n]o language" in a multiemployer plan's SPD "suggests that [a participant is] not at liberty to effect such a change" in holding that a participant was not precluded from switching from disability benefits to early retirement benefits upon reaching the plan's early retirement age with the years of service required for early retirement.[242]

In *Bower v. Bunker Hill Co.*, the Ninth Circuit reversed a district court because of its failure to consider statements in an SPD in determining the duration of health benefits for retirees. The SPD said health benefit eligibility was based on pension benefit eligibility, which was unquestionably for life, rather than for the duration of a collective bargaining agreement, and the SPD failed to specify that contract expiration was a "circumstance" which would result in discontinuance of benefits. The SPD also assured retirees that even on their death, their children and spouse would continue to be covered by health benefits. The Ninth Circuit said that these statements and omissions in the SPD suggested that an ambiguous provision in the plan itself may not have been intended to limit the duration of the retirees' health benefits to the duration of the collective bargaining agreement.[243] In *Eardman v. Bethlehem Steel Corp.*, the employer argued that the arbitrary and capricious standard should sustain its interpretation that it reserved authority to reduce retiree health benefits by instituting new employee premiums for continued coverage, increased deductibles, and new certification requirements for certain types of in-patient care. The district court held that the interpretation of the plan's amendment

---

benefits (primary), workmen's compensation or other legislated benefits" to which the employer made contributions); *Horn & Hardart Co. v. Ross*, 395 N.Y.S.2d 180, at 181 (Sup. Ct. App. Div. 1977) (power to terminate a plan short of full funding for $100 per month benefits limited because of promise of lifetime pensions in plan booklet with power to terminate plan short of full funding never "brought home" to plan participants); *Central Tool Co. v. IAM Nat'l Pension Fund*, 523 F.Supp. 812, 2 EBC 2019, at 2023 (D.D.C. 1981), *rev'd on other grounds*, 811 F.2d 651, 8 EBC 1268 (D.C. Cir. 1987) (restricting multiemployer plan provision cancelling past service credits on an employer's withdrawal from the plan because vested benefits are "generally understood" as not remaining subject to conditional divestment, with this understanding "buttressed by an examination of the plan's booklet" which did not "suggest[] the possibility of divestment by virtue of the [plan's] forfeiture provisions"); *Keding v. Barton*, 154 N.W.2d 172 (Iowa 1967) (using employee booklet to interpret whether a right to an immediate distribution of profit-sharing benefits on termination of employment was "vested" within the "practical meaning" of the parties against an amendment making such distributions discretionary).

241 752 F.2d 1293, 6 EBC 1046, at 1051 (8th Cir. 1985) (*en banc*), *cert. denied*, 471 U.S. 1102 (1985).

242 717 F.2d 988, 4 EBC 2233, at 2235 (6th Cir. 1983).

243 725 F.2d 1221, 5 EBC 1180 (9th Cir. 1984).

authority was arbitrary because it was not consistent with the "clearly explained" nonterminability of benefits after retirement as described in the SPD and in other oral and written statements by Bethlehem Steel's personnel representatives.[244] In *Musto v. American General Corp.*, a summary plan description statement that amendments or a termination of health benefits for retirees would be made "if necessary" was used to imply a requirement of "good faith and cause" into a reservation of "at-will" amendment authority in the plan itself.[245]

In *Latrobe Steel Co.*, an employer contended that eligibility for a special early retirement benefit available under the United Steelworkers' pension plan could be discontinued based on an employee's refusal to accept a recall *after* taking the early retirement. Since the plan itself was not clear, the arbitrator examined the SPD, and found that it did not describe a recall obligation after retirement. The arbitrator emphasized that the SPD must be used as a guide to interpretation since it was prepared by the Company, and under ERISA Section 102(b), is affirmatively required to describe the circumstances that may result in a "*loss of benefits*."[246] In *Blau v. Del Monte Corp.*, the Del Monte Corporation failed to prepare and distribute *any* SPD for a severance pay plan. Because the employer would have been required to describe the plan's benefit terms understandably and accurately and to set out all circumstances for loss or denial of the benefits in the SPD, the Ninth Circuit found the lack of an SPD "alter[ed] the very balance of knowledge and rights" which Congress had sought to "balance somewhat more equally" through disclosure. The lack of disclosure was therefore a factor which "weigh[ed] heavily" against Del Monte's imposition of a condition on the benefits that was not evident from the face of the plan.[247]

Statements in an SPD can also affect the standard to which a fiduciary is held in interpreting the plan. In *Hepler v. CBS, Inc.*, the Washington Court of Appeals noted a statement in an SPD that participants "have a right to expect fiduciaries—that is, the people who are responsible for the management of the . . . plan—to act . . . *in your best interest.*" While the court did not elaborate, it was obviously not in the participant's best interest to interpret the plan's definition of "compensation" as being limited to an imputed artificial salary base

---

[244] 607 F.Supp. 196, 5 EBC 1985, at 2001 n.25 (W.D.N.Y. 1984). And see *Hansen v. White Farm Equipment Co.*, 42 B.R. 1005, 5 EBC 2130 (N.D. Ohio 1984), *rev'd and remanded on other grounds,* 788 F.2d 1186, 7 EBC 1411 (6th Cir. 1986) (using booklets to help determine whether salaried employees' health and welfare benefits vested against amendment on retirement); *Mioni v. Bessemer Cement Co.*, 6 EBC 2677 (W.D. Pa. 1985) (using SPD promises of lifetime health insurance benefits in retirement with "no indication [in the SPD] that benefits would be terminated upon expiration" of the collective bargaining agreement to interpret employer's contractual obligation); *District 29, UMWA v. Royal Coal Co.*, 6 EBC 2117 (S.D. W.Va. 1985) ("[n]othing in . . . the Summary Plan Descriptions clearly discloses to plan beneficiaries that their entitlement to health benefits may be forfeited if their last signatory employer subsequently fails to become signatory to successor collective bargaining agreements").

[245] 615 F.Supp. 1483, 6 EBC 2071, at 2076 and 2087 (M.D. Tenn. 1985).

[246] 5 EBC 1277, at 1281 (Hannan, Arb., 1984) (emphasis in original).

[247] 748 F.2d 1348, 6 EBC 1264, at 1269 (9th Cir. 1984), *cert. denied*, 474 U.S. 865 (1985).

that was lower than the participant's actual compensation from sales commissions.[248]

The interpretive weight accorded statements and omissions in a summary plan description under ERISA is perhaps most dramatically illustrated by the fact that misleading statements, or nondisclosure of a condition or limitation, in an SPD can form the basis for estoppel—even when an underlying plan provision unambiguously requires a denial of benefits.[249]

Statements in an SPD can also be extrinsic evidence *against* an employee's interpretation of a plan. In *Struble v. New Jersey Brewery Employees' Welfare Fund*, the SPD was even clearer than the plan in providing that retirees' medical insurance benefits ended on the expiration of their former employer's contribution obligation to a multiemployer plan. The SPD stated that "[benefits for] you and your dependents will terminate if . . . your Employer ceases to contribute towards the insurance."[250] Similarly in *Sharron v. Amalgamated Insurance Agency Services, Inc.*, the Eleventh Circuit rejected a district court's interpretation of a plan based on an SPD when the district court focused on only one page in the SPD in finding that a denial of disability benefits could not be based on a break in service. Other parts of the SPD clearly showed that the plan's break-in-service rule applied to disability benefit entitlement as well as to retirement benefits under the plan. The Eleventh Circuit therefore reviewed the "pamphlet as a whole" to determine its interpretive effect.[251]

b. Use of other written and oral statements. Letters to participants, informational fliers and brochures, and other written and oral statements can also serve as extrinsic evidence in plan interpretation. In *Apponi v. Sunshine Biscuits, Inc.*, employees alleged their employer stated to union representatives in bargaining that an age 55 and 15 years of service early retirement pension would not be interpreted to require an employee to still be in service at age 55 to obtain the benefits. The Sixth Circuit stated:

> "If company representatives did make the statements they were alleged to have made during the labor negotiations, then the company . . . will simply be held to its word."[252]

The use of extrinsic evidence in plan interpretation is also illustrated by:

• Oral statements that past service with another company would

---

[248] 6 EBC 1426, at 1430 n.1 (Wash. Ct.App. 1985), *cert. denied*, 474 U.S. 946 (1985) (emphasis added).

[249] See ch. 8, sec. I.A.

[250] 732 F.2d 325, 5 EBC 1676, at 1680 (3d Cir. 1984).

[251] 704 F.2d 562, 4 EBC 2178, at 2182 (11th Cir. 1983). See also *Noell v. American Design, Inc., Profit Sharing Plan*, 764 F.2d 827, 6 EBC 1833 (11th Cir. 1985) (ambiguity in provisions for forfeiture of benefits vested above the ERISA minimum requirements resolved against participant when SPD explained the forfeiture provision clearly).

[252] 652 F.2d 643, 2 EBC 1534, at 1540 (6th Cir. 1981).

count "for all purposes connected with employment benefits"—used in interpreting "continuous service" under the plan of a company that had acquired another company with whom a participant had substantial past service;[253]

- A written statement in an employer's application for determination of tax-qualified status that benefits were based on "total compensation"—used in interpreting the scope of "monthly compensation" under a plan;[254]
- Written statements that employees were "laid off" for unemployment compensation purposes—used in interpreting whether the employees were "discharged" within the meaning of a plan;[255]
- Oral assurances to union officials of adequate funding for "full benefits" that would be "good as long as you live"—used in interpreting an employer's obligation to fund benefits on a "sound actuarial basis" to require the *maximum* deductible contributions allowed under the pre-ERISA Code;[256] and
- Oral assurances that changing from a plan with benefits provided under fully paid individual annuity contracts to a noninsured trusteed plan would have no effect on the security of retirees' pensions—used in interpreting an employer's contractual obligation to complete the funding of benefits after plan termination.[257]

Oral and written assurances to employees that health benefits will last throughout their retirement have also been extensively used in construing whether health benefits for retirees continue after the expiration of collective bargaining agreements covering active workers.[258] Similar representations to *salaried* employees in exit interviews, group meetings, and plant closing presentations have weighed in interpreting employers authority to amend salaried plans to reduce health benefits after an employee's retirement.[259]

Actions by employers or plan trustees can also function as the equivalent of oral or written statements. In *Luli v. Sun Products Corp.*, a plan required an employer's consent for a participant to obtain a "mutually satisfactory" early retirement benefit. The consent was interpreted to have been given when the employer closed the plant at

---

253 *Walker v. Western Southern Life Ins. Co.*, 391 So.2d 925, at 927 (La.App. 1980).

254 *Korn v. Levine Bros. Iron Works Corp.*, 574 F.Supp. 836, 4 EBC 2533, at 2536 (S.D.N.Y. 1983).

255 *Cook v. Pension Plan for Salaried Employees of Cyclops Corp.*, C.A. No. C-1-82-615 (S.D. Ohio Oct. 5, 1984). *Cook* was, however, reversed with no mention of these statements in the reversal as a factor in plan interpretation. See 801 F.2d 865, 7 EBC 2278 (6th Cir. 1986).

256 *IAM Lodge No. 1194 v. Sargent Indus.*, 522 F.2d 280, at 283 (6th Cir. 1975).

257 *Hoefel v. Atlas Tack Co.*, 581 F.2d 1 (1st Cir. 1978), *cert. denied,* 440 U.S. 913 (1979).

258 See *UAW v. Cadillac Malleable Iron Co.*, 3 EBC 1369 (W.D. Mich. 1982), *aff'd,* 728 F.2d 807, 5 EBC 1283 (6th Cir. 1984); *Bower v. Bunker Hill Corp.*, 725 F.2d 1221, 5 EBC 1180 (9th Cir. 1984); *Food & Commercial Workers Local 150A v. Dubuque Packing Co.*, 756 F.2d 66, 6 EBC 1391 (8th Cir. 1985); *Mioni v. Bessemer Cement Co.*, 6 EBC 2677 (W.D. Pa. 1985).

259 See *Eardman v. Bethlehem Steel Corp.,* 607 F.Supp. 196, 5 EBC 1985 (W.D.N.Y. 1984); *Musto v. American General Corp.*, 615 F.Supp. 1483, 6 EBC 2071 (M.D. Tenn. 1985).

which the participants worked since this demonstrated that it was satisfactory to the employer for the employees to retire.[260] In *Evans v. Mo-Kan Teamsters Pension Fund*, a district court weighed plan trustees' acceptance of contributions on an employee's behalf against the trustees' interpretation that the employee was not working "in the jurisdiction of the fund" during that period.[261]

c. Individual benefit statements. Extrinsic statements on the exact amount of a participant's benefits and the number of his or her years of service for benefit accruals and vesting can also be found in "individual benefit statements." Individual benefit statements are typically computer print-outs or fill-in-the blank forms distributed annually to participants with individual accrued benefits and years of service for vesting printed or marked in. Although often provided before ERISA, ERISA Section 105 specifically requires:

> "Each administrator of an employee benefit plan [to] furnish to any plan participant or beneficiary who so requests in writing, a statement indicating, on the basis of the latest available information—
> "(1) the total benefits accrued, and
> "(2) the nonforfeitable pension benefits, if any, which have accrued, or the earliest date on which benefits will become nonforfeitable."

In single-employer plans, a participant generally need not make the written request referred to in Section 105 because individual statements are automatically furnished to all participants annually. However, this does not diminish the importance Congress accorded to the accuracy of the statements made therein.[262]

Individual benefit statements on the amount of a participant's

---

[260] 398 N.E.2d 553 (Ohio 1979). But see *Fielding v. Int't Harvester Co.*, 815 F.2d 1254 (9th Cir. 1987) (*contra* reasoning of *Luli*).

[261] 519 F.Supp. 9 (W.D. Mo. 1980), *aff'd*, 655 F.2d 900 (8th Cir. 1981). See also *Sanchez v. Trustees of the Pension Plan*, 359 So.2d 1279 (La. 1979) (weighing acceptance of contributions for employees who were major shareholders in a corporation to determine whether the employees were covered under the discretionary authority the trustees had to cover nonhourly employees under a multiemployer plan); *Hodgins v. Central States Pension Fund*, 624 F.2d 760 (6th Cir. 1980) (plan's continued acceptance of contributions on an employee's behalf considered as evidence that his status had not changed to noncovered self-employment).

Continued payment of health benefits during strikes when no contract is in effect is another type of action that has been considered in determining whether the duration of health benefits for retirees is bounded by the duration of the collective bargaining agreements that initially created them, or is a "lifetime" benefit. See *Bower v. Bunker Hill Co.*, 725 F.2d 1221, 5 EBC 1180 (9th Cir. 1984); *UAW v. Cadillac Malleable Iron Co.*, 3 EBC 1369 (W.D. Mich. 1982), *aff'd*, 728 F.2d 807, 5 EBC 1283 (6th Cir. 1984); *Food & Commercial Workers Local 150A v. Dubuque Packing Co.*, 756 F.2d 66, 6 EBC 1391 (8th Cir. 1985); *Mioni v. Bessemer Cement Co.*, 6 EBC 2677 (W.D. Pa. 1985).

[262] In remarks congratulating Representative John Erlenborn on his contributions to ERISA, Representative John Dent stated:
"The gentleman from Illinois (Mr. Erlenborn) was a great advocate of what I think is one of the greatest reforms in the whole bill. The gentleman insisted from the very beginning that a complete and full disclosure of a pension participant's standing within that pension plan be made available, and that it should be written in such a way that an individual would understand exactly what his position was, what his entitlement was, and exactly where he stood at the moment of his inquiry."
3 ERISA Leg. Hist. 4665. See also *Barrowclough v. Kidder, Peabody & Co.*, 752 F.2d 923, 6 EBC 1170 (3d Cir. 1985) (stressing importance Congress attached to individual annual reports of accrued and vested rights).

ERISA §209 also requires statements of deferred vested benefits to be provided after any participant's separation from service.

benefits and his or her vested status have not often appeared as extrinsic evidence in employee benefit litigation. More ancillary information in individual statements has appeared, but has not carried great weight in interpretation. In *Lewis v. Fulton Federal Savings & Loan Pension Plan,* individual benefit statements included approximate lump sum values of benefits based on a six percent interest assumption. The court held the statements did not to bind the plan from changing the interest assumption for "actuarially equivalent" lump sums to 13 and 14 percent interest rates, with the result that participants received much lower lump sums than appeared on the face of the individual benefit statements.[263] In *Fogel v. Goodelman,* an individual benefit statement for a profit-sharing plan stated that the vested portion of the employee's account could be received "[i]n the event you terminate your employment." The plan actually provided that such a distribution was discretionary until age 60. The court held this was "merely an incomplete statement" which could not be used to interpret an unambiguous plan provision. The employee also had not shown reliance on the statement as required for estoppel.[264]

However, in *Musto v. American General Corp.,* individual benefit statements issued "[a]t least once yearly" "emphasized that ... employees would *not* be required to contribute for continued life and medical coverage after retirement." This statement was used to interpret whether the employer had reserved "at-will" authority to amend the retirees' benefits after their retirement to institute new employee contributions.[265]

5. *Exceptions to Arbitrary and Capricious Review*

Beyond the refinements of the arbitrary and capricious standard discussed above, four exceptions to review of plan interpretations under the arbitrary and capricious standard are recognized.

a. Issues of trustee authority and procedural requirements. Interpretations of rules or provisions by trustees or plan administrators that "govern their own position"[266] or "authority"[267] under a plan are subject to direct contractual review. Once it is determined that the trustees or plan administrator have acted within the scope of their authority and

---

[263] 4 EBC 2071 (N.D. Ga. 1983).

[264] 420 N.Y.S.2d 844 (Sup.Ct. 1979), *aff'd,* 424 N.Y.S.2d 522 (App.Div. 1980).

[265] 615 F.Supp. 1483, 6 EBC 2071, at 2074 (M.D. Tenn. 1985).

[266] *Harm v. Bay Area Pipe Trades Pension Fund,* 701 F.2d 1301, 4 EBC 1253, at 1255 n.3 (9th Cir. 1983), citing *Culinary & Serv. Employees Union v. Hawaii Employee Benefit Admin.,* 688 F.2d 1228 (9th Cir. 1980) (using contract interpretation, instead of arbitrary and capricious standard, to review plan rule on the appointment and removal of plan trustees).

[267] *Central Hardware Co. v. Central States Pension Fund,* 770 F.2d 106, 6 EBC 2525, at 2528 (8th Cir. 1985), *cert. denied,* 475 U.S. 1108 (1986), citing in support, *Central States Pension Fund v. Central Transport Inc.,* 698 F.2d 802, 3 EBC 2624 (6th Cir. 1983), *rev'd on other grounds,* 472 U.S. 559, 6 EBC 1665 (1985). See also *McDaniel v. Nat'l Shopmen Pension Fund,* 6 EBC 2700 (W.D. Wash. 1985) (whether cancellation of past service credits on employer's withdrawal from plan was outside the scope of trustees' authority under terms of plan is subject to direct contractual review).

according to the rules governing the exercise of their authority under the plan, review of their actions reverts to the arbitrary and capricious standard—unless another exception applies.[268]

This rule is sometimes followed without expressly designating it as an exception to arbitrary and capricious review. In *Birmingham v. SoGen-Swiss International Corp. Retirement Plan*, the Second Circuit took a strict, obviously contractual view of who had authority to make a plan interpretation when a new corporate board of directors, after a takeover, attempted to override an outgoing retirement committee's interpretation that no actuarial reduction was required in pension benefits unless the early retirement occurred *before* age 55. The new corporate board claimed that all retirement committee decisions were "subject to" its approval under the plan. But the Second Circuit held that this authority was "limited" as a matter of contract to cases "where the Retirement Committee plainly exceeded its authority or violated the terms of either the plan or ERISA." The new board's approval was therefore not required, with the result that the retirement committee's interpretation was the effective interpretation at the time of the plan's termination.[269]

b. Single-employer collective bargaining exception. A universally practiced, but often unstated, exception to the "arbitrary and capricious" standard is that it gives way to direct contractual review for collectively bargained single-employer plans. While the "arbitrary and capricious" standard is often phrased in broad terms, it has never been applied when trustees or a plan administrator do not first have broad interpretive authority under the terms of the plan. As a matter of practice, unions negotiating single-employer plans generally relinquish authority to administer the plan to the sponsoring employer, but almost never allow the employer-appointed plan administrator or trustee to have "conclusive," "binding," or "final" authority over interpretations of the plan's terms. Instead, the plan administrator or trustee renders an initial determination concerning a plan's terms, and when there is a dispute, the terms of the plan are subject to *de novo* interpretation by a neutral arbitrator under the collective bargaining agreement's grievance and arbitration procedure. When the grievance and arbitration procedure does not apply, or is not mandatory, for example, because the claimant is a retiree, the interpretive issue is reviewed in court either under Section 301 of the LMRA or Section 502(a)(1)(B) of ERISA as a *de novo* contractual issue. The standard of review under ERISA cannot be any lower than in review of a collective bargaining agreement under Section 301 of the LMRA because of a clear statement in the ERISA Conference Report that actions brought under ERISA Section 502(a)(1)(B) to enforce "the terms of the plan" are "to

---

[268] *Central Hardware Co. v. Central States Pension Fund, supra.*

[269] 718 F.2d 515, 4 EBC 2369, at 2375 (2d Cir. 1983).

be regarded in similar fashion to those brought under section 301 of the Labor-Management Relations Act."[270]

This exception to the arbitrary and capricious standard is extensively evidenced in decisions on whether health benefits for retirees under negotiated health and welfare plans are "lifetime" benefits, or whether they end with the expiration date of the active workers' collective bargaining agreement with the employer. In these decisions, interpretations by employer-appointed plan administrators have not been mentioned, much less deferred to under an "arbitrary and capricious" standard.[271] Pension cases also demonstrate this exception to arbitrary and capricious review. In *Tolbert v. Union Carbide Corp.*, the Fourth Circuit examined whether a participant was entitled to a disability pension when he fell off a roof while on layoff. The issue was resolved under Section 301 of the LMRA as one of the "unforeseeable contingencies" under collective bargaining agreements which was not excluded, and which was covered by the purpose of the disability benefit.[272]

Collectively bargained plans are not necessarily the only plans covered by this exception to arbitrary and capricious review. Any plan that does not provide a plan administrator or trustees with absolute or conclusive discretion over the interpretation of the plan may be subject to a stricter contractual standard of review.[273]

c. Insurance contracts. State common law decisions on the interpretation of insurance contracts have long favored the expectations of the insured in claims under auto, life, health, and annuity insurance contracts. In *McLaughlin Estate v. Connecticut Gen. Life Ins. Co.*, a

---

[270] Conf. Rep., at 327, 3 ERISA Leg. Hist. 4594.

[271] See *UAW v. Cadillac Malleable Iron Co.*, 3 EBC 1369 (W.D. Mich. 1982), *aff'd*, 728 F.2d 807, 5 EBC 1283 (6th Cir. 1984); *UAW v. Yard-Man, Inc.*, 716 F.2d 1476, 4 EBC 2108 (6th Cir. 1983), *cert. denied*, 465 U.S. 1007 (1984); *UAW v. Federal Forge, Inc.*, 583 F.Supp. 1350, 5 EBC 1573 (W.D. Mich. 1982); *UAW v. Roblin Indus., Inc.*, 561 F.Supp. 288, 4 EBC 1316 (W.D. Mich. 1983); *UAW v. New Castle Foundry, Inc.*, 4 EBC 2455 (S.D. Ind. 1983); *Bower v. Bunker Hill Co.*, 725 F.2d 1221, 5 EBC 1180 (9th Cir. 1984), *and on remand*, C.A. C-82-412-RJM (E.D. Wash. Feb. 4, 1986); *Mioni v. Bessemer Cement Co.*, 6 EBC 2677 (W.D. Pa. 1985); *Food & Commercial Workers Local 150A v. Dubuque Packing Co.*, 756 F.2d 66, 6 EBC 1391 (8th Cir. 1985); *Policy v. Powell Pressed Steel Co.*, 770 F.2d 609, 6 EBC 2249 (6th Cir. 1985).

[272] 495 F.2d 719, at 723 (4th Cir. 1974). See also *Apponi v. Sunshine Biscuits, Inc.*, 652 F.2d 643, 2 EBC 1534 (6th Cir. 1981); *Hoefel v. Atlas Tack Corp.*, 581 F.2d 1 (1st Cir. 1978); *Union Central Life Ins. Co. v. Hamilton Steel Prod., Inc.*, 448 F.2d 501 (7th Cir. 1971); *Luli v. Sun Products Corp.*, 398 N.E.2d 553 (Ohio 1979); *Siss v. U.S. Steel Corp.*, 339 N.E.2d 279 (Ill. App. 1975); *Terones v. Pacific States Steel Corp.*, 526 F.Supp. 1350 (N.D. Cal. 1981); *Murphy v. Heppenstall Co.*, 635 F.2d 233, 2 EBC 1891 (3d Cir. 1980), *cert. denied*, 454 U.S. 1142 (1982); *In re Alan Wood Steel Co.*, 4 B.C.D. 850, 1 EBC 2166 (Bankr. E.D. Pa. 1978); *UAW v. H.K. Porter Co.*, 1 EBC 1277 (E.D. Mich. 1976).

[273] In *Hepler v. CBS, Inc.*, 696 P.2d 596, 6 EBC 1426, at 1430 (Wash. Ct.App. 1985), *cert. denied*, 474 U.S. 946 (1985), the Washington Court of Appeals found a summary plan description that promised participants, "You have a right to expect fiduciaries—that is, the people who are responsible for the management of the . . . plan—to act . . . in your best interests." This is hardly compatible with a standard of review that permits fiduciaries to interpret the plan to deny benefits when an equally reasonable interpretation could grant benefits to the participants in whose best interests the plan is to be managed. The *Hepler* court retained the arbitrary and capricious standard, but found the fiduciary's interpretation arbitrary and capricious because the plan would have failed to comply with ERISA §402's requirement for an exact description of "the basis on which payments are made . . . from the plan" if the fiduciary's interpretation had been upheld.

federal district court, interpreting a group health insurance plan provided by Connecticut General for employees of Trans World Airways, cited the principle that:

> "If semantically permissible, an insurance contract will be given such interpretation as will fairly achieve its object of securing indemnity for the insured for the losses to which the insurance relates."[274]

While an insurer's interpretation may be subject to the "arbitrary and capricious" standard of review when challenged as an ERISA fiduciary violation, the interpretation of individual and group insurance policies remains subject to state common law rules for insurance contracts when challenged as such. This effectively provides an exception to arbitrary and capricious review. This exception continues to be available under ERISA because ERISA expressly saves from its sweeping federal preemption state insurance laws of general application. In *Lee v. Dayton Power & Light Co.*, a federal district court thus found that Ohio decisional law on the interpretation of insurance contracts remained applicable to an employee benefit plan that provided benefits through insurance contracts. The Ohio decisional law fell under the exception to preemption of state law for "any law of any state which regulates insurance," with "laws" defined to include court decisions, as well as statutes and regulations.[275]

The state insurance law alternative, or exception, is generally

---

[274] 565 F.Supp. 434, 4 EBC 1879, at 1883 (N.D. Cal. 1983) (quoting and citing earlier cases). And see, e.g., *Matter of Erie Lackawanna Railway Co.*, 548 F.2d 621 (6th Cir. 1977) (interpreting group life insurance contract to avoid forfeiture); *Union Central Life Ins. Co. v. Hamilton Steel Prod., Inc.*, 448 F.2d 501 (7th Cir. 1971) (construing group annuity insurance policy to avoid forfeiture); *Bush v. Metropolitan Life Ins. Co.*, 656 F.2d 231 (6th Cir. 1981) (construing group disability benefits policy); *Conn. Gen. Life Ins. Co. v. Craton*, 405 F.2d 41 (5th Cir. 1968) (construing group disability benefits policy); *Suddeth v. Piedmont Health Care Corp.*, 8 EBC 1406 (S.C. Ct.App. 1987) (principle that ambiguities in insurance contracts resolved against insurers applied to whether reconstructive breast surgery following a masectomy was cosmetic, and thus excluded from coverage; citing other cases following the same principle).

[275] 604 F.Supp. 987, at 994 n.3 (S.D. Ohio 1985). See *Presti v. Conn. Gen. Life Ins. Co.*, 605 F.Supp. 163 (N.D. Cal. 1985); *McLaughlin Estate v. Conn. Gen. Life Ins. Co., supra*, 4 EBC at 1884-90; *Trogner v. New York Life Ins. Co.*, 633 F.Supp. 503, at 509-10 (D.Md. 1986); *Eversole v. Metropolitan Life Ins. Co.*, 500 F.Supp. 1162, at 1166-70 (C.D. Cal. 1980); *Cate v. Blue Cross & Blue Shield*, 434 F.Supp. 1187, at 1190 (E.D. Tenn. 1977). And see generally *Metropolitan Life Ins. Co. v. Massachusetts*, 471 U.S. 724, 6 EBC 1545 (1985) (state insurance law mandating inclusion of mental health benefits in all group insurance policies not preempted by ERISA because of savings clause in ERISA §514(b)(2)(A)). But compare *Pilot Life Ins. Co. v. Dedeaux*, 481 U.S. ___, 8 EBC 1409 (1987) (state common law tort and contract remedies for bad faith denial of a claim for benefits under an insured employee benefit plan are not saved from ERISA preemption by express savings provision for state laws and decisions regulating insurance when (1) state law remedies for bad faith breaches of contract were not "specifically directed toward [the insurance] industry," (2) the state law "does not define the terms of the relationship between the insurer and insured," and (3) Congress "clearly" intended "that the federal remed[ies] displace" state law remedies).

Even if *Dedeaux* could somehow be read as preempting state law decisions on the *interpretation* of insurance contracts, the arbitrary and capricious standard would not necessarily supplant the state law decisions under ERISA's federal common law. The arbitrary and capricious standard is a trust law standard of review. But insurance contract plans are expressly exempted from the requirement that they be in trust form by ERISA §403. But compare R. Mandel, "Must Claims Denials Be Upheld Unless Arbitrary and Capricious—What Standard of Review Applies to Group Policies Issued to ERISA Plans?," 14 Forum 457, at 460 (Spring 1984) (article by assistant general counsel for Metropolitan Life Insurance Company arguing that arbitrary and capricious standard should supplant state decisional law on the interpretation of insurance contracts).

more important in the area of health, disability, and death benefit plans than pension plans because such benefits are more often provided through insurance contracts. However, some pension plans, particularly of small employers, continue to be group annuity or retirement income insurance contracts, or an aggregation of individual insurance contracts.[276]

d. Class interpretations. Class interpretations are interpretations of a plan in which the "gravamen of the complaint" is that the trustees have sacrificed the interests of plan participants in interpreting the plan in favor of the interests of the employer because of substantial cost savings for the employer under a restrictive interpretation. The fiction that forms the basis for the deference in the arbitrary and capricious standard—that a trustee is engaged in balancing twofold obligations to current and future claimants—may be tolerable when a participant's claim is a "personal claim" for benefits that is relatively insignificant to an employer's total funding obligations. In these instances, the costs to the employer from an interpretation granting a benefit may generally be outweighed by the adverse message a miserly interpretation will send to current personnel about how they will later be treated.

But as the class of participants affected by a plan interpretation grows, the fiction that a fiduciary is balancing current and future *claimants'* interests must finally give way to the reality that the interests are the class of claimants' versus the employer's. The employer-appointed plan administrator or trustee has the same difficulty maintaining loyalty to the participants' interests in these situations as when he or she is deciding whether to invest plan assets in the employer's securities under heavy pressure from the employer to do so. Another distinguishing characteristic of class interpretations is that the interpretation is often so broad that the administrator or trustee is effectively denying benefits to future as well as current claimants, thus undercutting the argument that the administrator or trustee is balancing current versus future claimants' interests.

In *Struble v. New Jersey Brewery Employees' Welfare Fund,* the Third Circuit held that the arbitrary and capricious standard must give way to a stricter standard of review when a claim for benefits passes from what can reasonably be considered a "personal claim" to one where the gravamen of the complaint is that interests of participants have been sacrificed in favor of the interests of nonbeneficiaries (e.g., generally, the employer's interest in a decrease in future contribution obligations, or in a potential reversion of plan assets). In *Struble,* the Third Circuit applied this stricter standard of review to the issue of whether a surplus of plan assets under a multiemployer health plan

---

[276] Group insurance contracts must, however, be distinguished from group deposit administration contracts with insurers that provide investment services, but do not themselves insure the plan's benefits. See *Powell v. Chesapeake & Potomac Tel. Co.,* 780 F.2d 419, 6 EBC 2754 (4th Cir. 1985), *cert. denied,* 476 U.S. ___ (1986).

should be applied to continue retiree health benefits after the expiration of the employers' contribution obligations to the plan, or should be refunded to the employers.[277] In *Eardman v. Bethlehem Steel Corp.*, a district court similarly distinguished the arbitrary and capricious standard as limited to "personal claims" for benefits, rather than a class-wide interpretation concerning whether amendments to over 18,000 retirees' health benefits were permissible under a plan's amendment authority. The employer's financial self-interest in curtailing the benefits, and thus in favor of an expansive interpretation of the amendment authority, was substantial.[278]

Other decisions have indirectly recognized a class interpretation distinction. Even in a decision generally considered unfavorable to participants' rights, an employer's authority to terminate health benefits for all retired salaried employees was examined with no mention of the arbitrary and capricious standard, or of other deference to the plan administrator's interpretation.[279] Similarly, in interpreting the term "partial termination" under plans, which by definition presents a class interpretation issue, courts have generally referred only to the IRS's rulings on the meaning of the term, and have not applied the arbitrary and capricious standard to the plan administrator's interpretation of the term.[280] The issue of whether an employer has an obligation under a plan to complete the funding of benefits after a plan's termination is likewise examined as a contractual matter, including under nonbargained plans.[281] Whether a nonbargained plan provides for a reversion of any excess plan assets to an employer on termination has also been resolved as a contractual issue, without reference to a plan administrator's interpretations.[282]

However, in *Edwards v. Wilkes-Barre Publishing Co. Pension Trust*, the Third Circuit, which earlier decided *Struble*, applied the arbitrary and capricious standard to a claim in which the complaint's gravamen was that a class of participants' interests were being sacrificed to an employer's. *Edwards* concerned a trustee interpretation that uncompensated time on strike should be credited as service under a plan that based benefits on an average of final pay. The result of the trustees' interpretation was that accrued benefits for participants who had gone out on strike and who had been permanently replaced would

---

[277] 732 F.2d 325, 5 EBC 1676, at 1683 (3d Cir. 1984).

[278] 607 F.Supp. 196, 5 EBC 1985, at 2001 n.25 (W.D.N.Y 1984).

[279] *Hansen v. White Farm Equipment Co.*, 788 F.2d 1186, 7 EBC 1411 (6th Cir. 1986), *rev'g and remanding,* 42 B.R. 1005, 5 EBC 2130 (N.D. Ohio 1984). See also *Musto v. American General Corp.*, 615 F.Supp. 1483, 6 EBC 2071 (M.D. Tenn. 1985); *Bower v. Bunker Hill Co.*, 725 F.2d 1221, 5 EBC 1180 (9th Cir. 1984) ("[a]lthough not covered by the union agreement, nonunion employees had always received benefits identical to those provided union members"; no suggestion that the determination of their rights should be under a lower, arbitrary and capricious standard).

[280] See cases at ch. 11, sec. I, except *Taylor v. Food Giant, Inc., Salaried Employees Pension Plan*, 6 EBC 1291 (N.D. Ga. 1984), which used the arbitrary and capricious standard.

[281] See *Matter of M&M Transp. Co.*, 3 B.R. 722, 2 EBC 2486 (S.D.N.Y. 1980).

[282] See *Pollock v. Castrovinci*, 476 F.Supp. 606, 1 EBC 2091, at 2098 (S.D.N.Y. 1979), *aff'd*, 622 F.2d 575 (2d Cir. 1980) ("stripped of its ERISA garb, this action presents only an issue of contract interpretation"), and cases cited in ch. 12, sec. IX.C.

be lower than they had *before* they left active work. Although the employer would be the beneficiary of this interpretation because of the lowering of accrued benefits, and hence, decreased future funding obligations, the Third Circuit stated that "between two reasonable interpretations," it is for the trustees [who were appointed by the employer] to choose." The court further stated that the trustees were under no obligation "to interpret the Plan in such a way as to benefit any particular group of beneficiaries to the detriment of others," and "[i]f trustees choose an interpretation that results in a greater amount of benefits to be paid to members of one group, the result is less money to pay the benefits of non-members." No mention was made of the *Struble* distinction (although *Struble* was cited), nor was any explanation offered for exactly how an interpretation in favor of the strikers would have been to the detriment of nonmembers, or how the nonmembers, rather than the employer, were going to benefit from the restrictive interpretation.[283]

Similarly, in *Jung v. FMC Corp.*, the Ninth Circuit expressly rejected the argument that *Struble* always requires a stricter standard when a class interpretation pits the interests of plan participants and an employer. The plan in *Jung* was an unfunded severance pay plan, with the issue being whether the employer had to pay severance benefits on the sale of a division to another company if the purchasing company reemployed all the division's employees. An interpretation in favor of the employees had a direct cost to the employer, and an interpretation against the employees would directly benefit the employer. The Ninth Circuit retained the arbitrary and capricious standard of review in spite of *Struble*, but it conceded that "less deference" should be provided under it when an employer-appointed plan administrator or trustee is balancing claimants' interests and the employer's interests, with "substantial outlays" for the employer from an interpretation in the claimants' favor.[284]

---

[283] 757 F.2d 52, 6 EBC 1395, at 1398 and 1399 (3d Cir. 1985), *cert. denied,* 474 U.S. 843 (1985). As discussed in ch. 4, sec. IV.A, the *Edwards* court overlooked the prohibition in ERISA §204(b)(1)(G) against ever reducing a participant's accrued benefits on account of an increase in credited service or age.

[284] 755 F.2d 708, 6 EBC 1485, at 1488 (9th Cir. 1985). See also *Dockray v. Phelps Dodge Corp.*, 801 F.2d 1149, 7 EBC 2327 (9th Cir. 1986) ("less deference" due employer-appointed plan administrator's interpretation denying early retirement benefits on ground that benefit only applied to employees forced by employer to leave work when "serious conflict" of interest and "divided loyalty" had been engendered by bitter strike, and plan administrator had contradictorily denied group health benefits on grounds that "no work [was] available" for the permanently replaced strikers; "less deference" means that district court should be "appreciably more critical" of the plan administrator's reasoning and "less willing to resolve all ambiguities" in the employer's favor); *Ahne v. Allis Chalmers Corp.*, 640 F.Supp. 912 (E.D. Wis. 1986) (but interpretation still not arbitrary and capricious even with less deference). Cf. *Adams v. Gen. Tire & Rubber Co. Supplemental Unemployment Ben. Plan,* 794 F.2d 164 (4th Cir. 1986) (employer-appointed fiduciary had duty after expiration of collective bargaining agreement to act "solely in the interest" of employees already on layoff and entitled to supplemental unemployment benefits under plan terms).

The *Restatement of Trusts* basically makes the same point as *Jung* and *Dockray*, stating that in determining whether a fiduciary has abused discretion, "the existence or nonexistence of an interest in the trustees conflicting with that of the beneficiaries" is a relevant circumstance. *Restatement (Second) of Trusts,* §187, comment (d). Accord *III Scott on Trusts,* §187, p. 1524. Similarly, in *Maggard v. O'Connell*, 671 F.2d 568 (D.C. Cir. 1982), the U.S. Court of Appeals for

6. *De Novo Review of Statutory Issues*

As described in the introductory material to section III, *de novo* review applies when an issue of statutory construction overlaps with an issue of plan interpretation. This can function as another exception to arbitrary and capricious review of plan interpretations.

B. Factual Determinations

1. *Substantial Evidence*

Under the arbitrary and capricious standard of review, a plan administrator's or trustees' factual determinations are sustained if they are supported by "substantial evidence." As summarized by one court:

> "The court must determine whether the Trustees' decision is based on substantial evidence in the record taken as a whole. 'Substantial evidence' is evidence that a reasonable mind would accept as sufficient to support a particular conclusion. It consists of somewhat more than a scintilla but may be less than a preponderance of the evidence. If the decision of the Trustees is supported by substantial evidence, that decision must be sustained even if the court may believe that substantial evidence supports a contrary result."[285]

It is astounding that this highly deferential standard, used for review of factual determinations by public agencies, has been adopted for decisions of private employer-appointed administrators of pension, health, and welfare plans when a preponderance of the evidence test would apply if the same facts were determined by a private insurance company under a health, disability, or annuity contract with the employee.[286] The insurance contract analogy was, however, rejected before ERISA for plans not in the form of insurance contracts in favor of this

---

the District of Columbia Circuit stated that when there are "danger signals," for example, that trustees have an "undue bias towards particular private interests," review with a "stern hand and a flinty eye" follows. 671 F.2d at 571 and 572.

Even with "less deference," the standard of review adopted in *Jung* is still at odds with the contractual standard of review that applied to the interpretation of severance pay plans before ERISA. See Note, "Severance Pay, Sales of Assets, and the Resolution of Omitted Cases," 82 Colum. L. Rev. 593 (April 1982) (discussing the resolution of the same sale of assets issue under a contractual standard of review in state courts and in arbitration).

[285] *Persio v. Combs*, 2 EBC 2239, at 2239 (W.D. Pa. 1981) (case citations omitted). See also *LeFebre v. Westinghouse Elec. Corp.*, 747 F.2d 197, 5 EBC 2521 (4th Cir. 1984) (trustees will only be reversed on a finding of fact if there is a "clear error of judgment"); *Brown v. Retirement Committee of Briggs & Stratton Retirement Plan*, 797 F.2d 521 (7th Cir. 1986) (substantial evidence test applied); *Roberson v. Gen. Motors Corp., Detroit Diesel Allison Div.*, 801 F.2d 176 (6th Cir. 1986) (upholding rejection of certain evidence of disability presented by plan participant under arbitrary and capricious standard); *Horn v. Mullins*, 650 F.2d 35 (4th Cir. 1981); *Boyd v. Brown & Williamson Tobacco Corp.*, 2 EBC 2266 (W.D. Ky. 1981). And see the cases cited at the beginning of sec. III on the full articulation of the arbitrary and capricious standard, and the cases cited below.

[286] See *Couch on Insurance* 2d (rev. ed.) §79:314–19. The insured generally has the burden of proving facts necessary to establish a claim by a preponderance of the evidence, with the insurer having the burden of proof on facts necessary to establish exclusions and limitations under a policy. *Id.*

deferential standard.[287] The substantial evidence standard has carried over under ERISA, largely without further discussion of its sharp contrast with the standard of review applicable to factual determinations under insurance contracts.[288]

The only major variation from the substantial evidence test that has been suggested for ERISA claims is that a court may take into account the greater possibility of bias against individual claimants, or claimants in general, than when an administrative law judge has tenure and is insulated from outside pressures. In *Maggard v. O'Connell*, the U.S. Court of Appeals for the District of Columbia Circuit held that when "danger signals" of administrative irregularity are detected, such as bias in favor of particular private interests, evidence that the decisionmaker did not really take a hard look at the salient issues, or a history of inconsistent or *ad hoc* judgments, the substantial evidence test under ERISA may be restricted to factual determinations that are satisfactory when reviewed by a court with a "stern hand and flinty eye."[289]

The context in which the substantial evidence test is applied under ERISA may also vary from its normal context. ERISA contemplates less adversarial proceedings than occur before many public agencies, with plan administrators or trustees having duties to assist participants in framing and developing their claims. When this assistance is not provided, the substantial evidence test may not be appropriate for review of a factual determination that was made without the benefit of a presentation of the participant's claim in the most favorable light.[290]

a. Procedural requirements. To achieve the deference normally allowed under the substantial evidence test, the overriding requirement is that plan fiduciaries meet "elemental requirements of fairness."[291] In *Sturgill v. Lewis*, the District of Columbia Circuit stated:

> "[T]he proceedings before the Trustees should [therefore] normally include, in addition to notice, a hearing at which the applicant is confronted by the evidence against him, an opportunity to present evidence in his own behalf, articulated findings, conclusions having a substantial basis in the evidence taken as a whole, and a reviewable record."

The court then stated that:

> "If the Trustees for some reason are unable or unwilling to comply with these fairness requirements, . . . it may become necessary to reconsider

---

[287] See, e.g., *Beam v. Int'l Org. of Masters, Mates & Pilots*, 511 F.2d 975 (2d Cir. 1975).

[288] But see *Toland v. McCarthy*, 499 F.Supp. 1183, 2 EBC 2335 (D. Mass. 1980) (questioning how substantial evidence test became applicable to the "decisions of a private institution such as the trustees of an employee benefit fund").

[289] 671 F.2d 568, at 572 (D.C. Cir. 1982). And see *Blankenship v. UMW 1950 Pension and Benefit Trusts*, 4 EBC 2385 (D.D.C. 1983).

[290] *Toland v. McCarthy*, 499 F.Supp. 1183, 2 EBC 2335, at 2344–45 (D. Mass. 1980).

[291] *Sturgill v. Lewis*, 372 F.2d 400, at 401 (D.C. Cir. 1966).

our ruling in *Danti* [*v. Lewis,* in favor of the substantial evidence test]."[292]

Under ERISA, the courts have generally not required oral hearings, but have focused on the following procedural standards and rules as "elemental requirements of fairness" needed to support the deference of the substantial evidence test:

(1) *Full and fair review.* The opportunity for a "full and fair review" of a denied claim requires that "specific reasons" for an initial factual determination be detailed in a preliminary denial letter. The participant, or his or her attorney, must then be allowed to examine all of the evidence on which the determination is based so that the participant can "submit issues and comments in writing" before the final plan determination is made.[293]

(2) *Fair development of evidence.* The trustees or other factfinder have a duty to ensure a "fair development" of evidence to support a participant's claim. In most instances, the factfinder can substitute the claimant's efforts for his own by specifying "with some detail what type of information would help to resolve the question, and how the applicant should present such information."[294] In some cases, however, instruction is not enough. In *Toland v. McCarthy,* the trustees of a plan determined that a participant had been a supervisor, rather than a production worker, for a number of years, and therefore was ineligible for pension credits for those years, but the trustees did not seek to verify their determination of his supervisory status with the participant's employers during those years. The *Toland* court held the trustees "had a duty to take an initiative to cause reasonably available evidence ... to be developed."[295]

---

[292] *Id.* And see *Danti v. Lewis,* 312 F.2d 345 (D.C. Cir. 1962).

[293] *Grossmuller v. UAW,* 715 F.2d 853, 4 EBC 2082 (3d Cir. 1983); *Freeman v. IBEW Local 613 Pension Fund,* 3 EBC 1865 (N.D. Ga. 1982). See also 29 C.F.R. 2560.503-1(f) and (g), and *Toland v. McCarthy, supra,* 2 EBC at 2344-45.

[294] *Wolfe v. J.C. Penney Co.,* 710 F.2d 388, 4 EBC 1795, at 1799 (7th Cir. 1983). And see *LeFebre v. Westinghouse Elec. Corp.,* 747 F.2d 197, 5 EBC 2521 (4th Cir. 1984); *Freeman v. IBEW Local 613 Pension Fund,* 3 EBC 1865 (N.D. Ga. 1982), and 29 C.F.R. 2560.503-1(f)(3).

[295] 499 F.Supp. 1183, 2 EBC 2335, at 2341 (D. Mass. 1980). In *Berry v. CIBA-GEIGY Corp.,* 761 F.2d 1003, 6 EBC 1481 (4th Cir. 1985), the Fourth Circuit suggested that whether trustees can simply tell a participant what information to secure, or must themselves ensure the fair development of evidence, hinges on whether the plan, or ERISA, commits the trustees to act only with a full "evidentiary foundation." 6 EBC at 1484. For example, if a plan provides that a participant shall receive disability benefits "for as long as the Participant continues to be Totally Disabled," a full evidentiary foundation may be required before a participant is taken off the disability rolls. *Id.* Similarly, when ERISA's recordkeeping requirements require a plan to maintain records of participant's credited service, it may not be appropriate to put the burden on the participant if the records were not maintained or are missing. In *Berry,* the Fourth Circuit found abundant reliable evidence that the participant was not disabled and no duty on the trustees to lay a full evidentiary foundation before taking him off the disability rolls. In *LeFebre v. Westinghouse Elec. Corp.,* 747 F.2d 197, 5 EBC 2521 (4th Cir. 1984), the Fourth Circuit also found trustees had no duty to gather additional evidence on a participant's behalf when the participant had counsel at the claims stage and the trustees had abundant, reliable evidence that the participant was not

(3) *Oral hearings.* While the Department of Labor's regulations do not require oral hearings as a part of a full and fair claims procedure, they also do not rule out oral hearings when issues, such as credibility, would make an oral hearing a significant aid in a fair determination.[296] Pre-ERISA case law suggests that an oral hearing is required in certain circumstances for a plan to meet "elemental requirements of fairness"[297] unless the claimant has only a "weak case."[298] Post-ERISA cases suggest that an oral hearing is not generally required,[299] but an opportunity to present evidence in person may be required when adverse evidence is taken from third parties appearing in person (or over the phone).[300]

(4) *Competent determinations.* Although generally not described as a separate procedural requirement, the ERISA prudent man standard requires that a factfinder act with the "care, *skill*, prudence and diligence . . . that a prudent man *acting in a like capacity and familiar with such matters* would use in the conduct of an enterprise of a like character and with like aims."[301] Thus, a plan fiduciary as a factfinder must take the difficulty or technicality of the issues into account and take appropriate steps to ensure that a fair and competent determination is made.[302]

(5) *Explanatory statements.* When a claim is denied after review within a plan, a final "explanatory statement" is required with

---

disabled. In *Toland v. McCarthy,* on the other hand, a full evidentiary foundation was required for the determination of a participant's years of credited service.

[296] 29 C.F.R. 2560.503-1(g)(1) (a full and fair review "shall include but not be limited to . . . submi[ssions of] issues and comments in writing").

[297] *Sturgill v. Lewis, supra,* 372 F.2d 400, at 401 (D.C. Cir. 1966). And see R. Thomas, "Due Process, Hearings, and Pension and Welfare Claims Denials Under ERISA," 28 Lab. L.J. 276 (1977), citing *Russell v. Princeton Laboratories, Inc.*, 231 A.2d 800 (N.J. Sup.Ct. 1967); *Schillinger v. McCory,* 55 Lab. Cas. ¶12,041 (N.Y. Sup.Ct. 1967); and *Weber v. Bell Tel. Co.*, 203 A.2d 554 (Pa. Super.Ct. 1964), as other cases requiring oral hearings to support the substantial evidence test.

[298] *Lugo v. Employees Retirement Fund,* 366 F.Supp. 99 (E.D.N.Y. 1974), *aff'd,* 529 F.2d 251 (2d Cir.), *cert. denied,* 429 U.S. 826 (1976).

[299] See *Boyd v. Brown & Williamson Tobacco Corp.*, 2 EBC 2266 (W.D. Ky. 1981); *Grossmuller v. UAW,* 715 F.2d 853, 4 EBC 2082, at 2086 n.5 (3d Cir. 1983) ("written record will suffice").

[300] See *Grossmuller v. UAW, supra,* 4 EBC at 2086–87.

[301] ERISA §404(a)(1)(B) (emphasis added).

[302] To deal with competence, many plans use the results of other proceedings to decide certain facts under the plan. As a prime example, "disability" is often determined according to the results of Social Security disability proceedings. A plan may provide that the decisions of Social Security or other proceedings are conclusive for purposes of the plan. See *Norman v. UMWA,* 755 F.2d 509 (6th Cir. 1985); *Crusto v. Clothing Workers,* 524 F.Supp. 130, 2 EBC 2104 (E.D. La. 1981). Plan trustees may rely on the results of other proceedings or the determinations of other experts in other instances, but they may not make them conclusive for purposes of the plan if the plan provides that in the final instance they are to use their own judgment. See *Freeman v. IBEW Local 613 Pension Fund,* 3 EBC 1865 (N.D. Ga. 1982); *Cohen v. Kralstein,* 62 Lab. Cas. ¶10,731 (N.Y. Sup.Ct. 1970) (following *III Scott on Trusts* (3d ed.) at 1518–19); and N. Levin, *Guidelines for Fiduciaries of Taft-Hartley Trusts* (IFEBP 1980), at 102 and 105. But compare *Andersen v. CIBA-GEIGY Corp.*, 759 F.2d 1518, 6 EBC 1565 (11th Cir. 1985) (disregarding improper delegation of duty to make decision in determining whether a plan interpretation was arbitrary and capricious). Also, note that no §404 or §503 violations have been found on the basis that a plan's review procedure consists of the *same* person or committee reviewing his or its own initial determinations. See ch. 14, sec. I.A.

"specific reasons" for the denial. The statement need not review *all* of the favorable and unfavorable evidence unless a "substantial interest" is being denied because of "marginal" ineligibility. In the latter case, the explanatory statement or the administrative record must show consideration of all evidence in the claimant's favor, even when other, unfavorable evidence may constitute "substantial evidence" to support the trustees' denial.[303]

(6) *Body of precedent.* Adequate "explanatory statements" for *other* benefit denials are also required since they allow the participant and the court a "body of precedent" to compare with his or her denial in determining whether a plan is being consistently administered.[304]

(7) *Judicial review of record.* On review, a court will consider only the record that was before the trustees at the time of the final denial. If a participant presents additional evidence in court that goes beyond an insignificant strengthening of the participant's claim, the evidence will generally be excluded from consideration, but the court may in its discretion "remand to the fiduciary to make an initial assessment" of the evidence and a redetermination of whether the claim should be granted.[305]

Technically, single-employer plans that adopt the collective bargaining agreement's grievance and arbitration procedure for processing claims are exempt from the more detailed ERISA claims procedure requirements set out in the Department of Labor's regulations, including providing "specific reasons" for denials, and the opportunity to inspect the evidence before the plan and to submit comments and other evidence in writing. To come under this exception, the collective bargaining agreement must specifically provide that benefit claims are subject to the grievance and arbitration procedure. The grievance and

---

[303] *Beggs v. Mullins*, 499 F.Supp. 916, at 920 (S.D. W.Va. 1980). See also *Brown v. Retirement Committee of Briggs & Stratton Retirement Plan*, 797 F.2d 521 (7th Cir. 1986) (plan provided fair claims procedure when employee had opportunity to submit documentary evidence, committee considered the evidence, and committee sent employee copy of minutes of hearing that showed evidence it relied on and its assessment of all the evidence).

[304] See *Richardson v. Central States Pension Fund*, 645 F.2d 660, 2 EBC 1477 (8th Cir. 1981).

[305] *Wolfe v. J.C. Penney Co.*, 710 F.2d 388, 4 EBC 1795, at 1800 (7th Cir. 1983); and see *Wardle v. Central States Pension Fund*, 627 F.2d 820, 2 EBC 1633 (7th Cir. 1980), *cert. denied*, 449 U.S. 1112 (1981); *Berry v. CIBA-GEIGY Corp.*, 761 F.2d 1003, 6 EBC 1481 (4th Cir. 1985); *Weeks v. Coca-Cola Bottling Co.*, 491 F.Supp. 1312 (E.D. Ark. 1980).

New theories or arguments may be distinguished from new evidence. See *Offutt v. Prudential Ins. Co.*, 735 F.2d 948 (5th Cir. 1984); *Wolf v. Nat'l Shopmen Pension Fund*, 728 F.2d 182, 5 EBC 1257 (3d Cir. 1984) (claims exhaustion does not require "issue or theory exhaustion").

When *trustees* seek to support an adverse determination with additional evidence, the evidence is also excluded from consideration by the court, but there may be an opportunity for the trustees to take the claim back and redetermine it based on a supplemented record. See *Offutt v. Prudential Ins. Co., supra*; *Sturgill v. Lewis*, 372 F.2d 400 (D.C. Cir. 1966)—both suggesting that when trustees assert an alternative ground for a denial in court, the court may remand the claim. New arguments by plan trustees based on the same evidence may again be distinguished from the introduction of new evidence. See *Offutt, supra*. In *Phillips v. Kennedy*, 542 F.2d 52, 1 EBC 1418 (8th Cir. 1976), new evidence was submitted to the court by both parties when neither side objected.

arbitration procedure must also be described in the plan's summary plan description and must not "contain any provision, [or be] administered in a way, which unduly inhibits or hampers the initiation or processing of plan claims."[306] In *Grossmuller v. UAW*, however, the Third Circuit found that a collectively bargained grievance and arbitration procedure had been administered to deny a participant a "full and fair opportunity." While the Department of Labor's more detailed claims procedure requirements on confronting the evidence were not directly applicable, the Third Circuit measured whether the participant had a full and fair opportunity against the regulatory requirements that participants be provided specific written reasons for benefit denials and a description of material that could support or validate the claim.[307]

b. Remedies for procedural violations. When a court finds that a plan's claims procedures are not sufficiently fair to support use of the "substantial evidence" test for review of a factual determination, the remedy can range from (1) sending the claim back to the plan for a redetermination by the same plan fiduciaries under a proper procedure (in some cases with a continuation of benefits in the interim), (2) reviewing the administrative record under a very strict substantial evidence test, with the addition of new evidence, if necessary, to (3) a *de novo* redetermination by the court of the facts.[308]

"Ordinarily, a claimant who suffers because of a fiduciary's failure to comply with ERISA's procedural requirements is entitled to no substantive remedy."[309] In *Berry v. CIBA-GEIGY Corp.*, for example, the Fourth Circuit stated that if a district court believes that a plan administrator or trustee lacked adequate evidence to make a determination, the proper course for the district court is to remand for a new determination based on a complete record, rather than for the court to allow new evidence and hear it *de novo*.[310] In *Wolfe v. J.C. Penney Co.*, a plan administrator's failure to specify what type of "medical information" a participant should supply to support a claim that he was terminated because of "injury or sickness," rather than "substandard job performance," and the failure of the plan administrator to fulfill its

---

[306] 29 C.F.R. 2560.503-1(b)(1) and (2).

[307] 715 F.2d 853, 4 EBC 2082, at 2086 (3d Cir. 1983).

[308] Damages for mental distress and other personal consequences of improper claims handling are discussed in ch. 14, sec. II.F.

[309] *Blau v. Del Monte Corp.*, 748 F.2d 1348, 6 EBC 1264, at 1269 (9th Cir. 1984), *cert. denied,* 474 U.S. 865 (1985). See also *Hancock v. Montgomery Ward Long Term Disability Plan*, 787 F.2d 1302, at 1308 (9th Cir. 1986) (substantive remedies are available under ERISA for procedural defects only when the defects cause a "substantive violation or themselves work[] a substantive harm," quoting *Ellenburg v. Brockway, Inc.*, 763 F.2d 1091 (9th Cir. 1985); *Hancock* plaintiff showed no prejudice from alleged inadequacy of letters from plan administrator explaining insufficiency of medical evidence plaintiff submitted on disability).

[310] 761 F.2d 1003, 6 EBC 1481, at 1483 (4th Cir. 1985) (citing *Wardle v. Central States Pension Fund*, 627 F.2d 820, 2 EBC 1633 (7th Cir. 1980), *cert. denied,* 449 U.S. 1112 (1981); *Phillips v. Kennedy*, 542 F.2d 52, 1 EBC 1418 (8th Cir. 1976)). The *Berry* court distinguished lack of adequate evidence to make a determination from cases in which fiduciaries commit a "clear error" or act in bad faith, in which event a "reversal, rather than a remand, is within the discretion of the district court." 6 EBC at 1483 n.3.

own "limited duty" to develop affirmative evidence in support of the participant's claim, made the plan's claims procedure inadequate. But the Seventh Circuit did not redetermine the claim. Instead, it remanded it to the plan administrator for a "new determination" based on a full, properly developed record.[311]

Sending a claim back for review under a proper procedure can in some circumstances provide a substantive remedy by requiring benefits to continue at least until a new determination can be made. In *Grossmuller v. UAW*, a plan revoked a participant's disability benefits based on information that he was gainfully employed (the information included a movie of him tending bar), but the plan's fiduciaries did not provide the participant with an opportunity to review the evidence or to contest it. The Third Circuit found the plan's claims procedures inadequate and did not foreclose a redetermination of the participant's ineligibility under a proper procedure, but it ordered continuation of his disability benefits in the interim.[312] In *Freeman v. IBEW Local 613 Pension Fund*, a court awarded back benefits and a continuation of benefits because of a plan's failure to provide specific reasons and to permit review of pertinent documents before disqualifying participants from disability benefits. In contrast to *Grossmuller*, the court did not state whether the plan might later redetermine their ineligibility under proper procedures.[313]

An intermediate ground between a remand to trustees and a *de novo* determination of facts was set out in *Maggard v. O'Connell.* In *Maggard*, the U.S. Court of Appeals for the District of Columbia Circuit directed a district court to proceed to a determination of a participant's years of credited service under the substantial evidence test, but with a "stern hand and flinty eye," and if necessary, by adding to the record, because the plan's history of *ad hoc* and inconsistent determinations defeated the presumption of administrative regularity.[314] This intermediate ground could also be required when explanatory statements have not been provided for grants and denials of *other* participants' benefit claims, thus denying a participant a "body of precedent" with which to compare his or her denial. A remand to the plan in this instance obviously cannot produce a body of precedent that was never developed.

At the other end of the spectrum from a mere procedural remand is a *de novo* determination of the facts. In *Hayden v. Texas-U.S. Chemical Co.*, a plan's claims procedure was inadequate because it did not provide a claimant with specific reasons for the conclusion that he was not totally and permanently disabled, the administrator was tardy in consideration of the claim, and the plan failed to provide the claimant with an opportunity for a full and fair review of the initial denial.

---

[311] 710 F.2d 388, 4 EBC 1795, at 1797 and 1798 (7th Cir. 1983).

[312] 715 F.2d 853, 4 EBC 2082 (3d Cir. 1983).

[313] 3 EBC 1865 (N.D. Ga. 1982).

[314] 671 F.2d 568, at 572 (D.C. Cir. 1982).

In view of these defects, the court examined the evidence itself, and concluded the plan's decision was arbitrary and capricious.[315]

c. Substantial evidence when no procedural impediment exists. When no procedural defect exists, or when a procedural defect is corrected after a remand with a participant still being denied the benefits, the substantial evidence test presents a tough hurdle for a participant to overcome. In *Beam v. International Organization of Masters, Mates and Pilots*, a participant had "third degree burns which covered 25% of his body," but "substantial evidence" supported the trustees' determination that "chronic alcoholism," rather than "solely" the burns, was the cause of death. On this basis, his widow was denied accidental death benefits.[316] In *Freeman v. IBEW Local 613 Pension Fund*, a court stated that it did not agree with all four determinations by an employer-appointed physician that participants were not totally disabled under a new reevaluation program for disability retirees, but except for procedural defects in the plan's claims procedure, it would have been forced to sustain each given the deference in the "substantial evidence" test.[317]

Some determinations of fact, on the other hand, cannot pass muster even under substantial evidence. In *Phillips v. Kennedy*, a general description by a union dispatcher of an employee as a "supervisor" (which could start a break in service under a pre-ERISA plan) was "largely negated" by other evidence and by the local union's treatment of the employee as an hourly employee during the 10-year period in question. The trustees' finding of supervisory status was thus insufficiently supported on the record before them.[318] More objectively determinable facts, e.g., mathematical issues, are also not susceptible to conclusory approval under substantial evidence. In *Chastain v. Delta Air Lines, Inc.*, a determination that a deceased participant's children were not eligible for benefits under a disability and death benefits plan because less than one-half of their support came from their father

---

[315] 557 F.Supp. 382, 4 EBC 1304 (E.D. Tex. 1983). In *Cohen v. Kralstein*, 62 Lab.Cas. ¶10,731 (N.Y. Sup.Ct. 1970), a New York court found that plan trustees improperly delegated a decision on whether a participant was to be credited with certain years as covered service to the plan's administrative director, and hence, looked at the participant's evidence *de novo*, following *III Scott on Trusts* (3d ed.) at 1518–19 (if trustee fails to use his own judgment under a power conferred on him by the settlor, court may interpose). In *Toland v. McCarthy*, 499 F.Supp. 1183, 2 EBC 2335 (D. Mass. 1980), the court reserved the question of whether it should make a determination about a participant's work history itself when the plan's trustees failed to cause reasonably available evidence to be developed.

[316] 511 F.2d 975, at 980 (2d Cir. 1975).

[317] 3 EBC 1865, at 1870 (N.D. Ga. 1983). See also *Persio v. Combs*, 2 EBC 2239 (W.D. Pa. 1981) (conflicting records and evidence on service to be credited to participant, but substantial evidence supported trustees' denial); *Torimino v. UFCW Pension Fund*, 548 F.Supp. 1012, 3 EBC 2374 (E.D. Mo. 1982), *aff'd*, 712 F.2d 882, 4 EBC 1903 (8th Cir. 1983) (conflicting evidence on whether participant with "severe injury to his lower back" was disabled, but adequate enough to support trustees' decision that he was not disabled under substantial evidence test).

[318] 542 F.2d 52, 1 EBC 1418, at 1421 (8th Cir. 1976). See also *Horn v. Mullins*, 650 F.2d 35 (4th Cir. 1981) (trustees' factual determination that back injury did not "result from" a mine accident occurring 48 hours earlier reversed as not supported by substantial evidence).

could not be sustained when the plan used a faulty measure to determine the total costs of their support.[319]

Even under substantial evidence, determinations of fact must also be made according to standards that are consistent with those applied in other determinations of the same or similar facts. In nonbargained and bargained plans alike, past practice may thus be used to ascertain whether a determination, such as of credited service or disability, has been made according to consistent standards, and also to determine whether other discretion under the plan may have been used in other instances to waive slight shortfalls in service or in lieu of the same type of proof that is being required for the current claimant.

2. Exceptions to Substantial Evidence

As in plan interpretation, exceptions to the "substantial evidence" test are established for collectively bargained plans that do not provide plan administrators with conclusive or final authority over the determination of facts under the plan, and for plans that provide benefits under individual or group insurance contracts.[320]

The determination of facts applicable to an entire class of participants could also be separated for review under ERISA's stricter fiduciary standards. However, in *Foltz v. U.S. News & World Report*, a district court stated that the arbitrary and capricious standard for determination of facts would apply when retirees from the U.S. News & World Report profit-sharing plan alleged their non-publicly traded shares of company stock were intentionally or negligently undervalued when the shares were cashed-out at retirement.[321]

If trustees or a plan administrator establish a new factual "presumption" relating to the proof of facts for an entire class, such as that it will be presumed that all disabled participants are no longer disabled *unless* they submit new evidence of their continuing disability, the new factual presumption may have to be examined separately for breach of fiduciary duty under ERISA's strict standards.[322]

3. Separating Statutory and Common Law Issues

Because the substantial evidence test is a tough hurdle for participants, it is always preferable for a participant to frame issues in the alternative in a manner which accepts the fiduciary's factual determinations as much as possible, and focuses instead on plan interpretation, or a statutory or common law violation. In *Richardson v. Central*

---

[319] 496 F.Supp. 979 (N.D. Ga. 1980).

[320] See sec. III.A.5 above.

[321] 613 F.Supp. 634, 6 EBC 1761 (D.D.C. 1985), *on remand from*, 760 F.2d 1300, 6 EBC 1534 (D.C. Cir. 1985).

[322] See sec. III.C on review of exercises of discretion under the terms of plans. But see *Freeman v. IBEW Local 613 Pension Fund*, 3 EBC 1865 (N.D. Ga. 1982).

States Pension Fund, for example, factual determinations that supported the trustees' conclusion that a participant had been "self-employed" were basically accepted, but the proper interpretive standards for the trustees to use in determining whether those facts amounted to being "self-employed" were challenged on the ground that the standards used were incorrect under Illinois common law, which the plan had adopted as its interpretive reference.[323] Similarly, in *Helms v. Monsanto Co.*, a doctor, jointly selected by a claimant and the company to determine whether the claimant had a "total disability" within the meaning of a plan, found that the claimant had retinitis pigmentosa, a progressive eye disease culminating in blindness, but found that he was not "totally disabled" because under the plan, a participant had to be prevented by the disability from engaging in "any occupation or employment for remuneration or profit." The doctor determined that this phrase could only be satisfied by a lack of "conscious life." Without contesting the doctor's findings of fact, the Eleventh Circuit followed state law cases and Social Security disability cases to determine that the phrase used under the plan meant "physical inability to follow any occupation from which [the claimant] could earn a *reasonably substantial income*," and concluded that the doctor's interpretive standard would render the disability provision "totally meaningless."[324]

Care should also be taken to distinguish factual determinations subject to the substantial evidence test from statutory and common law questions subject to *de novo* review. For example, whether a participant has a "year of service" with an employer contributing to a multiemployer plan may depend on the "fact" of what job he or she held with the employer and whether the employer had a contribution obligation during that period. But it also depends on whether the plan meets ERISA's minimum standards for measuring a "year of service" and whether the fiduciaries have kept records necessary to administer the trust's terms, as required under ERISA.[325] A plan rule limiting

---

[323] 645 F.2d 660, 2 EBC 1477 (8th Cir. 1981).

[324] 728 F.2d 1416, at 1420 and 1421 (11th Cir. 1984) (emphasis added). See also *Farrow v. Montgomery Ward Long Term Disability Plan,* 222 Cal. Rptr. 325 (Cal. App. 1986) (adopting burden of proof allocation from Social Security Act disability cases because plan's definition of disability was "quite similar," thus requiring plan to provide specific examples of jobs the claimant could hold once she proved that she could not do her previous job). But compare *Brown v. Retirement Committee of Briggs & Stratton Retirement Plan,* 797 F.2d 521 (7th Cir. 1986) (state law cases defining disability under insurance contracts not required to be followed by pension plan administrator); *Pokratz v. Jones Dairy Farm,* 771 F.2d 206, 6 EBC 2097 (7th Cir. 1985) (rejecting claim of participant who had retinitis pigmentosa that he was disabled under nearly identical plan language to that in *Helms*); *LeFebre v. Westinghouse Elec. Corp.*, 747 F.2d 197, 5 EBC 2521 (4th Cir. 1984) (participant with retinitis pigmentosa also unsuccessful on disability claim under substantial evidence test).

[325] See ERISA §209(a)(1) and §107, 29 C.F.R. 2530.200b-3(a) and (b), and Prop. Regs. 29 C.F.R. 2530.209-2 and -3. And see *Holt v. Winpisinger,* 811 F.2d 1532, 8 EBC 1169 (D.C. Cir. 1987) (factual issues related to statutory issue of when a person is "employed" for purposes of counting vesting service must be separated from factual issues subject to substantial evidence test); *Combs v. King,* 764 F.2d 818 (11th Cir. 1985) (employer contributing to a multiemployer plan has duty under ERISA §209 to maintain adequate records of the number of hours worked by its employees sufficient to determine the benefits that may become due to each employee; when such records are not maintained, employer assumes burden of disproving the accuracy of the trustees' reasonable estimates).

methods of proof of disputed years of service to employer records, Social Security records, union records, and affidavits from co-employees to the exclusion of other forms of proof may also be arbitrary if applied to employees who necessarily have worked for short periods with a vast number of employers, some of whom may have made incomplete Social Security contributions or otherwise have kept inadequate records.[326]

Factual determinations by a plan's trustees may also be redetermined without the deference of substantial evidence when the disputed facts are a part of a separable ERISA claim. In *Amaro v. Continental Can Co.*, the Ninth Circuit held that even the findings of a neutral arbitrator are not binding on a related, but distinct ERISA Section 510 cause of action for intentional interference with the attainment of pension rights. The Ninth Circuit stated that the arbitrator's findings, which concerned whether layoffs were in violation of certain collective bargaining obligations or were due to changing market conditions, would be admissible as evidence on whether the layoffs were for the purpose of interfering with pension rights, but would only be accorded such weight as the court "deems appropriate."[327]

C. Exercises of Discretionary Authority

The most sweeping type of discretionary authority under the terms of any pension plan is the authority to rewrite the rules, or in other words, to amend the plan. Plan amendment authority is discussed in Chapter 9. However, other discretionary authority may exist under a plan. Such authority can permit fiduciaries to effectively establish exceptions to plan rules, or to implement general plan rules according to criteria largely of their own devising without directly writing the rules into the plan itself. Most decisions on the exercise of such discretionary authority under pension plans involve denials of lump sum benefits under plan provisions where lump sum options are in the "discretion" of a plan administrator, the trustees, or a retirement committee.[328] A plan administrator or trustees may also have discretion under the terms of the plan, or in practice, to selectively waive or alter certain benefit requirements,[329] or to consider employees in a relatively

---

326 See *Cohen v. Kralstein*, 62 Lab. Cas. ¶10,731 (N.Y. Sup.Ct. 1970) (plan rules on methods of proof arbitrary when applied to handcraft baking industry in New York City where employees worked for a vast number of small employers; rules on proof also discriminated against employees of small employers and in favor of the employees of large, well-established baking companies, from which all the employer-appointed trustees had been drawn).

327 724 F.2d 747, 5 EBC 1215, at 1221 (9th Cir. 1984). But compare *Burke v. Latrobe Steel Co.*, 775 F.2d 88, 6 EBC 2328 (3d Cir. 1985) (participant may be entitled to remedies in ERISA action for breach of fiduciary duty in plan interpretation that were not available before arbitrator, but suggesting that all overlapping contract or factual determinations made in the preceding arbitration will be accepted).

328 See, e.g., *Morse v. Stanley*, 732 F.2d 1139, 5 EBC 1602 (2d Cir. 1984) (lump sum options in the "sole discretion" of the trustees).

329 See *Bruder v. Pension Plan for Employees of Holscher-Wernig, Inc.*, 599 F.Supp. 347 (E.D. Mo. 1984) (exception to definition of "compensation" made for one employee to enable him

open-ended status, such as on "leave of absence," that will result in continued credit for pensions past an employee's last day of active work.[330] A plan also may provide authority for trustees to discretionarily waive or adjust certain requirements for "good cause,"[331] "hardship," disability,[332] or other exceptional conditions. Many plans make certain early retirement benefits contingent on the discretionary "consent" of the sponsoring employer to the employee's retirement.[333] Plan trustees also may have discretion over whether certain types of employees are covered under the plan, for example, whether employees outside of a bargaining unit are covered under a multiemployer plan.[334]

The full scope of discretionary authority may not be apparent from the face of the plan. Particularly after ERISA's "written plan" requirement went into effect, trustees have been known to respond to requests for a discretionary exception to a benefit requirement by saying that they may have made such exceptions in the past, but ERISA's "written" plan requirement and the Code's "definitely determinable" benefits requirement have restricted or eliminated their previous discretionary authority. Whether this is so may only be gathered from actual practice both before and after ERISA.[335]

In the past, discretionary authority frequently existed to increase or decrease interest rates and to alter mortality assumptions used in computing lump sum options, actuarially equivalent early retirement benefits, joint and survivor benefits, and other options from a single-life annuity form.[336] As discussed in Chapter 4, for plan years after December 31, 1983, discretion to change actuarial assumptions used in computing the amount of benefits under benefit options has been limited by a requirement that the assumptions must be specified in the

---

to obtain some benefits not extended to a second employee who would receive some benefits without the exception); *Faunce v. American Can Co.*, 407 A.2d 733 (Me. 1979) (waiver by personnel manager of 2-month deficiency in qualifying for early retirement benefits). The estoppel cases discussed in ch. 8 also demonstrate actual or apparent authority to selectively waive or alter benefit requirements.

[330] See *Hardy v. H.K. Porter Co.*, 417 F.Supp. 1175 (E.D. Pa. 1976), *aff'd in part, rev'd in part,* 562 F.2d 42 (3d Cir. 1977).

[331] See *Shishido v. SIU-Pacific District PMA Plan*, 587 F.Supp. 112, 5 EBC 1067 (N.D. Cal. 1983).

[332] See *Valle v. Joint Plumbing Industry Board*, 623 F.2d 196, 3 EBC 1026 (2d Cir. 1980).

[333] See, e.g., *Petrella v. NL Indus., Inc.*, 529 F.Supp. 1357, 3 EBC 1210 (D.N.J. 1982).

[334] *Sanchez v. Trustees of the Pension Plan*, 359 So.2d 1279 (La. 1978) (acceptance of contributions for employees, who were major shareholders in a small company, foreclosed reversal of trustees' position on their coverage when trustees had discretion to cover nonhourly employees under multiemployer plan).

[335] See *Genter v. Acme Scale & Supply Co.*, 776 F.2d 1180 (3d Cir. 1985) (although in violation of ERISA and fiduciary duties, neither written plan nor SPD advised employees of employer's selectively practiced discretion to double their life insurance benefits under plan immediately after a salary increase to above $20,000, rather than only at the end of the year, as stated under the terms of the plan).

[336] See, e.g., *Lewis v. Fulton Federal Savings & Loan Pension Plan*, 4 EBC 2071 (N.D. Ga. 1983).

plan.[337] The consequence of this is that the assumptions may henceforth only be changed by plan amendment.[338]

The scope of permissible discretion under tax-qualified plans may be further narrowed in the future. The IRS has proposed regulations under the Code's "definitely determinable" benefits and contributions allocation requirement that would, after a transition period, require objective, ascertainable criteria to be used in determining the availability of *all* benefit options under plans, including lump sum options and early retirement benefits that often have depended on exercises of discretionary consent.[339]

1. Arbitrary and Capricious Standard

The standard of review for exercises of discretionary authority is the "arbitrary and capricious" standard. In *Fine v. Semet*, a discretionary decision to deny a lump sum payment of benefits to a partner departing from the law firm sponsoring the plan was examined by the Eleventh Circuit to determine whether the decision was "arbitrary and capricious." Although the denial was challenged under ERISA Section 404(a)(1)'s "high" standard of fiduciary duty, the Eleventh Circuit expressly stated that "ERISA does not require a more stringent standard of review than the arbitrary and capricious standard" for such exercises. The court then upheld the denial because of the plan's asserted need to maintain "diversification of its assets," which the plan trustees claimed could not be done without holding onto the assets in the departing partner's individual account.[340] In *Morse v. Stanley*, the Second Circuit dealt with a discretionary denial of lump sum payments to participants who went to work for employers engaged in competition with the employer sponsoring the plan. The denial of lump sum benefits was analyzed not for whether the decision was "solely in the interest" of participants, or for the "exclusive purpose of providing benefits to participants," as the language of Section 404(a)(1) directs, but only for whether the denials were "arbitrary and capricious." The Second Circuit held the denials were not arbitrary because of secondary benefits to the plan from a policy that penalized competition with the sponsoring employer.[341] Analyzing the issue under the more precise language in Section 404(a)(1), one lower court concluded that such

---

[337] Rev. Rul. 79-90, and Code §401(a)(25), as added by the 1984 Retirement Equity Act. And see ch. 4, sec. IV.B.3.

[338] A plan can avoid the need for frequent amendments to an interest assumption by adopting a variable standard, such as a designated percentage of the prime interest rate of a named bank or banks, but the variable standard must be stated in the plan and must be outside of the employer's or plan fiduciaries' discretion once adopted, except by plan amendment. See Rev. Rul. 79-90.

[339] Prop. Regs. 1.401(a)-4 and 1.411(d)-4, 51 Fed. Reg. 3798 (Jan. 30, 1986). And see sec. III.C.2 below.

[340] 699 F.2d 1091, 4 EBC 1273, at 1275 (11th Cir. 1983).

[341] 732 F.2d 1139, 5 EBC 1602 (2d Cir. 1984). See also *Pompano v. Michael Schiavone & Sons, Inc.*, 680 F.2d 911, 3 EBC 1545 (2d Cir. 1982), *cert. denied*, 459 U.S. 1039 (1982) (approving denial of lump sum benefits under the arbitrary and capricious standard).

"trickling down" effects in favor of a plan could not sustain benefit denials when the policy against competition was obviously instituted primarily for the employer, and at best "incidentally" for the plan.[342] The "arbitrary and capricious" standard has also been applied to discretionary increases in interest rates used in computing "actuarially equivalent" lump sum options.[343]

While *Fine* and *Morse* and the lump sum interest rate cases can be read to make judicial review of any exercise of discretionary authority a rubber stamp, closer examination of these and other cases reveals standards that have substance, but that may be applied more leniently in lump sum benefit option cases because of the courts' view that no "loss" of benefits generally occurs from the denial of lump sum benefits.[344] These standards are that an exercise or nonexercise of discretion:

(1) Must be in accord with the purpose for which the discretionary authority was provided;

(2) Must be consistent with other exercises of discretion under the authority;

(3) Must be based on distinguishing criteria that are rationally related to legitimate plan purposes and that do not on their face or in operation prefer or discriminate against particular participant groups; and

(4) Must, as a fiduciary's decision, be based on professional consideration of the request, and of alternatives to a denial that

---

[342] *Cohen v. Stanley*, 566 F.Supp. 246, 4 EBC 1985, at 1992 (S.D.N.Y. 1983), *rev'd sub nom. Morse v. Stanley.*

[343] *Lewis v. Fulton Federal Savings & Loan Pension Plan*, 4 EBC 2071 (N.D. Ga. 1983) (change from 6% interest rate for computing lump sum value of benefits in annuity form to 13.65% and then 14.5% interest rates not arbitrary and capricious, even though lump sum amounts cut in half by change).

As discussed before, discretionary changes in interest rates used for lump sum and other benefit options have prospectively been limited by Rev. Ruls. 79-90 and 81-12 and by Code §401(a)(25), as amended by the 1984 Retirement Equity Act.

[344] See *Morse v. Stanley, supra*, 5 EBC at 1610 (no "denial" or "loss" of benefits where lump sum option was discretionary and "ultimately [the participants] will receive *all* of their benefits, with interest, upon reaching age 65"). And see *Pompano v. Michael Schiavone & Sons, Inc., supra*, 3 EBC at 1548 (no "substantive denial" under the facts when participant denied discretionary lump sum "mode" of benefits). In contrast to these decisions, the Senate Report on the 1984 Retirement Equity Act recognizes that lump sum benefits are very important for participants with substandard mortality, which includes members of many minority groups, as well as participants with health problems:

"[F]or a participant or beneficiary with substandard mortality, [for example], the elimination of [a lump sum option] could eliminate a valuable right even if a benefit of equal actuarial value (based on standard mortality) is available under the plan."

S. Rep. 98-575, 98th Cong., 2d Sess., at 30, reprinted in [1984] U.S. Code Cong. & Ad. News 2547, at 2576.

Lump sum benefits are also favored by participants who need money now or who hope to outdo the interest assumption used in discounting annuity benefits to lump sum form. They also are favored by participants who have doubts about the security of their deferred benefits under a former employer's continuing control. For profit-sharing and stock bonus plans, claims to lump sum benefits are particularly strong because this is the traditional form of benefit payment under such plans.

may serve the same plan purposes, but that are less harsh on participants' expectations.[345]

These standards parallel those developed in cases under Section 302(c)(5) of the Labor Management Relations Act reviewing plan provisions designed by plan trustees under their discretionary authority.[346] They also basically parallel standards developed under the common law of trusts.[347]

a. Purpose of discretionary authority. Discretionary authority under a pension plan inherently leaves courts with a less definite standard for review than when a fiduciary is interpreting an objective benefit requirement, or finding facts to apply against an objective plan rule. But the purposes put forward as the trustees' or plan administrator's basis for deciding whether or not to exercise discretionary authority may be reviewed for consistency with the plan's overall benefactory purposes and any more specific express or implied purposes for the particular discretionary authority.[348] In *Shishido v. SIU-Pacific District-PMA Plan,* a plan provided that 20 years of credited service had to be accumulated for a pension within a 30-year period, but the 30-year period could be extended for disability, or for "other good cause." The district court found, "It is manifest that the drafters of the Agreement contemplated that there could be extraordinary circumstances which would warrant extension of the period." As a result, the court found it "illogical" and "inconsistent" for the plan trustees to refuse to exercise this discretion for a participant who had been prevented from working in covered employment during a six-year period due to an unconstitutional blacklist in effect from 1951 to 1956. Presumably, the authority to extend the period for "good cause" was in the plan so that it could be exercised in such deserving circumstances.[349]

A plan's fundamental purpose of providing retirement income to employees and their families can serve as a more general aid in a determination of whether discretionary authority has been exercised

---

[345] See below, and see, e.g., *Pompano v. Michael Schiavone & Sons, Inc., supra,* 3 EBC at 1547 (lump sum criteria must be in accord with "major purpose" of the plan: assurance of a monthly income that one can retire on); *Fine v. Semet,* 4 EBC at 1277 (facial inconsistency with past exercises of discretion shifts burden to trustees to show a denial is not arbitrary); *Morse v. Stanley, supra,* 5 EBC at 1608 (trustees have duty to deal impartially and even-handedly among plan participants).

[346] See ch. 8, sec. VIII, and ch. 9, sec. II.B.

[347] The *Restatement of Trusts,* for example, provides:

"In determining the question [of] whether [a] trustee is guilty of an abuse of discretion in exercising or failing to exercise a power, the following circumstances may be relevant: (1) the extent of the discretion conferred upon the trustee by the terms of the trust; (2) the purposes of the trust; (3) the nature of the power; (4) the existence or nonexistence, the definiteness or indefiniteness, of an external standard by which the reasonableness of the trustee's conduct can be judged; (5) the motives of the trustee in exercising or refraining from exercising the power; [and] (6) the existence or non-existence of an interest in the trustee conflicting with that of the beneficiaries."

Restatement (Second) of Trusts, §187, comment (d).

[348] See *Restatement (Second) of Trusts,* §187, comment (d).

[349] 587 F.Supp. 112, 5 EBC 1067, at 1073 (N.D. Cal. 1983).

consistently with its purpose within the plan.[350] In close cases, courts may also consider that even when a plan provides discretionary authority, trustees and plan administrators may be "naturally disinclined" to use it.[351]

b. Consistency with other exercises. Within the purpose for a grant of discretionary authority, the arbitrary and capricious standard requires consistency. A line drawn for one participant must be consistent with the line drawn for others. Frequently, a discretionary decision is not arbitrary because the claimant's circumstances are simply not as compelling as when the discretionary authority has been favorably exercised for others, with the distinguishing criteria used in determining what is compelling being consistently applied and not being themselves arbitrary and capricious. In *Petrella v. NL Industries, Inc.*, all employees who were within three months of age 55 or older were offered a discretionary early retirement benefit when their division was sold to another company. The district court found this line had been used and applied consistently in the past and had been applied consistently in the case at hand. As discussed below, the line drawn was also found to be rational.[352]

In other cases, however, consistency has not been found. In *Hardy v. H.K. Porter Co.*, discretionary authority was used to grant extended "leaves of absence" to some participants in a plan "solely" to qualify them for early retirement benefits requiring service until age 60, but the same treatment was denied other participants in a practically identical situation without a showing of a consistent or rational basis for the distinction.[353] In *Kann v. Keystone Resources, Inc., Profit Sharing Plan*, a district court did not find consistency when lump sum payments had been made to participants who acted "no differently" than the plaintiff.[354]

A limitation on consistency as a restraint on arbitrary and capricious action is that past exercises rarely estop plan trustees from

---

[350] See the discussion above of the plan's retirement income purpose as a guide in plan interpretation.

[351] *Maggard v. O'Connell*, 671 F.2d 568, at 571 (D.C. Cir. 1982). And see *Russell v. Princeton Laboratories, Inc.*, 231 A.2d 800 (N.J. 1967) ("dollar interest" of administrators of profit-sharing plan in forfeitures under a plan also "does not encourage judicial deference" to their decisions).

[352] 529 F.Supp. 1357, 3 EBC 1210 (D.N.J. 1982).

[353] 417 F.Supp. 1175 (E.D. Pa. 1976), *aff'd in part, rev'd in part,* 562 F.2d 42 (3d Cir. 1977). In *Hardy*, the employer argued that putting certain employees on a leave of absence was not done within its discretion *under the plan*, but was done in its discretion as their employer, and hence, that it need not be done uniformly. The court, however, found that because the employer granted the leaves solely to qualify employees for pension benefits under the plan, the authority had to be considered discretion under the plan. See also Rev. Rul. 81-106.

[354] 575 F.Supp. 1084, 5 EBC 1233, at 1242 (W.D. Pa. 1983). See also *Associated Milk Producers v. Nelson*, 624 S.W.2d 920 (Tex. Ct.App. 1981) (discretionary forfeiture of pension benefits for dishonest conduct—making political contributions in violation of federal election laws—impermissible when four other employees who engaged in the same conduct not similarly treated). And cf. *U.S. Steel Pension Fund v. McSkimming*, 759 F.2d 269, 6 EBC 1621 (3d Cir. 1985) (employer's decision to treat a similarly situated employee differently than other employees who were granted discretionary consent for a "mutually satisfactory" early retirement pension found by arbitrator to violate fiduciary duties under ERISA; Third Circuit denied enforcement of the award because arbitrator lacked authority to make ERISA determinations, and did not draw "essence" of decision from the contract).

changing their discretionary criteria, and thereby distinguishing past favorable exercises.[355] But when discretionary criteria are changed, the burden on the trustees to establish the rationality and nondiscriminatory effects of the new criteria, and professional consideration of the new criteria before adopting them, may be greater.[356]

c. Rational and nondiscriminatory criteria. Even when consistently applied, discretionary criteria must be rationally related to legitimate overall plan purposes or the more specific purpose of the discretionary authority they purport to serve, and must not have unrelated discriminatory or preferential effects among different participant groups, either on their face or in operation. In *Petrella v. NL Industries, Inc.*, the line drawn between employees over age 55 and employees below that age for purposes of discretionary early retirement benefits was held to be rational because older employees had less employment mobility than younger employees after the sale of their division to another company.[357]

Discretionary criteria that are unrelated to the purpose of the specific discretionary grant are often purported to serve some broader purpose of the plan. Commonly, this is protecting the plan's overall funding. The courts have long recognized that general financial concerns could lend support to practically any benefit denial, whether under discretionary authority or otherwise.[358] However, in *Pompano v. Michael Schiavone & Sons, Inc.*, a policy of denying lump sum benefits to retirees with benefits worth over $3,000 was upheld as rational based on the trustees' concern with the costs of liquidating assets to cash out larger lump sum benefits and their concern with adverse selection against the plan if all participants in poor health or with substandard mortality were permitted to exercise this option.[359] In *Fine v. Semet*, trustees successfully argued that a need to maintain "diversification" of a plan's assets was the basis for denying a request for lump sum benefits to a departing law firm partner. Previous requests for lump sum benefits, which had been routinely granted, were distinguished as

---

[355] See *Morse v. Stanley*, 732 F.2d 1139, 5 EBC 1602, at 1606 (2d Cir. 1984) (past practice does not cause trustees to don a "discretionary strait-jacket"). See also *Fine v. Semet*, 699 F.2d 1091, 4 EBC 1273 (11th Cir. 1983); *Hackett v. PBGC*, 486 F.Supp. 1357, 2 EBC 2522 (D. Md. 1980); and sec. III.C.2.

[356] See *Fine v. Semet, supra*; *Frary v. Shorr Paper Products, Inc.*, 494 F.Supp. 565, 2 EBC 2268 (N.D. Ill. 1980).

[357] 529 F.Supp. 1357, 3 EBC 1210 (D.N.J. 1982).

[358] In *Donovan v. Carlough*, for example, a district court stated:

"Every time the Trustees make a decision to deny benefit applications, they are preserving the Fund's financial resources. Were the Court to defer to this argument, Trustee denials of benefits could never be deemed arbitrary and capricious."

576 F.Supp. 245, 5 EBC 1400, at 1405 (D.D.C. 1983). And see *Elser v. IAM Nat'l Pension Fund*, 684 F.2d 648, 3 EBC 2155 (9th Cir. 1982), *cert. denied*, 464 U.S. 813 (1983); *Snyder v. Titus*, 513 F.Supp. 926, 2 EBC 1269 (E.D. Va. 1981); *Robinson v. UMW Health & Retirement Funds*, 640 F.2d 416, 2 EBC 1086 (D.C. Cir. 1981), *rev'd on other grounds*, 455 U.S. 562, 3 EBC 1129 (1982); *Fase v. Seafarers Welfare & Pension Plan*, 432 F.Supp. 1037 (E.D.N.Y. 1977), *aff'd*, 589 F.2d 112, 1 EBC 1474 (2d Cir. 1978).

[359] 680 F.2d 911, 3 EBC 1545 (2d Cir. 1982), *cert. denied*, 459 U.S. 1039 (1982).

involving lesser amounts that had not had the effect on "diversification" that this grant would have.[360] In *Morse v. Stanley*, trustees were upheld in their contention that a criteria or policy of denying lump sum payments to employees who left to compete with the employer furthered a legitimate plan purpose because of the effects competition could have on the employer as the plan's source of funds.[361]

One problem with criteria that serve overall financial purposes is that while the purposes may be legitimate in general, the criteria seem to so often function as a means of penalizing persons who leave professional partnerships, employees who go to work for competitors, employees who are no longer union members, or simply lower paid or otherwise disfavored employees who lack influence in plan administration.[362] In essence, "bad boy" and other disloyalty clauses, which ERISA outlawed as the basis for the forfeiture of accrued pension benefits, have been moved into remaining areas of discretion under plans (as well as into nondiscretionary provisions for the forfeiture of benefits and benefit options that are not protected as a part of the participant's vested "accrued benefit").[363]

Close examination could, however, reveal that criteria put forward by a plan's trustees are not rationally related to the proper pension purpose they purport to serve, or while contributing slightly to a proper purpose, they are overdrawn. This type of review has not materialized in lump sum cases, apparently because of the courts' view that participants denied lump sums are generally not "losing" a valuable right. For example, the court in *Fine* could have questioned whether the "diversification" the trustees contended was necessary for the plan could not as well be achieved with a smaller amount of plan assets. The dissent in *Fine* illustrates how the trustees' facially plausible rationale looks when examined more closely.[364] In *Teskey v. M.P. Metal Products, Inc.*, the Seventh Circuit applied a similar analysis in holding that a plan's denial of lump sum benefits on account of a need to maintain liquidity, while plausible in general, was a feeble excuse when nearly all of the plan's assets were already liquid.[365]

Likewise, the contention in *Morse v. Stanley* that denying lump sum benefits to employees who work for competitors of their former employer serves a legitimate pension plan interest may be questioned on rationality grounds. In *Frary v. Shorr Paper Products, Inc.*, a district court stated that it is "generally recognized" that the purpose of penalties for competition is to protect the employer, and found that the denials of lump sum benefits had not been shown to serve any legitimate purpose of the plan. The court suggested that the proper place for

---

[360] 699 F.2d 1091, 4 EBC 1273 (11th Cir. 1983).

[361] 732 F.2d 1139, 5 EBC 1602 (2d Cir. 1984).

[362] See the cases above, and the cases cited in ch. 5, sec. V, on permitted forfeitures.

[363] *Id.*

[364] 699 F.2d 1091, 4 EBC 1273 (11th Cir. 1983).

[365] 795 F.2d 30, 7 EBC 1950 (7th Cir. 1986).

implementing such a policy is in an employment agreement, rather than under general discretionary authority in a pension plan.[366] Anticompetitive lines under discretionary authority can also be irrational on the same grounds that forfeitures based on express plan rules have been held to be irrational, i.e., if the departing employee is simply "one more salesman seeking orders in an industry which is admittedly highly competitive,"[367] if an anticompetitive line applies even when an employee has been discharged or constructively discharged by an employer,[368] if it extends to a type of employment the employer does not engage in or to employment in a geographic area or market where the employer does not operate,[369] or if the anticompetitive rule exacts a loss of benefits that is more than reasonably necessary to compensate the plan for any competitive effects.[370] An anticompetitive line can also be irrational when it is not disclosed to participants beforehand so that the rule or policy can serve its asserted function of encouraging employees to stay with and not compete against the employer.[371]

In making discretionary changes to interest rates for lump sum benefits, considerable latitude may similarly exist, but a new interest rate established under discretionary authority must still be reasonable.[372] However, in *Lewis v. Fulton Federal Savings & Loan Pension Plan*, a district court did not closely examine whether new 13.65 percent and then 14.5 percent interest rates were still reasonable once it concluded that *some* change in the plan's interest rate from its prior level of 6 percent was called for.[373] Over the same time periods, the PBGC's interest rates for immediate annuities, which are based on a survey of the rates on which insurers are selling immediate annuities, were 10.5 percent and 10.75 percent.[374]

---

366 494 F.Supp. 565, 2 EBC 2268, at 2271 (N.D. Ill. 1980). In *Morse v. Stanley*, a slightly more plausible showing was made than in *Frary* of secondary effects on the profit-sharing plan as the employees who left had apparently taken substantial business accounts with them that could affect the employer's future ability to make profits and thus substantial contributions out of profits to the plan. Exercising discretion under a plan to protect an employer as the future source of funding for a plan is, however, questionable if the employer does not have a contractual obligation to continue maintaining the plan, or even to make a fixed contribution from profits.

367 *Ellis v. Lionikis*, 394 A.2d 116, at 119 (N.J. App.Div. 1978) (the company's sales in Ellis' territory actually increased after his departure).

368 See ch. 5, sec. V (on permitted forfeitures of vested benefits), and *Morse v. Stanley, supra* (also suggesting the discharge or constructive discharge exception).

369 See ch. 5, sec. V.

370 *Id.*

371 Compare *Morse v. Stanley, supra*, with *Hillis v. Waukesha Title Co.*, 576 F.Supp. 1103 (E.D. Wis. 1983); *Chambless v. Masters, Mates & Pilots Pension Plan*, 772 F.2d 1032, 6 EBC 2209 (2d Cir. 1985); *Frary v. Shorr Paper Products Inc.*, 494 F.Supp. 565, 2 EBC 2268 (N.D. Ill. 1980). And see ch. 9, sec. V, on advance notice of adverse plan amendments.

372 See ch. 6, sec. III.B.

373 4 EBC 2071 (N.D. Ga. 1983). Compare *Dooley v. American Airlines, Inc.*, 797 F.2d 1447 (7th Cir. 1986) (summary judgment not proper against plaintiffs on claim that change from fixed interest rate to a variable standard that reached 16% was unreasonable and in breach of fiduciary duty when PBGC rate at same time was 11%); *UAW District 65 v. Harper & Row Publishers, Inc.*, 576 F.Supp. 1468, 4 EBC 2586 (S.D.N.Y. 1983).

374 See *Lewis v. Fulton Federal Savings & Loan Pension Plan, supra*, and 29 C.F.R. 2619, Appendix B, for the table of the PBGC's rates. And see ch. 6, sec. III.B, on the use of the PBGC's rates as the upper bounds of reasonability.

A line drawn under discretionary authority can also be arbitrary, even if rationally related to legitimate plan purposes, when it discriminates against individuals or groups of individuals, on its face or in operation. In *Winpisinger v. Aurora Corp.*, a multiemployer board of trustees exercised discretionary authority to amend a plan to add a provision cancelling previously granted past service credits on the withdrawal of an employer for those employees who were not union members before the withdrawal. The trustees identified the legitimate purpose to be served as protecting the plan's funding, which the amendment would do. The court, however, focused on the fact that the trustees were protecting the fund by establishing a new "preference[] amongst [the plan] participants" that focused the burden of improving the plan's funded status on a discrete group of participants. The court stated:

> "[T]he fiduciary is forbidden from granting preference as between a plan's participants ... [he or she] owe[s] a duty of fairness to all—not just some of the covered employees.... [Fiduciaries are therefore] required to exercise their discretion in a non-discriminatory manner."[375]

To the extent the *Winpisinger* decision rejects the "arbitrary and capricious" standard of review in favor of closer scrutiny under ERISA's express language for fiduciary duties, the decision has not been followed.[376] But the more central point that lines drawn under discretionary authority must not create discriminatory preferences is widely recognized. In *Morse v. Stanley*, the Second Circuit found that trustees have a duty to deal "impartially" and "even-handedly" with the entire employee group under any discretion they have.[377] In *Petrella v. NL Industries, Inc.*, the district court recognized that discretion must be exercised not only rationally, but also in a manner that does not result in "prohibited discrimination."[378] In *Fine v. Semet*, the district court explicitly rejected *Winpisinger* to the extent it can be read to demand absolutely no preferences (on the ground that some preference is almost inevitable), but accepted that dissimilar treatment cannot be based on improper discriminatory purposes.[379]

At some point, discretion under a plan can also be so fraught with discriminatory or preferential potential as to be inherently discriminatory. In *Steidtmann v. Koelbel & Co.*, an employer reserved discretion to vary the date of its annual contributions to an incentive pay plan, and at the same time, required employment on the date it finally set for an employee to receive *any* allocation of the annual contributions. An employee repeatedly asked when the date was expected to be so he could remain until then, but was given evasive answers until he finally

---

[375] 456 F.Supp. 559, 1 EBC 2201, at 2207 and 2214 (N.D. Ohio 1978).

[376] See nn. 90 and 91 above.

[377] 732 F.2d 1139, 5 EBC 1602, at 1608 (2d Cir. 1984).

[378] 529 F.Supp. 1357, 3 EBC 1210, at 1218 and 1220 (D.N.J. 1982).

[379] 514 F.Supp. 34, 2 EBC 1103 (S.D. Fla. 1981), *aff'd*, 699 F.2d 1091, 4 EBC 1273 (11th Cir. 1983). See also ch. 9, sec. II.B, on discriminatory exceptions under plan amendments.

left. The Colorado Court of Appeals held the employer could not have both the discretion to set the date and the right to deny any payments for the entire year because of lack of employment on one date because of the potential for evasion and self-dealing if this were permitted.[380]

Favorable exercises of discretion can be arbitrary and capricious if nondiscriminatory treatment inherently cannot be extended to other participants, or if the exercise is detrimental to the other participants' rights. In *In re Braniff Airways, Inc.*, fulfillment of one group of participants' requests for discretionary lump sum benefits before a final termination allocation of a plan's limited assets would have discriminated in favor of the one group, who would have received full payment of their benefits, at the expense of others, who would have been left with still less assets in the plan to pay their benefits.[381] Similarly, in *Lewis v. Fulton Federal Savings & Loan Pension Plan*, the court stated that maintaining an unreasonable low interest rate for computing and paying lump sum benefits could constitute a breach of fiduciary duty because of the preferential effect it could have in unreasonably depleting the plan assets remaining for other participants.[382]

d. Professional consideration. ERISA Section 404(a)(1)(B) requires fiduciaries to act with the "care, skill, prudence and diligence" of a person acting in a like capacity and in a like enterprise who is "familiar with such matters." This requires not just legitimate purposes, but professional inquiry and consideration of the rationality of means to ends, and of alternatives that would permit achievement of the same ends while allowing participants to have their benefits, or benefit options, as anticipated. To a large extent this requirement overlaps with rationality and the consideration of alternative means with less preferential or discriminatory effects. But it reemphasizes that trustees cannot assert a need for "diversification" that has only surface rationality, or that was devised as a *post hoc* rationale, but rather must show consideration of their position and of alternatives before the fact. To illustrate, in *Frary v. Shorr Paper Products, Inc.*, the district court stated that "the record [which showed that a policy of denying lump sum benefits to employees who went to work for competitors was not reduced to writing and had never been applied previously] suggests that defendants' avowed policy was no policy at all, but rather a *post hoc* rationalization for its attempt to improperly punish plaintiff for his alleged breach of his contract of employment with Shorr Paper."[383]

---

380 506 P.2d 1247 (Colo. App. 1973). *Steidtmann* did not involve a Code §401(a) qualified plan. If a qualified plan had been involved, the plan would have also violated the Code's definite determinability requirement, which requires that allocations of contributions to a qualified profit-sharing plan be made at regular intervals. See Rev. Rul. 80-155.

381 4 EBC 1116 (Bankr. N.D. Tex. 1982).

382 4 EBC 2071, at 2079 (N.D. Ga. 1983).

383 494 F.Supp. 565, 2 EBC 2268, at 2273 (N.D. Ill. 1980). The requirement that the rationale for an exercise of discretion must be one that was developed and considered before the fact, along with alternatives, is most developed in decisions on plan amendments. See ch. 9, sec. II.B.

2. Separating Statutory and Common Law Issues

When an undisclosed but concrete standard is put forward as the basis for an exercise of discretion, such as that employees who go to work for competitors are denied discretionary lump sum benefits, a fundamental fiduciary and disclosure question is why the standard was not disclosed to participants in the plan and in the SPD. In *Frary v. Shorr Paper Products*, the district court said:

> "[B]asic notions of fairness dictate that any rule or policy of Plan Administration be in a form which makes them knowable to the Plan's participants."[384]

If the plan provision conferring discretionary authority turns on "hardship" or "good cause," what is required to convince a fiduciary to exercise the discretion may be fairly obvious. But when a concrete and basically unrelated standard is applied under general discretionary authority, fairness dictates that the standard be made known to participants in advance so they can conform their actions to the rule.

The failure to put in writing a concrete standard used in the exercise of discretionary authority raises questions of compliance with both ERISA Section 402(b)(4)'s requirement that a plan "specify the basis on which payments are made to and from the plan," and also Section 102(b)'s requirement that the SPD describe the plan's provisions for qualification for benefits *and* the circumstances that may result in disqualification. However, in *Morse v. Stanley*, the Second Circuit distinguished criteria for granting or denying discretionary lump sum options where no "loss" of benefit value occurs if the lump sum option is denied, from criteria that cause an irretrievable loss of benefit value, holding that the former criteria need not be disclosed in an SPD, nor presumably in the plan itself or any other published form.[385] Outside of the narrow sphere of claims where no "loss" of benefit value occurs, however, trustees have a clear obligation to disclose concrete criteria used under discretionary authority.[386]

More fundamentally, trustees have a duty to disclose all the areas of their express or implied discretion under the plan. In *Valle v. Joint Plumbing Industry Board*, the Second Circuit held the trustees of a

---

[384] 494 F.Supp. 565, 2 EBC 2268, at 2273 (N.D. Ill. 1980). See also *Kosty v. Lewis*, 319 F.2d 744, at 748 (D.C. Cir. 1963), *cert. denied,* 375 U.S. 964 (1964) ("trust relationships operate within some limitations of fundamental fairness," which are exceeded when trustees fail to provide notice of plan rules so that participants may retire under old rules or else attempt to comply with the new rule).

[385] 732 F.2d 1139, 5 EBC 1602 (2d Cir. 1984). See also *Pompano v. Michael Schiavone & Sons, Inc.*, 680 F.2d 911, 3 EBC 1545, at 1548 (2d Cir. 1982), *cert. denied,* 459 U.S. 1039 (1982) (no "substantive denial" of ERISA benefits involved under the facts when participant denied lump sum mode of payment); *Dooley v. American Airlines, Inc., supra,* (implicit discretion to change interest rate under plan language providing for "actuarially equivalent" lump sums not barred by ERISA §402(b)(4) written plan or Code's definite determinability requirement when it occurred before effective date of Rev. Rul. 79-90).

[386] See *Morse v. Stanley, supra*; *Pompano v. Michael Schiavone & Sons, Inc., supra.* If disclosure is not required because no "loss" of benefits occurs on a denial, failure to reduce a discretionary policy to writing can still go to whether the "avowed policy" is a "post-hoc" rationale. See *Frary v. Shorr Paper Products, Inc., supra,* 2 EBC at 2273.

multiemployer plan had a duty to disclose that two of the years required under a new requirement of 15 contributory years of service for a pension could be waived in the trustees' discretion for disability.[387] In *Genter v. Acme Scale & Supply Co.*, an employer and plan administrator failed to advise participants in the SPD or written plan of a discretionary practice of increasing certain participants' life insurance after their salary increased, rather than waiting until the end of the year in which the salary increase occurred as provided under the terms of the plan. The Third Circuit held this violated ERISA's fiduciary duties and the SPD and written plan requirements. In view of the participant's death, it could never be known whether he would have availed himself of this opportunity had it been disclosed. But the Third Circuit held that the crucial point was that if he had been properly informed of the opportunity, he might have increased his life insurance coverage from $10,000 to $20,000 prior to his death. Therefore, based on the omission where there was a duty to disclose, summary judgment was granted in the amount of the increased coverage in favor of his estate.[388]

A failure to contemporaneously provide "specific reasons" later asserted at trial as the basis for a benefit denial can violate ERISA Section 503's claims procedures and can also be evidence of a *post hoc* construction of a legitimate rationale for a denial. In *Short v. Central States Pension Fund*, the Eighth Circuit found that to comply with the ERISA Section 503 claims procedure requirements, the trustees must state their "specific reasons" for a denial of a claim for benefits in writing *at the time* of the denial. The court stated:

> "A post hoc attempt to furnish a rationale for a denial . . . to avoid reversal on appeal, and thus meaningful review, diminishes the integrity of the Fund and its administrators. ERISA and its accompanying regulations were intended to help claimants process their claims. . . ."[389]

The failure to provide reasons for a denial prevents a participant from demonstrating conformity with the criteria being used. If it has occurred in the past, it also means that the plan does not have records of the specific reasons used when exercises of discretion have been either favorably extended or denied other participants. The plan administrator or trustees have thus not developed the "body of precedent" that ERISA's claims procedure was expected to bring about as an aid for themselves and for participants and the courts in reviewing the consistency of plan administration.[390] "Ordinarily," the failure to follow claims procedure requirements does not lead to a direct substantive

---

387 623 F.2d 196, 3 EBC 1026 (2d Cir. 1980).

388 776 F.2d 1180 (3d Cir. 1985).

389 *Short v. Central States Pension Fund*, 729 F.2d 567, 5 EBC 2552, at 2559 (8th Cir. 1984).

390 See *Richardson v. Central States Pension Fund*, 645 F.2d 660, 2 EBC 1477, at 1480 (8th Cir. 1981).

remedy,[391] but it may weigh in the degree of scrutiny given to undocumented claims by plan administrators or trustees of "consistent" past applications of discretion. Procedural violations can also weigh in the degree of scrutiny given to claims that the rationality and nondiscriminatory effects of *new* criteria used under discretion were considered before the fact—as required for the action not to be "in contravention of fiduciary duties."[392]

The Internal Revenue Code's nondiscrimination requirement significantly limits the discretion permitted trustees or an employer under a tax-qualified plan. To meet the Code's nondiscrimination requirement, a subsidized early retirement benefit that depends on the "consent" of the employer must be administered according to "set" criteria that are uniformly applied, and that do not in operation produce discrimination in favor of the prohibited group of employees.[393] Similarly, for a lump sum benefit provided in the discretion of a plan's trustees or a retirement committee, the discretion must not be exercised "primarily" in favor of the prohibited group of employees. Such discrimination can be measured by whether the percentage of prohibited group employees receiving the lump sum benefits is "significantly higher" than the percentage of rank and file employees.[394]

To meet the Code's "definitely determinable" benefits requirement, open-ended classifications, such as a "leave of absence," which may function as discretionary authority, must also be administered according to "established" criteria that extend uniformly to all employees covered by the plan, are applied consistently to employees in similar circumstances, and do not otherwise primarily advantage the prohibited group of employees under the plan.[395] Regulations, still in proposed form at the date of this writing, would go one step farther in giving substance to the Code's definite determinability requirement by providing that the availability of benefit options must always be determined under ascertainable criteria stated in the plan.[396] If a plan states that it is to be interpreted as a tax-qualified plan, as most do, these rules bear directly on the interpretation of the scope of discretion afforded the trustees or employer under a plan, and in most circuits, they bear on this issue even without a specific plan interpretation

---

[391] *Blau v. Del Monte Corp.*, 748 F.2d 1348, 6 EBC 1264, at 1268–69 (9th Cir. 1984), *cert. denied,* 474 U.S. 865 (1985).

[392] *Id.*, and see sec. III.A.3.h on the effect of procedural defects in review of plan interpretations. But see *Pompano v. Michael Schiavone & Sons, Inc., supra,* (lack of specific reasons for denial of lump sum benefits at the time of the denial has no effect on court's review if it determines that no "substantive" loss of benefits resulted from denial of discretion).

[393] Rev. Rul. 58-151, as amplified by Rev. Rul. 58-604. When no prohibited group employees are in a plan, e.g., because the plan is a collectively bargained plan covering only hourly employees, these standards do not apply. Rev. Rul. 58-604.

[394] Rev. Rul. 85-59.

[395] Rev. Rul. 81-106.

[396] Prop. Regs. 1.401(a)-4 and 1.411(d)-4, 51 Fed. Reg. 3798 (Jan. 30, 1986). Although this regulation could be made final at any time, it is not proposed to actually become *effective* until the second plan year after Jan. 30, 1986, for nonbargained plans, or for collectively bargained plans, not until the earlier of the third plan year after Jan. 30, 1986, or the second plan year after the expiration of the collective bargaining agreement in effect on Jan. 30, 1986.

proviso.[397] In every case, noncompliance with the nondiscrimination requirements also raises tax-qualification issues.

Common law principles can also apply to exercises of discretionary authority. Generally, no matter how routine an exercise of discretion has been in the past, courts are reluctant to bind a plan under estoppel or to find a modification by past practice of a requirement that the discretion be favorably exercised, for example, by granting a lump sum option, or an early retirement benefit requiring employer consent.[398] However, in some cases, common law principles estop or modify a discretion requirement, *or* estop or modify other plan requirements that have been bypassed through routine application of the discretion. In *Hardy v. H.K. Porter Co.*, a plan's requirement that participants be in service at age 60 for an early retirement benefit was found to have been modified by the employer's past practice of discretionarily placing employees on leaves of absence "solely" to qualify them for the benefit.[399] Acts can also function as statements to satisfy a plan's discretion or consent requirements. In *Luli v. Sun Products Corp.*, an employer's consent for a discretionary early retirement was found to be given by its act of shutting down a plant.[400] In *Sanchez v. Trustees of Pension Plan,* discretion to cover nonhourly employees as participants under a multiemployer plan was found to have been exercised by the plan trustees' knowing acceptance of contributions on behalf of certain nonhourly employees for a number of years.[401]

---

[397] See *Petrella v. NL Indus., Inc.*, 529 F.Supp. 1357, 3 EBC 1210 (D.N.J. 1982), and sec. III.A.3.e, on plan interpretation.

[398] See *Fine v. Semet*, 699 F.2d 1091, 4 EBC 1273 (11th Cir. 1983) (although routinely granted in the past, discretion still must be exercised for lump sum option); *Hackett v. PBGC*, 486 F.Supp. 1357, 2 EBC 2522 (D. Md. 1980) (although routine in the past, consent still required for early retirement benefit requiring employer consent); *Morse v. Stanley*, 732 F.2d 1139, 5 EBC 1602, at 1606 (2d Cir. 1984) (past practice does not create "discretionary strait-jacket").

[399] 417 F.Supp. 1175 (E.D. Pa. 1976), *aff'd in part, rev'd in part,* 562 F.2d 42 (3d Cir. 1977).

[400] 398 N.E.2d 553 (Ohio 1979). But see *Fielding v. Int'l Harvester Co.*, 815 F.2d 1254 (9th Cir. 1987) (contra reasoning of *Luli* without citing or distinguishing).

[401] 359 So.2d 1279 (La. 1978).

8

Estoppel, Separate Contracts, Misrepresentation, Unjust Enrichment, and Reform in Equity

I. Equitable Relief for Misstatements and Omissions in an SPD

ERISA's stringent requirements for adequate disclosure in a summary plan description (SPD) make the SPD the "key document in disputes over benefit entitlement."[1] Under ERISA Section 102, an employer must prepare an SPD that understandably, comprehensively, and accurately describes the benefit provisions of a plan, and that affirmatively and specifically sets forth the negative circumstances, or drawbacks, that may result in ineligibility, loss, or disqualification from the promised benefits.[2] Because of this statutory obligation, statements in the SPD, or the omission of negative circumstances in an SPD, are strong extrinsic evidence in the interpretation of ambiguous plan provisions. If a plan provision is unambiguous, SPD statements or omissions can estop application of the plan provision under a court's authority to provide "appropriate equitable relief." The SPD may, in other words, "effectively become the terms of the plan."[3]

---

[1] E. Miller and M. Dorenfeld, "ERISA: Adequate Summary Plan Descriptions," 14 Hous. L. Rev. 835, at 835 (1977).

[2] See ch. 7, sec. III.A.4.a.

[3] E. Miller and M. Dorenfeld, "ERISA: Adequate Summary Plan Descriptions," 14 Hous. L. Rev. 835, at 848 (1977). And see *Bachelder v. Communications Satellite Corp.*, 8 EBC 1609 (D. Me. 1987) (SPD unambiguously promising cash distributions by the last day of the year constituted the governing plan instrument or document when plan itself did not specify date of distribution).

A. Range of Judicial Remedies

An SPD that is at odds with the provisions of a plan, or that is otherwise misleading or incomplete, is a fiduciary violation and also a violation of Section 102 of ERISA. "[A]ppropriate equitable relief" is available under ERISA Section 502(a)(3) for both violations. Equitable relief, including estoppel, may also be provided under the federal common law of ERISA Section 502(a)(1)(B).

Most commonly, statements in SPDs are used in interpretation of ambiguous plan provisions, as discussed in Chapter 7. But when the related plan provision is unambiguous and contradictory, SPD statements and omissions can estop application of the contradictory plan provision. In *Zittrouer v. Uarco Inc. Group Ben. Plan*, a health insurer plan was estopped from asserting an exclusion, unambiguously contained in the full plan document, for convalescent care which did not begin until after age 70 because the exclusion was not disclosed, or suggested, in the SPD.[4] Similarly, in *Hillis v. Waukesha Title Co.*, a pension plan was estopped from asserting a forfeiture provision for competition with the employer when an SPD had not been distributed to the participant. The court stated:

> "[W]here a plan participant is reasonably unaware of a benefit forfeiture clause, and where the plan administrator fails to take any steps to advise the participant of the clause, the forfeiture may not be enforced against the participant."[5]

In *McKnight v. Southern Life & Health Ins. Co.*, an employee was held entitled to benefit accrual credit for two early periods of service that had been interrupted by breaks in service before the period of service during which the employee vested. The Eleventh Circuit found the employee was entitled to the credit under a literal interpretation of the plan's break-in-service rules, and alternatively, under the summary plan description of the break rules. Although both had the same result, the two versions were at odds so that the SPD could not be used for interpretation of the plan. But the court found that even if the trustees' adverse interpretation of the plan were correct, the SPD still controlled, holding:

> "It is of no effect to publish and distribute a ... summary booklet designed to simplify and explain a voluminous and complex document, and then proclaim that any inconsistencies will be governed by the plan. Unfairness [would] flow to the employee for reasonably relying on the summary booklet."[6]

In *Winston v. Trustees of Hotel & Restaurant Employees & Bartenders*

---

[4] 582 F.Supp. 1471 (N.D. Ga. 1984).

[5] 576 F.Supp. 1103, at 1109 (E.D. Wis. 1983).

[6] 758 F.2d 1566, 6 EBC 1707, at 1711 (11th Cir. 1985). See also *Chambers v. Kaleidoscope, Inc. Profit Sharing Plan*, 650 F.Supp. 359, 7 EBC 2628, at 2634 (N.D. Ga. 1986) ("any inconsistencies between the plan summary and the plan document that inure to the employer's benefit should be resolved in favor of the plan summary," following *McKnight*).

International Welfare Fund, a participant who was disabled by a heart attack at age 62 was entitled to extended medical, hospital and disability benefits according the SPD. The trustees, however, claimed that under the plan itself, the extended benefits were only for beneficiaries after a participant's death. The trustees for unexplained reasons never introduced the plan into evidence, but the court stated that even if the plan was different, the booklet said it was describing the plan's benefits, and estoppel principles would therefore prevent the trustees from "denying the correctness of their own publication."[7] In *Genter v. Acme Scale & Supply Co.*, an employer and plan administrator failed to advise participants in an SPD or written plan of a discretionary practice of increasing certain participants' life insurance in the middle of a year after their salary increased, rather than waiting until the end of the year in which the salary increase occurred, as provided under the terms of the plan. The Third Circuit held this violated their fiduciary duties and the statutory SPD and written plan requirements. In view of the participant's death, it could never be known whether he would have availed himself of this opportunity had it been disclosed. But the Third Circuit held that the crucial point was that if he had been properly informed of the opportunity, he might have increased his life insurance coverage from $10,000 to $20,000 prior to his death. Based on the omission of information there was a duty to disclose, the court granted summary judgment in the amount of the increased coverage in favor of his estate.[8]

An appropriate equitable remedy for an SPD violation can also be more limited. In *Corley v. Hecht Co.*, an SPD stated that "[t]he low cost of [life insurance requiring employee contribution] is made possible by the company paying the difference between your contribution and the total cost of the plan." This statement was found under a "common sense reading" to mean that the employer did not consider its payments as a loan, and did not expect reimbursement for its payments in the event of experience dividends. The employer had, however, been receiving reimbursement for its payments from experience dividends as permitted under its formal contract with the insurer. The district court found the SPD in violation of Section 102(a)(1), but limited the appropriate equitable remedy to prohibiting the return to the employer of experience dividends still owed by the insurer, while allowing the employer to keep the dividends it received earlier.[9]

Potentially, a fiduciary who does not prepare an accurate and

---

[7] 441 N.E.2d 1217, at 1221 (Ill. App. 1982). And see *Bachelder v. Communications Satellite Corp.*, 8 EBC 1609 (D. Me. 1987) (SPD unambiguously promising cash distributions by last day of the year constituted the governing plan instrument or document when plan itself did not specify date of distribution).

[8] 776 F.2d 1180 (3d Cir. 1985).

[9] 530 F.Supp. 1155, 2 EBC 2397, at 2405 (D.D.C. 1982). And see *Bruch v. Firestone Tire & Rubber Co.*, 640 F.Supp. 519 (E.D. Pa. 1986) (no estoppel because of SPD's failure to illustrate extent of actuarial reductions for early retirement under deferred vested pension when SPD otherwise distinguished between eligibility requirements for early retirement benefits subject to a lesser reduction and requirements for deferred vested benefits).

complete SPD may be personally liable either to the plan for benefits that have to be paid out beyond those anticipated under the plan's terms, or directly to the affected participants and beneficiaries.[10] In *Allen v. Atlantic Richfield Retirement Plan*, a district court stated:

> "Clearly . . . part of the fiduciary's duty under [Section 404] is to provide employees with a comprehensive explanation of the contents of the plan."[11]

B. Reliance as an Element for Estoppel or Other Appropriate Equitable Relief

Reliance is not technically required to establish a Section 102 violation, but it is clearly relevant in determining "appropriate equitable relief," under ERISA Section 502(a)(3) or under the federal common law of Section 502(a)(1)(B). Of course, if a plan can be *interpreted* to provide benefits consistently with the representations in the SPD, no showing of reliance is required.

Estoppel, or "appropriate equitable relief" in the form of benefit payments, may *not* be forthcoming when a participant knows that a statement in an SPD is not true or that it is inconsistent with the plan's terms. Thus, while various notices posted for employees may clearly indicate that an employee is covered by a plan, the notices cannot estop the plan if the court finds that the employee otherwise knew and understood that he was not covered.[12] Participants may also constructively be on notice of inconsistent plan terms if they ratified a collective bargaining agreement containing the plan terms and cannot reasonably expect that the employer unilaterally modified the terms in the SPD. In *Michota v. Anheuser-Busch, Inc.*, participants who had

---

[10] See E. Miller and M. Dorenfeld, "ERISA: Adequate Summary Plan Descriptions," 14 Hous. L. Rev. 835, at 842–49 (1977). Generally, fiduciaries are insured against such liability, with the insurance premiums paid by the plan (with the insurer then required to have recourse against the fiduciary) or by the employer (with or without recourse), or else the fiduciaries have indemnity agreements with the employer or employers.

[11] 480 F.Supp. 848, 1 EBC 1523, at 1526 (E.D. Pa. 1979), *aff'd*, 633 F.2d 209 (3d Cir. 1980). And see *Blau v. Del Monte Corp.*, 748 F.2d 1348, 6 EBC 1264 (9th Cir. 1984), *cert. denied*, 474 U.S. 865 (1985) (fiduciaries act arbitrarily and capriciously in administration of the plan when reporting and disclosure duties are not fulfilled).

[12] *Stutelberg v. Farrell Lines, Inc.*, 529 F.Supp. 566, 3 EBC 1124 (S.D.N.Y. 1982), *aff'd*, 697 F.2d 297 (2d Cir. 1982). See also *Kamenstein v. Jordan Marsh Co.*, 623 F.Supp. 1109, 6 EBC 2611 (D. Mass. 1985) (failure to disclose according to ERISA requirements not actionable when participant has actual knowledge of plan provisions); *Nachwalter v. Christie*, 611 F.Supp. 655, at 662-63 (S.D. Fla. 1985), *aff'd*, 805 F.2d 956, 7 EBC 2675 (11th Cir. 1986) (oral agreement to value account balance of law firm partner/plan trustee as of certain date prior to precipitous drop in value of plan assets at variance with terms of plan not binding when plaintiff knew plan's terms; to hold otherwise would permit the "collusion" and "exact evil" ERISA's written plan requirements were designed to prevent); *Rubin v. Decision Concepts, Inc.*, 566 F.Supp. 1057 (S.D.N.Y. 1983) (failure to distribute summary of material modification of plan not actionable when participant received memo that in combination with the SPD was enough to let him know that new plan was a restatement of former profit-sharing plan and not an additional profit-sharing plan); *Ridens v. Voluntary Separation Program*, 610 F.Supp. 770 (D. Minn. 1985) (no estoppel when employee knew what severance pay plan said and did not reasonably rely on inconsistent oral representations made by employee without actual or apparent authority over plan).

not received a summary of a plan amendment were held to have "adequate constructive notice as a matter of law" when they ratified the amendment in their collective bargaining agreement. The Third Circuit stated:

> "A necessary corollary to the rule that all terms of a collective bargaining agreement are binding on the individual members of the . . . unit, is the concept that [they] have notice of the terms therein set forth."[13]

However, the fact that a catch-all notice may be contained in an SPD that the full plan is available for inspection is generally not enough to constitute constructive notice of inconsistent terms.[14]

Reliance on, or injury from, the SPD statement or omission must also be shown.[15] In *Hillis v. Waukesha Title Co.*, the "showing of injury" was the plaintiff's statement of the importance of pension benefits to him, and his testimony that he would not have separated from service when he did if he had known of the forfeiture-for-competition clause contained in the plan. The *Hillis* court stated that requiring a "showing of injury" was not to establish a sharp barrier to relief, but was to cull "mere procedural violations" of the reporting and disclosure requirements that do not result in "cognizable injury."[16] A prime example of this is when an SPD has not been distributed, but no benefit denials are linked to the nondisclosure.[17]

Generally, it should be possible to establish detrimental reliance, as in other employment-related estoppel cases, by showing that a participant continued to work as an employee after a representation in an SPD was made. The showing of reliance, or injury, thus need not be proof that a participant would have left on a certain date to take a high-paying job with another company "but for" the SPD statement,

---

[13] 755 F.2d 330, 6 EBC 1161, at 1166 (3d Cir. 1985).

[14] See sec. I.C below on disclaimers of inaccuracy.

[15] See *Hillis v. Waukesha Title Co.*, 576 F.Supp. 1103 (E.D. Wis. 1983); *Burud v. Acme Elec. Co.*, 591 F.Supp. 238, 5 EBC 1793 (D. Alas. 1984).

[16] 576 F.Supp. at 1109–1110. See also *Baker v. Lukens Steel Co.*, 793 F.2d 509, 7 EBC 2039, at 2043 (3d Cir. 1986) (summary of material modification required to be distributed under ERISA on plan amendment deleting early retirement benefits available on plant closing; but for estoppel based on the nondisclosure, participants must show reliance, e.g., that they "did not leave their jobs for other employment or even search for such employment because of misinformation concerning their status"); *Ruotolo v. Sherwin-Williams Co.*, 622 F.Supp. 546 (D. Conn. 1985) (not disclosing that employee's disability benefits would be reduced by 70% of any earnings violated SPD requirements; but employee must show reliance on the nondisclosure to recover lost benefits; this was left open, the employee having claimed that he might have chosen early retirement benefits that were not subject to such an offset had he known of its existence under the disability plan).

[17] See the cases cited in ch. 14, sec. VII, in which penalties generally have not been imposed under ERISA §502(c) for reporting and disclosure violations because of lack of "prejudice" to participants. Other decisions express more reluctance concerning the scope of appropriate relief even when benefit denials are linked to nondisclosure. In *Petrella v. NL Indus., Inc.*, 529 F.Supp. 1357, 3 EBC 1210 (D.N.J. 1982), a company denied benefits under severance pay and vacation pay plans for which no summary plan descriptions had been distributed on a sale of a division to another company. The company's motion for summary judgment on the disclosure violations was denied, but the court said the disclosure violations would not result in a "grabbag" of compensatory damages, but "at most" an injunctive remedy or other equitable relief. 3 EBC at 1222. But see *Blau v. Del Monte Corp.*, 748 F.2d 1348, 6 EBC 1264 (9th Cir. 1984), *cert. denied*, 474 U.S. 865 (1985), for a nearly identical situation where the nondisclosure was weighed in holding that a plan interpretation was arbitary and capricious.

but rather may be proof of reliance and injury using inferences drawn from everyday experience.[18]

Reliance may thus generally be inferred based on a continuation of work, but it is not automatic, or irrefutable. In *Govoni v. Bricklayers, Masons and Plasterers Local No. 5 Pension Fund*, the First Circuit rejected a participant's claim that estoppel precluded application of a pre-ERISA break-in-service rule because the rule was not disclosed in his SPD. The First Circuit found the plaintiff had failed to show "significant reliance upon, or possible prejudice flowing from, the faulty plan description." In *Govoni*, the participant's break in service occurred *before* ERISA, and thus before the more liberal ERISA break-in-service rules described in the SPD went into effect. Therefore, the participant could not have been relying on the SPD's omission *at the time* the break occurred. The participant still claimed he might not have retired when he did if he had known that the SPD was inaccurate, but the record showed he was informed of the trustees' position before he retired, and his retirement was, moreover, not irreversible.[19] Similarly, in *Risch v. Waukesha Title Co.*, an employee received an SPD with notice of a forfeiture for competition provision *before* he left to go to work for a competitor. The court found that although the SPD had been prepared late, in violation of ERISA, and with the result that the participant had no notice of the provision during a significant period when he continued to work for the employer, no injury or prejudice resulted when he had notice of the forfeiture provision before he left.[20]

---

[18] See sec. II.D below on the reliance requirement for estoppel of a pension plan. See also *Genter v. Acme Scale & Supply Co.*, 776 F.2d 1180 (3d Cir. 1985) (estate of employee awarded $10,000 in increased life insurance when SPD and written plan failed to disclose discretion exercised for certain other employees to increase benefits immediately upon a salary increase, rather than at the end of the year; although employee had died and it therefore could not be known whether he would have availed himself of this opportunity had it been disclosed, crucial point was that he would have had the opportunity to do so); *Shea v. Teacher's Retirement System of City of New York*, 381 N.Y.S.2d 266 (App. Div. 1976), *app. dismissed*, 387 N.Y.S.2d 837 (Ct. App. 1976) (relief provided a deceased teacher's estate based on a misleading description of death benefit options in an employee booklet; the dissent in *Shea* complained that the teacher's reliance on the booklet was entirely inferred since no direct evidence showed she had read the booklet, or relied on it, in making her choice). But compare *Lee v. Union Elec. Co.*, 789 F.2d 1303, 7 EBC 1636 (8th Cir. 1986), *cert. denied*, 479 U.S. ___ (1986) (SPD adequately explained need for participant to affirmatively elect survivor's annuity for spouse in the event of death before retirement; but even if SPD's explanation of survivor's benefit options was inadequate, evidence must be introduced that the participant had an interest in providing benefits to his spouse to establish detrimental reliance).

[19] 732 F.2d 250, 5 EBC 1389, at 1392 (1st Cir. 1984).

[20] 588 F.Supp. 69 (E.D. Wis. 1984). See also *Freund v. Gerson*, 610 F.Supp. 69, 6 EBC 1796, at 1798 (S.D. Fla. 1985) (no reliance on SPD that did not disclose forfeiture-for-competition clause when participant was notified of the clause at the time he gave notice he was leaving and before he turned down a $15,000 raise and the opportunity to manage an office nearer his home if he stayed; court found that the plaintiff, an accountant, had been "scheming" his departure with a substantial portion of the firm's business "for some time," and had "his mind made up" regardless of the presence or absence of the pension forfeiture, which caused the loss of $4,448 in benefits); *Reynolds v. Bethlehem Steel Corp.*, 619 F.Supp. 919 (D. Md. 1984) (even if participant relied on mistaken approval of lump sum payment of benefits, reasonable reliance on expectation of lump sum payment ended once he was informed that benefits would not be paid in a lump sum, employer offered him his job back, and participant elected not to return).

C. Disclaimers of Accuracy or Completeness in an SPD

A reliance-related issue in SPD litigation is whether the statutory and federal common law consequences of a misleading, incomplete, or inaccurate SPD can be overcome by a boilerplate disclaimer in the SPD booklet. A typical disclaimer reads:

> "This booklet is not a part of and does not modify or constitute any provisions of the plan described herein, nor does it alter or affect in any way the rights of any participant under the plan. The plan and all descriptions and outlines thereof are governed by the formal plan document. A copy of this plan is on file at the office of the company and may be inspected, upon request, during normal business hours of any regular working day."[21]

Disclaimers can also be less strongly worded. For example:

> "The purpose of this summary is to describe the Plan to you in nontechnical terms. It is intended to give you enough information to answer most of the questions you are likely to have. However, if we covered every detail of the Plan, it would no longer be a summary, but as technical as the full text itself; so if you have a specific question you should consult the Plan document."[22]

Before ERISA, disclaimers of the completeness or accuracy of statements in an SPD were sometimes effective[23] and sometimes not.[24] Since an employer was under no statutory obligation to prepare an understandable, complete, and accurate SPD (or to prepare an SPD at all), a well-worded disclaimer might limit the responsibility an employer was seen as having voluntarily undertaken with publication of a summary booklet.[25] However, many courts rejected this view when the representations in an SPD were "clear," and the employer knew the

---

21 *Trombly v. Marshall*, 502 F.Supp. 29, 2 EBC 2500, at 2501-02 (D.D.C. 1980), *vacated in unpublished order* filed June 12, 1980.

22 *Anderson v. Alpha Portland Indus., Inc.*, 752 F.2d 1293, 6 EBC 1046, at 1051 n.13 (8th Cir. 1985) (*en banc*), *cert. denied*, 471 U.S. 1102 (1985). And see the disclaimer in *Hurd v. Hutnik*, 419 F.Supp. 630, 1 EBC 1382, at 1390 (D.N.J. 1976).

23 See *Spitznass v. First Nat'l Bank of Oregon*, 525 P.2d 1318 (Ore. 1974); *Anthony v. Ryder Truck Lines, Inc.*, 466 F.Supp. 1287, 1 EBC 1961 (E.D. Pa. 1979); *Joy Mfg. Co. v. Stohl*, 222 S.E.2d 888 (Ga. App. 1975); *Adams v. Hercules, Inc.*, 265 S.E.2d 781 (Ga. 1980); *Van Orman v. American Ins. Co.*, 680 F.2d 301, 3 EBC 1653 (3d Cir. 1982); *Gross v. Univ. of Chicago*, 302 N.E.2d 444 (Ill.App. 1973).

24 See *Hurd v. Hutnik*, 419 F.Supp. 630, 1 EBC 1382 (D.N.J. 1976); *Horn & Hardart Co. v. Ross*, 395 N.Y.S.2d 180 (Sup.Ct. App.Div. 1977); *Bauer v. Ins. Co. of N. America*, 351 F.Supp. 873 (E.D. Wis. 1972); *Gladden v. Pargas, Inc.*, 575 F.2d 1091 (4th Cir. 1978).

25 See *Spitznass v. First Nat'l Bank of Oregon, supra*; *Adams v. Hercules, Inc., supra*; *Van Orman v. American Ins. Co., supra*. See also *Kolentus v. Avco Corp.*, 798 F.2d 949 (7th Cir. 1986) (employee could not rely on general statements in pre-ERISA SPD that benefits were to be received as long as employee lived to require employer to complete the funding of all vested benefits after plan termination; SPD did not purport to set forth complete plan provisions on termination and plaintiff's "asserted reliance on the summary booklets [was] neither reasonable nor foreseeable in light of the admonition prefacing each of the booklets" that the booklet only covered the "high points" and that "should any questions arise the Agreement Covering Pensions shall govern," 798 F.2d at 955 and 958—citing still other cases, pro and con, on the effect of pre-ERISA disclaimers; *however*, the Seventh Circuit recognized that "one of the major changes" brought about by ERISA was that "it mandates disclosure of circumstances under which benefits may be terminated," 798 F.2d at 960).

booklets were customarily used by participants *as if* they were the terms of the plan.[26]

Some commentators continue to cite the pre-ERISA decisions as precedent on whether disclaimers are effective after ERISA,[27] but ERISA's statutory requirements that an SPD be prepared and that it meet the understandability, completeness, and accuracy standards of Sections 102(a) and (b) have fundamentally altered the issues involved in these cases.[28] Congress' intent, as evidenced in the legislative history and in the express requirements of ERISA Section 102, is that understandable, complete, and accurate information about a plan's benefits must be provided to participants and beneficiaries in an SPD. The SPD requirements are to remove the discrepancies between, in Senator Javits' words, "nicely phrased booklets" and the "cold legal phrasing" in the plan itself.[29] To allow a plan to avoid this statutory duty through a boilerplate disclaimer of completeness or accuracy would be to reallow the equivocation that Section 102 sought to remove from summary booklets issued to employees.

Accordingly, disclaimers are held to be invalid to the extent that they limit ERISA's statutory disclosure responsibilities. In *Zittrouer v. Uarco Inc. Group Ben. Plan*, a beneficiary was denied benefits for her stay in a convalescent home under a plan provision that unambiguously required the stay in such a facility to begin before age 70 for the benefits to be due. The summary plan description mentioned numerous limits on the health plan's benefits, but did not mention, or suggest, this limitation. Despite the discrepancy, the plan argued that an express disclaimer in the SPD stating that it "describe[d] the highlights" of the plan, with the benefits being "described fully in the Plan Document," meant that it had never represented that the SPD contained *all* the plan's benefit limitations. The court held:

> "By law defendant is required to include within the summary plan 'circumstances which may result in disqualification, ineligibility, or denial or loss of benefits. . . .' 29 U.S.C. §1022(b). Defendant's failure to do so is at best gross negligence and at worst intentional deception through concealment or inaction. The fact that defendant's summary plan included the quoted disclaimers does not relieve defendant of the statutory requirement of disclosure. To allow a plan to avoid statutory requirements of disclosure by including disclaimers of this sort would negate one of ERISA's major goals, protection of participants and beneficiaries. The

---

[26] See *Hurd v. Hutnik*, 1 EBC at 1393 and 1403; *Bauer v. Ins. Co. of N. America, supra*; *Gladden v. Pargas, Inc., supra*. And see *Shea v. Teacher's Retirement System of the City of New York*, 381 N.Y.S.2d 266 (App. Div. 1976), *app. dismissed*, see 387 N.Y.S.2d 837 (Ct. App. 1976) (emphasizing employer's knowledge of an employee booklet's "prospective use").

[27] See B. Creed, *ERISA Compliance: Reporting and Disclosure* (PLI 1979), at 52.

[28] A number of cases based on pre-ERISA facts continue to be before the courts for which the pre-ERISA decisions carry greater weight. See *Kolentus v. Avco Corp., supra*; *Van Orman v. American Ins. Co., supra*; *Anthony v. Ryder Truck Lines, Inc., supra*; *Adams v. Hercules, Inc., supra*. SPDs meeting the ERISA requirements were generally not required to be distributed until November of 1977. See 29 C.F.R. 2520.104b-2(f).

[29] 3 ERISA Leg. Hist. 4750.

> court holds that disclaimers of this sort are invalid in light of ERISA's requirements of disclosure."[30]

The plan in *Zittrouer* went on to argue that estoppel should still not apply—even if the omission was in violation of its statutory duties—because *reliance* on the SPD was not justified due to the disclaimer, and was especially not justified when the beneficiary had been represented in her dealings with the plan both by her niece's husband, who was a group insurance claims manager for Kemper Insurance, and one of his work colleagues. To this, the court responded:

> "[T]he fact that they were experienced in insurance, particularly group insurance, means that they were probably aware of ERISA's disclosure requirements and that they were, therefore, justified in assuming that any exclusion such as this would be included in the summary plan because it was required by law."[31]

Similarly, in *Winston v. Trustees of Hotel & Restaurant Employees & Bartenders International Welfare Fund*, a participant was entitled to extended medical, hospital, and disability benefits under an SPD's representations, but not under the terms of the plan. While the SPD contained a disclaimer that the description was still "governed by and . . . subject in every respect to the provisions of the Plan," the court held this was not "sufficient warning" that the benefits under the plan could be different than in the summary description, and therefore, applied estoppel to prevent the trustees from "denying the correctness of their own publication."[32] In *Anderson v. Alpha Portland Industries, Inc.*, the Eighth Circuit also rejected an employer's claim that a disclaimer prohibited the use of an SPD's statements in interpretation of whether arbitration was required for retirees as a part of the plan's claims procedure. The court noted first that the disclaimer was not prohibitively worded, and second, that it would be inconsistent with the purposes of ERISA Section 102 to hold that the plan was so completely integrated as to exclude from use as extrinsic evidence a description of the plan that is statutorily required to be accurate.[33]

In *Bower v. Bunker Hill Co.*, the issue of a disclaimer was again addressed, but the Ninth Circuit concluded that "the adequacy of such a disclaimer is a factual dispute." In *Bower*, the question was whether medical benefits for retirees were "lifetime" benefits, or whether they were limited to the duration of the collective bargaining agreement for

---

[30] 582 F.Supp. 1471, at 1475 (N.D. Ga. 1984).

[31] *Id.*

[32] 441 N.E.2d 1217, at 1220-21 (Ill.App. 1982).

[33] 752 F.2d 1293, 6 EBC 1046, at 1051 n.13 (8th Cir. 1985) (*en banc*), *cert. denied,* 471 U.S. 1102 (1985). See also *McKnight v. Southern Life & Health Ins. Co.*, 758 F.2d 1566, 6 EBC 1707, at 1711 (11th Cir. 1985) (employer argued that in the event of conflict between the plan and the summary, the plan should prevail; Eleventh Circuit held "[s]uch an assertion defeats the purpose of the summary[; i]t is of no effect to publish and distribute a plan summary booklet designed to simplify and explain a voluminous and complex document, and then proclaim that any inconsistencies will be governed by the plan[; u]nfairness will flow to the employee for reasonably relying on the summary booklet"). But cf. *Tinsley v. General Motors Corp.*, 622 F.Supp. 1547 (N.D. Ind. 1985) (disclaimer held effective, but text of SPD was identical to plan so that it could not have misled the participant in any event).

active workers. The plan's SPD was introduced by the retirees as extrinsic evidence of the benefits' lifetime status, but the employer argued that any inferences of meaning and intent from the SPD were negated by a disclaimer on the last page of the booklet. The Ninth Circuit reversed the lower court's grant of summary judgment in the employer's favor based on the disclaimer, finding that although set off from the text, the disclaimer was in substantially smaller type so that its effectiveness could only be resolved after a full evidentiary hearing.[34] Since, less than one month earlier, the Ninth Circuit had stated, "We do not believe that Congress intended that [ERISA's] minimum standards could be eliminated by contract,"[35] it is difficult to understand how the effectiveness of a disclaimer of Section 102's disclosure responsibilities could be a factual dispute, but the Ninth Circuit nevertheless held it was.

Two issues not yet addressed in the courts may further establish the invalidity of disclaimers:

(1) *Compliance With the Labor Department's SPD Regulations.* While the regulations do not prohibit disclaimers *per se*, they do require that limitations on a plan's benefits be contained directly in the text describing the benefit offer, or else be directly cross-referenced in the description of the benefit offer.[36] The type of overall limitation that a disclaimer attempts to effect, namely, that there may be other unspecified limitations on a benefit, is not in compliance with this regulation.

(2) *Exculpation of Fiduciaries From Liability for Breach of Fiduciary Duty.* Section 410(a) of ERISA voids as against public policy any plan provision "which purports to relieve a fiduciary from responsibility or liability" for breach of fiduciary duty. As described before, preparation and distribution of an understandable, complete, and accurate SPD is a fiduciary duty.[37] As an attempt to limit a fiduciary's potential liability for breach of this duty, a disclaimer may thus also run afoul of Section 410(a).

D. Jurisdiction When Benefits Are Provided Under an SPD, But Not Under the Plan

An issue that has troubled some courts in SPD litigation is the basis of the court's jurisdiction when an employee, or beneficiary, is entitled to benefits under representations or misleading omissions in an SPD, but not under the terms of the plan. In *O'Brien v. Sperry Univac*, a district court held that a claim based on a misrepresentation

[34] 725 F.2d 1221, 5 EBC 1180, at 1183 (9th Cir. 1984).

[35] *Amaro v. Continental Can Co.*, 724 F.2d 747, 5 EBC 1215, at 1220 (9th Cir. 1984).

[36] See 29 C.F.R. 2510.102-2(b).

[37] See *Allen v. Atlantic Richfield Retirement Plan, supra; Blau v. Del Monte Corp., supra.*

of benefits in an SPD was not "under the terms of the plan" and therefore dismissed the complaint as lacking subject matter jurisdiction under Section 502(a)(1)(B) of ERISA.[38]

This view has not warranted discussion in other cases and was firmly rejected in *Gors v. Venoy Palmer Market.* In *Gors*, a plan provided that 10 years were required for full vesting in benefits, with only a 50 percent vested interest in benefits being provided after five years. But the SPD stated that an employee was completely vested after five years. The employer moved to dismiss the employee's claim for estoppel based on the SPD as lacking subject matter jurisdiction under Section 502(a)(1)(B). The court denied the motion, finding:

> "Section [502](a)(1)(B) does not require a limited construction excluding claims involving a challenge to the plan based on the summary plan description. Any attempt to establish a right to benefits will involve a determination of the terms of the plan, which, in turn, may require a consideration of whether a summary plan description served to modify the existing plan. In this case, plaintiff will be entitled to greater benefits if this Court determines that the existing plan has been modified to provide for complete vesting of benefits after five years.
>
> "It is only logical that plan participants should be the proper ones to bring suit if they have suffered because of a misleading and damaging summary plan description. They are the parties affected and the intended beneficiaries of the statute, and, as plaintiff points out, the dissemination of erroneous and misleading information about plan requirements is as damaging to the purposes of the Act as the failure to provide any information at all. In some instances, the consequences resulting from misrepresentation might be worse than those resulting from a failure to speak at all. In any case, Congress could not have intended that federal courts strictly police the one situation and totally ignore the other."[39]

Although not mentioned in *O'Brien* or *Gors*, the other jurisdictional basis for a benefit claim supported under an SPD description, but not under the terms of a plan, is under ERISA Section 502(a)(3) for "appropriate equitable relief" for a violation of ERISA Section 102 and the fiduciary responsibilities of Section 404(a)(1).[40]

---

[38] 458 F.Supp. 1179, 1 EBC 1940 (D.D.C. 1978). Accord *Guthrie v. Dow Chemical Co.*, 445 F.Supp. 311 (S.D. Tex. 1978); *Matter of Eli Witt*, 20 B.R. 778 (Bankr. M.D. Fla. 1982). A similar holding in *Trombly v. Marshall*, 502 F.Supp. 29, 2 EBC 2500 (D.D.C. 1980), was vacated in an unpublished order filed June 12, 1980.

[39] 578 F.Supp. 365, at 368-69 (E.D. Mich. 1984). *Gors* was cited with approval by the Eighth Circuit in *Anderson v. Alpha Portland Indus., Inc.*, 752 F.2d 1293, 6 EBC 1046, at 1051 n.12 (8th Cir. 1985) (*en banc*), *cert. denied*, 471 U.S. 1102 (1985). See also *Bachelder v. Communications Satellite Corp.*, 8 EBC 1609 (D. Me. 1987); *Ogden v. Michigan Bell Tel. Co.*, 595 F.Supp. 961, 5 EBC 2281, at 2288 (E.D. Mich. 1984).

[40] See *Hillis v. Waukesha Title Co., supra* (estopping undisclosed forfeiture provision as "appropriate equitable relief" under §502(a)(3)).

II. Estoppel Based on Other Statements

A. Under Single-Employer Plans

"The doctrine of estoppel is accepted in labor relations and in pension benefits cases"[41] —except when an oral misrepresentation is made to a high-level employee with dominion over a plan.[42] In *Hurd v. Hutnik*, the court thus stated:

> "[A] court of equity will not permit the reasonable and justified expectations of ... employees, knowingly wielded by the employers for whom they labored for so many years, to be frustrated."[43]

Estoppel requires a "showing that the party to be estopped knows the facts; that it intend[ed] its conduct to be relied upon; that the party asserting estoppel is ignorant of the facts; and that it has relied upon the [other party's] conduct to its injury."[44]

As discussed before, estoppel can be based on statements or omissions in an SPD. Other statements, written and oral, can also form the basis for estoppel. In *Apponi v. Sunshine Biscuits, Inc.*, management representatives of Sunshine Biscuits allegedly told union representatives in collective bargaining that an age 55 and 15 years service pension would *not* be interpreted to require an employee to be in service at age 55. The Sixth Circuit stated:

> "If company representatives did make the statements they were alleged to have made during the labor negotiations, then the company shall be precluded from arguing that it is not liable. The company will simply be held to its word."[45]

---

[41] *Terones v. Pacific States Steel Corp.*, 526 F.Supp. 1350, at 1356 (N.D. Cal. 1981). And see *Dockray v. Phelps Dodge Co.*, 801 F.2d 1149, 7 EBC 2327 (9th Cir. 1986); *Ogden v. Michigan Bell Tel. Co., supra* ("employer representations and employee expectations [may] define the terms of a benefit plan beyond the language in the [singular] document creating the plan"; such claims considered under federal common law of ERISA §502(a)(1)(B)); *Landro v. Glendenning Motorways*, 625 F.2d 1344 (8th Cir. 1980) (promissory estoppel states claim under ERISA's federal common law); *Brunt v. Charter Corp.*, 3 EBC 1201 (E.D. Pa. 1982) (accord with *Landro*); *O'Grady v. Firestone Tire & Rubber Co.*, 635 F.Supp. 81 (S.D. Ohio 1986) (recognizing equitable estoppel claim under ERISA common law against employer based on misrepresentations of health benefit coverage by agent of employer who was a fiduciary for the plan); *Murphy v. Curran Contracting Co.*, 648 F.Supp. 986 (N.D. Ill. 1986) (estoppel or waiver must be alleged when integration proviso of plan requires modifications to be in writing and participant's suit is based on alleged oral agreement); and the cases cited in the succeeding text.

[42] *Nachwalter v. Christie*, 805 F.2d 956, 7 EBC 2675, at 2679 (11th Cir. 1986) ("[r]eading the 'written agreement' provision of [ERISA] in light of [the] requirement of formal written amendment procedures necessitates ... conclusion that ... ERISA precludes oral modifications of employee benefit plans"; district court and Eleventh Circuit emphasized that the equitable problem was that the plaintiff was the co-owner of the sponsoring employer and a trustee of the plan, and that by honoring oral agreements with him, other employees without dominion over the plan could be denied plan assets for their retirement—resulting in the "collusion" and "exact evil" the written plan requirement was designed to prevent, 611 F.Supp. 655, at 662 (S.D. Fla. 1985)).

The wording of the Eleventh Circuit's decision in *Nachwalter* may be overbroad. The claim could readily have been dismissed based on a lack of reasonable reliance.

[43] 419 F.Supp. 630, 1 EBC 1382, at 1403 (D.N.J. 1976).

[44] *Terones v. Pacific States Steel Corp., supra*, 526 F.Supp. at 1356. And see *Dockray v. Phelps Dodge Co., supra.*

[45] 652 F.2d 643, 2 EBC 1534, at 1540 (6th Cir. 1981).

In *Hardy v. H.K. Porter Co.*, an employer argued that a requirement that participants be in service at age 60 to secure an early retirement benefit applied to a group of employees who were just short of the age when their plant closed. The evidence showed, however, that other employees in similar circumstances had been granted leaves of absence until they reached age 60, "solely" to qualify them for the pension. The court found that:

> "In the exercise of its discretion Porter has dispensed with the condition of employment until age sixty.... As to those employees the pension plan offer was, in effect, modified." [46]

A large number of estoppel cases have focused on representations that years of past service will be credited employees for pension purposes. In *Landro v. Glendenning Motorways, Inc.*, a promise that years of past service under a union plan would be credited an employee when he became a salaried employee provided the basis for estoppel.[47] In *Oates v. Teamsters Affiliates Pension Plan*, a promise of credit under a union staff employees' plan for past service with a union that was about to affiliate with the Teamsters estopped the plan from denying the credit.[48] In *Novembre v. Local 584 Pension Fund*, representations to employees that their past service under another plan would be credited under "reciprocal" agreements after their local union merged with another and they came under a different plan estopped the denial of the promised credits.[49]

Estoppel has also applied to:

- A representation that a condition of service until age 60 would be waived for an employee with 20 years of service and a heart condition;[50]
- An erroneous representation of the amount of a participant's early retirement benefits under which the employee had already retired;[51]

---

[46] 417 F.Supp. 1175 (E.D. Pa. 1976), *aff'd in part, rev'd in part,* 562 F.2d 42 (3d Cir. 1977). Although the plan in *Hardy* expressly provided that discretion was to be exercised uniformly for participants in substantially identical situations, the same is required under ERISA as a fiduciary duty, and also under the Code to meet the "definitely determinable" benefits requirement. See *Petrella v. NL Indus., Inc.*, 529 F.Supp. 1357, 3 EBC 1210 (D.N.J. 1982); *Fine v. Semet,* 699 F.2d 1091, 4 EBC 1273 (11th Cir. 1983), and Rev. Rul. 81-106.

[47] 625 F.2d 1344 (8th Cir. 1980). And see *Vastoler v. American Can Co.*, 700 F.2d 916 (3d Cir. 1983) (reversing summary judgment against employee on identical issue and remanding for trial). See also *Anthony v. Ryder Truck Lines, Inc.*, 611 F.2d 944, 1 EBC 1961 (3d Cir. 1979) (letter representing that years of service under an acquired company's pension plan would count under the new employer's plan held to potentially form the basis for estoppel).

[48] 482 F.Supp. 481 (D.D.C. 1979). But see *Yglesias v. United Paper Workers Pension Fund,* 2 EBC 1851 (E.D.N.Y. 1981).

[49] 4 EBC 1286 (D.N.J. 1981), *aff'd,* 4 EBC 1289 (3d Cir. 1982), *cert. denied,* 459 U.S. 1172 (1983). And cf. *Spitznass v. First Nat'l Bank of Oregon,* 525 P.2d 1318 (Ore. 1974) (although individual annual reports clearly stated that employee's past service would be counted, plan not estopped when employee failed to show that plan trustee was responsible for preparation of the individual reports; employer might be liable if employee could show that employer's head timekeeper was responsible).

[50] *Sessions v. So. Cal. Edison Co.*, 118 P.2d 935 (Cal. Dist. Ct.App. 1941).

[51] *Sanders v. United Distributors, Inc.*, 405 So.2d 536 (La.App. 1981).

- A promise by a personnel manager that a two-month deficiency in age and service credits for an early retirement pension would be waived on a plant closing;[52]
- A published schedule erroneously showing an employee with 22 years of credited service, when the plan's trustees did nothing over a five year period to correct the schedule, even though they had adequate records in their possession to do so;[53]
- A representation to a corporate officer before his termination after a corporate takeover that his profit-sharing benefits would not be withheld based on the prior corporate board's failure to formally approve annual contributions to the plan;[54]
- A promise to an independent contractor that he would be covered under a multiemployer plan if he made contributions on his own behalf;[55]
- The failure of plan trustees to designate an employer as a "new contributing employer" until two years after a sale of assets when the trustees had a duty to make such a designation immediately and notify the participants because of the effect it could have in canceling their past service credits if their employer later withdrew from the plan;[56] and
- The failure of trustees to communicate a plan procedure for making up employer contributions with employee contributions before retirement when an employee was prepared to make the contributions himself and remained willing to do so after retirement.[57]

Numerous other decisions have applied estoppel to general promises of pensions made to employees technically not covered by a plan.[58]

---

52 *Faunce v. American Can Co.*, 407 A.2d 733 (Me. 1979).

53 *Dorward v. ILWU-PMA Pension Plan*, 452 P.2d 258 (Wash. 1969).

54 *Kann v. Keystone Resources, Inc. Profit Sharing Plan*, 575 F.Supp. 1084, 5 EBC 1233 (W.D. Pa. 1983).

55 *Scheuer v. Central States Pension Fund*, 358 F.Supp. 1332 (E.D. Wis. 1973), and 394 F.Supp. 193 (E.D. Wis. 1975), *aff'd*, 570 F.2d 347 (7th Cir. 1977).

56 *Lix v. Edwards*, 147 Cal.Rptr. 294, at 299 (Cal. Ct.App. 1978) (trustees could not "lock[] the barn door after the horse got out").

57 *Moch v. Durkin*, 297 N.Y.S.2d 865 (Sup. Ct. 1969).

58 See *Lowe v. Feldman*, 168 N.Y.S.2d 674 (Sup.Ct. 1957), *aff'd*, 174 N.Y.S.2d 949 (App.Div. 1958) (union estopped from taking union member's dues, part of which went into a pension fund, for over 29 years, with knowledge that he only worked one day a week, and then claiming at retirement that pension benefits did not extend to such "casual" employees); *Fries v. UMWA*, 333 N.E.2d 600 (Ill. App. 1975) (estoppel of union based on representations to labor arbitrator that he would receive pension at retirement even though he was not covered by union's or employer association's staff plans); *Feinberg v. Pfeiffer Co.*, 322 S.W.2d 163 (Mo. App. 1959) (company estopped from reneging on promise of pension for 40-year office manager made in corporate resolution near the end of her employment); *Langer v. Superior Steel Corp.*, 161 A. 571 (Pa. Super.Ct. 1932), *rev'd on other grounds*, 178 A. 490 (Pa. 1935) (estoppel of company when promise of $100 per month pension made at conclusion of employee's service conditioned on his not working for a competitor; reversed on finding that president of company who wrote the letter lacked authority to do so without corporate board approval); *Hunter v. Sparling*, 197 P.2d 807 (Cal. Dist. Ct.App. 1948) (completion of two-installment pension required where company promised employee a "large payment" on his retirement and the promise had been reduced to a fixed amount at retirement with the company attempting to back out on the second payment); *Specht*

As discussed in Chapter 9, estoppel has also been applied to limit plan amendments reducing benefits based on representations that benefits would be maintained as is, including representations inferred largely from the overall circumstances.[59]

B. Judicial Reluctance to Apply Estoppel to Multiemployer Plans

When it is sometimes said that estoppel does not apply to pension claims, the reference is generally to a relatively narrow line of cases involving jointly administered multiemployer plans (commonly called Taft-Hartley plans). In recent years, this line of cases has become still narrower. The cases cited most often for judicial reluctance to apply estoppel to Taft-Hartley multiemployer plans are *Moglia v. Geoghegan* and *Thurber v. Western Conference of Teamsters' Pension Plan.* In *Moglia,* the Second Circuit refused to apply estoppel based on a plan's acceptance of employer contributions on an employee's behalf for over 12 years because his employer had never signed a written contribution agreement with the plan, as required under Section 302(c)(5) of the Labor Management Relations Act.[60] In *Thurber,* the Ninth Circuit refused to apply estoppel to an alleged representation by a firm that administered the multiemployer plan that a break in service would be "healed."[61] Other cases have refused to apply estoppel based on an acceptance of contributions—as in *Moglia*—combined with representations that individuals would be considered "employees," instead of supervisors or self-employed.[62] Estoppel has also been denied based on a representation allegedly made by a plan administrator that an employee would be vested under a "new law" (ERISA), when he actually would not vest without further service.[63]

In 1985, the Second Circuit, in *Chambless v. Masters, Mates & Pilots Pension Plan,* reiterated its reluctance to apply estoppel to a multiemployer plan. The court stated that the actuarial soundness of such plans is too important "to permit trustees to obligate the fund to pay pensions to persons not entitled to them under the express terms of the plan." In *Chambless,* other elements for estoppel were missing as

---

v. Eastwood-Nealley Corp., 111 A.2d 781 (N.J. Super. 1955) (promise of a pension estopped company from withdrawing commitment).

[59] See ch. 9, sec. III.E.

[60] 403 F.2d 110 (2d Cir. 1968), *cert. denied,* 394 U.S. 919 (1969).

[61] 542 F.2d 1106 (9th Cir. 1976) (*per curiam*).

[62] *Phillips v. Kennedy,* 542 F.2d 52, 1 EBC 1418 (8th Cir. 1976); *Reiherzer v. Shannon,* 581 F.2d 1266, 1 EBC 1175 (7th Cir. 1978); *Aitken v. IP & GCU-Employer Retirement Fund,* 604 F.2d 1261 (9th Cir. 1979).

[63] *Haeberle v. Buffalo Carpenters Pension Fund Trustees,* 624 F.2d 1132, 3 EBC 1019 (2d Cir. 1980).

a statement assuring a participant that he could go to work for noncontributing employers in the maritime industry without any "union problem" was made by a union dispatcher who was not a plan trustee, and who did not appear to have authority to speak for plan trustees.[64]

The theory of the courts has been that "absent extraordinary circumstances," estoppel should not be applied to an LMRA Section 302(c)(5) multiemployer trust because of the potential for "corruption and jeopardy [to the] actuarial soundness" of plans that Congress sought to counteract under Section 302(c)(5) by requiring that the plans be jointly administered with an equal number of employer trustees, and by requiring that payments be made to and from the plan only on the basis of the plan's "express" written terms. The courts' fear seems primarily to be that if estoppel were allowed, persons with actual or apparent authority would deliberately make statements to bind the plan, and other employers would have to pay for them, or if they did not, that the actuarial soundness of the plan would be put in jeopardy, with other employees in effect paying for the misrepresentations.[65]

Although the written plan requirement in Section 302(c)(5) is now duplicated under ERISA Sections 402(a)(1) and (b)(4) for all plans, the same concerns are generally not present under single-employer plans.[66] In single-employer plans, the union as such is generally not involved in administration of the plan, and so statements by union representatives cannot be relied on by plan participants as the basis for estoppel of the plan. On the other hand, if an employer makes representations about benefits, it cannot shift the cost of its representations to other employers, and it will be required, through ERISA's funding requirements, to gradually make up any actuarial loss to the plan from its representations.

Even for multiemployer plans, the *Moglia* and *Thurber* line of cases is subject to exception. In *Scheuer v. Central States Pension Fund*, estoppel was applied to a multiemployer plan based on the plan's acceptance of contributions and a union business agent's representations to an independent contractor that he would be covered by the plan if he made the contributions.[67] In *Hurd v. Hutnik*, estoppel required employers to continue funding benefits promised under a multiemployer plan even after its termination when clear and consistent representations, "knowingly wielded" by the employers, had been made

---

[64] 772 F.2d 1032, 6 EBC 2209, at 2217 (2d Cir. 1985), quoting *Phillips v. Kennedy, supra*, 1 EBC at 1420 n.8.

[65] *Aitken v. IP & GCU-Employer Retirement Fund, supra*, 604 F.2d at 1267. See also *Chambless v. Masters, Mates & Pilots Pension Plan, supra; Operating Engineers Pension Trust v. Beck Eng'g & Surveying Co.*, 746 F.2d 557 (9th Cir. 1984).

[66] But see *Nachwalter v. Christie*, 611 F.Supp. 655, at 662-63 (S.D. Fla. 1985), *aff'd*, 805 F.2d 956, 7 EBC 2675 (11th Cir. 1986) (oral agreement to value account balance of law firm partner/plan trustee as of certain date prior to precipitous drop in value of plan assets in variance of terms of single-employer plan not binding when plaintiff knew plan's terms; to hold otherwise would permit the "collusion" and "exact evil" ERISA's written plan requirements were designed to prevent).

[67] 358 F.Supp. 1332 (E.D. Wis. 1973), and 394 F.Supp. 193 (E.D. Wis. 1975), *aff'd*, 570 F.2d 347 (7th Cir. 1977).

to participants for 14 years that benefits from the plan would be for life.[68] Other cases have estopped multiemployer plans when trustees were directly responsible for misrepresentations, or else failed to disclose an administrative rule of the plan to participants.[69]

More recently, the Third Circuit has permitted estoppel of multiemployer plans when the elements for estoppel are present and there is no indication of corruption or that estoppel will jeopardize the "actuarial soundness" of the plan. In *Rosen v. Hotel & Restaurant Pension Fund*, a plan's acceptance of an employee's personal contributions in lieu of his employer's thus estopped the plan from denying the employee credit for those years because of the lack of employer contributions.[70] In *Novembre v. Local 584 Pension Fund*, representations by union officers, who were also plan trustees, that "reciprocal" service credit would be granted employees on their entry into a new plan after the merger of their union local with another estopped their new plan from denying such credit.[71] In neither case did the courts find a danger of corruption or a substantial issue of actuarial soundness that might bar estoppel.[72]

C. Estoppel-Like Holdings That Benefit Denials Are Arbitrary and Capricious

As a functional, but unstated, alternative to estoppel, particularly in multiemployer plans, benefit denials have been found to be arbitrary and capricious based on misleading statements or nondisclosure, even though the denials are in accord with the plan language. In *Rosen v.*

---

[68] 419 F.Supp. 630, 1 EBC 1382, at 1403 (D.N.J. 1976).

[69] See *Dorward v. ILWU-PMA Pension Plan*, 452 P.2d 258 (Wash. 1969) (estopping multiemployer plan from denying participant service credits that had been listed on a schedule for almost 5 years when trustees had the necessary information to check the schedule and the participant had relied on its accuracy); *Lix v. Edwards*, 147 Cal.Rptr. 294 (Cal. Ct.App. 1978) (estopping trustees of multiemployer plan from designating an employer as a "new contributing employer" 2 years after a change in ownership when trustees had duty to notify employees immediately of such a designation because of its potential effect on their past service credits if the new employer withdrew from the plan within 5 years); *Moch v. Durkin*, 297 N.Y.S.2d 865 (Sup. Ct. 1969) (estopping multiemployer plan from denying participant the opportunity to make up unpaid employer contributions after his retirement when the plan's procedures for making such contributions were not communicated to him before retirement); *Carlsen v. Masters, Mates & Pilots Pension Plan*, 403 A.2d 880 (N.J. 1979) (estopping multiemployer plan from forfeiting employee's benefits based on his unavailability for work when plan and the union led him to believe that reinstating his union membership would cure any defect); *Pizzirusso v. Graziano*, 125 BNA Pens. Rep. D-1 (E.D.N.Y. 1976) (failure of union and plan trustees to disclose what constitutes a contributing employer to uneducated, non-English speaking participant estopped trustees of multiemployer plan from applying break-in-service rule to participant's service with a noncontributing employer). See also *Sanchez v. Trustees of Pension Plan*, 359 So.2d 1279 (La. 1978) (acceptance of contributions for employees who were major shareholders in a contributing company foreclosed reversal of trustees' position on their coverage when trustees had discretion under the terms of the plan to treat nonhourly employees as participants).

[70] 637 F.2d 592, 2 EBC 1054 (3d Cir. 1981), *cert. denied*, 454 U.S. 898 (1981).

[71] 4 EBC 1286 (D.N.J. 1981), *aff'd*, 4 EBC 1289 (3d Cir. 1982), *cert. denied*, 459 U.S. 1172 (1983).

[72] See also *Hodgins v. Central States Pension Fund*, 624 F.2d 760 (6th Cir. 1980) (concurring opinion) (setting out basically the same approach). Still earlier, in *Aitken v. IP & GCU-Employer Retirement Fund*, 604 F.2d 1261 (9th Cir. 1979), the Ninth Circuit endorsed this approach, but declined to overturn its own precedent in *Thurber*. 604 F.2d at 1267–68.

Hotel and Restaurant Pension Fund, after finding the plan estopped by its acceptance of Rosen's contributions in lieu of his employer's contributions for one period of service, the Third Circuit found that the plan's denial of credit for a second period during which the employer failed to make contributions was not estopped, but was arbitrary and capricious because the plan's trustees had a fiduciary duty to notify Rosen that his employer's delinquency was denying him benefit credits. The Third Circuit stated:

> "Continued eligibility is the core of the trustee beneficiary relationship and those responsible for the fund are required to notify [participants] when their employer jeopardizes their eligibility."[73]

In *Branch v. White,* multiemployer plan trustees used local union meetings as the exclusive means for distributing a booklet describing the plan. Bargaining unit employees who were not members of the union thus never received the summary booklet and were not informed that $2 per month employee contributions were required for participation in the plan. The court held the trustees had an equitable duty under state trust law to ensure that *all* potentially eligible employees had notice of the plan's requirements. As a remedy, the employees were allowed to obtain credits by retroactive payments of the required employee contributions.[74] In *Hodgins v. Central States Pension Fund,* lack of notice to a participant that gradual changes in his job duties had made him a noncovered "supervisor" and thus had started a break in service under a plan was held to make application of the plan's break rule arbitrary and capricious as to the individual participant.[75]

Other "arbitrary and capricious" decisions, and in particular, a line of cases holding benefit denials arbitrary and capricious because of lack of advance notice of plan amendments, can also be seen as functional equivalents of estoppel.[76]

D. Actual or Apparent Authority and Detrimental Reliance

In single-employer plans where estoppel is seldom rejected out of hand and in multiemployer plans where it may be reluctantly or indirectly applied, plaintiffs must still always show that a representation was made, the actual or apparent authority of the person making it to speak on behalf of the plan, and reasonable and detrimental reliance on the representation.

Generally, it has been held that employees should know both in single-employer and in multiemployer plans that union officers and

---

[73] 637 F.2d 592, 2 EBC 1054, at 1060 (3d Cir. 1981), *cert. denied,* 454 U.S. 898 (1981). See also *Taylor v. Amalgamated Meat Cutters,* 619 S.W.2d 120 (Tenn. Ct.App. 1981) (trustees had duty to notify participant that his employer had failed to make contributions when participant had right to make up the contributions himself).

[74] 239 A.2d 665 (N.J. Sup.Ct. App.Div. 1968).

[75] 624 F.2d 760 (6th Cir. 1980).

[76] See ch. 9, sec. V.

union business agents lack authority to bind a plan by their representations—unless they are also plan trustees or appear to have some other authority over the plan.[77] Somewhat similarly, an employer contributing to a multiemployer plan generally lacks actual or apparent authority to speak on behalf of the multiemployer plan.

In single-employer plans, someone other than the employer, e.g., a bank, may often nominally be the plan's trustee or administrator, but it is recognized that the employer retains actual or apparent authority to bind the plan. However, when employees are represented by a union, statements made by the employer to individual employees outside of collective bargaining negotiations may sometimes be disregarded, either because of lack of reasonable reliance or because of the parol evidence rule. In *Belland v. PBGC*, a district court thus held that employees should know not to rely on individual representations made to them by an employer before a collective bargaining agreement is concluded when the union is their exclusive bargaining representative and the employer's representations are not reflected in the final bargaining agreement. The court also criticized the employees for not knowing that the parol evidence rule precludes enforcement of oral promises made *prior to* the adoption of an unambiguous and completely integrated written agreement.[78]

For reliance to be reasonable, an employee must not know, or constructively know, that a representation is inconsistent with a plan's terms. In *Stutelberg v. Farrell Lines, Inc.*, various notices posted for employees stated that an employee was covered by the plan, but the notices could not form the basis for estoppel where the employee was shown to have otherwise known and understood that he was not covered by the plan.[79] Similarly, in *Michota v. Anheuser-Busch, Inc.*, employees who ratified a collective bargaining agreement with a plan

---

[77] See *Chambless v. Masters, Mates & Pilots Pension Plan*, 772 F.2d 1032, 6 EBC 2209 (2d Cir. 1985); *Chamberlin v. Bakery & Confectionery Union*, 99 LRRM 3176 (N.D. Cal. 1977); *McHugh v. Teamsters Pension Trust Fund of Philadelphia*, 638 F.Supp. 1036 (E.D. Pa. 1986); *Sobie v. ITU Pension Plan*, 4 EBC 2524 (N.D. Ohio 1983); *Galvez v. Local 804 Welfare Trust Fund*, 543 F.Supp. 316, 3 EBC 1857 (E.D.N.Y. 1982); *Knoll v. Phoenix Steel Corp.*, 465 F.2d 1128 (3d Cir. 1972), *cert. denied*, 409 U.S. 1126 (1973). But see *Scheuer v. Central States Pension Fund*, *supra* (recognizing that in a multiemployer plan, the complexity of the fund arrangements and the breadth of the trustees' discretion may encourage participants to rely on understandable statements from union officials; also placing emphasis on a statement in plan's summary booklet that suggested that union representatives were acting as the fund's representatives); *Novembre v. Local 584 Pension Fund*, 4 EBC 1286 (D.N.J. 1981), *aff'd*, 4 EBC 1289 (3d Cir. 1982), *cert. denied*, 459 U.S. 1172 (1983) (statements by union officers who were also plan trustees bound plan, even though it was not entirely clear in which capacity they were speaking).

[78] 4 EBC 1162 (D.D.C. 1983), *aff'd on other issues*, 726 F.2d 839, 5 EBC 1109 (D.C. Cir. 1984), *cert. denied*, 469 U.S. 880 (1984).

[79] 529 F.Supp. 566, 3 EBC 1124 (S.D.N.Y. 1982), *aff'd*, 697 F.2d 297 (2d Cir. 1982). See also *Nachwalter v. Christie*, 611 F.Supp. 655, at 662-63 (S.D. Fla. 1985), *aff'd*, 805 F.2d 956, 7 EBC 2675 (11th Cir. 1986) (oral agreement to value account balance of law firm partner/plan trustee as of certain date prior to precipitous drop in value of plan assets at variance with terms of plan not binding when plaintiff knew plan's terms; to hold otherwise would permit the "collusion" and "exact evil" ERISA's written plan requirements were designed to prevent); *Kamenstein v. Jordan Marsh Co.*, 623 F.Supp. 1109, 6 EBC 2611 (D. Mass. 1985) (failure to disclose according to ERISA requirements not actionable when participant has actual knowledge of plan provisions); *Rubin v. Decision Concepts, Inc.*, 566 F.Supp. 1057 (S.D.N.Y. 1983) (failure to distribute summary of material modification of plan not actionable when participant received memo that in combination

amendment contained in it were precluded from claiming they lacked notice of the amendment even though they had never received a summary description of it. The Third Circuit held they had "adequate constructive notice [of the amendment] as a matter of law" on ratifying the contract, stating:

> "A necessary corollary to the rule that all terms of a collective bargaining agreement are binding on the individual members of the unit, is the concept that [they] have notice of the terms therein set forth."[80]

At the same time, notice of the terms of an unratified plan provision cannot be based on its availability to employees for inspection when employees reasonably rely on representations of its content, and do not otherwise know about the inconsistent plan terms. In *Zittrouer v. Uarco Inc. Group Ben. Plan*, an employer argued that a beneficiary's representatives could have inspected the full plan instead of relying on statements in the plan's SPD that did not disclose that entering a convalescent home after age 70 was a circumstance under which benefits were not paid. The court held that ERISA's disclosure requirements "justified" her representatives' assumption that a significant "exclusion such as this would be included in the summary plan [description] because it was required by law." Thus, their reliance on the SPD was reasonable despite the availability of the full plan for inspection.[81]

The burden in establishing detrimental reliance, or injury, for estoppel is generally less difficult than has been stated in some cases, such as *Boase v. Lee Rubber & Tire Co.*, where the Third Circuit seemed to presume that employees "in the twilight of their careers" cannot detrimentally rely on misrepresentations of benefits because they have nowhere else to go anyway.[82] Most courts now infer reliance on a representation from a continuation of employment after the representation is made. They do not require a showing of exactly what other employment or course of action a participant would have taken if the representations had not been made. This conforms with the general view that the consideration necessary to make an employee benefit offer enforceable as a contract need not be great, and need not be proof

---

with the SPD was enough to let him know that new plan was a restatement of former profit-sharing plan and not a second profit-sharing plan); *Ridens v. Voluntary Separation Program*, 610 F.Supp. 770 (D. Minn. 1985) (no estoppel when employee knew what severance pay plan said and did not reasonably rely on inconsistent oral representations made by another employee without actual or apparent authority over plan).

[80] 755 F.2d 330, 6 EBC 1161, at 1166 (3d Cir. 1985). Compare *Valle v. Joint Plumbing Industry Board*, 623 F.2d 196, 3 EBC 1026 (2d Cir. 1980), and *Agro v. Joint Plumbing Industry Board*, 623 F.2d 207, 3 EBC 1036 (2d Cir. 1980), where a plan claimed employees had notice of plan amendments from discussions at union meetings, but the amendments themselves were not in any contract the employees had ratified. See also *Barrett v. Thorofare Markets, Inc.*, 452 F.Supp. 880 (W.D. Pa. 1978) (suggesting potential violation of a disclosure duty if employer or union are "aware of an ambiguity and knew or should have known that a significant portion of the Union membership would misunderstand their rights thereunder" and no clarifying disclosure is made).

[81] 582 F.Supp. 1471, at 1475 (N.D. Ga. 1984). And see sec. I.C above on disclaimers in SPDs.

[82] 437 F.2d 527, at 534 (3d Cir. 1970). And see *Craig v. Bemis*, 517 F.2d 677 (5th Cir. 1975) (also setting an apparently next-to-impossible standard for proof of detrimental reliance).

that an employee would definitely have left a job "but for" the benefit offer. In *Vinyard v. King*, the Tenth Circuit, for example, stated that the consideration necessary to require an employer's adherence to promises made in a personnel policy handbook distributed to employees

> "can be quite small and can even consist of the employee continuing to work and foregoing the option of quitting."[83]

Along this line, the Third Circuit later found potential detrimental reliance on a representation that years of past service would be credited an employee after he changed from an hourly to a salaried position because he continued working after the representation was made, and he must have had other job opportunities (although he did not show specific offers).[84] Similarly, the Eighth Circuit has found reliance on corporate representations that one-half of profits were being annually contributed to a profit-sharing plan based on "countless" statements by the company that the profit-sharing plan encouraged employees to remain with the company and to do extra work. In light of these statements, employees were not required to prove "exactly what job opportunities" they gave up, or specifically "what extra work" they performed.[85] Without even this detail, other courts infer reliance from the fact that employees continue working after a representation is made.[86]

A representation made shortly before an employee is to retire may, however, raise questions about whether the continuation of employment for a very short period is sufficient to constitute detrimental reliance. For example, a continuation of employment for *one* week after a representation was made has been held to be insufficient reliance.[87] On the other hand, the continuation of employment clearly does not have to be equal to the period on which the benefits subject to the

---

[83] 728 F.2d 428 (10th Cir. 1984) (following Oklahoma common law as expressed in *Langdon v. Saga Corp.*, 569 P.2d 524 (Okla.App. 1976), which involved the consideration necessary to support severance and vacation pay promises in an employee handbook). And see, e.g., *Lampley v. Celebrity Homes, Inc.*, 594 P.2d 605 (Colo.App. 1979) (same view of consideration under Colorado law); *Hinkeldey v. Cities Service Oil Co.*, 470 S.W.2d 494 (Mo. 1971) (same under Missouri law); *Anthony v. Jersey Central Power & Light Co.*, 143 A.2d 762 (N.J. 1958) (same in New Jersey); *Hadden v. Consolidated Edison Co.*, 312 N.E.2d 445 (N.Y. Ct.App. 1974) (same in New York); *Kulins v. Malco, A Microdot Co.*, 459 N.E.2d 1038 (Ill.App. 1984) (same in Illinois).

[84] *Vastoler v. American Can Co.*, 700 F.2d 916 (3d Cir. 1983). See also *Baker v. Lukens Steel Co.*, 793 F.2d 509, 7 EBC 2039, at 2043 (3d Cir. 1986) (summary of material modification required to be distributed under ERISA on plan amendment deleting early retirement benefits available on plant closing; but for estoppel, participants have to show reliance, e.g., that they "did not leave their jobs for other employment or even search for such employment because of misinformation concerning their status").

[85] *Monson v. Century Mfg. Co.*, 739 F.2d 1293, 5 EBC 1625, at 1631 (8th Cir. 1984).

[86] See *Novembre v. Local 584 Pension Fund*, 4 EBC 1286 (D.N.J. 1981), *aff'd*, 4 EBC 1289 (3d Cir. 1982), *cert. denied*, 459 U.S. 1172 (1983); *Kann v. Keystone Resources, Inc. Profit Sharing Plan*, 575 F.Supp. 1084, 5 EBC 1233 (W.D. Pa. 1983); *Kulins v. Malco, A Microdot Co.*, 459 N.E.2d 1038 (Ill.App. 1984).

[87] *Hayes v. Plantations Steel Co.*, 438 A.2d 1091 (R.I. 1982) (no reliance when employee planned to retire anyway and statement made one week before his retirement).

representation are based.[88] When a representation is made very shortly before an employee is to retire, detrimental reliance may also hinge on whether there is some *other* action the employee could have taken, instead of retiring, if the statement had not been made. In *Sanders v. United Distributors, Inc.*, reliance was based on an employee's option to continue working, instead of taking early retirement, if a representation of a higher amount of benefits than actually provided him under the plan had not been made.[89] On the other hand, in *Haeberle v. Buffalo Carpenters Pension Fund Trustees,* no reliance was found when an employee failed to show that he would have done anything except retire with or without a representation that he was already vested under the "new law" (ERISA).[90] Reliance on promises made near retirement may also be based on agreements concerning postretirement conduct by the employee.[91]

Ideally, of course, support for reliance is always as specific as possible, with examples of other job opportunities foregone, or of other specific reliance. In *Nevada Public Employees Retirement Board v. Byrne,* an employee showed he had sold his house and purchased a retirement home in reliance on representations concerning the amount of his retirement benefits.[92]

---

[88] See, e.g., *Kann v. Keystone Resources, Inc. Profit Sharing Plan, supra* (employee continued to work for 2 years after statement made, but benefits subject to the representation covered 6-year period).

[89] 405 So.2d 536 (La.App. 1981). See also *Hillis v. Waukesha Title Co.,* 576 F.Supp. 1103 (E.D. Wis. 1983) (reliance based on employee's option to continue working if he had known that a noncompete forfeiture would apply if he left for work with a competitor); *Sessions v. So. Cal. Edison Co.*, 118 P.2d 935 (Cal. Dist. Ct.App. 1941) (reliance based on evidence that plaintiff would not have ceased employment when he did except for promise that age 60 condition on right to early retirement benefits would not apply to him); *Dorward v. ILWU-PMA Pension Plan,* 452 P.2d 258 (Wash. 1969) (had employee known that credits listed for him in a schedule were not correct, he might not have retired at age 65). Accord *Feinberg v. Pfeiffer Co.*, 322 S.W.2d 163 (Mo. App. 1959).

The cases discussed in ch. 9, sec. V, on whether denials of benefits are arbitrary and capricious because of a lack of advance notice of a plan amendment without a grace period to retire, or an opportunity to conform to the new rule, are also instructive on the reliance required in near-retirement estoppel cases.

[90] 624 F.2d 1132, 3 EBC 1019 (2d Cir. 1980). See also *Govoni v. Bricklayers, Masons and Plasterers Local No. 5 Pension Fund,* 732 F.2d 250, 5 EBC 1389 (1st Cir. 1984) (plaintiff was informed that break-in-service rule would cancel pre-ERISA service before his retirement and went ahead and retired anyway); *Galvez v. Local 804 Welfare Trust Fund,* 543 F.Supp. 316, 3 EBC 1857 (E.D.N.Y. 1982) (complaint for estoppel dismissed when it failed to allege "that in 1979, when Galvez received notice of his ineligibility, he could not have returned to work, acquired the necessary pension credits and cured his change of position in reliance on [a union business agent's] statement"); *Reynolds v. Bethlehem Steel Corp.*, 619 F.Supp. 919 (D. Md. 1984) (even if participant relied on mistaken approval of lump sum payment of benefits, reasonable reliance on expectation of lump sum payment ended once he was informed that benefits would not be paid in a lump sum, employer offered him his job back, and participant elected not to return).

[91] See *Specht v. Eastwood-Nealley Corp.*, 111 A.2d 781 (N.J. Super. App.Div. 1955) (reliance based on promise not to disclose business information after retirement or to otherwise interfere with the business); *Langer v. Superior Steel Corp.*, 161 A. 571 (Pa. Super.Ct. 1932), *rev'd on other grounds,* 178 A. 490 (Pa. 1935) (reliance based on agreement not to work for competitor after retirement).

[92] 607 P.2d 1351 (Nev. 1980). See also *Hayes v. Nat'l Con-Serv., Inc.,* 523 F.Supp. 1034, 2 EBC 1965 (D. Md. 1981) (employees alleged they failed to set up IRAs because of employer's promise to set up a pension plan).

III. Separate Contracts for Promised Benefits

Rather than estoppel of a *plan* per se, or holding a benefit denial to otherwise be arbitrary and capricious, liability is also sometimes based on a separate contract, or agreement, with an employer. In *Miller v. Dictaphone Corp.*, judgment was rendered against a company, rather than its pension plan, when the company in a letter to employees promised unreduced early retirement benefits. The plan itself provided for actuarial reductions for early retirement. Efforts by the company to retract the letter were held to come too late as substantial performance had already been rendered, with the letter establishing a separate contract for the difference in benefits from the employer.[93] In *Aronson v. Servus Rubber Division*, recovery of profit-sharing contributions for two highly paid employees was based on separate employment agreements with the company after the company modified its plan to generally preclude the payments for employees at their plant. The court distinguished this "contract" recovery from an "ERISA [plan] recovery," and ruled in the employees' favor under its pendent state law jurisdiction that attached based on the unsuccessful ERISA claims.[94] In *In re Alan Wood Steel Co.*, individual employment contracts with salaried employees who had been recruited from other companies (some of which provided that service with the other companies was to count for both vesting and benefit accruals, and some of which provided that it would count only for benefit accruals) established separate contracts for the difference between the promised benefits and the benefits the plan provided under its terms.[95] In *Amato v. Western Union International, Inc.*, the Second Circuit found that the purchaser of a company might be bound by a promise in the sales agreement that benefits under the seller's pension plan would not be reduced following the sale. The plan participants were entitled to bring an action to enforce this promise based on their rights as third-party beneficiaries, or under promissory estoppel.[96]

Contractual liability has also been found when estoppel could be applied to a plan, but would not provide an adequate remedy. In *Monson v. Century Mfg. Co.*, company officers and plan fiduciaries for a single-employer profit-sharing plan repeatedly represented to employees, including through a summary booklet about the plan, that the

---

[93] 334 F.Supp. 840 (D. Ore. 1971). In a second decision based on the same facts, *Dictaphone Corp. v. Clemons*, 488 P.2d 226 (Colo. 1971), it was unclear whether the court held the employer liable under a separate contract or estopped the plan based on the employer's representation.

[94] 730 F.2d 12, 5 EBC 1343, at 1347 (1st Cir. 1984), *cert. denied*, 469 U.S. 1017 (1984).

[95] 12 B.R. 964 (E.D. Pa. 1981).

[96] 773 F.2d 1402, 6 EBC 2226 (2d Cir. 1985). The Second Circuit found no need to determine whether the estoppel and third-party beneficiary causes of action arose under federal common law or state law because the same principles apply in either case. Accord *Holliday v. Xerox Corp.*, 555 F.Supp. 51, 4 EBC 1221 (E.D. Mich. 1982). But compare *Jackson v. Martin Marietta Corp.*, 805 F.2d 1498, 7 EBC 2767 (11th Cir. 1986) (ERISA preempts state law claim for breach of contract based on promise at job interview in 1977 that pension service would date from 1959); and cases cited at n. 104.

company was contributing one-half of its pretax profits to the plan, when, in fact, only one-third of its profits were being contributed. The employees did not sue the plan because the money had not been contributed, but sued the company for breach of contract, and the company, its officers, and plan fiduciaries for fraud and breach of ERISA fiduciary duty.[97] In *Hayes v. National Con-Serv, Inc.*, an employer failed to establish a pension plan as agreed. Recovery thus could not be against the unestablished plan, but was obtained against the employer under both contract and equity.[98]

IV. Fiduciary Liability for Misrepresentations or Nondisclosure

Intentional or negligent misrepresentations of benefits by plan fiduciaries present claims for breach of fiduciary duty under ERISA. Such actions have, however, generally not reached the stage for decisions on the merits.[99] Some of the pre-ERISA cases discussed in the section below on intentional or negligent misrepresentations by nonfiduciaries would, however, now be claims for breach of fiduciary duty as the personnel managers and other parties in those actions would now be ERISA fiduciaries. The remedy in actions based on a fiduciary's misleading statements is not necessarily limited to personal fiduciary liability, but can be estoppel of the denial of benefits, or a holding that a denial is arbitrary and capricious.

Without a misrepresentation by a fiduciary, the courts have generally found *no* fiduciary duty to offer individually-tailored explanations of a plan's benefits when an adequate SPD has been distributed, and no change in the plan's terms has occurred.[100] However, a fiduciary can

---

[97] 739 F.2d 1293, 5 EBC 1625 (8th Cir. 1984). See also *In re White Motor Corp.*, 731 F.2d 372, 5 EBC 1558 (6th Cir. 1984) (side-letter between company and union required company to fully fund all promised pension benefits).

[98] 523 F.Supp. 1034, 2 EBC 1965 (D. Md. 1981).

[99] But see *Freund v. Marshall & Ilsley Bank*, and *Monson v. Century Mfg. Co.*, at nn. 101-02; *Chambers v. Kaleidoscope, Inc. Profit Sharing Plan*, 650 F.Supp. 359, 7 EBC 2628, at 2634 (N.D. Ga. 1986) (employee entitled to rely on fiduciary's materially misleading, $27,000 overstatement of employer's contributions to a defined contribution plan in annual financial report distributed to participants; fiduciary consequently personally liable for the amount of the overstatement). See also *Kuntz v. Reese*, 785 F.2d 1410, 7 EBC 1227 (9th Cir. 1986), *vacating*, 760 F.2d 926, 6 EBC 1780 (9th Cir. 1985), *cert. denied*, 479 U.S. ___ (1986) (allegation that plan administrator misrepresented a plan's benefits states claim for breach of fiduciary duty if plaintiff is a participant in the plan); *Ogden v. Michigan Bell Tel. Co.*, 571 F.Supp. 520, 4 EBC 2540 (E.D. Mich. 1983), and 8 EBC 1481 (E.D. Mich. 1987) (allegedly fraudulent statements by plan fiduciary present claim for breach of fiduciary duty); *Whitaker v. Texaco, Inc.*, 566 F.Supp. 745, 4 EBC 1762 (N.D. Ga. 1983) (alleged misrepresentations by fiduciary about lump sum benefits state claim for breach of fiduciary duty). And compare *Provience v. Valley Clerks Trust Fund*, 509 F.Supp. 388, 2 EBC 1618 (E.D. Cal. 1981) (holding, after removal to federal court, that state law claims for fraud and bad faith denial of benefits by plan fiduciaries are not preempted by ERISA and sending the claims back to state court for decision), with *Provience*, 163 Cal. App. 3d 249, 6 EBC 1153, at 1156 (Cal. Ct.App. 1984) (holding that the same state law claims were preempted by ERISA because the state court's decision "would effectively regulate the way the Fund processes its claims").

[100] See *Hopkins v. FMC Corp.*, 535 F.Supp. 235, 3 EBC 1814 (W.D.N.C. 1982) (no duty to individually explain how plan applies to participant when SPD is adequate and employee never

have a duty to speak up in certain circumstances. In *Freund v. Marshall & Ilsley Bank*, fiduciaries loaned most of a plan's assets to the company sponsor and failed to notify participants about the potential effects on the loans of a sale of the company in a leveraged buy-out in which the purchaser's creditors obtained security interests to virtually all of the company's assets that had priority over the plan's unsecured claims. Although no express disclosure requirements had been violated, this silence breached ERISA's fiduciary duties because the participants had the right to withdraw their money under the terms of the plan, and could have done so before the sale took place, or before the plan's loans turned bad.[101] In *Monson v. Century Mfg. Co.*, plan fiduciaries were liable to participants when they either directly participated in a company's fraudulent misrepresentations about the amount of profits being contributed to a profit-sharing plan, or stood by and failed to take any action to remedy the other fiduciaries' breaches of fiduciary duty.[102]

V. Liability of a Nonfiduciary for Intentional or Negligent Misrepresentations

A nonfiduciary, such as a personnel manager without discretionary authority over benefit claims, or a union officer, may be liable for intentional or negligent misrepresentations of plan benefits.[103] Such actions are generally under non-preempted state law.[104] As an example,

---

asked a question); *Allen v. Atlantic Richfield Retirement Plan*, 480 F.Supp. 848, 1 EBC 1523 (E.D. Pa. 1979), *aff'd*, 633 F.2d 209 (3d Cir. 1980) (individual disclosure not required); *Aronson v. Butcher Workmen's Local 174 Welfare Fund*, 3 EBC 2134 (S.D.N.Y 1982) (Congress did not intend additional disclosure duties beyond adequate SPD and timely summaries of material modification); *Hester v. Brada Miller Freight System, Inc.*, 3 EBC 1871 (E.D. Mich. 1982) (no duty to individually notify participants of conversion rights under group life insurance policy); *Castello v. Gamache*, 593 F.2d 358 (8th Cir. 1979) (same); *Sleichter v. Monsanto Co.*, 612 F.Supp. 856 (E.D. Mo. 1985) (no duty to disclose early retirement incentive program improvements in advance of implementation when program still in formative stage at time employee retired with no certainty of implementation and no misrepresentations are made to employee about the status of corporate deliberations on the program); *Nostrame v. Consolidated Edison Co.*, 504 F.Supp. 507, 2 EBC 1025 (S.D.N.Y 1980) (no duty to notify departing employee of pending ERISA-required changes under which he would have vested with slightly more service); *Lehner v. Crane Co.*, 448 F.Supp. 1127 (E.D. Pa. 1978) (no duty to personally notify departing employee of pending benefit improvements).

[101] 485 F.Supp. 629, 1 EBC 1898 (W.D. Wis. 1979). See also *McNeese v. Health Plan Marketing, Inc.*, 647 F.Supp. 981 (N.D. Ala. 1986) (fiduciary breach from failure to notify employees of their employer's failure to contribute to health plan).

[102] 739 F.2d 1293, 5 EBC 1625 (8th Cir. 1984). A number of other cases have recognized a fiduciary duty to provide advance notice of adverse plan amendments, beyond ERISA's minimum disclosure requirements, when participants could have retired or could have conformed their actions to the new rule. See ch. 9, sec. V.B.

[103] See *Aitken v. IP & GCU-Employer Retirement Fund*, 604 F.2d 1261, at 1269 (9th Cir. 1979); *Thurber v. Western Conference of Teamsters' Pension Plan*, 542 F.2d 1106, at 1109 n.5 (9th Cir. 1976) (*per curiam*).

[104] See *Walker v. Mountain States Tel. & Telegraph Co.*, 645 F.Supp. 93, 7 EBC 2623 (D. Colo. 1986) (early retirees were not "participants" in voluntary early retirement incentive plan that had not been extended to employees in their job class at the time of their retirement; after reaching this conclusion, court reversed its earlier dismissal of state common law claims for fraud, breach of contract, and constructive fraud since Congress' decision to limit ERISA actions to

before the district court in *Novembre v. Local 584 Pension Fund* determined it could apply estoppel following the Third Circuit's *Rosen* decision, the court found the union liable for misrepresentations by its officers that pension credits for years of past service would be provided under "reciprocal" agreements with a new multiemployer plan which, in fact, never existed. The court stated:

> "As to the unions, the same policy considerations [that at first made the court reluctant to apply estoppel to the multiemployer plan] do not apply. Insofar as they are concerned this is a simple case of misrepresentation with all of the essential elements having been proved and the appropriate burden satisfied.... [T]he necessary elements for a fraud action are a false representation, knowledge or belief by the defendant of the falsity, and intention that the plaintiff act thereon, reasonable reliance in acting thereon by the plaintiff and resultant damage.
>
> "The Court has already indicated that there was a misrepresentation. Mr. McKinley admits that the representation was untrue in that he knew that there was no reciprocal agreement.
>
> "Those persons acting on behalf of the unions were authorized to do so. It was intended that the audience rely upon the representations.
>
> "Their reliance, as already indicated, was reasonable. And they sustained damages as a result of the loss of their pension benefits."[105]

Similarly, in *Monson v. Century Mfg. Co.*, a company was liable for intentional misrepresentation, as well as for breach of contract, when it repeatedly represented to employees that one-half of pretax profits were being contributed to a profit-sharing plan, when, in fact, it was

---

participants necessitates conclusion that claims by nonparticipants are not preempted); *Coleman v. Gen. Elec. Co.*, 643 F.Supp. 1229 (E.D. Tenn. 1986) (employees lacked standing *under ERISA* to bring suit against buyer of plant for alleged misrepresentations in comparison of buyer's and seller's benefit plans); *Schlansky v. United Merchants & Mfrs., Inc.*, 443 F.Supp. 1054, 1 EBC 1871 (S.D.N.Y 1977) (negligent misrepresentation by employer that years of service with predecessor employer would count under plan, if proven, constitutes claim under state tort law); *Kennedy v. Sale*, 689 S.W.2d 890, 6 EBC 1505 (Tex. 1985) (misrepresentation of preexisting condition coverage under group insurance contract by insurance agent in meeting with employees states claim under Texas consumer protection statute and in fraud).

But compare *Jackson v. Martin Marietta Corp.*, 805 F.2d 1498, 7 EBC 2767 (11th Cir. 1986) (ERISA preempts state law claim for breach of contract based on promise at job interview in 1977 that pension service would date from 1959); *Ogden v. Michigan Bell Tel. Co.*, 8 EBC 1481 (E.D. Mich. 1987) (former employees' claims that fiduciaries misrepresented when a voluntary early retirement incentive program would become effective dismissed upon determination that the representations were made by employer in nonfiduciary capacity; as a result, court at first reversed earlier rulings, 595 F.Supp. 961, 5 EBC 2281 (E.D. Mich. 1984), and 571 F.Supp. 520, 4 EBC 2540 (E.D. Mich. 1983), that ERISA preempted the employees' state common law claims, see 8 EBC 1219; however, the court later changed course again and held that the plaintiffs' state law fraud and misrepresentation claims were preempted because ERISA §510 "governs business activity of a non-fiduciary nature" and the plaintiffs' complaint was that Michigan Bell "acted wrongfully to deprive them of rights and benefits under [an ERISA] plan"). *Ogden* may be unsound because the court then found *no* §510 violation even when common law misrepresentation might have occurred.

[105] 4 EBC 1279, at 1286 (D.N.J. 1981), *modified for other reasons,* 4 EBC 1286 (D.N.J. 1981), *aff'd,* 4 EBC 1289 (3d Cir. 1982), *cert. denied,* 459 U.S. 1172 (1983). See also *Goins v. Teamsters Local 639,* 598 F.Supp. 1151 (D.D.C. 1984) (claim that union business agent fraudulently or negligently stated that new 10-year minimum requirement for disability benefits would not apply to employees who already had 5 years as required under unamended plan is state law claim); *Southern California Clerks Pension Fund v. Bjorklund,* 5 EBC 1285 (9th Cir. 1985) (rejecting employer defense to a delinquent contribution claim on basis that he had falsely been promised a pension, but noting that in state court, the employer had already obtained a judgment for fraud against the local union for the value of the promised pension).

contributing only one-third.[106] In *Stanger v. Gordon*, compensatory and punitive damages were awarded an employee based on his employer's willful misrepresentations that the employee would have an absolute right to profit-sharing benefits on termination of employment when there were, in fact, numerous forfeiture provisions in the plan.[107]

A more individual undertaking of assistance or advice may also lead to tort liability for negligence. In *Boucher v. Valus*, the supervisor of a company's insurance department undertook to inform an employee about insurance coverage for the treatment at a convalescent center of the employee's son, but supplied misinformation. The court found the company liable for the supervisor's negligence because one of the supervisor's duties was to supply such advice when requested, but he had not checked or made reasonable inquiries to get the proper information, even though he knew the employee intended to immediately rely on the information he supplied.[108] In *Gediman v. Anheuser Busch, Inc.*, an employee sought advice from his employer about differences between an immediate or deferred lump sum distribution of benefits after early retirement. The employer in turn obtained the information from the company's pension consultant. A memo from the consultant said that if the employee deferred benefits for two years, tax advantages would accrue, although the death benefit would not be "as much." In fact, the death benefit was less than one-half of the amount otherwise immediately available. Judge Friendly, for the Second Circuit, found that the employer was liable for the difference when the employee died after selecting the deferred benefit option, stating that "[h]aving undertaken to advise," the employer was "bound to advise clearly," taking into account the "frailties of human understanding."[109]

In certain circumstances, a general undertaking of assistance may also create a duty to disclose more obvious and pertinent points without a direct question. In *Erion v. Timken Co.*, an employer was held liable for failure to advise an employee in a retirement counseling meeting that survivor's benefits were being added to the plan and would be available to him if he waited just one week longer to retire. Although the employer contended it was internal company policy to only respond to direct inquiries in such meetings, the court held the

---

[106] 739 F.2d 1293, 5 EBC 1625 (8th Cir. 1984).

[107] 244 N.W.2d 628 (Minn. 1976). See also *Spitznass v. First Nat'l Bank of Oregon*, 525 P.2d 1318 (Ore. 1974) (although individual annual reports clearly stated that employee's past service would be counted, plan not estopped when he failed to show that plan trustee was responsible for preparation of the individual statements; however, employer could be liable if employee could show that employer's head timekeeper was responsible).

[108] 298 A.2d 238 (Conn. Cir. Ct. 1972).

[109] 299 F.2d 537, at 546 (2d Cir. 1962). But see *Cunha v. Ward Foods, Inc.*, 804 F.2d 1418, 7 EBC 2747 (9th Cir. 1986) (recovery for pre-ERISA negligent misrepresentations that noninsured plan would be secure limited to recovery of employee contributions, plus interest, under Hawaii common law, when employer terminated plan 3 years later with plan assets far short of paying all promised benefits—under pre-ERISA allocation schedule, all plan assets went to retired employees; Ninth Circuit rejected contention that younger employees were entitled to a "benefit-of-the-bargain" recovery when the misrepresentation was not intentional; court did not discuss why employees were not entitled to recovery of the *employer* contributions made on their behalf, with interest).

company had by its offer undertaken a duty to at least bring the "more obvious and pertinent points" to the employee's attention (without playing twenty questions).[110]

VI. Unjust Enrichment

Restitution may be available when a plan, or an employer, will "unjustly benefit," or an employee will "unjustly suffer loss,"[111] because the employee has rendered performance:

- Under an illusory promise in a pension plan;
- Under a misrepresentation or mistake concerning a benefit provision; or
- Toward satisfaction of a condition that has been discharged by impracticability or prevention.[112]

Restitution of the value of the employee's performance in these circumstances is generally measured by the contributions made on the employee's behalf, with interest.

Under ERISA, federal courts "will not lightly create additional rights [based on unjust enrichment] under the rubric of federal common law" where "Congress established [such] an extensive regulatory network."[113] But unjust enrichment may be available "to fill in interstitially or otherwise effectuate the statutory pattern enacted in the large by Congress."[114] Following this framework, courts have generally disfavored unjust enrichment claims under ERISA when the plan provision under which the "unjust enrichment" allegedly took place is unrescinded for any of the three reasons stated before, and is specifically permitted under ERISA. In *UAW v. Dyneer Corp.*, employees challenged an employer's recoupment of "excess" plan assets after the employer terminated a plan and satisfied then-existing contractual liabilities to employees. The court rejected the employees' unjust enrichment claim on the ground that no "unjust" enrichment *could* occur

---

[110] 368 N.E.2d 312, at 317 (Ohio Ct.App. 1976). See also *O'Hara v. United Gas Improvement Co.*, 31 Pa.D.&C.2d 567 (1963) (company officials visited terminally-ill employee in hospital to talk about his condition and benefits, but were under specific instructions to "under no circumstances ... initiate" discussion of his taking an immediate disability retirement so that benefits would be provided his wife when he died; court found that there comes a point when the circumstances require such advice); *Berry v. Playboy Enterprises Inc.*, 480 A.2d 941, 5 EBC 2682 (N.J. Super.Ct. App.Div. 1984) (triable issue of fact on whether employer undertook to generally advise new employee on employment and benefit options and then failed to tell her of a specific way to secure immediate health coverage).

[111] J. Calamari and J. Perillo, *Contracts*, at 570-1 (West 2d ed. 1977) (quoting *Restatement of Restitution*, §1 (1937)).

[112] *Id.*, at 570.

[113] *Van Orman v. American Home Ins. Co.*, 680 F.2d 301, 3 EBC 1653, at 1662 (3d Cir. 1982).

[114] *Airco Indus. Gases v. Teamsters Health & Welfare Fund*, 618 F.Supp. 943, 6 EBC 2409, at 2416 (D. Del. 1985) (quoting *Van Orman v. American Ins. Co.*, *supra*, 3 EBC at 1662, and thus finding a cause of action for an employer to recover mistaken contributions to a multiemployer plan).

when Section 4044(d)(1) of ERISA expressly permits recovery of excess assets by an employer when the plan provides for it, and the plan provision providing for it is not rescinded.[115] In *Van Orman v. American Ins. Co.*, the Third Circuit similarly refused to recognize unjust enrichment when unrescinded plan provisions entitled an employer to use excess plan assets existing under a plan that had not been terminated to fund benefits for a new group of employees.[116]

A. From Illusory Promises

An at-will amendment to a pension plan under authority to amend the plan "at any time and for whatever reason" can manifest that the unamended promise never constituted a firm "offer," but was instead illusory. Restitutionary recovery for unjust enrichment on the ground that a promise of benefits was illusory is discussed in Chapter 9 on plan amendments.

B. Based on Misrepresentation or Mistake

Restitutionary recovery can also be provided when a plan administrator or plan trustees admit a mistake of fact or law concerning the effect of a plan's provisions on an individual or a class of individuals, or when a mutual mistake or misrepresentation of fact or law is not freely admitted by the trustees or administrator, but is proven in court.[117] In *Chase v. Western Teamsters Pension Fund Trustees*, the Ninth Circuit carefully distinguished the reluctance of courts to order receipt of pension benefits contrary to a multiemployer plan's terms under estoppel, from restitution of contributions made on the employees' behalf, with interest. The court stated that neither the Labor Management Relations Act nor ERISA "prevents [the employees] from seeking recovery of the contributions made" based on a misrepresentation or mistake.[118] The *Chase* court cited numerous cases on the return to *employers* of contributions made to a multiemployer plan by mistake under the authority of ERISA Section 403(c)(2)(A)(ii), emphasizing that the mistake may be either one of fact or law, and that there is no limitation under the statute on the number of mistaken contributions that may be recovered if the refund is accomplished within six months after the mistake is determined by the plan administrator.[119] (For

---

[115] 4 EBC 1486 (N.D. Ohio 1983), *aff'd,* 5 EBC 2605 (6th Cir. 1984).

[116] 680 F.2d 301, 3 EBC 1653 (3d Cir. 1982).

[117] See *Peckham v. Painters Union Pension Fund Trustees,* 719 F.2d 1063, 4 EBC 2361, *modified on allowance of interest,* 724 F.2d 100, 4 EBC 2654 (10th Cir. 1983); *Chase v. Western Teamsters Pension Fund Trustees,* 753 F.2d 744, 6 EBC 1007 (9th Cir. 1985).

[118] *Id.*, 6 EBC at 1011 (citing *Thurber v. Western Conference of Teamsters' Pension Plan,* 542 F.2d 1106, at 1109 n. 4 and 5 (9th Cir. 1976) (*per curiam*); *Moglia v. Geoghegan,* 403 F.2d 110, at 116 n. 3, *cert. denied,* 394 U.S. 919 (1968)).

[119] However, other courts have held that ERISA confers no statutory or federal common law right for an employer to recover mistaken contributions. Instead, such refunds must be conferred

single-employer plans, a refund to an employer under Section 403(c)(2)(A)(i) is limited to contributions made within one year of a determination of a mistake of fact.) In *Chase,* the Ninth Circuit held that although the plaintiff taxicab owner-drivers were not employers, it was satisfied that the general equitable principles and limitations in Section 403(c)(2)(A) should apply to restitutionary suits by employees based on mistake.[120]

While rejected by the Ninth Circuit in *Chase,* employee suits for unjust enrichment based on misrepresentation or mistake may alternatively not be limited by ERISA Section 403(c)(2)(A) at all. Section 403(c)(2)(A) is tailored to limiting potential corruption of a plan in favor of *employers,* while at the same time allowing some restitutionary recovery. Indeed, the distinctions in Section 403(c)(2)(A) between single-employer and multiemployer plans make little or no sense as applied to suits by employees. In *Novembre v. Local 584 Pension Fund,* a district court ordered restitutionary recovery to employees to the extent of the contributions made on their behalf, plus interest, without mentioning Section 403(c)(2)(A), when trustees of the plan misrepresented to the employees that reciprocal credit for their service under another plan would be provided. The *Novembre* court, which was at first unwilling to apply estoppel because the plan was a multiemployer plan, provided recovery based on the misrepresentation, and the consequent unilateral mistake of the employees, to the extent of the contributions, plus interest, to prevent unjust enrichment [121]

When an *employer* recovers contributions under ERISA Section 403(c)(2)(A) based on mistake, the employees for whose benefit those contributions were made may have a claim against the employer for unjust enrichment or to establish a constructive trust.[122]

---

by the plan's terms or in the trustees' discretion—subject to the statutory limits in §403. See *Dime Coal Co. v. Combs,* 796 F.2d 394, 7 EBC 2068 (11th Cir. 1986); *Whitworth Bros. Storage Co. v. Central States Teamsters Pension Fund,* 794 F.2d 221 (6th Cir. 1986); *Crown Cork & Seal Co. v. Teamsters Pension Fund,* 549 F.Supp. 307, 3 EBC 2398 (E.D. Pa. 1982), *aff'd,* 720 F.2d 661, 4 EBC 2655 (3d Cir. 1983); *McHugh v. Teamsters Pension Trust Fund of Philadelphia,* 638 F.Supp. 1036 (E.D. Pa. 1986); *IBEW Local 995 v. Gulino,* 594 F.Supp. 1265 (M.D. La. 1984).

120 And see *Peckham v. Painters Union Pension Fund Trustees, supra* (ordering return of contributions to self-employed individuals as "participants," instead of as "employers," when contributions made based on mistake and no showing that refund of contributions would jeopardize plan's actuarial soundness; interest disallowed following Prop. Treas. Reg. 1.401(a)-3(b)(2)(ii)(A)).

121 4 EBC 1279, *modified for other reasons,* 4 EBC 1286 (D.N.J. 1981), *aff'd,* 4 EBC 1289 (3d Cir. 1982), *cert. denied,* 459 U.S. 1172 (1983). See also *Airco Indus. Gases v. Teamsters Health & Welfare Fund,* 618 F.Supp. 943, 6 EBC 2409 (D. Del. 1985) (holding that §403(c) does not create a cause of action for employers; instead employers may bring suit under federal common law for unjust enrichment from mistaken contributions, with their recovery limited by §403(c)).

122 See *Moglia v. Geoghegan, supra,* 403 F.2d at 116 n.3; *Chamberlin v. Bakery & Confectionery Union,* 99 LRRM 3176, at 3180–81 (N.D. Cal. 1977).

C. From Impracticability and Prevention

Restitutionary recovery can also be available to the extent justice requires when fulfillment of a condition for pension benefits is rendered "impracticable" by events whose nonoccurrence was a basic assumption of the parties,[123] or when fulfillment of a condition is "prevented" by actions of the employer.

"Impracticability" applies where a "basic assumption" of the parties' contract has been defeated.[124] The basic assumption must be one shared by both parties, or one that one party had, and the other party represented or implied it shared.[125]

Prevention is, in a sense, impracticability actively created by the other party to the contract. An implied promise exists in every contract that the parties will do nothing to prevent the performance of the other party.[126] Williston states:

> "It is a principle of fundamental justice that if a promisor is himself the cause of the failure ... of a condition upon which his own liability depends he cannot take advantage of the failure."[127]

It is, moreover, "as effective an excuse of performance of a condition that the promisor has hindered performance as that he has actually prevented it."[128] Exceptions to the doctrine of prevention apply when the other party "could not or would not have performed his promise anyway," or "where the action which prevents or hinders the other's performance was permitted by the express or implied terms of the contract, so that the risk of its non-happening was a risk ... assumed by the plaintiff."[129]

Impracticability and prevention seem to almost perfectly describe the effects plant closings and mass layoffs have on employee opportunities to attain pension entitlement. For example, one law review note states:

> "[W]here ... employees, in exchange for a pension, made wage concessions ... it is likely they expected [at least an opportunity] to receive the promised pension benefits. The opportunity ... [is thus] basic to their decision to work for [the] company at that wage."[130]

---

[123] The older common law cases refer to "impossibility," but "impracticability" connotes the greater flexibility now accorded the concept. *Restatement (Second) of Contracts,* §261, comment (d) (1981 ed.).

[124] *Restatement (Second) of Contracts,* §261, comments (a) and (b). And see U.C.C. §2-615, and *Restatement (Second) of Trusts,* §65A and §167.

[125] *Id.* If an employer *represents* that it shares an assumption, an action may also be present, and often more easily established, under estoppel.

[126] *Restatement (Second) of Contracts,* §205, comment (d) and §245.

[127] *Williston on Contracts,* §677.

[128] *Id.*, at §677A. And see *Restatement (Second) of Contracts,* §205 and §245.

[129] L. Simpson, *Contracts,* at 382 (West 2d ed. 1965).

[130] Note, "Employees' Rights to Employer Contributed Pension Benefits After a Plant Shutdown," 1984 Utah L. Rev. 807, at 821.

The courts, however, have generally not been receptive to unjust enrichment claims based on impracticablity or prevention either because they do not consider it a "basic assumption" of the parties that such events would not occur, or more rhetorically, because "quantum meruit is not a surrogate for the specifics of the contract."[131] Thus, courts have usually held that plant closings and work force reductions are a part of everyday life, that the employer did not promise employees they could remain in employment until the conditions for pension benefits were fulfilled, and that employees have therefore assumed the risk of a shortfall in service from these events.[132] In a sense, this may sidestep the issue since employers and employees alike may acknowledge that the risk is on employees as far as their general employment contract, or lack thereof, but both may also typically, if somewhat contradictorily, assume the nonoccurrence of major business contractions for pension planning purposes. In particular, employers generally fund plans based on actuarial assumptions that such events, i.e., major business changes, will not occur,[133] and generally also do not disclose such events in the SPD as potential "circumstances" that may result in a loss or denial of benefits.[134] Most employees, similarly, have thought about losing their jobs, but not about the effect of a job loss on their opportunities for pension benefit entitlement. A distinction between assumptions of risk as far as an employment contract and as far as a pension plan can, therefore, be realistic in terms of both parties' expectations.[135]

Reflecting such a distinction, unjust enrichment based on impracticability and prevention has been accepted in a small number of pension cases. The most cited is *Lucas v. Seagrave Corp.* In *Lucas*, 30 out of 65 participants in a pre-ERISA pension plan that provided vesting only at retirement age were discharged short of that age within a one-year period after the Seagrave Corp. bought their division and assumed control of its pension plan. The plaintiffs showed that the new employer's windfall from the unexpectedly high pension forfeitures resulting from its discharges of them had produced funding credits against

---

[131] *Craig v. Bemis*, 517 F.2d 677, at 686 (5th Cir. 1975).

[132] See *Craig v. Bemis, supra*; *Lovetri v. Vickers, Inc.*, 397 F.Supp. 293 (D. Conn. 1975); *Luli v. Sun Products, Inc.*, 398 N.E.2d 553 (Ohio 1979); *Shaw v. Kruidenier*, 470 F.Supp. 1375 (S.D. Iowa 1979); *United Steelworkers Local No. 2098 v. Int'l Systems & Controls Corp.*, 566 F.2d 1135 (10th Cir. 1977). In *Schneider v. Elec. Auto-Lite Co.*, 456 F.2d 366 (6th Cir. 1972), the Sixth Circuit held that even assuming employment through a certain date was required for a year's vacation pay, a *pro rata* portion of that pay must be considered due when "the company's action in closing a plant prevented employees from working until the December 31st date." 456 F.2d at 372. The court refused, however, to apply the same reasoning to eligibility requirements under the employer's pension plan.

[133] See M. Bernstein, "Employee Pension Rights When Plants Shut Down," 76 Harv. L. Rev. 952, at 967–72 (1963).

[134] See 29 C.F.R. 2520.102-3(l). Some plans and summary plan descriptions have specific provisions for plant shutdowns and work force reductions. When this is the case, their nonoccurrence is not a basic assumption of either party for purposes of pension entitlement.

[135] See *Lucas v. Seagrave Corp.*, 277 F.Supp. 338, at 346 (D. Minn. 1967) (distinguishing assumption of risk of a layoff from assumption of risk of loss of pension benefits); *Lemmon v. Cedar Point, Inc.*, 406 F.2d 94 (6th Cir. 1969) (distinguishing employer's right to terminate employee under employment contract from consequences of the termination under stock option plan); and cases cited below.

the employer's future contributions sufficient to eliminate all employer contributions from the time the company acquired the division. The district court emphasized that this had occurred because the employees' continued performance was "unwanted and, indeed, [had been] prevented by the employer." Without a restitutionary recovery, the employer would retain the "full benefit of the employees' past service, [the] favorable tax treatment on contributions, [and would] recapture ... the accumulated pension credits created by [the] forfeitures." While the court did not technically hold that this was unjust enrichment, but rather rejected the employer's motion for summary judgment, the court's strongly worded opinion left little doubt on how it would rule.[136] In *Kenneke v. First National Bank of Chicago*, the Illinois Appellate Court followed *Lucas* in rejecting an employer's motion for summary judgment on an unjust enrichment claim. In *Kenneke*, a termination of all the employees of a newspaper was held to be an extraordinary contingency not foreseen in collective bargaining negotiations over pensions, with the employer otherwise being unjustly enriched by an actuarial surplus created by its own actions.[137]

In *Fredericks v. Georgia Pacific Corp.*, an employee who forfeited 90 percent of his benefits from a stock bonus plan because of his resignation also survived a motion to dismiss on an unjust enrichment count when he alleged that he was "constructively discharged" and that it would be unjust for Georgia Pacific to benefit from its own inequitable conduct.[138] "Noncompete" provisions in pension plans have also often been construed as containing a constructive condition that such forfeitures will *not* occur if the "competition" is precipitated by a discharge or constructive discharge of the employee.[139] Similarly, in *Hillis v. Waukesha Title Co.*, a district court found that "[b]y firing Hillis on December 23, 1977" after the employer learned Hillis intended to leave, the plan administrator "sought to *prevent* Hillis from securing a Company contribution on his behalf for the year 1977." Without elaboration on whether it was acting under ERISA Section 510 or the contract law doctrine of prevention (or tortious interference with contract), the court ordered the 1977 contribution to be allocated to Hillis when it enjoined the plan from enforcing an undisclosed forfeiture for competition clause.[140]

While not litigated, impracticability may be particularly likely to

---

[136] 277 F.Supp. 338, at 345 (D. Minn. 1967).

[137] 434 N.E.2d 496 (Ill.App. 1982).

[138] 331 F.Supp. 422 (E.D. Pa. 1972), *app. dismissed,* 474 F.2d 1338 (3d Cir. 1972).

[139] See *Lojek v. Thomas*, 716 F.2d 675, 4 EBC 2321 (9th Cir. 1983); *Post v. Merrill Lynch, Pierce, Fenner & Smith*, 421 N.Y.S.2d 847 (N.Y. 1979); *Kroeger v. Stop & Shop Co.*, 432 N.E.2d 566 (Mass. App.Ct. 1982). Cf. *Morse v. Stanley*, 732 F.2d 1139, 5 EBC 1602 (2d Cir. 1984). Without phrasing their decisions in terms of impracticability or prevention, a number of courts distinguish voluntary and involuntary absences from work in determining whether application of a break-in-service rule is arbitrary and capricious, thereby implying a constructive condition that avoiding the break in service must not be impracticable or prevented by actions of the employer. See ch. 5, sec. III.A.4.a.

[140] 576 F.Supp. 1103, at 1105 and 1110 (E.D. Wis. 1983).

apply when a classic impracticability event, such as fire, other destruction of a plant, an "act of God," or government regulation makes completion of conditions for pension rights impracticable.

When unjust enrichment theories are disfavored by a court, an alternative is to frame the claim under the most analogous statutory or plan provision, and to emphasize the same points that would be made in an unjust enrichment action. Code Section 411(d)(3), requiring that all tax-qualified plans provide for nonforfeitability of benefits accrued on a termination or partial termination of a plan, is analogous to impracticability or prevention with recovery in quasi-contract ("to the extent [the benefits are] funded").[141] Section 510 of ERISA can provide still broader relief, that is, recovery may be without the "to the extent funded" limitation, and possibly also with back pay and reinstatement, if an employer or another party *intentionally* hinders or prevents fulfillment of the conditions for benefits, e.g., by discharging an employee or employees, for the purpose of interfering with the attainment of those rights.[142] The facts that would otherwise establish unjust enrichment may also form the basis for an ERISA Section 404(a)(1) fiduciary action, or an action under Section 403(c)(1)'s prohibition on "inurement" of a plan's assets for the benefit of the employer.[143]

VII. Reform of Plans in Equity

In rare circumstances, pension plans are reformed in equity when a plan provision, as written, is the product of fraud, misrepresentation, mistake, or undue influence.[144] For example, mistake has been applied to reform a plan provision allowing unilateral termination of a plan by an employer that was surreptitiously written in by the sponsoring employer, without agreement from the union with whom the employer negotiated the plan.[145]

Generally, however, courts are cautious about reforming contracts, including pension plans.[146] But the same results can sometimes be obtained under legal theories courts are less reluctant to use, namely, by plan interpretation, by estoppel, by rescission of a plan provision

---

[141] See ch. 9, sec. VIII, and ch. 11, sec. I.

[142] See ch. 10, sec. I.

[143] See ch. 9, secs. II.B and VIII.

[144] See *Hackett v. PBGC*, 486 F.Supp. 1357, 2 EBC 2522 (D. Md. 1980) (but none of these present).

[145] See *Steelworkers Local 2341 v. Whitehead & Kales Co.*, 94 Lab. Cas. ¶13,600 (E.D. Mich. 1982); *Delgrosso v. Spang & Co.*, 769 F.2d 928, 6 EBC 1940 (3d Cir. 1985), *cert. denied*, 476 U.S. ___ (1986) (reforming unilaterally-drafted plan that contradicted pension part of collective bargaining agreement; also ordering that independent plan administrator be appointed to reform plan provisions so that excess assets would not just go to unvested participants).

[146] See McClintock, *Equity*, §242 (2d ed. 1977), *Hackett v. PBGC*, *supra*; *United Steelworkers v. North Bend Terminal Co.*, 752 F.2d 256, 6 EBC 1299 (6th Cir. 1985); *Chesser v. Babcock & Wilcox*, 753 F.2d 1570, *reh. denied*, 760 F.2d 281 (11th Cir. 1985) (no equitable reformation of 30-year early retirement benefit requirement when participants had 25 + years and were involuntarily laid off).

based on misrepresentation or mistake, with recovery to the extent necessary to prevent unjust enrichment, or in a jointly administered multiemployer plan, by a declaration that a plan provision as written, or as applied under particular facts, is "arbitrary and capricious."

VIII. Reform of Structural Defects in Jointly Administered Plans

Under Section 302(c)(5) of the Labor Management Relations Act of 1947 (commonly called the Taft-Hartley Act),[147] the courts have found authority to correct, and for all practical purposes, to reform, "structural defects" in jointly administered multiemployer plan rules that are denying benefits to an unusually high percentage of participants, or that on their face, or in operation, are denying benefits to individuals, or groups of individuals, on arbitrary grounds. Section 302(c) of the LMRA prohibits transfers of money or other things of value from employers, or their representatives, to unions, or their representatives. As an exception to this general prohibition, Section 302(c)(5) allows transfers of money to union-sponsored pension and welfare funds if certain conditions are met, namely:

(1) The fund must be established as a trust;

(2) It must provide that payments are only to be made to the trust on the "detailed basis" "specified in a written [contribution] agreement with the employer";

(3) It must have an equal number of employer representatives as plan trustees with any deadlocks on issues of plan administration resolved by an impartial arbitrator; and

(4) It must be structured "for the sole and exclusive benefit" of employees, their families and dependents.

The last requirement that a jointly administered trust must be structured "for the sole and exclusive benefit" of employees, their families, and dependents has given rise to federal court litigation to redress structural defects that are rendering a plan arbitrary and capricious. The courts have recognized that the purpose of this litigation is often to reform unambiguous terms of Taft-Hartley plans to meet the "sole and exclusive benefit" requirement. Because this involves extraordinary equitable jurisdiction, with a somewhat "ambiguous" legislative history behind it, this power is used only when a plan's benefit requirements are clearly arbitrary.[148] The arbitrary and capricious

---

[147] 29 U.S.C. §186(c)(5).

[148] *Alvares v. Erickson*, 514 F.2d 156, 1 EBC 1121, at 1127 (9th Cir. 1975).

standard of review used in this context is a restrained standard, reflecting the need to implement Section 302(c)(5)'s "sole and exclusive benefit" mandate while at the same time "respecting the trustees' need for discretion in conceiving [plan rules] to maximize employee welfare."[149]

In 1982, the Supreme Court held in *UMW Health & Retirement Funds v. Robinson* that this arbitrary and capricious standard of review does not apply to those plan provisions which are the product of collective bargaining. By the sweep of its language, the Court questioned whether Section 302(c)(5)'s "sole and exclusive benefit" standard was ever intended to do more than prevent outright diversion of plan funds to nonparticipants, thus implying that even plan rules designed by plan trustees might not be reviewable under Section 302(c)(5) except to sanction diversion.[150] Every circuit that has addressed the issue since has, however, limited *Robinson* to its holding, namely, that collectively bargained plan amendments are not subject to review under the Section 302(c)(5) arbitrary and capricious standard.[151] However, in *Central Tool Co. v. IAM Nat'l Pension Fund*, the U.S. Court of Appeals for the District of Columbia Circuit upheld a cancellation of past service credits on an employer's withdrawal from a multiemployer plan with *no* review for arbitrary and capricious action—even though the past service was cancelled under a plan provision that the plan's trustees had designed and adopted. Since the provision authorizing the cancellation was in the plan at the time the employer agreed to the collective bargaining agreement requiring it to contribute to the plan, the court held that the provision was collectively bargained, and thus, excepted from review for reasonableness under the Supreme Court's ruling.[152]

One reason for the general reluctance to go any further than the strict holding in *Robinson* is found in *NLRB v. Amax Coal Co.*, where the Supreme Court recognized in 1981, shortly before *Robinson* was decided, that Congress in enacting nearly identical language to Section 302(c)(5) under ERISA's Section 404(a)(1) standard "essentially codified the strict fiduciary standards that a Section 302(c)(5) trustee must meet."[153] In adopting this language, Congress was, moreover, aware that the identical language under Section 302(c)(5) had been construed to permit review of benefit provisions in Taft-Hartley plans for arbitrary and capricious benefit requirements. In the debates over ERISA, Representative Carl Perkins twice mentioned scores of letters seeking his assistance because of denials of benefits from the United Mine

---

[149] *Hurn v. Plumbing, Heating & Piping Industry Trust*, 703 F.2d 386, 4 EBC 1811, at 1814 (9th Cir. 1983).

[150] See 455 U.S. 562, 3 EBC 1129, at 1133 (1982).

[151] See *Chambless v. Masters, Mates & Pilots Pension Plan*, 772 F.2d 1032, 6 EBC 2209 (2d Cir. 1985); *Sellers v. O'Connell*, 701 F.2d 575, 4 EBC 1312 (6th Cir. 1983); *Murn v. UMW 1950 Pension Trust*, 718 F.2d 359, 4 EBC 2388 (10th Cir. 1983); *Hurn v. Plumbing, Heating & Piping Industry Trust*, 703 F.2d 386, 4 EBC 1811 (9th Cir. 1983); *Short v. UMW 1950 Pension Trust*, 728 F.2d 528, 5 EBC 1532 (D.C. Cir. 1984).

[152] 811 F.2d 651, 8 EBC 1268 (D.C. Cir. 1987). And see ch. 9, sec. II.A.

[153] 453 U.S. 322, 2 EBC 1489, at 1493 (1981).

Workers health and retirement funds "on account of rigid, arbitrary and unreasonable eligibility standards,"[154] and favorably discussed recent class action suits "confirm[ing] what many of us had believed for quite some time. That is, that the eligibility standards of the [United Mine Workers health and retirement funds were] being administered in an arbitrary and capricious fashion."[155] He further stated:

> "I am hopeful that this legislation will take a giant step forward, not only in making welfare and pension benefits to miners administered in a fair and equitable manner and with assurances of security, but also the thousands of other workers in other fields of labor who have had similar experiences."[156]

Based on the recodification of the LMRA Section 302(c)(5) standard under ERISA Section 404(a)(1), the Ninth Circuit has adopted the Taft-Hartley cases as direct precedent for ERISA fiduciary claims when plan provisions have been designed or amended by a plan's trustees.[157] Section 302(c)(5) continues to apply as well in cases involving Taft-Hartley plans so long as the plan provision is not the product of collective bargaining.[158]

Substantively, the case law under Section 302(c)(5) begins with a series of decisions in the District of Columbia Circuit concerning eligibility requirements and procedures of the United Mine Workers pension and welfare plans.[159] As the cases evolved in the District of Columbia and other circuits, the basic rule emerged that for a Taft-Hartley plan to be for the "sole and exclusive benefit" of participants and beneficiaries, a "rational nexus" must exist between the plan's legitimate purposes and any exclusionary requirements that deny benefits to employees for whom substantial contributions to the fund have been made.[160] The plan's primary legitimate objective, or purpose, is the provision of pension benefits to "as many intended employees as is

---

[154] 2 ERISA Leg. Hist. 3368 and 3 ERISA Leg. Hist. 4658.

[155] 3 ERISA Leg. Hist. 4658.

[156] *Id.*

[157] See *Elser v. IAM Nat'l Pension Fund*, 684 F.2d 648, 3 EBC 2155 (9th Cir. 1982), *cert. denied*, 464 U.S. 813 (1983); *Harm v. Bay Area Pipe Trades Pension Fund*, 701 F.2d 1301, 4 EBC 1253 (9th Cir. 1983); *Fentron Indus. v. Shopmen's Pension Fund*, 674 F.2d 1300, 3 EBC 1373 (9th Cir. 1982); *Brug v. Carpenters Pension Trust*, 669 F.2d 570, 3 EBC 1240 (9th Cir. 1982).

The use of the Taft-Hartley cases as precedent under ERISA in cases involving non-Taft-Hartley plans, (i.e., collectively bargained and nonbargained single-employer plans) does not extend, as under §302(c)(5) of the LMRA, to review of the *initial* terms of a plan, since until a single-employer plan is designed, no one is generally a plan fiduciary. In a collectively bargained single-employer plan, collectively bargained plan amendments are also not subject to review under the Taft-Hartley precedents because of the collective bargaining exception announced in *UMW Health & Retirement Funds v. Robinson*. See ch. 9, sec. II.A.1.

[158] See cases at nn. 151 and 157 above.

[159] See *Kosty v. Lewis*, 319 F.2d 744 (D.C. Cir. 1963), *cert. denied*, 375 U.S. 964 (1964); *Roark v. Lewis*, 401 F.2d 425 (D.C. Cir. 1968); *Gaydosh v. Lewis*, 410 F.2d 262 (D.C. Cir. 1969); *Roark v. Boyle*, 439 F.2d 497 (D.C. Cir. 1970); *Lavella v. Boyle*, 444 F.2d 910 (D.C. Cir. 1971). Ironically, these cases do not *directly* state that the court's jurisdiction is based on §302 of the LMRA, leaving open the possibility that they were decided under the common law of trusts within the court's diversity jurisdiction. The analysis, however, laid the foundation for all §302(c)(5) cases.

[160] See, e.g., *Roark v. Lewis, supra; Rehmar v. Smith*, 555 F.2d 1362, 1 EBC 1799 (9th Cir. 1977).

economically possible."[161] A rational nexus with this purpose does not require defined benefit plans to establish and maintain a "precise fit" between contributions made to the plan on an individual's behalf and the individual's benefit entitlement. It does not, in other words, require the plan to become a defined contribution plan with immediate vesting and no forfeitures. But the rational nexus requirement does set an outer limit on the degree of arbitrariness which can be introduced into a plan with this retirement income purpose.[162]

Under the rational nexus test, when an exclusionary plan requirement denies benefits to an "unusually high" percentage of plan participants, a presumption of arbitrariness is created. The plan's trustees may rebut the presumption if they show the "reasonableness of the requirement" under all the circumstances.[163] Even if forfeitures caused by a plan provision are not "unusually high," a presumption of arbitrariness is established when an exclusionary requirement creates an arbitrary forfeiture, such as through the application of a break-in-service rule to an employee who is *involuntarily* absent from work, e.g., because of a layoff or disability. In *Lee v. Nesbitt*, the Ninth Circuit thus stated that it is arbitrary

> "to impose a requirement that [a participant] continue to work to retirement, even though no work was available."[164]

Plan provisions that cancel years of past service credit if an employee's employer withdraws from a multiemployer plan also generally create a presumption of arbitrariness since the cause of the cancellation, the employer's withdrawal from the plan, is an event over which the employees generally have no control.[165]

---

[161] *Elser v. IAM Nat'l Pension Fund*, 684 F.2d 648, 3 EBC 2155, at 2162 (9th Cir. 1982), quoting *Ponce v. Construction Laborers Pension Trust*, 628 F.2d 537, 2 EBC 1777 (9th Cir. 1980), in turn quoting *Gaydosh v. Lewis*, 410 F.2d 262 (D.C. Cir. 1969). And see *Mosley v. NMU Pension & Welfare Plan*, 438 F.Supp. 413 (E.D.N.Y. 1977). See also *Struble v. New Jersey Brewery Employees' Welfare Fund*, 732 F.2d 325, 5 EBC 1676, at 1683 (3d Cir. 1984).

[162] *Central Tool Co. v. IAM Nat'l Pension Fund*, 523 F.Supp. 812, 2 EBC 2019, at 2024 (D.D.C. 1981), *rev'd on other grounds*, 811 F.2d 651, 8 EBC 1268 (D.C. Cir. 1987). And see *Harm v. Bay Area Pipe Trades Pension Fund*, 701 F.2d 1301, 4 EBC 1253 (9th Cir. 1983); *Elser v. IAM Nat'l Pension Fund*, 684 F.2d 648, 3 EBC 2155 (9th Cir. 1982), *cert. denied*, 464 U.S. 813 (1983).

[163] See *Ponce v. Construction Laborers Pension Trust*, 628 F.2d 537, 2 EBC 1777 (9th Cir. 1980) (presumption of arbitrariness created when less than 4% of a plan's participants vested under a 15-year vesting requirement), and 774 F.2d 1401, 6 EBC 2468 (9th Cir. 1985), *cert. denied*, 479 U.S. ___ (1986) (affirming district court decision on remand that increasing dollar amount of benefits in the face of "unusually high" lack of vesting of participants on whose behalf the contributions were made was arbitrary); *Miranda v. Audia*, 681 F.2d 1124, 3 EBC 1847 (9th Cir. 1982) (presumption of arbitrariness under nearly identical vesting requirement and facts, but presumption rebutted by showing of reasonableness for particular plan).

[164] 453 F.2d 1309, at 1312 (9th Cir. 1972). And see *Van Fossan v. Teamsters Local 710 Pension Fund*, 649 F.2d 1243, 2 EBC 1457, at 1462 n.21 (7th Cir. 1981) (break-in-service provision not arbitrary and capricious *per se*, "only the application of such a rule to a circumstance *beyond the employee's control*" is arbitrary). Other decisions following the voluntary/involuntary distinction are discussed above in ch. 5, sec. III.A.4, and below in ch. 9, sec. II.B.1.

[165] See ch. 4, sec. III.C.6. When an employer's withdrawal from a plan is caused by the bargaining unit employees' decertification of a union, it may appear to be a voluntary event, but the employees adversely affected by the past service cancellation may be only a minority of the employees voting on the issue, thus making the withdrawal and cancellation an event over which the affected employees have no individual control. See *Elser v. IAM Nat'l Pension Fund, supra*, 3 EBC at 2160.

Rules that single out groups of employees who have substantially greater service than other employees receiving benefits, but who lack an arbitrary characteristic, such as having their very last year of work before retirement or before disability with a contributing employer (a "signatory" last year of service requirement) can also shift the burden to the trustees to disprove the arbitrariness of the requirement.[166] Along the same line, a requirement of unbroken service over a longer period immediately preceding retirement can raise a presumption of arbitrariness if participants without that characteristic have substantially greater service, but in a broken skein.[167] A requirement of employment on one particular day to receive credit for years of past service may also be arbitrary when it is "well known" to plan trustees that the selected date will exclude most "travelers," i.e., union members who frequently work within the jurisdiction of the plan, but who have a different home local.[168]

As discussed further in Chapter 9, plan amendments that strip participants of vested rights, or plan amendments that are put into effect without advance notice to enable participants to conform their service to the new rule, can also raise a presumption of arbitrariness—even if the plan amendment is reasonable on a purely prospective basis.[169] More general considerations on the arbitrariness of plan amendments are the evidence before the trustees on the financial need and financial advantages for the plan from a plan amendment, and the trustees' consideration of alternative means to obtain equivalent financial advantages—particularly those which do not deny benefits to participants with substantial service toward a benefit, or which do not deny benefits to participants who are involuntarily separated from service by reason of a reduction in the work force or disability. Plan amendments are also examined for whether they effectively carve out discriminatory preferences or exceptions that deprive nonunion plan participants of benefits, while providing benefits to union members with the same or lesser service.[170]

Once a presumption of arbitrariness under a plan provision is established, the burden of proof shifts to the plan's trustees, but the mere invocation of "financial considerations" is not sufficient justification

> "as *every* exclusive eligibility requirement would have the virtue of saving money. To be sure, actuarial soundness is of legitimate concern to a

---

[166] *Roark v. Lewis*, 401 F.2d 425 (D.C. Cir. 1968); *Roark v. Boyle*, 439 F.2d 497 (D.C. Cir. 1970); *Teston v. Carey*, 464 F.2d 765 (D.C. Cir. 1972); *Pete v. UMWA Welfare & Retirement Fund*, 517 F.2d 1275, 1 EBC 1239 (D.C. Cir. 1975) (*en banc*); *Seafarers Pension Plan v. Sturgis*, 630 F.2d 218, 2 EBC 2347 (4th Cir. 1980).

[167] *Malone v. Western Conference of Teamsters Pension Trust*, 168 Cal.Rptr. 210 (Cal. Ct.App. 1980). But compare *Roark v. Boyle, supra.*

[168] *Int'l Ass'n of Heat & Frost Insulators v. Graham*, 81 Lab. Cas. ¶13,142 (Tex. Civ.App. 1976).

[169] See ch. 9, secs. IV and V.

[170] Review of plan amendments for arbitrary and capricious action is discussed in ch. 9, sec. II.B.

fund's trustees, but financial integrity must be secured by methods dividing beneficiaries from non-beneficiaries on lines reasonably calculated to further the fund's purposes."[171]

Examples of successful rebuttals by trustees have been:

- That eligibility rules other than the one challenged had been relaxed to counter "unusually high" exclusions under a plan and that the change the plaintiffs sought would have only an insignificant effect on the number of benefit denials;[172]
- That a changed early retirement standard was necessary to discourage workers from voluntarily taking actions that shifted the burden of supporting the fund to other employees;[173]
- That restrictions in vesting rules prompted by financial concerns, while discriminatory in their impact against casual and part-time seamen, were necessary to preserve benefits for qualified full-time seamen.[174]

Even when a requirement is held to be arbitrary, trustees may be given an opportunity to reformulate the rule in a nonarbitrary manner, rather than the court reformulating the rule or striking it down in its entirety.[175]

---

[171] *Robinson v. UMW Health and Retirement Funds of America*, 640 F.2d 416, 2 EBC 1086, at 1091 (D.C. Cir. 1981), *rev'd on other grounds*, 455 U.S. 562, 3 EBC 1129 (1982). And see *Elser v. IAM Nat'l Pension Fund, supra*; *Fase v. Seafarers Welfare & Pension Plan*, 432 F.Supp. 1037 (E.D.N.Y. 1977), *aff'd*, 589 F.2d 112, 1 EBC 1474 (2d Cir. 1978); *Winpisinger v. Aurora Corp.*, 456 F.Supp. 559, 1 EBC 2201 (N.D. Ohio 1978) (financial concerns must be addressed by means which do not create undue preferences among plan participants); *Central Tool Co. v. IAM Nat'l Pension Fund*, 523 F.Supp. 812, 2 EBC 2019 (D.D.C. 1981), *rev'd on other grounds*, 811 F.2d 651, 8 EBC 1268 (D.C. Cir. 1987) (reduction in benefits following employer withdrawal to be accomplished by least drastic means and only "to the extent necessary"). See also *Donovan v. Carlough*, 576 F.Supp. 245, 5 EBC 1400 (D.D.C. 1983).

[172] *Miranda v. Audia*, 681 F.2d 1124, 3 EBC 1847 (9th Cir. 1982). See also *Mestas v. Huge*, 585 F.2d 450, at 453 (10th Cir. 1978) (miner with 17½ years of service challenged all or nothing 20-year vesting requirement as unreasonable rule for trustees to adopt instead of a graduated vesting schedule; court held trustees had "several rational alternatives," including their rule and the plaintiff's proposed rule, and selected one, "leaving no basis for judicial intervention"). But compare *Ponce v. Construction Laborers Pension Trust*, 774 F.2d 1401, 6 EBC 2468 (9th Cir. 1985), *cert. denied*, 479 U.S. ___ (1986).

[173] See *Gaydosh v. Lewis*, 410 F.2d 262 (D.C. Cir. 1969); *Saunders v. Teamsters Local 639 Pension Trust*, 667 F.2d 146, 2 EBC 1961 (D.C. Cir. 1981) (but rationale did not apply to a disabled miner who met all the requirements for early retirement, except age, before the change).

[174] *Mosley v. NMU Pension and Welfare Plan*, 451 F.Supp. 226 (E.D.N.Y. 1978). See also *Johnson v. Botica*, 537 F.2d 930 (7th Cir. 1976) (valid factual basis existed for plan rule conditioning past service credits on two quarters of contributory service under plan, even though employee's failure to meet requirement was involuntary, since contributory service is essential to support the plan's benefits on a sound actuarial basis).

[175] See *Johnson v. Botica*, 537 F.2d 930, at 937-38 (7th Cir. 1976).

9

Plan Amendments Under the Fiduciary Standard, Federal Common Law, and Special Rules

I. Limits of ERISA's Minimum Standard Protections

ERISA's minimum standards protect plan participants against amendments that adopt more restrictive vesting schedules or that decrease any participant's "accrued benefit." These protections have been discussed in Chapters 4 and 5. The chief limitation on the minimum standard protections is, as discussed there, that before the effective dates of the 1984 Retirement Equity Act, ERISA Section 204(g) did not clearly protect subsidized early retirement benefits or benefit options that did not fit squarely within ERISA's definition of "accrued benefit." Thus, the House Ways and Means Committee stated:

> "The term 'accrued benefit' refers to pension or retirement benefits and is not intended to apply to certain ancillary benefits, such as medical insurance or life insurance, which are sometimes provided in conjunction with a pension plan, and are sometimes provided separately. . . . Also, the accrued benefit to which the vesting rules apply is not to include such items as the value of the right to receive benefits commencing at an age before normal retirement age, or so-called social security supplements which are commonly paid in the case of early retirement but then cease when the retiree attains the age at which he becomes entitled to receive current social security benefits, or any value in a plan's joint and survivor annuity provisions to the extent that exceeds the value of what the participant would be entitled to receive under a single life annuity."[1]

[1] H.R. 93-807, at 60, 2 ERISA Leg. Hist. 3180. See also 2 ERISA Leg. Hist. 3306.

With the effective dates of the 1984 REA amendments, the protection of accrued benefits against benefit-reducing amendments has been clarified and extended to include amendments that would otherwise reduce or eliminate an early retirement benefit or a retirement-type subsidy. Optional benefit forms that do not include a subsidy, such as actuarially equivalent lump sum options and joint and survivor's options, may also not be eliminated by plan amendment, unless specifically permitted under to-be-issued Treasury regulations.[2]

If a plan amendment is not covered by the pre-REA protections, or the post-REA clarification and modification, other considerations can still limit the amendment. These are:

(1) Whether the amendment is in breach of fiduciary duty;

(2) Whether the amendment is in breach of the employer's duty to bargain or the union's duty of fair representation; or for a nonbargained plan, whether it is in breach of an implied contractual duty of good faith and fair dealing;

(3) Whether the amendment is in breach of any contractual limits contained in the plan, as interpreted by the disclosure in the SPD and other extrinsic evidence; or whether the amendment is estopped by promissory representations and assurances concerning plan amendments;

(4) Whether the amendment impairs "vested" rights in a contractual sense;

(5) Whether advance notice of the amendment has been provided so that participants have the maximum opportunity to conform their actions to the new rule;

(6) Whether the effects of the amendment, and ways around it, have been fully explained to participants, with any related discretionary authority exercised consistently; and

(7) Whether the amendment results in unjust enrichment of the employer.

In addition to these federal common law considerations, special ERISA and Internal Revenue Code provisions on partial terminations of plans from amendments reducing benefits, on inurement of plan assets to the benefit of an employer, and on reversions of plan assets to an employer to the extent excess assets result from a plan amendment further limit the retroactive effects a plan amendment is permitted to have. ERISA and the Code also provide special rules on plan amendments that merge two plans or transfer assets or benefit liabilities from one plan to another. These rules are designed to prevent dilution of the assets backing a participant's benefits as a result of such amendments.

Plan amendments on the eve of benefit entitlement can also violate Section 510 of ERISA if they are for the purpose of interfering

---

[2] See ch. 4, sec. IV.B.3.

with the attainment of benefit rights. Age, race, and sex discrimination protections, and Code Section 401(a)(4)'s prohibition of discrimination in favor of highly compensated employees can further limit plan amendments that focus on benefits primarily used by protected classes of employees. These limits on plan amendments are discussed in Chapter 10.

II. Plan Amendments and Fiduciary Duties

A. When Is a Plan Amendment a Fiduciary Function

The initial question on whether a plan amendment is in breach of fiduciary duty is not the stringency, or lack thereof, of the arbitrary and capricious standard of review that is generally used for benefit claims alleging fiduciary violations, but is whether the act of amending a plan is a fiduciary function. The key language in the ERISA Section 3(21)(A) definition of a fiduciary is "discretionary authority or discretionary control" respecting "administration" or "management of [the] plan," or discretionary authority or control respecting "management or disposition of [the plan's] assets." This language is broad enough on its face to encompass plan amendments, but at the same time, it does not absolutely compel their inclusion as fiduciary functions.

In *Moore v. Reynolds Metals Co. Retirement Program*, the Sixth Circuit held that until a plan is established, discretionary authority or control over the administration or management of a plan cannot exist. Therefore, no one is generally a fiduciary under ERISA in designing a plan's initial terms.[3] However, once a plan is established, decisions to amend the plan are, at least potentially, exercises of discretionary authority or control over the management or administration of the plan, and also over the disposition of its assets. It may seem anomalous that an initial decision of plan design may *not* be a fiduciary function, but a later decision to amend the plan may be. As a matter of policy, the major difference is that after a plan is established, there is a trust *res* and employees have provided their labor in reliance on receiving part of that *res* under the terms of the initial benefit offer. Whether or not a benefit has vested or has become an "accrued benefit," the employer has then created expectations that the terms for the benefit will be continued, or improved—or if benefits, or benefit options, have to be reduced for business reasons, that the burden of such reductions will be spread evenly.

---

[3] 740 F.2d 454, 5 EBC 1873 (6th Cir. 1984), *cert. denied,* 469 U.S. 1109 (1985). But see *Brock v. Hendershott*, 8 EBC 1121 (S.D. Ohio 1987) (union officials who arranged for dental plans to specify a dental service-provider in which they had an indirect financial interest when the dental plans were first "established" in collective bargaining were fiduciaries for plans because of resulting disposition of plan assets). An exception could also apply when a plan is first established in a skeletal trust form, with benefit provisions later being designed and adopted by the plan's trustees, as is the practice in the establishment of multiemployer plans.

The broad definition of a "fiduciary" under ERISA supports the view that plan amendments are fiduciary functions. A fiduciary under ERISA is colloquially described in the legislative history as "one who occupies a position of confidence or trust" under a plan.[4] Persons with authority to amend benefits for which employees have already rendered service are necessarily occupying a position of confidence or trust.

1. Collectively Bargained Amendments

The issue of whether plan amendments are fiduciary functions has been examined in two of the three major situations in which plan amendments occur. In *UMW Health & Retirement Funds v. Robinson*, the Supreme Court determined that a collectively bargained plan amendment is *not* subject to review for arbitrary and capricious action under Section 302(c)(5) of the Labor Management Relations Act. The *Robinson* decision weighed the interests protected by Section 302(c)(5) against the strong policy of the National Labor Relations Act in favor of collectively bargained resolutions of issues concerned with wages and other terms and conditions of employment, with the latter, NLRA policy prevailing.[5] Following *Robinson*, the primacy of national labor relations policy over the interests that would be served by review of collectively bargained plan amendments for compliance with fiduciary duties has been widely recognized under ERISA. In *Sutton v. Weirton Steel Division*, for example, the Fourth Circuit followed *Robinson* in rejecting a claim of breach of ERISA fiduciary duties in the adoption of a collectively bargained amendment restricting certain early retirement benefits. The amendment had been made in anticipation of a corporate sale that otherwise might have triggered benefit entitlement.[6]

2. Trustee-Designed Amendments

At the opposite end of the spectrum from the *Robinson* collective bargaining exception are plan amendments designed and adopted by

---

[4] S.Rep. 93-127, at 28, 1 ERISA Leg. Hist. 614, and 2 ERISA Leg. Hist. 3307 (Material in the Nature of a Committee Report, introduced by Rep. Perkins, chairman of the House Education and Labor Committee).

[5] 455 U.S. 562, 3 EBC 1129 (1982).

[6] 724 F.2d 406, 5 EBC 1033 (4th Cir. 1983), *cert. denied,* 467 U.S. 1205 (1984). See also *White v. Distributors Ass'n Warehousemen's Pension Trust,* 751 F.2d 1068 (9th Cir. 1985); *Flight Officers, Inc. v. United Air Lines, Inc.*, 756 F.2d 1274, 6 EBC 1086 (7th Cir. 1985); *Short v. UMW 1950 Pension Trust,* 728 F.2d 528, 5 EBC 1532 (D.C. Cir. 1984); *Music v. Western Conference of Teamsters Pension Trust,* 712 F.2d 413 (9th Cir. 1983); *Evans v. Bexley,* 750 F.2d 1498, 6 EBC 1418 (11th Cir. 1985). But see *Brock v. Hendershott,* 8 EBC 1121 (S.D. Ohio 1987) (union officials who arranged for dental plans to specify a dental service-provider in which they had an indirect financial interest when the dental plans were first "established" in collective bargaining were fiduciaries for plans because of resulting disposition of plan assets—despite *Robinson* exception).

plan trustees. This is the most common manner by which multiemployer plans are amended.[7] It is unquestionable that plan trustees are acting in a fiduciary capacity in making such amendments. In *Elser v. IAM National Pension Fund*, for example, the trustees of a multiemployer plan adopted a provision canceling past service credits previously granted employees if their employer later withdrew from the plan. The plan amendment was subject to review for breach of fiduciary duty under ERISA.[8]

When an amendment is made by plan trustees, but is later ratified by the union and employers in collective bargaining, review for breach of fiduciary duty under ERISA and Section 302(c)(5) still applies.[9] Similarly, if an amendment that is an "outgrowth of collective bargaining" is arbitrary and capricious when *combined with* a trustee-designed plan provision, review for breach of fiduciary duty and Section 302(c)(5) also applies.[10] However, in *Central Tool Co. v. IAM Nat'l Pension Fund*, the U.S. Court of Appeals for the District of Columbia Circuit upheld a cancellation of past service credits on an employer's withdrawal from a multiemployer plan without review for arbitrary and capricious action—even though the past service was cancelled under a plan provision that the plan's trustees had designed and adopted. Since the provision authorizing the cancellation was in the plan at the time the employer agreed to the collective bargaining agreement requiring it to contribute to the plan, the court held that the provision was collectively bargained, and thus, excepted from review for reasonableness under the Supreme Court's holding in *UMW Health & Retirement Funds v. Robinson.*[11]

---

[7] See GAO, "Effects of the 1980 Multiemployer Pension Plan Amendments Act on Plan Participants Benefits" (GAO/HRD-85-58), Appendix I (plan trustees establish benefit provisions in 95% of surveyed multiemployer plans).

[8] 684 F.2d 648, 3 EBC 2155 (9th Cir. 1982), *cert. denied,* 464 U.S. 813 (1983). Numerous other decisions recognize that when plan trustees amend a plan, the amendment is subject to review for breach of ERISA's standard of fiduciary duty, as well as for compliance with the "sole and exclusive benefit" standard established under LMRA §302(c)(5) (assuming the plan is administered jointly by labor- and management-appointed trustees). See *Chambless v. Masters, Mates & Pilots Pension Plan,* 772 F.2d 1032, 6 EBC 2209 (2d Cir. 1985); *cert. denied,* 475 U.S. 1012 (1986); *Sellers v. O'Connell,* 701 F.2d 575, 4 EBC 1312 (6th Cir. 1983); *Murn v. UMW 1950 Pension Trust,* 718 F.2d 359, 4 EBC 2388 (10th Cir. 1983); *Hurn v. Plumbing, Heating, & Piping Industry Trust,* 703 F.2d 386, 4 EBC 1811 (9th Cir. 1983); *Winpisinger v. Aurora Corp.,* 456 F.Supp. 559, 1 EBC 2201 (N.D. Ohio 1978). Compare *Short v. UMW 1950 Pension Trust, supra* (multiemployer plan amendment not subject to review for breach of duty when amendment made in collective bargaining, rather than by the plan's trustees).

[9] See *Chambless v. Masters, Mates & Pilots Pension Plan,* 571 F.Supp. 1430, at 1444 n.21 (S.D.N.Y. 1983), *aff'd,* 772 F.2d 1032, 6 EBC 2209 (2d Cir. 1985), *cert. denied,* 475 U.S. 1012 (1986) (rejecting inclusion under *Robinson* exception of amendment made by plan trustees and later "ratified" by employers and the union in collective bargaining). Accord *Hurn v. Plumbing, Heating & Piping Industry Trust,* 703 F.2d 386, 4 EBC 1811, at 1814 (9th Cir. 1983).

[10] *Chambless v. Masters, Mates, & Pilots Pension Plan, supra,* 6 EBC at 2216.

[11] 811 F.2d 651, 8 EBC 1268 (D.C. Cir. 1987). Compare *Chambless v. Masters, Mates & Pilots Pension Plan, supra.*

3. Amendments by an Employer to a Nonbargained Plan

The resolution of whether plan amendments are fiduciary decisions in the two situations presented by *Robinson* and *Elser* effectively reduces the issue to amendments to plans that are not collectively bargained (or that are no longer collectively bargained). In nonbargained plans, the reservation of amendment authority generally militates against review of amendments under a fiduciary or any other standard. The plan may provide: "The Board of Directors of the Employer shall have the right to amend the plan in any and all respects at any time or from time to time." The only express limit may be a proviso that none of ERISA's statutory protections for accrued benefits or vesting rules and schedules may be abridged. Subject to the specific ERISA protections, the employer thus offers benefits under the plan, and generally emphasizes those benefits in recruiting and attempting to retain employees, but under the plan's language, the employer ostensibly retains the power to revoke the benefits "at will."[12]

At-will amendment authority is not confined to nonbargained plans. Multiemployer plans are also likely to provide plan trustees with virtually identical amendment powers.[13] However, despite the language, multiemployer plan trustees' amendments are subject to review for breach of fiduciary duty. It is also clear that the NLRA and national labor policy considerations that support the collective bargaining exception established in *Robinson* do not support a parallel exception for amendments to nonbargained plans. An employer's at-will authority to amend a plan is not subject to the inherent restraints on arbitrary and capricious action that exist when plan amendments can only be made in "informed and intense" collective bargaining with the representative of the employee/participants in the plan.[14]

a. ERISA's fiduciary definition. If the common law of trusts prevailed, the issue of whether amendments to nonbargained plans are fiduciary decisions would be resolved by the "hat" an employer purported that it would wear in making amendments. Under trust law, the settlor (which for nonbargained plans is the employer) "has the power to modify [or revoke] the trust if and to the extent that by the terms of the trust he reserved such a power."[15] The settlor does not become a fiduciary by exercising such a power if the language and the circumstances show that the power is reserved solely for the settlor's benefit.[16] Thus, by reserving an unlimited power to amend a plan to itself as a

---

[12] See J. Calamari and J. Perillo, *Contracts* (West 2d ed. 1977), at 216 (with surprising frequency, employers reserve "at will" amendment authority under pension plans); and *Musto v. American General Corp.*, 615 F.Supp. 1483, 6 EBC 2071, at 2079 (M.D. Tenn. 1985) (unqualified amendment clause makes benefits ostensibly "mere gratuities terminable at the will of the employer").

[13] See, e.g., *Winpisinger v. Aurora Corp.*, 456 F.Supp. 559, 1 EBC 2201 (N.D. Ohio 1978).

[14] See *UMW Health & Retirement Funds v. Robinson, supra,* 3 EBC at 1132.

[15] *Restatement (Second) of Trusts,* §§330 and 331 (1959).

[16] See *II Scott on Trusts,* §185 (3d ed. 1967).

settlor, without accompanying circumstances or representations indicating that the power will be exercised subject to a fiduciary standard of duty, an employer could insulate plan amendments from fiduciary review.

The issue under ERISA is not what would happen under the common law of trusts, but a statutory issue of whether the power to amend a plan is among the functions described in ERISA Section 3(21)(A).[17] The functions described there are fiduciary functions regardless of exculpatory drafting, formal title, or the hat a person or entity purports to wear in exercising discretionary authority or control over an employee benefit plan.[18] The scope of the functions described in ERISA Section 3(21)(A) is, moreover, "broad."[19] Congress intended that the definition of fiduciary encompass anyone "who occupies a position of trust or confidence" with respect to a plan.[20] Congress recognized that this would alter the allowance under the common law of trusts for a settlor to exculpate certain functions by trust drafting.[21] However, recognizing the "special nature" of employee benefit plans and that "the typical employee benefit plan . . . is quite different from the testamentary trust both in purpose and nature,"[22] Congress intended to ensure that positions of trust or confidence under a plan would be subject to a fiduciary standard of duty under ERISA, without the possibility of insulating or immunizing important responsibilities according to the formal title of the person or entity designated by a settlor to carry out the function under the trust or plan document.[23]

In addition to this congressional intent, case law under predecessor legislation to ERISA included the power to amend a plan within the scope of "administration" and "management." In *Hales v. Winn-Dixie Stores, Inc.*, a corporate employer was considered the "administrator" of a plan under the Welfare and Pension Plans Disclosure Act because its power to appoint and remove trustees and "to amend,

---

[17] See ch. 7, sec. II.A.

[18] Conf. Rep., at 302, 3 ERISA Leg. Hist. 4569.

[19] *Chicago Board of Options v. Conn. Gen. Life Ins. Co.*, 713 F.2d 254, 4 EBC 1927, at 1932 (7th Cir. 1983); *Donovan v. Mercer*, 747 F.2d 304, 5 EBC 2512, at 2514 (5th Cir. 1984).

[20] S. Rep. 93-127, at 28, 1 ERISA Leg. Hist. 614, and Material in the Nature of a Committee Report, 2 ERISA Leg. Hist. 3307.

[21] S. Rep. 93-127, at 29, 1 ERISA Leg. Hist. 615, and Material in the Nature of a Committee Report, 2 ERISA Leg. Hist. 3308.

[22] Conf. Rep., at 302, 3 ERISA Leg. Hist. 4569. And see S. Rep. 93-127, at 29, 1 ERISA Leg. Hist. 615, Material in the Nature of a Committee Report, 2 ERISA Leg Hist. 3308, *Donovan v. Mazzola*, 716 F.2d 1226, 4 EBC 1865 (9th Cir. 1983), *cert. denied*, 464 U.S. 1040 (1984); *Eaves v. Penn*, 587 F.2d 453, 1 EBC 1592 (10th Cir. 1978); *Marshall v. Teamsters Local 282 Pension Trust*, 458 F.Supp. 986, 1 EBC 1501 (E.D.N.Y. 1978).

[23] *Eaton v. D'Amato*, 581 F.Supp. 743, 3 EBC 1003, at 1006 (D.D.C. 1980). And see *Eaves v. Penn*, *supra*, and *Chicago Board of Options, v. Conn. Gen. Life Ins. Co., supra*. In *Thornton v. Evans*, 692 F.2d 1064, 3 EBC 2241 (7th Cir. 1982), the Seventh Circuit further recognized that "application of traditional trust law principles may, in some instances conflict with Congress' desire to eliminate barriers to the protections and enforcement of rights in ERISA-covered benefit plans." 3 EBC at 2255. Similarly, in *Free v. Briody*, 732 F.2d 1331, 5 EBC 1442 (7th Cir. 1984), the Seventh Circuit stated that "Congress intended to codify the principles of trust law with whatever alterations were needed to fit the needs of employee benefit plans." 5 EBC at 1448.

modify, or terminate the Program and trust instruments" gave it "ultimate control over how the Program monies will be managed and disposed of."[24] In determining the scope of plan "administration" under LMRA Section 302(c)(5)(B), a "distinction has been drawn between ordinary and extraordinary matters." But courts have held that amendments to a plan's benefit terms are not extraordinary, and thus, are within the scope of administration.[25] In contrast, an amendment to a trust agreement to require an employer to make contributions after the expiration of its collective bargaining obligation may be extraordinary.[26]

Reflecting this broad usage of plan administration in the debates over ERISA, Representative Carl Perkins, the chairman of the House Education and Labor Committee, twice discussed denials of benefits from the United Mine Workers welfare and retirement plans "on account of rigid, arbitrary and unreasonable eligibility standards."[27] Representative Perkins stated that recent class action suits striking down such standards as arbitrary and capricious "confirm what many of us had believed for quite some time. That is, the eligibility standards of [the United Mine Workers welfare and retirement funds were] being *administered* in an arbitrary and capricious fashion."[28]

The routine inclusion of amendments by plan trustees to jointly administered multiemployer plans as fiduciary functions under ERISA provides another point of reference on the scope of ERISA's fiduciary functions. The significance of these decisions may be obscured because in most instances the courts immediately recognize such amendments as fiduciary decisions without referring to a specific ERISA Section 3(21)(A) function.[29] But the Sixth Circuit has suggested that such amendments are fiduciary functions because they represent an exercise

---

[24] 500 F.2d 836, at 843 (4th Cir. 1974). See also *Anderson v. Seaton*, 143 N.E.2d 59 (Ill.App. 1957) (under state common law, benefits committee with power to amend plan subject to corporate board approval was charged with "administration" of plan).

[25] See *Geigle v. Flacke*, 768 F.2d 259, 6 EBC 1929 (8th Cir. 1985), *reh. denied*, 6 EBC 1933 (8th Cir. 1985).

[26] See *Ader v. Hughes*, 570 F.2d 303 (10th Cir. 1978); *Farmer v. Fisher*, 586 F.2d 1226 (8th Cir. 1978).

[27] 2 ERISA Leg. Hist. 3368 and 3 ERISA Leg. Hist. 4658.

[28] 3 ERISA Leg. Hist. 4658 (emphasis added). Rep. Perkins further stated:

"I am hopeful that this legislation will take a giant step forward, not only in making welfare and pension benefits to miners *administered* in a fair and equitable manner and with assurances of security, but also the thousands of other workers in other fields of labor who have had similar experiences."

Id. (emphasis added).

[29] See, e.g., *Chambless v. Masters, Mates & Pilots Pension Plan*, 772 F.2d 1032, 6 EBC 2209 (2d Cir. 1985), *cert. denied*, 475 U.S. 1012 (1986); *Geib v. New York State Teamsters Conference Pension Fund*, 758 F.2d 973, 6 EBC 1475 (3d Cir. 1985); *Struble v. New Jersey Brewery Employees' Welfare Fund*, 732 F.2d 325, 5 EBC 1676 (3d Cir. 1984); *Winpisinger v. Aurora Corp.*, 456 F.Supp. 559, 1 EBC 2201 (N.D. Ohio 1978); *Goins v. Teamsters Local 639*, 599 F.Supp. 141 (D.D.C. 1984); *In re Des Moines Iron Workers Pension Trust*, 4 EBC 2364 (Heinsz, 1983) (deadlock between union and management trustees over benefit increase resolved by reference to trustees' fiduciary duty to participants to increase benefits when money is available).

of control respecting the "management" of the plan and the "disposition of [its] assets."[30] Once plan amendments are recognized as within ERISA's fiduciary functions when made to a jointly administered plan, it is difficult to see how they can be outside the same functions when the amendment is to a unilaterally administered plan.

Commentators have also taken the position that nonbargained plan amendments are potentially fiduciary functions under ERISA. In *Employee Benefits Law*, Jeffrey Mamorsky writes:

> "Members of the company's board of directors are fiduciaries to the extent that they perform fiduciary functions such as the selection and retention of other plan fiduciaries. *The power to amend or terminate a plan* may also be sufficient to give the board of directors fiduciary status, since almost any plan amendment and any decision to terminate a plan could be regarded as an exercise of discretionary control regarding *management* of the plan."[31]

The same position has been taken less equivocally based on the ERISA Section 402(b)(3) requirement that a plan must name the persons who can amend it and specify a procedure for plan amendments. This requirement makes the identified persons "named fiduciaries" within the meaning of ERISA Section 402(a)(2), and thus fiduciaries under ERISA Section 3(21)(A).[32]

Corporate representations about internal divisions of responsibilities may also support a broad understanding of "administering" a plan. For example, IBM's Notice of 1986 Annual Meeting and Proxy Statement states:

> "The Retirement Plans Committee [which is a standing committee composed of members of IBM's Board of Directors] has the responsibility of administering the IBM Retirement Plans, including selection of investment managers, determination of investment guidelines within which they operate, reviewing their performance, and amending the plans."

b. Decisions under ERISA on the applicability of the fiduciary standard to nonbargained plan amendments. The courts are divided on whether an amendment to a nonbargained plan is a fiduciary function (except that the decision to terminate a plan entirely has uniformly been held not to be a fiduciary function). In *Chicago Board of Options v. Connecticut Gen. Life Ins. Co.*, the Seventh Circuit held that an

---

[30] *UAW v. Greyhound Lines, Inc.*, 701 F.2d 1181, 4 EBC 1105, at 1109 (6th Cir. 1983) (but arbitrator was still not fiduciary because of arbitral immunity doctrine).

[31] At 12-7 (Law Journal Seminars-Press 1983 ed.) (emphasis added). See also R. Gilbert, "Fiduciaries Under ERISA," 43 Inst. on Fed. Tax'n (1985), at 33-11 (corporate directors "may be fiduciaries by virtue of their authority to amend the terms of a plan").

[32] See J. Lee, 308 Tax Mgmt. (BNA), "(ERISA)—Fiduciary Responsibilities and Prohibited Transactions," at A-11, B-4, B-5, and B-16, and Conf. Rep., at 297, 3 ERISA Leg. Hist. 4564, and 2 ERISA Leg. Hist. 3309. "Named fiduciaries" are fiduciaries who have specific, identified duties under a plan. Outside of identification, the primary significance of classifying someone as a "named fiduciary," rather than as any other fiduciary, is that they ordinarily will not be liable for breaches of fiduciary duty outside their specific area of responsibility. See 29 C.F.R. 2509.75-8, Q&A D-4. A corporate board's power to select and retain a plan's fiduciaries, which Jeffrey Mamorsky mentions, makes the corporation a named fiduciary, but it does not create liability outside of this specific area of responsibility.

insurance company was a fiduciary under ERISA because it had discretionary authority over plan management and disposition of plan assets by virtue of its unilateral authority to amend the terms of an annuity contract issued to an employer. An amendment to the annuity contract by the insurer to limit the amount a plan participant could withdraw from the insurer's guaranteed investment account was therefore subject to review for breach of fiduciary duty.[33] In *Hickerson v. Velsicol Chemical Corp.*, the Seventh Circuit likewise held that an employer had a fiduciary duty in amending a profit-sharing plan to convert the plan to a defined benefit plan to avoid the suggestion of "self-interested plan administration" and therefore had a duty to preserve a market rate of interest earnings on the participants' existing profit-sharing account balances until the account balances were distributed.[34]

In *Dependahl v. Falstaff Brewing Corp.*, an employer amended a severance pay plan immediately before a large layoff of employees to institute a new 15 years of service requirement for severance benefits. The amendment was held to be in breach of fiduciary duty. The district court said that the holding did not mean that "an employer may never cut back on benefits previously provided to an employee," but it was a breach of fiduciary duty when an amendment divested employees of benefits to which they would "otherwise" shortly have become entitled.[35] In *Helmetag v. Consolidated Rail Corp.*, the railroad assets of a company in Chapter 11 reorganization were sold to Conrail, with the company's pension plan being transferred to and then merged with Conrail's plan. A plan amendment by Conrail under which plan participants who continued working for the bankrupt company (which had some residual operations) would have their benefit accruals frozen but, at the same time, could not retire and begin drawing their benefits while continuing to work for the company was held to be in breach of fiduciary duty because it penalized their continued employment with

---

[33] 713 F.2d 254, 4 EBC 1927 (7th Cir. 1983). See also *Leigh v. Engle*, 727 F.2d 113, 4 EBC 2702, at 2722 (7th Cir. 1984) (reaffirming this as the holding in *Chicago Board of Options*); *Ed Miniat, Inc. v. Globe Life Ins. Group, Inc.*, 805 F.2d 732, 7 EBC 2414 (7th Cir. 1986).

[34] 778 F.2d 365, 6 EBC 2545, at 2556 (7th Cir. 1985), *cert. denied*, 479 U.S. ___ (1986). Similarly, in *Eaves v. Penn*, 587 F.2d 453, 1 EBC 1592 (10th Cir. 1978), a plan amendment converted a profit-sharing plan, which had limited investments in employer stock, into an ESOP, which would invest only in employer stock. The Tenth Circuit held the amendment was in breach of fiduciary duty because it diverted existing plan assets from the payment of benefits. The Tenth Circuit emphasized that it was not holding that a plan could never be amended to change it into an ESOP, but it was holding that this amendment amounted to an investment of plan assets that jeopardized the security of the participants' benefits. The court expressly rejected the defendant's argument that he could not be a fiduciary because he was wearing his corporate hat as an officer and director of the sponsoring company when he was "recommending, designing, and implementing the plan amendment." 1 EBC at 1596. See also *Werschkull v. United California Bank*, 149 Cal.Rptr. 829 (Cal.App. 1978) (plan amendment transferring excess plan assets from one plan for credit against employer's contributions to another plan disposed of plan assets in violation of fiduciary duty); *Delgrosso v. Spang & Co.*, 769 F.2d 928, 6 EBC 1940 (3d Cir. 1985), *cert. denied*, 476 U.S. ___ (1986) (employer's amendment to collectively bargained plan to insert provision for reversion of excess plan assets was in breach of fiduciary duty when employer lacked authority under collective bargaining agreement to make such amendments).

[35] 491 F.Supp. 1188, at 1197 (E.D. Mo. 1980), *aff'd in part, rev'd in part*, 653 F.2d 1208, 2 EBC 1521 (8th Cir. 1981), *cert. denied*, 454 U.S. 1084 (1981).

the bankrupt employer without providing them with any additional benefits.[36]

Other cases have found that an amendment to a plan states a claim for breach of fiduciary duty under ERISA, but either have not reached the issue of whether a breach of duty occurred, or have reached it and found no breach.[37] The power to amend a plan has also often been considered as a major criterion in determining whether a person or entity is an ERISA fiduciary in cases where a plan amendment is itself not the issue.[38]

An opposing view has also emerged. In *Sutton v. Weirton Steel Division*, the Fourth Circuit consolidated district court decisions that involved identical amendments to a collectively bargained plan and a nonbargained plan. Focusing primarily on the collectively bargained amendment, the court summarily held that the unilateral amendment by the employer to benefits under the nonbargained, salaried employees' plan was not to be reviewed for breach of fiduciary duty. The court followed the exception established in *Robinson* for plan amendments that result from "informed and intense" bargaining with the representative of the employees, but did not delve into how this exception had become applicable to a unilateral plan amendment.[39]

In *Amato v. Western Union International, Inc.*, a district court held that a plan amendment eliminating an unreduced early retirement benefit from a nonbargained plan was not a fiduciary decision. The district court followed *Sutton*, but again did not discuss the jump from an exception for collectively bargained amendments to one for unilateral amendments. The court, however, indicated in quoting from the *Sutton* decision that it considered the amendment "reasonable business behavior," as distinct from what it considered to be within the scope of plan administration or management or disposition of plan assets.[40] On appeal, the Second Circuit affirmed, holding that in

---

[36] 5 EBC 1617 (E.D. Pa. 1984).

[37] See *Jiminez v. Pioneer Diecasters, Inc., Pension Plan*, 549 F.Supp. 677, 3 EBC 2192 (C.D. Cal. 1982) (plan amendment deleting lump sum option established potential claim for breach of fiduciary duty, but no decision on the merits); *Cator v. Herrgott & Wilson, Inc.*, 609 F.Supp. 12, 6 EBC 1921 (N.D. Cal. 1985) (finding fiduciary duties in plan amendment adding interim valuation date for profit-sharing plan account balances, but holding that no breach of fiduciary duty occurred under the facts). See also *Bigger v. American Commercial Lines, Inc.*, 652 F.Supp. 123, 8 EBC 1424 (W.D. Mo. 1986) (participants in spin-off plan had standing to challenge spin-off as in breach of fiduciary duty when entire excess retained in other plan: "[t]he court does not see how any important decision regarding a plan's assets, especially if made in the interest of someone other than the participants as alleged here, could be exempted from [§404's] comprehensive standard").

[38] See *U.S. Steel Corp. v. Pennsylvania Human Relations Comm.*, 669 F.2d 124, 2 EBC 2393 (3d Cir. 1982) (employer with power to amend terms of employee health plan is a fiduciary); *Monson v. Century Mfg. Co.*, 739 F.2d 1293, 5 EBC 1625 (8th Cir. 1984) (person's role in crafting plan amendments is an indicia of fiduciary status); *Bradshaw v. Jenkins*, 5 EBC 2755 (W.D. Wash. 1984) (employer's fiduciary status established "by virtue of its authority ... to appoint [and] to remove the trustees [and] to amend the terms of the Plan"). Accord *Robbins v. First American Bank*, 514 F.Supp. 1183, 2 EBC 1576 (N.D. Ill. 1981).

See also the cases and authorities cited in ch. 12, secs. I.C. and IX.

[39] 724 F.2d 406, 5 EBC 1033 (4th Cir. 1983), *cert. denied*, 467 U.S. 1205 (1984).

[40] 596 F.Supp. 621, 5 EBC 2718, at 2722 (S.D.N.Y. 1984).

amending the nonbargained plan, the company "officers acted on behalf of a corporate employer and not as Plan fiduciaries." The Second Circuit, however, cautioned that plan fiduciaries who make plan amendments on behalf of a corporate employer must be cognizant of whether in exercising their fiduciary authority they are cooperating in making or implementing an amendment in a manner that breaches their duties to plan participants. For example:

> "To the extent that defendants, wearing their hats as Plan fiduciaries, cooperated in creating ... a surplus and diverting it from being held solely for the benefit of plaintiffs [and their class of participants], or misled plaintiffs with respect to their rights under the Plan, a valid claim for breach of fiduciary duty is stated."[41]

The Second Circuit's broad reading of the ERISA Section 403(c)(1) prohibition on any "inurement" of a plan's assets to the benefit of an employer, announced in the same opinion and discussed in section VIII.A below, also provides a fiduciary restraint on plan amendments—whether or not the Second Circuit calls the act of amending a plan a fiduciary function.

Other courts have held that plan amendments are not fiduciary functions. In *Shaw v. IAM Pension Plan*, a plan amendment phasing out an automatic cost-of-living adjustment under a pension plan for union staff employees was held not to state a claim for breach of fiduciary duty when the amendment was adopted by a union convention (with the union in this instance acting as the sponsoring employer), and the plan's trustees lacked discretionary authority to alter the amendment in any way.[42]

In contrast to the division among the courts on plan amendments, the decision to *terminate* a plan entirely has uniformly been held not to

---

[41] 773 F.2d 1402, 6 EBC 2226, at 2240 and 2241 (2d Cir. 1985). See also *Monson v. Century Mfg. Co.*, 739 F.2d 1293, 5 EBC 1625 (8th Cir. 1984) (fiduciaries who knew of and kept silent about employer's misrepresentations on amount of profits being contributed to plan breached fiduciary duties).

[42] 563 F.Supp. 653, 4 EBC 1737 (C.D. Cal. 1983), *aff'd,* 750 F.2d 1458, 6 EBC 1193 (9th Cir. 1985). The amendment in *Shaw* was nevertheless prohibited as a decrease in accrued benefits. See ch. 4, sec. IV.B.1. See also *Phillips v. Amoco Oil Co.*, 614 F.Supp. 694 (N.D. Ala. 1985), *aff'd,* 799 F.2d 1464, 7 EBC 2246 (11th Cir. 1986) (no fiduciary duty for company selling a division to secure for the division employees by plan amendment or otherwise comparable early retirement and other contingent benefits under purchaser's retirement plans); *Coleman v. Gen. Elec. Co.*, 643 F.Supp. 1229 (E.D. Tenn. 1986) (no fiduciary duties in negotiating terms for sale of business); *United Steelworkers 2116 v. Cyclops Corp.*, 653 F.Supp. 574, 8 EBC 1194 (S.D. Ohio 1987) (no fiduciary violation in business sale and transfer of share of plan assets and liabilities allocable to transferred employees to buyer's plan on basis that did "not destroy[] any vested or accrued benefits"); *Dougherty v. Chrysler Motors Corp.*, 8 EBC 1217 (E.D. Mich. 1987) (no fiduciary breach by seller of business in not ensuring that buyer would increase benefits beyond levels existing at time of sale); *Cattin v. Gen. Motors Corp.*, 641 F.Supp. 591, 7 EBC 2151 (E.D. Mich. 1986) (no fiduciary breach when years of service with subsidiary not counted for early retirement benefit vesting after employees were transferred to wholly-owned subsidiary).

In *Moore v. Reynolds Metals Co. Retirement Programs*, 740 F.2d 454, 5 EBC 1873 (6th Cir. 1984), *cert. denied,* 469 U.S. 1109 (1985), the Sixth Circuit made the same jump as in *Amato* from the *Robinson* and *Sutton* collective bargaining exception to an exception for a nonbargained plan provision. But in *Moore*, no "amendment" to the plan appears to have been made. Rather the plaintiff challenged an original plan provision as a breach of fiduciary duty. The original terms of a plan are not subject to the same expectational interests as when participants have rendered service under a provision that is later amended. Nor can the design of the original terms of a plan generally be seen as "administration" or "management" of the plan. See sec. II.A above.

involve fiduciary duties—at least if the plan's assets are sufficient to pay all benefit liabilities under the plan.[43] Plan amendments shortly before a termination to install a provision under which an employer will take back "excess" plan assets after all benefit liabilities have been satisfied have, with some notable exceptions, also generally been held not to involve fiduciary duties.[44]

B. Standard of Review for Breach of Fiduciary Duty

1. Arbitrary and Capricious Standard

When a plan amendment is reviewed to see if its adoption constitutes a breach of fiduciary duty, the standard of review is generally the arbitrary and capricious standard. But recitation of the words "arbitrary and capricious" does not elucidate the types of amendments most likely to be found in breach of fiduciary duty. The application of the arbitrary and capricious standard to plan amendments is most developed in decisions arising under the longstanding requirement of Section 302(c)(5) of the LMRA that plans be structured for the "sole and exclusive benefit" of employees and their families.[45] After ERISA, these Section 302(c)(5) cases, commonly referred to as Taft-Hartley decisions, remain directly applicable to jointly administered plans, and also have been expressly adopted by the Ninth Circuit as direct precedent for breach of fiduciary duty claims under ERISA Section 404(a)(1).[46] Regardless of the circuit, the principles of the Taft-Hartley decisions are certain to be examined in any claim for breach of fiduciary duty from a plan amendment since the "rational nexus" test, which these cases develop, has been adopted under ERISA as the general standard for review of the exercise of any discretionary authority over benefits under a plan.[47]

The overriding requirement of the Taft-Hartley decisions is a rational nexus between the plan amendment and the pension plan's

---

[43] See cases cited in ch. 12, sec. I.C. However, decisions implementing the termination, such as the choice of an interest rate for any lump sum payments to close out the plan, are fiduciary functions. *Id.*

[44] See ch. 12, sec. IX.C.3. Plan amendments *after* a plan termination have not been subject to fiduciary review, but they have been held invalid as a matter of trust and/or contract law and also because it would defeat Congress' intent under ERISA §403(c)(1) and §4044(d) "if retroactive amendments after termination could alter substantive rights of the pension plan." *Audio Fidelity Corp. v. PBGC*, 624 F.2d 513, 2 EBC 1856, at 1859 (4th Cir. 1980). And see *Plumbers & Steamfitters Local 530 Annuity Fund v. Shaffer*, 457 F.Supp. 954 (W.D. Pa. 1978) (pre-ERISA trust law prevents post-termination amendments).

[45] In Taft-Hartley plans, review for arbitrary and capricious action extends to the plan's original provisions as well as to plan amendments (so long as the plan provision, or amendment, is not collectively bargained). A Taft-Hartley *plan* must be "for the sole and exclusive benefit" of participants, whereas the ERISA sole and exclusive benefit standard applies only to actions by plan fiduciaries.

[46] See cases at ch. 8, sec. VIII (on reform of plan provisions under §302(c)(5) of the Labor Management Relations Act).

[47] See ch. 7, sec. III (on the adoption of the arbitrary and capricious standard under ERISA), and ch. 7, sec. III.C (on review of exercises of discretionary authority).

central purpose of providing retirement benefits to as many covered employees as is economically possible:

> "The trustees, although possessing the power to amend the provisions of a pension plan, must do so in a way calculated to achieve legitimate ends; the standard is, at its core, a requirement that the trustees have a rational basis for taking any action which affects the rights of pension plan participants under an existing plan.
>
> "[This] necessitates a reasoned exercise of discretion."[48]

In determining whether an exercise of discretion is reasoned, the rational nexus test focuses on:

(1) The factual information before the trustees concerning the plan's financial status and the likely financial effects of an amendment;

(2) The trustees' consideration of alternatives that could achieve the same legitimate ends;

(3) How the amendment affects participants with substantial service toward a benefit;

(4) How the amendment affects different participant groups, e.g., whether it denies pensions to certain participants, while continuing to grant pensions to others who "worked a substantially lesser period of time," or otherwise creates any other undue preference between different participant groups; and

(5) How the amendment affects participants who are, or in the future will be, involuntarily separated from service, e.g., by involuntary layoff or disability.[49]

In reviewing for a rational nexus, courts have thus not required employers sponsoring single-employer plans or multiemployer plan trustees to refrain from amendments that reduce plan costs to within limited means—unless the participants' rights are vested or otherwise statutorily, contractually, or equitably protected. For example, in *Moore v. Reynolds Metals Co. Retirement Program*, the Sixth Circuit stated, "Clearly, a company such as Reynolds Aluminum is entitled to determine without judicial interference the *amount* of money it desires or can afford to appropriate for ... benefits."[50] But protecting the business part of a decision to amend a plan, namely, the *amount* of money to be appropriated, has not extended to enabling an employer or

---

[48] Comment, "The Arbitrary and Capricious Standard Under ERISA," 23 Duq. L. Rev. 1033, at 1054 (Summer 1985).

[49] Whether participants have vested rights sufficient to withstand the application of a restrictive plan amendment and whether the application of an amendment is arbitrary and capricious because of lack of advance notice to participants before the effective date of the amendment are discussed separately in secs. IV and V below.

[50] 740 F.2d 454, 5 EBC 1873, at 1874 n.3 (6th Cir. 1984), *cert. denied*, 469 U.S. 1109 (1985) (emphasis added). Decisions on amendments to multiemployer plans under §302(c)(5) of the Labor Mangement Relations Act and under ERISA also reflect this view as a multiemployer plan's means are inherently limited to the plan's assets and the contribution rate established in collective bargaining. But within these limited means, plan trustees must establish benefit terms and make plan amendments subject to a fiduciary standard of duty.

multiemployer plan trustees to impose undue burdens on one group of participants in the implementation of a cost reduction, or to justify decisions on the basis of costs when, in fact, the costs of a provision are unknown and uninvestigated at the time.

Applying nearly all of these standards, the Second Circuit in *Chambless v. Masters, Mates & Pilots Pension Plan* reviewed an amendment adopted by a multiemployer plan board of trustees that completely forfeited early retirement benefits of retired plan participants who went back to work for any period of time with maritime industry employers who did not contribute to the plan. The forfeiture of early retirement benefits effected by the amendment could have the further effect of reducing the participants' benefits in absolute dollar amount on reaching the plan's normal retirement age. This was because compensation for purposes of the plan's benefit formula was defined as the highest five years in the 10 years *before* retirement, rather than in the 10 years before retirement *or* an earlier separation from service.

On review, the Second Circuit found the trustees had failed to substantiate a claim of financial necessity for the amendment. Financial necessity was "unsupported by any actuarial data"—an actuarial valuation the plan pointed to for support "was not even transmitted to the Plan until . . . approximately six months *after* the Trustees' action that was assertedly 'based in part' upon it," and a letter to plan participants sent a month before the amendment had stated the plan was "financially sound." The trustees, moreover, did not "even assert that alternative solutions were considered," and the record was "devoid of evidence showing [how] the Amendment benefited the Plan or its participants."[51] In holding the amendment arbitrary and capricious, the Second Circuit further emphasized the particularly onerous interaction between the amendment and the definition of average compensation used in determining benefits, the lack of adequate advance notice to participants of this interaction, and a general policy against exacting forfeitures based on an employee attempting to improve his economic position, whether by accepting work with a contributing or a noncontributing employer.[52]

Chambless' emphasis (1) on the evidence before the trustees *at the time* of the amendment concerning financial necessity and the likely financial benefits for the plan from the amendment, and (2) on the

[51] 772 F.2d 1032, 6 EBC 2209, at 2214-15 (2d Cir. 1985), *cert. denied,* 475 U.S. 1012 (1986).

[52] 6 EBC 2215-17. The Second Circuit distinguished *Morse v. Stanley,* 732 F.2d 1139, 5 EBC 1602 (2d Cir. 1984), which had permitted a plan to deny lump sum distributions of benefits to participants leaving to work for competitors, as a case that did not involve a "forfeiture" since an actuarially equivalent amount remained available to the participants at a later date. The Second Circuit still apparently overlooked ERISA minimum standard violations in a compensation definition that (1) caused accrued benefits to decrease after a separation from service, and (2) caused accrued benefits to decrease below the dollar amount available at early retirement. See ERISA §§204(b)(1)(A)-(C), and 26 C.F.R. 1.411(a)-7(b)(6) (example (4)).

trustees' consideration of alternatives, is found in numerous other decisions. In *Elser v. IAM National Pension Fund,* a cancellation of employees' past service credits on their employer's withdrawal from a multiemployer plan under an amendment adopted two years before the withdrawal was arbitrary and capricious, even though concerns with preserving the financial integrity of the fund were legitimate in the abstract, because the trustees never calculated the unfunded liability resulting from the employer's withdrawal, and thus had no evidence on the extent the employer's withdrawal actually threatened the financial soundness of the fund.[53] In *Blankenship v. Boyle,* a decision to *increase* plan benefits was similarly taken without thorough consideration of the implications of the action:

> "No detailed projections of the Fund's long-term ability to pay were made, nor were possible alternative changes in benefit payments considered [such as broadening eligibility]. The trustees took no contemporaneous steps partially to offset the additional payout by eliminating unnecessary administrative expenses or by investing cash in income-producing securities. In short, the increase was handled as an arrangement between labor and management with little recognition of its fiscal and fiduciary aspects."[54]

Consideration of alternatives is further emphasized in *Struble v. New Jersey Brewery Employees' Welfare Fund.* In *Struble,* management-appointed trustees voted to give a surplus of plan assets back to employers, rather than to use it to continue to fund the health benefits of retired employees. The Third Circuit stated that in examining

> "whether the [trustees] acted with the requisite prudence and with complete and undivided loyalty to the beneficiaries in voting to credit the Employers with the Blue Cross surplus . . . [w]e must consider, for example, whether the [trustees] voted as they did on the instructions of the Employers; whether they took time to investigate the merits of alternative courses of conduct; and whether they consulted with others, for example their attorneys [before acting]. We do not intend this list of considerations to be exhaustive."[55]

Substantial credit toward a benefit can also create a "protectible interest" that heightens the need for thorough consideration of a plan's

---

[53] 684 F.2d 648, 3 EBC 2155 (9th Cir. 1982), *cert. denied,* 464 U.S. 813 (1983).

[54] 329 F.Supp. 1089, 1 EBC 1062, at 1078 (D.D.C. 1971). See also *Rettig v. PBGC,* 744 F.2d 133, 5 EBC 2025 (D.C. Cir. 1984) (government agency failed to show that regulation restricting pension benefit insurance was product of "actually weighing" costs against considerations in favor of insuring benefits). Other decisions state that actuarial evidence is necessary when a rule is alleged to be compelled by financial necessity, as opposed to a choice between policies or a decision based on behaviorial predictions. *Harm v. Bay Area Pipe Trades Pension Plan,* 701 F.2d 1301, 4 EBC 1253, at 1257, n. 7 (9th Cir. 1983); *Eddington v. CMTA-Indep. Tool & Die Craftsmen Pension Trust,* 794 F.2d 1383 (9th Cir. 1986).

Still other decisions recognize that almost every restrictive revision or interpretation of a plan's rules has the virtue of saving a plan some money. But if saving a plan some money was sufficient justification for any rule restriction, judicial review for arbitrary and capricious action would quickly become meaningless. See *Elser v. IAM Nat'l Pension Fund, supra; Donovan v. Carlough,* 576 F.Supp. 245, 5 EBC 1400, at 1405 (D.D.C. 1983); *Rhoton v. Central States Pension Fund,* 717 F.2d 988, 4 EBC 2233, at 2236 (6th Cir. 1983); and cases cited in ch. 8, sec. VIII (on reform of structural defects under Taft-Hartley plans).

[55] 732 F.2d 325, 5 EBC 1676, at 1684 (3d Cir. 1984) (citations omitted).

financial constraints, the financial benefits of the amendment, and alternative amendments that will achieve the same cost reduction objective. In *Goins v. Teamsters Local 639*, a multiemployer plan provided disability benefits if a participant had five years of credited service and became disabled. The plaintiff had five years of service, and was thus protected against future disability. But in 1978 the plan was amended to require 10 years of service to qualify for the disability protection. The *Goins* court did not find that the plaintiff had a "vested" right in the disability protection, but it found that the participant had acquired a "protectible interest" once he had five years of service that had to be outweighed by other considerations. The court stated that the "extent to which a pension plan participant has satisfied the benefit criteria bears on the degree of deference which should be paid to a decision to revise those criteria." Against this protectible interest, the trustees had not offered a sufficient explanation for the change: They had been generally apprehensive about the costs of disability benefits, but they had not studied the issue, and did not give special attention to the interests of participants who had disability coverage before the amendment.[56]

Plan amendments are upheld as not in breach of fiduciary duty when financial need, the financial effects of an amendment, and alternatives are considered before the fact, and the amendment is not otherwise arbitrary. In *Adams v. New Jersey Brewery Employees' Pension Fund Trustees*, a plan amendment cancelling past service credits on an employer's withdrawal from a multiemployer plan was not arbitrary when the financial imbalance to the plan (the liabilities from the grant of past service credits to the employer's employees less the value of the employer's contributions) was documented and the amendment was not otherwise arbitrary.[57] In *Geib v. New York State Teamsters Conf. Pension Fund*, a plan amendment suspending benefits if an early retiree accepted employment in the same industry and geographic area covered by the plan was not arbitrary and capricious when it was adopted in response to the plan's financial constraints and was a rational means to conserve plan assets to provide the pensions still offered by the plan.[58] In *Mosley v. NMU Pension & Welfare Plan*, plan trustees were faced with a sharp decline in the maritime industry, and thus in the plan's contribution base, and a steep increase in the excess of plan liabilities over plan assets (to a level of $550 million in liabilities compared to $106 million in assets). In this context, the trustees did not act arbitrarily in eliminating an age 60 and 15 years service early retirement benefit for participants who did not have both the age and

---

[56] 599 F.Supp. 141, at 145 (D.D.C. 1984). See also *Dependahl v. Falstaff Brewing Corp.*, 491 F.Supp. 1188 (E.D. Mo. 1980), *aff'd in part, rev'd in part,* 653 F.2d 1208, 2 EBC 1521 (8th Cir. 1981), *cert. denied,* 454 U.S. 1084 (1981) (breach of fiduciary duty to cut benefits to which employees would shortly have become entitled for the employer's benefit alone), and sec. IV.B below (on inexorably vested rights).

[57] 670 F.2d 387, 3 EBC 1083 (3d Cir. 1982). See also ch. 4, sec. III.C.6.

[58] 758 F.2d 973, 6 EBC 1475 (3d Cir. 1985).

service within an eight-month grace period after adoption of the amendment. The trustees also did not act arbitrarily in amending the plan to require more days of maritime work for each year of service for vesting, even though the effect of this change was more severe on "casual" seamen than full timers.[59] In *Cator v. Herrgott & Wilson, Inc.*, the addition of a new interim date for valuing a profit-sharing plan's assets was not arbitrary and capricious when the value of the plan's assets had declined sharply since the last valuation date, so that a retiring company president would otherwise have received $72,000 more than under the interim valuation, with the remaining participants having commensurately less in their account balances as a result.[60]

Despite documented financial need, irrational or discriminatory preferences and exceptions under an amendment designed to reduce plan costs can make the amendment arbitrary and capricious. In a collectively bargained plan, such preferences are most likely to be against individuals in the bargaining unit who are not union members, or who are in the process of leaving the bargaining unit. In a nonbargained plan, the preferences are most likely to be in favor of highly paid employees or against rank and file employees. In both cases, discrimination may also sometimes occur along age, race, or sex-based lines. In *Winpisinger v. Aurora Corp.*, a district court held that trustees cannot establish a "preference[ ] amongst [the] plan participants" that focuses the burden of improving the plan's funding status on participants in one discrete group, instead of "evenly on all participants in the Fund."[61] The court stated that the fiduciaries

> "owed a duty of fairness to all—not just some of the covered employees. [Fiduciaries are] required to exercise their discretion in a non-discriminatory manner."[62]

To the extent the *Winpisinger* decision contains language rejecting the arbitrary and capricious standard of review in favor of closer scrutiny under ERISA's express language for fiduciary duties, the decision has not been followed.[63] But the more central point of the opinion that

---

[59] 451 F.Supp. 226 (E.D.N.Y. 1978). See also *Gaydosh v. Lewis*, 410 F.2d 262, at 264 (D.C. Cir. 1969) (trustees did not act arbitrarily when faced with "fast diminishing Fund" by amending plan to require service in the coal industry immediately prior to date the plan was established for entitlement to benefits); *Palino v. Casey*, 664 F.2d 854, 2 EBC 2169 (1st Cir. 1981) (trustees' restriction of extended health care coverage after employment in construction industry ceased not arbitrary when based on consideration of changes in employment availability in industry, financial drain on plan from the extended coverage, and fear that participants who were actually self-employed were using it to provide their health coverage); *Johnson v. Botica*, 537 F.2d 930 (7th Cir. 1976) (valid factual basis existed for plan rule conditioning past service credits on two quarters of contributory service under plan, even though employee's failure to meet the requirement was involuntary, because of need for contributory service to support the plan's benefits on an actuarially sound basis).

[60] 609 F.Supp. 12, 6 EBC 1921 (N.D. Cal. 1985).

[61] 456 F.Supp. 559, 1 EBC 2201, at 2214 (N.D. Ohio 1978).

[62] 1 EBC at 2214. And see 1 EBC at 2207.

[63] See ch. 7, sec. III, on the adoption of the "arbitrary and capricious" standard of review for benefit claims.

lines drawn under discretionary authority cannot create discriminatory preferences is widely recognized.[64]

An amendment that adversely affects the rights of participants who are involuntarily absent from employment because of job termination or disability is less likely to withstand challenge than an amendment that "discourages workers from taking voluntary action which shifts the burden of supporting the Fund to other employees."[65] Thus, numerous decisions hold that the application of a break-in-service rule to forfeit a participant's benefits is arbitrary when "no work was available" for the participant to do to avoid the break,[66] or when the break rule is applied to an absence otherwise "beyond the employee's control."[67] Similarly, changing the requirements for a benefit when a participant met "all eligibility requirements then in effect, save [the attainment of a stated] age," and cannot return to work because no work is available or because he or she is disabled, is generally arbitrary.[68] Forfeitures "exacted from an employee for attempting to improve his position by accepting work with a competitor of his [former] employer" are also disfavored.[69]

Disclosure to participants of the potential for future amendments to a benefit can affect whether a plan amendment is arbitrary and capricious. In *Winpisinger v. Aurora Corp.*, the district court emphasized "unequivocal" language in the multiemployer plan and the summary booklet describing the plan's vesting requirements, and refused to "read" broad discretionary amendment authority in a manner that would "subsume in a detailed plan a *hidden* power to cancel express benefits through retroactive modification."[70] The application of an amended rule to a period of service or event that occurred before *notice*

---

[64] See *Elser v. IAM Nat'l Pension Fund*, 684 F.2d 648, 3 EBC 2155, at 2162 (9th Cir. 1982), *cert. denied*, 464 U.S. 813 (1983) (arbitrariness of cancellation of past service credits established, in large part, by fact that one group of employees would lose benefits while others who "worked a substantially lesser period of time for a contributing employer" would still receive them). See also *Morse v. Stanley*, 732 F.2d 1139, 5 EBC 1602, at 1608 (2d Cir. 1984) (trustees have duty to deal "impartially" and "even-handedly" with entire employee group under any discretionary authority); *Petrella v. NL Indus. Inc.*, 529 F.Supp. 1357, 3 EBC 1210, at 1218 and 1220 (D.N.J. 1982) (discretion under plan must be exercised rationally and in manner that does not result in "prohibited discrimination"); *Fine v. Semet*, 514 F.Supp. 34, 2 EBC 1103 (S.D. Fla. 1981), *aff'd*, 699 F.2d 1091, 4 EBC 1273 (11th Cir. 1983) (not feasible to demand absolutely no preferences, but dissimilar treatment cannot be irrational or serve discriminatory purposes); *Adams v. New Jersey Brewery Employees' Pension Fund Trustees*, 670 F.2d 387, 3 EBC 1083, at 1091 (3d Cir. 1982) (examining whether "exceptions" to an amendment were "irrational" in a sense that encompasses discrimination). Decisions striking down "signatory" last year of service requirements for benefits can also be seen as demanding that plan rules be neither arbitrary nor discriminatory. See ch. 8, sec. VIII.

[65] *Goins v. Teamsters Local 639*, 599 F.Supp. 141, at 145 (D.D.C. 1984). And see *Adams v. New Jersey Brewery Employees' Pension Fund Trustees, supra.*

[66] *Lee v. Nesbitt*, 453 F.2d 1309, at 1312 (9th Cir. 1972).

[67] *Van Fossan v. Teamsters Local 710 Pension Fund*, 649 F.2d 1243, 2 EBC 1457, at 1462 n.21 (7th Cir. 1981). And see ch. 5, sec. III.A.4.a.

[68] See *Saunders v. Teamsters Local 639 Pension Trust*, 667 F.2d 146, 2 EBC 1961, at 1963 (D.C. Cir. 1981). And see sec. IV below on the protection of vested rights.

[69] *Chambless v. Masters, Mates & Pilots Pension Plan*, 772 F.2d 1032, 6 EBC 2209, at 2216 (2d Cir. 1985), *cert. denied*, 475 U.S. 1012 (1986). And see ch. 5, sec. V, on forfeitures of vested rights.

[70] 456 F.Supp. 559, 1 EBC 2201, at 2209 (N.D. Ohio 1978) (emphasis added).

of the amendment is provided a participant can also make an amended rule arbitrary and capricious as applied to the individual participant (as discussed in sec. V below).

Benefit increases can also be examined under the arbitrary and capricious standard, although they are seldom held to be arbitrary. In *Toensing v. Brown*, plan trustees were held not to have acted arbitrarily in adopting a higher benefit increase for active employees than for retirees.[71] However, in egregious cases, courts have considered whether the trustees' choice of an increase in the dollar amount of benefits over a liberalization of vesting requirements is arbitrary.[72] Also, a failure to increase benefits or to liberalize vesting requirements can be arbitrary when a plan has enough assets to do so and is otherwise accumulating unnecessary reserves.[73]

2. A Stricter Standard of Review

A stricter standard of review than "arbitrary and capricious" can apply to review of a plan amendment if the "gravamen" of a plaintiff's claim is that plan fiduciaries "have sacrificed valid participant interests to advance the interests of non-beneficiaries," e.g., the employer's.[74] In *Struble v. New Jersey Brewery Employees' Welfare Fund*, management-appointed trustees voted to give a surplus of plan assets back to contributing employers, rather than to use it to continue health benefits for retired participants. The Third Circuit stated that in this instance the "strict" standard of review from ERISA Section 404(a)(1) applies, rather than the arbitrary and capricious standard, which applies to cases involving "personal claims" for benefits.[75]

Without explaining it in this manner, other courts follow the same distinction. In *Dependahl v. Falstaff Brewing Corp.*, a plan amendment drastically restricted eligibility for severance benefits on the eve of a mass reduction in the employer's workforce with the financial gain from the amendment going to the employer "alone." The amendment

---

[71] 528 F.2d 69, 1 EBC 1083 (9th Cir. 1975). See also *Tomlin v. Board of Trustees*, 586 F.2d 148, 1 EBC 1302 (9th Cir. 1978) (not arbitrary to improve provisions for normal and early retirement benefits by adding credit for reciprocal service under related plans without providing same improvement for disability pensions).

[72] See *Ponce v. Construction Laborers Pension Trust*, 628 F.2d 537, 2 EBC 1777 (9th Cir. 1980) (increasing benefit amounts for small group of participants instead of broadening vesting rules that were excluding an unusually high percentage of participants from benefits raised presumption of arbitrariness), and 774 F.2d 1401, 6 EBC 2468 (9th Cir. 1985) (affirming district court's decision on remand that trustees' action was, in fact, arbitrary). See also *Blankenship v. Boyle*, 329 F.Supp. 1089, 1 EBC 1062, at 1078 (D.D.C. 1971).

[73] See *Riley v. MEBA Pension Trust*, 570 F.2d 406, 1 EBC 1757, at 1763 (2d Cir. 1977), *modified on other grounds after remand*, 586 F.2d 968, 1 EBC 1763 (2d Cir. 1978); *In re Des Moines Iron Workers Pension Trust*, 4 EBC 2364 (Heinsz, 1983) (fiduciaries have duty to increase benefits when plan assets allow them to do so). Cf. *Mestas v. Huge*, 585 F.2d 450, at 453 (10th Cir. 1978) (trustees may have "duty to liberalize and maximize benefits to the extent allowed by the Fund," but duty not applicable when plan was on a "pay-as-you-go basis at the time, with all money coming in . . . being paid out in benefits").

[74] *Struble v. New Jersey Brewery Employees' Welfare Fund*, 732 F.2d 325, 5 EBC 1676, at 1683 (3d Cir. 1984).

[75] *Id.*, 5 EBC at 1683. And see ch. 7, sec. III.A.5.d.

was reviewed under ERISA's strict fiduciary standard and was found to be in breach of duty.[76] Likewise, in *Hickerson v. Velsicol Chemical Corp.*, the Seventh Circuit held that an employer violated a fiduciary duty by amending a profit-sharing plan to convert it to a defined benefit plan without preserving a market rate of interest on participants' existing account balances. No reference was made to applying an "arbitrary and capricious" standard to determine whether the employer's initial offer of a five percent interest rate sufficed.[77]

III. Labor Law and Contract Restraints on Plan Amendments

A. Collectively Bargained Single-Employer Plans

Amendments to collectively bargained single-employer plans, including an amendment terminating a plan, are subject to the NLRA's duty to bargain, unless the union unmistakably surrenders a unilateral right to amend the plan to the employer.[78] When plan amendments are subject to bargaining, the union will in the normal course refuse to bargain away existing benefits or rights, whether or not "accrued" in the ERISA sense. However, with adverse business conditions, unions sometimes make concessions that do not preserve all benefits that participants considered earned.[79] When a union does so, it is subject to

---

[76] 491 F.Supp. 1188, at 1197 (E.D. Mo. 1980).

[77] 778 F.2d 365, 6 EBC 2545 (7th Cir. 1985), *cert. denied,* 479 U.S. ___ (1986). See also *Eaves v. Penn*, 587 F.2d 453, 1 EBC 1592 (10th Cir. 1978) (reviewing plan amendment converting a profit-sharing plan to an ESOP to shift more plan assets to investments in employer stock under the strict ERISA standard). Accord *Werschkull v. United California Bank*, 149 Cal.Rptr. 829 (Cal.App. 1978) (reviewing amendment shifting excess plan assets to another plan of the employer under strict state law fiduciary standard). On the same basis, amendments redirecting excess plan assets to an employer immediately before a plan termination may also be subject to strict review. The opposing interests in this situation are, in fact, identical to those in *Struble*. But see cases cited in ch. 12, sec. IX.C.3.

[78] See, e.g., *Terones v. Pacific States Steel Corp.*, 526 F.Supp. 1350 (N.D. Cal. 1981) (unless union clearly and unmistakably surrenders a unilateral right to the employer, plan termination subject to bargaining duty); *T.T.P. Corp.*, 190 NLRB 240, 77 LRRM 1097 (1971) (plan termination subject to bargaining, even when plan is unilaterally established and not an express part of collective bargaining agreement); *Laborers Health & Welfare Fund v. Advanced Lightweight Concrete Co.*, 779 F.2d 497 (9th Cir. 1985) (unilateral changes in pension agreement may not be made until (1) agreement has expired and (2) employer has bargained to impasse on proposed changes; employer may then unilaterally implement its best offer); *Delgrosso v. Spang & Co.*, 769 F.2d 928, 6 EBC 1940 (3d Cir. 1985), *cert. denied,* 476 U.S. ___ (1986) (employer did not have authority under collective bargaining agreement to unilaterally amend plan to insert provision enabling it to obtain a reversion of excess plan assets). But cf. *RCA Corp. v. Professional Engineers Local 241*, 700 F.2d 921, 4 EBC 1258 (3d Cir. 1983) (ordering arbitration of whether changes in actuarial assumptions for computing lump sum benefits were subject to bargaining duty or whether collective bargaining agreement made such changes administrative functions within employer's unilateral control); *United Steelworkers 2116 v. Cyclops Corp.*, 653 F.Supp. 574, 8 EBC 1194 (S.D. Ohio 1987) (no collective bargaining violation in sales agreement transferring plan assets and liabilities to buyer when seller thereby fulfilled all its pension obligations under the collective bargaining agreement).

[79] See, e.g., *Sutton v. Weirton Steel Division*, 724 F.2d 406, 5 EBC 1033 (4th Cir. 1983), *cert. denied,* 467 U.S. 1205 (1984).

the duty of fair representation.[80] If the burden of concessions is not spread reasonably evenly among all plan participants, but instead focuses on one benefit, such as an unreduced early retirement benefit, that is particularly important and valuable to employees who have nearly all the years required for the benefit, those employees may claim that the union has acted hostilely to their interests.[81] Any concessionary agreement (as well as any agreement improving benefits) must also comply with the substantive requirements of the NLRA on not discriminating for or against union membership.[82] As discussed below, a union is also without authority to negotiate away vested rights.[83]

The bilateral restrictions on plan amendments inherent in collective bargaining disappear if the collective bargaining agreement expires and the employer, after bargaining to impasse over proposed amendments, unilaterally puts the proposed amendments into effect (or if an employer declares bankruptcy and executory parts of a pension agreement are approved for rejection by a federal bankruptcy court).[84] Fiduciary, contractual, and quasi-contractual considerations on plan amendments may then parallel those for a nonbargained plan.

B. Multiemployer Plans

In multiemployer plans, the plan's benefit terms are typically not produced by collective bargaining.[85] Instead, collective bargaining establishes the rate of employer contributions, leaving the plan's trustees

---

[80] See *UMW Health & Retirement Funds v. Robinson*, 455 U.S. 562, 3 EBC 1129, at 1135 (1982).

[81] The duty of fair representation requires the union to act without hostility to, or discrimination against, any particular group of employees in the bargaining unit. *Steele v. Louisville & N. Ry. Co.*, 323 U.S. 192 (1944); *Vaca v. Sipes*, 386 U.S. 171 (1967). But it is inevitable that all employees' interests cannot be satisfied; therefore, a "wide range of reasonableness" is permitted. *Ford Motor Co. v. Huffman*, 345 U.S. 330, at 338 (1953), and see *Sutton v. Weirton Steel Division*, *supra* (no breach of duty of fair representation when union compromise to save several thousand jobs was not arbitrary, discriminatory, or in bad faith—even though it did affect some participants more than others). The duty of fair representation may also be violated by negligent actions, inaction, or mistatements that result in harm to employees. Cf. *Brown v. UAW*, 689 F.2d 69, 3 EBC 2101 (6th Cir. 1982) (union failure to monitor employer contributions to a plan could be negligence, but no harm to employees when employer could not have made contributions in any event; exact degree of negligence to establish breach of duty of fair representation not addressed). But see *Flight Officers, Inc. v. United Air Lines, Inc.*, 756 F.2d 1274, 6 EBC 1086 (7th Cir. 1985) (only intentional or deliberate misconduct breaches duty of fair representation).

[82] *UMW Health & Retirement Funds v. Robinson, supra*, 3 EBC at 1135. And see *Chambless v. Masters, Mates & Pilots Pension Plan*, 571 F.Supp. 1430, at 1444 n.21 (S.D.N.Y. 1983), *aff'd*, 772 F.2d 1032, 6 EBC 2209 (2d Cir. 1985), *cert. denied*, 475 U.S. 1012 (1986).

[83] See sec. IV below. A discrimination claim can arise when participants are disproportionately saddled with the burden of benefit reductions on the basis of age, race, or sex, or are left without benefit improvements because of the same factors. See *UMW Health & Retirement Funds v. Robinson, supra*, 3 EBC at 1135 (1982). And see ch. 10, secs. III and IV.

ERISA §510's prohibition of intentional interference with the attainment of rights under an employee benefit plan, and the ERISA and Code rules on partial terminations of plans by amendments reducing benefits, on inurement of plan assets to the benefit of an employer, and on reversions of excess assets resulting from restrictive plan amendments can also apply despite the exemption from fiduciary duties established in *Robinson*. See ch. 10, sec. I, and sec. VIII below.

[84] See ch. 12, sec. I.D.

[85] See GAO, "Effects of the 1980 Multiemployer Pension Plan Amendments Act on Plan Participants Benefits" (GAO/HRD-85-58), Appendix I.

with the responsibility of working out the benefits that can be provided based on the agreed contribution rates and the plan's existing assets and liabilities. As discussed before, the amendments the trustees make to the plan's benefit terms are unquestionably subject to the fiduciary standard of ERISA Section 404(a)(1) as well as to the "sole and exclusive benefit" standard of Section 302(c)(5) of the LMRA.[86]

When a multiemployer plan amendment is in fact the product of collective bargaining, instead of an amendment made by the plan's trustees, under *UMW Health & Retirement Funds v. Robinson* neither the fiduciary standard nor Section 302(c)(5) applies to review of the amendment.[87] However, as with negotiated amendments to single-employer plans, the union will again, in the normal course, refuse to bargain away earned benefits, whether or not they were "accrued" in an ERISA sense. The duty of fair representation, vested rights protections, and age, race, and sex discrimination prohibitions also offer general protections against concessionary amendments that are hostile to the interests of any one group of participants.

C. Implied Good Faith and Fair Dealing Duty Under Nonbargained Plans

In nonbargained plans, the absolute language employers typically use to reserve authority to amend plans seems to militate against any contractual restriction on plan amendments. The plan's amendment authority may provide that "The Board of Directors of the Employer shall have the right to amend the plan in any and all respects at any time and from time to time." The only proviso, which is sometimes only implied by operation of law, may be that none of the specific statutory protections of ERISA for "accrued benefits" or for vesting rules and schedules are to be violated.

The contractual problem with giving literal effect to an unfettered reservation of amendment authority is that it means that the employer has never made an "offer" of the benefits and benefit rights not specifically protected by ERISA. Rather, the employer has only outlined a "proposal" of an offer.[88] The "offer" is made by the employee's satisfaction of all conditions for the proposed benefit, with the employer accepting the offer by not having amended the proposal immediately before the conditions are met.[89] Put more succinctly, John Calamari and Joseph Perillo state that although employers propose benefits with a reservation of "at will" amendment authority "with surprising frequency," "[s]uch an offer is an illusory promise."[90]

---

[86] See sec. II.A.2 above.

[87] *Id.*

[88] See *Restatement (Second) of Contracts,* §45.

[89] *Id.*

[90] J. Calamari and J. Perillo, *Contracts* (West 2d ed. 1977), at 216.

Even before ERISA, the view of the courts under the common law was against interpretations of plans as offering illusory promises:

> "[W]henever the sense of the plan will allow, pension plans will be construed to create contractual rights."[91]

As stated in the *Restatement of Contracts*:

> "[A]n interpretation which gives a reasonable, lawful, and effective meaning to all the terms is preferred to an interpretation which leaves a part unreasonable, unlawful or of no effect."[92]

Similarly, in interpreting collective bargaining agreements:

> "Contractual provisions are construed so as to make none nugatory and the promises contained therein *illusory*."[93]

A less direct factor in favor of implying a reviewable standard into the reservation of amendment authority is that if *none* is implied, and the promise of benefits thus remains an illusory promise, recovery may be had under unjust enrichment to the extent necessary to prevent injustice.[94]

To avoid a construction which leads to an illusory promise, a plan's "at will" amendment authority must be limited by a standard that a court can review and enforce. The prime candidates for limiting a plan's amendment authority from absolute, unreviewable terms are a "good faith and fair dealing" standard, or alternatively, the "arbitrary and capricious" standard for fiduciary duties. Implying a standard of "good faith and fair dealing" is not unusual. The *Restatement of Contracts* provides that it is implied into every contract, including a commercial contract, which reserves to one party a power to determine whether the other's performance is satisfactory.[95] Similarly, reservations of standardless authority in insurance and other adhesion contracts are commonly construed to imply a good faith and fair dealing standard, and thus not to defeat reasonable expectations.[96]

The courts have recognized that if literal effect were given to certain boilerplate provisions in pension plans, substantive benefit provisions would be rendered illusory. The first plan provisions to be so limited were interpretive authority provisions that gave nonreviewable, conclusive authority to plan administrators' or trustees' interpretations of plan terms. Such authority was narrowly construed to prevent an undermining of the plan's substantive benefit offers by requiring the administrator's or trustees' interpretation to pass the arbitrary and

---

[91] Note, "Pension Plans and the Rights of the Retired Worker," 70 Colum. L. Rev. 909, at 917 (1970) (citing *Magee v. San Francisco Bar Pilots Benev. & P. Ass'n*, 198 P.2d 933 (Cal. App. 1948).

[92] *Restatement (Second) of Contracts*, §203.

[93] *Cordovan Assoc., Inc. v. Dayton Rubber Co.*, 290 F.2d 858, at 861 (6th Cir. 1961) (emphasis added).

[94] See sec. VII below.

[95] *Restatement (Second) of Contracts*, §205.

[96] See *In re Erie Lackawanna Railway Co.*, 548 F.2d 621 (6th Cir. 1977) (implying good faith and sufficient cause standard under at-will termination clause of group life insurance contract).

capricious standard of review,[97] or put still another way, to be justified in terms of a "fair pension plan."[98] Many courts later further discounted the literal terms of such interpretive authority by interpreting plans "in favor of the employee" and "to avoid forfeiture" either within the arbitrary and capricious standard of review or under a direct contractual standard.[99]

A more directly related area where standardless boilerplate reservations of authority have been limited by courts is to protect vested rights against plan amendments. In *Cantor v. Berkshire Life Ins. Co.*, the Ohio Supreme Court thus held that the vested benefits of a group of retirees were protected against plan amendments, stating:

> "Even where an employer declares the plan is within the absolute discretion of the directors, the court will interpret the plan ... so as to give effect to its general purpose of securing the loyalty and continued service of the employees, and the employer may not defeat the employee's reasonable expectations of receiving the promised reward....
>
> "Therefore, whether a retirement plan is contributory or noncontributory, *and even though the employer has reserved the right to amend or terminate the plan*, once an employee ... has complied with all the conditions ..., his rights become vested and the employer cannot divest the employee of his rights thereunder."[100]

1. Disclosure of At-Will Authority

ERISA enhanced the support for interpreting plans as making firm, reviewable "offers" of all benefits described therein, as opposed to mere "proposals," or illusory promises. "The purpose of ERISA [was] to make the pension promise ... real rather than illusory." Accordingly, the view throughout ERISA is opposed to the treatment of employee benefits as gratuities.[101] However, if a power to amend a plan is unlimited, earning a benefit remains the employer's gratuity since the employer can change the benefit terms at will at any moment before they become vested.[102] Supporting the view that an illusory promise is not permissible, ERISA Sections 402(a)(1) and (b)(4) require a written plan that specifies the basis on which payments will be made from the plan. Still more specifically, ERISA Section 402(b)(3) provides that while a right to amend can be reserved, the plan must identify the persons with such authority and must establish a written

---

[97] See ch. 7, sec. II.C.1.

[98] *General Electric v. Martin*, 574 S.W.2d 313, at 317 (Ky.App. 1978). And see, e.g., *Lowe v. Feldman*, 168 N.Y.S.2d 674, at 684 (Sup.Ct. 1957), *aff'd*, 174 N.Y.S.2d 949 (App.Div. 1958) (arbitrary refusals of benefits not permitted where retirement plan is "contract" supported by "consideration of continued service," not a "benefaction").

[99] See ch. 7, sec. II.C.2.

[100] 171 N.E.2d 518, at 521-22 (Ohio 1960) (emphasis added), in part quoting *Bird v. Conn. Power Co.*, 133 A.2d 894, at 897 (Conn. 1957). And see sec. IV below.

[101] H.R. Rep. 93-533, at 10, 2 ERISA Leg. Hist. 2357. And see ch. 7, sec. II.C.3, on Congress' view of employee benefits as deferred wages, rather than gratuities from employers.

[102] See *Fickling v. Pollard*, 179 S.E. 582, at 583 (Ga.App. 1935) (pension benefits subject to an employer's unlimited reservation of authority to amend are a "gratuitous arrangement," a "mere gift" from the employer). Accord *Menke v. Thompson*, 140 F.2d 786, at 790 (8th Cir. 1944).

"procedure" under which amendments to the plan will be made. If a plan's amendment authority is written, but completely "at will," whether the plan sets a written "procedure" for plan amendments is in doubt since no standards have been established which participants can refer to in determining the circumstances under which amendments to the plan may or may not be made.[103]

Perhaps the strongest argument in favor of implying at least a good faith and fair dealing restraint on authority to amend a plan arises when a reservation of unlimited, at-will authority is not disclosed to participants in the plan's SPD in a manner that "brings home" the scope of the reserved power and dispels any expectations of participants that such authority will be exercised only under a good faith and fair dealing standard. ERISA's SPD requirements effectively require a reservation of an absolute right to amend a benefit "at any time and for whatever reason" to be understandably disclosed in the SPD because it is a "circumstance" that may result in a loss or denial of benefits "that a participant might otherwise reasonably expect the plan to provide on the basis of the description of benefits" in the SPD.[104]

Use of legal or technical jargon in describing an employer's reserved authority in an SPD may also have to be limited if the full import of an at-will reservation of amendment authority is to be understood by participants (who may be accustomed to seeing such reservations in consumer contracts and insurance policies, with a duty of good faith and fair dealing nevertheless implied). Thus, to effectively reserve at-will amendment authority, an employer may not describe its amendment authority in the same boilerplate language used under the plan, but may be required to provide clarifying examples and illustrations to make the significance of the reserved authority concrete for the average plan participant.[105]

---

[103] See generally Conf. Rep., at 297, 3 ERISA Leg. Hist. 4564 (written plan requirements established so employee can determine "exactly" what his rights under plan are).

Under the Internal Revenue Code, a right to amend may be reserved, see 26 C.F.R. 1.401-1(b)(2), but when such a right is not subject to a standard other than an employer's unfettered discretion, the benefits described in the plan may fail to be "definitely determinable" as required under 26 C.F.R. 1.401(b)(1)(i) and (ii). Proposing one dollar amount or set of benefit terms today is practically meaningless if the next day a lower dollar amount or more restrictive benefit terms can be substituted without any standard outside the employer's sole discretion governing the alteration. See generally Rev. Rul. 74-385, 79-90, 85-130, and Prop. Regs. 1.401(a)-4, 51 Fed. Reg. 3798 (Jan. 30, 1986).

[104] 29 C.F.R. 2520.102-3(l). In ERISA Technical Release 84-1, the Department of Labor recognized that an employer's reservation of authority to terminate a plan constitutes a "circumstance" that may result in the loss or denial of benefits. The Technical Release provides that the SPD must contain a "summary of any plan provisions governing the rights of the plan sponsor or others to terminate the plan, *and the circumstances, if any, under which the plan may be terminated.*" ERISA Technical Release No. 84-1 (May 4, 1984), reprinted in 11 BNA Pens. Rep. at 653-54 (May 14, 1984) (emphasis added).

[105] See 29 C.F.R. 2520.102-2(a). The Labor Department's regulations further provide that any such limitations on a plan's benefits shall not be "minimized, rendered obscure or otherwise made to appear unimportant." 29 C.F.R. 2520.102-2(b). Many summary plan descriptions say that "accrued benefits" are protected against decreases from plan amendment, thus implying that other benefits may not be. However, this may not clarify the complete lack of protection under a reservation of at-will amendment authority for other benefits or benefit rights.

These SPD requirements can be seen as developing the application of basic contract law. The contract law rule is that a unilateral contract offer becomes irrevocable as soon as an offeree begins performance. This is because of the "obvious injustice" when an offeree begins performance, only to have the offeror substantially retract or modify the offer.[106] Irrevocability yields to the offeror's reservation of authority to amend the offer after the offeree's performance begins, but only if the reservation of such authority is made "manifest" to the offeree.[107] The SPD requirements can be seen as specifying more precisely than the common law exactly how manifest the reservation must be if it is to be effective in overriding the basic contract rule.

Combining practically all of these elements, a federal district court in *Musto v. American General Corp.* found that while retiree health benefits were not "vested" against any and all plan amendments under the terms of a plan, a standard of "good faith and cause" had to be implied into a reservation of at-will amendment authority. The factors the court cited in reaching this conclusion were:

(1) The need to reconcile the plan's clear and express offer of benefits with the at-will amendment authority in a manner that avoids an illusory or nugatory promise;

(2) ERISA's policies in favor of secure retirement income and its policy against treatment of employee benefits in a manner that reduces them to gratuities;

(3) The failure of the plan to specify an amendment procedure as required by ERISA Section 402(b)(3), which while not rendering the amendment authority unenforceable, required a showing of good faith and cause prior to invocation of the amendment authority; and

(4) A statement in the summary plan description repeating the plan's amendment authority, but suggesting that changes would be made in the plan only "if necessary."[108]

2. *Implementing a Good Faith and Fair Dealing Standard*

In implementing a good faith and fair dealing standard, the same factors used in determining whether actions are arbitrary and capricious apply. In *Kulins v. Malco, A Microdot Co.*, the duty of good faith and fair dealing was thus applied to an amendment to a severance pay plan that reduced the level of benefits for each year of service, including years of service before the amendment. Although the benefits

---

[106] L. Simpson, *Contracts* (West 2d ed. 1965), at 37–38. And see *Restatement (Second) of Contracts,* §45.

[107] *Restatement (Second) of Contracts,* §45, illustration 2. And see *Williston on Contracts* (3d ed.), §43; and Corbin, *Contracts* (1962 Supp.), §178 (stressing importance of bringing the reservation to the attention of the other party).

[108] 615 F.Supp. 1483, 6 EBC 2071, at 2076 (M.D. Tenn. 1985).

for years before the amendment were not "accrued" or "vested" benefits in the ERISA sense, and as with normal retirement benefit accruals, could be reduced prospectively, the court found that the benefits due for past years of service could not be reduced because it would violate the employer's implied covenant of "good faith" to use the plan's amendment authority to make such a reduction on the eve of a termination of employment that the employer knew would trigger severance benefits.[109] The analysis in *Kulins* is virtually identical to *Dependahl v. Falstaff Brewing Corp.*, where an employer amended a plan to restrict the eligibility requirements for severance benefits on the eve of a mass discharge of employees. But in *Dependahl*, the plan amendment was a breach of fiduciary duty.[110]

Similarly, in *Dhayer v. Weirton Steel Division*, a district court equivocated on whether the arbitrary and capricious standard or an implied contractual standard of reasonableness applied to an employer's amendment of a "plant shutdown" early retirement pension offered under a nonbargained pension plan. But the court analyzed the amendment along the same lines under both standards. The court did not find a breach under either standard because the amendment was a clarification of the unamended plan adopted in anticipation of a sale of the division, which affected all employees equally, did not affect any unconditional rights, and contained a limited degree of grandfathering in the event of a later plant shutdown by the purchaser.[111]

Under a good faith and fair dealing standard, the right to amend a plan may also be limited once there is no intent to continue the plan. In *Matter of Bankers Trust Co. (Fifth Avenue Coach Lines)*, a "last minute" amendment to a plan before termination redirecting plan assets from participants in the plan to employees of a subsidiary who had previously not been covered was invalid when at the time of the amendment there was no intent to continue the plan, and thus no intent to support the new employees' inclusion under the plan with additional contributions. The court stated that although "an extremely liberal" interpretation of the amendment authority might have allowed such an amendment, it was an amendment that the participants "could not reasonably have contemplated," and one that would "do[ ] violence to the fair intent . . . of the plan."[112]

Good faith and fair dealing, or alternatively, the arbitrary and capricious standard, have also been used as the basis to protect

---

[109] 459 N.E.2d 1038, at 1045 (Ill.App. 1st Dist. 1984).

[110] 491 F.Supp. 1188 (E.D. Mo. 1980), *modified on other grounds*, 653 F.2d 1208, 2 EBC 1521 (8th Cir. 1981), *cert. denied*, 454 U.S. 1084 (1981).

[111] 571 F.Supp. 316, 4 EBC 2413, at 2421 and 2425 (N.D. W.Va. 1983), *aff'd on other grounds sub nom., Sutton v. Weirton Steel Division*, 724 F.2d 406, 5 EBC 1033 (4th Cir. 1983), *cert. denied*, 467 U.S. 1205 (1984).

[112] 52 Lab. Cas. (CCH) ¶51,367 (N.Y. Sup. Ct. 1965). Accord *Kulins v. Malco, A Microdot Co.*, *supra*. But compare cases cited in ch. 12, sec. IX.C.3, generally permitting employers to amend plans immediately before plan termination to redirect "excess" plan assets from employees to the employer.

"vested" rights against plan amendments—even when a plan's amendment authority is ostensibly unlimited.[113] While not finding benefits "vested" against any and all amendments, in *Musto v. American General Corp.*, the district court applied a stringent "good faith and cause" standard requiring an employer to show "necessity . . . [a] sufficiently compelling financial reason to amend the level of benefits promised . . . on which employees have justifiably relied" before the employer could use its at-will amendment authority to reduce health benefits of participants who had already retired. The court stated that this standard required the employer to show "that the contractual promises previously made are now avoidable because of some unforeseen contingency that threatens the financial basis of the entire corporation." The fact that the cost of the health insurance plan had increased fourfold over the past five years was not sufficient when the company was profitable and the retirees had years of "sweat equity" in the promise of health benefits in retirement.[114]

D. Other Contractual Limits

More specific restrictions on plan amendments than an implied good faith and fair dealing standard are sometimes found under the terms of plans, or under separate contracts with employers. Such limits often parallel the ERISA protections against plan amendments affecting vested rights or decreasing accrued benefits, but the language may predate ERISA or it may go further than ERISA, particularly when combined with extrinsic evidence of a broader intent. Specific procedural requirements for plan amendments may also be stated in a plan.

The substantive or procedural limits on the authority an employer or trustee wields under plan documents raise "issues of law."[115] Thus, the arbitrary and capricious standard is not appropriate to review of these issues. But once it is determined that an employer or trustee has acted within its authority under the plan, actions under the authority are reviewed under the arbitrary and capricious standard.

In *Keding v. Barton*, a profit-sharing plan thus provided that once a participant had a "vested equitable interest," his or her rights could not be altered by plan amendment. The Iowa Supreme Court determined that the practical meaning the parties placed on the term "vested equitable interest" was broad and that it included a right to an immediate distribution of a participant's account on a termination of

---

[113] See *Cantor v. Berkshire Life Ins. Co.*, 171 N.E.2d 518, at 522 (Ohio 1960), and sec. IV below.

[114] 615 F.Supp. 1483, 6 EBC 2071, at 2083–84 and 2087–88 (M.D. Tenn. 1985).

[115] See *Central Hardware Co. v. Central States Pension Fund*, 770 F.2d 106, 6 EBC 2525, at 2528 (8th Cir. 1985), *cert. denied*, 475 U.S. 1108 (1986), citing as support, *Central States Pension Fund v. Central Transport Inc.*, 698 F.2d 802, 3 EBC 2624 (6th Cir. 1983), *rev'd on other grounds*, 472 U.S. 559, 6 EBC 1665 (1985). See also *McDaniel v. Nat'l Shopmen Pension Fund*, 6 EBC 2700 (W.D. Wash. 1985) (whether cancellation of past service credits on employer's withdrawal from plan was outside of scope of trustees' authority under terms of plan subject to direct contractual review).

employment. The employer's right to amend the plan therefore did not extend to making any distribution before retirement age discretionary when an employee already had a vested benefit under the plan.[116] In *Hauck v. Eschbacher*, a plan provided that it could be amended from time to time, but that no amendment would reduce a participant's accrued benefits "to less than he would have been entitled if he had resigned from the employ of the Employer on the day prior to the effective date of such amendment." The employer adopted an amendment establishing a new three-year postemployment competition restriction applicable to those participants who vested under a more liberal vesting schedule than required by ERISA. The employer argued that the amendment was not a reduction in the "amount" of benefits as contemplated by the amendment authority limitation. Without reaching the issue of the applicability of ERISA Section 204(g), the Eighth Circuit held as a matter of contract that elimination of entitlement for an employee who violated the restriction would be "nothing more than a one hundred percent reduction in accrued benefits," and therefore held that contractually the amendment could not be applied to employees who had separated from service when a more limited, one-year restriction was in effect.[117]

Similarily, in *Ingram Mfg. Co.*, an arbitrator determined that an employer violated a collective bargaining agreement obligation to "continue to maintain a pension program with benefits comparable to the program presently in effect" when the employer increased the interest assumption for computing lump sum benefits from 3½ percent to 6½ percent, thus cutting lump sum benefits nearly in half. The arbitrator's decision was bolstered by oral assurances that the cash-out option would be retained in the same form as in the past.[118] In *Amato v. Western Union International, Inc.*, the Second Circuit found that the purchaser of a company might be bound by a promise in its sales agreement that benefits under the seller's pension plan would not be reduced following the sale. The plan participants were entitled to enforce this promise as third-party beneficiaries, or alternatively, under promissory estoppel based on separate oral assurances to them by the purchaser.[119]

---

[116] 154 N.W.2d 172, at 175 (Iowa 1967).

[117] 665 F.2d 843, 2 EBC 2202, at 2206 (8th Cir. 1981). See also *Rochester Corp. v. Rochester*, 450 F.2d 118, at 119 (4th Cir. 1971) (plan provided that no plan amendments were to "impair the interest in the Trust of any member created by or resulting from prior contributions"; Fourth Circuit held a participant's deferred vested benefits could not be impaired under this language by addition of a new forfeiture provision for postemployment competition); and cases cited in ch. 12, secs. I.E. and IX.C.

[118] 72 LA 47 (Caraway, 1978). Compare *Sherwood Medical Indus.*, 81-1 ARB (CCH) ¶8031 (Teple, 1980), and *Grand Union Co.*, 82-2 ARB (CCH) ¶8433 (Sands, 1982), both permitting changes in actuarial assumptions for lump sum benefits when contracts reserved power to make such changes for the employer or an employer-appointed retirement committee. And cf. *RCA Corp. v. Professional Engineers Local 241*, 700 F.2d 921, 4 EBC 1258 (3d Cir. 1983) (ordering arbitration of whether changes in actuarial assumptions violated contract or were within employer's unilateral powers).

[119] 773 F.2d 1402, 6 EBC 2226 (2d Cir. 1985). The Second Circuit found no need to determine whether the estoppel and third-party beneficiary causes of action lodged under federal common law or state law because the same principles would apply in either case.

Summary plan descriptions can provide extrinsic evidence on the scope of a plan's amendment authority. In *Amato*, the plan stated that the employer reserved the right to amend a plan "at any time or from time to time." The SPD repeated the reservation, but it also stated the company's intent to continue the plan "indefinitely and to meet any foreseeable situations," with the employer reserving the right "to change or even terminate the plan" only to "protect against any unforeseen situations." The Second Circuit held that although there could be no "separate contract claim based solely on the language of the summary plan description," the right to amend or terminate the plan was "not so unambiguous" as to preclude use of the SPD statements in interpretation of the scope of the employer's reserved authority.[120] In *Horn & Hardart Co. v. Ross*, "lifetime pensions" of $100 per month were offered in a plan and plan booklet, but "the power to terminate" the plan short of full funding for the benefits was not "brought home" to the employees in the plan booklet. The power to terminate the plan was therefore limited by the plan's and booklet's representation of "lifetime" benefits and the lack of disclosure in the booklet of what the termination power could mean.[121] In *Winpisinger v. Aurora Corp.*, a district court emphasized "unequivocal" language in a section of a multiemployer plan and a summary booklet describing the plan's vesting requirements, and therefore refused to "read" the plan's broad discretionary amendment authority in a manner that would "subsume in a detailed plan a *hidden* power to cancel [the] express benefits through retroactive modification."[122]

Interpretation of a plan's amendment authority can be guided by other types of extrinsic evidence. In *Eardman v. Bethlehem Steel Corp.*, oral assurances to employees in group meetings and exit interviews that health benefits in retirement were for life were used in determining that a plan's amendment authority did not authorize reducing the benefits once an employee had retired.[123] In *Hoefel v. Atlas Tack Co.*, oral assurances that an amendment changing a plan from one in which benefits were provided entirely through the purchase of fully paid-up individual annuity contracts to an uninsured trusteed

---

[120] *Id.*, 6 EBC at 2241 and 2242. The Second Circuit did not discuss the effect of the plan's apparent noncompliance with the SPD requirement on eliminating technical jargon by providing concrete illustrations and examples of circumstances that may limit benefits, or the plan's apparent failure to cross-reference the amendment authority in the description of the promised early retirement benefit as a circumstance that could limit the benefit.

[121] 395 N.Y.S.2d 180, at 181 (Sup.Ct. App.Div. 1977) (the cited opinion affirms a decision of the Industrial Board of Appeals and does not indicate whether the Board limited the plan as a matter of interpretation or estoppel). See also *Hurd v. Hutnik*, 419 F.Supp. 630, 1 EBC 1382 (D.N.J. 1976) (dealing with similar facts and resolving issue under promissory estoppel); *Bryant v. Int'l Fruit Products Co.*, 793 F.2d 118, 7 EBC 1688 (6th Cir. 1986) (plan amendment to install reversion provision precluded by limitations on the power to amend described in earlier plan, as buttressed by statements in SPDs).

[122] 456 F.Supp. 559, 1 EBC 2201, at 2209 (N.D. Ohio 1978) (emphasis added).

[123] 607 F.Supp. 196, 5 EBC 1985 (W.D.N.Y. 1984).

plan would have no effect on the security of retirees' pensions were used in interpreting the employer's contractual obligation to complete the funding of the benefits after the plan's termination.[124]

Procedural requirements for plan amendments must be satisfied if a plan amendment is to be effective. As described above, ERISA Section 402(b)(3) requires every employee benefit plan to identify the persons with authority to amend a plan, and to specify the "procedure" under which amendments will be made.[125] In *Maas v. Dubuque Packing Co.*, the Eighth Circuit held that a joint labor-management administrative board had the authority under a plan's terms to determine whether the employer could unilaterally terminate the plan after a certain date, or whether that date had been extended by a memorandum of agreement between the bargaining parties.[126] In *Burud v. Acme Electric Co.*, a challenge by employees to an employer's compliance with corporate law requirements for notice to all directors of the board meeting at which a plan was terminated survived a motion to dismiss when one out of three board members responsible for such decisions had not been notified of the meeting.[127] If a plan does not have a "procedure" for making plan amendments, the violation of ERISA Section 402(b)(3) may result in a more stringent "good faith and cause" standard being applied to review the amendment.[128]

E. Estoppel

Estoppel can be applied to limit plan amendments "to the extent necessary to avoid injustice."[129] In *Kulins v. Malco, A Microdot Co.*, promissory estoppel, as well as an implied covenant of good faith and fair dealing, limited an employer's authority to amend a severance pay plan to decrease benefits for all years of service. Based on promissory estoppel, the amendment was limited to only future years of service because employees had worked for years in reliance on the promise of

---

[124] 581 F.2d 1 (1st Cir. 1978), *cert. denied,* 440 U.S. 913 (1979).

[125] Whether the plan's procedures have been followed in making an amendment is subject to direct contractual review, even if the arbitrary and capricious standard is otherwise applicable to benefit decisions by the plan's fiduciaries. See n. 115 *supra,* and *Harm v. Bay Area Pipe Trades Pension Fund,* 701 F.2d 1301, 4 EBC 1253, at 1255 n.3 (9th Cir. 1983) (provisions governing exercises of authority under plans subject to direct contractual review).

[126] 754 F.2d 287, 6 EBC 1385 (8th Cir. 1985), *reh. denied, but clarified,* 757 F.2d 194, 6 EBC 1390 (8th Cir. 1985).

[127] 591 F.Supp. 238, 5 EBC 1793 (D. Alas. 1984). The district court left open the possibility that the employer could prove a "custom of informality within the closely held corporation" as to such "meetings and notice."

[128] See *Musto v. American General Corp.*, 615 F.Supp. 1483, 6 EBC 2071 (M.D. Tenn. 1985).

[129] *Restatement (Second) of Contracts,* §87 provides:

"[A]n offer which the offeror should reasonably expect to induce action or forbearance of a substantial character . . . and which does induce such action or forbearance is binding as an option contract *to the extent necessary to avoid injustice.*"

Emphasis added.

severance benefits and the employer was only attempting to cut back its entire severance obligation shortly before terminating their employment.[130] In *Hurd v. Hutnik*, a promise of "lifetime" pensions, "knowingly wielded by . . . employers" for over of 14 years, estopped employers when they were later able to convince the union to "sell [its] old people down the river," by agreeing to a termination of a multiemployer plan, thereby halting the employer contributions needed to complete the funding of the retirees' "lifetime benefits," while putting active workers under a new plan.[131] In *Weesner v. Electric Power Board of Chattanooga*, oral and written assurances to employees that retirement benefits would not be altered if they voted to come under Social Security estopped an employer from amending a pension plan two years later to offset the employees' primary Social Security benefits from a minimum pension benefit offered under the plan. The court stated that it would not allow the "reasonable expectations of receiving the promised reward" to be defeated.[132]

However, in *Chambless v. Masters, Mates & Pilots Pension Plan*, a union dispatcher allegedly assured a participant that he could go to work for noncontributing employers in the maritime industry without any "Union problem." The participant claimed he took this to mean that a plan amendment forfeiting early retirement benefits in the event of such reemployment would not apply to him. The Second Circuit refused to estop application of the plan amendment because (1) the union dispatcher was not a plan fiduciary, (2) his assurance was only a general statement that did not specifically relate to the pension plan, and (3) the court was generally reluctant to apply estoppel to a multiemployer plan.[133]

An SPD's nondisclosure or inadequate disclosure of an employer's power to amend a plan can also be the basis for estoppel of a plan amendment.[134] In most cases, however, courts have not needed to use

---

[130] 459 N.E.2d 1038 (Ill.App. 1st Dist. 1984).

[131] 419 F.Supp. 630, 1 EBC 1382, at 1403–04 (D.N.J. 1976). See also *Horn & Hardart Co. v. Ross*, 395 N.Y.S.2d 180 (Sup.Ct. App.Div. 1977) (limiting a single-employer plan sponsor's ability to deny "lifetime" pensions not funded at the time of plan termination when the significance of the termination authority was never "brought home" to participants as a limitation on the plan's promise of benefits).

[132] 344 S.W.2d 766, at 768 (Tenn. Ct.App. 1961). And cf. *Bell v. Amcast Indus. Corp.*, 607 F.Supp. 486, 6 EBC 1472 (S.D. Ohio 1985) (remanding claims for breach of contract, estoppel, and fraud to state court based on amendment to a severance pay plan immediately before a plant shutdown in breach of alleged oral representations made by the employer to induce the employees to stay on until the full shutdown).

[133] 772 F.2d 1032, 6 EBC 2209, at 2217 (2d Cir. 1985), *cert. denied*, 475 U.S. 1012 (1986). An action for misrepresentation may still exist when the speaker lacks authority to bind a plan. See *Goins v. Teamsters Local 639*, 598 F.Supp. 1151 (D.D.C. 1984) (misrepresentation claim founded on alleged statements by union business agent that plan amendment requiring 10 years of service as precondition for disability benefits would not apply to those participants who already had 5 years of service as required under the preamendment plan).

[134] See *Hurd v. Hutnik, supra*, 1 EBC at 1393 and 1403–04. See also *Horn & Hardart Co. v. Ross*, 395 N.Y.S.2d 180 (Sup.Ct. App.Div. 1977) (unclear whether court used estoppel or plan interpretation as the basis to require employer to complete the funding of promised benefits after termination of single-employer plan). Similarly, in *Miller v. Dictaphone Corp.*, 334 F.Supp. 840 (D. Or. 1971), a district court held that a letter to participants promising unreduced early retirement benefits, with no reservation of a power to amend the offer in the letter, bound an

estoppel because the plan language reserving the amendment authority has been found to be "not so unambiguous" as to exclude consideration of the SPD's disclosure or nondisclosure in interpreting the plan.[135]

Promises that a plan *will* be amended to improve benefits can also form the basis for estoppel. In *Novembre v. Local 584 Pension Fund,* a multiemployer plan was estopped from denying participants reciprocal service credits for service under another multiemployer plan when union officials, who were also plan trustees, promised that the plan would be amended to provide such credits if the participants' union local merged with theirs.[136] However, in *Chesser v. Babcock & Wilcox,* the Eleventh Circuit found no detrimental reliance on representations that a plan would probably be amended in effects bargaining over a plant's closing to provide additional credit to enable certain participants to qualify for 30-year early retirement pensions. The employees' allegations that if the representations had *not* been made they would have organized opposition to the agreement and that this might have resulted in the agreement not being ratified were not sufficient.[137]

IV. Vested Rights Protection Against Adverse Amendments Under Contract and Trust Law

Common law contract and trust law protections for "vested" rights back up the ERISA minimum standard protections against decreases in accrued benefits and changes in vesting rules and schedules and can extend them in certain situations where the ERISA rules do not apply.[138] As described in Chapter 4, prior to the 1984 Retirement Equity Act amendments, the protection of "accrued benefits" from decreases from plan amendments was generally interpreted narrowly with respect to early retirement benefits, and it continues to be interpreted narrowly for disability benefits and certain other ancillary benefit rights. In addition, in cases still dealing with pre-ERISA facts, the common law contract and trust rules are the only available participant protections.

ERISA's Conference Report states that early retirement benefits

---

employer to the terms in the letter—despite an express reservation of such amendment authority under the plan. In *Miller,* a separate contract with the employer was established by the letter. In *Dictaphone Corp. v. Clemons,* 488 P.2d 226 (Colo. 1971), it was unclear whether the court held the employer liable in contract or whether the plan was bound by estoppel. (In a single-employer plan, this difference may often be inconsequential in terms of recovery and who actually pays.)

[135] See *Eardman v. Bethlehem Steel Corp.,* 607 F.Supp. 196, 5 EBC 1985, at 1985 (W.D.N.Y. 1984); *Amato v. Western Union Int'l, Inc.,* 773 F.2d 1402, 6 EBC 2226, at 2242 (2d Cir. 1985); *Winpisinger v. Aurora Corp.,* 456 F.Supp. 559, 1 EBC 2201 (N.D. Ohio 1978); *Musto v. American General Corp.,* 615 F.Supp. 1483, 6 EBC 2071 (M.D. Tenn. 1985).

[136] 4 EBC 1286 (D.N.J. 1981), *aff'd,* 4 EBC 1289 (3d Cir. 1982), *cert. denied,* 459 U.S. 1172 (1982). And see 4 EBC 1279 (D.N.J. 1981).

[137] 753 F.2d 1570, *reh. denied,* 760 F.2d 281 (11th Cir. 1985).

[138] See ch. 4, sec. IV.B, and ch. 5, sec. IV, on the ERISA minimum standard protections for accrued benefits and vesting schedules and rules.

and ancillary benefit rights are generally not within ERISA's definition of an "accrued benefit," and are thus not required to "vest" at the times specified under the ERISA minimum standard schedules. But such benefits may vest contractually under the terms of a plan. ERISA's vesting requirements, therefore, do not "preclude" the vesting of such benefits, "they merely state that vesting is not [statutorily] required."[139]

The courts have long abhorred plan amendments that retroactively divest employees of benefits they thought were vested, even if a plan's amendment authority could literally be interpreted to permit amendments after vesting. In *Cantor v. Berkshire Life Ins. Co.*, the Ohio Supreme Court stated:

> "[W]hether a ... plan is contributory or noncontributory and even though the employer has reserved the right to amend or terminate ..., once an employee has complied with all the conditions ..., his rights become vested, and the employer cannot divest the employee of his rights thereunder."[140]

In negotiated single-employer plans, the protection of vested rights against plan amendment manifests itself as a contractual limitation and as a limitation on the union's bargaining authority. A union thus cannot bargain away vested rights of active workers, of former employees who no longer have recall rights, or of retirees.[141] As a

---

[139] *Kulins v. Malco, A Microdot Co.*, 459 N.E.2d 1038, at 1043 (Ill.App. 1st Dist. 1984). See also *Hansen v. White Farm Equipment Co.*, 42 B.R. 1005 (N.D. Ohio 1984), *rev'd and remanded on other grounds,* 788 F.2d 1186, 7 EBC 1411 (6th Cir. 1986) (ERISA's vesting requirements do not foreclose possibility that other benefits may be vested contractually); *Fine v. Semet*, 699 F.2d 1091, 4 EBC 1273 (11th Cir. 1981) ("[a]ny right to earlier benefits and a particular amount of payment must be found in the individual agreements"); *Sutton v. Weirton Steel Division*, 724 F.2d 406, 5 EBC 1033 (4th Cir. 1983), *cert. denied,* 467 U.S. 1205 (1984) ("right[s] to payment of benefits before normal retirement age must be found in [the] agreement").

[140] 171 N.E.2d 518, at 522 (Ohio 1960). And see *Sheehy v. Seilon, Inc.*, 227 N.E.2d 229, at 230 (Ohio 1967) (once vested, employee may not be deprived of benefits "notwithstanding a proviso in the contract of employment to the contrary").

[141] See *Allied Chemical Workers v. Pittsburgh Plate Glass*, 404 U.S. 157, 1 EBC 1019, at 1029 n.20 (1971) ("[u]nder established contract principles, vested retirement rights may not be altered without the pensioner's [individual] consent"); *Hauser v. Farwell, Ozmun, Kirk & Co.*, 299 F.Supp. 387, at 393 (D. Minn. 1969) ("a Union has no authority on behalf of its membership to bargain away vested or accrued rights"); *Bianchin v. McGraw Edison Co.*, 438 F.Supp. 585 (W.D. Pa. 1976); *Bomhold v. Pabst Brewing Co.*, 5 EBC 2315 (C.D. Ill. 1984); *UAW v. Yard-Man, Inc.*, 716 F.2d 1476, 4 EBC 2108 (6th Cir. 1983), *cert. denied,* 465 U.S. 1007 (1984).

An exception may apply in bankruptcy. See *In re Century Brass Products, Inc.*, 795 F.2d 265, 7 EBC 1801 (2d Cir. 1986), *cert. denied,* 479 U.S. ___ (1986) (reductions in retiree benefits may be a mandatory subject of bargaining when employer has filed a bankruptcy petition and alterations in retirees' benefits "vitally affect" chances for a successful reorganization, and thus, active employees' wages and benefits; however, if union has a conflict of interest in representing retirees in such bargaining, a separate retiree representative may have to be appointed).

Another area where the protection of vested rights does *not* apply is to the funding necessary to support vested benefits. A union can agree to modify an employer's future funding obligations to a level that leaves a plan with less assets to pay all vested benefits on termination, or it can settle claims for unpaid contributions or underfunding at a level below 100% payment. See *Adams v. Gould, Inc.*, 687 F.2d 27, 3 EBC 1913 (3d Cir. 1982), *cert. denied,* 460 U.S. 1085 (1983) (characterizing settlement of funding claim as working out details of an arbitral award, but court would in any event have held that participants only had "vested" right to participate in distribution of plan assets, not a right to a "sum certain"). And see *Dwyer v. Climatrol Indus., Inc.*, 544 F.2d 307, 1 EBC 1265 (7th Cir. 1976) (modification of employer's future funding obligation did not bargain away "vested" rights). The union may not, however, agree to a modification of the allocation order for existing plan assets in a manner that impairs vested rights. See *Hauser v. Farwell, Ozmun, Kirk & Co., supra.* But compare *Finnell v. Cramet, Inc.*, 289 F.2d 409 (6th Cir.

corollary, benefit improvements for retirees or for workers no longer in the bargaining unit are not a mandatory subject for collective bargaining.[142] Both these rules recognize that for workers who are no longer in the bargaining unit and for retirees, the union:

> "[D]oes not have the same interest in the enforcement of those contractual rights on the behalf of individual retirees' that it has in the terms and conditions of employment of active workers."[143]

Under nonbargained plans, the vested rights rule protects vested rights against amendments even when the employer reserves general at-will amendment authority under the plan's terms. Thus, unless a very specific contrary intent is expressed, the contractual rule is that once benefit rights have firmed up, or "vested," by fulfillment of the conditions for benefits, the benefits are not subject to change by future unilateral amendments made at the will of an employer.[144]

Courts have been more reluctant to find contractually "vested" rights under multiemployer plans that can withstand any and all amendments by plan trustees. But the same protection of vested rights against adverse plan amendments emerges as a restraint on "arbitrary and capricious" action.[145] The most fundamental part of this protection is that "pension rights [must] vest [against adverse plan amendments] at the date [a retiree] applies for benefits if the applicant meets all eligibility criteria *then in effect*."[146] In addition, if a participant meets all eligibility criteria, except that he or she has not applied for a benefit, the participant must be given either "advance notice or a grace period within which [to] elect to retire and protect their fully earned rights."[147] When a participant meets all eligibility requirements, except for the attainment of a stated age, a more circumstantial analysis has applied to determine whether benefits are "sufficiently vested" to make application of a restrictive amendment arbitrary and capricious, examining in particular:

1961) (permitting negotiated plan amendment immediately before plan termination that reallocated plan assets so that nonvested participants received no payments of their accrued benefits).

[142] See *Allied Chemical Workers v. Pittsburgh Plate Glass, supra.*

[143] *UAW v. Yard-Man, Inc., supra*, 4 EBC at 2115. For active workers, the vested rights protection sets a floor on concessionary bargaining.

[144] See *Cantor v. Berkshire Life Ins. Co., supra; Schofield v. Zion's Co-op Mercantile Inst.*, 39 P.2d 342, at 347 (Utah 1934); *Tilbert v. Eagle Lock Co.*, 165 A. 205 (Conn. 1933); *Sheehy v. Seilon, Inc.*, 227 N.E.2d 229 (Ohio 1967); *Rochester Corp. v. Rochester*, 450 F.2d 118 (4th Cir. 1971); *Genevese v. Martin Marietta Corp.*, 312 F.Supp. 1186 (E.D. Pa. 1969) (if rights "firmed up" on employee's side, amendment authority ineffective to vary terms of payment). See also cases discussed below (e.g., *Denzer* and *Morales*).

[145] When an amendment to a multiemployer plan is not designed by the plan trustees, but is instead produced in collective bargaining, the same contractual and labor law standards apply as for amendments to vested rights under negotiated single-employer plans. See *Short v. UMW 1950 Pension Trust*, 728 F.2d 528, 5 EBC 1532 (D.C. Cir. 1984).

[146] *Kiser v. Huge*, 517 F.2d 1237, at 1247 (D.C. Cir. 1974) (emphasis added). And see *Danti v. Lewis*, 312 F.2d 345 (D.C. Cir. 1962); *Brug v. Carpenters Pension Trust*, 669 F.2d 570, 3 EBC 1240 (9th Cir. 1982), *cert. denied*, 459 U.S. 861 (1982).

[147] *Agro v. Joint Plumbing Industry Board*, 623 F.2d 207, 3 EBC 1036, at 1040 (2d Cir. 1980). And see *Kosty v. Lewis*, 319 F.2d 744 (D.C. Cir. 1963), *cert. denied*, 375 U.S. 964 (1964); *Norton v. IAM Nat'l Pension Fund*, 553 F.2d 1352 (D.C. Cir. 1977).

(1) The financial necessity for the rule change;[148]

(2) Whether the participant had advance notice of the amendment to allow the maximum opportunity to conform with the new rule;[149] and

(3) Whether the participant is involuntarily absent from service so that he or she cannot comply with the new rule.[150]

A. When Particular Benefit Rights Are Vested

Early retirement benefits, lump sum options, disability benefits, and health benefits are often susceptible to varying interpretations about exactly when, if ever, the rights become vested against adverse plan amendments. Since the issue of whether such rights are vested so as to withstand adverse amendments is a contractual issue (even if not expressly stated as such for a multiemployer plan), statements and omissions in the summary plan description and other extrinsic evidence can play an important role in interpretation. In *Eardman v. Bethlehem Steel Corp.*, Bethlehem Steel amended health insurance benefits of over 18,000 retirees to institute (1) retiree contributions as a condition for continued coverage, (2) increased deductibles, and (3) new certification requirements for certain types of in-patient care. The plan's amendment authority stated that an Insurance Board had the right to amend or terminate the benefits program provided that no termination would deprive any participants of any benefits to which they were theretofore entitled. The district court found that this was "not so unambiguous" as to exclude the use of extrinsic evidence. The extrinsic evidence, including the plan's SPD, was overwhelming that retirees had *not* been told the employer intended to reserve authority to amend the benefits after their retirement. Rather, the employer's representations had all stated, or implied, the opposite, namely, that the benefits would not be altered *once* an employee retired. Properly interpreted, the court held the reservation did not encompass authority to reduce or cancel health benefits after retirement.[151]

---

[148] See *Mosley v. NMU Pension and Welfare Plan*, 451 F.Supp. 226 (E.D.N.Y. 1978).

[149] See *Agro v. Joint Plumbing Industry Board*, *supra*, and cases cited below in sec. V.B.

[150] See *Lavella v. Boyle*, 444 F.2d 910 (D.C. Cir. 1971) (*per curiam*), *cert. denied*, 404 U.S. 850 (1971); *Saunders v. Teamsters Local 639 Pension Trust*, 667 F.2d 146, 2 EBC 1961 (D.C. Cir. 1981).

[151] 607 F.Supp. 196, 5 EBC 1985, at 1985, 1995, and 2001 (W.D.N.Y. 1984). See also *Mioni v. Bessemer Cement Co.*, 6 EBC 2677 (W.D. Pa. 1985); *District 29, UMWA v. Royal Coal Co.*, 6 EBC 2117 (S.D. W.Va. 1985); *Bower v. Bunker Hill Co.*, 725 F.2d 1221, 5 EBC 1180 (9th Cir. 1984)—all considering statements made in summary plan descriptions in determining whether health benefits of retirees were vested against alteration after retirement. And compare *Struble v. New Jersey Brewery Employees' Welfare Fund*, 732 F.2d 325, 5 EBC 1676 (3d Cir. 1984) (employees' SPD considered, but SPD even clearer than plan in stating that retiree health benefits were not vested); *Hansen v. White Farm Equipment Co.*, 42 B.R. 1005, 5 EBC 2130 (N.D. Ohio 1984), *rev'd*, 788 F.2d 1186, 7 EBC 1411 (6th Cir. 1986) (handbook statements considered, but decision reversed on appeal because of district court's presumption that benefits were vested).

See also *Keding v. Barton*, 154 N.W.2d 172, at 175 (Iowa 1967) (considering employee booklet description, protection of participants' "vested equitable interests" under terms of plan against

1. Early Retirement Benefits

Although the plan's exact terms and disclosure are crucial in each case, early retirement benefits have generally not been found to be vested before a participant meets *both* the age and service requirements for the benefit. In *Bencivenga v. Western Pennsylvania Teamsters Pension Fund*, the Third Circuit permitted a plan amendment reducing an age 55 early retirement benefit for a participant who already had the 15 years of service required for the benefit and who would have met the age 55 requirement by just growing older—whether or not he was in service. The court held that growing older was an additional condition for a "vested" right that could withstand such an amendment.[152] Similarly, in *Short v. UMW 1950 Pension Trust*, an employee who developed black lung disease at age 46 had the 20 years of service necessary to be entitled to a pension at age 55. However, a collectively bargained amendment changed the rules for computing credited years of service and added a new requirement of eight years of signatory service, leaving him short of the benefit on two counts. The U.S. Court of Appeals for the District of Columbia Circuit held that the employee's rights before the amendment were not completely vested, and therefore, that the amendment was not an impermissible alteration of vested rights.[153] *Bencivenga* and *Short* both may be at odds with the understanding of employees and benefit specialists alike that a benefit "vests" once it requires no more service and can therefore withstand a separation from service before the date on which the benefits will begin. In *Nachman Corp. v. PBGC*, the Supreme Court favorably quoted Dan McGill's explanation of a vested right:

"In essence . . . , the vesting of a pension benefit simply means that the

---

alteration by plan amendment had broad "practical meaning" covering right to lump sum distribution). In *McCoy v. Mesta Machine Co.*, 260 BNA Pens. Rep. D-1 (W.D. Pa. 1979), a plan contained express language that no vested rights would be conferred prior to meeting both age and service conditions for an early retirement benefit *and* actually retiring. The court did not indicate whether such language was in the SPD, but the implication was that if adequately communicated to the participant, such language might prevent vesting before actual retirement.

Other types of oral and written assurances on the vested status of health benefits in retirement were also considered in *UAW v. Cadillac Malleable Iron Co.*, 3 EBC 1369 (W.D. Mich. 1982), *aff'd*, 728 F.2d 807, 5 EBC 1283 (6th Cir. 1984); *Food & Commercial Workers Local 150A v. Dubuque Packing Co.*, 756 F.2d 66, 6 EBC 1391 (8th Cir. 1985); *Mioni v. Bessemer Cement Co., supra*; *Bower v. Bunker Hill Co., supra*.

152 763 F.2d 574, 6 EBC 1799 (3d Cir. 1985). A concurring opinion found a contractually vested right, but read the plan's amendment authority to still permit amendments reducing the benefit amount.

153 728 F.2d 528, 5 EBC 1532 (D.C. Cir. 1984). In *Rothlein v. Armour & Co.*, 377 F.Supp. 506 (W.D. Pa. 1974), a district court held that an early retirement pension requiring the attainment of age 55, the completion of 20 years of service, *and* a termination of employment because of a permanent reduction in the employer's work force was not vested until a participant met *all* the conditions, including a termination of employment for the stated reason. And cf. *Van Fossan v. Teamsters Local 710 Pension Fund*, 649 F.2d 1243, 2 EBC 1457 (7th Cir. 1981) (plaintiff's rights, if any, to early retirement pension requiring age 57 and 20 years of credited service were not vested against application of break-in-service forfeiture of credit until participant had *both* the age and service).

realization of the benefit is no longer contingent upon the individual's remaining in the service of the employer to normal retirement age."[154]

While courts have been reluctant to find "vested" rights under multiemployer plans, multiemployer plan participants have actually been better protected against the type of adverse amendments that occurred in *Bencivenga* and *Short*—at least when the participant is unable to return to work to complete service required under an amended benefit requirement and the plan's financial circumstances are not exceedingly dire. In *Lavella v. Boyle*, a participant was thus "sufficiently vested" in an age 55 retirement benefit when he met the previous 20 years of service requirement for the benefit, but lacked attainment of the stated age. The court emphasized that the participant could not conform to a new rule requiring 20 years service in the 30 years before age 55 because he had black lung disease and could no longer return to work.[155] Similarly, in *Saunders v. Teamsters Local 639 Pension Trust*, an amendment to an age 60 retirement benefit to require plan participation immediately before age 60 was arbitrary and capricious when it was applied to a participant who met the previous conditions for the benefit, save attainment of the stated age, and could not return to active service because of a partial disability.[156]

In contrast, in *Gaydosh v. Lewis*, a coal miner who retired voluntarily at the age of 56 was not "vested" in retirement benefits requiring 20 years of service and age 60, even though he had the 20 years, when the trustees found a change in the rules necessary to "preserv[e] a fast diminishing fund." A new rule requiring service in the coal industry immediately prior to 1946 was therefore not arbitrary and capricious as applied to Gaydosh.[157] In *Mosley v. NMU Pension & Welfare Plan*, trustees who faced a sharp decline in the maritime industry and thus in their plan's contribution base—along with a steep increase in the excess of the plan's total accrued liabilities over plan assets (to a level of $550 million in liabilities compared to $106 million in assets)—also did not act arbitrarily in eliminating an age 60 and 15 years service early retirement pension for plan participants who did not have *both* the age

---

[154] 446 U.S. 359, 2 EBC 1431, at 1439 n.27 (1980), quoting D. McGill, *Preservation of Pension Rights* (Richard D. Irwin 1972), at 6. For plan amendments after July 30, 1984 (or for a collectively bargained plan, generally after April 1, 1985), ERISA §204(g), as amended by the 1984 Retirement Equity Act, would require a reversal of both *Bencivenga* and *Short*. See ch. 4, sec. IV.B.3. Moreover, in *Amato v. Western Union Int'l, Inc.*, 773 F.2d 1402, 6 EBC 2226 (2d Cir. 1985), the Second Circuit held that ERISA §204(g), even before REA, prohibited such amendments because of their indirect effect in decreasing the participant's accrued benefits.

[155] 444 F.2d 910, at 912 (D.C. Cir. 1971) (*per curiam*), *cert. denied,* 404 U.S. 850 (1971).

[156] 667 F.2d 146, 2 EBC 1961 (D.C. Cir. 1981). In *Short v. UMW 1950 Pension Trust, supra,* the U.S. Court of Appeals for the District of Columbia distinguished *Lavella* and *Saunders* as only applying to trustee-designed amendments to multiemployer plans, rather than to a collectively bargained amendment, as in *Short.*

[157] 410 F.2d 262, at 264 (D.C. Cir. 1969). In addition to the fact that he retired voluntarily, another salient point in *Gaydosh* is that the participant had *no* contributory service under the plan. Rather, on the establishment of the UMWA pension plan, the trustees adopted a sweeping rule to provide retirement benefits to long-term coal miners who had no contributory service, apparently without sufficient records to determine how many coal miners could qualify. As the trust funds diminished, the trustees altered the initial rule to also require service in the coal industry immediately before a certain date.

and service for retirement before the end of an eight-month grace period after adoption of the amendment.[158]

2. Lump Sum Distributions

Vested rights to lump sum distributions of benefits may be found under the terms of plan. In *Denzer v. Purofied Down Corp.*, a plan provided for payment of the balance of a participant's profit-sharing account on the date of the participant's termination from service. A plan amendment delaying such distributions until age 65 was ineffective for a participant who had a vested right to an immediate distribution on termination prior to the amendment based both on his service for over the 10-year period required for vesting and his termination from employment before the date the amendment was adopted.[159] However, when lump sum distributions are discretionary before retirement age, but have routinely been granted, courts have been reluctant to find a "vested" right to such a distribution based on past practice, so long as the practice has been changed for rational and nondiscriminatory reasons.[160] Vested rights have also been held not to be altered by changes in actuarial assumptions used to compute lump sum distributions or benefit amounts under optional benefit forms—unless the previously used actuarial assumptions were specifically stated in the plan.[161]

---

[158] 451 F.Supp. 226 (E.D.N.Y. 1978).

[159] 474 F.Supp. 773, 1 EBC 1768 (S.D.N.Y. 1979). See also *Morales v. Plaxall, Inc.*, 541 F.Supp. 1387, 3 EBC 1972 (E.D.N.Y. 1982) (right to immediate distribution of profit-sharing account on separation from service cannot be altered to the extent participant has a vested right to benefits before the amendment); *Keding v. Barton*, 154 N.W.2d 172 (Iowa 1967) (emphasizing "practical meaning" of the parties, right to immediate distribution of profit-sharing account on termination of employment was vested against an amendment making such distributions discretionary to the extent a participant already had vested rights under the plan's terms). In *Kilman v. Du-All Plate Corp.*, 6 EBC 1370 (3d Cir. 1984) (unpubl.), however, the Third Circuit distinguished a vested right to 100% of a promised benefit from a vested right to a distribution of the benefit in lump sum form at a particular time. The court held that an employee who was 100% vested in the amount of his benefits thus did not necessarily have a vested right to a distribution of the benefits in a lump sum form prior to actual termination of employment. The Third Circuit distinguished *Denzer* as only holding that the right to a particular form of distribution becomes vested on a termination of employment, although the court acknowledged that *Denzer* may be read to vest all related benefit rights after the normal period required under a plan for vesting. *Morales* and *Keding* were not discussed. See also *Taylor v. ITU Pension Plan*, 1 EBC 2123 (D. Md. 1979) (no breach of fiduciary duty in amendment eliminating right to withdraw lump sum equal to one-half of employer's contributions in lieu of all other pension rights after an employee had withdrawn from plan for a period of six months; the three plaintiffs were not "vested" under the old rule in that none had been withdrawn from the plan for the requisite period; harm from the amendment also mitigated by benefit improvements adopted at the same time); *Joy Mfg. Co. v. Stohl*, 222 S.E.2d 888 (Ga.App. 1975) (amendment eliminating lump sum option available on termination of employment held reasonable under plan that did not provide any vesting before such a termination).

[160] See *Fine v. Semet*, 699 F.2d 1091, 4 EBC 1273 (11th Cir. 1983), and ch. 7, sec. III.C.1.

[161] See *Lewis v. Fulton Federal Savings & Loan Pension Plan*, 4 EBC 2072 (N.D. Ga. 1983). The addition of a new interim valuation date for a participant's profit-sharing plan account balance before distribution has also been held not to affect any "vested" interest in having the account valued only annually when *any* distribution of the account balance before age 65 was discretionary and when the value of the plan's assets had declined sharply since the last annual valuation date so that a distribution preserving the prior rule would have depleted $72,000 from other participants' accounts. *Cator v. Herrgott & Wilson, Inc.*, 609 F.Supp. 12, 6 EBC 1921 (N.D. Cal. 1985).

3. Disability Benefits

Exactly when a disability benefit is vested against amendment depends on interpretation. A disability benefit provision may, for example, create a vested right based on service for a "qualifying time," such as a period of 10 years, before disability occurs, or it may make disability both the morning and evening star of vesting in the disability benefit's terms.[162] But even when vesting is contingent on the actual occurrence of disability, plan rules cannot be altered once a participant becomes disabled and applies for the benefits.[163]

4. Health Benefits

Health benefits under a pension plan, or under a separate health plan, can also vest contractually, but have rarely been held to vest prior to retirement (assuming the plan offers health benefits in retirement). Thus, the elimination of extended health care coverage during layoffs or during periods when there is a shortage of work covered under a multiemployer plan has been held not to affect any vested rights—even for participants currently receiving the extended benefits—and has also been held not to otherwise be arbitrary when the amendments are justified on actuarial grounds and notice is provided participants far enough in advance of the effective date so they can attempt to secure other coverage.[164]

As a result of the 1984 REA amendments to ERISA, reductions in, alterations of conditions for receipt, and complete elimination of benefit options, including lump sum options, are now subject to minimum standard protections under ERISA §204(g)(2), as amended. See ch. 4, sec. IV.B.3.

[162] Compare *Terpinas v. Seafarer's Int'l Union*, 722 F.2d 1445 (9th Cir. 1984) (disability benefits "vested" against amendment after the 10 years required as "qualifying time," even though disability had not occurred), with *Coleman v. Kroger Co.*, 399 F.Supp. 724 (W.D. Va. 1975) (employee who was not disabled at time of amendment did not have a vested interest in continuation of prior terms); *Vaughan v. Metal Lathers' Local 46 Pension Fund*, 626 F.2d 237 (2d Cir. 1980) (same as *Coleman*, even though participant became disabled only one month *after* amendment). See also *Goins v. Teamsters Local 639*, 599 F.Supp. 141 (D.D.C. 1984) (disability benefits not vested after 5 year qualifying period, but "protectible interest" created after the 5-year period deserved special consideration in making any plan amendment); *Swackard v. Commission House Drivers Local 400*, 647 F.2d 712, 2 EBC 1317, at 1318 (6th Cir. 1981), *cert. denied,* 454 U.S. 1033 (1981) (application of an entirely different interpretation of a condition for disability benefits, which the Sixth Circuit characterized as effectively a plan amendment, requiring 15 consecutive years of service for a participant who already had 15 accumulated years, as required in the past, was arbitrary and capricious because it "amount[ed] to a retroactive application of a [new] 'break in service' rule").

[163] See *Brug v. Carpenters Pension Trust*, 669 F.2d 570, 3 EBC 1240 (9th Cir. 1982), *cert. denied,* 459 U.S. 861 (1982) (plan provision including clerical staff employees of a union under plan's benefit coverage, including disability benefit coverage, could not be rescinded for an employee whose disability had already been incurred and who had filed an application for the benefits). But see *Freeman v. IBEW Local 613 Pension Fund*, 3 EBC 1865 (N.D. Ga. 1982) (permitting plan to add a periodic reevaluation requirement for disability benefits and to apply it to persons already receiving benefits because disability benefits never "vest").

[164] See *Palino v. Casey*, 664 F.2d 854, 2 EBC 2169 (1st Cir. 1981) (elimination of extended health coverage during slack periods in construction industry permitted as not affecting vested rights and not unreasonable when notice provided prior to effective date of change and the change was actuarially justified, even though plaintiff was unable to secure alternate individual coverage because of his wife's pregnancy). See also *Bridge, Structural and Ornamental Iron Workers Local 111 v. Douglas*, 646 F.2d 1211, 2 EBC 1470 (7th Cir. 1981), *cert. denied,* 454 U.S. 866 (1981) (reduction in extended health benefits from 3 months to 31 days following employer's withdrawal

While the outcome still depends on each plan's exact language, most recent decisions have found health benefits in retirement to be vested once an employee retires, unless both the plan and the SPD establish that such benefits are still subject to amendment after retirement.[165] However, even if participants could have retired prior to an amendment reducing health benefits, one court has held that health benefits are only vested against amendment for those participants who have actually retired.[166]

B. Inexorably Vested Rights

When benefit rights are not fully vested as a matter of contract at the time of a plan amendment, the remaining conditions for vesting may compel the conclusion that they are tantamount to being vested or that they would inexorably vest with the passage of time. In *Stacey v. Combs*, an employee with a permanent disability was "certain" to vest under a plan provision counting time receiving workmen's compensation toward a five-year "signatory" service requirement for an age 55 and 20 years of service pension. A plan amendment to eliminate the workmen's compensation time credit was arbitrary and capricious as applied to him because he was "inexorably vested."[167]

---

from multiemployer plan did not affect vested rights and was not unreasonable under the facts); *Pierce v. NECA-IBEW Welfare Trust Fund*, 620 F.2d 589, 2 EBC 2470 (6th Cir. 1980), *cert. denied*, 449 U.S. 1015 (1980) (basically the same facts and holding as in *Douglas*).

[165] See *Sheehy v. Seilon, Inc.*, 227 N.E.2d 229 (Ohio 1967); *UAW v. White Farm Equipment Co.*, 5 EBC 2449 (D. Minn. 1984); *Eardman v. Bethlehem Steel Corp.*, 607 F.Supp. 196, 5 EBC 1985 (W.D.N.Y. 1984); *UAW v. Yard-Man, Inc.*, 716 F.2d 1476, 4 EBC 2108 (6th Cir. 1983), *cert. denied*, 465 U.S. 1007 (1984); *UAW v. Cadillac Malleable Iron Co.*, 728 F.2d 807, 5 EBC 1283 (6th Cir. 1984); *District 29, UMWA v. Royal Coal Co.*, 6 EBC 2117 (S.D. W.Va. 1985); *Food & Commercial Workers Local 150A v. Dubuque Packing Co.*, 756 F.2d 66, 6 EBC 1391 (8th Cir. 1985); *Mioni v. Bessemer Cement Co.*, 6 EBC 2677 (W.D. Pa. 1985); *Weimer v. Kurz-Kasch, Inc.*, 772 F.2d 669, 6 EBC 2258 (6th Cir. 1985); *Policy v. Powell Pressed Steel Co.*, 770 F.2d 609, 6 EBC 2249 (6th Cir. 1985). See also *Bower v. Bunker Hill Co.*, 725 F.2d 1221, 5 EBC 1180 (9th Cir. 1984); *Musto v. American General Corp.*, 615 F.Supp. 1483, 6 EBC 2071 (M.D.Tenn. 1985) (health benefits in retirement not "vested" *per se*, but subject to stringent test on neccessity for amendments).

But compare *Turner v. Teamsters Local 302*, 604 F.2d 1219 (9th Cir. 1979); *UAW v. Roblin Indus., Inc.*, 561 F.Supp. 288, 4 EBC 1316 (W.D.Mich. 1983); *UAW v. New Castle Foundry, Inc.*, 4 EBC 2455 (S.D. Ind. 1983); *Struble v. New Jersey Brewery Employees' Welfare Fund*, 732 F.2d 325, 5 EBC 1676 (3d Cir. 1984); *Anderson v. Alpha Portland Indus. Inc.*, 647 F.Supp. 1109, 7 EBC 2534 (E.D. Mo. 1986); *Box v. Coalite, Inc.*, 643 F.Supp. 709, 7 EBC 2180 (N.D. Ala. 1986)—all permitting curtailment or elimination of retiree health benefits. In *Hanson v. White Farm Equipment Co.*, 788 F.2d 1186, 7 EBC 1411 (6th Cir. 1986), a district court's adoption of a presumption that retiree health benefits are vested and may not be terminated even under unambiguous authority in a plan was reversed and remanded for a determination of the parties' intent without regard to such a presumption.

[166] See *Bomhold v. Pabst Brewing Co.*, 5 EBC 2315 (C.D. Ill. 1984) (union could bargain away health and welfare benefits of employees who could have retired prior to the changes because their rights had not vested, even though they would have been vested had they retired). And cf. *Eardman v. Bethlehem Steel Corp., supra*; *Sheehy, v. Seilon, Inc., supra*. But compare *Bower v. Bunker Hill Co.*, 124 LRRM 2483 (E.D. Wash. 1986) (employees with deferred pension benefits had vested rights to health benefits on their later retirement).

[167] 671 F.2d 602, 3 EBC 1080, at 1082 (D.C. Cir. 1982). Similarly, in *Lavella v. Boyle*, 444 F.2d 910, at 912 (D.C. Cir. 1971) (*per curiam*), *cert. denied*, 404 U.S. 850 (1971), a participant was "sufficiently vested" when he met all eligibility requirements for benefits then in effect, save the attainment of the stated age when the benefits would begin, and could not return to work to meet additional requirements because of a disability.

However, in *Short v. UMW 1950 Pension Trust,* the District of Columbia Circuit fashioned a collective bargaining exception to this case. In *Short,* an employee developed black lung disease at age 46. Under the plan's rules in effect at that time, he would inexorably vest in a pension requiring 20 years of service once he reached age 55. However, a new collective bargaining agreement changed the rules for computing credited years of service and added a new requirement of eight years of signatory service. The court found that his rights before the amendment were not completely "vested," and rejected the argument that they were "inexorably vested" under *Stacey,* holding that *Stacey* defines arbitrary and capricious action by plan trustees, but does not apply when an amendment is collectively bargained.[168]

V. Notice of Plan Amendments

A. Summaries of Material Modification

Under ERISA, a summary of material modification is required whenever "significant changes are made to a plan." "[A] change in the information required by [ERISA] Section 102(b) . . . to be included in the summary plan description" is always significant.[169] This means that any amendment to a plan's benefit offer, whether it is a benefit increase or improvement, or a decrease or restriction, and any change in the circumstances that may result in disqualification, loss, or denial of benefits must be disclosed in a summary of material modification.[170] The summary of material modification is required to be distributed to participants within 210 days after the end of the plan year in which the plan amendment or other change is adopted.[171] Effective in 1986, the Single Employer Pension Plan Amendments Act of 1986 (SEPPAA) amends ERISA Section 204 to also require 15 days *advance* notice to

---

[168] 728 F.2d 528, 5 EBC 1532 (D.C. Cir. 1984). How close an employee is to vesting may still heighten the scrutiny given to claims for breach of the duty of fair representation, age, race, or sex discrimination claims, or ERISA §510 claims of intentional interference with rights. See ch. 10 on discrimination and noninterference with the attainment of rights.

[169] 42 Fed. Reg. 14267 (March 15, 1977) (preamble to final regulations), and 29 C.F.R. 2520.104b-3(a).

[170] 29 C.F.R. 2520.104b-3(a). A summary of material modification is also required for any change in a plan's procedures for presenting claims, any change in the remedies available under a plan for redress of denied claims, any change in the plan administrator or the plan's trustees, any change in the type of administration of the plan or the source of financing for the plan, any change in the identity of any organization through which benefits are provided, and any change in the period used as the plan year or the period used as the basis for records kept under the plan. *Id.*, and see ERISA §102(b) and 29 C.F.R. 2520.102-3.

Changes to plan provisions that are not directly required to be described in an SPD may still be required to be disclosed in a summary of material modification because of past practice. See *Burud v. Acme Elec. Co.*, 591 F.Supp. 238, 5 EBC 1793 (D. Alas. 1984) (plan amendment allowing trustees to invest up to 100% of plan assets in employer securities required to be disclosed in summary of material modification when a summary had previously been provided when the plan was amended earlier, in response to participant complaints, to limit such investments).

[171] 29 C.F.R. 2520.104b-3(a).

participants of plan amendments providing for "significant reduction[s] in the rate of future benefit accrual[s]."[172]

Like the SPD, summaries of material modification, and presumably SEPPAA's advance 15-day notice, must be "written in a manner calculated to be understood by the average plan participant," and must be accurate and comprehensive in describing the changes effected by the plan amendment.[173]

When a plan amendment is not disclosed within these time limits, or is inadequately disclosed, appropriate equitable relief may include estoppel of the application of the amendment, or a declaration that its application is arbitrary and capricious. In *Chambless v. Masters, Mates & Pilots Pension Plan*, the Second Circuit held that a summary notice of a plan amendment was inadequate when it failed to explain "the full import of the interaction" between the amendment, which forfeited early retirement benefits for work with noncontributing employers, and the plan's benefit formula, which based benefits on compensation during the highest five years within the 10 years *prior to* retirement. Because of the forfeiture of early retirement rights, this 10-year period would be postponed to the 10-year period before age 65, which for some participants could result in a decrease in the absolute dollar amount of benefits because of a decreased compensation average, in addition to the loss of their early retirement benefits before that time. The lack of a full explanation of this interaction violated the ERISA summary of material modification requirement for a "clear [and] timely explanation" of a new circumstance that could result in a loss or denial of benefits. As a result, the Second Circuit affirmed the district court's holding that applying the amendment to a participant who lacked this notice before going to work for a noncontributing employer was arbitrary and capricious.[174]

Under pre-ERISA common law, it is also established that the duty to explain an amendment can extend to explaining options *around* the

---

[172] ERISA §204(h), as amended by §11006 of P.L. 99-272. For plan amendments significantly reducing future benefit accruals adopted between Jan. 1, 1986, and April 7, 1986, the notice requirement is satisfied if notice is provided within 60 days after April 7, 1986. See §11006(b) of P.L. 99-272.

[173] 29 C.F.R. 2520.104b-3(c). And see 42 Fed. Reg. 14273 (March 15, 1977) (summary must be "comprehensive [and] accurate," as well as written in understandable manner for the average participant). See also *Chambless v. Masters, Mates & Pilots Pension Plan*, 772 F.2d 1032, 6 EBC 2209 (2d Cir. 1985), *cert. denied*, 475 U.S. 1012 (1986).

[174] *Id.*, 6 EBC at 2217. See also *Baker v. Lukens Steel Co.*, 793 F.2d 509, 7 EBC 2039, at 2043 (3d Cir. 1986) (summary of material modification disclosing plan amendment deleting early retirement benefit available on plant closing required to be distributed; but for participants to obtain estoppel based on the nondisclosure, reliance must be shown, e.g., that they "did not leave their jobs for other employment or even search for such employment because of misinformation concerning their status"). And cf. *UAW, District 65 v. Harper & Row Publishers, Inc.*, 576 F.Supp. 1468, 4 EBC 2586, at 2596 (S.D.N.Y. 1983) (even when summary of material modification not required under ERISA, court examined explanation given participants on plan termination about a lump sum option and found "information supplied to [the participants] may have been insufficient to enable them to make an informed decision"). But compare *Rubin v. Decision Concepts, Inc.*, 566 F.Supp. 1057 (S.D.N.Y. 1983) (failure to distribute summary of material modification of plan not actionable when participant received memo that in combination with the SPD was enough to let him know that new plan was a restatement of former profit-sharing plan and not a second profit-sharing plan).

amendment that may previously have been little used or needed. In *Valle v. Joint Plumbing Industry Board*, a plan amendment created a requirement of 15 years of service with a contributory employer for a benefit, which was a longer period of contributory service than under the previous plan rule. The Second Circuit held the amendment imposed a duty on the trustees to explain to employees who were just short of the required contributory service that two of the years might be waived for disability under another provision of the plan, or that two years could be obtained toward the new requirement simply by working one *day* in each of two years.[175]

B. Requirements Under Common Law

Ordinarily, compliance with the ERISA time limits for distribution of an adequate summary of material modification satisfies a fiduciary's duty of disclosure. But the courts have recognized that "particularly egregious circumstances" can require more timely disclosure.[176] Even before the 1986 SEPPAA amendment, an adverse plan amendment or other change reducing benefits that a participant could avoid or seek to ameliorate with advance notice of the change or amendment was held to present a particularly egregious circumstance requiring disclosure. In *Freund v. Marshall & Ilsley Bank*, profit-sharing plan fiduciaries failed to notify participants that a sale of the sponsoring company would subordinate loans the fiduciaries had made to the company with most of the plan's assets to a level below the security interest of the heavily leveraged buyer's creditors. Although no statutory disclosure requirement had yet been violated, this lack of notice was a breach of fiduciary duty because plan participants had the right to withdraw money from their accounts, and could have done so before the acquired company started failing had they known the "full facts concerning the sale."[177]

In *Helmetag v. Consolidated Rail Corp.*, the railroad assets of a company in Chapter 11 reorganization were sold to Conrail, with the company's pension plan merged with Conrail's. An amendment to the merged plan by Conrail provided that participants who continued working for the reorganized company would have their accrued benefits frozen, but could not retire under a 30 years of service and age 60 pension while still working for the reorganized company (a condition

---

[175] 623 F.2d 196, 3 EBC 1026 (2d Cir. 1980). And cf. *Janowski v. Teamsters Local No. 710 Pension Fund*, 673 F.2d 931, 3 EBC 1225 (7th Cir. 1982), *vacated and remanded on standing and attorney's fee award*, 463 U.S. 1222 (1983) (plan's first ERISA summary plan description failed to fully explain options to computation of benefits under amended benefit formula, but injunction improper when explanation had since been provided).

[176] *Leonard v. Drug Fair, Inc.*, 2 EBC 1118, at 1119 (D.D.C. 1980).

[177] 485 F.Supp. 629, 1 EBC 1898, at 1915 (W.D. Wis. 1979). See also *McNeese v. Health Plan Marketing, Inc.*, 647 F.Supp. 981 (N.D. Ala. 1986) (fiduciary breach from failure to notify employees of employer's failure to contribute to health plan).

that would not apply to work with any other company). The amendment was a breach of fiduciary duty because it penalized the participants' continued employment with the company without providing them with any additional benefits and was instituted without any notice to them when they were deciding whether to stay with the company or to go to work for Conrail.[178] In *New York State Teamsters Conference Pension v. Hoh*, an amendment expanded a plan provision suspending benefits for reemployment with a contributing employer after retirement to a suspension of benefits for reemployment with any employer in the industry, trade or craft, and geographic area covered by the plan, whether or not the employer was a contributing employer. Although the amendment was not "*per se* unreasonable," application of the amendment to a participant who had already retired before the amendment was arbitrary and capricious "since, to be effective, notification of rule changes, necessary to allow the employee to satisfy eligibility requirements, must be made *prior* to retirement." Without such notice, application of the amendment would "retroactively divest [Hoh] of earned benefits." The court left open whether such an amendment might still be permissible given sufficiently compelling "actuarial concerns."[179] In *McCoy v. Mesta Machine Co.*, lack of advance notice of a plan amendment that restricted eligibility for an unreduced early retirement benefit was a breach of fiduciary duty when an employee met the preamendment requirements for the early retirement benefit and could have gone ahead and retired with advance notice of the pending change. The court held that the failure of the fiduciaries "to accord any notice of [the] impending change[ ] or a period of grace to enable Plaintiff to elect to take [the] 70/80 retirement was unreasonable, and, therefore, constituted a breach of fiduciary duty."[180]

A fiduciary duty to provide advance notice of adverse plan amendments was also well-established before ERISA under Section 302(c)(5) of the LMRA and the common law of trusts, although in some decisions, the courts left an opening, as in *Hoh*, for the plan to show sufficiently compelling actuarial concerns to overcome the advance

---

[178] 5 EBC 1617 (E.D. Pa. 1984).

[179] 561 F.Supp. 679, at 684–85 (N.D.N.Y. 1982) (emphasis in original). But see *Geib v. New York Teamsters Pension Fund*, 758 F.2d 973, 6 EBC 1475 (3d Cir. 1985) (allowing the same amended suspension of benefits rule as in *Hoh* to apply to early retirees who retired before the rule was adopted).

[180] 213 BNA Pens. Rep. D-1, at D-5 (W.D. Pa. 1978), *modified*, 260 BNA Pens. Rep. D-1 (W.D. Pa. 1978). And see *Palino v. Casey*, 664 F.2d 854, 2 EBC 2169, at 2173 (1st Cir. 1981) (suggesting that notice of health benefit reduction within ERISA's pre-1986 requirement of 210 days after end of plan year in which amendment adopted would not meet fiduciary requirement of fundamental fairness); accord *Pierce v. NECA-IBEW Welfare Trust Fund*, 488 F.Supp. 559 (E.D. Tenn. 1978), *aff'd*, 620 F.2d 589, 2 EBC 2470 (6th Cir. 1980) (*per curiam*), *cert. denied*, 449 U.S. 1015 (1980). See also *Rosen v. Hotel & Restaurant Pension Fund*, 637 F.2d 592, 2 EBC 1054 (3d Cir. 1981) (denial of pension credits on account of employer's delinquency in making contributions to multiemployer plan arbitrary and capricious under ERISA because of failure to provide advance notice to employee that employer was delinquent).

Prior to a defined benefit plan termination, participants must have notice of the intent to terminate the plan—whether or not a summary of material modification is due under the 210 days after the end of the plan year rule (or after 1985, under the 15 days advance notice rule). See ch. 12, sec. II.A.

notice requirement. In *Kosty v. Lewis,* the U.S. Court of Appeals for the District of Columbia Circuit held that an employee who could have retired under an existing plan rule requiring 20 years of service had to be provided with notice and an opportunity to retire *before* a plan amendment requiring 20 years of service within the last 25 years before retirement could be put into effect. The court hesitated to find the participant's rights "vested," but stated:

> "[T]rust relationships operate within some limitations of fundamental fairness. These were ... exceeded here by the failure of the Trustees to accord any notice or grace period which would have afforded some reasonable possibility for an employee ... to have elected to retire and take the pension available immediately prior to the change.... To have made no effort at all in such direction [was] arbitrary and capricious action by those who owed him adherence to a different—and higher—standard of conduct."[181]

In addition to instances when a participant could have retired with notice, if a "new rule [is] intended to shape employees' incentives, it [can] rationally be applied only to future events."[182] In *Burroughs v. Operating Engineers Pension Fund,* application of a plan amendment altering a plan's break-in-service rule was thus "fundamentally unfair" and arbitrary and capricious when the amended rule was applied retroactively to create a break in service in a period when a participant had no notice of the new rule, and thus no opportunity to conform his service to "protect [himself] from its impact."[183] In *Agro v. Joint Plumbing Industry Board,* a plan amendment required a longer 15-year period of service with contributing employers for a pension. The amendment was arbitrary and capricious when applied to a participant who could have continued working for contributing employers to meet the new requirement if he had notice of the amendment. Instead, notice was only mailed six years after the amendment was adopted, by which time the participant had already worked for three years abroad in noncontributory service. Application of a second amendment altering the "years" component in the plan's benefit formula from years of union membership to years of contributory service was also arbitrary when the participant was not provided advance notice of this change so that he could retire under the old formula.[184] In *Norton v. IAM National Pension Fund,* a plan amendment canceling past service credits

---

[181] 319 F.2d 744, at 748 (D.C. Cir. 1963), *cert. denied,* 375 U.S. 964 (1964).

[182] 58 ALR Fed. at 210.

[183] 542 F.2d 1128, 1 EBC 1258, at 1261 (9th Cir. 1976), *cert. denied,* 429 U.S. 1096 (1977).

[184] 623 F.2d 207, 3 EBC 1036 (2d Cir. 1980). See also *Valle v. Joint Plumbing Industry Board,* 623 F.2d 196, 3 EBC 1026 (2d Cir. 1980); *Harris v. Joint Plumbing Industry Board,* 474 F.Supp. 1284 (S.D.N.Y. 1979); *Kraft v. Felder,* 452 F.Supp. 933 (S.D.N.Y. 1978); *Mitzner v. Jarcho,* 403 N.Y.S.2d 490 (Ct.App. 1978)—all involving arbitrary applications of the same undisclosed amendments to the Joint Plumbing Industry Plan.

But see *Baker v. Lukens Steel Co.,* 793 F.2d 509, 7 EBC 2039 (3d Cir. 1986) (amendment deleting early retirement benefit available on plant closing or layoff was not arbitrary and capricious under *Agro v. Joint Plumbing Industry Board* because of lack of advance notice when participants were not retroactively stripped of benefits; the essential benefit requirement of a plant closing or layoff had not occurred prior to the amendment; however, the lack of disclosure of the amendment did violate ERISA's summary of material modification requirement).

on an employer's withdrawal from a multiemployer plan was likewise arbitrary and capricious when applied to employees of an employer that had already withdrawn from the plan *before* the amendment was adopted. Application of the amendment was also arbitrary because employees of the employer who were eligible to retire were not provided with notice and an opportunity to go ahead and retire without loss of their past service credits before the employer's withdrawal.[185]

An exception to the advance notice requirement for adverse amendments arises when a participant otherwise has advance notice of an amendment. Thus, union members who were not provided with summary notice of a plan amendment by plan trustees were held to have "adequate constructive notice of the amendment as a matter of law" when they had ratified a contract containing the amendment.[186] However, no advance notice has been found when plan trustees assert that a plan amendment was discussed at union meetings, but no ratification of a contract containing the amendment occurred at the meetings and the plaintiffs testified that such discussions either did not occur or did not occur at any union meetings they attended.[187]

Courts have not been as receptive to claims of breach of fiduciary duty from lack of advance notice when plan amendments increase or improve benefits and notice is provided as required by the ERISA minimum standards. In *Lehner v. Crane Co.*, no breach of fiduciary duty was found when an employee terminated his employment without notice of a plan amendment that became effective three days later that would have increased his pension benefits from $242 per month to $440 per month.[188] In *Nostrame v. Consolidated Edison Co.*, no fiduciary duty was found to warn an employee of pending ERISA compliance

---

[185] 553 F.2d 1352 (D.C. Cir. 1977). Advance notice has also been required when a change in a participant's job duties jeopardizes benefit rights. See ch. 5, sec. III.A.4.a.

[186] *Michota v. Anheuser-Busch, Inc.*, 755 F.2d 330, 6 EBC 1161, at 1166 (3d Cir. 1985). See also *Rubin v. Decision Concepts, Inc.*, 566 F.Supp. 1057 (S.D.N.Y. 1983) (failure to distribute summary of material modification of plan not actionable when participant received memo that in combination with the SPD was enough to let him know that new plan was a restatement of former profit-sharing plan and not a second profit-sharing plan), and cases cited in ch. 8, sec. II.D (on reliance).

[187] See *Valle v. Joint Plumbing Industry Board*, 623 F.2d 196, 3 EBC 1026 (2d Cir. 1980); *Agro v. Joint Plumbing Industry Board*, 623 F.2d 207, 3 EBC 1036 (2d Cir. 1980). See also *Branch v. White*, 239 A.2d 665 (N.J. Sup.Ct. App.Div. 1968) (arbitrary and capricious to hand booklets out at union meetings, but not distribute them to employees who were not union members so that they, too, might know plan rules); *Michota v. Anheuser-Busch, Inc., supra* (concurring opinion) (emphasizing that former employees who are no longer in the bargaining unit would still not have constructive notice of a plan amendment through contract ratification); *Barrett v. Thorofare Markets, Inc.*, 452 F.Supp. 880 (W.D. Pa. 1978) (if union officials or employer mislead employees about an ambiguous plan provision during ratification process, breach of duty may occur).

[188] 448 F.Supp. 1127 (E.D. Pa. 1978). In so holding, the court emphasized that although the amendment had been in the works for some time, and had been approved by the corporation's board several days before the employee's termination, word of the amendment had not reached plant managers, and no one who knew Lehner was about to retire knew about the amendment. The court also emphasized that Lehner had given notice two weeks before his termination, so that a permanent replacement for his job could be chosen, thus making his decision to retire irreversible even if notice had been provided as soon as the amendment was adopted by the corporate board.

amendments which would have vested his accrued benefits with just five more months of service.[189]

However, if an employee inquires, or if disclosure of an employee's options is undertaken as a personnel or plan administration function, nondisclosure of pending benefit improvements may be a breach of fiduciary duty. In *Erion v. Timken Co.*, failure to disclose a pending improvement in survivor's benefits was a breach of fiduciary duty when a company posted a notice inviting employees to consult with the company's insurance office before retiring, and the benefits advisor, pursuant to an internal company policy of only responding to direct questions, remained silent and did not tell an employee about the improvement that would be available if he waited just one week to retire.[190]

VI. Exercises of Related Discretionary Authority Around an Amendment

Plan administrators and trustees sometimes retain discretionary authority to waive, alter, or circumvent an amended benefit requirement, either by express discretion, by interpretation of other open-ended terms, such as "leave of absence," or simply by a practice of making "exceptions."[191] If such discretionary authority is exercised inconsistently or discriminatorily, a breach of fiduciary duty arises. In *Valle v. Joint Plumbing Industry Board*, plan trustees thus had a duty to explain to participants that while a plan amendment required a longer 15-year period of contributory service for benefits, the trustees retained discretionary authority to waive up to two of those years for disability.[192] The trustees presumably would be required to exercise this authority under the generally applicable standards for such discretion, namely, according to the purpose of the authority, consistently with other exercises, and according to rational and nondiscriminatory criteria.[193]

In certain circumstances, a *favorable* exercise of discretionary authority after or in anticipation of a decision to amend or terminate a plan can be in breach of fiduciary duty. In *In re Braniff Airways, Inc.*, an employer planned to terminate a plan, but plan trustees retained discretionary authority under the plan's terms to grant participants lump sum payments before the date of termination. Exercise of this

---

[189] 504 F.Supp. 507, 2 EBC 1025 (S.D.N.Y. 1980). See also *Sleichter v. Monsanto Co.*, 612 F.Supp. 856 (E.D. Mo. 1985) (no duty to disclose early retirement incentive program improvements in advance of implementation; new program still in formative stage at time employee retired with no certainty of implementation, and with no misrepresentations made to the employee about the status of corporate deliberations on the program).

[190] 368 N.E.2d 312 (Ohio Ct.App. 1976).

[191] See ch. 7, sec. III.C.

[192] 623 F.2d 196, 3 EBC 1026 (2d Cir. 1980).

[193] See ch. 7, sec. III.C.1.

authority in favor of one group of participants would, however, be a breach of fiduciary duty because it would enable those participants to receive a full lump sum payment of their benefits to the detriment of remaining plan participants.[194]

VII. Unjust Enrichment From Plan Amendments

Federal courts "will not lightly create additional rights [based on unjust enrichment] under the rubric of [ERISA] federal common law" where "Congress established [such] an extensive regulatory network."[195] But unjust enrichment may be applied "to fill in interstitially or otherwise effectuate the statutory pattern enacted in the large by Congress."[196]

An amendment under "at-will" authority to amend a plan can manifest that an unamended benefit description never constituted an "offer," but was instead an "illusory promise."[197] Employees who have rendered service under an illusory promise may be entitled to recover the value of their performance if the employees will otherwise "unjustly suffer loss," or if the employer will otherwise "unjustly benefit."[198] In *McCoy v. Mesta Machine Co.*, a federal district court granted recovery for unjust enrichment when an early retirement benefit was amended under at-will authority *after* a participant met the age and service conditions for the benefit, but before he actually retired. The court stated that the "key element for [its] consideration" was not whether the benefits "vested" before retirement, but whether the employer's "retaining the benefits would be unjust" when no advance notice of the amendment had been provided so the employee would have the opportunity to retire first.[199] In *Novembre v. Local 584 Pension Fund*, unjust enrichment was applied when representatives of a plan and the sponsoring union local promised employees that the plan would be amended to provide reciprocal credits for service under a separate plan if the employees' local union merged with theirs. The

---

[194] 4 EBC 1116 (Bankr. N.D. Tex. 1982).

[195] *Van Orman v. American Ins. Co.*, 680 F.2d 301, 3 EBC 1653, at 1662 (3d Cir. 1982).

[196] *Airco Indus. Gases v. Teamsters Health & Welfare Fund*, 618 F.Supp. 943, 6 EBC 2409, at 2416 (D. Del. 1985) (quoting *Van Orman, supra*, 3 EBC at 1662, and thus finding a cause of action for an employer to recover mistaken contributions to a multiemployer plan). See generally ch. 8, sec. VI.

[197] While employers retain authority to amend pension and other fringe benefit offers at-will "[w]ith surprising frequency[, s]uch an offer is an illusory promise." J. Calamari and J. Perillo, *Contracts* (West 2d ed. 1977), at 216.

[198] *Id.*, at 570–71. Alternatively, the duty of good faith and fair dealing may be implied into the reservation of amendment authority to make the benefit offer nonillusory. See secs. III.C and III.D above.

[199] 213 BNA Pens. Rep. D-1 (W.D. Pa. 1978), *modified*, 260 BNA Pens. Rep. D-1 (W.D. Pa. 1979). In the modified order, the court continued to find the same basis for unjust enrichment, but found that the particular participant was not entitled to a recovery because his benefits under another early retirement option were greater than under the unamended option. Under the terms of the plan, he could not be entitled to both benefits.

plan's unjust enrichment was measured by the contributions received by the plan on the participants' behalf after the statements, plus interest.[200]

However, in *Amato v. Western Union International, Inc.*, a district court, addressing an at-will amendment eliminating early retirement benefits, categorically rejected an unjust enrichment claim under ERISA.[201] The participants claimed unjust enrichment because the amendment eliminated an unreduced early retirement benefit for which they had completed substantial service and which had already been fully funded as an "accrued liability" of the plan. On appeal, the Second Circuit narrowed the district court's holding, rejecting unjust enrichment only "in the circumstances of the case," and in particular, in view of the remedies the Second Circuit provided through an expansive interpretation of ERISA's protections for accrued benefits and against inurement of plan assets to the benefit of an employer. Under these circumstances, the Second Circuit saw "no need" to develop ERISA common law on unjust enrichment.[202]

VIII. Special ERISA and Code Rules on Plan Amendments

A. Partial Terminations, Noninurement, and Reversions of Excess Assets

ERISA and Internal Revenue Code provisions on partial terminations of plans resulting from amendments eliminating or reducing benefits, on noninurement of plan assets to the benefit of the employer, and against reversions of excess assets resulting from plan amendments reducing or eliminating benefits can apply when a relatively well-funded defined benefit plan is amended to eliminate or reduce benefits that technically are not protected as "accrued benefits," but that have been wholly or partly funded as "accrued liabilities" of the plan.[203] The partial termination rule can also apply to amendments to

---

[200] 4 EBC 1279 (D.N.J. 1981), *modified* (to provide more complete relief under estoppel), 4 EBC 1286 (D.N.J. 1981), *aff'd*, 4 EBC 1289 (3d Cir. 1982), *cert. denied*, 459 U.S. 1172 (1983). In *Kulins v. Malco, A Microdot Co.*, 459 N.E.2d 1038 (Ill.App. 1st Dist. 1984), promissory estoppel seemed to substitute for unjust enrichment when a severance pay plan was amended to decrease severance benefits for all years of an employee's service on the eve of a large-scale termination of employees. The amendment was estopped insofar as its application to years of service rendered before the amendment because it would "run counter to fundamental principles of equity and justice" for employees to work for years in reliance on a promise of severance benefits only to have an employer use general amendment authority to cut back its obligations immediately before they come due. 459 N.E.2d at 1045.

[201] 596 F.Supp. 621, 5 EBC 2718 (S.D.N.Y. 1984).

[202] 773 F.2d 1402, 6 EBC 2226, at 2243 (2d Cir. 1985).

[203] 26 C.F.R. 1.412(c)(3)-1(c)(1) and (f)(2) provide that all of a plan's benefits, whether or not they are "accrued benefits," must be funded as "accrued liabilities" based on the actuarial expectation of future payment.

defined contribution plans decreasing employer contributions to the plan.

At the date of this writing, *Amato v. Western Union International, Inc.*, is the only case to deal with all three of these ERISA and Code provisions. In *Amato*, MCI acquired Western Union International from Xerox through a purchase of all of Xerox's stock in the subsidiary. Immediately after taking control of Western Union, MCI used the amendment authority under the Western Union pension plan to eliminate an unreduced early retirement benefit. After the amendment, early retirement benefits were only available with a full actuarial reduction. The plaintiff-employees focused on the fact that the benefits, and in fact, the entire plan, were already funded. The amendment thus did not improve the plan's funding of other current benefit obligations to the participants, but served only to free plan assets for use in reducing MCI's subsequent contributions to the plan.[204]

1. Partial Terminations

Code Section 411(d)(3) requires that every tax-qualified plan contain a plan provision making benefits accrued nonforfeitable to the extent funded, regardless of the plan's normal vesting rules, on a "partial termination" of the plan. A plan amendment reducing benefits can constitute a "partial termination." Three ERISA committee reports state identically:

> "Examples of a partial termination might include, under certain circumstances, a large reduction in the work force, *or a sizable reduction in benefits under the plan.*"[205]

The IRS's regulations defining "partial termination" refine this to provide that when plan amendments "cease or decrease future benefit accruals under [a defined benefit] plan," and "as a result of such cessation or decrease, a potential reversion to the employer, or employers, maintaining the plan . . . is created or increased," a partial termination can occur, requiring immediate vesting of the eliminated or reduced benefits to the extent funded.[206] Without a potential reversion of excess assets, a reduction of benefits can still cause a partial termination of either a defined benefit plan or a defined contribution plan if the benefit reduction causes prohibited discrimination in favor of the

---

[204] See 596 F.Supp. 621, 5 EBC 2718 (S.D.N.Y. 1984), and 773 F.2d 1402, 6 EBC 2226 (2d Cir. 1985).

[205] S. Rep. 93-383, at 50, 1 ERISA Leg. Hist. 1118, H.R. Rep. 93-807, at 65, 2 ERISA Leg. Hist. 3185, and H.R. Rep. 93-779, at 64, 2 ERISA Leg. Hist. 2653. And see "Material in the Nature of a Committee Report Explaining H.R. 12906," introduced by Rep. Carl Perkins, chairman of the House Education and Labor Committee, 2 ERISA Leg. Hist. 3330.

[206] 26 C.F.R. 1.411(d)-2(a)(1) and (b)(2). The protection of early retirement benefits and retirement-type subsidies provided under ERISA §204(g)(2), as amended by the 1984 Retirement Equity Act, is distinguished from the partial termination right by the requirement that the affected participants' benefits must vest immediately on a partial termination, to the extent funded. In contrast, under §204(g)(2), benefits vest when the original conditions for the benefit have been fulfilled, but with no "to the extent funded" limitation. See ch. 4, sec. IV.B.3.

highly compensated employees in the plan, or increases the potential for such discrimination.[207]

On the partial termination claim in *Amato* (based on the employer's amendment eliminating unreduced early retirement benefits), the district court first held that a partial termination could only vest "accrued benefits." Then, assuming *arguendo* that the early retirement benefits were accrued benefits, or that a partial termination was not so limited, the court still refused to consider the IRS regulations on when a partial termination occurs, relying on the Third Circuit's decision in *United Steelworkers v. Harris & Sons Steel Co.* for the proposition that tax regulations cannot be used to interpret the contractual requirements of a plan.[208] On appeal, the Second Circuit reversed, holding that it was error to ignore the IRS regulations and rulings on partial terminations. The Second Circuit also held that if a partial termination did occur from the amendment, it was not necessary for the benefits to be "accrued benefits." Rather the early retirement benefits would become nonforfeitable to the extent funded at the time of the amendment as determined under an ERISA Section 4044 termination allocation of the plan's assets, as provided under the plan.[209]

A number of other types of amendments reducing benefits can potentially result in partial terminations. Before ERISA, "freezing" a defined benefit plan, that is, halting all future benefit accruals, but permitting years of service to continue to count for vesting, was considered a benefit curtailment partial termination.[210] Under ERISA, a

---

[207] See 26 C.F.R. 1.411(d)-2(b)(1) and IRS Doc. 6678, "Plan Termination Standards" (4-81), reprinted at ¶107,402 P-H Pension & Profit Sharing.

[208] 596 F.Supp. 621, 5 EBC 2718 (S.D.N.Y. 1984). And see *United Steelworkers v. Harris & Sons Steel Co.*, 706 F.2d 1289, 4 EBC 1396 (3d Cir. 1983). A more general discussion of the significance of *Harris & Sons* is contained in the ch. 7 section on the use of relevant administrative agency regulations and rulings in plan interpretation.

[209] For this purpose, the liabilities for the early retirement benefits are placed under priority category (6) as other forfeitable benefits offered under the plan. The court stated that in this manner "as long as assets [are] available, they [will] be used to meet participants' benefit expectations based upon the Plan's full benefit structure [before the amendment]." *Amato v. Western Union Int'l, Inc.*, 773 F.2d 1402, 6 EBC 2226, at 2240 (2d Cir. 1985). The Second Circuit did not discuss *exactly* how the plan's liabilities for the forfeitable early retirement benefits would be calculated, or how the benefits would be paid on an individual basis, but the plaintiffs contended they should receive fractions, e.g., 70/75 of the unreduced early retirement benefit if a participant had 70 of the required 75 points for the benefit at the time of the amendment.

See also ch. 12, sec. IV.A, for a brief discussion of methods for valuing early retirement benefit liabilities. The interest rate used in computing the present value of the plan's benefit liabilities is also a critical element in determining the extent benefits are funded on a partial termination. See ch. 11, sec. I.E.

Procedural avenues for enforcing partial termination requirements are discussed in ch. 11, sec. I.F. One distinctive feature from the discussion there is that on a plan amendment reducing benefits, the sponsoring employer generally files an application for a determination of the plan's tax-qualified status, thereby giving participants an opportunity to file comments on the partial termination issue within 45 days after the application is filed. If the IRS does not declare a partial termination, review of the adverse determination may be sought in the U.S. Tax Court. In addition to this route, participants can bring suit in federal district court under ERISA §§502(a)(1)(B) and (a)(3) to enforce the plan terms that require benefits to be nonforfeitable on a partial termination (as occurred in *Amato, supra*).

[210] See C. Gilchrist, 312 Tax Mgmt. (BNA), "(ERISA)—Plan Terminations: Corporate Acquisitions," at A-5.

partial termination generally occurs only if the freeze creates or increases a potential reversion to the employer.[211] If a freeze results in greater forfeitures of benefits by rank and file employees, which serve primarily to secure the benefits of prohibited group employees, a partial termination can also occur.[212] A sharp reduction in the level of future benefit accruals under a plan, such as by an increase in a Social Security offset, an increase in the covered compensation level used under an excess plan, or the introduction of employee contributions into a previously noncontributory plan, are other candidates for partial termination declarations.[213]

A partial termination can also occur on the reduction of an employer's contribution obligation to a money purchase pension plan. In IRS Document 6678, the IRS states that an amendment ceasing future contributions to a money purchase pension plan, without terminating the plan *per se*, can create a potential reversion because future forfeitures may then go directly to the employer, rather than being used to reduce future employer contributions *to the plan*. A less steep reduction in contributions to a money purchase plan could also result in a partial termination if it is likely that the forfeitures in any future year will exceed the reduced level of employer contributions.

A reduction in contributions to a profit-sharing plan resulting in, or accompanied by, an increase in forfeitures allocated to the prohibited group of employees, can also result in a partial termination. In Revenue Ruling 73-535, the IRS examined whether a reduction in an employer's profit-sharing contributions from 15 percent of participant compensation to six percent resulted in a partial termination. The IRS concluded that no partial termination occurred because the plan's participation requirement had concomitantly been reduced from five years of service to one year, with the result that participation in the plan nearly doubled and the employer's total contributions to the plan actually increased. But "by implication, the ruling suggests that the reduction in the contribution formula by itself would have been a partial termination."[214]

2. *Noninurement*

ERISA Section 403(c)(1) provides that "the assets of [a] plan shall never *inure* to the benefit of any employer."[215] When benefits that have

---

[211] IRS Doc. 6678, "Plan Termination Standards" (4-81).

[212] *Id.*

[213] See S. Lewis, "Partial Terminations of Qualified Plans—An Evolving Doctrine," 13 Comp. Plan. J. 223 (July 5, 1985).

[214] *Id.*, 13 Comp. Plan. J. at 227.

[215] Emphasis added. Express exceptions to ERISA §403(c)(1) permit assets to "inure" to the benefit of an employer on termination of a plan if the conditions in §4044 are satisfied, and also permit "mistaken" contributions and overpayments of withdrawal liability to be returned to an employer within certain periods.

been fully or partially funded as accrued liabilities of a plan are reduced, the assets already contributed for those benefits can inure to the benefit of the employer either as a set-off against subsequent employer contributions to the plan or as a potential reversion.

In *Amato*, the employer's amendment eliminating early retirement benefits that were already funded caused plan assets to "inure" to the benefit of the employer within the dictionary definition of "to become of advantage."[216] The previously contributed assets could serve after the amendment as a reserve or set-off against the employer's future contribution obligations under the plan or might revert to the employer on a plan termination. However, the district court concluded it would be "anomalous" if ERISA's noninurement protection served to protect benefits that were not directly protected as "accrued benefits" under ERISA. The district court added that if such an amendment were permissible when a plan is underfunded, but prohibited as inurement of assets when the plan is well-funded, this might encourage underfunding of plans. On appeal, the Second Circuit disagreed and held that "inurement" means to "become of advantage," as provided in the dictionary, stating:

> "[Section 403(c)(1)] protects the policy interest that employers not be permitted to eliminate certain kinds of non-accrued benefits solely for the purpose of using existing [plan] assets to meet other obligations under the pension plan."

The court was "unpersuaded" by the district court's argument that finding inurement might encourage underfunding in view of the floor established by ERISA's minimum funding requirements.[217]

3. Reversions of Excess Assets Resulting From Plan Amendments

IRS regulations on the recovery by an employer of excess assets on a plan termination arising from "erroneous actuarial computations" provide that excess assets that may potentially revert to an employer cannot include any excess assets "accumulated as a result of a change in the benefit provisions or in the eligibility requirements of the plan."[218] In *Amato*, neither the district court nor the Second Circuit applied this rule to the employer's elimination of the plan's unreduced

---

[216] *Webster's New Collegiate Dictionary* (1975 ed.).

[217] 773 F.2d 1402, 6 EBC 2226, at 2238 (2d Cir. 1985). See also *Hickerson v. Velsicol Chemical Corp.*, 778 F.2d 365, 6 EBC 2545 (7th Cir. 1985), *cert. denied*, 479 U.S. ___ (1986) (employer amending plan has fiduciary duty to avoid suggestion of "self-interested plan administration" and inurement of plan assets to employer's benefit; therefore in amending profit-sharing plan to convert it to defined benefit plan, earnings on account balances existing at time of amendment must not be fixed at below market rates of interest without allowing participants the opportunity to withdraw the funds from their accounts). But see *United Steelworkers 2116 v. Cyclops Corp.*, 653 F.Supp. 574, 8 EBC 1194 (S.D. Ohio 1987) (no inurement to seller of business in transfering share of plan assets with accrued liabilities allocable to transferred employees to plan of buyer).

[218] 26 C.F.R. 1.401-2(b)(1).

early retirement benefit because no plan termination had occurred. The district court, however, emphasized:

> "Treas. Reg. 1.401-2(b)(1) provides that, upon termination, an employer may recover any balance remaining in the fund as a result of *actuarial error* . . . , but [it] may *not* recover [that part of] a surplus that has accumulated 'as a result of a change in the benefit provisions or in the eligibility requirements of the plan.'"[219]

On appeal, the Second Circuit did not comment on the issue. But the Second Circuit's decision on inurement establishes virtually the same limitation.[220]

B. Plan Merger and Asset or Liability Transfer Rules

1. Single-Employer Plans

Plan amendments merging two plans or transferring assets and benefit liabilities of some participants from one plan to another can dilute the security of participants' benefits as measured by the difference in the amount of the benefits that would be paid them if the plan terminated immediately before or immediately after the plan merger or asset or liability transfer. For example, when a plan that is 100 percent (or fully) funded for all its accrued liabilities is merged with a 50 percent funded plan, as may occur after the acquisition of a business, the security of the benefits of the participants in the fully-funded plan may be diluted.

But, as one commentator has written, "[t]he drafters of ERISA, being aware that the rights of employees were often being sacrificed in the process of a corporate acquisition or reorganization, included a provision to protect those rights."[221] ERISA Section 208, and Code Section 414(l), thus provide that:

> "A pension plan may not merge or consolidate with, or transfer its assets or liabilities to, any other plan . . . unless each participant in the plan would (if the plan then terminated) receive a benefit immediately after the merger, consolidation, or transfer which is equal to or greater than the benefit he would have been entitled to receive immediately before the merger, consolidation, or transfer (if the plan had then terminated). . . ."[222]

Representative Al Ullman, the Chairman of the House Ways and Means Committee, explained this requirement in the floor debate on ERISA:

---

[219] 5 EBC at 2724 n.7 (emphasis in original). And see generally *Lynch v. Dawson Collieries, Inc.*, 485 S.W.2d 494 (Ky. 1972); *Kruzynski v. Richards Brothers Punch Co.*, 211 BNA Pens. Rep. D-8 (E.D. Mich. 1978); *Pollock v. Castrovinci*, 476 F.Supp. 606, 1 EBC 2091 (S.D.N.Y. 1979), *aff'd*, 622 F.2d 575 (2d Cir. 1980).

[220] See *Amato v. Western Union Int'l, Inc.*, 773 F.2d 1402, 6 EBC 2226, at 2238 (2d Cir. 1985).

[221] L. Kilian, "Analyzing the Effects of a Merger, Acquisition or Spin-Off on a Qualified Retirement Plan," 55 J. Tax. (July 1981), at 36.

[222] Code §401(a)(12) requires the same language to appear in all tax-qualified plans.

"Provision is made to prevent mergers and consolidations of plans from reducing the rights of participants. This is achieved by specifying that immediately after the merger each participant would be entitled to receive a benefit equal to or greater than the benefit he would have been entitled to receive immediately before the merger had the plan been terminated."[223]

ERISA Section 208 and the legislative history can be read as bestowing a permanent right to plan assets under the preamendment schedule in the event of any subsequent termination. However, the IRS's regulations provide that while a merged plan must construct, or maintain the data to construct, a special allocation schedule, if the plan does not terminate within five years after the merger, the special allocation schedule may be disregarded and the records for it thrown away.[224] The special allocation schedule is not required to be maintained at all if a plan merger occurs and the sum of the assets of both plans is greater than the sum of the present value of both plans' accrued benefits.[225]

For a spin-off of part of the benefit liabilities of a plan to a new plan (e.g., in conjunction with the spin-off of a subsidiary), the regulations provide that assets must actually be allocated to the spun off plan equal to the termination basis value of the benefits of the participants who are to be under the new plan.[226] For this purpose, "benefits on a termination basis" include not only all accrued benefits under the plan, but also the actuarial value of all early retirement benefits for which the age or service requirements are not complete, as well as the actuarial value of preretirement survivor's annuity coverage.[227] A special allocation schedule need not be maintained in this instance because the termination basis allocation must actually occur in the process of spinning off the plan.

When benefit liabilities are transferred to another existing plan, the transfer is broken into two steps for purposes of the regulations. First, the transfer is treated as a spin-off of a new plan. Assets are therefore required to be allocated to participants' benefits on a termination basis. Second, the transfer of these assets and the associated benefit liabilities to the second plan is treated as a merger of the spin-off plan plan and the second plan. This requires that a special allocation schedule be maintained for the new participants, based on the assets that they are bringing into the plan; for the existing participants, a schedule is required based on the assets that are in the plan

---

[223] 2 ERISA Leg. Hist. 3429. See also H.R. Rep. 93-779, at 28, 2 ERISA Leg. Hist. 2617, H.R. Rep. 93-807, at 29, 2 ERISA Leg. Hist. 3149, Material in the Nature of a Committee Report Explaining H.R. 12906, 2 ERISA Leg. Hist. 3318, and Conf. Rep., at 385, 3 ERISA Leg. Hist. 4652.

[224] 26 C.F.R. 1.414(l)-1(e), (i), and (j).

[225] 26 C.F.R. 1.414(l)-1(e).

[226] 26 C.F.R. 1.414(l)-1(n)(1).

[227] *Id.*, and see 26 C.F.R. 1.414(l)-1(b)(5) and Rev. Rul. 86-48. Note that ERISA §208 and Code §414(l) both provide protection for the "benefit" a participant would have been entitled to receive on a termination, not just for the portion of the "accrued benefit" the participant would be entitled to receive.

before the transfer actually occurs. These special schedules may be disregarded if the transferee plan does not terminate within the succeeding five years.[228]

2. Multiemployer Plans

Mergers of multiemployer plans and transfers of benefit liabilities or assets from one multiemployer plan to another can also occur when local unions merge or spin-off, or when employees change collective bargaining representatives.

Originally, ERISA Section 208 was to apply to multiemployer plan mergers and interplan asset and liability transfers "to the extent determined by the Pension Benefit Guaranty Corporation." The PBGC, however, never issued the regulations. When MPPAA was enacted in 1980, Congress filled the void by establishing four requirements under Section 4231 of ERISA Title IV for mergers or transfers of assets or liabilities between two multiemployer plans:

(1) Notice must be given the PBGC 120 days before the merger or transfer;

(2) An actuarial valuation of the assets and benefit liabilities of each plan must be made before the merger or transfer;

(3) No participant or beneficiary's "accrued benefits" may be lower immediately after the effective date than before; and

(4) Neither plan's benefits may be "reasonably expected" to become subject to suspension under the insolvency provisions established by MPPAA.[229]

Section 4231 alters the protection against dilution found in ERISA for single-employer plan participants. Under Section 4231, a participant's accrued benefit must not be lowered, but a special allocation schedule in the event of a subsequent termination is not required to be maintained. Instead, the requirement that neither of the plans' benefits may reasonably be expected to become subject to suspension under the multiemployer plan insolvency rules substitutes for more direct protection against dilution.

The period during which benefits may not be reasonably expected to become subject to the insolvency provisions is not specified in the

---

[228] 26 C.F.R. 1.414(l)-1(o). And see *United Steelworkers 2116 v. Cyclops Corp.*, 653 F.Supp. 574, 8 EBC 1194 (S.D. Ohio 1987) (buyer and seller complied with §208 asset and liability transfer rules when each participant would receive a benefit immediately after the transfer equal to or greater than the benefit he or she would have received immediately before). But compare *Dougherty v. Chrysler Motors Corp.*, 8 EBC 1217 (E.D. Mich. 1987) (plan complied with §208 when pension liability and assets sufficient to provide "accrued benefits" transferred to different plan).

[229] See 29 C.F.R. 2672 for the PBGC's regulations under ERISA §4231, and 29 C.F.R. 2670.3 for related definitions. "*De minimis*" plan mergers and asset or liability transfers are exempt from these rules. See 29 C.F.R. 2672.6 for definition of *de minimis.* Even if not *de minimis*, the multiemployer asset and liability transfer rules do not apply to transfers under reciprocity agreements. ERISA §4234(c).

statute, but it is specified in PBGC regulations as five years.[230] The regulations provide a safe harbor under which plans that are parties to a *transfer* of assets and liabilities will not be considered to be reasonably expected to become subject to the insolvency provisions within five years if:

(1) The transferor and the transferee plan are expected to satisfy minimum funding standards (including reorganization funding standards if applicable) for the first five plan years after the transfer;
(2) Each plan's assets immediately after the transfer are sufficient to meet expected benefit payments in the first five years after the transfer;
(3) Contributions to each plan in the first plan year after the transfer are expected to be sufficient to meet benefit payments in the year without drawing on any other plan assets; and
(4) Future contributions are expected to equal both unfunded accrued benefits and future normal costs.[231]

Plan mergers and "non-significant" asset and liability transfers are not subject to this safe harbor.[232] But they are subject to a special rule under which the plan, or plans in the case of a nonsignificant transfer, are not considered to be reasonably expected to become subject to the insolvency provisions if:

(1) The fair market value of plan assets immediately after the merger, or nonsignificant transfer, equals or exceeds five times the benefit payments in the last plan year ending before the effective date of the merger; or
(2) Expected plan assets plus expected plan contributions and investment earnings exceed expected benefit payments and expenses in each of the first five plan years beginning after the effective date of the merger or transfer.[233]

A separate statutory section, ERISA Section 4232, applies to mergers, spin-offs, and transfers of assets and liabilities between multiemployer and single-employer plans. After such a merger, spin-off, or transfer, no participant's "accrued benefit" may be lower than before. When a single-employer plan is spun off from a multiemployer plan, the multiemployer plan must also remain liable in the event of a termination within a period of five years for the lesser of (1) the unfunded benefit liabilities spun off by the multiemployer plan or (2) the spun off plan's remaining insufficiency to the PBGC after assessment of up to 30 percent of the single-employer plan sponsor's net worth.

---

[230] 29 C.F.R. 2672.5(a).

[231] *Id.* While ERISA §4231 does not expressly include the reasonable expectation of a benefit reduction in reorganization, the safe harbor tests bear on this possibility.

[232] "Non-significant" is defined in 29 C.F.R. 2670.3.

[233] 29 C.F.R. 2672.5(b).

MPPAA added unique new rules *requiring* transfers of assets and liabilities if there is a certified change in the collective bargaining representative of employees covered by a multiemployer plan and as a result of the change those employees will participate in a different multiemployer plan. A change in collective bargaining representatives generally results in either a complete or partial withdrawal of the employer from the plan and thus triggers withdrawal liability for the employer. However, under ERISA Section 4235, the plan from which the employer is withdrawing as a result of the change in bargaining representation must transfer the assets and liabilities attributable to nonforfeitable benefits of the employer's bargaining unit employees to the employees' new multiemployer plan.[234] If the transfer involves an excess of liabilities over assets, the amount of the employer's withdrawal liability is reduced by the excess. The transferee plan may appeal the transfer to the PBGC on the ground that it will incur "substantial harm as a result" of the transfer (i.e., if the liabilities to be transferred are well in excess of the assets).[235]

In addition to review for compliance with the statutory provisions on multiemployer plan mergers and asset and liability transfers, the decisions of multiemployer plan trustees who initiate or approve a merger or asset and liability transfer are subject to review for breach of fiduciary duty if they have not acted "solely in the interest" of their own participants and beneficiaries as required by ERISA Section 404(a)(1).[236] In contrast, the protection of the fiduciary standard of duty may, or may not, be present in a merger or transfer of assets and liabilities between two single-employer plans, depending on whether the court views the sponsoring employers' actions in amending the plans to provide for such a merger or asset and liability transfer to be fiduciary functions.

---

[234] And see generally *TIME-DC, Inc. v. ILA Local 1730 Management-Labor Welfare & Pension Funds,* 756 F.2d 939, 6 EBC 1374 (2d Cir. 1985).

[235] ERISA §4235(b)(3). And see *IAM Nat'l Pension Fund v. Central States Pension Fund,* 643 F.Supp. 746, 7 EBC 2600 (D.D.C. 1986) (multiemployer plan can only contest transfer of liabilities and assets to it after certified change in collective bargaining representative within the prescribed 60-day period after notice of the pending transfer). Certain other exceptions are also provided. See §§4235(e)(1) and (f).

[236] ERISA §4231, as amended by MPPAA, was expressly intended to reverse the result in *Cutaiar v. Marshall,* 590 F.2d 523, 1 EBC 2153 (3d Cir. 1979), in which a transfer of assets between a pension plan and a related welfare plan was held to violate the *per se* prohibitions on transactions between plan fiduciaries and related parties in interest in ERISA §406. However, the general ERISA §404(a)(1) standard of fiduciary duty was not intended to be overridden.

10

Protection Against Interference With Benefit Rights and Discrimination

I. ERISA Section 510

A. Interference With the Attainment of Pension Rights

ERISA Section 510 has potentially very broad application to individual and classwide discharges and layoffs, plant closings, corporate sales and mergers, and restrictive plan amendments that have been timed to interfere with the attainment of benefit rights under a plan. Under Section 510:

> "It shall be unlawful for any person to discharge, fire, suspend, expel, discipline, or discriminate against a participant or beneficiary . . . for the purpose of interfering with the attainment of any right to which such participant may become entitled under the plan [or] this title . . . ."[1]

The chief advantage for participants of Section 510 over the fiduciary standard in ERISA Section 404(a)(1) is that it is not conditioned on the function—e.g., the act of discharging or laying off employees, or amending a plan—being a "fiduciary" function. Instead, the cause of action is against any "person" who performs one of the enumerated actions "for the purpose of interfering" with the attainment of pension or other employee benefit rights.[2] Section 510 is, moreover, a remedial provision which is to be liberally construed.[3] Whether a discharge or

---

[1] 29 U.S.C. §1140.

[2] "Person" is defined in ERISA §3(9) as any "individual, partnership, joint venture, corporation, mutual company, joint-stock company, trust, estate, unincorporated organization, association, or employee organization."

[3] *Kross v. Western Elec. Co.*, 701 F.2d 1238, 4 EBC 1265 (7th Cir. 1983).

other discrimination violates fiduciary obligations or contractual rights is not dispositive of whether a Section 510 violation has occurred,[4] although some courts would require a participant to exhaust all contractual remedies before pursuing a Section 510 action.[5]

Section 510 applies to interference with the attainment of *any* rights under an employee benefit plan, not just the attainment of the minimum vesting rights created under Title I of ERISA. Thus, interference with the attainment of a right to unreduced early retirement benefits requiring 30 years of service, or interference with the attainment of rights under a long-term disability or health care plan, is prohibited under Section 510 to the same extent as interference with the attainment of the vested rights required under ERISA Section 203.[6] Section 510 is also broad in scope in that it applies to discharges or other discrimination which occurred after September 2, 1974, but before the ERISA Title I minimum standards generally became effective in 1976.[7] Section 510 also protects participants from retaliation "for exercising any right" under a plan or under Title I, such as the right to file a claim or a lawsuit, or to request documents from a plan.[8]

The focus of Section 510 is on interference with the attainment of benefit rights under a plan. In *McClendon v. Continental Group, Inc.*, a district court said that Section 510 prohibits discrimination on the basis of "one's proximity to [eligibility for employee] benefits."[9] In *Lojek v. Thomas*, the Ninth Circuit discussed this focus further:

> "ERISA's legislative history ... reveals that Congress was concerned with the acts of unscrupulous employers who discharged and harassed their employees in order to keep them from obtaining vested pension rights. Senator Hartke, speaking in support of sanctions for interference with protected rights made it clear:
>
> 'Most collective bargaining agreements protect employees against discharge without good cause and provide effective enforcement machinery in arbitration proceedings whose results are enforceable under section 301 of the Labor-Management Relations Act. But roughly half of all pension participants are not unionized and so they lack protection. Especially vulnerable are managers and executives whose substantial pension

---

[4] *Amaro v. Continental Can Co.*, 724 F.2d 747, 5 EBC 1215 (9th Cir. 1984); *Gavalik v. Continental Can Co.*, 3 EBC 1311 (W.D. Pa. 1982); *Kross v. Western Elec. Co., supra.*

[5] See ch. 14, sec. I.A.

[6] See *Ursic v. Bethlehem Steel*, 4 EBC 1537 (W.D. Pa. 1983), *aff'd*, 719 F.2d 670, 4 EBC 2297 (3d Cir. 1983) (interference with 30-year unreduced early retirement pension prohibited); *Folz v. Marriott Corp.*, 594 F.Supp. 1007, 5 EBC 2244 (W.D. Mo. 1984) (interference with attainment of rights to long-term disability and health care benefits prohibited).

[7] *Baeten v. Van Ess*, 474 F.Supp. 1324, 1 EBC 2046 (E.D. Wis. 1976).

[8] See *McGinnis v. Joyce*, 507 F.Supp. 654, 2 EBC 1485 (N.D. Ill. 1981) (suit alleging retaliation for exercise of ERISA rights to information about employers contributing to multiemployer plan). But see *Bittner v. Sadoff & Rudoy Indus.*, 728 F.2d 820, 5 EBC 2670 (7th Cir. 1984) (employee fired for seeking damages for emotional distress and punitive damages not discharged for exercise of rights *under ERISA* because court found these remedies are not available under ERISA and employer would not have fired the employee based on filing of benefit claim alone).

[9] 602 F.Supp. 1492, 6 EBC 1113, at 1121 (D.N.J. 1985).

potentialities provide an incentive to their discharge before vesting.' "[10]

The "unscrupulous" action of discharging employees to interfere with the attainment of rights under a plan can be very business-like and without personal animus to individual employees. Any cliffs in vesting where an employee is entitled to nothing one day, and the next day to a benefit worth several thousand dollars, present economic incentives for interference. When a large group of employees are all about to become vested in a benefit at approximately the same time (e.g., because they were all hired at about the same time), an employer's economic incentives for interference multiply, and potentially can tip the scales in a decision about when to close a marginally profitable facility or department.[11]

The Senate Finance Committee and the House Ways and Means Committee recognized the potential for abuse when vesting is based on cliff schedules, and for this reason originally favored only gradual vesting schedules, which were seen as attenuating an employer's incentives to discharge or layoff employees just before they became vested.[12] In the final Act, however, cliff vesting schedules were permitted under the minimum standards, and also were allowed for benefits such as unreduced early retirement benefits that are not required to vest according to the minimum standard schedules. The incentives for abuse under such cliffs were left to be controlled by Section 510.

Discharges and permanent or indefinite layoffs are the "prototypical" means by which an employer or other person may attempt to interfere with the attainment of rights to which a participant is about to become eligible.[13] In addition, as Senator Vance Hartke stated in the floor debates, Section 510 also covers "constructive discharges," e.g., making working conditions so intolerable that the employee will be forced to leave, if the loss of pension or other employee benefits is a motivating factor for the employer's actions.[14] Section 510 "discrimination" can also arise from a failure to recall or rehire employees if the selection of employees for recall or rehire is to interfere with the

---

[10] 716 F.2d 675, 4 EBC 2321, at 2326 (9th Cir. 1983) (emphasis omitted). Senator Hartke's statement appears at 2 ERISA Leg. Hist. 1774-75. See also S.Rep. 93-127, at 35-36, 1 ERISA Leg. Hist. 621-22, 2 ERISA Leg. Hist. 1641 and 1811, and 3 ERISA Leg. Hist. 4753 (statements of Senator Javits on the purpose of §510), 3 ERISA Leg. Hist. 4745 (statement of Senator Williams), and 2 ERISA Leg. Hist. 3491 (statement of Rep. Wright).

[11] Smaller amounts can also affect the timing of discharges. See GAO, "Tax Revenues Lost and Beneficiaries Inadequately Protected When Pension Plans Terminate" (GAO/HRD 81-117 September 30, 1981), at 14-17 (describing instances where participants appear to have been discharged shortly before vesting in profit-sharing contributions, with the forfeitures going to the officers who discharged them, but not mentioning ERISA §510 as a potential remedy).

[12] See S.Rep. 93-383, at 20 and 46, 1 ERISA Leg. Hist. 1088 and 1114, and H.R. Rep. 93-807, at 55, 2 ERISA Leg. Hist. 3175.

[13] *Goins v. Teamsters Local 639*, 598 F.Supp. 1151, at 1154 (D.D.C. 1984).

[14] 2 ERISA Leg. Hist. 1174-75. Constructive discharges to interfere with rights have also been recognized in court cases as potential §510 claims, but the facts presented in the cases have not established §510 violations. See *Lojek v. Thomas*, *supra* (recognizing §510 claim but concluding employee not constructively discharged); *Donnelly v. Aetna Life Insurance Co.*, 465 F.Supp. 696 (E.D. Pa. 1979) (same); *Crouch v. Mo-Kan Iron Workers Welfare Fund*, 740 F.2d 805, 5 EBC 1971 (10th Cir. 1984) (remanding for determination of facts).

attainment of rights under a plan (even if the initial layoff or discharge was not for this purpose). In *Baeten v. Van Ess*, it was alleged, but not proven, that discrimination in a company's rehiring of strikers was to interfere with the attainment of pension rights.[15] In *Franci v. Avco Corp.*, it was alleged and proven in an ADEA action that older employees whose fringe benefit costs were higher were discriminated against in recalls.[16]

Section 510 can likewise apply to a suspension, expulsion, disciplinary action, or any other form of discrimination, which is "for the purpose" of interfering with pension rights. However, only one of these, that no person shall "discriminate" against a participant or beneficiary is susceptible to broad interpretation. The others all concern specific changes in the employment relationship. In *West v. Butler*, the Sixth Circuit held that "discriminate" is to be interpreted in the same manner, that is, the discrimination must affect the employment relationship "in some substantial way." Measured under this standard, secondary picketing of a coal mine was not purposeful interference with the attainment of pension rights, even though it caused the mine to cut back production, and thus reduced employer contributions to a plan that were based on each ton of coal mined. According to the Sixth Circuit, Section 510's reference to discrimination was "aimed solely at protecting individual rights," rather than overall "fiscal integrity" or "financial security" of pension funds. Therefore, secondary picketing was not "the threat [to employee benefit rights] Congress sought to address when it enacted §510."[17] Somewhat similarly, in *Phillips v. Amoco Oil Co.*, it was not discrimination under Section 510 for an employer to agree to the sale of a division on terms that did not provide for a continuation of benefits that division employees had not yet vested in when the sale of the division was motivated by "legitimate business concerns" and Section 510 creates no duty for the employer to sell the division only on terms that protect the employees' "inchoate" pension interests.[18] But a Section 510 claim is stated by an allegation that an employer reduced monthly salaries in anticipation of a mass layoff that would cause severance benefits to become due based on the employees' last month's salary.[19]

As discussed below, Section 510 can also apply in some circumstances to plan amendments made in anticipation of the attainment of rights.

---

15 474 F.Supp. 1324, 1 EBC 2046 (E.D. Wis. 1976).

16 538 F.Supp. 250 (D. Conn. 1982).

17 621 F.2d 240, 2 EBC 1985, at 1990 (6th Cir. 1980).

18 614 F.Supp. 694, at 722 and 723 (N.D. Ala. 1985) *aff'd.* 799 F.2d 1464, 7 EBC 2246 (11th Cir. 1986). And see *West v. Greyhound Corp.*, 813 F.2d 951, 8 EBC 1569 (9th Cir. 1987) (no §510 violation in successor employer's refusal to hire union employees who had refused to agree to concessions in pension benefits for predecessor employer). See also *Goins v. Teamsters Local 639 Pension Fund*, 598 F.Supp. 1151 (D.D.C. 1984) (alleged misrepresentation of benefits by union business agent not actionable under §510).

19 *Ahne v. Allis Chalmers Corp.*, 640 F.Supp. 912 (E.D. Wis. 1986).

B. Proof That an Action Was "For the Purpose of Interfering"

The Ninth Circuit offered this observation about age discrimination claims in *Cancellier v. Federated Department Stores*:

> "Because the attribute [age] with which the statute is concerned comes to each of us in time, it will inevitably be present in a multitude of employee discharges. It will be a factor in many and a determining factor in some. It is only this last group that can obtain relief under the ADEA, even though, in the broad sense it aims to benefit the entire aged employment force."[20]

The same observation can be made for Section 510 actions. Section 510 is not a panacea for every employee who was ever discharged just short of vesting in a normal or early retirement benefit.

The major legal issue under Section 510 is the showing of "purpose" needed to establish a violation. When a discharge, layoff, plant closing, or plan amendment occurs shortly before an employee was to become entitled to a benefit, a complaint may be drafted alleging that the occurrence, or at least the timing, of the action was to interfere with the proximate attainment of pension rights. From there, whether the "purpose" of interference must be exclusive, primary, or just a factor in the timing or occurrence of the action to violate Section 510 is the critical element that is not directly spelled out in the statute or in the ERISA committee reports.

The floor debates on ERISA, however, describe the required "purpose" in more detail. Senator Jacob Javits analogized Section 510's protections to those existing for race and sex discrimination. Under Title VII, race or sex does not have to be the "sole" basis for discrimination, but rather must be a "but-for" cause.[21] Senator Hartke stated that Section 510 was designed to parallel Section 8(a)(3) of the NLRA,[22] which provides that it shall be an unfair labor practice to discriminate "in regard to hire or tenure . . . or any term or condition of employment to encourage or discourage [union] membership." Under Section 8(a)(3), as with race and sex discrimination, the discriminatory purpose is not required to be the "sole" purpose, but must be a "substantial" or "motivating" factor in the action. As an affirmative defense, the employer may then show by a preponderance of the evidence that the same decision or action would have occurred in the absence of any interfering purpose.[23]

Case law under ERISA on the "purpose" required to establish a Section 510 violation has been slow in developing. Under Section 510, it was first established that the participant has the burden of proof.[24]

---

[20] 672 F.2d 1312, at 1316 (9th Cir. 1982), *cert. denied*, 459 U.S. 859 (1982).

[21] See 2 ERISA Leg. Hist. 1641 and *McDonald v. Santa Fe Trail Transp. Co.*, 427 U.S. 273, at 282 n.10 (1976); *Albemarle Paper Co. v. Moody*, 422 U.S. 405, at 425 (1975).

[22] 2 ERISA Leg. Hist. 1774–75.

[23] *NLRB v. Transp. Management Corp.*, 462 U.S. 393, at 400–01 (1983).

[24] *Dependahl v. Falstaff Brewing Corp.*, 491 F.Supp. 1188 (E.D. Mo. 1980), *modified on other grounds*, 653 F.2d 1208, 2 EBC 1521 (8th Cir. 1981), *cert. denied*, 454 U.S. 1084 (1981); *Baeten v.*

What that burden is directed to showing has been described in more detail in some cases. In *Titsch v. Reliance Group, Inc.*, a district court found that the loss of pension benefits must be a "motivating factor behind [the] termination of employment," and not a "mere consequence." But at the same time, it need not be the "sole" or "single" motivation.[25] In *Watkinson v. A&P Co.*, no cause of action was held to exist if a "mere consequence" of a discharge is a loss of pension benefits. Instead, the plaintiff must show "specific intent" of the employer or other person to interfere with the attainment of pension rights. In *Watkinson*, "specific intent" was defined by reference to the *Titsch* statement that the plaintiff must show that the loss of pension benefits was a "motivating factor . . . behind the termination."[26] In *Gavalik v. Continental Can Co.*, the Third Circuit relied on *Titsch* and *Watkinson* in holding that Section 510 does not require plaintiffs to show that they would have retained their jobs "but for" the consideration of their impending benefit entitlement. Rather, it is sufficient to show that interference with their benefit entitlement was a determinative factor in the layoffs.[27]

A stricter test than the "determining" or "motivating factor" test may apply for plan amendments. In *Aronson v. Servus Rubber Division*, plaintiffs claimed that a plan amendment ending their participation in a plan after their plant was sold, but while some of the plant's employees were still employed in winding up operations, was for the purpose of interfering with their right to a year-end allocation of profit-sharing contributions under the plan. The First Circuit stated that since plan amendments almost inevitably interfere with the attainment of someone's rights, the plaintiffs would have to show "invidious intent," a standard it did not define precisely. However, the court did suggest that Section 510 could cover a plan amendment where the employer was "discriminatorily modif[ying] the plan, intentionally benefitting, or injuring, certain identified employees or a certain group of employees." In *Aronson* the line established by the independent business decision to sell the plant's assets with only 11 of 64 employees thereafter remaining employed in winding up operations, provided a "readily apparent business justification" for the amendment that was sufficient to counteract any inference of invidious discrimination.[28]

Proof of a Section 510 violation may vary depending on whether an individual or a classwide discharge or other discrimination interfering with benefit rights is alleged. In an individual case, the employee must initially show, by direct or circumstantial evidence, that interference with the attainment of his or her rights was more than a mere side consequence of a discharge. He or she must then also show that any

---

Van Ess, 474 F.Supp. 1324, 1 EBC 2046 (E.D. Wis. 1979); *Gates v. Life of Montana Ins. Co.*, 638 P.2d 1063 (Mont. 1982).

[25] 548 F.Supp. 983, at 985 (S.D.N.Y. 1982).

[26] 585 F.Supp. 879, 5 EBC 1945, at 1948 (E.D. Pa. 1984).

[27] 812 F.2d 835, 8 EBC 1047 (3d Cir. 1987).

[28] 730 F.2d 12, 5 EBC 1343, at 1346–47 (1st Cir. 1984), *cert. denied*, 469 U.S. 1017 (1984).

"legitimate" reasons put forward by the employer for the job action, which are sufficient standing alone, are pretextual. In a classwide discharge, the issue is likely to be whether the interference purpose was a "substantial" or "determining" factor in the job action, with the employer acknowledging that it was aware of pension cost savings from the action, but arguing that consideration of this factor did not rise to this unlawful level in the decision-making process.

Because pension costs increase with age, age discrimination actions overlap with potential individual and class Section 510 actions. Since the "determining" factor test used under Section 510 is derived from the ADEA (and Title VII), proof in these parallel ADEA actions may be nearly identical to proof under Section 510. ADEA actions alleging age discrimination based on higher pension costs are discussed in section III.B below.

Proof in actions alleging Section 510 violations from plan amendments presents special issues because of the different "invidious intent" standard for finding a Section 510 violation from a plan amendment.

1. Individual Discharges

In *Ursic v. Bethlehem Mines*, an individual plaintiff with 29 years, five months, and 11 days of service prevailed in a Section 510 action alleging that his discharge was for the purpose of interfering with the attainment of a right to a 30-year pension. The court found that the reason given by the employer for the discharge—that the employee had been taking work tools home without authorization—was "pretextual" and that the real reason for the discharge was that he was within "hailing distance" of the 30-year unreduced early retirement right. Interference with the attainment of the 30-year right did not stem from personal animus or retaliation, but rather appeared to be based on the cost-consciousness of one of the managers and the fact that the plaintiff would have been the first employee to become entitled to this benefit before age 50.[29]

In *Folz v. Marriott Corp.*, a Section 510 action was based on an employee's claim that he was dismissed once his employer learned he had multiple sclerosis so the employer could avoid paying him long-term disability benefits of 60 percent of his salary (up to $750 per week) until age 65 and health insurance benefits when the multiple sclerosis began to prevent him from working. The discharge also caused the employee to fall short of vesting in profit-sharing benefits of more than $21,000. The company claimed that the employee was not terminated to prevent him from attaining these rights, but was terminated because of "poor performance," with prior warnings having been given. As in *Ursic*, the court found that the company's reasons were

---

[29] 4 EBC 1537, at 1539-40 (W.D. Pa. 1983), *aff'd,* 719 F.2d 670, 4 EBC 2297 (3d Cir. 1983).

pretextual, and that the real reason was to avoid the costs the employee's illness would have under the employee benefit plans. In making this determination, the court described the factors it considered somewhat more systematically than the court in *Ursic*, stating that it focused on:

(1) *Timing.* Prior to notifying the employer of his illness, no poor performance ratings or warnings had been given during the employee's 18-year career.

(2) *Long history of good performance.* Until the employer became aware of the illness, it was acknowledged that the employee had a history of good performance.

(3) *The manner in which the discharge was handled.* Standard operating procedure was to place an employee on probation after the types of warnings that were given this employee, rather than simply to discharge him.

(4) *Substantial economic incentive.* The costs of the long-term disability benefits and medical benefits and the amount at stake in the profit-sharing plan were substantial. There was a significant economic incentive for the employer to interfere.[30]

In more abbreviated form, a district court found in *Hillis v. Waukesha Title Co.* that "[b]y firing Hillis on December 23, 1977," after the employer learned Hillis intended to leave, the plan administrator "sought to *prevent* Hillis from securing a Company contribution on his behalf for the year 1977." Without further elaboration on whether it was acting under Section 510, the common law contract doctrine of prevention, or tortious interference with contract, the court ordered the 1977 contribution made to Hillis when it also enjoined the plan from enforcing an undisclosed forfeiture for competition clause.[31]

Other individual plaintiffs have not been as successful in Section 510 actions, usually falling short in presenting evidence from which an inference of purposeful interference can be drawn. In *Dependahl v. Falstaff Brewing Corp.*, an employee who first survived a motion to dismiss, lost after trial on a Section 510 claim based on his termination after nine years and one month of service under a plan requiring 10 years for vesting. The employee failed to carry his initial burden of proof in showing that the discharge was motivated by interference with vesting.[32] Similarly, in *Gates v. Life of Montana Ins. Co.*, an employee

---

[30] 594 F.Supp. 1007, 5 EBC 2244 (W.D. Mo. 1984).

[31] 576 F.Supp. 1103, at 1105 and 1110 (E.D. Wis. 1983) (emphasis added). See also *Zipf v. AT&T Co.*, 799 F.2d 889, 7 EBC 2289 (3d Cir. 1986) (denying employer's motion for summary judgement on claim that employee was terminated to prevent her from obtaining disability benefits when employee testified that her supervisor had told her that this was the reason and when she had handwritten notes prepared by him after the termination that attempted to create a record to justify the company's action); *K Mart Corp. v. Ponsock*, 8 EBC 1548 (Nev. 1987) (compensatory and punitive damages awarded under state law for unjust dismissal of employee who was only 6 months shy of vesting under 10-year cliff vesting schedule).

[32] 491 F.Supp. 1188 (E.D. Mo. 1980), *modified on other grounds*, 653 F.2d 1208, 2 EBC 1521 (8th Cir. 1981), *cert. denied*, 454 U.S. 1084 (1981).

with three years and three months of service was fired short of a four years of service requirement for vesting under a profit-sharing plan. His Section 510 claim failed when he presented no evidence from which a reasonable inference of an interference purpose could be drawn.[33]

2. Class Discharges

When a class of individuals is discharged at the same time, or systematically over a period of time, the plaintiffs' case is more likely to turn on a showing that the dollars-and-cents savings for the employer in pension costs were a substantial or determining factor in the occurrence or timing of the job action. *Gavalik v. Continental Can Co.*, *Amaro v. Continental Can Co.*, and *McClendon v. Continental Group, Inc.* were the first reported cases in which Section 510 interference has been alleged in mass layoffs and plant closings. In these cases, the plaintiffs alleged that Continental Can systematically selected plants for closing or "shrinking" based on computer printouts showing whether employees would shortly qualify for an unreduced early retirement pension requiring 20 years of service and a combination of age and service equalling 65 points.[34] As expressed by the court in *McClendon v. Continental Group, Inc.*, the plaintiffs allege a program under which

> "hundreds of Continental employees who were close to satisfying, but had not yet satisfied, the requirement for [early retirement] benefits . . . were selectively laid off in order to deprive them of [the] benefits to which they were about to become entitled."

The court further noted that:

> "Defendant admits that 'Continental undeniably did look at pension costs when deciding what plants to shut down and cap [i.e., shrink by attrition].' "

In response, Continental argued "the decision to cap and shrink was not made *solely* on the basis of pension costs."[35] However, as described before, the test under Section 510 is not "solely" but whether interfering with the attainment of rights was a determining factor in the decisions.

---

[33] 638 P.2d 1063 (Mont. 1982). See also *Moore v. Home Ins. Co.*, 601 F.2d 1072 (9th Cir. 1979) (employee with 12 years of service who was discharged 7½ months before ERISA's minimum vesting standards became effective failed to prove that his dismissal violated a state common law duty of fair dealing in employment when court found significant weaknesses in his job performance that could account for the dismissal standing alone).

In *Savodnik v. Korvettes, Inc.*, 488 F.Supp. 822 (E.D.N.Y. 1980), an individual plaintiff's cause of action survived a motion to dismiss (on a claim brought under state common law for tortious discharge) when he alleged that his firing after 13 years of service was for the purpose of interfering with his attainment of a vested pension right after 15 years; the case apparently never came to trial thereafter.

[34] See *Gavalik v. Continental Can Co.*, 3 EBC 1311 (W.D. Pa. 1982); *Amaro v. Continental Can Co.*, 724 F.2d 747, 5 EBC 1215 (9th Cir. 1984); *McClendon v. Continental Group, Inc.*, 602 F.Supp. 1492, 6 EBC 1113 (D.N.J. 1985).

[35] 6 EBC at 1115 and 1124 (emphasis added).

Without apparent regard to this distinction, the *Gavalik v. Continental Can Co.* plaintiffs lost at trial. The district court found that (1) the plant shutdown pensions cost Continental Can between $40,000 and $100,000 for each employee with the age and service to be eligible for 70/75 or Rule of 65 early retirement benefits, (2) a sophisticated management system was developed by Continental Can to minimize such costs by shifting work to keep employees who were already eligible for the benefits employed while removing work from other employees before their eligibility was achieved, and (3) a "motivating factor" in the decisions to close a steel pail line and to lay off other employees was to prevent the employees from attaining eligibility for the 70/75 and Rule of 65 benefits. But then, without further discussion, the court simply concluded that Continental's actions did not violate ERISA Section 510.[36] On appeal, the Third Circuit reversed and remanded, holding that the plaintiffs needed only to show that interference with their benefit entitlement was a determinative factor in the layoffs. The court held, moreover, that once a classwide discriminatory policy or practice is proven, individual class members are presumed to be the victims of the policy—unless the employer can prove that an individual layoff or other job action would have occurred in the absence of the discriminatory policy or practice.[37]

3. Plan Amendments

Proof that a plan amendment is for the purpose of interfering with the attainment of pension rights may require a more stringent showing of invidious intent. In *Aronson v. Servus Rubber Division,* a plan amendment excluded employees at one plant from a profit-sharing plan one month before the year-end allocation of contributions. The amendment was held not to violate Section 510 because it had a "readily apparent business justification" based on "independently established lines"—the plant at which the employees worked had been sold and they were among only a few employees involved in winding up operations. The First Circuit, however, indicated that "invidious intent" might be shown by a plan amendment which "discriminatorily modified [a plan provision] intentionally benefitting, or injuring certain identified employees or a certain group of employees."[38]

"Invidious intent" may be in the eye of the beholder, but the type of intent the First Circuit was looking for may have been present in *Dependahl v. Falstaff Brewing Corp.* In *Dependahl,* an eleventh hour amendment to a severance pay program just before a large layoff of employees was found to be a breach of fiduciary duty under Section 404(a)(1) because it divested employees of benefits to which they would "otherwise" have become entitled, and was made in anticipation of so

---

[36] C.A. 81-1519 (W.D. Pa. Sept. 24, 1985).

[37] 812 F.2d 835, 8 EBC 1047 (3d Cir. 1987).

[38] 730 F.2d 12, 5 EBC 1343, at 1346–47 (1st Cir. 1984), *cert. denied,* 469 U.S. 1017 (1984).

doing. No "independently established lines" justified the amendment. Although *Dependahl* thus involved a potential Section 510 violation, the amendment was struck down as a Section 404(a)(1) fiduciary violation with the court then not needing to reach the Section 510 issue.[39]

C. Remedies for Section 510 Interference

When a Section 510 violation has occurred, recovery may be against the "person" responsible for the interference.[40] This is generally the employer, rather than the plan or plan fiduciaries. The remedy in a Section 510 case is an "appropriate equitable remedy" under the authority of Section 502(a)(3) to redress violations of Title I. This requires that the employee be "made whole" for the pension rights that have been interfered with. It can also require an award of front pay and back pay. In *Folz v. Marriott Corp.*, the employer contended that remedies under Section 510 were limited to reinstatement as a plan participant and that other remedies such as employment reinstatement and back pay were not appropriate. The district court rejected this, holding that its equitable power was "broad enough to recreate the circumstances that would have existed absent the employer's illegal conduct." The court followed ADEA and Title VII cases in determining that it must make the employee "whole" for the injuries caused by the discrimination. Reinstatement was not feasible because the employee had held a high-level management position requiring constant communication and cooperation and an antagonistic relationship had developed in the course of the dispute. Accordingly, the court awarded front pay as well as back pay, with the front pay going to the employee's projected date of retirement (even though there was a substantial possibility because of the nature of his illness that the employee would not be able to continue working that long). In addition to back pay and

---

[39] 491 F.Supp. 1188 (E.D. Mo. 1980), *modified on other grounds,* 653 F.2d 1208, 2 EBC 1521 (8th Cir. 1981), *cert. denied,* 454 U.S. 1084 (1981). See also *Kulins v. Malco, A Microdot Co.*, 459 N.E.2d 1038 (Ill.App. 1984) (under contract and estoppel, retroactive application of amendment reducing severance benefits on the eve of a large termination of employees precluded without reference to either §404(a)(1) or §510); *Norton v. IAM Pension Fund,* 553 F.2d 1352 (D.C. Cir. 1977) (pre-ERISA plan amendment cancelling all past service credits on employer's withdrawal from a multiemployer plan held arbitrary and capricious as applied to employees of employer who withdrew from the plan *before* the amendment was adopted); *Hurd v. Hutnik,* 419 F.Supp. 630, 1 EBC 1382, at 1393 and 1404-05 (D.N.J. 1976) (estopping plan amendment terminating multiemployer plan short of full funding for retirees' benefits when employers convinced union "to sell [its] old people down the river" by terminating the plan, and thus discontinuing contributions to it—while putting active workers under another plan—in derogation of "clear and consistent" representations to retirees during their working careers that "lifetime" pensions would be provided).

But see *Cator v. Herrgott & Wilson, Inc.*, 609 F.Supp. 12, 6 EBC 1921 (N.D. Cal. 1985) (addition of new interim valuation date for profit-sharing plan account balances 30 days before retirement of company president not arbitrary and capricious even though action was specifically initiated to deal with his pending retirement because value of plan assets had declined sharply since last annual valuation date and company president otherwise would have received $72,000 more at the expense of remaining participants).

[40] See *Bittner v. Sadoff & Rudoy Indus.*, 490 F.Supp. 534 (E.D. Wis. 1980).

front pay and continuation of the long-term disability and health insurance coverage, the court also vested the employee's profit-sharing account and ordered reinstatement of certain stock options that had been lost because the employee had gone to work for a competing hotel after his discharge in violation of a noncompetition clause in the stock option plan.[41]

II. Code Section 401(a)(4) Discrimination

Even after enactment of ERISA's detailed minimum standards, most of which are replicated as tax-qualification requirements, the linchpin of pension law for many tax lawyers is still the requirement in Section 401(a)(4) of the Internal Revenue Code that a plan must not discriminate in contributions or benefits in favor of employees who are members of the "prohibited group" of officers, shareholders, and highly compensated employees.[42] Section 1.401-1(b)(3) of the Internal Revenue regulations provides:

> "[A] plan is not for the exclusive benefit of employees in general if, *by any device whatever*, it discriminates either in eligibility requirements, contributions or benefits in favor of officers, shareholders ... or the highly compensated employees."[43]

The Code's discrimination prohibition is not a product of ERISA, but has been a part of the Internal Revenue Code since the 1942 Revenue Act.[44] The purpose of the requirement is not to prevent highly compensated employees from receiving substantial pension benefits, but to require the plan, on its face and in operation, to provide benefits on substantially the same basis to other employees—so that the plan is not primarily a tax shelter for the prohibited group. The Code's nondiscrimination rule differs from ERISA Section 510 (and the ADEA and Title VII) in that it provides only a backhanded protection for lower paid employees against discrimination. Discrimination against participants who are *not* officers, shareholders, or highly compensated employees is not prohibited as such. Rather, discrimination *in favor of* the select employees is banned. In many instances, however, the effect of this rule is to prohibit discrimination against rank and file employees—at least as a group.

The application of the Code's nondiscrimination standard is spelled out in three specific Code provisions:

---

[41] 594 F.Supp. 1007, 5 EBC 2244 (W.D. Mo. 1984). See also *Bittner v. Sadoff & Rudoy Indus., supra.*

[42] The determination of which employees are in the "prohibited group" is discussed in ch. 2, sec. I, and in ch. 3, sec. V (for collectively bargained plans).

[43] Emphasis added.

[44] See B. Wolk, "Discrimination Rules for Qualified Retirement Plans," 70 Va. L. Rev. 419, at 426-28 (April 1984) (describing the origin of the nondiscrimination requirement).

(1) Code Section 410(b) establishes standards for nondiscriminatory coverage of employees;
(2) Code Section 401(a)(5) permits and at the same time limits the use of Social Security integration in benefit formulas; and
(3) Code Section 411(d)(1) requires that vesting be nondiscriminatory.

The Code Section 411(d)(3) requirement that participants' benefits become vested on the termination or partial termination of a plan,[45] and the Code Section 416 rules for top-heavy plans can also be seen as applications of the basic Section 401(a)(4) nondiscrimination standard to vesting and Social Security integration.

Even when a plan does not discriminate under these specific statutory rules, it may still be discriminatory if other plan provisions cause it to depart from the basic nondiscriminatory paradigm of providing benefits as a level percentage of total compensation for all covered employees. The detailed rules on Social Security integration in Revenue Ruling 71-446 are, for example, not a blanket endorsement of offset and excess formulas at the maximum permissible limits regardless of the results produced in actual operation:

> "[S]ection 401(a)(5) specifies certain provisions which of themselves are not discriminatory. However, this does not mean that a plan containing these provisions may not be discriminatory in actual operation."[46]

Similarly, even though a plan satisfies the Section 411(b) requirements for benefit accruals for each year of participation, the plan may still be discriminatory under Section 401(a)(4) "with regard to its benefit accrual rates."[47]

To determine whether other aspects of a plan cause it to depart too far from the nondiscrimination standard, the IRS's regulations state that plans will generally be viewed "as a whole."[48] But the IRS's rulings and pronouncements show that particular types of plan provisions are considered so ripe with discrimination that they will not be approved simply because the plan "as a whole" may contain other aspects which are not discriminatory. Thus:

(1) A benefit formula based on an average of final pay must use at least a three-year average of compensation as a deterrent to manipulation of compensation to favor the prohibited group, or to disfavor other employees;[49]

---

[45] Vesting on termination or partial termination is not just to prevent discrimination. See ch. 11, sec. I. Rules on the reallocation of plan assets when the assets are short of paying all accrued benefits on termination and special "early termination" limits on benefits for the 25 highest paid employees act as further extensions to the requirement that all employees' benefits must become nonforfeitable on termination to prevent discrimination. See Rev. Rul. 80-229 and 26 C.F.R. 1.401-4(c).

[46] 26 C.F.R. 1.401-1(b)(3).

[47] Prop. Regs. 1.411(d)-1(e).

[48] 26 C.F.R. 1.401-4(a)(2)(iii).

[49] Rev. Rul. 71-330.

(2) A plan's definition of "compensation" is examined for the inclusion of types of compensation, such as unfunded deferred compensation or bonuses, that are only or primarily available to prohibited group members, and for the exclusion of other types of compensation, such as overtime, that are only or primarily available to nonprohibited group members;[50]

(3) Defined contribution plan formulas that match a percentage of employee contributions with employer contributions are examined for discrimination in operation;[51]

(4) Defined contribution plan formulas that allocate each year's contributions, or that reallocate forfeited profit-sharing accounts, by weighing past years of service, rather than by use of a formula based on current pay, are subject to special scrutiny;[52]

(5) Credit under a defined benefit plan for years of past service is reviewed for discrimination in operation in total benefits as a percentage of compensation;[53]

(6) Credit for "leaves of absence" or under other open-ended categories must be predicated on an established policy uniformly applied and must not otherwise give rise to discrimination;[54]

(7) Credit, or the denial of credit, for work after a plan's normal retirement age is reviewed for discrimination in operation;[55]

(8) Offsets of benefits from other qualified plans, or from nonqualified plans, e.g., an offset of benefits from a separate disability benefit plan, are examined to determine whether the remaining qualified plan benefits are nondiscriminatory;[56]

(9) Estimates of Social Security benefits used in offset formulas must comply with certain rules to prevent overintegration, and thus discrimination, through use of the estimates;[57]

(10) Plan provisions forfeiting annual defined contribution plan contributions because of lack of employment on one date, e.g., December 31, are examined closely for discrimination in operation;[58]

---

[50] See ch. 3, sec. IV.

[51] Rev. Rul. 80-307.

[52] See ch. 3, sec. VI.

[53] Rev. Rul. 81-248, and see Rev. Rul. 70-77.

[54] Rev. Rul. 81-106.

[55] See Rev. Rul. 74-342.

[56] Rev. Rul. 76-259 and Rev. Rul. 81-33.

[57] Rev. Rul. 84-46.

[58] Rev. Rul. 76-250.

(11) Provisions forfeiting benefits vested under standards more liberal than the ERISA minimum standards because of competition with the employer are permitted, but reviewed for discrimination;[59]

(12) Early retirement or other benefit options that depend on the "consent" of the employer or other discretionary action cannot provide more than the actuarial equivalent of the participant's normal retirement benefit and must not be available "primarily" to prohibited group employees when the percentage of prohibited group employees taking advantage of the benefit is compared to the percentage of rank and file employees;[60]

(13) Any provisions for loans from a plan must be available on a uniform, nondiscriminatory basis and will still be examined for discrimination in operation;[61]

(14) Other devices that permit prohibited group employees to cash out their benefits on better terms than nonprohibited group employees, e.g., by a redemption of shares under a stock bonus plan at a higher price, or with less restrictions, may also be discriminatory.[62]

Plan amendments inevitably receive particularly strict review for discrimination. An isolated change highlights the issue of who the change is for more than when a plan provision is first adopted within an entire package of provisions whose effect cannot be entirely foreseen. In *Epstein v. Commissioner*, a plan amendment including bonuses in "compensation" under a plan's benefit formula was held to be discriminatory, whether or not it would have been discriminatory if in the plan from the start, since at the time the amendment was made it was clear that it was designed to favor the prohibited group of employees.[63]

---

[59] Rev. Rul. 85-31.

[60] See Rev. Rul. 85-59, and Rev. Rul. 58-151, as amplified by Rev. Rul. 58-604. When no prohibited group employees are covered under a plan, e.g., a collectively bargained plan covering only hourly employees, the Rev. Rul. 58-151 standards do not apply. Rev. Rul. 58-604.

The future of early retirement, lump sum, and other benefit options requiring "consent" of an employer, or "mutually satisfactory" conditions is, at the date of this writing, clouded by proposed IRS regulations that would require plans to eliminate any plan provision that requires employer consent or the exercise of discretion with respect to the availability of any alternative forms of benefits to satisfy both the Code's definitely determinable benefit requirement and ERISA §204(g), as amended by the Retirement Equity Act. See Prop. Regs. 1.401(a)-4 and 1.411(d)-4, 51 Fed. Reg. 3798 (Jan. 30, 1986). In lieu of open-ended discretion, plans could adopt objective and clearly ascertainable criteria, for example, on the insurability of an employee if the purpose of the discretion has been to ensure that only employees in good health receive lump sum benefits. This antidiscretion regulation is proposed to become effective for nonbargained plans in the second plan year after Jan. 30, 1986, and for collectively bargained plans, in the earlier of the third plan year after Jan. 30, 1986, or the second plan year after the expiration of the collective bargaining agreement in effect on Jan. 30, 1986.

[61] IRS Pub. 778, part 5(o). See also Code §72(p), as amended by §1134 of P.L. 99-514 (setting specific dollar limits and rules on loans from plans).

[62] *Friedman & Jobusch Architects & Engineers v. Commissioner*, 627 F.2d 175 (9th Cir. 1980).

[63] 70 T.C. 439 (1978).

Conversely, a plan amendment reducing or eliminating a benefit or benefit option that was used primarily by employees who are *outside* of the prohibited group of employees can also raise questions of discrimination. In enacting the 1984 Retirement Equity Act, which placed minimum standard restrictions on such amendments, the Senate Finance Committee stated that under present law:

> "[T]he reduction of a benefit or elimination of an option is prohibited under a qualified plan if it results in discrimination in favor of employees who are officers, shareholders, or highly compensated."[64]

III. Age Discrimination

The Age Discrimination in Employment Act prohibits a refusal to hire, a discharge, or any other form of discrimination with respect to "compensation, terms, conditions, or privileges of employment because of [an] individual's age."[65] The standard of proof in ADEA cases, as in Section 510 suits under ERISA, is that age must be shown to be a "determining factor" in the decision or action. The employee need not prove that age was the "sole" factor in a discharge or other form of discrimination, but must prove that age "made a difference" in the decision in the sense that "but for" the presence of age, the discrimination would not have occured.[66]

The drawback in the ADEA's application to certain types of pension claims is a "bona fide" employee benefit plan exception in Section 4(f)(2). This exception provides that it is not age discrimination for an "employer to observe the terms of . . . any bona fide employee benefit plan which is not a subterfuge to evade the purposes of [the Act]."[67] As discussed further below, this bona fide plan exception is not as broad as it at first appears. The exception does not apply to job actions where employees are selected for a layoff or discharge on the basis of higher pension costs, or on the basis of eligibility for pension benefits. Nor does it apply where an offset or denial of other benefits, such as severance benefits, is based on pension eligibility at the time of a layoff or discharge. Age discrimination in these instances relates to pension benefits, but it does not come about by "observ[ing] the terms of [the] plan." Rather, higher costs or eligibility for benefits under a plan, both

---

[64] S.Rep. 98-575, at 27, reprinted in [1984] U.S. Code Cong. & Ad. News, 98th Cong., 2d Sess. 2547, at 2573.

[65] 29 U.S.C. §623(a)(1).

[66] *Cancellier v. Federated Department Stores*, 672 F.2d 1312, at 1316 (9th Cir. 1982), *cert. denied*, 459 U.S. 859 (1982). This standard has been adopted in every circuit. See *Loeb v. Textron, Inc.*, 600 F.2d 1003 (1st Cir. 1979); *Bentley v. Stromberg-Carlson Corp.*, 638 F.2d 9 (2d Cir. 1981); *Smithers v. Bailar*, 629 F.2d 892 (3d Cir. 1980); *Spagnuolo v. Whirlpool Corp.*, 641 F.2d 1109 (4th Cir. 1981); *Haring v. CPC Int'l, Inc.*, 664 F.2d 1234 (5th Cir. 1981); *Ackerman v. Diamond Shamrock Corp.*, 670 F.2d 66 (6th Cir. 1982); *Golomb v. Prudential Ins. Co.*, 688 F.2d 547 (7th Cir. 1982); *Tribble v. Westinghouse Elec. Corp.*, 669 F.2d 1193 (8th Cir. 1982), *cert. denied*, 460 U.S. 1080 (1983); *Kelly v. American Standard, Inc.*, 640 F.2d 974 (9th Cir. 1981); *Kentroti v. Frontier Airlines, Inc.*, 585 F.2d 967 (10th Cir. 1979); *Anderson v. Savage Laboratories, Inc.*, 675 F.2d 1221 (11th Cir. 1982); *Cuddy v. Carmen*, 694 F.2d 853 (D.C. Cir. 1982).

[67] 29 U.S.C. §623(f)(2).

of which are age-related factors, have been used as the basis for discriminatory treatment *outside* the terms of the plan.

A. Pension Benefits as a Remedy

When employees are discharged, laid off, or otherwise discriminated against on the basis of age, lost pension and other employee benefits can be included in back pay, and may also be awarded as a part of a front pay remedy if reinstatement is not a viable option.[68]

Even without pension benefits as an express part of a remedial court order, hours of service for which back pay is awarded, or agreed to by an employer in a settlement, may be required to be credited for years of service for vesting and years of participation for benefit accruals under the Department of Labor's hours of service regulations.[69] Under the regulatory elapsed time alternative to counting hours of service, periods for which back pay is awarded, or agreed to by an employer in settlement, are not required to be credited for vesting years of service,[70] but they may be required to be credited for benefit accruals.[71]

B. Selectivity in Layoffs, Discharges, or Recalls Based on Higher Pension Costs for Older Workers

Costs under defined benefit plans generally increase with age because of the shorter period before the benefits become payable and the greater likelihood that an older worker is, or will become, vested. According to Dan McGill, the additional effective compensation from a defined benefit plan providing one percent of a final average of salary for each year of service may be less than .2 percent of compensation for a worker age 30, but more than 19 percent of compensation for a worker age 64.[72] Further increases in the costs of pensions for older workers can come about from unreduced early retirement benefits that

---

68 See, *Loeb v. Textron, Inc., supra*; *Hoffman v. Nissan Motor Corp.*, 511 F.Supp. 352 (D.N.H. 1981); *Bleakley v. Jekyll Island-State Park Authority*, 536 F.Supp. 236 (S.D. Ga. 1982)—each including pension benefits in back pay awards even when the employee was not vested at date of trial. And see *Ventura v. Federal Life Ins. Co.*, 571 F.Supp. 48, 4 EBC 1623 (N.D. Ill. 1983) (including pension benefits in award of front pay).

69 See 29 C.F.R. 2530.200b-2(a)(3) (defining "hour of service" for vesting years of service and benefit accrual years of participation), 29 C.F.R. 2530.200b-3(d)(3)(i) (including such hours under equivalencies based on "hours worked" and "regular time hours"), and 29 C.F.R. 2530.200b-3(e)(1) (including such hours under equivalencies based on days, weeks, or months in which an employee has an hour of service). But see 29 C.F.R. 2530.200b-3(f) (not specifically including back pay under equivalencies based on total earnings or total earnings from the performance of duties during a computation period).

70 See 26 C.F.R. 1.410(a)-7(d).

71 See 26 C.F.R. 1.410(a)-7(e)(2) and 29 C.F.R. 2530.204-3(a).

72 D. McGill, *Fundamentals of Private Pensions* (Richard D. Irwin 5th ed. 1984), at 276-277. This estimate is apparently without taking preretirement vesting into account, which would increase the percentage for the younger employee. The cost of a $100 per month life annuity starting at age 65 is on the order of 1⁄13 as much for an age 30 worker as for an age 64 worker if

are generally not obtainable until the worker is past age 45 or 50 and has 25 or 30 years of service. Other employee benefit costs that may be higher for older workers include health and life insurance premiums, the cost of vacation benefits under graduated vacation schedules based on years of service, and the cost of service-related bonuses and severance payments.

Because these age-related employee benefit costs can cumulatively be substantial, proof that they were considered in a job action is frequently a part of the proof in an age discrimination claim. When consideration of such costs is shown, the bona fide plan exception is not a defense because rather than observing the terms of employee benefit plans, the employer is allegedly basing layoffs or dismissals on the higher costs of benefits for older workers under the plans. For example, in *Franci v. Avco Corp.*, an ADEA violation was found when it was shown that company vice-presidents were directed to cut specified amounts of overall salaries from their division budgets by layoffs. Because fringe benefit costs of older workers, and in particular their pension costs, were higher, the managers selected a disproportionate number of older workers for layoff. In *Franci*, the plaintiffs were also able to produce direct evidence that top management viewed the layoffs as a "fortuitous" occasion for thinning the ranks of older persons. Although no written criterion for selecting employees for layoff was supplied when the amounts of divisional budget cuts to be made were given the vice-presidents, higher salaries and fringe benefit costs made older workers the almost inevitable choice.[73]

In *Adama v. Doehler-Jarvis*, a Michigan state age discrimination action, the plaintiffs alleged their plant was closed and much of the work transferred to another location because of the pension costs associated with the plant's older workforce. A jury found in favor of the employees, but on review by the Michigan Court of Appeals, the case was remanded because of the admission of hearsay. In discussing the substantive standard to be used on remand in finding an age discrimination violation, the court stated the plaintiffs could prevail if the consideration of pension costs, the age-related factor, "was afforded such weight in relation to other factors considered so as to have been a major determinative factor, one that made a 'significant' difference in the decision [to close the plant]."[74]

A refusal to rehire or recall older employees because of higher pension costs (usually because of their proximity to eligibility for an early retirement benefit) is also a violation of the ADEA (and of ERISA Section 510). In *Franci v. Avco Corp.*, plaintiffs were able to

---

both employees are assumed to be vested and an equal flat dollar benefit is promised (as compared to McGill's 1% of a final average of salary). See "The Costs of Employing Older Workers," 98th Cong., 2d Sess., at 49 (Comm. Print for the Senate Special Committee on Aging 1984).

[73] 538 F.Supp. 250 (D. Conn. 1982).

[74] 320 N.W.2d 298, at 302 (Mich. Ct.App. 1982), *rev'd*, 353 N.W. 2d 48 (Mich. 1984), *award aff'd with adjustments*, 376 N.W. 2d 406 (Mich. Ct. App. 1985). And cf. *Allen v. American Home Foods, Inc.*, 644 F.Supp. 1553 (N.D. Ind. 1986) (alleging that plant was closed because of older employees' higher pension costs in violation of ADEA).

show that after first selecting them for layoff because of their higher age-related pension and other fringe benefit costs, the employer refused to recall or rehire them when new openings became available, and instead recruited younger employees for the positions.[75]

Despite higher pension costs, individual plaintiffs have generally not been successful in proving that such costs made a significant difference in their discharges. In *Kerwood v. Mortgage Bankers Ass'n*, an older executive alleged that salary and pension cost savings were the reason for his dismissal when a new executive took over the association's staff, but the action failed when the association was able to show sufficient nondiscriminatory reasons to support the dismissal standing alone, and the employee was not able to show they were pretextual.[76]

One departure from the reasoning normally applied in both individual and classwide cases is found in *Mastie v. Great Lakes Steel Corp.* The plaintiffs in *Mastie* alleged that their higher salaries and pension costs, which correlated with their older ages, were factors in their employer's decision to discharge them ahead of other supervisors. The court disagreed, finding that the pension costs for them were not higher because they were already entitled to unreduced early retirement benefits with the cost to the employer of future benefit accruals actually being outweighed by the savings from postponement of the unreduced payments. The court went further, however, to say that consideration of individual-by-individual labor costs, as opposed to the use of generalizations based on age, should not violate the ADEA.[77]

The *Mastie* decision generally appears to be rejected on the point that individual assessments of labor costs cannot violate the ADEA when age-related costs are subsumed within the individual labor costs. In *Adama v. Doehler-Jarvis*, the Michigan Court of Appeals accepted *Mastie*, but *sub silentio* altered it to hold that while age-related costs can be considered, it violates the ADEA if they are "afforded such weight in relation to other [legitimate] factors so as to be a major determinative factor . . . in the decision."[78] In *Marshall v. Arlene Knitwear, Inc.*, a federal district court, somewhat more forcefully, stated

---

[75] 538 F.Supp. 250 (D. Conn. 1982).

[76] 494 F.Supp. 1298 (D.D.C. 1980). See also *Tice v. Lampert Yards, Inc.*, 761 F.2d 1210 (7th Cir. 1985) (57-year-old millshop foreman failed to prove that his termination was pretext to deny him pension benefits for which he had 9 years of service under plan requiring 10 years for vesting; independent plan administrator had determined after his discharge that plaintiff did, in fact, have 10th year of service under ERISA's 1,000 hours standard for measuring a year of service); *Christensen v. Equitable Life Assurance*, 767 F.2d 340 (7th Cir. 1985) (52-year-old division manager who was replaced by younger employee showed negative effects on amount of his pension from his early departure, but failed to show that employer terminated him to reduce the payments); *Pirone v. Home Ins. Co.*, 559 F.Supp. 306 (S.D.N.Y. 1983) (no evidence to indicate that impact of termination of three employees on costs of retirement plan was considered, and sufficient nondiscriminatory reasons supported their discharge); *Stanojev v. Ebasco Services, Inc.*, 643 F.2d 914 (2d Cir. 1981) (preparation of figures on pensions to be paid employee using three alternative retirement dates did not lead to inference that age-related costs were a factor in employee's dismissal).

[77] 424 F.Supp. 1299 (E.D. Mich. 1976).

[78] 320 N.W.2d 298, at 302 (Mich. Ct.App. 1982).

that "[w]here economic savings and expectation of longer future service are directly related to an employee's age it is a violation of the ADEA to discharge the employee for those reasons."[79] The *Arlene Knitwear* standard has been adopted by the Second and Eighth Circuits.[80] The underlying equities may also favor this view. When an employer maintains a benefit program with built-in age-related costs, it is disingenuous for the employer to use those higher age-related costs as a basis for discharging an employee since they are either the employer's own creation, or under collective bargaining, the employer's agreed contractual obligations.

C. Selectivity in Layoffs, Recalls, or Receipt of Other Benefits Based on Pension Eligibility

Pension benefits have frequently been a part of age discrimination cases because of the selection of employees for discharge or layoff based on their *eligibility* for immediate pension benefits. Use of pension eligibility as a selection factor is a patently age-related criterion. As a result, courts have uniformly held that use of eligibility for early or normal retirement benefits for selecting employees for discharge or layoff violates the ADEA.[81] The bona fide plan exception does not apply in these cases because the employers are not "observ[ing] the terms" of a bona fide plan, but are instead using an age-related factor as the basis for selecting *which* employees to force out. An employer also may not distinguish between the rights of employees who are being discharged or laid off, as by requiring older employees to take early retirement benefits while allowing other employees to remain on layoff for possible recall.[82]

A common practice, until recently, has been the use of eligibility for pension benefits as the basis for an offset of severance benefits by the amount of pension benefits that employees who are discharged or laid off are eligible to receive immediately. Rather than as an offset, severance benefits are, in some cases, flatly denied if an employee is

---

[79] 454 F.Supp. 715, at 728 (E.D.N.Y. 1978), *aff'd in part, rev'd in part,* 608 F.2d 1369 (2d Cir. 1979).

[80] See *Geller v. Markham,* 635 F.2d 1027 (2d Cir. 1980), *cert. denied,* 451 U.S. 945 (1981); *Leftwich v. Harris-Stowe State College,* 702 F.2d 686 (8th Cir. 1983). See also *Laugeson v. Anaconda Co.,* 510 F.2d 307, at 316–17 (6th Cir. 1975). But as in *Mastie,* a district court in *Donnelly v. Exxon Research & Eng'g Co.,* 12 FEP Cases 417 (D.N.J. 1974), *aff'd,* 521 F.2d 1398 (3d Cir. 1975), allowed an older employee to be terminated under a policy requiring that the employee's productivity equal 75% of salary, even though the employee argued this had a disparate impact on older workers when age-related benefits and components of salary were included.

[81] See *McCorstin v. U.S. Steel Corp.,* 621 F.2d 749 (5th Cir. 1980) (age discrimination occurs when availability of early retirement benefits is used in selecting employees for reduction-in-force); *EEOC v. Baltimore & Ohio RR Co.,* 632 F.2d 1107 (4th Cir. 1980), *cert. denied,* 454 U.S. 825 (1981) (age discrimination when entitlement to pension benefits is used in selecting employees for work force reduction). See also *EEOC v. City of Altoona,* 723 F.2d 4, 4 EBC 2670 (3d Cir. 1983), *cert. denied,* 467 U.S. 1204 (1984); *Popko v. City of Clairton,* 570 F.Supp. 446, 4 EBC 2285 (W.D. Pa. 1983); *EEOC v. City of New Castle,* 4 EBC 2291 (W.D. Pa. 1983).

[82] *EEOC v. Chrysler Corp.,* 546 F.Supp. 54, 3 EBC 2029 (E.D. Mich. 1982), *aff'd,* 733 F.2d 183, 5 EBC 1875 (6th Cir. 1984). And see *Franci v. Avco Corp.,* 538 F.Supp. 250 (D. Conn. 1982).

eligible for immediate pension benefits. Whether as an offset or a flat denial, this practice violates the ADEA because it denies severance benefits to older workers based on an age-related factor—their immediate pension eligibility.[83] Employers have contended this practice is not an ADEA violation because they are merely observing the terms of a bona fide plan, namely, the severance pay plan, but the courts have uniformly held that the bona fide plan exception is limited to retirement plans and employee benefit plans that *necessarily* have age-related costs, such as health insurance plans and defined benefit pension plans. A severance pay plan is not considered such a plan, and hence, an age-discriminatory offset from or a flat denial of severance benefits is not protected by Section 4(f)(2).[84]

A policy of denying employees who are eligible for immediate pension benefits the option of using their accrued vacation or sick leave before retiring under a pension plan may also violate the ADEA if other employees are permitted such an option on separation from service.[85]

D. "Bona Fide" Plan Exception

Even when alleged age discrimination is from an employer "observ[ing] the terms of [an] employee benefit plan," the bona fide plan exception is narrow. The major limitation on the exception was enacted in 1978 in reaction to the Supreme Court's decision in *United Air*

---

[83] *EEOC v. Westinghouse Elec. Corp.*, 725 F.2d 211, 4 EBC 2684 (3d Cir. 1984), *cert. denied,* 469 U.S. 820 (1984); *EEOC v. Borden's Inc.*, 724 F.2d 1390, 5 EBC 1122 (9th Cir. 1984); *EEOC v. Curtiss-Wright Corp.*, 3 EBC 1999 (D.N.J. 1982); *EEOC v. A&P Co.*, 618 F.Supp. 115, 6 EBC 2338 (N.D. Ohio 1985); *Malone v. Borden, Inc.*, 6 EBC 1341 (3d Cir. 1984) (unpub.); *EEOC v. Westinghouse Elec. Corp.*, 632 F.Supp. 343, 7 EBC 1318 (E.D. Pa. 1986) (also holding denial of severance benefits to laid off employees who were eligible to retire to be "willful" age discrimination for purposes of awarding plaintiffs liquidated damages under the ADEA, applying the elucidation of willfulness in *Trans World Airlines, Inc. v. Thurston*, 469 U.S. 111 (1985), and finding that the employer had known or shown reckless disregard for whether the conduct violated the ADEA; note that this is a separate case from the *Westinghouse* case cited above). See also 29 C.F.R. 860.120(a)(1). But compare *Britt v. E.I. du Pont de Nemours & Co.*, 768 F.2d 593, 6 EBC 1912 (4th Cir. 1985) (not an ADEA violation to condition severance benefits on postponement of pension benefits for the period of regular pay covered by the severance benefits at least when severances are voluntary so that severance pay functions as an inducement to voluntarily leave work, rather than as a fringe benefit); *EEOC v. Firestone Tire & Rubber*, 42 FEP Cases 1328 (W.D. Tenn. 1987) (no ADEA violation when denial of "severance" awards offered under terms of pension plan to certain pension-eligible employees found to be a denial of a "minimum pension trust distribution and not severance pay at all").

[84] See cases at n. 83 above. Even if a severance pay plan were covered by §4(f)(2), to avoid being a "subterfuge" for age discrimination, the offset would have to be justified on the basis of equalizing costs under the severance plan for older and younger workers, without consideration of the higher pension costs of the older workers. See 29 C.F.R. 860.120(d). If an offset runs in the opposite direction, i.e., if a pension plan provides that pension benefits are offset by the amount of severance benefits for which an employee is eligible, the plan is not in compliance with Rev. Rul. 78-178 (see ch. 3, sec. X) and the plan may also run afoul of the "subterfuge" limitation of the bona fide plan exception to the ADEA. See sec. III.D.3 below.

[85] See cases at n. 83, and cf. *Alford v. City of Lubbock*, 664 F.2d 1263 (5th Cir. 1982), *cert. denied,* 456 U.S. 975 (1982) (policy of denying accrued sick leave pay to severed employees if they were ineligible to participate in pension plan, based on the age at which they were hired, violated ADEA); *EEOC v. Air Line Pilots Ass'n*, 661 F.2d 90 (8th Cir. 1981) (requirement that vacation time be used *before* forced retirement at age 60 did not violate ADEA, but only because rule applied equally regardless of age, and employees required to retire precisely at age 60).

Lines, Inc. v. McMann. In *McMann,* the Supreme Court held that a mandatory retirement age provision under a bona fide pension plan was not a "subterfuge" to evade the purposes of the ADEA if the provision was established long before the ADEA and had simply been continued after its enactment. In response, Congress modified the bona fide plan exception to prohibit any plan provisions requiring mandatory retirement before age 70.[86] Basically, this left only two common types of pension plan provisions under the bona fide plan exception that would otherwise be considered to patently discriminate on the basis of age. These are plan provisions:

(1) Excluding an employee hired less than five years before a defined benefit plan's normal retirement age from participation in the plan, or

(2) Stopping benefit accruals under a defined benefit plan, or employer contributions under a defined contribution plan, at a plan's normal retirement age.[87]

Except for these specifically permitted plan provisions, both of which are prohibited for plan years beginning in 1988,[88] an employer must be able to show that an otherwise discriminatory provision fits within three elements if it is to be sustained under the "bona fide" plan exception. As stated by the EEOC:

> "Since section 4(f)(2) is an exception from the general non-discrimination provisions of the Act, the burden is on the one seeking to invoke the exception to show that every element [of the exception] has been clearly and unmistakably met. The exception must be narrowly construed. The ... key elements of the exception [are]: (i) What a 'bona fide employee benefit plan' is; (ii) what it means to 'observe the terms' of such a plan; and (iii) what kind of plan, or plan provision, [is] considered 'a subterfuge to evade the purposes of [the] Act.'"[89]

---

[86] See *United Air Lines, Inc. v. McMann,* 434 U.S. 192, 1 EBC 1556 (1977). The 1986 Age Discrimination in Employment Amendments Act removed the age 70 ceiling on the age discrimination prohibition. See P.L. 99-592, §2(c) (deleting age 70 ceiling from 29 U.S.C. §631(a)). This reform applies to involuntary retirement under the terms of bona fide retirement plans. See 29 U.S.C. §623(f)(2) (cross-referencing 29 U.S.C. §631(a)).

[87] See 29 C.F.R. 860.120(f)(1)(iv) and ch. 4, secs. I.B and III.C.1 for a more complete description of these exceptions and their limitations.

[88] See ch. 4, sec. III.C.1. Even the specifically protected plan provisions halting benefit accruals at normal retirement age or excluding workers from participation based on the age when they are hired may be examined for compliance with each of the three elements described below *if* the plan provisions are amendments to a plan adopted after the ADEA was enacted in 1967. See R. Blum and C. Kolm, 363 Tax Mgmt. (BNA), Age and Sex Discrimination and Employee Benefit Plans, at A-9. Cf. *Crosland v. Charlotte Eye, Ear & Throat Hosp.*, 686 F.2d 208, 3 EBC 1954 (4th Cir. 1982). In like manner, amendments lowering mandatory retirement ages under plans have been found to fall outside protection of the the bona fide plan exception as subterfuges when the amendments were made *after* the ADEA was enacted. See *EEOC v. Home Ins. Co.*, 553 F.Supp. 704 (S.D.N.Y. 1982), *on remand from,* 672 F.2d 252, 3 EBC 1058 (2d Cir. 1982).

[89] 29 C.F.R. 860.120(a)(1). And see *EEOC v. Home Ins. Co.*, 672 F.2d 252, 3 EBC 1058 (2d Cir. 1982) (employer has burden of proving that actions fall within each of the three elements of the exception); *EEOC v. Westinghouse Elec. Corp.*, 725 F.2d 211, 4 EBC 2684 (3d Cir. 1983), *cert. denied,* 469 U.S. 820 (1984) (employer must demonstrate the three elements); *Sexton v. Beatrice Foods Co.*, 630 F.2d 478 (7th Cir. 1980) (given the ADEA's remedial purpose, exceptions to be narrowly construed); *EEOC v. Eastern Airlines*, 27 FEP Cases 1686 (5th Cir. 1981), *cert. denied,* 454 U.S. 818 (1981).

As examples of this analysis, if a plan provision offsets benefits from a retirement plan of a former employer following a corporate sale or merger, with a resulting discriminatory impact on future accruals on the basis of age, or if unreduced early retirement benefits that older workers are about to become eligible for are reduced or eliminated as a cost-cutting measure (a measure which is restricted since 1985 by amendments to ERISA Section 204(g)), each of these three elements must be established to insulate the otherwise discriminatory action under Section 4(f)(2).

1. What Is a Bona Fide Plan

An employer usually has little difficulty in bringing a plan under the first part of the bona fide plan exception. A plan is "bona fide" when it (1) genuinely exists and (2) pays "substantial benefits."[90] For a plan to genuinely exist, employees must be provided with an accurate written description of the plan and must be notified promptly of any changes in the plan.[91] While these requirements are satisfied by compliance with ERISA's disclosure requirements,[92] noncompliance may thus have ADEA consequences, as well as consequences under ERISA.

Some employees have argued that a plan does not pay "substantial" benefits if the benefits are inadequate to support them in retirement. In *Sikora v. American Can Co.*, two employees whose benefits under a plan were barely 10 percent of their final salaries questioned whether the plan's benefits were substantial enough for the plan to be considered bona fide. The Third Circuit vacated the district court's conclusory determination that it was bona fide, and remanded for a determination with factual findings.[93] In addition to low benefits, *Sikora* also suggests that a low early or normal retirement age under a plan, e.g., age 55, could be another factor to consider in determining whether a plan is a bona fide *retirement* plan.[94] Most courts, however, answer the question of whether a plan's benefits are substantial with an automatic "yes."[95]

---

[90] *EEOC v. Home Ins. Co.*, 672 F.2d 252, 3 EBC 1058, at 1065-66 (2d Cir. 1982). And see *Marshall v. Hawaiian Tel. Co.*, 575 F.2d 763 (9th Cir. 1978); *Jensen v. Gulf Oil Refining & Marketing Co.*, 623 F.2d 406 (5th Cir. 1980).

[91] 29 C.F.R. 860.120(b). But see *Brennan v. Taft Broadcasting Co.*, 500 F.2d 212 (5th Cir. 1974) (rejecting this as a necessary requirement).

[92] 29 C.F.R. 860.120(b).

[93] 622 F.2d 1116 (3d Cir. 1980). And see *Raymond v. Bendix Corp.*, 15 FEP Cases 49 (E.D. Mich. 1977).

[94] *Sikora v. American Can Co., supra.* If not considered in determining whether a plan is "bona fide," a lack of substantial benefits or a low retirement age could make a plan more susceptible to a determination that a discriminatory provision is a "subterfuge" for age discrimination. See R. Blum and C. Kolm, 363 Tax Mgmt. (BNA), Age and Sex Discrimination and Employee Benefit Plans, at A-6 and A-8.

[95] See *Leece v. State of Wisconsin*, 26 FEP Cases 1117 (W.D. Wis. 1981) (rejecting claim that $481 per month was not "substantial"); *Brennan v. Taft Broadcasting Co.*, 500 F.2d 212 (5th Cir. 1974); *Marshall v. Hawaiian Tel. Co.*, 575 F.2d 763 (9th Cir. 1978); *Carpenter v. Continental Trailways*, 635 F.2d 578 (6th Cir. 1980), *cert. denied*, 451 U.S. 986 (1981).

2. Observing the Terms of a Bona Fide Plan

For the "bona fide" plan exception to insulate a plan provision that otherwise discriminates on the basis of age, the otherwise discriminatory action must be "actually prescribed" and nondiscretionary under the plan's terms.[96] The requirement that an otherwise discriminatory action must "actually [be] prescribed" under the plan serves to provide employees with the "opportunity to know of the policy and to plan (or protest) accordingly."[97] It also "assures that the particular plan provision will be equally applied to all employees of the same age" and thus ensures against "individual, discretionary acts of discrimination."[98] Under this requirement, for example, plan provisions that stop benefit accruals after normal retirement age or that exclude older workers from participation because of their age when hired must be nondiscretionary. When a plan provision discriminates on the basis of age, but the age discrimination is not clear from the face of the plan, the discrimination could also be considered not to be "actually prescribed" in the plan. Thus, a provision for an offset of benefits from under another plan that discriminates on the basis of age, but that is neutral on its face, may fall outside of the exception because of the "observ[ing] the terms" requirement.

3. When a Plan, or Plan Provision, May Be a Subterfuge to Evade the ADEA's Purposes

The existence of a bona fide plan, and observance of its actually prescribed, nondiscretionary terms, still does not resolve whether a plan provision, or an amendment to a provision, is a "subterfuge to evade the purposes of [the ADEA]."[99] If a plan provision, or amendment, is shown to otherwise discriminate on the basis of age, the employer has the burden of proving that the provision or amendment is not a subterfuge to evade the ADEA's purposes.[100]

Showing discrimination based on age is, of course, the first step for a plaintiff faced with a plan provision or amendment that he or she believes is discriminatory. A facially neutral provision, or facially neutral plan amendment, can be shown to discriminate on the basis of age based on disparate impact, as in race and sex discrimination cases.[101]

---

[96] 29 C.F.R. 860.120(c). But see *Sexton v. Beatrice Foods Co.*, 630 F.2d 478, at 486 (7th Cir. 1980) (plan must "expressly sanction" the discriminatory treatment for an employer to be observing its terms, but noting that earlier cases on mandatory retirement ages under plans permitted employers to retire employees under express, but discretionary plan provisions).

[97] 29 C.F.R. 860.120(c).

[98] *Id.*

[99] *EEOC v. Home Ins. Co.*, 672 F.2d 252, 3 EBC 1058, at 1066 (2d Cir. 1982). And see 29 C.F.R. 860.120(d).

[100] 29 C.F.R. 860.120(a)(1).

[101] See *EEOC v. Borden's, Inc.*, 724 F.2d 1390, 5 EBC 1122 (9th Cir. 1984); *Leftwich v. Harris-Stowe State College*, 702 F.2d 686 (8th Cir. 1983); *Geller v. Markham*, 635 F.2d 1027 (2d Cir. 1980), *cert. denied*, 451 U.S. 945 (1981); *Kelly v. American Standard, Inc.* 640 F.2d 974 (9th

For example, a plan provision offsetting benefits accrued under a former employer's pension plan after a corporate sale or merger may appear facially neutral, but the effect may be to virtually eliminate future benefit accruals for older workers if the former employer's pension plan provided a higher rate of benefit accruals.[102]

Once a *prima facie* case that a plan provision or amendment discriminates on the basis of age is established, the burden of proof shifts and the sponsoring employer must prove that the provision or amendment is not a "subterfuge" by showing valid, non-age-related business reasons for the provision or amendment.[103] Valid business reasons will generally be the equalization of costs for employees in the older age group.[104] The employer can show cost equalization by proving that the costs for older employees are not below, or have not been reduced below, the level for employees in the five-year age bracket immediately preceding theirs.[105]

The basic problem with an ADEA challenge to a discriminatory defined benefit plan provision or amendment is that employers may be able to show that the defined benefit plan remains more costly overall for older workers, even with the amendment or plan provision. The employer may thus claim that regardless of whether an amendment discriminates on the basis of age, the plan is still satisfactory under cost-equalization. The employer must, however, be able to prove this, and more specifically, must be able to prove that the age-related cost reductions are not any more extensive than needed to equalize costs with the *next* preceding age group.[106] It is also questionable whether an employer can play off remaining costs against a plan amendment that by itself sharply discriminates on the basis of age. Salaries, too, are usually higher for older workers, but this does not mean that a 10 percent pay cut can apply only to workers over age 55 and not violate the ADEA. Along the same line, the EEOC's rules concerning health insurance coverage suggest that reductions may not be "concentrated on certain items so as to make coverage less attractive to older workers," apparently regardless of whether costs are equal even after the concentrated reductions.[107]

The question of whether a discriminatory plan amendment may be tested apart from a plan's remaining costs to determine whether it is a subterfuge has not been addressed because cases have not advanced

---

Cir. 1981); *Flight Officers, Inc. v. United Air Lines, Inc.*, 572 F.Supp. 1494, 4 EBC 2401 (N.D. Ill. 1983); *EEOC v. City of New Castle*, 4 EBC 2291 (W.D. Pa. 1983).

[102] See ch. 4, sec. IV.B.2.

[103] *EEOC v. Home Ins. Co., supra*, 3 EBC at 1066–69.

[104] 29 C.F.R. 860.120(d).

[105] 29 C.F.R. 860.120(d)(3).

[106] Differences in defined benefit plan pension costs for workers in succeeding 5-year age brackets are not as sharp as between workers age 30 and age 64, but still can be on the order of 60% more for workers in the next higher 5-year age bracket. See "The Costs of Employing Older Workers," 98th Cong., 2d Sess., at 51 (Comm. Print for the Senate Special Committee on Aging 1984).

[107] 29 C.F.R. 860.120(f)(1)(ii).

to that stage. In *Flight Officers, Inc. v. United Air Lines, Inc.*, a district court rejected a disparate impact claim from a pension plan amendment that changed a contributory plan to a noncontributory plan and credited years of service under the contributory plan only to the extent that an employee actually contributed to the plan. Prospectively, all years of service were to be credited since the plan had become noncontributory. It was alleged that this distinction favored younger employees, but the court had difficulty finding a rational discriminatory nexus with age. Rather the only "discrimination" appeared to be that the employees who had not made employee contributions before the plan amendment were now predominantly older workers.[108]

Beyond the question of exactly how cost-equalization applies to plan amendments, a "subterfuge" may also require knowledge or willfulness. In *Germann v. Levy*, lower life insurance benefits for employees who were past the age of 60 that exceeded differences justified by cost equalization did not lead to a "subterfuge" violation of the ADEA when the court viewed "subterfuge" as requiring knowledge or willfulness. Under the *Germann* plan, medical insurance was maintained at the same levels at all ages, but after age 60, life insurance coverage was reduced from $20,000 to $1,000. The court found this reduction went beyond that required by cost-equalization (although the cost of both the medical and life insurance coverage increased with age, they did not increase enough to justify this reduction). However, because the employer was not shown to have known the facts about the costs and the plan was an insurance policy that the company had not designed, the court refused to find a "subterfuge."[109]

IV. Race and Sex Discrimination

Under Title VII of the Civil Rights Act, 42 U.S.C. Section 2000e, *et seq.*, it is an unlawful employment practice:

> "[T]o discriminate against any individual with respect to his compensation, terms, conditions or privileges of employment, because of such individual's race, color, religion, sex, or national origin; or . . . to limit, segregate, or classify . . . employees . . . in any manner which would deprive or tend to deprive any individual of employment opportunities or otherwise adversely affect his status as an employee, because of such individual's race, color, religion, sex, or national origin."[110]

The U.S. Supreme Court's decisions in *Los Angeles Water & Power v. Manhart* and *Arizona Comm. for Deferred Compensation Plans v. Norris* prohibit the use of sex-based mortality assumptions in computing either employee contributions under a contributory pension plan or

---

[108] 572 F.Supp. 1494, 4 EBC 2401 (N.D. Ill. 1983).

[109] 553 F.Supp. 700 (N.D. Ill. 1982).

[110] 42 U.S.C. §2000e-2(a).

benefit payouts under any type of pension plan.[111] Both decisions also firmly establish the application of Title VII to discrimination under pension plans on the basis of race, sex, national origin, or religion (hereafter only race and sex are referred to). ERISA's legislative history is also crystalline in establishing that ERISA is not intended to preempt or impair the application of Title VII to employee benefit plans, including pension plans.[112] In contrast to the ADEA, moreover, Title VII contains no exception for observing the terms of a bona fide "employee benefit plan." Thus, Title VII's prohibitions apply to employee benefit plans to the same extent they apply to discrimination in any term or condition of employment.

A. Pension Benefits as a Remedy

Under Supreme Court precedent, successful Title VII claimants are entitled to "make whole" relief.[113] Consistent with this principle, numerous decisions have awarded pension benefits to victims of race or sex discrimination when it is shown that but for the discrimination, the plaintiffs would have received such benefits.[114]

Even without pension benefits as an express part of a remedial court order, hours of service for which back pay is awarded, or agreed to by an employer in a settlement, may be required to be credited for years of service for vesting and years of participation for benefit accruals under the Department of Labor's hours of service regulations. Under the regulatory elapsed time alternative to counting hours of service, periods for which back pay is awarded, or agreed to by an employer in settlement, are not required to be credited for vesting years of service, but they may be required to be credited for benefit accruals.[115]

---

[111] 435 U.S. 702, 1 EBC 1813 (1978) (*Manhart*), and 463 U.S. 1073, 4 EBC 1633 (1983) (*Norris*).

[112] See 2 ERISA Leg. Hist. 1862–63 (colloquy between Senators Mondale and Williams), 3 ERISA Leg. Hist. 3518–19 (colloquy between Representatives Abzug and Dent), and 3 ERISA Leg. Hist. 3475–76 (statement of Representative Schroeder).

[113] *Franks v. Bowman Construction Co.*, 424 U.S. 747, 763–70 (1976); *Albemarle Paper Co. v. Moody*, 422 U.S. 405, 418–21 (1975).

[114] See *EEOC v. St. Joseph Paper Co.*, 557 F.Supp. 435 (W.D. Tenn. 1983) (including order that employee be vested when reinstatement not appropriate); *Gates v. ITT Continental Baking Co.*, 581 F.Supp. 204 (N.D. Ohio 1984); *Berkman v. City of New York*, 580 F.Supp. 226 (E.D.N.Y. 1983); *Ingram v. Madison Square Garden Center*, 482 F.Supp. 426 (S.D.N.Y. 1979); *EEOC v. Kallir, Phillips, Ross, Inc.*, 401 F.Supp. 66 (S.D.N.Y. 1975), *aff'd*, 559 F.2d 1203 (2d Cir.), *cert. denied*, 434 U.S. 920 (1977); *Laffey v. Northwest Airlines, Inc.*, 366 F.Supp. 763 (D.D.C. 1973) and 374 F.Supp. 1382 (D.D.C. 1974), *vacated and remanded in part, aff'd in part*, 567 F.2d 429 (D.C. Cir. 1976), *cert. denied*, 434 U.S. 1086 (1978); *Tidwell v. American Oil Co.*, 332 F.Supp. 424 (D. Utah 1971). But compare *Whatley v. Skaggs Co.*, 707 F.2d 1129 (10th Cir. 1983), *cert. denied*, 464 U.S. 938 (1983) (profit-sharing contributions not included as remedy when employee voluntarily resigned before vesting, apart from the discrimination).

[115] See sec. III.A above (on remedies for age discrimination) for citations.

B. Disparate Treatment Under Plan Provisions

Manhart and *Norris* establish that disparate treatment under a plan, e.g., through the use of sex-distinct mortality assumptions for computing required employee contributions, or benefit payouts under optional forms of benefits, violates Title VII.[116] The use of different vesting schedules or retirement ages for men and women, or different conditions for death benefits for their spouses has also been found to violate Title VII.[117]

Under the 1978 Pregnancy Discrimination Amendments to Title VII, "women affected by pregnancy, childbirth or related medical conditions [are required to be] treated the same for all employment-related purposes, including receipt of benefits under fringe benefit programs, as other persons [with] similar [temporary or long-term inabilities to work]."[118] This amendment requires coverage of pregnancy and childbirth under health, disability, sick leave, and extended leave of absence plans whenever similar conditions are covered. If continued accumulation of pension credits is a benefit provided under a pension or profit-sharing plan for periods of disability, illness, or leave, such credits are also required for women who are similarly disabled or on leave because of pregnancy and childbirth.[119]

Racial discrimination under the express terms of a plan also violates Title VII, but it has been less prevalent. The use of race-based mortality tables for life insurance was largely discontinued by the 1950's.[120] Different vesting rules, retirement ages, or conditions for death benefits based on race do not seem to have ever been used outright under the terms of employee benefit plans.[121]

---

[116] See also the cases cited in *Norris* to the same effect, and ch. 6, sec. III.D, on the impact of the *Norris* decision on benefit payouts under different optional benefit forms.

[117] See *Chastang v. Flynn & Emrich Co.*, 541 F.2d 1040 (4th Cir. 1976) (different vesting requirements); *Rosen v. Public Service Elec. & Gas Co.*, 477 F.2d 90 (3d Cir. 1973) (different vesting and retirement age rules); *Fillinger v. East Ohio Gas Co.*, 4 FEP Cases 73 (N.D. Ohio 1971) (different retirement ages); *Bartmess v. Drewrys U.S.A., Inc.*, 444 F.2d 1186 (7th Cir. 1971), *cert. denied*, 404 U.S. 939 (1971) (different retirement ages); *Fitzpatrick v. Bitzer*, 390 F.Supp. 278 (D. Conn. 1974), *aff'd in part, rev'd in part*, 519 F.2d 559 (2d Cir. 1975), *aff'd in part, rev'd in part*, 427 U.S. 445 (1976) (different retirement ages); *Mixson v. Southern Bell Tel. Co.*, 334 F.Supp. 525 (N.D. Ga. 1971) (different conditions for death benefits). See also 29 C.F.R. 1604.9(f). Cf. *American Finance System, Inc. v. Harlow*, 65 F.R.D. 94 (D. Md. 1974) (alleging Title VII discrimination from earlier distribution dates of profit-sharing accounts for women following voluntary terminations).

[118] 42 U.S.C. §2000e(k), as amended by P.L. 95-555.

[119] See *Zichy v. Philadelphia*, 36 FEP Cases 1637 (E.D. Pa. 1979), and 29 C.F.R. 1604, Appendix, Q&A 17.

[120] See Amicus Brief of Eight Individual Actuaries, at 8, submitted to the Supreme Court in *Norris, supra*, Docket No. 82-52. And see J. Magee, *Life Insurance* (3d ed. 1957), at 657 and 730 (indicating that the practice diminished in the 1950's, but was still not extinct unless specifically prohibited under state law).

[121] In *Peters v. Missouri-Pacific RR Co.*, 483 F.2d 490 (5th Cir. 1973), *cert. denied*, 414 U.S. 1002 (1973), race discrimination under Title VII was found when black firemen were subject to mandatory retirement under a pension plan at age 65 while the white firemen's unions all had been able to negotiate an age 70 mandatory retirement age under separate pension plans.

C. Disparate Impact Under Plan Provisions

Potential disparate impact claims under pension and profit-sharing plans may be divided into three groups:

(1) *Disparate impact of coverage requirements.* If women or minorities are bunched in certain departments or job classifications, e.g., temporary or part-time work, or the shipping or clerical departments, that are excluded from pension coverage a disparate impact claim could arise, even if the plan's coverage requirements are not along patently racial or sexual lines.[122]

(2) *Disparate impact of coverage under a different plan with different benefits or benefit requirements.* Similarly, if women or minorities are bunched in certain departments or job classifications that are under a different plan that is less advantageous in terms of benefits or has more restrictive benefit requirements, such as in the years required for vesting, or in early retirement benefits, a disparate impact claim under Title VII could also arise.[123]

(3) *Disparate impact under the terms of one plan.* Even within a single plan, eligibility, vesting or benefit accrual requirements equally applicable to all workers could have a disparate impact among groups of workers along basically racial or sexual lines. Thus, the hours of work required for maximum benefits under a plan could be set just beyond the grasp of women or minority employees who have work assignments with limited hours, or the years required for vesting in unreduced early retirement benefits could be beyond the years customarily worked in occupations predominantly held by women and minorities.

A common query in each of these three situations may be whether the lines drawn under a plan, or plans, are another manifestation of job discrimination in placing employees in certain positions, e.g., in the jobs not covered by a plan, or in jobs that have high occupational turnover, and not promoting or transferring women or minority employees thereafter. If this type of job discrimination exists, the disparate impact of facially neutral pension plan provisions may be part of the proof of discrimination and damages in a broader job discrimination action. For example, in *Wilburn v. Steamship Trade Ass'n of Baltimore, Inc.*, black employees alleged, but were unable to prove, that

---

[122] A tax-qualified plan must meet either a percentage test for coverage or must cover a classification of employees that does not discriminate in favor of highly compensated employees. See ch. 2, sec. II. Neither standard directly tests for race or sex discrimination in exclusions from coverage.

[123] When an employer covers employees under two different plans and seeks to satisfy the Code's coverage requirements by aggregating the coverage under the two plans, the plans must be "comparable" under tests set out in Rev. Rul. 81-202. See ch. 2, sec. II.E. Those tests, however, permit substantial variations in the terms of the two plans and do not test for race or sex discrimination in placing employees under one plan or the other.

race discrimination in work assignments prevented them from working the number of hours required under a multiemployer plan for the maximum level of pension benefits.[124]

Assuming that discrimination in placing employees in certain jobs, or in the allocation of work, does not exist (or cannot be proven) the question becomes when a Title VII claim can be based on the disparate impact of facially neutral lines under a pension plan, or plans, standing alone. Following *Griggs v. Duke Power Co.*, a *prima facie* violation of Title VII is established by showing that discrete policies or practices that are neutral on their face nonetheless discriminate in impact against a particular group.[125] When such a showing is made, the employer may show that the practice or policy bears a demonstrable relationship to successful job performance.[126] For pension benefits, the analogous rebuttal would be that the pension practice or policy bears a demonstrable relationship to rewarding job performance. *Griggs* thus recognizes that "Congress directed the thrust of the Act to the consequences of employment practices, not simply the motivation";[127] proof of discriminatory motivation is, in fact, not required. Rather, once the plaintiff shows a substantial disproportionate impact from criteria used in employment, the employer must show job-relatedness or business necessity. Moreover, even if an employer can show this, criteria will not survive Title VII scrutiny if alternative criteria exist with an equivalent degree of job relatedness and lesser adverse impact.

Equally or more pertinent to an employer's defense against most claims of disparate impact under pension plans is that Section 703(h) of the Civil Rights Act provides:

> "Notwithstanding any other provision of this title, it shall *not* be an unlawful employment practice for an employer to apply different standards of compensation, or different terms, conditions, or privileges of employment pursuant to a bona fide seniority or merit system, or a system which measures earnings by quantity or quality of production or to employees who work in different locations, provided that such differences are not the result of an intention to discriminate because of race, color, religion, sex, or national origin . . . ."[128]

Cases applying Title VII to facially neutral pension requirements are relatively rare, but they reveal the contours of successful and unsuccessful claims and defenses. In *Marcoux v. State of Maine*, women "corrections officers" guarded women felons serving sentences of over five years at one prison facility, while male "prison guards" guarded male felons serving similar sentences at another facility. The women "corrections officers," however, did not come under the same special early retirement pension provisions applicable to "prison guards." The

---

[124] 376 F.Supp. 1228 (D. Md. 1974).

[125] 401 U.S. 424, at 430-31 (1971).

[126] *Id.*

[127] 401 U.S. at 432 (1971).

[128] 42 U.S.C. §2000e-2(h) (emphasis added).

State of Maine contended that the early retirement benefits were not discriminatorily provided because they also were not applicable to male "corrections officers" who worked at the same facility as the women. Thus, the state contended, the early retirement benefits were provided on the basis of job classification, rather than sex. The district court found, however, that the female "corrections officers" performed equal work under similar working conditions on jobs requiring equal skill, effort, and responsibility as those of the male "prison guards." The male "corrections officers" with whom the women had been grouped were not performing substantially equal jobs as they were not guarding dangerous felons. The court thus found that the State of Maine failed to prove that the adverse distinction in pension benefits was based on job classification and location, instead of sex.[129]

On the other hand, in *Dobbs v. City of Atlanta*, the provision of two more lucrative pension plans with earlier retirement ages for policemen and firefighters than for other city employees was not discriminatory, even though, because of past discrimination, the police and firefighters were predominantly white. The Fifth Circuit held that the differences in benefits did not constitute unlawful continuation or perpetuation of the past discrimination when there were no current barriers to blacks obtaining police and firefighter work, when the differences in benefits were prospectively neutral and rational because of the different risks and demands of police and fire work, and when the past discrimination in job allocation was not reinforced by new plan provisions.[130] Somewhat similarly, in *Simmons v. S.C. State Ports Authority*, black employees alleged that race discrimination caused their jobs to be classified as "temporary" jobs, which in turn were excluded from coverage under a pension plan. Although the discrimination in job classifications had been discontinued, they alleged the effects of the practice lingered under the pension plan. The district court, however, held that the statute of limitations barred the claim since it was in essence based on job discrimination that was beyond the limitations period.[131]

In *Carpenter v. Stephen F. Austin State University*, black and female job applicants were channeled into lower paid maintenance and clerical jobs which were all classified as hourly positions. Until 1964, when Title VII became effective, hourly positions were excluded from the university's retirement plan. After 1964, new hourly hires were automatically included in the pension plan, but employees hired before 1964 were required to choose between foregoing pension coverage entirely or contributing, *in one lump sum,* all employee contributions that would have been due if their past years of service had been covered by

---

[129] 35 FEP Cases 553, at 565 (D. Me. 1984). The court discounted that four women had become prison guards as "insignificant as far as removing the taint of unlawful gender-based discrimination." *Id.*, at n.7. The district court's decision was affirmed in 1986. See 7 EBC 2338 (1st Cir. 1986).

[130] 606 F.2d 557 (5th Cir. 1979).

[131] 495 F.Supp. 1239 (D.S.C. 1980), *aff'd,* 3 EBC 2413 (4th Cir. 1982).

the plan. The employees claimed this facially neutral requirement inhibited entry into the plan and had a disparate impact on blacks and women because they composed over 75 percent of the hourly group. The district court and the Fifth Circuit, however, held that the pre-1964 exclusion of hourly paid employees from the retirement plan was without an intent to discriminate (even though the channeling of blacks and women into lower paid hourly jobs had been discriminatory) because the exclusion of all hourly employees from the retirement plan had been based on administrative cost considerations and the belief that hourly employees "would not want" the employee contributions required for plan participation to be deducted from their weekly paychecks. In finding a lack of intent to discriminate, both courts discounted the fact that certain white hourly paid supervisors had been selectively reclassified as salaried employees to enable them to participate in the plan. Because of the lack of intent, the lingering effects of the pre-1964 exclusion did not constitute a continuing violation of Title VII.[132]

The Fifth Circuit did reject the employer's Section 703(h) seniority exception defense to the claim of discrimination from the requirement of a lump sum contribution for hourly employees hired before 1964 because the requirement was not directly based on the statutory criteria.[133]

However, a Title VII violation from the disparate impact of the lump sum contribution requirement still did not result because the requirement applied equally to white male hourly employees who had been excluded from the plan before 1964. Moreover, if less employee contributions had been required, hourly employees would have been favored over salaried employees who had been in the plan all along.[134]

---

[132] 706 F.2d 608 (5th Cir. 1983), *reh. denied,* 712 F.2d 1416 (5th Cir. 1983).

[133] In *California Brewers Ass'n v. Bryant,* 444 U.S. 598 (1980), by contrast, a 45 weeks of work requirement in a single year to become a "permanent" employee, with greater benefits under vacation pay and supplemental unemployment benefit plans from that status, was a "component" of a seniority system. The Supreme Court did not mention whether eligibility to participate in a pension plan followed the same distinction (the 45 weeks of work requirement may have run afoul of ERISA's minimum participation requirements), but the opinion provides no basis to distinguish consequences under a pension plan when they flow directly from a *bona fide* seniority system classification. The opinion did not distinguish the vacation and supplemental unemployment benefit advantages under the 45 weeks of work requirement from more traditional seniority protections against layoffs and promotion and transfer opportunity rights. Cf. *Teamsters v. U.S.,* 431 U.S. 324, at 343 (1977) (eligibility for pensions was based on years of service as determined under seniority system, but challenged part of seniority system did not relate to pension eligibility).

In *Carpenter v. Stephen F. Austin State Univ.,* 706 F.2d 608 (5th Cir. 1983), the plaintiffs also challenged the disparate impact of a second distinction drawn by the university under which an optional pension plan with vesting after one year and other advantages was offered academics and highly paid administrative employees, but not all salaried employees or any hourly employees. This distinction was found to be subject to a §703(h) defense because it was "attributable to a system that awarded more favorable benefits to higher level employees on the basis of their 'quality of production,' and [was] without intention to discriminate on the basis of race or gender." 706 F.2d at 628 n.10 (citing *Dobbs v. City of Atlanta, supra*).

[134] The court mentioned, but did not fully discuss, less onerous alternatives to the all-or-nothing lump sum contribution rule that would have enabled the hourly employees to contribute employee contributions for only part of their past service, or have allowed them to start under the plan as if they were post-1964 hires. See 706 F.2d at 629 n.11.

In so holding, the Fifth Circuit expressed general reservations about the extent to which disparate impact claims apply to fringe benefit programs. The court quoted from *Los Angeles Water & Power v. Manhart*, in which the Supreme Court stated that "assuming disparate-impact analysis applies to fringe benefits . . . , *some* disproportionate impact on one group or another" is "inevitabl[e]" from facially "completely neutral provisions."[135] In *Carpenter*, the Fifth Circuit emphasized that even under disparate impact analysis, the relationship between a facially neutral provision and the disproportionate impact must be analogous to height requirements producing a disproportionate impact against women, or high school diploma requirements disproportionately impacting blacks, before a *prima facie* claim is established that will shift the burden to the employer to show job-relatedness, or a Section 703(h) defense. A "happenstance that the group to which a rule applies is composed mostly of women and blacks does not give rise to Title VII liability, even under disparate impact."[136]

D. Intentional Discrimination

The overriding limitation to the Section 703(h) seniority and work classification exceptions—and also to any more general reluctance to apply disparate impact to employee benefit plans—is that any disproportionate impact must always be without an "intention to discriminate" on the basis of race or sex.[137] Sometimes employers may openly say that a classification used under a pension plan is not based on quantity or quality of production, but is because women or minorities don't need or appreciate deferred pension benefits, e.g., because their husbands will take care of them, or for minorities, because they don't value retirement benefits as highly as current compensation.[138]

The proof of "intent" sufficient to take a classification out from under Section 703(h) is still developing. Discriminatory intent under Section 703(h) is a "question of fact" requiring proof of "actual motive."[139] This intent may be established by direct evidence or by the circumstances, for example, if the history of the pension plan reveals changes or amendments creating or reinforcing a disproportionate impact on the basis of race or sex that could not have occurred without "conscious regard" to race- or gender-based impact and that do not serve a "separate and distinct" business purpose.[140] In a technical area

---

[135] 435 U.S. 702, 1 EBC 1813, at 1816 n.20 (1978) (emphasis in original).

[136] 706 F.2d at 630.

[137] See generally *Teamsters v. U.S.*, 431 U.S. 324 (1977).

[138] But see *Carpenter v. Stephen F. Austin State Univ.*, 706 F.2d 608 (5th Cir. 1983) (no discriminatory intent when "the defendant had determined at the time [before Title VII] that these lower paid employees [over three-quarters of whom were black or female] would not want deductions made from their wages" for retirement).

[139] *Pullman-Standard v. Swint*, 456 U.S. 273, at 290 (1982).

[140] See generally *Sears v. Atchison, Topeka & Santa Fe Ry. Co.*, 645 F.2d 1365 (10th Cir. 1981), *cert. denied*, 456 U.S. 964 (1982) (changes in seniority system that could not have occurred

like pensions, courts may as in *Manhart* be inclined to believe that "some disproportionate impact" is "inevitabl[e]," and thus, not intentional.[141] But the degree of inevitability of discrimination under facially neutral *pension* plan provisions may not be as great as it appears in the abstract. An employer will generally be aware that employees in a department with occupationally high turnover are not going to vest under a 30-year requirement for early retirement benefits, or that under a plan with a high Social Security offset or excess benefit level, lower paid employees are not going to receive significant benefits. The employer is also likely to know who those employees are, e.g., that black employees in the shipping department will not receive pension benefits because of the level at which a Social Security offset or excess formula is set.[142] Such awareness may bring an employer close to a "conscious regard" for race- or gender-based impact in the design of the plan. The open question may then be how receptive courts are to claims that such features of plans serve "separate and distinct" business purposes.

---

without "conscious regard" to race may show intent); *James v. Stockham Valves & Fittings Co.*, 559 F.2d 310 (5th Cir. 1977), *cert. denied,* 434 U.S. 1034 (1978) (lack of "separate and distinct" functional business basis for classifications weighs in whether seniority system is bona fide).

[141] *Los Angeles Water & Power, Inc. v. Manhart, supra,* 1 EBC at 1816 n. 20.

[142] If this seems to impute a degree of awareness that employers may lack, it may be remembered that, in contrast to health insurance plans, pension plans are generally designed with employer input on the vesting and Social Security integration options to be used under the plan. The options are generally discussed with a benefits specialist or attorney who will tell the employer that under a Social Security offset or excess formula his employees making less than a certain amount will receive disproportionately less, or no, benefits. The employer presumably knows who those employees are.

11

Work Force Reductions and Partial Terminations

The business section of any newspaper reveals the frequency with which large reductions in employment occur through plant closings and mass layoffs. With attention often focused on the ERISA Title IV rules for complete pension plan terminations, what passes less noticed is that most of these plant closings and work force reductions take place without a complete pension plan termination. In single-employer plans, plants, divisions, and entire subsidiaries may be shut down with no termination of the pension plan. Similarly, in multiemployer plans, contributing employers can go out of business by the dozens each year with no termination of the overall plan.

For participants in single-employer plans, the closing of a plant, or a mass reduction in the work force, means the loss of their jobs, and frequently, for older workers, the loss of any real prospects for future employment. As far as pension benefits, it means the loss of any opportunity to vest in unvested normal or early retirement benefits. If a plant closes when an employee has eight years of service, the opportunity to vest in benefits under a 10-year cliff vesting schedule is lost. Similarly, any chance for early retirement benefits is lost if a plant closes when an employee has 23 years of service and the early retirement provision requires 25 years.

For participants in multiemployer plans, the effects of a plant's closing or the discharge of a large percentage of an employer's work force can vary. A carpenter who is a participant in a multiemployer plan may be able to find work with another union contractor who contributes to the same multiemployer plan. Even if the carpenter has to move out of the area covered by the plan to find work, if he or she can find work with a union contractor who contributes to a multiemployer plan affiliated with the same international union, the plans may have reciprocity agreements that will tie service for vesting and benefit accruals together. However, these opportunities are not always present. A carpenter, forced out of work by changing industry conditions, may go to work as a millwright in a factory that has a single-employer plan with no reciprocity agreements, he may go to work for an employer who has no plan, or he may retire because of inability to find work. When an entire industry is in flux, the carpenter, along with 15 to 20 percent of the participants in the plan, may be excluded from the plan. Yet, if he is a year or two short of vesting or early retirement, no accommodation may be made to secure his pension benefits.[1]

In these situations, the participants' expectations of becoming entitled to pension benefits have been dashed. Participants assume the risk of shortfalls in service for pension benefit vesting due to discharges "for cause" or "voluntary" quits, but few expect that they will be left short of benefit entitlement because their plant closed or their trade or craft became obsolete. Perhaps most important, as Merton Bernstein discussed over 20 years ago, the pension plan's actuary has probably not assumed mass layoffs and plant closings in constructing turnover assumptions for funding the plan either. Given this, the plan may actually reap a windfall from assets that have been set aside on the assumption that most of these employees would have the opportunity to continue in service long enough to vest in normal or in early retirement benefits.[2] In light of the assumptions on both sides, the retention of these assets for use in reducing the employer's subsequent contribution obligations, or the reallocation of the forfeited account balances to other participants' accounts in profit-sharing plans, may be said to "cheat the affected laid off employees of their hard-earned retirement benefits."[3]

In many instances, laid-off participants are, of course, only temporarily laid off and are recalled by their employer after a period of time, or in the case of a multiemployer plan, are hired by another employer contributing to the plan (or to another plan with a reciprocity agreement with the first). When a participant is recalled or rehired, the questions basically are:

(1) What vesting and benefit accrual credits did the participant have before the layoff;

(2) How did the layoff affect those credits and accruals (e.g., was

---

[1] With the expansion of unions, such as the Teamsters, beyond the occupations reflected in their names, multiemployer plans increasingly encompass service and industrial workers. Laid off and discharged participants who are in these occupations may be no more likely to find work with another employer covered by the plan than they are to work for any other employer.

[2] See M. Bernstein, "Employee Pension Rights When Plants Shut Down," 76 Harv. L. Rev. 952, at 967-72 (1963).

[3] Brief of IRS, at 18, in *Tipton & Kalmbach, Inc. v. Commissioner*, 83 T.C. 154, 5 EBC 1976 (1984).

the layoff so long that a disqualifying break in service occurred under the plan);

(3) What, if any, additional credits are due for some part or all of the layoff for vesting and/or benefit accruals; and

(4) How soon are new credits for vesting and accrual to recommence for work after the recall or rehire?

The answers to these questions are discussed above in Chapters 4 and 5, in the sections on counting years of participation for benefit accrual and years of service for vesting.

I. Partial Terminations of Plans

When participants are discharged or laid off en masse, and are not subsequently recalled or rehired, Section 411(d)(3) of the Code, and the related regulations, provide a powerful remedy for any shortfall in service normally required for vesting through declaration of a "partial termination." Section 411(d)(3) provides:

> "Notwithstanding the provisions of subsection (a) [the minimum vesting standards], a trust shall not constitute a qualified trust under section 401(a) unless the plan . . . provides that . . . upon its termination or partial termination . . . the rights of all affected employees to benefits accrued to the date of such termination, partial termination, or discontinuance, to the extent funded as of such date, . . . are nonforfeitable."

ERISA added the term "partial termination" to the preexisting Code provision requiring nonforfeitability on "termination" of a plan. But the rule that benefits must become nonforfeitable on a "partial termination" of a pension plan was actually developed before ERISA in regulations and Revenue Rulings issued under the preexisting Code Section 401(a)(7).[4] The concept of a partial termination is also rooted in the doctrines of impracticability and prevention in contract law.[5] In effect, a partial termination provides for recovery to prevent unjust enrichment when unexpected events, such as plant closings, interfere with the opportunity to vest under the normal schedule—to the extent the benefits are already funded. In *Tipton & Kalmbach, Inc. v. Commissioner*, the Tax Court recognized that Section 411(d)(3) thus serves a broad "ameliorative purpose." According to the Tax Court, Congress thereby

> "sought to protect employees from forfeiting their retirement benefits upon termination of a plan. . . . Where a significant percentage of plan participants are discharged, the effect is the same [as on a complete termination:] unless the discharge is a partial termination, a significant

---

[4] See 26 C.F.R. 1.401-6(b)(2) and Rev. Ruls. 72-439, 72-510 (superseded by Rev. Rul. 81-27), and Rev. Rul. 73-284.

[5] See ch. 8, sec. VI.C, and M. Bernstein, "Employee Pension Rights When Plans Shut Down," 76 Harv. L. Rev. 952 (1963).

percentage of plan participants are compelled to forfeit accrued but nonvested retirement benefits."[6]

Other courts have recognized that Section 411(d)(3), and its predecessor Section 401(a)(7), were enacted to protect the rights of nonvested participants when they are deprived of the opportunity to vest by events that are not normally anticipated, and that would, without a partial termination determination, permit the employer to enjoy a "windfall" reduction in its subsequent funding obligations based on the unanticipated forfeitures.[7]

ERISA's legislative history does not set out exact guidelines on the circumstances which are to prompt a "partial termination." Although references to partial terminations appear throughout the legislative history, the only attempt to give concrete meaning to the term is an identical parenthetical appearing in three committee reports, stating:

> "Examples of a partial termination might include, under certain circumstances, a large reduction in the work force, or a sizable reduction in benefits under the plan."[8]

Congress thus left the detailed construction of the term "partial termination" to the IRS. The IRS's regulations implementing Section 411(d)(3) are, however, similarly circumstantial, providing:

> "Whether or not a partial termination of a qualified plan occurs (and the time of such event) shall be determined by the Commissioner with regard to all the facts and circumstances in a particular case. Such facts and circumstances include: the exclusion, by reason of a plan amendment or severance by the employer, of a group of employees who have previously been covered by the plan; and plan amendments which adversely affect the rights of employees to vest in benefits under the plan."[9]

As discussed in more detail below, the IRS's "facts and circumstances" test has evolved in numerous Revenue Rulings, court decisions, and private letter rulings into a more objective test for whether a "significant percentage" or a "significant number" of participants have been excluded from a plan by a plant closing, permanent layoff, transfer of work to another location, or otherwise (such as when a group of participants is excluded from a plan as a result of a collective bargaining agreement placing them under another plan). As stated in Revenue

---

[6] 83 T.C. 154, 5 EBC 1976, at 1980 (1984).

[7] *United Steelworkers v. Harris & Sons Steel Co.*, 706 F.2d 1289, 4 EBC 1396, at 1404-05 (3d Cir. 1983). And see *Tionesta Sand & Gravel, Inc. v. Commissioner*, 73 T.C. 758 (1980), *aff'd*, 642 F.2d 444 (3d Cir. 1981). Cf. *Union Central Life Ins. Co. v. Hamilton Steel Prod., Inc.*, 448 F.2d 501, at 507 (7th Cir. 1971).

[8] S. Rep. 93-383, at 50, 1 ERISA Leg. Hist. 1118, H.R. Rep. 93-807, at 65, 2 ERISA Leg. Hist. 3185, and H.R. Rep. 93-779, at 64, 2 ERISA Leg. Hist. 2653; and see "Material in the Nature of a Committee Report Explaining H.R. 12906," introduced by Rep. Perkins, chairman of the House Education and Labor Committee, 2 ERISA Leg. Hist. 3330.

[9] 26 C.F.R. 1.411(d)-2(b)(1). As the regulations and legislative history both suggest, a "sizable reduction in benefits" under a plan can also result in a partial termination. This was at one time called a benefit "curtailment" partial termination and is discussed in ch. 9 on plan amendments. For a defined benefit plan, this type of partial termination is generally confined, under a special rule in the regulations, to instances where the reduction in benefits creates, or increases, a potential reversion to the employer maintaining the plan. See 26 C.F.R. 1.411(d)-2(b)(2).

Ruling 81-27, the test for a significant percentage or number is moreover

> "[i]rrespective of whether the significant decrease in participation in the plan was the result of adverse economic conditions or causes within the control of the employer."

Thus, in *Tipton & Kalmbach, Inc. v. Commissioner*, the Tax Court flatly rejected an employer's argument that a partial termination should not occur because a downturn in its business was not within its control. The Tax Court held that a partial termination is not dependent on a finding of fault or abusive intent or purpose on the part of the employer.[10]

While the decline in participation need not be the fault of the employer, the courts and the IRS have at the same time sought to limit partial terminations to events that are not within the employees' own control or volition. In *Weil v. Terson Co. Retirement Plan Committee,* the Second Circuit emphasized that the exclusion of a significant percentage or number of participants from a plan must be *"in connection with a major corporate event."* If employees leave voluntarily, or for reasons unrelated to the corporate event, a partial termination either would not occur, or if it otherwise occurred, would not apply to those employees.[11] Similarly, in a General Counsel Memorandum, the IRS concluded that a partial termination did not occur when strikers refused an offer of reemployment at the conclusion of an apparently unsuccessful strike, because the reduction in the percentage of participants was not the result of "employer-initiated action," but rather resulted from a decision within the employees' own "volition." The Memorandum concluded that employee-participants "do not need protection [under Section 411(d)(3)] if the reason retirement benefits are forfeited is the result of voluntary employee behavior that did not occur as a result of employer-initiated action."[12]

Although this voluntary/involuntary distinction is in accord with the common law roots of Section 411(d)(3) in impracticability and prevention, the distinction between the two is often blurred (as a closer examination of the stipulated facts in the General Counsel Memorandum might have shown). It also may be out of line with earlier Revenue Rulings. In Revenue Ruling 72-439, a union negotiated a separate pension plan for members of the bargaining unit; the collective bargaining agreement provided that the employer was to amend its profit-sharing plan to prospectively exclude those employees from further participation in that plan. While this exclusion was arguably the result of "voluntary" employee action, a partial termination resulted. In the same Ruling, the partial termination occurred, moreover, *despite the fact* that the employer provided that the employees' future service with

---

[10] 83 T.C. 154, 5 EBC 1976 (1984).

[11] 750 F.2d 10, 5 EBC 2537, at 2540 (2d Cir. 1984) (emphasis in the original).

[12] GCM 39344 (March 6, 1985), reprinted in 12 BNA Pens. Rep., at 474 (April 1, 1985).

the employer would still count for vesting in the benefits they had accrued under the profit-sharing plan.[13] Similarly, in Revenue Ruling 73-284, an employer changed its business location, but offered employees jobs at the new location 100 miles away. Again the exclusion from the plan was arguably due, at least in part, to the employees' "voluntary" decision not to relocate, but a partial termination occurred.

A. Significant Percentage Test

What constitutes a "significant percentage" has gradually emerged in Revenue Rulings and court decisions. In Revenue Ruling 73-284, a partial termination occurred when 12 of 15 participants, or 80 percent of the participants, were "effectively excluded" from a plan when they did not relocate to an employer's new business location 100 miles away.[14] In Revenue Ruling 72-439, a partial termination occurred where 120 of 170 participants, or 70.6 percent, in a profit-sharing plan were excluded from participation upon coming under a collectively bargained plan. In Revenue Ruling 81-27, a partial termination occurred where 95 of 165 participants, or 57.6 percent, were excluded from participation in a plan when an employer dissolved one of two divisions of its business. In *Tipton & Kalmbach, Inc. v. Commissioner*, the Tax Court affirmed the IRS's determination of two successive partial terminations in which 34 percent of the participants in a profit-sharing plan were excluded in one year, and 51 percent of the remaining participants were excluded the next year, due to a downturn in the employer's business.[15] In *Weil v. Terson Co. Retirement Plan Committee*, 104 of 386 participants in a plan, or 27 percent, were excluded as the result of a shutdown of 2 of 16 divisions of a company. The district court determined that no partial termination had occurred,[16] but on appeal, the Second Circuit reversed and remanded for further consideration by the district court. While not providing precise guidelines, the Second Circuit twice emphasized that the question was whether a significant number of employees had been excluded "in connection with a major corporate event."[17] In an amicus brief, the Treasury Department "strongly suggested" that 27 percent was significant under the circumstances.[18] Finally, in a 1978 private letter ruling, the IRS stated, "as a matter of general information," that the exclusion of 400

---

[13] Such credit is now required under ERISA's minimum standards. See ch. 5, sec. III.A.1.

[14] The addition of an equal number of replacement employees did not subtract from the number of excluded employees used in testing for a partial termination. Rev. Rul. 73-284, and see W.R. Culp, Jr., "Not All Reductions in Covered Employees Result in Partial Terminations of a Plan," 63 J. Tax. 294 (Nov. 1985).

[15] 83 T.C. 154, 5 EBC 1976 (1984). See also PLR 7909084 (Nov. 30, 1978) (78 of 160 participants, or 49%, declared partial termination).

[16] 577 F.Supp. 781, 5 EBC 1265 (S.D.N.Y. 1984).

[17] 750 F.2d 10, 5 EBC 2537, at 2540 (2d Cir. 1984).

[18] See GCM 39344 n.5 (March 6, 1985), reprinted in 12 BNA Pens. Rep., at 475 n.5 (April 1, 1985).

of 1,800 participants, or 22.2 percent, from a plan when a division closed "constituted a partial termination."[19]

In five recent court cases and a special IRS ruling, partial terminations were determined *not* to have occurred. In *Ehm v. Phillips Petroleum Co.*, a partial termination was determined not to have occurred when 415 out of 16,444 participants were excluded from a thrift plan by the closing of the employer's Kansas City refinery. The district court found that the percentage, 2.5 percent, was not significant under the IRS's rulings and other federal district court decisions.[20] In *Wishner v. St. Luke's Hospital Center*, a district court determined that the exclusion of 57 of 1,529 participants, or 3.7 percent, when their community out-patient health facility disassociated from St. Luke's Hospital, was not a "significant percentage," and thus, not a partial termination.[21] In *Beck v. Shaw Industries, Inc.*, a district court ruled that the exclusion of 100 of 1,599 participants, or 6.2 percent, was not a partial termination, noting that the percentage was not "significant" under existing rulings and that the dismissals were not the result of a shutdown of a separate "division" of the employer, although they did result from sale of an entire plant.[22] In *Babb v. Olney Paint Co.*, 14 out of 109, or 12.8 percent, of the participants in both a pension and a profit-sharing plan were excluded from participation when their division was spun off as a separate corporate entity, but the Fourth Circuit found no partial termination.[23] In *Taylor v. Food Giant, Inc., Salaried Employees Pension Plan*, no partial termination occurred when 44 of 344 participants, or 12.8 percent, were excluded from a plan by the sale of a corporate division to another company.[24] Finally, in a special ruling issued in 1978, the IRS determined that the exclusion of 2 out of 12 participants, or 16.7 percent, from a profit-sharing plan was not a partial termination.[25]

Despite the indications in *Babb*, *Taylor*, and the special ruling, partial terminations have sometimes been declared by IRS key district offices with percentages as low as 10 percent.[26] But as a general benchmark, although never quite stated as an outright rule, 20 percent is the dividing line for a partial termination on a percentage basis, *if* certain other factors are present. The IRS states that the Revenue Rulings described above with percentages above 50 percent represent "clear-

---

[19] PLR 7902030 (Oct. 10, 1978).

[20] 583 F.Supp. 1113, 5 EBC 1857 (D. Kan. 1984). See also *Bruch v. Firestone Tire & Rubber Co.*, 640 F.Supp. 519 (E.D. Pa. 1986) (no fiduciary duty to consider if partial termination occurred when 228 out of 10,500 participants, or 2%, excluded by sale of 5 plants).

[21] 550 F.Supp. 1016, 3 EBC 2621 (S.D.N.Y. 1982).

[22] 2 EBC 2366 (N.D. Ga. 1981).

[23] 764 F.2d 240, 6 EBC 1756, at 1758 (4th Cir. 1985). While the results would appear to be the same in either case, it is worth noting that in determining the percentage of participants excluded, the Fourth Circuit did not count two excluded participants whose interests in the plans were "fully vested."

[24] 6 EBC 1291 (N.D. Ga. 1984).

[25] Special Ruling dated Sept. 1, 1978, reprinted in CCH Pension Plan Guide, at ¶17,367S.

[26] See 462 BNA Pens. Rep. 1477 (Sept. 19, 1983) (reporting speech by Peter Turza of Gibson, Dunn and Crutcher to National Association of Manufacturers' conference).

cut" examples of partial terminations regardless of other circumstances.[27] But when 20 percent of the participants in a plan are excluded, the IRS states the fact that the exclusion was the result of the "elimination of a division, a plant closing, or the discontinuance of a particular product" weighs in favor of the partial termination determination.[28] Similarly, in *Weil,* with a 27 percent exclusion, the central factor emphasized by the Second Circuit was whether the employees were discharged or laid off *"in connection with a major corporate event."*[29]

Other factors bearing on whether a partial termination occurs with exclusions of around 20 percent are:

- Increased discrimination in favor of prohibited group employees from the exclusion of participants who are primarily rank and file employees, e.g., by the reallocation of forfeitures to highly compensated employees' accounts under a profit-sharing plan;[30] and
- The potential for a reversion of "excess" assets under a defined benefit plan.[31]

Plan amendments immediately before or after a plant closing or work force reduction that either restrict eligibility for benefits or decrease benefit amounts may also weigh in favor of a partial termination.[32]

A factor weighing against the occurrence of a partial termination is the number of excluded employees who are later recalled; however, the mere possibility that employees will later be recalled or rehired is

---

[27] IRS Doc. 6678, "Plan Termination Standards" (4-81), reprinted at ¶107,402 P-H Pens. & Profit Sharing.

[28] See IRS Doc. 6678, "Plan Termination Standards" (4-81). Twenty percent has also been recognized in a number of articles as generally being the lower percentage that causes a partial termination to occur because of its appearance in IRS forms and documents, such as IRS Doc. 6678, and its appearance in other parts of ERISA as a measure of substantial change in a plan. See ERISA §4043(b)(3), §4062(e), and 29 C.F.R. 2615.14. And see W.R. Culp, Jr., "Not All Reductions in Covered Employees Result in Partial Terminations of a Plan," 63 J. Tax. 294 (Nov. 1985); S. Lewis, "Partial Terminations of Qualified Plans," 13 Comp. Plan. J. 223 (July 5, 1985), M. Macris, "Partial Terminations of Qualified Plans," 11 J. Pens. Plan. & Compl. 49 (Spring 1985), and S. Offer, "Partial Terminations of Qualified Plans," 9 Tax. Law. 240 (Jan.-Feb. 1981).

Percentages lower than 20% may be most likely to result in a partial termination if prohibited discrimination under a profit-sharing plan occurs through the exclusion of nonvested rank and file employees with reallocation of their forfeited account balances to prohibited group employees' accounts otherwise occurring, or when a potential reversion of "excess" assets under a defined benefit plan is created or increased.

[29] 750 F.2d 10, 5 EBC 2537, at 2540 (2d Cir. 1984) (emphasis in original). Along the same lines, the IRS's first proposed regulations on partial terminations emphasized whether a "readily identifiable group of employees" had been excluded, using an example where one of an employer's three factories closed. See 28 Fed. Reg. 3406 (1963). Only more general language was included when the regulations were made final. See 28 Fed. Reg. 10120 (1963).

[30] IRS Doc. 6678, "Plan Termination Standards" (4-81).

[31] *Id.*, and see *Tipton & Kalmbach, Inc. v. Commissioner,* 83 T.C. 154, 5 EBC 1976, at 1980 (1984) (reversion potential a factor, but not an essential one because of broader ameliorative purpose of partial termination authority).

[32] See 26 C.F.R. 1.411(d)-2(b)(1). In certain circumstances, a plan amendment restricting eligibility or decreasing benefits may by itself lead to a partial termination declaration (at one time called a benefit "curtailment" partial termination). See ch. 9, sec. VIII.A.

not consequential.[33] Under the IRS's pre-ERISA regulations, a second negative factor arose if the buyer of a plant, division, or subsidiary reemployed the excluded participants and credited their years of service for vesting under a "comparable" plan.[34] Although this continues to be mentioned,[35] it is no longer a consideration. Credit for vesting under a buyer's plan only affects how likely it is that participants will incur a second loss of benefits on a subsequent discharge or layoff from employment with the buyer, it does not diminish the first loss of benefits earned under the seller's plan.[36]

A different type of factor that could cause relatively low percentages to produce a partial termination occurs when a company reduces operations on a *protracted* basis. For example, if a "significant percentage" reduction in a single year is 20 percent when it occurs "in connection with a major corporate event," a 25 percent reduction over a two-year period could be considered a significant percentage if it is in connection with a major corporate event, such as a systematic reduction in an employer's operations.[37] The IRS was scheduled to rule on whether such a partial termination, or partial terminations, occurred under the Great A&P Tea Company's pension plan when "[b]etween 1970 and 1979 A&P reduced the number of its retail stores from 4,500 to 1,500 and the number of its employees from 130,000 to 63,000."[38] A&P later completely terminated the plan to obtain a reversion of over $200 million in "excess" plan assets, but the results of the partial termination determination have not been reported.[39] In *Weil v. Terson Co. Retirement Plan Committee*, however, a district court refused to look at reductions over a protracted period (from 1975 to 1981) as a circumstance in determining whether a partial termination occurred. It found that the years up to 1980 had been the subject of previous, negative IRS determinations. The court reasoned that since the IRS district office had focused on one-year periods in making its determinations, the court also would not look at the percentage over a longer than one-year period. On appeal, the Second Circuit did not question this part of the district court's holding.[40]

Actually, in an A&P-type case, where reductions in participation

---

[33] See 11 BNA Pens. Rep. 649 (May 14, 1984) (remarks of Sam Berger, IRS attorney, at Washington employee benefits forum), and *Tipton & Kalmbach, Inc. v. Commissioner, supra,* 5 EBC at 1981 (mere possibility that employees may later be rehired is not consequential).

[34] 26 C.F.R. 1.401-6(b)(1).

[35] See J. Mamorsky, *Employee Benefits Law* (Law Journal Seminars-Press 1982 ed.), at 13-26.

[36] See 26 C.F.R. 1.411(d)-3(b), IRS Doc. 6678, and 12 BNA Pens. Rep. 484 (April 1, 1985) (letter of Ronald A. Pearlman, Assistant Secretary of the Treasury for Tax Policy, to Rep. Edward A. Roybal) (full vesting required on a partial or complete termination regardless of whether excluded participants come under a "comparable" plan).

[37] This is the PBGC's criteria for a reportable event. See ERISA §4043(b)(3) and 29 C.F.R. 2615.14.

[38] *Walsh v. A&P Co.*, 4 EBC 2577, at 2579 (3d Cir. 1983).

[39] See *Walsh v. A&P Co.*, 4 EBC 1055, at 1074 (D.N.J. 1983), *aff'd,* 4 EBC 2577 (3d Cir. 1983).

[40] 577 F.Supp. 781, 5 EBC 1265 (S.D.N.Y. 1984), *aff'd,* 750 F.2d 10, 5 EBC 2537 (2d Cir. 1984).

culminate in a *complete termination* of the plan, a separate partial termination declaration may be unnecessary. On a complete termination, the accrued benefits of participants who were previously excluded from the plan should become nonforfeitable to the extent benefits are funded, unless the period of the participant's separation has already exceeded his or her previous years of service under the plan so that a forfeiture occurred under the plan's break-in-service rules before the date of termination.[41]

B. Significant Number Test

While less developed in court decisions, the IRS's test for a partial termination is for a "significant percentage" *or* a "significant number." Revenue Ruling 82-27, in fact, referred to the discharge of 95 of 165 participants as a "significant number" rather than "percentage." While the IRS may not have intended this to mean that a partial termination occurs *whenever* 95 or more participants are discharged, the legislative history's repeated reference to "a large reduction in the work force" indicates that the absolute number of employees, rather than the percentage, can be the critical element. In two private letter rulings, the IRS also focused on the "number," rather than the "percentage." In PLR 7909084 (November 30, 1978), the exclusion of 78 of 160 participants was stated "as a matter of general information" to be "such a substantial number" that a partial termination occurred. Similarly, in PLR 7902030 (October 10, 1978), the exclusion of 400 out of 1800 participants was, again "as a matter of general information," "such a substantial number" as to constitute a partial termination.[42]

In *Ehm v. Phillips Petroleum Co.*, however, a district court rejected a partial termination claim based on a "significant number" when 415 out of 16,444 participants were excluded from Phillips Petroleum's nationwide thrift plan upon the closing of its Kansas City refinery. The court stated that although none of the rulings or cases dealt with this large a number, it was "not persuaded that this difference alone provides an adequate basis for disregarding the significant percentage test."[43] As noted before, the percentage of *all* participants excluded in *Ehm* was low, 2.5 percent, and thus was not "significant" under the percentage test. In *Beck v. Shaw Industries, Inc.*, a district court approved a plan administrator's decision that 100 participants was not a significant "number or percentage." The plan administrator

---

[41] See ch. 12, sec. III, and GCM 39310 (April 4, 1984) (on complete or partial termination, nonvested and partially vested participants must vest unless their benefits have already been "forfeited" or cashed-out).

[42] And see IRS Doc. 6678 (4-81) (also distinguishing the "number" from the "percentage").

[43] 583 F.Supp. 1113, 5 EBC 1857 at 1859 (D. Kan. 1984). See also *Bruch v. Firestone Tire & Rubber Co.*, 640 F.Supp. 519 (E.D. Pa. 1986) (rejecting exclusion of 228 participants as a significant number even though their exclusion was in connection with a major corporate event—the sale of 5 plants comprising a plastics division to another company).

in *Beck* had a concurring determination letter from an IRS key district office to back him up.[44]

In *Weil v. Terson Co. Retirement Plan Committee*, 104 participants were excluded with the closing of two divisions. The district court never discussed the "significant number" test, but focused exclusively on the percentage test.[45] On appeal, the Second Circuit reversed and remanded for a determination of whether a "significant number" of employees had been excluded from the plan. Although the Second Circuit referred to a determination of whether this was a significant "number" three times, it is still not clear from the opinion whether the court recognized that the significant "number" test is distinct from the percentage test.[46] In *Tipton & Kalmbach, Inc. v. Commissioner,* the Tax Court did not need to reach the issue of whether the number might be significant by itself, but expressly reserved any holding on whether the number of participants excluded from a plan might be significant independently, citing *Ehm* as a case where this issue had been raised.[47]

When this issue is finally fully addressed by the courts and the IRS, it would be incongruous to conclude that an employer with 20 participants in a plan is required to make benefits nonforfeitable on a "partial termination" when 4, or 20 percent, of the participants are discharged, while permitting an employer such as AT&T to exclude up to 24,000 participants with no partial termination of the plan, because the "percentage" may still be small. When the number of participants excluded is large in absolute numbers, a "large reduction in the work force" has taken place, regardless of the percentage. Not only are the benefits at stake larger, but the administrative expense of a partial termination declaration compared to the benefits it confers is far less than in a small defined benefit plan where a significant percentage, but very small number, of participants are excluded.

A factor that weighs in favor of determining that the exclusion of an absolute number of participants is significant is again whether the participants were excluded "in connection with a major corporate event," such as "the elimination of a division, a plant closing, or the discontinuance of a particular product."[48]

---

[44] 2 EBC 2366 (N.D. Ga. 1981).

[45] 577 F.Supp. 781, 5 EBC 1265 (S.D.N.Y. 1984).

[46] 750 F.2d 10, 5 EBC 2537 (2d Cir. 1984).

[47] 83 T.C. 154, 5 EBC 1976, at 1980 n.6 (1984). See also W.R. Culp, Jr., "Not All Reductions in Covered Employees Result in Partial Terminations of a Plan," 63 J. Tax. 294 (Nov. 1985) (in light of the legislative history, exclusion of 415 employees in *Ehm* should have been significant).

[48] See sec. I.A above.

C. Significant Percentages and Numbers in Multiemployer Plans

In multiemployer plans, the number rather than the percentage is likely to be critical to a partial termination declaration. In a large multiemployer plan, dozens of companies may go out of business or otherwise withdraw from a plan each year without a "significant percentage" of the plan's total participants being excluded. To date, however, the IRS has not declared a partial termination of a multiemployer plan in a published ruling, either on a percentage or a numerical basis—possibly because the participants can, at least in theory, still go to work for another company contributing to the plan, and thereby secure additional credits needed to vest. It also may be that the "to the extent funded" caveat is so much more limiting for multiemployer plans that the IRS has generally not found it valuable for participants to make the declaration.[49] However, when the right has value, and when it can be shown that work for other employers contributing to the plan is not available, a partial termination of a multiemployer plan should be declared on the same basis as for a single-employer plan. One recognized difference is that when a multiemployer plan contains distinct "benefit computation formulas" for different groups of participants, as multiemployer plans sometimes do, the determination of a partial termination may be based on whether a significant percentage or number of the group of participants under a particular benefit computation formula has been excluded from the plan.[50] A difference in past service credits granted different groups of participants might constitute a separate "benefit computation formula."[51]

The IRS had several candidates for a partial termination of a multiemployer plan on *either* a percentage or a numerical basis presented by the multiemployer plans that received contributions from work on the Trans-Alaska oil pipeline. Participation in the Alaska Hotel and Restaurant Employees Retirement Plan, for example, dropped more than 60 percent in two years, from 7,004 participants in 1977 to 2,683 participants in 1979.[52] Participation in the Alaska Laborers-Employers Retirement Fund, similarly, dropped 75 percent in one year, from 7,963 participants in 1978 to 1,982 participants in 1979.[53] But while the IRS was considering declaring a partial termination of these plans, a special proviso was enacted in the 1984 Deficit Reduction Act, introduced by the two Alaska senators and backed by the unions sponsoring the plans, that legislatively declared that a partial termination had not occurred.[54]

---

[49] See sec. I.E below.

[50] See 26 C.F.R. 1.413-1(c)(3) and (c)(5) (examples (2), (3), (4), and (5)).

[51] See *id.*

[52] See Washington Post, June 2, 1984, at D-10 ("Short-Term Pipeline Workers Could Get Surprise Pensions").

[53] *Id.*

[54] See P.L. 98-369, §552.

D. Whose Benefits and What Benefits Become Nonforfeitable

A partial termination causes the accrued benefits of all nonvested or partially vested participants who have benefits that have not been forfeited before the time the partial termination occurs to become nonforfeitable—to the extent funded—*regardless* of whether they are employed on the exact day of the partial termination. In General Counsel Memorandum 39310 (April 4, 1984), the IRS found that a participant who had not "forfeited" accrued benefits at the time of a partial termination under a plan's break-in-service rules was entitled to nonforfeitable benefits under Code Section 411(d)(3) even though she was no longer actively employed on the date the partial termination occurred.[55] This result follows what would occur on a complete termination—which is what a partial termination is to mirror.[56] *Weil v. Terson Co. Retirement Plan Committee*, however, suggests that participants who leave voluntarily, or who are discharged for cause, before, or even at the same time as, a partial termination may be denied the beneficial effects of the partial termination—even if their accrued benefits are not forfeited on the date of partial termination under the plan's break-in-service rules.[57]

An open question concerns whether the benefits that may become nonforfeitable on a partial termination are limited to "accrued benefits," as a strict reading of the term "benefits accrued" in Code Section 411(d)(3) might have it, or may include benefits such as unreduced early retirement benefits. If a defined benefit plan is well-funded, a partial termination clearly benefits participants who have less than the 10-year or other period required for vesting in accrued normal retirement age benefits. But many other excluded participants, while vested in normal retirement benefits, may be just short of vesting in unreduced (or only slightly reduced) early retirement benefits. On a complete termination, these participants would receive at least a part of their forfeitable early retirement benefits under the sixth priority category of Section 4044, which covers all forfeitable benefits, whether or not accrued—assuming that the plan's assets reach the sixth category.[58]

The IRS has not taken a position on whether early retirement benefits are covered by Code Section 411(d)(3),[59] but most sponsoring employers would undoubtedly argue that "benefits accrued" in Section 411(d)(3) is limited to the restrictive, technical definition of the term

---

[55] Reprinted at ¶17,504 CCH Pension Plan Guide. And cf. *Union Central Life Ins. Co. v. Hamilton Steel Prod., Inc.*, 448 F.2d 501 (7th Cir. 1971) (rights on termination applied to former employees not employed on the exact termination date, instead of basing their rights on an "artificial line[]").

[56] See ch. 12, sec. III.

[57] 750 F.2d 10, 5 EBC 2537, at 2540 (2d Cir. 1984), and see the material at the start of sec. I.

[58] See ch. 12, IV.A.

[59] See 26 C.F.R. 1.411(d)-2(a)(1) (repeating the statutory "benefits accrued" language without elucidation).

"accrued benefit." However, there is little indication Congress intended the two terms to be synonymous. Two committee reports and the House Education and Labor Committee's "Material in the Nature of a Committee Report Explaining H.R. 12906" referred to the benefits that become nonforfeitable on termination or partial termination as "accrued benefits" at one point, but as "accrued liabilities" at another.[60] The term "accrued liabilities" includes forfeitable early retirement benefits.[61] Moreover, the House Education and Labor Committee expressly provided that "[i]n the event of a partial termination, net assets of the plan are to be allocated on behalf of the participants and beneficiaries giving rise to the termination in accordance with priority classes as if a complete termination had occurred."[62] As previously noted, this type of allocation would cover otherwise forfeitable early retirement benefits under priority category (6), assuming there are sufficient plan assets to reach that category.[63]

A broad reading of "benefits accrued" is especially supported when the exclusion of a significant percentage or number of participants leaves a plan in a position where plan assets exceed benefit liabilities on a termination basis. Under 26 C.F.R. 1.411(d)-2(b)(2), a plan amendment decreasing benefits under a plan that leaves the plan with a potential reversion of "excess" assets can result in the declaration of a partial termination with respect to the reduced or eliminated benefits. This provision, previously called a benefit "curtailment" partial termination, is not limited to vesting in "accrued benefits." In *Amato v. Western Union International, Inc.*, the Second Circuit strongly suggested that a partial termination could occur from the elimination of unreduced early retirement benefits from a plan. In such a partial termination, the Second Circuit ruled, early retirement benefits that are still forfeitable at the time of the amendment are to be paid to the extent funded when the plan's assets are allocated according to ERISA Section 4044, with the early retirement benefits being placed in priority category (6). In this manner, the Second Circuit stated, "as long as assets [are] available, they [are] used to meet participant's benefit expectations based upon the plan's full benefit structure."[64] Making

---

60 See H.R. Rep. 93-807, 65, 2 ERISA Leg. Hist. 3185, H.R. Rep. 93-779, 2 ERISA Leg. Hist. 2653, and "Material in the Nature of a Committee Report Explaining H.R. 12906," 2 ERISA Leg. Hist. 3330; but see Conf. Rep., at 277, 3 ERISA Leg. Hist. 4544 (referring only to "accrued benefits").

61 See 26 C.F.R. 1.412(c)(3)-1(c)(1) and (f)(2), and see 26 C.F.R. 1.401-2(b)(2).

62 2 ERISA Leg. Hist. 3309.

63 Another indication of Congress' intent can be gleaned from the carryover of the term "benefits accrued" from pre-ERISA §401(a)(7). Before ERISA, the term "benefits accrued" did not have the technical meaning the term "accrued benefit" has under ERISA. Thus, by not changing the term "benefits accrued" in enacting ERISA and §411(d)(3), Congress carried over a potentially broader term.

64 773 F.2d 1402, 6 EBC 2226, at 2240 (2d Cir. 1985). See also *Tilley v. Mead Corp.*, 815 F.2d 989 (4th Cir. 1987) (§4044(a) requires allocation of plan assets to fund employees' contingent early retirement benefits requiring 30 years of service and attainment of age 62; plaintiffs with 30 years of service who were not age 62 and plaintiff with 28 years of service were thus entitled to allocation based on value of contingent right).

early retirement benefits nonforfeitable to the extent funded on a termination basis on a partial termination is also in accord with the common law roots of partial terminations in the doctrines of impracticability and unjust enrichment, and in furtherance of Congress' overall objective of ensuring that employees with long years of employment do not lose "anticipated retirement benefits" due to restrictive plan rules and circumstances beyond their control.[65]

Apart from the construction of Section 411(d)(3), nonforfeitability of early retirement benefits on a partial termination can be required as a matter of plan interpretation when a plan promises, as some do, that "benefits," instead of just "accrued benefits," will become nonforfeitable on a partial termination.

E. The Extent Benefits Are Funded

The main financial drawback to the rights conferred by a partial termination is they are only valuable if the benefits can be funded, in whole or in part, from the plan's existing assets. In *Weil v. Terson Co. Retirement Plan Committee,* the Second Circuit emphasized that the rights accorded under Section 411(d)(3) are limited "to the extent that the benefits [are] funded as of the date of [the partial] termination," and further suggested that the employees "must demonstrate funding of the benefits they seek," although it did not elaborate on the type of proof this may entail.[66]

Under a defined contribution plan, the "extent" benefits are funded is not a real limitation. Benefits accrued are equal to each individual's account balance, which is fully funded when contributions have been made as promised, and contributions plus earnings have been allocated to individual accounts as specified in the plan.

For a defined benefit plan, whether a partial termination is valuable for affected participants is not as simple. First, how valuable the right is depends primarily on how well-funded the plan is. For example, the received wisdom is that multiemployer plans are on the whole not as well-funded as single-employer plans, so partial terminations may generally be less valuable in multiemployer plans.[67] Second, the method used to determine the "extent" benefits are funded can alter how valuable the right is. On a complete termination, Section 4044 requires that the assets be distributed according to its priority categories, with nonvested benefits being placed in priority category (6).[68] But Section

---

[65] ERISA §2(a), 29 U.S.C. §1001(a). See also ch. 1, sec. I, on the remedial construction accorded ERISA where the statutory language and legislative history are susceptible to varying interpretation.

[66] 750 F.2d 10, 5 EBC 2537, at 2541 (2d Cir. 1984).

[67] But see Washington Post, Oct. 9, 1985, at F-3 (describing survey finding by the Martin E. Segal Co. that 73% of multiemployer plans are fully funded for all *vested* benefits—thus indicating that nonvested benefits would at least be *partially* funded in most cases).

[68] An argument can be made that the benefits that vest on a termination or partial termination should be in the higher priority category (5), but the PBGC's regulations on §4044 clearly

4044 is not directly applicable on a partial termination, and the IRS's regulations effectively make it only a "safe harbor" against a charge of Code Section 401(a)(4) discrimination in the determination of the extent that benefits are funded. Other asset allocation methods are acceptable on a partial termination as long as prohibited discrimination does not result.[69] The most commonly used alternative is a straight pro rata allocation of plan assets, dividing the assets according to the ratio the present value of the excluded participants' benefits bears to the present value of all other plan benefits. A second alternative is simply to fund the benefits of the excluded participants *in full*. This alternative has the drawback that it could invite a lawsuit by remaining participants for breach of fiduciary duty if the plan's terms do not require this and if it significantly dilutes the current funding for other participants' benefits.[70] (Over time, the employer's increased future funding obligations would make up any dilution.) As suggested, some plans also omit the "to the extent" funded limitation, in which case forfeitable benefits may be required to become nonforfeitable in full as a matter of plan interpretation.

When the terms of a plan provide for a Section 4044 allocation on a partial termination, the question is: Do the assets reach priority category (6) so that a partial termination is valuable for nonvested participants? As ERISA was originally enacted, this determination might have been simple as ERISA Section 103(d)(6) required the present value of the plan's benefits to be allocated each year by termination priority category with this allocation listed in Schedule B of the annual financial report. With this allocation in hand, the plan's assets could be compared to the values in the priority categories to determine the extent the plan's assets reach benefits in priority category (6). A partial termination might then be considered worth pursuing if the plan's assets covered a significant portion of the plan's category (6) benefits.

By regulation, however, the Department of Labor waived the requirement that the present value of benefits be allocated by termination priority category in Schedule B.[71] Consequently, only a rougher measure of the value of a partial termination can now be obtained from information in Schedule B. Item 6(d) of the [1985] Schedule B requires a value for all the plan's accrued liabilities for vested benefits, and Item 6(e) requires a value for the plan's accrued liabilities for nonvested benefits. Basically, for a partial termination to be valuable, the plan's assets should exceed the value in Item 6(d), and cover a significant

---

provide that these benefits are in category (6). See 29 C.F.R. 2618.2 (defining "nonforfeitable benefit") and 2618.15 and .16 (describing benefits in priority categories (5) and (6), respectively). And see *Amato v. Western Union Int'l, Inc.*, 773 F.2d 1402, 6 EBC 2226 (2d Cir. 1985), and ch. 12, sec. IV.A.

[69] See 26 C.F.R. 1.411(d)-2(a)(2).

[70] See S. Offer, "Partial Terminations of Qualified Plans," 9 Tax. Law. 240, at 244 (Jan.-Feb. 1981). Offer suggests a third alternative of making all benefits accrued nonforfeitable on a partial termination, but this seems to be indistinguishable from the second alternative.

[71] 29 C.F.R. 2520.104-42.

amount of the plan's benefits in Item 6(e) (which is still roughly equivalent to priority category (6)).

To complicate matters, however, three other variables can significantly affect whether the values in Schedule B accurately reflect the extent that nonvested benefits are funded on a termination basis. First, the information in a plan's Form 5500 may be out of date. The Schedule B actuarial information may actually be based on a valuation made more than a year and a half before the schedule is filed. Second, the interest rate used in discounting a plan's benefit liabilities to a present value in Schedule B can be significantly lower than would be used in valuing its benefits on a plan termination. As a result, a plan may appear under Schedule B to have higher benefit liabilities than it would actually have on a plan termination. A third variable is whether the accrued liabilities a plan lists in Items 6(d) and (e) include benefit liabilities based on projected salary increases. If projected salary increases are included, the benefit values in these items may again be higher than the plan's liabilities would be on a termination basis.

The significance of these last two variables can be assessed by examining the accountant's statement if it is prepared in accordance with FASB 35. Under FASB 35, the accountant's statement is required to contain a value for vested and nonvested benefits that does *not* reflect projected increases in salary, and the value is also required to be based on an interest rate which generally will be higher and more realistic in terms of current interest rates than the plan's funding interest rate (which may have been used as the basis for the Schedule B valuation).[72] Because these two changes will tend to decrease the valuation of the plan's benefit liabilities, the plan's assets will go further toward funding the lower priority nonvested benefits, and a partial termination will be worthwhile in more cases than might appear at first under Schedule B.

In comparing a plan's assets with its benefit liabilities, a current fair market value of the plan's assets should also be used. The value of the plan's assets appearing in Item 8(b) of the [1985] Schedule B should not be used for this purpose because under IRS regulations the value appearing in that item is only required to be within an 80 to 120 percent corridor of the current fair market value. A current fair market value may be found in Item 6(c) in Schedule B, in Item 13 of the Form 5500, and also in the accountant's statement.[73]

Although the Section 4044 allocation may be the best grounded in the regulations and legislative history, a pro rata allocation may be simpler administratively because benefit liabilities do not have to be

---

[72] See Financial Accounting Standards Board Opinion No. 35, paras. 18 and 20. The interest assumption in the accountant's statement will still not necessarily be as high as used on plan termination.

[73] A current fair market value may sometimes be disadvantageous to nonvested participants affected by a partial termination if a recent *downward* fluctuation in the value of the plan's assets has occurred which the Item 8(b) actuarial value would hold up. See D. McGill, *Fundamentals of Private Pensions* (Richard D. Irwin 5th ed.), at 392.

allocated according to the Section 4044 priority categories. It also offers a basis that assures that nonvested participants will receive at least some benefits from a partial termination determination. Use of the pro rata alternative, however, must not result in prohibited discrimination. Even under a pro rata method, the assumptions used in valuing the plan's benefit liabilities are again variables which can significantly increase or decrease the "extent" benefits are determined to be funded.

Under either the Section 4044 or pro rata approaches, if contributions to a plan are delinquent, or if a plan has not been funded in accordance with its contractual or minimum funding standard obligations, "make-up" contributions may be required to increase the plan's assets, and thus, the extent benefits are funded.[74]

F. Enforcement Procedures

No procedure for initiating a determination by the IRS of a partial termination is available to participants,[75] although the legislative history of ERISA reflects Congress' desire that one be established.[76] The IRS may, however, declare a partial termination on its own initiative. What this means is that if a participant lodges a complaint with the IRS District Director for the key district covering the plan, the IRS may issue such a determination. The drawback from the lack of a "procedure" for participants to initiate a determination is that if a District Director determines that a partial termination has not occurred, or simply takes no action on a complaint, the procedures for obtaining Tax Court review in Code Section 7476 do not apply, although the Tax Court conceivably could take jurisdiction in light of the legislative intent that the IRS establish a determination procedure for participants, and consequently, access to Tax Court review.

An employer sponsoring a plan may seek a determination of the occurrence, or not, of a partial termination by application to the IRS District Director for the key district covering the plan, with Tax Court review of the IRS's determination.[77] If a plan sponsor applies for such a determination, participants can file comments on the application within 45 days as "interested parties," and then may seek review in the Tax Court if the District Director's determination is unfavorable to their interests. As a practical matter, however, this option is rarely

---

[74] See H.R. Rep. 93-807, at 65, 2 ERISA Leg. Hist. 3185, H.R. Rep. 93-779, at 64, 2 ERISA Leg. Hist. 2653, and "Material in the Nature of a Committee Report Explaining H.R. 12906," 2 ERISA Leg. Hist. 3330 ("make-up" funding required to be included in determining the nonforfeitable amount).

[75] Rev. Proc. 80-30.

[76] See S. Rep. 93-383, at 113, 1 ERISA Leg. Hist. 1181, and H.R. Rep. 93-807, at 107, 2 ERISA Leg. Hist. 3227.

[77] Rev. Proc. 80-30.

open. Most plan sponsors do not apply for partial termination determinations in even obvious cases.[78] Even when an application for determination is filed, the "notice" required to be posted soliciting comments from interested parties is not required to indicate the subject matter of the application. As a result, many participants do not look at the application itself, and the matter is rarely put in the hands of a lawyer who might recognize the importance of the opportunity to comment before expiration of the 45-day period.[79]

In recognition of the gaps in the IRS's procedures, and consequently in the opportunity for participants to obtain Tax Court review, participants have increasingly initiated lawsuits to obtain federal district court determinations of the occurrence of partial terminations. Ordinarily, no private right of action exists to enforce pension provisions that are in the Code but that are not mirrored in Title I of ERISA. But Code Section 411(d)(3) is distinct in that it requires every tax-qualified plan to contain a plan *provision* providing for nonforfeitability of benefits accrued on a termination or partial termination. When the plan contains such a provision, as is usually the case, a private right of action exists under ERISA Section 502(a)(1)(B) and Section 502(a)(3) for participants to enforce "the terms of the plan." Thus, in the participant-initiated court cases cited above, the plaintiffs predicated their actions on the plan provisions requiring nonforfeitability on a partial termination, rather than on direct review for a violation of Code Section 411(d)(3).

One drawback to a district court action is that some courts may view the partial termination determination as a matter of plan interpretation with deference to the plan trustees' interpretation unless it is "arbitrary and capricious." The *Beck v. Shaw* decision indicates that the court viewed the partial termination issue as one where it should review the trustee's interpretation for "arbitrary and capricious" action.[80] In *Taylor v. Food Giant, Inc., Salaried Employees Pension Plan*, another district court expressly used the "arbitrary and capricious" standard to review plan trustees' interpretation of the partial termination provision, holding that the trustees could "*rationally* conclude" under the IRS guidelines and other court decisions that a partial termination had not occurred.[81] However, none of the other decisions have used the arbitrary and capricious standard. This latter view is consistent with the "class interpretation" exception from arbitrary and capricious review discussed in Chapter 7, and is also consistent with Congress' intent that the term "partial termination" be construed by the

---

[78] See J. Mamorsky, *Employee Benefits Law* (1984 ed.), at 13-26 ("as a practical matter, employers generally do not 'volunteer' partial terminations").

[79] The issue of whether a partial termination has occurred could also be raised through comments to the IRS when an employer submits an application for determination on any other type of amendment to the plan. See ch. 14, sec. IV.

[80] 2 EBC 2366 (N.D. Ga. 1981).

[81] 6 EBC 1291, at 1294 (N.D. Ga. 1984) (emphasis added).

IRS, without dilution by a second, restrictive filter of reinterpretations of IRS interpretations by employer-appointed plan administrators.

Apart from potential use of the arbitrary and capricious standard, a second drawback to a district court action is that a district court may simply be more reluctant than the IRS or the U.S. Tax Court to go beyond "clear-cut" cases, such as 50 percent exclusions, and find partial terminations in the more circumstantial areas of 20 percent exclusions or exclusions of 100 or more participants. Certainly, the initial lower court decision in *Weil* that no partial termination occurred with a 104 participant, or 27 percent, exclusion occasioned by the closing of two divisions, and the *Ehm* decision that no partial termination occurred with the exclusion of 415 participants were both based on facts that the IRS could easily have ruled the other way on.[82]

A further issue is whether a court will follow the IRS regulations and rulings on the interpretation of the term "partial termination." In cases alleging pre-ERISA partial terminations, some courts refused to do so.[83] The chief distinguishing factor in these cases, however, is that pre-ERISA Code Section 401(a)(7) did not require plans to contain a *provision* making benefits nonforfeitable on a "partial termination" of a plan, but only referred to nonforfeitability on a "termination." In 1963, the IRS extended "termination" by regulation to include a "partial termination." But most plans continued to lack the phrase under their terms, and the courts refused to follow the IRS's lead without a more precise plan provision to interpret. This view has *not* been carried over in any of the post-ERISA cases cited above where the IRS's regulations and rules have been used as the almost exclusive source of authority on the meaning of "partial termination."[84] If these regulations and rulings were not used, moreover, it would frustrate Congress' intent in requiring all qualified plans to contain a "partial termination" provision, thus deliberately requiring it to be part of the employer's contract with the employee, while leaving the exact construction of the term to the IRS.

---

[82] See, e.g., IRS Doc. 6678, Rev. Rul. 81-27, and PLR 7902030 (Oct. 10, 1978). In *Weil v. Terson Co. Retirement Plan Committee*, the IRS filed an amicus brief on appeal strongly suggesting that a partial termination had occurred.

[83] See *Craig v. Bemis Co.*, 517 F.2d 677 (5th Cir. 1975); *Shaw v. Kruidenier*, 470 F.Supp. 1375 (S.D. Iowa 1979); *United Steelworkers v. Harris & Sons Steel Co.*, 706 F.2d 1289, 4 EBC 1396 (3d Cir. 1983) (citing other cases with pre-ERISA facts).

[84] In *Weil v. Terson Co. Retirement Plan Committee*, 750 F.2d 10, 5 EBC 2537 (2d Cir. 1984), and *Amato v. Western Union Int'l, Inc.*, 773 F.2d 1402, 6 EBC 2226 (2d Cir. 1985), the Second Circuit twice instructed district courts to follow the IRS's regulations and rulings in interpreting the meaning of "partial termination" in post-ERISA cases. See also the other court decisions cited in sec. I.A above, and the discussion of the use of relevant administrative agency regulations and rulings in plan interpretation in ch. 7.

II. Other Grounds for Pension Benefits After a Work Force Reduction

Pension benefits may be secured on other grounds after a plant closing or work force reduction:

(1) If a court, or the IRS, determines that a partial termination has *not* occurred;

(2) When a partial termination is not valuable because of the "to the extent funded" limitation; or

(3) If a partial termination does not vest early retirement benefits.

When participants are represented by a union, the union may be able to negotiate, as a part of "effects" bargaining, a new provision for vesting of normal or early retirement benefits on a plant shutdown, or a "creep" provision under which employees who are laid off may receive additional vesting or accrual credits, for example, for two years after the plant closing or work force reduction. Similar types of provisions may be provided salaried or nonunion employees for consistency with the treatment afforded union employees or for personnel policy reasons.[85]

Absent the ability to obtain new provisions such as these, the next step for participants is an examination of compliance with ERISA's minimum standards, the exact terms of the existing plan, statements and omissions in the summary plan description, and any other written and oral statements by company officials or plan fiduciaries relating to the plan, or to the continuation of their employment.

Under the "elapsed time" method or an "hours counting" method for measuring "years of service" for vesting and "years of participation" for benefit accruals, short periods of vesting and benefit accrual credit may sometimes be overlooked by a plan administrator. These include periods of accrued vacation or sick leave that are paid, or for which payment is due, after a plant closing or reduction in force.[86] Periods which form the basis for severance pay, e.g., when one week of regular pay is due for each year of work, may also be required to be credited.[87] Earlier periods that may have been overlooked in crediting years of service include years of military service, whether in war or in peace, if surrounded by service with the employer.[88]

Compliance with the minimum standards can also interact with

---

[85] For examples where employers have agreed to similar provisions on plant closings, see Dept. of Labor, "Plant Closing Checklist: A Guide to Best Practice," at 40, 45, and 66 (examples involving the Brown & Williamson Tobacco Corp., the Dana Corp., and Goodyear's Lee Tire Division).

[86] 29 C.F.R. 2530.200b-2(b)(3). Under some hours-counting methods, these periods are not directly credited, but because of their omission a "year of service" for vesting must be based on a lower hours total than the standard 1,000 hours. See ch. 5, sec. III.B.1.

[87] See PLR 8031091 (May 9, 1980), reprinted at ¶17,372E CCH Pens. Plan Guide, and ch. 5, sec. III.B.1.

[88] See ch. 4, sec. III.B, and ch. 5, sec. III.

plan interpretation. For example, in *Cook v. Pension Plan for Salaried Employees of Cyclops*, a plan used the "elapsed time" method for crediting service for vesting. This required it to provide up to an additional year of credit whenever an employee separated from service "for any reason *other than* quit, retirement, discharge, or death." The Cyclops plan provided (although it was not required to) that the same service-counting rule applied to vesting in early retirement benefits. But when the employer closed a plant, the employer-appointed plan administrator denied the terminated employees the additional year of credit on the ground that they had been "discharged." The district court held that this interpretation was arbitrary and capricious since a "discharge" in labor-management relations means a discharge for cause, or for the "individual fault" of an employee. On appeal, however, the Sixth Circuit reversed, holding that under all the circumstances the plan administrator had sufficient leeway to make the interpretation he made.[89]

Plan interpretation can also require additional credits for participants by itself. For example, even when prospects for reemployment after a plant closing are nil, a plan provision for two years additional credit during periods of "layoff" may be interpreted to require additional credit for participants who are laid off as a result of a permanent plant closing.[90] As mentioned earlier, a plan may also provide that *all* benefits, including early retirement benefits, must become nonforfeitable on a partial termination, rather than limiting the nonforfeitability to "accrued benefits," or the plan's terms may not include the "to the extent" funded limitation on nonforfeitability of benefits on a partial termination.

Summary plan description statements, including the omission in an SPD of a description of important benefit limitations, are an essential guide in plan interpretation.[91] Apart from their interpretive use, an SPD that fails to accurately and understandably describe the circumstances that limit the plan's benefits violates Section 102 of ERISA. A court can provide "appropriate equitable relief" for such violations, including a statutorily based form of estoppel.[92]

Other written and oral statements can be used in interpreting a plan, or where a plan provision is unambiguous, can form the basis for estoppel. In *Apponi v. Sunshine Biscuits, Inc.*, an early retirement benefit requiring 15 years service and the attainment of age 55 while in service, although clear on its face, was held to be alterable through estoppel if participants could prove that employer representatives stated in collective bargaining that the age 55 *while in service* condition

---

[89] 801 F.2d 865, 7 EBC 2278 (6th Cir. 1986), *rev'g*, C.A. No C-1-82-615 (S.D. Ohio, Oct. 5, 1984). But compare 26 C.F.R. 1.410(a)-7(b)(2) and (d)(1)(i), and ch. 5, sec. III.B.2.

[90] See *Fitzsimons Steel Co., Youngstown Ohio*, 81-2 ARB (CCH) ¶8408 (Ruben, 1981).

[91] See ch. 7, sec. III.A.4.

[92] See ch. 8, sec. I.A.

would not apply.[93] Acts or inconsistent treatment of different groups of participants can also result in estoppel or waiver. In *Luli v. Sun Products, Inc.*, a plant closing acted to waive a requirement of employer consent to early retirement, or alternatively, constituted an implied consent.[94] In *Hardy v. H.K. Porter Co.*, extended leaves of absence granted some employees in past plant closings "solely" to qualify them for a pension requiring service until age 60 modified the condition for others.[95]

Other claims, described in Chapter 10, are based on a showing of purposeful interference with pension rights or discrimination with pension-related consequences in a plant closing or work force reduction. These are:

(1) *Section 510 of ERISA.* Whether a plant closing or work force reduction, or the timing of such, were for the purpose of interfering with the attainment of pension rights under the plan—in other words, whether cost savings from the nonattainment of pension rights were a determining factor in the decision to close a plant or to lay off workers, or in the timing of the decision to do so.[96]

(2) *Age, race, or sex discrimination.* Whether a plant closing or the selection of employees for a work force reduction discriminated on the basis of age, race, or sex, and thus also caused discrimination in the attainment of pension benefits.[97]

(3) *Code Section 401(a)(4) discrimination.* Whether a plant closing or work force reduction increased discrimination in the operation of the pension plan in favor of the "prohibited group" of employees.[98]

Multiemployer plan participants are sometimes faced with special problems after plant closings, such as plans that fail to credit periods of employer delinquency in making contributions to the plan prior to the plant closing, or multiemployer plans that attempt to *cancel* past service credits on an employer's complete cessation of contributions to the plan. These issues are discussed in Chapter 4.

---

[93] 652 F.2d 643, 2 EBC 1534 (6th Cir. 1981). In other instances, ambiguous age and service early retirement provisions have simply been interpreted as "vesting" on completion of the service requirement. See cases in ch. 5, sec. I.D.

[94] 398 N.E.2d 553 (Ohio 1979).

[95] 417 F.Supp. 1175 (E.D. Pa. 1976), *aff'd in part, rev'd in part,* 562 F.2d 42 (3d Cir. 1977).

[96] See ch. 10, sec. I.

[97] See cases in ch. 10, secs. III and IV.

[98] See ch. 10, sec. II. A particular potential for Code §401(a)(4) discrimination is created by requirements in many defined contribution plans that participants must be employed on a certain day in the plan year to receive the entire year's allocation of employer contributions. If rank and file employees disproportionately lose a year's contribution allocation under such a provision, while prohibited group employees disproportionately are retained long enough to receive the allocation, prohibited discrimination can result. See Rev. Rul. 76-250, and ch. 4, sec. III.E.

12

Single-Employer Plan Terminations

Pension plan terminations are among the most widely discussed pension topics. Numerous articles have focused on the billions of dollars in benefit liabilities that the collapse of a few large companies, e.g., International Harvester, Chrysler, Wheeling-Pittsburgh Steel, and LTV, and the termination of their pension plans would place on the Pension Benefit Guaranty Corporation, the federally chartered pension benefit insurance agency. Public attention has also focused on terminations of "overfunded" plans, where on-going companies, such as Harper & Row, A&P, United Air Lines, Exxon, and Phillips Petroleum, have terminated their pension plans to take back billions of dollars in "excess" plan assets.

Congress established the Pension Benefit Guaranty Corporation (PBGC) in 1974 to administer plan termination rules and a program of pension insurance established in Title IV of ERISA.[1] With certain limitations discussed below, the PBGC's insurance covers nonforfeitable pension benefits from almost all terminated "defined benefit" plans.[2] The program excludes terminated defined contribution plans, and contains 12 other exceptions to the PBGC's coverage.[3] Most of the exceptions merely repeat exclusions from ERISA's general coverage, such as the exclusions of church and governmental plans. The most significant other type of exception is for defined benefit plans of "professional service" corporations that never had more than 25 active participants.[4]

Pension benefit insurance for covered defined benefit plans is financed in two ways. Employers pay premiums to the PBGC on a per

[1] ERISA §§4001-4402, 29 U.S.C. §§1301-1461, as amended by the Multiemployer Pension Plan Amendments Act of 1980, P.L. 96-364, and the Single Employer Pension Plan Amendments Act of 1986, Title XI of P.L. 99-272.

[2] ERISA §§4021(a)(1) and (b)(1) and §4022.

[3] See ERISA §4021(b).

[4] ERISA §4021(b)(13).

participant basis (on January 1, 1986, the premium rate increased from $2.60 per participant per year to $8.50). In addition, an employer who sponsors a terminating plan is liable to make up any shortfall, or "insufficiency," between the plan's assets and the benefits the PBGC guarantees. ERISA limits this liability to 30 percent of the employer's net worth (plus, after January 1, 1986, 75 percent of the unfunded guaranteed benefits remaining after payment of the up to 30 percent of net worth liability). For all practical purposes, a separate insurance program now governs multiemployer defined benefit plans (discussed below in Chapter 13).

Congress did not find it necessary or feasible to insure defined contribution plans:

> "Money purchase, profit-sharing, and stock bonus plans are excluded from the insurance program since they generally are characterized by some type of promise with regard to contributions and no promise with regard to benefits—the participant is merely entitled to benefits determined by reference to his own account. Since no particular benefits are promised in these cases there appears to be no appropriate amount to insure."[5]

Put still another way, defined contribution plans are "fully funded" by definition, unless the promised contributions have not been made, or a breach of fiduciary duty has improvidently diminished the plan's investment earnings.

In contrast, defined benefit plans routinely operate on a less than fully funded basis. That is, they promise specific, "defined" benefits, but the promised benefits are not necessarily funded by concurrent employer contributions. This occurs because defined benefit plans frequently are created with large unfunded liabilities from grants of past service credits for participants who were employed before the plan was established. These liabilities may be amortized (or gradually paid off) over a 30-year period.[6] Further unfunded liabilities can arise from plan amendments improving past benefits. The liabilities from the application of the benefit improvements to existing credited service may also be amortized over 30-year periods.[7] Poorer experience than a plan's actuary expected, e.g., poorer investment performance than expected, can also lead to increases in unfunded benefit liabilities. A plan sponsor can amortize these actuarial losses over 15 years.[8]

When a defined benefit plan terminates after these liabilities have been created, but before the liabilities are fully amortized, the plan's assets may not be great enough to pay all the promised benefits. This

---

[5] S. Rep. 93-383, 81, 1 ERISA Leg. Hist. 1149.

[6] See ERISA §302(b)(2)(B)(ii) (Code §412(b)(2)(B)(ii)). A plan can amortize these liabilities over shorter periods (up to the deductible contribution limits in Code §404(a)(1)), or if the plan is a multiemployer plan or a single-employer plan with liabilities that were in existence before ERISA, over slightly longer 40-year periods. See ERISA §§302(b)(2)(B)(i) and (b)(6) (Code §§412(b)(2)(B)(i) and (b)(6)).

[7] See ERISA §302(b)(2)(B)(iii) (Code §412(b)(2)(B)(iii)).

[8] ERISA §302(b)(2)(B)(iv) (Code §412(b)(2)(B)(iv)).

shortfall can translate into tragic losses for employees, who were counting on *all* the retirement benefits promised by the plan. Congress addressed the issue of underfunding on plan termination by enacting Title IV's program of pension insurance for defined benefit plans, and also by requiring faster amortization of unfunded liabilities than the Internal Revenue Code required before ERISA's passage.[9]

I. The Decision to Terminate a Plan

A. Title IV Rules for Defined Benefit Plans

In contrast to most insurable events, Title IV of ERISA, as in effect until 1986, allowed a defined benefit plan termination subject to PBGC insurance to result from an entirely voluntary decision of the sponsoring employer to terminate the plan. A voluntary defined benefit plan termination could occur by following the procedure for plan termination set forth in the plan and satisfying certain procedural rules under Title IV of ERISA. For purposes of Title IV, a plan termination included, and still includes, any amendment converting a PBGC-covered defined benefit plan into a defined contribution plan.[10]

Before 1986, ERISA Section 4041, which governs voluntary terminations of single-employer plans, thus did not require an employer to be bankrupt, or even to show business hardship, to voluntarily terminate its pension plan. However, Sections 4062 and 4047 of Title IV did impose indirect limits, or disincentives, on voluntary terminations. Under ERISA Section 4062, the PBGC assesses up to 30 percent of a sponsoring employer's net worth to fund any insufficiency between the plan's assets on termination and the benefits the PBGC insures. Moreover, under Section 4047, the PBGC can disallow a plan termination if it is determined to be a manipulation of the insurance system, for example, a termination designed to dump liabilities on the PBGC when a sponsoring company's net worth is low. Both of these limits, though, only protect the PBGC's insurance obligations. Since the PBGC did not, and does not, insure all benefits, an employer could still usually discard unfunded benefits above the PBGC insured levels by terminating a plan. An employer with little or no net worth could also generally discard PBGC guaranteed benefits without significant restriction under Title IV.

The Single Employer Pension Plan Amendments Act of 1986

---

[9] See generally Conf. Rep., at 283, 3 ERISA Leg. Hist. 4550.

[10] ERISA §4041(e), formerly §4041(f). And see 26 C.F.R. 1.411(d)-2(c)(2)(i). On such an amendment, participants must be given a written election to either take a distribution of the plan's assets as allocated to their benefits under §4044 in the form of an annuity, or to have the assets transferred to their individual account under the new defined contribution plan. See PBGC Opinion Letters 76-12 and 76-30. Under the SEPPAA amendments to Title IV, an amendment converting a defined benefit plan to a defined contribution plan can take effect only after the requirements for a standard or a distress termination are followed. ERISA §4041(e), as amended.

(hereafter SEPPAA) places more direct limits on "voluntary" terminations of defined benefit plans. Effective for plan years beginning after December 31, 1985, Title IV, as amended by SEPPAA, divides defined benefit plan terminations into two types: (1) "standard" terminations, and (2) "distress" terminations. Under the standard termination rules, a plan can still be voluntarily terminated, but only if it has enough assets to pay *all* "benefit commitments" under the plan, which are defined as all nonforfeitable benefits under the plan, including nonforfeitable benefits that are not guaranteed by the PBGC.[11]

The only other possibility after SEPPAA is a distress termination. A distress termination can take place only if the plan sponsor (and each person who is a substantive member of any controlled group that includes the contributing sponsor [12]) satisfies one of three conditions, each indicative of business hardship. The conditions are that the sponsor (and each substantive member of any control group that includes the sponsor):

(1) Has filed, or has had filed against it, a petition seeking liquidation under the federal bankruptcy code or any similar state law;

(2) Has filed, or has had filed against it, a petition seeking reorganization under the federal bankruptcy code or any similar state law, *with* the bankruptcy court having approved the plan's termination; or

(3) Demonstrates to the satisfaction of the PBGC that it is unable to pay debts when due and to continue in business unless the plan is terminated, or that it is incurring unreasonably burdensome pension costs solely as a result of a decline in the active work force covered by all plans maintained by the contributing sponsor.[13]

If one of the distress termination criteria is satisfied, a distress termination can take place. The contributing sponsor and all members of any controlled group of which it is a member are then liable, as under prior law, for unfunded guaranteed benefits, with interest from the plan termination date, up to the ceiling of 30 percent of net worth.[14]

---

[11] ERISA §§4001(a)(16) and 4041(b), as amended.

[12] Common control is determined under the rules described in ch. 2. See ERISA §4001(a)(14) and ch. 2, sec. II.C. A substantive member of a controlled group is an owner of 5% or more of the total controlled group assets. ERISA §4041(c)(2)(C), as amended.

[13] ERISA §§4041(c)(2)(B)(i)-(iii), as amended.

[14] Net worth is clarified by SEPPAA to mean the sum of net worths greater than zero of the contributing sponsor and each member of any controlled group that includes the contributing sponsor. ERISA §4062(e), as amended. Net worth also includes the amount of any transfer of assets which the PBGC determines to have been improper, such as transfers of assets in anticipation of the assessment of net worth liability. *Id.* In addition, if the principal purpose of a transaction within 5 years of a plan termination is to evade liability under §§4061-68, the transaction may be ignored in determining liability. ERISA §4069, as amended. And see 131 Cong. Rec. H-13299 (daily ed. Dec. 19, 1985) (statement of Rep. Augustus Hawkins) (example may arise when a subsidiary with unfunded liabilities is sold to a buyer that does not have a reasonable prospect of funding the benefits).

In addition, Title IV, as amended by SEPPAA, provides that the contributing sponsor and all members of any controlled group are also liable for 75 percent of the unfunded guaranteed benefits remaining after payment of the up to 30 percent of net worth assessment. The 30 percent of net worth assessment is ordinarily due immediately. Payments under the 75 percent of unfunded guaranteed benefits liability may be made over time under commercially reasonable terms agreed to by the PBGC.[15]

When a plan terminated in a distress termination is insufficient to pay all PBGC guaranteed benefits, the plan must be involuntarily terminated by the PBGC.[16] Payments to the trustee of the involuntarily terminated plan must then also include all accumulated funding deficiencies of the plan, including previously waived funding requirements and amounts that would have been due if any extensions of amortization periods had not been granted.[17] Further contributions to fund "benefit commitments" must be made after a distress termination to a trust established pursuant to Section 4049 (according to rules described in section VII.C below).

In addition to employer-initiated standard or distress terminations, Title IV allows the PBGC to initiate "involuntary" terminations of defined benefit plans under ERISA Section 4042 if a plan:

(1) Has not met the minimum funding requirements of ERISA;
(2) Will be unable to pay benefits that are due;
(3) Distributes over $10,000 in benefits to a substantial owner, at a time when other nonforfeitable benefits are unfunded; or
(4) May reasonably be expected to place increasing long-run losses on the PBGC if the plan is not terminated.[18]

As mentioned before, an involuntary termination proceeding is also required to be instituted if an employer terminates a plan in a distress termination and the plan has insufficient assets to pay all PBGC guaranteed benefits.

B. Defined Contribution Plans

An employer can voluntarily terminate a defined contribution plan. Defined contribution plans are not subject to Title IV's procedural or substantive termination rules. But the discussions below on

---

[15] If neither the contributing sponsor nor any member of a controlled group that includes the contributing sponsor has pretax profits, the PBGC's repayment terms must provide that 50% of the payments due in the liability year ending in that tax year may be deferred. ERISA §4062(b)(2)(B).

[16] ERISA §4041(c)(3)(B)(iii)(I).

[17] ERISA §4062(d).

[18] SEPPAA amended the PBGC's involuntary termination authority to provide for institution of involuntary termination proceedings by the PBGC when a plan "will be" unable to pay benefits when due, instead of when it "is" unable to pay benefits when due. ERISA §4042(a)(2), as amended.

fiduciary duties, collective bargaining obligations, implied contractual limits, and procedural requirements can apply to their termination.

The Title IV rule that an amendment converting a defined benefit plan to a defined contribution plan constitutes a plan termination does not work in reverse. In *Hickerson v. Velsicol Chemical Corp.*, a plan amendment converting a profit-sharing plan to a defined benefit plan was held *not* to constitute a termination of the profit-sharing plan—which would have required an immediate distribution of all account balances under the terms of the plan. The Seventh Circuit recognized that pre-ERISA Code regulations on terminations required vesting of all nonvested participant accounts in such cases because a pension plan was not considered to be "comparable" to a profit-sharing plan, and thus not a continuation of it, but the Seventh Circuit held that those regulations are inapplicable after ERISA. Whether a termination occurred was to be determined according to whether the procedures in the plan for a termination were followed, or for purposes of the Code's rules, by the presence of prohibited discrimination, a large exclusion of participants, or a potential reversion of excess assets to the employer as a result of the amendment.[19]

C. Fiduciary Duties

The Department of Labor and most courts shade firmly toward excluding all decisions to terminate plans from the ERISA fiduciary standard. The Department of Labor's position was outlined in 1982 by Jeffrey Clayton, then administrator of the Department's Pension and Welfare Benefits Program, in testimony before the House Select Committee on Aging:[20]

> "One important consideration in [our general approach to the application of ERISA's fiduciary provisions] is the voluntary nature of the private employee benefit system in this country. ERISA provides certain protections for participants and beneficiaries if an employer has a plan. It does not, however, require any employer to have a plan; nor in general, does it prevent him from terminating a plan. The decision of the employer whether or not to have a plan is not a fiduciary decision. However, other decisions by the employer may indeed be fiduciary decisions.
>
> "ERISA recognizes that the employer can play two roles, both as plan sponsor and plan fiduciary. Section 408(c)(3) of ERISA specifically provides that:
>
> > 'Nothing in Section 406 shall be construed to prohibit any fiduciary from serving as a fiduciary in addition to being an officer, employee, agent, or other representative of a party in interest.'
>
> "It would seem to follow from this that ERISA envisions that there are times when the fiduciary can take off his fiduciary hat and act as an

---

[19] 778 F.2d 365, 6 EBC 2545 (7th Cir. 1985), *cert. denied*, 479 U.S. ___ (1986).

[20] This statement can be somewhat confusing as Mr. Clayton uses the "hat," rather than the proper "functional," approach to identifying fiduciary duties. See ERISA §3(21)(A) and ch. 7, sec. II.A.

officer of the company. Assessment of his conduct requires deciding when he is wearing his fiduciary hat and whether and when he may properly wear his company officer hat.

"It is hard to generalize, since every case depends on its special facts. It is clear that a person wears his fiduciary hat when he directs the use of plan funds. For example, if he causes the plan to purchase a certain stock, whether it is to aid the sale of the company or the avoidance of a take-over, he is wearing his fiduciary hat. Such activity must satisfy the fiduciary rules of ERISA, including acting prudently and for the exclusive purpose of providing benefits for participants and beneficiaries. In situations, however, where the corporate officer, although he is also a fiduciary of the plan, is not causing the plan to do anything, or in general is not conducting any activities that cause him to be a fiduciary, his actions may not be fiduciary activities and thus, he may not be subject to the ERISA rules of conduct.

"We have seen recently situations where employers have terminated plans in order to recover the extra assets of the plan that resulted from overfunding. As discussed above, ERISA in the absence of special circumstances, allows employers to terminate a plan. It also allows employers to receive plan funds by reversion in certain circumstances. The specific facts of any case, however, may result in a fiduciary violation. Thus, I would not want my remarks today to be interpreted as general approval of all such situations. Nevertheless, one must recognize that one consequence of a voluntary system must be the freedom to terminate plans."[21]

Most courts agree with Mr. Clayton's view that the decision to terminate a plan is not a fiduciary function—at least not when all unconditional and conditional benefit liabilities to employees can be satisfied from the plan's assets. The courts have thus approved plan terminations as not involving breaches of fiduciary duty, even when the intent of an employer is expressly to recoup a "surplus" of plan assets.[22]

However, fiduciary duties can apply to plan amendments made immediately before a plan's termination; and plan amendments after a plan's termination may be invalid *per se*.[23] Moreover, while the decision to terminate a plan may not be a fiduciary decision, functions

---

[21] Hearing on Pension Funding Problems Before the House Select Committee on Aging, 97th Cong., 2d Sess., at 106-07 (Comm. Pub. No. 355, June 7, 1982). In the committee print, every sentence in Mr. Clayton's testimony appears as a separate paragraph; the paragraph structure appearing above is supplied for readability.

[22] See *Pollock v. Castrovinci*, 476 F.Supp. 606, 1 EBC 2091 (S.D.N.Y. 1979), *aff'd*, 622 F.2d 575 (2d Cir. 1980); *In re C.D. Moyer Co. Pension Trust*, 441 F.Supp. 1128, 1 EBC 1363 (E.D. Pa. 1977), *aff'd*, 582 F.2d 1273 (3d Cir. 1978); *UAW District 65 v. Harper & Row Publishers, Inc.*, 576 F.Supp. 1468, 4 EBC 2586 (S.D.N.Y. 1983); *Washington-Baltimore Newspaper Guild v. Washington Star Co.*, 555 F.Supp. 257, 3 EBC 2609 (D.D.C. 1983), *aff'd*, 729 F.2d 863 (D.C. Cir. 1984). See also *Cunha v. Ward Foods, Inc.*, 804 F.2d 1418, 7 EBC 2747 (9th Cir. 1986) (decision to terminate a plan far *short* of full funding for promised benefits a business decision, not a breach of fiduciary duty).

Decisions to terminate plans, however, continue to be challenged as fiduciary violations. See, e.g., *Brunt v. Charter Corp.*, 3 EBC 1201 (E.D. Pa. 1982); *Air Line Pilots Ass'n v. United Air Lines, Inc.*, No. 85-C-4765 (N.D. Ill., filed July 26, 1985). In one case, a fiduciary violation theory provided the basis for a settlement allocating $50 million out of a potential reversion of $250 million to plan participants for benefit increases, even though the district court approving the settlement expressed grave doubts about whether the decision to terminate a plan involved fiduciary duties. See *Walsh v. A&P Co.*, 96 F.R.D. 632, 4 EBC 1055 (D.N.J. 1983), *aff'd* 4 EBC 2577 (3d Cir. 1983).

[23] See ch. 9, sec. II.A.3.

involved in the *implementation* of the decision are, e.g., ensuring the proper allocation of the plan's assets, choosing an interest rate for any lump sum payments from among reasonable interest rates, choosing an insurer for annuities to be purchased to close out the plan, and determining whether the statutory conditions for a reversion of excess assets to an employer have been satisfied.[24]

The dichotomy between the view that a decision to terminate a plan is not a fiduciary function and the view, discussed in Chapter 9, that a decision to amend a plan generally is, can be seen as similar to the dichotomy in labor law between the duty of an employer to bargain over decisions to close or relocate plant operations and its duty to bargain over changes in the terms and conditions of employment generally.[25] A distinction between the decision to amend a plan and the decision to terminate a plan may be further supported by the structure of ERISA Section 403(c)(1)'s prohibition on inurement of a plan's assets to the benefit of the employer. Under ERISA Section 403(c)(1), a plan's assets can never inure to the benefit of an employer through plan amendment or otherwise, but an express exception is provided when a plan is terminated with excess assets and the conditions set forth in Section 4044 for a reversion are satisfied.[26]

D. Collective Bargaining Obligations

The primary factor limiting many employers' ability to "voluntarily" terminate plans in either a standard or a distress termination is the presence of a union. When employees are represented by a union, the employer has a duty to bargain with the union over if, and when, a plan termination can take place.[27] If the collective bargaining agreement requiring maintenance of the plan has not expired, a termination is barred as a mid-term modification of the basic agreement, absent "clear and unequivocal" relinquishment to the employer of a right to unilaterally terminate the plan during the term of the agreement.[28]

---

[24] See letter of Dennis M. Kass, Assistant Secretary of Labor for Pension and Welfare Benefits, to former Rep. John N. Erlenborn, Chairman, Department of Labor Advisory Council on Employee Welfare and Pension Benefit Plans, reprinted in 13 BNA Pens. Rep. at 472-73 (March 17, 1986).

[25] See *Textile Workers Union v. Darlington Mfg. Co.*, 380 U.S. 263 (1965) (management has prerogative to close operations unless discriminatory motivation); *First National Maintenance v. NLRB*, 452 U.S. 666 (1981) (applying the management functions doctrine to partial plant closings).

[26] See *In re C.D. Moyer Co. Pension Trust*, 441 F.Supp. 1128, 1 EBC 1363 (E.D. Pa. 1977), *aff'd*, 582 F.2d 1272 (3d Cir. 1978) (terminations with reversions of excess assets are an express exception to the general rule prohibiting inurement of the plan's assets to the benefit of an employer during the on-going administration of a plan).

[27] See *Terones v. Pacific States Steel Corp.*, 526 F.Supp. 1350 (N.D. Cal. 1981); *T.T.P. Corp.*, 190 NLRB 240, 77 LRRM 1097 (1971) (finding duty to bargain over plan termination even when pension plan was not an express part of the collective bargaining agreement).

[28] *Terones v. Pacific States Steel Corp.*, *supra*, 526 F.Supp. at 1355. And see *Steelworkers Local 2341 v. Whitehead & Kales Co.*, 94 Lab. Cas. ¶13,600 (E.D. Mich. 1982) (unilateral termination provision drafted into plan by employer, but inconsistent with collective bargaining negotiations, invalid because of misrepresentation that new draft of plan contained only those changes negotiated by the parties).

However, if the long-run losses to the PBGC appear likely to increase, the PBGC can involuntarily terminate a plan, despite the employer's collective bargaining agreement and duty to bargain, leaving the union with only a remedy at law against the employer for damages for breach of contract.[29] An employer's collective bargaining agreement, including the pension part of the agreement, can also be rejected by a bankruptcy court under Section 365(a) of the Bankruptcy Code if the agreement is an "executory" contract, and meets certain criteria specified in Bankruptcy Code Section 1113, as amended by the 1984 Bankruptcy Amendments and Federal Judgeships Act.[30] Section 1113 requires the debtor-in-possession in a Chapter 11 reorganization to make a specific proposal to the union, ahead of rejection, detailing necessary changes in its collective bargaining agreement, with complete information provided the union to support the necessity of the changes. The debtor must confer with the union in good faith, attempting to reach mutually satisfactory modifications. The collective bargaining agreement can only be rejected if the bankruptcy court then finds that the union rejected the company's proposal without "good cause," and finds that the balance of the equities "clearly favors" rejection of the agreement.[31]

It is questionable whether a pension plan can be terminated by a bankruptcy court as an "executory contract" subject to the court's rejection authority. The legislative history describes an "executory contract" as "generally includ[ing] contracts in which performance remains due to some extent on both sides."[32] In *In re Alan Wood Steel Co.*, a bankruptcy court recognized that terminating a pension plan might not be within its power to reject executory contracts because a pension plan termination can effectively discard an employer's obligation to fund benefits due for service that has already been rendered, in addition to benefits for service to be rendered in the future.[33] *Alan*

SEPPAA amends Title IV specifically to provide that a plan termination cannot take place in violation of the terms of an existing collective bargaining agreement unless the PBGC institutes proceedings to involuntarily terminate the plan. ERISA §4041(a)(3), as amended. "This provision is an endorsement of judicial decisions such as *Terones* ... holding that a company cannot unilaterally terminate a collectively bargained plan ... in violation of any agreement between the parties." 131 Cong. Rec. H-13300 (daily ed. Dec. 19, 1985) (statement of Rep. Augustus Hawkins, Chairman, House Education and Labor Committee).

[29] See *PBGC v. Heppenstall Co.*, 633 F.2d 293, 2 EBC 1884 (3d Cir. 1980); *UAW v. White Farm Equipment*, 3 EBC 2380 (N.D. Ill. 1982).

[30] P.L. 98-353, §541. The statutory criteria supersede the criteria announced by the Supreme Court in *NLRB v. Bildisco & Bildisco*, 465 U.S. 513, 5 EBC 1015 (1984).

[31] Bankruptcy Code §1113, as amended by §541 of P.L. 98-353. For one of the first applications of this standard, see *In re Wheeling-Pittsburgh Steel Corp.*, 791 F.2d 1074, 7 EBC 1529 (3d Cir. 1986), *rev'g*, 6 EBC 1897 and 2038 (Bankr. W.D. Pa. 1985). And see *Century Brass Products, Inc. v. UAW*, 795 F.2d 265, 7 EBC 1801 (2d Cir. 1986), *cert. denied*, 479 U.S. ___ (1986) (union cannot bargain for retirees under §1113 when it has a conflict of interest in representing their interests over those of the active workers). In a Chapter 7 liquidation proceeding, executory contracts are automatically rejected unless the contract is assumed within 60 days of the bankruptcy filing. Bankruptcy Code §365(d)(1).

[32] S. Rep. 95-989, at 58, 95th Cong., 2d Sess.

[33] 4 B.C.D. 850, 1 EBC 2166 (Bankr. E.D. Pa. 1978). The legislative history of SEPPAA is also equivocal on whether a bankruptcy court's power to approve rejection of executory contracts includes the power to terminate a plan. See Jt. Explanatory Statement of Conference Committee,

Wood thus seemed to suggest that normally the rejection power might be limited to halting future benefit accruals under the plan, i.e., "freezing" the plan. But in *Alan Wood,* the court went on to allow the employer's pension plans to be terminated under its rejection authority because all of the employer's obligations based on nonexecutory performance would survive the plan's termination as contractual obligations of the employer to pay all unfunded benefits.[34] Without this caveat, another bankruptcy court in *In re The Bastian Co.* held that the power to reject executory contracts encompasses the power to terminate a pension plan.[35]

In determining whether to approve termination or modification of the executory provisions of a plan, a bankruptcy court can consider the burden on the employer and balance of equities from a pension plan *separately* from the rest of a collective bargaining agreement. The plan's benefits may also be compared with other plans in the industry and other plans of the employer, including plans for management employees, in weighing the burden of maintaining a plan against the equities in favor of its continuance.[36]

Even when a plan is terminated, or if only the purely executory provisions of the plan are rejected, a debtor-in-possession must still bargain with the union over new pension benefits.[37]

E. Implied Contractual Limits

Even nonbargained plans may be subject to an implied contractual duty of "good faith and fair dealing" in the adoption of plan amendments, including an amendment to terminate a plan.[38] More specific limits on plan terminations can arise from statements or omissions in

131 Cong. Rec. H-13252 (daily ed. Dec. 19, 1985) (distress termination provisions are not intended to make substantive changes in bankruptcy court's decision on whether to approve the termination of a plan, taking "no position on when or whether a pension plan is an executory contract").

[34] For a contractual claim to survive a plan termination is not to say that the claim will be paid on the same basis as if the plan had not been terminated. When claims survive only as unsecured general claims of creditors, payment on the dollar may be low.

[35] 6 EBC 1282 (Bankr. W.D.N.Y. 1985). As mentioned before, even if a plan cannot be terminated under the rejection power, the PBGC retains authority to involuntarily terminate the entire plan. This includes when a sponsoring employer is in bankruptcy. See ERISA §§4042(a), (e), and (f).

[36] See *In re Alan Wood Steel Co.*, 4 B.C.D. 850, 1 EBC 2166 (Bankr. E.D. Pa. 1978); *In re Blue Ribbon Trans. Co.*, 30 B.R. 783 (Bankr. D.R.I. 1983); *Matter of Connecticut Celery Co.*, 90 Lab. Cas. ¶12,515 (Bankr. D. Conn. 1980).

[37] See *NLRB v. Bildisco & Bildisco*, 465 U.S. 513, 5 EBC 1015 (1984). Because of this bargaining duty, it may often be uneconomical to terminate a plan only to renegotiate another one with lower future benefits. On termination of the first plan, the PBGC can assert a claim for guaranteed benefits of up to 30% of the employer's net worth, plus the additional claims for guaranteed benefits and unfunded benefit commitments established under SEPPAA. Employees may also assert claims for unfunded benefits on a contractual basis. In addition, contractual obligations for future pension benefits that are rejected in bankruptcy, and not resecured in bargaining after the rejection, can give rise to additional unsecured contract claims against the employer. See *In re Bildisco*, 682 F.2d 72, at 80 (3d Cir. 1982), *aff'd,* 465 U.S. 513, 5 EBC 1015 (1984).

[38] See ch. 9, sec. III.C.

a summary plan description, or from other written and oral statements to employees concerning the conditions under which a power to amend or terminate might be exercised.[39] In *Musto v. American General Corp.*, a district court found that while an employee health benefit plan reserved at-will amendment and termination authority for the employer, including authority to decrease retirees' health benefits, a standard of "good faith and cause" had to be implied into the reservation considering: (1) ERISA's policies in favor of secure retirement income, (2) the need to avoid an interpretation of the amendment/termination authority that would render the employer's benefit promises to retirees illusory, (3) the failure of the plan to specify an amendment/termination procedure as required by ERISA Section 402(b), and (4) a statement in the summary plan description that changes or the termination of the plan would occur only "if necessary."[40] In *Amato v. Western Union International, Inc.*, statements in a summary plan description that amendments to a pension plan would only be made in "unforeseen situations" and that the employer's intent was to "continue the plan indefinitely" were not strong enough to establish a separate contractual claim based "solely" on the summary plan description, but could be used to interpret an employer's obligations under an at-will reservation of amendment/termination authority.[41] In *Horn & Hardart Co. v. Ross*, "lifetime pensions" of up to a maximum of $100 per month were promised in a plan booklet, with "the power to terminate" the plan short of full funding of the promised benefits not "brought home" to employees. The power to terminate was therefore limited by the booklet's offer of lifetime benefits, and its lack of disclosure of what the termination power could mean.[42]

In ERISA Technical Release 84-1, the Department of Labor also recognized that a plan's potential termination constitutes a "circumstance" that may result in the denial or loss of promised benefits, and that therefore must be disclosed in an SPD. Consequently, the SPD must contain:

(1) A "summary of any plan provisions governing the rights of the plan sponsor or others to terminate the plan, and [a summary

---

[39] The absence of ambiguity in a plan's reservation to an employer of a power to terminate should seldom bar extrinsic evidence on the meaning and intent of the parties if it exists. See ch. 7, sec. III.A.4 (on the use of extrinsic evidence in plan interpretation).

[40] 615 F.Supp. 1483, 6 EBC 2071 (M.D. Tenn. 1985). See also *In re Erie Lackawanna Ry. Co.*, 548 F.2d 621 (6th Cir. 1977) (implying good faith and sufficient cause standard into at-will termination clause of pre-ERISA group life insurance contract).

[41] 773 F.2d 1402, 6 EBC 2226 (2d Cir. 1985).

[42] 395 N.Y.S.2d 180, at 181 (Sup.Ct. App.Div. 1977). See also *Hurd v. Hutnik*, 419 F.Supp. 630, 1 EBC 1382 (D.N.J. 1976) (same result under estoppel when employers contributing to a multiemployer plan made "clear and consistent" representations of "lifetime" pensions in plan booklets and otherwise, but then persuaded a union to "sell [its] old people down the river" by terminating the plan short of full funding for the retirees' benefits). But compare *Hamilton v. Travelers Ins. Co.*, 752 F.2d 1350, at 1351 (8th Cir. 1985) (termination of health plan not precluded by SPD that stated employer "may terminate the Plan in whole or in part at any time").

of] the *circumstances*, if any, under which the plan may be terminated";

(2) A "summary of any plan provisions governing the benefits, rights and obligations of plan participants under the plan on termination ... including ... a summary of any provisions relating to the accrual and the vesting of benefits under the plan upon termination"; and

(3) A "summary of any plan provisions governing the allocation and disposition of assets upon termination."[43]

Under ERISA Section 502(a)(3), courts are authorized to provide appropriate remedial relief for violations of the SPD requirements. One remedy for misleading or incomplete disclosure of the power to terminate a plan short of full funding for all benefits may be that of *Horn & Hardart Co. v. Ross*, where the court required the funding of promised benefits to be completed, rather than prohibiting the plan termination *per se*.

F. Procedural Requirements for a Termination Under a Plan's Terms

ERISA Section 402(b)(3) requires employee benefit plans to identify the persons with authority to amend the plan, including to terminate it, and to specify the "procedure" under which such amendments may be made.[44] Whether the p's and q's of a plan's amendment procedure have been followed in terminating a plan is subject to direct contractual review, even if an "arbitrary and capricious" standard is otherwise applicable to interpretations of the terms of the plan.[45] In *Burud v. Acme Electric Co.*, a challenge by employees to a corporation's compliance with state law requirements of notice to all directors of the corporate board meeting at which a plan was terminated survived a motion to dismiss when only two out of three board members received

---

[43] ERISA Technical Release No. 84-1 (May 4, 1984), reprinted in 11 BNA Pens. Rep. at 653-54 (May 14, 1984) (emphasis added). Technical Release 84-1 is not restricted to the future, but provides that any SPD or summary of material modification that fails to disclose the described information will be considered by the Department as not in compliance with the SPD requirements. And see *Kolentus v. Avco Corp.*, 798 F.2d 949 (7th Cir. 1986) (employee could not rely on general statements in pre-ERISA SPD that benefits were to be received as long as employee lived to require employer to complete the funding of all vested benefits upon plan termination; however, Seventh Circuit recognized that "one of the major changes" brought about by ERISA was that "it mandates disclosure of circumstances under which benefits may be terminated," 798 F.2d at 960).

[44] See *Musto v. American General Corp.*, 615 F.Supp. 1483, 6 EBC 2071 (M.D. Tenn. 1985) (plan terminations are included within the §402(b)(3) requirement that a plan specify the procedure for amendments). See also ERISA Technical Release No. 84-1 (May 4, 1984), reprinted in 11 BNA Pens. Rep. at 653-54 (May 14, 1984) (providing that the circumstances under which a plan may be terminated must be stated in the SPD, including a summary of plan provisions governing the rights of the plan sponsor or others to terminate the plan), and Rev. Rul. 85-6 (plan termination is a plan "amendment" within meaning of ERISA §204(g)).

[45] See *Harm v. Bay Area Pipe Trades Pension Fund*, 701 F.2d 1301, 4 EBC 1253, at 1255 n.3 (9th Cir. 1983); *Central Hardware Co. v. Central States Pension Fund*, 770 F.2d 106, 6 EBC 2525 (8th Cir. 1985), *cert. denied*, 475 U.S. 1108 (1986).

notice of the meeting.[46] In *Maas v. Dubuque Packing Co.*, the Eighth Circuit held that a joint labor-management administrative board had authority under the terms of a plan to decide whether an employer in turn had the authority to unilaterally terminate a plan after a certain date, or whether that date had been implicitly delayed by a general memorandum of agreement between the bargaining parties.[47]

II. Termination Dates

A. Defined Benefit Plans

The exact date of a plan's termination becomes important to many participants if a termination cannot be prevented. The PBGC does not generally insure benefits unless they are nonforfeitable under the terms of the plan before the date of termination. Nonforfeitability under the plan's terms is also an important dividing line in the ERISA Section 4044 priority categories for allocating a plan's assets among benefits, and in the obligation created by SEPPAA after 1985 to fund "benefit commitments," defined as all nonforfeitable benefits under the plan, whether or not guaranteed. If participants are still employed, a later termination date can allow them to obtain additional credit for meeting the plan's nonforfeitability (i.e., vesting) requirements, as well as additional credit for benefit accruals. Even without active employment, periods of layoff can result in additional credit for meeting vesting requirements, as well as credit for benefit accruals, under the provisions of many collectively bargained plans.[48] Without either active employment or a negotiated layoff provision, but with a later termination date, up to one year of service may still be required for vesting under plans that use the "elapsed time" regulation for crediting vesting service if the employees are considered to have separated from service for "any other reason" than a quit, discharge, death, or retirement.[49] Shorter periods of credit for vesting can be obtained under plans that count hours of service, or an equivalency to hours (e.g., days, weeks, or months of service within 12-month computation periods) for periods for which vacation pay, accrued sick leave, or severance pay are drawn

[46] 591 F.Supp. 238, 5 EBC 1793 (D. Alas. 1984).

[47] 754 F.2d 287, 6 EBC 1385 (8th Cir. 1985), *reh. denied, but opinion clarified,* 757 F.2d 194, 6 EBC 1390 (8th Cir. 1985).

[48] See, e.g., *Fitzsimons Steel Co., Youngstown, Ohio,* 81-2 ARB (CCH) ¶8408 (Ruben, 1981) (collectively bargained provision required up to 2 years credit for layoff, even though prospects for reemployment were nil).

[49] See ch. 5, sec. III.B.2. A plan's rules for measuring a year of participation for benefit accruals may follow the same standard. However, some plans modify the elapsed time method so that an additional year of credited service for absences for "any other reason" than a quit, discharge, or retirement does not apply for benefit accruals. The Tax Court has held that such modifications are permissible *so long as* the plan credits all periods of time that would be required to be credited under an hours-counting approach. See *Standard Oil Co. v. Commissioner,* 78 T.C. 541, 3 EBC 1276 (1982), and ch. 4, sec. III.D.2 (on the measurement of a year of participation).

after active employment ends—again assuming that the plan's termination date is late enough for these periods to count.[50]

Even when additional credits for vesting and benefit accruals cannot be gained on these grounds, a later termination date can still ameliorate the PBGC's "phase-in" of insurance on benefit increases made within five years of the plan termination. For example, just a few days or weeks more before a plan terminates can mean that a benefit increase has been in effect for two complete years, and is therefore 40 percent, instead of 20 percent, insured. A later termination date can also bring more participants into pay status, or make more participants eligible for pay status, for three years prior to the termination date, and thus put their benefits under category (3), where benefits above the PBGC's guarantee can be paid from a plan's assets even when the plan's assets are insufficient to cover all of the PBGC's guaranteed benefits. A later termination date also allows all retirees to draw full benefits for a longer period (once a plan terminates, benefits above the level provided under a final termination basis allocation of the plan's assets may be lost). Finally, a later termination date requires the employer to continue funding the plan, and thereby to fund more of the benefits already credited to participants under the plan. For all these reasons, the interests of employees and retirees are generally united in favor of the latest possible termination date.[51]

A defined benefit plan subject to Title IV is not terminated until the Title IV procedures for a termination are followed. Thus, even if the PBGC's Title IV insurance is not needed to pay a plan's benefits, the PBGC must still be notified of the plan termination in advance, and the Title IV procedures and notice requirements must be followed before the plan is actually terminated. Even when a company files for bankruptcy under Chapter 7 (liquidation) or Chapter 11 (reorganization) of the Bankruptcy Code, its pension plan does not automatically "terminate." The plan may be terminated in either situation, and inevitably will be in a liquidation, but the procedures in Section 4041 or Section 4042 must be followed before the plan is considered terminated under ERISA.[52]

---

[50] See ch. 5, sec. III.B.1.

[51] See *Braniff Int'l Corp. v. Interfirst Bank*, 24 B.R. 466, 3 EBC 2328, at 2333 (Bankr. N.D. Tex. 1982).

[52] However, in *In re Bastian Co.*, 6 EBC 1282 (Bankr. W.D.N.Y. 1985), a bankruptcy court held that the ERISA procedures are not the exclusive means for terminating a plan once a bankruptcy petition is filed. The court held it could authorize the termination of a plan *apart from* the ERISA §4041 procedures, with the termination then relating back to the date before the date of the bankruptcy filing. At the same time, the court suggested that without its approval, a bankrupt employer cannot terminate a plan *once* a bankruptcy petition is filed—even if the employer can, outside of bankruptcy, unilaterally terminate the plan. *Id.*

The power of a bankruptcy court asserted in *In re Bastian Co.* was ostensibly negated by a provision in SEPPAA that ERISA §§4041 and 4042 are the exclusive means to effect a plan termination. See §4041(a)(1), as amended. The legislative history however, is more equivocal on whether a bankruptcy court's power to terminate a plan as an executory contract—assuming a plan is an executory contract—is affected by this provision. Compare Jt. Explanatory Statement of Conference Committee, 131 Cong. Rec. H-13252 (daily ed. Dec. 19, 1985) (distress termination provisions are not intended to make substantive changes in bankruptcy court's decision on

1. Voluntary Terminations of Sufficient Plans Before SEPPAA

Under ERISA Section 4041, as in effect before SEPPAA, the administrator of a plan that is being voluntarily terminated proposes a termination date to the PBGC which "may not be earlier than" 10 days after the filing with the PBGC of a Notice of Intent to Terminate (which must include the information required on the IRS/PBGC Form 5310). As a part of the notice requirements, plan participants, including retirees, must be notified of the employer's intent to terminate the plan through posted or mail notice, and through notice to any union involved.[53] In Opinion Letter 82-25, the PBGC stated:

> "The section 4041(a) filing procedure must include notif[ication to] plan participants.... Thus participants normally can know *with certainty* whether they are still covered by an ongoing plan for purposes of ERISA.
>
> "On occasion, events involving a plan and its sponsor may be a reasonable basis for belief that the plan cannot continue indefinitely, that participants have no reasonable expectation of accruing additional benefits, or both. [However, a]s would be expected in view of the prior discussion, such events do not automatically constitute an ERISA termination."[54]

Once the notice requirements are satisfied, the PBGC has until 90 days after the proposed termination date to make a determination of whether the plan's assets are "sufficient" and to decide whether to approve the proposed date.[55]

Before SEPPAA, if a voluntarily terminated plan was found to be "sufficient," i.e., able to pay all PBGC guaranteed benefits out of plan assets, the PBGC could agree to the employer-proposed termination date, or it could refuse to agree to any date except a still later date. If no agreement could be reached, a court established the termination date.[56] However, regardless of an employer's or the PBGC's desires, the termination date for a "sufficient" plan could be no earlier than 10 days after the filing of the Notice of Intent to Terminate, including

---

whether to approve the termination of a plan, taking "no position on when or whether a pension plan is an executory contract"), with H.R. Rep. 99-266, 99th Cong., 1st Sess., at 41.

Regardless of whether *In re Bastian Co.* is correct, benefit accruals automatically stop in a Chapter 7 proceeding unless the plan is "assumed" within 60 days of the filing. As an "executory contract," future benefit accruals can also be "rejected" in a Chapter 11 proceeding. See sec. I.D above.

[53] See 29 C.F.R. 2616.4(c). Prior to Feb. 28, 1983, the regulations did not require notice to retirees and former employees.

[54] See PBGC Opinion Letter 82-25 (emphasis added).

[55] Under a 1985 regulation, an enrolled actuary and the plan's administrator could self-certify the sufficiency of a plan's assets to cover all benefits the PBGC guarantees. The plan administrator could then proceed to a more immediate distribution. 29 C.F.R. 2617.12(b) (issued Aug. 1, 1985).

[56] ERISA §4048(3), before the 1986 SEPPAA amendments. When a large group of employees is just short of vesting, ERISA §404(a)(1) actions for breach of fiduciary duty in the timing of the date of termination, or ERISA §510 actions for intentional interference with the attainment of pension rights, may also be present. In a sense, the PBGC's pre-SEPPAA authority to refuse to agree to anything except a later date allowed it leverage to achieve the same purposes as ERISA §§404(a)(1) and 510 without litigation—unless an employer forced the issue to court under ERISA §4048.

notice to participants.[57] A still later termination date might be secured by reviewing compliance with the plan's own procedures for a termination. Failure to follow the procedures set forth under the terms of the plan can require a duly-authorized resubmission of the Notice of Intent to Terminate to the PBGC.[58]

2. *Standard Terminations and Distress Terminations of Sufficient Plans After SEPPAA*

After SEPPAA, written notice to participants, beneficiaries, and any union representing plan participants is required 60 days before a standard or distress termination.[59] For a distress termination, the PBGC is also required to receive notice 60 days in advance. No leeway remains for the PBGC to refuse to agree to any except a later termination date in a standard termination.[60] In a distress termination of a plan with sufficient assets to pay all PBGC guaranteed benefits, the termination date is the date agreed to by the plan administrator and the PBGC, but the date can be no less than 60 days after written notice is provided plan participants.[61]

3. *Involuntary Terminations and Voluntary or Distress Terminations of Insufficient Plans*

The PBGC's financial interests in an involuntary termination, including an involuntary termination resulting from a distress termination in which the plan's assets are insufficient to pay all PBGC guaranteed benefits, are different than on the termination of a sufficient plan. In an involuntary termination, the PBGC faces funding part of the plan's benefits from its trust funds. As a result, the PBGC can have a financial interest in an early termination date. With an early termination date, the plan's insured benefits are less because less benefits have accrued, fewer participants have nonforfeitable benefits, and provisions, such as the five-year phase-in of benefit increases, have a greater effect in reducing insured benefit liabilities. An earlier termination date can, moreover, enable the PBGC to reach more of a sponsoring employer's assets under its authority to assess up to 30 percent of an employer's net worth, with net worth determined within 120 days

---

[57] ERISA §4041(a), before SEPPAA, and PBGC Opinion Letter 82-25. And see *Braniff Int'l Corp. v. Interfirst Bank*, 24 B.R. 466, 3 EBC 2328 (Bankr. N.D. Tex. 1982).

[58] See sec. I.F above on procedural requirements under a plan's terms for a termination.

[59] ERISA §§4041(a)(2) and 4001(a)(21), as amended. Generally, the SEPPAA amendments are effective as of Jan. 1, 1986—even though SEPPAA did not become law until April 7, 1986. However, the 60-day notice requirement is not effective for plans for which a notice of intent to terminate was filed before April 7, 1986. P.L. 99-272, §11019. A special rule applies to notice of standard plan terminations with reversion potentials of $1 million or more. See P.L. 99-272, §11008(d).

[60] ERISA §4048(a)(1), as amended.

[61] ERISA §4048(a)(2), as amended.

of the termination date.[62] Particularly if the sponsoring employer's net worth has been deteriorating, the PBGC may want as early a termination date as possible so that the 120-day period reaches back to a more prosperous time. On the other hand, if the employer's net worth has remained relatively constant, the additional employer contributions from a later date can in some instances outweigh the additional benefits the PBGC may have to guarantee. No absolute rules therefore exist in these cases. For financial and equitable reasons, the PBGC has sometimes sought a later termination date for an insufficient plan than an employer desired, although generally not as late a date as the participants have wanted.[63]

The PBGC can initiate an involuntary termination under ERISA Section 4042 when one of four conditions is present, each basically requiring that the plan or the sponsoring employer be in poor financial condition, with the PBGC's losses likely to increase without an involuntary termination of the plan. When the PBGC initiates an involuntary termination, it, rather than the employer, proposes the termination date. ERISA Section 4042 does not contain a 10- or 60-day prior notice requirement. Thus, the PBGC can propose a termination date that is simultaneous with its initiation of the involuntary proceeding, or even earlier. If the employer does not agree to the PBGC's proposed termination date, the date is set by a court pursuant to ERISA Section 4048(a)(4).

When a plan termination starts out as a voluntary termination, but the plan's assets are found to be insufficient, the PBGC must begin involuntary proceedings under Section 4042 to put the plan into a trusteeship.[64] After SEPPAA, the same rule applies for a distress termination in which the plan's assets are found to be insufficient to pay all guaranteed benefits.[65] A question arises then on whether the termination retains its "voluntary" character for the purpose of setting the termination date. If it does, the termination date can be no earlier than 10 days (or from 1986 on, 60 days) after the notice of intent to terminate was filed by the employer with the PBGC, with concurrent written notice given to participants.

Cases on whether Section 4041 still applies to the setting of the termination date for an insufficient plan are divided, but only on whether the PBGC can *elect* to retain the plan administrator's proposed voluntary termination date. This issue has arisen where the PBGC, for one reason or another, wants to retain the Section 4041 voluntary termination date, and the employer wants an earlier date. No cases suggest the PBGC cannot seek an earlier termination date if it elects, assuming participants had actual or constructive notice of the

---

[62] See ERISA §4062(b).

[63] See *Braniff Int'l Corp. v. Interfirst Bank*, 24 B.R. 466, 3 EBC 2328 (Bankr. N.D. Tex. 1982); *PBGC v. Broadway Maintenance Co.*, 707 F.2d 647, 4 EBC 1673 (2d Cir. 1983); *PBGC v. DiCenso*, 698 F.2d 199, 3 EBC 2616 (3d Cir. 1983).

[64] ERISA §4041(e), as amended.

[65] ERISA §4041(c)(3)(B)(iii), as amended.

plan termination on the date PBGC wants. In *Braniff International Corp. v. Interfirst Bank*, the bankruptcy court found that once the PBGC determines that a plan is insufficient, the termination loses its voluntary character entirely, with the consequence that the only relevance of its initiation as a voluntary proceeding is to establish a concrete date when participants had notice of an intent to terminate the plan.[66] On the other hand, in *PBGC v. Broadway Maintenance Co.* and *PBGC v. DiCenso*, the Second and Third Circuits found that the PBGC can elect to retain the Section 4041 voluntary termination date—except in those cases where the notice of intent to terminate was filed with the PBGC only because of the PBGC's threat to involuntarily terminate the plan.[67]

The courts have at the same time recognized that in an involuntary termination initiated by the PBGC or an involuntary termination after finding an insufficiency of plan assets, neither the PBGC nor the employer necessarily acts in the participants' behalf in setting the termination date for the insufficient plan. For this reason, and because of the "incomprehensible vagueness" of the role set for participants in involuntary termination proceedings, the courts have accepted the responsibility of protecting plan participants from "overly cautious use of the involuntary termination feature by the PBGC."[68] In resolving disputes over the date for an involuntary termination, the cases have further established that there are only two relevant considerations: "the expectations of participants and the financial implications . . . for [the] PBGC. . . . [T]he financial interests of the *employer* should play no role in setting of a termination date."[69]

The "expectations of participants" center on the time when all participants first had "no justifiable expectation in the plan's continuation."[70] When this occurs has been subject to different formulations. In *PBGC v. Dickens*, a district court focused on when employment, and thus benefit accruals under a plan, ended as the key to the extinction of

---

[66] 24 B.R. 466, 3 EBC 2328 (Bankr. N.D. Tex. 1982). Accord *PBGC v. Dickens*, 535 F.Supp. 922, 3 EBC 1460 (W.D.Mich.1982).

[67] 707 F.2d 647, 4 EBC 1673 (2d Cir. 1983), and 698 F.2d 199, 3 EBC 2616 (3d Cir. 1983), respectively.

In most instances, this seems to be a distinction without a substantive difference. The courts agree that the financial interests of the employer play no role in the establishment of an involuntary termination date. *PBGC v. Broadway Maintenance Co., supra*; *PBGC v. Heppenstall Co.*, 633 F.2d 293, 2 EBC 1884 (3d Cir. 1980). Thus, if the PBGC *wants* a termination date 10 or 60 days after the date voluntary notice was given, that is presumably the date that is most in the PBGC's financial interests. As opposed to an earlier termination date, it is also the date that is most in the participants' interest. The only way an employer could challenge this would seem to be to show that the participants had notice before that date *and* that the PBGC is not acting in its own financial interests. Thus, in *Braniff Int'l Corp. v. Interfirst Bank*, 24 B.R. 466, 3 EBC 2328 (Bankr. N.D. Tex. 1982), despite the court's finding that the PBGC did not have a right to automatically elect the §4041 date, the court set practically the same termination date. Presumably, the same occurred on remand of *PBGC v. Broadway Maintenance Co.*, where the PBGC's threat of an involuntary plan termination eliminated the PBGC's right to elect to retain the ERISA §4041 termination date.

[68] *PBGC v. Heppenstall Co.*, 633 F.2d 293, 2 EBC 1884, at 1890 and 1891 (3d Cir. 1980).

[69] *PBGC v. Broadway Maintenance Co., supra*, 4 EBC at 1677, following *PBGC v. Heppenstall Co., supra*, and *PBGC v. DiCenso, supra*.

[70] *PBGC v. Heppenstall Co., supra*, 2 EBC at 1890.

justifiable participant expectations in plan continuation, "assuming no retiree interests are involved." While the participants had no actual notice on that date that the PBGC was seeking to involuntarily terminate the *plan,* and the employer had also not notified the participants of any intent to voluntarily terminate the plan, the *Dickens* court held that the cessation of business operations established the latest date necessary to protect the employees' expectations.[71] In *PBGC v. Heppenstall Co.* and *PBGC v. Broadway Maintenance Co.*, however, the Third and Second Circuits focused on the time when participants had actual or constructive notice that the PBGC or the employer intended to terminate the *"plan."*[72] In *PBGC v. Broadway Maintenance Co.*, the Second Circuit stated that this date set the "earliest" time when the plan could be involuntarily terminated. The latest date would be the first date after this when the PBGC's financial exposure increased (presumably with some *de minimis* exception).[73] In *Braniff International Corp. v. Interfirst Bank*, a bankruptcy court also focused on "expectations" in the continuation of the *"plan,"* finding that this is not necessarily synonymous with expectations of continued employment, and specifically stating that it includes the expectations of retirees, which would apparently end only with notice specifically directed to them of the intent to terminate the plan.[74]

An important point on participant enforcement of these rules is that a plan's termination date does not automatically come before a court for the court to protect the participants' interests. When the PBGC and a plan administrator reach an agreement, courts are not presented with the question of the appropriate termination date—unless participants raise the issue. For example, in *PBGC v. Dickens*, whether participants had notice on the termination date the PBGC proposed only came before the court because the plan administrator wanted a still earlier date.[75] If the PBGC and plan administrator had agreed on a date, even a date preceding *any* notice to participants, the issue would not have been before the court. When the PBGC and plan administrator agree on an early termination date, participants can raise the issue of notice by appealing under the PBGC's administrative appeals procedures within a 45-day period after the decision is made, or within 45 days after the participant, exercising due diligence, learns

---

[71] 535 F.Supp. 922, 3 EBC 1460, at 1464 (W.D. Mich. 1982). And see *PBGC v. Maryland Glass Corp.*, 6 EBC 2332 (D. Md. 1985) (using date of cessation of production, rather than the date of cessation of all employment, including clean-up work, or the date of notice to participants of specific intent to terminate plan). Accord *Moore v. PBGC*, 566 F.Supp. 534 (E.D. Pa. 1983).

[72] See case citations above. In *PBGC v. Heppenstall Co.*, the court used the date the business closed as an outside parameter, but it was clear that employees had earlier notice of the plan termination and the question was *when* they had such notice. Accord PBGC Opinion Letter 82-25 (distinguishing expectations of future employment from expectations about plan termination).

[73] 4 EBC at 1678.

[74] 24 B.R. 466, 3 EBC 2328 (Bankr. N.D. Tex. 1982). Benefits received by retirees above the PBGC's guaranteed benefit levels after a plan's termination date can be recouped by the PBGC. Retirees can also benefit from a later termination date in other ways, primarily by moving more of their benefits under priority category (3).

[75] *PBGC v. Dickens, supra.*

of the decision. If the PBGC does not reconsider the date, participants can bring suit under ERISA Section 4003(f).[76]

B. Defined Contribution Plans

The Title IV rules on setting plan termination dates do not apply to money purchase pension plans (and defined benefit plans which are not covered under Title IV of ERISA, such as plans of professional service corporations that never have more than 25 active participants). But under ERISA Section 402(b)(3), a procedure for terminating a defined benefit or defined contribution plan must be stated in the plan itself, with the person or persons who are authorized to terminate the plan identified. The proper person or committee must therefore act to terminate the plan, adhering to all aspects of the termination procedure set out under the plan.[77] Until that procedure is followed, the employer's obligation to fund the plan continues. Thus, an employer who wants to stop those obligations has an incentive to follow the procedures in the plan for termination. In addition, ERISA Section 204(h), as amended by SEPPAA, now requires 15 days prior notice of any amendments significantly reducing benefits.[78] If this advance notice is not provided, a court may order "appropriate equitable relief" under ERISA Section 502(a)(3).

For profit-sharing and stock bonus plans, uncertainty can still surround when a plan "termination" has occurred. Under the Code, contributions to profit-sharing and stock bonus plans are only required to be "recurring and substantial" for a plan to remain tax-qualified. If a plan sponsor retains discretion to set the level of contributions to a profit-sharing or stock bonus plan annually with *no* fixed minimum contribution, the sponsor can effectively stop contributions to the plan without necessarily terminating it according to the plan's own procedures. It is also uncertain what relief a court could provide for failure to

---

[76] See 29 C.F.R. 2606.1(b)(6) and (7), and 2606.53 and 2606.5 on the filing period under the PBGC's appeals procedure. A shorter 30-day period may apply to administrative reconsideration of a PBGC determination on a voluntary termination date. See 29 C.F.R. 2606.1(b)(3) and 2606.33.

Whether exhaustion of the PBGC's administrative appeals procedure is required before instituting a law suit is not established. In *Moore v. PBGC*, 566 F.Supp. 534 (E.D. Pa. 1983), a participant, proceeding *pro se*, was unsuccessful in attempting to have a court set an involuntary termination date later than the date agreed on by the PBGC and his employer so that he would have the 30 years of service needed for an unreduced early retirement benefit. The participant apparently did not use the PBGC's appeals procedures, but without reference to this, the district court held it lacked authority to alter the date agreed on by the PBGC and the employer because it was based on the date the employer ceased business, and thus the date the participant ceased work. (The court did not cite or otherwise distinguish the cases that have held that an involuntary termination date can never be earlier than the date on which the participants, including retirees, had notice of the employer's or the PBGC's intent to terminate the *plan.*)

[77] But see *Chambers v. Kaleidoscope, Inc. Profit Sharing Plan*, 650 F.Supp. 359, 7 EBC 2628 (N.D. Ga. 1986) (abandoned money purchase pension plan terminated 1 year after end of last taxable year of employer for which contributions were made when no one was left with the authority to terminate plan).

[78] For plan amendments significantly reducing future benefit accruals adopted between Jan. 1, 1986, and April 7, 1986, this notice requirement is satisfied if notice is provided within 60 days after April 7, 1986. See §11006(b) of Title XI of P.L. 99-272.

give notice of a plan amendment significantly reducing benefits if the reduction in benefits is accomplished through preexisting discretion to contribute no percentage of profits, or only a very small percentage of profits, to the plan.

The Code recognizes the uncertainties surrounding termination dates of discretionary profit-sharing and stock bonus plans and instead uses the date when contributions to the plan are completely discontinued for purposes of the vesting on termination requirement (which is discussed next).

III. Vesting on Termination

Code Section 411(d)(3) provides that on the termination of a pension plan, or on the complete discontinuance of contributions to a profit-sharing or stock bonus plan, all benefits accrued must become nonforfeitable, regardless of a participant's place on a plan's normal vesting schedule, to the extent the benefits are funded by the plan's assets. If there is funding for the benefits, Section 411(d)(3) confers an important right for nonvested participants on termination.[79]

A. Defined Benefit Plans

For a defined benefit plan, the major caveat to the nonforfeitable rights conferred under Code Section 411(d)(3) is that they are only valuable for nonvested participants *to the extent* their benefits are funded when the plan's assets are allocated under the Section 4044 priority categories. As discussed further below, an allocation of assets to priority category (6), where the PBGC's regulations place forfeitable benefits, requires that benefits in all the preceding priority categories must first be paid in full.[80] This means the Section 411(d)(3) rights can have *no* value if the plan's assets do not reach category (6), or a widely varying partial value if the assets reach category (6), but do not cover all benefits in the category.

Section 411(d)(3)'s nonforfeitable rights cover nonvested participants who are employed on the date of plan termination, and also those nonvested participants who were laid-off or discharged before the date of a plan termination. This second group of employees can be particularly large if a plan's termination follows a decline of a business.

---

[79] Since Code §411(d)(3) requires the *terms* of all tax-qualified plans to provide for vesting on termination, a participant can enforce this requirement under ERISA §502(a)(1)(B)—even though the source of the requirement is the Internal Revenue Code. See ch. 11, sec. I.F. See also *Tionesta Sand & Gravel, Inc. v. Commissioner*, 73 T.C. 758 (1980), *aff'd*, 642 F.2d 444 (3d Cir. 1981) (plan may be disqualified if it fails to contain provision that benefits vest on termination or complete discontinuance of contributions, regardless of whether plan has actually failed to meet the substantive requirement).

[80] Whether the PBGC's regulations are in error in placing these benefits under priority category (6), instead of priority category (5), is discussed in sec. IV.A.

When a business is in decline, employees with less seniority, and thus, employees who are less likely to be vested, are generally laid off first, often before the pension plan's termination date. While Code Section 411(d)(3) speaks of "affected employees" receiving nonforfeitable benefits on a plan's termination, it does not require employment on the precise date of a plan's termination. Indeed, such a reading would make the provision a fortuitous right, and in some instances would practically invite employer abuse through layoffs or terminations of nonvested employees a few days, weeks, or months before the plan termination. Accordingly, the IRS reads Section 411(d)(3) to require vesting on termination for all employees *and* former employees who have not suffered a break in service forfeiting all of their benefits prior to the plan's termination date.[81] Independently, priority category (6) of ERISA Section 4044 requires payment of all "forfeitable" benefits under a plan to the extent funded at termination. As long as a break in service has not forfeited the benefits before a proposed termination date, the benefits remain "forfeitable" within the meaning of category (6), and on that basis must also be paid to the extent funded—with or without employment on the exact termination date.[82]

As discussed in Chapters 4 and 5, a break in service cannot forfeit accrued benefits under a defined benefit plan unless the number of consecutive years of break equals or exceeds the number of years of service for vesting accumulated before the break begins. When a participant has *any* nonforfeitable rights (e.g., is 25 percent vested after five years under a 5-to-15 year vesting schedule), a break in service can never forfeit the nonvested portion of the participant's accrued benefits.[83] Under the 1984 Retirement Equity Act amendments, moreover, a five-year floor is placed under the break-in-service rule of parity so that the benefits of a participant with four or less years of service cannot be forfeited until his or her break in service equals or exceeds five years.[84]

One question about vesting on termination under defined benefit plans concerns whether the forfeitable benefits that become nonforfeitable on a termination are limited to "accrued benefits"—as a strict reading of "benefits accrued" in Section 411(d)(3) might have it—or can include unreduced, or only slightly reduced, early retirement benefits for which a participant lacked either a service or age requirement at the date of termination. The IRS has not taken a position on the

---

[81] General Counsel Memorandum (GCM) 39310 (April 4, 1984), reprinted at ¶17,504 CCH Pension Plan Guide. And cf. *Union Central Life Ins. Co. v. Hamilton Steel Prod., Inc.*, 448 F.2d 501 (7th Cir. 1971) (rights on termination applied to former employees not employed on the exact termination date, instead of basing their rights on an "artificial line[]").

[82] When a proposed termination date is so late that a large number of participants' accrued benefits have been forfeited, it is possible that a partial termination of the plan occurred earlier. See ch. 11.

[83] See ERISA §203(b)(3)(D) and ch. 5, sec. III.A.4.b.

[84] ERISA §203(b)(3)(D)(i)(I), as amended.

benefits generally covered by Section 411(d)(3) on a termination.[85] However, in *Amato v. Western Union International, Inc.*, the Second Circuit suggested that a partial termination could require the vesting of unreduced early retirement benefits from a plan. In a partial termination, the Second Circuit ruled, early retirement benefits that are still forfeitable at the time of the amendment must be paid to the extent funded when the plan's assets are allocated according to ERISA Section 4044, with the early retirement benefits falling into priority category (6). In this manner, the Second Circuit stated, "as long as assets [are] available, they [are] used to meet participant's benefit expectations based upon the plan's full benefit structure."[86] As *Amato* indirectly indicates, the issue of whether early retirement benefits become nonforfeitable on a *termination* under Code Section 411(d)(3) to the extent funded is largely moot because ERISA independently requires payment of such benefits to the extent funded under the Section 4044 allocation of assets. Nonforfeitability of early retirement benefits on a termination can also be required as a matter of plan interpretation when a plan promises, as some do, that all "benefits," instead of just "accrued benefits," will become nonforfeitable on a termination.

B. Defined Contribution Plans

In a defined contribution plan, forfeitable as well as nonforfeitable accrued benefits should always be funded on termination, regardless of the priority category, because a participant's accrued benefits are simply the individual's account balance under the plan. The individual account is fully funded when contributions have been made as required by the plan, and contributions, earnings, and forfeitures properly allocated to participant's account as provided under the plan's terms.

The Code recognizes the potential uncertainty in termination dates of profit-sharing or stock bonus plans without substantial nondiscretionary contribution obligations by providing that for purposes of the Section 411(d)(3) nonforfeitable rights, the date of "complete discontinuance" of contributions to a profit-sharing or stock bonus plan is equivalent to the termination date, whether or not the plan has been terminated according to its own procedures. The IRS determines whether a cessation of contributions represents a "complete discontinuance," or a mere "suspension" of contributions, based on all the facts and circumstances, including but not limited to the employer's representations. For example, in Revenue Ruling 80-146, an employer discontinued contributions to a profit-sharing plan for five years due to an absence of profits, but the IRS found that a "complete discontinuance" had not occurred because it was reasonable, under the facts, to

[85] See 26 C.F.R. 1.411(d)-2(a)(1) (repeating the statutory "benefits accrued" language without further elucidation).

[86] 773 F.2d 1402, 6 EBC 2226, at 2240 (2d Cir. 1985). Also see the discussion in ch. 11, sec. I.D, on vesting in early retirement benefits on a partial termination.

expect future profits, and therefore, a recurrence of contributions to the plan from profits. In this Ruling, the employer had a definite contribution commitment for years in which there were profits. Had the employer's contribution commitment been discretionary *even when* profits recurred, the IRS's conclusion that this was a "mere suspension" might have been different.[87] If a suspension of contributions later becomes a complete discontinuance of contributions, the *date* of "complete discontinuance" for purposes of Code Section 411(d)(3) vesting must be no later than the last day of the taxable year of the employer following the last taxable year during which a substantial contribution was made to the plan.[88]

Under Code Section 411(d)(3), nonvested participants who have not forfeited the benefits in their individual accounts prior to a defined contribution plan's termination date (or the date of complete discontinuance of contributions to a profit-sharing or stock bonus plan) are to obtain nonforfeitable rights to their accounts, whether or not they are still employed on the exact termination date, or date of complete discontinuance.[89] In addition, by virtue of ERISA Section 403(d)(1), the ERISA Section 4044 asset allocation categories also apply to defined contribution plans. Ordinarily, the application of Section 4044 has little significance for a defined contribution plan, but in this instance it means that independently of Code Section 411(d)(3)'s vesting requirement, a defined contribution plan's assets must be allocated to all forfeitable individual accounts on termination, regardless of whether the participant is employed on the exact date of termination.

A major drawback to vesting on termination under defined contribution plans has been, and to an extent, still is, that whether a participant has incurred a break in service prior to a plan's termination date that forfeits accrued benefits may be determined under less liberal rules than for a defined benefit plan. Prior to the Retirement Equity Act amendments, defined contribution plans were permitted to provide that any nonvested portion of an individual account balance could be forfeited by a break in service of only one year.[90] Under the 1984 REA

---

[87] Other factors the IRS considers in determining whether contributions to a profit-sharing plan have been completely discontinued are whether the employer may be calling an actual discontinuance of contributions a suspension to avoid the requirement of full vesting, and whether contributions have been recurring and substantial in the past. 26 C.F.R. 1.411(d)-2(d)(1) and Rev. Rul. 80-277. A complete discontinuance of contributions may occur for purposes of Code §411(d)(3) even though some amounts are contributed to the plan, if the amounts are not substantial enough to reflect an intent on the part of the employer to continue the plan. 26 C.F.R. 1.411(d)-2(d)(1).

[88] 26 C.F.R. 1.411(d)-2(d)(2). And see *Chambers v. Kaleidoscope, Inc. Profit Sharing Plan*, 650 F.Supp. 359, 7 EBC 2628 (N.D. Ga. 1986) (abandoned profit-sharing plan terminated for purposes of vesting and distribution of benefits 1 year after end of tax year in which last contributions were made).

[89] GCM 39310 (April 4, 1984), reprinted at ¶17,504 CCH Pension Plan Guide.

[90] ERISA §203(b)(3)(C). When nonvested participants in a defined contribution plan have incurred a one-year break under a plan permissibly using the pre-REA rule before the date of a plan termination, other avenues for relief may still be available. First, the date of "complete discontinuance" of contributions for a profit-sharing or stock bonus plan for purposes of Code §411(d)(3) is not as fixed as for a defined benefit plan. As described before, when a suspension of contributions to a profit-sharing plan becomes a complete discontinuance, the IRS may look back

amendments, this period may be no less than five years.[91] But a forfeiture can still occur without a series of consecutive one-year breaks in service equal to or exceeding the participant's years of service for vesting—as required for a forfeiture to occur under a defined benefit plan.

IV. Allocating Plan Assets on Termination

Six priority categories in ERISA Section 4044(a) and the extent of a defined benefit plan's assets together determine how much of a participant's benefits are paid from plan assets on termination. Of the over 43,000 plans subject to PBGC insurance coverage that have terminated since ERISA, 98 percent have had sufficient assets to pay more benefits than the PBGC guarantees.[92] Thus, these priority allocation categories, rather than the PBGC's insurance limits, as such, generally determine the exact amount of benefits a participant receives on plan termination. Even in these "sufficient"plans, however, the PBGC's guaranteed benefit rules still figure prominently in the allocation of assets because they constitute the major dividing line between the fourth and fifth priority categories.

Basically, Section 4044's priority categories rank a plan's benefits in the order that they are to be paid from the plan's assets. Plan assets are allocated to the first, or highest, priority category of benefits until all benefits in that category are paid; assets are then allocated to the second priority category until all benefits in that category are paid, and so on—until the plan's assets run out. If a plan's assets are not enough to pay all of the benefits in a priority category, the assets are prorated among the benefits in that category (with a special provision, discussed below, applying to the allocation of assets among benefits in category (5)). Once a plan's assets are exhausted by benefit claims within a

---

to the end of the tax year after the last taxable year in which substantial contributions were made to the plan to set the date of complete discontinuance for purposes of Code §411(d)(3). See Rev. Rul. 80-277. Second, the IRS may also examine whether a partial termination occurred before the complete discontinuance, or it can require faster vesting on finding an abusive pattern of discharges slightly over a year before the §411(d)(3) date. See ch. 11 (on partial terminations) and Code §411(d)(1) (on vesting if there is a pattern of abuse). And see S. Lewis, "Partial Terminations of Qualified Retirement Plans," 13 Comp. Plan. J. 223 (July 5, 1985) (IRS frequently maintains that partial terminations occurred in the years before termination based on review of Application for Determination on Termination, which must list the number of participants in each of the five years before termination).

If it appears that discharges or the plan's termination date were purposefully timed to effect break-in-service forfeitures of accrued benefits before the plan's termination, a violation of ERISA §510 may also have occurred. See ch. 10, sec. I, and GAO, "Tax Revenues Lost and Beneficiaries Inadequately Protected When Private Pension Plans Terminate" (HRD-81-117 Sept. 30, 1981), at 14-17 (finding evidence that nonvested employees in profit-sharing plans have sometimes been let go shortly before plan terminations to create forfeitures). Some courts have also found it arbitrary and capricious to apply a break-in-service rule to forfeit benefits based on an *involuntary* absence from work. See ch. 5, sec. III.A.4.

[91] ERISA §203(b)(3)(C), as amended. This 5-year floor became effective with the first plan year beginning after Dec. 31, 1984, except for collectively bargained plans. See ch. 5, sec. III.A.4, and P.L. 98-397, §303(a).

[92] PBGC, Annual Report, FY 82, at 4 and 48.

priority category, no assets are allocated to any lower priority categories.[93]

When a plan's assets are enough to pay all the benefits in categories (1) through (4), including the uninsured benefits in both categories (3) and (4), the plan is considered "sufficient" in terms of the PBGC's guarantee of benefits. It could be argued that a plan is "sufficient" if there are enough assets to cover only the *insured* benefits in categories (1) through (4), but the legislative history is clear that a plan's assets are to be allocated in the order provided in Section 4044.[94]

The Section 4044 allocation schedule has two important related characteristics: First, a plan can have more than enough assets to cover the PBGC's guaranteed benefits in priority categories (1) through (4), but if a participant's uninsured benefits are in priority category (6), rather than category (5), and the plan's assets run out in category (5), the participant may still receive *no more* than the benefits the PBGC insures. Second, when a participant has uninsured benefits in a high priority category, namely, category (3) which basically covers the benefits of retirees, it is possible that the participant will receive *more* than the benefits the PBGC insures, even though the plan's assets are insufficient to pay all of the PBGC's guaranteed benefits.

The priority categories in Section 4044(a) apply to all defined benefit plans, including the professional service corporation plans that are excluded from the PBGC's insurance coverage.

A. The Six Priority Allocation Categories

Priority categories (1) and (2) cover, respectively, benefits attributable to "voluntary" and to "mandatory" employee contributions.[95] The vast majority of defined benefit plans are, however, completely "noncontributory," i.e., employees do not make contributions to the plan on *either* a voluntary or a mandatory basis. Voluntary employee contributions are almost universally handled through separate defined contribution plans, and only a small percentage of defined benefit

---

[93] Plans can have subcategories for allocating assets within the category where the assets run out, e.g., based on age or length of service. Such subcategories override the statute's method of prorating the assets among all benefits in the category (except under category (5))—so long as the subcategories do not produce discrimination in favor of the Code §401(a)(4) group of highly compensated employees. See ERISA §4044(b)(6). The priority categories themselves may not be altered by different plan provisions.

[94] See Conf. Rep., at 375, 3 ERISA Leg. Hist. 4642.

[95] "Mandatory" employee contributions are contributions that are required (1) as a condition of employment, (2) as a condition of participation in the plan, or (3) as a condition of receiving matching employer contributions. ERISA §4044(b)(5) and Code §411(c)(2)(C). The most prevalent type of mandatory contributions are employee contributions to savings plans that are required to obtain matching contributions from an employer.

"Voluntary" employee contributions must be completely voluntary. No "carrot" other than tax-free appreciation and convenient deposits may be attached. See ch. 1, sec. V.C.

plans require mandatory employee contributions.[96] Therefore, the assets allocated to these two priority categories are usually nil under a defined benefit plan.[97]

Priority category (3) covers benefits of retirees who have been in pay status for three years before a plan's termination. It also covers benefits of participants who *could have been* in pay status for the three years before termination, e.g., when an employee could have retired under an early or normal retirement provision, but instead chose to continue to work.[98] The amount of these participants' category (3) benefits is, however, limited to their benefits as determined under the lowest dollar level of benefits in effect under the plan during the *five* years before the termination.[99] Benefits in category (3) are, at the same time, not limited by the guaranteed benefit ceiling or the substantial owner limits on guaranteed benefits discussed below.[100] In some small plans, most of the plan's assets may in fact be allocated to category (3) to provide high benefits to retired owner-employees, or owner-employees who could have retired three years before the termination.

Category (4) covers all nonforfeitable benefits that are insured, and that are not already included in category (3). Some uninsured benefits are also included in category (4), namely, benefits that are not insured because of the substantial owner limits, and benefits that are not insured because of a limitation that applies the guaranteed benefit ceiling to a participant's *total* benefits from two or more terminated insufficient plans.[101]

Favorable reduction factors for early retirement benefits, e.g., a reduction in normal retirement benefits of .5 percent per month of early retirement down to age 60 and .25 percent per month more for still earlier retirements, can be a part of a participant's category (4) benefit, and thus a required part of any annuity or lump sum value distributed to cover the participant's benefits, if the participant has a

---

[96] See *LLC Corp. v. PBGC*, 703 F.2d 301, 4 EBC 1233 (8th Cir. 1983), for an example of a defined benefit plan requiring employee contributions.

[97] When a defined benefit plan requires mandatory employee contributions, 29 C.F.R. 2618.12 provides the rule for determining how much of a participant's benefits are attributable to the employee contributions. See also ERISA §204(c)(2)(B) (Code §411(c)(2)(B)), 26 C.F.R. 1.411(c)-1(c), and Rev. Ruls. 76-47 and 78-202 (providing additional conversion factors).

In the rare instances when a defined benefit plan accepts voluntary employee contributions, separate accounting is required. The benefits attributable to the voluntary employee contributions are the amounts credited to the separate account. See 29 C.F.R. 2618.11 and ERISA §204(b)(2)(A).

[98] 29 C.F.R. 2618.13(b)(1).

[99] 29 C.F.R. 2618.13(b)(3). PBGC Opinion Letter 79-8 provides several concrete examples applying what it calls the "two-step" analysis of (1) determining the participant's eligibility for pay status 3 years before the termination, and then (2) determining the amount of his or her category (3) benefits based on the lowest dollar benefit level in effect 5 years before the termination.

[100] See 29 C.F.R. 2618.13(a).

[101] See 29 C.F.R. 2618.14, and sec. VI.C (on the substantial owner limits).

nonforfeitable right to retire early before the date of plan termination.[102] Preretirement survivor's annuity coverage is also a nonforfeitable benefit that is required to be included under priority category (4). Before the Retirement Equity Act amendments to ERISA, this coverage was not required to be provided after a plan's termination under an express IRS ruling.[103] As a result of this ruling, preretirement survivor's annuity coverage was effectively considered neither a nonforfeitable nor a forfeitable benefit for purposes of the allocation of a plan's assets. However, under the 1984 REA amendments, preretirement survivor's coverage is automatic at any age when a participant has nonforfeitable benefits, and applies whether or not the participant is still in service with the employer at the time of death.[104] This preretirement coverage has thus become an indivisible part of the participant's nonforfeitable benefits under priority category (4), and according to the IRS, it must either continue after a plan's termination, or be a part of any lump sum distribution or any annuity purchased under the plan's allocation of assets to close out the plan.[105]

Priority category (5) covers all nonforfeitable benefits that are not insured by the PBGC which are not already covered under priority categories (3) and (4). Primarily, this category consists of benefits that are not insured because of the five-year phase-in and the PBGC's guaranteed benefit ceiling. It can also include Social Security supplements that are not insured because of the PBGC's definition of "pension" benefits. When a plan's assets are exhausted within category (5), a special rule provides that instead of simply prorating the assets among all benefits in category (5), the assets are allocated first to benefits determined under plan provisions in effect five years before the plan's termination. If assets remain after this first allocation, they are allocated to the benefits in category (5) resulting from the next earliest amendment of the plan, and so on, until the assets are exhausted.[106]

Inclusion in category (5) is significant. In a flat-dollar plan, substantial benefits that were ruled out by the five-year phase-in are in this category, such as those for the Braniff-Teamsters plan illustrated in section VI.B, below. In a nonbargained plan, the pension benefits of

---

[102] See sec. VI.A.1 below on the nonforfeitable benefits covered by the PBGC's guarantee. When a nonforfeitable benefit is guaranteed, it must be among the nonforfeitable benefits included under priority category (4). See also 29 C.F.R. 2617.4(a) and 2617.31.

[103] See Rev. Rul. 81-9 (situations 2 and 3). But compare 26 C.F.R. 1.401(a)-11(a)(1)(i)(D) (if a participant separates from service after a plan's qualified early retirement age and dies before his or her benefits commence, survivor's annuity coverage must be automatic; this coverage presumably was always required to either continue after plan termination or be a contingency covered by the annuity contract purchased to close out the plan).

[104] For purposes of the PBGC's guarantee, and hence, also for the purpose of priority category (4), the SEPPAA amendments also expressly provide that preretirement survivor's annuity coverage is not a forfeitable benefit solely because the participant has not died as of the termination date. ERISA §4022(d), as amended.

[105] See Temp. and Prop. Regs., 1.401(a)-11T, Q&A 10, 50 Fed. Reg. 29371 (July 19, 1985).

[106] ERISA §4044(b)(3). If some benefits in this priority category are in excess of the guaranteed benefit ceiling, they could be paid before benefits ruled out by the phase-in if they arise under plan provisions in effect for a longer period before the termination.

highly compensated employees that are in excess of the guaranteed benefit ceiling (and that are not already included in category (3)) are also in this category, sometimes with the benefit amounts in excess of the ceiling being on the order of $10,000 per month. Even when a plan's assets do not run out in category (5), they may not be enough to cover category (6) benefits in full, which means that only part payments of benefits in category (6) will be made, whereas full payment may apply for category (5) benefits.

According to the PBGC, benefits that become nonforfeitable on the termination of the plan (such as the benefits of an employee with eight years of service under a plan that requires 10 years of service for vesting) are not within category (5). The PBGC regulations exclude these benefits from the definition of "nonforfeitable benefit" and in this manner exclude them from category (5).[107] This position may be at odds with the language of Section 4044(a) that category (5) will cover "all other [other than insured] nonforfeitable benefits under the plan." Since Code Sections 401(a)(7) and 411(d)(3) require all qualified plans to include plan provisions under which accrued benefits become nonforfeitable "under the plan" on termination, these benefits fit within the statutory language for category (5). Where Congress intended to treat benefits that become nonforfeitable on termination on a less favorable basis than other nonforfeitable benefits, it used specific language, namely, "nonforfeitable benefits (other than benefits becoming nonforfeitable solely on account of the termination of a plan)," as in Section 4022(a), to do so.[108]

Category (6) covers "*all* other benefits under the plan,"[109] "whether forfeitable or nonforfeitable."[110] As mentioned above, because of the PBGC's position on the benefits in category (5), this necessarily includes accrued benefits that become nonforfeitable on account of the termination of a plan. Category (6) also includes as "forfeitable" benefits unreduced, or only slightly reduced, early retirement benefits and so-called Social Security supplements for participants who have not satisfied the age or service requirements for the benefits at the time of plan termination—for example, a participant who has 28 years of service out of a required 30 years for an early retirement benefit. While these benefits are not required to "accrue" from year to year, and arguably do not automatically become nonforfeitable under Code Section 411(d)(3) on termination (unless the plan so provides), they are clearly "forfeitable" benefits under the plan.[111] In *Amato v. Western*

---

[107] See 29 C.F.R. 2618.2 and 40 Fed. Reg. 51370 (Nov. 4, 1975).

[108] The deference accorded the PBGC's regulation might also be diminished by the fact that it is not directly related to the PBGC's operational or financial interests. Once a plan's assets reach category (5), the PBGC is no longer at risk. In a small nonbargained plan, the same results as would be produced by including these benefits in category (5) may sometimes be achieved through the nondiscrimination reallocations described in sec. IV.C below.

[109] ERISA §4044(a) (emphasis added).

[110] 29 C.F.R. 2618.16.

[111] See 29 C.F.R. 2619.16 and 26 C.F.R. 1.401-2(b)(2). Under the minimum funding requirements, these benefits are also required to be valued actuarially as accrued liabilities before the

Union International, Inc., the Second Circuit found that such early retirement benefits are covered by category (6) as it is "not limited to accrued benefits." The court stated that "as long as assets [are] available, they should be used to meet participants' benefit expectations based upon the Plan's full benefit structure."[112] Category (6) may also include the value of disability and death coverage that extends until a separation from service or retirement for participants who were promised such coverage under a plan's terms, but who were not "entitled" to the benefits before the date of termination.

Although more attention has recently focused on this area, it is doubtful that forfeitable benefits, other than the forfeitable accrued benefits that become nonforfeitable on termination, are in practice always paid under category (6). One reason for this is that the exact basis for valuing and paying forfeitable benefits, such as unreduced early retirement benefits for which either an age or service requirement has not been completed, is not spelled out in ERISA. The regulations are also unenlightening.[113] Two ways to value and pay early retirement benefits are, however, available. The first is to use the actuarial "accrued liability" generated by the offer of these benefits under the funding method the plan uses,[114] prorating the total accrued liability at the time of termination among participants according to their service, or combination of age and years of service, toward the benefit. A second basis is to derive the present value of the entire benefit for each participant and prorate this liability according to each participant's service toward the benefit.[115]

In Revenue Ruling 85-6, the IRS suggested that a third method may be permissible, at least in complying with the Retirement Equity Act requirement that no amendment to a plan, including an amendment terminating the plan, may reduce or eliminate subsidized early retirement benefits.[116] In Revenue Ruling 85-6, the IRS ruled that an early retirement benefit that is still forfeitable on termination may be satisfied by purchasing a contingent annuity contract that provides the benefit *only if* the participant subsequently satisfies all of the

---

required service is completed, and funded along with benefits that "accrue" from year to year. See 26 C.F.R. 1.412(c)(3)-1(c)(1) and (f).

112 773 F.2d 1402, 6 EBC 2226, at 2240 (2d Cir. 1985) (citing rejection by the ERISA Conference Committee of language that would have defined category (6) as "other accrued benefits" in favor of language covering "all other benefits under the plan"). See also *Tilley v. Mead Corp.*, 815 F.2d 989 (4th Cir. 1987) (§4044(a) requires allocation of plan assets to fund employees' contingent early retirement benefits requiring 30 years of service and attainment of age 62; plaintiffs with 30 years of service who were not age 62 and plaintiff with 28 years of service were thus entitled to allocation based on value of contingent right).

113 See 29 C.F.R. 2619.16.

114 See n. 111 (on the minimum funding requirements).

115 The second method seems to result in higher values. In *Tilley v. Mead Corp., supra*, plaintiffs had contingent rights to unreduced early retirement benefits requiring 30 years of service and age 62. The value of the benefits of the plaintiffs with 30 years of service who were younger than age 62 was computed by actuarially reducing their benefits only from age 62. The benefits of a plaintiff with 28 years who was already age 62 were valued by actuarially reducing from age 64 when he could have obtained the 30 years.

116 See ERISA §204(g)(2), as amended by P.L. 98-397, and see ch. 4, sec. IV.B.3.

pretermination age and service requirements for the benefit. For example, if a benefit requires 30 years of service and age 55, the annuity contract could require both conditions. No exception is provided if the employee has 29 years and the employer has closed down a business so that subsequent employment is unavailable. Alternatively, the ruling provides that a plan may be amended on plan termination to provide the benefits whether or not the full conditions are satisfied.[117] The latter method may be the only way to comply with both the REA amendments and the Section 4044 allocation rules because Section 4044 independently requires that all forfeitable benefits under a plan must be paid on termination, whether or not the conditions for nonforfeitability are subsequently satisfied.[118]

Obtaining an allocation of assets under priority category (6) for any forfeitable employment-based disability and lump sum death benefit protections offered under a plan may be more difficult. Such "incidental" benefits are currently generally ignored in asset allocations. An employer can argue that this coverage is like term insurance, and that the term expires with the termination of the plan. If the representations in the SPD on the discontinuance of coverage are consistent with this view, this could be a strong argument. But if the SPD promises coverage until the earlier of retirement or separation from service, rather than on a year-to-year basis until plan termination, these protections may have to be valued according to the period of employment they would otherwise have covered, and be paid as forfeitable benefits under the plan under priority category (6).

B. Priority Categories and Defined Contribution Plans

Under ERISA Section 403(d)(1), defined contribution plan assets must be allocated according to the Section 4044 priority categories on termination.[119] Section 4044's application to defined contribution plans does not have a great deal of significance since defined contribution plans have individual accounts, which, except for delinquent contributions, are by definition fully funded. Therefore, regardless of which priority category a participant's benefits were considered to fall under, they should be funded in the same amount as credited to the participant's individual account. As mentioned before, Section 4044's application to defined contribution plans is significant in one circumstance. Priority category (6) mandates payment of "forfeitable" as well as

---

[117] Prohibited discrimination must also not result, and the plan's assets must be allocated to the benefit in the same manner as for participants who satisfied the necessary conditions before the amendment. *Id.*

[118] The first alternative in Rev. Rul. 85-6 might be fair when a participant still has the opportunity to continue in employment after a plan's termination, but when no employment is available after a plan's termination, it is not a fair rule. In either instance, requiring completion of the requirements under the terms of the plan to receive any allocation would effectively undermine priority category (6) of ERISA §4044.

[119] The Secretary of Labor has authority under ERISA §403(d)(1) to issue regulations permitting different allocation categories for defined contribution plans, but has not done so.

nonforfeitable benefits.[120] This means a participant's accrued benefits must be paid on termination as long as they have not already been forfeited by a disqualifying break in service prior to the date of plan termination.

On occasion, allocations of assets from small defined contribution plans are beset by discrepancies between the plan's assets before and after termination.[121] If detected, unaccounted for plan assets, or incorrect computations of the amount to be allocated to a participant's account, present standard fiduciary and benefit claims, as well as claims for violation of the asset allocation rules.

C. Nondiscrimination Reallocations

When a defined benefit plan's assets are not enough to pay all of the plan's accrued benefits (including those that became nonforfeitable on termination), the Code Section 401(a)(4) prohibition on discrimination in favor of highly compensated employees, as applied in Revenue Ruling 80-229, can require a reallocation of plan assets that in part overrides the ERISA Section 4044 allocation. Under Revenue Ruling 80-229, plan assets that would otherwise go to highly compensated employees' benefits in priority categories (4)(B), (5), and (6) must be reallocated to rank and file employees' benefits if rank and file employees as a group are not receiving at least the same percentage of their accrued benefits as members of the prohibited group.[122] The reason for this rule is that, particularly in small plans, there are often two distinct types of participants: Owner-employees who receive very high benefits, and rank and file employees who receive not only lower benefits, but who also frequently do not have enough service to be vested. But for Revenue Ruling 80-229, the allocation of assets in these types of plans under the Title IV priority categories might tend to produce discrimination in favor of the owner-employees in terms of the percentage of accrued benefits actually paid.[123] For example, most of the owner-employees' benefits above the insured benefit ceiling may be in category (5), whereas the accrued benefits of all nonvested rank and file employees would be in priority category (6). Thus, the owner-employees' higher priority category (5) benefits would otherwise have to be paid in full before the rank and file employees would receive anything.[124]

---

[120] See 29 C.F.R. 2618.16.

[121] See GAO, "Tax Revenues Lost and Beneficiaries Inadequately Protected When Pension Plans Terminate" (GAO/HRD 81-117 Sept. 29, 1981), at 9 and 13-15.

[122] See Rev. Rul. 80-229. And see ERISA §4044(b)(4) (specifically recognizing that these nondiscrimination reallocations can override the priority categories).

[123] As mentioned before, this reallocation can make up for the PBGC's placement of accrued benefits that become nonforfeitable on termination in priority category (6), rather than category (5).

[124] Discrimination in operation may also occur when benefits are all within category (5) if the prohibited group employees' benefits were in effect earlier than the rank and file employees' and thus fall under a higher sub-category in category (5).

The assets subject to reallocation under Revenue Ruling 80-229 are those which would otherwise have gone to prohibited group employees for (1) benefits in excess of the substantial owner limitations (which are in category (4)(B)),[125] (2) benefits in excess of the guaranteed benefit ceiling and phase-in limitations (in category (5)), and (3) all other prohibited group employee benefits falling under category (6)'s broad language.[126] What it takes for an employee to be considered "highly compensated" is discussed in Chapter 2, section I. The nondiscrimination rules also apply to collectively bargained plans, but in collectively bargained plans, there are often no highly compensated employees within the meaning of the Code. This is discussed in Chapter 3, section V.

D. Early Termination Restrictions and Reallocations

Another type of nondiscrimination rule under the Internal Revenue Code applies to an "early" termination of a plan, i.e., one within 10 years of a plan's establishment, or within 10 years of a plan amendment substantially increasing benefits. The early termination rule restricts assets that would go to benefits of a plan's "25 highest paid" employees under any priority category above certain dollar limits. These restricted assets may be reallocated to more fully fund rank and file employees' benefits.[127] The "early" termination rules are designed to discourage plans from being established, or amended to substantially increase benefits, and then terminated as soon as the highest paid employees have the benefits they want. To accomplish this, the rules limit the benefits of employees who were among the 25 highest paid employees of the employer at the inception of the plan.[128] For collectively bargained plans, the "25 highest paid employees" are determined in the same manner as are "highly compensated" employees, i.e., by reference to the salaries of *all* of an employer's employees, whether or not covered by the plan.[129] Generally, this means that the rule does not apply to collectively bargained plans that terminate early.

---

[125] Also included are those benefits which would be insured but for the special rule applying the guaranteed benefit ceiling to a participant's total benefits when the participant has benefits from two or more terminated insufficient plans.

[126] The rule excludes from reallocation all insured benefits in category (4) and all benefits of retired prohibited group employees, and would-be retirees, that are in category (3).

[127] 26 C.F.R. 1.401-4(c) and Rev. Rul. 80-229. And see *Victor v. Home Savings of America*, 645 F.Supp. 1486, 8 EBC 1020 (E.D. Mo. 1986) (upholding plan's compliance with IRS rules on nondiscrimination reallocations on early termination after benefit increases against retired employees' contention that their benefits were inalterable). The early termination limits may not be contained in a plan if the IRS has determined that they are not necessary to prevent discrimination, as it may do with some larger plans and collectively bargained plans. See 26 C.F.R. 1.401-4(c)(1).

[128] 26 C.F.R. 1.401-4(c)(2) and Rev. Rul. 80-229.

[129] See Rev. Rul. 71-438. In all cases, the rules only apply if the anticipated pension of an employee otherwise among the employer's highest paid employees is in excess of $1,500 per year. With current benefit levels, this requirement is generally easily satisfied, but in some plans it can mean that there are less than 25 such highest paid employees.

In the event of an early termination, the 25 highest paid employees' benefits are restricted to the benefits that can be funded with employer contributions equal to 20 percent of the first $50,000 of the employee's compensation multiplied by the number of years of the plan's existence, or $20,000 if this is greater. After two years, the 20 percent element usually controls. As the above indicates, the early termination limits are formulated only in terms of contributions. To provide a rough example of what these contributions translate to in benefits, contributions of $10,000 per year (20% × $50,000) for eight years will fund benefits of roughly $10,300 per year for an employee who is age 57 at the inception of the plan and age 65 after the eight years of contributions.[130] Under a 1984 amendment to the regulations, these early termination limits can be raised in certain instances.[131] For "substantial owners" who are among the 25 highest paid employees, the amended early termination regulations provide that the ERISA Title IV substantial owner limitations on insured benefits (i.e., the fractions described in section VI.C below) apply if they produce a higher limit.[132] Usually, they would not seem to do so. However, for employees who are among the 25 highest paid employees, but who are *not* substantial owners, the early termination limits are raised to the higher of the PBGC's guaranteed benefit ceiling or the contribution-based limits described above.[133] Since the guaranteed benefit ceiling in 1987 was $22,295 annually for a single-life annuity beginning at age 65 ($1,875.95 per month × 12), this limit is generally higher than the amounts provided in the prior regulations.

Either a $10,300 per year or a $22,295 per year benefit may seem like a generous "limit" for benefits under a plan that was in existence for less than 10 years. However, many plans provide past service credits so that an employee in an early terminated plan could be receiving credit for 25 or 30 more years of past service with the company (in addition to the less than 10 years of service since the plan was established). Under a 1½ percent of final pay plan, an employee with final earnings of $75,000 might thus otherwise receive $25–30,000 more annually than these early termination limits. When a plan has a number of employees with comparable salary and service histories, the plan assets subject to reallocation to more fully fund rank and file employees' benefits can be substantial.

Because the 25 highest paid employees are usually in a position to determine when a plan is terminated, and because these limits can be substantial in terms of restricting these employees' benefits, most plans are continued for at least 10 years, absent business necessity for a termination. However, when a plan is terminated early, regardless of

---

130 Assuming a 6% interest rate and the UP-1984 mortality table with a one-year setback.

131 26 C.F.R. 1.401-4(c)(7), as added by 49 Fed. Reg. 1182 (Jan. 10, 1984).

132 *Id.*

133 *Id.*

whether the termination is compelled by business necessity, benefits are limited under these rules.[134]

A less common type of early termination occurs when a plan amendment "substantially increases" benefits within the 10 years before a plan is terminated.[135] In this case, the 25 highest paid employees for the purpose of the early termination rules are determined as of the time of the plan amendment.[136] Benefit formulas based on percentages of salary are, however, almost self-adjusting because benefits increase with increases in salary. The need for plan amendments to substantially increase benefits is therefore not pronounced, and thus amendments substantially increasing benefits in the 10 years before terminations of salaried plans seem to be fairly rare.[137]

The "substantial increase" type of early termination could apply to collectively bargained plans in which flat dollar benefits are substantially increased in the 10 years before termination, e.g., from $5 to $15 per month per year of service. However, the rule for determining the 25 highest paid employees at the time of an amendment to a collectively bargained plan is based on *all* the employer's employees. As a result, there are usually no such employees under the plan. In addition, the levels of unrestricted benefits under the regulations for employees who are not substantial owners are high enough to make it unlikely that the rule will affect most negotiated plans.

When the "substantial increase" early termination limit applies, it works basically as when a plan is terminated within 10 years of its inception. The increase in benefits for the 25 highest paid employees is restricted to the increase in benefits that can be funded with contributions of 20 percent of up to the first $50,000 in compensation multiplied by the number of years that the increase has been in effect. The $20,000 minimum is, in effect, dropped.[138]

---

[134] Rev. Rul. 80-229.

[135] 26 C.F.R. 1.401-4(c)(5).

[136] *Id.*

[137] But see *Victor v. Home Savings of America, supra.* Technically, this early termination limit applies to "changes" which "substantially increase" the extent of possible discrimination; it is therefore not limited to plan "amendments." For example, if the salaries of the highest paid employees are substantially increased in the 10 years before termination, while rank and file employees' salaries are held constant, the limit might also apply.

[138] See 26 C.F.R. 1.401-4(c)(5). Under the amendments to the regulations, for an employee among the 25 highest paid employees who is also a substantial owner, the substantial owner fraction that applies in determining insured benefits in the case of an amendment is applied to the increase, if this produces a higher limit. See 26 C.F.R. 1.401-4(c)(5) and (7), and sec. VI.C below on the substantial owner limit. For employees who are among the 25 highest paid employees but not substantial owners, the guaranteed benefit ceiling applies to the employee's total benefits, before and after the change, if this produces a higher limit. *Id.*

E. Preferential Benefit Payments Before a Plan Termination

A non-Code provision that can provide another type of nondiscrimination reallocation is contained in the PBGC's regulations implementing ERISA Section 4044's asset allocation rules. Under these regulations, any distribution, transfer, or allocation of assets to a participant "made in anticipation of plan termination" is a violation of ERISA Section 4044 *if* the distribution exceeds the participant's entitlement under the Section 4044 priority categories. In determining whether a distribution was made "in anticipation of plan termination," the PBGC examines any change in standard operating procedures, past practice with regard to employee requests for a form of distribution, and whether the distribution is consistent with the plan's provisions.[139] In *In re Braniff Airways, Inc.*, a plan was to be terminated, but the trustees retained discretionary authority under the plan to grant participants lump sum payments of their benefits up to the date of termination. On a request by the plan's fiduciaries for instructions, a bankruptcy court held that exercise of this discretionary authority in favor of one group of participants immediately before the termination would be a breach of fiduciary duty, and also a violation of the PBGC's regulations, because it would allow one group of participants to receive full payment of their benefits at the expense of the remaining participants.[140]

Under ERISA Section 4045, a trustee of a terminated plan is also authorized to recover for the benefit of a plan certain large payments which were made within three years before a plan's termination—whether or not the payments were made in anticipation of termination. Recoverable payments are payments to a participant in excess of $10,000 during any 12-month period within the three years prior to the plan's termination or, if this leaves the participant with more money, only those payments over the same period in excess of the amount of benefits the participant was entitled to receive under a single-life annuity beginning at age 65.[141] Payments in excess of these amounts on account of death or total disability are not recoverable, and the recovery may also be waived by the PBGC if substantial economic hardship would result for the participant. The benefit rights of participants who have received large payments of this type are not eliminated, but rather the payments in excess of the statutory amounts are recoverable for reallocation under the priority categories. Some of the assets may then be allocated to the same participant's benefits. But for a plan that is not fully funded, recovery and reallocation under the Section 4044 categories may reduce large pretermination payments, and increase the benefits other participants receive. A trustee may first determine the

---

[139] 29 C.F.R. 2618.4.

[140] 4 EBC 1116 (Bankr. N.D. Tex. 1982).

[141] *Id.*, and see Conf. Rep., at 378, 3 ERISA Leg. Hist. 4645.

amount that would be allocated back to the participant under the allocation categories, and recover only the difference.[142]

When a terminated plan has insufficient assets to pay for all of the PBGC's guaranteed benefits, the PBGC is also authorized to recoup any benefit payments above the guaranteed benefit levels that were made by a plan administrator *after* the plan's termination date.[143] Generally, this recoupment only serves to reduce the PBGC's losses. SEPPAA contains related new rules on maintenance of a plan that is proposed to be terminated in a distress termination. These rules restrict the payment of benefits pending the required PBGC determinations of sufficiency or insufficiency to payment of benefits in annuity form (except for the payment of certain death benefits).[144]

F. Special Allocation Schedules After Plan Mergers or Transfers

Pursuant to ERISA Section 208, a special schedule for the allocation of assets on plan termination must be maintained for five years after a plan is merged with another plan or after a plan transfers benefit liabilities and assets to another plan. In the event that a termination occurs within five years after the plan merger or asset and liability transfer, the special schedule modifies the plan's allocation of assets based on the allocation that would have occurred if the plan had terminated the day before the plan merger or asset and liability transfer.[145]

V. Lump Sum Distributions on Plan Termination

A common misunderstanding among participants is that they will have an option on plan termination to receive a cash distribution of their benefits from the terminated plan's assets. After termination of a "sufficient" plan, trustees are required to "distribute" the plan's assets within 90 days of the PBGC's issuance of a notice of sufficiency.[146] However, this requirement only means that the plan must purchase annuity insurance contracts from an insurer for the plan's benefits to the extent they can be funded by the plan's assets. These insurance

---

[142] CCH's Pension Plan Guide suggests that the ERISA §4045 recovery is only applicable to involuntarily terminated plans for which a §4042 trustee (which is usually the PBGC) has been selected. See CCH Pension Plan Guide ¶10,186. The statute and the legislative history do not directly support this limitation.

[143] See 29 C.F.R. 2623.11 and .12. See also *Bechtel v. PBGC*, 5 EBC 1665 (D.D.C. 1984); and *Williams v. PBGC*, 5 EBC 1668 (D.N.J. 1984), both describing and affirming the PBGC's recoupment authority.

[144] ERISA §4041(c)(3)(D), as amended.

[145] See ch. 9, sec. VIII.B.

[146] 29 C.F.R. 2617.21.

contracts are, moreover, required to be "nonsurrenderable" so that a participant may not turn in the contract to the insurer for cash.[147]

Many plans do, however, provide lump sum options as an alternative to receipt of an annuity contract on termination. In some cases, only those benefits with an actuarial value below $3,500 are cashed out. ERISA provides that if the actuarial value of a benefit is $3,500 or less, the benefit can be cashed out involuntarily, i.e., the participant need not be given the annuity option.[148]

Whether a lump sum is offered as a voluntary option to an annuity, or is involuntarily provided participants whose benefits have a present value of $3,500 or less, the interest rate used in the lump sum computation, and in determining whether a participant is within the range for an involuntary cash-out, is obviously crucial. As discussed in Chapter 6, section III.B, interest rates used in providing actuarially equivalent options must always be "reasonable." Until recently, the PBGC's regulations for terminated "sufficient" plans provided that "normally" four different interest rates were reasonable in determining the amount of a lump sum benefit from a terminated plan, namely:

(1) The interest rate the plan used for funding;
(2) The interest rate the plan used for any lump sum options offered under the plan before plan termination;
(3) The interest rate used by the PBGC in valuing immediate annuities from terminated plans; or
(4) The interest rate on which an insurer's qualifying offer of annuities to discharge the plan's benefits is based.[149]

These "normally" reasonable interest rates could range widely. For example, in *UAW District 65 v. Harper & Row Publishers, Inc.*, Prudential offered Harper & Row a 15 percent interest rate as the basis for providing the Harper & Row plan's annuities on a group basis, at a time when the PBGC's immediate annuity interest rate, which is itself based on a survey of the rates insurers are using, was 10.75 percent, and when the plan's interest assumption for funding was 8 percent.[150] To see what is involved in this, if a 15 percent interest rate is used in computing the lump sum value of an immediate annuity for an age 65 participant, the lump sum value of the annuity is 19 percent less than when a 10.75 percent interest rate is used, and 30 percent less than if an 8 percent interest rate is used.[151]

For a deferred annuity, e.g., an annuity for a 45-year-old participant that is not payable until age 65, these percentage differences can be compounded. While the PBGC's regulations for lump sum payments from sufficient plans normally allow immediate annuity interest rates

---

[147] 29 C.F.R. 2617.14(b) and 2617.4.
[148] ERISA §203(e)(1), Code §411(a)(11)(A).
[149] 29 C.F.R. 2619.26(c)(2).
[150] 576 F.Supp. 1468, 4 EBC 2586 (S.D.N.Y. 1983).
[151] Assuming the 1971 GAM mortality table for an all-male workforce.

to be used to discount for a period of deferral, the PBGC itself always uses a lower rate to value deferred benefits, reflecting actuarial conservatism in predicting interest rates over longer periods of time.[152] Thus, while the PBGC's 1981 10.75 percent rate was appropriate for valuing an immediate annuity, an adjusted, lower rate was used to discount for any period before the benefits became payable.[153] In reviewing the reasonableness of Harper & Row's use of Prudential's 15 percent interest rate to cash out participants with immediate and deferred annuities in small amounts, the district court emphasized that the insurer's rate, as well as the PBGC rates, were just *"among"* the four indices which were "normally" acceptable, with the overriding requirement being that a "*reasonable* actuarial assumption" be chosen from among them. As such, the court concluded, Prudential's 15 percent bid to provide the plan group annuities was "only one fact which may be of limited usefulness in determining the reasonableness of [an] assumption."[154]

The 1984 Retirement Equity Act regulates this area more directly. Under REA, the interest rate an ongoing or a terminated plan can use for a voluntary or involuntary lump sum cash-out of benefits cannot exceed the interest rates the PBGC uses on plan termination.[155] Under temporary and proposed regulations, the IRS defined this to mean the PBGC's immediate annuity interest rate.[156] A strong argument can be made that this regulation does not go far enough for deferred annuities. As stated, the interest rates the PBGC uses for valuing deferred annuities on plan termination combine an immediate annuity interest rate with a generally lower interest rate for any period of deferral.[157] The use of these lower deferred annuity interest rates can substantially increase the value of accrued benefits that are not due for a number of years.[158]

Effective on January 1, 1987, the Tax Reform Act effectively modifies the IRS's temporary rule. The Act requires that the interest rates used in determining the present value of vested accrued benefits must be no greater than the PBGC's interest rates for valuing benefits in a lump sum form on plan termination, using the PBGC's deferred or

---

[152] See 29 C.F.R. 2619.45 and 29 C.F.R. Part 2619, Appendix B.

[153] *Id.*, and see ch. 6, sec. III.B.

[154] 576 F.Supp. 1468, 4 EBC 2586, at 2596 (S.D.N.Y. 1983).

[155] ERISA §203(e)(2) (Code §411(a)(11)(B)) and ERISA §205(g)(3) (Code §417(c)(3)), as amended.

[156] Temp. and Prop. Regs. 1.417(e)-1T(b)(2)(ii) and (e)(1), 50 Fed. Reg. 29371 (July 19, 1985).

[157] See 29 C.F.R. 2619.45 and 29 C.F.R. Part 2619, Appendix B.

[158] See ch. 6, sec. III.B. Regardless of the IRS's position under REA, the PBGC announced that it will require deferred annuity rates to be used in computing lump sum values for deferred benefits under terminated plans. Under draft regulations, and in a cross-claim filed in *UAW District 65 v. Harper & Row Publishers, Inc.*, the PBGC takes the position that unless interest rates that separately account for the period of deferral are used, a lump sum value is actuarially unreasonable. See draft PBGC regulations reprinted in 11 BNA Pens. Rep. 641 (May 7, 1984) and 11 BNA Pens. Rep. 505 (April 16, 1984) (describing the PBGC's cross-claim in *UAW District 65).*

immediate interest rate, whichever conforms with the deferred or immediate status of the benefit in question.[159] When still lower interest rates for either immediate or deferred annuities have been used by a plan for lump sum options available prior to plan termination (whether the rates are stated in the plan or are inferred from practice under the plan), draft PBGC regulations would require those lower rates to be used instead of the PBGC's published rates.[160]

Apart from whether the interest rate is reasonable, a duty may exist to disclose to participants the exact rate that is being used in computing any lump sum amount. In *UAW District 65 v. Harper & Row Publishers, Inc.*, Harper & Row gave employees with benefits valued at between $250 and $1,000 a voluntary option of taking a lump sum distribution, but failed to state that a 15 percent rate would be used both to value their benefits and to cash them out under this option. The court stated that "it appears that the information supplied to [the employees] may have been insufficient to enable them to make an informed decision" on whether to take the lump sum.[161]

VI. PBGC Insurance of Benefits From Insufficient Defined Benefit Plans

To be insured by the PBGC, a benefit must be from a defined benefit plan that is covered by the PBGC's insurance.[162] It must also be a *type* of benefit that the PBGC insures. The PBGC insures "pension" benefits to which a participant or beneficiary is "entitled" that are "nonforfeitable" other than "solely on account" of the plan's termination.[163] "Pension" benefits, "nonforfeitability," and "entitlement" are all technical terms that limit the PBGC's insurance. Even when a benefit is insured, two general limitations—a "phase-in" on benefit

---

[159] ERISA §§203(e)(2) and 205(g)(3) and Code §§411(a)(11)(B) and 417(e)(3), as amended by §1139 of TRA. If the present value of a participant's benefits is more than $25,000 (using the PBGC's rates), an interest rate not exceeding 120% of the appropriate PBGC rate can be used, if a plan so provides. *Id.* A plan amendment before the close of the first plan year beginning on or before Jan. 1, 1989, to take advantage of the statutory allowance for use of 120% of the PBGC's rates is not an impermissible cutback in benefits in violation of ERISA §204(g). §1139(d)(2) of TRA. And see IRS Notice 87-20, reprinted in 14 BNA Pens. Rep. at 123 (Jan. 26, 1987).

[160] See 11 BNA Pens. Rep. 641 (May 7, 1984). If the interest rate for computing lump sum equivalents of accrued benefits on termination is higher than the rate used for the same benefit option before termination, this may also be an ERISA §204(g) violation, as a plan amendment indirectly decreasing accrued benefits. See ch. 4, sec. IV.B.3, and ch. 6, sec. III.C.

[161] 576 F.Supp. 1468, 4 EBC 2586, at 2596 (S.D.N.Y. 1983). Particularly when disclosure of use of a high interest rate is not adequate, there may also be Code §401(a)(4) discrimination in operation if rank and file employees disproportionately take lump sum payouts in comparison to the number of prohibited group employees taking the option. See J. Mamorsky and D. Hulbert, "Employers' Entitlement to Excess Pension Assets," N.Y.L.J., Sept. 19, 1983, at 21, and 26 C.F.R. 1.401-1(b)(3) ("if, by any device whatever, [the plan] discriminates ... in favor of [prohibited group employees]").

[162] See ERISA §4021(b) and the introductory material to ch. 12 on exclusions from the PBGC's coverage of defined benefit plans.

[163] See ERISA §4022(a) and §§4001(a)(8) and 4002(a)(2).

increases made within five years of the plan termination and a "ceiling" on insured benefits—can lower the amount of benefits that are insured. A third limitation for "substantial owners" of the company sponsoring a terminated plan can also lower the insured amount.

The PBGC's guarantee limitations remain relevant even if a plan's assets are "sufficient" to cover all of the PBGC guaranteed benefits. This is because they constitute a major dividing line in the ERISA Section 4044 priority categories under which a plan's assets are allocated. As a result, many participants receive benefits as limited by the PBGC guarantees, even though their plan's assets are more than "sufficient" to pay all the PBGC's guaranteed benefits.[164]

A. Nonforfeitable Pension Benefits to Which a Participant Is Entitled

The three requirements for a benefit to be insured by the PBGC are:

(1) The benefit must be nonforfeitable *other than* solely on account of the termination of the plan;[165]
(2) The benefit must be a pension benefit;[166] and
(3) The benefit must be one to which the participant is entitled, other than for submission of a formal application, retirement, or completion of a required waiting period.[167]

1. Nonforfeitable Benefits

A large group of benefits is ruled out of the PBGC's insurance coverage at the start by the requirement in ERISA Section 4022(a) that benefits must be nonforfeitable "other than . . . solely on account of the termination of a plan." Code Section 411(d)(3) requires nonvested benefits to become nonforfeitable, to the extent funded, on the termination of any plan. Thus, an employee who has eight years of service in a plan requiring 10 years for vesting obtains a nonforfeitable right to his or her accrued benefits on the plan's termination. However, the right is only "to the extent funded." By virtue of Section 4022(a), the PBGC does not insure further funding for these benefits.[168]

A benefit can be "nonforfeitable" even if it is not one that is required to vest under the ERISA minimum vesting schedules. For example, an early retirement benefit requiring 30 years of service may

---

[164] Conversely, when a plan is insufficient, participants with benefits in category (3) can still receive benefits above the PBGC's guarantee because of the way the priority categories are structured. See sec. IV.A above.

[165] ERISA §4022(a).

[166] ERISA §4002(a)(2).

[167] ERISA §4001(a)(8). And see 29 C.F.R. 2613.3.

[168] More precisely, there is nothing for the PBGC to insure. Under Code §411(d)(3), benefits that are otherwise not vested become nonforfeitable on termination only "to the extent funded."

be nonforfeitable for purposes of the PBGC's insurance. But whether a benefit, such as an early retirement benefit, is nonforfeitable under a plan's terms is construed strictly. For example, an early retirement benefit may require 30 years of service plus the attainment of age 55 *while in service.* The PBGC will not insure this benefit for a participant who has enough service but who has not reached the specified age on the date of termination on the ground that the benefit was not completely nonforfeitable under the terms of the plan as of the date of plan termination.[169]

The requirement of nonforfeitability under a plan's *terms* also crops up in a slightly different context. Hundreds, and perhaps thousands, of plans terminated after ERISA's effective dates without being amended to comply with ERISA.[170] The most obvious result of this is that these plans may not have complied with one of ERISA's vesting schedules. Noncompliance can also mean that a plan did not satisfy ERISA's minimum participation rules, its benefit accrual requirements, or its joint and survivor's benefit provisions. Thus, benefits that should have been nonforfeitable under ERISA's requirements may not have been nonforfeitable under the plan's terms before termination. To deal with the effects of this unexpectedly widespread noncompliance with ERISA under the PBGC's insurance program, amendments to ERISA Section 4001(a)(8) and Section 4022(a), tucked away in the 1980 Multiemployer Pension Plan Amendments Act, expressly require the PBGC to read ERISA minimum standards into terminated plans. Technically, these MPPAA amendments apply only to plans that terminate after September 26, 1980.

For plans terminated before that time, it can be argued that the PBGC should have been reading the minimum standards into plans all along. Under basic ERISA enforcement principles widely applied in cases where the PBGC was not involved, such as *Duchow v. New York Teamsters Pension Fund*[171] and *Nedrow v. MacFarlane & Hays Co. Plan and Trust,*[172] courts have conformed unamended plans to ERISA's requirements, or have nullified plan provisions to the contrary. In perhaps the closest case to this issue that involved the PBGC, *Michota v. Anheuser-Busch, Inc.*, a district court would have required the PBGC to guarantee benefits denied under a plan provision that the court found to be "arbitrary and capricious" under Section 302(c)(5) of the Labor Management Relations Act.[173] On review, the Third Circuit reversed the arbitrary and capricious holding, and thus did not reach

---

[169] PBGC Opinion Letter 76-69, and see 29 C.F.R. 2613.5(a)(3) and 2613.6(a).

[170] See 126 Cong. Rec. 23288 (Aug. 26, 1980) (statement by Sen. Williams, explaining the need for the MPPAA amendments described below). See also 126 Cong. Rec. 23041 (Aug. 25, 1980) (statement by Rep. Frank Thompson), and *Rettig v. PBGC,* 744 F.2d 133, 5 EBC 2025 (D.C. Cir. 1984).

[171] 691 F.2d 74, 3 EBC 2312 (2d Cir. 1982).

[172] 476 F.Supp. 934 (S.D. Mich. 1979). Other cases implying ERISA vesting rules into unamended plans are cited throughout ch. 5.

[173] 526 F.Supp. 299 (D.N.J. 1980), *rev'd on other grounds sub nom. Adams v. New Jersey Brewery Employees' Trust Fund,* 670 F.2d 387, 3 EBC 1083 (3d Cir. 1982).

the question of how the PBGC's guarantee obligation applies in such cases. Alternatively, a participant in an unamended plan can sue his or her employer for the value of the lost insurance resulting from the employer's failure to amend the plan as required by ERISA.

Although not spelled out in its regulations, PBGC practice until 1984—apparently under the nonforfeitability or entitlement rules—was to deny participants with deferred benefits at the date of a plan termination the right to elect a joint and survivor's form of benefits on their later retirement—unless the plan expressly provided that the joint and survivor's form was the normal form in which benefits were to be paid without *any* election by the participant.

Also apparently under the nonforfeitability requirement, the PBGC has in the past denied insurance for preretirement survivor's annuity coverage—even if a participant had reached the plan's qualified early retirement age and elected preretirement survivor's coverage before the plan terminated. The IRS and the PBGC both initially construed ERISA's preretirement survivor annuity requirement to apply only while the participant was still employed and the plan still in existence.[174] Thus, unless a participant's death while under the coverage occurred before plan termination, so that the spouse was already "entitled" to the benefits, the preretirement coverage expired at plan termination. With the 1984 Retirement Equity Act amendments, the IRS recognized that this rule must change. Under REA, preretirement survivor's benefits are automatic (rather than elective) for death *at any age* after a participant obtains nonforfeitable benefits, without regard to whether a participant is still in service under the plan.[175] The IRS's temporary regulations implementing these changes thus provide that preretirement survivor's annuity coverage must continue after plan termination, including under insufficient plans placed under the PBGC's trust.[176]

2. Pension Benefits

In addition to being nonforfeitable, a benefit must be a "pension" benefit to be insured by the PBGC. The PBGC's authority for limiting insurance to only pension benefits is based on a statement of purpose in Section 4002(a)(2) that the purpose of the PBGC insurance is to

---

[174] See Rev. Rul. 81-9 (situations 2 and 3) (ruling that a terminated plan need not continue to provide this election after the termination date when a participant is still employed, and moreover, that it need not continue to provide the preretirement survivor's annuity coverage even to those participants who had elected the coverage before the plan's termination). But compare 26 C.F.R. 1.401(a)-11(a)(1)(i)(D) (if a participant separates from service after the qualified early retirement date and dies before retirement, survivor's annuity coverage must be automatic; this coverage presumably was always required either to continue after plan termination or to be a contingency covered by any annuity contract purchased to close out the plan).

[175] The SEPPAA amendments to Title IV also expressly provide that qualified preretirement survivor's annuity coverage is not a forfeitable benefit for purposes of the PBGC's guarantee solely because the participant has not died as of the plan's termination date. ERISA §4022(d), as amended.

[176] Temp. and Prop. Regs., 1.401(a)-11T, Q&A 10 and 11, 50 Fed. Reg. 29371 (July 19, 1985).

insure "pension" benefits. It is also based on a Conference Report statement that "nonbasic" benefits, which are defined under Section 4001(a)(7) as benefits that the PBGC is not required to insure, "may include both what are sometimes called ancillary benefits and what are called supplemental benefits."[177]

The most widespread consequence of the pension benefit limitation is that the PBGC does not insure, or in other words, will not pay, benefits in *lump sum* form, even if a participant has a nonforfeitable right to a lump sum option under the terms of a plan.[178] When the total value of a benefit is $1,750 or less, the PBGC may, but is not required to, pay the benefit in lump sum form.[179]

On the basis that they are not "pension" benefits, the PBGC also does not insure so-called Social Security supplements, which a few plans provide early retirees until they reach age 65 or 62, to the extent that the dollar amount of the Social Security supplement *plus* the lifetime early retirement benefit exceeds the dollar amount of the participant's benefits available at normal retirement age.[180] Insurance for these benefits can be further reduced by the PBGC's guarantee ceiling, described below.[181]

The "pension" benefit distinction can also exclude an array of disability, death, and health benefits that are sometimes provided under pension plans. The exact dividing line between a pension benefit and disability, death, and health benefits is difficult to draw, and the PBGC's basis for excluding these benefits seems to more frequently cross over to whether the participant is "entitled" to the benefit on the date of the plan's termination.

3. *Entitlement*

The requirement that a participant or beneficiary must be "entitled" to a benefit for it to be insured first arose in a PBGC regulation defining a "nonforfeitable benefit,"[182] and in a separate regulatory entitlement requirement.[183] The Multiemployer Pension Plan Amendments Act of 1980 expressly added the entitlement requirement to the definition of a "nonforfeitable benefit" in ERISA Section 4001(a)(8). The significance of this requirement can be subtle. Whereas the Title I definition of "nonforfeitable" speaks in terms of whether a claim to an immediate or deferred benefit "arises from the participant's service . . . is unconditional, . . . and . . . legally enforceable against the plan,"[184] the PBGC's definition requires that a participant also be "entitled" to the

[177] Conf. Rep., at 366, 3 ERISA Leg. Hist. 4633.

[178] See 29 C.F.R. 2613.2 and 2613.8.

[179] See 29 C.F.R. 2613.8(b)(1).

[180] See 29 C.F.R. 2613.4(a)(1).

[181] See sec. VI.C.

[182] 29 C.F.R. 2613.6(a).

[183] 29 C.F.R. 2613.5(a)(3).

[184] ERISA §3(19).

benefit "*other than for* the submission of a formal application, retirement or completion of a required waiting period."[185] The impact of this is greatest in the case of disability or death benefits. As defined in Title I, it is possible for a participant to have a nonforfeitable right to a disability or death benefit *before* disability or death occurs. But with the entitlement requirement, these benefits are usually not insured *unless* disability or death occurs before the plan terminates since the participant or beneficiary is not entitled to the benefit on that date "*other than for*" an application, retirement, or a required waiting period.

The major types of disability, death, and health care benefits the PBGC does not insure either because they are not "pension" benefits, or because the participant is not "entitled" to the benefits, are:

(1) *Disability benefits*—unless the disability began before the termination of the plan and is "total and permanent";[186]

(2) *Death benefits payable in a single installment* (or "substantially so," e.g., in two or three installments)—unless the death occurs before the plan's termination, or unless payment is "substantially derived" from a reduction in pension benefits payable directly to the participant or to a surviving beneficiary;[187] and

(3) *Retiree health benefits* (e.g., payment of the 1985 $15.50 per month Medicare Part B premium for retirees, which is sometimes included in pension plans)—unless the benefits were in pay status before the plan termination (or could have been in pay status except for an application, retirement, or satisfaction of a required waiting period), or unless the benefits are an option to a pension benefit payable directly to the participant.[188]

Under the "entitlement" requirement, the PBGC also does not insure early retirement benefits that depend on the "consent" of an employer unless the employer's consent is obtained before the plan's termination—regardless of whether the consent has been withheld contrary to past practice, or is given *after* the plan's termination.[189]

While the PBGC interprets entitlement under plans strictly,[190] it may be noted that it also retains authority to find entitlement "on the

---

185 29 C.F.R. 2613.7(a) and 2613.5(a)(3), and ERISA §4001(a)(8).

186 29 C.F.R. 2613.7(a) (apparently based on "pension" benefit and "entitlement"). But note that a disability does not have to be diagnosed before a plan termination if it "began" before.

187 See 29 C.F.R. 2613.4(a)(2)(i) and (c)(1) (apparently based on "pension" benefit and "entitlement"). And see 29 C.F.R. 2613.8(a) (providing that when the PBGC does guarantee a death benefit, it may choose to pay it only in annuity form).

188 See 29 C.F.R. 2613.5(a)(2) and (3) (on "entitlement") and 29 C.F.R. 2613.2 (definition of "pension" benefit).

189 See *Hackett v. PBGC*, 486 F.Supp. 1375, 2 EBC 2522 (D. Md. 1980). But compare *Luli v. Sun Products, Inc.*, 398 N.E.2d 553 (Ohio 1979) (implying such consent from act of closing a plant in case in which the PBGC was not a party).

190 See *Hackett v. PBGC, supra.*

basis of the provisions of the plan and the circumstances of the case."[191]

B. Five-Year Phase-In of Benefit Increases

Despite the limitations described above, most nonforfeitable benefits from terminated defined benefit plans are insured. But other limitations can significantly lower the insured *amount.*

For rank and file participants, the major limitation on the amount of insured benefits is a "phase-in" of insurance for increases in the amount of benefits resulting from plan amendments within five years of a plan's termination. Insurance on benefit increases made in this period is phased-in under a formula that insures the greater of 20 percent of the increase in the amount of benefits or up to $20 per month for each year that the amendment was adopted or was in effect, beginning with whichever was later, before the date of the plan's termination.[192] To illustrate, if a plan amendment increasing the amount of benefits under a plan is adopted, or is in effect, for less than a full year before a plan's termination, the increase in the amount of benefits resulting from the amendment is not insured at all.[193] If an amendment is adopted, or is in effect, for more than one year, but less than two, 20 percent of the increased amount, or up to $20 per month, if greater, is insured. If an amendment is adopted or is in effect for more than two years, but less than three, 40 percent, or up to $40 per month, if greater, is insured. And so on—until the PBGC's insurance reaches 100 percent when an amendment is adopted or is in effect for five or more years before the plan's termination.

For participants in plans that promise flat-dollar benefits, such as $15.00 per month per year of service, instead of a percentage of salary, the five-year phase-in can be very significant. To keep up with inflation, or to improve benefits in real terms over inflation, plans that specify flat-dollar amounts *have* to be amended. In contrast, benefits under a plan based on a percentage of salary are largely self-adjusting as benefit amounts increase with salary increases, which in turn reflect both cost-of-living and merit increases. Despite this disparity, the phase-in does *not* apply to increases in benefits resulting from increases in salary under an unamended salary-based formula,[194] but does apply to *each* amendment to a flat-dollar plan. For a flat-dollar plan

---

[191] 29 C.F.R. 2613.5(b). The PBGC also has general discretionary authority to insure benefits that do not fall within the strict letter of *any* of its rules. See ERISA §4022(c).

[192] ERISA §4022(b)(1)(B) and (b)(7).

[193] See 29 C.F.R. 2621.6(c). And see *Lear Siegler, Inc., v. PBGC,* 1 EBC 2010 (E.D. Mich. 1979) (plan amendment increasing benefits that went into effect May 1, 1975, not insured when plan terminated April 30, 1976). As of Jan. 1, 1986, SEPPAA reverses the result in *Lear Siegler* by amending ERISA §4022(b)(7) to count each 12 months "beginning with" the later of the date on which an amendment is made or first becomes effective as a full year for phase-in (rather than each 12 months "following" the date). And see H.R. Rep. 99-266, at 58, 99th Cong., 1st Sess. (stating that even under prior law, *Lear Siegler* was wrong).

[194] See S. Rep. 93-383, at 83, 1 ERISA Leg. Hist. 1151.

that has had a number of recent increases in benefits, such as one that Braniff International maintained for members of its Teamsters' Union bargaining unit prior to the plan's termination in 1982, the effect of the phase-in can be dramatic, as the table below shows:

PLAN BENEFIT

	Level in Effect Per Month	With 20 Years of Service[a]	Years in Effect Prior to Termination	Increase Within 5 Years of Termination	Phased-In Increase		PBGC Insured Benefit
1/1/77	$ 8.35	$167	5+	None	100%		$167.00
1/1/79	15.00	300	3	$133	60% × $133	=	79.80
1/1/80	18.00	360	2	60	$20 × 2 yrs[b]	=	40.00
1/1/81	22.00	440[c]	1	80	$20 × 1 yr[b]	=	20.00
					Total PBGC Insured Benefit		$306.80

[a] Based on information from the PBGC and assuming a participant with 20 years of service.

[b] For these increases, $20 per month times the number of years in effect is greater than 20 percent of the increase times the years in effect.

[c] The total plan benefit prior to termination was $440.00, or $133.20 more than the PBGC insured benefit.

The PBGC's regulations provide that the five-year phase-in applies not just to conventional increases in the *amount* of benefits under the plan, but to any plan amendment that has the *effect* of increasing the amount of benefits under the plan, including plan amendments that liberalize vesting or conditions for beginning participation requirements, or amendments that create new benefit options.[195] In *Rettig v. PBGC*, plan participants, whose company did not provide for any preretirement vesting before ERISA, successfully challenged this interpretation insofar as it applied to the vesting amendments mandated by ERISA on the grounds that ERISA's vesting rules are not within the plain statutory language for increases in the *amount* of benefits, nor were they within its intended scope as they were not the type of voluntary, potentially abusive plan amendments that Congress sought to control when it phased-in the PBGC's insurance.[196]

The phase-in of benefits to the extent of 20 percent of the increased amount or $20 per month may be disallowed entirely if the

[195] 29 C.F.R. 2621.2 and 2621.5.

[196] 744 F.2d 133, 5 EBC 2025 (D.C. Cir. 1984). Except for approximately 20,000 participants in plans terminated before Dec. 31, 1981, the effect of phasing-in ERISA-mandated vesting amendments has itself phased out because of the time that has passed since ERISA became effective and because amendments to §§4001(a)(8) and 4022(a) in the Multiemployer Pension Plan Amendments Act indirectly sped up the starting date for the phase-in of amendments required by ERISA.

However, the problem may repeat itself if the PBGC applies the phase-in regulation to (1) the faster vesting required under TEFRA after 1982 for top-heavy plans, and (2) the new preretirement survivor's benefits and changes in break-in-service and participation rules required under the 1984 Retirement Equity Act. The Conference Report on the 1986 Tax Reform Act specifically states that the faster 5-year cliff or 7-year graded vesting required by the Act effective in 1989 is not to be subject to the PBGC's phase-in if a plan terminates within 5 years of the new rules' effective date. Conf. Rep. on P.L. 99-514, H. R. Rep. 99-841, at II-427.

PBGC finds that a plan termination is not for a "reasonable business purpose" (which does not include a business purpose of obtaining the payment of benefits from the PBGC).[197] For "substantial owners" of the sponsoring employer, separate limitations, discussed below, apply in lieu of the five-year phase-in.

C. Insured Benefit Ceiling and Substantial Owner Limits

The second limitation on the amount of PBGC-insured benefits is a guaranteed benefit ceiling. This ceiling is equal to the *lower* of a dollar amount, which is adjusted each year with changes in the Social Security taxable wage base, *or* 100 percent of the participant's average monthly wages over the five highest paid years of employment. If the guaranteed benefit ceiling applies at all, the dollar amount is usually the lower of the two. Originally, the dollar amount of the guaranteed benefit ceiling was $750 per month, but each year the dollar ceiling is adjusted for changes in the Social Security wage base. By 1987, the ceiling had thus reached $1,857.95 per month or $22,295 per year.[198] Once a plan terminates, the dollar amount of the ceiling remains fixed based on the guarantee ceiling for the year the plan terminated. Thus, for participants in plans that terminated in 1978, the dollar ceiling on insured benefits is still $1,074 per month. The same dollar ceiling established by the year of plan termination applies to participants in a terminated plan who do not reach retirement age until a number of years after the year of plan termination.

The insured benefit ceiling may appear so high that it could only affect the insured benefits of very highly paid and generously pensioned employees.[199] But the ceiling drops if early retirement and joint and survivor's benefits are a part of a participant's pension. For early retirement benefits, the ceiling is reduced by 7⁄12 of one percent for each month before age 65, down to age 60, that the benefits are to begin (to reflect the longer period of time they are likely to be paid). For early retirement benefits beginning at age 60, the resulting reduction in the amount of the ceiling is thus 35 percent. Another 4⁄12 of one percent is taken off for each month before age 60 that benefits begin, for a total reduction of 55 percent in the amount of the ceiling if benefits begin at age 55.[200] Similarly, when benefits are paid on a joint and 50 percent survivor basis (with 50 percent of the participant's benefit continuing

---

[197] ERISA §4022(b)(7).

[198] See 13 BNA Pens. Rep. 1976 (Nov. 24, 1986) (reporting on PBGC announcement). The PBGC guaranteed benefit ceiling for earlier years is contained in 29 C.F.R. Part 2621, Appendix A.

[199] Under a formula providing 1½% of a final average of salary for each year of credited service, a participant would need 30 years of service and a final average salary in excess of $45,000 to reach the $1,857.95 per month insured benefit ceiling applicable in 1987. Not only do few people earn this much, but few people have 30 years of service under one pension plan.

[200] 29 C.F.R. 2621.4(c).

to be paid to a surviving spouse), the ceiling is reduced by 10 percent.[201] If the spouse is younger than the participant, one percent more is taken off for each year's difference in age.[202] Thus, if benefits from a terminated plan are to begin at age 55, and are to be paid on a joint and 50 percent survivor basis with the spouse three years younger than the participant, the 1987 \$1,857.95 insured benefit ceiling drops to a \$732.96 per month benefit ceiling ((\$1,857.95 × (1 − .55) × (1 − .10%) × (1 − .03%) = \$732.96).[203]

Benefits payable to "substantial owners" are limited by the guarantee ceiling, and also by a special rule. Substantial owners are employees who own 10 percent or more of the company sponsoring the terminated plan.[204] Under ERISA Section 4022(b)(5)(B), the insured benefits of substantial owners are limited by a fraction, the numerator of which is the number of years of the substantial owner's active participation in the plan (not including credits for past service before the plan was established), and the denominator of which is 30. This fraction is multiplied by the amount of the substantial owner's benefits—as *first* limited by the guarantee ceiling.[205] If the benefits of a substantial owner have been increased by a plan amendment, instead of applying the five-year phase-in, another fraction is used to limit the insured benefits under the benefit increase. This fraction is produced by dividing the number of years of active participation since the plan amendment by 30, with this fraction multiplied by the amount of the increase to determine the part of the benefit increase that is insured for the substantial owner.[206]

While the substantial owner limitations can result in sharper percentage reductions in insured benefits for substantial owners than for other participants, Congress determined this was necessary to discourage abuse of the insurance program (substantial owners are usually the people who decide to terminate a plan). Moreover, because of the structure of the priority categories for allocating a plan's assets, the substantial owner limitations can have little actual effect if a plan is just barely "insufficient" in terms of the PBGC's guarantees.[207]

---

[201] 29 C.F.R. 2621.4(d)(2).

[202] 29 C.F.R. 2621.4(e). Survivor's benefits that pay more than 50% of the participant's benefits to a survivor reduce the ceiling further. See 29 C.F.R. 2621.4(d)(2).

[203] See 29 C.F.R. 2621.4(a) and (b). If a plan pays a Social Security supplement that stops when the person becomes eligible for Social Security benefits, any part of the supplement not already excluded from insurance as not being a "pension" benefit is converted to a lifetime annuity and added to the early retirement benefit for purposes of testing the participant's benefits against the insured benefit ceiling. See 29 C.F.R. 2623.5 (examples 3, 4, and 5).

[204] See ERISA §4022(b)(5)(A).

[205] *Id.*, and see 29 C.F.R. 2621.7(b).

[206] ERISA §4022(b)(5)(C), 29 C.F.R. 2621.7(c), and Conf. Rep., at 369, 3 ERISA Leg. Hist. 4636 (establishing, perhaps more clearly than the statute, that the benefit increases of substantial owners are not phased-in, but rather are subject to the special rule for substantial owners in §4022(b)(5)(C)).

[207] See sec. IV.A above on the benefits in priority categories (3) and (4).

VII. Post-SEPPAA Funding Obligations for Benefit Commitments

A. Benefit Commitments

SEPPAA establishes new rules for the funding of benefit commitments. Benefit commitments are all nonforfeitable benefits under a plan, including those that are not guaranteed by the PBGC because of the five-year phase-in of benefit increases, the guaranteed benefit ceiling, and the substantial owner limits. Benefit commitments also include promises of nonforfeitable benefits, such as early retirement supplements provided until Social Security benefits begin, that are not within the scope of "pension" benefits as defined for purposes of the PBGC's guarantee—*if* the participant met all the conditions for entitlement to the benefit prior to the termination date except for retirement, the submission of a formal application, completion of a required waiting period subsequent to application for benefits, or the designation of a beneficiary.[208]

B. Funding for Benefit Commitments Before Standard Terminations

Under the 1986 SEPPAA amendments to Title IV, a standard termination cannot take place *until* all PBGC guaranteed benefits and all benefit commitments under a plan are funded.[209] To ensure compliance, an enrolled actuary must certify to the PBGC that the plan's assets are sufficient to pay all benefit commitments under the plan.[210] At the same time, a plan administrator must send a notice to each participant and beneficiary specifying the amount of such person's benefit commitments, including the length of service, age, wages, and other assumptions, e.g., the interest rate, on which the amount and the present value of the benefit commitments to the individual have been determined.[211]

C. Funding for Benefit Commitments After Distress Terminations

Under SEPPAA, a "distress" termination can take place *before* all benefit commitments under a plan have been funded. However, a sponsoring employer, and any members of a controlled group of which the sponsoring employer is a member, who continue in business must take

---

[208] ERISA §4001(a)(16), as amended.

[209] ERISA §4041(b), as amended.

[210] ERISA §4041(b)(2)(A), as amended.

[211] ERISA §4041(b)(2)(B), as amended. And see ERISA §4041(b)(1)(D) (when final distribution of assets occurs, plan must be sufficient for all benefit commitments).

on additional funding obligations to complete the funding of all benefit commitments under the plan. For unfunded benefit commitments, the sponsor of a plan terminated in a distress termination, and any member of a controlled group of which the sponsoring employer is a part, is therefore to contribute to a trust—to be established by the PBGC pursuant to Section 4049—75 percent of the plan's outstanding liabilities for benefit commitments in excess of the plan's funded guaranteed benefit liabilities (after all statutory assessments are paid), or if less, 15 percent of the total actuarial present value of all benefit commitments.[212] Payment of this liability may be made over time under commercially reasonable terms agreed to by the Section 4049 fiduciary appointed by the PBGC.[213] If neither the plan nor any member of a controlled group has pretax profits, 75 percent of the payments due the Section 4049 trust in a year can be deferred.[214] For a distress termination pursuant to a notice of intent to terminate filed before January 1, 1987, a transition rule provides that no payment of benefit commitments liability to a Section 4049 trust is due before January 1, 1989.[215]

Not later than 30 days after the end of each year for which benefit commitments liability payments are due a Section 4049 trust,[216] the PBGC is to distribute payments from the trust's funds to participants and beneficiaries whose benefit commitments were not completely funded on termination. The amount of the annual payments is derived by multiplying the balance of the assets in the trust by the fraction produced by dividing the value of the individual's outstanding benefit commitments, including interest, by the total value of the outstanding benefit commitments of the plan, including interest.[217]

VIII. Additional Claims for Uninsured and Unfunded Benefits

Benefits that are not insured by the PBGC and that are not paid from a benefit commitments trust or under the Section 4044 allocation

[212] ERISA §4062(c)(1), as amended. If the principal purpose of a transaction occurring within 5 years of a distress termination is to evade liability under ERISA §4062, the transaction may be ignored in determining liability to the benefit commitments trust. ERISA §4069, as amended. Such evasion could occur, for example, if a subsidiary with unfunded liabilities is sold to a buyer that does not have a reasonable prospect of funding the benefits or paying the ERISA §4062(c) liability. See 131 Cong. Rec. H-13299 (daily ed. Dec. 19, 1985) (statement of Rep. Hawkins).

[213] If an employer's liability to the §4049 trust, as determined under the 75 and 15% tests, is less than $100,000, the liability may be paid, with interest, in 10 equal annual installments. ERISA §4062(c)(2)(B), as amended.

[214] ERISA §4062(c)(2)(C), as amended. Pretax profits are defined in ERISA §4062(e)(2), as amended.

[215] P.L. 99-272, §11012(d).

[216] Liability payment years are the consecutive one-year periods following the end of the last plan year preceding the plan termination date, excluding the first such year if it ends less than 180 days after the termination date. ERISA §4062(e)(3), as amended.

[217] ERISA §4049(c)(1), as amended.

of a plan's existing assets may sometimes be secured through additional claims, primarily against the sponsoring employer. The Third Circuit established in *Murphy v. Heppenstall Co.* that neither the PBGC's insurance nor its statutory claim to 30 percent of an employer's net worth limit other valid statutory or contractual claims of employees.[218]

A. Contractual Rights to Benefits

Under *Murphy v. Heppenstall Co.*, employees have a right to recover directly "any additional benefit to which [an] employer has contractually obligated itself," unless the employer's contractual liability for the promised benefits is expressly limited in the plan, or collective bargaining agreement, to the plan's existing assets.[219] Many collectively bargained single-employer plans do not disclaim contractual liability beyond the plan's assets for nonforfeitable benefits, and in any case, a disclaimer of such liability must be explicit in its terms to be effective.[220] A disclaimer of liability beyond the plan's assets under an employer-drafted plan may, moreover, be ineffective if the collective bargaining agreement contractually obligates the employer to pay the promised benefits, and the union has not acquiesced in the employer-drafted limitation in the plan.[221] A disclaimer of liability for benefits beyond the plan's assets on termination may also be required to be adequately disclosed in the plan's SPD as a significant limitation on the plan's benefits.[222]

---

[218] 635 F.2d 233, 2 EBC 1891 (3d Cir. 1981), *cert. denied,* 454 U.S. 1142 (1982). See also *Matter of M&M Transp. Co.*, 3 B.R. 722, 2 EBC 2486 (S.D.N.Y. 1980); *In re Alan Wood Steel Co.*, 4 B.C.D. 850, 1 EBC 2166 (Bankr. E.D. Pa. 1978), and 4 B.C.D. 921, 1 EBC 2166 (Bankr. E.D. Pa. 1978); *In re J.L. Thomson Rivet Corp.*, 19 B.R. 385, 3 EBC 1582 (Bankr. D. Mass. 1982); *In re White Motor Corp.*, 731 F.2d 372, 5 EBC 1558 (6th Cir. 1984) (side-letter between company and union required funding of all promised benefits). This rule has a common sense rationale. Congress did not intend for the PBGC's insurance to override greater obligations, but instead intended it to provide a basic "backup" or "safeguard" when a plan lacks enough assets on termination to pay all benefits and the plan sponsor has disclaimed liability beyond the plan's assets—or has not disclaimed such liability, but is a penniless creditor. See 2 ERISA Leg. Hist. 3371 (statement of Rep. Perkins).

[219] 2 EBC at 1896, and see *In re Alan Wood Steel Co., supra.*

[220] Compare *Hoefel v. Atlas Tack Corp.*, 581 F.2d 1 (lst Cir. 1978) (using oral assurances to construe employer's obligation); *UAW v. H.K. Porter Co.*, 1 EBC 1277 (E.D. Mich. 1976) (in view of vesting provisions, any limit on payment must be explicit in its terms); *Delaware Trust Co. v. Delaware Trust Co.*, 222 A.2d 320 (Del. Ch. 1966), with *United Steelworkers v. Crane Co.*, 605 F.2d 714, 1 EBC 1313 (3d Cir. 1979) (disclaimer of liability for further contributions after termination effective); *United Steelworkers v. North Bend Terminal Co.*, 752 F.2d 256, 6 EBC 1299 (6th Cir. 1985) (even though no express disclaimer, no obligation to complete funding when contract only provided for employer "to make contributions to a pension plan"); *Piech v. Midvale-Heppenstall Co.*, 594 F.Supp. 290 (E.D. Pa. 1984) (limitation of contractual obligation to assets in plan effective); *In re Johnson Steel & Wire Co.*, 61 B.R. 203 (Bankr. D. Mass. 1986) (limitation effective).

[221] *Murphy v. Heppenstall Co., supra; Local 1574 Machinists v. Gulf & Western Mfg. Co.*, 417 F.Supp. 191 (D. Me. 1976).

[222] See ERISA Technical Release No. 84-1 (May 4, 1984), reprinted in 11 BNA Pens. Rep. at 653-54 (May 14, 1984), and 29 C.F.R. 2520.102-3(l) and 2520.102-2(b). And see *Horn & Hardart Co. v. Ross*, 395 N.Y.S.2d 180, at 181 (Sup.Ct. App.Div. 1977) (limiting power to terminate plan short of full funding when limitation on payment of benefits on termination to plan's assets was not "brought home" to participants); *Hurd v. Hutnik*, 419 F.Supp. 630, 1 EBC 1382 (D.N.J. 1976);

B. Claims for Unpaid Contributions, Systematic Underfunding, and Fiduciary Violations

Whether or not a disclaimer of contractual liability for nonforfeitable benefits exists, a sponsoring employer is liable after termination (as well as before, but generally without as pressing consequences) for (1) unpaid contributions to the plan,[223] and (2) systematic underfunding of the plan in violation of ERISA's minimum funding requirements or higher contractual obligations.[224] Fiduciary violations in investments or administrative expenses constitute a third type of claim that can result in liability on the part of the plan's fiduciaries to restore lost profits to the plan. The plan's fiduciaries may include the employer if the employer is directly or indirectly responsible for the breach; and nonfiduciaries, including the employer, may be liable if they profited from a breach of fiduciary duty.[225]

Claims for unpaid contributions include the amount of contributions that are "due," in addition to those that are "delinquent," and also include interest from the due date. Revenue Ruling 79-237 provides that when a defined benefit plan terminates in the middle of a plan year, contributions are due for the part of the plan year in which the plan was maintained.[226] The contributions may not be "delinquent" for tax purposes until two and a half months after the end of the plan year, with routine extensions adding another six months to this.[227] Interest should begin on the day when a contribution first became a charge to the plan's funding standard account—generally the first day

---

Hoefel v. Atlas Tack Corp., supra. But compare *Kolentus v. Avco Corp.,* 798 F.2d 949 (7th Cir. 1986) (employee could not rely on general statements in pre-ERISA SPD that benefits were to be received as long as employee lived to require employer to complete the funding of all vested benefits upon plan termination; SPD did not purport to set forth complete plan provisions on termination, and stated that formal plan's terms controlled in the event of a conflict; however, Seventh Circuit recognized that "one of the major changes" brought about by ERISA was that "it mandates disclosure of circumstances under which benefits may be terminated," 798 F.2d at 960.

[223] See *In re J.L. Thomson Rivet Corp., supra*; *In re Alan Wood Steel Co., supra,* 1 EBC at 2173; *PBGC v. Greene,* 570 F.Supp. 1483, 4 EBC 1169 (W.D. Pa. 1983), *aff'd,* 727 F.2d 1100 (3d Cir. 1984), *cert. denied sub nom. Allen v. PBGC,* 469 U.S. 820 (1984); *Stopford v Boonton Molding Co.,* 265 A.2d 657 (N.J. 1970).

[224] See *Matter of M&M Transp. Co., supra,* and H.R. Rep. 93-807, at 65, 2 ERISA Leg. Hist. 3185 (employer still liable to "make-up" funding after plan termination).

[225] When terminated plans are insufficient, the PBGC generally has itself appointed by a district court, or under an agreement with the plan administrator, as the trustee of the plan and regularly brings claims on all of these bases, in addition to asserting its statutory net worth liability claim. See, e.g., *PBGC v. Greene, supra* (breach of fiduciary duties by imprudent loans before plan termination and failure to collect unpaid contributions). And see *ERISA Litigation* (PLI 1982), at 105-06 and 118-19 (citing cases from presentation by Henry Rose, then-PBGC General Counsel).

[226] The portion of annual contributions needed to amortize previously waived minimum funding requirements over 15 years is, however, due as if the plan were in existence for the entire plan year. See Rev. Rul. 79-237 and Prop. Regs. 1.412(b)-4(b), 47 Fed. Reg. 54093 (Dec. 1, 1982).

For defined contribution plans, a more technical rule applies which looks only at whether the plan termination occurred before or after the date specified in the plan on which contributions are due. If the termination date is a day or week before, *no* contributions are due for that year. See Rev. Rul. 79-237.

[227] See Code §412(c)(10). The IRS has proposed regulations which will gradually eliminate the routine 6-month extension. See 47 Fed. Reg. 54093 (Nov. 29, 1982).

of the plan year in a defined benefit plan—and should accrue at the rate of interest used in determining the plan's funding.[228]

Contributions required under ERISA's minimum funding standards have sometimes been waived by the IRS under Code Section 412(d) for the year or several years prior to a plan termination based on a finding by the IRS of "substantial business hardship." Generally, waived contributions do not automatically come due on termination of a plan, unless the IRS requires this as a condition of obtaining the waiver.[229] As a matter of practice, the IRS began in the early 1980's to make this a condition,[230] but in 1982, three "insufficient" plans were terminated by companies that had obtained waivers of contributions in excess of $45 million without this condition.[231] Even without a condition in the IRS's waiver, the IRS does not have the authority to waive contractual funding obligations. Rather, it can only waive the statutory violation and resulting excise taxes from noncompliance with the minimum funding standards.[232]

To determine whether a plan has been systematically underfunded in violation of ERISA's minimum funding requirements or higher contractual funding obligations requires the services of an actuary. As far as compliance with ERISA's minimum funding requirements, the funding "method" itself is usually not in issue. It will usually be one of the generally permissible methods listed in ERISA, and will have been approved by the IRS in its general terms (however, funding of early retirement benefits, death benefits, and disability benefits is subject to varying practice even under the same "funding method," and may never have been examined by the IRS).[233]

---

[228] See Code §412(b)(5).

[229] SEPPAA provides that the full amount of any accumulated funding deficiencies or waived minimum funding requirements comes due on a distress termination of a plan that has insufficient assets to pay all PBGC guaranteed benefits. See ERISA §§4062(a)(3) and (d), as amended, and 131 Cong. Rec. H-13252-53 (daily ed., Dec. 19, 1985). If the waived funding requirements are substantial, collection of this liability could increase a plan's assets enough to pay all PBGC-guaranteed benefits plus some uninsured, previously unfunded benefits.

[230] After SEPPAA, any application to the IRS for a funding waiver by a plan sponsor with outstanding minimum funding waivers in excess of $2 million must be accompanied by notice to the union and to the PBGC, with an opportunity for both to submit comments to the IRS on appropriate conditions for the waiver. The IRS is also expressly authorized to place a lien on the employer's assets to secure eventual payment of any waived amount. ERISA §306 and Code §412(f)(3), as amended by SEPPAA.

[231] Statement of Edwin M. Jones, PBGC Executive Director, before the Subcommittee on Labor-Management Relations of the House Education and Labor Committee, Sept. 28, 1983.

[232] See *UAW v. Keystone Consolidated Indus.*, 793 F.2d 810, 7 EBC 1705 (7th Cir. 1986), *vacating and withdrawing*, 782 F.2d 1400, 7 EBC 1059 (7th Cir. 1986), *cert. denied*, 479 U.S. ___ (1986) (IRS waiver of minimum funding based on employer's unilateral application is *not* allowed to override employer's collectively bargained contribution obligations). But compare *McMahon v. McDowell*, 794 F.2d 100, 7 EBC 1859 (3d Cir. 1986), *cert. denied*, 479 U.S. ___ (1986) (no breach of fiduciary duties arises from failure to collect contributions when employer has secured an IRS funding waiver for contributions to a nonbargained plan).

[233] See *PBGC v. George B. Buck Consulting Actuaries, Inc.*, C.A. No. 85-1913 (W.D. Pa., filed Aug. 22, 1985), summarized in 12 BNA Pens. Rep. 1162 (Aug. 26, 1985) (complaint alleging actuarial malpractice from failure to use reasonable actuarial methods and assumptions for funding early retirement benefits due on a plant shutdown), *dismissed pursuant to settlement*, see 13 BNA Pens. Rep. 267 (Feb. 10, 1986).

The plan's actuarial assumptions may be less insulated from review. Actuarial assumptions, and in particular, the interest rate, expected retirement age, turnover assumption, and any salary increase assumptions, must reflect the "best estimate of anticipated experience under the plan."[234] Instead of meeting this standard, actuarial assumptions will in some cases have been designed to produce very low contribution requirements for an employer. Generally, a degree of latitude is accorded actuarial assumptions, but "[t]he use of more aggressive assumptions (i.e., larger expected investment earnings, later retirement, etc.) [which produce lower employer contributions] may be hard to justify for a company in financial trouble."[235]

When an employer is contractually obligated to fund a plan on an "actuarially sound" or more specific basis stated in a plan or collective bargaining agreement, the question of whether the plan was underfunded may be raised above compliance with ERISA's *minimum* funding requirements.[236]

Fiduciary violations constitute a third type of liability that is not affected by a disclaimer of contractual liability for unfunded benefits. Violations of the ERISA fiduciary standards can result in fiduciaries being held personally liable for losses to a plan resulting from the transactions which were in breach of fiduciary duty, and may result in other "appropriate" equitable or remedial relief.[237] A sponsoring company may itself be a fiduciary, or may be indirectly liable for fiduciary violations under indemnification agreements with corporate officers who are plan fiduciaries. A company will also be considered a plan fiduciary, regardless of whether it is named as one, to the extent that its officers or agents recommend, influence, or help implement a high-risk or otherwise imprudent investment strategy that is designed, for example, to reduce required contributions or to otherwise divert plan assets to the employer's use. Assets may be less directly diverted to an employer's use through investments in a company's creditors, suppliers, or customers to obtain collateral benefits for the company. A sponsoring employer may also be liable to the extent that it profits

---

[234] Code §412(c)(3). And see Rev. Rul. 78-331 (assumption that employees retire at plan's normal retirement age may be unreasonable if it ignores frequency of early retirement), and PLR 8552001 (Aug. 13, 1985), reprinted at ¶17,377H CCH Pension Plan Guide (interest assumption for funding can be unreasonable when it ignores plan's actual investment experience).

The IRS has also issued audit guidelines for use by employee benefit specialists in its district offices in testing the reasonableness of actuarial assumptions used for minimum funding. See 11 BNA Pens. Rep. 1644 (Dec. 24, 1984).

[235] M. Johnston, "Actuarial Considerations," in *ERISA and Bankruptcy* (PLI 1983), at 221.

[236] See *United Steelworkers v. Crane Co.*, 605 F.2d 714, 1 EBC 1313 (3d Cir. 1979) (employer failed to amortize past service benefits over 25 years as required under pension agreement); *IAM Lodge 1194 v. Sargent Indus.* 522 F.2d 280 (6th Cir. 1975) (oral assurances of adequate funding for "full pensions" "good as long as you live" used to construe contractual obligation to fund on a "sound actuarial basis" to require employer to make the *maximum* deductible contributions allowed under the Code). See also *Briggs v. Michigan Tool Co.*, 369 F.Supp. 920 (E.D. Mich. 1974); *Matter of M&M Transp. Co.*, 3 B.R. 722, 2 EBC 2486 (S.D.N.Y. 1980).

[237] ERISA §§502(a)(2) and 409. And see *PBGC v. Greene, supra*; *Chambers v. Kaleidoscope, Inc. Profit Sharing Plan*, 650 F.Supp. 359, 7 EBC 2628, at 2634 (N.D. Ga. 1986) (fiduciaries liable for failure to protect profit-sharing plan's assets and to ensure that the plan received the money required to be contributed).

from "party-in-interest" transactions, such as loans from the plan's assets, or transactions which have the effect of loans, such as the acceptance by plan fiduciaries of contributions in the form of common or preferred stock of questionable value in lieu of cash contributions, regardless of whether the employer has acted as a fiduciary for the plan on the transaction.[238]

As a rough benchmark of the significance poor or imprudent investments can have on a plan's assets, a one-half percent difference in a plan's investment return can make a 10 percent difference in a plan's ability to pay promised benefits over time.[239] A Department of Labor study has found that one out of three plans exhibit signs of fiduciary violations based solely on review of information in their annual financial reports.[240] Although many of these potential violations might turn out on further review to be groundless or unprovable, or technical violations where losses to the plan are only slight, others are consequential.

C. Making Claims Against Bankrupt Employers

When a company files for bankruptcy under Chapter 7 or Chapter 11 of the Bankruptcy Code—which may occur before or after a plan termination—claims for additional funds due a plan from the employer are entitled to certain priorities under the Bankruptcy Code, but to a large extent are unsecured claims of general creditors.[241]

Under Bankruptcy Code Section 507(a)(4), "claims for contributions to employee benefit plans ... arising from services rendered

---

[238] Contributions of overvalued stock or other consideration in lieu of cash may also be handled as a funding claim.

[239] See D. McGill, *Fundamentals of Private Pensions* (Richard D. Irwin 5th ed.), at 344.

[240] See DOL Joint OIG-LMSA Task Force, "Report, Evaluation and Recommendations, ERISA Enforcement" (May 1, 1982), at 54.

[241] This section does not discuss pension claims under state law alternatives to the federal Bankruptcy Code, i.e., state laws on assignments for the benefit of creditors, on bulk asset transfers, and on dissolutions of insolvent corporations (without a preceding Chapter 7 liquidation). For a general discussion of these laws and how they compare with federal bankruptcy, see B. Weintraub and A. Resnick, *Bankruptcy Law Manual* (Warren, Gorham & Lamont 1980), ch. 10. If state law priorities or the treatment of contingent claims are less favorable to participants than the federal Bankruptcy Code, an involuntary Chapter 7 proceeding can be commenced so that the federal Bankruptcy Code's provisions apply. *Id.*

In some cases, state laws for collection of unpaid wages and benefits (including through personal liability of corporate officers and shareholders) are more favorable than the federal Bankruptcy Code priorities, but questions of ERISA preemption arise in the application of such laws to claims for money due ERISA-covered employee benefit plans. See *McMahon v. McDowell*, 794 F.2d 100, 7 EBC 1859 (3d Cir. 1986), *cert. denied*, 479 U.S. ___ (1986) (Pennsylvania wage claim law preempted by ERISA insofar as its application to unpaid pension contributions). But compare *Sasso v. Vachris*, 484 N.E.2d 1359, 6 EBC 2393 (N.Y. Ct.App. 1985) (state law remedies against 10 largest shareholders of closely held company for unpaid contributions to employee benefit plans not preempted by ERISA; state law does not "relate[] to" terms of employee benefit plan, but rather provides "additional enforcement mechanism"; legislative history of 1980 amendments to ERISA for multiemployer plans also shows that ERISA mechanisms for collecting delinquent contributions are supplement to state law remedies); *Amalgamated Ins. Fund Trustees v. Danin*, 8 EBC 1588 (D. Mass. 1986) (corporate officer with significant ownership interest and operational control of corporation's day to day functions who made decision not to pay may be liable for delinquent contributions to plan under "expansive" ERISA definition of "employer").

within 180 days before the date of the filing of the petition or the date of the cessation of the debtor's business, whichever occurs first," are entitled to fourth priority among all unsecured claims of creditors.[242] It has been argued that the Section 507(a)(4) priority should only cover the "normal cost" component of plan contributions due a plan for this 180-day period, since any "past service" component is attributable to earlier service.[243] *In re Columbia Packing Co.* specifically rejects this argument. In this case, a debtor attempted to distinguish the past service component of its required contributions as not having been earned by services during the 180-day period prior to its bankruptcy filing for purposes of the Section 507(a)(4) priority. The bankruptcy court held that the past service component must be included because it was a present cost of doing business and of the employees' services, even if it paid for already granted pension credits. The court did, however, limit the Section 507(a)(4) priority in a major respect by holding that since the plan's annual contributions were based on an actuarial valuation that assumed 201 active workers, whereas only an average of 137 were still at work during the 180-day period, the plan's contributions for services in the 180-day period had to be prorated. The formula the court arrived at was:

> X (the annual minimum contribution) × 180 days/365 days (the priority period) × 137 active employees (during the 180-day period)/201 active employees (anticipated under the actuarial valuation) = Fourth priority claim.[244]

Instead of a fourth priority, claims based on an employer's contractual obligation to pay unfunded benefits after a plan termination might be considered to be entitled to third priority under Bankruptcy Code Section 507(a)(3). Section 507(a)(3) covers:

> "[C]laims for wages, salaries, or commissions, including vacation, severance, and sick leave pay . . . earned by an individual within 90 days before the date of the filing of the petition or the date of the cessation of the debtor's business, whichever occurs first."[245]

The basis for placing contractual claims for unfunded benefits in the third priority, rather than the fourth, would be that the distinction between the third and fourth priorities is not a "wage" versus "employee benefit" distinction, as evidenced by the inclusion of vacation,

---

[242] 11 U.S.C. §507(a)(4). The 180-day period may be from any earlier date of cessation of the business to prevent delay in filing for bankruptcy from defeating the statutory priorities. *In re Helleman*, 4 EBC 1514 (Bankr. C.D. Ill. 1983); *In re Bodin Apparel, Inc.*, 6 EBC 1217 (Bankr. S.D.N.Y. 1985).

[243] See H. Novikoff and B. Polebaum, "Pension-Related Claims in Bankruptcy Code Cases," 40 Bus. Law. 373, at 407 (1985), and R. Soble, J. Eggersten, and S. Bernstein, "Pension-Related Claims in Bankruptcy," 56 Am. Bankr. L.J. 155, at 164 n.54 (1982).

[244] 6 EBC 1633 (Bankr. D.Mass. 1985). The priority was also limited by the §507(a)(4)(B) cap of $2,000 per employee for third and fourth priority claims. This cap is described in the text below.

[245] 11 U.S.C. §507(a)(3).

severance, and sick pay benefits in the third priority, nor do the enumerated benefits represent the extent of benefits under the third priority as evidenced by the word "including."[246] Rather, the distinction between the third and the fourth priorities can be seen as being between whether the payments are due employees directly from the employer, or are due employees only through the intermediary of an employee benefit trust.[247] Because contractual claims for unfunded benefits can be considered due employees directly, it can be argued that they are within the third priority—at least to the extent earned in the 90-day period before the earlier of the date of bankruptcy filing or the cessation of the business.[248] The sounder alternative, however, seems to be to treat contractual claims as additional contribution obligations. This is generally more desirable for participants because the longer 180-day period covered by the fourth priority should outweigh any difference in the amount paid per dollar on claims for a fourth versus the third priority claim. Claims for funds from an employer based on fiduciary violations could also be seen as contribution obligations, and thus within the fourth priority, at least to the extent that the fiduciary violations occurred within the 180-day period, or depleted contributions due during that period.

The total amount of claims for any individual employee under *both* the third and fourth priorities may in no event exceed $2,000, *including* all other claims for wages, salary and benefits, such as severance and vacation pay under the third priority.[249] Under Section 507(a)(4)(B), moreover, the $2,000 is *first* reduced by the wage and benefit claims in the third priority. Priority is then given to claims in the fourth priority *only* to the extent of the remaining amount. Thus, if wage and other benefit claims in the third priority are substantial, the amount of pension claims accorded priority under the fourth priority may be limited.[250]

In Chapter 7 liquidations and Chapter 11 reorganizations in which a pension plan is not terminated until after the bankruptcy filing (or is not terminated at all, for example, in a successful Chapter 11 reorganization), contribution obligations that arise *after* the date of bankruptcy filing may be expenses of administration under Bankruptcy Code Section 503. If they are so treated, they are accorded first priority among the claims of all unsecured creditors under Section 507(a)(1) of the

---

[246] See R. Soble, J. Eggersten and S. Bernstein, "Pension-Related Claims in Bankruptcy," 56 Am. Bankr. L.J. 155, at 161.

[247] *Id.*

[248] *Id.*

[249] See Bankruptcy Code §507(a)(4)(B).

[250] By way of reference, the PBGC's claim on 30% of a company's net worth for any insufficiency has seventh priority among unsecured creditors claims as a tax "due and owing" the United States. See ERISA §4068(c)(2), Bankr. Code §507(a)(7), and *PBGC v. Washington Group, Inc.*, 8 EBC 1351 (M.D. N.C. 1987). If the PBGC's claim is perfected prior to the filing of a Chapter 11 petition, it may be treated as a tax lien, and thus come before *all* priority claims—as well as before secured and judgment creditors. See "Pension-Related Claims in Bankruptcy," *supra*, at 170-71, and 14 BNA Pens. Rep. 393 (March 30, 1987) (statement of Gary Ford, PBGC General Counsel, before ABA section meeting).

Code, with no comparable limitation to the $2,000 limitation applicable to third and fourth priority claims. In *In re Columbia Packing Co.*, the court applied the first priority administrative expense to contributions due a plan by looking at the minimum annual contribution, multiplying it by the number of days between the filing of the petition and the termination of the plan divided by 365, with this result then multiplied by the average number of active employees during the administrative period divided by the number of active employees that the actuarial valuation had assumed.[251]

If provisions of a plan are rejected as executory agreements under Bankruptcy Code Section 365(a), the "actual, necessary costs" of services rendered prior to rejection are still entitled to first priority as administrative expenses.[252] Unless a plan's benefits are exorbitant, it appears that all of the claims incurred up to the date of rejection should therefore still be considered an "actual, necessary cost[]" of administration, and should thus retain the administrative expense priority.[253] If a plan's benefits are exorbitant, the priority of a small *part* of the claims arising from services during the period between the filing and the rejection could be determined as if a breach had taken place just before the filing.[254]

The fundamental starting point for participants when a company with a terminated or soon-to-be terminated plan goes into bankruptcy is to ensure that proofs of claim have been filed in a Chapter 7 liquidation for all money due the plan or participants, and filed in a Chapter 11 reorganization if the claims are not already properly scheduled. When a plan of reorganization is confirmed, any debts arising from claims existing before confirmation of the reorganization plan are discharged, whether or not a claim has been filed.[255] When a company is liquidated, claims are not "discharged,"[256] but as a practical matter, unfiled claims may be worth much less because the corporation's assets will have been distributed according to the plan of liquidation, and ordinarily, the corporation will be dissolved under state law, or will continue to exist only as a corporate shell.

In both a Chapter 7 liquidation and a Chapter 11 reorganization, the debtor files a schedule of all claims against it, including contingent, unliquidated, and disputed claims. Thereafter, notice is given to all listed creditors. In a Chapter 7 proceeding, the claimant, or an agent for the claimant, must file a proof of claim, whether or not the debtor has already scheduled the claim.[257] Particularly for contingent and

---

[251] 6 EBC 1633 (Bankr. D. Mass. 1985).

[252] See Bankruptcy Code §503(b).

[253] See D. Lewis and R. Schiffer, "Bankruptcy Code Plays a Part in Contract Negotiations," Legal Times, (Oct. 31, 1983), at 18, and 2 *Collier on Bankruptcy*, at ¶365.02 (15th ed. 1983) ("fair value" received remains an administrative expense after rejection of executory lease agreements).

[254] See Bankruptcy Code §365(g).

[255] Bankruptcy Code §1141(d)(1).

[256] See Bankruptcy Code §727(b).

[257] Bankr. Rule 3002.

unliquidated claims, this may mean filing a proof of a claim that the debtor failed to schedule, or scheduled but listed at a low amount. In a Chapter 11 proceeding, proofs of claim need not be filed *unless* the claim:

(1) Is not scheduled by the debtor;

(2) Is listed as disputed, contingent, or unliquidated; or

(3) Is scheduled at a different amount than the creditor claims is due.[258]

As this suggests, the Bankruptcy Code uses a very broad definition of the term "claim." Contingent, unliquidated, and disputed claims are explicitly included.[259] Thus, the fact that a claim for additional funds for a pension plan is not certain or that it may be objected to by the debtor, trustee in bankruptcy (or debtor-in-possession in a reorganization), or other creditors is no reason for the claim not to be filed as long as it is reasonably supportable. The bankruptcy court will resolve the controversy over the proper amount, or whether any amount is due.

Since most pension claims are for money due the plan, the plan's trustees' have the responsibility to ensure that proofs of claim are filed properly and for the full amounts due the plan.[260] Contractual claims for unfunded benefits, as mentioned before, can be seen as running either to the plan or to the participants directly. But in either case, it should be the plan trustees' responsibility to ensure that proofs are filed for these claims since it would impractical, as well as uneconomical, for each participant to have to hire a bankruptcy lawyer. When the plan's trustees do not act, a breach of fiduciary duty under ERISA Section 404(a)(1) occurs. With the breach, personal liability and appropriate equitable relief under ERISA Sections 502(a)(2) or (a)(3) become available to redress the violation.[261] If trustees are not filing claims, or are not filing claims for the full amounts that are due a plan, an order required them to do so may thus be sought under ERISA

---

[258] Bankr. Rule 3003. A tardy claim may be subordinated to the claims of all other creditors, regardless of the priority the claim would otherwise have. Under the Bankruptcy Rules, the time for filing proofs of claim in a Chapter 7 case is 90 days after the first meeting of the creditors. Bankr. Rule 3002. When a claimant had notice or knowledge of the bankruptcy proceeding (which will invariably be the case for single-employer pension claims because of the close relationship between the employer and the plan) tardily filed claims are subordinated to the claims of all other creditors. Bankruptcy Code §726(a)(3).

In a Chapter 11 proceeding, the rules on tardily filed claims are less rigid. The time for filing proofs for claims that have not been properly scheduled by the debtor, or which are disputed, contingent, or unliquidated, is set by the bankruptcy court, and may be extended for "cause shown." Bankr. Rule 3003.

[259] See Bankr. Code §101(4), and H.R. Rep. 95-595, at 309, 95th Cong., 1st. Sess. (claim in bankruptcy "contemplates all legal obligations of the debtor, no matter how remote or contingent").

[260] See *In re Alan Wood Steel Co.*, 4 B.C.D. 850, 1 EBC 2166 (Bankr. E.D. Pa. 1978).

[261] In addition to violating ERISA §404(a)(1), unfiled claims, or claims for less than the full amounts due the plan, can also constitute prohibited transactions under §406 if the result is an extension of credit or transfer of assets from the plan to the employer or another "party in interest."

Equitable and remedial relief can extend to nonfiduciary creditors or holders of equity interests who profited from the fiduciary's failure to file.

Section 502(a)(2) or (a)(3), in addition to an order for recovery of any monies that may already have been lost as a result of inaction or delay. If this process is too cumbersome, or costly, a union or the trustee in bankruptcy may be the next best candidates to file proofs of claim directly on behalf of the plan, or all participants. A union is a proper claimant or agent if payments are due under a collective bargaining agreement.[262] The trustee in bankruptcy may also file proofs of claim, although it is "questionable" whether the trustee has a "duty to do so."[263] In a reorganization, it is similarly doubtful whether a debtor-in-possession has a duty to file the claims on behalf of a plan or its participants, but it may do so.[264] Plan participants may themselves act as agents for the plan (and, of course, may act on their own behalf where monies are arguably due them directly) in filing proofs of claim.[265] A power of attorney is required before a person acting as an agent can vote on a creditor's committee, vote for or against a trustee, or vote on whether to accept or reject a plan of reorganization, but no formal agency is required to file a proof of claim.[266] The Department of Labor may also be able to assist participants in the filing of proofs of claims pursuant to ERISA Sections 502(a)(2) and (5), or else to assist in forcing the trustees to accept their responsibility to do so.

IX. Overfunded Plans and Excess Asset Reversions

Newspaper and magazine articles and a continuing series of court cases challenging corporate take backs of millions of dollars in "excess" assets after pension plan terminations have brought excess asset reversions to the public's attention. Reversions of excess assets to employers after plan terminations are not new,[267] but high interest rates under which annuities have been available for purchase to discharge a plan's benefit liabilities have increased the number of plans which have excess assets when they are terminated, and also the magnitude of the excesses. Although the element of surprise can be overdone, in part, "[t]he issue ... very baldly stated, is who is to get the dollars that nobody [wholly] expected to find in the till?"[268]

---

[262] See *In re Schatz Federal Bearings Co.*, 5 B.R. 549 (Bankr. S.D.N.Y. 1980); *In re Shearon*, 10 B.R. 626 (Bankr. D. Neb. 1981).

[263] See Cowans, *Bankruptcy Law and Practice*, at 658 (West 1983 interim ed.) and Bankr. Rule 3004.

[264] See Bankr. Rule. 3004.

[265] Official forms are provided for filing proofs of claim. See Official Bankruptcy Forms Nos. 19-21.

[266] See Bankr. Rule 9010.

[267] See 2 ERISA Leg. Hist. 1791-92 (remarks of Sen. Percy) and 3 ERISA Leg. Hist. 4710-11 (remarks of Rep. McClory), both commenting unfavorably on the reversion of excess assets to the Elgin Watch Co. after termination of an overfunded plan, and 470 BNA Pens. Rep. 1724 (Nov. 14, 1983) (reporting statement by Solomon Weinberger, principal with the actuarial firm of William M. Mercer, Inc., that reversions have been going on for years without their recent notoriety).

[268] *In re Washington Star Newspaper Retirement Plan*, 4 EBC 2441, at 2441 (Gellhorn, 1983).

From 1980 to 1986, over 1,220 plans with 1.4 million participants have been terminated with reversions to sponsoring employers totaling over $12 billion.[269] Based on 1980 annual financial report data, almost 2,500 pension plans would have excess assets of over $1 million if they were terminated.[270] Plans of two-thirds of the top Fortune 100 companies would have at least some excess assets if they were terminated.[271] IBM is said to have a potential reversion of $3 billion if it ever terminated its plan.[272] And Exxon, United Air Lines, and Phillips Petroleum are at the time of this writing in the process of terminating plans to take back well over $1 billion, $962 million, and $400 million in excess assets, respectively.[273]

As examples of how much in excess assets there can be on a termination compared to the plan's benefit liabilities, the benefit liabilities of the Harper & Row Publishers' pension plan on termination were only $7.3 million while the plan's assets were $16.9 million, more than *double* the benefit liabilities.[274] The Great A&P Tea Company's pension plan benefit liabilities were roughly $300 million on termination while the plan's assets were over $550 million.[275]

The presence of "excess" assets says nothing about whether a participant's benefits are high, adequate, or low. Rather, it only means that a plan has more assets than may be technically required to provide whatever benefits have accrued or are otherwise forfeitable benefits under the terms of the plan at the date of termination. The question of who is to get the "excess" plan assets is also a question of tax policy, as well as of labor, pension, and contract law. This is because excess assets are the result not only of the employer's contributions to the plan, plus earnings, but also of the deferral of taxation on those contributions, plus the tax-exempt status of earnings. When excess assets revert to an employer, the excess assets are taxed as ordinary income of the company, but the result is not a wash for the federal treasury. Part of the net reversion is still the result of the tax advantages extended to qualified plans, in the same way that part of a distribution from an IRA, also taxed as ordinary income when it comes out, is still

---

269 See 14 BNA Pens. Rep. 204 (Feb. 16, 1987) (reporting data prepared by the PBGC).

270 See 462 BNA Pens. Rep. 1484 (Sept. 19, 1983) (reporting statement of Roger Thomas, House Aging Committee pension counsel before the Dept. of Labor ERISA Advisory Council, Sept. 14, 1983).

271 Hearing on Pension Funding Problems, *supra* note 21, at 209 (testimony of Lawrence N. Margel, vice president and chief actuary, Towers, Perrin, Forster & Crosby).

272 J. Bulow, M. Scholes and P. Menell, "Economic Implications of ERISA," NBER Working Paper No. 927, at 24, (1982).

273 See 13 BNA Pens. Rep. 1087 (June 9, 1986) (Exxon), Washington Post, "'Recapturing of Pension Assets Stirs Debate," June 30, 1985, at G-1 (United Air Lines), and 13 BNA Pens. Rep. 1115 (June 16, 1986) (Phillips Petroleum).

274 See Hearing on Pension Funding Problems, *supra* note 21, at 147.

275 See Hearing on Pension Funding Problems, *supra* note 21, at 148, and *Walsh v. A&P*, 96 F.R.D. 632, 4 EBC 1055 (D.N.J. 1983) ($50 million of the $250 million excess was allocated to improving participants' benefits under a class-action settlement).

Overall, plans that have terminated with reversions since 1980 have had $25.6 billion in assets compared to $14.5 billion in benefit liabilities on termination. See 13 BNA Pens. Rep. 1879 (Nov. 3, 1986).

partly the product of the tax advantages for IRAs. Indeed, to the extent of the reversion of excess assets, the plan has functioned as a "tax-free IRA" for the employer.[276]

In recognition of these tax advantages, the Tax Reform Act of 1986 levies a 10 percent excise tax on the amount of any excess assets reverting to an employer after a plan termination. This tax is effective for terminations occurring after December 31, 1985.[277]

A. Sources of Excess Assets

Before examining the law on reversions of excess assets, it is worth looking at how excess assets come to be in a plan on termination. A common assumption is that excess assets are present on termination because the plan's fiduciaries have earned a lot more money through wise investments than needed to pay the plan's benefits. In a sense, this is true. Many plans have improved investment earnings, riding on surges in the stock market. And certainly if any plan with excess assets earned less on investments than it actually did, the excess assets would be less.

By and large, however, investment performance is not the primary reason for excess assets on plan termination. Even with improved recent investment performance, most plans have just average investment earnings over time.[278] Moreover, if investment performance was, in fact, the only cause of excess assets, excess assets would be contained by the "full funding limitation" on deductible contributions established by Code Sections 404(a)(1)(A) and 412(c)(7). Basically, the Code's full funding limitation provides that an employer's contributions to a pension plan are not deductible *once* a plan's assets equal or exceed its "accrued liability" for benefits.[279] If contributions are not deductible, they rarely are made. When no contributions are made, a plan's accrued liability continues to increase by the amount of the plan's normal cost in each year, plus interest on the accrued liability

---

[276] See "IRS, Pension Agency Disagree About New Device," Legal Times, Sept. 19, 1983, at 9 (quoting this as a tax lawyer's "joking" appellation for excess asset reversions).

Part of the tax advantage of an IRA or of a qualified plan is that the employee-taxpayer is likely to be in a lower bracket after retirement. While corporations do not retire, their effective tax brackets may become lower with time. Some corporations, in fact, have had sufficient net operating loss carryovers so that a substantial excess could be received with no tax at all.

[277] Code §4980, as amended by §1132 of TRA, P.L. 99-514. An exception to the tax, slated to expire in 1989, is provided if the excess assets are transferred by an employer to an ESOP that meets the requirements of Code §4975(e)(7), covers at least half of the participants in the terminated plan, and satisfies certain other rules. *Id.* The excise tax also does not apply on the termination of certain small plans that do not meet the minimum overall coverage and participation test requiring participation of the lesser of 50 employees or 40% of the employer's employees that becomes effective in 1989. Conf. Rep., H.R. Rep. 99-841, at II-423, and §1112(e)(3) of TRA.

[278] Until the recent bull market, when almost every investor did well, the major criticism of pension funds was how they so consistently underperformed market averages from the mid 1960's to the mid 1970's. See J. Rifkin and R. Barber, *The North Will Rise Again* (Beacon 1978), at 121-22.

[279] See 26 C.F.R. 1.404(a)-14(k) and Rev. Rul. 82-125.

and normal costs. Unless a plan's investment earnings are extraordinary, the plan's accrued liability will thus generally rise above the value of the plan's assets. In this manner, the full funding limitation should contain a significant excess above the plan's accrued liability.

Because significant excesses arise nevertheless, it becomes obvious that the *sine qua non* for a significant excess is that a plan's liabilities for benefits "on a termination basis" are less than its "accrued liability" on an ongoing basis. Two factors are central in creating a disparity between a plan's accrued liability and its liabilities on a termination basis. The first is that under all funding methods—except the "accrued benefit" (or "unit credit") cost method—a plan's "accrued liability" is measured not by reference to liabilities for accrued benefits, but by reference to projected benefits at normal retirement.[280] That is, rather than funding benefits as they accrue each year, most funding methods project the participant's ultimate accrued benefits, and then fund a portion of those projected benefits each year, using either a level dollar amount or a level percentage of pay.[281]

When a plan offers benefits under a flat-dollar formula, funding the plan by reference to projected benefits seem to create little disparity, since the projected benefits are essentially a straight multiple of the plan's annual accrued benefits. In a plan that provides benefits under a career average salary formula, the disparity between the accrued liability and liability on termination can be somewhat greater, because the plan's projected benefits are based partly on projected salary increases, which will not occur to increase accrued benefits if the plan is terminated sooner. This disparity increases to its greatest level in a plan that offers benefits under a final or highest average salary formula. Under these formulas, salary increases affect not just future years' benefits, but also benefits for years already worked under the plan. However, if the plan is terminated, accrued benefits are based only on salary up to the termination date.[282] Funding by reference to projected benefits in final or highest average salary plans thus generates an "accrued liability" that is much more than if the plan is terminated, and the participants' accrued benefits are determined, before those projected salary increases take effect.

The disparity between the plan's accrued liability, based on projected benefits, and its termination basis liability tends to be counteracted somewhat if the "level" method by which the projected benefits are funded is a level percentage of pay, rather than a level dollar

---

[280] See G. Ashley Cooper, "Financing Defined Benefit Plan," in F. Foulkes, *Employee Benefits Handbook* (Warren Gorham & Lamont 1982), at 11-21 to 26.

[281] *Id.*

[282] To illustrate this difference, under a final or highest average of salary formula, with a 4% annual salary increase assumption, the projected benefits of a participant 10 years away from retirement are 48% greater for years already worked than if the plan is terminated currently and his or her benefits are determined under the salary in effect at the date of termination. A 4% salary increase assumption is not uncommon. A&P's salary increase assumption was 6.5%, which projects 88% greater benefits at retirement for a participant now 55 than if the plan is terminated and current salaries used.

amount.[283] But Dan McGill shows that even with funding as a level percentage of pay, projected benefits in a "fairly typical" final or highest pay plan can so far outrun accrued benefits that a plan's "accrued liability" can be 25 to 30 percent more than its termination basis benefit liabilities solely for this reason.[284] If the plan has been in existence long enough to have amortized past service liabilities, and if the actuarial assumptions for earnings have panned out, the plan's assets thus *should* equal its "accrued liability," and therefore be 25 to 30 percent in excess of its termination liabilities—all as an inherent feature of the plan's funding method, rather than of unexpectedly high earnings.

The second factor in creating a disparity between a plan's accrued liability and its liability on a termination basis is the difference between the funding interest rates under which projected benefits are discounted to present value to determine the plan's "accrued liability" and the interest rates offered by insurers on group annuities which may be purchased to discharge the liabilities on termination. Many plans continue to use 5 and 6 percent interest rates to discount projected benefits to determine their "accrued liability," and thus normal funding costs. However, insurers in the early 1980's were willing to provide annuities to discharge the same benefit liabilities based on 9, 10, or in the case of Prudential's 1981 group annuity bid to Harper & Row, 15 percent interest rates. The result is that when a plan is terminated, the liabilities on termination may be much lower than they were using the plan's interest assumption.

Either of these factors—funding by reference to projected benefits that are greater than accrued benefits, or the difference between the interest rate used for funding and the interest rate used in discharging benefits on termination—can create excess assets. When the two factors are combined, and relatively high investment earnings over the past few years are added in, excess assets on termination can be extreme, as they were in both the Harper & Row and A&P plan terminations.[285]

---

[283] Funding as a level percentage of pay means the plan's normal costs remain lower until salaries in fact increase.

[284] See D. McGill, *Fundamentals of Private Pensions* (5th ed. 1984), at 418-31. See also D. Grubbs, "Termination of Pension Plans With Asset Reversion," 11 J. Pens. Plan. & Compl. 299 (Winter 1985), at 300:

"Most plans have funding policies designed to fund the projected benefits payable at retirement age based on [the] salary ... projected to be payable at that time. When a plan is terminated, the benefits are limited to those already accrued based on past salaries. The liabilities on plan termination ... are [thus] usually substantially less than the liabilities that were being funded to secure the projected benefits that would have been payable if the plan had continued. The existence of excess assets on plan termination is frequently a natural result of the decrease in liabilities caused by the event of termination. Thus, plan assets that were not excess in relation to the needs of an ongoing plan become excess assets if the plan is terminated."

[285] Another reason for excess assets that is more directly related to investment earnings is that plans may value their assets for purposes of the "full funding" limitation by averaging over a 5-year period. See 26 C.F.R. 1.412(c)(2)-1. In a rising market, this means that a plan's assets may be lower for the purpose of determining whether the full funding limitation has been reached than they are on a termination basis.

B. Who Receives a Windfall From Excess Assets

Beneath the strata of legal argument discussed below, one reason why the courts have not sought to grant employees more of the "excess" assets remaining on termination is the view that the employees couldn't reasonably have been counting on receiving any part of the excess assets. A number of cases have gone so far as to suggest that it would be a "windfall" if the employees obtained any part of the excess.[286] As described above, excess assets are usually *not* due to the employer's unusual investment acumen. Rather, they are due to the fact that employees don't receive, at plan termination, the full "accrued liability" the plan's funding targeted. While employees may not be experts on pension funding (particularly when it comes to the obscure difference between "accrued liability" and benefit liabilities on a plan termination), employees obviously are expecting benefits, including those benefits that are not technically "accrued benefits" at the date of a plan's termination. When a plan's formula is keyed to a *final* average of salary, employees are expecting that salary increases up to retirement will provide the final basis for their benefits. The other major component of excess assets arises from higher interest rates being used to discharge a plan's benefits than were used for funding. This reflects not an increase in long-term real interest rates, but rather higher anticipated deflation in the value of the fixed benefits the plan has offered than even the plan's actuary had assumed.

In short, both major sources of excess assets reflect worse benefit experience for participants in the plan than was expected in funding the plan's benefits. How receiving a part of this excess could be a "windfall" for employees is a question that the courts have not directly addressed. In contrast, in *Riley v. MEBA Pension Trust*, one of the earliest ERISA cases, Judge Friendly suggested that it would be an ERISA Section 404(a)(1) violation if benefits were ever kept "so meagre that unnecessary reserves were being accumulated" under a plan.[287]

Despite the factors which allow a plan's "accrued liability" to be more than its termination basis liability, plans do occasionally reach the full funding limitation. A&P's plan reached it, and as a result, A&P did not make contributions in 1979, 1980, and 1981. See Hearing on Pension Funding Problems, *supra* note 21, at 148. An equally interesting facet to this is that A&P was able to reach the full funding limitation, make no contributions for 3 years, while normal costs continued to add to the plan's accrued liabilities, and still wind up with assets nearly double the entire amount of its termination benefit liabilities.

[286] See *Washington-Baltimore Newspaper Guild v. Washington Star Co.*, 555 F.Supp. 257, 3 EBC 2609, at 2611 (D.D.C. 1983), *aff'd*, 729 F.2d 863 (D.C. Cir. 1984); *In re C.D. Moyer Co. Pension Trust*, 441 F.Supp. 1128, 1 EBC 1363, at 1367 (E.D. Pa. 1977), *aff'd*, 582 F.2d 1273 (3d Cir. 1978). But see *Bryant v. Int'l Fruit Products Co.*, 793 F.2d 118, 7 EBC 1688, at 1693 (6th Cir. 1986), *rev'g*, 604 F.Supp. 890, 6 EBC 1623 (S.D. Ohio 1985) (disagreeing with district court's characterization of the "windfall" for employees, the Sixth Circuit stated: "We do not believe this decision will result in a windfall for the plaintiffs. The plan was designed to provide some financial security for the employees, all of whom lost their jobs when the company ceased operations shortly after terminating the pension plan. On the other hand, permitting the company to recapture its [tax-deductible] contributions to the fund might well result in a windfall").

[287] 570 F.2d 406, 1 EBC 1757, at 1763 (2d Cir. 1977), *modified on other grounds after remand*, 586 F.2d 968, 1 EBC 1763 (2d Cir. 1978). See also *In re Des Moines Iron Workers Pension Trust*, 4 EBC 2364 (Heinsz, 1983) (fiduciaries have duty to increase benefits when plan assets allow them to do so). Cf. *Mestas v. Huge*, 585 F.2d 450, at 453 (10th Cir. 1978) (trustees may have "duty

This prediction has not come about to date, but the opposite suggestion of a "windfall" if employees receive any part of excess assets after benefits have been kept so low that unnecessary reserves accumulate seems equally unfounded.

C. Requirements for a Reversion of Excess Assets

The law on terminations of plans with excess assets is developing rapidly. Thus far, most of it is unfavorable to employees. No general fiduciary or other obligation prevents a company from terminating a plan for the express purpose of taking back excess assets.[288] However, five requirements do exist that must be satisfied before any "excess" assets may be taken back:

(1) "[A]ll liabilities of the plan to participants and their beneficiaries must be satisfied";
(2) The plan must specifically "provide[ ] for" the reversion of any excess assets to the employer (with an exception applying, even if the plan "provides for" an excess asset reversion, if the plan ever required employee contributions);
(3) The reversion must not "contravene any [other] provision of law";
(4) The excess assets must be the result of "erroneous actuarial computations"; and
(5) The plan termination must itself be authorized and the plan must actually be terminated.[289]

When these requirements are *not* met, the excess assets, or any part of them that is determined to be unavailable for reversion, are allocated to the plan's participants based on the ratio of the present value of the individual participant's benefits under all priority categories to the present value of all participants' benefits, multiplied by the excess assets which are not to revert.[290]

---

to liberalize and maximize benefits to the extent allowed by the Fund," but duty not applicable when plan was on a "pay-as-you-go basis at the time, with all money coming in . . . being paid out in benefits").

[288] See *Pollock v. Castrovinci*, 476 F.Supp. 606, 1 EBC 2091 (S.D.N.Y. 1979), *aff'd*, 622 F.2d 575 (2d Cir. 1980); *In re C.D. Moyer Co. Pension Trust*, 441 F.Supp. 1128, 1 EBC 1363 (E.D. Pa. 1977), *aff'd*, 582 F.2d 1273 (3d Cir. 1978); *Esteves v. GAF Corp.*, C.A. No. 82-4226 (D.N.J. Aug. 31, 1983); *UAW District 65 v. Harper & Row Publishers, Inc.*, 576 F.Supp. 1468, 4 EBC 2586 (S.D.N.Y. 1983); *Washington-Baltimore Newspaper Guild v. Washington Star Co.*, 555 F.Supp. 257, 3 EBC 2609 (D.D.C. 1983), *aff'd*, 729 F.2d 863 (D.C. Cir. 1984).

[289] ERISA §4044(d)(1) and 26 C.F.R. 1.401-2(b). See also ERISA §§403(c) and 408(b)(9) and Code §401(a)(2).

[290] 29 C.F.R. 2618.30 and 2618.32(a). And see Rev. Rul. 80-229 (providing that if excess assets go to participants, participants who are not members of the prohibited group may be entitled to a better-than-proportionate distribution under plans that use the maximum limits of Social Security integration to prevent overintegration of benefits provided under the plan).

To quote a related case, unless these requirements are met, "the language of ERISA makes abundantly clear that plan monies . . . shall be [used] for the exclusive benefit of the participants and beneficiaries," and thus are to be distributed in this manner. *Marshall v. Snyder*, 1 EBC 1878,

1. Satisfaction of All Benefit Liabilities

The first requirement for a reversion is that all "liabilities of the plan" must be satisfied. This encompasses all benefit liabilities covered under Section 4044(a)'s priority categories (1) through (6). Benefits in category (6) are not limited to "nonforfeitable" benefits, nor are they limited to "accrued benefits." Accrued benefits which become nonforfeitable on termination are thus in category (6). Early retirement benefits that are still forfeitable and that are not required to accrue from year-to-year under ERISA are also included in category (6). The value of disability or death benefit coverage offered under the terms of a plan up to a separation from service or retirement may also be in category (6).[291] Even if category (6)'s reference to "all other benefits under the plan" were held *not* to cover some of these benefits, Section 4044(d)(1)'s reference to *"all* liabilities of the plan to participants and their beneficiaries" could require a plan to go farther before plan assets could revert to an employer. Under 26 C.F.R. 1.401-2(b)(2), the "liabilities" which are to be satisfied prior to a reversion must include all "contingent" obligations to those participants who "have not yet completed the required period of service."[292]

The interest rate used in determining lump sum values for benefits can also be significant in whether *all* of a plan's liabilities have been satisfied. Reasonable interest rates for lump sum distributions on the termination of sufficient plans have been discussed above in sec. V. A relatively high, but reasonable interest rate for lump sums can be justified when a plan's assets are not enough to pay *all* benefits because a relatively high interest rate in this case spreads the plan's assets farther, covering more of the plan's benefits. When a plan's assets can provide all plan benefits, this justification for a relatively high interest rate vanishes. In an overfunded plan, no other participant will be deprived of any benefits by the use of a lower, but reasonable rate. Therefore, an interest rate at the lower end of reasonableness may have to be the choice of plan fiduciaries *if* their decision on which interest rate to use to discharge benefits in lump sum form is to be "solely in the interest" of participants and beneficiaries.[293]

---

at 1887 (E.D.N.Y. 1979) (holding that the presence of excess plan assets cannot be used as a defense to a breach of fiduciary duties).

[291] See sec. IV.A above.

[292] See also *Shatto v. Evans Products Co.*, 728 F.2d 1224 (9th Cir. 1984).

[293] See letter of Dennis M. Kass, Assistant Secretary of Labor for Pension and Welfare Benefits, to former Rep. John N. Erlenborn, Chairman, Department of Labor Advisory Council on Employee Welfare and Pension Benefit Plans, dated March 13, 1986, reprinted in 13 BNA Pens. Rep. at 472-73 (March 17, 1986) (choice of interest rates for use in lump sum cash-out of benefits on plan termination is a fiduciary function).

Rev. Rul. 83-52, however, allows overfunded plans to use any rate acceptable to the PBGC to meet the Code §401(a)(2) requirement of satisfying all liabilities of the plan prior to a reversion. This ruling revoked Rev. Rul. 71-152, which previously required that lump sum payments from overfunded plans be determined on the basis of an interest assumption no higher than the rate used by the plan for funding. While Rev. Rul. 83-52 is, in a sense, a step backward, higher rates are only "normally" reasonable under the PBGC's regulations. Thus, Rev. Rul. 83-52 does not dispose of the Code §401(a)(2) issue, and it does not address the ERISA §404(a)(1) issue in the

2. Plan Provides for the Reversion

The second requirement for a reversion is that the plan must specifically "provide[ ] for" the reversion of excess assets to the employer. If a plan is silent, or is ambiguous with the summary plan description not adequately disclosing that the excess goes to the employer, the plan may be considered not to "provide[ ] for" the reversion as required by Section 4044(d)(1)(C). Prior to ERISA, no statute required that plans "provide[ ] for" a reversion, and excess assets sometimes reverted to employers when plans were silent.[294] But when a plan is silent now, or when it does not expressly provide for a reversion, the unavailability of a reversion is clear.[295] In *Bryant v. International Fruit Products Co.*, a nonbargained plan did not "provide[] for" a reversion when the plan amendment to install the reversion provision violated earlier express limits on the power to amend and was at odds with SPD descriptions that "assured the participating employees that, once contributed, no money paid into the fund could ever be reclaimed by the company."[296] In *In re Washington Star Newspaper Retirement Plan*, Arbitrator Walter Gellhorn found that when a written plan neither unambiguously compels nor precludes a reversion, the retirement income purpose of the plan and the underlying realities of the employer-employee relationship, in which benefits are costed-out, and higher wages or other benefits foregone based on those costs, leads to the conclusion that the excess assets should go to the employees.[297]

Court cases have not thoroughly addressed the effect that an SPD's disclosure, or nondisclosure, can have on an ambiguous, or even an unambiguous provision for a reversion.[298] However, in ERISA Technical Release 84-1, the Department of Labor found that a plan's termination provisions constitute a "circumstance" which may result in the denial or loss of benefits that a participant otherwise might reasonably expect on the basis of the description of benefits. Technical Release

---

choice of an interest rate. See also sec. V above on reasonable interest rates for determining lump sum benefits on termination.

[294] See J. Mamorsky and D. Hulbert, "Employers' Entitlement to Excess Pension Assets," N.Y.L.J., Sept. 19, 1983, at 21 (citing one example, *In re Marine Midland Trust Co.*, 144 N.Y.S.2d 4 (Sup.Ct. 1955)).

[295] See *Kruzynski v. Richards Bros. Punch Co.*, 211 BNA Pens. Rep. D-8 (E.D. Mich. 1978).

[296] 793 F.2d 118, 7 EBC 1688, at 1692-93 (6th Cir. 1986), *rev'g*, 604 F.Supp. 890, 6 EBC 1623 (S.D. Ohio 1985). See also cases at n. 308.

[297] 4 EBC 2441 (Gellhorn, 1983).

[298] Compare *Corley v. Hecht Co.*, 530 F.Supp. 1155, 2 EBC 2397 (D.D.C. 1982) (requiring disclosure in SPD of employer's right to recoup surplus under group life insurance contract); *Bryant v. Int'l Fruit Products Co.*, *supra* (decision that plan did not "provide[ ] for" reversion of excess assets when plan amendment to install reversion provision was not permitted under earlier express limitations on the power to amend buttressed by descriptions in employees' handbook about the plan that "assured the participating employees that, once contributed, no money paid into the fund could ever be reclaimed by the company"), with *Eagar v. Savannah Foods & Indus. Inc.*, 605 F.Supp. 415 (N.D. Ala. 1984) (plan that said assets would revert and SPD that said they would not reconciled in favor of terms of plan; court emphasized lack of employee reliance on SPD statement). Disclosure in a plan's SPD was discussed in *Van Orman v. American Ins. Co.*, 680 F.2d 301, 3 EBC 1653 (3d Cir. 1982), but it was discussed in the context of pre-ERISA rules, not the more stringent ERISA disclosure requirements.

84-1 therefore specifically requires SPDs to contain a summary of plan provisions governing the rights of the plan sponsor to terminate the plan, and the circumstances under which those rights may be exercised. The Technical Release further provides that the SPD must contain a summary of plan provisions governing the allocation and disposition of assets on plan termination.[299]

The need for disclosure of a reversion clause may be particularly acute in salary-based plans because such plans develop excess assets as a routine, inherent part of their funding methods.[300] Rather than disclosure of this incentive to terminate the plan, the more likely situation is that the SPD emphasizes benefits based on salary up to retirement, with no reference to the employer's incentive to terminate the plan before that time if excess assets have accumulated based on the funding of those projected benefits. Individual benefit statements may also have reinforced participant expectations of benefits based on salary up to retirement. In such cases, it is possible that the plan may be considered not to "provide[ ] for" the reversion, despite an ambiguous, or even a clear-cut provision in the plan document, or alternatively, not to "provide[ ] for" a reversion until benefits based on projected salaries at retirement are paid.[301]

Notwithstanding any plan provision "provid[ing] for" a reversion, if a plan requires, or has ever required, employee contributions as a condition of participation in the plan or as a condition of employment, the excess assets must be divided between excess assets attributable to the employees' contributions and excess assets attributable to the employer's contributions.[302]

3. *Reversion Does Not Contravene Any Provision of Law*

The third requirement for a reversion is that it must not "contravene any provision of law." Under "any provision of law," amendments that insert a reversion clause after a termination are invalid *per se*.[303] Similarly, amendments inserting a reversion provision in anticipation of a termination may be invalid under federal common law principles. In *Matter of Bankers Trust Co. (Fifth Avenue Coach Lines)*, the right to amend a plan to redirect plan assets was held to assume an intent to

---

[299] Reprinted in 11 BNA Pens. Rep. at 653-54 (May 14, 1984). Technical Release 84-1 is not limited to the future, but covers all existing SPDs. Lack of disclosure in an existing SPD can be remedied by a summary of material modification with the required disclosure.

[300] See 29 C.F.R. 2520.102-2(b) and 2520.102-3(l) (the SPD shall describe "circumstances which may result in ... loss ... of any benefits that a participant might otherwise reasonably expect the plan to provide on the basis of the description of benefits").

[301] Alternatively, the plan could be considered to "provide[ ] for" the reversion, but the requirement that the reversion "not contravene any [other] provision of law" could be abridged by the SPD violation.

[302] ERISA §4044(d)(2) and 29 C.F.R. 2618.31. And see S. Rep. 93-127, 1 ERISA Leg. Hist. 616. But see *LLC Corp. v. PBGC*, 703 F.2d 301, 4 EBC 1233 (8th Cir. 1983) (eviscerating this rule when employees made 6% mandatory employee contributions, but the employer "carried the risk" of providing the specified benefits).

[303] See *Audio Fidelity Corp. v. PBGC*, 624 F.2d 513, 2 EBC 1856 (4th Cir. 1980).

continue the plan.[304] Late amendments might also be invalid under ERISA Section 510 when the excess assets were present before the amendment, and the amendment thus "interferes" with benefit rights to which participants would otherwise have become entitled under ERISA Title IV.[305] If excess assets already exist at the time of a plan amendment, the amendment also "disposes" of those assets, thus making it subject to ERISA Section 404(a)(1)'s fiduciary standard of whether the amendment, and hence disposition of assets, is "solely in the interest" and for the "exclusive benefit" of participants and beneficiaries. This is a standard which an amendment to insert a reversion provision shortly before a plan termination should not be able to satisfy.

To date, however, amendments inserting reversion provisions shortly before terminations have been subject to mixed treatment in the courts. Some decisions give little consideration to whether the amendment was in anticipation of the termination, and thus may be *ultra vires* as a matter of common law, or to whether the amendment interfered with rights to which participants would "otherwise" have become entitled.[306] To deal with the patent fiduciary problem in adopting an amendment that "disposes" of excess assets by giving them all to the employer rather than the participants, some courts have distinguished the disposition of "excess" assets from the disposition of other plan assets as far as fiduciary duties, a distinction which finds no support in the statute or legislative history.[307] Other more recent decisions, however, have focused on whether such amendments are in breach of any other provision of the plan, or of a collective bargaining obligation.[308]

---

[304] 52 Lab. Cas. (CCH) ¶51,367 (N.Y. Sup.Ct. 1965). See also *Kulins v. Malco, A Microdot Co.*, 459 N.E.2d 1038 (Ill.App. 1st Dist. 1984) (amendment to severance pay plan to cut benefits on eve of layoffs constrained by promissory estoppel and contractual requirement of good faith).

[305] See *Dependahl v. Falstaff Brewing Corp.*, 491 F.Supp. 1188 (E.D. Mo. 1980), *modified on other grounds*, 653 F.2d 1208, 2 EBC 1521 (8th Cir. 1981), *cert. denied*, 454 U.S. 1084 (1981) (amendment to severance pay plan lengthening eligibility requirement immediately before layoffs interfered with rights to which participants would otherwise have become entitled).

[306] See *In re C.D. Moyer Co. Pension Trust*, *supra* (allowing amendment 18 days before plan termination); *Pollock v. Castrovinci*, *supra* (permitting amendment immediately before plan termination); *Washington-Baltimore Newspaper Guild v. Washington Star Co.*, *supra* (amendment to "clarify" authority to take reversion made nearly simultaneously with plan termination); *Walsh v. A&P Co.*, 96 F.R.D. 632, 4 EBC 1055 (D.N.J. 1983) (amendment less than 6 months before termination). See also *Chait v. Bernstein*, 645 F.Supp. 1092, 8 EBC 1126 (D.N.J. 1986) (decision by bankruptcy receiver to amend plan to add reversion provision immediately before plan termination not subject to review for breach of fiduciary duty; insurance company official who grossly mismanaged the company would have been prime beneficiary of the excess assets if the reversion provision had not been inserted).

[307] See *In re C.D. Moyer Co. Pension Trust*, *supra*; *Esteves v. GAF Corp.*, C.A. No. 82-4226 (D.N.J. Aug. 31, 1983). But compare *Marshall v. Snyder*, 1 EBC 1878, at 1887 (E.D.N.Y. 1979); *Werschkull v. United California Bank*, 149 Cal. Rptr. 829 (Cal. App. 1978).

[308] See *Bryant v. Int'l Fruit Products Co.*, 793 F.2d 118, 7 EBC 1688, at 1692-93 (6th Cir. 1986), *rev'g*, 604 F.Supp. 890, 6 EBC 1623 (S.D. Ohio 1985) (plan did not provide for reversion of excess assets when plan amendment to install reversion provision 1 month before plan termination was not permitted by earlier express limitations on the power to amend as buttressed by descriptions in employees' handbook that "assured the participating employees that, once contributed, no money paid into the fund could ever be reclaimed by the company"); *Delgrosso v. Spang & Co.*, 769 F.2d 928, 6 EBC 1940 (3d Cir. 1985), *cert. denied*, 476 U.S. ___ (1986) (amendment to plan by employer to install reversion provision was unauthorized under pension

Not contravening "any provision of law" may also include not violating ERISA Section 102 and the regulations on the content of the SPD, and thus may double-over with the "provides for" requirement to cover nondisclosure or implied affirmative representations in an SPD that create legitimate employee expectations of benefits beyond those which are technically "accrued benefits" or otherwise in category (6) as of the date of termination.[309]

4. Erroneous Actuarial Computations

The fourth condition for a reversion is that the excess assets must result from "erroneous actuarial computations."[310] If part of a plan's overfunding is willful (for example, through the use of actuarial assumptions that pad a plan's excess assets and thereby create a "tax-free IRA" for the employer), rather than being based on the plan actuary's "best estimate of anticipated experience under the plan,"[311] *or* if part of the excess arises from a plan amendment reducing benefits, e.g., a reduction in a plan's nonaccrued benefits or a change in eligibility provisions, that part of the excess is not to revert, and should therefore go to the participants.[312] The requirement that excess assets must be the result of "erroneous actuarial computations" to revert is a

---

part of collective bargaining agreement and therefore constituted breach of fiduciary duty); *Wright v. Nimmons*, 641 F.Supp. 1391, 7 EBC 2184 (S.D. Tex. 1986) (amendment to excess asset distribution provision of plan of closely held company ineffective when it occurred subsequent to constructive termination of plan—which occurred at the time when all employees were discharged—and violated plan provisions restricting amendments that would diminish beneficial interest of any participant or that would vest in the company any interest in plan assets); *Unitis v. JFC Acquisition Co.*, 643 F.Supp. 454, 7 EBC 2217 (N.D. Ill. 1986) (accord with *Delgrosso, supra*, on reversion provisions in violation of collective bargaining agreements). But compare *Schuck v. Gilmore Steel Corp.*, 784 F.2d 947, 7 EBC 1455 (9th Cir. 1986) (collective bargaining agreement allowed employer to write its own trust provisions; therefore, reversion provision did not violate agreement). See also *Struble v. New Jersey Brewery Employees' Welfare Fund*, 732 F.2d 325, 5 EBC 1676 (3d Cir. 1984) (management-appointed trustees who voted to dispose of a surplus in a terminated health plan's assets by giving the assets back to contributing employers, rather than using them to continue benefits to retired participants for as long as possible, had burden of proof that they did not act in breach of their fiduciary duties); *Werschkull v. United California Bank, supra* (amendment transferring excess assets from plan for credit against contributions to another plan disposed of plan assets in violation of fiduciary duty).

Plan amendments adopting reversion provisions in 1975 or 1976 may not be subject to the same analysis because prior to that time it was not generally necessary for a plan to "provide[ ] for" a reversion, as is now required by ERISA §§4044(d)(1) and 403(c)(1). An amendment at that time can therefore sometimes be seen as maintaining the status quo, rather than changing existing contingent rights under the plan. Cf. *In re C.D. Moyer Co. Pension Trust, supra* (1976 amendment).

[309] The PBGC's preamble to the regulations on not "contraven[ing] any provision of law" states that the language does not preclude equitable theories. See 46 Fed. Reg. 49843 (Oct. 8, 1981). See also 470 BNA Pens. Rep. 1736 (Nov. 14, 1983) (reprinting letter from Rep. Edward Roybal, chairman of the House Select Committee on Aging, to Secretary of Labor Raymond Donovan on this point).

[310] 26 C.F.R. 1.401-2(b).

[311] Code §412(c)(3).

[312] 26 C.F.R. 1.401-2(b). And see generally *Lynch v. Dawson Collieries, Inc.*, 485 S.W.2d 494 (Ky. 1972); *Kruzynski v. Richards Bros. Punch Co.*, 211 BNA Pens. Rep. D-8 (E.D. Mich. 1978); *Pollock v. Castrovinci*, 476 F.Supp. 606, 1 EBC 2091 (S.D.N.Y. 1979), *aff'd*, 622 F.2d 575 (2d Cir. 1980); *Amato v. Western Union Int'l, Inc.*, 596 F.Supp. 621, 5 EBC 2718 (S.D.N.Y. 1984), *rev'd on other grounds*, 773 F.2d 1402, 6 EBC 2226 (2d Cir. 1985).

Code requirement that is not directly replicated in the Title I provisions of ERISA. Therefore, enforcing this requirement would seem to initially present the same problems discussed in Chapter 14, section IV, regarding private enforcement of Code requirements for qualified plans. Thus far, however, the courts have proceeded with an at least cursory examination of this requirement under ERISA Section 4044(d)(1). This is because many plans contain language directly paralleling the Code requirements, thus making noncompliance a violation of the Section 4044(d)(1)(C) rule that the plan must "provide[] for" the reversion.[313]

Plan amendments reducing benefits at any time in the past may thus result in part of the excess assets being considered due to deliberate action of the employer, rather than "erroneous actuarial computations."[314] Under the erroneous actuarial computation requirement, it is likewise difficult to see how that part of excess assets arising in a salary-based plan because the plan's funding method is deliberately targeted to benefits based on projected salaries, rather than salary at termination, can be considered an *"erroneous"* actuarial computation. When a plan is terminated by an employer before those salary increases take place, considering the part of the excess resulting from funding based on future salaries an "erroneous actuarial computation," is like saying it is an "error" after deliberately stopping a trip half way that there is more gas in the tank than would be left after the full trip.[315]

When a plan's interest rate assumption for funding has been kept low to avoid the full funding limitation and thus to obtain further tax deductions and tax-free appreciation on contributions, the resulting part of the excess may also not be an "erroneous" actuarial computation. Some difference with the interest rates that insurers are using to offer group annuities may generally be acceptable—to encourage greater contributions to underfunded plans. But once a plan is substantially overfunded on a termination basis (and particularly with the two-to-one asset to benefit liability ratios often existing in overfunded

---

[313] See *UAW v. Dyneer Corp.*, 747 F.2d 335, 5 EBC 2605 (6th Cir. 1984); *UAW District 65 v. Harper & Row Publishers, Inc.*, 576 F.Supp. 1468, 3 EBC 2586 at 2595 (S.D.N.Y. 1983), and the cases cited above.

Another avenue for obtaining judicial review of compliance with this requirement is to file written comments with the IRS within 45 days after the date a plan files an Application for Determination Upon Termination. If the IRS does not respond favorably to comments suggesting that some or all of the excess is not due to erroneous actuarial computations, a declaratory judgment action can be filed in the U.S. Tax Court. See ch. 14, sec. IV.

[314] 26 C.F.R. 1.401-2(b)(1).

[315] *In Kruzynski v. Richards Bros. Punch Co.*, 211 BNA Pens. Rep. D-8 (E.D. Mich. 1978), the court found that the plan's actuary "knowingly suggested such yearly contributions despite the fact that they left the Plan in a continually overfunded state." The court concluded that this was "no actuarial mistake." 211 BNA Pens. Rep. at D-9.

plans), maintaining a low interest assumption may be deliberate padding of the excess assets, with the employer having no intention of leaving those assets in the plan to provide benefits.[316]

Perhaps because sorting out precisely what part of an excess is deliberate and what part is erroneous may be difficult, the courts have not closely examined how much of an excess is due to "erroneous actuarial computations," but rather have simply followed, at least in the absence of strong evidence otherwise, an IRS ruling that any excess resulting from use of an approved method of funding and actuarial assumptions that are not unreasonable is due to "erroneous actuarial computations."[317] One problem with following the IRS's rulings on the meaning of "erroneous actuarial computation" or "actuarial error" when these phrases or a similar phrase appear in a plan or SPD, is that a technical definition of this phrase is being adopted that may go against the "reasonable understanding" of employees.[318]

5. Plan Termination Is Authorized and the Plan Is Actually Terminated

A basic antecedent for a reversion, which can be considered a fifth requirement, is that the termination must be authorized under the plan, and a "termination" of the plan must actually occur. Terminations of plans with excess assets have generally involved nonbargained plans. Under such plans, the employer has usually reserved authority to amend or terminate the plan at will. However, even under such authority, an implied limitation may be that a termination of the plan will not occur absent financial hardship for the employer from maintaining the plan. Such an implied limitation is in accord with the ordinary understanding of plan participants and may be further supported by statements in SPDs that the employer expects to continue the plan "indefinitely" absent unforeseen circumstances or business hardship from maintaining the plan.[319] The Internal Revenue Code's requirement that a qualified plan be "permanent" has also long been seen as requiring that there be a valid business reason for a termination consistent with the assumption that the plan was designed for the exclusive benefit of employees and was intended to be permanent.[320]

---

[316] In cases where the employer is undergoing a major business contraction, it may be important to check whether actuarial turnover assumptions have been adjusted to reflect current experience, or have been left "as is" to increase the excess assets.

[317] See *UAW v. Dyneer Corp.*, 747 F.2d 335, 5 EBC 2605 (6th Cir. 1984); *UAW District 65 v. Harper & Row Publishers, Inc., supra.* And see Rev. Rul. 83-52 and 26 C.F.R. 1.401-2(b) for the IRS's interpretation of this term.

[318] See the discussion in ch. 7 on the use of reasonable understanding in plan interpretation.

[319] See sec. I.E above.

[320] See, e.g., Rev. Rul. 69-24.

If a plan termination is authorized, the occurrence of the termination may seem to be a foregone conclusion, but when a company terminates a defined benefit plan to obtain excess assets and immediately, or shortly thereafter, starts another defined benefit plan, whether a "termination" occurred may be questioned.[321] Under ERISA Section 4021(a), a plan that covers "substantially the same employees" and provides "substantially the same benefits" is considered a continuation of the predecessor plan for the purposes of Title IV. Under ERISA Section 4047, the PBGC may also disallow terminations "as a result of such circumstances as the [PBGC] determines to be relevant." Under these provisions, the PBGC was at one time opposing reversions where an employer immediately establishes another defined benefit plan, which in the early years of its existence may be underfunded, and thus a potential burden for the PBGC.[322] If a defined benefit plan is replaced by a defined contribution plan, the "termination" of the defined benefit plan may not be questioned,[323] but the employees may be dissatisfied, with the result that this option is often not open to employers as a practical matter.

Under "Guidelines" developed jointly by the IRS, the Department of Labor, and the PBGC, and issued on May 23, 1984, terminations followed by a reestablishment of the same, or practically the same, defined benefit plan are now recognized by all the agencies, including the PBGC, as distinct steps that will not be pulled together under a "substance-over-form" or "step transaction" doctrine so long as slightly faster funding rules are adopted for the new plan and no further termination/reestablishment transactions occur in the next 15 years.[324]

Another means for taking excess assets out of a defined benefit

---

[321] If a plan has not "terminated" because another defined benefit plan is started soon after, the exceptions to ERISA for reversions to an employer on plan termination cannot apply, and the reversion of assets may violate Code §401(a)(2)'s prohibition against diversion of the plan's assets, ERISA §403(c)(1)'s provision that the plan's assets shall never inure to the benefit of the employer, ERISA §406's provisions on prohibited transactions, and ERISA §404(a)(1)'s fiduciary requirement that dispositions of plan assets be "solely in the interest" and for the "exclusive benefit" of participants and beneficiaries. See 470 BNA Pens. Rep. 1724 (Nov. 14, 1983) (reporting presentation by Morton Klevan, Department of Labor PWBP deputy administrator, on the consequences of a plan "termination" being deemed *not* to have occurred).

[322] See S. Sacher and G. Jerome, "Reversion Termination Controversy," Nat'l L. J., Jan. 2, 1984, 15-18.

[323] See ERISA §4041(e), formerly §4041(f).

[324] See PBGC, IRS and Labor Department Guidelines on Asset Reversions, reprinted in 11 BNA Pens. Rep. at 724 (May 28, 1984). Whether or not a plan "termination" occurs for these purposes, an employer who establishes another defined benefit plan may have to credit service under the terminated plan for vesting, and possibly for all purposes, under the new plan. See 26 C.F.R. 1.411(a)-5 (requiring credit for vesting under either a new defined benefit or defined contribution plan for service under a "predecessor" plan). And see ERISA §210(b)(1) (Code §414(a)(1)) and Conf. Rep., at 264 and 270, 3 ERISA Leg. Hist. 4531 and 4537 (requiring that service be credited for vesting, accruals, and all other purposes, where a *successor* employer only nominally terminates a plan—*a fortiori,* the same should apply where the *same* employer only nominally terminates a plan).

plan is to spin-off a retirees' plan from what is left as an active workers' plan, with all the excess assets being put in the retirees' plan, and only the retirees' plan then being terminated.[325] The advantage in this method for an employer is that the active workers' defined benefit plan is not terminated, and thus employee dissatisfaction with a defined contribution plan is avoided, as is the question of whether the reestablishment of another defined benefit plan might nullify the "termination" of the first plan. The legal questions concerning spin-off terminations and reversions are not too different that those presented in the termination of an overfunded plan generally. Each of the five requirements described above must still be satisfied. Moreover, the preliminary act of spinning off a part of the plan's assets, unlike the final decision to terminate the retirees' plan, may be seen as a fiduciary function since it "disposes" of plan assets *before* a plan termination that could otherwise go to increase or to continue to secure the benefits of the active participants in the nonterminated plan.[326] For a time, the PBGC was opposing spin-offs on the grounds that they constitute only a partial termination of a plan, and that they increase the potential burden on the PBGC if funding for the active workers' plan falters.[327] Under the 1984 Guidelines, however, the PBGC withdrew its opposition to spin-off terminations as long as:

(1) Notice of the proposed transaction is provided participants 10 days before the date of the transaction;

(2) All benefits of participants in the nonterminated (active workers') plan become fully vested;

(3) Annuity contracts are purchased to secure all current benefits of participants in the nonterminated plan;

(4) Slightly faster funding rules are adopted for future benefit accruals under the nonterminated plan; and

---

[325] For a detailed early description of this device, see 470 BNA Pens. Rep. 1738 (letter of William T. Coleman to John Chapoton, Oct. 11, 1983).

[326] See *Bigger v. American Commercial Lines, Inc.*, 652 F.Supp. 123, 8 EBC 1424 (W.D. Mo. 1986) (participants in spin off plan have standing to challenge spin-off as in breach of fiduciary duty when entire excess retained in other plan: "[t]he court does not see how any important decision regarding a plan's assets, especially if made in the interest of someone other than the participants as alleged here, could be exempted from [§404's] comprehensive standard"); *Werschkull v. United California Bank*, 149 Cal.Rptr. 829 (Cal.App. 1978); *Eaves v. Penn*, 587 F.2d 453, 1 EBC 1592 (10th Cir. 1978); *Cutaiar v. Marshall*, 590 F.2d 523, 1 EBC 2153 (3d Cir. 1979). But see *Foster Corp. Employees' Pension Plan v. Healthco, Inc.*, 753 F.2d 194, 6 EBC 1187 (1st Cir. 1985) (no breach of fiduciary duty in not transferring portion of excess assets along with assets and liabilities spun off in sale of corporate division when employees would not necessarily receive any increase in benefits even if the assets were transferred).

[327] See "IRS, Pension Agency Disagree About New Device," Legal Times, Sept. 19, 1983, at 2, and S. Sacher and G. Jerome, "Reversion Termination Controversy," Nat'l L.J., Jan. 2, 1984, 15-18. The IRS was at one time considering amending its regulations on asset and liability transfers to require that a part of the excess be left in the active workers' plan.

(5) No future termination/reestablishment or spin-off termination with respect to the nonterminated plan occurs in the next 15 years.[328]

---

[328] PBGC, IRS and Labor Department Guidelines on Asset Reversions, reprinted in 11 BNA Pens. Rep. at 724 (May 28, 1984). The annuity contract must cover all benefits that would be provided on a termination basis allocation of the plan's assets. See ch. 9, sec. VIII.B; 26 C.F.R. 1.414(l)-1(n); and Rev. Rul. 86-48 (benefits on a termination basis include value of early retirement benefits and preretirement survivor's annuity coverage).

See also *Interco v. PBGC*, 620 F.Supp. 689, 6 EBC 2433 (E.D. Mo. 1985) (upholding Guidelines' requirement that nonvested active employees become vested and that annuities be purchased to cover all active employees' current benefits before spin-off termination and reversion takes place), and PBGC Opinion Letters 85-11 and 85-21, reprinted in 13 BNA Pens. Rep. at 26 and 30 (Jan. 6, 1986) (Guidelines' requirement of vesting and annuitization of benefits under the nonterminated plan after a spin-off is not required if a pro rata portion of excess assets is retained in (or spun off to, as the case may be) the nonterminated plan, with pro rata determined by the proportion the accrued benefits of participants in the nonterminated plan bear to total accrued benefits under the plan before the spin-off).

Contract language could require more than the Guidelines on a spin-off/termination. See *Foster Corp. Employees' Pension Plan v. Healthco, Inc.*, 753 F.2d 194, 6 EBC 1187 (1st Cir. 1985) (in a spin-off of plan assets and liabilities as a part of a sale of a division to another company, parol evidence established that intent of the parties was to transfer only so much assets as needed to fully fund benefit liabilities to the division employees, even though ambiguity existed in sales contract on whether portion of assets and liabilities "attributable to" division employees included a pro rata share of surplus assets).

13

Multiemployer Plan Reorganization, Insolvency, and Termination Rules

The Multiemployer Pension Plan Amendments Act of 1980 (MPPAA)[1] revamped the ERISA Title IV insurance program for multiemployer plans. As originally enacted, ERISA's multiemployer insurance program closely paralleled the single-employer insurance program. It permitted voluntary terminations and provided insurance for benefits under a terminated multiemployer plan at the single-employer levels. The PBGC could assess up to 30 percent of the net worth of employers who withdrew from a plan within five years of the termination to pay for any insufficiency between the plan's assets and the assets needed to pay the PBGC guaranteed benefits.[2] However, under ERISA's terms, Congress delayed the effective date for the multiemployer insurance program until January 1, 1978, and then postponed it again until 1980, with the PBGC providing insurance to multiemployer plans on a discretionary basis in the interim.[3]

The need of multiemployer plan participants for benefit insurance tends to be reduced by one characteristic of multiemployer plans: Because many employers contribute to a plan, it is not dependent on the economic fortunes of a single employer. In fact, in enacting ERISA, Congress "was guided by the concept that [a multiemployer] plan, if sufficiently comprehensive in size or scope, would be unlikely to terminate because its existence did not depend on the economic fortunes of one employer or employer entity."[4] But a down-side of multiemployer plans, which drew more attention as the mid 1970's recession set in, is

---

[1] P.L. 96-364, primarily codified at 29 U.S.C. §1301, *et seq.*

[2] See ERISA §4064, as originally enacted, on employer liability. The same statutory sections on voluntary terminations and the insurance level for benefits from terminated plans would also have applied. See ERISA §§4041 and 4022.

[3] The original and four later deferrals of the effective date of this program are described in *PBGC v. R.A. Gray & Co.*, 467 U.S. 717, 5 EBC 1545, at 1546-47 (1984).

[4] 2 ERISA Leg. Hist. 3306 (statement of Rep. Perkins).

that multiemployer plans generally have a larger percentage of unfunded liabilities (compared to all the plan's liabilities) than most single-employer plans. Increasingly, multiemployer plans also seemed to be in cyclical or sunset industries, or industries in which the sponsoring unions were losing ground. The fear resulting from this was that if large numbers of contributing employers went out of business, without a comparable number of entrants into the plan under new collective bargaining agreements, a relatively small number of employers would be left to support the entire plan's unfunded liabilities. The remaining employers would not be willing to pay higher contributions to support unfunded liabilities that stemmed mostly from service with unrelated employers. They, too, would then insist on negotiating out of their pension agreements. Thus, the contribution base for an entire plan might collapse.

ERISA's original multiemployer insurance provisions seemed as if they might actually encourage this process. Withdrawal liability was *only* to be imposed if an employer contributed to a plan within the five years before the plan's termination. It was feared that this reward for an early withdrawal might spur employers to withdraw before what they anticipated was the beginning of the five-year period.[5] A 1978 study by the PBGC seemed to confirm the problems that many multiemployer plans were confronting and indicated that this scenario of anticipatory early withdrawals was a distinct possibility under ERISA's original insurance provisions. The PBGC study found that multiemployer plans covering about 1.6 million workers and retirees—out of 8 million total multiemployer plan participants—were already experiencing financial difficulties and, without a change in the law or in current conditions, could be expected to terminate within 10 years.[6]

In the face of this, Congress overhauled the multiemployer insurance program that ERISA originally contained. The chief reform was the imposition of withdrawal liability *whenever* an employer withdraws from a multiemployer plan (with no 30 percent of net worth limitation on the liability). Congress also eliminated the possibility of employers collectively wiping out liabilities through voluntary terminations—a right which single-employer plan sponsors enjoyed until 1986. It thus made the event when the PBGC steps in with insurance "insolvency," rather than plan "termination," with continued funding of all benefit liabilities of terminated plans being required until the benefits are funded, or until all employers withdraw and pay withdrawal liability. Congress also created an intermediate status for multiemployer plans called "reorganization" that requires increased employer contributions,

---

[5] See *PBGC v. R.A. Gray & Co.*, 467 U.S. 717, 5 EBC 1545, at 1547 (1984) (reviewing the arguments about the "vicious downward cycle" that could ensue under PBGC's original multiemployer provisions); see also Joint Explanation of Senators Harrison Williams and Russell Long, chairmen of the Sen. Comms. of Labor and Human Resources and Finance, 126 Cong. Rec. 20189, at 20192 (July 29, 1980).

[6] See PBGC, Multiemployer Study Required by P.L. 95-214, Appendix (1978), and see H.R. Rep. No. 96-869 (Part I), 55-56, reprinted in [1980] U.S. Code Cong. & Ad. News, at 2934.

and allows plans to reduce benefits to a limited extent to prevent, or at least forestall, insolvency. It also created a slightly different intermediate stage if all employers withdraw from a plan, called a "termination by mass withdrawal," in which benefits must be reduced if necessary to bring the plan's benefit liabilities into long-term equilibrium with the plan's assets, including withdrawal liability claims. Finally, despite a statement in ERISA's legislative history that multiemployer plan participants would not be made "second-class citizens,"[7] Congress lowered the guarantee of benefits from multiemployer plans that become "insolvent" below the levels that prevail for benefits from terminated single-employer plans. This lower guarantee is to reduce the costs of the insurance program and to create incentives for employees to "resist"—by unspecified means—declines in a plan's financial status.[8]

The most controversial feature of MPPAA is the assessment of "withdrawal liability" *whenever* an employer withdraws from a multiemployer plan. Methods for computing the amount of an employer's withdrawal liability are not discussed here, although definitions of "complete" and "partial" withdrawals are set out in Chapter 5.

To provide an indication of the numbers of participants and plans that may be affected by these provisions, over 500,000 employers contribute to about 2,000 multiemployer plans covering an estimated 8 million workers and retirees. Of the 500,000 employers, the PBGC estimates that about 25,000 will be required to pay withdrawal liability in any year.[9] It has been estimated that the reorganization provisions will affect 500,000 participants within the next 20 years, that 10 plans per year will terminate by mass withdrawals, and that 13 plans with 65,000 participants will become subject to the insolvency provisions in the next 20 years.[10] In the five years since MPPAA was enacted, two plans with 12,000 participants have actually become subject to the Act's insolvency provisions.[11]

I. Benefit Reductions in Reorganization

Besides withdrawal liability, reorganization is the chief mechanism installed by MPPAA to prevent or forestall multiemployer plan insolvency.[12] The reorganization rules have not drawn as much attention partly because they are a less dramatic change in the law for

---

[7] 3 ERISA Leg. Hist. 4767 (statement of Sen. Javits).

[8] See Jt. Explanation, *supra*, 126 Cong. Rec. 20189, at 20192 (July 29, 1980), and H.R. Rep. 96-869 (Part II), at 59, reprinted in [1980] U.S. Code Cong. & Ad. News, at 3046.

[9] 48 Fed. Reg. 27092 (June 13, 1983).

[10] See 126 Cong. Rec. 12225 (May 22, 1980) (statement of Rep. Frank Thompson), and 50 Fed. Reg. 31171 (Aug. 1, 1985) (estimate of expected number of terminations by mass withdrawal in PBGC explanatory statement to final regulations on notice after terminations by mass withdrawal).

[11] GAO, "Effects of [MPPAA] on Plan Participants Benefits" (GAO/HRD-85-58), at 33.

[12] ERISA §4241.

employers and partly because they generally only became effective in 1983.[13]

Aptly enough, a plan is in "reorganization" when its "reorganization index" is greater than zero.[14] The reorganization index compares a plan's "vested benefits charge," the amount necessary to amortize unfunded benefits in pay status over 10 years and all other unfunded vested benefits over 25 years, with the plan's net funding charge determined under the regular ERISA minimum funding requirements.[15] If the vested benefits charge is greater than the net funding charge, the reorganization index is greater than zero, and the plan goes into reorganization. Basically, the reorganization index indicates that a plan is facing such heavy outlays for retirees that the contributions required under ERISA's regular funding requirements will not sustain the plan in the long run.[16] A plan may be terminated after reaching reorganization, or it may be terminated and then only later reach reorganization.

When a plan goes into reorganization, contributing employers' contributions must be redetermined under a new "minimum contribution requirement" (or MCR), which is essentially the "vested benefit charge" described before (i.e., the amount necessary to amortize pay status benefits over 10 years and all other vested benefits over 25 years).[17] However, in an equivocal fashion, Congress determined that this new minimum contribution requirement might sometimes result in "inappropriately high and escalating pension costs,"[18] and so it provided an "overburden" credit, and a cap on increases, both of which can reduce the reorganization MCR.[19]

A multiemployer plan is required to notify employers and the

---

[13] See ERISA §4402(e)(3) (the reorganization rules generally took effect only with the expiration of the *last* collective bargaining agreement requiring contributions to the plan that was in effect on Sept. 26, 1980).

[14] ERISA §4241(a).

[15] ERISA §4241(b).

[16] The derivation of this index is not self-evident. But when a plan's vested benefits charge exceeds the plan's net charge under the minimum funding standards, it means that the 10- and 25-year amortization of these unfunded benefits, standing alone, exceeds the plan's normal cost *plus* the 30- and 40-year amortization of all unfunded benefits required under the minimum funding standards. This is a fairly extreme condition. Moreover, ERISA §4241(b)(7) provides that a plan's assets are first to be applied to pay status benefits, thus reducing the 10-year amortization component considerably over the figure that would be obtained if a pro rata allocation of the plan's assets were used.

[17] ERISA §4243.

[18] See Jt. Explanation, *supra*, 126 Cong. Rec., at 20199 (July 29, 1980).

[19] See ERISA §4244 ("overburden" credit) and §4243(d) (cap). A plan is "overburdened" when the number of plan participants in pay status exceeds the average number of active participants in that year and the preceding two years. ERISA §4244(b). If overburdened, the overburden credit, which offsets the new vested benefits charge, is equal to one-half of the average guaranteed benefit of pay status participants, multiplied by the number of pay status participants in excess of active participants. ERISA §4244(d).

The "cap" on the new minimum contribution requirement is the greater of 107% of the net charge to the funding standard account under the regular minimum contribution requirements in the preceding plan year, or the funding standard account net charge without any credits. ERISA §4243(d). For a discussion of the reorganization MCR and both the overburden credit and cap, see A. Fink, "[MPPAA]-The New Funding Requirements and Related Provisions," in *Eleventh Annual Employee Benefits Institute* (PLI 1981), at 65-82.

union, but not individual participants, when it goes into reorganization.[20] It is also required to limit the payout of benefits to annuity form, except for death benefits and lump sum benefits of less than $1,750.[21] More important for most plan participants, a plan in reorganization is permitted to reduce benefits *retroactively* by amendment of the plan. The main reason plan trustees might want to reduce benefits retroactively would be to prevent or forestall the plan's insolvency. But reducing benefits can also reduce the contributions required to be paid by contributing employers under the new reorganization minimum contribution requirement by reducing the plan' vested benefit charge.[22] Whether or not this is a lawful objective, this latter incentive for benefit reductions is limited because, even with an amendment reducing benefits, the new minimum contribution rate can never be less than the greater of the contribution rate calculated without the amendment, or the contribution rate in the last plan year when the amendment was not effective.[23] However, if the contribution base units for a plan, e.g., the hours of service of covered employees, are declining, an employer's contribution rate *per* base unit might otherwise be much higher, so that even with this restriction, benefit reductions can still be in the interest of contributing employers.

The chief limitation on benefit reductions in reorganization is that they can apply only to benefits that are not "eligible for" the PBGC's guarantee of benefits from insolvent multiemployer plans, i.e., benefits accrued under plan amendments in effect for less than five years.[24] Once a benefit or benefit increase has been in effect for five years, it is generally "eligible for" the PBGC's guarantee (although perhaps not fully guaranteed), and thus it may not be reduced in reorganization.[25] Other statutory limitations on benefit reductions in reorganization are:

(1) Six-months notice must be given participants before the first day of the plan year in which the amendment reducing benefits is to be adopted (to give participants an opportunity to plan for the change, and to protest);[26]

(2) The accrued benefits of retirees and inactive workers may not be reduced "to a greater extent proportionally" than the reduction applicable to the accrued benefits of active workers.[27] Moreover, benefits of active workers that are not accrued benefits, such as forfeitable early retirement benefits, and the currently promised rate of future benefit accruals must also be

---

20 ERISA §4242(a)(2).

21 ERISA §4241(c).

22 ERISA §4244A(a)(2).

23 ERISA §4244A(b)(1)(C).

24 ERISA §§4244A(a)(1) and 4022A(b). To be eligible for such a reduction, the amendment also must not have been made before March 27, 1980. ERISA §4244A(a)(1).

25 *Id.*

26 ERISA §4244A(b)(1)(A), and see §4244(b)(2) (information on "rights and remedies" to be included in the notice).

27 ERISA §4244A(b)(1)(B)(i).

reduced "at least to an extent equal" to the reduction in accrued benefits applying to inactive workers and retirees;[28] and

(3) Any reduction that involves a change in the form of benefits or of eligibility requirements for benefits *cannot* apply to pay status participants, or to participants within five years of the plan's normal retirement age.[29]

Finally, but perhaps most important, under ERISA Section 404(a)(1)'s fiduciary standard, any reduction in benefits must be "solely in the interest" of participants and beneficiaries. This means that a plan's trustees must be prepared to show that any reduction in benefits will prevent or substantially forestall insolvency. Significantly, in expressing disapproval of the House provision introducing the possibility of benefit reductions in reorganization, Senator Robert Dole stated that "the PBGC itself informed the Finance Committee that this provision would have no substantial effect on plan solvency."[30] If the effect of the reductions is simply to *forestall* an eventual insolvency, the plan's fiduciaries must weigh the fact that when a reduction in benefits is made in reorganization, the five-year complete exclusion of benefit increases from the PBGC's guarantee dates from that point, rather than what may be a substantially later date at which the plan becomes insolvent or terminates by mass withdrawal.

Another type of benefit reduction that can occur in reorganization (and that is also permitted whether or not a plan is in reorganization) is a retroactive plan amendment under Code Section 412(c)(8) (ERISA Section 302(c)(8)) on a finding by the Secretary of Treasury of "substantial business hardship."[31] Under this benefit reduction authority, a multiemployer plan can be amended to reduce benefits retroactively to the start of the plan year beginning two years before the plan year in which the amendment is adopted, or in other words, almost three years earlier. For a multiemployer plan this requires a finding by the Secretary that 10 percent or more of the employers contributing to the plan are unable to make the otherwise required contributions without "substantial business hardship," and that a funding waiver is unavailable or inadequate.[32]

Under ERISA Sections 4243(a) and 4244A(a)(3), a substantial

---

[28] ERISA §4244A(b)(1)(B)(ii). The application of both these requirements may be elaborated by Treasury regulations. ERISA §4244A(b)(1)(B). And cf. *Winpisinger v. Aurora Corp.*, 456 F.Supp. 559, 1 EBC 2201 (N.D. Ohio 1978) (applying similar rule under the ERISA §404(a)(1) fiduciary standard to forbid creation of undue preferences among employee groups in implementing cost reductions).

[29] ERISA §4244A(b)(1)(B)(iii).

[30] 126 Cong. Rec. 23284 (Aug. 26, 1980).

[31] Substantial business hardship is defined in Code §412(d)(2) (ERISA §302(d)(2)). The statutory delegation of this authority was transferred to the Secretary of Treasury under Reorganization Plan No. 4 of 1978. See 5 U.S.C.A. App. 1.

[32] ERISA §§302(c)(8), and 303(a) and (b). And see ERISA §204(g)(1). A single-employer plan may make such an amendment within 2½ months after the close of the plan year for which it is to have retroactive effect upon similar findings of "substantial business hardship" and that a funding waiver is unavailable or inadequate. However, the 2 year versus 2½ months disparity makes this a much broader provision for multiemployer plans. Effectively, as much as 3 years of

business hardship amendment also reduces the vested benefits charge, and thus, the required employer contributions under the reorganization MCR. However, the notice and other requirements on a benefit reduction in reorganization, e.g., proportionality, do not seem to apply in this case. But the same fiduciary issue posed above applies, requiring that the fiduciaries, in addition to showing substantial business hardship, be able to show that these reductions will prevent insolvency or substantially postpone it, and not merely reduce benefits while also dating the five-year exclusion of benefit increases under the PBGC's guarantee back to an earlier period.

Because of the protest that benefit reductions generate, and for the reasons stated above, it seems unlikely that many plans will reduce benefits in reorganization. Rather, trustees are likely to generally postpone actions reducing benefits until insolvency actually occurs, and MPPAA can be pointed to as *mandating* the reductions.

In this regard, starting with the end of the plan year in which a plan enters reorganization, and every three years thereafter (as long as the plan is still in reorganization), the plan is required to project whether it "may become insolvent" in the succeeding three-year period. If the plan may become insolvent, it is to give notice to the PBGC, the IRS, contributing employers, the union, and participants and beneficiaries.[33] Then, at least two months before the start of the projected insolvency plan year, the plan is required to give notice to all of these parties of the "resource benefit level," in other words, the amount of benefits that it will be able to pay in the first insolvency plan year.[34] Participants and beneficiaries in pay status, or who are expected to reach pay status during the first insolvency year, are required to receive personal notice of the individual monthly benefits the plan expects they will receive during the year.[35] This type of personal notice is also required for plans that terminate by mass withdrawal and that are, or later become, insolvent.[36]

When a plan in reorganization is terminated by the withdrawal of every employer from the plan, the rules on "mass withdrawals," discussed next, override, and the plan is no longer in reorganization.[37]

---

benefits can be retroactively reduced in a multiemployer plan, compared to 14½ months in a single-employer plan.

33 ERISA §§4245(d) and (e).

34 ERISA §§4245(e)(2) and (b)(2).

35 See 29 C.F.R. 2674.4(d) and .5(c).

36 See 29 C.F.R. 2675.7(b).

37 ERISA §4241(d).

II. Benefit Reductions After Mass Withdrawal Terminations

A plan termination by "mass withdrawal" occurs when *every* employer has withdrawn from a plan, or when all employers have otherwise ceased to have an obligation to contribute to a multiemployer plan.[38] A termination by "mass withdrawal" is somewhat of a misnomer. The employers contributing to the plan need not withdraw *en masse.* Rather, a plan is considered terminated by a mass withdrawal whenever *every* employer has withdrawn from the plan, whether the withdrawals occur singly or in bunches, and whether they occur by mutual agreement or by the individual decision of each employer.[39] While it is not absolutely clear from the face of the statute, a termination can also become a termination by "mass withdrawal" when a plan is terminated by an amendment halting all accruals and vesting under the plan, and later *all* employers, some of whom initially may have continued to contribute to the plan, withdraw.[40]

The term mass withdrawal should not be confused with another, almost identical concept in MPPAA. As stated, for a mass withdrawal termination to occur "*every*" employer in the plan must withdraw, or "*all*" employers' obligations to contribute to the plan must have ceased.[41] What is confusing is that MPPAA also contains several provisions covering instances where "substantially all" employers withdraw pursuant to an agreement or arrangement. For example, a *de minimis* rule on withdrawal liability does not apply to an employer who withdraws in a year when "substantially all" of the employers withdraw, nor does it apply to an employer who was a party to an agreement or arrangement under which "substantially all" of the employers withdrew from a plan over a longer period.[42] An agreement is presumed, and, unless a preponderance of the evidence shows otherwise, proven, if substantially all of the employers withdrew within three years.[43] In some of these cases, a "mass withdrawal" termination may not have occurred—because *some* employers are still in the plan. Conversely, a mass withdrawal termination could conceivably occur over a three-year or longer period with no agreement, or with the first or the last employers not having been party to any agreement.[44]

---

[38] ERISA §4041A(a)(2).

[39] See *id.*

[40] See Jt. Explanation, *supra,* 126 Cong. Rec., at 20202 (July 29, 1980).

[41] ERISA §4041A(a)(2) (emphasis added).

[42] ERISA §4209(c).

[43] ERISA §4209(d).

[44] Compare ERISA §4041A(a)(2) with ERISA §§4209(c)(1) and (2) and §4209(d).

Under §4219(c)(1)(D), a 20-year cap on withdrawal liability payments is not available *both* where a mass withdrawal termination occurs and where "substantially all" of the employers have withdrawn pursuant to an agreement—with a presumption of an agreement where substantially all of the employers withdraw within 3 years. Similarly, the grandfathering of the single-employer insurance level under ERISA §4022A(h) for participants in pay status, or within 3 years of the plan's normal retirement age, on July 29, 1980, is not available *both* where a mass withdrawal

For a plan to terminate by mass withdrawal, an agreement will almost invariably have to be reached at some point with the union affiliated with the plan (except in the extremely rare case when *every* employer contributing to the plan happens to have decertified the union or to have relocated or ceased all operations covered by their collective bargaining obligations). For this reason, the PBGC estimates that "no more than" 10 multiemployer plans will terminate by mass withdrawal each year.[45]

A plan that is terminated by mass withdrawal has lost all future sources of contributions that can be adjusted depending on the plan's experience. Instead, the plan only has its existing assets and fixed withdrawal liability claims. On account of these characteristics, MPPAA prescribes special steps to bring benefits into a long-term equilibrium with the plan's assets and withdrawal liability claims, regardless of whether the plan is then in reorganization or is insolvent.[46] As for a plan in reorganization, a plan terminated by mass withdrawal must immediately limit the payment of benefits to payments in annuity form (except for death benefits that were nonforfeitable before the termination and lump sum benefits with a value of less than $1,750).[47] Next, in contrast to the permissive benefit reductions in reorganization, a plan terminated by mass withdrawal *must* reduce benefits within six months after the plan year in which the mass withdrawal occurs to a point where they can be sustained in the long-run.[48] To do this, the plan must value its assets (including withdrawal liability claims) and all nonforfeitable benefits under the plan. If the value of the nonforfeitable benefits is greater than the assets, the plan *must* reduce all benefits not "eligible for" the PBGC's guarantee to the point, or as close to the point as possible, where benefits "eligible for" the PBGC's guarantee can be sustained in the long-run.[49]

Benefits eligible for the PBGC's guarantee, and thus not subject to this mandatory reduction, are more than just those benefits that are guaranteed. The only benefits not eligible for the PBGC's guarantee are nonpension benefits and benefit increases in effect for less than five years.[50] Thus, benefits eligible for the PBGC's guarantee can be considerably more than the final product of the PBGC's guarantee for insolvent multiemployer plans (described in section IV below). As under the reorganization rules, reductions in benefits down to those

---

termination occurs and where substantially all of the employers in a plan withdraw pursuant to an agreement. ERISA §4022A(h)(3).

[45] 50 Fed. Reg. 31171 (Aug. 1, 1985) (explanatory statement to final regulations at 29 C.F.R. Part 2675).

[46] ERISA §§4041A(c) and (d). In addition, a 20-year cap on payments of withdrawal liability, which a plan is permitted to adopt, and a mandatory *de minimis* limitation on withdrawal liability, no longer apply on a termination by mass withdrawal. ERISA §§4219(c)(1)(D) and 4209(c) and (d).

[47] ERISA §§4041A(c)(2) and (f)(1).

[48] ERISA §§4041A(d) and 4281(c).

[49] *Id.*

[50] See ERISA §4281(c)(2)(B), and preamble to Prop. Regs., Part 2675, 51 Fed. Reg. 24536 (July 7, 1986).

eligible for the guarantee must be proportional for all participants' benefits.[51] If insolvency later occurs, a second stage of suspensions of pay status benefits is required which may bring benefits down to the guaranteed level; such suspensions must likewise be in substantially uniform proportions both for participants currently in pay status and for all other participants who enter pay status while the plan is insolvent.[52]

As this suggests, it is possible that reductions in benefits that are not eligible for the PBGC's guarantee will not be enough to bring a plan terminated by mass withdrawal into a long-run balance, but rather will just slow a slide into insolvency. If the plan, usually farther down the road, becomes insolvent, benefits in pay status are then suspended down to the plan's "resource benefit level" for the insolvency year, unless this is lower than the level of guaranteed benefits. The PBGC notes that "typically, when a plan that has terminated by mass withdrawal becomes insolvent, it will continue to be insolvent in subsequent plan years (because there is no on-going [increasable] funding for the plan)."[53] If a plan terminated by mass withdrawal does become insolvent, a MPPAA provision grandfathering the single-employer guaranteed benefit levels for participants who were already in pay status on July 29, 1980, or within three years of pay status on that date, does not apply.[54]

Under PBGC regulations, notice must be given to employees of "mass withdrawal" benefit reductions within 45 days after the adoption of the required plan amendment, which in turn must occur within six months after the end of the plan year in which the termination by mass withdrawal occurs.[55] This requires personal notice to participants who are in pay status or who are "reasonably expected" to enter pay status within the plan year. Notice by posting or publication must be provided all other participants. The notice must contain a "description of the effect of the plan amendment on the benefits to which it applies."[56] If the plan later becomes insolvent, notice is generally required 60 days before the second-stage suspensions of pay status benefits. The notice to pay status participants and those reasonably expected to enter pay status must specify the benefits expected to be paid during the coming insolvency year and must also specify the guarantee level, if this is still lower. Notice to all other participants is not required to be this specific until they approach pay status.[57]

---

[51] ERISA §§4281(c)(2)(C) and 4244A(b)(1)(B).

[52] ERISA §§4281(d)(4) and 4245(c)(2).

[53] Preamble to Prop. Regs., Part 2675, 48 Fed. Reg. 27092 (June 13, 1983).

[54] ERISA §4022A(h)(3).

[55] 29 C.F.R. 2675.2 and ERISA §4281(c)(2)(D).

[56] 29 C.F.R. 2675.2(c) and (e)(2).

[57] 29 C.F.R. 2675.4, .5(b), .6, and .7(b).

III. Multiemployer Plan Partitions and Benefit Reductions

Under ERISA Section 4233, the PBGC, on its own initiative or on the application of a plan sponsor, can "partition" a multiemployer plan if a major contributing employer's bankruptcy under Chapter 11 of the Bankruptcy Code threatens to make the entire plan insolvent. Under ERISA Section 4233(b), the PBGC must find that:

(1) The employer's bankruptcy has or will substantially reduce contributions to the plan;

(2) The plan is likely to become insolvent without partitioning;

(3) Contributions will have to be increased significantly in reorganization; and

(4) A partition will significantly reduce the likelihood that the overall plan will become insolvent.[58]

Notice that a partition is being considered is also required to be given participants whose vested benefits may be affected.[59]

If a plan is partitioned, liabilities for vested benefits attributable to service with the bankrupt employer are transferred to a new partitioned plan whose only sponsor is the bankrupt employer. Only those liabilities for vested benefits "directly attributable to service with the employer" are transferred.[60] Thus, if an employee has worked for other employers under the multiemployer plan, his or her benefits have to be prorated for this purpose. Along with the transfer of attributable liabilities, an "equitable share" of the plan's assets is also transferred to the new partitioned plan; the plan can then only look to the assets of the bankrupt employer, and to the PBGC, for further resources.[61]

A plan created in this manner is considered terminated *ab initio* so that any service with the bankrupt employer is no longer required to augment service for vesting or benefit accruals under the plan.[62] A plan created by partition is also treated as a terminated *multiemployer* plan for insurance purposes if it is initially or later becomes insolvent, even though after the partition there is just a single employer sponsoring it.[63] The mass withdrawal termination rules for immediate reductions in benefits down to benefits eligible for the multiemployer guarantee must also be immediately applied, unless and until the partitioned plan becomes insolvent and suspensions of pay status benefits down to the "resource benefit level," or the PBGC guaranteed benefit level, if

---

58 ERISA §§4233(b)(1)-(4).

59 ERISA §4233(b).

60 ERISA §4233(d).

61 ERISA §§4233(d) and (e)(2).

62 ERISA §4233(e) and ERISA §§203(b)(1)(G)(ii) and 204(b)(3)(A).

63 ERISA §4233(e).

higher, are required.[64] Because of the criteria for partitioning, a plan created by partition will almost invariably be insolvent at the start, or will become insolvent within a short period after the partition—unless the bankrupt employer is successfully reorganized under Chapter 11.

The justification for partitioning is to cut the larger plan's losses and thus to save the benefits of a greater number of participants from reduction and suspension. But to achieve this greater good, partitioning places an inordinate burden on the employees who happened to have substantial service with the bankrupt employer.[65] Because of this, the findings the PBGC is required to make before partitioning a plan may be subject to close scrutiny. As with involuntary terminations of single-employer plans, the courts may protect participants against overly precipitous use of the partition power.[66]

A related feature of the multiemployer plan insurance program is the PBGC's retention of authority under ERISA Section 4042 to involuntarily terminate an entire multiemployer plan, as it may involuntarily terminate a single-employer plan. The PBGC may do this when a multiemployer plan is not meeting the minimum funding requirements, when it will be unable to pay benefits when due, when the long-run loss to the corporation may increase unreasonably unless the plan is terminated, or when another reportable event described in Section 4043(b)(7) has occurred.[67] On approval of the involuntary termination by a U.S. district court, or by agreement with the plan's administrator, the PBGC may also have itself or another party appointed as the plan's trustee.[68]

The effect of an involuntary termination of a multiemployer plan is, however, no longer as drastic as under the single-employer insurance program. While an involuntary termination stops new vesting and benefit accruals under the plan, it does not stop the contributing employers' obligation to continue funding existing benefit liabilities, nor does it result in any immediate reductions or suspensions in benefits—unless the plan is otherwise in reorganization or insolvent. The chief reasons for the action would seem to be (1) to stop continued accruals under a plan that is already heading rapidly for insolvency, and (2) to substitute the PBGC for trustees who are mismanaging a deteriorating plan. With regard to the latter, the PBGC has separate authority to petition a court to have itself, or another party, appointed trustee over a multiemployer plan that is in reorganization, without necessarily involuntarily terminating the plan, or it may petition to have itself, or another party, appointed trustee over a plan that has already been

---

64 ERISA §4233(e)(2).

65 See Jt. Explanation, *supra*, 126 Cong. Rec., at 20199 (July 29, 1980) (partition authority to be used only when "it is very clear that the failure to partition will result in the insolvency of the multiemployer plan").

66 See ch. 12, sec. II.A.3, on involuntary single-employer plan terminations.

67 ERISA §4042(a).

68 ERISA §4042(b)(1).

terminated by mass withdrawal.[69] If the PBGC has occasion to use the involuntary termination authority after MPPAA for the first reason alone, courts should protect plan participants against overly cautious, i.e., precipitous, use of the authority.[70]

IV. Insolvency and PBGC Benefit Guarantees

The bottom line guarantee for participants in multiemployer plans is the PBGC's benefit insurance on plan insolvency. This guarantee is, however, generally lower than the guarantee of benefits from terminated single-employer plans.[71] A multiemployer plan is insolvent when its "available resources," basically all of its marketable assets, are not sufficient to pay pay-status benefits as they come due during a plan year.[72] Obviously, a plan is in dire financial straits when *all* of its marketable assets are not enough to pay just the benefits coming due in one plan year.

When a plan is insolvent, benefits in pay status must be reduced to the point where the plan's marketable assets will be sufficient to pay the benefits due in that plan year.[73] These reductions, or more technically "suspensions," must apply in "substantially uniform proportions" to the benefits of all persons in pay status.[74] If the suspensions necessary to achieve balance with the plan's marketable assets would reduce benefits below the guarantee level, the PBGC provides "financial assistance" to the plan to maintain benefits at the guarantee level (or it may petition to take over the plan itself under its involuntary termination authority and provide the benefits directly).[75]

An insolvent plan may at first have enough marketable resources to pay reduced benefits at levels slightly above the guarantee (and hence, also without any financial assistance). As suggested, the benefits that are not paid in insolvency are technically "suspended," and may be prospectively restored, in whole or in part, if the plan's financial status later improves.[76] But unless an industry, or union, is in only a temporary decline, pay status benefits are likely to be "suspended" down to the guarantee level in the next year or two, if they are not already at that level in the first year of insolvency, and are then likely to remain permanently suspended at that level as all other vested participants in the plan gradually come into pay status.

---

[69] ERISA §4042(b)(2)(B).

[70] See ch. 12, sec. II.A.3, on judicial review of involuntary termination dates.

[71] Compare ch. 12, sec. VI.

[72] ERISA §§4245(b)(1) and (3).

[73] ERISA §4245(a).

[74] ERISA §4245(c)(2). The Secretary of Treasury is authorized to issue regulations allowing variances from the requirement that the suspensions be in "substantially uniform proportions," based on such factors as different contribution rates from different employers. *Id.*

[75] ERISA §§4245(a) and (f), 4261, 4022A, 4061, and 4042.

[76] See ERISA §§4245(c)(4) and (5). See also ERISA §4245(c)(6).

An insolvent plan can continue to have some new resources in addition to the financial assistance provided by the PBGC. Employers who have already withdrawn from the plan must continue to make their quarterly annual withdrawal liability payments to the insolvent plan. Employers who have not withdrawn must continue to pay the "reorganization" minimum contribution requirements, described above, although some protection against further increases in their contribution obligations due to continuing declines in an insolvent plan's contribution base is provided.[77] It seems likely that once insolvency occurs, or appears imminent, all employers who are still in the plan will weigh the financial benefits of withdrawing versus continuing to pay this reorganization MCR.[78] If every employer later withdraws, the plan is terminated by mass withdrawal, as discussed in section II above.

As with the PBGC's single-employer benefit guarantee, the multiemployer benefit guarantee on plan insolvency first excludes:

(1) Benefits that are not "pension" benefits;

(2) Benefits that are not "nonforfeitable," or that only became nonforfeitable on the plan's termination (assuming the plan has been or will be terminated); and

(3) Benefits that a participant is not "entitled" to before any termination.[79]

After these exclusions, the similarity with the single-employer benefit guarantee largely ends. In contrast to the phase-in of insurance on benefit increases made within five years of the termination of a single-employer plan, the multiemployer program provides *no* insurance on any benefit increases made by plan amendment within five years of the *earlier* of (a) the first year of plan insolvency, (b) the first year in which benefits were reduced in reorganization, or (c) the date of the termination of the plan if it is terminated by mass withdrawal.[80]

The insurance on the remaining benefits is also more limited than for single-employer plans. For multiemployer plans, the PBGC's insurance is capped at 100 percent of the first $5 per month of benefits per year of credited service, and 75 percent of the next $15 per month per year of credited service.[81] No insurance is provided on any benefits

---

[77] ERISA §4243(c)(2)(B).

[78] In some cases, the protection in insolvency for employers against future increases in contribution obligations from a declining contribution base could make staying in the plan less costly than paying withdrawal liability. Certain limitations on withdrawal liability, namely, the 20-year cap that some plans provide and the *de minimis* rule for small amounts of withdrawal liability, no longer apply if "substantially all" of the employers withdraw.

[79] ERISA §4022A(a), and see ch. 12, sec. VI.A.

[80] ERISA §§4022A(b)(1)(A) and (B). One compensatory feature is that the date for calculating the 5-year exclusion may generally be *later* than the date used in calculating the 5-year phase-in for a voluntarily terminated single-employer plan. Under MPPAA, a plan's financial status must decline substantially before reorganization or insolvency will occur. This decline may take a number of years, and frequently no benefit increases will have occurred in the final 5-year period.

[81] ERISA §4022A(c)(1). For plans that did not meet the Internal Revenue Code's pre-ERISA funding standards, or that have not had an asset to benefit payment ratio of 8 to 1 for three consecutive years after ERISA was enacted, the 75% limit on benefits between $5 and $20 per

promised under a plan that exceed $20 per month per year of credited service.[82] And unlike the single-employer insured benefit ceiling, *no* provision is made for adjustment of these set dollar figures for increases in the Social Security wage base or any other index.[83] These benefit levels are, however, *not* adjusted down if a plan provides unreduced early retirement benefits or subsidized joint and survivor's benefits. Thus, if a plan provides $20 per month benefits at age 65 and provides the same dollar benefits for participants with 25 years of service who are age 55, with a 100 percent survivor's benefit, the same $16.25 per month per year of credited service insurance limit applies.[84]

Technically, the PBGC's guaranteed benefit ceiling also applies to benefits from insolvent multiemployer plans.[85] But with an effective guarantee limitation of $16.25 per month per year of credited service ($5 × 100% + $15 × 75%), a participant would have to have over 100 years of credited service before the $1,875.95 per month benefit ceiling existing in 1987 would come into play.[86]

To illustrate what the multiemployer guarantees mean, if a multiemployer plan offering the same $22.00 per month per year of credited service benefit as the Braniff-Teamsters' single-employer plan (described in Chapter 12, section VI.B) became insolvent, a participant with 20 years of credited service would only be guaranteed, at maximum, benefits of $16.25 per month per year of credited service, for a total benefit of $325.00 per month—instead of the plan's promised $440 per month. If the $22.00 per month benefit level was the result of a benefit increase (or increases) which was adopted in the five years before the *earlier* of a reorganization year in which benefits were reduced, insolvency, or a termination by mass withdrawal, the guarantee could be still lower because of the five-year exclusion. Assuming that the $22.00 per month benefit was the result of an increase from $18.00

month is lowered to 65%. ERISA §§4022A(c)(2), (5), and (6). Plans should be able to determine now whether the 75% limit would apply in the event of insolvency. If the 65% limit would apply currently, this might still be reversed if the asset to benefit payment ratio for the plan later improves.

A slight bright spot for some participants in the PBGC guarantee is that the monthly benefits used in calculating the guaranteed amount are determined without regard to any cancellation of past service credits that occurred on their employer's withdrawal from the plan. See ch. 4, sec. III.C.6, on past service cancellations. But if the participant's entire benefit, determined with the cancellation, is lower than the guaranteed benefits determined without it, the lower of the two dollar amounts controls. ERISA §§4022A(c)(3)(A)(ii) and (c)(4)(C), and 4022A(d).

[82] ERISA §4022A(c)(1).

[83] The dollar amounts can also be reduced without an act of Congress if the PBGC determines that a premium increase is necessary to maintain the current guarantee level, and Congress rejects or takes no action on the increase. The guarantee levels are then to be reduced to the level the PBGC determines is supportable under the existing premium. ERISA §4022A(f)(2).

The flip-side is that if experience shows that Congress set the guarantee level too low given existing premiums, an increase in the guarantee may be made. The PBGC is to study whether the guarantee level can be increased without increasing premiums and report to Congress in September 1985, and every 5 years thereafter. ERISA §§4022A(f)(1) and (3).

[84] See ERISA §4022A(c)(1)(3).

[85] See ERISA §4022B(a).

[86] See 13 BNA Pens. Rep. 1976 (Nov. 24, 1986) (reporting PBGC announcement of its 1987 single-employer insured benefit ceiling). The only case in which this dollar ceiling might apply is to a participant who is receiving insured benefits from a second insolvent multiemployer plan or a terminated single-employer plan.

per month three years before insolvency, with no earlier increases within the five-year period, the $4.00 per month increase would not be eligible for insurance, and the $18.00 per month benefit would be reduced under the formula to $14.75 per month ((100% × $5) + (75% × the remaining $13.00))—yielding a guaranteed benefit of $295 per month for a 20-year participant. In an extreme case, where a series of sharp benefit increases had become effective in the five years before the earlier of the first plan year in which benefits were reduced in reorganization, insolvency, or the date of a termination by mass withdrawal, the insurance could be still lower. The only benefit that was in effect under the Braniff-Teamsters' plan for more than five years was $8.35 per month. If this were the case for a multiemployer plan, that $8.35 benefit alone would then be eligible for insurance, and the $8.35 would be further reduced to $7.51 per month ((100% × $5) + (75% × $3.35)). This would leave a 20-year participant with an insured benefit of $150 per month, instead of the $440 per month this hypothetical plan was promising. It seems unlikely that many plans that become insolvent will have had a series of sharp benefit increases like this in the five years before insolvency, but it is possible that such a series of increases could have occurred in the five years before an *earlier* termination by mass withdrawal, or a reorganization in which benefits were reduced.[87]

A grandfather clause in MPPAA preserves the PBGC's benefit guarantee at the single-employer guarantee levels *if* a participant's benefits were in pay status on July 29, 1980, *or* if the participant had a nonforfeitable benefit and was within 36 months of the plan's normal retirement age on that date.[88] The grandfather rule does not apply if the plan terminates by a "mass withdrawal" of every employer, or if "substantially all" of the employers withdraw from the plan pursuant to an agreement or arrangement to withdraw.[89]

Under ERISA Section 4022A(g)(2), the PBGC must offer an elective supplemental program of insurance for benefits above the multiemployer guarantee level. However, coverage under the supplemental program is only available to plans that have a ratio of assets to pay status benefits of at least 15 to 1 when the application for supplemental

---

[87] Presumably, however, a plan in poor-enough financial condition to be approaching reorganization, insolvency, or the point at which a mass withdrawal may be an attractive option for contributing employers, will *generally* have refrained from instituting sharp benefit increases like those under the Braniff-Teamsters plan within the 5-year period.

[88] ERISA §§4022A(h)(1) and (2). A plan's "normal retirement age" may be lower than age 65. See, e.g., *Nichols v. Trustees of Asbestos Workers Pension Plan,* 1 EBC 1868 (D.D.C. 1979) (unless a "normal retirement age" is identified as such in the plan, the normal retirement age may be the *earliest* age at which benefits are available on an unreduced basis; in *Nichols,* this was age 65 *or* any earlier age when the participant had 25 years of service). See also ch. 5, sec. I.A.

[89] ERISA §4022A(h)(3). Grandfathering of the single-employer insurance levels also expires in the plan year after an insolvent plan terminates by mass withdrawal or the year after substantially all of the employers withdraw pursuant to an agreement or arrangement to withdraw—if either occurs after the plan first becomes insolvent.

coverage is made. The supplemental insurance also requires an additional insurance premium.[90] To ameliorate extreme hardship, the PBGC has discretion, apart from this supplemental program, to insure additional benefits.[91]

Even though a multiemployer plan "termination" is no longer the "insurable event," the plan termination date is still significant for active employees in insolvent plans. By itself, "insolvency" does not stop the service of active employees whose employers have *not* withdrawn from an insolvent plan from counting toward vesting and for additional benefit accruals. Benefit accruals remain at the level set under the terms of the plan (unless the rate for benefit accruals has been reduced by plan amendment in reorganization), even though receipt of the full amount may be unlikely to ever occur because of the suspensions of pay status benefits required by the plan's insolvency.

Continued credits for vesting and accruals only stop when the plan is terminated.[92] If this does not occur before, or shortly after, a plan becomes insolvent, and the long-run loss to the PBGC appears likely to increase, the PBGC could involuntarily terminate the plan. But until it does so (and unless a retroactive termination date is used when it does), vesting and benefit accrual credits for active employees whose employers have not withdrawn continue to be required.[93]

V. Voluntary Terminations by Plan Amendment

Under MPPAA, voluntary terminations of multiemployer plans can still occur apart from any financial distress of the plan or its sponsoring employers simply by amendment, including an amendment converting the plan to a defined contribution plan.[94] But after MPPAA, a voluntary termination is like a "freeze" of a single-employer plan. As in a freeze, all future benefit accruals under the plan stop, but the employers' obligation to fund the plan's existing unfunded liabilities continues, through contributions or through the payment of withdrawal liability, until the plan is either "fully funded," or until a reorganization, insolvency, or mass withdrawal alters the employers' contribution obligations. Unlike a freeze of a single-employer plan,

---

[90] ERISA §§4022A(g)(2) and (3), and see Prop. Regs. Parts 2691-2695, 48 Fed. Reg. 4632 (Feb. 1, 1983).

[91] ERISA §4022A(g)(1).

[92] A terminated plan is defined in ERISA §4041A(a)(1) as one which provides that service no longer counts for any purpose. On vesting credit, see also ERISA §§203(b)(1)(G)(i) and (ii), as added by MPPAA. Benefits accruals may be halted if the employers are no longer "maintaining" the plan. See ERISA §§204(b)(3)(A) and 202(b)(1).

[93] See ERISA §4042(a) (on the PBGC's involuntary termination authority) and §203(b)(1)(G)(ii) (on the effect of a voluntary or involuntary termination on crediting service for vesting).

[94] ERISA §§4041A(a)(1) and (3).

however, a multiemployer plan termination also halts all new years of service for vesting.[95]

The term "fully funded" is used in ERISA Section 4041A(e) to mark the point when employers' contribution obligations, or obligations to pay withdrawal liability, end after a voluntary termination. But fully funded is not defined in Title IV. However, a special Code provision, added by MPPAA, provides that in determining the full funding limitation for a multiemployer plan, the accrued liability of the plan does "not include benefits which are not nonforfeitable under the plan after the termination of the plan (taking into consideration Section 411(d)(3) [which provides for nonforfeitability under the plan on a termination or partial termination of the plan])."[96] What this seems to mean is that a plan cannot be fully funded until benefits that become nonforfeitable on termination, as well as those that were nonforfeitable prior to the termination, are funded. Until a voluntarily terminated plan is "fully funded" in this manner, the employers' obligation to make contributions, or to pay withdrawal liability continues, and the plan must continue to pay benefits in full, including non-basic benefits—unless and until reorganization, insolvency, or a mass withdrawal intervenes.

The date of voluntary termination of a multiemployer plan can be crucial, as it is for single-employer plans, in determining the amount of a participant's benefits, and whether the participant is vested other than solely on account of the plan's termination. However, in contrast to the PBGC's pre-SEPPAA power to approve or withhold approval of voluntary single-employer termination dates (subject to judicial resolution if no agreement was reached), the termination date of a multiemployer plan is fixed by statute. ERISA Section 4041A(b)(1) provides that the termination date is the later of the date of adoption or effectiveness of an amendment that (1) provides that participants will receive no credit under the plan for any purpose for service with any employer, or (2) converts the plan to a defined contribution plan. For a plan terminated by mass withdrawal, the termination date is the earlier of (1) the date on which the last employer withdraws from the plan or (2) the first day of the plan year for which no employer contributions are required. Issues such as the number of participants who would vest if the multiemployer termination date was set slightly later are thus not relevant. However, compliance with the PBGC's notice requirements for a plan termination, and compliance with the plan's own requirements for a termination, may still be examined.[97]

If a voluntarily terminated multiemployer plan has excess assets

---

95 See n. 92 above.

96 Code §412(b)(7)(E).

97 See 29 C.F.R. Part 2673, and ch. 12, sec. I.F, on procedural requirements under a plan's terms for a single-employer plan termination.

on termination, no reversion of excess assets appears to be permitted under Section 302(c)(5) of the Labor Management Relations Act.[98]

VI. Additional Participant Claims

When benefits are permissibly or mandatorily reduced or suspended under MPPAA, additional claims for benefits, like those discussed previously for single-employer plans, can still be brought by participants based on higher contractual and quasi-contractual obligations to pay promised benefits, or to collect or obtain redress for unpaid contributions, underfunding, and fiduciary violations.

A. Contractual Promises of Benefits

Contractual claims based on the contributing employers' failure to disclaim liability beyond a multiemployer plan's assets are rare in the multiemployer area—because the contribution agreement generally expressly limits the employer's contractual liability.[99] But quasi-contractual obligations may still arise. In *Hurd v. Hutnik,* contributing employers were liable beyond their contribution obligations to a multiemployer plan because of the consistency of representations in the plan, and in plan booklets, that retirees would receive "lifetime pensions."[100] In *Hurd,* the court found a contractual limitation on employer liability, but held that giving it effect would negate the "clear and consistent" representations of "lifetime" benefits on which retirees had justifiably relied, without adequate notice of the limitation.[101]

After MPPAA, similar issues can arise when a plan, or its summary plan description, does not adequately disclose the limitations on participants' benefits if their plan enters reorganization, becomes insolvent, or terminates by mass withdrawal. The guarantee limitations in MPPAA and the possibility of earlier benefit reductions are substantial limitations on the benefits offered by a multiemployer plan. An

---

[98] Section 302(c)(5) of the LMRA provides that contributions must be made to a jointly administered trust for the sole and exclusive benefit of employees. Unlike ERISA, it provides no exception to this commitment under which a plan may "provide[ ] for" excess plan assets to revert to employers. But see *Struble v. New Jersey Brewery Employees' Welfare Fund,* 732 F.2d 325, 5 EBC 1676 (3d Cir. 1984) (sharply questioning whether employer-appointed trustees acted in breach of fiduciary duty in voting to give an excess of assets existing at the termination of a health plan to employers, but not suggesting that §302(c)(5) establishes an absolute bar to such a reversion).

[99] See, e.g., *Connolly v. PBGC,* 581 F.2d 729, 1 EBC 1410 (9th Cir. 1978), *cert. denied,* 440 U.S. 935 (1979).

[100] 419 F.Supp. 630, 1 EBC 1382 (D.N.J. 1976). And see *Alderney Dairy Co. v. Hawthorn Mellody, Inc.*, 643 F.2d 113, 2 EBC 1049 (3d Cir. 1981) (concerning whether a successor employer, or its predecessor, was liable under the settlement which followed the *Hurd v. Hutnik* decision).

[101] 1 EBC at 1393 and 1404.

accurate description in the SPD of these limitations is therefore required under ERISA Section 102 and 29 C.F.R. 2520.102-3(d) as "circumstances which may result in ... denial or loss of benefits." The limitations, moreover, must not be "minimized, rendered obscure or otherwise made to appear unimportant."[102] The Department of Labor's position on this is made clear by a technical release, in which the Department stated that an SPD must describe the plan's provisions on termination, and those governing the payment of benefits on termination, in addition to describing the PBGC's guarantee limitations.[103] For multiemployer plans, the benefit reductions and suspensions that can take place in insolvency, reorganization, or after a mass withdrawal must also be considered "circumstances" limiting benefits that must be described. If participants do not receive this explanation, and as a result maintain reasonable and justifiable expectations that their benefits will not be reduced or suspended except in the circumstances that are described in their booklets, "appropriate equitable relief" may be available under ERISA Section 502(a)(3) for the disclosure violation.

The Department of Labor has recognized that its model statement for inclusion in SPDs on the PBGC's insurance at 29 C.F.R. 2520.102-3(m)(3) "no longer provides an accurate statement of the PBGC guaranty program" for multiemployer plans.[104] But to date it has not issued a revision. A model statement that was under consideration would have described the five-year exclusion of benefit increases, but not the $5 per month and 75 percent limitations on the multiemployer guarantee, or the circumstances which can lead to a reduction or suspension just above the guarantee level.[105] The position the Department of Labor takes, or fails to take, through a model statement is, however, not dispositive of whether a violation of the SPD requirements occurs. The Department's regulations already separately require an accurate statement in the SPD of the PBGC's insurance limitations and of circumstances that can limit benefits above those levels.[106] The issue when such limits on a plan's benefits are not disclosed is whether, as the *Hurd v. Hutnik* court stated, "equity will ... permit reasonable and justified expectations of ... employees, knowingly wielded by the employers for whom they labored for so many years, to be frustrated." [107]

---

[102] 29 C.F.R. 2520.102-2(b).

[103] ERISA Technical Release No. 84-1 (May 4, 1984), reprinted in 11 BNA Pens. Rep. 653-54 (May 14, 1984).

[104] Letter from Jeffrey N. Clayton, Administrator, Dept. of Labor Pension and Welfare Benefit Programs, to Robert E. Nagle, Executive Director, Pension Benefit Guaranty Corporation, dated Jan. 25, 1982.

[105] *Id.* But see 29 C.F.R. 2674.3(b)(5) (describing both in a model notice of the PBGC's insurance limitations to be given participants in insolvent plans).

[106] 29 C.F.R. 2520.102-3(l) and (m)(2).

[107] *Hurd v. Hudnik, supra,* 1 EBC at 1403.

B. Underfunding, Unpaid Contributions, and Fiduciary Violations

Other participant claims discussed in the single-employer plan termination chapter are also relevant to multiemployer plans. These include claims for underfunding because of unreasonable actuarial assumptions, claims for delinquent contributions (or delinquent withdrawal liability), and claims based on fiduciary violations in investments of the plan's assets. These additional claims, even if successful, may in many cases only postpone a multiemployer plan's insolvency by a matter of days or months, and thus only postpone reductions or suspensions down to the guarantee level by the same periods. But receiving higher benefits for this time, while not optimal, may be significant for retired participants.

As in single-employer plans, a multiemployer plan's funding method is likely to be considered reasonable if it is one of those described in ERISA's minimum funding standards. However, the reasonableness of the actuarial assumptions used under the method may be subject to question. In addition to the interest rate, retirement age, turnover, and mortality assumptions, another critical assumption in multiemployer plans is the number of contribution base units, e.g., hours of service, expected to be rendered under the plan. If there is an unreasonable overestimation of the plan's contribution base units, the contribution rate may be unreasonably low, and thus violative of minimum funding standards.[108]

Delinquent contributions are a common problem among multiemployer plans. In determining whether trustees have fulfilled their fiduciary duties to collect such contributions, courts focus on whether the plan has a systematic auditing procedure for reviewing the number of contribution base units reported by an employer as having been rendered under a plan, and a systematic collection procedure.[109] Failure to collect delinquent contributions can constitute a "prohibited transaction" under ERISA, or in other words, a *per se* fiduciary violation, when the lack of "systematic, reasonable, and diligent efforts" to collect delinquent contributions is found to constitute an effective "extension of credit" to a prohibited party-in-interest to the plan, namely, the

---

[108] The GAO reports that many multiemployer plans lack even basic participant data, e.g., on age and length of service, necessary to perform accurate actuarial valuations. See GAO, "Incomplete Participant Data Affect Reliability of Values Placed by Actuaries on Multiemployer Pension Plans" (GAO/HRD-84-38 September 6, 1984).

[109] See, e.g., *Nedd v. UMWA*, 556 F.2d 190 (3d Cir. 1977), *remanded sub nom. Ambromovage v. UMW*, 3 EBC 1873 (M.D. Pa. 1982), *aff'd*, 726 F.2d 972, 5 EBC 1042 (3d Cir. 1984) (failure to collect delinquent contributions violated fiduciary duties union assumed with its dominance of the fund, but liability set off by loans from union to the plan); *Nichols v. Trustees of Asbestos Workers Pension Plan*, 3 EBC 1726 (D.D.C. 1982) (failure to develop adequate system for determining and collecting payments due plan under reciprocity agreements violates ERISA §404(a)(1)).

employer.[110] After MPPAA, withdrawal liability is another type of contribution obligation that plans must systematically attempt to collect.[111]

Fiduciary violations may, of course, also have occurred in investments or in administrative expenditures from a multiemployer plan's assets.

By the time a plan winds down to a point when benefit reductions in reorganization, or suspensions in insolvency, take place, some of these additional claims may be foreclosed by ERISA's statute of limitations. ERISA contains no general statute of limitations for Title I violations, but for fiduciary violations, the statute of limitations is the *earlier* of six years after the last act which constituted a violation, or three years after the plaintiff had actual knowledge of the violation, or else could have obtained knowledge of the violation from a report filed with the Secretary of Labor.[112] Even if a claim for underfunding or a fiduciary violation is not foreclosed by a limitations period, if the claim is only brought after reductions in reorganization or suspensions in insolvency take place, recourse against contributing employers or other parties who profited from the violations, e.g., from the noncollection of delinquent contributions, may be difficult simply because many employers will have gone out of business. If relief is effectively limited to persons who are fiduciaries, limitations in their liability insurance and their inability to otherwise satisfy substantial personal judgments may come into play as a nonstatutory type of limitations period.

---

[110] See Prohibited Transaction Exemption ("PTE") 76-1, 41 Fed. Reg. 12740 (March 26, 1976). And see *Marshall v. Wilson,* C.A. No. 3-76-373 (E.D. Tenn. 1976) (Department of Labor complaint alleging ERISA §404(a)(1) violation for systematic failure to collect delinquent contributions according to the standards established in PTE 76-1; consent order entered before trial).

[111] Other issues on withdrawal liability involve the reasons for a plan's adoption of permissive relief provisions for withdrawal liability. If a plan adopts one of MPPAA's permissive relief provisions (for example, the higher *de minimis* limitation or the 20-year cap on withdrawal liability payments) a Title I fiduciary action may concern whether the action was "solely in the interest" of participants. ERISA §4219, as amended by MPPAA, provides that it is not a prohibited transaction to act or withhold action as *permitted* by MPPAA's withdrawal provisions. But this merely establishes that permissive actions are not *per se* fiduciary violations. It does not address the overriding "solely in the interest" and "exclusive purpose" standards for fiduciaries. In other instances, such as the use of an unreasonably high interest assumption for computing withdrawal liability, Title I fiduciary and MPPAA actions may both be present.

In cases involving permissive plan rules and procedures on withdrawal liability, the chief issue may be how receptive courts are to "trickle-down" arguments, e.g., that a higher *de minimis* limitation discourages existing contributors from taking more drastic action to reduce withdrawal liability, despite the clear loss in plan assets from the rule. Cf. *Marshall v. Mercer,* 4 EBC 1523 (N.D. Tex. 1983), *rev'd and remanded on other issues,* 747 F.2d 304, 5 EBC 2512 (5th Cir. 1984) (fear of forcing employer into bankruptcy by collecting contributions not sufficient, "interest" must serve the plan participants' interests).

[112] ERISA §413, and see generally ch. 14, sec. II.D.

14

Claims Procedures, Causes of Action, and Disclosure to Participants

I. Procedures for Claiming Benefits Promised Under a Plan's Terms

Every employee benefit plan must contain a procedure for handling claims for benefits offered under the terms of the plan. ERISA Section 503 provides:

> "In accordance with regulations of the Secretary of Labor, every employee benefit plan shall—
>
> "(1) provide adequate notice in writing to any participant or beneficiary whose claim for benefits under the plan has been denied, setting forth the specific reasons for such denial, written in a manner calculated to be understood by the participant, and
>
> "(2) afford a reasonable opportunity to any participant whose claim for benefits has been denied for a full and fair review by the appropriate named fiduciary of the decision denying the claim."[1]

For a claims procedure to be "reasonable" under ERISA Section 503, the Department of Labor's regulations provide that it must be described in the plan's summary plan description. As an overall constraint, the procedure also must not "contain any provision," *or* be "administered in a manner," that "unduly inhibits or hampers the initiation or processing of claims."[2] For a collectively bargained single-employer plan that is *not* jointly administered, the collective bargaining agreement's grievance and arbitration procedure constitutes a "reasonable" claims procedure, so long as the procedure is specifically described in the summary plan description as applying to claims for

[1] 29 U.S.C. §1133.

[2] 29 C.F.R. 2560.503-1(b)(1).

benefits under the terms of the plan and the procedure does not "contain any provision," or is not "administered in a manner," which "unduly inhibits or hampers the initiation or processing of claims."[3]

For all other types of plans (i.e., nonunion and jointly administered Taft-Hartley plans—generally, multiemployer plans), the Department of Labor's regulations outline more detailed standards for a "reasonable" claims procedure. Under the regulations, once a claim for benefits is filed, a plan must make an initial determination of the claim within 90 days after the day the claim is filed, with a possible extension for "special circumstances" (which must be explained to the claimant) of another 90 days.[4] When a claim for benefits is denied, the plan administrator must explain the specific reasons for the denial *in writing*, in a manner calculated to be understood by the participant, with specific references to the plan rules on which the denial is based. If additional information could support, or perfect, a claim, the denial letter must describe the type of material or information needed and explain why it is necessary. The denial letter must also describe the procedure for obtaining review of the initial determination.[5]

A participant must be able to obtain a "full and fair" review of a denied claim from a "named fiduciary" of the plan. This may, however, be the same plan administrator, or committee, who denied the claim initially.[6] The plan must provide the participant with at least 60 days to request this review and to submit additional material or information to support the denied claim. The participant, or an authorized representative of the participant, must be allowed to review "pertinent documents," such as plan records and individual worksheets, to prepare the claim for review.[7]

The Department of Labor's regulations do not require an oral hearing on review, but they also do not rule out the possibility that an oral hearing may be required in certain circumstances (e.g., where credibility is an issue).[8] Oral hearings, and a reviewable record covering the hearing, were required before ERISA in certain circumstances as "elemental requirements of fairness."[9] If an opportunity for an oral

---

[3] 29 C.F.R. 2560.503-1(b)(2).

[4] 29 C.F.R. 2560.503-1(e).

[5] 29 C.F.R. 2560.503-1(f).

[6] See *Denton v. First Nat'l Bank of Waco*, 765 F.2d 1295, 6 EBC 1980, *reh. denied*, 772 F.2d 904 (5th Cir. 1985); *Brown v. Retirement Committee of Briggs & Stratton*, 797 F.2d 521 (7th Cir. 1986).

[7] 29 C.F.R. 2560.503-1(g)(1)(ii). See also *Lee v. Dayton Power & Light Co.*, 604 F.Supp. 987 (S.D. Ohio 1985) (plan's duty to allow inspection or copying extends to manuals and tables used in determining Social Security amounts for offsets), and Prop. Regs. 29 C.F.R. 2530.209-2(f) and -3(f).

[8] See 29 C.F.R. 2560.503-1(g)(1)(iii) and ch. 7, sec. III.B.1.

[9] *Sturgill v. Lewis*, 372 F.2d 400 (D.C. Cir. 1966). See also R. Thomas, "Due Process, Hearings, and Pension and Welfare Claims Denials Under ERISA," 28 Lab. L.J. 276 (1977), citing *Russell v. Princeton Laboratories*, 231 A.2d 800 (N.J. Sup. Ct. 1967); *Schillinger v. McCory*, 55 Lab. Cas. ¶12,041 (N.Y. Sup.Ct. 1967); and *Weber v. Bell Telephone Co.*, 203 A.2d 554 (Pa. Super.Ct. 1964), as requiring oral hearings to support the substantial evidence test. But see *Lugo v. Employees Retirement Fund*, 366 F.Supp. 99 (E.D.N.Y. 1974), *aff'd*, 529 F.2d 251 (2d Cir.), *cert. denied*, 429 U.S. 826 (1976) (oral hearing not required when participant has only a "weak" claim).

hearing is not provided when it is appropriate, a court may send the claim back to the plan with an order that an oral hearing be held. Alternatively, the lack of an oral hearing, and a reviewable record, could lead a court to take a closer look at a plan's findings of fact, or application of the terms of the plan to the facts, than under the usual "arbitrary and capricious" and "substantial evidence" tests for review.[10]

A final decision on a denied claim must be rendered by the plan's named fiduciary within 60 days of the request for review, unless special circumstances require another 60 days. However, if a plan committee or board of trustees with review authority only meets quarterly, the decision may be made at the next quarterly meeting, or if an appeal is received less than 30 days before that meeting, at the following quarterly meeting.[11]

As with an initial decision on a claim, a decision on review of a denied claim must be in writing, and must be written in a manner calculated to be understood by the participant. If the claim has been denied on review, the letter must include the specific reasons for the decision and specific references to the plan rules on which it is based.[12] In *Richardson v. Central States Pension Fund*, the Eighth Circuit elaborated on the need for specific reasons for a decision, rather than "bald-faced" conclusions, stating that the purpose of the requirement is to help the claimant prepare for further administrative review, if available, as well as for possible resort to the federal or state courts, *and* also to help the plan "build a body of precedent that will ultimately bring about a form of consistency otherwise lacking in the administration of the [plan]."[13]

The effects of an inadequate claims procedure vary on a case-by-case basis from a remand to the plan for a determination under a proper claims procedure, to a more "flinty eye" in reviewing the plan's decision, or, finally, to *de novo* review of the participant's claim by the court. These remedies have been discussed separately for plan interpretation issues and factual questions in Chapter 7.

If a claim is sent back to a plan and ultimately is granted under proper procedures, benefits generally date from the time when they would have been granted had the plan used a proper claims procedure initially. In addition, interest may be awarded to make the participant whole for the improper benefit denial. In cases of willful, malicious,

---

[10] See n. 9 above, ch. 7, secs. III.A.3.h and III.B.1.b, and R. Ekman, "The Resolution of Contested Employee Benefit Claims," 17 IFEBP Digest 10 (June 1980) (arbitrary and capricious standard of review and substantial evidence tests "presume[] that the trustees have acted in accordance with review procedures meeting the minimum standards of fairness").

[11] 29 C.F.R. 2560.503-1(h)(1).

[12] 29 C.F.R. 2560.503-1(h)(3).

[13] 645 F.2d 660, 2 EBC 1477, at 1480 (8th Cir. 1981).

wanton, or oppressive denials of claims, extra-contractual compensatory damages and punitive damages *could* be available, although the decisions are generally against such awards.[14]

A. Exhaustion as a Requirement for Court Action

Exhaustion of a plan's internal claims procedure is an established prerequisite to bringing a civil action under ERISA Sections 502(a)(1)(B) or 502(a)(3) to enforce the terms of the plan. ERISA does not expressly require that a participant exhaust a plan's Section 503 claims procedure before going to court, but the courts have required exhaustion on the basis of "sound policy" because it enables them to obtain the assistance of plan administrators and trustees in developing a record and refining their reasons for an interpretation or decision.[15] The failure of a participant to exhaust a plan's claims procedure before going to court usually means that the suit is dismissed without prejudice, or is stayed, with the claim 'remanded' to the plan for a determination.[16] Occasionally, however, a failure to exhaust has led to a dismissal with prejudice when the plan's 60 or more day time period for requesting review of the denied claim expired before the filing of the lawsuit.[17]

Before bringing a benefit denial to a lawyer, it is not unusual for participants to allow a 60 or more day period to pass. Because of the exhaustion requirement, this oversight can delay judicial review, or in the worst case, preclude it. An attorney representing a claimant should therefore immediately seek review of the denied claim within the plan if the time period has not expired (some plans have much longer time periods than the minimum 60 day period). If the period has expired, review may be sought anyway. Since the courts' exhaustion requirement is not a statutory prerequisite to suit under ERISA, but is a judicially created policy to assist the courts in obtaining more reasoned opinions on the merits from plans, a court may look askance at a plan's refusal to provide review outside of its limited time period and treat it as an effective denial of the claim on review, or as having demonstrated

---

[14] See sec. II.F below.

[15] *Amato v. Bernard*, 618 F.2d 559, 2 EBC 2536 (9th Cir. 1980). And see *Denton v. First Nat'l Bank of Waco*, 765 F.2d 1295, 6 EBC 1980, *reh. denied*, 772 F.2d 904 (5th Cir. 1985); *Kross v. Western Elec. Co.*, 701 F.2d 1238, 4 EBC 1265 (7th Cir. 1983); *Ridens v. Voluntary Separation Program*, 610 F.Supp. 770 (D. Minn. 1985); *Worsowicz v. Nashua Corp.*, 612 F.Supp. 310 (D.N.H. 1985); *Sample v. Monsanto Co.*, 485 F.Supp. 1018 (E.D. Mo. 1980); *Mahan v. Reynolds Metals Co.*, 569 F.Supp. 482 (E.D. Ark. 1983), *aff'd*, 739 F.2d 388 (8th Cir. 1984); *Bowler Contract Hauling, Inc. v. Central States Pension Fund*, 547 F.Supp. 783, 3 EBC 2318 (S.D. Ill. 1982); *Imler v. Southwestern Bell Tel. Co.*, 650 P.2d 712, 3 EBC 2147 (Kan.App. 1982).

[16] See *Amato v. Bernard*, *supra*; *Kross v. Western Elec. Co.*, *supra*; *Challenger v. Ironworkers Local No. 1*, 619 F.2d 645, 2 EBC 1711 (7th Cir. 1980); *Sample v. Monsanto Co.*, *supra*; *Chambers v. European Am. Bank & Trust Co.*, 601 F.Supp. 630 (E.D.N.Y. 1985); *Fox v. Merrill Lynch & Co.*, 453 F.Supp. 561, 1 EBC 1976 (S.D.N.Y. 1978); *Lucas v. Warner & Swasey Co.*, 475 F.Supp. 1071, 1 EBC 1924 (E.D. Pa. 1979); *Tatterson v. Koppers Co.*, 458 A.2d 983 (Pa. Super. Ct. 1983).

[17] See *Taylor v. South Central Bell*, 422 So.2d 528 (La. App. 1982); *Gray v. Dow Chemical Co.*, 615 F.Supp. 1040 (W.D. Pa. 1985), *aff'd*, 791 F.2d 917 (3d Cir. 1986) (one of two claims time-barred because of expiration of period for requesting review).

the futility of review. Other points to check when a participant is ostensibly outside the time period for requesting review are:

(1) Whether a request for review was in fact made in some manner by the participant, or by letters or telephone calls of the attorney;[18]

(2) Whether a request for review was made and was denied by the plan's inaction beyond the period for response on a request for review;[19]

(3) Whether the plan's procedures for obtaining review of a denied claim were adequately communicated to the participant;[20] and

(4) Whether use of those procedures is demonstrably futile.[21]

A trial court's determination of whether the exhaustion requirement has been satisfied, or is futile, is generally within its discretion and is not subject to review on appeal.[22]

The exhaustion requirement has been held to require only "claim" exhaustion, not exhaustion of every "issue" or "theory." Thus, when a participant or beneficiary exhausts a plan's claims procedure, but fails to raise a specific theory at the claims stage to support a claim, the theory is not foreclosed, and the claim will not ordinarily be sent back to the plan for reconsideration.[23]

---

[18] See *Adams v. Joy Mfg. Co.*, 6 EBC 2594 (D.N.H. 1985) (lawyer's communication of employee's demands effectively constituted claim and request for review); *Turrill v. Life Ins. Co. of N.A.*, 753 F.2d 1322, 6 EBC 1325 (5th Cir. 1985) (course of dealing established that providing employer, rather than insurer, with proof of disability constituted claim under plan).

[19] If a decision after a request for review is not made within the time periods for processing a claim, it is "deemed denied on review." 29 C.F.R. 2560.503-1(h)(4), and see *Adams v. Joy Mfg. Co., supra* (inaction on claim for over 180 days functioned as denial under DOL regulations).

[20] See *Adams v. Joy Mfg. Co., supra* (exhaustion not required when employees not told of claims procedure for obtaining review of denied claim); *Gray v. Dow Chemical Co., supra* (failure to give notice of procedure for obtaining review in denial letter extended time period for filing request for review, although defect did not constitute exhaustion). See also *Tomczyscyn v. Teamsters Local 115 Health & Retirement Fund*, 590 F.Supp. 211 (E.D. Pa. 1984); *Brown v. Babcock & Wilcox Co.*, 589 F.Supp. 64 (S.D. Ga. 1984).

[21] See *Korn v. Levine Bros. Iron Works Corp.*, 574 F.Supp. 836, 4 EBC 2533 (S.D.N.Y. 1983) (plaintiff's attempts to obtain relief demonstrated trustees' awareness of claim and futility of further proceedings within the plan); *Lieske v. Morlock*, 570 F.Supp. 1426 (N.D. Ill. 1983) (repeated refusals to honor plaintiffs' requests for lump sum benefits and refusals to reply to their requests for information demonstrated futility of administrative remedies); *Boesl v. Suburban Trust & Sav. Bank*, 642 F.Supp. 1503 (N.D. Ill. 1986) (denial of meaningful access to review and futility excused failure to exhaust on breach of fiduciary duty, §510, and fraud claims); *DePina v. Gen. Dynamics Corp.*, 8 EBC 1453 (D. Mass. 1987) (futility excused exhaustion; remand to plan "would cause [plaintiff] to expend needless resources for what appears to be a certain denial of his appeal"); *Elby v. Livernois*, 194 N.W.2d 429 (Mich. Ct.App. 1972) (exhaustion not required when administrative board for review of claims denials is but a "creature" of the employer).

But see *Denton v. First Nat'l Bank of Waco, supra* (exhaustion not futile even though committee reviewing denied claim composed of same persons who initially turned down the claim); *Brown v. Retirement Committee of Briggs & Stratton*, 797 F.2d 521 (7th Cir. 1986) (review by *same* person or committee who made initial benefit decision does not make administrative appeal futile).

[22] *Janowski v. Teamsters Local 710 Pension Fund*, 673 F.2d 931, 3 EBC 1225 (7th Cir. 1982), *vacated and remanded on standing and attorney's fee award,* 463 U.S. 1222, 4 EBC 2004 (1983).

[23] See *Wolf v. National Shopmen Pension Fund*, 728 F.2d 182, 5 EBC 1257 (3d Cir. 1984) (claim not sent back). However, if an issue involves new factual information, some courts may send the issue back to develop a record and gain the benefit of the trustees' consideration. See *Phillips v. Kennedy*, 542 F.2d 52, 1 EBC 1418, at 1421 n. 10 (8th Cir. 1976).

Exhaustion of a plan's claims procedure is not a prerequisite to court action to remedy statutory violations if the violation is independent of the correct interpretation of the plan's terms. For example, a Section 404(a)(1) fiduciary claim or a Section 510 claim for interference with the attainment of rights under the plan may not require exhaustion if the claim of a statutory violation is independent of any claim arising under the terms of the plan. Statutory claims of this type can, however, be very similar to claims arising under the terms of the plan which require exhaustion. To date, the courts have drawn the line between claims that are independent and those that are not in slightly different ways. Claims for Section 510 interference with the attainment of rights appear generally to be more likely to be characterized as independent of claims under the terms of a plan[24] than are claims of fiduciary violations in interpreting the plan.[25]

---

[24] Compare *Amaro v. Continental Can Co.*, 724 F.2d 747, 5 EBC 1215 (9th Cir. 1984) (exhaustion not required on §510 claim that is not just an assertion of rights under the terms of the plan); accord *Zipf v. AT&T Co.*, 799 F.2d 889, 7 EBC 2289 (3d Cir. 1986); *Grywczynski v. Shasta Beverages, Inc.*, 606 F.Supp. 61, at 64 (N.D. Cal. 1984) (emphasizing unlikelihood that §510 claim fell within Pension Committee's authority to decide questions "arising under the Plan"); *Gavalik v. Continental Can Co.*, 812 F.2d 835, 8 EBC 1047 (3d Cir. 1987); *McClendon v. Continental Group, Inc.*, 602 F.Supp. 1492, 6 EBC 1113 (D.N.J. 1985); *Garry v. T.R.W., Inc.*, 603 F.Supp. 157 (N.D. Ohio 1985) with *Kross v. Western Elec. Co.*, 701 F.2d 1238, 4 EBC 1265 (7th Cir. 1983) (§510 claim that is not separable from a claim under the terms of the plan requires exhaustion, even though remedy of rehiring employee was not within arbitrator's authority); *Mason v. Continental Group, Inc.*, 763 F.2d 1219, 6 EBC 1933 (11th Cir. 1985), *cert. denied*, 474 U.S. 1087 (1986) (White, J., dissenting from denial of certiorari in light of conflict between the circuits) (following *Kross* in holding that §510 claim requires exhaustion of arbitration procedures on all issues that are "grist for the arbitration mill"); *Delisi v. United Parcel Serv., Inc.*, 580 F.Supp. 1572 (W.D. Pa. 1984) (accord with *Kross* when grievance for wrongful discharge was closely intertwined with §510 claim; and apparently dismissing with prejudice for failure to exhaust grievance procedure). See also *Allen v. American Home Foods, Inc.*, 644 F.Supp. 1553 (N.D. Ind. 1986) (dismissing ADEA claims that could have been brought as §510 claims when participants did not exhaust plan's procedures; following *Kross* as controlling within Seventh Circuit, but indicating in footnote that *Kross* should be reconsidered).

[25] Compare *Delgrosso v. Spang & Co.*, 769 F.2d 928, 6 EBC 1940 (3d Cir. 1985), *cert. denied*, 476 U.S. ___ (1986) (exhaustion not required on fiduciary claim about distribution of excess assets that is not the same as an ordinary dispute over right to pension or its amount); *Air Line Pilots Ass'n v. Northwest Airlines, Inc.*, 627 F.2d 272, 2 EBC 1665 (D.C. Cir. 1980) (exhaustion not required on breach of §404(a) fiduciary duties claims that are independent of correct construction of the plan); *Lewis v. Merrill Lynch & Co.*, 431 F.Supp. 271, 1 EBC 1737 (E.D. Pa. 1977) (breach of fiduciary duty claim does not require exhaustion), with *Fox v. Merrill Lynch & Co.*, 453 F.Supp. 561, 1 EBC 1976 (S.D.N.Y. 1978) (although based on the same facts as in *Lewis v. Merrill Lynch & Co.*, *supra*, holding that §404(a)(1) claim was not separable from claim under the terms of the plan and therefore required exhaustion); *Viggiano v. Shenango China Division*, 750 F.2d 276, 5 EBC 2481 (3d Cir. 1984) (whether employer had obligation to continue insurance premiums during strike subject to arbitration and exhaustion requirement, even though cause of action pleaded as a fiduciary violation); *Lindahl v. American Tel. & Tel. Co.*, 609 F.Supp. 267 (N.D. Ill. 1985). A number of other decisions have applied the exhaustion requirement to claims that are framed, or that could be framed, as claims for breach of fiduciary duty without discussing this issue. See most of the cases cited in nns. 15 through 17.

But exhaustion of a plan's internal remedies is never required for a breach of fiduciary duty based on alleged noncompliance with a statutory requirement. See *Janowski v. Teamsters Local No. 710 Pension Fund*, *supra* (alleged violations of ERISA benefit accrual rules not subject to exhaustion requirement at least when issue "is solely a question of statutory interpretation and does not require a factual record"); *Barrowclough v. Kidder, Peabody & Co.*, 752 F.2d 923, 6 EBC 1170 (3d Cir. 1985) (action for failure to provide individual statement of accrued benefits and vested rights not subject to exhaustion); *Clouatre v. Lockwood*, 593 F.Supp. 1136 (M.D. La. 1984) (exhaustion not required in suit alleging ERISA §503 violation from plan's failure to disclose specific reasons for a benefit denial).

B. Arbitration as a Claims Procedure Step

Plan provisions requiring arbitration of all claims under the terms of a plan present a second type of exhaustion issue. Arbitration is often desirable for participants because of its speed, lower costs, and lower attorney's fees (or no attorney's fees if a union provides representation). Arbitration may also be desirable for claims "under the terms of a plan" because an arbitrator may be more willing than a court to examine the plan administrator's or trustees' factual determinations and interpretation of the plan *de novo*, whereas a court will generally use the "arbitrary and capricious" standard for review.

In spite of the points in favor of arbitration, participants in many cases prefer direct access to the federal or state courts. An underlying premise of labor arbitration is that a union, equally experienced in the arbitral process, is willing to provide representation, and is committed to the individual's cause. Particularly in jointly administered Taft-Hartley plans, where the union by appointment of plan trustees is involved in the plan's administration, this commitment to the individual's cause may be absent once the plan trustees initially decide to deny the individual's claim. In single-employer plans as well, some claims are not popular with the union. Even when a collective bargaining agreement or pension plan allows a participant to secure an outside lawyer, or other representative, and individually take the claim to arbitration, there may be concern about whether the arbitral process will work as well without union representation. Other concerns that lead participants to bypass arbitration are whether the arbitrator can consider statutory grounds that support but are not dispositive of a claim and whether the arbitrator will be able to provide as complete a remedy as allowed under ERISA Section 502(a)(3)'s provision for "appropriate equitable relief," including an award of prejudgment interest and, under Section 502(g), attorney's fees. Litigation may also permit broader discovery than is allowed in practice in arbitration.[26]

The Department of Labor's regulations on a "reasonable" Section 503 claims procedure establish that a grievance and arbitration procedure can *only* be substituted for the claims procedure outlined in the regulations when (1) the plan is collectively bargained, and (2) the plan is *not* a collectively bargained Taft-Hartley plan.[27] In nonbargained plans or Taft-Hartley plans, an agreement to arbitrate a claim voluntarily may still be permissible, but only if the participant knows that it is

---

[26] Section 9(a) of the National Labor Relations Act provides that an individual can pursue a grievance without union assistance if the resolution of the grievance is not inconsistent with the terms of the collective bargaining agreement and the collective bargaining representative has the opportunity to be present. It is "unusual," although "not without precedent," for collective bargaining agreements to allow employees to individually take claims to arbitration. A. Lewis, "The Duty of Fair Representation," in ABA Lab. & Empl. Law Sec., *A Review of the NLRA* (ABA 1984), at 158. Attorney's fees may also be available. See *Consolidated Labor Union Trust v. Clark*, 7 EBC 2605 (Fla. Dist.Ct.App. 1986) (participant entitled to attorney's fees incurred in arbitration in which she prevailed on application to court; arbitration is within ambit of "any action" contemplated by ERISA §502(g)(1) authority to award attorney's fees).

[27] 29 C.F.R. 2560.503-1(b)(2).

neither a mandatory part of the claims procedure nor a prerequisite to court action.

Despite the clarity of the Department of Labor's regulations, a line of cases has required claims for benefits to be submitted to arbitration under both Taft-Hartley plans and nonbargained plans. In *Challenger v. Ironworkers Local No. 1*, the Seventh Circuit held that a claim for benefits from a Taft-Hartley plan could be subject to mandatory arbitration.[28] In *Fox v. Merrill Lynch & Co.*, a district court held that arbitration of a claim under a nonbargained plan was mandatory because of a standardized employment contract that called for arbitration.[29] These cases do not discuss the Department of Labor's claims procedure regulations. They therefore offer weak support for future decisions. The Department of Labor's regulations are supported by the express policy in ERISA Section 2(b) of providing "ready access to the Federal courts" and the legislative history of ERISA. The Senate-passed version of ERISA would have required all plans to include arbitration as a voluntary option for participants under what is now Section 503, but would have allowed it to be a *mandatory* claims procedure step only if the arbitration provision was collectively bargained and the Secretary of Labor specifically found that the collectively bargained arbitration procedure was "reasonably fair and effective," a thinly veiled warning that use of collectively bargained grievance and arbitration procedures would not usually be permitted to be mandatory under Taft-Hartley plans.[30] The conferees rejected the Senate provision only because the voluntary arbitration requirement for all participants might have been "too costly."[31] In promulgating the Section 503 regulations, the Department of Labor essentially followed

---

[28] 619 F.2d 645, 2 EBC 1711 (7th Cir. 1980). *Taylor v. Bakery & Confectionery Union Fund,* 455 F.Supp. 816 (E.D.N.C. 1978), is sometimes cited with *Challenger* as support for requiring arbitration of a benefits claim under a Taft-Hartley plan, but while the *Taylor* court required exhaustion, it made no mention of arbitration, and in fact, stated that the plan complied with the Department of Labor's regulations.

[29] 453 F.Supp. 561, 1 EBC 1976 (S.D.N.Y. 1978). See also *Barrowclough v. Kidder, Peabody & Co.*, 752 F.2d 923, 6 EBC 1170 (3d Cir. 1985) (claims to enforce rights to benefits under the terms of a plan may be subject to arbitration agreement covering all disputes arising out of employment relationship; opinion does not discuss DOL claims procedure regulations although plan was not a collectively bargained single-employer plan); *Scheider v. U.S. Steel,* 486 F.Supp. 211 (W.D. Pa. 1980) (similar holding under U.S. Steel plan covering salaried employees which contained an arbitration provision). It is not clear from the *Scheider* opinion that the plaintiffs were salaried employees, but according to U.S. Steel's attorney, they were. Telephone conversation with James Carney, Aug. 26, 1981. *Gordon v. U.S. Steel,* 2 EBC 1853 (D. Utah 1981), is sometimes cited with *Scheider,* but the case is ambiguous, because the plaintiff, a retired coal miner, wanted to take his claim to arbitration. *Sample v. Monsanto Co.,* 485 F.Supp. 1018 (E.D. Mo. 1980), appears to be another case in this line, in this instance requiring a participant to go to medical arbitration on a claim of total disability; the *Sample* opinion does not indicate whether the plan was collectively bargained, but the lack of any reference to a union or collective bargaining agreement indicates that it was not.

The American Arbitration Association has published arbitration rules for employee benefit plan claims which in the introduction suggest that arbitration can be made either optional or mandatory under a nonbargained plan. See AAA, "Employee Benefit Plan Claims Arbitration Rules," at 3.

[30] See H.R. 2, with amendments, as passed by the Senate, 3 ERISA Leg. Hist. 3813-15.

[31] 3 ERISA Leg. Hist. 4769 (statement of Sen. Javits).

the Senate bill with respect to including collectively bargained arbitration provisions as a mandatory part of a "reasonable" claims procedure. But in Taft-Hartley plans, where the union's interest, along with the employers', is often aligned against the individual benefit claimant, the Department decided that a collectively bargained grievance and arbitration procedure does not constitute a "reasonably fair and effective" procedure for claims under those plans.[32]

Even when arbitration can be a part of a collectively bargained single-employer plan's claims procedure, there are established exceptions to the requirement that a claim under the terms of a plan has to be submitted to arbitration. First, the plan or the collective bargaining agreement must *provide* that benefit claims are subject to the grievance and arbitration procedure. The fact that an employee benefit plan is established pursuant to collective bargaining and that a grievance and arbitration procedure is contained in the collective bargaining agreement does not necessarily lead to the conclusion that employee benefit claims are subject to the grievance and arbitration procedure.[33] In other cases, use of the grievance and arbitration procedure may be optional,[34] or certain types of claims may fall outside its scope.[35] Second, the summary plan description for the plan must specifically describe the grievance and arbitration procedure as the procedure for

---

[32] See 42 Fed. Reg. 27427 (May 27, 1977) (preamble to final claims procedure regulations, stating that dual roles of unions in representing employees and participating in the operation of Taft-Hartley plans led the Department of Labor to exclude Taft-Hartley plans from the regulatory provision allowing arbitration as a claims procedure step). See also 161 BNA Pens. Rep. A-7 (Oct. 31, 1977) (reporting statement of Steven Sacher, former Labor Department associate solicitor, that exclusion of Taft-Hartley plans is because of Labor Department view that unions' institutional interest in multiemployer plans does not permit them to zealously represent individual claimants in arbitration).

A reference in the ERISA Conference Report to claims for benefits under the terms of a plan being treated by the courts "in similar fashion to those brought under Section 301 of the LMRA," 3 ERISA Leg. Hist. 4745, has sometimes been construed as offering support for mandatory arbitration under Taft-Hartley, as well as collectively bargained single-employer, plans. However, under §301, the courts develop federal substantive law to resolve labor contract disputes "fashion[ed] from the policy of our national labor law." *Textile Workers Union v. Lincoln Mills of Alabama*, 353 U.S. 448, at 456 (1957). The policy of the LMRA from which this federal substantive law is fashioned is expressly in favor of arbitration, see LMRA §203(d), 29 U.S.C. §173(d), whereas the express policy of ERISA is in favor of "ready access to the Federal courts." ERISA §2(b).

[33] See 29 C.F.R. 2560.503-1(b)(2); *UAW v. Allis-Chalmers Corp.*, 643 F.Supp. 342, 7 EBC 2347 (E.D. Wis. 1986) (collective bargaining agreement excepted benefit entitlement issues from arbitration requirement); *Brown v. Babcock & Wilcox Co.*, 589 F.Supp. 64, at 67 (S.D. Ga. 1984) ("[n]owhere in the Plan . . . is there reference to mandatory arbitration procedures to resolve eligibility disputes"); *Lindahl v. American Tel. & Tel. Co.*, 609 F.Supp. 267 (N.D. Ill. 1985) (accord); *Sreckovic v. Int'l Harvester Co.*, 601 F.Supp. 332 (N.D. Ill. 1984) (arbitration not required under terms of collectively bargained pension plan); *Bonin v. American Airlines, Inc.*, 621 F.2d 635, (5th Cir. 1980) (arbitration not required when pension plan's terms establish its independence from the collective bargaining agreement's dispute procedure); but compare *Bonin*, 562 F.Supp. 896, 4 EBC 1671 (N.D. Tex. 1983) (on remand, holding that it is not arbitrary and capricious for plan administrator to follow an arbitrator's determination in a separate proceeding that a participant was discharged "for cause" in deciding whether the participant is eligible for disability benefits).

[34] See *McClendon v. Continental Group, Inc.*, 602 F.Supp. 1492, 6 EBC 1113 (D.N.J. 1985) (precatory language under pension agreement that differences "may" be taken up as grievances does not show that union has agreed to arbitrate all differences).

[35] See *Murphy v. Heppenstall Co.*, 635 F.2d 233, 2 EBC 1891 (3d Cir. 1981), *cert. denied*, 454 U.S. 1142 (1982) (claim for full funding of benefits after plan termination not subject to exhaustion when it was not within the intended scope of the claims procedure); *Delgrosso v. Spang &*

benefit claims.[36] Third, the grievance and arbitration procedure must not "contain any provision" or be "administered in a manner" which unduly inhibits or hampers the initiation or processing of claims.[37]

Even when a grievance and arbitration procedure meets these three requirements, retirees and participants who are no longer members of the bargaining unit may not be required to arbitrate their claims on the ground that the union no longer has the interest in representing them that it has in representing still-active bargaining unit participants.[38] For active participants, an exception may also apply based on futility if a union fails to process, or is only going through the motions of processing, a claim or otherwise displays a "community of interest" with the employer or plan.[39] Whether exhaustion is excused because of futility is within the discretion of the trial court.[40]

As mentioned earlier, exhaustion is also not required, and thus arbitration is not required, if a claim for benefits is based on a statutory violation that is independent of the correct construction of the plan.[41] If a participant's cause of action includes claims that depend on the correct interpretation of the plan, the court may require exhaustion of the arbitration procedure to resolve those issues, while retaining jurisdiction over the statutory issues.[42]

When a benefit claim is permissibly arbitrated, the general labor law rule is that a court reviews the arbitrator's decision only to determine whether the arbitrator exceeded his or her authority, whether the arbitration was procedurally fair, whether the decision draws its essence from the contract, and whether the decision violates a law or public policy.[43] However, in the debates on ERISA, Senator Jacob Javits stated that plan participants would still have the "same right to

---

Co., 769 F.2d 928, 6 EBC 1940 (3d Cir. 1985), *cert. denied*, 476 U.S. ___ (1986) (exhaustion not required on fiduciary claim about distribution of excess assets that is not the same as an ordinary dispute over right to pension or its amount); *Berry v. Playboy Enterprises, Inc.*, 480 A.2d 941, 5 EBC 2682 (N.J. Sup.Ct. App.Div. 1984) (allegations of negligence and misrepresentation may be beyond the scope of bargaining agreement and hence not subject to a plan's grievance and arbitration procedure).

[36] 29 C.F.R. 2560.503-1(b)(1) and *Anderson v. Alpha Portland Indus. Inc.*, 752 F.2d 1293, 6 EBC 1046 (8th Cir. 1985) (*en banc*), *cert. denied*, 471 U.S. 1102 (1985).

[37] 29 C.F.R. 2560.503-1(b)(2).

[38] See *Anderson v. Alpha Portland Indus. Inc.*, *supra*; *Weimer v. Kurz-Kasch, Inc.*, 773 F.2d 669, 6 EBC 2258 (6th Cir. 1985); *Justice v. Union Carbide Corp.*, 405 F.Supp. 920 (E.D. Tenn. 1975), *aff'd*, 551 F.2d 1078 (6th Cir. 1977); *Hazen v. Western Union Telegraph Co.*, 518 F.2d 766 (6th Cir. 1975). But see *Republic Steel Corp. v. Maddox*, 379 U.S. 650 (1965) (permanently laid off employee must still use grievance and arbitration procedure in claim for unpaid severance benefits).

[39] *Hauser v. Farwell, Ozmun, Kirk & Co.*, 299 F.Supp. 387, at 392 (D. Minn. 1969). And see *Taylor v. Bakery & Confectionery Union Fund*, 455 F.Supp. 816 (E.D.N.C. 1978); *Glover v. St. Louis-San Francisco Ry.*, 393 U.S. 324 (1969); *Vaca v. Sipes*, 386 U.S. 171 (1967).

[40] *Janowski v. Teamsters Local 710 Pension Fund*, 673 F.2d 931, 3 EBC 1225 (7th Cir. 1982), *vacated and remanded on standing and attorney's fee award*, 463 U.S. 1222, 4 EBC 2004 (1983).

[41] See *Amaro v. Continental Can Co.*, 724 F.2d 747, 5 EBC 1215 (9th Cir. 1984), and sec. I.A above.

[42] *Amaro v. Continental Can Co.*, *supra*; *Air Line Pilots Ass'n v. Northwest Airlines, Inc.*, 627 F.2d 272, 2 EBC 1665 (D.C. Cir. 1980).

[43] See *United Steelworkers v. Enterprise Wheel & Car Corp.*, 363 U.S. 593, at 597 (1960); *W.R. Grace & Co. v. Rubber Workers*, 461 U.S. 757 (1983).

go to court as on the basis of race or sex discrimination."[44] Following the Supreme Court's reasoning in *Alexander v. Gardner-Denver Co.* on the effect of prior resort to arbitration on a Title VII discrimination claim,[45] the Ninth Circuit stated in *Amaro v. Continental Can Co.* that it takes a strict view on whether an arbitrator has exceeded his or her authority and decided ERISA questions. According to *Amaro*, interpreting a statute, and particularly a remedial statute such as ERISA that confers "individual" rights, is a "task for the judiciary, not an arbitrator," whose job is only to decide the collective "law of the shop."[46] In *Amaro*, the Ninth Circuit thus stated that even the factual findings of a neutral arbitrator are not binding on a related, but distinct ERISA Section 510 cause of action for intentional interference with the attainment of pension rights. The arbitrator's findings, which concerned whether layoffs of employees were in violation of certain collective bargaining obligations or were due to changing market conditions, would be admissible as evidence on whether the layoffs were for the purpose of interfering with pension rights, but they would be accorded only such weight as the court "deems appropriate."[47]

Two additional wrinkles complicate the effect of arbitration on benefit claims under ERISA. First, the Department of Labor in promulgating its Section 503 claims procedure regulations purposefully refused to take a position on whether arbitration would be as "binding" on nonstatutory issues, when permitted, as it is generally in labor arbitration.[48] In this regard, in *Alexander v. Gardner-Denver Co.*, prior resort to arbitration was held not to preclude or bind judicial review on *all* issues related to a later Title VII claim. However, in *Fox v. Merrill Lynch & Co.*, a district court distinguished *Alexander v. Gardner-Denver* on the basis that Congress did not intend for nonstatutory pension claims under ERISA to have as high a priority as Title VII discrimination claims.[49]

Second, under Section 503, the person who decides the claim must be a "named fiduciary."[50] An arbitrator's decision on a claim may thus be reviewable as a fiduciary's decision under Section 404(a)(1), rather than just under the general labor rule for whether the decision is

[44] 2 ERISA Leg. Hist. 1642.

[45] 415 U.S. 36 (1974).

[46] 724 F.2d 747, 5 EBC 1215, at 1218 and 1220 (9th Cir. 1984), quoting *Alexander v. Gardner-Denver Co., supra.* See also *U.S. Steel Pension Fund v. McSkimming,* 759 F.2d 269, 6 EBC 1621 (3d Cir. 1985); *Hansen v. Bd. of Trustees of Northwest Marine Ben. Trust,* 7 EBC 2350 (W.D. Wash. 1986).

[47] 5 EBC at 1221. And see Senator Javits' statement, *supra.* But compare *Burke v. Latrobe Steel Co.*, 775 F.2d 88, 6 EBC 2328 (3d Cir. 1985) (although ERISA fiduciary and §510 claims not precluded because of prior arbitration, Third Circuit indicated that it would accept all determinations of overlapping facts as binding).

[48] See 42 Fed. Reg. 27427 (May 27, 1977) (regulatory preamble stating that reference to whether arbitration is binding in proposed regulations was deliberately deleted because regulations are only to establish when arbitration is permissible, not substantive effect of arbitration on participant's claim).

[49] 453 F.Supp. 561, 1 EBC 1976 (S.D.N.Y. 1978).

[50] Likewise, ERISA §3(21)(A) states that anyone who exercises discretionary authority over the administration of a plan is a "fiduciary."

procedurally fair and "draws its essence" from the contract. This is apparently the position of the Department of Labor, despite consternation among arbitrators about their liability under this potentially higher standard.[51] However, as a result of the general public policy favoring arbitration, a greater degree of deference is likely to be paid to a neutral arbitrator's decision than to a plan administrator's or plan committee's, particularly if an oral hearing was held and detailed findings made based on a reviewable record.[52]

II. ERISA Title I Causes of Action for Participants

ERISA's stated policy is to provide participants with "ready access to the Federal courts."[53] To implement this, ERISA Section 502(a) establishes four causes of action to enable participants and beneficiaries to enforce both their rights under the terms of plans and their statutory rights under ERISA.

(1) Under ERISA Section 502(a)(1)(B), a participant or beneficiary whose claim for benefits "under the terms of a plan" has been denied can bring a civil action against a plan "to recover benefits due him under the terms of the plan," "to enforce his rights under the terms of the plan," i.e., by injunction, or "to

---

[51] See Department of Labor Advisory Opinion (AO) 79-66A (Sept. 14, 1979), reprinted in 260 BNA Pens. Rep. R-9 (Oct. 8, 1979), AO 81-50A (June 4, 1981), reprinted in 348 BNA Pens. Rep. R-1 (June 29, 1981), and AO 78-14 (July 27, 1978), reprinted in 210 BNA Pens. Rep. R-4 (Oct. 16, 1978). See also *Helms v. Monsanto Co.*, 728 F.2d 1416 (11th Cir. 1984) (reviewing medical doctor's decision as an "arbitrator" under the ERISA fiduciary standard); *UAW v. Greyhound Lines, Inc.*, 701 F.2d 1181, 4 EBC 1105 (6th Cir. 1983) (arbitrator may himself be immune from personal liability under arbitral immunity, but this may not foreclose action against plan fiduciaries for following decision if it is arbitrary and capricious under the ERISA fiduciary standard). Cf. *Mahan v. Reynolds Metals Co.*, 739 F.2d 388 (8th Cir. 1984) (*per curiam*), *aff'g*, 569 F.Supp. 482 (E.D. Ark. 1983) (employee bound by arbitrator's decision on ground that it was not arbitrary and capricious under ERISA fiduciary standard; Eighth Circuit refused to rule on district court's alternative holding that the arbitrator's decision was *res judicata* even if arbitrary and capricious under this standard).

[52] See *Delaney v. Union Carbide Corp.*, 749 F.2d 17, 5 EBC 2491 (8th Cir. 1984) (decision of medical arbitration board established pursuant to collective bargaining agreement binding to the same degree as in any LMRA §301 action); *Burke v. Latrobe Steel Co., supra* at n. 47; *Barrowclough v. Kidder, Peabody & Co.*, 752 F.2d 923, 6 EBC 1170 (3d Cir. 1985) (claims to enforce rights to benefits under terms of a plan may be subject to arbitration agreement covering all disputes arising out of employment relationship); *Wilson v. Fischer & Porter Co. Pension Plan*, 551 F.Supp. 593 (E.D. Pa. 1982) (arbitrator's decision in class grievance on method for calculating benefits held to bar subsequent individual action challenging interpretation under ERISA—even when arbitrator's opinion expressly excepted the plaintiff from the grievant class); *King v. James River-Pepperell, Inc.*, 592 F.Supp. 54, at 56 (D. Mass. 1984) (employee who settled grievance for unjust dismissal barred from bringing subsequent ERISA action "seek[ing] identical relief" by alleging that his dismissal was for the purpose of interfering with his attainment of disability benefit rights); *Bonin v. American Airlines, Inc.*, 562 F.Supp. 896, 4 EBC 1671 (N.D. Tex. 1983) (adoption by plan trustees of arbitrator's findings in separate arbitration, without reevaluation, is not arbitrary and capricious).

[53] ERISA §2(b).

clarify his rights to future benefits under the terms of the plan"—even before a formal denial has taken place.[54]

(2) ERISA Section 502(a)(3) enables a participant or beneficiary to bring a civil action against a plan, a fiduciary, or any other responsible person to enjoin violations of Title I of ERISA or of the terms of the plan and to obtain other appropriate equitable relief to enforce Title I or the terms of the plan.

(3) ERISA Section 502(a)(2) enables participants or beneficiaries to bring a civil action to hold fiduciaries responsible through personal liability or such other equitable or remedial relief as a court finds appropriate for any losses to a plan resulting from a breach of fiduciary duty.

(4) ERISA Section 502(a)(1)(A) and Section 502(c) enable a participant or beneficiary to bring an action to collect up to $100 per day from a plan administrator, and to obtain such other relief as a court deems proper when a plan administrator fails to furnish information to a participant or beneficiary required to be furnished under Title I within 30 days of a request.[55]

Special causes of action to enforce the ERISA Title IV plan termination rules for single-employer defined benefit plans and the reorganization, plan insolvency, and plan termination rules for multiemployer plans are discussed below.

A. Jurisdiction

Federal court jurisdiction over actions under ERISA Section 502(a) is without regard to the amount in controversy or diversity of citizenship among the parties.[56] The federal courts' jurisdiction is *exclusive* for all Section 502(a) causes of action—except actions to enforce the terms of a plan under ERISA Section 502(a)(1)(B). In the latter actions, the state courts have concurrent jurisdiction.[57] However, when a Section 502(a)(1)(B) action is commenced in state court, the defendant has the option of removing the action to federal court under 28 U.S.C. Section 1441.[58]

---

[54] See *Janowski v. Teamsters Local 710 Pension Fund*, 673 F.2d 931, 3 EBC 1225 (7th Cir. 1982), *vacated and remanded on other grounds*, 463 U.S. 1222, 4 EBC 2004 (1983); *Hauck v. Eschbacher*, 665 F.2d 843, 2 EBC 2202 (8th Cir. 1981).

[55] A fifth, but less commonly used, cause of action in §502(a)(4) enables a participant to obtain "appropriate relief" for a plan administrator's failure to furnish an individual statement of deferred vested benefits on the participant's separation from service, as required under ERISA §105(c).

[56] ERISA §502(f).

[57] ERISA §502(e)(1).

[58] See *Leonardis v. Local 282 Pension Fund*, 391 F.Supp. 554, 1 EBC 1098 (E.D.N.Y. 1975); *McConnell v. Marine Engineers Beneficial Ass'n.*, 526 F.Supp. 770 (N.D. Cal. 1981); *Buck v. Plumbers & Pipefitters Nat'l Pension Fund*, 70 F.R.D. 530 (E.D. Tenn. 1976); *Ziskind v. Retail Clerks Int'l Ass'n.*, 3 EBC 1012 (E.D. Cal. 1982). But see *Lederman v. Pacific Mutual Life Ins. Co.*, 494 F.Supp. 1020, 2 EBC 2195 (C.D. Cal. 1980) (removal not allowed because of Congress' intent that state courts have concurrent jurisdiction over §502(a)(1)(B) actions).

If a complaint is filed in state court which could be pleaded as an ERISA claim, but which in fact pleads only state law claims, the federal courts of appeals have been divided on whether removal is allowed. Under one line, removal is not allowed on the ground that federal preemption may preclude some or all of the participant's state law claims. Instead, federal preemption must be raised by the defendant as a defense to the state law action, with the preemption issue to be decided by the state court.[59] Other circuits have permitted removal on the ground that federal court jurisdiction is not avoided by "artfully" failing to plead essential federal issues or by failing to plead as federal issues claims that necessarily arise under federal law.[60] In *General Motors Corp. v. Taylor* and *Metropolitan Life Ins. Co. v. Taylor*, the U.S. Supreme Court resolved this conflict by holding that a complaint filed in state court can be removed to federal court if ERISA not only preempts the action, but under Section 502(a) also affirmatively provides a federal cause of action.[61]

B. Service of Process and Venue

Service of process may be made on a defendant in an ERISA Title I action in any district nationwide in which the defendant resides or may be found.[62] Service of process on a defendant plan is made by serving the agent for service of process named in the plan's summary plan description.[63] Except in actions that are exclusively to enforce the terms of a plan under Section 502(a)(1)(B), a copy of the complaint is also required to be served by certified mail on both the Secretary of Labor and the Secretary of the Treasury, who may then intervene in the action.[64]

Under ERISA Section 502(e)(2), venue is proper in any district:

(1) Where a plan is administered;

(2) Where the breach of the terms of the plan or ERISA took place; or

(3) Where a defendant resides or "may be found."

Where a plan is administered has been interpreted narrowly by looking

---

[59] *Powers v. Health & Welfare Trust*, 719 F.2d 760, 4 EBC 2552 (5th Cir. 1983); *Taylor v. General Motors Corp.*, 763 F.2d 216, 7 EBC 1027 (6th Cir. 1985); *Bell v. Amcast Indus. Corp.*, 607 F.Supp. 486, 6 EBC 1472 (S.D. Ohio 1985).

[60] *Clorox Co. v. U.S. District Court for the Northern District of California*, 779 F.2d 517, 6 EBC 2770 (9th Cir. 1985); *Lafferty v. Solar Turbines Int'l*, 666 F.2d 408, 3 EBC 1001 (9th Cir. 1982); *Roe v. General American Life Ins. Co.*, 712 F.2d 450 (10th Cir. 1983); *Rodriguez v. Food Employees Local 196*, 1 EBC 1001 (E.D. Pa. 1977).

[61] 481 U.S. ___, 8 EBC 1417 (1987).

[62] ERISA §502(e)(2).

[63] ERISA §502(d)(1).

[64] ERISA §502(h).

at the physical location of the administrative office of the plan.[65] However, in *Varsic v. U.S. District Court,* the Ninth Circuit stated that "may be found" has the same broad meaning in ERISA as under other statutes—a defendant "may be found" in a district if personal jurisdiction over the defendant can be obtained in the district based on the "minimum contacts" test in *International Shoe Co. v. Washington.*[66] Under this test, if a plan is named as a defendant, venue will generally be proper in any district where employees of a sponsoring employer perform work and earn benefits.[67] Section 502(e)(2)'s reference to whether "a" defendant may be found in a district is also literally applied. If one defendant may be found in the district, venue is proper for all other defendants.[68] When a participant is retired, and only receives, or fails to receive, benefits in a district, with no other plan participants actively working and earning benefits in the district, the minimum contacts for a plan to be "found" in a district may be missing.[69] Even in such districts, however, it is possible that venue could be based on a "breach" of the terms of the plan or ERISA having taken place in the district when, for example, the retiree fails to receive his or her benefit check, or fails to receive the proper amount of benefits, in the district.[70]

Venue is more restricted when a bank is one of the defendants. ERISA's liberal venue provisions have consistently been held to be overridden by the National Bank Act venue provisions which limit venue to the district in which a defendant bank is established—which is generally the district of the bank's home office.[71] However, if a bank has branched into the district in question, the National Bank Act's

---

[65] See *Boyer v. J.A. Majors Co. Employees' Profit Sharing Plan,* 481 F.Supp. 454 (N.D. Ga. 1979) (plan not "administered" in Northern District of Georgia when plan records kept, plan assets deposited, and administrative actions taken in Texas); accord *Bostic v. Ohio River Co. Pension Plan,* 517 F.Supp. 627, 2 EBC 1670 (S.D. W.Va. 1981). But compare *Sprinzen v. Supreme Court of New Jersey,* 478 F.Supp. 722 (S.D.N.Y. 1979) (venue proper based on plan administration in New York when documents and records kept in New York, many employees responsible for program worked in New York, and many beneficiaries resided in New York—even though plan's principal office was in New Jersey).

[66] 607 F.2d 245, 1 EBC 1844 (9th Cir. 1979); and see *International Shoe Co. v. Washington,* 326 U.S. 310 (1945).

[67] See *Varsic v. U.S. District Court, supra; IAM Nat'l Pension Fund v. Wakefield Indus. Inc.,* 699 F.2d 1254, 4 EBC 1201 (D.C. Cir. 1983); *Ballinger v. Perkins,* 515 F.Supp. 673, 2 EBC 1454 (W.D. Va. 1981); *Turner v. CF&I Steel Corp.,* 510 F.Supp. 537, 2 EBC 1397 (E.D. Pa. 1981); *Fulk v. Bagley,* 88 F.R.D. 153 (M.D.N.C. 1980).

[68] *Turner v. CF&I Steel Corp, supra.*

[69] See *Higman v. Amsted Indus.,* 2 EBC 1948 (E.D. Pa. 1981) (no minimum contacts when retiree only receives benefits in a district).

[70] Compare *Bostic v. Ohio River Co. Pension Plan,* 517 F.Supp. 627, 2 EBC 1670 (S.D. W.Va. 1981), with *Boyer v. J.A. Majors Employees' Profit Sharing Plan,* 481 F.Supp. 454 (N.D. Ga. 1979) (breach did not occur in district even when trustees had stopped payment on a check which participant had received and deposited in a bank in the district).

[71] See *Ewton v. Employees' Profit Sharing Retirement Plan,* 416 F.Supp. 1055, 1 EBC 2044 (S.D. Fla. 1976); *Amalgamated Local Union 355 v. Dooley Bros.,* 1 EBC 1687 (E.D.N.Y. 1977); *Allen v. Wachovia Bank & Trust Co.,* 470 F.Supp. 18, 1 EBC 1443 (E.D. N.C. 1978); *Boyer v. J.A. Majors Co. Employees' Profit Sharing Plan,* 481 F.Supp. 454 (N.D. Ga. 1979); *UAW v. Allis Chalmers Corp.,* 447 F.Supp. 766 (E.D. Wis. 1978).

restriction of venue to the district in which the bank is established may be "waived."[72]

In suits to review a final order of the Secretary of Labor, to restrain the Secretary of Labor from taking action contrary to ERISA, or to compel the Secretary of Labor to take action required under ERISA, venue is also more restricted—being limited to the District of Columbia, or to the district in which the participant's plan has its principal office.[73]

Once venue is properly established, the forum will not be changed on grounds of inconvenience unless the balance of relevant factors in favor of a different forum is strong.[74]

C. Actions by "Participants" or "Beneficiaries"

ERISA Section 502 authorizes civil actions by plan "participants" or their "beneficiaries." ERISA Section 3(7) defines "participant" as "any employee or former employee of an employer . . . who is or may become eligible to receive a benefit of any type from an employee benefit plan which covers employees of such employer. . . ." Similarly, Section 3(8) defines a "beneficiary" as a "person designated by a participant, or by the terms of an employee benefit plan, who is or may become entitled to a benefit thereunder."

The scope of "participant" is liberally construed in claims for benefits based on statements or omissions in SPDs that do not accurately reflect the terms of plans.[75] A broad view has also been taken in restitutionary claims in which an employee who has been determined by plan trustees to fall outside the coverage of the plan alleges unjust enrichment of the plan from the contributions made on his or her behalf by mistake or because of misrepresentations.[76] In contrast, courts have narrowly construed the term "participant" in actions in which nonvested former employees who have no expectation of returning to employment seek $100 per day penalties as provided under ERISA Section 502(c) on account of a plan administrator's failure to furnish documents required to be available on request to a participant or beneficiary.[77]

---

[72] See *Allen v. Wachovia Bank & Trust Co., supra.*

[73] ERISA §502(k).

[74] See, e.g., *Robbins v. Hernstrom*, 2 EBC 1102 (N.D. Ill. 1981); *Combs v. Pelbro Fuel, Inc.*, 4 EBC 2610 (D.D.C. 1983); *C&S Wholesale Grocers, Inc. v. New England Teamsters Pension Fund*, 4 EBC 1097 (D. Vt. 1982).

[75] See ch. 8, sec. I.D.

[76] See *Peckham v. Painters Union Pension Fund Trustees*, 653 F.2d 424, 2 EBC 1323 (10th Cir. 1981); *Chase v. Western Teamsters Pension Fund Trustees*, 753 F.2d 744, 6 EBC 1007 (9th Cir. 1985).

[77] *Weiss v. Sheet Metal Workers Local 544 Pension Trust*, 719 F.2d 302, 4 EBC 2273 (9th Cir. 1983), *cert. denied*, 466 U.S. 972 (1984) (unvested former employee who does not show significant probability that he will return to work to secure the service needed to vest lacks standing as participant to pursue claim for $100 per day penalties for plan administrator's failure to furnish documents on his pension status); *Saladino v. ILGWU Retirement Fund*, 754 F.2d 473, 6 EBC 1041 (2d Cir. 1985) (former employee pursuing $100 per day penalties lacked "colorable claim" to

Participants who are receiving benefits in annuity or installment form, but who claim they are entitled to greater amounts, are participants or beneficiaries under ERISA Section 502. A requirement that employees sign waivers of rights to claim additional benefits as a condition to commencing receipt of undisputed benefit amounts has, moreover, been held to violate ERISA's nonforfeitability rules.[78] However, Department of Labor regulations indicate that a "participant" may not include a person whose *entire* benefit rights are fully guaranteed by an insurance company if a contract, policy, or certificate evidencing the benefits has been distributed to the individual and the rights are legally enforceable at the sole option of the individual.[79]

A remaining issue on the meaning of "participant" concerns former employees who have received a lump sum payment of vested benefits, but who thereafter assert claims to additional benefits. In *Kuntz v. Reese*, former employees who received lump sum payments of their vested benefits alleged that plan administrators had misrepresented to them that their participation under a plan would commence immediately after they were hired and also misrepresented the amount of the plan's benefits. The Ninth Circuit first held that the former employees were still plan participants for purposes of bringing suit under ERISA because denying their standing would enable an employer to defeat the right to sue by distributing "whatever lump sum he wishes."[80] On a petition for rehearing, the Ninth Circuit vacated its prior opinion and held that because the former employees did not claim that they were eligible for more benefits *under the terms of the plan*, but only sought damages from a breach of fiduciary duty, they could not be considered plan participants. The Ninth Circuit was careful to note that this rationale would not apply if the plaintiffs had claimed that their benefits were improperly computed or determined in violation of law so that they did not receive their entire vested interest.[81] In *Yancy v. American Petrofina, Inc.*, the Fifth Circuit similarly

---

vested benefits and did not reasonably expect to return to covered employment to vest); *Nugent v. Jesuit High School of New Orleans*, 625 F.2d 1285, 2 EBC 1173 (5th Cir. 1980) (unvested former employee with no reasonable expectation of returning to employment lacked standing as a participant to pursue $100 per day penalties). But see *Hager v. Veco Corp.*, 1 EBC 1827 (N.D. Ill. 1979) (participant for purposes of securing documents and $100 per day penalties includes a former employee who received a "final" distribution of his interest in a plan; narrow construction would empower employer to defeat rights by making distribution and then not be held accountable for whether it was the entire interest).

[78] *Bruchac v. Universal Cab Co.*, 580 F.Supp. 295, 5 EBC 1697 (N.D. Ohio 1984) (allowing waivers would violate ERISA's nonforfeitability requirement). Conditioning receipt of undisputed benefit amounts on a signed waiver of other rights may also violate ERISA's anti-assignment rule.

[79] 29 C.F.R. 2510.3-3(d)(2)(ii)(A). The cited regulations define "participant covered under the plan" for purposes of ERISA §3(3). This definition is not necessarily determinative of the meaning of "participant" under ERISA §3(7) and §502. However, the courts have looked to this set of regulations in cases described next concerning whether an individual who has received a lump sum distribution is still a participant under ERISA §502.

[80] 760 F.2d 926, 6 EBC 1780, at 1785 (9th Cir. 1985).

[81] 785 F.2d 1410, 7 EBC 1227 (9th Cir. 1986), *cert. denied*, 479 U.S. ___ (1986), and see 29 C.F.R. 2510.3-3(d)(2)(ii)(B). See also *Lovetri v. Vickers, Inc.*, 397 F.Supp. 293 (D. Conn. 1975) (holding, based on pre-ERISA facts, that election of a cash option for undisputed benefits does not estop former employees from pursuing claims for disputed benefits); *Bricklayers Health & Welfare Trust v. Brick Masons Health & Welfare Trust Fund*, 656 F.2d 1387, 2 EBC 1921 (9th

held that a participant who received a lump sum distribution for all vested benefits lacked standing under ERISA to claim he lost future benefits because a breach of fiduciary duty in increasing the interest assumption for lump sums had precipitated his retirement before the increase in the interest rate took effect.[82]

D. Statutes of Limitation and Laches

Except for breach of fiduciary duty actions, ERISA contains no express statute of limitations for actions brought under Section 502(a). Under ERISA Section 413, a cause of action to redress a breach of fiduciary duty must be commenced within the "*earlier* of:

"(1) [S]ix years after (A) the date of the last action which constituted a part of the breach or violation, or (B) in the case of an omission, the latest date on which the fiduciary could have cured the breach or violation, *or*

"(2) [T]hree years after the earliest date (A) on which the plaintiff had actual knowledge of the breach or violation, or (B) the date on which a report from which he could reasonably be expected to have obtained knowledge of such breach or violation was filed with the Secretary [of Labor] under [Title I]."[83]

Section 413 provides an exception to the three-year element of this limitations period "in the case of fraud or concealment" by allowing a six-year period after the date of discovery of the breach or violation in which to bring an action.

In actions alleging imprudent investments or expenditures of a plan's assets, the courts have interpreted Section 413 to recognize that fiduciary breaches generally carry with them "continuing obligations" to cure the breach of duty. Therefore, the courts look for the fiduciary's

---

Cir. 1981) (former participants whose coverage under health benefit plan ended when their employers withdrew from plan had standing as participants to sue plan for transfer to their new plan of pro rata share of unallocated reserve assets).

[82] 768 F.2d 707, 6 EBC 2198 (5th Cir. 1985). See also *Joseph v. New Orleans Elec. Pension & Retirement Plan*, 754 F.2d 628, 6 EBC 1252 (5th Cir. 1985), *cert. denied*, 474 U.S. 1006 (1985) (retirees who accepted lump sum payments of benefits no longer participants for purpose of pursuing ERISA fiduciary claim that benefit increases for retirees should have extended to them as well); *Freeman v. Jacques Orthopaedic & Joint Implant Surgery Medical Group, Inc.*, 721 F.2d 654 (9th Cir. 1983) (former employee who waived participation in plan and later contended waiver should be invalid because employer had misrepresented the costs of participation is not an ERISA participant for purpose of bringing misrepresentation suit); *Walker v. Mountain States Tel. & Telegraph Co.*, 645 F.Supp. 93, 7 EBC 2623 (D. Colo. 1986) (early retirees were not "participants" in voluntary early retirement incentive plan that had not been extended to employees in their job class at the time of their retirement); *Stanton v. Gulf Oil Corp.*, 792 F.2d 432, 7 EBC 1873 (4th Cir. 1986) (employee who took early retirement was never a "participant" in a severance pay plan that took effect immediately thereafter). But compare *Ogden v. Michigan Bell Tel. Co.*, 8 EBC 1481 (E.D. Mich. 1987) (former employees who claimed fiduciaries misrepresented when a voluntary early retirement incentive program would go into effect had standing as participants under ERISA to bring suit; indirectly disagreeing with *Kuntz*). See also *Bigger v. American Commercial Lines, Inc.*, 652 F.Supp. 123, 8 EBC 1424 (W.D. Mo. 1986) (participants in spin-off plan were still participants in former plan within the meaning of §3(7) for purposes of challenging the spin off).

[83] Emphasis added.

last opportunity to cure a breach before starting the six-year element of the Section 413 period.[84] The three-year element has also not been invoked unless a plaintiff had actual knowledge of the entire breach,[85] or unless a report filed with the Secretary of Labor "shouted" the breach of duty.[86] A pleading of fraud or concealment that is not dismissable on a motion for summary judgment may also extend the three-year period to six years after discovery of the breach or violation.[87]

For benefit claims based on the terms of a plan, the courts have almost uniformly held that the most analogous state statute of limitations is to be applied to test the timeliness of an action—even though many claims for benefits under the terms of a plan are framed, at least in the alternative, as claims for breach of fiduciary duty. In *Miles v. New York Teamsters Pension Fund*, the Second Circuit held that the applicable limitations period for a benefit claim that included an allegation that plan trustees' actions were arbitrary and capricious was the most analogous *state* statute of limitations—which in New York was a six-year state statute of limitations for contracts.[88] Similarly, in *Jenkins v. Teamsters Local 705 Pension Plan*, the Seventh Circuit held

---

[84] See *Donovan v. Bryans*, 566 F.Supp. 1258, 4 EBC 1772 (E.D. Pa. 1983); *Buccino v. Continental Assurance Co.*, 578 F.Supp. 1518, 5 EBC 1225 (S.D.N.Y. 1983) (citing other cases).

[85] See *Katsaros v. Cody*, 744 F.2d 270, 5 EBC 1777 (2d Cir. 1984) (actual knowledge of breach of fiduciary duty in making loans did not arise when plaintiffs learned of existence of loans, but arose when they learned loans would not be repaid); *Brock v. Nellis*, 809 F.2d 753, 8 EBC 1206 (11th Cir. 1987) (actual knowledge limitation did not begin to run when Labor Department first knew real estate price was excessive when Labor did not yet know of defendants' involvement in the "transgressions"); *Foltz v. U.S. News & World Report, Inc.*, 627 F.Supp. 1143, 7 EBC 1229 (D.D.C. 1986); *Donovan v. Roseman*, 3 EBC 1117 (S.D. Fla. 1982).

[86] Compare *Brock v. TIC Int'l Corp.*, 785 F.2d 168, 7 EBC 1041 (7th Cir. 1986) (Posner, J.) (filing of report "shout[ing]" imprudence starts 3-year period immediately), with *Fink v. Nat'l Savings & Trust Co.*, 772 F.2d 951, 6 EBC 2269 (D.C. Cir. 1985) (disclosure of transaction that is not inherently a statutory breach does not communicate the breach); *Donovan v. Roseman, supra*; *Davidson v. Cook*, 567 F.Supp. 225, 4 EBC 1816 (E.D. Va. 1983), *aff'd*, 734 F.2d 10, 5 EBC 1440 (unpub.) (4th Cir. 1984); *Donovan v. Tricario*, 5 EBC 2057 (S.D. Fla. 1984), *aff'd sub nom. Brock v. Tricario*, 768 F.2d 1351 (11th Cir. 1985).

Reports to the Department of Labor that are not a part of a plan's regular Title I filings, as well as reports filed with other agencies, such as applications for determination filed with the IRS, do not start the 3-year element of the §413 limitations period. See *Struble v. New Jersey Brewery Employees' Welfare Fund*, 732 F.2d 325, 5 EBC 1676 (3d Cir. 1984) (rejecting 3-year limitation in suit by participants when participants had no way of knowing a letter "report[ing]" trustees' action had been sent to the Labor Dept.); *Marshall v. Mercer*, 4 EBC 1523 (N.D. Tex. 1983), *rev'd on other grounds*, 747 F.2d 304, 5 EBC 2512 (5th Cir. 1984) (filing of report with the Internal Revenue Service does not start §413 limitations period applicable to Title I reports filed with the Department of Labor); *Donovan v. Unicorn Group*, 3 EBC 1665 (S.D.N.Y. 1982) (3-year period based on actual knowledge or report filed with Department of Labor did not start when defendant introduced no evidence showing Labor Department had actual knowledge of FBI or SEC investigations of the same activities).

[87] See *Buccino v. Continental Assurance Co.*, 578 F.Supp. 1518, 5 EBC 1225 (S.D.N.Y. 1983) (if fraud or concealment allegation cannot be disposed of on motion for summary judgment, 3-year element of §413 period cannot be applied—at least not until after trial); *Donovan v. Cody*, 5 EBC 1773 (E.D.N.Y. 1984) (when facts in complaint suggest fraud or concealment, 6-year period may apply in spite of absence of specific pleading of fraud or concealment). And cf. *Kuntz v. Reese*, 760 F.2d 926, 6 EBC 1780 (9th Cir. 1985), *vacated and withdrawn on other grounds*, 785 F.2d 1410, 7 EBC 1227 (9th Cir. 1986), *cert. denied*, 479 U.S. ___ (1986) (pleading of fraud or concealment triggers 6-year exception).

[88] 698 F.2d 593, 4 EBC 2160 (2d Cir. 1983), *cert. denied*, 464 U.S. 829 (1983).

that the most analogous limitations period for a benefit claim under ERISA Section 502(a)(1)(B) was a ten-year period for contracts.[89]

Some states have shorter statutes of limitations for wage claims than for written contracts, but in an action to recover pension benefits, the most analogous limitations period has been held to be the longer period for written contracts.[90] When a state statute provides a short limitations period for written contracts, for example, a one- or three-year period that may be considered to undercut the purpose and policies of ERISA, a court may look back to ERISA Section 413 for a more appropriate limitations period.[91]

Written contract limitations periods may not provide the most analogous limitations period for certain types of benefit claims. If rights are based entirely on oral promises, e.g., that certain years of service will be credited for benefits, shorter limitations periods for oral contracts might apply.[92] Claims for misrepresentation by plan fiduciaries may be controlled by the ERISA Section 413 periods or by state

---

[89] 713 F.2d 247, 4 EBC 2315 (7th Cir. 1983). See also *Nolan v. Aetna Life Ins. Co.*, 588 F.Supp. 1375 (E.D. Mich. 1984) (applying 6-year state limitations period for contracts to §502(a)(1)(B) claim); *Haynes v. O'Connell*, 599 F.Supp. 59 (E.D. Tenn. 1984) (applying 6-year state period for contracts); *Morgan v. Laborers' Pension Trust Fund*, 433 F.Supp. 518 (N.D. Cal. 1977) (applying 4-year state statute); *Ferguson v. Greyhound Retirement & Disability Trust*, 613 F.Supp. 323 (W.D. Pa. 1985) (state law limitations period for contracts applied to disability benefits claims); *Holliday v. Xerox Corp.*, 555 F.Supp. 51, 4 EBC 1221 (E.D. Mich. 1982) (applying statute of limitations for contract actions). Accord *Cowden v. Montgomery Co. Society for Cancer Control*, 591 F.Supp. 740 (S.D. Ohio 1984); *Burud v. Acme Elec. Co.*, 591 F.Supp. 238, 5 EBC 1793 (D. Alas. 1984); *Meyer v. Phillip Morris, Inc.*, 569 F.Supp. 1510 (E.D. Mo. 1983).

When a plan is administered and the sponsoring company headquartered in a state other than the state in which an action is brought, the "most appropriate" state statute of limitation may be that of the state in which the company is headquartered and from which its plan is administered—even though venue is proper in the state in which the action is brought. *Jenkins v. Teamsters Local 705 Pension Plan, supra*, 4 EBC at 2318.

ERISA's limitations period for fiduciary claims has been used in some benefit claims cases without discussion of analogous state law alternatives. See *Edwards v. Wilkes-Barre Publishing Co. Pension Trust*, 757 F.2d 52, 6 EBC 1395 (3d Cir. 1985), *cert. denied*, 474 U.S. 843 (1985) (applying 3-year §413 limitations period to claims of ERISA vesting and benefit accrual standard violations instead of 6-month NLRA limitations period that company contended should apply); *Sparks v. Ryerson & Haynes, Inc.*, 638 F.Supp. 56 (E.D. Mich. 1986) (applying 3-year §413 period to claim that health benefits for retirees were impermissibly reduced by a negotiated plan amendment over 6-month NLRA period that defendant sought; 6-year state law period for contracts discussed as an alternate limitations period for LMRA count, but not for ERISA count); *Ballinger v. Perkins*, 515 F.Supp. 673, 2 EBC 1454 (W.D. Va. 1981) (applying 6-year element of §413 limitation period to benefit claim without discussion of most analogous state statutory period).

[90] See *Carpenters Local 1846 v. Pratt Farnsworth, Inc.*, 609 F.Supp. 1302 (E.D. La. 1984). But see *Salyers v. Allied Corp.*, 642 F.Supp. 442 (E.D. Ky. 1986) (5-year Kentucky statutory period for redressing withholding of personal property applied in lieu of 15-year statute for written contracts in ERISA action alleging that offset from disability benefits of full amount of workmen's compensation benefits was arbitrary and capricious interpretation of plan).

[91] See *Dameron v. Sinai Hospital of Baltimore, Inc.*, 595 F.Supp. 1404, 5 EBC 2321 (D. Md. 1984); cf. *Kuntz v. Reese*, 760 F.2d 926, 6 EBC 1780 (9th Cir. 1985), *vacated and withdrawn on other grounds*, 785 F.2d 1410, 7 EBC 1227 (9th Cir. 1986), *cert. denied*, 479 U.S. ___ (1986). On examination of all the cases cited in n. 90 above, no case has been found in which a court used a *shorter* state law period than the period provided by application of §413.

[92] See *Miller v. Int'l Harvester Co.*, 811 F.2d 1150 (7th Cir. 1987) (2-year state statute for employment actions not based on written contract applied to action to redress oral misrepresentation of pension eligibility from time employer told employee that representation was a mistake and would not be honored); *Sheeran v. General Elec. Co.*, 593 F.2d 93 (9th Cir. 1979).

law limitation periods for injury to personalty based on misrepresentation.[93]

Actions to redress ERISA minimum standard violations are controlled by the *longer* of the fiduciary limitations period or the state written contract period.[94]

For pension benefit claims, the courts have also uniformly held that any limitations period does not begin to run until participants have clear notice of the "repudiation" of their claim. This generally occurs only when they retire, apply for, and are denied benefits. The Fifth Circuit has thus stated:

> "[A] cause of action does not accrue until a claim is denied.... To hold otherwise would put an almost intolerable burden on employees covered by pension plans. It would require individuals who are unversed in the law to be constantly vigilant.... Moreover, claims filed before a pension actually has been denied might be challenged for lack of ripeness."[95]

The rule that a limitations period on a benefit claim does not start to run until the benefits are denied also recognizes that fiduciaries have continuing duties to review their positions on benefit entitlement before final disposition of claims, and implicitly recognizes the practical consideration that participants are reluctant to sue a plan (in effect, their employer) while they are still employed.

Because ERISA does not contain an express statute of limitations for Section 510 actions for purposeful interference with pension rights, the most analogous state law period in such actions may be the state's

---

[93] Compare *Kuntz v. Reese, supra* (applying §413 period, rather than shorter state period, in action for misrepresentation by plan fiduciaries), with *Whitaker v. Texaco, Inc.*, 566 F.Supp. 745, 4 EBC 1762 (N.D. Ga. 1983) (applying state statutory period for injury to personalty).

[94] See *Edwards v. Wilkes-Barre Publishing Co. Pension Trust, supra* at n. 89; *Fraver v. North Carolina Farm Bureau Mut. Ins. Co.*, 643 F.Supp. 633 (E.D.N.C. 1985), *rev'd on other grounds*, 801 F.2d 675, 7 EBC 2137 (4th Cir. 1986), *cert. denied*, 480 U.S. ___ (1987) (3-year contract period and 3-year period for statutory actions used for action to enforce ERISA minimum standards on forfeitures for competition); *Dameron v. Sinai Hospital of Baltimore, Inc.*, 595 F.Supp. 1404, 5 EBC 2321 (D. Md. 1984), *aff'd*, 815 F.2d 975 (4th Cir. 1987) (fiduciary and state written contract periods in congruence; therefore, state law period not at odds with ERISA).

[95] *Paris v. Wolf, Inc., Profit Sharing Plan*, 637 F.2d 357, 2 EBC 1244, at 1247 (5th Cir. 1981), *cert. denied*, 454 U.S. 836 (1981) (in large part quoting *Morgan v. Laborers Pension Trust Fund*, 433 F.Supp. 518, at 522 n.5 (N.D. Cal. 1977)). And see *Miles v. New York Teamsters Pension Fund*, 698 F.2d 593, 4 EBC 2160 (2d Cir. 1983), *cert. denied*, 464 U.S. 829 (1983); *Edwards v. Wilkes-Barre Publishing Co. Pension Trust*, 757 F.2d 52, 6 EBC 1395 (3d Cir. 1985), *cert. denied*, 474 U.S. 843 (1985); *Tanzillo v. Teamsters Local 617*, 769 F.2d 140 (3d Cir. 1985); *Dameron v. Sinai Hospital of Baltimore, Inc.*, 595 F.Supp. 1404, 5 EBC 2321 (D. Md. 1984), *aff'd*, 815 F.2d 975 (4th Cir. 1987); *Jenkins v. Teamsters Local 705 Pension Plan*, 713 F.2d 247, 4 EBC 2315 (7th Cir. 1983); *Reiherzer v. Shannon*, 581 F.2d 1266, 1 EBC 1175 (7th Cir. 1978); *Menhorn v. Firestone Tire & Rubber Co.*, 738 F.2d 1496, 5 EBC 2193 (9th Cir. 1984); *Holt v. Winpisinger*, 811 F.2d 1532, 8 EBC 1169 (D.C. Cir. 1987) (statute of limitations begins to run when benefit request is denied); *Jackson v. American Can Co.*, 485 F.Supp. 370 (W.D. Mich. 1980); *Whitaker v. Texaco, Inc.*, 566 F.Supp. 745, 4 EBC 1762 (N.D. Ga. 1983). More technically, the limitations period may not start until the benefit claim is denied *and* administrative remedies are exhausted. See *Dameron v. Sinai Hospital of Baltimore, Inc., supra.*

Some cases also suggest that the due date of each disputed monthly payment creates a distinct cause of action. See *Dameron v. Sinai Hospital of Baltimore, Inc.*, 815 F.2d 975 (4th Cir. 1987) ("series of successive breaches" arise from denial of full monthly payments); *Connell v. U.S. Steel*, 371 F.Supp. 991 (N.D. Ala. 1974).

limitations period for contracts or for employment termination actions.[96] A failure to distribute documents, such as an SPD, may be controlled by the fiduciary limitations period or an analogous state limitations period.[97] For the $100 per day penalties under ERISA Section 502(c), the state written contract period, rather than any shorter period for actions brought under state penalty statutes, has been applied.[98]

Laches, rather than a statute of limitations, could apply if a court determines that a benefit claim is more equitable than legal in nature. Generally, however, the courts have not used laches to test the timeliness of benefit claims (even though many courts see *all* pension claims as more equitable than legal in nature in determining the availability of a jury trial). In *Dameron v. Sinai Hospital of Baltimore, Inc.*, laches was applied because a district court considered the plaintiff's claims to be equitable, but the court still referred to the analogous state law limitations period, finding no reason for delay beyond this period and no effective rebuttal of presumed prejudice to the defendant when the suit was filed beyond this period. On appeal, *Dameron* was reversed by the Fourth Circuit insofar as it applied laches in an ERISA contract and minimum standard violation action.[99]

E. Right to a Jury Trial

To date, the weight of judicial authority is against the right to a jury trial for ERISA causes of action.[100] However, in *Sixty-Five Security Plan v. Blue Cross of New York*, a district court stated that the

---

[96] Compare *Gavalik v. Continental Can Co.*, 812 F.2d 835, 8 EBC 1047 (3d Cir. 1987) (6-year state period for wrongful discharge and employment discrimination actions governed §510 action); *Corkery v. SuperX Drugs Corp.*, 602 F.Supp. 42 (M.D. Fla. 1985) (period applicable for employment termination actions); with *Delisi v. United Parcel Service, Inc.*, 580 F.Supp. 1572 (W.D. Pa. 1984) (contract period).

[97] Compare *Kuntz v. Reese*, *supra*, with *Burud v. Acme Elec. Co.*, 591 F.Supp. 238, 5 EBC 1793 (D. Alas. 1984) (most analogous state statute is to be applied in action alleging failure to distribute summary of plan amendment).

[98] *Abbott v. Drs. Ridgik, Steinberg & Assocs., P.A.*, 609 F.Supp. 1216, 6 EBC 2289 (D.N.J. 1985).

[99] 815 F.2d 975 (4th Cir. 1987), *aff'g in part, rev'g in part*, 595 F.Supp. 1404, 5 EBC 2321 (D. Md. 1984). In *Anderson v. Automotive Industries Pension Fund*, 2 EBC 2278 (N.D. Cal. 1981), another defendant raised the issue of laches, but the district court held it had not met its burden of proving "unreasonable delay" and "prejudice."

[100] Decisions favoring a right to a jury trial are: *Haytcher v. ABS Indus., Inc.*, 7 EBC 2158 (N.D. Ohio 1986); *Bower v. Bunker Hill Co.*, C.A. No. C-82-412 (E.D. Wash. Feb. 4, 1986); *Paladino v. Taxicab Indus. Pension Fund*, 588 F.Supp. 37, 5 EBC 1757 (S.D.N.Y. 1984); *Ovitz v. Jefferies & Co.*, 553 F.Supp. 300, 3 EBC 2601 (N.D. Ill. 1982); *Pollock v. Castrovinci*, 476 F.Supp. 606 (S.D.N.Y. 1979), *aff'd*, 622 F.2d 575 (2d Cir. 1980); *OCAW Local 4-23 v. Texaco*, 88 F.R.D. 86 (E.D. Tex. 1980); *Bouton v. Central States Pension Fund*, 1 EBC 1498 (E.D. Tenn. 1978); *Stamps v. Michigan Teamsters Joint Council*, 431 F.Supp. 745, 1 EBC 1734 (E.D. Mich. 1977).

Decisions denying a right to a jury trial are: *Turner v. CF&I Steel Corp.*, 770 F.2d 43, 6 EBC 2101 (3d Cir. 1985), *cert. denied*, 474 U.S. 1058 (1986); *Blau v. Del Monte Corp.*, 748 F.2d 1348, 6 EBC 1264 (9th Cir. 1984), *cert. denied*, 474 U.S. 865 (1985); *Katsaros v. Cody*, 744 F.2d 270, 5 EBC 1777 (2d Cir. 1984), *cert. denied*, 469 U.S. 1072 (1984); *Berry v. CIBA-GEIGY Corp.*, 761 F.2d 1003, 6 EBC 1481 (4th Cir. 1985); *Wardle v. Central States Pension Fund*, 627 F.2d 820, 2 EBC 1633 (7th Cir. 1980), *cert. denied*, 449 U.S. 1112 (1981); *Calamia v. Spivey*, 632 F.2d 1235, 2 EBC 1321 (5th Cir. 1980); *In re Vorpahl*, 695 F.2d 318, 3 EBC 2597 (8th Cir. 1982); *Hollenbeck v. Falstaff Brewing Corp.*, 605 F.Supp. 421 (E.D. Mo. 1984), *aff'd*, 780 F.2d 20 (8th Cir. 1985);

"right to a jury trial of ERISA claims is by no means settled."[101] The division on whether a jury trial may be obtained for an ERISA claim focuses on claims for benefits under Section 502(a)(1)(B), since both the action and the relief thereunder may be, but are not necessarily, characterized as legal. When the nature of the action and the relief are equitable, as in a Section 502(a)(2) suit alleging imprudent investments or expenditures of a plan's assets by plan fiduciaries, with restitution sought as a remedy, there is agreement that a jury trial is not available.[102]

Some pro-jury courts have looked at the specific nature of the claims and relief sought, regardless of whether Section 502(a)(1)(B) or 502(a)(3) is involved, before deciding whether to grant a jury trial, recognizing that some allegations under Section 502(a)(3) may also be more legal than equitable in nature.[103] But most pro-jury trial courts would confine the right to a jury to Section 502(a)(1)(B) claims based on an ERISA Conference Report statement that actions under Section 502(a)(1)(B) are to be regarded "in similar fashion to those brought under Section 301 of the Labor Management Relations Act of 1947."[104] As these courts, and some of the courts that have rejected a jury right under ERISA, have recognized, Section 301 of the Labor Management Relations Act (which enables unions and retirees to enforce the terms of collectively bargained agreements) is a contract enforcement section that confers a right to a jury trial. Still more pertinently, Section 301 has often been found to confer a right to a jury trial in actions to

---

Gilliken v. Hughes, 609 F.Supp. 178, 6 EBC 1745 (D. Del. 1985); *Kolata v. UMW Pension Trust*, 533 F.Supp. 313, 3 EBC 1501 (S.D. W.Va. 1982), *aff'd*, 696 F.2d 990, 3 EBC 2458 (4th Cir. 1982); *Cowden v. Montgomery Co. Society for Cancer Control*, 591 F.Supp. 740 (S.D. Ohio 1984); *Diano v. Central States Pension Fund*, 551 F.Supp. 861, 3 EBC 2395 (N.D. Ohio 1982); *Burud v. Acme Elec. Co.*, 591 F.Supp. 238, 5 EBC 1793 (D. Alas. 1984); *Rubin v. Decision Concepts, Inc.*, 566 F.Supp. 1057 (S.D.N.Y. 1983); *Foulke v. Bethlehem 1980 Salaried Pension Plan*, 565 F.Supp. 882, 4 EBC 1848 (E.D. Pa. 1983); *Rice v. Hutton*, 487 F.Supp. 278 (W.D. Mo. 1980); *Gavalik v. Continental Can Co.*, 3 EBC 2023 (W.D. Pa. 1982); *Porter v. Central States Pension Fund*, 98 LRRM 3210 (N.D. Iowa 1978).

[101] 583 F.Supp. 380, 5 EBC 1430, at 1437 (S.D.N.Y. 1984) (convening jury, but reserving decision on effect of its verdict until after trial). However, the judge who decided *Sixty-Five Security Plan, supra*, subsequently granted a motion to strike a jury demand in *Nobile v. Pension Committee of Pension Plan*, 611 F.Supp. 725 (S.D.N.Y. 1985), in which a spouse claimed his wife was not given enough information by plan fiduciaries to enable her to make a reasoned decision about survivor's benefit options.

[102] See, e.g., *Katsaros v. Cody, supra* (no jury trial on fiduciary mismanagement of assets claim); *Donovan v. Wheeler*, 4 EBC 1079 (D.N.H. 1983); *Donovan v. Cody*, 5 EBC 1773 (E.D.N.Y. 1984); *Donovan v. Roseman*, 3 EBC 1117 (S.D. Fla. 1982).

See also *Crews v. Central States Pension Fund*, 788 F.2d 332, 7 EBC 1642 (6th Cir. 1986) (suit by owner-employee to recover contributions to pension fund made on his own behalf allegedly under a mistake was essentially equitable action for restitution for which there is no right to a jury).

[103] See *Pollock v. Castrovinci, supra* (jury trial granted on both §§502(a)(1)(B) and 502(a)(3) claims which "stripped of . . . ERISA garb" were basically questions of "contract"); *Sixty-Five Security Plan v. Blue Cross of New York, supra* (provisionally granting jury trial, but reserving final decision on whether §502(a)(3) claims and relief were more legal than equitable).

[104] See, e.g., *Stamps v. Michigan Teamsters Joint Council, supra*, and Conf. Rep., at 327, 3 ERISA Leg. Hist. 4594.

enforce employee benefit provisions of collective bargaining agreements.[105] Similarly, in pre-ERISA suits to enforce the terms of nonbargained plans and in suits under state law to enforce collectively bargained plans, employee benefit claims were sometimes submitted to juries.[106]

The far larger number of courts, however, categorically reject the right to a jury trial for *all* ERISA benefit claims. These courts reason that employee benefit claims were traditionally considered "equitable" before ERISA. Consequently, they have held that the Conference Report statement directing the courts to regard cases under Section 502(a)(1)(B) in similar fashion to those brought under Section 301 of LMRA is not specific enough to require jury trials.[107] Some confusion about the uniformity of traditional pre-ERISA practice may exist because many widely publicized benefit claims were brought before ERISA under Section 302(e) of the Labor Management Relations Act to enforce Section 302(c)(5)'s requirement that plans be structured solely for the benefit of employees and their families. These claims were, and are, essentially actions for equitable reformation of the terms of the plan, and they were treated as equitable claims, in terms of both the action and the available relief,[108] with no right to a jury arising.[109] As described above, however, other pre-ERISA cases allowed juries in contract enforcement actions.

Courts disallowing a right to a jury on benefit claims have been forced to draw finer lines as the cases on jury trials proceed. In *Bugher v. Feightner*, the Seventh Circuit (which decided *Wardle v. Central States Pension Fund*, the leading case denying a right to a jury trial) found a right to a jury for an employer faced with an action by a plan under ERISA Section 502(a)(3) and LMRA Section 301 to collect delinquent contributions. In *Bugher*, the Seventh Circuit maintained its position that the denial of a jury for the participant in *Wardle* was proper on the basis that benefit claims had a "different historical background" from contribution actions in that benefit claims were "traditionally" treated as equitable claims before ERISA.[110] *May v. Interstate Moving & Storage Co.*, shows how blurry the *Bugher* distinction can become. In *May*, the Tenth Circuit held that if an employer's

---

[105] See *Bower v. Bunker Hill Co., supra*; *Haytcher v. ABS Indus., Inc., supra*; *Stamps v. Michigan Teamsters Joint Council, supra*; *Pollock v. Castrovinci, supra*; *Hazel v. Lynch Corp.*, C.A. No. IP 84-1352-C (S.D. Ind. Jan. 17, 1986); *Bugher v. Feightner*, 722 F.2d 1356, 4 EBC 2604 (7th Cir. 1983), *cert. denied*, 469 U.S. 822 (1984); *A.I.W. v. General Elec. Co.*, 471 F.2d 751 (6th Cir. 1973); *May v. Interstate Moving & Storage Co.*, 739 F.2d 521 (10th Cir. 1984).

[106] See *Apponi v. Sunshine Biscuits, Inc.*, 652 F.2d 643, 2 EBC 1534 (6th Cir. 1981); *Scheuer v. Central States Pension Fund*, 358 F.Supp. 1332 (E.D. Wis. 1973) and 394 F.Supp. 193 (E.D. Wis. 1975), *aff'd on other grounds*, 570 F.2d 347 (7th Cir. 1977); *Tanuggi v. Grolier, Inc.*, 471 F.Supp. 1209, 1 EBC 1889 (S.D.N.Y. 1979); *Salvatori v. Rubin*, 283 S.E.2d 326 (Ga. Ct.App. 1981); *Bierley v. American Cast Iron Pipe Co.*, 374 So.2d 1341 (Ala. 1979) (jury question would have been present if an ambiguity in the terms of the plan).

[107] See *Wardle v. Central States Pension Fund, supra*; *Calamia v. Spivey, supra*.

[108] See *Sellers v. O'Connell*, 701 F.2d 575, 4 EBC 1312 (6th Cir. 1983).

[109] *Souza v. Western Teamsters Pension Trust*, 663 F.2d 942, 2 EBC 2322 (9th Cir. 1981).

[110] 722 F.2d 1356, 4 EBC 2604, at 2608 (7th Cir. 1983), *cert. denied*, 469 U.S. 822 (1984).

contribution obligation under a bargaining agreement requires resolution of an ambiguity in the pension part of the agreement about whether part-time employees are "casual" employees for whom contributions are required, the ambiguity is a jury question under ERISA.[111] However, if the part-time employees themselves raise the issue of their coverage under the plan, it appears that a jury trial would be denied them under ERISA.

Whatever the ultimate outcome of the jury trial issue under ERISA, jury trials remain available under Section 301 of the LMRA, and under any non-preempted state law causes of action that an employee or former employee may have.[112] When a jury is convened in an ERISA Section 502(a)(1)(B) or an LMRA Section 301 action, however, all issues will not be submitted to the jury. As the Sixth Circuit stated in *Apponi v. Sunshine Biscuits, Inc.*, in remanding a pre-ERISA pension case brought under state law for a jury trial:

> "The respective roles of judge and jury in contract cases depend on the circumstances. Ordinarily, the construction of a written contract is a matter of law to be decided by a judge. However, while it is the function of a court to construe a contract, it is the province of the jury to ascertain and determine the intent and meaning of the contracting parties in the use of uncertain or ambiguous language. . . .
>
> "[I]ssues as to waiver or estoppel are [also] classic examples of disputed fact which are amenable to decision by a jury."[113]

Juries may also be convened to determine damages from tort-like benefit denials.[114]

---

[111] 739 F.2d 521 (10th Cir. 1984).

[112] See n. 105 above on jury trials under LMRA §301. Examples of nonpreempted state law causes of action for which a jury trial may remain available are actions for breach of an insurance contract or for breach of a separate contractual agreement with an employer. See *Trogner v. New York Life Ins. Co.*, 633 F.Supp. 503 (D. Md. 1986) (right to a jury in action alleging breach of insurance contract to provide employee benefits).

[113] *Apponi v. Sunshine Biscuits, Inc., supra*, 2 EBC at 1541 n.12 (citations omitted). And see *Apponi v. Sunshine Biscuits, Inc.*, 809 F.2d 1210, 8 EBC 1397 (6th Cir. 1987), *reh. denied*, 8 EBC 1567 (6th Cir. 1987) (holding on appeal of decision on remand that Sixth Circuit's prior mandate contemplates jury trial on all elements of waiver and estoppel, e.g., whether representations were made by person with authority and whether they were intended to be relied on); *Paladino v. Taxicab Industry Pension Fund*, 588 F.Supp. 37, 5 EBC 1757 (S.D.N.Y. 1984) (whether participant had a break in service is a question of fact for jury because right to pension arises out of contract; questions of fact are separated from questions of entitlement for presentation to jury); *Bower v. Bunker Hill Co., supra*, (claim that health benefits are vested is a contractual issue under ERISA that plaintiffs are entitled to have tried by a jury insofar as any factual questions necessary for contract interpretation); *Haytcher v. ABS Indus., Inc.*, 7 EBC 2158 (N.D. Ohio 1986) (claims for breach of fiduciary duty to be tried by court after resolution by jury of contract claims).

[114] See *Holmes v. Oxford Chemicals, Inc.*, 510 F.Supp. 915, 2 EBC 1167 (M.D. Ala. 1981), *aff'd*, 3 EBC 1667 (11th Cir. 1982) (sustaining $25,000 jury award based on tort of outrage when a plan administrator offset Social Security disability benefits from benefits under the pension plan, even though administrator knew the participant was not currently receiving the Social Security benefits); *Bower v. Bunker Hill Co., supra* (amount of plan participants' damages from a breach is question for jury).

F. Remedies for Benefit Denials

An order directing a plan to pay benefits is the basic remedy in employee benefits litigation. If benefit payments have been missed because of an unlawful denial, the remedy can include a monetary judgment or an order directing that back benefits be paid in a lump sum. Prejudgment interest from the date of the benefit application is routinely included to make participants whole. In *Short v. Central States Pension Fund*, the Eighth Circuit described the reasons for awarding prejudgment interest:

> "Zorn [the plaintiff] was entitled to benefits upon the processing of his application. Essentially, the Fund has retained money which rightfully belongs to Zorn. To allow the Fund to retain the interest it earned on funds wrongfully withheld would be to approve of unjust enrichment. Further the relief granted would fall short of making Zorn whole because he has been denied the use of money which was his."[115]

Usually, no lump sum payments of future benefits will be awarded as a remedy unless a lump sum option is provided under the terms of the plan.[116] However, in certain cases, a lump sum payment of future benefits could be obtained based on a total anticipatory breach, even though no lump sum form is offered under the terms of the plan.[117]

To make an individual whole, other compensatory damages could be awarded. For example, if a participant has been forced to borrow at higher interest rates than the prejudgment rate or has been forced to liquidate assets at a disadvantageous price, extra-contractual compensatory damages could be awarded if such consequences were within the

---

[115] 729 F.2d 567, 5 EBC 2552, at 2560 (8th Cir. 1984). See also *Dependahl v. Falstaff Brewing Corp.*, 653 F.2d 1208, 2 EBC 1521 (8th Cir. 1981), *cert. denied*, 454 U.S. 968 (1981); *Valle v. Joint Plumbing Industry Board*, 623 F.2d 196, 3 EBC 1026 (2d Cir. 1980); *Blanton v. Anzalone*, 760 F.2d 989, 6 EBC 1610 (9th Cir. 1985); *Kann v. Keystone Resources, Inc., Profit Sharing Plan*, 575 F.Supp. 1084, 5 EBC 1233 (W.D. Pa. 1983); *Grossmuller v. Budd Co. Retirement Plan*, 547 F.Supp. 111, 4 EBC 1937 (E.D. Pa. 1982); *Donovan v. Carlough*, 581 F.Supp. 271, 5 EBC 1406 (D.D.C. 1984); *Baeten v. Van Ess*, 474 F.Supp. 1324, 1 EBC 2046 (E.D. Wis. 1979).

The prejudgment interest rate is based on the last 52-week Treasury bill rate, as provided under 28 U.S.C. §1961, before the plaintiffs' claim for benefits was made. See *Kann v. Keystone Resources, Inc. Profit Sharing Plan, supra*; *Blanton v. Anzalone, supra*. *Dameron v. Sinai Hospital of Baltimore, Inc.*, 626 F.Supp. 1012, 6 EBC 2742 (D. Md. 1986), used the last 52-week rate before the date of judgment. In a few cases, state law pre- or post-judgment interest rates have been used. See *Donovan v. Carlough, supra*; *Dependahl v. Falstaff Brewing Corp., supra* (using state law interest rate because 28 U.S.C. §1961 at the time of the decision used state law postjudgment interest rates); *Valle v. Joint Plumbing Industry Board, supra* (using state law interest rate for pre-ERISA claim). The sounder view under ERISA appears to be to use the last 52-week Treasury bill rate. See *Kann v. Keystone Resources, Inc. Profit Sharing Plan, supra*, 5 EBC at 1244.

[116] See, e.g., *Tanuggi v. Grolier, Inc.*, 471 F.Supp. 1209, 1 EBC 1889 (S.D.N.Y. 1979) (no money damages available as remedy before retirement age when plan provided no right to preretirement lump sum payment).

[117] See *Stopford v. Boonton Molding Co.*, 265 A.2d 657 (N.J. 1970) (lump sum awarded when employer's actions in terminating plan and repudiating obligation to continue paying plaintiff $296 per month amounted to total anticipatory breach; when such breaches occur, plaintiffs will not be left with prospect of having to take future piecemeal actions to enforce their rights); *Hauck v. Eschbacher*, 665 F.2d 843, 2 EBC 2202 (8th Cir. 1981) (citing *Stopford* and other decisions, but not finding such a breach when plan fiduciaries themselves sought declaratory judgment on their ability to apply 3-year noncompetition clause to benefits accrued before clause adopted, with no indication that they would not abide by court's decision).

reasonable contemplation of the parties at the time the plan was adopted.

Mental and emotional distress may also accompany a benefit denial that is contrary to the terms of a plan or otherwise in violation of law. In *UAW v. Federal Forge, Inc.*, a district court found that an award for mental or emotional distress may be proper when an employer wrongfully terminates health insurance of retirees if the mental and emotional distress accompanying a wrongful termination of the insurance could reasonably have been contemplated by the parties when the plan was adopted.[118] However, in *Massachusetts Mutual Life Ins. Co. v. Russell*, the Supreme Court rejected a participant's claim for mental and emotional distress damages arising from a plan's failure to process her claim in good faith and in a fair and diligent manner.[119] The Court held that the participant's claim that plan fiduciaries could be liable for such damages in an ERISA Section 502(a)(2) action as "appropriate relief under [ERISA S]ection 409" for breach of fiduciary duty ran contrary to the "plan-related" context of ERISA Section 409, which focuses on requiring fiduciaries who breach their duties to restore "losses to the plan."[120] But as the Court's opinion noted, and as the concurrence of four justices emphasized, the claimant, for unexplained reasons, had disclaimed reliance on ERISA Section 502(a)(3), which authorizes "other appropriate equitable relief [for participants and beneficiaries] to redress" any act or practice which violates Title I of ERISA or the terms of the plan.[121] Since *Russell*, decisions have been mixed on the availability of extra-contractual damages under ERISA Section 502(a)(3).[122]

The courts are also divided on whether punitive damages are available in litigation under Section 502(a). Until 1985, the majority of decisions held that punitive damages were available under ERISA "if a plaintiff proves that there has been a willful, malicious, wanton, or

---

[118] 583 F.Supp. 1350, 5 EBC 1513 (W.D. Mich. 1984). See also *Bobo v. 1950 Pension Plan*, 548 F.Supp. 623 (W.D.N.Y. 1982) (awarding damages for mental anguish); *Hazel v. Lynch Corp.*, *supra* (claim for mental distress damages may be brought under §301 of the LMRA when matters of mental concern were within the reasonable contemplation of the parties when executing the agreement, following *UAW v. Federal Forge, supra*).

The mental and emotional distress caused by pension benefit denials was recognized in the legislative history of ERISA. Rep. Dominick Daniels cited instances where workers went out to their garages and hung themselves after learning that they would not receive pension benefits. 3 ERISA Leg. Hist. 4717.

[119] 473 U.S. 134, 6 EBC 1733 (1985). The plan took 132 days to reinstate the claimant's disability benefits. She alleged this caused her husband to have to cash out his retirement savings and aggravated a psychological condition that caused her back problems.

[120] 6 EBC at 1736-37. The Court rejected the claim that further remedies for participants should be implied under §409, finding a "stark absence" of the legislative intent required to support such an implication. 6 EBC at 1740.

[121] 6 EBC at 1735 n.5 and 1741-45. The concurrence emphasizes that the majority's broad language against implied remedies of extra-contractual and punitive damages under ERISA should not be read to resolve whether such damages may be available under §502(a)(3).

[122] Compare *Haytcher v. ABS Indus., Inc.*, 7 EBC 2158 (N.D. Ohio 1986) (extra-contractual damage claims under §§502(a)(3) and 502(a)(1)(B) not subject to motion to dismiss after *Russell* when contract violation alleged to be "willful"), with *Hutchinson v. Benton Casing Service, Inc.*, 619 F.Supp. 831 (S.D. Miss. 1985) (after *Russell* extra-contractual damages are not allowed under §502); *Sokol v. Bernstein*, 803 F.2d 532, 7 EBC 2321 (9th Cir. 1986).

oppressive breach of fiduciary duty."[123] However, in *Massachusetts Mutual Life Ins. Co. v. Russell* the Supreme Court rejected a punitive damages claim (as well as the claim for extra-contractual compensatory damages) based on the plan's alleged failure to process her claim in good faith and in a fair and diligent manner. The Court again held that the participant's assertion that plan fiduciaries could be liable for such damages under ERISA Section 502(a)(2) as "appropriate relief under [ERISA S]ection 409" ran contrary to the focus of Section 409 on requiring a fiduciary who is in breach of duty to restore "losses to the plan."[124] But as the Court noted, and as the concurrence of four justices again emphasized, the claimant disclaimed reliance on ERISA Section 502(a)(3), which authorizes "other appropriate equitable relief [for participants and beneficiaries] to redress" any violation of Title I of ERISA or of the terms of the plan.[125] Since *Russell*, courts have tended to reject punitive damages under Section 502(a)(3) as well, although some ambiguously suggest reservation of the issue in areas where punitive damages traditionally have been awarded under state law.[126]

---

123 *Gilliken v. Hughes*, 609 F.Supp. 178, 6 EBC 1745, at 1749 (D. Del. 1985). And see *Scott v. Gulf Oil Corp.*, 754 F.2d 1499 (9th Cir. 1985); *Monson v. Century Mfg. Co.*, 739 F.2d 1293, 5 EBC 1625 (8th Cir. 1984); *Winterrowd v. David Freedman & Co.*, 724 F.2d 823, 5 EBC 1221 (9th Cir. 1984); *Korn v. Levine Bros. Iron Works Corp.*, 574 F.Supp. 836, 4 EBC 2533 (S.D.N.Y. 1983); *Jiminez v. Pioneer Diecasters, Inc., Pension Plan*, 549 F.Supp. 677, 3 EBC 2192 (C.D. Cal. 1982); *Bittner v. Sadoff & Rudoy Indus.* 490 F.Supp. 534 (E.D. Wis. 1980); *Eaton v. D'Amato*, 581 F.Supp. 743, 3 EBC 1003 (D.D.C. 1980); *Baeten v. Van Ess*, 474 F.Supp. 1324, 1 EBC 2046 (E.D. Wis. 1979); *Free v. Gilbert Hodgman, Inc.*, 3 EBC 1010 (N.D. Ill. 1982); *Kann v. Keystone Resources, Inc. Profit Sharing Plan*, 575 F.Supp. 1084, 5 EBC 1233 (W.D. Pa. 1983); *Miner v. Typographical Union Negotiated Pension Plan*, 601 F.Supp. 1390, 6 EBC 1208 (D. Colo. 1985) (citing still other decisions, pro and con).

Punitive damages were held not to be available in: *Dependahl v. Falstaff Brewing Corp.*, 653 F.2d 1208, 2 EBC 1521 (8th Cir. 1981), *cert. denied*, 454 U.S. 1084 (1981) [but compare *Monson v. Century Mfg. Co., supra* (8th Cir. 1984), and *Hollenbeck v. Falstaff Brewing Co.*, 780 F.2d 20 (8th Cir. 1985) (reserving issue)]; *Lewis v. Fulton Federal Savings & Loan Pension Plan*, 4 EBC 2071 (N.D. Ga. 1983); *Walker v. Jaffe*, 5 EBC 2736 (W.D. Tex. 1983); *Whitaker v. Texaco, Inc.*, 566 F.Supp. 745, 4 EBC 1762 (N.D. Ga. 1983); *Diano v. Central States Health & Welfare Fund*, 551 F.Supp. 861, 3 EBC 2395 (N.D. Ohio 1982); *Meyer v. Phillip Morris, Inc.*, 569 F.Supp. 1510 (E.D. Mo. 1983).

124 473 U.S. 134, 6 EBC 1733, at 1736-37 (1985).

125 6 EBC at 1735 n.5 and 1741-45.

126 Compare *Powell v. Chesapeake & Potomac Tel. Co.*, 780 F.2d 419, 6 EBC 2754 (4th Cir. 1985), *cert. denied*, 476 U.S. ___ (1986) (mishandling of disability benefit claim by allegedly withholding benefit payments without justification and demanding unnecessary medical reports does not provide the basis for punitive damages under §502(a)(3), although footnote suggests there may be exceptions for fraud or malice); *Unitis v. JFC Acquisition Co.*, 643 F.Supp. 454, 7 EBC 2217 (N.D. Ill. 1986) (punitive damages denied under facts, but if fiduciary's actions constitute an independent tort, e.g., fraud or misrepresentation, they may be awarded); *Wilson v. Pye*, 6 EBC 2761, at 2765 (N.D. Ill. 1986) (punitive damages "are [after *Russell*] probably never recoverable by an ERISA participant or beneficiar[y; i]f they are recoverable at all, it is when a fiduciary flagrantly violates a longstanding duty toward an individual beneficiary under state trust law"); *Haytcher v. ABS Indus., Inc.*, 7 EBC 2158 (N.D. Ohio 1986) (punitive damage claims under §§502(a)(1)(B) and 502(a)(3) not subject to motion to dismiss after *Russell* when contract violation alleged to be "willful"), with *Sommers Drug Stores Co. Employees Profit Sharing Trust v. Corrigan Enterprises, Inc.*, 793 F.2d 1456, 7 EBC 1782 (5th Cir. 1986), *cert. denied*, 479 U.S. ___ (1987) (no punitive damages under §502(a)(3)); *Foltz v. U.S. News & World Report, Inc.*, 627 F.Supp. 1143, 7 EBC 1229 (D.D.C. 1986) (punitive damages not allowed under §502(a)(3) because "redress" language in §502(a)(3) cannot allow a court to do more than make a participant "whole"); *Kleinhans v. Lisle Savings Profit Sharing Trust*, 8 EBC 1038 (7th Cir. 1987) (punitive damages not available under ERISA §502(a)(3) because not generally available under common law of trusts for breach of fiduciary duty); *Boesl v. Suburban Trust & Sav. Bank*, 642 F.Supp. 1503 (N.D. Ill. 1986) (no punitive damages for ERISA violations).

Regardless of how sweepingly *Russell* is ultimately read, extra-contractual and punitive damages remain available on claims brought under non-preempted state common law[127] and under state insurance law.[128] Extra-contractual, but not punitive, damages may be available in LMRA Section 301 actions.[129] Awards of back pay and front pay (which are extra-contractual as far as the terms of the plan) may also be made under ERISA Section 510 when an employee is shown to have been discharged to prevent the attainment of a right to benefits under the terms of a plan. For unjust enrichment, employer contributions on an employee's behalf may be returned, with interest. Statutory penalties of $100 per day are also provided under ERISA Section 502(c) for delay in furnishing information required to be furnished under Title I.[130]

---

[127] See *Monson v. Century Mfg. Co.*, 739 F.2d 1293, 5 EBC 1625 (8th Cir. 1984) (punitive damages awarded when corporation and corporate officers, as well as plan fiduciaries, fraudulently misrepresented to plan participants that one-half of employer's profits were being contributed to plan when only one-third were); *K Mart Corp. v. Ponsock*, 8 EBC 1548 (Nev. 1987) (compensatory and punitive damages awarded under state law for unjust dismissal of employee who was only 6 months shy of vesting under 10-year cliff vesting schedule); *Werschkull v. United California Bank*, 149 Cal.Rptr. 829 (Cal.App. 1978) ($550,000 in punitive damages awarded under state law when employer-appointed trustees fraudulently concealed plan amendment diverting plan assets); *Stanger v. Gordon*, 244 N.W.2d 628 (Minn. 1976) (punitive damages assessed against employer for willful misrepresentation that no forfeiture provisions existed under plan); *Whitaker v. Texaco, Inc.*, 566 F.Supp. 745, 4 EBC 1762 (N.D. Ga. 1983) (punitive damages may be available on pre-ERISA claims brought under state law). See also *Masi v. Ford City Bank & Trust Co.*, 779 F.2d 397 (7th Cir. 1985) (bank that functioned as fiduciary for money held in trust in IRA accounts under Code §408(a), enacted as a part of ERISA, may by liable for punitive damages for willful or wanton conversion of funds).

Other cases are divided on whether state laws of general application on fraud, bad faith and emotional distress are preempted by ERISA or might provide an alternative basis for extra-contractual recovery if no recovery is permitted under ERISA. Compare *Provience v. Valley Clerks Trust Fund*, 509 F.Supp. 388, 2 EBC 1618 (E.D. Cal. 1981) (not preempted); *Holmes v. Oxford Chemicals, Inc.*, 510 F.Supp. 915, 2 EBC 1167 (N.D. Ala. 1981), *aff'd*, 3 EBC 1667 (11th Cir. 1982), with *Dependahl v. Falstaff Brewing Corp.*, *supra* (preempted), and cases at n. 128 below. Cf. *Aitken v. IP & GCU-Employer Retirement Fund*, 604 F.2d 1261 (9th Cir. 1979) (state law remedies not precluded when no relief available under §302(c)(5) of the Labor Management Relations Act).

[128] See *Powell v. Chesapeake & Potomac Tel. Co.*, 780 F.2d 419, 6 EBC 2754 (4th Cir. 1985), *cert. denied*, 476 U.S. ___ (1986) (punitive damages may be awarded against insurers under non-preempted state insurance law, but punitive damages are unavailable when insurer acted only as provider of administrative services to a plan which is not in the form of an insurance contract). Accord *Trogner v. New York Life Ins. Co.*, 633 F.Supp. 503 (D. Md. 1986).

But compare *Pilot Life Ins. Co. v. Dedeaux*, 481 U.S. ___, 8 EBC 1409 (1987) (state common law *tort and contract* remedies for bad faith denial of a claim for benefits under an insured employee benefit plan are not saved from ERISA preemption by express savings provision for state laws and decisions regulating insurance when (1) state law remedies for bad faith breaches of contract were not "specifically directed toward [the insurance] industry," (2) the state law "does not define the terms of the relationship between the insurer and insured," and (3) Congress "clearly" intended "that the federal remed[ies] displace" state law remedies); *Howard v. Parisian, Inc.*, 8 EBC 1033 (11th Cir. 1987) (ERISA preempts state law claim for bad faith refusal to pay health benefits against nonfiduciary insurance company acting as plan administrator for a self-funded health plan, following *Powell v. Chesapeake & Potomac Tel. Co.*, *supra*, that the insurance law savings clause is inapplicable in such cases).

[129] See *Hazel v. Lynch Corp.*, C.A. No. IP 84-1352-C (S.D. Ind. Jan. 17, 1986); *Haytcher v. ABS Indus., Inc.*, 7 EBC 2158 (N.D. Ohio 1986) (extra-contractual but not punitive damages allowed under LMRA §301); *UAW v. Federal Forge, Inc.*, 583 F.Supp. 1350, 5 EBC 1513 (W.D. Mich. 1984) (citing split between the circuits on issue of extra-contractual damages under LMRA §301).

Double and treble damage awards may also be available under the ADEA, FLSA, and RICO. See secs. VI.C and E below.

[130] See sec. VII below. The presence of the $100 per day statutory penalties has been held to bar any additional punitive damages for delay in furnishing requested documents. See *Meyer v.*

G. Attorney's Fee Awards

Under ERISA Section 502(g)(1), reasonable attorney's fees and costs may be awarded to either party in an ERISA Section 502 action. On occasion, attorney's fee awards under Section 502(g)(1) have been fairly substantial. For example, in *Dependahl v. Falstaff Brewing Corp.*, $149,000 in attorney's fees was awarded to prevailing participants.[131] In *Corley v. Hecht Co.*, over $148,000 in fees were awarded.[132] However, as these are some of the largest published awards under ERISA, Section 502(g)(1) has obviously not functioned to make participants' attorneys rich. But it is intended "to enable pension claimants to obtain competent counsel and to distribute the economic burden of litigation in a fair manner."[133]

Most circuits have adopted a five factor test first announced by the Tenth Circuit in *Eaves v. Penn* in determining whether to award attorney's fees in an ERISA Section 502 action. The factors are:

(1) The degree of the respective parties' culpability or bad faith;

(2) The ability of the respective parties to satisfy an award of fees;

(3) Whether an award would deter others from acting wrongfully in similar circumstances;

(4) Whether the claimant has sought to benefit all beneficiaries of the plan or to resolve a significant legal question; and

(5) The relative merits of the parties' positions.[134]

It is not necessary for each of the five questions implicit in these factors to be answered affirmatively for attorney's fees to be awarded to a prevailing participant. For example, attorney's fees may be

---

Phillip Morris, Inc., 569 F.Supp. 1510 (E.D. Mo. 1983); *Wilson v. Pye*, 6 EBC 2761 (N.D. Ill. 1986). But cf. *Kuntz v. Reese*, 760 F.2d 926, 6 EBC 1780 (9th Cir. 1985), *vacated and withdrawn on other grounds*, 785 F.2d 1410, 7 EBC 1227 (9th Cir. 1986), *cert. denied*, 479 U.S. ___ (1986).

131 653 F.2d 1208, 2 EBC 1521 (8th Cir. 1981), *cert. denied*, 454 U.S. 1084 (1981).

132 4 EBC 1155 (D.D.C. 1983).

133 *Gennamore v. Buffalo Sheet Metals, Inc. Pension Plan*, 568 F.Supp. 931, 5 EBC 1268, at 1272 (W.D.N.Y. 1983) (in turn citing *Ford v. New York Teamsters Pension Fund*, 506 F.Supp. 180, 2 EBC 1013 (W.D.N.Y. 1980), *aff'd*, 642 F.2d 664, 2 EBC 1016 (2d Cir. 1981)).

134 See *Eaves v. Penn*, 587 F.2d 453, 1 EBC 1592 (10th Cir. 1978); *Gray v. New England Tel. & Tel. Co.*, 792 F.2d 251 (1st Cir. 1986); *Chambless v. Masters, Mates & Pilots Pension Plan*, 815 F.2d 869 (2d Cir. 1987) (adopting 5-factor test in Second Circuit); *Ursic v. Bethlehem Mines*, 719 F.2d 670, 4 EBC 2297 (3d Cir. 1983); *Davidson v. Cook*, 567 F.Supp. 225, 4 EBC 1816 (E.D. Va. 1983), *aff'd*, 734 F.2d 10, 5 EBC 1440 (unpubl.) (4th Cir. 1984), *cert. denied*, 469 U.S. 899 (1984); *Ironworkers Local 272 v. Bowen*, 624 F.2d 1255 (5th Cir. 1980), and 695 F.2d 531, 4 EBC 1015 (11th Cir. 1983); *Marquardt v. North American Car Corp.*, 652 F.2d 715, 2 EBC 1545 (7th Cir. 1981); *Janowski v. Teamster Local No. 710 Pension Fund*, 673 F.2d 931, 3 EBC 1225 (7th Cir. 1982); *Lawrence v. Westerhaus*, 749 F.2d 494 (8th Cir. 1984); *Hummell v. S.E. Rykoff & Co.*, 634 F.2d 446, 2 EBC 1416 (9th Cir. 1980); *Gordon v. U.S. Steel*, 724 F.2d 106, 5 EBC 1062 (10th Cir. 1983) (clarifying applicability of the 5-factor test in the Tenth Circuit).

But compare *Central States Pension Fund v. Hitchings Trucking, Inc.*, 492 F.Supp. 906 (E.D. Mich. 1980) (criticizing *Eaves* test as containing "needless strictures" and arguing for straightforward presumption in favor of awards to prevailing parties), and Student Symposium, "Attorney's Fees Under ERISA," 71 Cornell L. Rev. 1037, at 1050-51 (July 1986) (arguing that ERISA §502(g)(1) should function only as a "weak fee-shifting provision" in favor of "those whose financial position is so weak that they cannot [otherwise] bring suit"; at same time, arguing that test for awarding fees to prevailing defendants should be frivolousness or bad faith, rather than 5-factor test).

awarded when the claimant's suit does not benefit other participants in the plan.[135] Some courts have gone still farther to state that attorney's fees will ordinarily be awarded prevailing participants under the five factors unless such an award would be unjust.[136] However, attorney's fees are rarely, if ever, awarded to participants for noble, but losing efforts.[137] But attorney's fees can be awarded when a plaintiff settles for a significant "portion of what he brought suit to recover" if the parties settle on everything except fees.[138]

For attorney's fees to be assessed *against* a participant-plaintiff who does not prevail, the same five factors have been applied. The courts have stated, however, that "[a]lthough the five factors ... do not explicitly differentiate between plaintiffs and defendants, consideration of these factors will seldom dictate an assessment of attorney's fees against ERISA plaintiffs."[139] The courts have singled out typical differences in culpability, in the participant's ability to satisfy an award of fees, in the deterrence factor, and in the benefit to other participants as leading to this result.[140]

---

[135] See *Chambless v. Masters, Mates & Pilots Pension Plan, supra* (attorney's fees awarded to prevailing plaintiff despite plan's argument that suit was not "brought" to confer a common benefit on a group of plan participants); *Ford v. New York Teamsters Pension Fund, supra* (attorney's fees awarded even though decision in plaintiff's favor did not benefit any other participants); accord *Korn v. Levine Bros. Iron Works Corp.*, 574 F.Supp. 836, 4 EBC 2533 (S.D.N.Y. 1983); *Lawrence v. Westerhaus*, 749 F.2d 494 (8th Cir. 1984) (award in suit where all participant obtained was a remand of his claim to the plan on a procedural issue); *Sokol v. Bernstein*, 803 F.2d 532, 7 EBC 2321 (9th Cir. 1986); *Groves v. Johns Manville Corp. Modified Retirement Plan*, 803 F.2d 109, 7 EBC 2359 (3d Cir. 1986). But compare *McKnight v. Southern Life & Health Ins. Co.*, 758 F.2d 1566, 6 EBC 1707 (11th Cir. 1985) (no attorney's fee award even though participant prevailed when employer had substantial argument and no benefit conferred on other participants).

[136] See *Smith v. CMTA-IAM Pension Trust*, 746 F.2d 587, 5 EBC 2428 (9th Cir. 1984) (given ERISA's remedial purpose of protection of employee rights, participant succeeding on any significant issue is as a general rule entitled to award of attorney's fees); *McConnell v. MEBA Medical & Benefits Plan*, 778 F.2d 521 (9th Cir. 1985) (denial of attorney's fees by district court an abuse of discretion when no special circumstances exist to make an award to prevailing plaintiff unjust); *Birmingham v. SoGen-Swiss Int'l Corp. Retirement Plan*, 718 F.2d 515, 4 EBC 2369 (2d Cir. 1983); *Landro v. Glendenning Motorways, Inc.*, 625 F.2d 1344 (8th Cir. 1980).

[137] See *Miles v. New York Teamsters Pension Fund*, 698 F.2d 593, 4 EBC 2160 (2d Cir. 1983), *cert. denied*, 464 U.S. 829 (1983) (although success not "indispensable" in theory, rarely will a losing party be entitled to fees), and Student Symposium, "Attorney's Fees Under ERISA," 71 Cornell L.Rev. 1037, at 1048-49 (July 1986) (denial of fees for "wholly unsuccessful" plaintiff "will never constitute an abuse of discretion that is reversible on appeal; citing other decisions denying fees to unsuccessful plaintiffs). See also *Janowski v. Teamsters Local 710 Pension Fund*, 812 F.2d 295, 8 EBC 1503 (7th Cir. 1987) (denying any award of attorney's fees after adverse ruling on remand of plaintiffs' standing to raise the one issue they had previously prevailed on).

[138] *Smith v. CMTA-IAM Pension Trust, supra*, 5 EBC 2428, at 2431.

[139] *Marquardt v. North American Car Corp.*, 652 F.2d 715, 2 EBC 1545, at 1548 (7th Cir. 1981). And see *Carpenters So. Cal. Admin. Group v. Russell*, 726 F.2d 1410, 5 EBC 1611, at 1616 (9th Cir. 1984) (the 5 factors determine whether fees are awarded to prevailing defendants, but application of the factors "very frequently suggest[s] that attorney's fees should not be charged against ERISA plaintiffs"); *Operating Eng. Pension Trust v. Gilliam*, 737 F.2d 1501, 5 EBC 1908 (9th Cir. 1984).

[140] See *id.*, *Dennard v. Richards Group, Inc.*, 681 F.2d 306, 3 EBC 1769 (5th Cir. 1982) (5 factors apply, but when defendants are indemnified for their legal fees, and plaintiff's challenge is in good faith, it normally does not serve ERISA's remedial purposes to award fees to prevailing defendants), accord *Nachwalter v. Christie*, 805 F.2d 956, 7 EBC 2675 (11th Cir. 1986); *Clouatre v. Lockwood*, 593 F.Supp. 1136 (M.D. La. 1984). See also *Vintilla v. U.S. Steel Corp. Plan for Employee Benefits*, 642 F.Supp. 295, 8 EBC 1123 (W.D. Pa. 1986) (awarding attorney's fees to prevailing plan when participants' action, while not in bad faith, was "ill-conceived" and "highly speculative," and participants had ability to pay fees); *Operating Eng. Pension Trust v. Gilliam, supra* (fee award to prevailing defendant where action "grossly unfair" and plaintiff Trust Fund

When fees are awarded in favor of a participant-plaintiff, time spent on distinct nonprevailing claims, or on non-ERISA claims, may be subtracted from the fee award. In *Teamsters Local 710 Pension Fund v. Janowski*, the Supreme Court vacated a Seventh Circuit decision for reconsideration in light of *Hensley v. Eckerhart*, a civil rights action that distinguished time spent on *distinct* nonprevailing or nonstatutory issues.[141] In *Davidson v. Cook*, attorney's fees were also awarded, but not for duplicative work by separate teams of attorneys, or for work in pursuit of distinct unsuccessful claims.[142]

In reviewing an attorney's fee request and determining whether to apply a multiplier to a lodestar figure, the courts following the Supreme Court's vacation of *Teamsters Local 710 Pension Fund v. Janowski* apparently are also to consider the factors outlined in *Hensley v. Eckerhart*. These include (1) the documentation supporting the hours, (2) what the hours were expended doing, (3) the reasonableness of the hourly rates, (4) the contingent nature of the case, (5) the results obtained, (6) the quality of the work, and (7) the novelty or complexity of the facts or issues in the case. Despite ERISA's reputation as a complex statute, multipliers on lodestar figures in ERISA cases either have not been awarded or have not been high, although this may simply reflect a lack of complexity in particular cases.[143]

---

had "substantial ability" to satisfy award); Student Symposium, "Attorney's Fees Under ERISA," 71 Cornell L. Rev. 1037, at 1047 (July 1986) (citing *American Communications Ass'n v. Retirement Plan for Employees of RCA Corp.*, 507 F.Supp. 922 (S.D.N.Y. 1981), and *Wishner v. St. Luke's Hosp. Center*, 550 F.Supp. 1016, 3 EBC 2621 (S.D.N.Y. 1982), as holding that a plaintiff's inability to pay may be sufficient ground by itself for denying fees to a prevailing defendant).

Some decisions have gone still farther to suggest that the issues raised in a participant's action must show that the suit was motivated by bad faith. See *Lojek v. Thomas*, 716 F.2d 675, 4 EBC 2321 (9th Cir. 1983); *Lewis v. Fulton Federal Savings & Loan Pension Plan*, 4 EBC 2071 (N.D. Ga. 1983), both declining to award attorney's fees against participants when their suits were not motivated solely by self interest or bad faith. However, in *Bittner v. Sadoff & Rudoy Indus.*, 728 F.2d 820, 5 EBC 2670, *opinion amended*, see 5 EBC viii-ix (7th Cir. 1984) (Posner, J.), the Seventh Circuit expressly rejected a district court's use of a "frivolous" standard, suggesting instead a test analogous to the Equal Access to Justice Act test under which substantial justification for the participant's claim, or special circumstances that make an award unjust, such as a participant's financial situation if an award were made, are required to deny an award to a prevailing defendant.

[141] 463 U.S. 1222, 4 EBC 2004 (1983), *vac'g*, 673 F.2d 931, 3 EBC 1225 (7th Cir. 1982); and see *Hensley v. Eckerhart*, 461 U.S. 424 (1983). But see *Smith v. CMTA-IAM Pension Trust, supra* (hours working on alternate theories that the court rejected or did not reach generally will be compensated, citing *Hensley*, 461 U.S. at 435); *Dameron v. Sinai Hospital of Baltimore, Inc.*, 644 F.Supp. 551 (D.Md. 1986), *aff'd*, 815 F.2d 975 (4th Cir. 1987) (fees awarded for all time spent on case, even though court did not reach some legal theories and rejected others).

[142] 567 F.Supp. 225, 4 EBC 1816 (E.D. Va. 1983). See also *Holmes v. Oxford Chemicals, Inc.*, 510 F.Supp. 915, 2 EBC 1167 (M.D. Ala. 1981), *aff'd*, 3 EBC 1667 (11th Cir. 1982) (fees awarded for time spent on an ERISA claim, but not for time spent on state law claims; because the participant's attorney did not keep time records on this basis and because there were basically two claims in the action, total time was split in half for purpose of awarding attorney's fees); *Aronson v. Servus Rubber Division*, 730 F.2d 12, 5 EBC 1343, at 1347 (1st Cir. 1984), *cert. denied*, 469 U.S. 1017 (1984) (recovery of profit-sharing contributions under separate employment contracts with the employer that were distinct from the plan distinguished as a "contract" recovery, as opposed to an "ERISA [plan] recovery"; attorney's fee authority of ERISA §502(g) therefore not a basis for an award); *Fase v. Seafarers Welfare & Pension Plan*, 589 F.2d 112, 1 EBC 1474 (2d Cir. 1978) (denying attorney's fees when prevailing plaintiff obtained none of his relief under ERISA).

[143] See, e.g., *Ursic v. Bethlehem Mines*, 719 F.2d 670, 4 EBC 2297 (3d Cir. 1983); *Katsaros v. Cody*, 4 EBC 2698 (E.D.N.Y. 1984), *aff'd in part, rem'd in part*, 744 F.2d 270, 5 EBC 1777 (2d Cir. 1984); *Davidson v. Cook*, 594 F.Supp. 418, 5 EBC 2161 (E.D. Va. 1984); *Corley v. Hecht Co.*, 4 EBC 1155 (D.D.C. 1983). But compare *Dameron v. Sinai Hospital of Baltimore, Inc., supra*

III. Other Plaintiffs in ERISA Title I Actions

Besides participants and beneficiaries, other potential plaintiffs under Section 502(a) are (1) the plan's fiduciaries, (2) the Department of Labor, (3) the union, and (4) the employer. The IRS also has authority, as discussed below, to enforce some Title I and all tax-qualification requirements, but not under Section 502(a).

A. Plan Fiduciaries

The primary nonparticipant advocates for the interests of participants and beneficiaries in Section 502(a) litigation would seem to be the plan's fiduciaries since they have a duty to act solely "in the interest" of the participants and their beneficiaries. Although the *plan* itself is not a proper plaintiff under Section 502(a),[144] plan fiduciaries are specifically named as potential plaintiffs in Section 502(a)(3), which covers causes of action to enjoin or obtain other appropriate equitable relief for a violation of the terms of a plan or a violation of Title I. Fiduciaries are also named as potential plaintiffs in Section 502(a)(2), which covers causes of action to obtain appropriate relief for another fiduciary's breach of fiduciary duty.

While a legal obligation exists under ERISA Section 405 for fiduciaries who are not involved in a violation of fiduciary duty to take action to remedy other fiduciaries' breaches,[145] fiduciaries, as a practical matter, rarely sue other fiduciaries.[146] The most common type of suit that fiduciaries actually bring are suits against employers who are

---

(upward adjustment of 10% to lodestar for "risk" with "absolutely no guarantee" of compensation and unique skills and experience brought to bear in "difficult and novel case"); *Miles v. New York Teamsters Pension Fund*, 3 EBC 1513 (W.D.N.Y. 1982), *vacated on other grounds*, 698 F.2d 593 (2d Cir. 1983) (applying 1.5 multiplier to lodestar); *Janowski v. Teamsters Local No. 710 Pension Fund, supra* (initially applying 2.0 multiplier to lodestar).

[144] See *Pressroom Union Printers Fund v. Continental Assurance Co.*, 700 F.2d 889, 4 EBC 1112 (2d Cir. 1983) (plan not proper plaintiff in suit alleging fiduciary violations); *Industrial Local 44-A Health Fund v. Webb*, 562 F.Supp. 185, 4 EBC 1616 (N.D. Ill. 1983) (plan not proper plaintiff in suit for alleging fiduciary violations from excessive compensation for two trustees' services); *Mobil Oil Corp. Employees Savings Plan v. Vickery*, 99 F.R.D. 138, 4 EBC 2506 (S.D.N.Y. 1983) (plan not proper plaintiff in suit for declaratory judgment to determine whether participant or his divorced spouse had right to benefits; leave granted in light of *Pressroom Union Printers Fund, supra*, for Mobil Oil to be substituted as plaintiff in its role as fiduciary for the plan); *Rheingold Breweries Pension Plan v. PepsiCo., Inc.*, 2 EBC 2406 (S.D.N.Y. 1981).

[145] See also 29 C.F.R. 2509.75-5, Q&A FR-10.

[146] But see *Clayton v. A.G. Becker Paribus*, C.A. 84-1262 (D. Idaho, filed June 21, 1984), summarized at 11 BNA Pens. Rep. 863 (July 2, 1984) (suit by a former Department of Labor pension administrator as a plan fiduciary against other fiduciaries for breach of duty). In *Blackmar v. Lichtenstein*, 603 F.2d 1306, 1 EBC 1679 (8th Cir. 1979), a trustee, who was a law professor, was removed as a fiduciary after initiating suit against former plan trustees and the sponsoring employer; the Eighth Circuit held that, once removed, he lacked standing under ERISA as a fiduciary to challenge his removal. See also *Authier v. Ginsberg*, 757 F.2d 796, 6 EBC 1420 (6th Cir. 1985) (fiduciary whose employment was allegedly terminated for being too vigilant in exercise of fiduciary duty would have state law cause of action for wrongful discharge in Michigan before ERISA, but ERISA preempted cause of action—even though cause of action the fiduciary had under ERISA was not clear; court suggested that there might be a cause of action under ERISA §409(a) against the other fiduciary for discharge in breach of fiduciary duty).

delinquent in making contributions to multiemployer plans. Delinquent contributions to multiemployer plans are specifically a violation of Title I under ERISA Section 515. (Special remedies, not available in other Section 502(a) actions, are provided, including liquidated damages, generally not in excess of 20 percent of the delinquent amount, and nondiscretionary attorney's fee awards.) Another type of fiduciary versus fiduciary suit that has arisen is an action in which fiduciaries sue a service-provider who has not performed services, which may include fiduciary functions, to the satisfaction of the other fiduciaries.[147]

B. The Department of Labor

The Department of Labor (or more technically, the Secretary of Labor) is a potential plaintiff under Section 502(a):

(1) *Title I Violations.* Under Section 502(a)(5), the Department of Labor can bring an action to enjoin or obtain other appropriate relief for any violation of Title I. For violations of Parts 2 and 3 of Title I (covering participation, vesting, benefit accrual, joint and survivor's benefits, nonalienation of benefits, and funding standards), the Department must be requested to bring the action by the Secretary of the Treasury or by one or more participants, beneficiaries, or fiduciaries of the plan.[148]

If a request for enforcement relating to Parts 2 or 3 of Title I comes from a participant or beneficiary, the Department is required to find that the "violation affects, or such enforcement is necessary to protect, claims of participants or beneficiaries to benefits under the plan" before taking action.[149] Such a finding does not, however, require the Department to act.[150]

With or without a participant request or a request from the Secretary of the Treasury, the Department of Labor has authority under Section 502(a)(5) to enforce the Part 1 reporting

---

[147] See *Schulist v. Blue Cross of Iowa*, 553 F.Supp. 248, 4 EBC 1193 (N.D. Ill. 1982), *aff'd*, 717 F.2d 1127, 4 EBC 2237 (7th Cir. 1983). If an action is determined to be for breach of nonfiduciary contractual obligations, the plan's remedy may be under state contract law rather than ERISA. *Id.*

[148] See ERISA §502(b)(1). The Department of Labor is willing to take informal action on behalf of participants in some cases in which it will not bring suit. A participant information and assistance program is operated out of the Office of Technical Assistance of the Department of Labor's Pension and Welfare Benefit Administration in Washington (Room N-5658, 200 Constitution Ave., N.W., Washington, D.C. 20216, telephone 202/523-8776).

[149] ERISA §502(b)(1)(B). The Department of Labor's procedure for handling requests for enforcement action from participants, beneficiaries, or fiduciaries is set forth in 29 C.F.R. 2560.502-1.

[150] 29 C.F.R. 2560.502-1(b). For examples of Department of Labor actions to enforce participants' benefit rights, see *Donovan v. Carlough*, 576 F.Supp. 245, 5 EBC 1400 (D.D.C. 1983); *Winer v. Edison Bros. Stores Pension Plan*, 593 F.2d 307, 1 EBC 1191 (8th Cir. 1979); *Winpisinger v. Aurora Corp.*, 456 F.Supp. 559, 1 EBC 2201 (N.D. Ohio 1978) (Department of Labor intervention in suit).

and disclosure requirements, the Part 4 fiduciary standards, and ERISA Section 510 on noninterference with the exercise or attainment of rights under Title I or the terms of a plan.[151]

(2) *Fiduciary Violations.* Under ERISA Section 502(a)(2), the Secretary of Labor, along with participants, beneficiaries, and fiduciaries, has authority (with or without a participant request) to seek appropriate relief for a fiduciary's breach of duty as provided in Section 409.

The Department of Labor's initiation of any type of action (or intervention in any action) is a major litigation development because of the deference likely to be shown to the Department's interpretation of obligations arising from Title I. Particularly if there are potential fiduciary violations in investments, enlisting one of the Department of Labor's regional offices to investigate can also be beneficial for participants because of the Department's expertise and because of the costs of an extensive investigation. If the Department decides not to file suit, the record of the investigation may be made available to participants and their attorneys.[152]

C. Unions

Since unions, like "plans," are not listed among the potential plaintiffs in Section 502(a), unions are generally not permissible plaintiffs in actions under ERISA Section 502(a).[153] An exception to this rule may apply in actions to redress breaches of fiduciary duty in investments of a plan's assets, or in administrative expenses.[154]

Whether a union can be a plaintiff in an ERISA action makes little practical difference. A union can do everything *except* stand in as the plaintiff, and can always find a participant to appear as the named plaintiff. Moreover, when a pension issue arises under the terms of the

---

[151] While §502(a)(5) is almost identically worded to §502(a)(3), it does not directly empower the Secretary to bring an action to enjoin or obtain other appropriate equitable relief for a violation of "the terms of the plan." However, if a plan's administrator or other fiduciaries are acting in disregard of a plan's terms, the Department of Labor can bring an action for a violation of the §404(a)(1)(D) fiduciary duty to act "in accordance with the documents and instruments of the plan governing the plan. . . ."

[152] See ERISA §504(a), and Conf. Rep., at 329, 3 ERISA Leg. Hist. 4596.

[153] In *UAW District 65 v. Harper & Row Publishers, Inc.*, 576 F.Supp. 1468, 4 EBC 2586 (S.D.N.Y. 1983), a district court followed *Pressroom Union Printers Fund v. Continental Assurance Co.*, 700 F.2d 889, 4 EBC 1112 (2d Cir. 1983), in holding that a union was not a proper plaintiff in an ERISA action. See also *Utility Workers Union v. Consumers Power Co.*, 453 F.Supp. 447 (E.D. Mich. 1978), *aff'd*, 637 F.2d 1082 (6th Cir. 1981), *vacated on other grounds*, 451 U.S. 1014 (1981); *Espinosa v. Crowe*, 2 EBC 1907 (D. Mass. 1981); *New Jersey State AFL-CIO v. New Jersey*, 747 F.2d 891, 5 EBC 2465 (3d Cir. 1984) (state labor organization not a participant or beneficiary entitled to sue under ERISA). But compare *Bridge, Structural & Iron Workers Local 111 v. Douglas*, 646 F.2d 1211, 2 EBC 1470 (7th Cir. 1981), *cert. denied*, 454 U.S. 866 (1981) (union allowed to sue under ERISA without discussion of issue of standing); *Fentron Indus., Inc. v. Shopmen's Pension Fund*, 674 F.2d 1300, 3 EBC 1323 (9th Cir. 1982) (allowing employer to serve as a plaintiff in a §502(a) action because the employer's injuries from a cancellation of its employees' past service credits fell within the "zone of interests" that Congress intended to protect when it enacted ERISA).

[154] *Walker v. Jaffe*, 5 EBC 2736 (W.D. Tex. 1983).

collective bargaining agreement, the union can be the named plaintiff under Section 301 of the LMRA.[155]

The NLRA duty of fair representation creates no duty for a union to bring, or provide backing for, claims on behalf of former employees or retirees, whether under ERISA or otherwise.[156] However, if a claim is undertaken on their behalf, the union has a duty to carry it through.[157]

D. Employers

Like plans and unions, employers are not listed among the parties empowered to sue under ERISA Section 502(a).[158] Nevertheless, in *Fentron v. Shopmen's Pension Fund*, the Ninth Circuit held that an employer could be within the "zone of interests" Congress intended to protect, and therefore could be an ERISA plaintiff.[159] Most other courts have disagreed with this decision.[160]

A unique aspect to an employer's standing under ERISA Section 502(a) is that in a single-employer plan, the employer always has a dual role as a named fiduciary for the plan through its power to select the plan's trustees and its power to amend the plan. If an employer is a fiduciary under the plan, it can sue under ERISA Section 502(a)(2) and (3) in that capacity.[161] Even when the employer is not a named fiduciary to the plan, the employer almost always has the ability in a single-employer plan to initiate suit under ERISA Section 502(a) through its control of persons who are fiduciaries, much as the union has the capacity to initiate suit through participants.

While in a position to initiate suit on behalf of participants and beneficiaries, the employer, like the plan's fiduciaries, is unlikely to do so if the plan is a single-employer plan since it is more likely to be in fact, or in substance, one of the defendants on any participant claim. If the "plan" is required to pay, the employer's contribution obligations increase over what they would otherwise be. Even for personal liability running only to plan fiduciaries, the employer may be indirectly liable

---

[155] See, e.g., *In re Schatz Federal Bearings Co.*, 5 B.R. 549 (Bankr. S.D.N.Y. 1980) (recognizing union as creditor in bankruptcy proceeding based on its contractual rights under LMRA §301 to enforce claims for unpaid contributions to a plan). A union can also challenge certain contract violations relating to employee benefit plans as unfair labor practices before the NLRB. See *Capitol City Lumber Co. v. NLRB*, 721 F.2d 546, 4 EBC 2530 (6th Cir. 1983) (employer's failure to make contributions to plan challengable as unfair labor practice since it represents a failure to bargain over a change in terms and conditions of employment).

[156] See *UAW v. Yard-Man, Inc.*, 716 F.2d 1476, 4 EBC 2108 (6th Cir. 1983).

[157] See *Toensing v. Brown*, 528 F.2d 69, 1 EBC 1083 (9th Cir. 1975).

[158] See *Tuvia Convalescent Center, Inc. v Hospital Employees*, 717 F.2d 726, 4 EBC 2223 (2d Cir. 1983); *Modern Woodcrafts, Inc. v. Hawley*, 534 F.Supp. 1000, 3 EBC 1169 (D. Conn. 1982); *Niagara Paper Corp. v. Paper Industry Pension Fund*, 5 EBC 1496 (D. Minn. 1983), *aff'd on other rulings*, 800 F.2d 742, 7 EBC 2313 (8th Cir. 1986).

[159] 674 F.2d 1300, 3 EBC 1323 (9th Cir. 1982).

[160] See, e.g., *UAW District 65 v. Harper & Row Publishers, Inc.*, 576 F.Supp. 1468, 4 EBC 2586 (S.D.N.Y. 1983); *Niagara Paper Corp. v. Paper Industry Pension Fund, supra.*

[161] See *Great Lakes Steel Division v. Deggendorf*, 716 F.2d 1101, 4 EBC 2093 (6th Cir. 1983); *Mobil Oil Corp. Employees Savings Plan v. Geer*, 535 F.Supp. 1052, 3 EBC 1251 (S.D.N.Y. 1982).

through an indemnification arrangement, or through payment of increased premiums to maintain fiduciary insurance.

Employers have been active in one area of pension benefit litigation, namely, challenges to cancellations of past service credits by multiemployer plans on the withdrawal of the employer from the plan. The *Fentron* decision was rendered in this context. In another decision on the same issue, an employer lacked standing under ERISA, but was allowed to challenge the plan provision under the LMRA.[162]

E. The IRS

The IRS has no authority under ERISA Section 502(a) to bring actions on behalf of participants. The IRS thus cannot directly enforce even those parts of Title I that are within its regulatory jurisdiction. It can, however, request the Department of Labor to enforce the Title I provision, or it can intervene or file an *amicus* brief in an action brought by a participant.[163]

The IRS has other indirect enforcement authority that relates to Title I of ERISA, but that is established outside of ERISA Section 502. As its overall club, the IRS can disqualify a plan that violates any of the Code requirements for qualification, including the Title I minimum standards that are paralleled in the Code, as well as the requirements that are not paralleled in Title I (such as nondiscrimination in favor of the prohibited group and the requirement that benefits vest on partial termination or termination of the plan). An employer's challenge to such disqualfication may then be litigated by the IRS in the Tax Court if the employer, or affected employees, refuse to pay the taxes that follow disqualification. Under Code Section 4971, the IRS also has authority to impose excise taxes on employers who do not make contributions required under the minimum funding standards of ERISA.[164] Finally, under Code Section 4975, the IRS has authority to impose excise taxes for certain types of prohibited transactions. The initial tier of excise taxes is five percent of the amount involved in the underfunding of a plan or in a prohibited transaction. If the underfunding or prohibited transaction is not corrected, a 100 percent excise tax is imposed.

In one sense, all of the IRS's indirect Title I enforcement authority is *negative*. That is, the excise taxes for underfunding and for prohibited transactions do not increase plan participants' benefits, but

---

[162] See *Niagara Paper Corp. v. Paper Industry Pension Fund, supra*. And see *Central Tool Co. v. IAM Nat'l Pension Fund*, 523 F.Supp. 812, 2 EBC 2019 (D.D.C. 1981), *rev'd on other grounds*, 811 F.2d 651, 8 EBC 1268 (D.C. Cir. 1987) (employer had standing under the LMRA to challenge cancellation of employees' past service credits on the employer's withdrawal from multiemployer plan).

[163] See ERISA §502(h) (Secretary of Treasury may intervene in all Title I actions except actions under fiduciary provisions or actions to enforce the terms of a plan under §502(a)(1)(B)).

[164] And see *Anthes v. Commissioner*, 4 EBC 2265 (T.C. 1983) (penalty for underfunding is excise tax under §4971, and not plan disqualification, as minimum funding standards are not qualification requirements under Code §401(a)).

rather only go to the Treasury. Similarly, disqualification of a plan does not protect or enhance participants' benefits, but rather protects the Treasury from depletion of its coffers through tax advantages for plans that do not meet the ERISA minimum standards and other Code requirements for tax-qualification.

Beneath the negative surface of these actions, however, are positive features which can benefit participants. In practice, the threat of plan disqualification usually leads to corrective action. Only if the noncompliance extends beyond the period for which retroactive correction of noncompliance is permitted under Code Section 401(b) are participants faced with the prospect that the IRS's actions will remain negative. The IRS's discretion to protect innocent plan participants even in these instances is discussed in the next section. The IRS's excise taxes are similarly all negative on the surface. However, the imposition of the five percent tax may not be a great expense for the corrective effects it produces. To avoid the second-tier 100 percent excise tax that follows, most employers quickly make up the underfunding or reverse the prohibited transaction that caused the initial excise tax to be imposed.

IV. Participant Enforcement of the Code's Tax Qualification Requirements

The Internal Revenue Code requirements for tax qualification of pension or profit-sharing plans are, for the most part, mirrored in Title I provisions of ERISA. However, certain requirements are contained only in the Code, most notably:

(1) Section 401(a)(4)'s prohibition against discrimination in favor of the prohibited group of employees;
(2) Section 410(b)'s related requirements for nondiscriminatory coverage;
(3) Section 411(d)(1)'s provision for faster vesting when there is a "pattern of abuse;"
(4) Section 411(d)(3)'s requirement for vesting of benefits on the termination or partial termination of a plan to the extent funded; and
(5) Section 416's requirements for "top heavy" plans, which require both faster vesting and minimum nonintegrated benefits for non-key employees.

Participants and beneficiaries are not provided with an express private right of action to enforce Code requirements that are not mirrored in Title I.[165] Moreover, although the legislative history of ERISA

---

[165] See *Reklau v. Merchants Nat'l Corp.*, 808 F.2d 512, 8 EBC 1001 (7th Cir. 1986) (Code qualification provisions are not directly enforcable under ERISA §502; employee had charged that

indicates that Congress intended for participants to be able to initiate a determination by the IRS of a plan's compliance with Code requirements that are not paralleled in Title I, and then to be able to obtain Tax Court review of the IRS's determination if it is not in their favor, the IRS has never established such a procedure.[166]

Several avenues are nevertheless open for participant enforcement of these requirements. First, certain Code requirements, although not in Title I, are required to be contained in provisions in the plan itself.[167] Code Section 411(d)(3) thus requires that the plan provide that benefits become nonforfeitable, to the extent funded, on the termination or partial termination of the plan. Similarly, Code Section 401(a)(10) requires that tax-qualified plans contain the top heavy provisions for faster vesting and minimum nonintegrated benefits, and also the statutory rule for determining whether the plan is top heavy. With such plan provisions, participants can enforce "the terms of the plan" under ERISA Section 502(a)(1)(B) or Section 502(a)(3).

A second alternative for enforcement of Code requirements is through interpretation of related plan provisions. For example, a plan's provisions on coverage can be interpreted to avoid discrimination within the meaning of Code Section 410(b) and 401(a)(4), and thus to avoid the adverse tax consequences of plan disqualification. Supporting this interpretive principle, many plans contain express language stating that the plan is to be interpreted to be a qualified plan. On this basis, the Tenth Circuit in *Crouch v. Mo-Kan Iron Workers Welfare Fund* construed an ambiguous coverage provision to include a secretary because otherwise a violation of Code Section 410(b) and discrimination under Code Section 401(a)(4) would have resulted from inadequate coverage of rank and file employees. The Tenth Circuit stated:

> "Because the pension plan states that it is to be construed to meet the requirements of ERISA [including the tax-qualification requirements], and there are obvious and significant benefits to meeting those requirements, we conclude that we must construe the plan as including [the] plaintiff as a participant."[168]

---

faster vesting than 10 year cliff was required by the Code to prevent discrimination; he had 8.58 years of service); *Cicatello v. Brewery Workers Pension Fund,* 434 F.Supp. 950, at 957 (W.D.N.Y. 1977), *aff'd,* 578 F.2d 1366 (2d Cir. 1977).

166 The Senate Finance Committee and House Ways and Means Committee reports both stated that the Committees expected the IRS to establish a procedure under which participants, or noncovered employees, could initiate determinations of a plan's compliance with Code requirements not contained in Title I. See S. Rep. 93-383, at 113, 1 ERISA Leg. Hist. 1181, and H.R. Rep. 93-807, at 107, 2 ERISA Leg. Hist. 3227.

167 A plan may be disqualified simply for not containing this provision, apart from the plan's compliance with the requirement in operation. See *Tionesta Sand & Gravel, Inc. v. Commissioner,* 73 T.C. 758 (1980), *aff'd,* 642 F.2d 444 (3d Cir. 1981).

168 740 F.2d 805, 5 EBC 1971, at 1975 (10th Cir. 1984). And see *Dennard v. Richards Group, Inc.,* 681 F.2d 306, 3 EBC 1769 (5th Cir. 1982) ("any relevant" regulations or rulings formulated by IRS to be considered in interpretation). But see *United Steelworkers v. Harris & Sons Steel Co.,* 706 F.2d 1289, 4 EBC 1396 (3d Cir. 1983) ("normally" tax regulations and rulings do not bear on plan interpretation). This division of authority is discussed in ch. 7, sec. III.A.3.e.

The route followed in *Crouch* may be useful for employees in areas such as coverage where the IRS's rules are relatively clear-cut. If there is room for doubt, courts may be less willing than the IRS or Tax Court to develop a novel application of the Code's requirements under a general interpretation proviso.

A third enforcement alternative for Code requirements for participants (and for noncovered employees) is through the submission of written comments to the IRS at the time an employer files an application for determination of a plan's tax-qualified status. If such comments are submitted, review of an IRS determination that is adverse to the employee can be obtained in the Tax Court under Code Section 7476.[169] Applications for determination are *routinely* filed by employers for the initial qualification of a pension or profit-sharing plan, for determinations on plan amendments—whether the amendment is voluntary or is required by a change in the law or the IRS's rulings—and for determinations of a plan's tax-qualified status on termination. Notice of an employer's application for determination is required to be provided plan participants and noncovered employees who are interested parties within the meaning of 26 C.F.R. 1.7476-1(b). The required "notice" may, however, be satisfied by a bulletin board posting which need not describe the subject matter of the plan provision or amendment for which a determination is sought.[170] But the requirement that at least this notice be provided interested parties is strictly construed.[171]

With notice, participants and other interested parties have the opportunity to review the employer's application for a determination and to submit written comments to the IRS district director before whom the application is pending within 45 days of the date the application is received by the district director.[172] When a participant submits comments on an application for determination, and the IRS's determination remains adverse to the participant's comments, the participant has the right to petition the Tax Court for review of the determination by filing a petition within 90 days after the date notice of the adverse determination is mailed by the IRS to the participant.[173] Review in the Tax Court is limited to the administrative record and the issues raised in the participant's comments.[174] It is questionable

---

[169] In addition to enforcement of Code requirements that are not in Title I, the ability to obtain Tax Court review could be significant on some regulatory issues that can be raised in an ERISA §502(a)(3) action as well. For example, the Tax Court apparently takes a dimmer view than some courts of the IRS's authority under its Title I "elapsed time" regulations to require more for a "year of service" than the completion of 1,000 hours. Compare *Automated Packaging Systems, Inc. v. Commissioner*, 70 T.C. 214, 1 EBC 1834 (1978) (concurring opinion), with *Swaida v. IBM Retirement Plan*, 570 F.Supp. 482, 4 EBC 2017 (S.D.N.Y. 1983), *aff'd*, 728 F.2d 159, 5 EBC 1120 (2d Cir. 1984), *cert. denied*, 469 U.S. 874 (1984).

[170] See 26 C.F.R. 1.7476-2(b), 26 C.F.R. 601.201(o)(3)(xvi), and Rev. Proc. 80-30. Former employees and retirees are not required to receive the notice to interested parties. 26 C.F.R. 1.7476-1(b).

[171] See *Hawes v. Commissioner*, 73 T.C. 916 (1980) (consideration of plan amendments by IRS and opportunity for comments reopened when participant not given required notice of application for determination); *Steffen Ins. Agency Retirement Plan v. Commissioner*, 2 EBC 1518 (T.C. 1981) (employer's declaratory judgment action challenging IRS determination dismissed when notice not provided interested parties; Congress intended to give employees the "opportunity to be informed and heard as to the employer's retirement plans").

[172] 26 C.F.R. 601.201(o)(3)(xvi)(h), (o)(5)(i)(a), and (o)(10)(ii).

[173] 26 C.F.R. 1.7476-3(a).

[174] See *Thompson v. Commissioner*, 71 T.C. 32, 1 EBC 2040 (1978).

whether the right to obtain Tax Court review extends to IRS determinations on whether a plan discriminates in operation, even if that issue was raised in a participant's comments.[175]

A fourth avenue that employees can pursue to enforce tax qualification requirements, particularly when an employer is not seeking or has already obtained a favorable determination letter, is to file complaints about perceived tax qualification problems in the operation of the plan with the IRS district office covering the plan. The IRS has no formal procedures for handling such complaints, nor is there any requirement that the IRS notify the participant or other employee of the action it takes on the complaint. However, such a complaint should generally result in the IRS at least considering the matter and notifying the participant of its decision.[176] Review in the Tax Court is not available if the IRS decides to do nothing, or decides that no violation has occurred, because of the absence of any regulatory procedure that triggers the Tax Court's Code Section 7476 jurisdiction.

In raising tax qualification issues, participants have to be concerned that they could conceivably obtain no remedy for themselves, and only jeopardize the plan's tax qualification over a retroactive period. The effect of a retroactive disqualification of a plan is to disallow the employer's tax deductions for contributions to the plan and to tax earnings on those contributions to the employer in all open tax years (generally, three years, unless there was a "willful" attempt to evade taxation[177]) during which the noncompliance existed. The employer's deductions may be preserved, and contributions, plus earnings, instead taxed as income to the employee/participants in the disqualified plan to the extent the participants were vested in the year in which the nonqualified contributions were made.[178] If employee/participants were not vested in that current year, but later vest, the employer's deduction may be taken in the year in which the employee/participant constructively has income from the nonqualified contributions.

---

[175] *Id.* Similarly, while participants are free to submit comments on discrimination in operation at the time of an application for determination on a plan amendment, the IRS is not required to make a determination on an operational issue unless the noncompliance is clear from the facts in the employer's application. *Id.*

[176] To enhance the chances that a district director will look into a matter, copies of the complaint or information could be sent to the IRS's national Employee Plans and Exempt Organizations office, and to the participant's congressional representatives.

[177] Code §6501. A 6-year statute of limitations applies if 25% or more of a taxpayer's gross income is unreported as a result of noncompliance.

[178] See Code §§402(b) and 83. And see *Ludden v. Commissioner*, 68 T.C. 826, 1 EBC 1787 (1977), *aff'd*, 620 F.2d 700, 2 EBC 2329 (9th Cir. 1980) (television performers Allen Ludden and Betty White's vested benefits taxed when 3-person pension plan they controlled failed to secure contributions for the only nonprohibited group participant under the plan causing the plan to be retroactively disqualified). However, if benefits are vested, but still subject to a substantial risk of forfeiture, the contributions cannot be taxed as current income to the employee. 26 C.F.R. 1.402(b)-1(a) and 26 C.F.R. 1.83-3(b), (c), and (d).

While retroactive disqualification is ominous, it is "rarely applied." Rather, it is generally used for its "*in terrorem*" effect in obtaining retroactive correction of noncompliance.[179] In other instances, neither retroactive disqualification nor retroactive correction of the noncompliance is available because of a prior, erroneous IRS determination of compliance. Specifically, the principles related to retroactive disqualification are:

- When a plan sponsor has obtained a favorable determination letter that is not caveated for discrimination in the plan's operation:

  "Except in rare or unusual circumstances, the revocation or modification of a ruling will not be applied retroactively with respect to the taxpayer to whom the ruling was originally issued or to a taxpayer whose tax liability was involved in such ruling if (1) there has been no misstatement or omission of material facts, (2) the facts subsequently developed are not materially different from the facts on which the ruling was based, (3) there has been no change in the applicable law, (4) the ruling was originally issued with respect to a prospective or proposed transaction, and (5) the taxpayer directly involved in the ruling acted in good faith in reliance upon the ruling and the retroactive revocation would be to his detriment."[180]

  A favorable determination of the plan's qualified status can, however, always be revoked or modified *prospectively.*

- When (1) no determination letter has been secured, (2) a determination letter is caveated for discrimination in operation, or (3) the facts or the law have changed, noncompliance may be retroactively cured without the loss of tax advantages if an amendment correcting the noncompliance is adopted by the end of the employer's tax filing period for the tax year in which the noncompliance first occurred.[181] If the noncompliance extends farther back, the employer can preserve the tax advantages for one plan year by correcting the noncompliance for all years in which it occurred by the end of the employer's filing period for the tax year coincident with or within which the preserved plan year ends.[182]

---

[179] See R. Blum, "What Happens on Plan Disqualification," in ALI-ABA, *Pension and Profit-Sharing and Other Deferred Compensation Plans,* Vol. 1 (ALI-ABA 1985), at 100.

[180] Rev. Proc. 83-36, secs. 14 and 15, and 26 C.F.R. 601.201(l)(5). And compare *Boggs v. Commissioner,* 784 F.2d 1166, 7 EBC 1113 (4th Cir. 1985) (retroactive disqualification an abuse of discretion when no material change in facts occurred since favorable determination letter issued); *Lansons, Inc. v. Commissioner,* 69 T.C. 773 (1978), *aff'd,* 622 F.2d 774 (5th Cir. 1980) (finding no material change in facts on which determination letter was issued to support retroactive disqualification); *Emergency Professional Group, Inc. v. Commissioner,* 3 EBC 1588 (T.C. 1982), with *Wisconsin Nipple & Fabricating Corp. v. Commissioner,* 581 F.2d 1235, 1 EBC 1169 (7th Cir. 1978) (permitting retroactive revocation of determination letter when subsequent Revenue Ruling established that a plan such as petitioner's was discriminatory prior to the period for which IRS revoked plan's qualification).

[181] Code §401(b) and 26 C.F.R. 1.401(b)-1(c).

[182] Rev. Rul. 82-66. It is not clear that Rev. Rul. 82-66 applies to discrimination in operation.

- Retroactive disqualification for other open tax years may be limited in the IRS's discretion.[183] The IRS's determination in this regard will not be disturbed by the courts unless it is an abuse of discretion.[184] IRS pronouncements and court decisions state that protecting the interests of "innocent plan participants," avoiding inequitable results, and maintaining consistency with the treatment extended other sponsoring employers are all factors in determining the extent to which a plan is to be retroactively disqualified.[185] Particular emphasis is placed on the effect of retroactive disqualification on "innocent plan participants." Retroactive disqualification may be "fractionalized" to obtain correction of the noncompliance for innocent plan participants, while disallowing remaining tax advantages for contributions made on behalf of highly compensated employees who were in positions of control over the plan.[186] Voluntary correction of noncompliance without conditioning it on a stipulation by the IRS that retroactive disqualification will not apply is also a factor in favor of exercising discretion not to retroactively disqualify a plan.[187]

---

[183] Code §7805(b) and 26 C.F.R. 1.401(b)-1(e).

[184] See, e.g., *Boggs v. Commissioner*, 784 F.2d 1166, 7 EBC 1113 (4th Cir. 1985); *Sutherland v. Commissioner*, 78 T.C. 395, 3 EBC 1182 (1982).

[185] See *Automobile Club of Michigan v. Commissioner*, 353 U.S. 180, at 184 and 186 (1957), and General Counsel Memorandum (GCM) 39385 (July 19, 1985), reprinted in CCH Pension Plan Guide at ¶17,508.

[186] See GCM 37856 (Feb. 16, 1979), as summarized in GCM 39385, *supra* (singling out "innocent plan participants" for §7805 relief if defects cured, instead of using total retroactive disqualification). The ERISA Non-Compliance Enforcement Program (ENCEP), which was established by the IRS under its §7805 authority to encourage plans to come into belated compliance with ERISA, further establishes the IRS's emphasis on corrective action at least insofar as innocent plan participants are concerned. See IRS Notice 80-7, reprinted in 294 BNA Pens. Rep. R-4 (June 9, 1980), and Employee Plans Restoration Guidelines (Document 6651), reprinted in 313 BNA Pens. Rep. R-7 (Oct. 20, 1980).

In the event of coverage violations resulting in disqualification of a plan, the Tax Reform Act specifically provides that *only* highly compensated employees are to be taxed on their vested benefits. Code §402(b)(2), as added by §1112(c) of P.L. 99-514.

[187] See *Ludden v. Commissioner, supra.* Robert Blum suggests that if innocent plan participants are ever adversely affected by a retroactive disqualification, they may have a cause of action against the sponsoring employer and the plan's fiduciaries for failing to maintain the plan's qualified status. He also suggests that the summary plan description may provide a separate ground for action as the SPD is unlikely to have informed participants that the plan could be retroactively disqualified with adverse tax consequences for vested participants. See R. Blum, "What Happens on Plan Disqualification," *supra*, at 87 and 88.

An "innocent," but adversely affected plan participant would also have a cause of action in the Tax Court, Court of Claims, or federal district court as a taxpayer against the IRS for failing to exercise its discretion according to its own pronouncements about protecting innocent plan participants. Because some possibility remains, however remote, that the IRS could penalize innocent plan participants, participants raising retroactive compliance issues can seek written assurance from the IRS that this will not occur before providing specific information to the IRS. Even before then, the employer can be given the opportunity to retroactively amend the plan to correct the noncompliance.

V. Separate ERISA Title IV Causes of Action

Participants who are "adversely affected by [an] action" of the PBGC, including a determination by the PBGC of the amount of their guaranteed benefits, may seek judicial review under ERISA Section 4003(f).[188] However, unless futile, participants may be required to first exhaust the PBGC's administrative appeals remedies.[189] For adverse determinations of the amount of guaranteed benefits, this requires an administrative appeal within 45 days of the date the PBGC notifies the participant of the adverse determination.[190] If the administrative appeal is to no avail, Section 4003(f) provides the means for an action against the PBGC for violation of its Title IV obligations. After April 7, 1986, it is also the exclusive means for challenging PBGC actions as a *trustee* of a terminated insufficient plan or a benefits commitments trust.[191]

ERISA Section 4070, as amended by the Single Employer Pension Plan Amendments Act of 1986 (SEPPAA), establishes a second Title IV cause of action under which any adversely affected person, or any employee organization representing such a person, can bring an action to enjoin a violation of the Title IV conditions for standard, distress, and involuntary terminations, or a violation of the Title IV rules on the payment of liability to a benefit commitments trust after a distress termination and on the distribution of benefits therefrom. Section 4070 provides the federal courts with exclusive jurisdiction over such actions. Venue is proper in any district where the plan is administered, where the violation took place, or where a defendant resides or may be found.[192] In contrast to Section 4003, Section 4070 expressly allows discretionary awards of attorney's fees to prevailing, or substantially prevailing, parties. The statute of limitations for such actions is six years after the cause of action arises, or if *later*, three years after the date the plaintiff acquired or should have acquired actual knowledge of a violation (in the case of fraud or concealment by the defendant, a

---

[188] Adverse PBGC actions may include the setting of termination dates and questionable practices and regulations, such as the PBGC's denial of insurance for benefits in plans not amended to comply with ERISA. See ch. 12, sec. VI.A.1. Other adverse PBGC actions turn on interpretation of a plan's terms in conjunction with a regulatory provision. These mixed plan interpretation and regulatory questions include whether a benefit is "nonforfeitable" under the plan, and whether a benefit is one to which a participant is "entitled" under the terms of the plan—other than for submission of a formal application, retirement or completion of a waiting period.

[189] See 29 C.F.R. 2606.7.

[190] See 29 C.F.R. 2606.1(b)(6) and (7), 2606.51, and 2606.53. A shorter 30-day period applies to administrative reconsideration of a PBGC determination on a voluntary termination date. See 29 C.F.R. 2606.1(b)(3) and 2606.33. See also proposed PBGC regulations, 48 Fed. Reg. 22330 (May 18, 1983), reprinted in 445 BNA Pens. Rep. 926 (May 23, 1983), which would simplify and consolidate the PBGC's administrative procedures for all types of determinations.

[191] ERISA §4003(f)(4). Prior to SEPPAA, actions against the PBGC for a breach of its duties as a §4042 plan trustee might be brought under ERISA §502 or under state trust law, as well as under §4003(f).

[192] Service of a copy of the complaint must also be made on the PBGC, with the PBGC then having the right to intervene. ERISA §4070(d).

longer six-year period applies after the date the plaintiff acquired or should have acquired actual knowledge).[193]

Under ERISA Section 4301, as amended by the 1980 Multiemployer Pension Plan Amendments Act (MPPAA), participants and other parties have a third cause of action against a multiemployer plan, the plan's trustees, contributing employers, and potentially, arbitrators for any act or omission violating MPPAA's withdrawal liability, reorganization, insolvency, or mass withdrawal rules. This cause of action is thus a MPPAA compliance cause of action. For example, a plan in reorganization might improperly reduce benefits accrued under plan provisions that were in effect *more than* five years before the plan went into reorganization. Similarly, a multiemployer plan might fail to provide the required notice before making reductions in reorganization or benefit suspensions in insolvency. The federal courts have exclusive jurisdiction over such actions under Section 4301 (except that actions by fiduciaries to collect the withdrawal liability established under MPPAA may also be brought in state court). Venue in such actions is in the district court where the plan is administered or where a defendant resides or may be found. Attorney's fees may be awarded in the court's discretion to the prevailing party. ERISA Section 4301 also sets a limitations period for redressing violations of the MPPAA provisions. Like ERISA Section 4070, it uses the *later* of six years after the date on which the cause of action arose, or three years after the plaintiff either had actual knowledge or should have acquired actual knowledge of a violation.

When a multiemployer plan termination, reorganization, or insolvency issue goes beyond compliance with MPPAA's requirements to a permissive area, the action *might* be brought under Section 4301 if it indirectly relates to MPPAA's provisions, but such actions seem to more generally arise under ERISA as a question of whether an act or omission, which is permissive under MPPAA, was "solely in the interest" and for the "exclusive purpose" of providing benefits to participants. For example, if a plan adopts an amendment reducing benefits in reorganization, this may be permissible under MPPAA, and therefore not actionable under Section 4301, but the amendment may still violate the "solely in the interest" and "exclusive benefit" standards of ERISA Section 404(a)(1) under the facts and circumstances, and thus may be actionable under ERISA Sections 502(a)(2) and (a)(3).[194] Multiemployer plan participants also still have a cause of action against the PBGC under Section 4003(f) for any adverse action the PBGC takes, or fails to take, that is detrimental to their rights.

---

[193] ERISA §4003(f)(5), as amended. This limitations period contrasts with the ERISA §413 limitations period for breach of fiduciary duty actions which uses the *earlier* of 6 years after a cause of action arose, or 3 years after the plaintiff gained actual knowledge of the violation (with an extension to 6 years in the case of fraud or concealment).

[194] See ch. 13, sec. I, for an example of a potential fiduciary violation from such an amendment.

VI. Other Causes of Action for Benefit Claims

In addition to those causes of action set forth in Section 502(a) of ERISA, participants retain other causes of action for the enforcement of benefit rights.

A. Sections 301 and 302 of the LMRA

Rights arising under a collectively bargained plan may be enforced by the union representing the employees under Section 301 of the Labor Management Relations Act.[195] Retirees, beneficiaries, and former employees who are no longer a part of the bargaining unit can individually enforce their rights under the collective bargaining agreement under Section 301.[196] Individuals who are still within the bargaining unit can enforce their rights individually in a hybrid duty of fair representation/Section 301 enforcement action if the union's failure to enforce the contract right is a breach of its duty of fair representation.[197]

Participants in jointly administered plans subject to Section 302(c)(5) of the LMRA can bring actions under Section 302(e) of the Act to enjoin structural defects in the plan's rules [198]—although that course of action has now been limited under *UMW Health & Retirement Funds v. Robinson* if the plan provision in question is the result of collective bargaining.[199] Actions to enforce the terms of a jointly administered plan can also generally be brought under Section 301 of the LMRA even when the terms of the plan are not the product of express bargaining between the union and the employers.[200]

Duty of fair representation claims and hybrid duty of fair representation/Section 301 enforcement actions have been sharply limited by the six-month limitations period for bringing such actions adopted

---

195 Exhaustion of the collective bargaining agreement's grievance and arbitration procedure may be required before any court action is taken if the grievance and arbitration procedure is expressly applicable to employee benefit claims. See sec. I.B above. A union can also challenge certain contract violations relating to employee benefit plans as unfair labor practices before the NLRB. See *Capitol City Lumber Co. v. NLRB*, 721 F.2d 546, 4 EBC 2530 (6th Cir. 1983) (employer's failure to make contributions to plan challengable as unfair labor practice since it represents a failure to bargain over a change in terms and conditions of employment).

196 See *Sheeran v. General Elec. Co.*, 593 F.2d 93 (9th Cir. 1979); *Rehmar v. Smith*, 555 F.2d 1362, 1 EBC 1799 (9th Cir. 1976); *Apponi v. Sunshine Biscuits, Inc.*, 652 F.2d 643, 2 EBC 1534 (6th Cir. 1981); *UAW v. Yard-Man, Inc.*, 716 F.2d 1476, 4 EBC 2108 (6th Cir. 1983); *Allied Chemical Workers v. Pittsburgh Plate Glass*, 404 U.S. 157, 1 EBC 1019 (1971); *Smith v. Evening News Ass'n*, 371 U.S. 195 (1962); *Lewis v. Benedict Coal Corp.*, 361 U.S. 459 (1960).

197 See *Vaca v. Sipes*, 386 U.S. 171 (1967); *Hines v. Anchor Motor Freight, Inc.*, 424 U.S. 554 (1976); *DelCostello v. Teamsters*, 462 U.S. 151 (1983).

198 See *Lugo v. Employees Retirement Fund*, 366 F.Supp. 99 (E.D.N.Y. 1974), *aff'd*, 529 F.2d 251 (2d Cir.), *cert. denied*, 429 U.S. 826 (1976) (actions for violations of §302(c)(5) are brought under §302(e)).

199 455 U.S. 562, 3 EBC 1129 (1982). And see ch. 8, sec. VIII, and ch. 9, sec. II.A.

200 See *Rehmar v. Smith*, 555 F.2d 1362, 1 EBC 1799 (9th Cir. 1976); *Reiherzer v. Shannon*, 581 F.2d 1266, 1 EBC 1175 (7th Cir. 1978) (citing split in court decisions, but not needing to reach issue in light of availability of ERISA §502(a)(1)(B) cause of action).

by the Supreme Court in *DelCostello v. Teamsters*.[201] However, whether this six-month limitation applies to duty of fair representation claims related to collectively bargained *pension* rights remains an open issue.[202]

B. Non-Preempted State Law

When a state law claim does not duplicate any ERISA claim, the state law cause of action may not be preempted by ERISA. In *Amato v. Western Union International, Inc.*, the Second Circuit found no need to decide whether claims, based on a written sales agreement and oral assurances that the buyer of a business would not reduce pension benefits after the sale, were under ERISA's federal common law or under non-preempted state law because state law would provide the principles for decision in either case.[203] In *Aronson v. Servus Rubber Division*, profit-sharing contributions were recovered from an employer based on individual employment agreements of two highly paid employees requiring the contributions to be made, with jurisdiction premised on the federal court's pendent state law jurisdiction.[204]

Somewhat similarly, if a misrepresentation of a plan's benefits is made by a person who is not a fiduciary of a plan, a state law misrepresentation claim may be made.[205] The absence of preemption under

---

[201] 462 U.S. 151 (1983).

[202] Compare *Adams v. Gould, Inc.*, 739 F.2d 858, 5 EBC 1878 (3d Cir. 1984), *cert. denied*, 469 U.S. 1122 (1985) (applying 3-year limitation period from ERISA §413 instead of 6-month *DelCostello* period to claim that union allowed employer to pay less than its agreed contributions to pension plan); *Local Union 1397 v. United Steelworkers*, 748 F.2d 180 (3d Cir. 1984) (reiterating position in *Adams v. Gould, Inc.* in *dicta*); *O'Hare v. General Marine Trans. Co.*, 740 F.2d 160 (2d Cir. 1984), *cert. denied*, 469 U.S. 1212 (1985) (applying 6-year New York period for contracts to claim by pension plan trustees for delinquent contributions); *Sparks v. Ryerson & Haynes, Inc.*, 638 F.Supp. 56 (E.D. Mich. 1986) (using 3-year period for ERISA breach of fiduciary duty actions, instead of *DelCostello* period, for claim that vested health benefits of retirees were impermissibly reduced by negotiated plan amendment); *Haytcher v. ABS Indus., Inc.*, 7 EBC 2158 (N.D. Ohio 1986) (following *Adams v. Gould, Inc.* in rejecting application of *DelCostello* to a §301 action for pension benefits in favor of 3-year ERISA limitations period), with *Flight Officers, Inc. v. United Air Lines, Inc.*, 756 F.2d 1262, 6 EBC 1075 (7th Cir. 1985) (6-month *DelCostello* period applied to claim that pension plan amendment was in breach of duty of fair representation with period beginning with date contract was signed); *Goins v. Teamsters Local 639*, 598 F.Supp. 1151 (D.D.C. 1984) (6-month limitations period applied, but opinion suggests that starting point was date of benefit denial instead of date of plan amendment). And cf. *Young v. Great A&P Tea Co.*, 120 LRRM 2471 (W.D. Pa. 1984), *aff'd*, 120 LRRM 2504 (3d Cir. 1985), *cert. denied*, 474 U.S. 947 (1985) (applying 6-month *DelCostello* limit in §301 suit for failure to pay accrued vacation benefits); *Gibson v. AT&T Technologies, Inc.*, 120 LRRM 2064 (N.D. Ill. 1985), *aff'd*, 782 F.2d 686, 121 LRRM 2626 (7th Cir. 1986) (applying 6-month limit in action alleging employer withheld information about plant closing leading employees to leave earlier and take "SIPP" benefits [benefits under a voluntary incentive program to encourage technologically displaced employees to go elsewhere for work] thereby denying them layoff allowance available on plant closing—in one instance, with a $51,000 difference in benefits).

[203] 773 F.2d 1402, 6 EBC 2226 (2d Cir. 1985). Accord *Holliday v. Xerox Corp.*, 555 F.Supp. 51, 4 EBC 1221 (E.D. Mich. 1982), *aff'd*, 732 F.2d 548, 5 EBC 1705 (6th Cir. 1984).

[204] 730 F.2d 12, 5 EBC 1343 (1st Cir. 1984), *cert. denied*, 469 U.S. 1017 (1984). See also *PBGC v. Greene*, 570 F.Supp. 1483, 4 EBC 1169 (W.D. Pa. 1983) (if state law claim is not preempted and is included in a suit with ERISA claims, federal courts have pendent jurisdiction to retain the state law claim); and ch. 8, sec. III. But compare *Jackson v. Martin Marietta Corp.*, 805 F.2d 1498, 7 EBC 2767 (11th Cir. 1986) (ERISA preempts state law claim for breach of contract based on promise during job interview in 1977 that pension service would date from 1959).

[205] See ch. 8, sec. V.

ERISA for state domestic relations laws[206] and state law causes of action for breaches of insurance contracts and misrepresentations by insurers[207] has been described in earlier chapters.

State law causes of action can also apply to the exclusion of any ERISA cause of action for breach of fiduciary duties if *all* the acts or omissions constituting the claim occurred before January 1, 1975.[208] Under this standard, some courts hold that the "mere formal[ity]" of a benefit denial after January 1, 1975, does not necessarily lead to ERISA jurisdiction if the benefit denial was pursuant to an unambiguous and nondiscretionary plan provision adopted before the ERISA effective date.[209] But other courts have stated that "the grant or denial of pension benefits is itself the [last] 'act or omission,'" not the "metaphysical [earlier] operation," for example, of a break-in-service rule.[210]

C. ADEA Actions

As discussed in Chapter 10, the Age Discrimination in Employment Act can provide the basis for pension-related claims if, for example, the terms of a plan discriminate on the basis of age, of if the costs of benefits under a plan, or eligibility for benefits, is used as a selection factor in determining which employees to lay off. If both an ADEA and an ERISA action are available based on the same set of facts (for example, a claim that the timing of a plant closing was based on the higher pension costs of older workers at the plant), the ADEA can provide advantages in terms of the availability of a jury trial and the availability of liquidated damages for willful violations in an amount equal to the compensatory damages resulting from the age discrimination.[211]

The ADEA requires that charges of age discrimination be filed with the EEOC within 180 days of the date of the alleged unlawful practice, or within 300 days in a state where deferral to a state agency is required.[212] The statute of limitations for filing a court action under

---

[206] See ch. 6, sec. IV.A.

[207] See ch. 7, sec. III.A.5.c, and ch. 8, secs. IV and V.

[208] ERISA §514(b)(1).

[209] See *Menhorn v. Firestone Tire & Rubber Co.*, 738 F.2d 1496, 5 EBC 2193, at 2197 (9th Cir. 1984). But see *Jameson v. Bethlehem Steel Corp. Pension Plan*, 6 EBC 1893 (3d Cir. 1986), *cert. denied*, 479 U.S. ___ (1987) (when cause of action accrues after ERISA effective dates, but pre-ERISA "acts or omissions" determine entitlement, federal courts have jurisdiction, with substantive rules determined by state law; disagreeing on jurisdictional issue with *Menhorn, supra*).

[210] See *Tanzillo v. Teamsters Local 617*, 769 F.2d 140, at 144 (3d Cir. 1985).

[211] See 29 U.S.C. §§626(b) and (c)(2). See also B. Schlei and P. Grossman, *Employment Discrimination Law* (BNA 1983 ed.), at 494-95 and 524, and *EEOC v. Westinghouse Elec. Corp.*, 632 F.Supp. 343, 7 EBC 1318 (E.D. Pa. 1986) (holding denial of severance benefits to pension eligible employees to be "willful" age discrimination for purposes of awarding plaintiffs liquidated damages under the ADEA, applying the elucidation of willfulness in *Trans World Airlines, Inc. v. Thurston*, 469 U.S. 111 (1985), and finding that the employer had known or shown reckless disregard for whether the conduct violated the ADEA).

[212] 29 U.S.C. §626(d).

the ADEA is two years from when the cause of action accrued, or three years if the discrimination was willful.[213]

A central question in the application of these time periods is when the cause of action accrues—whether it accrues when an age discriminatory amendment is made to a plan, when the provision first applies to an employee, or when benefits under the plan become due. In *EEOC v. Westinghouse Electric Corp.*, the Third Circuit followed ERISA cases in which causes of action have been held to accrue for the purpose of a statute of limitations only when the benefits become due.[214] As discussed in the next section, the same approach has been followed in Title VII cases in which a plan provision is alleged to discriminate on the basis of race or sex.

On the other hand, if the alleged age discrimination does not arise directly from the terms of the plan, but is, for example, in the use of pension eligibility or pension costs as a selection factor in determining which employees to layoff or terminate, a cause of action may accrue at the time the layoff or job termination occurs. The difference in this case is that costs or eligibility for benefits under a plan have been used as unlawful criteria in selecting employees for layoff or termination, not that benefits under the terms of the pension plan are discriminatory.

D. Title VII of the Civil Rights Act

In contrast to the ADEA, Title VII of the 1964 Civil Rights Act does not provide for a jury trial, or for liquidated damages for willful violations.[215] However, like the ADEA, Title VII requires causes of action alleging discrimination to be commenced within certain limited time periods. A charge must be filed with the EEOC within 180 days, or within 300 days in a state where deferral to a state agency is required. A court action must then be filed within 90 days after the issuance of a right to sue letter by the EEOC.[216]

When a cause of action arises is a central question in how these limitations periods apply. In *Bartmess v. Drewrys U.S.A. Inc.*, the

---

[213] 29 U.S.C. §626(e). See also *Trans World Airlines, Inc. v. Thurston*, 469 U.S. 111 (1985) (recognizing division among the circuits on whether "willful" has the same meaning for purposes of the ADEA limitations period as for obtaining liquidated damages, but not resolving issue).

[214] 725 F.2d 211, 4 EBC 2684 (3d Cir. 1984), *cert. denied*, 469 U.S. 820 (1984); and see *EEOC v. Home Ins. Co.*, 553 F.Supp. 704, 3 EBC 2435 (S.D.N.Y. 1982) (to the same effect following Title VII cases); *EEOC v. Westinghouse Elec. Corp.*, 42 FEP Cases 1203 (D.N.J. 1987) (2-year ADEA limitation period starting from date benefits denied applied to action to redress denial of severance pay for early retirees). See also sec. II.D above for pension cases in addition to those cited by the Third Circuit in *EEOC v. Westinghouse*.

[215] See generally B. Schlei and P. Grossman, *Employment Discrimination Law* (BNA 1983 ed.), at 695-97. However, punitive damages and extra-contractual compensatory damages for mental or emotional distress may be available in actions under the Civil Rights Act of 1866, 42 U.S.C. §1981. *Id.*

[216] 42 U.S.C. §§2000e-5(e) and (f)(1). Actions by the EEOC against private employers are not subject to a statute of limitations. See *Occidental Life Ins. Co. v. EEOC*, 432 U.S. 355 (1977). But laches could apply in certain cases. Cf. *EEOC v. A&P Co.*, 34 FEP Cases 1412 (3d Cir. 1984) (problematic whether laches applies, but doctrine inapplicable under facts).

Seventh Circuit suggested that maintenance of a discriminatory pension plan was a continuing violation for which an action could be brought at the time of retirement, as opposed to the type of single, isolated act for which the cause of action should accrue when the plan, or plan amendment, was first conceived, or when the participant first came under the plan or amendment.[217] This is in accord with the general treatment of pension claims,[218] and with the treatment of claims of age discrimination under the terms of a pension plan under the ADEA.[219]

On the other hand, if a Title VII claim is essentially a charge of discrimination in regard to hiring, discharge, promotion, or transfer, and the alleged discrimination has effects under a pension plan (as opposed to a claim that the design of the plan is itself a part of the discrimination), the cause of action may accrue when the discriminatory act occurred.[220]

E. FLSA, RICO, and Other Federal Law Actions

Fair Labor Standards Act actions related to pension and profit-sharing plans are discussed in Chapters 2 and 3. The statute of limitations for Fair Labor Standards Act violations is two years, or three years for a willful violation. Liquidated damages in an amount equal to unpaid back wages, along with attorney's fees, may be recovered in FLSA actions.[221] Other federal laws with benefit implications, discussed in the text above, include the Veterans Readjustment Assistance Act, the Bankruptcy Code, and the Equal Pay Act.

Some plaintiffs with pension claims have also used the Racketeer Influenced and Corrupt Organizations Act (RICO)[222] to attempt to obtain treble damages for false representations that are communicated by mail or wire for the purpose of executing a scheme or conspiracy to deprive them of their benefits. To date, there are few published decisions applying RICO to pension plans.[223]

---

[217] 444 F.2d 1186 (7th Cir. 1971), *cert. denied,* 404 U.S. 939 (1971). And see *Long v. Florida,* 805 F.2d 1542, 7 EBC 2648 (11th Cir. 1986) (each month's retirement check, if computed on a discriminatory basis, constitutes an actionable event); *Hannahs v. New York State Teachers' Retirement System,* 26 FEP Cases 527 (S.D.N.Y. 1981) (time periods begin to run at retirement when benefits are due); *Mixson v. Southern Bell Tel. Co.,* 334 F.Supp. 525 (N.D. Ga. 1971) (because of continuing nature of violation, time periods may not begin to run as long as benefits are still due "but for" the discriminatory plan provision); *American Finance System, Inc. v. Harlow,* 65 F.R.D. 94 (D.Md. 1974) (following *Mixson*).

[218] See sec. II.D.

[219] See sec. VI.C.

[220] See *Simmons v. South Carolina State Ports Auth.,* 3 EBC 2413 (4th Cir. 1982).

[221] 29 U.S.C. §§255(a) and 216(b). And see generally BNA Wage & Hour Man. 98:197-213.

[222] 18 U.S.C. §§1961-68. And see generally *Sedima v. Imrex Co.,* 473 U.S. 479 (1985).

[223] See *McClendon v. Continental Group, Inc.,* 7 EBC 2370 (D.N.J. 1986) (denying employer's motion to dismiss RICO claim on ground that no "pattern of racketeering" was shown in alleged nationwide scheme to deprive employees of pension rights through selective layoffs and plant closings prior to benefit eligibility); *Crawford v. La Boucherie Bernard Ltd.,* C.A. No. 83-0780 (D.D.C., Aug. 15, 1984), summarized at ¶23,666W CCH Pens. Plan Guide, *aff'd,* 815 F.2d 117 (D.C. Cir. 1987) (participants can sue fiduciaries on behalf of plan under RICO for fraudulent

VII. Gathering Pension Information

For lawyers representing participants, the summary plan description (SPD), the plan itself, the letter from the plan denying the claim, and any other information or representations concerning the plan's benefits are standard items in initially reviewing the potential of a benefit claim.

ERISA requires plan administrators to automatically furnish the plan's SPD to each participant within 90 days after he or she becomes covered by the plan, or in the case of a beneficiary, begins receiving benefits from the plan.[224] Summaries of any material modification in the terms of the plan which affect the information in the summary plan description are to be furnished automatically within 210 days after the close of the plan year in which the modification was made.[225] Notice of any plan amendments significantly reducing benefits is required 15 days prior to the effectiveness of the amendment.[226] Updated summary plan descriptions are required to be provided after five years, if modifications have been made to the plan.[227]

ERISA Sections 104(b)(2) and (4) provide that a plan must make available for inspection or, at the request of a participant, furnish a copy of:

- The plan itself;[228]
- "[T]he bargaining agreement, trust agreement, contract, or other instruments under which the plan is established or operated";[229]
- The "annual report";[230] and

---

conversion of plan assets; no reason to distinguish profit-sharing plans from other entities entitled to recovery under RICO). See also *Bigger v. American Commercial Lines, Inc.*, 652 F.Supp. 123, 8 EBC 1424 (W.D. Mo. 1986) (no RICO claim in spin off of plan since single scheme is not a RICO racketeering "pattern"); *Otto v. Variable Annuity Life Ins. Co.*, 808 F.2d 512, 8 EBC 1593 (7th Cir. 1986), *modified on other grounds*, 8 EBC 1605 (7th Cir. 1987) (no RICO claim from failure to fully disclose method of crediting interest under a fixed annuity plan when complaint failed to identify the RICO "enterprise").

224 ERISA §§101(a) and 104(b)(1)(A). For persons who were already participants or beneficiaries when ERISA was enacted, an SPD in compliance with the ERISA requirements of understandability, completeness, and accuracy should generally have been furnished in late 1977. See 29 C.F.R. §2520.104-6.

225 ERISA §104(b)(1).

226 ERISA §204(h), as amended by §11006 of the Single Employer Pension Plan Amendments Act of 1986 (enacted as Title XI of P.L. 99-272).

227 ERISA §104(b)(1). Even if no modifications are made, a new SPD is required to be distributed to participants every 10 years. *Id.*

228 In some cases, the plan document is included as an appendix to the summary plan description. But usually the two are separate, and the plan document is not automatically distributed.

229 The trust agreement for a plan may include the plan document, or it may be separate from it. The trust part of the agreement is concerned with the establishment of a valid trust, duties of trustees, committee structures, investment functions and, possibly, policies. Other instruments under which a plan is operated may include documents on the allocation of fiduciary duties under the plan, day-to-day administration of the plan, investment management and policies, and service-provider or consulting contracts.

230 This refers to the plan's Form 5500 Annual Return/Report of Employee Benefit Plan, with Schedule A (insurance information) and Schedule B (actuarial information), and also the accountant's statement and opinion, the actuary's statement, and any trustees' report.

- "[A]ny terminal report."[231]

A participant has the right to the assistance of counsel in the inspection of these plan documents and records.[232] When copies of documents are requested, charges may be imposed, but they must not exceed the actual cost incurred, and in no event may they exceed 25 cents per page.[233]

If a participant's or beneficiary's claim for benefits from a plan has been denied, the participant or beneficiary is to receive a written explanation of the denial from the plan administrator, with references to the plan provisions on which the denial is based.[234] Documents specifically related to the benefit denial, such as plan records and worksheets on credited service and individual benefit computations, may then be inspected and copied under the right of the participant, or an authorized representative, to review "pertinent documents" to a denied claim.[235] If the claim is denied on review, the participant should then receive a second letter, usually from a plan committee, reviewing any additional information or reasons submitted by the participant in support of the claim and explaining the plan's reasons for the denial.[236]

Participants also usually have in their possession annual individual benefit statements which list their accrued benefits and state whether those benefits are vested (and if not, when they will be). These statements are required to be furnished *on request* under ERISA Section 105, but are furnished automatically by most plans.[237] If a participant has left the job, or incurred a one-year break in service, a statement of his or her accrued benefits and the vested percentage of those

---

For plans with less than 100 participants, the annual report form is a shorter Form 5500-C. For such plans, a form with information paralleling that required by the Form 5500 is required to be filed triennially.

[231] This appears to refer primarily to the Notice of Intent to Terminate that employers sponsoring defined benefit plans are required to file with the PBGC on IRS/PBGC Form 5310 (Application for Determination Upon Termination), with attachments as specified in the instructions to Form 5310. Defined contribution plans also use the Form 5310 to obtain assurance from the IRS of a plan's tax qualified status before termination of the plan. "[A]ny terminal report" may also cover any final reports on the termination of a plan prepared, for example, by the plan's accountant or actuary.

[232] See Department of Labor *amicus curiae* brief in *Lee v. Woodward & Lothrop, Inc.*, C.A. No. 79-1460 (D.D.C. 1979), summarized at 249 BNA Pens. Rep. A-21 (July 23, 1979); case dismissed following employer's agreement to permit participant to have representative present, see 252 BNA Pens. Rep. at A-14 (Aug. 13, 1979).

[233] 29 C.F.R. 2520.104b-30(b). When participants under a plan are spread over more than one geographic area, each geographic area is to have these documents available for inspection and copying. 29 C.F.R. 2520.104b-1(b)(3).

[234] 29 C.F.R. 2560.503-1(f).

[235] 29 C.F.R. 2560.503-1(g)(1)(ii). See also *Lee v. Dayton Power & Light Co.*, 604 F.Supp. 987 (S.D. Ohio 1985) (plan's duty to allow inspection or copying extends to manuals and tables used in determining Social Security amounts for offsets), and Prop. Regs. 29 C.F.R. 2530.209-2(f) and 3(f).

A parallel right to obtain pertinent documents should be available under any collectively bargained grievance and arbitration procedure. See American Arbitration Association, "Voluntary Labor Arbitration Rules," at 7-8 (arbitrator's authority to subpoena documents and witnesses determined under state law).

[236] 29 C.F.R. 2560.503-1(h)(3).

[237] Some multiemployer plans may not furnish individual benefit statements either automatically or on request because §105(d) requires multiemployer plans to furnish the statements "only to the extent provided in regulations" and the regulations are still only in proposed form. See 45

benefits should have been furnished automatically.[238] A participant may also have been furnished with election materials on the plan's joint and survivor's benefit options (with dollar amounts of the participant's benefits and information on reductions in those benefits to provide joint and survivor's options) both before retirement and at retirement.

Summaries of the plan's annual financial reports (called "SARs") are to be furnished to every plan participant within 210 days after the end of each plan year. For defined benefit plan participants, these summaries may have little information relevant to benefit claims, but for defined contribution plans, the statements provide a record of the employer's contributions to the plan and the plan's financial performance, which in turn determines the value of the individual's account.

Although not required to be furnished automatically, participants often have in their possession a variety of other information about a plan, including correspondence with the company or plan, notes from individual or group meetings about employee benefits, company magazine and newsletter clippings, bulletin board notices, leaflets, and other types of handout material. *All* information that has been communicated to employees concerning the plan is important for purposes of contract interpretation and estoppel.[239] Even when these materials are not dispositive of a claim, they can put an issue in the perspective of how the plan was presented to participants on a less formal basis than in the plan document or even the SPD.

Applications for determinations filed with the IRS are required to be made available by plans for inspection by participants.[240] Notices to the other federal agencies are also available through the agencies either as information available only to participants or as information open for public inspection on filing a Freedom of Information Act request.[241] When a fiduciary claim has previously been investigated by the Department of Labor, the Department is authorized under Section 504(a) and the ERISA Conference Report "to make available to persons covered by the plan . . . information concerning any matter which has been the subject of investigation."[242]

A union also has a right, independent of any of the above, to

---

Fed. Reg. 52824 (Aug. 8, 1980). And see 45 Fed. Reg. 51231 (Aug. 1, 1980) (proposed single-employer individual benefit statement regulations).

[238] See ERISA §§105(c) and 209.

[239] See, e.g., *Eardman v. Bethlehem Steel Corp.*, 607 F.Supp. 196, 5 EBC 1985 (W.D.N.Y. 1984).

[240] See 26 C.F.R. 601.201(o)(3). Applications for determination can provide extrinsic evidence on a claim. See *Korn v. Levine Bros. Iron Works Corp.*, 574 F.Supp. 836, 4 EBC 2533 (S.D.N.Y. 1983) (application used in intepreting plan's definition of compensation). Applications may also be useful in explaining complex plan provisions. For example, the application for determination is required to explain how the plan's integration provisions, if any, comply with the limits on Social Security integration.

[241] See ERISA §106 and 29 C.F.R. 2603.

[242] Conf. Rep., at 329, 3 ERISA Leg. Hist. 4596.

obtain information, including pension information, needed to enable it to bargain effectively over wages and working conditions.[243]

Once a court action is filed, information that was not available before, or that was not clearly available, may, of course, be obtained through discovery. Key information that may not have been available to the participant previously includes records of past grants and denials of similar benefit claims, records of trustees' meetings, records of corporate board meetings, and memos and correspondence between corporate officers and the plan's administrator or trustees, or between any of these parties and the plan's attorneys, actuaries, or other service-providers. Several decisions have held that plans may not claim the attorney-client privilege against their own participants.[244] There are also no generally recognized privileges applicable to communications between a plan and its actuaries or accountants.[245]

Statutory penalties are provided for failure to furnish information required under ERISA Title I. A plan administrator can be held liable for up to $100 per day for each day of delay if copies of documents required to be furnished under ERISA Title I are not furnished within 30 days after a request. A court may also order "such other relief as it deems proper."[246] Courts have, however, been reluctant to apply the $100 per day penalties except in instances when the participant can show some prejudice to his or her rights, e.g., detrimental reliance or delay in the resolution of a claim.[247]

---

[243] See, e.g., *Cone Mills Corp. v. NLRB*, 413 F.2d 445 (4th Cir. 1969) (right to obtain data on pension costs and actuarial assumptions). Prior to discovery, the union's right to information for bargaining may make it the only party with a right to obtain a list of employees and retirees by age, sex, and years of service and other detailed information on layoffs and pension costs necessary to fully evaluate a Title VII discrimination, §510, or partial termination claim, all of which are discussed in chs. 10 and 11.

[244] See *Mioni v. Bessemer Cement Co.*, 4 EBC 2390 (W.D. Pa. 1983); *Washington-Baltimore Newspaper Guild, Local 35 v. Washington Star Co.*, 543 F.Supp. 906, 3 EBC 1741 (D.D.C. 1982); *Donovan v. Fitzsimmons*, 90 F.R.D. 583, 2 EBC 1393 (N.D. Ill. 1981). In *Washington-Baltimore Newspaper Guild*, a district court required disclosure of communications between an employer and its attorney about a plan when the attorney represented both the employer and the plan's fiduciaries.

[245] Information obtained from a plan may in some instances be valued more for making issues understandable than for any directly adverse effects on the plan's or employer's position. For example, an actuary's letters, memos, and reports to corporate officers and plan administrators may have more understandable explanations than available elsewhere on the effects, in terms of pension cost reductions, of plant closings and layoffs, or on the considerations behind the selection of one funding method or set of actuarial assumptions over others.

[246] ERISA §502(c). The "plan administrator," and not the plan, is the proper defendant in a suit for failure to provide employee benefit plan information on request. See *Boyd v. Philippine Airlines Pension Plan*, 3 EBC 1114 (D.D.C. 1982); *Turner v. CF&I Steel Corp.*, 510 F.Supp. 537, 2 EBC 1397 (E.D. Pa. 1981); *Crawford v. Armour & Co. Salaried Pension Plan*, 3 EBC 2335 (W.D. Pa. 1982).

[247] Compare *Chambers v. Kaleidoscope, Inc. Profit Sharing Plan*, 650 F.Supp. 359, 7 EBC 2628 (N.D. Ga. 1986) (to the extent injury must be shown under §502(c), plaintiff did so by showing that she was deprived of information about her benefits and whether part of them had been misappropriated; plan administrator's argument that she could always have obtained the information through discovery rejected because ERISA does not require participants to engage in litigation to obtain documents; $100 per day can be adjusted down to reflect court's view of injury sustained); *LeFebre v. Westinghouse Elec. Corp.*, 549 F.Supp. 1021, 3 EBC 2353 (D. Md. 1982), *rev'd on other grounds*, 747 F.2d 197, 5 EBC 2521 (4th Cir. 1984) ($74,000 awarded for failure to furnish SPD automatically and after request); *Kulchin v. Spear Box Co. Retirement Plan*, 208 BNA Pens. Rep. D-9 (S.D.N.Y. 1978) ($10,000 penalty for failure to provide form plan administrator asserted was required for lump sum benefits); *Bemis v. Hogue*, 635 F.Supp. 1100 (E.D.

If a document, such as an SPD, is to be furnished automatically, the $100 per day penalty may be triggered, but not until a separate written request for the document is made.[248] Similarly, if a plan administrator fails to provide specific reasons for a benefit denial, this could be a failure to supply information resulting in $100 per day penalties, but only if the reasons are not supplied within 30 days after a separate written request by the participant.[249]

Mich. 1986) (employee entitled to penalty when plan administrator failed to respond to claim for benefits and requests for information—irrespective of whether he was prejudiced or whether administrator acted in good faith); *Wright v. Nimmons*, 641 F.Supp. 1391, 7 EBC 2184 (S.D.Tex. 1986) (employees entitled to penalties where failure to respond to requests for information was malicious and without justification); with *Kann v. Keystone Resources, Inc. Profit Sharing Plan*, 575 F.Supp. 1084, 5 EBC 1233 (W.D. Pa. 1983) (no penalty because delay not in bad faith); *Pollock v. Castrovinci*, 476 F.Supp. 606, 1 EBC 2091 (S.D.N.Y. 1979), *aff'd*, 622 F.2d 575 (2d Cir. 1980) (no penalty because no prejudice from delay); *Boyd v. Cervantes*, 3 EBC 1796 (D.D.C. 1982) (technical violation, but timely response difficult because of extensiveness of request); *King v. Wagner Elec. Corp. Retirement Plan*, 1 EBC 1629 (E.D. Mo. 1979) (no showing of pecuniary damage or prejudice); *Medley v. Holly Farms Poultry*, 1 EBC 1004 (M.D.N.C. 1977) (innocent and understandable delay given regulatory confusion); *Bonin v. American Airlines, Inc.*, 562 F.Supp. 896, 4 EBC 1671 (N.D. Tex. 1983) (employer misconceived duty in confusion overly newly enacted law); *Lee v. Dayton Power & Light Co.*, 604 F.Supp. 987 (S.D. Ohio 1985) (disclosure violation in refusal to furnish manual with charts needed to check calculation of retirement benefits, but no discretionary award of penalties); *Bruch v. Firestone Tire & Rubber Co.*, 640 F.Supp. 519 (E.D. Pa. 1986) (no penalty when employees failed to show harm and, after their employment ended, were no longer participants in severance pay plan); *Chambers v. European Am. Bank & Trust Co.*, 601 F.Supp. 630 (E.D.N.Y. 1985) (no penalty for untimely provision of copies of plan and trust agreement when no prejudice to participant and no bad faith; citing still other cases in support).

The presence of the statutory penalties has been held to bar any additional punitive damages for delay in furnishing requested documents. See *Meyer v. Phillip Morris, Inc.*, 569 F.Supp. 1510 (E.D. Mo. 1983); *Wilson v. Pye*, 6 EBC 2761 (N.D. Ill. 1986). But cf. *Kuntz v. Reese*, 760 F.2d 926, 6 EBC 1780 (9th Cir. 1985), *vacated and withdrawn on other grounds*, 785 F.2d 1410, 7 EBC 1227 (9th Cir. 1986), *cert. denied*, 479 U.S. ___ (1986).

[248] See *Petrella v. NL Indus., Inc.*, 529 F.Supp. 1357, 3 EBC 1210 (D.N.J. 1982) (SPDs never furnished, but not requested either, therefore no $100 a day penalty); and compare *LeFebre v. Westinghouse Elec. Corp.*, 549 F.Supp. 1021, 3 EBC 2353 (D. Md. 1982), *rev'd on other grounds*, 747 F.2d 197, 5 EBC 2521 (4th Cir. 1984) ($74,000 penalty for SPDs not furnished automatically and then also not furnished after request). However, notwithstanding the lack of a specific request, equitable and injunctive relief may be available under §502(a)(3) for a failure to furnish an SPD automatically. See, e.g., *Hillis v. Waukesha Title Co.*, 576 F.Supp. 1103 (E.D. Wis. 1983).

[249] *Clouatre v. Lockwood*, 593 F.Supp. 1136 (M.D. La. 1984); *Bemis v. Hogue, supra*; *Kleinhans v. Lisle Savings Profit Sharing Trust*, 8 EBC 1038 (7th Cir. 1987) ($100 per day penalties not available when plan administrator simply fails to respond to claim for benefits; but they may be available when a particpant requests an explanation of the reasons for the denial and the administrator fails to respond). But compare *Groves v. Johns Manville Corp. Modified Retirement Plan*, 803 F.2d 109, 7 EBC 2359 (3d Cir. 1986) (failure to provide reasons for benefit denial and to allow review of pertinent documents not a basis for $100 per day penalties because §503 claims procedures are directed to plans, not plan administrators, and §502(c) penalties should not, in any event, be imposed for failure to comply with regulatory rules not specifically stated in statute); *Chambless v. Masters, Mates & Pilots Pension Plan*, 571 F.Supp. 1430 (S.D.N.Y. 1983) (§502(c) penalties may not be imposed for failure to release information about past denials of benefits to other claimants).

Appendix

List of Parallel ERISA/U.S.C. Sections

	ERISA	U.S.C.
Short title and table of contents	1	
Title I — Protection of Employee Benefit Rights		
Subtitle A — General Provisions		
Findings and declaration of policy	2	1001
Definitions	3	1002
Coverage	4	1003
Subtitle B — Regulatory Provisions		
Part 1 — Reporting and Disclosure		
Duty of disclosure and reporting	101	1021
Plan description and summary plan description	102	1022
Annual reports	103	1023
Filing with Secretary and furnishing information to participants	104	1024
Reporting of participant's benefit rights	105	1025
Reports made public information	106	1026
Retention of records	107	1027
Reliance on administrative interpretations	108	1028
Forms	109	1029
Alternative methods of compliance	110	1030
Repeal and effective date	111	1031
Part 2 — Participation and Vesting		
Coverage	201	1051
Minimum participation standards	202	1052
Minimum vesting standards	203	1053
Benefit accrual requirements	204	1054
Requirement of joint and survivor annuity and preretirement survivor annuity	205	1055
Other provisions relating to form and payment of benefits	206	1056
Temporary variances from certain vesting requirements	207	1057

	ERISA	U.S.C.
Part 6 — Continuation Coverage Under Group Health Plans		
Plans must provide continuation coverage to certain individuals	601	1161
Continuation coverage	602	1162
Qualifying event	603	1163
Applicable premium	604	1164
Election	605	1165
Notice requirements	606	1166
Definitions	607	1167
Regulations	608	1168
Title II — Amendments to the Internal Revenue Code Relating to Retirement Plans		
Amendment of Internal Revenue Code of 1954	1001	
Subtitle A — Participation, Vesting, Funding, Administration, etc.		
Part 1 — Participation, Vesting, and Funding		
* * *		
Minimum vesting standards	1012	
Minimum funding standards	1013	
* * *		
Effective dates and transitional rules	1017	
* * *		
Part 5 — Internal Revenue Service		
* * *		
Authorization of appropriations	1052	
Subtitle B — Other Amendments to the Internal Revenue Code Relating to Retirement Plans		
* * *		
Prohibited transactions	2003	
Limitations on benefits and contributions	2004	
* * *		
Salary reduction regulations	2006	
* * *		
Title III — Jurisdiction, Administration, Enforcement; Joint Pension Task Force, Etc.		
Subtitle A — Jurisdiction, Administration, and Enforcement		
Procedures in connection with the issuance of certain determination letters by the Secretary of the Treasury	3001	1201

	ERISA	U.S.C.
Date of termination	4048	1348
Distribution to participants and beneficiaries of liability payments to section 4049 trust	4049	1349

Subtitle D — Liability

	ERISA	U.S.C.
Amounts payable by the corporation	4061	1361
Liability for termination of single-employer plans under a distress termination or a termination by the corporation	4062	1362
Liability of substantial employer for withdrawal from single-employer plans under multiple controlled groups	4063	1363
Liability on termination of single-employer plans under multiple controlled groups	4064	1364
Annual report of plan administrator	4065	1365
Annual notification to substantial employers	4066	1366
Recovery of liability for plan termination	4067	1367
Lien for liability	4068	1368
Treatment of transactions to evade liability; effect of corporate reorganization	4069	1369
Enforcement authority relating to terminations of single-employer plans	4070	1370

Subtitle E — Special Provisions for Multiemployer Plans

Part 1 — Employer Withdrawals

	ERISA	U.S.C.
Withdrawal liability established	4201	1381
Determination and collection of liability; notification of employer	4202	1382
Complete withdrawal	4203	1383
Sale of assets	4204	1384
Partial withdrawals	4205	1385
Adjustment for partial withdrawal	4206	1386
Reduction or waiver of complete withdrawal liability	4207	1387
Reduction of partial withdrawal liability	4208	1388
De minimis rule	4209	1389
No withdrawal liability for certain temporary contribution obligation periods	4210	1390
Methods for computing withdrawal liability	4211	1391
Obligation to contribute; special rules	4212	1392
Actuarial assumptions, etc.	4213	1393
Application of plan amendments	4214	1394
Plan notification to corporation of potentially significant withdrawals	4215	1395
Special rules for section 404(c) plans	4216	1396
Application of part in case of certain pre-1980 withdrawals	4217	1397
Withdrawal not to occur merely because of change in business form or suspension of contributions during labor dispute	4218	1398
Notice, collection, etc., of withdrawal liability	4219	1399
Approval of amendments	4220	1400
Resolution of disputes	4221	1401
Reimbursements for uncollectible withdrawal liability	4222	1402
Withdrawal liability payment fund	4223	1403
Alternative method of withdrawal liability payments	4224	1404
Limitation on withdrawal liability	4225	1405

Table of Cases

Cases are referenced to chapter and footnote number(s), e.g., 2:21 indicates the case is cited in chapter 2, footnote 21. Names of cases discussed in text are italicized; the corresponding footnote number indicating the location of the discussion in text also is italicized, to distinguish the discussion from other footnotes which merely cite the case.

A

B

C

D

E

F

G

H

I

Ludden v. Commissioner, 68 T.C. 826, 1 EBC 1787 (1977), *aff'd*, 620 F.2d 700, 2 EBC 2329 (9th Cir. 1980) 14: 178, 187

Lugo v. Employees Retirement Fund, 366 F.Supp. 99 (E.D.N.Y. 1974), *aff'd*, 529 F.2d 251 (2d Cir.), *cert. denied*, 429 U.S. 826 (1976) 7: 298; 14: *9*, 198

Luli v. Sun Products Corp., 398 N.E.2d 553 (Ohio 1979) 5: 44; 7: 61, *260*, 272, *400*; 8: 132; 11: *94*; 12: 189

Lynch v. Dawson Collieries, Inc., 485 S.W.2d 494 (Ky. 1972) 9: 219; 12: 312

M

M&M Trans. Co.; Matter of, 3 B.R. 722, 2 EBC 2486 (S.D.N.Y. 1980) 1: 13; 7: 281; 12: 218, 224, 236

Maas v. Dubuque Packing Co., 754 F.2d 287, 6 EBC 1385 (8th Cir. 1985), *reh. denied, opinion clarified*, 757 F.2d 194, 6 EBC 1390 (8th Cir. 1985) 9: 126; 12: *47*

Maggard v. O'Connell, 671 F.2d 568 (D.C. Cir. 1982) 7: 55, 88, *201*, 284, *289*, *314*, 351

Mahan v. Reynolds Metals Co., 569 F.Supp. 482 (E.D. Ark. 1983), *aff'd*, 739 F.2d 388 (8th Cir. 1984) 14: 15, 51

Malhiot v. So. Cal. Retail Clerks Union, 735 F.2d 1133 (9th Cir. 1984) 7: 87, 92

Malone

—v. Borden, Inc., 6 EBC 1341 (3d Cir. 1984) (unpub.) 10: 83

—v. Western Conference of Teamsters Pension Trust, 168 Cal.Rptr. 210 (Cal. Ct.App. 1980) 8: 167

Manitowoc Eng'g Co. v. Powalisz, 7 EBC 1174 (E.D. Wis. 1987) 6: 116

Marcoux v. State of Maine, 35 FEP Cases 553 (D. Me. 1984), *aff'd*, 7 EBC 2338 (1st Cir. 1986) 10: *129*

Marine Midland Trust Co.; In re, 144 N.Y.S.2d 4 (Sup.Ct. 1955)) 12: 294

Marquardt v. North American Car Corp., 652 F.2d 715, 2 EBC 1545 (7th Cir. 1981) 14: 134, 139

Marshall

—*v. Arlene Knitwear, Inc.*, 454 F.Supp. 715 (E.D.N.Y. 1978), *aff'd in part, rev'd in part*, 608 F.2d 1369 (2d Cir. 1979) 10: *79*

—v. Davis, 517 F.Supp. 551, 2 EBC 1721 (W.D. Mich. 1981) 1: 13

—v. Hawaiian Tel. Co., 575 F.2d 763, 1 EBC 1664 (9th Cir. 1978) 10: 90, 95

—v. Kelly, 465 F.Supp. 341, 1 EBC 1850 (W.D. Okla. 1978) 1: 13

—v. Mercer, 4 EBC 1523 (N.D. Tex. 1983), *rev'd and remanded sub nom. Donovan v. Mercer*, 747 F.2d 304, 5 EBC 2512 (5th Cir. 1984) 13: 111; 14: 86

—v. Snyder, 1 EBC 1878 (E.D.N.Y. 1979) 12: 290, 307

—v. Teamsters Local 282 Pension Trust, 458 F.Supp. 986, 1 EBC 1501 (E.D.N.Y. 1978) 9: 22

—v. Wilson, C.A. No. 3-76-373 (E.D. Tenn. 1976) 13: 110

Martin v. Bankers Trust Co., 565 F.2d 1276, 1 EBC 1793 (4th Cir. 1977) 7: 10

Martinez v. Swift & Co., 656 F.2d 262, 2 EBC 1747 (7th Cir. 1981) 7: 99

Masi v. Ford City Bank & Trust Co., 779 F.2d 397, 6 EBC 2821 (7th Cir. 1985) 14: 127

Mason v. Continental Group, Inc., 763 F.2d 1219, 6 EBC 1933 (11th Cir. 1985), *cert. denied*, 474 U.S. 1087 (1986) 14: 24

Massachusetts Mutual Life Ins. Co. v. Russell, 473 U.S. 134, 6 EBC 1733 (1985) 14: *119*, *120*, *121*, *124*, *125*

Massengill v. Aetna Life Ins. Co., 405 So.2d 516 (La. 1981) 3: 182

Mastie v. Great Lakes Steel Corp., 424 F.Supp. 1299 (E.D. Mich. 1976) 10: *77*

Matthews v. Swift & Co., 465 F.2d 814 (5th Cir. 1972) 7: *53*

May v. Interstate Moving & Storage Co., 739 F.2d 521 (10th Cir. 1984) 14: *111*, 105

McCarthy v. Marshall, 723 F.2d 1034, 4 EBC 2545 (1st Cir. 1983) 4: 114

McClendon v. Continental Group, Inc., 602 F.Supp. 1492, 6 EBC 1113 (D.N.J. 1985), and 7 EBC 2370 (D.N.J. 1986) 10: *9*, 34, *35*; 14: 24, 34, 223

McConnell

—v. MEBA Medical & Benefits Plan, 778 F.2d 521 (9th Cir. 1985) 14: 136

—v. Marine Engineers Beneficial Ass'n, 526 F.Supp. 770 (N.D. Cal. 1981) 14: 58

McCorstin v. U.S. Steel Corp., 621 F.2d 749 (5th Cir. 1980) 10: 81

McCoy v. Mesta Machine Co., 213 BNA Pens. Rep. D-1 (W.D. Pa. 1978), *modified*, 260 BNA Pens. Rep. D-1 (W.D. Pa. 1979) 5: 43; 7: 58, 160; 9: 151, *180*, *199*

McDaniel v. Nat'l Shopmen Pension Fund, 6 EBC 2700 (W.D. Wash. 1985) 4: 203; 7: 267; 9: 115

McDonald v. Santa Fe Trail Transp. Co., 427 U.S. 273 (1976) 10: 21

McGinnis v. Joyce, 507 F.Supp. 654, 2 EBC 1485 (N.D. Ill. 1981) 10: 8

McHugh v. Teamsters Pension Trust Fund of Philadelphia, 638 F.Supp. 1036 (E.D. Pa. 1986) 2: 77; 8: 77, 119

McKnight v. Southern Life & Health Ins. Co., 758 F.2d 1566, 6 EBC 1707 (11th Cir. 1985) 4: 161, *169*; 8: *6*, 33; 14: 135

McLaughlin Estate v. Connecticut Gen. Life Ins. Co., 565 F.Supp. 434, 4 EBC 1879 (N.D. Cal. 1983) 7: 31, 32, 36, 165, *274*, 275

McLean v. Central States Pension Fund, 762 F.2d 1204, 7 EBC 1440 (4th Cir. 1985) 6: 244

McMahon v. McDowell, 794 F.2d 100, 7 EBC 1859 (3d Cir. 1986), *cert. denied*, 479 U.S. ___ (1986) 12: 232, 241

McNeese v. Health Plan Marketing, Inc., 647 F.Supp. 981, 8 EBC 1154 (N.D. Ala. 1986) 8: 101; 9: 177

Medley v. Holly Farms Poultry, 1 EBC 1004 (M.D.N.C. 1977) 14: 247

Meinhard v. Salmon, 249 N.Y. 458, 164 N.E. 545 (1928) 7: 25

Menhorn v. Firestone Tire & Rubber Co., 738 F.2d 1496, 5 EBC 2193 (9th Cir. 1984) 7: *11*, 12, 18, 98; 14: 95, 209

Menke v. Thompson, 140 F.2d 786 (8th Cir. 1944) 9: 102

Mestas v. Huge, 585 F.2d 450 (10th Cir. 1978) 8: 172; 9: 73; 12: 287

Metropolitan Life Ins. Co.

—v. Massachusetts, 471 U.S. 724, 6 EBC 1545 (1985) 1: 22; 7: 275

N

O

P

Q

R

S

Z

Index

A

D

E

J

K

L

M

T

U

V

W

Y

About the Author

Stephen R. Bruce is a lawyer in Washington, D.C., who specializes in employee benefits law. He is a graduate of the University of North Carolina at Chapel Hill, where he majored in economics, and the Georgetown University Law Center (cum laude). Mr. Bruce represents individual employees and unions in disputes involving pension and health benefits. He has testified on pension policy before Congress and has written and consulted with journalists on a number of articles about pension benefits.